LAW IN ACTION
A SOCIO–LEGAL READER

by

STEWART MACAULAY
Malcolm Pitman Sharp Hilldale Professor
of the University of Wisconsin–Madison
Theodore W. Brazeau Bascom Professor of Law
University of Wisconsin Law School

LAWRENCE M. FRIEDMAN
Marion Rice Kirkwood Professor of Law
Stanford University

ELIZABETH MERTZ
Professor of Law
University of Wisconsin Law School
Senior Research Fellow, American Bar Foundation

FOUNDATION PRESS

2007

© 2007 By FOUNDATION PRESS
        395 Hudson Street
        New York, NY 10014
        Phone Toll Free 1–877–888–1330
        Fax (212) 367–6799
        foundation–press.com
Printed in the United States of America

ISBN 978–1–59941–080–7

 TEXT IS PRINTED ON 10% POST CONSUMER RECYCLED PAPER

ACKNOWLEDGMENTS

Many people have helped us produce this book, and we want to thank them warmly. Molly Heiler did battle with the permissions-to-reprint monster and lent her expert skill to proof reading. Josh Cutler got the various copyright holders paid. We paid them from funds provided by Foundation Press and Stewart Macaulay's Theodore Brazeau Professorship. We thank the Press and the Brazeau family for making this kind of book possible. John Stookey, our good friend and coauthor on an earlier collection of teaching materials in law and society, did not participate in this version of the book. Nonetheless, his work on an earlier edition clearly affected what we have done here. In Chapter Two, we draw on an explanation of statistics and social science methods as they are applied to study of the legal system that originally appeared in that earlier book. We want to thank Herbert M. Kritzer and the late Jacqueline Macaulay for help in drafting our attempt to introduce these mysteries to law students. We thank Charles Camic for his helpful comments about the section on the work of Max Weber. Bonnie Shucha, Head of Reference and Michael Morgalla, Faculty Liaison, of the University of Wisconsin Law Library tracked down material from a wide variety of sources, and the staff of the Stanford Law Library also was extremely helpful. Mary Tye, Assistant to Lawrence M. Friedman, also deserves special thanks. Ms. Jennifer Mertz–Shea did a great deal of proof reading, and we thank her for her important, if not exciting, contribution to the project. Mark Suchman and Catherine Albiston have used the earlier collection of teaching materials by Macaulay, Friedman and Stookey, and they shared their course plans with us. We also have learned much from our friends at that remarkable institution, the American Bar Foundation. Blackwell Publishers prints and distributes *The Law & Society Review* and *Law & Social Inquiry*. We thank them for permissions to reprint so much from these key journals in our field. Macaulay and Friedman began teaching a law and society course in the mid–1960s. We must thank the many students both at Stanford and Wisconsin who have taken our courses and taught us much about what lurked in the field. Macaulay taught such a course jointly with, first, Jack Ladinsky and then with Howard Erlanger. Both sociologists contributed to his understanding of the field in important ways.

The following acknowledgments recognize the permissions granted by the various copyright holders of the material that we reproduce and excerpt:

Albiston, Catherine R., Bargaining in the Shadow of Social Institutions: Competing Discourses and Social Change in Workplace Mobilization of Civil Rights, 39 Law & Society Review 11 (2005). Reprinted by permission of Blackwell Publishers. 4.14

Bonnett, Dawn R., The Use of Colossus to Measure the General Damages of a Personal Injury Claim Demonstrates Good Faith Claims Handling, 53 Cleveland State Law Review 107 (2005). Excerpts reprinted by permission of the Law Review.

Bullis, Connie A. and Phillip K. Tompkins, The Forest Ranger Revisited: a Study of Control Practices and Identification, 56 Communication Monographs 287 (1989). Reprinted by permission of the publisher Taylor & Francis Ltd. http://www.informaworld.com. 5.7

Cohen, Julius, Reginald A. Robson, Alan P. Bates, Parental Authority: The Community and the Law. Copyright © 1958 by Rutgers, the State University. Reprinted by permission of Rutgers University Press. 3.6

Conley, John M. and Scott Baker, Review Essay: Fall from Grace or Business as Usual? A Retrospective Look at Lawyers on Wall Street and Main Street, 20 Law & Social Inquiry 783 (2005). Reprinted by permission of Blackwell Publishing. 5.11

Cooperrider, Luke, Review of Cohen, Robson and Bates, 57 Michigan Law Review 1119 (1959). Reprinted by permission.

Darley, John M., Paul H. Robinson and Kevin M. Carlsmith, The Ex Ante Function of the Criminal Law, 35 Law & Society Review 165 (2001). Reprinted by permission of Blackwell Publishers. 4.18

Edelman, Lauren B., Sally Riggs Fuller, and Iona Mara–Drita, Diversity Rhetoric and the Managerialization of Law, 106 American Journal of Sociology 1589 (2001). Copyright © 2001. University of Chicago Press. 3.10

Forbath, William, Law and the Shaping of Labor Politics in the United States and England in Tomlins, Christopher L., and Andrew J. King, eds. Labor Law in America: Historical and Critical Essays. Pp. 201–222 © 1992 The Johns Hopkins University Press. 6.1

Friedman, Lawrence M., American Legal Culture: The Last Thirty–Five Years, 35 St. Louis Law Journal 529 (1991). Reprinted with permission of the St. Louis University Law Journal © 1991 St. Louis University School of Law, St. Louis, Missouri. 3.9

Friedman, Lawrence M., The Deterrence Curve. Reprinted with permission from The Legal System: A Social Science Perspective. © 1975 Russell Sage Foundation, 112 East 64th Street, New York, N.Y. 10021. 4.3

Friedman, Lawrence M., Legal Culture and the Welfare State, in G. Teubner (ed.) Dilemmas of Law in the Welfare State (1985). Excerpted by permission of the publisher, W. de Gruyter. 3.8

Friedman, Lawrence M., Legal Rules and the Process of Social Change, 19 Stanford Law Review 786 (1967). Reprinted by permission. 5.4

Friedman, Lawrence M. and Jack Ladinsky, Social Change and the Law of Industrial Accidents, 67 Columbia Law Review 50 (1967). Copyright © 1967 Columbia Law Review. 3.3

Friedman, Lawrence M. and Robert V. Percival, A Tale of Two Courts: Litigation in Alameda and San Benito Counties, 10 Law & Society Review 267 (1976) Excerpt reprinted by permission of Blackwell Publishers.

Galanter, Marc, Judicial Mediation in the United States, 12 Journal of Law and Society 1 (1985). Excerpt reprinted by permission.

Galanter, Marc, Why the Haves Come Out Ahead: Speculations on the Limits of Legal Change, 9 Law & Society Review 95 (1974). Excerpts reprinted by permission of Blackwell Publishers.

Gibbs, Jack, Deterrence Theory and Research. Reprinted from the NEBRASKA SYMPOSIUM ON MOTIVATION, volume 33, by permission of the University of Nebraska Press. Copyright © 1986 by the University of Nebraska Press. 4.1

Givelber, Daniel J., William J. Bowers and Carolyn L. Blitch, Tarasoff, Myth and Reality: An Empirical Study of Private Law in Action, 1984 Wisconsin Law Review 443. Copyright © 1984 by the Board of Regents of the University of Wisconsin System. Reprinted by permission of the Wisconsin Law Review. 4.17

Gluckman, Max, The Technical Vocabulary of Barotse Jurisprudence, 61 American Anthropologist 743 (1959). Reprinted by permission. 6.4

Goldman, Sheldon, Elliot Slotnick, Gerard Gryski and Sara Schiavoni, W. Bush's Judiciary: The First Term Record, 88 Judicature 244 (May–June 2005). Reprinted by permission. 5.8

Grasmick, Harold G. and Robert J. Bursik, Jr., Conscience, Significant Others and Rational Choice: Extending the Deterrence Model, 24 Law & Society Review 837 (1990). Reprinted by permission of Blackwell Publishers. 4.5

Gross, Samuel R., The American Advantage: The Value of Inefficient Litigation, 85 Michigan Law Review 734 (1987). Excerpt reprinted with permission of the University of Michigan Law Review.

Gusfield, Joseph R., Moral Passage: The Symbolic Process in Public Designations of Deviance, 15 Social Problems 175 (1967). Copyright © Social Problems (1967). Reprinted by permission of the Journal, The Society for the Study of Social Problems and the author. 4.13

Hickman, Laura J. and Sally S. Simpson, Fair Treatment or Preferred Outcome? The Impact of Police Behavior on Victim Reports of Domestic Violence Incidents, 37 Law & Society Review 607 (2003). Reprinted by permission of Blackwell Publishers. 2.2

Hodgson, Jacqueline, The Police, The Prosecutor and The Juge D'Instruction: Judicial Supervision in France, Theory and Practice, 41 British Journal of Criminology 342 (2001). Reprinted by permission. 5.1

Horney, Julie and Cassia Spohn, Rape Law Reform and Instrumental Change in Six Urban Jurisdictions, 25 Law & Society Review 117 (1991). Reprinted by permission of Blackwell Publishers. 4.15

ACKNOWLEDGMENTS

Jacob, Herbert, Silent Revolution. Copyright © 1988. University of Chicago Press. Reprinted by permission. 3.11

Kagan, Robert A., Adversarial Legalism: The American Way of Law. Copyright © 2001, by the President and Fellows of Harvard University. Reprinted by permission of the Harvard University Press. 2.8

Kagan, Robert A., The Routinization of Debt Collection: An Essay on Social Change and Conflict in Courts, 18 Law & Society Review 323 (1984). Reprinted by permission of Blackwell Publishers. 3.13

Kaufman, Herbert, The Forest Ranger: A Study in Administrative Behavior, Copyright © 1960 Johns Hopkins Press, Baltimore, published for Resources for the Future, Inc. Reprinted from pp. 91–99, 101–107, 126–40, 142–45, 149–53, by permission. 5.6

Leo, Richard A., Miranda's Revenge: Police Interrogation as a Confidence Game, 30 Law & Society Review 259 (1996). Reprinted by permission of Blackwell Publishers 2.3

Macaulay, Stewart, Images of Law in Everyday Life: The Lessons of School, Entertainment and Spectator Sports, 21 Law & Society Review 185, 188, 189–92 (1987). Reprinted by permission of Blackwell Publishers. 2.1, 4:11

Macaulay, Stewart, Law and the Behavioral Sciences: Is There Any There There? 6 Law & Policy 149, 152–55 (1984) Excerpts reprinted by permission. 1

Macaulay, Stewart, Lawyers and Consumer Protection Laws, 14 Law & Society Review 115 (1979). Reprinted by permission of Blackwell Publishing. 5:14

Macaulay, Stewart, Long–Term Continuing Relations: The American Experience Regulating Dealerships and Franchises, in C. Joerges (ed.) Franchising and the Law: Theoretical and Comparative Approaches in Europe and the United States, at 179–237. Reprinted by permission of Nomos Verlagsgessellschaft. 3.12

Macaulay, Stewart, Non-Contractual Relations in Business: A Preliminary Study, 28 American Sociological Review 55 (1963). Reprinted with permission of the author. 2.4

Markovitz, Inga, Last Days © 1992 by the California Law Review, Inc. Reprinted from California Law Review, Vol. 80, No. 1, pp. 79–80 & 99–107, by permission of the California Law Review, Inc. 5 6.3

Martin, Elaine, Men and Women on the Bench: Vive la Difference? 73 Judicature 204, 208 (1990). Excerpt reprinted by permission of the publisher.

Mather, Lynn, Craig A. McEwen, and Richard J. Maiman, Divorce Lawyers at Work: Varieties of Professionalism in Practice (2001). Reprinted by permission of Oxford University Press, Inc. 2.6

ACKNOWLEDGMENTS

Matsuda, Mari, Law and Culture in the District Court of Honolulu, 1844-1845: A Case Study of the Rise of Legal Consciousness; 32 American Journal of Legal History 16 (1988). Excerpt reprinted with permission of the publisher.

Mayhew, David R., Congress: The Electoral Connection (2d ed. 2004). Copyright © 2004. Reprinted by permission of Yale University Press 2.7

McCann, Michael, William Haltom, and Anne Bloom, Java Jive: Genealogy of a Juridical Icon, 56 University of Miami Law Review 113 (2001). Reprinted by permission. 3.5

McKillop, Bron, Anatomy of a French Murder Case, 45 American Journal of Comparative Law 527 (1997) Reprinted with permission of The University of Michigan Law Review. 5.2

Merry, Sally Engle, Going to Court: Strategies of Dispute Management in an American Urban Neighborhood, 13 Law & Society Review 891 (1979). Reprinted by permission of Blackwell Publishers. 3.1

Mertz, Elizabeth, Language, Law, and Social Meanings: Linguistic/Anthropological Contributions to the Study of Law, 26 Law & Society Review 413 (1992). Reprinted by permission of Blackwell Publishers. 6.5

Mertz, Elizabeth, Teaching Lawyers the Language of Law: Legal and Anthropological Translations, 34 John Marshall Law Review 91 (2000). Reprinted by permission. 6.6

Milgram, Stanley, Obedience to Authority: An Experimental View, abridged from pp. 1, 2–5, 7–8 in Obedience to Authority: An Experimental View by Stanley Milgram. Copyright © 1974 by Stanley Milgram. Reprinted by permission of the author and Harper & Row Publishers, Inc. 4.10

Nadler, Janice, Flouting the Law, 83 Texas Law Review 1399 (2005). Reprinted by permission of © the University of Texas Law Review. 4.9.

Posner, Richard A., Case Against Strict Constructionism: What am I? A Potted Plant? The New Republic, Sept. 18, 1987, at 23. Reprinted by permission of The New Republic, © 1987, The New Republic, LLC. 5.10

Reichman, Nancy J. and Joyce S. Sterling, Gender Penalties Revisited. Reprinted by permission of the authors. 5.12

Rheinstein, Max (ed), Max Weber on Law in Economy and Society. Copyright © 1954, by the President and Fellows of Harvard University. Harvard University Press. Reprinted by permission of the publisher. 3.2

Rosenberg, Gerald N., Tilting at Windmills: Brown II and the Hopeless Quest to Resolve Deep-Seated Social Conflict Through Litigation, 24 Law and Inequality 31 (2006). Reprinted by permission of the publisher. 4.16

Ross, H. Laurence, Settled Out of Court: The Social Process of Insurance Claims Adjustment. Copyright © 1980 by Transaction Publishers. Reprinted by permission of the publisher. 2.5

Ross, H. Laurence, Interrupted Time Series Studies of Deterrence of Drinking and Driving, in John Hagen (ed.) Deterrence Reconsidered: Methodological Innovations (1982). Reprinted by permission of Sage Publications.   4.4

Sarat, Austin and William L. F. Felstiner, Law and Strategy in The Divorce Lawyer's Office, 20 Law & Society Review 93 (1986). Reprinted by permission of Blackwell Publishers. 5.15

Schultz, Mark F., Fear and Norms and Rock & Roll: What Jambands Can Teach Us About Persuading People to Obey Copyright Law, 21 Berkeley Technological Law Journal 651 (2006). Reprinted by permission of the journal and the author. 4:7

Shamir, Ronen, Formal and Substantive Rationality in American Law: A Weberian Perspective, 2 Social & Legal Studies 45 (1993). Excerpt reprinted by permission of Sage Publication Ltd.   Copyright (© Sage Publications, 1993).

Suchman, Mark C. and Lauren B. Edelman, Legal Rational Myths: The New Institutionalism and the Law and Society Tradition, 21 Law & Social Inquiry 903 (1997). Reprinted by permission of Blackwell Publishers. 4.12

Suchman, Mark C. and Mia L. Cahill, The Hired Gun as Facilitator: Lawyers and the Suppression of Business Disputes in Silicon Valley, 21 Law & Social Inquiry 679 (1996). Reprinted by permission of Blackwell Publishers. 5.13

Sunstein, Cass R., David Schkade, & Lisa Michelle Ellman, Ideological Voting on Federal Courts of Appeals: A Preliminary Investigation, 90 Virginia Law Review 301 (2004). Reprinted by permission. 5.9

Tittle, Charles R. and Alan R. Rowe, Moral Appeal, Sanction Threat, and Deviance: An Experimental Test, 20 Social Problems 488 (1973). © Social Problems. Reprinted by permission of Social Problems, The Society for the Study of Social Problems and the authors. 4.6

Tyler, Tom R., Public Mistrust of the Law: A Political Perspective Originally published in the University of Cincinnati Law Review. 66 University of Cincinnati Law Review 847 (1988). Reprinted by permission. 4.8.

Weisberg, Robert, The Death Penalty Meets Social Science: Deterrence and Jury Behavior Under New Scrutiny 4:2 Reprinted with permission, from the *Annual Review of Law and Social Science*, Volume 1 © 2005 by Annual Reviews www.annualreviews.org.

Whitman, James Q., Harsh Justice: Criminal Punishment and the Widening Divide between America and Europe (2003). Reprinted by permission of Oxford University Press, Inc. 6.2

TABLE OF CONTENTS

TABLE OF CONTENTS

TABLE OF CONTENTS

TABLE OF ARTICLES
CITED OR REPRINTED

Writings we reproduce in whole or substantial part are indicated in one type face and those where we only offer an excerpt or citation are indicated in another. Those reproduced as major readings are cited in this table by chapter and article number and then by page. For example, (2:12 – 34) would indicate Reading 12 in Chapter 2 which appears on page 34. Those excerpted or only cited are indicated by chapter number and then page. For example, 5 : 555 would indicate that the citation is in chapter 5 on page 555.

TABLE OF ARTICLES CITED OR REPRINTED

TABLE OF ARTICLES CITED OR REPRINTED

LAW IN ACTION
A SOCIO–LEGAL READER

*

CHAPTER 1

Introduction

This is a book of readings about law, legal systems, and legal institutions. But it is a book with a particular slant. The readings primarily approach that system from an *outside* rather than an *inside* perspective. The *inside* perspective focuses on legal rules and procedures the way that lawyers and judges usually see them—from *within* the legal system, so to speak—and it usually accepts them more or less at face value. This introduction will try to explain what we mean by the outside perspective. It will also give a brief account of the history and present status of outside approaches to law.

I. The Outside Point of View

When we say "the outside point of view," we mean, roughly, looking at legal phenomena from the standpoint of one or more of the social sciences: sociology, anthropology, economics, psychology, political science, and perhaps others. Of course, these are all quite different fields, and each has its own slant, its own special way of looking at human behavior and human thought. An economist might be interested, for example, in asking whether it makes more sense to give companies subsidies as an incentive to refrain from dumping toxic wastes rather than using a regime of fines and criminal sanctions. An anthropologist might be interested in how cultures differ in the ways they handle disputes between husband and wife. A psychologist might want to find out how juries actually go about making their decisions. A political scientist might wonder how lobbyists affect the votes of legislators. A sociologist might ask how race and gender affect the behavior of judges and juries. Each field has its own little stock of favorite questions (and answers), and its own pet methods.

But the social sciences do have certain traits in common. Perhaps the most important is a commitment to empirical observation and scientific measurement, as far as this is possible. Related to this is a commitment to objectivity and neutrality, again, as far as possible. Sophisticated social scientists are not naïve about science and its limits. They know that they themselves are only human. They realize that they have prejudices and values, just as everyone else. They know too that these prejudices and values can affect their work. The best of them will try very hard to keep their personal values from prejudicing their work.

There are some critics who think that objectivity and scientific neutrality are delusions; that "value free" social science is a myth, or, worse, a fraud. There is a grain of truth in this accusation. A social scientist does not pick her topics at random; values, attitudes, viewpoints and prejudices play a role in these decisions about what to do and how to do it; and values, attitudes,

1

viewpoints and prejudices inevitably color the way questions get asked and even how data get analyzed. Actually, we owe this insight itself to social science—in particular, to the sociology of knowledge and the sociology of science. The social sciences use many methods, but all of them are flawed or limited. None can promise to produce pure, objective, uncontrovertible truth.

Moreover, our subject matter—law and legal systems—is particularly cantankerous and resistant. It is very hard to study law scientifically. The things that we want to describe and analyze, often enough, are not tangible objects that can be measured with practical yardsticks. They involve morals, ideas, attitudes, personal privacy, economic interests, and other tangled and delicate stuff. Doing research on law and legal behavior is not like studying, say, the muscular structure of rodents. The legal process is, in part, a labeling process—it is a set of social constructs, ideas and concepts. Raw material from the real world—whatever that might mean—gets transformed and twisted and renamed and reconceived when it enters the world of the legal order. It is easier, for example, to study accidents than to study torts. Judgments of judges, jurors or lawyers transform a collision between two autos—an objective event—into a "tort." This is a legal concept. Furthermore, people inside the legal system often manipulate data and ideas. They may produce a picture that is not at all like the picture and the perceptions of the people who actually lived through the collision or were affected by it.

The people who make and run the legal system in any society are not a random cross-section of the public. In our society, for most of our history, these people—the judges, lawyers, legislators and others—have been white males who belonged to the upper middle-class. They made the law more or less in their image. The situation today (2007) is quite different. Almost half of all law students now are women. Women are lawyers, judges, law professors, and deans. Members of racial minorities have also gained more representation. This is one kind of progress for women and minorities—filling the roles that once belonged exclusively to men. But some women and minority group members have gone further. They have challenged core assumptions and concepts that underlie law and legal institutions. Theorists and practitioners have had to confront the experience of subordinated groups. The voices of sexual minorities and other disadvantaged people have also begun to be heard. Much of the scholarship, of course, is deeply controversial. But legal scholarship, and law-and-society scholarship, can only benefit when it is forced to confront underlying assumptions, ruling ideas and habits. Law-and-society scholarship has had to learn, the hard way, how much gender, race, class, and lifestyle colored the way that people, including legal officials and scholars, have looked at the world.

Still, having said all this, we have to reject the deep skepticism about what law-and-society studies show. Felice Levine has expressed a more optimistic view:

> [O]ne learns from the various critiques and ... these critiques are not necessarily separate and apart from science, but part of the dialogue of

doing science in a better way. For those who value the process of learning and the value of understanding without any illusion of absolute certainty of what we know, such critiques are instructive and integral to the activity and integrity of science itself. We must keep in mind that science is a social process and, like all social processes, it is dynamic, even at times erratic, but capable of change. Thus, the critiques are grist for doing science in a more profound way.[1]

After all, despite all the doubting and theorizing, there is a big difference between honest research on law and no research at all; between trying to interpret data fairly and combing through data to find an example or two in support of some political or ideological position. There is a big difference, on the one hand, between measuring litigation rates and trying to interpret the zigs and zags in the data, and, on the other, fulminating about a "litigation explosion." (Or just making up the data out of one's head or offering colorful anecdotes.)

In any specific study or research project, there are bound to be problems and failings. But this is no reason to discard the whole enterprise. One test of fairness is whether the researcher is willing to accept results that are surprising or that contradict the researcher's own desires and expectations. Social science is far from perfect, but it is, after all, a kind of science. In science a "theory" is something testable, a guide to research, an idea that leads the researcher in a particular direction. Or it may be a general concept that sums up and explains a mass of data. Legal scholars often use "theory" in a different way. They describe a philosophical or political position which has not been and cannot be tested.

In any event, the social sciences have over the years developed a toolbox of traditions, methods and credos. (These are, to be sure, sometimes in conflict with each other.) The social scientific study of law borrows from this toolbox. There are also *distinctive* traditions, methods, and credos relating to the social scientific study of law. What they have in common is the "outside" approach to the legal system. "Insiders," mostly lawyers, law professors and judges, are not usually well-trained in the social sciences. They have practical experience and insights, but the insights are not always entirely accurate.

A researcher, using the tools of social science, can often gain valuable insights into a society, community, or group dynamics that "insiders" overlook or take for granted—although the researcher, who might well be an "outsider," also risks projecting his or her own values or prejudices onto that society, community or group. However, trained anthropologists and other social scientists try hard to put aside cultural prejudices in order to understand other societies in less biased or "ethnocentric" ways. The tools of social science can also be turned back on parts of our own society—the legal system, for example—to acquire new insights and analytic clarity.

---

1. Felice J. Levine, " 'His' and 'Her' Story; The Life and Future of the Law and Society Movement," 18 *Florida State University Law Review* 69, 86 (1990).

Law professors, lawyers and judges (and often the public) are concerned not so much with empirical, measurable reality, with what is going on in the world, as they are with what is on the books, what is right and wrong, what is legally correct or incorrect. To be sure, most legal questions do have—and must have—some sort of answer. A woman who runs a consulting business out of her home asks a tax lawyer whether she can deduct some of her heating bills as business expenses. She expects a professional answer—she wants to be told that she can deduct, she can't or whether it depends on this or that factor. She expects that answer to come from the law, although she may not be clear about where one finds that or what it consists of. She is asking an inside question, and she demands an inside answer.

There also is a very large normative element in discussions of law. People argue and discuss what *should* be legal or illegal and what is morally, politically or otherwise right or wrong. Indeed, lawyers and lay people alike often fudge or confuse legal correctness and ethical rightness. Is it a good thing to put murderers to death? Should we let teachers in public schools offer prayers in class? These are normative or ethical questions about what should be done. But they also happen to be legal issues in this country. It is not easy to keep the two dimensions apart, if we assume that they should be kept apart.

To take one example, the Bill of Rights forbids cruel and unusual punishment. Many opponents of the death penalty say that it is cruel and unusual and therefore forbidden. But in some ways this is a rather odd statement. After all, the justices of the Supreme Court in a number of cases have specifically held that the death penalty is not cruel and unusual punishment. And the Supreme Court has the last word on the official meaning of the Constitution.

However, the person who insists that, despite the Supreme Court's decisions, the death penalty is cruel and unusual is saying: "I think that the death penalty is wrong and should be abolished." But she is also saying something more about law, the role of the Supreme Court, the Constitution, and what the correct reading of the Constitution ought to be. She is making a point about the differences between legal and moral validity. The point may be, and often is, inchoate and confused. However, that people make this point is an important social fact about such things as values, beliefs, ideals and attitudes. These are basic to any legal system.

Of course, the social scientist has no way to suggest an answer to the question of whether the death penalty is constitutional. She can only discuss and describe why people think it is or it is not. She can only tell us which people (or judges) think that it is valid, and which ones do not. She can tell us how opinion varies from men to women, whites to blacks, young to old, and the like. She can compile and analyze data on the actual impact of the death penalty. She can show where movements for and against the death penalty come from, politically or historically speaking, and so on.

4

These are not trivial contributions to the debate itself, and they are not frivolous or unimportant questions for researchers. Some of us (including the editors of this book) think that understanding the factual and social underpinnings of the legal system is very important indeed. In a society that thinks that it is committed to the rule of law—whatever that may mean—grasping the nature of the legal system, explaining it, observing it in action, is absolutely crucial.

It would seem easier to defend the death penalty if you could prove that it saved lives by deterring murderers. Moreover, people who are in favor of the death penalty would be a lot more comfortable if they could prove that no innocent people had been or were likely to be put to death by mistake. Better yet if we could show that racial discrimination was not involved in the choice of which convicted murderers get the death penalty and which do not.

However, it is possible that we cannot prove or disprove any of these propositions. What do we do if we cannot answer such questions? Is common sense good enough? Do we keep putting people to death unless the opponents can make a stronger case? Who has the burden of proof? Suppose we could show that the death penalty deters, but only somewhat. Moreover, suppose we could show that there is some racial discrimination but not an enormous amount. Who decides how much is too much? Obviously, the social sciences do not and cannot give us answers to such questions. Nonetheless, without data and research, without the perspective of the social sciences, it is easy to ignore these issues and reduce the whole matter to political sloganeering.

Law, however, is not just social engineering. Law is one way of declaring what is morally right and wrong. The death penalty is an important symbol of a society's abhorrence of murder. Capital punishment could be viewed as a factor in reinforcing all of the norms in the culture that keep individuals to some degree safer in their daily lives. Some people may simply feel better if they see that those who commit horrible murders pay the ultimate price. Indeed, for them, putting murderers to death may be part of what the legal system must do to gain and retain legitimacy. (In some cultures, for example, it is legitimate for a victim's family to seek revenge, and, arguably, our culture does not totally condemn a person who takes revenge on a rapist or killer). Many people, however, have a strong moral objection to the death penalty. They see the symbolism and the lesson as all wrong: the death penalty, along with violence in film and television, teaches that killing is an appropriate solution to problems. Other opponents point to instances where people on death row have been shown to be innocent. Still others have shown that the actual process in death penalty cases is frequently flawed. What the death penalty actually symbolizes, how people perceive it, and how it operates—and on whom—are also empirical questions.

In other words, we think that a law-and-society perspective can do much to clarify and improve debates about issues such as the death penalty. However, if we are realistic, we have to ask, who is the audience for this kind of scholarship? The Supreme Court? The President? Legislators? The Supreme Court, at times, seems to ignore or distort social science findings to suit preconceived policy positions. The President, members of Congress, and local legislators are interested in getting elected or reelected. Sometimes it seems that the only social science studies that they care about are public opinion polls. Interest groups look for data and findings that they can use that suit their cause as they battle to get their way in the legislative market-place. Sometimes interest groups even buy the social science findings that they want. These groups ignore or distort data that comes out the "wrong way."

Claims about facts do not *by themselves* automatically change the world. The social study of law *also* includes the study of the way that law gets made and remade. Good empirical studies have an influence, but so do other things such as colorful anecdotes, scandals, conventional wisdom, popular stereotypes, and sometimes outright lies. We should neither claim too much nor too little for the impact on society of our enterprise—of our ongoing attempt to understand how the law actually works.

II. The Riddle of Legal Autonomy

It is one thing to describe a legal system from the outside. It is quite another to say that the outside viewpoint *explains* what makes a legal system tick much better than any inside explanation. Which approach gives you a better handle on how legal systems work hinges on whether or not legal systems are autonomous.

An "autonomous" legal system would be "one that is independent of other sources of power and authority in social life," according to Richard Lempert and Joseph Sanders.[2] A legal action in an autonomous system is "influenced only by the preestablished rules of the legal system." It defines events "in its own terms," and is "independent of society's other mechanisms of social control." Lempert and Sanders also insist that an autonomous system is "self-legitimating." Its "rules and rulings are accepted because they are legal" and not because of some other reason. An autonomous legal system is not legitimated by political, social or ethical considerations. And in an autonomous system, such outside factors do not influence what the legal system does. We will not enter into a long discussion of legal autonomy here. Nobody thinks that the legal system is *totally* autonomous and completely independent of the society in which it is imbedded. Nobody really thinks that a legal system goes entirely its own way, deciding everything according to legal criteria with no room for political pressure, ethical considerations, economic consequences and the like. A totally autonomous legal system would be very undesirable. Such a system also is probably impossible, at least in any society that we know about.

However, is our legal system *partially* autonomous? Is there something tough, unyielding and resistant to external influences, something self-contained about law? Does law march to its own drummer at least sometimes?

---

2. *An Invitation to Law and Social Science* 402 (1986).

Does it follow its own internal program when it can? Many law professors, and probably many lay people, seem to think so. Yet the real question is *how* autonomous? How much of the system is self-generated, technocratic, traditional, insulated from the outside world, and how much is not?

A judge may say that he decides cases "according to the law," and he does not let any other consideration sway him. The head of an agency like the Food and Drug Administration may say that FDA has decided to ban a "morning after" pill because this is the legally correct thing to do under the agency's rules and procedures. The commissioner can insist that political pressures or public opinion had nothing to do with the decision. The judge and the commissioner are claiming political independence and some sort of autonomy. It is not easy to know whether they are telling the truth or even whether they really *think* that they are telling the truth.

Many of us tend to be cynical about statements such as the ones the judge and the commissioner made. But surely some actors feel (and behave?) this way sometimes. The exact situation makes a difference. Birth control pills are controversial, but routine decisions about food dyes are much less so. The *structure* of the legal system may also make a difference. If the director of an agency is likely to be shot at dawn if she does something that displeases the head of state, she is unlikely to make herself a martyr. However, if a judge has life-tenure as our federal judges do, or if an agency head cannot be removed by the President or governor, it may be a different story.

What does seem fairly clear is that legal systems as a whole cannot be autonomous *in the long run*. Sooner or later their shape will get bent more or less in the direction of their society regardless of any technical, traditional or historical elements. Medieval law looked, smelled, and acted medieval. The law of the Trobriand Islanders or the ancient Egyptians fit with the structure and culture of those societies. The law of modern free-market states is full of rules that support or presuppose free markets. Modern legal systems contain an endless list of prescriptions and institutions concerning clean air and water, toxic waste, gene splicing, computer hacking. All of these are specific to the age in which we live. We cannot label these legal arrangements as autonomous.

How could it be otherwise? Legal systems do not exist to answer abstract questions. They solve (or mis-solve) real problems. Legislators react to demands of their constituents and lobbyists. Judges decide real cases between real people who live in real time and who have real problems. These problems necessarily are problems of the society in which the litigants, constituents, and lobbyists live, and not those of any other society. And the outcomes or solutions to the problems, too, will take on the coloration of the society and the culture that supplies both questions and answers.

Social scientists who study law tend to emphasize the role of the culture, the society, and the world outside the courtroom, legislative hall or police station. In other words, they tend to explain happenings within the system in terms of social forces—political pressures, internalized values, cultural norms, economic interests and so on. They tend to deemphasize "internal" aspects of the system—the technical stuff of the law. Law professors, and others who make their living explaining the law, traditionally have taken an "inside" point of view. Insiders are bound up in their daily work with details of law. They tend to explain what happens in the system in such terms.

Some of the biases of the editors of this book should be obvious by now. We would not have put this book together if we did not believe that an external perspective on the legal system offers important benefits not available to those using an internal point of view. But nobody can prove that the outside approach is a better one or measure the exact degree to which legal systems respond or relate to their specific societies. Nor can we presuppose that each legal system is as autonomous as every other one. It is *possible* that American law is more legalistic than the law of some other country or society. It is also possible that some subfields of law are more autonomous than others. A person who favors an outside approach must still consider the degree to which *internal* legal doctrines influence the output of a legal system. It would be foolish to assume that legal thought never makes a difference. After all, the language of doctrine is an integral part of the culture of law. Similarly, it would be foolish to assume that legal thought explains everything, or even most things, about a legal system.

The problems raised in this introduction will not be solved here or anywhere. They will run through almost every page of the readings that follow.

III. Complexity and Change

Legal systems, we must remember, are incredibly complicated. They also change over time. And they are also culture-bound or at least tied to specific cultures. These are three elementary but crucial facts about legal systems throughout the modern world.

The complexity of any legal system is obvious. The law is an enormous and complicated business. Nobody knows all of American law, even all of American tax law or even all of American law relating to taxes on corporations. There is simply too much of it. Law is conventionally divided into subfields such as personal injury law, divorce law, food and drug law, copyright law, criminal law, tort law, and so on. These subfields, taken together, cover or touch on almost every conceivable aspect of life. This fact—the sheer size and scope of the legal system—is true of every modern society. But there is an added wrinkle to the law of the United States. Americans live in a federal system. The country is blessed (if that is the word) with 50 legal systems, one for each state. In addition, there is the national (federal) system of laws and courts, not to mention various territorial systems, and the system in the District of Columbia. There is also a system of courts for some of the native American peoples—there is, for example, a Navajo Supreme Court. And there are distinct legal systems in Puerto Rico, Guam, and the Virgin Islands.

To complicate matters further, there are also thousands of cities, towns, townships, counties, and special subdivisions (sewer and school districts, port authorities, and so on) that have the power to make rules and regulations or municipal ordinances. Every state, every city, and above all the federal government has an enormous number of administrative agencies, large and small. For example, on the federal level, we can point to the Securities and Exchange Commission, the Food and Drug Administration, the Social Security Administration and so forth. On the state level, we find medical and dental licensing boards and highway commissions as well as human rights commissions, occupational safety and health boards and the like. On the local level, zoning and school boards are at work. These also churn out rules, regulations, decisions and orders beyond counting.

And of course this vast body of legal material is constantly changing. Each rule and regulation as well as each published court decision is at least a minor change, a footnote, in the immense book of the laws. The pace of social change has increased enormously in our times, and the pace of legal change has increased along with it. So many legal issues are new: in vitro fertilization, copyright problems relating to computer software and others. There is a Department of Homeland Security in Washington, D.C., and a body of law devoted to the "war on terror," most of which didn't exist before 2001.

Finally, law is a remarkably parochial discipline. Chemical engineering or molecular biology is more or less the same subject in China or Honduras as it is in the United States. Even the social sciences tend to transcend national boundaries. Economics can be studied anywhere, and while the emphasis may be different, the core of the discipline will be more or less the same. If you learn any subject in one country, it will at least give you a foothold anywhere else. However, a knowledge of French law does not equip you to practice law, say, in Iran or Japan. Every country has its own official legal system. No two are the same or even approximately the same. They vary according to differences in the culture, traditions, economics, and politics of the particular countries. There is, therefore, an immense number of legal systems all over the world. Even so tiny a country as Andorra or so new a country as East Timor has its own unique system of law.

A "science" of law should in theory have principles or generalizations that go beyond a particular legal system. Do any such principles exist? Can we say anything of value about legal systems in general?[3] Or about some subgroup such as legal systems in Western industrial countries, for example?

Most of these questions have no answers that would command general agreement. It is difficult to compare systems of law or even parts of them in a systematic empirical way. There are theoretical and practical obstacles. But in an age of global communication and global economics, the legal systems of the

---

3. There have been some attempts to offer such generalizations. For example, Donald Black, *The Behavior of Law* (1976) offers a number of propositions. For a critical analysis of this work, see Gloria T. Lessan and Joseph F. Sheley, "Does Law Behave? A Macrolevel Test of Black's Propositions on Change in Law," 70 *Social Forces* 655 (1992).

world are becoming more and more interconnected. This trend is likely to continue. Law, and its study, are likely to become at least a bit less parochial. So, too, the social study of law.

IV. Private Government

Thus far we have spoken mostly about official, formal legal systems. These systems are what law students generally study and what most legal scholars write about. But the formal legal system, as it exists on paper, is not the real living and lived system of law. The social study of law is concerned with the whole system and all its working parts. It looks at the formal and informal, official and unofficial, and legitimate and illegitimate aspects.

The real legal system differs from its official picture in at least two significant ways. First, it contains much behavior that is informal and unofficial and which cannot be deduced from the official texts of the rules. These informal and unofficial elements are everywhere. They surround, supplement, supplant and complement the official and formal elements. In criminal law, this is the world of plea bargaining ("copping a plea") and the dozens of arrangements, shortcuts, rules of thumb and patterns of behavior that people inside the system know about, but that law school courses seldom mention or develop. It is the world in which the police sometimes beat prisoners and in which the police sometimes let other prisoners go free. It is the world in which some police officers even take bribes.

Second, everywhere in society we find law-like systems or institutions that exist side-by-side with or acting as rivals to the official system. There are, for example, what we might call "private governments."

> We live in a world of "legal pluralism" where rules are made and interpreted and sanctions imposed by many public and private governments which are only loosely coordinated.... Examples of private governments range from the Mafia to the American Arbitration Association. Trade associations, sports leagues, church groups, neighborhood organizations and many other "private" units such as business corporations exercise what are, effectively, legal powers. They make rules ... they interpret them in their day-to-day operations; they offer benefits ... and they may suspend or expel members, associations or employees as a sanction.[4]

Throughout this book, we will see examples of informal patterns of legal behavior, and we will also see examples of pluralism and of "private governments." Some patterns amount to what we might even call legal subcultures. No society of any size—and the United States is certainly a big and heterogeneous society—has a single general culture. In the United States, for example, ideas and behaviors differ as between men and women, young and old, black

---

4. Stewart Macaulay, "Law and the Behavioral Sciences: Is There Any There There?" 6 *Law and Policy* 249 (1984).

and white, Protestant and Catholic, and within communities of Asian Americans or Armenian–Americans. They differ also within communities of auto dealers, jazz musicians, nurses, cab drivers, gang members and heroin addicts—any community or group that can be described at all has its own "dialect" of culture. The same is true of *legal* culture. Any society will have many legal cultures, and they will not necessarily be consistent with each other. This adds another layer of complexity to our subject, but throughout this book of readings, these subcultures will figure very prominently. The legal system cannot be understood without them.

V. Law-and-Society Scholarship

The study of the relationship between law and society, practically speaking, goes back to the 19th century, when modern social science began to develop. Sir Henry Maine, whose book, *Ancient Law,* appeared in 1861, was one of the pioneers. Maine looked at the law in a broad historical sweep, and he tried to discern relationships between types of legal systems and types of society (or types of social structure). Karl Marx, another seminal if controversial 19th century figure, wrote little explicitly about law. He considered law as a by-product of economic structure and an instrument of repression in the hands of social and economic elites. His general approach has continued to be influential with neo-Marxists and others. Emile Durkheim (1858–1917), another of the founding figures of modern social thought, has had particular influence on the sociology of crime and deviance.[5]

Max Weber (1864–1920) is probably is the most important historical figure in the development of the sociology of law. Weber himself was trained as a lawyer. Concepts developed by Weber still are extremely useful in law-and-society scholarship, and we will meet some of them later in these materials.[6]

After the death of Weber, the social study of law seemed to enter a kind of dormancy phase. The work done in the next 30 or so years hardly compares to that done during the golden age of Weber and Durkheim. There were, however, some important contributions from anthropologists who were studying law.[7] But neither legal academics nor the bulk of social scientists paid much attention to the relationship between legal and social systems—whether in America or in other societies.

5. See Kai Erikson, *Wayward Puritans* 6–13 (1966).

6. Another classical figure worth mention is Eugen Ehrlich (1862–1922), whose fame rests on the concept of "living law." Ehrlich was one of the first jurists seriously interested in the rules people followed in their everyday lives as opposed to the rules "in the books."

7. One notable example was Bronislaw Malinowski's *Crime and Custom in Savage Society* (1926). Another classic of legal anthropology, *The Cheyenne Way: Conflict and Case Law in Primitive Jurisprudence* (1941), deserves special mention because it was a rare collaboration between a law professor (Karl Llewellyn) and a social scientist (E. Adamson Hoebel, an anthropologist). See John M. Conley & William M. O'Barr, "A Classic in Spite of Itself: *The Cheyenne Way* and the Case Method in Legal Anthropology," 29 *Law & Social Inquiry* 179 (2004).

Fortunately, the field came into its own in the second half of the 20th century. Social science in general had a boom period after the Second World War. In the United States, such dramatic decisions as *Brown v. Board of Education* (1954) refocused attention on the social importance of law. In addition, private foundations began to invest money in socio-legal research, which provided yet another stimulus.

The last 40 years have been a time of steady and impressive growth in the field. In many ways, law-and-society studies are flourishing. The Law and Society Association, the umbrella group for scholars in the field in the United States, is more than 40 years old. It was founded by a handful of social scientists, aided and abetted by an aberrant law professor or two.[8] Much of the founding energy was generated at the University of Wisconsin, and Professor J. Willard Hurst of the Law School was a potent influence. Hurst himself was a legal historian, but his influential works on that subject pointed the way to the social study of law in American society.[9]

Today, the Law and Society Association (LSA) has well over 1,000 members, holds annual meetings, and publishes a journal, the *Law & Society Review*. Another leading journal in the field is *Law & Social Inquiry*, a publication of the American Bar Foundation. Other journals on the subject published in the United States include *Law & Policy,* as well as the *Journal of Empirical Legal Studies* and the *Annual Review of Law and Social Science,* both of which appeared in the early years of the 21st century. There are also journals on specialized subjects. For example, *Law and Human Behavior* concentrates on articles about psychology and law. The *Journal of Law and Economics* does the same for economists who look at law.

The field shows considerable vitality in many other countries as well. The Japanese counterpart to the Law and Society Association, established long before LSA, has hundreds of members. There are a number of national law-and-society organizations in Europe, and journals on the subject are published in, for example, Australia, Canada, France, Germany, the Netherlands, Italy, Japan and the United Kingdom. There is considerable activity in other countries too—for example, Spain and Mexico. At one time there was an active law-and-society group in Poland, and the fall of Communism has opened the door to further development in that country. There are, however, somewhat distinctive national styles. Many continental scholars who teach and write about law-and-society come from backgrounds in legal philosophy and tend to be more interested in large questions of theory rather than the nitty-gritty of empirical research. To be sure, there is also a tradition of empirical research in Europe, but the United States seems to be the leader in

---

8. On the history of the law and society movement and the Association, see Bryant Garth and Joyce Sterling, "From Legal Realism to Law and Society: Reshaping Law for the Last Stages of the Activist State," 32 *Law and Society Review* 409 (1998).

9. See, e.g., J. Willard Hurst, *The Growth of American Law: The Law Makers* (1950); J. Willard Hurst, *Law and the Conditions of Freedom in the Nineteenth–Century United States* (1956). See, for an assessment of Hurst's work, the collection of essays in 18 *Law and History Review*, No. 1 (Spring 2000).

research on the law in action. There is in this global world more and more interest in issues that transcend national boundaries. And today scholars of foreign law—those who study Japan, France, Russia or Latin America, for example—are more likely to be using a sociological approach than would have been true in past decades.

Law-and-society studies on the whole have not made as much of a dent in legal education as one might have expected. The Law and Society Association is flourishing, but the majority of its members are not legally trained and not associated with law schools. They are social scientists in political science, sociology, psychology, anthropology and economics departments. There is a scattering of philosophers, historians and others. A fair number of colleges and universities have departments of legal studies or offer courses and programs on criminal justice, business law or the like. In some of these programs, law-and-society studies form an important component. Probably there are over 1,500 people working in all sorts of disciplines. These scholars generate a substantial output of essays, review articles, research projects and monographs every year. There are, in addition, many criminologists, historians and other scholars who write about subjects that have intimate connections with the legal system but who do not identify themselves as law-and-society scholars. Their work is, of course, nonetheless extremely relevant.

With all of this output, it is fair to ask what the field has accomplished. What do we know that we did not know before? What are the insights, the contributions to understanding? A fair number of scholars have tried to come up with a general survey of the field, a synthesis or even some sort of general theory.[10] In the vast body of work, as Stewart Macaulay has put it: "social science and law has washed up a few shining nuggets."[11] He summed up some of the basic insights that the field has contributed, as follows:

> 1. *Law is not free.* There are barriers to access to the legal system which some people can jump far more easily than others.... When we turn to social regulation, we find that it involves costs which some can pass along to others. It usually is fruitful to ask who benefits from and who pays for any type of legal action. Often we will find that regulation operates as a kind of regressive taxation, burdening the have-nots far more than the haves.

10. See, for example, Richard Lempert and Joseph Sanders, *An Invitation to Law and Social Science: Desert, Disputes, and Distribution* (1986); Lawrence M. Friedman, *The Legal System: A Social Science Perspective* (1975); Roger Cotterrell, *The Sociology of Law: An Introduction* (2d ed. 1992); Donald Black, *Sociological Justice* (1989); Reza Banakar, *Merging Law and Sociology: Beyond the Dichotomies in Socio–Legal Research* (2003).

11. Stewart Macaulay, "Law and the Behavioral Sciences: Is There Any There There?"

6 *Law & Policy* 149, 152–55 (1984). Frank Munger, "Mapping Law and Society," in *Crossing Boundaries: Traditions and Transformations in Law and Society Research* 21, 42–55 (Austin Sarat et al. eds., 1998), looked at Macaulay's seven propositions and reported that fourteen years after he wrote, "our vision of the contemporary law and society field are remarkably consistent with the earlier empirical results summarized by Macaulay...."

2. *Law is delivered by actors with limited resources and interests of their own in settings where they have discretion.* "Street-level bureaucrats" such as police, assistant prosecuting attorneys, caseworkers, clerks of court, those handling intake at administrative agencies and many more, have discretion although no one planned it that way. This is true for a number of reasons. Policies conflict and the rules may be unclear. As a result, those who deal with the public may have a choice of goals to pursue or rationalizations for whatever they want to do to serve the public or their own self interest. Those who do the day-to-day work of a legal agency often are hard to supervise because they control the official version of events by writing reports in the files. Resource constraints often make it impossible to "go by the book" since officials cannot do everything mandated. If those enforcing a law cannot carry out all their duties, they must choose which of them, under what circumstances, they will attempt to implement. Those choices of "street-level bureaucrats" are unlikely to be random or neutral in their impact. They will be affected by folk wisdom or bias, reward and punishment structures, and self-interest.

3. *Many of the functions usually thought of as legal are performed by alternative institutions, and there is a great deal of interpenetration between what we call public and private sectors....*

4. *People, acting alone and in groups, cope with law and cannot be expected to comply passively.* Many people are able to ignore most legal commands, or redefine them to serve self-interest or "commonsense," and live with a vague and often inaccurate sense of the nature of law and legal process—all without encountering serious problems. There is great opportunity for evasion in a society that values privacy, civil liberties, and limited investment in government. Coping with the law can become a game that offsets any sense of obligation. Many participants in social fields and networks pass along techniques of evasion, legitimate breaking the law, honor the crafty, and even sanction those who would comply. The law is frequently uncertain and plausible arguments can be fashioned to rationalize much of what many people want to do. This means that there is great opportunity for bargaining in the shadow of the law or in the shadow of questionable assumptions about the law. Thus, people's view of the likely legal consequences of action at best affect but do not determine their behavior. Sometimes, however, the command of the law rings loud and clear and has direct impact on behavior. In short, the role of law is not something that can be assumed but must be established in every case.

5. *Lawyers play many roles other than adversary in a courtroom.* Lawyers' self-interest, and their view of what is best for a client, often dictates that litigation should be avoided, and lawyers seek other ways to provide service to clients. They tend to know who makes decisions and what kinds of appeals, legal and other types, are likely to be effective. They know how to bargain and how to manipulate situations so that

accommodations can be reached. Often they serve as coercive mediators, acting in settings where their profession itself is a tacit threat of trouble if people do not behave reasonably. Instead of pursuing only their client's immediate interest, lawyers often act as what Justice Brandeis called "counsel for the situation," seeking what they see as the best long term solution for all concerned. Other lawyers, with more or less success, seek to transform clients' perceptions about what is just, or at least tolerable. Often they deal with bruised egos and manage public relations far more than they vindicate clients' rights.... [T]he wide variety of roles played by lawyers is a factor in making the functioning of social institutions far more complex than formal descriptions assume. For example, many lawyers' stock in trade includes their contacts with officials, knowledge of acceptable rhetoric, and awareness of mutually advantageous possibilities. Thus, they are able to cut through formal channels and get things done. When this happens regularly, behavior in a corporation or a public agency no longer follows official procedures....

6. *Our society deals with conflict in many ways, but avoidance and evasion are important ones....* We may pass symbolic laws declaring the good, the true and the beautiful, but we leave enforcement to local option. We find social consensus at a high level of abstraction and so keep our doctrines ambiguous or contradictory. This avoids the costs of definition and of deciding that some interpretations of values are right while others are wrong. Thus, a simple means-and-ends view of law should be suspect....

7. *While law matters in American society, its influence tends to be indirect, subtle and ambiguous.* It is easy to find gaps between the promise and performance of our law. Americans are selectively law abiding.... Nonetheless, law matters in a number of ways. For example, many ideas that are part of our common normative vocabulary are crystallized in law, and they both help rationalize action and affect our expectations about the social world.... While the ability of the legal system to prompt social change that is unwanted by a large or powerful minority may be limited, often law can be the focus of a social movement, forcing reformers to define goals and select means to obtain them. Even failed reform efforts may influence the behavior of both proponents and opponents. Moreover, law can restrain power in many situations. For many reasons, those with power hesitate to exercise it too crudely. The effort to cloak an exercise of power with a mantle of right or to cover up abuses are costly exercises which, at times, deter action. Law and lawyers have helped gain accommodations for some of the less powerful by using legal symbols and procedures. In this culture even the counterattacks by the powerful have to be rationalized in legal rhetoric. This effort may affect both the form and substance of the way such battles are fought and resolved.

Stewart Macaulay is one of the editors of this book; naturally, he thinks highly of the field, and is cautiously impressed with its accomplishments. Not everybody agrees.[12] Some scholars think that the field is guilty of repetitiveness, triviality, spinning wheels.[13] Also, in the last generation or so, there are scholars who have raised some fairly fundamental questions about social science in general, and about the value of empirical research. This has spilled over into socio-legal research as well. Some qualitative scholars espouse what they call a more "interpretive," self-conscious style of examining legal phenomena while others do not. Regardless of orientation, qualitative researchers tend to pay more attention to the cultural meanings and ideologies that underlie legal phenomena; their work, though not quantitative, is nonetheless fundamentally empirical in nature. We will return to these issues at various points. After going through the material, readers should be able to judge for themselves whether the law-and-society enterprise has been worthwhile, and whether some or all of the criticisms directed at it are well-taken.

The various social sciences, after all, do not agree on methods, approaches, and points of view. In many ways, the economists stand apart from the other social scientists. In the law school world, "law and economics" refers to a movement which attempts to use the tools of neoclassical economics to critique legal rules in terms of efficiency and wealth-maximization. Some of its practitioners seem to feel that the other social sciences are weaklings, that they lack a solid unitary theory to give them backbone, and that many social sciences are tilted politically to the left.[14] On the other hand, some of the leading figures in law and economics work with theory rather than data. (Politically, too, they tilted to the right). But in recent years, many of the younger economists interested in law have shown much greater interest in grounding their work in a solid empirical basis. They are also reaching increasingly beyond a narrower economic scope in their efforts to understand law.

VI. What Lies Ahead?

In Chapter 2, we will deal with descriptions of the legal system. The general idea is that there are different ways of describing legal systems involving different methods and approaches. These affect the way one actually sees a legal system.

Chapter 3 asks the question: where does law come from? We examine ideas about the social sources of law, and the way different social contexts shape the form (and relative formality) of legal responses. The chapter also asks more particular questions about the emergence of laws, legal doctrines and legal institutions. How do we explain, say, why American courts began to

---

12. See, for example, Austin Sarat and Susan Silbey, "The Pull of the Policy Audience," 10 *Law & Policy* 97 (1988); David M. Trubek, "Where the Action Is: Critical Legal Studies and Empiricism," 36 *Stanford Law Review* 575 (1984).

13. Richard Abel, "Redirecting Social Studies of Law," 14 *Law & Society Review* 805 (1980).

14. See Richard A. Posner, "The Sociology of the Sociology of Law: A View from Economics," 2 *European Journal of Law & Economics* 265 (1995).

pay attention to gender discrimination, or why Congress passed a law outlawing discrimination on the basis of sex? This chapter will deal with pressure groups, public opinion, and related subjects, all of them touching on the question of where law comes from. It concludes by examining the way that society and law are in an influential ongoing interaction with each other.

Chapter 4, in a way, turns the question of Chapter 3 upside down. It asks about the impact of law. Congress passes a law, the President issues an executive order, or a court comes out with a decision. What happens next? What effect does any one of these have on the way people think or behave? The question of impact is actually quite complex, and it includes a whole range of subquestions. For example, it includes the much debated question of deterrence. Does the death penalty have any effect on the murder rate? How would social scientists go about answering this question? In this chapter, too, we ask how messages from the legal system get communicated to at least some of the public. We also examine the effect that the way these messages get transmitted has on obedience or disobedience to law. Questions of impact draw our attention to the limits of effective legal action. How much can lawmakers change the world by changing the law?

Chapter 5 deals with the structure of the legal system—its organizational shape—and what difference this structure might make. The chapter also introduces readers to the sociology of legal roles. That is, we look at the social organization and impact of the work of the main players and actors inside the system, especially judges and lawyers.

Most of the readings in the book have been written by Americans and are about the American legal system. There were always connections between legal systems, but in this global era the connections are denser and more complex. Chapter 6 invites us to look outside the United States and across history. It considers, first, the question of how different histories impact the development of law. It then turns to examine legal cultures—how they differ, how they are interrelated—including the impact of globalization on the legal order. Chapter 6 concludes by considering the interaction of language and culture in law.

In some ways this book is modeled after the typical law school casebook which provides raw materials and questions, but hesitates to give answers. The student is supposed to work out at least tentative answers for herself. The main points are not neatly summarized at the end of each section and chapter.

And the book also is not a "reader" in the social science tradition. The materials are used to develop certain major themes. There is a strong overall structure reflecting the judgments—perhaps the biases—of the authors. Opposing views are frequently paired. If you work with this book, you will have to deal with controversy and important questions that have no certain, fixed and knowable answers. This reflects, of course, the law school style of teaching. We think that it leads to active class participation and discussion. The many notes and citations after each article are meant to help students see what is at issue as well as making suggestions for those who might want to pursue some of these matters in more detail. (Some of the notes that introduce new topics begin with underlined headings as guideposts for the reader.)

We have taught from these materials as they took shape over time. For us, the book works. Generally, students respond favorably to the course. Some law students are a bit leery of the social science vocabulary and methods at first. Some students trained in the social sciences worry that they are not sure footed enough on the paths of the law. Our experience is that as the course rolls on, the students deal with common problems and distinctions between law students and others tend to blur and disappear.

We are amused that some law professors who are ready, willing and able to master the black arts of the Internal Revenue Code or the tangled web of the Rule Against Perpetuities, seem to turn pale when confronted with simple tables and graphs. And sociologists who think nothing of invading the world of medicine or religion sometimes treat the legal domain as if it were a cave inhabited by fire-eating dragons.

We have tried to avoid the more exotic methods and vocabulary of social science. Sometimes we offer explanations in notes and questions after readings. The law, too, is kept clean and simple. We feel that this book can be taught even by a law professor with little background or experience in the social sciences. Social scientists without legal training can also cope quite nicely. Perhaps the ideal teacher would have training or sophistication in both realms. More and more, law schools are hiring professors with doctorates in social science fields as well as law degrees. (Indeed, this describes one of the editors of this book). Nonetheless, such people are and will be rare enough so that this area is likely to remain open to amateurs in one field or another for a long time to come. That indeed is part of its charm and its potency.

CHAPTER 2

The Legal System at Work: What We Know and How We Know It

I. Introduction

One elementary job of the law-and-society movement—in some ways the fundamental job—is to describe exactly how the legal system works. The official pictures of the legal system—the way it would be described in an old-fashioned civics book for high school students; or the way it is supposed to work—is a long way from the messy reality of the living law. Nor does the way the law works fit with what most lay people (and probably most lawyers) think of it; and certainly, living law is not law as we see it on TV or in the movies.

The public has a lot of ideas about law, most of them unexamined, many of them probably wrong; and a lot of these ideas are quite negative. Some people think we would be better off as a society without so many lawyers, and without all the litigation that is choking the courts, ruining businesses, and so on. Some people feel that big government is eroding our freedoms. There is no reason why conventional wisdom should be necessarily <u>wrong</u>, but often enough it is not based on facts or on solid investigations.

But people, as we said, do have their ideas about law, legal systems, lawyers, legal process, and the like. Where do these ideas come from? The first part of this chapter asks this question. The rest of the chapter is devoted to a few examples of attempts to describe the legal system in action. Among other things, we want to raise the question: what is a scholar doing when he or she is attempting to describe the legal system? In what sense can a snapshot of the legal system in operation be "true"? There is an old saying that the camera does not lie; but cameras in fact do lie, or can be made to lie; and even when a photograph is not doctored, everything depends on the light, the size of the lens, and the skill and purpose of the photographer. In our exploration of the job of "describing" the legal system, we will also raise and discuss some fundamental issues of method.

II. Where do Ideas About Law & the Legal System Come From?

(2.1) Images of Law in Everyday Life: The Lessons of School, Entertainment and Spectator Sports

Stewart Macaulay

21 *Law & Society Review* 185 (1987).

One of the sources of our beliefs about authority, law, and the legal system, is what we learn in and from school. Writers reflecting on the functions of education distinguish what schools attempt to teach from lessons that students may learn just from going to school. Just as the sociology of law has long distinguished the law in action from the law on the books, the sociology of education distinguishes the announced curriculum from the curriculum in action. Schools are supposed to pass on knowledge and ways of thinking. Throughout our history, Americans have called for schools to train young people so they have good work habits. . . .

But that is not the only agenda in school; there is a hidden curriculum as well. Students learn about coping with multiple authority structures. Administrators, teachers, coaches, and even other students all make demands. Some students get along by going along. Others practice passive resistance or evasion. Only a few rebels openly challenge the system. . . . I will consider, in turn, the formal and hidden curricula.

A. *Teaching about the Legal System*

Schools attempt to teach aspects of the legal system. . . . Insofar as they say anything at all, textbooks offer a simplified, formal picture of government, courts, trials, lawyers, and police. They present theoretical explanations of the functions of government agencies as if they were empirical descriptions of how, say, the police actually operate. There may be some change taking place today. Many have attacked the "dumbing down" of textbooks and called for them to deal with difficult issues. . . . Modern high school history books deal largely with institutions rather than individuals. Branding a president or senator a hero or a villain might offend some parents or newspaper columnists. There is little, if any, consideration of the political philosophy of the framers of the Constitution. The books report no fundamental conflicts of value or interest. In this "natural disaster" theory of history, things just happen, and the books make no attempt to explain why. History is just one damn thing after another.

Furthermore, the books say Americans always solve problems: Monopolies threatened America in the late nineteenth century. Congress responded with the Sherman Act, and the implicit message is that the statute resolved all the difficulties. It was hard for farmers to get goods to market in the same era, and so Congress naturally responded by creating the Interstate Commerce Commission. Again, the implicit message is that the ICC solved all the problems.

Textbooks are not this way by accident. They are created by private publishers who must market them profitably. In many states, government agencies adopt texts for use in the schools. Adoptions spell profit; rejections make success difficult if not impossible. Vigorous political struggles take place over the content of these books. People demanding the teaching of creation science and attacking secular humanism pull one way, while those concerned with the treatment of women and people of color push the other....

B. *That's Entertainment!*

School is not the only place Americans learn about the legal system and coping with authority. We go to the movies and watch television, and many dramatic shows involve law. Indeed, old films and TV series never die. Cable television and VCRs recycle them over and over again. Many Americans are able to discuss plots, characters, and actors from ten to twenty years of western, cop, private eye, and other films and TV series. We must wonder about the lessons learned here. For example, *Star Chamber* appeared a few summers ago. In this film an evil creep is tried for killing little old ladies to steal their Social Security payments. He evades just punishment by asserting his constitutional rights. The Warren court's rules about criminal prosecution force the judge to throw out the case. But then the judge discovers that other judges have solved the problem by direct action: They hire hit men to kill the creeps. The *Wall Street Journal*'s (August 17, 1988:22) editorial writers seemed to approve of this solution: "Even in our chic New York uptown theater, the audience cheered when the judges' hit man blew away the little-old-ladies-killer." Perhaps everyone who saw the film took it as just a movie. Perhaps not.

More Americans learn about their legal system from television and film than from firsthand experience. Few of us have ever been in a squad car, a jail, a courtroom, a lawyer's office, an administrative hearing, or a legislative committee meeting. Most of us know these places only from film and TV, but there is a lot of such teaching material around.

However, film and TV offer entertainment and not social science. Viewers who rely only on these reports for information are badly misled. Entertainment programs misrepresent the nature and amount of crime in the United States. Murder makes a much better show than embezzlement or fraud, and so drama tells us that society is a great deal more violent than official statistics indicate. Entertainment rarely shows street crime other than drug offenses. Television also offers a number of false or doubtful propositions. For example, it tells us that criminals are white males between the ages of twenty and fifty, that bad guys usually are businessmen or professional criminals, and that crime is almost always unsuccessful in the end.

Television and film also often misrepresent the roles of actors in the legal system. With few exceptions, police are in action constantly. Car chases, running after criminals on foot, and gunfights are all in a day's work. Lawyers are portrayed atypically....

Entertainment also presents important issues of civil liberties in distorted ways. Often the audience knows that the villain committed the crime, and we have no reason to worry about mitigating factors. We are the eyewitnesses, and matters are clear cut. Trials would be a waste of time. Television crime is solved by killing or capturing the guilty party. Leading characters often administer retribution on the spot. The hero shoots bad guys in a gunfight or sees them incinerated when their car goes off the road in a high-speed chase. We see arrests but seldom arraignments, pretrial motions, plea bargaining, or jury selection. Film and TV do not tell us about sentences or what part of a sentence is likely to be served.

However, occasionally TV and film do show their versions of trials. Messages about due process often conflict. On one hand, the defense lawyer as a champion of the innocent is a stock character. In these shows, the important message is that the police and prosecutor can be wrong. Sometimes the defendant is taking the rap for another, but usually the drama turns on the wrongly accused facing a mistaken or corrupt prosecution....

[Macaulay also discusses the lessons of spectator sport for U.S. public legal culture.]

... I drew several contradictory conclusions from my survey of writing about education, television and film, and spectator sport. On one hand, these reflections of legal culture tell us that we should comply with law, respect authority, and accept society as it is. At the same time, we see good guys who rationalize evasion and shading of the law and who successfully challenge authority. We also see society and those who hold official positions as corrupt. I'll first tell one side of this story and then the other.

These cultural sources offer strong lessons about the importance of fitting into society as it exists without raising questions. They teach us about some laws and reinforce our sense that certain interests are important. For example, at least the express messages are that murder is bad, private property should be respected, and people should keep promises. Furthermore, teachers, script writers, coaches, and commentators usually take the basic assumptions of society as given. Education, TV and film and spectator sports all rest on assumptions that are not debated. For example, there are hierarchies of authority, and those on top can and should direct those under them. Many also learn that you can't fight the teacher, the coach, the principal; the cops, or city hall. Beginning in kindergarten, if not preschool, parents and teachers tell us that we get along if we go along. Of course, some rebel and enjoy making trouble. However, the rest see what happens to them. If authority is able to apply sanctions to the troublemakers, the rest of us receive a strong message about the wisdom of taking the path of least resistance.

Whatever the accepted leeways and evasions, the rules are the rules. Although we may debate the designated hitter rule in baseball's American League, few think about whether three strikes should be an out. Few argue that a field goal in football should count other than three points or that a runner must stay in bounds. In short, we receive a powerful message that those in charge can act, and we accept the basic rules that constitute the game without debate.

These cultural sources also tell us that bad people cause problems, rather than society and its institutions. We all faced the terrible teacher or the arbitrary coach during our school days. Few of us knew enough to make more than a vague, negative indictment of our school or schools in general. Drama offers bad police and officials, but it seldom suggests that the institutions of government themselves are flawed. We even accept owners and schools responding to losing sports teams by firing the coach, although that seldom solves the problem. . . .

We must study the symbols related to law found in American culture. Children's schooling, private eye television shows, and spectator sports all display these templates, themes, or story lines. I'm not suggesting that we waste time on trivial matters. The familiar images shown again and again on film and television and both the formal and hidden curricula of our schools reflect, teach, and reinforce what most people know about things legal. And these ideas and attitudes matter.

NOTES AND QUESTIONS

1.   Macaulay argues that schools as well as the mass media "educate" us about law and legal process. Not much has been written about the impact of schools. The role of movies and television seems a bit more obvious. It seems reasonable to expect that people get many of their ideas about law and legal process from movies and television; and that the mass media are in some ways as powerful in "educating" people as the schools and churches. Exactly what, though, do they learn from movies and television? In "Law, Lawyers, and Popular Culture," 98 *Yale Law Journal* 1579, 1588 (1989), Lawrence Friedman points out that popular culture stresses criminal justice, a point that Macaulay also makes. Friedman says: "No songs have been composed about the Robinson–Patman Act, no movies produced about capital gains tax;" and there is little or nothing, too, in movies or TV about "Medicare, dog licenses, zoning laws, or overtime parking. On the other hand, television would shrivel up and die without cops, detectives, crimes, judges, prisons, guns and trials."

He goes on to say: "Suppose our legal sources were all destroyed in a nuclear nightmare which wiped out the West Digest, the Federal Register, the revised statutes ... and all casebooks;" and the only sources that a later generation, "digging in the ruins," could recover was the "archives of NBC television." The "diggers would certainly get a distorted picture of the legal system. They would learn little or nothing about property law, tax law, regulation of business, and very little about tort law or even family law; but they would find an enormous amount of material on police, murder, deviance, rape, and organized crime.''

2. Note the paradox implicit in the material presented thus far: in schools, students get an inaccurate picture of the legal system—a picture which is usually much too bland and tidy; the media present a different, and very sensational picture, which is in some ways the opposite—and this too is wildly inaccurate.

3. <u>Why do the media distort the legal system?</u> Obviously, the drive to make money is an enormous influence, probably a decisive influence, on the media. Trials are powerful dramas, and they make for good television shows, or movies. Hearings before the Securities and Exchange Commission are boring; nobody would watch a program that focused on administrative procedures.

Steven Garber and Anthony G. Bower looked at newspaper coverage of a set of U.S. trials, occurring between 1985 and 1996, in which plaintiffs brought lawsuits for product liability injuries against auto companies. Basically, newspapers <u>did not</u> report on cases where the auto company won. A number of factors seemed to account for newspaper coverage: big awards and punitive damages, for example—also, whether somebody died in the accident, and whether the cars in question had been recalled. Steven Garber and Anthony G. Bower, "Newspaper Coverage of Automotive Product Liability Verdicts," 33 *Law & Society Review* 93 (1999).

One can think of good reasons why newspapers would find these cases more interesting than the ones they ignore. Still, is it possible that the media <u>deliberately</u> mislead the public? Do they manipulate the data? This charge has been made, particularly with regard to tort law. Businesses that have been on the receiving end of tort suits have been clamoring, sometimes quite successfully, for "reform" that would limit tort claims against them. Their cause is helped by campaigns to persuade the public that the system has gone amok. Attacks on civil juries, as Stephen Daniels has argued ["The Question of Jury Competency and the Politics of Civil Justice Reform: Symbols, Rhetoric, and Agenda Setting," 52 *Law and Contemporary Problems* 269, 309 (1989)], are "an integral part of a concerted campaign aimed at the enactment of substantial change in the civil justice system that would benefit the insurance industry, physicians, certain manufacturers, and others." The strategy used includes "horror stories" about the behavior of courts and juries—stories which are "grossly inaccurate and distorted," and sometimes even "fabricated." On this point, see also William Haltom and Michael McCann, *Distorting the Law: Politics, Media, and the Litigation Crisis* (2004), and Chapter 3, Reading 3.5. But why do people believe these "horror stories"?

Political scientist Ross Cheit has urged further study of this issue, with regard to newspaper reporting on child sexual abuse. His research on newspapers in Rhode Island found patterns of distorted reporting of child sexual abuse cases:

> This study ... demonstrates two implications of dwelling on atypical cases.... First, the coverage of child sexual abuse gives an exaggerated sense of "stranger danger" by highlighting stories about strangers and almost never mentioning anything that would suggest incest.... Second, disproportionate coverage to long sentences leaves the mistaken impression that those are common outcomes and that the criminal justice system is much more stringent than it is in fact.

Ross Cheit, "What Hysteria? A Systematic Study of Newspaper Coverage of Accused Child Molesters," 27 *Child Abuse & Neglect* 607, 619 (2003). Cheit notes a similarity "to the impressions of the criminal justice system conveyed by newspaper reporting" in that they are based on a few atypical examples:

> The most unusual cases receive the most coverage, while the most common cases receive little or no coverage. The coverage of child sexual abuse cases also suffers from the same defects of most crime reporting: it focuses too much on arrests and arraignment without reporting on disposition or sentences, or providing a sense of system-wide outcomes.

Id. at 620. Here we find some themes reminiscent of McCann and Haltom's findings. Cheit did not find that sensationalism for commercial purposes was typical of newspaper coverage in these cases, but recommended further study at a national level to clarify the wider picture. With child abuse cases, there are many interesting questions as to why the public accepts particular pictures of what is happening, ranging from whether they are influenced by cultural conceptions surrounding families and children to how deliberate political efforts might be impacting public perceptions. What kinds of factors would you want to examine?

4. <u>Film versus television</u>: It is easy to lump movies and television together, in discussing the influence and the role of the mass media. But the movies may present quite different images of law than ordinary television does. Naomi Mezey and Mark C. Niles make this point in their article, "Screening the Law: Ideology and Law in American Popular Culture," 28 *Columbia Journal of Law and the Arts* 91 (2005). Both types of medium, according to Mezey and Niles, convey important ideological messages. But they argue that movies have more freedom than does television. Movies do not depend on advertisers, for one thing. They range from block-busters to small "art" movies produced by independents. This means that there is a broad spectrum of views. Television, on the other hand, has a "fairly narrow ideological range," probably because it is "almost entirely dependant on corporate advertisers" (id., at 170). Hence, Mezey and Niles conclude, you are more likely to find a movie that mounts a powerful critique of institutions, including legal institutions—or that levels a political attack on aspects of American society, than you are to find a television show with a similarly critical message. See also John Denvir, *Legal Reelism: Movies as Legal Texts* xiii (1996), for an argument that American films have been a source of critique.

Does this seem correct to you? Under this theory, would you expect there to be a difference between cable and network television shows? Mezey and Niles note that there is "more daring programming" on cable channels, in part because they have a more diverse set of relationships with advertisers than does network television. However, even the History Channel has had to pull programming because of issues with the sponsors of a particular show. Id. Nonetheless, there are literally dozens and dozens of cable channels, and the "ideology" of Fox News is not the same as the ideology of CNN, or of Comedy Central. One can also ask, what is it that people learn from talk radio? Or from daytime soap operas? Mezey and Niles conclude that the broad spectrum of interests and positions represented in the mass media is far too complicated to sum up "monolithically." They stress that it is important to analyze differences in context such as "structures of production, profits, and narrative."

There is a growing literature on the way law is represented in popular cultural forms such as film. One ongoing debate in the literature is the question of whether films actually have an impact on public attitudes, in addition to reflecting and depicting society. See Michael Asimow, "Bad Lawyers in the Movies," 24 *Nova Law Review* 533 (2000); see generally, e.g., Tara Emmers–Sommer and Mick Allen, "Surveying the Effect of Media Effects: A Meta–Analytic Summary of the Media Effects Research in Human Communications Research," 25 *Human Communications Research* 478 (1999). Michael Asimov points out an interesting example of the way that formal regulation itself can interrupt the relationship between film and social trends. During the late 1920s, under mounting threat of censorship by the federal government, the film industry imposed its own set of censoring regulations known as the "Hays Code." Michael Asimow, "Divorce in the Movies: From the Hays Code to Kramer v. Kramer," 24 *Legal Studies Forum* 221 (2000). Because the Code heavily limited the kinds of stories that could be told about divorce, Asimov notes that films about marriage failed to reflect or speak to social trends for some time.

5. <u>Live television coverage and public knowledge</u>: Is the level of knowledge about the legal system going up? There is much more live coverage of aspects of the American legal system than there was some decades ago. Hearings on the nomination of Supreme Court justices are now broadcast live. Members of the public could, if they wished, hear the back-and-forth between Senators and the (successful) nominee for Chief Justice (Roberts) in 2005; and later, the (also successful) nominee for Associate Justice, Samuel Alito. Some trials are televised, and can be seen on Court TV.

Sensational trials are also covered by what one might call "tabloid TV," as well as in newspapers and magazines. Scott Peterson was accused of killing his wife, Laci, who was pregnant, and dumping her body in San Francisco Bay, just before Christmas, 2002. The case, and the subsequent trial, were covered in enormous detail in the press and on TV. Peterson was convicted in December, 2004, and sentenced to death. Probably many more people in the country could identify Scott Peterson at the time than could identify their

Congressman. The Peterson case was, of course, only one example of a whole series of dramatic murder trials that captured the public imagination, and which provide fodder for "tabloid TV."

What, do you suppose, is the impact of the kind of coverage the Peterson case received? Do trials of this sort give the public a better picture of how the system operates, or do they just further distort reality, and project false images?

6. Public and legal professionals' opinion on law: Despite all of the coverage in newspapers, TV and on the internet, how much do people actually know about legal affairs? An opinion poll in February 2004 asked people to name the Vice President of the United States—77% could do so. But only 22% could name the Chief Justice (Rehnquist) of the United States. An earlier poll, in 1989, asked people if they could name a Justice of the Supreme Court other than the Chief Justice. 23% could name Sandra Day O'Connor; but in next place came Anthony Kennedy—7% of respondents could name him. Only 3% could identify Justice Breyer. (Source: AEI Public Opinion Study, Public Opinion on the Supreme Court, http://www.aei.org/publicopinion 16; as updated January 9, 2006).

Nonetheless, the public does generally hold the Supreme Court in high esteem. See www.pollingreport.com/Court.htm, 3.2.2007 (reporting that Gallup polls show generally positive approval ratings for the Supreme Court). The same may be true for courts in general; one study indicates that people who have actual experience with courts feel more favorably toward them than those who do not have such experience. See Herbert M. Kritzer and John Voelker, "Familiarity Breeds Respect: How Wisconsin Citizens View Their Courts," 82 *Judicature* 58 (1998). Other studies have indicated that, although people may be disappointed in the outcome of their cases in court, many of them somehow maintain faith in the system of justice as a whole, including the courts. See note 5, Reading 3.8.

People do not, however, feel quite so kindly about lawyers. One sign of the low state of opinion about lawyers is the incredible proliferation of lawyer jokes. It is fair to say that almost none of these jokes is complimentary. For a careful study of these jokes, and what they mean, see Marc Galanter, *Lowering the Bar: Lawyer Jokes and Legal Culture* (2005). Where do these negative ideas come from? Galanter has cataloged and traced hundreds of lawyer jokes. There are, to be sure, jokes about doctors, priests, psychiatrists, and so on; but nothing like the flood of jokes about lawyers. On the legal profession in general, see below, at Chapter 5.

The discussion thus far has been about popular legal culture—what lay people think and know about law. There are over a million lawyers in the United States, and they, together with judges and other members of the legal profession, have their own viewpoints, attitudes, assumptions, and prejudices—in short, their own legal culture.

Research on lawyers and judges has given us some indications about the legal culture of these professionals. One recent study emphasizes how attorneys' experiences in particular practice settings affect their views of law and legal representation. Gwyneth Williams, "Looking at Joint Custody through the Language and Attitudes of Attorneys," 26 *Justice System Journal* 1 (2005). See also discussions in Chapter 5. Research also indicates that attorneys' legal culture changes over time. Fore example, in her interview study of Illinois attorneys, Susan Shapiro quotes an older lawyer who mourns the inroads he has experienced on his role as a problem-solver in all kinds of cases, from those involving families to business law:

> Years ago, it never bothered me that, if there was a family dispute . . . if the two of them came in the office and I tried to resolve it. It never bothered me that two brothers owned a business and they were having troubles within themselves, that I wouldn't pull them into the office and try to knock heads and get the thing resolved. And it might even wind up drafting some type of an agreement between the two of them. . . . In a certain sense, I feel it's extremely unfortunate. I think that I could avoid a lot of the litigation that's going on. . . . In the past, you were always looked at as the family attorney, as the attorney for the business. The kids got in trouble, why, you always were called and you found a way of taking care of this and that. . . . And you could sit in the shareholder meetings and let 'em holler at each other. And you could make the decision for 'em and everything else and not feel that you were getting into some kind of a conflict. . . . I think that's part of my responsibility in having gotten to that point with the family. But in today's world, . . . with the concept of the development of some of the conflicts of interests, the smartest thing would be just to wash your hands and walk away from it. I have a hard time doing that.

Susan Shapiro (quoting attorney), *Tangled Loyalties: Conflict of Interest in Legal Practice* 82 (2002). This a distinctly anti-formalist view of the law, which takes a dim view of efforts to impose "black-letter" conflict of interests rules from above onto the practice of law on the ground. Shapiro's book offers a detailed examination of how attorneys negotiate between the messy everyday problems of their real-world practices and the formal rules that regulate their conduct (which remain important in many ways despite all the difficulties of translation). There are also interesting literatures on the legal cultures of legal professionals in other kinds of practice settings, such as "cause" lawyers, and others (and see Reading 2.6 and notes, as well as readings in Chapter 5).

One might wonder to what extent and how might these or other professional views "trickle down" to people outside the profession? How much, do you imagine, do the views of legal professionals influence the coverage of law, and attitudes toward law, expressed in newspapers, magazines, on television, and in the movies? One mechanism by which this can occur is through organized efforts by parts of the bar; as we will see in Chapter 3, one example of this can be found in the arena of "tort reform," where the plaintiffs' bar did attempt (ineffectively) to influence public opinion about tort law and their role as attorneys (Reading 3.5 and notes). Another mechanism is laypeople's own personal experience with lawyers and the legal system. As Sarat and Felstiner documented some time ago, some divorce attorneys convey to their clients an image of the legal system as unpredictable—dependent on hard-to-predict differences among judges and other "ground-level" factors. (See Chapter 5, Reading 5.5.)

7. Law in everyday experience and "legal consciousness": There are many ways for laypeople to learn first-hand about the legal system. Almost everybody has some experience with traffic and parking tickets. In the early 21st century, there were millions of people whose experience also included jail time, or probation, or juvenile court; or who were jurors or witnesses in a trial, or who were questioned or deposed in connection with a civil case. Many people have used lawyers—to buy or sell a house, to get a divorce or to cope with child custody or support. Business people have to deal with licensing and other government agencies. Old people cope with the Medicare system. Some taxpayers are audited every year.

Regardless of what people know about the legal system, or how it impinges on their lives, what determines how they actually use it? The police constitute a branch of the legal system with which people often come into contact. Working class and poor people may be more familiar with the police than with most parts of the government; they often try to make use of the police to cope with neighborhood problems, or to deal with with family disputes. See Barbara Yngvesson, *Virtuous Citizens, Disruptive Subjects: Order and Complaint in a New England Court* (1993). Yngvesson talks about how people sometimes go to the lower courts with such problems as neighborhood fights and teenage runaways. There they confront the clerks of court—and it is the clerks who, very often, handle the situation. What the citizens think of the law and know about the law is thus determined in large part by the work of these clerks. (And see Chapter 3, Reading 3.1).

Patricia Ewick and Susan Silbey, in The *Common Place of Law: Stories from Everyday Life* (1998), took a look at the role of "legality" in everyday life. Legality they defined as "the meanings, sources of authority, and cultural practices that are commonly recognized as legal, regardless of who employs them or for what ends." The authors recognized that there is "a sense of the legal that exists independently of its institutional manifestation." (p. 22). They define "three predominant types of legal consciousness" (p. 47). People's relationship to legality can be "before the law," that is, as a source of authority which is formal, hierarchical, and separate from ordinary life; "with the law," meaning that people use law, deploy it, treat it as a tool, a means to an end; and "against the law," that is, resisting and getting around the law. In other words, they are trying to capture the slippery and multiform ways in which ordinary people experience "legality," and try to cope with it.

See also the discussion of work by Sally Engle Merry and others in Chapter 3, notes accompanying Reading 3.9. Merry described the ways that citizens in a northeastern city, who had experience in the lower criminal and civil courts, understood the legal system—as well as how their court experiences affected that understanding.

8.   The push and pull of legal ideas in legal consciousness: Ewick and Silbey's book, mentioned above, helped stimulate a "wave of scholarship about legal consciousness." This statement comes from Anna–Maria Marshall and Scott Barclay, "In Their Own Words: How Ordinary People Construct the Legal World," 28 *Law & Social Inquiry* 617 (2003). Their essay is an introduction to a symposium issue with the same title. In their essay, Marshall and Barclay remark that in "legal consciousness research, the push and pull of legal ideas lie at the heart of modern explanations of the texture of law in our everyday existence. On one side is the pull of the law in constructing and constraining individual actions and decisions." The constraints are legal rules and regulations, and "social norms designed to maintain existing arrangements of power and order." Ordinary people have "acquiesced or grown accustomed to these formal rules that govern behavior." The rules and norms help shape everyday life; they make the status quo seem natural and normal.

On the other hand, there is also the "push" factor—"individuals' own interpretations of law," which gives the law in action a "dynamic force." Even as "legality constrains the range of accepted options ... people nevertheless have opportunities to redefine and challenge those constraints;" hence "legality provides a means of resistance," as well as a force that upholds and strengthens existing forces.

What are the "push" and the "pull" factors that mold legal consciousness and legal action with regard to, say, the death penalty? the abortion controversy? the rights of handicapped people?

For an empirical study of "legal consciousness" with regard to one particular issue, see Laura Beth Nielsen, "Situating Legal Consciousness: Experiences and Attitudes of Ordinary Citizens about Law and Street Harassment," 34 *Law and Society Review* 1055 (2000).

9.   In Chapter 3, we will deal with the difference between "legal consciousness" and "legal culture," another commonly used concept in law and society studies. On legal culture, see Lawrence M. Friedman, "The Place of Legal Culture in the Sociology of Law," in Michael Freeman, ed., 8 *Law and Sociology* 185 (Current Legal Issues, 2005); for a critique of the concept, see Roger Cotterrell, "The Concept of Legal Culture," in David Nelken, ed., *Comparing Legal Cultures*, at 13 (1997); see also Lawrence M. Friedman, "The Concept of Legal Culture: A Reply," in Nelken, ed., p. 33; and David Nelken, "Using the Concept of Legal Culture," 29 *Australian Journal of Legal Philosophy* 1 (2004).

III. The Formal Legal System in Operation

(A) Criminal Processes

(2.2) Fair Treatment or Preferred Outcome? The Impact of Police Behavior on Victim Reports of Domestic Violence Incidents

Laura J. Hickman and Sally S. Simpson

37 *Law & Society Review* 607 (2003).

[There has been an ongoing effort for a number of years now to address the problem of domestic violence through the legal system. A core debate revolves around whether the police should be required to arrest abusers once they have been called by a domestic violence victim. On the one hand, some scholars argue that mandatory arrest disempowers the victims by taking away their choice as to whether to press charges. On the other hand, some express concern that victims' fear might prevent them from truly expressing their preferences. In an attempt to measure the efficacy of police procedures, researchers have tried to discern what factors influence whether a victim will call for help a second time if the domestic violence continues. Hickman and Simpson point out that research has proceeded along two separate lines—(1) a focus on whether the victim obtained her preferred outcome (arrest or non-arrest); and (2) a focus on how the police treated the victim. The authors here bring these two separate lines of inquiry together, asking whether a desired outcome or favorable treatment by police (procedural justice) mattered more in a victim's future decision to call for help.]

Hypotheses

  . . . A common assertion is that domestic violence victims (and victims in general) who have negative experiences with police will refrain from calling them for assistance in the future. It is argued that bad experiences with police lead to negative expectations about future interaction and thus decisions not to seek police involvement. . . . There are two common hypotheses about how police behavior may impact victim attitude or expectations, which in turn impact reporting. One hypothesis is that police demeanor toward victims, . . . increases or decreases future reporting behavior. For example, victims who perceive that police are hostile or blaming are less likely to call them for assistance than victims who perceive that police are caring, supportive, and concerned. . . . Hereafter, we refer to this as the process hypothesis. The second hypothesis concerns attitudes or expectations formed as a result of the outcome of police involvement, e.g., whether offenders are arrested or ordered away from victims, and how this police action fits with victims' preference of outcomes. According to this hypothesis, victims who get the outcome they want from police are more likely to utilize them in the future than victims whose preference did not match the outcome. This assertion (we refer to it as the outcome hypothesis) commonly appears in arguments against the adoption of mandatory arrest laws. . . .

These two hypotheses are repeatedly mentioned in the victim reporting and domestic violence literature. Yet they are not well developed, discussed relative to one another, or combined into a single hypothesis about possible interactive effects of both the process and outcome of police involvement on future reporting behavior. Rather than serving as the focus of empirical investigation, these hypotheses are often proposed to account for unexpected research results. . . .

As an introduction to this line of empirical investigation, we present an exploratory analysis of the possible impact of police behavior on the subsequent reporting of female domestic violence victims. This study tests the two predominant hypotheses, i.e., the process and outcome hypotheses. The initial challenge is determining how to operationalize the two hypotheses in a manner consistent with their discursive definitions in the available literature. Fortunately, the meaning of the outcome hypothesis is straightforward, making a measurement scheme clear. This hypothesis, articulated in opposition to mandatory arrest laws, states that a call to police will be more likely when the outcome of a previous call was consistent with a victim's preference.

In theoretical terms, the outcome hypothesis can be understood as reflective of a social learning process. . . . Social learning theory predicts that behavior will be elicited and strengthened if it has been positively or negatively reinforced. In this case, victims will be more apt to call the police if, in previous encounters, police actions were consistent with their preferences. Importantly, social learning theory would not give greater weight to one outcome over another (i.e., arrest, mediation, or separation). . . . Therefore, victims who received a preferred outcome, regardless of what it is, should be more apt to call the police again under conditions of revictimization.

Another way to theoretically contextualize the outcome hypothesis is to situate it within an instrumental view of procedural justice . . . According to this viewpoint, disputants define procedural justice primarily in control terms, i.e., procedures will be viewed as fair to the extent that disputants maintain significant control over important life decisions. Fair procedures, according to this theory, are those in which disputant preferences are exercised. Thus, when police act according to the preferences of victims, the victims are more satisfied with the procedure (i.e., the police) and more apt to think it fair. This condition increases the likelihood that victims will utilize the police again in response to future victimization . . .

With regard to the process hypothesis, a measurement strategy is not as self-evident because it has been articulated in number of different ways. . . . Overall, it seems that the commonality in the numerous descriptions is whether police treat victims fairly during their interaction. Consequently, testing the process hypothesis requires operationalization of the term fair treatment.

Theories of procedural justice provide explicit criteria to assess whether individuals perceive fair treatment from authorities.... Tyler and Lind[1] decompose procedural justice into three factors that represent independent influences on individual perception of fair treatment: standing, neutrality, and trust. The standing component of procedural justice refers to the extent to which individuals are treated as valued group members—with politeness, dignity, and respect. The neutrality component refers to perceptions about authorities' bias, honesty, and use of accurate and full information to make decisions. Trust refers to perceptions of the intentions of the authorities to act fairly, show concern for individual needs, and behave in an ethical manner.... Consistent with the policy debates, we focus on whether receiving procedural or distributive justice from the police affects the likelihood that domestic violence victims will utilize the police again following subsequent victimization.

Methodology

[Five experiments were conducted by the National Institute of Justice, called Spouse Assault Replication Program Experiments. Hickman and Simpson chose the Metro–Dade County (Florida) experiment for their own work. The experiment was designed to test whether "arrest produced a deterrent effect" on abusers, comparing cases in which an arrest was made with cases where one was not. Data were collected from August 1987 to July 1989. The cases selected were cases where the police thought there was "probable cause" to arrest for a misdemeanor battery offense against a spouse. All were cases where the victim was an adult woman; there was no violence against the police; and there were no "warrants, injunctions, or criminal protective orders against either the suspect or the victim."

The cases had been randomly assigned to two categories. In one, the suspect was handcuffed, arrested, and held in jail—average jail time was 14.6 hours. In the other category, the victims were given a "brochure on their legal rights." The police then left.

Hickman and Simpson used "victim interview data" as the basis of their study. There were 907 eligible cases; 594 victims completed the "initial interview;" 65% of these completed a "six-month follow-up interview." This came to 42% of the 907 originally eligible cases.]

Sample Description

Because of the focus of the present research, we identified the subsample of victims who suffered some form of subsequent victimization that may or may not be reported to police. In both the initial interview and six-month follow-up interview, victims were asked whether there had been any form of revictimization since the experimental incident. Specifically, in both interviews victims were asked four questions about the behavior of the offender

---

1. T. R. Tyler & E. A. Lind, "A Relational Model of Authority to Groups," in M. Zanna, ed., *Advances in Experimental Psychology* (1992).

following the initial experimental incident, and these were classified into four categories of revictimization. Since the experimental incident, had the offender (1) hit, slapped, or tried to hurt the victim; (2) hit, slapped, or tried to hurt a family member; (3) made any threats to physically harm the victim, a family member, or damage property; and/or (4) actually damaged property?

Of the 594 interviewed victims, 396 did not answer yes to any of these questions in either the initial or the follow-up interview (or did not complete the follow-up interview), and we thus excluded them from our subsample, leaving 198 remaining cases. Of those, we excluded 18 cases because they were missing data on the dependent variable. Thus, the subsample we used in the present study consisted of 180 cases. Of the 180 cases in the revictimized subsample, follow-up interviews are missing for 46 women. We retain these cases because all had been revictimized before the initial interview and therefore had the opportunity to consider calling police for help in light of their experiences with police during the experimental incident.

One considerable restriction on the generalizability of our findings is the large amount of missing data that plagues the Dade County victim interview data. The question that arises relates to how well this group of located, cooperative victims represents the full group of 907 eligible victims. Victims who could not be located or refused to cooperate may be more seriously victimized, may live in greater fear of the offender, may be more likely to be homeless, or may experience more household instability than those present in the sample. As a result, this study's sample may underrepresent high-risk victims. We found no significant differences between the demographic characteristics of victims who completed and those who did not complete the follow-up interview. In a comparison of the characteristics of the group of all 907 eligible victims to the 594 who completed the initial interview, we uncovered significant differences in victim employment status and race. Employed victims (likely those with a higher level of stability) were more likely to participate in the initial interview, as were blacks and Hispanics relative to whites. Given that race effects have been found in some victim reporting studies, ... we understand that any race effects we uncovered in this study may be due to biases built into our sample. Yet given the exploratory nature of this study, the Dade County data provided a reasonable first test of the process and outcome hypotheses....

Of the 180 women in our sample, the majority were either black (41%) or Hispanic (23%) (See Table 1). Offenders and victims were from the same racial group in 87% of the cases. Victims ranged in age from 18 to 80, with an average age of 32. Most (69%) had achieved at least a high school diploma and were employed at the time of the experimental incident (63%), working on average about 40 hours per week. About one in three stated that they were not dependent at all on the offender for financial support, while a similar share stated that they were totally or very dependent on the offender. Most offenders (81%) were husbands or ex-husbands (4%) of the victim. Generally, the relationships were lengthy, with the mean length of relationship being nearly nine years. Nearly 90% of the victims were living with the offender at the time of the experimental domestic violence incident.

Table 1.   Victim Sample Demographic Characteristics

Victim Sample Characteristics	Number N = 180[1]	Valid Percent[2]
Race/Ethnicity		
Black	73	40.8
White	60	33.3
Hispanic	41	22.8
Other	5	2.8
Intraracial Relationship	156	86.6
Relation to Offender		
Current or Former Wife	152	84.5
Current or Former Girlfriend	28	15.6
Education		
Some High School/Equivalent	54	30.7
Graduated High School	60	34.1
Trade School or Some College	45	25.6
Graduated College	17	9.7
Employed at Least Part–Time	113	62.8
Unemployed	67	37.2
Financial Independence of Offender		
Totally or Very Dependent	66	36.6
Moderately Dependent	29	16.1
Somewhat or Not at All Dependent	85	47.2
	Mean	s.d.
Age	32	8.5
Length of Relationship in Years	9.9	8.3

[1]May not total 180 due to missing data.
[2]May not total 100% due to rounding.

For most of the women in the sample, the experimental incident was not the first time they had suffered victimization at the hands of this partner. In the six months prior to the experimental incident, about 65% had been hit, slapped, or hurt in some way. Also during this period, 20 (11%) reported that other family members had been hit or hurt, and a little more than half of these were children. About one in three women stated that the offender had damaged property, and 40% reported that the offender had issued threats to harm them, other family members, or to damage property. Overall, almost 75% stated that the offender had engaged in at least one of these four abusive behaviors in the six months prior to the experimental incident. Of these, 40% stated that police were called in response at least once. Most of these calls came from the victim herself (76%), with the remaining reported by another family member (11%), the offender (8%), or "someone else" (17%). Regarding the experimental incident, most women (70%) stated that they had been the one who called police. Thus, it is clear that the sample contains a group of women who were exposed to repeated victimization of various types and, on at least some occasions, most were willing to call police for assistance.

Outcome and Process Measures

According to the outcome hypothesis, reporting of future domestic violence incidents is dependent upon whether victims have received their preferred outcome from police. In the Dade County experiment, the two possible outcomes were arrest and nonarrest. In the initial interview, victims were asked whether they wanted police to arrest the suspect in response to the experimental incident. Recall that arrest and nonarrest were randomly assigned outcomes. We considered victims to have received their desired outcome when they answered yes to the arrest preference question and the offender was arrested. We also considered those who answered no and the offender was not arrested to have received their preferred outcome. Victims not receiving their outcome preference consisted of (1) those who answered yes to the arrest preference question, but the offender was not arrested, and (2) those who answered no, but the offender was arrested. We constructed a dichotomous variable where (1) indicated that the victim received her outcome preference and (0) indicated that she did not. We recognize that this is a rather simplistic method of measuring victim preference. Our intention was to test the hypothesis as it has been asserted in the literature. Among those arguing against mandatory arrest laws, the relationship between victim preference and official reporting is discussed almost exclusively in terms of this arrest/nonarrest dichotomy ... rather than as a range of outcomes victims may desire.

We used a measurement model developed by Tyler and Lind (1992) to test the process hypothesis. While the Dade County data do not contain a complete specification of this model, several similar measures are available. In the initial interview, victims were first asked to rate how carefully police listened to their side of the story, from "very carefully" (4) to "not at all carefully" (1). This item is similar to Tyler and Lind's (1992) "consideration of views" measure. We took another indicator from victim ratings of how seriously the police officers took their situation, from "very seriously" (4) to "not at all seriously" (1). This is similar to Tyler and Lind's (1992) "dignity and respect" measure. The third indicator, similar to Tyler and Lind's "concern for needs" concept, was a dichotomous variable regarding whether victims felt the police officers really wanted to help (1) or did not (0). Using these three indicators, we created a procedural justice scale variable by computing the average of the standardized scores for each of the four indicators on each case (alpha = 0.84).

Victims were also asked to rate on a four-point scale how satisfied they were with police, from very satisfied (4) to very dissatisfied (1). While victim satisfaction is important to procedural justice, for our purposes its meaning is not clear. Victims may feel very satisfied with police because they received fair treatment (process hypothesis) or because they received the outcome they wanted (outcome hypothesis). To examine whether victim satisfaction fits with the procedural justice indicators, we conducted a principal components factor analysis utilizing varimax rotation. The results revealed that all four indicators loaded together on a single factor (Satisfaction = 0.878, Careful = 0.862, Serious = 0.859, and Help = 0.847). Despite these factor loadings, we have reasons to question the face validity of victim satisfaction as an exclusive indicator of procedural justice and not distributive justice, as articulated in the outcome hypothesis. Thus, we did not include victim satisfaction in the procedural justice scale item but examined it as an independent variable.

Dependent Variable

In a general sense, the dependent variable of this study is clear—whether the victim called police or not in response to revictimization. Most victims, however, suffered more than one type of revictimization, and many suffered repeated revictimizations of the same type. The initial interview data did not distinguish reporting in individual incidents but asked victims whether they reported any of the potentially numerous repeat victimizations. The follow-up interview asked victims to state whether they reported only the first of potentially many victimizations since the initial interview. Consequently, we created a single dichotomous variable indicating whether victims reported at least one revictimization incident occurring before either interview. We included type and frequency of revictimization as control variables.

Control Variables

Demographic Characteristics

While the previous research is mixed on whether race plays a role in domestic violence victim reporting, there is reason to include race/ethnicity as a control in our analysis. Importantly, race and ethnicity may influence procedural justice judgments.... We included three dichotomous variables to represent each of the most prominent racial groups—black, Hispanic, and white. The null findings in previous research related to socioeconomic status overall may be because social class itself does not have a direct impact on victim reporting. It may be that a victim's financial dependence upon the offender has a direct impact and that socioeconomic status is related to victim reporting through financial dependence.... To take this argument into account, we included a variable that contains data on how victims rate their financial independence on a five-point scale, ranging from "totally dependent" (1) to "not at all dependent" (5) on the offender.

In general, other demographic variables have not been found to be important in the existing literature on domestic violence victim reporting. Because marital status is fairly invariant in the data set, we did not include marital status as a control variable. One variable that has been found to be important in the general victim reporting literature is age.... Given the paucity of studies that explore victim reporting in domestic violence cases, we included victim age in the analysis. Similarly, we included a continuous measure of relationship length to account for its potential influence on a victim's decision whether to call police.

Victimization History

To account for the nature and extent of victimization prior to the experimental incident, we included one variable that captured the frequency of each of the four types of victimization in the six months prior to the experimental incident. Some researchers have found that previous calls to police may be the most predictive variable in a model of victim reporting behavior.... Therefore, we created a dichotomous variable capturing whether the victim had reported any incident prior to the experimental incident to police (1) or did not (0).

Experimental Incident Characteristics

The eligibility requirement of the Dade County experiment required that the incident consist of a misdemeanor-level battery, resulting in either minor or no injury. Several characteristics of the experimental incident may be relevant for future victim reporting.... Charlotte (North Carolina) SARP Experiment data ... found that both victim and offender alcohol and drug use influenced the frequency of police utilization. Thus, we included a variable containing a victim self-report of drug or alcohol use at the time of the experimental incident. To some extent, this variable also controlled for the possibility that victim perceptions of police behavior were altered due to substance use. We included a second variable capturing victim perception of the offender's alcohol or drug use prior to the experimental incident. The data did not permit controls for alcohol and drug use during subsequent victimizations. In addition, we included a control for whether the victim reported the experimental incident to police (1) or it came to police attention in some other way (0). Aside from victim outcome preference, a specific action (arrest or nonarrest) taken by police may have some influence over whether victims choose to report subsequent victimizations. Thus, we included a variable indicating whether police did (1) or did not (0) arrest the offender following the experimental incident.

The Dade County experiment contained a second experiment that assigned victims in the original experiment to receive (or not receive) follow-up services from a special police unit.... [P]olice follow-up services were associated with official reporting of subsequent victimization. Thus, we included a dichotomous variable indicating whether victims responded that they were contacted by the special police unit following the experimental incident.

Revictimization

Previous studies using similar samples, ... found no relationship between victim injury and reporting. It may be that the pattern of offender behavior, rather than injury in individual incidents, has greater impact on the reporting decisions of women with more extensive victimization histories.

Thus, we included five variables that captured the type and frequency of victimization since the experimental incident. Four of these variables contained the frequency of each victimization type since the experimental incident. An additional variable captured whether the victim had suffered some injury as the result of being hit or hurt at any point following the experimental incident. To account for the different time periods over which victims were interviewed, we included a variable capturing the number of days from the experimental incident to the last interview.

Models to be Estimated

. . . We grouped the control variables in a meaningful way and conducted separate logistic regression analyses for each set of variables. We then selected the significant control variables from these grouped models and placed them in two separate theoretical models. Because the purpose of control variables is to examine the impact of theoretical variables while holding other potential influences constant, this method is not ideal. It does, however, allow some consideration of a number of factors within the restrictions placed on the analyses by a relatively small sample size. Since our goal was to test the specific predictions of the process and outcome hypotheses, we applied one-tailed significance tests to theoretical variables.

Results

Of the sample of 180 women, 61 chose to report while 119 refrained from reporting one or more victimizations suffered during the follow-up period. The simple bivariate relationships among the variables provided some support, albeit modest, for the outcome hypothesis and no support whatsoever for the process hypothesis. In our sample, 102 (57%) stated that they had received their preference of outcomes, and 77 (43%) stated that they did not (see Table 2). Consistent with the outcome hypothesis, the results show that those victims who received their preference were more likely to report subsequent victimization (39%) than those who did not (26%). While the chi-square and gamma statistics were not significant, the bivariate relationship was in the predicted direction and approached significance ($p < 0.057$). Similarly, those who did not receive their preference were more likely to refrain from reporting (74%) than those who received their preferred outcome (61%) following the experimental incident. Overall, however, the majority of women did not report their revictimization to police.

As shown in Table 3, we found that the procedural justice scale variable was in the direction opposite that predicted by the process hypothesis. Those who chose to report subsequent victimization had a lower average value for perception of procedural justice than those who did not. Similarly, the bivariate relationships between victim reporting and the three individual variables making up the procedural justice scale variable was not in the direction predicted by the process hypothesis. For example, among victims who reported subsequent victimization, nearly 30% stated that they felt police really wanted to help, listened to them very carefully, and took their situation very seriously. This compares to around 70% on each of these items among the victims who chose not to report subsequent victimization. As with the three indicators of procedural justice, 28% of the victims who felt very satisfied with police overall reported repeat victimization to police, but a much greater share (72%) feeling very satisfied with police chose not to report subsequent incidents.

Table 2. Bivariate Relationship Between Reporting and Outcome Hypothesis Variables

	Received Preference	Did Not Receive Preference	Row Total
Victim Report	40 (39%)	20 (26%)	60
No Victim Report	62 (61%)	57 (74%)	119
	102	77	179

$$\chi^2 = 3.45,\ \dagger\,p = 0.063;\ gamma = 0.295,\ \dagger\,p = 0.057$$

$\dagger\,p < 0.10.$

Table 3. Bivariate Relationship Between Reporting and Process Hypothesis Variables

	Victim Report	Victim No Report	Row Total
Police Wanted to Help	M = 0.68	M = 0.84	(N = 173)
No (0)	18 (48.6%)	19 (51.4%)	37
Yes (1)	39 (28.7%)	97 (71.3%)	136

$$\chi^2 = 5.25,\ *\,p = 0.022;\ gamma = -0.404,\ *\,p = 0.032$$

	Victim Report	Victim No Report	Row Total
Carefulness of Listening	M = 3.25	M = 3.46	(N = 178)
Not at All (1)	5 (38.5)	8 (61.5)	13
Not Very (2)	5 (50.0)	5 (50.0)	10
Somewhat (3)	20 (40.8)	29 (59.2)	49
Very Careful (4)	30 (28.6)	75 (71.4)	105

$$\chi^2 = 3.65,\ p = 0.301;\ gamma = -0.244,\ \dagger\,p = 0.078$$

	Victim Report	Victim No Report	Row Total
Seriousness of Situation	M = 3.08	M = 3.38	(N = 178)
Not at All (1)	9 (45.0)	11 (55.0)	20
Not Very (2)	6 (50.0)	6 (50.0)	12
Somewhat (3)	16 (36.4)	28 (63.6)	44
Very Serious (4)	29 (28.4)	73 (71.6)	102

$$\chi^2 = 3.98,\ p = 0.264;\ gamma = -0.250,\ \dagger\,p = 0.063$$

	Victim Report	Victim No Report	Row Total
Procedural Justice Scale	- 0.2112 (0.9185)[1]	0.0991 (0.8218)	(N = 180)

[1] This row indicates the mean and standard deviation (in standard scores) for the procedural justice scale variable.

$\dagger p < 0.10;\ *\,p < 0.05.$

Control Variable Models

The demographic control variable model contained race/ethnicity, financial dependence, age, and relationship length. The logistic regression analysis revealed none of these demographic variables to be significantly predictive of reporting (see Table 4). The victimization history control model contained five control variables capturing elements of victimization experience in the six months prior to the Dade County experimental incident. These variables were victim reports of the frequency with which the offender hit or hurt her, hit or hurt a family member, made threats, and damaged property. In addition, this model included whether victims called police to report any of these victimizations. We found no variables to be significant at the standard 0.05 level (see Table 4).

Table 4. Logistic Regression Control Variable Models

Control Variables	B	s.e.	p Value	Exp. (B)
Demographic Model				
Financial Independence	0.0814	0.1147	0.4777	1.0848
White Victim	−0.5727	0.3976	0.1497	0.5640
Hispanic Victim	−0.5959	0.4483	0.1837	0.5511
Victim Age	−0.0198	0.0251	0.4311	0.9804
Relationship Length	−0.0025	0.0026	0.3305	0.9975
Model Constant	0.2210	0.7669		
Victimization History Model				
Hit, Hurt Pre–Experiment	−0.0569	0.0350	0.1041	0.9447
Family Hit, Hurt Pre–Experiment	−0.0935	0.1391	0.5015	0.9107
Threaten Pre–Experiment	0.0000	0.0117	0.9959	1.0001
Damage Property Pre–Experiment	0.0540	0.0375	0.1502	1.0555
Report to Police Pre–Experiment	0.6512	0.3745	0.0821†	1.9178
Model Constant	−0.7761	0.2079		
Experimental Incident Model				
Victim Using Alcohol, Drugs	0.4006	0.4330	0.3549	1.4927
Offender Using Alcohol, Drugs	0.1324	0.3541	0.7085	1.1415

Control Variables	B	s.e.	p Value	Exp. (B)
Offender Arrested	−0.2538	0.3294	0.4410	0.7759
Police Follow–Up Contact	0.1584	0.3271	0.6282	1.1717
Report to Police	0.5808	0.3710	0.1175	1.7874
Model Constant	−1.1420			
Revictimization Model				
Victim Hit, Hurt in Follow–Up	0.3679	0.1356	0.0067**	1.4446
Family Hit, Hurt in Follow–Up	0.2943	0.2446	0.2288	1.3422
Threatened in Follow–Up	0.0021	0.0296	0.9446	1.0021
Damage Property in Follow–Up	0.3158	0.1671	0.0587†	1.3714
Victim Injured in Follow–Up	0.1437	0.3933	0.7148	1.1545
Number of Days in Follow–Up	0.0013	0.0016	0.4175	1.0013
Model Constant	−1.9968	0.4895		

† $p < 0.10$; ** $p < 0.01$.

The third control variable model included variables related to the Dade County experimental incident that may influence the future reporting of domestic violence victims. Two of these variables captured whether the victim stated that she or the offender had been using alcohol or drugs before the experimental incident. Another captured whether the victim was the person who had notified police following the experimental incident. The two remaining variables captured activities related to the Dade County experiment—whether the offender was arrested following the experimental incident and whether the victim received follow-up services from the special police unit. As with the previous two control variable models, none of these variables were found to be significant (see Table 4).

The final control variable model captured the characteristics of revictimization(s) victims may have suffered between the experimental incident and the final victim interview. Specifically, this revictimization model contained victim reports of the frequency with which the offender hit or hurt her, hit or hurt a family member, made threats, and damaged property. Also included in this model was a variable indicating whether the victim suffered any injury as the result of any revictimization incident. An additional variable included in this model captured the length in days from the experimental incident to the last interview. The results of this model indicated that only the frequency of being hit or hurt during the follow-up period significantly increased the likelihood of victim reporting (see Table 4).

Outcome and Process Hypotheses Models

Because the only significant variable from the control variable models was the frequency of the victim being hit or hurt during the follow-up period, this variable is the sole companion of the theoretical variables in the process and outcome models. As shown in Table 5, the results of the logistic regression analysis support the outcome hypothesis. Victim preference of outcome was a significant predictor (employing a one-tailed test) of victim reporting behavior, and the relationship was in the predicted direction. The lone significant control variable, the frequency of being hit or hurt, remained an important predictor of victim reporting behavior. However, the results of the logistic regression do not support the process hypothesis. The procedural justice scale variable was a significant predictor (employing a one-tailed test) but influenced reporting in a direction opposite that predicted by the process hypothesis (see Table 5). The frequency of being hit or hurt remained a significant predictor of reporting behavior.

Given the exploratory nature of this research, the direction of the procedural justice variable warrants further investigation. For the procedural justice scale variable and each of the three individual procedural justice variables, ratings of police fairness were consistently lower among those who called police to report revictimization than those who did not. Why might those who feel more fairly treated by police refrain from using them again and those who feel unfairly treated by police make greater use of them? The answer to this question is not readily apparent. One possible explanation relates to social desirability and the timing of the revictimization. One could argue that nonreporting victims inflated their ratings as a form of compensation for "disappointing" the interviewers by not calling police in the subsequent incident(s) discussed in the initial interview. This explanation is unlikely because questions relating to police ratings came before questions about revictimization and reporting in the initial interview. The scripted introduction to the interview did not state that questions would be asked about subsequent reports to police. Thus, it is unlikely that nonreporting victims engaged in this type of inflation.

Table 5. Logistic Regression Outcome Hypothesis and Process Hypothesis Models

Outcome Hypothesis Model

Variables	B	s.e.	p Value	Exp. (B)
Victim Preference	0.5844*	0.3461	0.0456	1.7939
Victim Hit, Hurt in Follow–Up	0.4372**	0.1238	0.0004	1.5484
Model Constant	−1.6851	0.3340		

* $p < 0.05$; † $p < 0.10$; ** $p < 0.01$.

Process Hypothesis Model

Variables	B	s.e.	p Value	Exp. (B)
Procedural Justice Scale	−0.333*	0.187	0.037	0.717
Victim Hit, Hurt in Follow–Up	0.440**	0.126	0.000	1.552
Model Constant	−1.335	0.251		

* $p < 0.05$; † $p < 0.10$; ** $p < 0.01$.

43

In the Portland, Oregon Domestic Violence Experiment, researchers found that victims rated the performance of responding police officers higher when these officers were followed by specialized officers providing follow-up services (Jolin and Clava-detscher 1995). It is possible that such a "halo" effect around the officers responding to the experimental incident was produced when victims received contact from Dade County's specialized police unit. This explanation is unlikely because a t-test revealed no significant difference between the mean ratings of victims who received and did not receive these services ($t = 0.973, p = 0.332$).

Another possibility is that victims receiving their preferred outcome are likely to rate police fairness higher than victims who do not. Those victims who stated that they received their preference of outcomes perceived a higher level of procedural justice (N = 102, M = 0.1021) than victims who did not (N = 77, M = −0.1283). However, because victim preference is positively associated with reporting, a relationship between victim preference and procedural justice ratings cannot account for our unanticipated negative procedural justice outcome.

To explore other possibilities, we conducted an ordinary least-squares regression analysis using the procedural justice scale variable as the dependent variable. We incorporated several categories of variables that could influence procedural justice judgments, including demographics, victimization history, and characteristics of the experimental incident. In addition to the variables already discussed, we included an additional variable that captured whether the victim resided with anyone other than the offender. The data set did not identify these other residents, who may have been children, parents, friends, boarders, or other relatives. Victim satisfaction may also be an important predictor of procedural justice judgments and was also included in the model. We conducted diagnostics on the independent variables and ruled out high multicollinearity.

Table 6. Linear Regression of Variables Associated With Procedural Justice Judgments

Variable Name	B	s.e.	Beta	t
Victim Using Alcohol, Drugs	0.037	0.112	0.017	0.332
Offender Arrested	0.114	0.087	0.066	1.306
Victim Injured in Follow–Up	−0.177†	0.091	−0.100	−1.932
White Victim	−0.222*	0.105	−0.122	−2.108
Hispanic Victim	−0.249*	0.114	−0.121	−2.182
Financial Independence	−0.052†	0.030	−0.094	−1.714
Victim Preference	−0.060	0.089	−0.035	−0.675
Hit, Hurt Pre–Experiment	−0.001	0.006	−0.016	−0.299
Report to Police (Experiment)	−0.051	0.096	−0.027	−0.536
Victim Living With Others	−0.036	0.110	−0.017	−0.324
Satisfaction with Police	0.635**	0.046	0.743	13.843
Constant	−1.587			

$R^2 = 0.609, R_{adj}^2 = 0.583, F = 23.461$ **
$* p < 0.05; † p < 0.10; ** p < 0.01.$

According to the linear regression analyses, procedural justice judgments were significantly related to several variables (see Table 6). Race and ethnicity were predictive, in that white and Hispanic victims perceived a significantly lower level of procedural justice from police than did black victims. In addition, victims who felt more satisfied with police perceived a significantly higher level of procedural justice than did victims who felt less satisfied.

For purposes of exploration, two other variables are note-worthy particularly because of the negative direction of their effects (although failing to meet a strict $p < 0.05$ criterion). Victims who indicated less financial independence from the offender gave police higher fairness ratings than victims who felt more financially independent. In addition, victims who were injured as a result of revictimization perceived a lower level of procedural justice than victims were not injured from a revictimization incident. It is possible that these five variables, in combination, may be responsible for the negative association between procedural justice judgments and victim reporting. To explore this possibility, we estimated a final model. We included these variables with those already identified as predictive of victim reporting in the separate tests of the process and outcome hypotheses, after ruling out the existence of high multicollinearity (see Table 7).

Table 7. Logistic Regression Results of Process Hypothesis Model Containing Variables Associated With Procedural Justice Judgments

Variables	B	s.e.	p Value	Exp. (B)
Procedural Justice Scale	−0.541*	0.317	0.044	0.582
Victim Preference	0.733*	0.377	0.026	2.082
Hit, Hurt in Follow–Up	0.396**	0.140	0.005	1.485
Injury in Follow–Up	0.081	0.386	0.833	1.085
Financial Independence	0.141	0.120	0.237	1.152
Satisfaction With Police	0.212	0.277	0.444	1.237
White Victim	−0.392	0.413	0.343	0.676
Hispanic Victim	−0.839	0.488	0.086	0.432
Constant	−2.609	1.055		

* $p < 0.05$; ** $p < 0.01$.

The analysis revealed that, even while controlling for the effects of other variables associated with procedural justice ratings, the counter-theoretical finding could not be eliminated. Yet further exploration of the process hypothesis produced an interesting result for the outcome hypothesis. Controlling for the influence of procedural justice judgments, victim preference became a more important predictor of reporting behavior. The original outcome hypothesis model revealed that the odds of victim reporting were increased by 79% when victims received their preference of outcomes (see Table 5). The "combined" model containing both procedural justice and victim preference variables revealed that the odds of victim reporting were increased by 108% when victims received their preference of outcomes (see Table 7). This finding suggests that omitting the procedural justice variable, along with other variables related to procedural justice, had a suppression effect on the victim preference variable.

Discussion and Conclusions

The goal of this research was to conduct an exploratory investigation of the often-asserted link between domestic violence victims' perceptions of police behavior and their subsequent utilization of police in response to revictimization. Results indicate that victims were more apt to call police upon further victimization when police had acted in a manner consistent with their preferences (i.e., the outcome hypothesis was supported). Conversely, we found no support for the process hypothesis. Instead, we found that victims who felt unfairly treated by police were more likely to call them in the future, compared to victims who felt fairly treated. In exploring this surprising result, we found that victims who felt more satisfied with police rated procedural fairness higher than victims who felt less satisfied. Satisfaction was not related to victim reporting and did not explain the counter-theoretical findings.

Holding a host of factors constant, including preference, white and Hispanic victims perceived themselves to be less fairly treated by police than did black victims; yet once these differences were controlled, procedural justice was still negative and significantly related to victim reporting of subsequent victimization. Given that our missing data were patterned by race (whites were significantly less likely to participate in the initial interview than blacks and Hispanics), we are hesitant to speculate about race/ethnicity effects in our models. If, however, we have discerned real race differences, our findings are inconsistent with both procedural justice and distributive justice predictions (i.e., blacks should perceive less procedural justice than whites and procedural justice should positively affect victim reporting).

Why might black victims perceive greater procedural justice than whites? One possibility is that black women (especially in poor communities) rely more on police to intervene in domestic violence incidents than do whites ... Even though the black community may view police as racist and oppressive, police may be one of the few institutional resources that low-income black women have at their disposal.... White victims, on the other hand, have more resources available to them, which lessen their dependence on police. Hispanics, due to cultural circumstances (including communication barriers, fear of immigration authorities, and religious teachings), may be less able to communicate with police and more afraid to report victimization to them....

Given that black victims are significantly more likely to perceive procedural justice in their encounters with police than white or Hispanic victims, what can account for the negative relationship between procedural justice and reporting? This too may also be race-related. Although black women may perceive higher levels of procedural justice than other victims, they may find themselves in a gender-race quandary, caught between loyalty to one's minority group (and partner) and self-preservation.... Thus, the group most likely to perceive procedural justice in their encounters with police (blacks) are also not as likely to call police for help.

Clearly, there is a need for more research focusing on the process hypothesis. As noted, the present sample suffers from a considerable missing data problem, and the extent to which our findings are impacted is unknown. But at a minimum, this work calls into question untested assumptions about victim reporting behavior. If these counter-theoretical findings are replicated, domestic violence researchers will need to carefully consider its present use. Theoretical work should focus on why unfair, rather than fair, treatment by police may be positively associated with domestic violence victim reporting or whether this is a spurious relationship explained by other factors. This task may require further exploration of whether procedural justice is the best operationalization of fair treatment or if some other measurement is more applicable in the special case of repeat victims of domestic violence.

While our exploratory study supported the outcome hypothesis, the results suggest that its articulation in the extant domestic violence literature may be somewhat simplistic. Victim preference has been very narrowly defined according to arrest versus nonarrest dichotomies, but victims may be interested in a host of additional outcomes. And contrary to unicausal statements about victim preference, our findings suggest that other factors may influence reporting as well. One explanation for the simplistic articulation of both the process and outcome hypotheses is that they have largely been framed as part of a public policy debate about what law enforcement should do in response to domestic violence.... Some factors that may be related to victim reporting behavior cannot be influenced by law enforcement policy and thus have not been the focus of attention. The policy debate has largely centered on the impact of mandatory arrest policies that restrict police discretion in the use of arrest in domestic violence cases. Because this restriction bars consideration of victim preference, critics of mandatory arrest argue that victims are disenfranchised.... Supporters of mandatory arrest policies would counter with concerns about the vulnerability of victims (and their preferences) to coercion and danger posed by the offender.... In this view, a potential increase in future reporting gained by giving active consideration to victim preferences would be seen as an inadequate tradeoff for fewer arrests of domestic violence offenders. Clearly, policy implications stemming from the replication of our findings raise complicated issues.

The present study provides one of the first pieces of evidence on whether and how victim perception of police behavior, both toward victims themselves and on their behalf, may influence future reporting. While this investigation found evidence in favor of the outcome hypothesis and counter to the process hypothesis, this research is exploratory and tentative. Continued empirical examination is vital to the understanding of how police may influence the reporting behavior of domestic violence victims and whether such influences may account for counter-theoretical findings in other domestic violence research.

NOTES AND QUESTIONS

1. Statistical Research Methods: Scholars in the law-and-society movement produce a body of knowledge about the legal system, and they draw what they consider to be a realistic picture of how this system operates. They use various methods to do this, and an important part of the whole enterprise is studying and developing and elaborating various research methods. We will identify and discuss various social science methods as we encounter them.[2] Here we introduce basic concepts of research using statistical methods.

A. The Research Question. Research aims to answer a research question. Empirical research tries to answer the question in terms of information and data gathered by the researcher. It is always useful to ask what the question is that motivates the research. What is the research question in the article by Hickman and Simpson?

B. Hypotheses. A hypothesis is a proposed answer to the research question—it is an informed guess as to what the research will find, a guess that subsequent empirical research will try to test.

For example, suppose the research question is whether race influences whether juries give some murderers the death penalty and not others. We review earlier studies, existing data, and our own insights, and advance the hypothesis that race does impact capital sentences, and that an African-American murderer is more likely to get the death penalty than a Caucasian murderer. But socio-legal phenomena are complex. There are probably other factors related to whether the murderer will get the death penalty or not. Age and gender might be important. The type of murder might matter—was it during a hold-up? Was it a domestic killing? Any serious attempt to understand this phenomenon—the death penalty—will consider a range of potential contributory factors. Once these have been controlled for in the analysis, we can better discern whether race has an impact. (As it turns out, scholars who have examined this question from multiple methodological angles have concluded that race matters in death penalty sentencing—but that it is important to consider the race of the victim as well as the race of the perpetrator.)

C. Variables. A hypothesis is a guess or a conjecture that typically connects two or more variables. A variable is simply something that can take on different values. In our example, whether someone gets the death penalty

---

2. A useful guide is Earl Babbie, *The Practice of Social Research* (10th ed., 2004). See also Michael O. Finkelstein and Bruce Levin, *Statistics for Lawyers* (2nd ed., 2001), and John Monahan and Laurens Walker, *Social Science in Law: Cases and Materials* (6th ed., 2006).

is a variable. You either get it or you don't. Race is a variable; defendants can be white, black, and so on. Age is a variable—you can be young, old, or in between.

When we test a hypothesis, we are assuming we can explain or predict one variable by finding a relationship between it and one or more other variables. Thus, we have hypothesized that race, and perhaps other factors such as gender and age, will explain or predict who will get the death penalty.

We distinguish between dependent and independent variables. What we are trying to explain is the dependent variable. The variables we use to explain the dependent variable are referred to as independent variables. (In popular speech, we often speak about cause and effect). The decision to give the death penalty is, in our example, the dependent variable; race, gender, and age are independent variables.

In Hickman and Simpson, what are the dependent and the independent variables?

Notice that the nature of variables differ. Some have an arithmetic relationship. For example, consider the age of those convicted of murder: if one person is 50 years old, he is twice as old as another person who is 25. However, investigators often use variables that do not have this kind of counting relationship. Whether or not a court sentences a convicted murderer to death is such a variable. We might code "1" for yes and "0" for no (or we can think of "1" as indicating presence of the variable and "0" indicating absence), and use these values in our analysis. Often social scientists say that transforming yes/no answers into numbers involves using a "dummy variable" because the investigator transforms the data into a numerical form necessary for statistical analysis. Hickman and Simpson use several such dummy variables.

We also might want to assess the influence of the religion of those convicted and on death sentences. We could code as follows: "Roman Catholic = 1; Protestant = 2; Jewish = 3; other = 4; and no religion = 5." This would create a nominal scale where the numbers only served to keep what is different apart and join together what is considered equivalent. While we can use such nominal values in our analysis, we cannot use the values on our 1 to 5 scale as we would use 1 and 0 to indicate whether a court imposed a death sentence. We must also remember that having no religion is not 5 times more or less of anything than being Roman Catholic. Moreover, by coding two people as falling into category 1, we have treated a devout Roman Catholic man and a woman who occasionally attended Mass as if the differences in their religious practices made no difference.

Finally, we can have an ordinal scale which expresses the order of a number in a series. For example, we might ask judges who presided at murder trials to rank the attorneys for convicted murderers as, say, poor, just adequate, competent, very good, and outstanding. We might code these responses as –2, –1, 0, +1 and +2. Again, we must wonder whether a judge who ranked one lawyer as "very good" and another as "outstanding" was asserting that the second lawyer was twice as good as the first.

D.   Operationalization and Data Collection. After a hypothesis has been formulated, the author must decide how to measure the variables and how data will be collected to test the hypothesis. As we learned in Hickman and Simpson, deciding how to measure a variable is called "operationalizing" the variable. For example, those coding observed data may be told to count a person with characteristics A, B and C as falling into category #2 of the variable under study. Some of those assigned to category #2 will also have characteristic D while others will not. Social scientists might argue about whether the investigator really measured the category #2 variable if those with characteristics A, B and C were lumped together with characteristics A, B, C and D. How did Hickman and Simpson operationalize each of their variables? What data did they collect? Do you see any problems with their operationalizations or data collections that might bias their results?

E.   Analysis. One of the primary uses of statistics in social science research is to determine the extent to which independent variables are related to dependent variables. In considering Hickman and Simpson, we are interested in how well the various independent variables allow us to predict whether a particular domestic violence situation will result in a report to the police. There are a large number of statistical measures that attempt to answer such a question. Different types of measures are appropriate for different types of variables. We cannot go into them fully in this course. However, the reader of social science research does need to be aware of at least three general forms of statistical analysis: (1) tests of significance, (2) measures of the degree of association (correlations), and (3) measures of the nature of association (multiple regression).

Tests of significance ask whether we can account for the relationship between variables by mere chance association. Much social research deals with a limited sample of the relevant events. For example, Hickman and Simpson did not study all domestic violence situations in all locations but only those from a particular time in a particular location. Social scientists use a variety of statistical techniques to indicate whether the relationship between the variables is "statistically significant." These techniques determine the probability that the observed relationship would be found in the sample if, in fact, there was no relationship between these variables in the entire population. Suppose, for example, we studied samples of men and women law professors of the same age and with similar experience. We found that the women were paid an average of $1,000 a year less than the men. Suppose our sample consisted of five professors. Now suppose, instead, it consisted of 500. We would run a test of significance to determine the probability that we would find such a salary difference in our samples if there were no such difference in the entire population of men and women law professors. We very likely would find that the sample of five would not yield significant results, but our sample of 500 might well do so.

A conventional practice is to require that *p* (the probability that a particular result was obtained by chance) must be less than .05 ("*p* < .05" indicates that the probability that the observed difference would occur by chance is one in twenty) for the result to be called statistically significant. This is not a law of nature but a custom as to where a line is to be drawn. If the chances are less than one in twenty that the result was obtained by chance, one can reason as if it is not, without offending other members of the statistical guild. There is some variation among scholars in how stringent a definition of statistical significance they use.

Demanding significance at the .05 level may be too conservative and cause a misinterpretation of our data. Social scientists often talk of Type I and Type II errors. We make a Type I error when we accept results that actually are the product of chance. We make a Type II error when we reject results that actually would be obtained with another sample. An investigator can minimize Type I errors by lowering her test for significance to, for example, .01 (or 1 in a 100) rather than .05 (or 1 in 20). However, this move will increase the likelihood of Type II error.

But how should we treat a result that is not statistically significant by whatever test we deem appropriate under the circumstances—our study of five law professors, for example? Statistical logic does not permit us to say that the result was caused by chance. Chance is only an explanation that we have not ruled out. If we drew a different sample (a larger one, for example), we might find a significant result. We can illustrate the point by an analogy: Suppose a defendant is tried for first degree murder. The judge instructs the jury that it must determine whether the evidence establishes guilt beyond a reasonable doubt. The jury returns a "not guilty" verdict. We cannot say that we know that the defendant did not commit first degree murder. All we know is that the prosecution failed to prove that the defendant did.[3]

When an investigator fails to obtain significant results, the investigator may still theorize about relationships with the same freedom as a scholar or journalist who does not purport to use statistics. Moreover, the "not significant" results may still serve as scraps of evidence "suggesting" certain relationships. However, such arguments are entitled to just as much but no more weight than other theoretical or speculative work.

Which of the independent variables in Hickman and Simpson are significantly related to the decision whether to report domestic violence?

A measure of the degree of association asks how much a particular independent variable helps us to predict a dependent variable. While these measures can be expressed in different ways, the conventional way to express them is in decimal form varying between 0 and 1. (0 indicates that a

---

3. Jurors in Scotland are given three options: they can render a verdict of guilty, not guilty or not proven. "Not statistically significant" is roughly analogous to the Scottish verdict of not proven. The Scottish verdict is controversial. Some argue that it is a second class acquittal that leaves a cloud over the accused; some argue that it allows a jury to evade the duty to decide cases; others defend it as a way accurately to reflect the jury's judgment about the case. See *The Guardian*, June 1, 1993, at 18.

particular independent variable does not help us to predict the dependent variable at all. Conversely, a 1 indicates that knowing the independent variable allows us to predict the dependent variable perfectly.)

Measures of the degree of association rest on correlations. Correlation means that two things occur together—when one thing is found, another will be found as well. Summer and heat are positively correlated. Two things are negatively correlated when the presence of one is associated with the absence of the other. Summer and snow are negatively correlated. Lack of correlation means that whether one thing occurs or does not occur when we find the other depends on chance. Notice that a correlation does not mean necessarily that one thing causes the other. For example, suppose we found that longer prison sentences are positively correlated with high crime rates. The correlation itself tells us nothing about whether harsh sentences cause increasing crime, increasing crime causes harsh sentences, some unknown third factor causes both heavy sentences as well as high amounts of crime, or one or more unknown factors cause the sentences while one or several other unrelated factors cause the crime, and the correlation is but a coincidence. We must explain correlations on the basis of logic, theory, hunch or other data. Correlations do not speak for themselves.

We can illustrate correlations and make some further points by considering a simple graph. Suppose we are interested in whether the percentage of left-handed pitchers on major league baseball teams is related to the percentage of games that the teams won. Suppose, very improbably, we found that teams that had 100% left-handed pitchers won 100% of their games; those with no left-handed pitchers won none; those with 50% left-handers won 50% of their games and so on. We could represent this by the line of stars on the following table:

		20	40	60	80	100
	100%					*
% left handed	80%	+			*	
pitchers on a	60%		+	*		
team	40%		*	+		
	20%	*			+	
% of games won by a team	0%	20	40	60	80	100

If these percentages were so neatly correlated, we would say that "r = +1.00." We would speak of the "positive slope" of the correlation because a line connecting the points on the graph would run upward to indicate the more we have of one thing, the more we have of another.

Suppose we found the absolute opposite situation. The more left-handed pitchers on a team, the fewer games the team won. Assume that teams with all left-handed pitchers lost all their games; those with 80% won only 20%; those with none at all won all their games. Here "r = –1.00." A line plotted on the graph would have a "negative slope," as the plus signs in the graph indicate. Of course, in neither case would our data prove whether left-handed pitchers had anything to do with winning or losing. The team with all left-handed pitchers, for example, could also have the best batters in the league. These batters could be the cause of the team's success.

Finally, suppose that half the teams in the major leagues had 10% left-handed pitchers on their pitching staffs and half had 90%. The same number of teams from each group won 20%, 40%, 60%, 80% or 100% of their games. There is no correlation at all between the two factors—the percentage of left-handed pitchers seems to have nothing to do with the number of games a team wins—and so we would say that "r = 0.00." If we plotted the percentage of left-handed pictures and the percentage of victories, our marks would scatter without pattern on our chart.

Of course, we seldom find sets of data yielding such neat patterns as in our first two examples. Most sets of data, when plotted on graphs, produce a scattered array of points. One can try to draw a straight line through the array so that the line comes as close as possible to all the points. If there is no relationship between the variables being considered, the "best-fitting" straight line will be a horizontal line as in our third example. If there is a relationship, we will get a line somewhere between the horizontal and the diagonal. Calculating the "r" statistic involves assessing how well a straight line fits the data. The value of "r" is called the correlation coefficient. It is a measure of the degree in which one thing goes with or does not go with another. It is expressed as a measure of how far the degree of correlation is from +1.00, 0.00 or –1.00, or how far it is from the three lines described above.

We often deal with more complex relationships, and want to know how much of the variation concerning one variable can be attributed to each of several other variables or to an interaction among them. We need a measure of the nature of the association among variables. To do this, we could turn to a multiple regression analysis such as Hickman and Simpson used.

Suppose, in addition to the percentage of (A) left-handed pitchers, we think the percentage of games a baseball team wins (the dependent variable) might be affected by independent variables such as (B) whether the team plays its home games on natural grass rather than an artificial surface, (C) how much it pays its players, (D) how much it spends on finding and developing new young players, (E) how many players leave the team and sign as free agents with other teams, (F) the population of the area in which the team markets its products (such as television rights and the right to use the team logo on caps and jackets), (G) the batting averages of its regular players other than pitchers, and (H) the percentage of players whose astrological sign is Taurus.

We might want to know how much of the variation (the percentage of wins by each team in the league) is explained by some combination of these factors. First, we would create an equation that, on the basis of theory or intuition, seemed to express likely relationships. For example, we might think that all of the eight factors we suggested contributed to the percentage of games a team won, but some of them may contribute much more than others. We could express this as:

% wins = __ Left-handed Pitchers __ Grass + __ Pay + __ Development + __ Free Agents + __ Population + __ Batting Averages + __ Taurus.

Second, we would calculate a weight for each of our predictor variables—that is, how much of the variance can we attribute to factor A, how much to factor B and so on? We would then fill in the blanks in our equation with values which when added together predict the percentage of wins. Finally, we might try other equations that combined the factors differently. Then we would look for the best "fit" of our data to our theories—we would ask which equations seemed to express sensible relationships in light of the values which we entered.

There are a number of common problems encountered when using regression analysis. We can illustrate one by pointing out that factor (F), the population of the area in which the team markets its products is likely to be closely related to the amount of money the team has to spend. The available income, in turn, will be related to how much the team can pay its players (C) and spend on player development (D). Unless we separate the influence of such confounding factors, we are likely to over-or underestimate the impact of each of these three factors on each team's success. Finkelstein and Levin[4] explain a particularly severe version of the problem as follows:

> Suppose that in a wage regression model almost all high-paid employees were men with special training and almost all low-paid employees were women without training. Sex and special training are then highly correlated. Data exhibiting such correlations are said to be collinear; where one factor is nearly a linear function of several other factors, the data are said to be multicollinear, a not uncommon occurrence in a multiple regression equation....
>
> [T]he effect [of multicollinearity] is simply to increase the standard errors of the coefficients, thus making significance tests less powerful and coefficient estimates less reliable.
>
> The reason for the unreliability is not hard to see. In the example, if sex and special training were perfectly correlated it would be impossible to distinguish their separate effects on wages because they would always move together. When explanatory factors are highly but not perfectly correlated, assessment of their separate effects depends on the few cases in which they do not move in tandem. The enlarged standard errors of the coefficients reflect the smallness of the effective sample size.

Stewart Macaulay[5] adds a note of caution: regression analysis is not a form of magic. It has to be used intelligently. For example, it can be misleading, if the data are not randomly selected from the population being

---

4. Michael O. Finkelstein and Bruce Levin, *Statistics for Lawyers* 374–75 (2d ed. 2001).

5. Stewart Macaulay, "Law and the Behavioral Sciences: Is There Any There There?" 6 *Law & Policy* 149, 159–161 (1984).

studied. Getting a good random sample is not easy, especially in studies of the legal system. Regression analysis, with its impressive equations and coefficients, gives off a flavor of enormous precision. But the equation may be based on guesses and estimates, and matters of judgment. The problem is particularly severe when "regression analysis is applied to macrodata gathered by public agencies. Too often these data are a mess." The reader should approach studies using regression analysis with appropriate caution, always asking: where do these numbers come from? And what do they really show?

2.   Hickman and Simpson were careful scholars, with quantitative skills. But, as with most empirical research, it is still important to ask how far we can generalize their study. Notice that they were studying a group of women victims in southern Florida. How do we know that the situation in, say, North Dakota is not entirely different? And how do we know that the situation ten years later is the same; or if it was the same, ten years before their study? Domestic violence has a history, which some historians have been trying to study. See Elizabeth Pleck, *Domestic Tyranny: The Making of Social Policy against Family Violence from Colonial Times to the Present* (1987); Linda Gordon, *Heroes of Their Own Lives: The Politics and History of Family Violence: Bost, 1880–1960* (1988). Of course, every methodology has its limits. That is why it can be very useful to look at studies that use differing methods to study the same question—or that combine multiple kinds of methods within a single study.

Children as well as adults can be abused; see, for example, Stephen Robertson, *Crimes Against Children: Sexual Violence and Legal Culture in New York City, 1880–1960* (2005). Legal professionals facing cases involving child abuse have also turned to social science for help, raising some equally complicated questions around how to generalize from research findings. See, e.g, Thomas Lyon, "False Denials: Overcoming Methodological Biases in Abuse Disclosure Research," in M. Pipe, M. Lamb, Y. Orbach, and A. Cederborg, *Disclosing Abuse: Delays, Denials, Retractions and Incomplete Accounts* (2007).

3.   Studying Police Practices: Notice that the police have an enormous amount of discretion in domestic violence cases—they can arrest, but they can also choose not to arrest. The formal law may seem clearly cut, on matters of crime and punishment; but in practice, the police make many decisions that cannot be easily reviewed, and in fact are not. Even when a police officer stops you and accuses you of speeding, you have a decent chance of arguing your way out of a ticket, especially if you have an appealing story. The police officer, in short, has wide discretion as to how to handle the situation in these situations of what Joseph Goldstein, in a classic article, called "low-visibility decisions." Joseph Goldstein, "Police Discretion Not to Invoke the Criminal Process: Low–Visibility Decisions in the Administration of Justice," 69 *Yale Law Journal* 543 (1960).

There are also manuals and rules about the way police should behave toward citizens—requiring courtesy, avoiding offensive language, and the use of unnecessary force. But these too are "low-visibility" matters; and many people feel the police often abuse their discretion in their manner and behavior, as well as in actual decisions whether to arrest or not. See Carroll Seron, Joseph Pereira, and Jean Kovath, "Judging Police Misconduct: 'Street–Level' versus Professional Policing," 38 *Law & Society Review* 665 (2004).

Hickman and Simpson are describing an experiment—one which is examining the hypothesis that differing approaches to arresting a man who has been violent against his wife or girl friend may have an impact on whether or not he will repeat his violence in the future. Arrest or non-arrest are normally within the discretion of the police. What factors determine whether they will use arrest? This was studied by Sarah Fenstermaker Berk and Donileen R. Loseke, in " 'Handlin' Family Violence: Situational Determinants of Police Arrest in Domestic Disturbances," 15 *Law & Society Review* 317 (1981). Their data were drawn from incidents in Santa Barbara County, California, in the 1970's. They analyzed 262 police reports. They found four significant variables influenced the decision to arrest. If the woman was willing to sign a "citizen's arrest warrant," that was a strong positive factor. When both the man and the woman were present when the police arrived, arrest was likely if the woman complained of violence, and if the man had been drinking. But the police were <u>less</u> likely to arrest if the woman had called them in, than if neighbors had complained of a disturbance.

4. <u>Policy and Social Science</u>: The Berk and Loseke study is quantitative and rigorous. But, like many such studies, this does not mean that the authors are unaware of the policy implications; very often, in studies of this sort, the author or authors are quite willing to draw policy conclusions. Berk and Loseke recommend, at the end of their article, close attention to the training and education of the police; they also call for "massive changes in prosecutorial and judicial practices. In a judicial system which seldom tries spouse abuse offenders and rarely convicts them, women are seldom protected from violent reprisals." Hickman and Simpson, though not as explicit, clearly have a policy aim in view: the goal is to craft ways to improve the enforcement of laws against domestic violence.

How should the courts respond to social scientific studies that bear on policy issues? The Supreme Court, for example, has wrestled with whether a city can put restrictions on "adult" businesses. Some cities have tried to control concentrations of "adult" businesses. This is a restriction on freedom of speech; but the cities have justified it by arguing that "adult" businesses have bad effects on neighborhoods—they become high crime areas, it is argued. But is this the case? Daniel Linz et al., in "An Examination of the Assumption that Adult Businesses Are Associated with Crime in Surrounding Areas: A Secondary Effects Study in Charlotte, North Carolina," 38 *Law & Society Review* 69 (2004), claimed, in a quantitative study, that a cluster of "adult erotic dance clubs" (with names like Baby Dolls, Leather 'n Lace North, and Twin Peaks) had no impact on crime rates in their surrounding neighborhoods. (McDonalds and Kentucky Fried Chicken were used as "control sites"—they showed in fact higher crime rates in their neighborhoods than the dance clubs). How much weight should the Supreme Court, or other courts, put on this study? It is, after all, a single study of a single city in a single state. The authors think, however, that the study "could have the effect of shifting the burden of proof to municipalities to demonstrate that their theory of adverse secondary effects is correct." Do you agree?

By contrast to this study of the impact of adult businesses, there have been a number of studies of domestic violence and police practices in a number of different localities, using a variety of samples and methods. This has contributed to a developing line of research on the impact of legal reforms in this area, along a number of dimensions. For examples of recent research on mandatory arrest, see, e.g., David Eitle, "The Influence of Mandatory Arrest Policies, Police Organizational Characteristics, and Situational Variables on the Probability of Arrest in Domestic Violence Cases," 51 *Crime and Delinquency* 573 (2005) (large-scale quantitative study finding, contra some other studies, that mandatory arrest policies modestly reduce racial disparities in arrest for domestic violence, using); Mary Finn and Pamela Bettis, "Punitive Action or Gentle Persuasion: Exploring Police Officers' Justifications for Using Dual Arrest in Domestic Violence Cases," 12 *Violence Against Women* 268 (2006) (small-scale interview study with police officers); Keith Guzik, "The Forces of Conviction: The Power and Practice of Mandatory Prosecution upon Misdemeanor Domestic Battery Suspects," 32 *Law & Social Inquiry* 41 (2007) (ethnographic study showing abusers' violence is repeatedly redefined and displaced, as they are processed through the court setting). For an overview of the baseline research in this area, see Lisa Frohmann and Elizabeth Mertz, "Legal Reform and Social Construction: Violence, Gender and the Law," 19 *Law & Social Inquiry* 829, 835–841 (1994) (summarizes development of research on mandatory arrest from initial Minneapolis study through subsequent challenges to early findings).

There is similarly a growing social science literature on closely related issues such as "no-drop" policies for prosecutors in domestic violence cases (requiring that accused offenders be prosecuted) and on the differing gender dimensions of domestic violence against women and against men. See Amy Busch and Mindy Rosenberg, "Comparing Women and Men Arrested for Domestic Violence: A Preliminary Report," 19 *Journal of Domestic Violence* 49 (2004); Michael Johnson, "It's Not About Gender—Or Is It?," 67 *Journal of Marriage and Family* 1126 (2005). With subjects like domestic violence, which have been studied in multiple ways, it is often possible to assess the findings of an individual study within the broader context provided by other research. See http://www.elsblog.org/the_empirical_legal_studi/2006/06/combining_quant. html, for an argument that combining methods yields more robust results; for an example of research employing triangulated comparisons in the area of domestic violence, see Carolyn Hoyle, *Negotiating Domestic Violence: Police, Criminal Justice, and Victims* (2000).

(2.3) Miranda's Revenge: Police Interrogation as a Confidence Game

Richard A. Leo

30 *Law and Society Review* 259 (1996).

[In the famous case of *Miranda v. Arizona,* decided in 1966, the United States Supreme Court held that the police must warn anybody they arrest that they have a right to remain silent, and a right to call a lawyer, before answering any questions. The case has been controversial from the start: does it hamstring the police? Does it unduly favor criminals?

The police do comply with the decision, in the sense that they routinely give suspects the warning. Nonetheless, Richard Leo found that 78% of custodial suspects waived their rights; 64% provided "incriminating statements, admissions of guilt, or full confessions." Why? The answer, Leo feels, lies in the "nature of contemporary interrogation strategies, which are based on the manipulation and betrayal of trust." Contemporary police interrogation "bears many of the essential hallmarks of a confidence game."]

I. Methodology and Data Collection

The interrogation room is—and historically has always been—the most private social space in an American police station. It is traditionally located at the rear of the station house, carefully secluded from the view of civilian outsiders and the distractions of police insiders. What happens inside the interrogation room—the drama of custodial questioning, the art and science of police technique, and the confession of guilt—has long remained a mystery not only to the public but also to academic criminologists, sociologists, and legal scholars. Notwithstanding the many, often sensational, portrayals of interrogation scenes in American cinema, we know very little about how custodial police questioning is routinely conducted in America. Even among the most professional police departments, contemporary interrogation practices remain shrouded in secrecy.

Because police interrogation remains an intentionally hidden institutional practice, it is an unusually difficult subject for social scientists to research, especially through observational methods....

The analysis reported here is based on 9 months (more than 500 hours) of fieldwork inside the criminal investigation division (CID) of a major, urban police department that I identify by the pseudonym "Laconia," where I contemporaneously observed 122 interrogations involving 45 detectives. In addition, I viewed 30 videotaped custodial interrogations performed by a police department I identify by the pseudonym of "Southville" and another 30 videotaped interrogations performed by a police department I identify by the pseudonym of "Northville." In total, then, I observed, either contemporaneously or by videotape, 182 police interrogations of custodial suspects. For each interrogation, I recorded my observations qualitatively in the form of field notes and quantitatively with a 47–question coding sheet. In addition, I interviewed, both formally and informally, numerous detectives at all three police departments. Finally, I attended a half-dozen interrogation training courses taught by private training firms as well as by local and federal police agencies. . . .

II.   Police Interrogators as Confidence Men

A.   The Sociology of the Confidence Game

Confidence games are as old as Western civilization. Memorialized in fiction, popular biographies, and cinema, archetypical images of confidence men—typically as charming tricksters, clever manipulators, and betraying seducers—have long been salient in American folklore. . . .

The essence of a confidence game is the exchange of trust for hope. The confidence man, as the name suggests, attempts to induce confidence from an unknowing (if self-interested) victim by offering him the prospect of a better life, typically through financial gain. Drawing on his repertoire of tricks, the confidence man carefully contrives and frames the situation to set up the mark, sometimes even rehearsing and making up his particular roles. The confidence man must vary his personality and adapt his technique to fit the particular event, enticing the mark by holding out something he very much desires. The confidence man preys on the psychological vulnerabilities of the mark—usually greed, vanity, ignorance, or loneliness—through false representations, artifice, and subterfuge, eventually eliciting from the mark both his money and his trust. Once he has fleeced the mark, however, the confidence man must "cool him out"—assuage his anger so that the mark does not attempt retribution or complain to the police. Ultimately, then, the defining characteristic of a confidence game is the exploitation and betrayal of another person's trust for some kind of gain. Unlike other criminals, however, the confidence man never uses force to separate a mark from his money; rather, the confidence man thrives by his wits alone. The only weapons a confidence man has are his words and the images they offer. . . .

For the confidence game is, after all, a structured social interaction with an underlying logic and sequence of events. It typically moves from the initial contact phase to the money-extracting phase to the cooling-out phase. Whether the confidence man relies on the sheer force of his personality or outright trickery, he must move the mark through each of these stages. The successful confidence man must therefore draw not only on his histrionic talents but also on the logic and characteristics of the game. The confidence man does so by cleverly constructing a situation that seems authentic to the victim. The confidence man then uses the elements of the situation to carefully create and exploit the role obligations of the mark. These obligations are based on informal social understandings built into the particular confidence game. Drawing on these everyday understandings of the situation, the confidence man obtains compliance by appealing to the mark's desires or personal vulnerabilities, as well as to his sense of obligation within the situation. To succeed, then, the confidence man must manipulate not only the mark but also the structure of his subsequent social interaction with the mark.

Although interrogation is fundamentally an information-gathering activity, it closely resembles the process, sequence, and structure of a confidence game. To understand either the confidence game or police interrogation, then, one must analyze not merely its individual players but also its structure and sequence. In the past 30 years, police interrogators have refined their skills in human manipulation and become confidence men par excellence. In the course of my fieldwork numerous detectives described this sentiment, whether they invoked the metaphor of the confidence trick, the poker bluff, skilled salesmanship, or some related metaphor to describe their activities. As one police instructor in an interrogation training class I attended proudly declared, "We are con men . . . and con men never tell the mark they've been had." Or as another detective privately told me:

> The bottom line is that getting a confession comes down to bait and switch. It's like handing candy to a child and then gradually taking it away. You keep giving the suspect a little bit of the truth, and eventually they get so wrapped up in their lies that they confess. It's really all just one big con game.

In the remainder of this article, I develop this argument by analyzing the similarities between the confidence game and police interrogation through several stages of detective work: from "qualifying" the suspect, to "cultivating" the suspect, to "conning" the suspect into giving up the confession, to "cooling out" the suspect. Like the confidence game, police interrogation consists of an underlying sequence and structure of events; the whole of interrogation adds up to more than the sum of its individual parts. That structure and that sequence, of course, remain hidden from the suspect; it becomes visible only to repeat players, though they too—just like marks who return to the confidence operator only to be beaten again—sometimes fall prey to the very same tricks once more. Police interrogators, like confidence men, attempt to induce compliance from their suspects by offering them hope. The detective sells this bargain by exploiting the suspect's trust, ignorance, and sense of obligation within the situation. The essence of the con that is police interrogation ultimately lies in convincing the suspect that he and the interrogator share a common interest, that their relationship is a symbiotic rather than an adversarial one. . . .

Like the confidence man, the detective begins by qualifying or sizing up his suspect. This involves two consecutive stages of police work for the interrogating detective: he must first size up the suspect and the case against the suspect *prior to* any custodial questioning; second, the detective will psychologically size up the suspect during interrogation. The purpose of the first sizing up is to construct a working profile of the suspect as well as a situational profile of the particular crime for which the suspect has been arrested; the purpose of the second sizing up is to figure out how the detective can manipulate the suspect into confessing.

Prior to any questioning, the detective has already "worked up the suspect's case." The detective has read the police report and possibly contacted the arresting or reporting officer for any clarifications as well as any fellow detectives who may have experience with the suspect; the detective has certainly contacted the victim; taken any witness statements; examined any property found in evidence; and usually has done any other preparatory work necessary to learn as much about the case as is reasonably possible. In addition, the detective has run the rapsheets of both the suspect and the victim to examine their arrest/conviction records, another factor that helps in sizing up both the suspect and the case prior to any questioning. . . .

Having sized up both the likelihood of the suspect's guilt and the "righteousness" of the victim, as well as the seriousness of the case, the detective enters the interrogation ready to size up the suspect on another level: the psychology of his personality and his vulnerability to various forms of manipulation. As one skillful female detective told me:

> I guess everyone has their own technique and strategies, but the first thing you have to do is meet with the person that you are going to interview and then you can determine what kind of strategy you are going to use—if it's going to be the mother approach, the mean approach, the sullen approach, the real friendly approach. It varies from person to person, and while you are interviewing the person, you are formulating questions in your mind as you speak.

The detective sizes up the suspect with what police almost universally refer to as their sixth sense, a heightened intuition about, and ability to analyze, human behavior based on occupational life experiences. The sixth sense of the police interrogator is identical to the grift sense of the confidence man. The detective analyzes the suspect's behavior, his body movements, and demeanor, as well as the content of his responses to different types of questions or appeals, in order to discern the suspect's apparent manner of lying and truth-telling as well as his apparent psychological vulnerabilities. The detective's goal in sizing up the suspect is to figure out strategically how he or she can "break" the suspect during interrogation to eventually elicit a confession.

In sizing up the suspect, the detective may conduct a "pre-interview" of sorts, asking the suspect essentially nonaccusatorial questions in order to observe his verbal and nonverbal baseline responses to stressful as well as nonstressful stimuli. As a homicide interrogator told me:

> In essence we are doing a pre-interview once we start talking to the guy. We don't jump right into the crime, we're talking to the guy basically getting his story, oftentimes it's his alibi, his denial. During that denial phase is when we use these techniques to determine what kind of person he is, you know, how he responds, and during his denial I am using things and keeping mental notes because in that denial there are things that I'm going to use against him later on to get him to break, and that's when I

gather information about his background, his family, his girlfriends, who he looks up to, those kinds of things.

To this end, interrogators may draw on the methods of Behavioral Analysis and/ or Neuro–Linguistic Programming, "two psychological strategies that, many police believe, teach interrogators to read the behavior of their subjects like human lie-detectors" . . . Fashioned by the Chicago-based interrogation training firm Reid & Associates, the Behavioral Analysis Interview consists of a structured set of nonaccusatorial hypothetical questions, ranging from general questions such as why the suspect thinks someone would have committed the crime to more specific questions such as whether the suspect would be willing to take a polygraph. . . .

According to the theory of Behavioral Analysis, guilty suspects react defensively and with discomfort to these questions; they equivocate, stall, and provide evasive or noncommittal answers. By contrast, innocent suspects are thought to produce cooperative, direct, and spontaneous responses to these questions.

Like the Behavioral Analysis Interview, Neuro–Linguistic Programming is another method of detecting truth and deception (again equated with innocence and guilt) on the basis of behavioral responses to nonaccusatory questions. According to Neuro–Linguistic Programming, a relationship exists between the positioning and movement of the eyes and the brain's sensory process mechanisms. Many interrogators believe that one can easily and reliably determine the suspect's predominant system of information processing (visual, auditory, or kinesthetic) by watching and studying the suspect's eye movements, which become windows into the suspect's soul. By analyzing the suspect's eye movements in relation to his primary sensory orientation, the interrogator can determine whether the suspect is lying or responding truthfully. For example, if a visually oriented person looks up and to the left, he is most likely telling the truth; but if his eyes look up and to the right or if he is staring straight ahead and not focused, he is most likely lying. In addition, once a pattern of eye movement has been established, a movement in the opposite direction is believed to indicate deception. Symptoms such as a break in eye contact, looking away at the ceiling or floor, pupil dilation, closed eyes, squinting eyes, and rapid blinking of the eyes are considered likely indicators of deception. . . .

C. "Cultivating" the Suspect

The next stage of the confidence game is to "cultivate" the mark, which confidence men accomplish through strategies of manipulation and control well known to students of "compliance professionals". . . . Masters of influence and suggestion, confidence men draw on a variety of psychological techniques that resemble common methods of persuading and manipulating others. Like a salesman, the confidence man must be a convincing talker who knows his product and can shift roles easily. . . . For like the salesman, the confidence man attempts to trade on certain weaknesses of human nature. . . .

Once the interrogator's belief in the suspect's guilt is confirmed the detective's goal becomes to cultivate the suspect to respond to his overtures. If detectives draw on the methods or general principles of Behavioral Analysis and/or Neuro–Linguistic Programming to qualify the suspect, they use many of the tactics I have described elsewhere as "conditioning" . . . to cultivate the suspect. The goal here is to establish a pattern of psychological dependence on the interrogator that leads to a "yes or submissive mood." To achieve this "conditioned reflex," police carefully stage-manage the physical and social aspects of the interrogation setting. In addition, police use positive and negative reinforcement to condition the suspect to feel emotionally compelled to cooperate with the interrogator's requests for information. . . .

Of course, even before questioning the suspect, the detective structures the custodial environment so as to facilitate conversation. The detective often brings the suspect from the jail to the interrogation room in the criminal investigation division, politely introduces himself (shaking the suspect's hand), inquires about the suspect's well-being, careful to project a friendly and sincere image, perhaps even joking a little with the suspect, and then provides the suspect with coffee before leaving him to "stew" in the interrogation room.

For example, in one interrogation I observed:

[T]he detective went down to the jail, very politely and graciously introduced himself and his partner to the suspect, apologized for having to handcuff the suspect, brought him up to the interview room in C.I.D, took off the cuffs, offered the suspect a cup of coffee, and then let him wait for 15 minutes.

The secluded interrogation room—with its barren and remote interior—is ecologically structured to avoid distractions and promote intimate conversation. Posted on the interrogation room door will be a sheet with the suspect's name written on it as well as the crime for which he is under investigation, and when the detective returns, he will bring in a thick case folder with the suspect's name prominently featured on it. An entry from my field notes describing an interrogator who uses this technique:

He puts the suspect's name on a sheet on the door, which the suspect then looks at before entering the interrogation room, which makes the suspect's interrogation look more serious than it really is. . . . He also lets the suspect sit in the room for 5–15 minutes, so as to create the impression that it isn't so important to the investigator whether he talks. He also brings in a stack of reports, so as to suggest that the suspect has a lot of evidence against him.

All these ploys are, of course, intended to raise the suspect's anxiety level and thus facilitate the process of eliciting inculpatory admissions. Once inside the interrogation room, the detective again strives to maintain a positive rapport with the suspect, even while asking the background questions necessary to fill out the top part of the *Miranda* form. During the process of asking the suspect these "routine booking questions," the detective may talk to him about where he lives. who else lives in his household, his employment history or prospects, sporting events. or any other subject that may be the basis of rapport-building conversation.

The first step in cultivating the suspect is successfully negotiating the *Miranda* waiver. Detectives will use subtle psychological strategies to predispose a suspect toward voluntarily waiving his or her *Miranda* warnings. For example, the detective may precede the reading of the *Miranda* warnings with a discussion of the importance of truth-telling. In one interrogation I observed:

> The detective said that he wanted to hear the suspect's side of the story but that he could do so only if the suspect gave us permission to talk to him. The suspect immediately denied any wrongdoing. The detective responded that we could not listen to his side of the story just yet. As he was to do many times throughout the interrogation, the detective emphasized that it would be important for the suspect to tell the truth, so that he could clear himself if he was not guilty. This would be his only opportunity to tell his side of the story, however, the detective said. But he first had to read the *Miranda* warnings, which he said were no big deal since the suspect had seen them before on television.

Or the detective may subtly nod his head up and down as he reads to the suspect the waiver statement that follows the warnings. In another interrogation I observed:

> Detective H moves his head in a slight up-down motion as he is reading the warnings, so as to subtly induce a waiver by subconsciously conveying the message that the suspect should mirror him and also wave his head up and own in a motion signifying "yes."

Or the detective may lightly refer to the warnings as a formality that the suspect is well aware of from television and can probably recite better than the investigator. In another interrogation I observed, the detective began by stating:

> In order for me to talk to you specifically about the injury with [victim's name], I need to advise you of your rights. It's a formality. I'm sure you've watched television with the cop shows, right, and you hear them say their rights and so you can probably recite this better than I can, but it's something I need to do and we can this out of the way before we talk about what's happened.

Or the detective may inform the suspect that this is going to be his one and only chance to tell the police his side of the story. In another interrogation I observed:

> The detective began by telling the suspect that he just wanted the suspect's side of the story. "You're implicated," he said, "whether or not

you're actually guilty." Then he confronted the suspect with the evidence against him. "Everyone says you did it, Everyone is pointing to you. You are a suspect, and that is why we have placed you under arrest for the murder of [victim's name]. If you did it accidentally, if you did it in self-defense, if someone else was in the room, we need to know, because all the evidence points to that happening. We need to get your side of the story, but first we have to advise you of your rights." The detective then read the suspect his *Miranda* rights.

Once *Miranda* has been successfully negotiated and the suspect has indicated a willingness to speak, the detective presses the suspect to respond to his questions truthfully. Prior to asking the suspect factual questions, many detectives first tell the suspect that they are not going to "jerk around" or lie to the suspect, so the suspect also should not jerk around or lie to them; or that the one thing the detective will not do is take a lie to the district attorney; or that lying to the detective will only make matters worse for the suspect. The detective might add that he has extensive experience investigating this kind of crime and can easily tell when a suspect is lying to him. Although the detectives I observed almost always appeared well versed in the facts of the suspect's case, they repeatedly emphasized the psychological importance of creating an appearance of knowing more than the suspect does about the case, so that the suspect does not think he can fool the detective.

Following this admonition about the important of telling the truth the interrogator usually begins by simply asking the suspect what happened. I often observed suspects telling stories or issuing denials that appeared to contradict either the victim's version of the events or the existing inculpatory evidence against the suspect. The detective's response was typically to point out the logical or factual inconsistencies between the suspect's account and the evidentiary record, pressing the suspect for an account of the events that comports with the facts as the detective knows or perceives them. During this process, detectives use strategies of positive and negative reinforcement to condition the suspect to respond truthfully. For example, when the suspect appears to be telling the truth, the detective may compliment him, praising him for being a "man about the situation" or an unusually honest person; when the suspect appears not to be speaking truthfully, the detective may repeatedly tell the suspect he is lying and that no one will believe his story. In addition, the detective may offer positive and negative reinforcement through his body movements and the manipulation of physical space. For example, some detectives move closer to the suspect when they believe the suspect is not responding truthfully, and pull back when they believe the suspect is telling the truth. Or the detective may mirror a suspect's body language— placing a hand on his cheek when the suspect places a hand on his cheek or turning right when the suspect turns right, for example....

A very common strategy among detectives is to tell the suspect that they are here to discuss why, not whether, the suspect committed the crime. In the words of one interrogator:

> I say, "I'll let you talk, but don't tell me you didn't do it, because you did it. You know you did it, we know you did it, everybody knows you did it. It ain't a question of who did it, I'm telling you it's not a mystery, you did it."

However, if cultivating the suspect to issue a version of the events that comports with the detective's beliefs initially fails, the detective may take a "denial statement" from the victim, hoping to catch the suspect in a lie that the detective can use as psychological leverage to induce a true statement from the suspect later in the interrogation.

D.   "Conning" the Suspect: Eliciting the Confession

The detective often begins custodial questioning by telling the suspect that his job is merely to discover the facts and that the interrogation session will be the suspect's only opportunity to tell the police the truth. Emphasizing that there are two sides to every story, the detective suggests, whether implicitly or explicitly, that the suspect needs to collect or rebut the charges against him if he wishes for the police to know the true version of what happened during the alleged crime. The detective attempts to establish common ground with the suspect by convincing him that the detective, in his role as fact-finder, can help the suspect only if he speaks truthfully. Underscoring that his role is merely to get the facts and report them to other, more influential actors within the criminal justice system, the detective portrays himself as the suspect's friend and ally, if not the suspect's advocate, implicitly seeking the suspect's trust and confidence. "There are degrees of innocence and degrees of guilt, and we need to know your level of participation," the interrogator may tell the suspect, suggesting that the suspect's story, if it is truthful, can be shaped and packaged by the detective to minimize the suspect's culpability. The catch, however, is that the suspect must be truthful. What is important, the detective informs the suspect, is not what the suspect tells the detective so much as what the detective tells the district attorney. For it is the district attorney, not the detective, who exercises the real power over the suspect's fate in the criminal justice system. It is the district attorney who will, at his complete discretion, decide whether and to what degree the suspect will be charged with the alleged offense. But how the district attorney reacts to the information the detective relays to him depends on what the suspect tells the detective. Following this suggestion, the detective may repeat several times that the suspect's degree of truthfulness and cooperation with the detective will determine how the district attorney approaches the case. An example from my field notes illustrates this point well:

> Sergeant D tried to sell suspect B on the idea that remorse was in his self-interest because the district attorney would go favorably on him if he was cooperative. Sergeant D drew out a little box chart on a piece of paper and said that the district attorney would, for example, X the 90–months box if the suspect did not cooperate, but only X the 10–month box if he did. That if the district attorney thought suspect B was full of shit, he wouldn't think twice about pressing for the maximum sentence. The

66

district attorney's decision, then, was dependent on suspect B's honesty and cooperativeness, especially since suspect B won't be clogging up the judicial system and he will be taking responsibility for his actions, Sergeant D told him.

Detectives are careful to qualify their appeals and make no explicit promises of leniency, but what the detective communicates to the suspect is, in effect, a hint or suggestion of leniency in exchange for truthful cooperation. If the detective believes the suspect is lying, the detective will conjure an image of the district attorney as a cynical and punitive figure, who has heard every cock-and-bull story enough times to know when an accused suspect is lying and when he should be "charged to the max." On the other hand, if the detective believes the suspect is telling the truth, he will conjure an image of the district attorney as an understanding and forgiving person who realizes that reasonable people sometimes make mistakes. . . .

The detective's next strategy may be to invoke the sensibilities and powers of a hypothetical judge and jury against which to evaluate the plausibility of the suspect's claims. In the detective's persuasive appeals to his expertise, to the weight of the incriminating evidence (whether real or fabricated) against the suspect, or to the suspect's self-interest, the detective may repeatedly conjure images of the judge and jury as future questioners of the suspect's motives and integrity unless he comes clean and admits to his crimes in the present. If the detective believes the suspect is not speaking truthfully, the detective portrays the judge as a stern and unforgiving figure who, like the district attorney, is cynical about defendants who plead their innocence despite overwhelming evidence of their guilt. For example, in one audio-recorded interrogation that I observed, the detective told the suspect:

> You know a thing the judge takes into consideration for sentencing is remorse or guilt in the person who did the crime. And somebody who doesn't feel sorry for what happened, who doesn't feel remorseful for what happened, the judge is going to feel they really need to be punished. They can't admit to what they did, that it was wrong, that they made a mistake. But this person didn't think he did anything wrong. I guess we'll just lock him up because he didn't do anything wrong. Or they say, look he knows he made a mistake, he knows he did something wrong.

Unlike the district attorney, however, the suspect realizes (or is told) that the judge carries sentencing powers. Although he often intones these words and delivers this appeal in a friendly and sympathetic manner, the detective's intent is to raise the suspect's anxiety about the perceived negative consequences of failing to provide the detective with inculpatory admissions.

Detectives, however, appeal more to juries in their persuasive efforts than to either the district attorney or the judge, perhaps because of the popular, and sometimes quite vivid, representations of the jury in American cinema. Detectives typically portray juries, in their role as fact-finders, as reasonable people who judge the suspect's credibility based on the consistency and plausibility of his denials; however, detectives also typically portray juries, in

67

their role as adjudicators of guilt, as angry about high levels of crime in our society and as especially punitive toward dishonest and remorseless defendants. In one audio-recorded interrogation I observed, for example, the detective made the following appeal:

> DETECTIVE: If you take this to a jury trial, they're going to hit you hard. They're going to slam you real hard. He's trying to lie to us, he must think we're stupid. Ladies and gentlemen of the jury, we have the evidence that shows he broke the window. He says "no, I didn't do it." Now do you want to be lenient with this guy?

> The suspect interjects: No, I'm not going to go for this one.

> DETECTIVE: Fine, we'll take it to a jury trial, but they're going to say he's guilty, he's guilty. You had a chance to tell the truth. They'll say: he had a chance. The sergeants talked to him and gave him an opportunity to explain how it happened, to give his side of the story, and what did he do? He lied. That's what he's going to say. He's going to say you lied. You had a chance to tell the truth but you lied. That's exactly what he's going to say.

With these images in place, the detective may repeatedly ask the suspect how he or she plans to prove their innocence to the jury in light of the evidence against them; or how the suspect expects the jury to react to his obviously inconsistent or contradictory alibi; or how the suspect expects the jury to treat an obviously guilty defendant who refuses to be truthful about or acknowledge responsibility for his actions (oftentimes the detective has caught the suspect in a lie and repeatedly uses this fact to challenge the suspect's perceived integrity in the eyes of the imagined jury unless the suspect comes forward with the whole truth); or what the suspect would do if he were in the jury's shoes and the facts were as the detective believes (and everyone else will also believe) them to be....

Through the use of these appeals, detectives often effectively reverse denials and elicit admissions, for they exploit not merely the suspect's trust but, like any good confidence operator, the mark's ignorance as well. To be successful, this confidence trick necessarily relies on the ignorance of its victim. For the detective can only persuade the suspect that his best interests dictate confessing if the suspect actually believes (or comes to believe) that he must prove his innocence to a jury; in fact, however, the prosecution bears the entire burden of proving the suspect's guilt in a criminal proceeding. Nor could this confidence trick succeed if the suspect realized that, despite the dramatic images of testimony and cross-examination, virtually all criminal cases never see the light of a jury trial but are instead resolved by backroom plea bargaining.

Perhaps most fundamentally, however, this confidence trick can only work if the detective mystifies the real nature of his relationship to the suspect. Although the suspect may convince a detective of his innocence and earn his subsequent release, it remains true that in most instances the detective is not a friend or protector of the suspect any more than he is a neutral fact-finder. In the adversary system, the purpose of the interrogation is, for the most part, to incriminate rather than to exculpate the criminal suspect. The suspect who admits to his crimes naively believes that by confessing to the interrogator his situation will be improved or that he will feel better or that this is the first step in turning his life around or that his family and friends will treat him with greater respect. The suspect may also confess out of a sense of obligation and reciprocation to the detective, who is offering to help him out.

Of course, some suspects are con-wise enough to see through the detectives' confidence tricks and scripted performances, just as some potential marks see through the guises of the con artist. The suspect may, for example, remind the detective that he doesn't have to prove his innocence to the police; or tell the detective that confessing will only earn him a prison sentence; or insist that he will prevail if his case is taken to a jury trial. And, of course, some suspects choose not to speak to the police altogether. Although the skillful interrogator is a confidence artist par excellence, he operates at a double disadvantage that distinguishes him from his real-world counterpart. First, unlike the confidence man, the detective does not get to choose his victims. Second, *Miranda* requires that the detective forewarn the suspect of the confidence game of police interrogation prior to its inception: "Anything you say can and will be used against you in court of law" flatly announces to the suspect that the detective's purpose is to incriminate him. Moreover, the suspect is told that he may remain silent and is entitled to state-appointed legal representation before any questioning. . . .

Most suspects who confess, however, do not appear to see through the con. The detective has treated the suspect in a polite, sympathetic, and sincere manner. Moreover, the detective, who embodies the authority of a police officer even if he is attired in civilian clothes, has convinced the suspect that he was acting in his best interest and thus doing the right thing when he confessed to his crimes. In exchange for the suspect's inculpatory admissions, the suspect received the hope of a better situation, perhaps even the promise of a better life. He has just been conned. The next step in the police interrogation, as in the classic confidence game, thus involves cooling out the suspect so that, having incriminated himself in the most fundamental and damning manner possible, he remains convinced (if only for a short while) that he did the right thing. For eventually the suspect will realize that he has been conned—whether this occurs immediately after he made his admissions; or when he is returned to jail and contemplates the significance of what just happened; or when he first speaks to the public defender's office and is chastised by his attorney for waiving his *Miranda* rights. Another example from my field notes:

> The detective asked the suspect why he "fessed up" to this at the end of the interrogation. The suspect remarked, "I've been conned, ... No," the detective responded, "You've just been tricked into telling the truth."

Like confidence men, police interrogators also maintain a generally cynical, if dualistic, view of human nature. It is a truism among detectives that all suspects lie; as one detective told me, "you can tell if a suspect is lying by whether he is moving his lips." Detectives perceive their suspect as typically corrupted (sometimes violent) and remorseless individuals who given another opportunity, would unhesitatingly repeat their criminal acts. Though no detective would describe a suspect as a "lying dirty son-of-a-bitch not worth shit" during a taped interview, they sometimes referred to their suspects in similar language in informal conversations with me or with one another. . . .

Just as a confidence man believes that no honest person can "be cheated by his tricks," so too do contemporary police interrogators believe that no innocent person can be tricked into falsely confessing by their techniques. These beliefs, central to the respective folklores of both the confidence game and police interrogation, are frequently offered to rationalize the confidence operators' or police detectives' deceits. They are myths, however. Honest people are, in fact, sometimes swindled by confidence tricksters, just as innocent suspects sometimes do, in fact, falsely confess to police as the result of psychologically sophisticated interrogation techniques. . . . Virtually all of the police detectives in my study, however, denied the possibility of false confessions, and were altogether ignorant of recent, documented cases of false confessions to police.

E. Cooling Out the Suspect

. . . .

The criminal suspect who makes an inculpatory admission or confesses to the police is subsequently cooled out not because the detective fears retribution or that the suspect will file a complaint against him. Rather, the detective cools out the suspect because he wants the suspect both to accept responsibility for his actions and to leave the interrogation room certain in his belief that confessing to the police was the best course of action. The cooling-out phase of interrogation is essentially an exercise in positive reinforcement and morale-building. It serves not only to reassure the suspect who has just incriminated himself but also to leave him with a favorable impression of both the interrogation and the police. For, as every detective knows, once the suspect obtains counsel, he will challenge the legality of his confession statement both at the pretrial *Miranda* and the pretrial evidence suppression hearings. In addition, the defense attorney will privately chastise his or her client for speaking to the police, reminding the suspect of the literal words of the *Miranda* warnings, as well as the adverse significance of confessions. The cooling-out phase of police interrogation consists of complimenting the suspect for his actions and then portraying the confession in its best possible light. Following the suspect's initial admissions, the detective will repeatedly thank the suspect for his honesty and cooperation, perhaps even underscoring the suspect's virtuous behavior by favorably contrasting him to other suspects the detective has questioned. Trying to psychologically soothe the suspect during his admission, the detective emphasizes that the suspect just made a simple mistake, which was understandable under the circumstances, "but owning up to it is what is important." Following one confession I observed, for example, the two interrogating detectives pointed out to the suspect that everybody made mistakes, and they complimented her for cooperating with them, admitting her mistake, and then trying to do the right thing. She was not a criminal, they said, just "someone who happened to get involved in a bad situation." Consistent with his feigned role as the suspect's friend, the detective cools out the suspect by writing up the confession in a neutral tone that emphasizes the suspect's remorse. . . .

The detective may, once again, tell the suspect the district attorney, judge, and jury will weigh his truthfulness and good character when evaluating the case against him, once more implicitly suggesting a hint of leniency or reward for the suspect's cooperation. The detective may also tell the suspect that he will press the district attorney to drop one of the collateral offenses with which the suspect is charged, or perhaps even tell the district attorney that he believes the suspect should only be charged with a "lesser-included" offense. After the suspect reads over and signs the confession statement that the detective has just written, the detective walks the suspect back down to the jail, thanking him for his cooperation and wishing him well. The confidence game that is police interrogation has just been completed.

III. Conclusion: The Exercise of Power inside the Interrogation Room

. . . .

That contemporary American police interrogation resembles the structure and sequence of a classic confidence game helps us understand not only why custodial suspects waive their *Miranda* rights and admit to wrongdoing in such high numbers but also how police power is exercised inside the interrogation room. As we have seen, contemporary interrogation strategies are based fundamentally on the manipulation and betrayal of trust. Like confidence men, police interrogators attempt to induce compliance from their suspects by offering them the hope of a better situation in exchange for incriminating information. The interrogator exercises power through his ability to frame the suspect's definition of the situation, exploiting the suspect's ignorance to create the illusion of a relationship that is symbiotic rather than adversarial. In the exercise of his power, the interrogator relies on a series of appeals that mystify both the true nature of the detective's relationship to the suspect and the true extent of his influence with other actors in the criminal justice system.

Yet the detective's power in the interrogation room appears on equal footing with that of the suspect's. After all, the interrogator can only interrogate if, and to the extent that, the suspect consents to questioning; and the interrogator must implore the suspect to buy the goods the interrogator is selling. No longer premised on force or duress, police power inside the interrogation room is based on, and limited by, the social psychology of persuasion. The logic of interaction becomes consensual. As its basis shifts from coercion to persuasion, police power becomes more diffuse, more relational, and more unstable ...

Miranda's revenge, however, has been to transform police power inside the interrogation room without undermining its effectiveness.... *Miranda* warnings symbolically declare that police take individual rights seriously. At the same time, *Miranda* inspired police to create more sophisticated interrogation strategies, effectively giving them the license to act as confidence men and develop their skills in human manipulation and deception. In ways not captured by doctrinal analysis, *Miranda* has changed profoundly both the psychological context and the moral ordering of police interrogation. Driven by careful strategic considerations, police interrogators exercise power by manipulating custodial suspects' definition of the situation and of their role; by creating the appearance of a symbiotic rather than an adversarial relationship; by appealing to their insider knowledge and expertise; and by exploiting the suspects' ignorance, fear and trust. Despite the universalistic pretensions of *Miranda*, the exercise of police power inside the interrogation room rests more on particularistic appeals than on universal norms. That contemporary police interrogation resembles both the method and substance of a classic confidence game—and thus has become manipulative and deceptive to its very core—may be *Miranda's* most enduring legacy.

NOTES AND QUESTIONS

1. In this article, Leo refers to a classic article by Abraham S. Blumberg, "The Practice of Law as Confidence Game: Organizational Cooptation of a Profession," which appeared in 1 *Law and Society Review* 15 (1967). The thrust of Blumberg's article is that, in criminal cases, the defense lawyer is not really on the defendant's side; rather, the lawyer is a "double agent," whose loyalty is to the court organization and the system itself, as well as (or in place of) loyalty to the client. He "lives astride both worlds and can serve the ends of the two as well as his own."

This "double agent" role is particularly salient in the light of the prevailing practicing of *plea bargaining* or "copping a plea." Defendants feel they were "conned," or "manipulated," induced to plead guilty, and most often the main force in persuading them to do this was their own lawyer. Of the defendants Blumberg surveyed who pleaded guilty (many of whom still claimed to be innocent), most identified defense counsel as the person who first suggest a plea of guilty, and as the one who influenced the accused the most in the final decision to plead.

2. Plea Bargaining: Most of the serious criminal cases in the United States end up with a plea bargain, rather than with a trial. Plea bargaining is a practice in which a defendant agrees to plead guilty, giving up his right to a trial, in exchange for a promise to drop charges, reduce charges, or lower the sentence. It is a pervasive aspect of the criminal justice system. In the federal district courts, in 2004, out of 73,616 criminal defendants who were *convicted*, no less than 71,028 pleaded guilty or nolo contendere (that is, did not enter a

defense); only 2,276 were convicted by a jury, and 312 by a judge. (These figures are from the *Sourcebook of Criminal Justice Statistics Online*, http://www.albany.edu/sourcebook/pdf/t5222004.pdf, visited August 10, 2006). The results are no different in the states. In New York City, for example, in 2005, 57,099 felons were convicted in 2005; 55,944 pleaded guilty—this is more than 97% (figures from Division of Criminal Justice Services, New York State, http://criminaljustice.state.ny.us/crimnet/ojsa/dispos/nyc/htm, visited August 10, 2006). A few of these defendants may have pleaded guilty out of shame or remorse, but the vast majority are accounted for by plea bargaining.

On the historical origins of plea bargaining, and its uses in the past, see George Fisher, *Plea Bargaining's Triumph* (2003); Carolyn Ramsey, "The Discretionary Power of 'Public' Prosecutors in Historical Perspective," 39 *American Criminal Law Review* 1309 (2002); Lawrence M. Friedman, "Plea Bargaining in Historical Perspective," 12 *Law & Society Review* 247 (1979); John Padgett, "Plea Bargaining and Prohibition in the Federal Courts, 1908–1934," 24 *Law & Society Review* 413 (1990).

3. <u>Plea bargaining is controversial</u>: There are many objections to it. Samuel Krislov, "Debating on Bargaining: Comments from a Synthesizer," 13 *Law & Society Review* 573 (1979), sums up some of them. Some people object to the very notion of "haggling," either because it is "unseemly," or because it "produces differential results." Others argue that plea bargaining, which is informal, and takes place out of sight of the public, "undermines the appearance of justice." Some argue that it is coercive, that it "induces the accused either to plead guilty in return for a lighter sentence ... or to give up other rights in return for some advantage."

Plea bargaining can be attacked as either too harsh or too lenient—too harsh: in that it subverts due process, and shuts off a defendant's chance to prove his innocence; too lenient: in that it results in lighter sentences and fewer charges for people who are dangerous to the public, or are simply bad people. Very few people have a good word to say for plea bargaining, and their have been repeated attempts to abolish it or to limit its scope.

4. <u>Do other societies have plea bargaining</u>? The answer seems to be yes—though always with a difference. On England, see John Baldwin and Michael McConville, "Plea Bargaining and Plea Negotiation in England," 13 *Law & Society Review* 287 (1979). Baldwin and McConville claimed to find plea bargaining in England, where it was not supposed to exist; their study angered the establishment of the English legal profession. On Canada, see Hedieh Nasheri, *Betrayal of Due Process: A Comparative Assessment of Plea Bargaining in the United States and Canada* (1998).

Canada and England are common law jurisdictions. In many legal systems, there is no such thing as a guilty plea. The state is supposed to make its case, whether or not the defendant claims to be innocent. In such a system, of course, it would be difficult to have plea bargaining, in the literal American sense. Yet in the German criminal justice system, we find something rather like plea bargaining, as described in Máximo Langer, "From Legal Transplants to Legal Translations: The Globalization of Plea Bargaining and the Americanization Thesis in Criminal Procedure," 45 *Harvard International Law Journal* 1, 39–45 (2004). In Germany, during the 1970's, "judges, prosecutors and defense attorneys of the German criminal justice system began developing bargains, or *Absprachen,* on the quiet before and during trial." The practice arose because there were more and more cases, and some were long and difficult. Since the guilty plea does not exist, the "bargain" consists of an offer to "confess at trial, in exchange for a guarantee by the judge that the sentence will not exceed a certain limit or that a number of charges will be dismissed." The confession makes it easier to prove the state's facts, and this shortens the trial. Also, the judge plays an active role in the process.

Langer also finds an Italian equivalent, the *patteggiamento.* Under this system, defense and prosecution "can reach an agreement about a sentence and request that it be imposed by the judge." The device, however, is more limited in scope than the U.S. plea bargain, and is less flexible (id. at 46–53). Langer also finds something like American plea bargaining in Argentina.

Langer's article attacks the thesis that these procedures, which more or less resemble the plea bargain, are the result of American influence. If he is correct, how are we to explain them? Notice that in such countries as Germany and England, plea bargaining or its equivalent was for a long time a kind of guilty secret, not to be mentioned or discussed. Nobody who just read the penal codes and codes of criminal procedure—in the United States and elsewhere—would learn much, if anything, about plea bargaining or its equivalents. Why should this be so? How would you go about trying to account for the rise of plea bargaining or its equivalents in these various countries?

5. The *Miranda* warning: The *Miranda* decision has been controversial from the start; but the Supreme Court has never repudiated it; and the "Miranda warning" has, indeed, entered into popular culture, thanks to the movies and television. Ernesto Miranda himself had a long prison record. In 1972, he was released on parole. For a while, he cashed in on his celebrity, "selling autographed, preprinted *Miranda* warning cards for $1.50 apiece in downtown Phoenix." A year and a half later, he went back to prison for a parole violation; meanwhile, he had been arrested several times, and listened to the warnings which were named after him. In 1975, he was released from prison. About a month later, he died—stabbed in a brawl in a barroom. Two men were arrested; they heard the "Miranda warning," and "voluntarily waived their rights." But they did not confess. They were released "pending further investigation," whereupon "both disappeared and were never seen again." Gary L. Stuart, *Miranda: The Story of America's Right to Remain Silent* 95–99 (2004).

The opponents of *Miranda* argue that it hobbles the police. Did it play a role in the fact that nobody has been punished for killing Miranda himself? Is it possible that, even though they waived their rights, they were not subjected to the same kind of vigorous questioning that would have taken place before the *Miranda* decision?

Those who <u>like</u> the decision argue that the decision helps curb police brutality and cruel or manipulative questioning. What is Richard Leo's view of the impact of the decision? What evidence does he bring to bear on this question? See Paul G. Cassell & Richard Fowles, "Handcuffing the Cops? A Thirty–Year Perspective on Miranda's Harmful Effects on Law Enforcement," 50 *Stanford Law Review* 1055 (1998); John J. Donohue III, "Did Miranda Diminish Police Effectiveness?" (id. at 1147); Cassell & Fowles, "Falling Clearance Rates After Miranda: Coincidence or Consequence?" (id. at 1181).

In *Dickerson v. United States*, 530 U.S. 428 (2000), the Supreme Court, over two dissenting votes, reaffirmed the validity of the *Miranda* case, and held that it was a "constitutional decision" that could not be "overruled by an Act of Congress;" and that the case and its "progeny in this Court govern the admissibility of statements made during custodial interrogation."

6. <u>Research Method</u>: How would you describe Leo's research method? His equivalent of a "sample"? Like Hickman and Simpson, Leo limited his study to one jurisdiction—indeed, to one police station. Can you generalize from this kind of research? What are its limitations? What are its strengths?

(B) Contract Law

(2.4) Non–Contractual Relations in Business: A Preliminary Study

Stewart Macaulay

28 *American Sociological Review* 55 (1963).

What good is contract law? who uses it? when and how? Complete answers would require an investigation of almost every type of transaction between individuals and organizations. In this report, research has been confined to exchanges between businesses and primarily to manufacturers. Furthermore, this report will be limited to a presentation of the findings concerning when contract is and is not used and to a tentative explanation of these findings.

This research is only the first phase in a scientific study. The primary research technique involved interviewing 68 businessmen and lawyers representing 43 companies and six law firms.... All but two of the companies had plants in Wisconsin; 17 were manufacturers of machinery but none made such items as food products, scientific instruments, textiles or petroleum products. Thus the likelihood of error because of sampling bias may be considerable.[6]

---

6. However, the cases have not been selected because they did use contract. There is as much interest in, and effort to obtain, cases of nonuse as of use of contract. Thus, one variety of bias has been minimized.

. . . This study represents the effort of a law teacher to draw on sociological ideas and empirical investigation. It stresses, among other things, the functions and dysfunctions of using contract to solve exchange problems and the influence of occupational roles on how one assesses whether the benefits of using contract outweigh the costs.

To discuss when contract is and is not used, the term "contract" must be specified. This term will be used here to refer to devices for conducting exchanges. Contract is not treated as synonymous with an exchange itself, which may or may not be characterized as contractual. Nor is contract used to refer to a writing recording an agreement. Contract, as I use the term here, involves two distinct elements: (a) rational planning of the transaction with careful provision for as many future contingencies as can be foreseen, and (b) the existence or use of actual or potential legal sanctions to induce performance of the exchange or to compensate for non-performance.

These devices for conducting exchanges may be used or may exist in greater or lesser degree, so that transactions can be described relatively as involving a more contractual or a less contractual manner (a) of creating an exchange relationship or (b) of solving problems arising during the course of such a relationship. For example, General Motors might agree to buy all of the Buick Division's requirements of aluminum for ten years from Reynolds Aluminum. Here the two large corporations probably would plan their relationship carefully. The plan probably would include a complex pricing formula designed to meet market fluctuations, an agreement on what would happen if either party suffered a strike or a fire, a definition of Reynolds' responsibility for quality control and for losses caused by defective quality, and many other provisions. As the term contract is used here, this is a more contractual method of creating an exchange relationship than is a home-owner's casual agreement with a real estate broker giving the broker the exclusive right to sell the owner's house which fails to include provisions for the consequences of many easily foreseeable (and perhaps even highly probable) contingencies. In both instances, legally enforceable contracts may or may not have been created, but it must be recognized that the existence of a legal sanction has no necessary relationship to the degree of rational planning by the parties, beyond certain minimal legal requirements of certainty of obligation. General Motors and Reynolds might never sue or even refer to the written record of their agreement to answer questions which come up during their ten-year relationship, while the real estate broker might sue, or at least threaten to sue, the owner of the house. The broker's method of *dispute settlement* then would be more contractual than that of General Motors and Reynolds, thus reversing the relationship that existed in regard to the "contractualness" of the *creation* of the exchange relationships.

Tentative Findings

It is difficult to generalize about the use and nonuse of contract by manufacturing industry. However, a number of observations can be made with reasonable accuracy at this time. The use and nonuse of contract in creating exchange relations and in dispute settling will be taken up in turn.

The creation of exchange relationships. In creating exchange relationships, businessmen may plan to a greater or lesser degree in relation to several types of issues. Before reporting the findings as to practices in creating such relationships, it is necessary to describe what one can plan about in a bargain and the degrees of planning which are possible.

People negotiating a contract can make plans concerning several types of issues: (1) They can plan what each is to do or refrain from doing; e.g., S might agree to deliver ten 1963 Studebaker four-door sedan automobiles to B on a certain date in exchange for a specified amount of money. (2) They can plan what effect certain contingencies are to have on their duties; e.g., what is to happen to S and B's obligations if S cannot deliver the cars because of a strike at the Studebaker factory? (3) They can plan what is to happen if either of them fails to perform; e.g., what is to happen if S delivers nine of the cars two weeks late? (4) They can plan their agreement so that it is a legally enforceable contract—that is, so that a legal sanction would be available to provide compensation for injury suffered by B as a result of S's failure to deliver the cars on time. . . .

Most larger companies, and many smaller ones, attempt to plan carefully and completely. Important transactions not in the ordinary course of business are handled by a detailed contract. For example, recently the Empire State Building was sold for $65 million. More than 100 attorneys, representing 34 parties, produced a 400–page contract. Another example is found in the agreement of a major rubber company in the United States to give technical assistance to a Japanese firm. Several million dollars were involved and the contract consisted of 88 provisions on 17 pages. The 12 house counsel—lawyers who work for one corporation rather than many clients—interviewed said that all but the smallest businesses carefully planned most transactions of any significance. Corporations have procedures so that particular types of exchanges will be reviewed by their legal and financial departments.

More routine transactions commonly are handled by what can be called standardized planning. A firm will have a set of terms and conditions for purchases, sales, or both printed on the business documents used in these exchanges. Thus, the things to be sold and the price may be planned particularly for each transaction, but standard provisions will further elaborate the performances and cover the other subjects of planning. Typically, these terms and conditions are lengthy and printed in small type on the back of the forms. For example, 24 paragraphs in eight-point type are printed on the back of the purchase order form used by the Allis Chalmers Manufacturing Company. The provisions: (1) describe, in part, the performance required, e.g., "DO NOT WELD CASTINGS WITHOUT OUR CONSENT"; (2) plan for the effect of contingencies, e.g., ". . . in the event the Seller suffers delay in performance due to an act of God, war, act of the Government, priorities or allocations, act of the Buyer, fire, flood, strike, sabotage, or other causes beyond Seller's control, the time of completion shall be extended a period of time equal to the period of such delay if the Seller gives the Buyer notice in writing of the cause of any such delay within a reasonable time after the beginning thereof"; (3) plan for the effect of defective performances, e.g., "The buyer, without waiving any other legal rights, reserves the right to cancel without charge or to postpone deliveries of any of the articles covered by this order which are not shipped in time reasonably to meet said agreed dates"; (4) plan for a legal sanction, e.g., the clause "without waiving any other legal rights," in the example just given.

In larger firms such "boiler plate" provisions are drafted by the house counsel or the firm's outside lawyer. In smaller firms such provisions may be drafted by the industry trade association, may be copied from a competitor, or may be found on forms purchased from a printer. In any event, salesmen and purchasing agents, the operating personnel, typically are unaware of what is said in the fine print on the back of the forms they use. Yet often the normal business patterns will give effect to this standardized planning. For example, purchasing agents may have to use a purchase order form so that all transactions receive a number under the firm's accounting system. Thus, the required accounting record will carry the necessary planning of the exchange relationship printed on its reverse side. If the seller does not object to this planning and accepts the order, the buyer's "fine print" will control. If the seller does object, differences can be settled by negotiation.

This type of standardized planning is very common. Requests for copies of the business documents used in buying and selling were sent to approximately 6,000 manufacturing firms which do business in Wisconsin. Approximately 1,200 replies were received and 850 companies used some type of standardized planning. With only a few exceptions, the firms that did not reply and the 350 that indicated they did not use standardized planning were very small manufacturers such as local bakeries, soft drink bottlers and sausage makers.

While businessmen can and often do carefully and completely plan, it is clear that not all exchanges are neatly rationalized. Although most businessmen think that a clear description of both the seller's and buyer's performances is obvious common sense, they do not always live up to this ideal. The house counsel and the purchasing agent of a medium sized manufacturer of automobile parts reported that several times their engineers had committed the company to buy expensive machines without adequate specifications. The engineers had drawn careful specifications as to the type of machine and how it was to be made but had neglected to require that the machine produce specified results. An attorney and an auditor both stated that most contract disputes arise because of ambiguity in the specifications.

Businessmen often prefer to rely on "a man's word" in a brief letter, a handshake, or "common honesty and decency"—even when the transaction involves exposure to serious risks. Seven lawyers from law firms with business practices were interviewed. Five thought that businessmen often entered contracts with only a minimal degree of advance planning. They complained that businessmen desire to "keep it simple and avoid red tape" even where large amounts of money and significant risks are involved. One stated that he was "sick of being told, 'We can trust old Max,' when the problem is not one of honesty but one of reaching an agreement that both sides understand." Another said that businessmen when bargaining often talk only in pleasant generalities, think they have a contract, but fail to reach agreement on any of the hard, unpleasant questions until forced to do so by a lawyer. Two outside lawyers had different views. One thought that large firms usually planned important exchanges, although he conceded that occasionally matters might be left in a fairly vague state. The other dissenter represents a large utility that commonly buys heavy equipment and buildings. The supplier's employees come on the utility's property to install the equipment or construct the buildings, and they may be injured while there. The utility has been sued by such employees so often that it carefully plans purchases with the assistance of a lawyer so that suppliers take this burden.

Moreover, standardized planning can break down. In the example of such planning previously given, it was assumed that the purchasing agent would use his company's form with its 24 paragraphs printed on the back and that the seller would accept this or object to any provisions he did not like. However, the seller may fail to read the buyer's 24 paragraphs of fine print and may accept the buyer's order on the seller's own acknowledgment-of-order form. Typically this form will have ten to 50 paragraphs favoring the seller, and these provisions are likely to be different from or inconsistent with the buyer's provisions. The seller's acknowledgment form may be received by the buyer and checked by a clerk. She[7] will read the face of the acknowledgment but not the fine print on the back of it because she has neither the time nor ability to analyze the small print on the 100 to 500 forms she must review each day. The face of the acknowledgment—where the goods and the price are specified—is likely to correspond with the face of the purchase order. If it does, the two forms are filed away. At this point, both buyer and seller are likely to assume they have planned an exchange and made a contract. Yet they have done neither, as they are in disagreement about all that appears on the back of their forms. This practice is common enough to have a name. Law teachers call it "the battle of the forms."

Ten of the 12 purchasing agents interviewed said that frequently the provisions on the back of their purchase order and those on the back of a supplier's acknowledgment would differ or be inconsistent. Yet they would assume that the purchase was complete without further action unless one of the supplier's provisions was really objectionable. Moreover, only occasionally would they bother to read the fine print on the back of suppliers' forms. . . .

---

7. [Eds. Note] At the time of this study, clerks working for the firms where interviews were conducted were overwhelmingly women, holding a relatively low status job. Few, if any, had the legal training necessary to give them the ability to analyze the legal consequences of the terms and conditions on the back of the business forms which they had to process in great quantity; even a woman or a man who had such training would not have had the time to undertake this task adequately.

Sixteen sales managers were asked about the battle of the forms. Nine said that frequently no agreement was reached on which set of fine print was to govern, while seven said that there was no problem. Four of the seven worked for companies whose major customers are the large automobile companies or the large manufacturers of paper products. These customers demand that their terms and conditions govern any purchase, are careful generally to see that suppliers acquiesce, and have the bargaining power to have their way. The other three of the seven sales managers who have no battle of the forms problem, work for manufacturers of special industrial machines. Their firms are careful to reach complete agreement with their customers. Two of these men stressed that they could take no chances because such a large part of their firm's capital is tied up in making any one machine. The other sales manager had been influenced by a lawsuit against one of his competitors for over a half million dollars. The suit was brought by a customer when the competitor had been unable to deliver a machine and put it in operation on time. The sales manager interviewed said his firm could not guarantee that its machines would work perfectly by a specified time because they are designed to fit the customer's requirements, which may present difficult engineering problems. As a result, contracts are carefully negotiated.

A large manufacturer of packaging materials audited its records to determine how often it had failed to agree on terms and conditions with its customers or had failed to create legally binding contracts. Such failures cause a risk of loss to this firm since the packaging is printed with the customer's design and cannot be salvaged once this is done. The orders for five days in four different years were reviewed. The percentages of orders where no agreement on terms and conditions was reached or no contract was formed were as follows:

1953	75.0%
1954	69.4%
1955	71.5%
1956	59.5%

It is likely that businessmen pay more attention to describing the performances in an exchange than to planning for contingencies or defective performances or to obtaining legal enforceability of their contracts. Even when a purchase order and acknowledgment have conflicting provisions printed on the back, almost always the buyer and seller will be in agreement on what is to be sold and how much is to be paid for it. The lawyers who said businessmen often commit their firms to significant exchanges too casually, stated that the performances would be defined in the brief letter or telephone call; the lawyers objected that nothing else would be covered. Moreover, it is likely that businessmen are least concerned about planning their transactions so that they are legally enforceable contracts. For example, in Wisconsin [at the time of this study] requirements contracts—contracts to supply a firm's requirements of an item rather than a definite quantity—probably were not legally enforceable. Seven people interviewed reported that their firms regularly used requirements contracts in dealings in Wisconsin. None thought that the lack of legal sanction made any difference. Three of these people were house counsel who knew the Wisconsin law before being interviewed. Another example of a lack of desire for legal sanctions is found in the relationship between automobile manufacturers and their suppliers of parts. The manufacturers draft a carefully planned agreement, but one which is so designed that the supplier will have only minimal, if any, legal rights against the manufacturers. The standard contract used by manufacturers of paper to sell to magazine publishers has a pricing clause which is probably sufficiently vague to make the contract legally unenforceable. The house counsel of one of the largest paper producers said that everyone in the industry is aware of this because of a leading New York case concerning the contract, but that no one cares. Finally, it seems likely that planning for contingencies and defective performances are in-between cases—more likely to occur than planning for a legal sanction, but less likely than a description of performance.

Thus one can conclude that (1) many business exchanges reflect a high degree of planning about the four categories—description, contingencies, defective performances and legal sanction—but (2) many, if not most, exchanges reflect no planning, or only a minimal amount of it, especially concerning legal sanctions and the effect of defective performances. As a result, the opportunity for good faith disputes during the life of the exchange relationship often is present.

The adjustment of exchange relationships and the settling of disputes. While a significant amount of creating business exchanges is done on a fairly noncontractual basis, the creation of exchanges usually is far more contractual than the adjustment of such relationships and the settlement of disputes. Exchanges are adjusted when the obligations of one or both parties are modified by agreement during the life of the relationship. For example, the buyer may be allowed to cancel all or part of the goods he has ordered because he no longer needs them; the seller may be paid more than the contract price by the buyer because of unusual changed circumstances. Dispute settlement involves determining whether or not a party has performed as agreed and, if he has not, doing something about it. For example, a court may have to interpret the meaning of a contract, determine what the alleged defaulting party has done and determine what, if any, remedy the aggrieved party is entitled to. Or one party may assert that the other is in default, refuse to proceed with performing the contract and refuse to deal ever again with the alleged defaulter. If the alleged defaulter, who in fact may not be in default, takes no action, the dispute is then "settled."

Business exchanges in non-speculative areas are usually adjusted without dispute. Under the law of contracts, if B orders 1,000 widgets from S at $1.00 each, B must take all 1,000 widgets or be in breach of contract and liable to pay S his expenses up to the time of the breach plus his lost anticipated profit. Yet all ten of the purchasing agents asked about cancellation of orders once placed indicated that they expected to be able to cancel orders freely subject to only an obligation to pay for the seller's major expenses such as scrapped steel. All 17 sales personnel asked reported that they often had to accept cancellations. One said, "You can't ask a man to eat paper [the firm's product] when he has no use for it." A lawyer with many large industrial clients said,

> Often businessmen do not feel they have "a contract"—rather they have "an order." They speak of "cancelling the order" rather than "breaching our contract." When I began practice I referred to order cancellations as breaches of contract, but my clients objected since they do not think of cancellation as wrong. Most clients, in heavy industry at least, believe that there is a right to cancel as part of the buyer-seller relationship. There is a widespread attitude that one can back out of any deal within some very vague limits. Lawyers are often surprised by this attitude.

Disputes are frequently settled without reference to the contract or potential or actual legal sanctions. There is a hesitancy to speak of legal rights or to threaten to sue in these negotiations. Even where the parties have a detailed and carefully planned agreement which indicates what is to happen if, say, the seller fails to deliver on time, often they will never refer to the agreement but will negotiate a solution when the problem arises apparently as if there had never been any original contract. One purchasing agent expressed a common business attitude when he said,

> if something comes up, you get the other man on the telephone and deal with the problem. You don't read legalistic contract clauses at each other if you ever want to do business again. One doesn't run to lawyers if he wants to stay in business because one must behave decently.

Or as one businessman put it, "You can settle any dispute if you keep the lawyers and accountants out of it. They just do not understand the give-and-take needed in business." All of the house counsel interviewed indicated that they are called into the dispute settlement process only after the businessmen have failed to settle matters in their own way. Two indicated that after being called in, house counsel at first will only advise the purchasing agent, sales manager or other official involved; not even the house counsel's letterhead is used on communications with the other side until all hope for a peaceful resolution is gone.

Law suits for breach of contract appear to be rare. Only five of the 12 purchasing agents had ever been involved in even a negotiation concerning a contract dispute where both sides were represented by lawyers; only two of ten sales managers had ever gone this far. None had been involved in a case that went through trial. A law firm with more than 40 lawyers and a large commercial practice handles in a year only about six trials concerned with contract problems. Less than 10 per cent of the time of this office is devoted to any type of work related to contracts disputes. Corporations big enough to do business in more than one state tend to sue and be sued in the federal courts. Yet only 2,779 out of 58,293 civil actions filed in the United States District Courts in fiscal year 1961 involved private contracts. During the same period only 3,447 of the 61,138 civil cases filed in the principal trial courts of New York State involved private contracts. The same picture emerges from a review of appellate cases.[8] Mentschikoff has suggested that commercial cases are not brought to the courts either in periods of business prosperity (because buyers unjustifiably reject goods only when prices drop and they can get similar goods elsewhere at less than the contract price) or in periods of deep depression (because people are unable to come to court or have insufficient assets to satisfy any judgment that might be obtained). Apparently, she adds, it is necessary to have "a kind of middle-sized depression" to bring large numbers of commercial cases to the courts. However, there is little evidence that in even "a kind of middle-sized depression" today's businessmen would use the courts to settle disputes.

At times, relatively contractual methods are used to make adjustments in ongoing transactions and to settle disputes. Demands of one side which are deemed unreasonable by the other occasionally are blocked by reference to the terms of the agreement between the parties. The legal position of the parties can influence negotiations even though legal rights or litigation are never mentioned in their discussions; it makes a difference if one is demanding what both concede to be a right or begging for a favor. Now and then a firm may threaten to turn matters over to its attorneys, threaten to sue, commence a suit or even litigate and carry an appeal to the highest court which will hear the matter. Thus, legal sanctions, while not an everyday affair, are not unknown in business.

One can conclude that while detailed planning and legal sanctions play a significant role in some exchanges between businesses, in many business exchanges their role is small.

Tentative Explanations

Two questions need to be answered: (A) How can business successfully operate exchange relationships with relatively so little attention to detailed planning or to legal sanctions, and (B) Why does business ever use contract in light of its success without it?

Why are relatively non-contractual practices so common? In most situations contract is not needed.[9] Often its functions are served by other devices. Most problems are avoided without resort to detailed planning or legal

---

8. My colleague Lawrence M. Friedman has studied the work of the Supreme Court of Wisconsin in contracts cases. He has found that contracts cases reaching that court tend to involve economically-marginal-business and family-economic disputes rather than important commercial transactions. This has been the situation since about the turn of the century. Only during the Civil War period did the court deal with significant numbers of important contracts cases, but this happened against the background of a much simpler and different economic system. [This study has since

been published as *Contract Law in America: A Social and Economic Case Study* (1965) Eds.]

9. The explanation that follows emphasizes a considered choice not to plan in detail for all contingencies. However, at times it is clear that businessmen fail to plan because of a lack of sophistication; they simply do not appreciate the risk they are running or they merely follow patterns established in their firm years ago without reexamining these practices in light of current conditions.

sanctions because usually there is little room for honest misunderstandings or good faith differences of opinion about the nature and quality of a seller's performance. Although the parties fail to cover all foreseeable contingencies, they will exercise care to see that both understand the primary obligation on each side. Either products are standardized with an accepted description or specifications are written calling for production to certain tolerances or results. Those who write and read specifications are experienced professionals who will know the customs of their industry and those of the industries with which they deal. Consequently, these customs can fill gaps in the express agreements of the parties. Finally, most products can be tested to see if they are what was ordered; typically in manufacturing industry we are not dealing with questions of taste or judgment where people can differ in good faith.

When defaults occur they are not likely to be disastrous because of techniques of risk avoidance or risk spreading. One can deal with firms of good reputation or he may be able to get some form of security to guarantee performance. One can insure against many breaches of contract where the risks justify the costs. Sellers set up reserves for bad debts on their books and can sell some of their accounts receivable. Buyers can place orders with two or more suppliers of the same item so that a default by one will not stop the buyer's assembly lines.

Moreover, contract and contract law are often thought unnecessary because there are many effective non-legal sanctions. Two norms are widely accepted. (1) Commitments are to be honored in almost all situations.... (2) One ought to produce a good product and stand behind it. Then, too, business units are organized to perform commitments, and internal sanctions will induce performance. For example, sales personnel must face angry customers when there has been a late or defective performance. The salesmen do not enjoy this and will put pressure on the production personnel responsible for the default. If the production personnel default too often, they will be fired. At all levels of the two business units personal relationships across the boundaries of the two organizations exert pressures for conformity to expectations. Salesmen often know purchasing agents well. The same two individuals occupying these roles may have dealt with each other from five to 20 years. Each has something to give the other. Salesmen have gossip about competitors, shortages and price increases to give purchasing agents who treat them well. Salesmen take purchasing agents to dinner, and they give purchasing agents Christmas gifts hoping to improve the chances of making a sale. The buyer's engineering staff may work with the seller's engineering staff to solve problems jointly. The seller's engineers may render great assistance, and the buyer's engineers may desire to return the favor by drafting specifications which only the seller can meet. The top executives of the two firms may know each other. They may sit together on government or trade committees. They may know each other socially and even belong to the same country club. The interrelationships may be more formal. Sellers may hold stock in corporations which are important customers; buyers may hold stock in important suppliers.

Both buyer and seller may share common directors on their boards. They may share a common financial institution which has financed both units.

The final type of non-legal sanction is the most obvious. Both business units involved in the exchange desire to continue successfully in business and will avoid conduct which might interfere with attaining this goal. One is concerned with both the reaction of the other party in the particular exchange and with his own general business reputation. Obviously, the buyer gains sanctions insofar as the seller wants the particular exchange to be completed. Buyers can withhold part or all of their payments until sellers have performed to their satisfaction. If a seller has a great deal of money tied up in his performance which he must recover quickly, he will go a long way to please the buyer in order to be paid. Moreover, buyers who are dissatisfied may cancel and cause sellers to lose the cost of what they have done up to cancellation. Furthermore, sellers hope for repeat orders, and one gets few of these from unhappy customers. Some industrial buyers go so far as to formalize this sanction by issuing "report cards" rating the performance of each supplier. The supplier rating goes to the top management of the seller organization, and these men can apply internal sanctions to salesmen, production supervisors or product designers if there are too many "D's" or "F's" on the report card.

While it is generally assumed that the customer is always right, the seller may have some counter balancing sanctions against the buyer. The seller may have obtained a large down payment from the buyer which he will want to protect. The seller may have an exclusive process which the buyer needs. The seller may be one of the few firms which has the skill to make the item to the tolerances set by the buyer's engineers and within the time available. There are costs and delays involved in turning from a supplier one has dealt with in the past to a new supplier. Then, too, market conditions can change so that a buyer is faced with shortages of critical items. The most extreme example is the post World War II gray market situation when sellers were rationing goods rather than selling them. Buyers must build up some reserve of good will with suppliers if they face the risk of such shortages and desire good treatment when they occur. Finally, there is reciprocity in buying and selling. A buyer cannot push a supplier too far if that supplier also buys significant quantities of the product made by the buyer.

Not only do the particular business units in a given exchange want to deal with each other again, they also want to deal with other business units in the future. And the way one behaves in a particular transaction, or a series of transactions, will color his general business reputation. Blacklisting can be formal or informal. Buyers who fail to pay their bills on time risk a bad report in credit rating services such as Dun and Bradstreet. Sellers who do not satisfy their customers become the subject of discussion in the gossip exchanged by purchasing agents and salesmen, at meetings of purchasing agents' associations and trade associations, or even at country clubs or social gatherings where members of top management meet. The American male's habit of debating the merits of new cars carries over to industrial items.

Obviously, a poor reputation does not help a firm make sales and may force it to offer great price discounts or added services to remain in business. Furthermore, the habits of unusually demanding buyers become known, and they tend to get no more than they can coerce out of suppliers who choose to deal with them. Thus often contract is not needed as there are alternatives.

Not only are contract and contract law not needed in many situations, their use may have, or may be thought to have, undesirable consequences. Detailed negotiated contracts can get in the way of creating good exchange relationships between business units. If one side insists on a detailed plan, there will be delay while letters are exchanged as the parties try to agree on what should happen if a remote and unlikely contingency occurs. In some cases they may not be able to agree at all on such matters and as a result a sale may be lost to the seller and the buyer may have to search elsewhere for an acceptable supplier. Many businessmen would react by thinking that had no one raised the series of remote and unlikely contingencies all this wasted effort could have been avoided.

Even where agreement can be reached at the negotiation stage, carefully planned arrangements may create undesirable exchange relationships between business units. Some businessmen object that in such a carefully worked out relationship one gets performance only to the letter of the contract. Such planning indicates a lack of trust and blunts the demands of friendship, turning a cooperative venture into an antagonistic horse trade. Yet the greater danger perceived by some businessmen is that one would have to perform his side of the bargain to its letter and thus lose what is called "flexibility." Businessmen may welcome a measure of vagueness in the obligations they assume so that they may negotiate matters in light of the actual circumstances.

Adjustment of exchange relationships and dispute settlement by litigation or the threat of it also has many costs. The gain anticipated from using this form of coercion often fails to outweigh these costs, which are both monetary and non-monetary. Threatening to turn matters over to an attorney may cost no more money than postage or a telephone call; yet few are so skilled in making such a threat that it will not cost some deterioration of the relationship between the firms. One businessman said that customers had better not rely on legal rights or threaten to bring a breach of contract law suit against him since he "would not be treated like a criminal" and would fight back with every means available. Clearly, actual litigation is even more costly than making threats. Lawyers demand substantial fees from larger business units. A firm's executives often will have to be transported and maintained in another city during the proceedings if, as often is the case, the trial must be held away from the home office. Top management does not travel by Greyhound and stay at the Y.M.C.A. Moreover, there will be the cost of diverting top management, engineers, and others in the organization from their normal activities. The firm may lose many days work from several key people. The non-monetary costs may be large too. A breach of contract law suit may settle a particular dispute, but such an action often results in a "divorce" ending the "marriage" between the two businesses, since a contract action is likely to carry charges with at least overtones of bad faith. Many executives, moreover, dislike the prospect of being cross-examined in public. Some executives may dislike losing control of a situation by turning the decision-making power over to lawyers. Finally, the law of contract damages may not provide an adequate remedy even if the firm wins the suit; one may get vindication but not much money.

Why do relatively contractual practices ever exist? Although contract is not needed and actually may have negative consequences, businessmen do make some carefully planned contracts, negotiate settlements influenced by their legal rights and commence and defend some breach of contract law suits or arbitration proceedings. In view of the findings and explanation presented to this point, one may ask why. Exchanges are carefully planned when it is thought that planning and a potential legal sanction will have more advantages than disadvantages. Such a judgment may be reached when contract planning serves the internal needs of an organization involved in a business exchange. For example, a fairly detailed contract can serve as a communication device within a large corporation. While the corporation's sales manager and house counsel may work out all the provisions with the customer, its production manager will have to make the product. He must be told what to do and how to handle at least the most obvious contingencies. Moreover, the sales manager may want to remove certain issues from future negotiation by his subordinates. If he puts the matter in the written contract, he may be able to keep his salesmen from making concessions to the customer without first consulting the sales manager. Then the sales manager may be aided in his battles with his firm's financial or engineering departments if the contract calls for certain practices which the sales manager advocates but which the other departments resist. Now the corporation is obligated to a customer to do what the sales manager wants to do; how can the financial or engineering departments insist on anything else?

Also one tends to find a judgment that the gains of contract outweigh the costs where there is a likelihood that significant problems will arise.[10] One factor leading to this conclusion is complexity of the agreed performance over a long period. Another factor is whether or not the degree of injury in case of default is thought to be potentially great. This factor cuts two ways. First, a buyer may want to commit a seller to a detailed and legally binding contract, where the consequences of a default by the seller would seriously injure the buyer. For example, the airlines are subject to law suits from the survivors of passengers and to great adverse publicity as a result of crashes. One would expect the airlines to bargain for carefully defined and legally enforceable obligations on the part of the airframe manufacturers when they purchase

10. Even where there is little chance that problems will arise, some businessmen insist that their lawyer review or draft an agreement as a delaying tactic. This gives the business-man time to think about making a commitment if he has doubts about the matter or to look elsewhere for a better deal while still keeping the particular negotiations alive.

aircraft. Second, a seller may want to limit his liability for a buyer's damages by a provision in their contract.

For example, a manufacturer of air conditioning may deal with motels in the South and Southwest. If this equipment fails in the hot summer months, a motel may lose a great deal of business. The manufacturer may wish to avoid any liability for this type of injury to his customers and may want a contract with a clear disclaimer clause.

Similarly, one uses or threatens to use legal sanctions to settle disputes when other devices will not work and when the gains are thought to outweigh the costs. For example, perhaps the most common type of business contracts case fought all the way through to the appellate courts today is an action for an alleged wrongful termination of a dealer's franchise by a manufacturer. Since the franchise has been terminated, factors such as personal relationships and the desire for future business will have little effect; the cancellation of the franchise indicates they have already failed to maintain the relationship. Nor will a complaining dealer worry about creating a hostile relationship between himself and the manufacturer. Often the dealer has suffered a great financial loss both as to his investment in building and equipment and as to his anticipated future profits. A cancelled automobile dealer's lease on his showroom and shop will continue to run, and his tools for servicing, say, Plymouths cannot be used to service other makes of cars. Moreover, he will have no more new Plymouths to sell. Today there is some chance of winning a law suit for terminating a franchise in bad faith in many states and in the federal courts. Thus, often the dealer chooses to risk the cost of a lawyer's fee because of the chance that he may recover some compensation for his losses.

An "irrational" factor may exert some influence on the decision to use legal sanctions. The man who controls a firm may feel that he or his organization has been made to appear foolish or has been the victim of fraud or bad faith. The law suit maybe seen as a vehicle "to get even" although the potential gains, as viewed by an objective observer, are outweighed by the potential costs.

The decision whether or not to use contract—whether the gain exceeds the costs—will be made by the person within the business unit with the power to make it, and it tends to make a difference who he is. People in a sales department oppose contract. Contractual negotiations are just one more hurdle in the way of a sale. Holding a customer to the letter of a contract is bad for "customer relations." Suing a customer who is not bankrupt and might order again is poor strategy. Purchasing agents and their buyers are less hostile to contracts but regard attention devoted to such matters as a waste of time. In contrast, the financial control department—the treasurer, controller or auditor—leans toward more contractual dealings. Contract is viewed by these people as an organizing tool to control operations in a large organization. It tends to define precisely and to minimize the risks to which the firm is exposed. Outside lawyers—those with many clients—may share this enthusiasm for a more contractual method of dealing. These lawyers are concerned with preventive law—avoiding any possible legal difficulty. They see many unstable and unsuccessful exchange transactions, and so they are aware of, and perhaps overly concerned with, all of the things which can go wrong. Moreover, their job of settling disputes with legal sanctions is much easier if their client has not been overly casual about transaction planning. The inside lawyer, or house counsel, is harder to classify. He is likely to have some sympathy with a more contractual method of dealing. He shares the outside lawyer's "craft urge" to see exchange transactions neat and tidy from a legal standpoint. Since he is more concerned with avoiding and settling disputes than selling goods, he is likely to be less willing to rely on a man's word as the sole sanction than is a salesman. Yet the house counsel is more a part of the organization and more aware of its goals and subject to its internal sanctions. If the potential risks are not too great, he may hesitate to suggest a more contractual procedure to the sales department. He must sell his services to the operating departments, and he must hoard what power he has, expending it on only what he sees as significant issues.

The power to decide that a more contractual method of creating relationships and settling disputes shall be used will be held by different people at different times in different organizations. In most firms the sales department and the purchasing department have a great deal of power to resist contractual procedures or to ignore them if they are formally adopted and to handle disputes their own way. Yet in larger organizations the treasurer and the controller have increasing power to demand both systems and compliance. Occasionally, the house counsel must arbitrate the conflicting positions of these departments; in giving "legal advice" he may make the business judgment necessary regarding the use of contract. At times he may ask for an opinion from an outside law firm to reinforce his own position with the outside firm's prestige.

Obviously, there are other significant variables which influence the degree that contract is used. One is the relative bargaining power or skill of the two business units. Even if the controller of a small supplier succeeds within the firm and creates a contractual system of dealing, there will be no contract if the firm's large customer prefers not to be bound to anything. Firms that supply General Motors deal as General Motors wants to do business, for the most part. Yet bargaining power is not size nor share of the market alone. Even a General Motors may need a particular supplier, at least temporarily. Furthermore, bargaining power may shift as an exchange relationship is first created and then continues. Even a giant firm can find itself bound to a small supplier once production of an essential item begins for there may not be time to turn to another supplier. Also, all of the factors discussed in this paper can be viewed as components of bargaining power—for example, the personal relationship between the presidents of the buyer and the seller firms may give a sales manager great power over a purchasing agent who has been instructed to give the seller "every consideration." Another variable relevant to the use of contract is the influence of third parties. The federal government, or a lender of money, may insist that a contract be made in a particular transaction or may influence the decision to assert one's legal rights under a contract.

Contract, then, often plays an important role in business, but other factors are significant. To understand the functions of contract the whole system of conducting exchanges must be explored fully. More types of business communities must be studied, contract litigation must be analyzed to see why the nonlegal sanctions fail to prevent the use of legal sanctions and all of the variables suggested in this paper must be classified more systematically.

NOTES AND QUESTIONS

1. This article is a study of when business people use formal processes of law, and, more significantly, when they do not. Would it be accurate, however, to say that Macaulay's was a study of the "nonuse of law," or would it be more to the point to say that it was a study about informal rules, norms, and practices—which happen not to coincide with the rules "on the books?" Would it make sense to call the code that the Wisconsin business people follow "law," or perhaps, "living law?"

The Macaulay study has been much cited and much discussed. It is more than 40 years old. Is it still valid? In 1985, a symposium on the 20th anniversary of the publication of the article appeared in the *Wisconsin Law Review* ("Symposium–Law, Private Governance and Continuing Relationships"). At this point, Macaulay reassessed the article, in the light of experience since the 1960's. Business litigation had apparently increased. There were instances where long-term continuing relationships had collapsed; and the result was litigation. There was an energy crisis in the 1970's which led to litigation, and produced a number of appellate opinions. The decline of the American industrial economy, and the shift to new technologies, such as computers, created new issues which were also productive of controversy. But despite the increase in litigation, and a number of well-publicized cases, Macaulay felt that the basic findings of his study remained valid.

In Lane Kenworthy, Stewart Macaulay, and Joel Rogers, " 'The More Things Change . . . .': Business Litigation and Governance in the American Automobile Industry," 21 *Law & Social Inquiry* 631 (1996), the authors begin by pointing out that "Over the past generation, and particularly since the early 1970's, there has been an enormous increase in business litigation and other uses of law in the United States . . . Expenditures on legal services have increased among all three major categories of law 'consumers'—business, individuals, and government." But the biggest boom had been in business "consumption" of law, so that "business has . . . emerged as the primary consumer in the rapidly expanding legal services market." The authors took a close look at one sector of the economy—the automotive sector. They found that there was little litigation between manufacturers and suppliers in the auto industry. The big auto companies are powerful, and suppliers are not eager to sue them. The companies also controlled the drafting of form contracts. The relationship between the companies and their dealers was somewhat more litigious, but here too litigation seemed to decline in the late 1980's. The authors suggest that firms responded to litigation by "creating new mechanisms of dispute resolution aimed at avoiding lawsuits" (id. at 675). The companies, after all, do not like disputes and lawsuits, and they are eager to find ways to resolve disputes without courtroom battles.

2.   How far can we generalize the Macaulay study? It is, after all, about the United States—indeed, about only *one* of the United States, and at one point in time. Could it even be generalized to all of Wisconsin? Russell Korobkin, in "Empirical Scholarship in Contract Law: Possibilities and Pitfalls," 2002 *University of Illinois Law Review* 1033, points out that the Macaulay study was "limited to a nonrandom sample of lawyers and businesspeople doing business in Wisconsin;" and there was "no attempt to ensure that this sample was representative of the world of commercial contracting parties."

In order to know whether the study tells us something fundamental about modern legal systems, we would have to look at other times and other places. There have been some follow-up studies, for example, Britt–Mari Blegvad, "Commercial Relations, Contract, and Litigation in Denmark: A Discussion of Macaulay's Theories," 24 *Law & Society Review* 397 (1990); Penny–Anne Cullen, Bob Butcher, Richard Hickman and John Keast, "A Critique of Contractual Relationships in the Aerospace Industry: Collaboration v. Conflict," 1 *International Journal of Law in Context* 397 (2006). The follow-up studies generally support Macaulay's initial findings. For his response to Korobkin's point, see Stewart Macaulay, "Contracts, New Legal Realism, and Improving the Navigation of *The Yellow Submarine*," 80 *Tulane Law Review* 1161, 1182–83 n. 94 (2006). Macaulay explains how he tried to cope with the problem as he did the research, and he cites eight studies that reach similar results. It is often not possible to get a random sample as scholars research law-and-society questions. Sometimes we cannot identify the population from which to sample. For example, how could we identify all of the business corporations that had a cause of action for breach of contract but decided not to assert it? Even if we could identify a population to sample, often people see information about potential or actual legal affairs as highly confidential. Sometimes researchers are lucky to find someone willing to take the time to talk to them about such matters. Macaulay considers a number of the problems of interviewing people who have faced such challenges and their lawyers in the *Tulane Law Review* article.

Macaulay was studying a jurisdiction with a functioning court system, and one that is reasonably independent and impartial. There are many places where no such court system exists. Here it is even more certain that contractual behavior will depend heavily on norms, customs, mutual trust; or that devices will evolve to replace formal contract law. See John McMillan and Christopher M. Woodruff, "Dispute Prevention without Courts in Vietnam," 15 *Journal of Law, Economics, and Organization* 635 (1999). In Vietnam, at the time the authors wrote, firms felt that they could not rely on the courts to enforce contracts. They relied on other devices—they carefully scrutinized their trading partners; and they sometimes invoked community sanctions. For riskier ventures, the firms used more elaborate ways to reduce the risk, and make sure their trading partners carried through. The firms studied were, on the whole, quite small in comparison with American businesses.

(C) Tort Law

(2.5) Settled Out of Court: The Social Process of Insurance Claims Adjustment

H. Laurence Ross

(2d ed. 1980).

... The major thesis of this book is that legal relationships cannot be understood as a product of the formal law alone, but must be understood in terms of the interplay between the formal law and aspects of the situation in which the law is applied. The determination of legal rights is in the vast majority of cases undertaken by means of informal procedures, the character of which substantively changes the rights thus processed. Moreover, the changes are not random. Informality does not mean lack of structure. Informal procedures exhibit regularities that result from the goals and purposes of the people involved, and from sociologically comprehensible pressures and strains upon them.

The regularities induced from the observation of the day–to–day working out of legal relationships constitute the law in action. It is these regularities that have to be taken into account by the ordinary man and his attorney when the question of rights and duties becomes concrete. I propose that the legal critic and the social analyst ought to share this perspective....

The Tort Law in Action

In the insured claim, it is the adjuster's task to evaluate the case according to the criteria of formal law, and to negotiate a settlement that will be justified in the light of these criteria and avoid the expensive formal procedure of courtroom trial.

The formal law of torts specifies that someone injured in an automobile accident may recover from a driver if he can show, by the preponderance of evidence, that the driver violated his duty to conduct the vehicle in the manner of an ordinarily prudent person. The driver, however, need pay nothing if he in turn can show by the preponderance of evidence that the claimant also violated a similar duty. Various qualifications apply, depending on the jurisdiction. For example, a governmental or charitable organization may be excused from paying claims, or a husband may not be able to recover from his wife, or a guest from his host. In some exceptional states payment may be reduced rather than eliminated where the claimant's negligent behavior has contributed to the accident. The formal law prescribes a recovery sufficient to make the claimant "whole," repaying in cash for everything he has lost in the accident (regardless of whether or not some other source such as health insurance or sick leave has also compensated for the accident-related losses), and for pain, suffering and inconvenience in addition to more tangible losses.

The formal criteria might lead to the expectation that relatively few people injured in an automobile accident would receive reparation. Most drivers may be thought to be ordinarily prudent people, and even where one is not, formal law embodies the difficulty of affirmative proof of unreasonable behavior. Moreover, to the extent that numbers of negligent drivers are on the highway, an equivalent number of negligent claimants might be expected, who ought to recover nothing. On these assumptions one would expect most claimants to be denied completely, the balance recovering something more than their economic losses. In contrast, the actual picture of recoveries shows that most people injured in traffic accidents are paid, and those who are seriously injured are paid in the large majority of cases. The amount of recoveries fits the formal model only for small claims; [also] where injuries are serious, most claimants fail to recover even their out-of-pocket losses.

The reason the distribution predicted by knowledge of the formal law does not fit the observed distribution of claims settlements is that other factors influence the settlement process. Some of these have been described in this book. Among them are the attitudes and values of the involved personnel, organizational pressures, and negotiation pressures. They exert a direct effect on the enormous majority of bodily claims. . . .

The personalities—attitudes and opinions—of the personnel are perhaps the least significant of the factors mentioned. Generally speaking, adjusters approach their work with conventional business values. Other things equal, they will seek low, conservative settlements, although a sense of fairness makes them disinclined to settle for less than net out-of-pocket losses in a case that is deemed to warrant any settlement at all. The goal of paying no more and no less than these tangible losses is often achieved in routine cases settled directly with the claimant. This is a settlement that many adjusters would characterize as ideal. However, many settlements are made for amounts quite different from the ideal, reflecting pressures and constraints of the employee role and the negotiating situation. Personal dispositions may affect the style with which an adjuster responds to external demands, but they seem to be relatively unimportant in determining the outcome of claims.

Organizational pressure would seem to be a more important factor than personality in affecting the outcome of claims. Pressures from the supervisory structure can even lead adjusters to violate some of the most important company rules, such as those forbidding nuisance payments. Perhaps unexpectedly, the most insistent of organizational pressures is not to keep payments low, but to close files quickly. The closing of files represents for adjusters something of the same kind of central goal as the attainment of good grades represents for the college student, or number of placements for an employment counselor, or a high clearance rate for policemen. . . . [T]he chief effect of this pressure on the behavior of claims men is to increase the number and raise the level of payments. This effect is unexpected and unrecognized by many claims department executives, who are insulated from the front lines by organizational distance, but it is understandable as a means to alleviate specific and recurring pressures experienced by adjusters from their supervisors. The pressure to close files quickly also causes adjusters to simplify their procedures of investigation, as well as their thinking in evaluation. Although the textbooks and manuals propose elaborate and time-consuming routines, the case load prescribes short cuts and approximations. . . .

Another important factor affecting settlement outcomes, particularly with represented claimants, is the medium of negotiation. Negotiation is a social process with a strong implicit rule structure and a repertory of tactics different from those available in litigation. In the case at hand, the most effective tactics threaten recourse to the expense of formal trial, and these threats can be nailed down with commitments. Bodily injury claims negotiators are in roughly the same position as negotiators for two nations disputing a border city, where all involved know that each party can obliterate a major interior city of the other. In such a situation there is strong pressure for compromise, as opposed to an all-or-none disposition. It does not matter much that the formal law prescribes the latter.

As a consequence of these and other pressures, the tort law in action is differentiated from the formal law by its greater simplicity, liberality, and inequity. The concepts of the formal tort law are quite complex: definitions of both damages and negligence suggest the need for case-by-case consideration. The rule of contributory negligence as a bar to recovery makes the formal law appear close-fisted, though it may be lavish in the recovery that it grants a "blameless" victim of a "negligent" driver. Above all, the formal tort law—like the bulk of Anglo–American law—is equitable in its insistence that cases similar in facts be treated in a similar fashion. The law in action departs from the formal law on these three main dimensions.

In order to process successfully vast numbers of cases, organizations tend to take on the characteristics of "bureaucracy" in the sociological sense of the term: operation on the basis of rules, government by a clear hierarchy, the maintenance of files, etc. Such an organizational form produces competence and efficiency in applying general rules to particular cases, but it is not well suited to making complex and individualized decisions. One form of response of bureaucracies to such demands involves a type of breakdown. There will be long delays, hewing to complicated and minute procedures, and a confusion of means with ends. A common and perhaps more constructive response is to simplify the task. This was the tack taken by the claims men I studied. Phone calls and letters replaced personal visits; only a few witnesses, rather than all possible, would be interviewed; and the law of negligence was made to lean heavily on the much simpler traffic law.

Traffic laws are simple rules, deliberately so because their purpose is to provide a universal and comprehensible set of guidelines for safe and efficient transportation. Negligence law is complex, its purpose being to decide after the fact whether a driver was unreasonably careless. However, all levels of the insurance company claims department will accept the former rules as generally adequate for the latter purpose. The underlying reason for this is the difficulty if not impossibility of investigating and defending a more complex decision concerning negligence in the context of a mass operation. In the routine case, the stakes are not high enough to warrant the effort, and the effort is not made. The information that a given insured violated a specific traffic law and was subsequently involved in an accident will suffice to allocate fault. No attempt is made to analyze why this took place or how. The legal concepts of negligence and fault in action contain no more substance than the simple and mechanical procedures noted here provide.

The law of damages is also simplified in action. Although the measurement of special damages appears rather straightforward even in formal doctrine, some further simplification occurs in action when, for instance, life table calculations are used to compute future earnings. More important, the measurement of pain, suffering, and inconvenience is thoroughly routinized in the ordinary claim. The adjuster generally pays little attention to the claimant's privately experienced discomforts and agonies; I do not recall ever having read recitals of these matters in the statements, which are the key documents in the settlement process and in which all matters considered relevant to the disposition of a claim are recorded. The calculation of general damages is for the most part a matter of multiplying the medical bills by a tacitly but generally accepted arbitrary constant. This practice is justified by claims men on the theory that pain and suffering are very likely to be a function of the amount of medical treatment experienced. There is of course a grain of truth in this theory, but it also contains several sources of error. Types of injury vary considerably in the degree of pain and suffering, the necessity for treatment, and the fees charged for treatment; and the correlations between these elements are low. I believe that the more important reason for the use of the formula is again that all levels of the claims department find it acceptable in justifying payment over and beyond special damages. The formula provides a conventional measurement for phenomena that are so difficult to evaluate as to be almost unmeasurable. It provides a rule by which a rule-oriented organization can proceed, though the rule is never formalized. This simplification also meets the comparable needs of plaintiffs' attorneys and is acceptable to them as well. Because of the mutual acceptability of the formula, attorneys will try to capitalize on it by adding to the use and cost of medical treatment, a procedure known as "building" the file, and adjusters will argue concerning the reasonableness of many items that purport to be medical expenses and thus part of the base to which the formula is applied. The procedure is still far less complicated—and less sensitive—than that envisaged in the formal law. Thus again it appears that, relative to the formal law, the law in action is simple and mechanical. Although more individual consideration occurs in larger cases, the principle of simplification governs to a great degree the entire range of settled claims.

The tort law in action is more liberal than the formal law. The formal law of negligence appears to be very stingy from the victim's point of view.... The doctrine of contributory negligence is of course the main block to recovery in the formal tort law, and it is this doctrine that is most strongly attenuated in action.

The principal evidence of this attenuation is in the large number of claims on which some payment is made. Insurance company procedures create a file for nearly every accident victim involved with an insured car. Any reasonable estimate of the number of cases in which the insured is not negligent plus the number in which the claimant is contributorily negligent suggests that well under half of all claims deserve payment by formal standards.... [C]ontrary to formal expectations the majority of claims are paid, and where serious injuries are involved virtually all claimants recover something from someone else's liability insurance.... It is true that in larger claims particularly, the payments may not equal the economic loss experienced, but they may still exceed the level of payment required by the formal law with its rule of contributory negligence.

In small claims, a fair number of denials are successfully made. The adjuster rationalizes his actions on the basis of formal law and the company is shielded from reprisals by high processing costs for the claimant relative to the amount at stake. The adjuster closes his files by denial when he feels the formal law warrants this and also that the claimant will take his case no farther. When he believes that the formal law favors the claimant, and thus finds himself ethically obliged, or when he believes the claimant is determined to press the claim, a payment can be made of considerable magnitude relative to the economic loss involved, although collateral sources—e.g., Blue Cross and sick pay—are usually deducted from negotiated settlements.

In claims based on large losses, the claimant's threat to litigate becomes more credible, and denial thus becomes more difficult. However, the adjuster uses the uncertainty of the formal process as a tool to secure a discount from the full formal value of the claim. Although processing costs may be disregarded, most claimants seem to prefer a definite settlement for a lower amount of money to the gamble of trial for a higher amount of money. The company—like a casino, which is able to translate a large number of gambles into mathematical certainty—is indifferent between these outcomes and can demand a concession for the definite settlement....

The tort law in action may also be termed inequitable. It is responsive to a wide variety of influences that are not defined as legitimate by common standards of equity. The interviews and observations I conducted convinced me that the negotiated settlement rewards the sophisticated claimant and penalizes the inexperienced, the naive, the simple, and the indifferent. Translating these terms into social statuses, I believe that the settlement produces relatively more for the affluent, the educated, the white, and the city-dweller. It penalizes the poor, the uneducated, the [African American], and the countryman. It is also responsive to such matters as the appearances and personalities of the parties and witnesses to the accident. Above all, it rewards the man with an attorney, despite the adjuster's honestly held belief that the unrepresented claimant will fare as well. Apart from the discrimination embodied in allowing recovery of different levels of lost income, these differences are unjustified in formal law, yet their effect on negotiated settlements is considerable.

Although this research was based for the most part on experience in a single, narrow, area of the law, I believe that the distinctions noted here between the formal law and the law in action may be more generally applicable. Wherever law or any other body of rules is applied on a day-to-day basis by a bureaucracy, pressures similar to those observed here may be expected to be present and to produce similar results. Simplification is the essence of mass procedures, and one would expect to find a deemphasis upon sensitivity, individualization, and subtlety in such situations, regardless of the complexity of the philosophy underlying the procedure. Where every man has his day in court, where each is judged according to his ability, where the whole man is being treated, an examination of the machinery in action can be predicted to yield evidence of routinization, categorization, and regimentation. Liberality or something akin to it may also be expected when rules are applied by a bureaucracy, depending on the extent to which sheer volume is emphasized by the processor. The bureaucratic employee under these circumstances seeks a trouble-free and expeditious resolution of disputes, and this may lead more frequently than previously thought to a liberal treatment of the case. Finally, inequity in the sense of applying formally inapplicable criteria is also likely to mark a wide variety of situations in which bureaucracies apply rules. Cases that are alike according to the formal rules may be for many reasons dissimilar when regarded as material to be processed. Factors ranging from the bureaucrat's idiosyncratic whim to strong and systematic organizational pressures may be expected to affect both the process and the outcome wherever the formal law or other rule is put into action.

NOTES AND QUESTIONS

1. According to Ross, insurance companies frequently pay claims, even when it is pretty clear that the law would probably not force them to pay up, if the claim was filed in court. Why do they behave this way? What does this fact tell us about the role that legal rules play in the insurance settlement process?

Macaulay, too, described a situation in which business people also often fail to invoke their legal "rights." Defendants who "cop a plea" are yet another group that gives up "rights," in exchange for some presumed benefits. Are these situations comparable to the situation Ross describes?

2. Ross tells us about a system which relies heavily on informal norms rather than formal law to settle accident cases. But the formal law does have an impact. Exactly what is the impact of formal law on insurance settlements?

Daniel Kessler, in "Fault, Settlement, and Negligence Law," 26 *RAND Journal of Economics* 296 (1995), tried to study this actual impact on insurance settlements. He compared states that had three different kinds of rules: some states followed the doctrine of contributory negligence—that is, if a plaintiff was at fault at all, however slightly, he could not recover; in other states, the rule is "comparative negligence," which "generally apportions damages between the parties to an accident according to their relative fault." Some states have a modified comparative negligence system—if the plaintiff is more than 50% responsible, the plaintiff cannot recover at all.

Kessler found that plaintiffs settled for the most money in states with pure comparative negligence, less in states with modified comparative negligence, least in contributory negligence rules. But the relationship "between appraised fault and settlement amount is not nearly as strong as the articulated negligence doctrines suggest. In particular, legislatively specified bars to recovery in tort law are not enforced." (Id. at 309). How would you explain these findings?

3.   Ross suggests that the results of informal bargaining are something quite unfair to people who are injured. The problem, of course, is much more general. How can we make sure that people are fairly treated in informal settings, where the scope of the formal rules (assuming these are at least theoretically fairer) is in practice quite limited.

It is possible, of course, that the results of the informal norms are *more* equitable than the world of the formal norms. Can Macaulay's study be read in this way?

4.   The claims adjusters Ross describes are not lawyers, and have almost certainly never taken a course in tort law. Do they actually know what "the law" is supposed to be? And if not, does this help explain Ross' findings, and the general remarks he makes in the last paragraph of the excerpt?

Some small percentage of tort claims do go further, of course, and are put in the hands of a lawyer. The lawyer usually works on a contingent-fee basis—that is, the lawyer gets nothing if the case loses; and a stiff percentage (often one-third) if the case wins. Most of *these* cases, too, settle out of court. But now we have a go-between—the lawyer himself. What effect does the lawyer have on the terms of settlement? See Herbert M. Kritzer, "Contingent–Fee Lawyers and Their Clients: Settlement Expectations, Settlement Realities, and Issues of Control in the Lawyer–Client Relationship," 23 *Law & Social Inquiry* 795 (1998).

5.   On English practice in personal injury cases, see Hazel Genn, *Hard Bargaining: Out of Court Settlements in Personal Injury Actions* (1987).

6.   There have been changes in insurance industry practices since Ross conducted his study. First, insurance companies in most states can be liable for the bad faith processing of a claim, and losing such a suit can lead to punitive damages. This has prompted more supervision of claims adjusters and more effort to tell them what they can and cannot do. Adjusters can

challenge both liability and damages and not run afoul of the requirement of good faith, but they must have a reasonable basis for their challenges. They cannot use delay and low offers as tactics to minimize claims. Moreover, they cannot use the claimants' need for compensation as a part of their bargaining strategy.

The second major change is that computers have come to the adjustment of insurance claims. There are a number of programs available to evaluate claims and eliminate subjective judgments by adjusters from the process. By 2003, twelve of the twenty leading automobile insurers used Colossus, a program that recommends settlement amounts by comparing an accident claim with a database of similar cases. Dawn R. Bonnett, The Use of Colossus to Measure the General Damages of a Personal Injury Claim Demonstrates Good Faith Claims Handling, 53 *Cleveland State Law Review* 107, 112–113 (2005), describes how the data base is created:

> Once an insurer decides to license Colossus, it has quite a bit of work to do to implement the system. Different insurance companies have different settlement philosophies. Consequently, Colossus does not determine the value of an injury without using an insurer's data. While each company sets up the system differently, generally a company will conduct roundtables to "assess the claim value factors" in an injury claim. The insurance company's most skilled and experienced casualty claims professionals come together to "evaluate hypothetical injury claims." Next, the insurance company may conduct a closed claims study to compare the baseline values determined by the roundtables to its claims practice history. The insurer uses both the closed claim study and the roundtables to assign monetary values to injury severity.
>
> After CSC enters the insurer's data, the claims professional can evaluate an injury. The claims professional first begins the evaluation by entering claim data, such as the insured's name, claimant's name and age and the venue. Next, the claims professional enters all diagnosed and accident related injuries. Once the claims professional enters the correct injuries into the system, Colossus guides the claims professional through a series of questions regarding the treatment, prognosis, pre-existing conditions, and symptoms of the injury. Colossus has over 10,000 rules determining what questions the system will ask the user based on the prior entries by the claims professional. The program uses the type and length of treatment along with the documented subjective complaints to assess the injury. Colossus will also ask the claims professional if the injured party had difficulty doing certain activities during his/her recovery period. The claims professional can also enter information regarding a claimant's inability to continue certain hobbies in his/her life. Colossus then assigns severity points based on the totality of the entries submitted by the claims professional. Colossus, using the insurer's information regarding the value of injuries, then recommends a value for the injury claim. The claims professional then uses this information as a guide in determining the settlement value of the injury claim.

The insurance industry has saved a great deal of money by using Colossus. However, many plaintiffs' lawyers and insurance regulators have questioned how data bases are constructed and how the program has been used. In a bad faith in settlement action brought against Allstate, for example, testimony established that jury awards as well as any settlements of more than $50,000 were excluded from the database. Adjusters who offered more than the minimum amounts suggested by Colossus were disciplined. After four days of testimony, Allstate settled the case. See Jerry Guidera, " 'Colossus' at the Accident Scene: Insurers Use a Software Program to Pay Out Claims for Injuries, but Lawsuits Claim It's Misused," *Wall Street Journal*, Jan. 2, 2003, at C1. State trial lawyers' associations have sponsored seminars to explain the Colossus system and its impact on negotiating with adjusters. There have been a number of bad faith in settlement cases brought where the plaintiff alleged that the way the insurance company used Colossus itself constituted bad faith. How does the rise of programs such as Colossus affect the picture that Ross presents of the operation of the settlement of insurance claims by insurance companies?

(D) Family Law

(2.6) Divorce Lawyers at Work: Varieties of Professionalism in Practice

Lynn Mather, Craig A. McEwen, and Richard J. Maiman

(2001).

[This study of divorce lawyers was conducted in Maine and New Hampshire. The lawyers were drawn from three of New Hampshire's ten counties, and four of the sixteen counties of Maine. Most of the data came from "lengthy semistructured interviews with 163 divorce lawyers." These interviews were conducted in 1990–1991.]

Communities of Divorce Lawyers

Lawyers who find themselves regularly interacting with each other on different sides of divorce cases constitute a community of practice. Not all lawyers do divorce work although surprisingly many do it occasionally. For example, in our samples of divorce cases from docket records between 1984 and 1988, 45 percent of the names listed as attorneys of record in New Hampshire and 39 percent of the names in Maine had only one case sampled in any court. Another 21 percent of the lawyers in the New Hampshire dockets and 16 percent of names in Maine had only two cases. This suggests that large numbers of lawyers only do an occasional divorce. In New Hampshire, the 20 percent of divorce lawyers who did the most divorces handled 56 percent of the total representations in our sample, while in Maine they handled 65 percent of the cases. The large group of attorneys who occasionally represent divorce clients works at the margins of the community of divorce practice. . . .

In the next section we will first consider the general community of divorce lawyers and then the finer gradations within it. As we examine these communities, we will see more clearly how important they are in providing reference points for the crucial judgments of lawyers.

The General Community of Divorce Practice: The Norm of the Reasonable Lawyer

The general community of divorce practice stems from shared interest, experience and knowledge about divorce law and from repeated contact and reputation. In this community, lawyers depend on one another as negotiating and litigating partners and develop common expectations that serve to regularize behavior, rendering it more predictable and their work more manageable. The common norm of a "reasonable lawyer" defines both typical and expected behavior within the community of divorce practice. One-third of the attorneys we interviewed explicitly used the terms "reasonable" or "unreasonable" to characterize "types of divorce lawyers," and many more invoked the concept of reasonableness elsewhere in the interview or used another adjective like "realistic," "rational" or "practical" to distinguish among divorce attorneys.

The notion of the reasonable lawyer provides guidance to attorneys who must negotiate the abstract and conflicting demands of their professional role in the context of the special characteristics of divorce law. How does zealous advocacy get balanced with the need for professional independence and objectivity? How much should lawyers guide their clients and how much should they be guided by them? How can lawyers manage to serve clients with modest resources in the context of a time-consuming and expensive adversary process? Such questions are raised indirectly but not necessarily answered through the codes of professional responsibility. The informal practice-based norms of the reasonable lawyer, however, give a somewhat clearer, although still incomplete, operating definition of what it means to be a responsible professional in divorce practice.

A reasonable lawyer first and foremost knows divorce law, understands the range of likely outcomes and the criteria for them, and accepts the consequent reality that divorce cases generally should be settled. She willingly cooperates in negotiation because she knows the law of divorce well enough to understand that it does not lend itself to win-lose outcomes.

> You just need to be rational, and you've got to be reasonable and know what the law is, so you can advise your client what the law is and then, in my opinion, there's no divorce that should go through on a contested basis, unless someone is being unreasonable.

Furthermore, she recognizes likely and acceptable outcomes of divorce cases and thus can be counted on to counsel acceptance of a settlement close to the typical result. As one attorney said, "I think the lawyers who practice for any length of time in the family law area know that it's kind of like a bell-shaped curve, that most results fall in a fairly narrow range of percentiles."

. . .

Reasonableness thus requires experience and knowledge in divorce practice that help to diminish the likelihood of demands or offers that fall outside of the range of acceptability.

Being willing to settle does not mean that reasonable lawyers are pushovers, however. As one lawyer put it, "I'm not saying they roll over by any stretch of the imagination, but they're realistic." While advocating for the client's interests, the reasonable lawyer knows that not all issues in a divorce have equal weight. A lawyer commented, "you have to be a bulldog at times and other times you have to be a poodle too. Sometimes you've got to understand that this isn't worth fighting over." Another attorney explained: "Obviously, you have to rely on your own best judgment of what battles are worth fighting and what battles are not, and how far to fight them. And there are some lawyers in town who take zealous advocacy to a new high." Thus, the reasonable lawyer separates important from unimportant issues and demonstrates good judgment and common sense in evaluating a case. . . .

Second, reasonable divorce lawyers remain objective and refuse to take on the client's emotions and anger as their own. By contrast, lawyers who become overly identified with the client's position lose their professional independence and become "knights on white horses who tell their clients what they want to hear."

> There are lawyers who adopt immediately their client's idiosyncrasies and deal through the whole case with the other lawyer and other party like they're Saddam Hussein and get very upset at the other lawyer and very upset at the other party and take a completely subjective partisan view of the situation.

> Well, there are those who are the soul of reason and well-skilled, such, as I. There are the others who seem to become emotionally involved with their clients and their client's cause, and that gets in the way of negotiating a reasonable resolution.

The reasonable lawyer recognizes that he should not take on his client's cause as his own personal battle and that he should maintain a generally dispassionate and independent view of the case, the client, and the outcome.

This independence of judgment and refusal to invest their own emotions in the case help reasonable lawyers to maintain "control" over their clients. Rather than letting clients "call the shots," reasonable lawyers "set their client's expectations." Indeed, 31 percent of lawyers we interviewed specifically mentioned the issue of client control as a major dimension of variation among divorce attorneys. It is not enough for the reasonable lawyer herself to know the law, the system, and "what a case is worth." She must clearly work to teach her clients these lessons, or, at least, to distance herself from unreasonable client demands. As one lawyer explained: "The worst thing you want is a weak lawyer on the other side. He's going to waste your time. He'll do what his client tells him to do instead of telling his client what to do." Another lawyer similarly noted:

> There are some types who are, I guess I would characterize them as total advocates who don't strive for the fair resolution. They strive for, they'll go for just exactly what their client wants, even though it may be unreasonable, and they don't seem to be willing to bring their client around.

The reasonable lawyer rejects the "hired gun" role and instead guides the client firmly to want or at least to accept the kinds of outcomes that are likely.

Third, reasonable divorce lawyers demonstrate honesty, integrity, and openness in their relationships with other lawyers. These qualities are part of ... professional "etiquette", ... a set of norms that members create to define professional working relations with each other. One aspect of this etiquette is that lawyers are not to let disagreements over case outcomes turn into personal animosity. Another aspect is honesty and keeping your word in discussions with your peers. As one attorney put it, "Reasonable people are not going to play games, are not going to try to hide anything, are going to try to be straightforward." Finally, the norm of reasonableness means that lawyers are to share information with one another rather than forcing opposing counsel to use the court to obtain it. That is, to be reasonable means "that you don't make it difficult to get information that I am perfectly entitled to, and otherwise I am going to have to go to court to get it, and it is going to cost everyone time and money, and I am going to get it anyway."

In sum, many attorneys who regularly practice divorce law share common conceptions of reasonable conduct. The portrait of the reasonable divorce lawyer shows a tough-minded advocate committed to settlement as the best resolution in divorce (but willing to go to trial if necessary), knowledgeable about the law and likely legal outcomes, objective and independent in judgment, and willing to guide the client to a fair outcome. Collegiality does not get in the way of advancing the client's interests, but neither does thoughtless advocacy undermine the working relationships necessary within the community. Judgment and balance prevail in this view of the consummate, reasonable professional.

In contrast, "unreasonable" lawyers have been given nicknames by their colleagues that reflect a lack of judgment and balance: "Rambo," "hired gun," "gunslinger," "loose cannon," "jerk," "shoe-banger," "mouthpiece," "asshole," "shark," "pitbull," "mad dog," and "son of a bitch." These lawyers exacerbate rather than reduce conflict, rely heavily and inappropriately on the tools of litigation; and see negotiation as another battleground rather than a place for reasonable accommodation. These are the attorneys "who simply cannot walk by a fire without throwing some gasoline on it, whether they are in a divorce case or anything else." The gasoline consists of outrageous demands in settlement negotiation, vituperative comments and personal antagonism, dishonesty and unreliability, and over-reliance on civil litigation techniques of discovery and motion practice.

Those who violate the norm of the reasonable divorce lawyer may do so because they are outsiders to that community, sharing neither its standards nor its bonds of reciprocity.

> And then maybe the last category is the litigator who has more of a personal injury-type practice. Divorces come along every now and then. They take them, they haven't a clue as to what's been happening in the practice of family law. They think it's an automobile accident case and they treat it that way.

Although the greatest contrasts in practice may be between those inside and those outside the community of divorce practice, not all insiders share or live up to the same standards of reasonableness. Lawyers within this community quickly earn reputations and labels among their peers when they violate the norms. But no other efforts appear to be made to change their behavior.

Even the norm of the reasonable lawyer proves too general to apply perfectly to different practice settings within divorce law, however. The general community of divorce practice is itself divided into family law specialists and general practice attorneys (or other specialists) who interpret somewhat differently this ideal. These interpretations reflect the overlapping effects of specialization of practice, social class of clients, and gender of the attorney. . . .

Defining Lawyers' Expertise in Divorce Practice

. . . . We sought to understand the ways that divorce lawyers constructed their own versions of expertise in their day-to-day practices in part by asking our respondents to rate on a scale of one ("not important") to five ("essential") six skills that a divorce attorney might utilize. Although the list of skills is basic, it does provide a benchmark for establishing how divorce lawyers rank order them and for comparing the ratings by different communities of practice. Two-thirds of our lawyers expanded on their ratings, and we draw on those explanatory comments, along with their responses to several related questions, to explore what lawyers in divorce practice believe to be their special expertise.

Table 4.1 reports the mean scores that lawyers gave to each of these six skills. As these data show, there was a consensus within the divorce lawyer community on the two most important skills: the ability to listen sensitively to clients and to effectively negotiate problems. The lawyers we studied. . . . perceived their expertise to lie more in the area of interpersonal communication and negotiation than in technical legal knowledge. One of our lawyers said, "that is a good list" and commented perceptively, "It is interesting because what it makes me think about in that list is how much of that really you depend on experience. Except for the first one, which is just knowledge of the law, just about everything else I think really comes with doing a lot of divorces." This perspective on professional expertise emphasizes that the most salient professional knowledge is acquired largely through experience.

Table 4.1   Lawyers' Ratings of Importance of Skills in Day-to-Day Practice of Divorce Law, on a Scale of 1 (Not Important) to 5 (Essential)

Skill	Mean Rating
Being a Sensitive Listener to Client	4.30 (n = 157)
Being a Skillful Negotiator	4.27 (n = 157)
Being Expert in Divorce Law	3.97 (n = 157)
Being a Skillful Litigator	3.68 (n = 157)
Knowing the Judges	3.50 (n = 155)
Knowing the Other Lawyers	3.25 (n = 156)

Listening to Clients

When lawyers rated "being a sensitive listener to the client" as the most important skill in divorce law practice, they had several distinct versions of "sensitive listening" in mind. For some, the skill of listening to clients was essential because it furthered the instrumental purpose of eliciting information for the construction of the technical legal case. Listening to clients mattered, in other words, "in order to get everything I need out" or "to get at the bottom of the divorce ... [to know] how solid their position is on various issues." Recognizing the potential for emotions to block information gathering, as well as the need for adequate information for effective legal representation, some lawyers stressed the skill of listening for the information it revealed. As one explained, "You have to be skillful in picking out items. You have got to make damn sure you are listening to those things." Gathering this information required careful listening to clients, but not necessarily "sensitive" listening in the sense of having a good bedside manner. As another explained, "If you are saying, 'Does that imply being compassionate to the client so they think you are listening, so that they feel better?' I don't know. If it's being a good listener so that you hear, you receive what the client is telling you so that you can use that in your negotiation or your litigation, that is very important." A third lawyer noted wryly that "you don't have to listen sensitively about property."

Another reason to listen was to build a close and trusting relationship with clients, to strengthen their faith in their lawyer. "You need to let your clients know that you understand their problems ... that they are placing their trust in you and you are going to do everything that you can to get everything that they need." Good listening skills thus helped to define and strengthen the lawyer's role as fiduciary for the client, a critical part of professional responsibility, regardless of whether any information was gleaned through the listening process. As one lawyer said bluntly, listening is essential because "if you don't have that, you won't have clients."

The third way of understanding sensitive listening to clients was as a means of providing emotional support and help for them during the painful process of divorce. Sensitive listening allowed lawyers to befriend and assist clients in solving their problems and moving on with their lives. As one lawyer said, "There's a lot of emotional stuff going on, and I really like to become friends with my clients." Another explained, "Going through my own divorce gave me a great deal of empathy for what my clients have to go through, and when somebody cries in my office, I know how much it hurts." . . .

This version of listening thus differed significantly from the first two, which served the more narrow conception of the lawyer as a legal advocate who needs to know the facts and have the trust of the client. One attorney described this latter view as follows: "You've got to wear two hats. You've got to be a counselor as well as an attorney and the counselor being more of a personal counselor than a legal counselor." . . .

Those lawyers who held this broader view of professional responsibility and expertise—about a quarter of the lawyers we interviewed—generally saw their personal counseling skills as arising from practical experience, although a few sought out new training and collaboration with psychologists and family counselors.

More commonly, however, the lawyers that we interviewed insisted on distinguishing between what they perceived to be legal and nonlegal issues in a case and frequently diverted the latter by referring clients to professional counseling. This boundary of professional expertise—between divorce lawyers as experts in certain kinds of problems and counselors as experts in other areas—was constructed in lawyers' offices through discussions between attorneys and their clients. Although most lawyers knew they could not be too rigid or unsympathetic to their clients' concerns without calling into question their allegiance to clients, they worried that they lacked the qualifications and patience to give appropriate advice or to justify the time (and therefore money) required to do so.

Divorce lawyers who reported that they strongly discouraged clients from discussing emotional issues insisted that a conceptual boundary line separated the legal from the nonlegal sides of a case, and that an attorney's expertise did not extend to personal matters. They defined their professional role in terms of "helping with legal rights" or educating clients "as to what the law says, as to what I would predict a court would do." They were not there "to either judge my client's personal decisions or to assist them in making a personal decision." Although two-thirds of the lawyers who drew such lines acknowledged that they had to tolerate emotional content in the initial conference ("It's expected at the outset") or even through the first several meetings, they tended to believe that the skillful divorce lawyer guides the client to shift away from the personal issues to the legal ones that should preoccupy the attorney. The attorneys we interviewed thus positioned themselves across a broad continuum, ranging from those who felt they should counsel their clients about their personal problems to those who tried to confine discussions with clients to the legal issues. Thus, lawyers varied in the ways that they understood their own expertise and roles.

106

Negotiating Effectively

The data reported in Table 4.1 show "being a skillful negotiator" in a virtual tie with "being a sensitive listener to the client" for importance in the day-to-day practice of divorce law. As attorneys explained their numerical ratings, however, they suggested that negotiation, much like listening to clients, involves very little technical training and is instead something that lawyers learn as they engage in and reflect on their practices. Indeed, as one attorney said, skill in negotiation is "absolutely essential [because] that's 95 percent of what a divorce lawyer does." For the lawyers we talked with, negotiation skills were of a rough-and-ready sort, beginning with "being prepared," and continuing with being practical, listening well, and communicating clearly. In other words, lawyers' skill at negotiation in divorce had multiple meanings, but each of these rather generic qualities was gained through experience, not formal legal training.

Understanding the ability to negotiate as uniquely a lawyer's skill was made more difficult by the fact that often clients wanted to engage in negotiation themselves, and in some instances attorneys preferred them to do so. We questioned attorneys about how they viewed the client's role in negotiation. Fifty-five percent indicated that they encouraged clients to negotiate, 33 percent said that they permitted client negotiation, and 12 percent reported that they actively discouraged clients from negotiating on their own. Thus, a substantial majority of divorce lawyers, whether out of conviction, necessity, or both, saw a part for their clients to play in the process of negotiating a divorce. . . .

Expertise in Divorce Law, Litigation, and Local Knowledge of Judges and Lawyers

"Being expert in the law of divorce" ranked a fairly distant third among the six skills rated by our respondents and reported in Table 4.1. This rating tells us something about the relative lack of importance that practitioners ascribed to knowing the "black letter" of divorce law. Legal expertise clearly mattered in practice and thus the skill was rated "very important." But why was it not rated higher? The most straightforward explanation for considering substantive legal expertise to be less than essential in divorce work is that, as several respondents put it, "there just isn't much law" governing divorce, and what exists is "not that complicated." According to this view, any reasonably competent lawyer knows enough law already to handle divorce cases as part of a general practice. And when a more difficult question of divorce law does arise, the answer is not hard to find. As one lawyer explained, "That's why they have law libraries." Or as another said, "As long as you have the skills to look it up, you don't need to have everything right at your fingertips." A third lawyer noted that "anyone can become an expert in any area of the law, in other words, of knowing the law. And divorce law can probably be one of the easier ones." More than one respondent mentioned the standard treatise on their state's domestic relations law as the "one book" that was essential for the divorce lawyer to own.

107

By contrast. the few lawyers who rated "being expert in divorce law" as essential in day-to-day practice emphasized the constantly changing nature of the field and the need to stay abreast of new cases, statutes, and legal rules.

> You certainly have to be thoroughly familiar with the statutes. There aren't that many of them, but they are constantly updated so you have to read everything that comes in. The child support guidelines and the things that go into that are constantly changing so you always have to be alert to those changes. New cases are coming out every week from the Supreme Court. You should be reading all of those domestic cases, because that's what changes the law.

These lawyers saw much greater complexity in family law and more material to master than the great majority of their colleagues.

Although technical legal expertise is supposed to be central to the professional identities of lawyers, it was not seen that way by most of our respondents. A wide range of perceptions across different groups of lawyers also emerged in the ratings of three other skills related to legal training and advocacy—skill as litigators, knowledge of the judges, and knowledge of other lawyers.

Lawyers' ratings of "being a skillful litigator" placed it fourth in importance on our list, but as with the rating of technical legal expertise, there was wide variation in responses here. The most common reason given for the relative lack of importance of litigation skill was that so few divorce cases are tried. "If it comes down to that, it's [litigation skill] important but most of them don't." Several lawyers explicitly compared the small role played by litigation versus the necessity of being able to deal effectively with clients. For example, one of them noted: "That is not as important, although I certainly came to divorce work because I had the litigation skills, but so much of this practice is client dealings, and I would say 90 percent of the cases end up being settled by the parties and their lawyers." . . .

For many lawyers, litigation skills were considered relatively low in importance because negotiated settlements were seen as the preferred outcome in divorce cases—for both the clients and their children. From this perspective, then, several attorneys emphasized that the goal in marital practice is to avoid litigation, so "by the time you litigate in a sense it's almost a failure." Or as another one said, "Most cases don't get litigated so, in the cases that go to trial, it's essential. But not many of them go to trial if you're doing your job." "Doing your job," then, meant acting according to the norms of the reasonable lawyer and settling cases by negotiation. But this exact point led some lawyers to express another way of thinking about litigation skill. These attorneys emphasized the linkage between negotiation and litigation, noting, for example, that "if you are a better litigator, that gives you an advantage in the negotiations, an unspoken advantage," or that "the stronger the litigator that you are, the greater the respect somebody else has for you, so then the better the negotiator you are."

If litigation skills were not seen as vitally important elements of the professional expertise of divorce lawyers, it is not surprising that "knowing the judges" was viewed as relatively low in importance as well.... [I]f much of the law is relatively straightforward and few cases get tried, it is understandable that the lawyers we interviewed saw knowledge of the judges as less important than other skills. This item also showed the greatest variation out of the six skills in responses from our lawyers. While some lawyers largely discounted the role of the judge because of the frequency of settlement and attorneys' inability to control who the judge was, others thought it crucial. Lawyers who gave credence to this item explained that by knowing individual judges, they could shape a court presentation to avoid issues that might irritate them or construct arguments to appeal to their predilections. But such stories of biases were frequently contradicted by other lawyers who insisted that judges are evenhanded in deciding divorce cases. Thus, divorce lawyers had different views of the value of this form of local professional knowledge as an aspect of their expertise.

Another aspect of local professional knowledge—knowing the other lawyers—was rated lower still, but its average rating suggests that it was still seen as an "important" skill in day-to-day practice. Since law is a social process as well as an intellectual one, knowing one's colleagues presumably makes work easier, and—according to our lawyers—more effective. For one thing, lawyers said that they could more easily anticipate the course of a divorce case if they knew the lawyer on the other side, being familiar with his or her particular work style and preferences. An experienced attorney could predict the timing and cost of a case, depending on the identity of an opposing lawyer and thus better advise their clients....

The crucial skills in day-to-day divorce practice remained those of listening to clients and negotiating with opposing lawyers. Neither of these skills is taught formally to most lawyers, and neither is confined to them. Thus, what appear most important to divorce attorneys are skills that are difficult to claim exclusively as within their professional sphere. This would seem to make divorce lawyers especially sensitive and vulnerable to competition from nonlawyers such as mediators.

NOTES AND QUESTIONS

1.   Maine and New Hampshire are "contiguous, semirural New England states" (p. 195), with small populations and no big cities. Does it mean that we cannot generalize the results to big cities and populous states?

2.   The data in the book also rest largely on interviews. As the authors point out, this is both a strength and a weakness. A strength, in that these were experienced divorce lawyers, and valuable "informants" about their own work, and the work of other lawyers. They were reporting, too, on their own "understandings, perceptions, and beliefs." But "friendly critics" have reminded the authors of the "need to be skeptical" about whether the interviews "provide a window on actual practice."

Another issue is whether the lawyers told the authors "professionally acceptable" responses, rather than "what they really believed or actually did." The authors admit that this is a real problem, but they were confident that they heard "candid views." This was because of the fact that "not all lawyers responded in ways that flattered them or put their own conduct in the best light;" and also because they checked what they heard against data provided by court records, where this was possible (pp. 198–200).

3. The Shadow of the Law: In a well-known article by Robert Mnookin and Lewis Kornhauser, "Bargaining in the Shadow of the Law: The Case of Divorce," 88 *Yale Law Journal* 950 (1979), the authors make the point that parties to a divorce "do not bargain ... in a vacuum; they bargain in the shadow of the law. The legal rules governing alimony, child support, marital property, and custody give each parent certain claims based on what each would get if the case went to trial. In other words, the outcome that the law will impose if no agreement is reached gives each parent certain bargaining chips—an endowment of sorts."

Would the lawyers in Mather et al., agree with this statement? And what is the "law" that is casting a shadow here? Many of the rules that make up divorce "law" are exceedingly vague—custody awards are to be "in the best interests of the child," for example. Mnookin and Kornhauser admit that this standard, and some others, are "extraordinarily vague and allow courts broad discretion;" it is therefore hard to analyze the "effects of uncertainty on bargaining."

4. Do criminal defendants plea-bargain "in the shadow of the law?" What role does the "shadow of the law" play for Macaulay's business people, or for Ross' insurance claimants? Herbert Jacob, in "The Elusive Shadow of the Law," 26 *Law & Society Review* 565, 586 (1992) argues that the "expectation that bargaining occurs in the shadow of the law is not a general rule but one that is contingent on many conditions." His research led him to think that the "strength of the shadow of the law" depends on "the language in which a claim is initially framed," along with "the manner in which attorneys are used and the success of consultation with personal networks."

Herbert Kritzer, in *Let's Make a Deal: Understanding the Negotiation Process in Ordinary Litigation* (1991), argues that there are two different "shadows" of law. In tort cases, appellate decisions provide "*relatively* little basis for prediction," especially about how much money the plaintiff might get in a lawsuit. But there is another "shadow" of law: "the ability to impose costs on the opponent and the capability of absorbing costs."

5. Under an Indiana statute, courts are supposed to award custody "in accordance with the best interests of the child." The statute says explicitly that "there is no presumption favoring either parent;" rather, the court should consider "all relevant factors," and lists a number of these. Julie E. Artis, "Judging the Best Interests of the Child: Judges' Accounts of the Tender Years Doctrine," 38 *Law & Society Review* 769 (2004), interviewed judges in Indiana, and found that judges voiced support for the so-called

"tender years" doctrine—that is, that a child of "tender years" is better off with its mother, not its father. Many judges felt that "the mother has the stronger natural nurturing instinct," or that the "mother is a better caregiver." Artis found that judges did not think the statute restricted them in any way; and some of them "appeared to be unfamiliar with the statute!" Yet the words of the statute strongly suggest that the "tender years" doctrine is not to be considered law in Indiana.

Women judges were more likely than male judges to "explicitly embrace egalitarian notions of parenthood," and reject the "tender years" doctrine. When Artis looked at actual custody decisions, she found that mothers got custody in 82% of the cases. Judges who supported the tender years doctrine gave the mother custody of children 6 or younger 100% of the time; judges who felt otherwise gave the mother custody 84.2% of the time. It should be pointed out that these were custody decisions of only nine judges. What kind of methodological problem does this pose?

How important was the "shadow of the law" in these custody cases?

6. Emotion and Legal Practice: In another part of their book, Mather and her associates talk about how lawyers need to "shift a client's perspective from the emotional divorce to the pragmatic issues of the legal divorce, and then either to bolster a client's demands or to moderate them." Lawyers often face "difficult negotiations" with their own clients (p. 96). They try to persuade; they may use "professional knowledge and power over clients" to try to move them; they may talk about the law, about what the judge might do, they might talk about the "built-in delays of the court process or consciously stall case progress themselves" (p. 101). In extreme cases, they might threaten to quit the case altogether.

Other studies have also made the distinction between the "emotional divorce" and the "legal divorce." See, for example, John Griffiths, "What Do Dutch Lawyers Actually Do in Divorce Cases?" 20 *Law & Society Review* 135 (1986), for a similar discussion, based on a study of divorce lawyers in the Netherlands. Another study of American divorce lawyers is Austin Sarat and William L. F. Felstiner, *Divorce Lawyers and Their Clients: Power and Meaning in the Legal Process* (1995). They make a point quite similar to that made by Mather and her associates. Lawyers "use and communicate their knowledge of the legal process as a resource in educating clients about what is 'realistic' in the legal process of divorce. They use this knowledge strategically to move clients toward positions they deem to be reasonable and appropriate." But it is not "the technical world of law, of sophisticated interpretation of specialized rules, that lawyers describe in their efforts to give meaning to the legally realistic.... Rather, they speak in terms of a world of uncertain and competing interpretations, in which personal agendas, organizational needs, and individual personalities play central roles." In this kind of work, nothing is "guaranteed;" but the "best chance of success rests with those who are familiar with legal practice and who have a working relationship with officials who wield local power" (pp. 145–146).

Still another study of divorce in operation is Howard S. Erlanger, Elizabeth Chambliss, and Marygold S. Melli, "Participation and Flexibility in Informal Processes: Cautions from the Divorce Context," 21 *Law & Society Review* 585 (1987). This study was based on "in-depth interviews with the parties and lawyers," in twenty-five cases, all involving divorces where there were minor children, together with the court records. The cases were from Dane County (Madison) Wisconsin, in June or July, 1982. The authors found tremendous pressure to settle the cases. Many parties simply could not afford to go to court, or to pay big lawyer fees if the case dragged on. The lawyers added their own pressure; and sometimes judges too. One judge told the parties "If you can settle, we'll go on to court and get this thing over with today." Otherwise, it would drag on endlessly. Some clients just wanted to get the whole thing over, because it was emotionally draining; or because they had a new relationship; or just wanted to return to "some semblance of a stable life style." In general, lawyers described divorce work as "emotionally draining." One lawyer said, "Divorce is 99 percent psychotherapy, 1 percent law."

People sometimes think that the courtroom is the place for contested divorces; informal settlements for people who "agree." But settlements often seem quite coercive to the people involved. Some of them seem "no less imposed than judgments at trial." More than 90% of divorce cases settle out of court. This "opens the possibility that the shadow of the law, which presumably constrains negotiating parties, is instead cast by them. In other words, in litigation, judges may be following the patterns they see in informal settlements rather than the other way around." So, instead of talking about "bargaining in the shadow of the law," one might talk about "litigating in the shadow of informal settlement."

7. Informal Process: Some scholars have argued that negotiation and mediation impact women and men quite differently. Penelope E. Bryan, in "Killing Us Softly: Divorce Mediation and the Politics of Power," 40 *Buffalo Law Review* 441 (1992) suggests that mediation favors men over women. Men have more money and power, on the whole. Women have lower self-esteem, find the divorce process more draining, are more easily influenced, and tend to conform rather than to dominate and fight. Mediation "exploits wives by denigrating their legal entitlements;" it strips them of "authority," it encourages "unwarranted compromises," isolates them from their support systems, and puts them "across the table from their more powerful husbands," forced to "fend for themselves." See also Trina Grillo, "The Mediation Alternative: Process Dangers for Women," 100 *Yale Law Journal* 1545 (1991). John Conley and William O'Barr point to systematic linguistic disadvantages faced by women in informal disputing situations such as divorce mediation. *Just Words*, at 39–59. There have been a number of attempts to study the economic effects of mediation on divorce outcomes; the studies have come to mixed results. There is more agreement on the dangers of mediation for

women in abusive relationships, although some mediation proponents have advanced arguments to the contrary.

The "bargaining" that seems ubiquitous in the world of law takes many forms—there is bargaining with the other side; and there is bargaining between lawyer and client. How then would you describe the real world of divorce and custody law?

8.   A Note on Method: Mather and her associates, and Sarat and Felstiner, used in-depth interviews. There are a range of methods that can be used in the study of how legal systems operate—all of the methods of the social sciences. These can be more or less arranged in order from the most highly statistical and mathematical, to the least statistical and mathematical. Some social science methods are modeled more on the natural sciences, employing hypothesis testing and formal measurement, while others have developed (generally more qualitative) methods specifically geared toward studying the unique characteristics of human culture and social life. Some methods have a foot in both camps. For example, interviews can be used to provide both qualitative information about how people understand the world and their lives—and can also be used to test hypotheses. Interviews can be structured or non-structured—that is, they can employ more rigid sets of questions, or they can be loose and open-ended. In this latter kind of interview, the interviewer tries to let the subject talk more or less freely.

The methods used depend on what it is you are trying to study. Suppose you wanted to study the mind and the work of armed robbers. You can hardly get a random sample of armed robbers. A lucky (if that is the word) researcher might get access to one or two armed robbers, get them to talk, and ask them to suggest other subjects. This is a so-called "snowball" sample. Richard T. Wright and Scott H. Decker, in *Armed Robbers in Action: Stickups and Street Culture* (1997) wanted to study the life and work of hold-up men. The authors managed to reach a few subjects, who gave them other names; eventually, they interviewed eighty-six "currently active armed robbers" in the city of St. Louis. Their interviews were "semistructured and conducted in an informal manner, allowing the offenders to speak freely." An earlier study by the same authors, *Burglars on the Job: Streetlife and Residential Breakins* (1994), used similar methods. The results of this kind of study are difficult to quantify.

On the other hand, a structured interview (or, still more rigid, a "paper" or on-line survey) yields more easily quantified results—but may do a poor job of capturing how people actually think. (In "forced choice" surveys, people have to select one of several alternatives, none of which may make much sense to them.) Survey researchers sometimes attempt to modulate the shortcomings of their methodology by conducting preliminary, more open-ended interviews with members of the population they plan to survey. Ultimately, every method sacrifices some kinds of accuracy to achieve others. Obviously, if your goal is to study the mind and work of armed robbers, a less structured method would generate more information by imposing fewer of your own operating assumptions. It is also important to consider the impact of the method itself on the population you are studying. More formal, structured formats can cause people to withdraw or feel uncomfortable, thereby limiting the amount and kind of information generated. See Charles Briggs, *Learning How to Ask: A Sociolinguistic Appraisal of the Role of the Interview in Social Science Research* (1986).

It is for this reason that anthropologists developed the "participant observation" method, which generated in-depth "ethnographic" studies. Early anthropologists sought a better understanding of cultures with very different presuppositions than the anthropologists' own. This required a more in-depth immersion in the research site than is provided by many other social science methods. Anthropologists developed demanding requirements for ethnographers: the researcher must live or work inside the research setting for an extended period of time. In this way, there can be close, intensive observation of the society. For an example, see June Starr, *Dispute and Settlement in Rural Turkey: An Ethnography of Law* (1978). The ethnographer who spends a year, or two, or six, living with a community, presumably can gain insights into the culture and way of life that could not be captured through structured interviews. Ethnography avoids trying to squeeze the actions and thoughts of the subjects into categories that the researcher has devised in advance.

Ethnography has a long history in law-and-society studies. A famous instance was Karl N. Llewellyn and E. Adamson Hoebel, *The Cheyenne Way* (1941). Llewellyn was a law professor; Hoebel was a trained anthropologist. On ethnographic methods, and their value, see Christine Harrington and Barbara Yngvesson, "Interpretative Sociolegal Research," 15 *Law and Social Inquiry* 135 (1990). A useful collection is June Starr and Mark Goodale, eds., *Practicing Ethnography in Law: New Dialogues, Enduring Methods* (2002).

Ethnography, of course, presents its own problems. See Robert J. Thomas, "Interviewing Important People in Big Companies," 22 *Journal of Contemporary Ethnography* 80 (1993). John Van Maanen, in "The Fact of Fiction in Organizational Ethnography," 24 *Administrative Science Quarterly* 539, 549 (1979) points out that

> The results of ethnographic study are ... mediated several times over—First, by the fieldworker's own standards of relevance as to what is and what is not worthy of observation; second by the historically situated questions that are put to people in the setting; third, by the self-reflection demanded of an informant; and fourth, by the intentional and unintentional ways the produced data are misleading.

How does the use of hypotheses, and the testing of hypotheses, avoid these sources of error? Or does it? What sorts of errors are introduced by the testing of hypotheses that are avoided by ethnography?

(E) Legislation

(2.7) Congress: The Electoral Connection

David R. Mayhew[11]

(2004).

I have become convinced that scrutiny of purposive behavior offers the best route to an understanding of legislatures—or at least of the United States Congress. In the fashion of economics, I shall make a simple abstract assumption about human motivation and then speculate about the consequences of behavior based on that motivation. Specifically, I shall conjure up a vision of United States congressmen as single-minded seekers of reelection, see what kinds of activity that goal implies, and then speculate about how congressmen so motivated are likely to go about building and sustaining legislative institutions and making policy. At all points I shall try to match the abstract with the factual.

I find an emphasis on the reelection goal attractive for a number of reasons. First, I think it fits political reality rather well. Second, it puts the spotlight directly on men rather than on parties and pressure groups, which in the past have often entered discussions of American politics as analytic phantoms. Third, I think politics is best studied as a struggle among men to gain and maintain power and the consequences of that struggle. Fourth—and perhaps most important—the reelection quest establishes an accountability relationship with an electorate, and any serious thinking about democratic theory has to give a central place to the question of accountability....

My subject of concern here is a single legislative institution, the United States Congress. In many ways, of course, the Congress is a unique or unusual body. It is probably the most highly "professionalized" of legislatures, in the sense that it promotes careerism among its members and gives them the salaries, staff, and other resources to sustain careers. Its parties are exceptionally diffuse. It is widely thought to be especially "strong" among legislatures as a checker of executive power. Like most Latin American legislatures but unlike most European ones, it labors in the shadow of a separately elected executive. My decision to focus on the Congress flows from a belief that there is something to be gained in an intensive analysis of a particular and important institution. But there is something general to be gained as well, for the exceptionalist argument should not be carried too far. In a good many ways the Congress is just one in a large family of legislative bodies....

Even if congressmen are single-mindedly interested in reelection, are they in a position as individuals to do anything about it? If they are not, if they are

---

11. Second edition, 2004. The book was originally published in 1974. The second edition is identical to the first, except that the author contributed a new preface, and there was a short introduction by R. Douglas Arnold.

inexorably shoved to and fro by forces in their political environments, then obviously it makes no sense to pay much attention to their individual activities. This question requires a complex answer, and it will be useful to begin reaching for one by pondering whether individual congressmen are the proper analytic units in an investigation of this sort. An important alternative view is that parties rather than lone politicians are the prime movers in electoral politics. The now classic account of what a competitive political universe will look like with parties as its analytic units is Downs' *Economic Theory of Democracy.*[12] In the familiar Downsian world parties are entirely selfish. They seek the rewards of office, but in order to achieve them they have to win office and keep it. They bid for favor before the public as highly cohesive point-source "teams." A party enjoys complete control over government during its term in office and uses its control solely to try to win the next election.

The fact is that no theoretical treatment of the United States Congress that posits parties as analytic units will go very far. So we are left with individual congressmen, with 535 men and women rather than two parties, as units to be examined in the discussion to come....

Are, then, congressmen in a position to do anything about getting reelected? If an answer is sought in their ability to affect national partisan percentages, the answer is no. But if an answer is sought in their ability to affect the percentages in their own primary and general elections, the answer is yes. Or at least so the case will be presented here. More specifically, it will be argued that they think that they can affect their own percentages, that in fact they can affect their own percentages, and furthermore that there is reason for them to try to do so. This last is obvious for the marginals, but perhaps not so obvious for the nonmarginals. Are they not, after all, occupants of "safe seats"? It is easy to form an image of congressmen who inherit lush party pastures and then graze their way through careers without ever having to worry about elections. But this image is misconceived, and it is important to show why....

It is possible to conceive of an assembly in which no member ever comes close to losing a seat but in which the need to be reelected is what inspires members' behavior. It would be an assembly with no saints or fools in it, an assembly packed with skilled politicians going about their business. When we say "Congressman Smith is unbeatable," we do not mean that there is nothing he could do that would lose him his seat. Rather we mean, "Congressman Smith is unbeatable as long as he continues to do the things he is doing." If he stopped answering his mail, or stopped visiting his district, or began voting randomly on roll calls, or shifted his vote record eighty points on the ADA scale, he would bring on primary or November election troubles in a hurry. It is difficult to offer conclusive proof that this last statement is true, for there is no congressman willing to make the experiment. But normal political activity among politicians with healthy electoral margins should not

12. Anthony Downs, *An Economic Theory* of Democracy *(1957).*

be confused with inactivity. What characterizes "safe" congressmen is not that they are beyond electoral reach, but that their efforts are very likely to bring them uninterrupted electoral success. . . .

The next step here is to offer a brief conceptual treatment of the relation between congressmen and their electorates. In the Downsian analysis what national party leaders must worry about is voters' "expected party differential."[13] But to congressmen this is in practice irrelevant, for reasons specified earlier. A congressman's attention must rather be devoted to what can be called an "expected incumbent differential." Let us define this "expected incumbent differential" as any difference perceived by a relevant political actor between what an incumbent congressman is likely to do if returned to office and what any possible challenger (in primary or general election) would be likely to do. And let us define "relevant political actor" here as anyone who has a resource that might be used in the election in question. At the ballot box the only usable resources are votes, but there are resources that can be translated into votes: money, the ability to make persuasive endorsements, organizational skills, and so on. By this definition a "relevant political actor" need not be a constituent; one of the most important resources, money, flows all over the country in congressional campaign years. . . .

What a congressman has to try to do is to insure that in primary and general elections the resource balance (with all other deployed resources finally translated into votes) favors himself rather than somebody else. To maneuver successfully he must remain constantly aware of what political actors' incumbent differential readings are, and he must act in a fashion to inspire readings that favor himself. . . .

[There are] three kinds of electorally oriented activities congressmen engage in—advertising, credit claiming, and position taking. It remains only to offer some brief comments on the emphases different members give to the different activities. . . . Senators, with their access to the media, seem to put more emphasis on position taking than House members; probably House members rely more heavily on particularized benefits. But there are important differences among House members. Congressmen from the traditional parts of old machine cities rarely advertise and seldom take positions on anything (except on roll calls), but devote a great deal of time and energy to the distribution of benefits. In fact they use their office resources to plug themselves into their local party organizations. . . . On the other hand, congressmen with upper-middle-class bases (suburban, city reform, or academic) tend to deal in positions. In New York City the switch from regular to reform Democrats is a switch from members who emphasize benefits to members who emphasize positions; it reflects a shift in consumer taste. . . . The same difference appears geographically rather than temporally as one goes from the inner wards to the outer suburbs of Chicago. . . .

Congressional policy-making activities produce a number of specifiable and predictable policy effects. Taken together these effects display what might

13. Downs, *supra*, at 38–45.

be called an "assembly coherence"—an overall policy pattern that one might expect any set of assemblies constructed like the United States Congress to generate.

One effect is delay—or, more properly, since the eye of the beholder creates it, a widespread perception of delay. Not too much should be made of this, but it is fair to say that over the years Congress has often lagged behind public opinion in enacting major legislation. Thus a perceived "inaction" was the major source of dissatisfaction with Congress in a survey of a generally dissatisfied public in 1963....

Recurrent perceptions of congressional delay on nonparticularized matters should cause little surprise. Mobilization may be halfhearted; there are so many other things to do; some issues may be uncomfortable to vote on at all; a live issue may be better than alive program; the effects are not important anyway. A second effect is particularism—that is, a strong tendency to wrap policies in packages that are salable as particularized benefits. Not only do congressmen aggressively seek out opportunities to supply such benefits (little or no "pressure" is needed), they tend in framing laws to give a particularistic cast to matters that do not obviously require it. The only benefits intrinsically worth anything, after all, are ones that can be packaged. Thus in time of recession congressmen reach for "accelerated public works" bills listing projects in the various districts; presidents prefer more general fiscal effects. In the education field a congressional favorite is the "impacted areas" program with its ostentatious grants to targeted school districts; again presidents prefer ventures of more diffuse impact. Presidents are capable of closing a hundred veterans' hospitals like a shot in the interest of "efficiency"; congressmen combine to keep them open.... The quest for the particular impels congressmen to take a vigorous interest in the organization of the federal bureaucracy. Thus, for example, the Corps of Army Engineers, structured to undertake discrete district projects, must be guarded from presidents who would submerge it in a quest for "planning."

A third effect is the servicing of the organized. This takes two familiar forms. First there is a deference toward nationally organized groups with enough widespread local clout to inspire favorable roll call positions on selected issues among a majority of members. Thus under four presidents in a row—Harding through Roosevelt—Congress passed veterans' bonus bills, the presidents vetoed them, and the House voted decisively to override the vetoes. In recent years the National Rifle Association has weighed in against gun control legislation. Second, there is deference toward groups with disposable electoral resources whose representatives keep a close watch on congressional maneuvers. Clientelism at the committee level is the result with its manifestations across a wide range of policy areas. Agriculture is an obvious example. Clientelism, like particularism, gives form to the federal bureaucracy. Congressmen protect clientele systems—alliances of agencies, Hill committees, and clienteles—against the incursions of presidents and cabinet secretaries.

A fourth effect is symbolism. The term needs explication. It is probably best to say that a purely symbolic congressional act is one expressing an attitude but prescribing no policy effects. An example would be a resolution deploring communism or poverty. But the term symbolic can also usefully be applied where Congress prescribes policy effects but does not act (in legislating or overseeing or both) so as to achieve them. No doubt the main cause of prescription-achievement gaps is the intractability of human affairs. But there is a special reason why a legislative body arranged like the United States Congress can be expected to engage in symbolic action by this second, impure construction of the term. The reason, of course, is that in a large class of legislative undertakings the electoral payment is for positions rather than for effects. . . .

A special word may be in order here on the politics of transfer programs—that is programs giving governmental cash payments to individuals in defined subclasses of the population. What distinguishes American transfer programs is not that they are "redistributive"—they are not any more so than some other programs—but that they offer legislators no particularized benefits. Who gets a check of what size is clearly prescribed by law, so congressmen get no credit for the handing out of individual checks. In these circumstances what can be said about the politics? A first point is that Congress will favor the passage of transfer programs when they are championed by powerful interest groups against unorganized opposition; the obvious example is the veterans' bonus. A second point is that Congress will legislate incremental payment increases in existent programs where there is little organized sentiment for or against doing so. Hence the biennial hike in social security benefits. The public assistance program has been enriched in an absentminded way over the years, mostly through the medium of Senate floor amendments. A third point is that Congress will be reluctant to legislate new programs benefiting the unorganized over the opposition of the organized. The third point is important. For members deciding how to vote there is a lack of prospective performance credit to counterbalance the influence of organized opposition. Hence major transfer innovations are unlikely to spring from individualistic assemblies. The impetus comes from elsewhere—Bismarck introduced his innovations for regime reasons; Lloyd George, for party reasons; Roosevelt (social security), Johnson (medicare), and Nixon (family assistance), for presidential reasons. A fourth and last point is that the politics of transfers would be vastly different if congressmen were allowed to put their names on the checks.

NOTES AND QUESTIONS

1. Mayhew's work can be classified as an example of what has been called public choice theory. Roughly, this means using the tools of economics to explain the behavior of legislatures and other organs of government and law. Or, more specifically, it means assuming rational, maximizing behavior. The advantage of public choice theory is that it permits scholars to create

models of the behavior in question. This has made it extremely attractive to many political scientists, as well as to economists. See, in general, Robert D. Tollison, "Public Choice and Legislation," 74 *Virginia Law Review* 339 (1988).

2. Mayhew's work on Congress is empirical, in the sense that he gives examples, and bases his conclusions on what he knows about Congress; but it is not quantitative. In the preface to the second edition, published in 2004, Mayhew describes his work as a "theoretical work that obviously goes too far. It is an intentional caricature. I planned the book that way on the assumption that advancing a simple argument to its limits might have explanatory utility." What are the advantages and disadvantages of this kind of approach?

3. One of the classics in the field is *The Calculus of Consent*, by James Buchanan and Gordon Tullock, published in 1962. The book proposes to "examine the operation of a single collective decision-making rule, that of simple majority, under certain highly restricted assumptions." One of these assumptions is the usual economic assumption of rational behavior that tries to maximize whatever it is that the actor wants. What happens if you make this assumption about members of a legislature, where a majority of the votes decides most issues?

One thing that happens is *log-rolling*: members trade votes with each other. You vote for my bill, I'll vote for yours. With this in mind, consider a particular situation. Imagine a community of a hundred farmers, all of whom are connected to a highway by an access road. Now suppose a farmer wants to get his road repaired, at the expense of the town. This would benefit him greatly, while the cost would be spread to all of the farmers. If the farmers were to vote on this, they would all vote no, except for the one particular farmer. No road would ever get repaired. But if you bring log-rolling into the picture, the situation changes greatly. A farmer would enter into bargains with 50 other farmers—I'll vote for your repair, you vote for mine. They could ignore the other 49, but the other 49 would have to pay, with taxes, for the roads of this group of 51. But these 49 would be forming their own groups, in a similar fashion. The net result, according to Buchanan and Tullock, is that "each road in the township would be maintained at a level considerably higher and at a greater expense than is rational from the individual stand-point of the farmers living along it."

Buchanan and Tullock believe that they have identified a real flaw in legislative systems. The actual situation is, of course—as they themselves say—much more complicated than the story about the farmers would suggest. But they do think that "the operation of simple majority rule ... will almost always impose external costs on the individual." Or, to put it another way, a legislature with majority rule will end up spending far more money and engaging in far more projects than is rational and efficient. The result is a kind of "pork barrel" society. The solution? One answer to this dilemma would be to require more than a majority vote on certain issues. In fact, there are a few states in which it takes a two-thirds vote of the legislature to raise taxes; and another group, in which this is a requirement for at least some forms of taxation. The California Constitution (Art. 13a, § 3), for example, provides that "any changes in State taxes enacted for the purpose of increased revenues ... must be imposed by not less than two-thirds of all members elected to each of the two houses of the Legislature." Do you think this kind of law is a good idea? Who is likely to gain, and who is likely to lose, from a provision of this type?

Note that *no* state requires a two-third vote on any proposal to *spend* money. But Buchanan and Tullock's model is about spending, not taxation. Why do you think there are no "super-majorities" required under state law, when it comes to proposals to spend money?

4.   Empirical Research and Public Choice Theory: Buchanan and Tullock were not conducting an empirical study of a real-life legislature. Thomas Stratmann, "The Effects of Logrolling on Congressional Voting," 82 *American Economic Review* 1162 (1992) looked at the *actual* votes of members of Congress on subsidies involved in proposed amendments to the farm bill of 1985. His research supports Buchanan and Tullock: "Evidence is found that legislators trade votes and that legislators with intense preferences are most likely to trade votes."

Public choice or rational choice approaches are quite popular among political scientists. But there are those who resist the trend, and this resistance was summed up in Donald P. Green and Ian Shapiro, in *Pathologies of Rational Choice Theory: A Critique of Applications in Political Science* (1994). Their basic point was this: however seductive the models and theories of rational choice theory might be, they have failed to advance our understanding of "how politics works in the real world." Most of the propositions of the theory "have not been tested empirically." Those that have been tested have "either failed on their own terms or garnered theoretical support for propositions that, on reflection, can only be characterized as banal: they do little more than restate existing knowledge in rational choice terminology" (p. 6).

5.   Ethics and Politics: Mayhew's analysis does not leave much room for principled behavior—for members of the legislature who vote because of what they honestly believe is right, rather than what their voters might want. This kind of behavior surely exists; but it hard to turn it into a mathematical model. Is this a serious flaw in Mayhew's analysis? How often do you think members of Congress or a state legislature take a principled stand, in defiance of their voters?

6.   Political Parties: Neither Mayhew nor Buchanan and Tullock put the existence of political *parties* at the center of their analysis of Congress. Many political scientists feel that explanations of the way legislatures behave make no sense unless one takes political parties into account. Party systems differ from country to country. In the United States, the party system is weak. Legislators are much more independent of their party than are legislators in European parliamentary systems. A Congressman can defy his party, so long as the voters in his district keep on sending him to Congress. Of course, the party can punish him by keeping him off committees he might want to be on,

or by refusing to fund projects that help his district. Members of Congress often bargain with the President. They might agree to vote on some bill the President wants badly—in exchange for the President's support for some other bill, or some project, that the members' constituents want badly.

In countries with Parliamentary systems, the government party makes policy, and expects its members to vote as a bloc to support the government's programs. Parties are more programmatic than in the United States—and voters are usually less concerned with the candidate than with the position of the party. To be sure, in this age of television and the internet, the personality of candidates is more and more crucial, even in Parliamentary systems. In England, a voter does not vote for the Prime Minister directly; she votes for a party, and the majority party selects the Prime Minister. But more and more, the image and personality of the likely Prime Minister makes a difference in these elections.

In parliamentary systems, insofar as there is bargaining about votes, it is more likely to involve party officials and particular legislators. The President of the United States is elected for a four year term, and nothing can dislodge him, short of impeachment; a Prime Minister, on the other hand, can alienate members of his party, who can then call for a vote of no confidence. If this carries, a new election must be held.

This does not happen very often in two-party systems. But many parliamentary governments are coalitions of groups of parties, sometimes awkwardly cobbled together. A government of this kind can fall much more easily. It is also much more prone to hard bargaining among the various parties to the coalition.

7. <u>Legislative Committees</u>: Members of legislatures propose new laws, and vote on bills. But more important, perhaps, is the work they do on committees and subcommittees. Carl E. Van Horn, "Congressional Policymaking: Cloakroom Politics and Policy," in Christopher J. Deering, ed., *Congressional Politics* (1989), argues that committee work is at the very core of congressional lawmaking. Most of this activity takes place far from the public eye. Representatives can act in committee without too much concern for the wishes of their constituents. Interest groups can try to influence committees, by offering campaign contributions, workers who will participate in the next election, and votes from those in the district whom they claim to influence. Bargaining and compromise are the central features of committee politics.

Compromise often takes the form of vague laws—thus shoving the problem onto administrative agencies. There is also often gridlock in committees—it is easier to block action than to act. Van Horn concludes that "From the perspective of most members of Congress, cloakroom politics works rather well. By serving up short term fixes that satisfy constituents, current political problems are solved and others are avoided."

In theory, committees hold hearings to gather information which might help in drafting legislation. Sometimes, however, a committee may be headline news, get big TV coverage, and perhaps affect public attitudes. Some legislators have risen to national prominence as a result of mass media coverage of hearings. Legislators also try to get the attention of the media— appearing on programs like "Meet the Press." They may also attempt to get themselves labeled as experts on some subject—tax policy; or national security; or the armed forces, for example.

The chairs of key committees are very powerful personages, indeed. At one time, chairs were chosen strictly on the basis of seniority; but the system has become more complex, and this is no longer exclusively the case. For the recent history of Congress in general, see Nelson W. Polsby, *How Congress Evolves: Social Bases of Institutional Change* (2004).

Legislators have staffs who help them do their work. One crucial task is constituent service. A voter who is having a problem with veterans' benefits, or social security, might call on his or her Senator or representative. A member of the staff will call the agency in question, and ask about the situation. At the very least, this kind of telephone call evokes a prompt and detailed explanation of why the agency is doing what it is doing. The fact that a Senator or representative is taking an interest in the issue *might* prompt the agency to change its mind. It might be easier just to do what the member of Congress wants, than to explain why the agency is denying a benefit (for example). In close cases, this surely makes a difference.

8. Public Opinion: Survey research tends to find that people in the United States have a very low opinion of Congress—compared to the President, or the Supreme Court, for example. Why should this be the case? John R. Hibbing and Elizabeth Theiss–Morse argue that it is because "Congress embodies practically everything Americans dislike about politics. It is large and therefore ponderous; it is . . . independent and powerful; it is open and therefore disputes are played out for all to see; it is based on compromise and therefore reminds people that most issues do not have right answers." People are "disgusted by what they perceive to be undue interest-group influence in Congress;" Congress does not "represent real people." But, they say, much of "what the public dislikes about Congress is endemic to what a legislature is. Its perceived inefficiencies and inequities are there for all to see." *Congress as Public Enemy: Public Attitudes toward American Political Institutions* 60 (1995).

9. Lobbying: No discussion of the legislative process would be complete, or accurate, if it did not deal with the subject of lobbying, lobbyists, and the work of pressure groups and interest groups. "Lobbying" is a complex phenomenon. Some lobbies do no more than give the legislature information. This can be extremely valuable information—it can tell legislators what some important company, or group, thinks, and also how it believes law might impact that company or group. Lobbying of this kind is not only benign, it might be useful or even indispensable. Legislators need to know what their constituents think; and they often lack good information about the views of their constituents on certain issues, especially those that are not exactly headline news. Lobbyists can supply this information—and, perhaps, also seek

123

to persuade the legislators that the views of the lobbyists are the views of the whole electorate. See Eric M. Uslaner, "Legislative Behavior: The Study of Representation," in Samuel Long, ed., *Annual Review of Political Science* (1986).

Lobbyists do other things, too. They can work to mobilize voters in some district, at election time. Or, they might actually offer contributions to legislators. What do they get in return? Good will, certainly; a ready audience in Washington—and they no doubt hope the Congressman or Senator or state legislator will feel the urge to vote for bills the lobby wants, and vote against those it doesn't want. This activity might be part of an implicit bargain—or, at times, an explicit one. There are lobbyists, after all, who engage in the dark arts of bribery. In 2005–2006, there was a huge scandal over the activities of Jack Abramoff, a high-powered lobbyist, but also one of the practitioners of this dark art of corruption. Abramoff pleaded guilty to fraud, tax evasion, and bribery in January 2006. *Washington Post,* Jan. 4, 2006. His fall from grace ended the career of at least two prominent Congressmen who had been closely associated with him.

In any event, lobbying is big business. Before 1920, U.S. Steel was the only corporation which had a permanent office in Washington, D. C. This rose to 175 in 1968; and by 2005, more than 600. By 2003, Microsoft spent $10,000,000 on lobbying in Washington. Corporations are not the only organizations active in lobbying in Washington—so are unions, and associations representing every conceivable group, including civil rights groups. There are many prominent lobbying firms. Ex-members of Congress often work as lobbyists—more than 150 of them, in the early 21st century. Ronald G. Shaiko, "Making the Connection: Organized Interests, Political Representation, and the Changing Rules of the Game in Washington Politics," in Paul S. Herrnson, Ronald G. Shaiko, and Clyde Wilcox, eds., *The Interest Group Connection: Electioneering, Lobbying, and Policymaking in Washington* 1, 6–7, 13 (2d edition, 2005). See also John P. Heinz, Edward O. Laumann, Robert L. Nelson, and Robert H. Salisbury, *The Hollow Core: Private Interests in National Policy Making* (1993).

All of this activity no doubt has an effect on legislation. But lobbying activities are not confined to legislation. The United States Senate also must consent to the appointment of federal judges, and here too, lobbyists and interest groups increasingly have their say. See Gregory A. Caldeira, Marie Hojnacki and John R. Wright, "The Lobbying Activities of Organized Interests in Federal Judicial Nominations," 62 *Journal of Politics* 51 (2000). Does all this lobbying have an impact? On the possible impact, consider the material in Chapter 3.

Lobbying has a bad name; and the eruptions of scandals, like the Abramoff case, feed the bad reputation of this business. The federal government requires lobbyists to register, see the Lobbying Disclosure Act of 1995, 2 U.S.C.A. § 1601ff. The states, too, regulate lobbying extensively, see Adam J. Newmark, "Measuring State Legislative Lobbying Regulation, 1990–2003," 5

State Politics and Policy Quarterly 182 (2005). It is not clear whether or not these regulations are effective.

(F) Administrative Process

(2.8) Adversarial Legalism: The American Way of Law

Robert A. Kagan

(2001).

The Concept of Adversarial Legalism

In contemporary democracies law is inescapable. Even in an era of political liberalism and "deregulation," it constrains ever more aspects of social, economic, and governmental activity-usually, even if not always, for good reasons. The rule of law is a very good thing. Different nations, however, implement the rule of law in different ways. Compared to other economically advanced democracies, American civic life is more deeply pervaded by legal conflict and by controversy about legal processes. The United States more often relies on lawyers, legal threats, and legal contestation in implementing public policies, compensating accident victims, striving to hold governmental officials accountable, and resolving business disputes. American laws generally are more detailed, complicated, and prescriptive. Legal penalties in the United States are more severe. And American methods of litigating and adjudicating legal disputes are more costly and adversarial.

To encapsulate some of the distinctive qualities of governance and legal process in the United States, I use the shorthand term "adversarial legalism," by which I mean policymaking, policy implementation, and dispute resolution by means of lawyer-dominated litigation. Adversarial legalism can be distinguished from other methods of governance and dispute resolution that rely instead on bureaucratic administration, or on discretionary judgment by experts or political authorities, or on the judge-dominated style of litigation common in most other countries. While the United States often employs these other methods too, it relies on adversarial legalism far more than other economically advanced democracies.

American adversarial legalism has both positive and negative effects. Viewed in cross-national comparison, the legal system of the United States is especially open to new kinds of justice claims and political movements. American judiciaries are particularly flexible and creative. American lawyers, litigation, and courts serve as powerful checks against official corruption and arbitrariness, as protectors of essential individual rights, and as deterrents to corporate heedlessness. In so doing, they also enhance the political legitimacy of capitalism and of the system of government as a whole.

At the same time, however, adversarial legalism is a markedly inefficient, complex, costly, punitive, and unpredictable method of governance and dispute resolution. In consequence, the American legal system often is unjust—

not, by and large, in its rules and official decisions, but because the complexity, fearsomeness, and unpredictability of its processes often deter the assertion of meritorious legal claims and compel the compromise of meritorious defenses. Adversarial legalism inspires legal defensiveness and contentiousness, which often impede socially constructive cooperation, governmental action, and economic development, alienating many citizens from the law itself.

Do the negative aspects of American adversarial legalism "outweigh" its positive features? To pose the question in such global terms is not very useful. There is no way to count up and compare all the social costs and social benefits that a gigantic, multifaceted legal system send rippling through economic, political, and communal life. And even if one could make such a calculation, the question would remain, "Compared to what?" That is, would alternative ways of implementing public policy and resolving disputes yield higher aggregate benefits and lower social costs, or vice versa? That question too defies any easy answer, at least at that sweeping, system-wide level of analysis.

Other economically advanced democracies, particularly in Western Europe, structure legal and regulatory institutions and processes in ways that suggest plausible alternatives to American adversarial legalism. But the practice that works well in Amsterdam or London might not work so well in Seattle or Miami, and it may also entail a "downside" not revealed by current comparative studies. Moreover, adversarial legalism is deeply rooted in the political institutions and values of the United States. Americans are not likely to accept wholesale replacement of familiar legal rights and practices by legal institutions drawn from rather different political traditions. Some Western European legal and regulatory practices may achieve higher levels of legal certainty than American adversarial legalism, without nearly so much expenditure on lawyers and legal conflict, but those practices are nested in political systems that impose high taxes and expect deference to governmental bureaucracies—neither of which has much political appeal in the United States. For good and for ill, adversarial legalism is the American way of law, and it is likely to remain so.

The purpose of this book, therefore, is not to provide a definitive overall assessment of adversarial legalism, nor to call for its burial, nor particularly to praise it. Rather, my principal intent is descriptive and explanatory—to enhance social scientific understanding of American adversarial legalism's characteristic features; to show how and why it differs from the legal and regulatory systems of other economically advanced democracies; and to highlight ways in which, for all its strengths, it also frustrates the quest for justice. . . .

The United States . . . has a unique legal "style." That is the message of an accumulating body of careful cross-national studies. . . . The studies focus not merely on the formal law but on how the law is implemented in practice: Cumulatively, the studies compare national systems for compensating injured people, regulating pollution and chemicals, punishing criminals, equalizing educational opportunity, promoting worker safety, discouraging narcotics use, deterring malpractice by police officers, physicians, and product manufacturers, and so on. For one social problem after another, the studies show, the American system for making and implementing public policy and resolving disputes is distinctive. It generally entails (1) more complex bodies of legal rules; (2) more formal, adversarial procedures for resolving political and scientific disputes; (3) more costly forms of legal contestation; (4) stronger, more punitive legal sanctions; (5) more frequent judicial review of and intervention into administrative decisions and processes; (6) more political controversy about legal rules and institutions; (7) more politically fragmented, less closely coordinated decisionmaking systems; and (8) more legal uncertainty and instability.

Comparative studies are hardly necessary, moreover, to show that in no other democracy is litigation so often employed by contestants in political struggles over the delineation of electoral district boundaries, the management of forests, the breakup of business monopolies, the appropriate funding level for inner-city versus suburban public schools, or the effort to discourage cigarette smoking. In no other countries are the money damages assessed in environmental and tort suits nearly so high, or have major manufacturers been driven into bankruptcy by liability claims, or have disagreements over tort law generated such intense interest group clashes in the legislatures....

The United States has by far the world's largest cadre of special "cause lawyers" seeking to influence public policy and institutional practices by means of innovative litigation. In no other country are lawyers so entrepreneurial in seeking out new kinds of business, so eager to challenge authority, or so quick to propose new liability-expanding legal theories. Finally, referring merely to the last few years, the United States is remarkable in its propensity to stage highly publicized, knock-down-drag-out legal donnybrooks such as the investigation and impeachment trial of President Bill Clinton, the custody battle over the six-year-old Cuban refugee Elian Gonzales, the antitrust cases against Microsoft, and the multicourt battle over Florida's votes in the 2000 presidential election—struggles that inject huge televised doses of politicized legal argument into the nation's everyday experience.

What Is Adversarial Legalism?

All these legal propensities are manifestations of what I call "adversarial legalism"—a method of policymaking and dispute resolution with two salient characteristics. The first is *formal legal contestation*—competing interests and disputants readily invoke legal rights, duties, and procedural requirements, backed by recourse to formal law enforcement, strong legal penalties, litigation, and/or judicial review. The second is *litigant activism*—a style of legal contestation in which the assertion of claims, the search for controlling legal arguments, and the gathering and submission of evidence are dominated not by judges or government officials but by disputing parties or interests, acting primarily through lawyers. Organizationally, adversarial legalism typically is

127

associated with and is embedded in decisionmaking institutions in which *authority is fragmented* and in which *hierarchical control is relatively weak.*

These defining features of adversarial legalism have two characteristic consequences. The first is *costliness*—litigant-controlled, adversarial decision-making tends to be particularly complex, protracted, and costly. The second is *legal uncertainty*—when potent adversarial advocacy is combined with fragmented, relatively nonhierarchical decisionmaking authority, legal norms are particularly malleable and complex, and legal decisions are particularly variable and unpredictable. It is the combination of costliness and legal uncertainty that makes adversarial legalism especially fearsome and controversial....

Compared to European democracies, regulatory decisionmaking in the United States entails many more legal formalities—complex legal rules concerning public notice and comment, restrictions on ex parte and other informal contacts with decisionmakers, legalistically specified evidentiary and scientific standards, mandatory official "findings" and responses to interest group arguments. These legal devices facilitate interest group participation and judicial review of administrative decisions. But hierarchical authority is correspondingly weak. Policymaking and implementing authority is often shared by different agencies at the same or at different levels of government, with different interests and perspectives. Agency decisions are frequently challenged in court by dissatisfied parties and reversed by judges, who dictate further changes in administrative policymaking routines. Lawyers, scientists, and economists hired by contending industry and advocacy groups play a large role in presenting evidence and arguments. Overall, the clash of adversarial argument has a larger influence on decisions than in other countries' regulatory systems, where policy decisions are characterized by a combination of political and expert judgment and consultation with affected interests....

The Roots of Adversarial Legalism

In the most immediate sense adversarial legalism is a product of American legal culture. In most other nations, legal elites place great emphasis on legal consistency and stability. Law is viewed as a set of authoritative rules and principles, carefully worked out over time. In the United States, in contrast, law is more often viewed as the malleable (and fallible) output of an ongoing political battle to make the law responsive to particular interests and values. Many, perhaps most, American lawyers, judges, legal scholars, and politicians (many of whom are lawyers) see adversarial litigation as a vital tool for righting wrongs, curtailing governmental and corporate arbitrariness, and achieving a just society. Every working day, American lawyers talk about law, legal ethics, and legal processes in ways that reemphasize those values—and American lawyers work unusually long days.

But there is a competing strain in American legal culture. Many lawyers, judges, law professors, and politicians disparage and discourage adversarial legalism. They work hard at promoting compromise and encouraging cooperation. They believe in judicial restraint, not activism. Moreover, judges and lawyers who do favor the institutions, rules, and practices of adversarial legalism, even if they are in the ascendance at a particular political moment, cannot work their will, at least for very long, without the support or acquiescence of other political elites and ultimately of the voting public. . . .

Disorder in the Port

Even ice-cream cones are no good if you eat too many of them. Even one is bad if you eat it at the wrong time or place. In some times and places, judges shouldn't turn the world upside down. And if too many judges are striving to turn the world upside down, the world may not work so well. Adversarial legalism's sword, honed by distrust of authority, can be used against the trustworthy too. Adversarial legalism can be invoked by the misguided, the mendacious, and the malevolent as well as by the mistreated. Its complexity, costliness, and malleability can produce injustice as well as justice. The Port of Oakland's frustrating struggle to dredge its California harbor illustrates the other face of adversarial legalism.

In 1988 international shipping lines launched a new generation of huge, efficient, $40 million containerships. The new vessels furthered a technological revolution that in the last two decades has transformed international trade, moving cargo across oceans and continents with dramatically greater speed, reliability, and economy. Today, shoppers in Dutch food stores buy green beans and grapefruits shipped in refrigerated containers from Senegal and Florida. A moving inventory of shirts, jeans, and dresses, packed in containers in a Hong Kong warehouse, whisked from ship to train in Los Angeles, flows to the loading docks of shops in Cincinnati and Atlanta at transportation costs of pennies per garment. Technological change has brought order to the port: today's electronically coordinated, mechanized container ports bear little resemblance to the seaports of the past, notorious for costly delays, labor exploitation, pilferage, drunkenness, and crime. On both sides of the Atlantic and Pacific, local monopolies and stodgy oligopolies are threatened by distant competitors, spurring productivity and innovation. . . .

In the 1970s the Port of Oakland in San Francisco Bay initiated plans to deepen its harbor to forty-two feet in order to accommodate the larger ships of the future. In 1986 the U.S. Congress, which finances improvements in the national navigation system, authorized funding for the project. For the next eight years, however, a seemingly endless series of regulatory actions and lawsuits blocked the dredging of the harbor.

Before the early 1970s seas and harbors were used as free disposal sites for sewage sludge, garbage, and chemical wastes. Regulatory officials and environmentalists had little input into port expansion decisions. Dredging and disposal operations dislodged chemical wastes buried in urban rivers and bays, destroyed marshlands, and disrupted fisheries. . . . Today, however, dredging projects require a permit from the U.S. Army Corps of Engineers; pursuant to the National Environmental Policy Act, the Corps must first prepare and circulate a comprehensive analysis of all potential environmental impacts and methods of mitigating unavoidable adverse consequences. The Corps of Engineers' decisions, in turn, are checked by other governmental bodies—the U .S. Fish and Wildlife Service, the National Marine Fisheries Service, the relevant state department of fish and game, the U.S. Environmental Protection Agency, the state agency charged with protecting water quality, and the relevant state coastal zone management agency. Each of these agencies, responsible for enforcing a specific environmental statute, is legally instructed to object to or block dredging projects that fail to meet those statutory standards. There is a third level of legal control: citizens, local politicians, and environmental advocacy groups who think that the Corps or the other agencies have not fulfilled their statutory responsibilities are legally empowered to file a lawsuit and seek judicial review of their decisions.

In the Port of Oakland case, the Army Corps of Engineers issued an Environmental Impact Statement (EIS) in 1986. It approved disposal of the dredged harbor floor sands at an established dumping site in San Francisco Bay, near Alcatraz Island. Environmentalists, fishing interests, and state regulatory officials raised concerns about damage to water quality and fisheries. The Corps, in response, conducted further sediment tests and in September 1987 released a Supplementary EIS comparing various alternatives. It called for "special care" disposal and "capping" methods for about 21,000 cubic yards of sediment (less than 1 percent of the total project) to be dredged from certain contaminated areas, but concluded that in-Bay disposal of the bulk of noncontaminated sediments would have no adverse environmental effects. State and local regulatory agencies, however, had legal power to block in-Bay disposal under state environmental law, and they preferred disposal in the deeper waters of the Pacific Ocean.

Confronted with this regulatory deadlock, Port of Oakland officials in January 1988 proposed disposal at an ocean site designated 1M, although that would double the cost of dredging. New regulatory hurdles then arose. Fishermen claimed that disposal at IM would harm ocean fisheries. The Corps prepared another Supplementary EIS, which disputed the fishermen's claims. Nevertheless, the U.S. Environmental Protection Agency, statutory guardian of ocean waters, refused to issue a permit for IM, and an environmental advocacy group (that had opposed disposal at Alcatraz) prepared to bring a lawsuit challenging the Corps' Supplementary EIS; the environmentalists said the sediments should be dumped beyond the Continental Shelf, fifty miles out at sea. The Corps responded that it was legally precluded from authorizing disposal beyond the Continental Shelf because that would cost at least twice as much as IM without being demonstrably better in environmental terms. Prodded by increasingly anxious Port of Oakland officials, in March 1988 the Corps and the EPA negotiated a compromise, also agreed to by environmental groups and a federation of Pacific fishing associations. Ocean site BIB, ten miles off the coast, would be used for the first 500,000 cubic yards of the dredged material (except for sediments from the clearly contaminated area); further testing and study would precede any decision concerning disposal of the remaining 6.5 million cubic yards. The dredging machinery and barges moved into place.

When access to court is easy, however, compromise is unstable. In mid-April of 1988, just before the dredging commenced, the Half Moon Bay Fishermen's Marketing Association brought suit in federal court, alleging that the BIB disposal decision violated a number of federal regulatory provisions and would disrupt fisheries. The U.S. district court judge, and then the federal court of appeals, rejected the fishermen's legal claims. The dredging machinery completed one day of digging. Then, on May 16, 1988, a state court judge, responding to a new lawsuit based on another legal argument, held that the dredging permit had been issued without a requisite certification from the California Coastal Commission. The dredging stopped.

By that time, shipping lines using the Port of Oakland were screaming for deeper water. Desperate port officials announced an alternative plan to dispose of the first 500,000 cubic yards of dredged material in the Sacramento River Delta, where it would be used to reinforce levees. Local regulatory processes then creaked into action. The Port prepared a new EIS. After a year or so, a California regional water quality agency approved the plan, but the Contra Costa Water District challenged the Port's EIS in state court. Yet another year later, in July 1990, the court upheld the Delta plan. At that point, however, the Port of Oakland declined to go forward, since regulatory conditions designed to safeguard Delta water quality had pushed estimated disposal costs to $21 per cubic yard, ten times the cost of disposal at Alcatraz.

As Oakland officials searched for other disposal alternatives, new legal obstacles arose. The Water Quality Control Board for San Francisco Bay explicitly banned deposit of all new dredge project spoils in the Bay, as did the National Marine Fisheries Service, which cited dangers to already diminished salmon populations. Officials from the National Marine Sanctuaries program and other environmental groups objected to ocean disposal off the Continental Shelf. The EPA, having been burned by litigation, retreated into legalistic defensiveness, refusing to approve any new ocean disposal site. It noted that federal law required agency officials to make scientifically grounded findings about the environmental impact of ocean disposal, and yet the requisite mapping of the ocean bottom and currents had not even been initiated until 1990. No decision that would hold up in court, EPA indicated, could be made before 1994.

All this time, while possible environmental harms were debated and investigated, very tangible economic and social harms mounted. The powerful and costly hydraulic dredging equipment stood idle. Big ships that sought to call at Oakland, nearly scraping bottom (and thereby risking truly significant environmental harm), had to carry reduced loads and wait for high tides. Schedules of container trains and waiting warehouses and factories were disrupted. Shipping companies, facing higher costs and customer complaints, scrapped plans to expand operations at the Port of Oakland. The previously successful port lost money, and hence the municipal government lost revenues it needed to maintain social services. Port-related employment was adversely affected.

Finally, political pressure mounted, new studies were funded, new impact statements were prepared, and more regulatory hearings were held. In late 1992 partial "Phase I" dredging, encompassing 500,000 cubic yards of sediment, was at last permitted. The contaminated sediment (21,000 cubic yards) was deposited in a lined upland site. Regulation officials allowed the port to dump the other half-million cubic yards near Alcatraz in San Francisco Bay—just where the Port and the Corps of Engineers had first proposed in 1986 (U.S. Army Corps of Engineers, 1992a). (In the interim, additional sampling and testing costs incurred by the Port of Oakland and the Corps of Engineers had reached almost $4 million, or $8 a cubic yard for Phase I—more than double the cost of the actual barging and disposal operation). For the next six million cubic yards, a final decision did not come until late 1994, after a multimillion-dollar research and analysis program. The relevant agencies endorsed a much more expensive disposal plan: some dredged sediments would be barged by sea to the edge of the Continental Shelf, and some (in order to win the support of environmental groups) would be used to create new wetlands far up the Sacramento River Delta. Funding the wetlands disposal project required a $15 million appropriation from Congress and an additional $5 million from the California legislature—at an estimated cost of about $20 per cubic yard. In 1995 the port finally was dredged to the planned forty-two-foot depth.

The Pathologies of Adversarial Legalism

The legal procedures that for eight years blocked dredging in Oakland Harbor reflect fundamental ideals of pluralistic democracy—that public policy should be formulated and implemented only after full and fair deliberation; that meaningful attention should be given to the claims of the individuals and groups who are not politically powerful (such as the Half Moon Bay fishermen); that environmental protection should be given special weight in planning currently urgent development projects that might deprive future generations of irreplaceable ecological amenities; and that to vindicate those values, a variety of interest groups and agencies should be able to challenge official assumptions and judgments in court. But in the Port of Oakland story, the procedures designed to protect those values seemed to fall into the hands of the Sorcerer's Apprentice, multiplying themselves beyond control. Month after month, regulatory officials, scientists, and lawyers, arguing first in one legal forum, then in another, debated the propriety of decisionmaking procedures, the adequacy of sediment samples and tests for chemical contamination, and the reliability of environmental impact models. No proceeding produced any definitive finding that the proposed disposal plans were environmentally dangerous. But neither could any single court or agency authoritatively designate a single environmentally acceptable, economically sensible alternative.

In the Port of Oakland case, adversarial legalism's legal flexibility ... produced only a legal mess. The governing body of law, detailed and complex, generated only uncertainty, inconsistency, and legalistic defensiveness. When one agency found a plan legally acceptable, another would disagree. When one court upheld a regulatory decision, another overturned it. No agency could ever be sure that its legal rulings would hold up in court. The mere threat of adversarial litigation, with its capacity to impose further crippling delays, induced both the Port and the Corps of Engineers to accept successively more remote (and far more costly) disposal sites and methods, regardless of the merits of the objections. In the tangled web of adversarial legalism, mollusks received far more protection than human communities.

Rotterdam, Europe's largest seaport, must deal with far larger volumes of far more seriously contaminated dredged material. The Netherlands, like the United States, adheres to the London Dumping Convention preventing ocean disposal of toxics. There is a strong "green movement" that pushes officials to comply with national environmental laws, which, like those in the United States, call for detailed impact analyses and detailed mitigation plans. Thus the Port of Rotterdam has dealt with its massive dredging and disposal problems in an environmentally responsible manner. It has done so, however, far more expeditiously than the Port of Oakland, without resource-draining and dispiriting adversarial litigation.... The deadlock in Oakland, the Rotterdam experience suggests, is not inherent in the task. It stemmed from a particular institutional structure, characterized by fragmented authority, complex and constrictive legal rules, wide access to litigation, and unpredictable risks of judicial reversal.

Because it derives from basic structures of American government, the Oakland story is far from unique. The same kind of expensive, time-consuming, legally unpredictable, extortive, and economically destructive legal wrangling is a common occurrence in the United States. Virtually every major port-dredging plan, on the East Coast as well as the West, must slog though the quicksand of litigation or invest huge sums in "mitigation projects" extorted by the threat of litigation. Adversarial legalism recurs, imposing similar risks and costs and concessions, in virtually every kind of large-scale development or construction effort-from siting garbage dumps.... to building highways ... factories ... and housing projects.... The complexities and costly delays of adversarial legalism burden commercial disputes, criminal prosecutions, and rule making by regulatory agencies. Adversarial legalism slows down and imposes large expenses on American processes for compensating injured people, drawing electoral district lines, battling discrimination, caring for the mentally ill, choosing labor union representatives, preserving wildlife habitats, financing businesses, running hospitals and schools, and cleaning up chemical waste sites. No other country comes close.

The U.S. Superfund program for cleanup of hazardous waste disposal sites, one study noted, generates so much time-consuming litigation among former chemical waste disposers that "by mid–1990 ... after 10 years of program operation, only sixty-three of the more than twelve hundred National

Priorities List sites had been cleaned up".... As several studies of regulatory rulemaking have shown, new rules concerning workplace health risks.... hazardous air pollutants ... and motor vehicle safety features.... were bogged down in the federal bureaucracy for years, while administrators called for additional scientific research, economic analyses, and legal opinions, hoping to ward off judicial reversal—a threat that their counterparts in other economically advanced democracies do not experience....

In the Oakland Harbor saga, the American legal and regulatory system was not malfunctioning. It was being used as directed, or at least as officially permitted and encouraged. Each regulatory agency and interest group whose legal actions postponed harbor dredging was invoking regulatory standards, procedures, and analytical requirements that are written into law. The redundant reviews by a multiplicity of specialized agencies, along with the laws that enabled fishermen and county water districts to haul government officials into court, were consciously designed bulwarks against environmental heedlessness. Each of those laws, viewed on its own, seems rational and balanced, attentive to economic as well as to environmental values, well grounded in democratic opinion. Nevertheless, the cumulative outcome was irrational, unjust, and lamentably inefficient. And that is because the mechanisms of American adversarial legalism—the very kinds of mechanisms that sometimes block environmentally obtuse development projects, that yielded *Brown v. Board of Education* and the prison reform decisions, and that sometimes free the unjustly accused—produce irrational, unjust, and inefficient outcomes as well. Adversarial legalism is Janus-faced.

NOTES AND QUESTIONS

1. Kagan's book has been taken as a powerful indictment of "the American way of law." Certainly, the story of the dredging of Oakland harbor is a story of delay and inefficiency. But Kagan is careful to point out that there are good points as well as bad points. The good points are drawn, mostly, from other areas of law, rather than from the administrative process. For example, he mentions prison reform in Alabama. These reforms, which "dragged Alabama's correctional system into the twentieth century," were not "developed by a national ministry of justice or corrections ... or implemented through a hierarchically organized bureaucracy." Rather, they were the result of "adversarial legalism" (Kagan, p. 22).

Many scholars have criticized the administrative process in the United States. Theodore Lowi, in a classic work, *The End of Liberalism* (2nd ed., 1979), makes the argument that administrative discretion can be harmful to a democracy. Decisions are made by people who are not elected, and who are not accountable to anybody. He wants a system where laws that authorize administrators to regulate have to be very explicit, clear, and limiting. In a way, he is calling for *more* legalism. The issue for him is not efficiency, but equality and democracy.

How does this square with Kagan's approach? Note that the European countries, and Japan, which do not suffer from "adversarial legalism" in their regulatory and administrative life, typically give administrators much *more* discretion than is true in the United States.

2.   In *Going by the Book: The Problem of Regulatory Unreasonableness* (1982), Eugene Bardach and Robert Kagan collaborated on a study of the administrative process, focusing not on litigation and outside control, but on the work of inspectors and line administrators within agencies, such as OSHA (Occupational Safety and Health Administration). There were "good inspectors," and not-so-good inspectors. The good inspector does not alienate the company he or she is inspecting, and has the capacity to be "reasonable, to distinguish serious from nonserious violations, and to invest effort in the former." This inspector can be tough when necessary, but ideally should "win cooperation" through a "relationship of reciprocity." The inspector gives violators time and a chance to comply, and recognizes good faith efforts to conform to legal standards.

Note, though, that the subtitle of their book refers to "unreasonableness." They find that there are lots of bad inspectors. These tended to "go by the book," or behave in ways that were harsh, punitive, and unyielding. OSHA, for example, followed a policy of "unannounced inspections." Factory managers and safety engineers bitterly resented these intrusions. Unreasonable behavior by inspectors tended to lead to reactions of defensiveness. Then enforcement officials reacted with "enhanced mistrust and legalism;" the business people became "still more resentful" and resorted to "various forms of noncooperation and resistance" (pp. 106–107).

3.   Administrative Agencies in Action: There is a large and important literature on the way administrative agencies actually operate in practice. Stewart Macaulay, in "Business Adaptation to Regulation: What Do We Know and What Do We Need to Know," 15 *Law and Policy* 259–62 (1993), points out how much the "empirical picture" of administrative law differs from the "conventional picture." The "conventional picture" is something like this: Congress or another legislature passes a law, and gives some administrative agency a general mandate—for example, to see to it that prescription drugs cure us instead of killing us. The agency makes rules. Mostly, there is compliance. When there is non-compliance with the rules, the agency finds out, holds hearings, and imposes sanctions. Other people "learn of the proceedings and they are deterred from evasion. As a result, everyone lives happily ever after."

In fact, studies show that most regulatory agencies enforce the law selectively. They attack "critical problems of interest to the press, public and legislators;" and they react to "atrocity stories." Agencies also try to "get national corporations to change their standard practices so they comply with the regulations." The corporations try to protect their reputations and to avoid bad publicity. They may revise their own procedures to get the employees to carry out the regulatory policy. Thus a kind of "private government" supplements the "enforcement activities of the public one."

Agencies are often "reactive rather than proactive." They respond to complaints. A consumer protection agency might respond mostly to letters from customers; and their response, in turn, is to write a letter to the offending business. Agencies also "often engage in soft law enforcement," trying to teach people how to comply, and persuading them to comply. They might publish a booklet, or set up a "telephone hot line" to answer questions.

A lot of what agencies do is "implicit or explicit bargaining." Their behavior varies; but so too of the companies. There may be differences between large companies and small companies; and of course the type of business also matters greatly.

4. Kagan's point about "adversarial legalism" is explicitly comparative—he stresses the fact that this is a distinctively American trait; and he contrasts the experience of other countries. Here his work rests on a good deal of prior work, for example, Steven Kelman, *Regulating America, Regulating Sweden: A Comparative Study of Occupational Safety and Health Policy* (1980); David Wallace, *Environmental Policy and Industrial Innovation: Strategies in Europe, the USA and Japan* (1995). This work has continued, in some cases influenced by Kagan's work on "adversarial legalism" in the 1990's. See, for example, Marco Verweij, "Why Is the River Rhine Cleaner than the Great Lakes (Despite Looser Regulation)?" 34 *Law & Society Review* 1007 (2000). According to Verweij, both the Rhine countries and the United States use "command-and-control" approaches to protecting the environment; but the American approach "has been much more rigid, top-down, and legalistic than the water policies adopted in the Rhine countries." The U.S. authorities have paid less attention to the views of industry. U.S. "pollution values and technological standards have been more detailed and more stringent than European ones;" they have been more punitive. And in some of the countries along the Rhine, the approach in actual implementation has been more "flexible," despite the "strict command-and-control policies favored by central policymakers." (Id. at 1037–1038).

5. Notice that inefficiency in regulating can come from within the agency itself—from the way in which the agency makes and applies rules—or from outside factors, such as litigation. Which of these two factors do you think is more important for understanding the administrative process as a whole?

6. Notice, too, that most of the work discussed has *criticized* administrators or the system itself for slow, inefficient work—and for work that interferes unduly with the proper functioning of the agencies. The problem can lie in the very nature of bureaucracy, or in its tendency toward rule-bound behavior, rigidity, and red tape.

Agencies are also subject to *political* pressure: the Food and Drug Administration has to move very cautiously on any drug or device that has an impact on sexual behavior, for example, for obvious political reasons. Also, what happens if the administration itself does not approve of some or all of the goals of some agency? It certainly has the power to appoint administrators who will change these goals. *The New York Times*, Sept. 6, 2006, p. A14, reported the nomination, for Secretary of Transportation of Mary Peters. Ms. Peters had served earlier as head of the Federal Highway Administration. As administrator, she "helped push through a highway authorization bill that allows public highways to be turned over to private companies for maintenance and toll collection."

The President surely has the right to appoint administrators who back the President's policies; and who even (like Ms. Peters) work hard to change the agency along the lines of those policies. But there is a fine line between reshaping the agency, and intentionally subverting the activities of the agencies; between reforming the agency, and deliberately setting about* to wreck it. How often do you think this kind of "wrecking" happens? Under what political conditions? Is it necessarily illegitimate, or can it be defended?

7.   Regulation by administrative agency is pervasive in modern society. The federal government regulates stock exchanges and securities, banks, and airlines; it has huge agencies that deal with old age pensions, Medicare, and veterans' benefits. There is the Food and Drug Administration, and the National Labor Relations Board. The states have many agencies of their own; cities have zoning boards and boards of education. Styles of administrative behavior surely differ greatly depending on *what* is being regulated, and *who* is subject to the regulation. And this in turn depends on politics, public opinion, the legal culture, and many other factors.

Consider, for example, the rather sad and sordid history of welfare administration. See Joel Handler, *The Poverty of Welfare Reform* (1995), and Michael B. Katz, *In the Shadow of the Poorhouse: A Social History of Welfare in America* (rev. ed.,1996). A scholar writing about welfare administration in Indiana reports that programs are "plagued by scandals and allegations of mismanagement." The basic premises underlying the system are: keep taxes low, and protect "political patronage and the status quo." Money issues have "trumped humanitarian ones. Over and over, it has been necessary to force public officials to provide even those benefits that federal law requires." Sheila Suess Kennedy, "The Poor You Have Always With You," in David J. Bodenhammer and Hon. Randall T. Shepard, *The History of Indiana Law* 90, 104–105 (2006). Why do you think this situation exists in Indiana? Do you think a study in other states would show the same results?

No doubt there are systematic differences between welfare administration and, say, the regulation of big business. But the regulation of business, too, depends on the climate of opinion; and this can vary a great deal from period to period. See, for example, Joel Seligman, *The Transformation of Wall Street: A History of the Securities and Exchange Commission and Modern Corporate Finance* (rev. ed., 1995).

It may, in fact, be hard to make general statements about how administrative agencies work—there are simply too many of them; and they have different styles and cultures. Edward P. Weber, in *Pluralism by the Rules: Conflict and Cooperation in Environmental Regulation* (1998), found a good deal of "collaboration" despite "the significant obstacles posed by an adversarial political culture, a fragmented interest group system, and an open political system;" and this "collaboration" was "appearing where we would least expect it," that is, in the "most combative of all regulatory arenas," the area of "pollution control" (p. 256).

Which agencies would you expect to be the most "combative," and which ones would you expect to be the most "collaborative"? Why?

IV. A Summary Note: The Legal System in Operation—Bargaining, Discretion, and the Shadow of the Law

This chapter has contained a number of studies about the legal system as it actually operates, drawn from various fields of law. They present pictures of the legal system, but they are pictures very different from the pictures one would get from reading only the official materials: statutes, rules and regulations, court decisions—or, for that matter, police manuals of procedure. The pictures are also quite different from the pictures of "the law" that come from the movies, or TV, or which are taught in the schools. They also differ from the pictures presented by interest groups with an axe to grind. The pictures are, alas, fairly complex. Life influences law, which influences life, which influences law, and so on. But *three* factors emerged that were emphasized—bargaining, discretion, and the law itself.

Bargaining is pervasive in the legal system. Disputes get resolved informally. Defendants "cop a plea." Inspectors sometimes hold off on punishing a company, if the company proposes some sort of arrangement the inspectors find reasonable. Couples bargain with each other before entering the divorce court. Legislators engage in "log-rolling." Insurance companies settle with people who make claims against them. If we look only at the formal law, it seems much sharper and definitive. The winner takes all. You win your case or you lose it. Your claim is right, or your claim is wrong. But that is not how the world works.

The ideal bargain is also rather fair: you give some and you get some. Both sides gain. But this is an ideal picture that does not conform to the real world. The power and resources of the bargainers make a huge difference. They make a huge difference, too, if the case actually goes to court. This is a point made in the famous article by Marc Galanter, "Why the Haves Come Out Ahead: Speculations on the Limits of Legal Change," 9 *Law & Society Review* 95 (1974).

Discretion makes bargaining possible. Rules or laws which are not precise, which vest discretion in some civil servant, or police officer, for example, practically invite bargaining. But discretion is everywhere in the legal system, even where the formal law seems to preclude it. Discretion is the power to choose between alternatives, or to craft some arrangement, though usually there are limits—formal or informal—to the exercise of discretion.

These limits mean that the third element, the *law* itself, is a significant factor, despite the fact that bargaining and discretion are pervasive. How much of a factor is always an empirical question. In many situations, it seems to set boundaries, within which informal bargaining takes place. As we have seen, there is controversy over how much of a "shadow" the law actually casts, in various fields of law, and in various circumstances.

In any event, although the research discussed in this chapter presented many quite different views, and followed different methodologies, the combination of discretion, bargaining, and the shadow of the law runs through the whole chapter. How general a phenomenon do you think we are describing here? The proportions might be different, but do you think *all* modern systems have the three elements? What are the advantages, and the disadvantages of a system of law with these three elements, in the combination which the chapter suggests?

On these advantages and disadvantages, see Stewart Macaulay, "Business Adaptation to Regulation: What Do We Know and What Do We Need to Know?" 15 *Law and Policy* 259 (1993). Many people, he says, might "find a great deal wrong" with such a system. "Discretion, bargaining and other forms of adaptation defeat rational planning and coherent regulatory programs." A system of "selective and partial enforcement" means that policy is carried out in an incomplete way, and "unpredictably."

There are other problems: "agency employees may divert the goals of the organization to suit their own programs." Corruption is always a possibility. "Soft law enforcement" takes place "back-stage and the audience is composed only of the insiders." The public is kept in the dark; rights are not vindicated; bad actors are not held up to public scorn. Bargaining also tends to preserve the status quo; it favors "short-run adaptations rather than costly long-run solutions."

But is there a real alternative? Can we actually afford to "pay the price of complete application of all the laws in formal regulatory procedures"? And is it really possible to draft precise, accurate laws that "capture all of the nuances of real life." Usually, cooperation "is better than coercion." Coercion leads to "evasion or resistance." Negotiated results are perhaps more stable; people are more likely to acquiesce in them.

Moreover, is it possible that we "honor a certain amount of deviation in our society." We comply with laws which, we think, "make sense," but not those we "see as foolish." And, if "we have space for a range of deviation from the present wishes of the majority, it may help hold a multi-cultural society together." In regulatory matters, in the short-run, it might be "better if we can get a substantial amount of compliance from the largest businesses and leave smaller firms alone." Some laws reflect "aspirations" but full enforcement "might provoke a powerful minority with intensely held beliefs. Soft law enforcement may help us mark time until actual working assumptions come to match our aspirations crystallized in laws."

More research, of course, would be very welcome, in shedding light on the issues presented in this chapter. The themes of the chapter, however, will appear again and again in the material that follows in later chapters. They are building blocks of any theory about the relationship of law to society and society to law.

V. Note: Legal Culture—Descriptions of Whole Legal Systems

There are many ways to describe a legal system, as this chapter has tried to make clear. You can approach this task from many different disciplinary angles, using many different techniques, and with many different goals in mind.

The material in this chapter has been, for the most part, about specific *aspects* of a legal system; and the system in question has been the United States. None of the material has tried to describe, or characterize, the *whole* legal system of the United States. Of course, no such thing is possible; but perhaps it might be possible to isolate a few, fundamental traits of the American system—or any system—that would set it off from other societies. Perhaps Kagan comes closest, in his discussion of adversarial legalism.

As we will see in Chapters 3 and 6, the field of anthropology is probably the social science that has tackled legal systems in the most holistic way. Legal anthropologists have studied legal behaviors and concepts. For a time, the field focused especially on rule-making and dispute resolution. They honed their skills by studying small-scale societies and communities, including societies that did not have written laws or specialized legal professionals—and these anthropologists often found rather sophisticated ways of settling disputes in such societies. Legal anthropologists produced a rich literature, and a number of insights that have value beyond the particular society which was studied. In the process, they struggled to refine the difficult and sometimes controversial concept of "culture", which earlier generations of anthropologists used in their efforts to analyze whole social and legal systems.

It is obvious difficult to try to distill the essence of say, French or Japanese legal culture—or even the overall legal cultures of smaller-scale societies, which still had internal variations. Yet in scholarly journals, we constantly find questions, assertions, and discussions about the nature of modern legal cultures, at the national level. We mentioned Kagan and adversarial legalism. In fact, we hear over and over again that American legal culture is litigious, rights-conscious, and adversarial; Asian legal cultures— Japan, Korea, Taiwan—on the other hand, are said to be oriented more toward compromise, harmony, and the like. Here we see the seeds of one controversy over the culture concept—that it promotes stereotyping and oversimplified views of complex peoples and systems. Thus every proposition of this sort is contested. At the same time, scholars seeking to compare different parts of the world need some kinds of broader categories within which to perform comparative analyses. We will deal in more detail with issues of legal culture and legal tradition in Chapter 6.

*

CHAPTER 3

The Impact of Society on Law

I. Introduction

This chapter examines the social sources of law. How do forces in society influence or create particular kinds of law? Citizens of Western democratic states might view the answer to this as obvious: the official source of law in a democracy is the will of the people—of the majority of voters in that society. The will of the people is expressed through elections, according to this professed ideal. Political parties that fall into disfavor can be driven from office; organized groups of citizens can convey their wishes to political leaders. This approach to law looks to society, and to consensus on the part of the governed, as a source of law. As obvious as this approach may seem to some, we must remember that many other governmental systems, both past and present, hold quite different beliefs about the sources of law. Some look to religious sources, claiming that law reflects the will of God. Others think that rulers or leadership groups have the right to make laws without public consent, locating the source of law in elites such as kings, chiefs, or elders.

Even in democratic states such as the U.S., the official story is complex. On the one hand, it is commonly understood that our laws reflect the popular will. On the other hand, this does not mean that U.S. law is thought to be a mere reflex of "what the people want." Federal and state constitutions limit popular will, allocating power among the branches of government—and among local, state, and federal governments. For example, at both federal and state levels, bills of rights exist to defend minorities against the unchecked will of the majority. Thus the idea of the "rule of law" is both an expression of the ideal of popular sovereignty, and a denial of popular sovereignty as absolute. Notice, however, that the American Constitution claims to be rooted in the popular will—despite the fact that it is drenched in natural law ideology, and suffused with the notion that there are fundamental rights beyond the power of temporary majorities to change. Originally, of course the U.S. Constitution was adopted by means of a vote. On the other hand, it is quite difficult to amend.

We have been talking so far about the ideas held by members of society about their political and legal systems—about professed ideals. However, when social scientists study the influence of society on law, they focus on individual and group behavior, on culture and social structure, and on institutions, in addition to examining professed ideals. Of course, the professed ideals of a political system can profoundly influence how people behave; but so can other factors. In this chapter we focus on the multiple sources of law that social science has identified. For example, to what extent does formal law reflect informal "custom," or general "public opinion"? These seemingly simple concepts are actually quite complicated. Where do we draw the line between formal law and informal custom? In small communities, is there a clear line between custom and public opinion? Some scholars have urged that we reserve the word "law" for systems in which rules governing behavior are codified in writing, in which there is a separate legal profession, and where disputes are settled in distinctly formal legal settings. Others focus on function, defining law as the set of practices by which social order and control are accomplished in a given society. Under this definition, more informal resolution of disputes by leaders according to custom could also be viewed as "law."

Regardless of whether we are talking about customs or formal rules, we can still ask about the *source* of these norms governing people's behavior. How much of the content of norms and rules can be explained by the fact that the affected group of people is nomadic? lives on fish and game as opposed to settled agriculture? resides in a dangerous urban ghetto or elite city suburb? has a high infant mortality rate? is relatively isolated from or integrated into the wider global economy? lives in a closely-knit community with a lot of face-to-face contact? These kinds of questions direct our attention to the precise role of economic and social forces in forming customs and rules. Social scientists have engaged in vigorous debates about this issue. Some argue that the stated norms or rules of a community actually influence how people behave. Others view the rules as secondary attempts to legitimate or rationalize behavior that is really caused by economic necessity—by the material conditions of life. More complex models look at the way multiple sources of law interact with each other, from cultural and religious ideas about what is right, through social and kinship networks that shape our sense of obligation, to the economic and institutional structures that define how we live.

In this chapter we examine the impact of society on law. The first section of this chapter deals with the issue of formal and informal systems of social control. Under what conditions do groups resort to using formal court systems as opposed to informal sanctions? And where do we draw the line between informal and formal, in any case? In the second section we discuss how social changes in the United States have resulted in a fundamental change to our legal culture—to our expectations about and demands from the legal system. Section three examines a variety of social sources of law—from general public opinion through interest groups, elites, and social classes. To what extent is the American legal system democratic? Who, if anyone, controls the legal system? Our fourth section discusses case studies of the relationship between social change and legal change in the United States. Finally, we conclude by examining how law and society exist in an ongoing interaction, back and forth, with each other. Thus social change can influence legal change, which in turn affects social institutions, whose changed practices then become the basis for further legal shifts. This final section sets the scene for Chapter 4, which examines in more detail the impact of law on society.

II. Law as Part of a Complex System of Social Control: From Informal Social Sanctions to Formal Law

(3.1) Going to Court: Strategies of Dispute Management in an American Urban Neighborhood

Sally Engle Merry

13 *Law & Society Review* 891 (1979).

INTRODUCTION

In recent years, legal anthropologists have increasingly focused on the process by which disputes are settled, ... investigating the strategies actors use to manage disputes and the choices they make between alternative modes of dispute settlement. Of recurring interest are the conditions under which disputants resort to courts rather than more informal modes of dispute settlement such as gossip and scandal. Although we know something about the role of courts in dispute settlement strategies in relatively stable, homogeneous, and close-knit communities such as Mexican, Lebanese, and Turkish peasant villages, small Ghanaian towns, and Atlantic fishing villages, we know relatively little about the situation in complex, heterogeneous urban neighborhoods. This paper investigates the role of criminal courts in dispute management strategies in a polyethnic American urban neighborhood. Many of the poor, relatively uneducated residents of this neighborhood use criminal courts extensively as part of their arsenal for managing disputes, and have become quite sophisticated in manipulating the courts for their own ends.

A detailed analysis of disputing in this heterogeneous urban housing project supports [Richard D.] Schwartz's (1954)[1] hypothesis that disputants turn to formal mechanisms of social control in social settings where informal social controls are ineffective. However, despite frequent appeals to the criminal courts in disputes within ongoing relationships, the formal legal system fails to resolve most disputes in the sense of providing a mutually acceptable settlement that terminates the dispute. Consequently, courts come to serve simply as a sanction—a way of harassing an enemy—and an alternative to violence for those unable or unwilling to fight. Ultimately, the only resolution of disputes occurs through avoidance, the "exit" of one or both disputants from the neighborhood.

... My findings suggest that the nature of the social structure surrounding disputants significantly affects their strategies of dispute management....

The appeal to courts to settle disputes in a heterogeneous urban neighborhood conforms with the general hypothesis that formal mechanisms of social control assume greater importance when informal controls are not

---

1. This classic study is discussed in Note 1 below.

effective. Black suggests this relationship as a general theoretical proposition: "Law tends to become implicated in social life to the degree that other forms of social control are weak or unavailable."[2] However, Felstiner argues that in technologically complex, rich societies, such as the United States, disputants do not turn to courts to settle interpersonal disputes when economic stakes are low. The courts' specialized and alien rules demand hiring an expensive lawyer, and the backlog of cases slows down adjudication. Instead, they use avoidance, a strategy of "limiting the relationship with the other disputant sufficiently so that the dispute no longer remains salient." He argues that avoidance is a common and relatively inexpensive way of settling disputes in complex societies and criticizes Black's hypothesis, arguing that "... he does not consider the possibility that as 'communities' and their informal controls disappear, the need for any external civil dispute processing between individuals may also substantially fade." He points out, however, that we have very little data on patterns of self-help, negotiation, and avoidance and do not know if avoidance is an empirical reality or simply a sociological possibility. My study suggests that law intrudes into urban social life where informal controls are absent, as Black hypothesizes, but that because courts fail to settle cases, avoidance is ultimately the only successful mode of terminating disputes, as Felstiner argues.

The decision to appeal to court in this neighborhood depends to a great extent on the nature of the relationship linking the disputants and the wider network of social ties enveloping them. Unlike patterns of disputing described in small, close-knit, and isolated communities ..., residents use courts as a resource against insiders as well as outsiders. In small, bounded communities, disputants often fear that court action will disrupt important social ties and that the gains of an uncertain victory are not worth the cost of social opprobrium. Recourse to court also appears to be disruptive to social relationships within this urban setting, but the implications of such disruption are quite different in the urban context. If the hostility of neighbors is too intense, urbanites have the option of withdrawing from the social system, though usually at some cost, and initiating new social relationships elsewhere. Such a shift is far more difficult in an isolated, rural society.... Although studies have frequently discussed the significance of ongoing social relationships to modes of dispute processing, the crucial variable here is not the duration of a relationship in the past, but its future.

THE SOCIAL ORGANIZATION OF HETEROGENEITY

Dover Square is a pseudonym for a ten-year-old housing project of 1150 inhabitants in a polyethnic East Cost port city. Located in the inner city, Dover Square is surrounded by ethnic neighborhoods and the city's skid row.... The area has almost the highest crime rate in the city ... The

2. The reference is to the work of Donald Black, "The Boundaries of Legal Sociology, in D. Black and M. Mileski (eds.)", *The Social Organization of Behavior* 53 (1973). William Felstiner expressed strong disagreement with Black in his article, "Influences of Social Organization on Dispute Processing," 9 *Law & Society Review* 63, 70–86 (1986).

project was constructed on the rubble of a white ethnic neighborhood destroyed in conjunction with a major urban renewal project. It contains 300 low-rise garden apartments for families (two, three, and four-bedroom units). Dover Square houses a very heterogeneous population: 55 percent Chinese, 26 percent black, 9 percent white, and 9 percent Hispanic, living primarily in nuclear families. Although income ceilings restrict tenancy to families with low or moderate incomes, the occupations of the tenant families . . . are highly diverse, ranging from a few teachers and social workers to welfare families. This is not conventional public housing, but mixed housing for moderate-income families with 20 percent leased for poorer, public-housing tenants. Much of the population holds steady, semi-skilled jobs; 15 percent are on welfare. Sixty percent of the families have lived in the project since it opened. The rate of turnover is only five percent a year; yet this is not an urban ethnic village with deep roots in the past. The heterogeneity of the population and its limited history maintain an anonymity between ethnic groups and consequently undermine informal social control in the project as a whole. . . .

STRATEGIES OF DISPUTE MANAGEMENT

. . . Disputes in Dover Square are rarely settled by an agreement which satisfies both parties and terminates the conflict. Most disputes persist for years, with varying levels of salience and intensity, ending only when one of the disputants moves out of the project. . . .

Gossip is the most comment dispute management strategy employed by Dover Square residents. While gossip accompanies all kinds of disputes, it appears to have little impact within ethnic groups and virtually none across ethnic boundaries. It is most influential within the Chinese community, where some disputants manage their cases using gossip as their sole strategy, but even here is does not stop the errant husband from sleeping with white women or the stingy woman from failing to reciprocate enough tea cakes. One Chinese woman, for example, lived with both her handicapped husband and a lover, despite considerable gossip about this very irregular union. Gossip within the black community appears to have even less impact. A black woman, for example, discovered that the new redwood gate on her back fence had vanished and reappeared gracing the back fence of a black neighbor whose son had a reputation for stealing. She discussed the incident freely, and it became widely known throughout the black community. When the victim confronted the possessor of the gate, however, the latter claimed that her son had found it. Despite the widespread gossip and consensus that the boy had stolen the gate, it was not returned. . . .

A second common mode of managing disputes is actual or threatened violence. The injured party gathers friends and attacks the offender. This option demands skill in street fighting and/or a pool of readily mobilizable allies who can fight. It can only be used in disputes when the aggressor can be identified and located again if retaliation is not immediate.

Disputants also appeal to third parties outside their social system. Grievances about dogs, noise, and trash are regularly taken to the office of the project manager with requests for restraining or evicting the offender. The project managers perceive their role as purely custodial, however, and make no effort to mediate such disputes or to evict families on the basis of disputes with neighbors.... They listen sympathetically, but do not intervene.

The police are a frequent resource for stopping events perceived as crimes and for halting some kinds of offensive behavior by neighbors. If they arrive in time, they will stop the offending behavior, but their intervention rarely leads to significant or arbitration of the underlying conflict. One woman, for example, summoned the police to stop her Chinese neighbors from exploding firecrackers on their shared porch during Chinese New Year, unaware of how that holiday was traditionally celebrated. The police did stop the firecrackers but did not formulate a compromise which would avoid such conflicts in the future ...

A third outside party to which disputants appeal is the court. Courts are instruments of the state, but the mode of access to them and implications of turning to them differ significantly from calling the police. Once the police have stopped an altercation, their role, for the most part, is completed. But the consequences of filing criminal charges are more enduring....

RECOURSE TO COURT

Analysis of when and why disputants in Dover Square seek court intervention uncovers a complex pattern of moves and counter moves aimed at dispute resolution.... As disputants become more emotionally committed to the dispute, their moves and reactions to counter moves of their opponents intensify and often escalate in frequency and level of violence. Recourse to the courts and resort to violence are most frequent. The following cases illustrate the complexity of these patterns of interaction....

The Case of the Averted Robbery

An older white man averted a robbery by warning an elderly Chinese man that he suspected a group of youths was plotting to rob him on his way home from the laundromat. One of the youths, a white boy, was furious at the old man and verbally threatened and abused him. The older man then went to the courthouse and filed an application for a complaint against the youth. When the clerk of the court told him he could not made a strong case on the basis of a verbal assault, he changed the charge to physical assault, explaining to me that the judge would believe him, an older respectable citizen, not the youth who had a record. The case did not come to court, however, since the boy was on probation and his probation officer warned the boy not to give the older man any trouble or he would be in jail. The boy did not harass the older man any further, and was actually quite polite to him. The older man moved out of the project three months later, and had been planning his departure at the time of the incident. He told me that his plans to move had given him courage to confront the local gang of criminals.

The Case of the Revengeful Brothers

This final case suggests the conditions under which disputants resort only to violence and do not appeal to an outside third party. In this case the plaintiffs, young Chinese males, were able to fight and were wary of the court. A teenage white boy who lived in the project began to date a teenage Chinese girl, also a project resident. The boy tried to persuade this girl to work for him as a prostitute and introduced her to drugs such as Valium. The Chinese girl did spend at least one night out with a customer, to my knowledge. Late that night when she did not return home, her brothers came to look for her boyfriend, angry that he had turned their sister to drugs and prostitution. The boy was nowhere to be found. The next day the brothers did find him and beat him up. The white boy and Chinese girl were not seen together again.

These ... cases reveal a complex process of unfolding moves and counter moves in which some parties used violence and others resorted to the police and the courts. The threat of court did serve as a deterrent, since court action did occasionally lead to the imposition of sanctions. However, it was most effective when the accused already had a reputation for crime with the police.... [G]ossip has little impact in deterring misbehavior, although it did play an important role in providing information. In contrast, violence appears to be a very effective mode of dealing with disputes....

Striking differences existed between those who used the court and those who turned to violence. Courts were used by physically weaker individuals less capable of defending their interests by fighting.... [I]t was primarily women who went to court and men who resorted to violence. Of the four men who used the court, one was elderly and another a juvenile transvestite unskilled in fighting. Those who used violence were almost entirely young males experienced in street fighting.

Second, court use was disproportionately high among whites and low among Chinese. About half the blacks turned to court and half to violence, but three quarters of the whites used courts, and no Chinese did. This difference probably reflects each group's familiarity and past experience with American courts. Third, those with a criminal record or a history of arrests did not turn to the court but used violence instead.... Fourth, those who turned to court generally had some special, inside knowledge of court operations, either through a close friend or relative on the police force or the past encounters of kin with arrests and court appearances. One exception was a nun who was persuaded to press charges against an armed robber. However, an equal number with inside knowledge of the court chose violence instead, some because they had a record and did not expect to be treated favorably.

Special knowledge seems to be a precondition for using the court, but does not guarantee it. Here, in an interesting twist on Galanter's argument,[3] the "repeat players" who were knowledgeable about the courts were the

---

3. Galanter, "Why the Haves Come Out Ahead: Speculations on the Limits of Legal Change," 9 *Law & Society Review* 95 (1974).

"have-nots" rather than "haves." The youths involved in crime were often quite sophisticated about criminal courts. One youth, for example, said that he avoided kicking or knocking down old women when he robbed them since he believed that would change the charge from a minor one, larceny, to a more serious one, assault. Another youth pointed out that he sometimes committed crimes which a judge would find so improbable that he would be acquitted....

Chinese residents, on the other hand, had no experience in court and shied away from any involvement in American legal institutions. Because of immigration laws, in effect from 1882 to 1965, excluding most categories of Chinese immigrants, a large proportion of Chinese entered the country illegally and have studiously avoided American police and courts. Many spoke little or no English. Only in the last two years has this Chinatown had a Chinese-speaking lawyer.

The nature of the relationship between the disputants also influenced the decision to appeal to court. But it was neither the "relational distance" nor the ongoing quality of the relationship, but its future, which was most significant. Residents filed charges against opponents who were known personally but with whom their relationships were terminating or could easily be terminated. In each case in which a Dover Square resident took another to court, the relationship, despite its long duration, had a limited future. In [a conflict between a man and woman], for example, their relationship had ended. One boy took his friend to court over a bike after he had eased out of his friendships in the project. [Some] moved out of the project soon after taking their protagonists to court. In ten of the 15 moves using the court, one of the disputants subsequently moved out of the project or broke off his social relationships with its residents. In a neighborhood with such separate, disjunctive social worlds and so few institutions to tie neighbors together, it was sometimes possible to avoid an enemy without moving away. However, for neighbors or individuals involved in the same social networks, avoidance without physically leaving the project was difficult. Moving out of the project was usually an expensive and undesirable solution to conflicts, but it is generally easier to move away and construct a new set of relationships elsewhere in an urban setting than in isolated rural villages.

Residents' choice of court appeal was also influenced by the extent to which they were encapsulated in a cohesive community. Disputants who were not linked into a tightly knit ethnic community were more likely to appeal to court for settlement than those who were. This partially explains the substantial differences between ethnic groups in patterns of dispute management. The Chinese residents of Dover Square, who were closely tied to the cohesive Chinatown community, did not go to court to settle disputes within the group, while the black and white groups, neither of whom was involved in a close-knit social network and community, used courts to settle disputes between intimates as well as strangers.

150

Chinese residents of Dover Square were dependent on connections to Chinatown for jobs in Chinese restaurants and shops, where most of them worked, and for partners and capital if they chose to establish their own restaurant. This represented the only chance for economic mobility for Chinese who spoke no English. Chinese residents were socially tied to Chinatown as members of family associations, churches, political parties, martial arts clubs, and circles of friends and relatives. Most of their social and recreational life took place in Chinatown, whether shopping in Chinatown shops or attending large wedding banquets, family association outings, traditional holiday celebrations, or social gatherings of kin from the same village in China. Those who spoke no English were dependent on Chinatown for Chinese-speaking bankers, doctors, social workers, and lawyers. Community opinion was a powerful form of informal social control in Chinatown, and Dover Square residents took this into account when contemplating a deviant act such as dating a white person. Chinese residents could not easily escape the social consequences of their misdeeds against other Chinese without severing their ties to Chinatown altogether, a difficult and costly experience.

Moreover, heads of family associations and leaders of the Chinatown Benevolent Association served as mediators for internal disputes. Every individual belonged to a clan or family association which traditionally handled disputes between clan members. Cases between members of different clans and appeals from family associations were mediated by the Chinese Consolidated Benevolent Association, an umbrella organization that included all Chinatown associations but was controlled by the wealthy owners of Chinese restaurants and businesses. Decisions by these associations were not legally binding, but were enforced by social pressure and the considerable economic power of the merchants. The Benevolent Association even punished Chinese criminals for incidents in Chinatown. According to a Dover Square resident, for example, a Chinese youth who robbed a Chinese man on the main street of Chinatown was traced down through the girl he was visiting and punished by receiving a beating from representatives of the Benevolent Association.

Neither blacks nor whites were implicated in this kind of cohesive, organized community with its own community mediators. Their jobs, friends, churches, and voluntary associations were scattered throughout the black and white neighborhoods of the city, and no more than three or four residents participated in the same organization. Similarly, their networks of friends and kin extended to diverse neighborhoods. Only the Syrian–Lebanese residents shared ties to a small ethnic community as the Chinese did. Relations between black and white neighbors were fleeting: they expected that sooner or later they would move out of the project and never see one another again. In contrast, even if Chinese residents moved out, they were still implicated in ongoing relationships with their neighbors through ties to Chinatown organizations and social networks. Blacks and whites recognized no leaders with the ability to mediate disputes either within or between their groups and did not even agree who the overall leaders of the project were. Consequently, blacks and whites turned to the courts to manage disputes within the group, but Chinese did not.

These ethnic differences in use of the court also reflect different values about disputing. Most of those who appealed to the court, both black and white, belonged to cultures which value open confrontation in dealing with disputes, protecting one's rights, and avoiding exploitation by others. Chinese residents, in contrast, stressed the importance of pressing claims indirectly while preserving the pretense of amity and gossiping about one another's misdeeds.

THE ROLE OF THE COURT

When Dover Square residents take their cases to court, however, they do not always obtain a negotiated settlement. American criminal courts are not designed to settle interpersonal disputes in the sense that anthropologists conceive of settlement, but rather to determine if a law has been violated, and if so, to punish the offender. Anthropologists view dispute settlement as a restoration of harmony in social relationships, something which "makes the balance." In an American court, however, facts which are relevant to restoring a balance, such as the past history of the dispute and the community reputation of the disputants, may be excluded as irrelevant to the particular case. This style of court procedure contrasts markedly with the Zapotec court style ... in which the goal of the court proceeding is to arrive at a mutually acceptable compromise which restores equilibrium in social relationships rather than a verdict specifying a winner and a loser. American courts are—at least conceptually—formal, public, narrow in their conception of relevance, and "all-or-nothing" in their style of decision-making, in contrast to other modes of settlement, such as a Zapotec court or Kpelle moot, which are informal, define much more of the context and history of the dispute as relevant, seek a compromise decision and restitution, and operate with reference to community norms—not specialized, alien rules. This latter form of court can also exist in a complex urban setting such as a squatter settlement in Chile.

Because of the number of cases American courts must handle, they are unable to take the time for a full airing of the dispute. Judges often decide not to hear a case at all if the evidence seems inadequate.... Furthermore, since the judge is a stranger to the disputants, he cannot rely on his personal knowledge of the situation or on the opinions of their neighbors.... Of the ten cases actually taken to court whose outcome I discovered, six ended before adjudication, and one was handled by a probation officer. In only three did the judge make a decision.

Even the decisions the judges did make did not always address the fundamental conflict between the disputants and succeed in restoring harmony. In one case, for example, although the court's decision appears to be reasonable and conciliatory, it failed to deal with the underlying issues of the conflict and was not carried out.

Bill, a 15–year–old, appeared one day in the project with a new ten-speed bike. His friend, Vernon, aged 20, asked if he could ride it, and Bill refused. Vernon then grew abusive, pushed Bill around, insulted him, took the bike, and rode off on it. Bill never saw the bike again. A policeman standing across the street watching the incident approached Bill and urged him to file a complaint against Vernon for stealing his bike. Vernon was suspected by the police of being responsible for many crimes in the project. Bill agreed, although he was somewhat afraid of Vernon, who was a leader of the youth group and had a reputation as a tough person. Both Bill and Vernon lived in Dover Square and had been friends for years, but in the last few months before this incident, Bill had been gradually withdrawing from the local youth group and had formed his own group of gay male friends. Consequently, although his relationship with Vernon was of long duration it had a limited future.

The judge required Vernon to repay Bill for the bike within a certain time period and continued the case until then. However, one day before that deadline Vernon had paid Bill none of the money and did not have it. As a clerk explained the system to me, unless Bill reappeared in court on the day of the deadline and reported that he had not received his money, the case would be automatically dismissed. Bill was too frightened of Vernon and his threats of violence to do that. Furthermore, he was angry less about the bike than about Vernon's abusive treatment of him, and since the bike had been stolen in the first place, Bill was more interested in revenge for the insult than in restitution of the bike.

Cases taken to court in Dover Square rarely produce an outcome which settles the dispute and restores good relations. At least for this low-income population, the court serves as a sanction, a way of harassing an enemy, rather than as a mode of airing and resolving disputes. It serves as an alternative to violence for those unable or unwilling to fight.

CONCLUSION

Disputants in Dover Square thus use courts frequently, but rarely successfully, as a mode of settling disputes. Although courts are used where informal sanctions are absent, they cannot fill this vacuum effectively. Rather, courts function as a potential sanction by intimidating one's opponent, and as an alternative to street violence. Courts are used extra-legally, not as a forum for adjudicating disputes according to shared legal principles but as a weapon marshaled by disputants to enhance their power and influence. Disputes taken to court are not adjudicated, but ... "negotiated." Negotiation, as used in this sense, is simply a discussion between the parties in which they must come to a mutually satisfactory agreement based on their relative strength. The disputant's ability to appeal to court and probability of success in that arena influences his or her relative power to "negotiate" a settlement. The victor is the contender with the greater power, not the party with superior rights.

Although the court is employed in disputes within ongoing social relationships, it is primarily used in those with a limited future. An ongoing relationship has both duration in the past and potential for the future. A relationship with a long past has little binding power if the participants expect that they will never see one another again. Conversely, even a relationship of relatively short duration may have considerable force if the participants realize they will have to deal with one another for a long period of time in the future. A limited future changes the calculations of costs and gains, making confrontation cheaper....

The extent to which individuals must take account of one another in the future depends, in turn, on the degree to which they are implicated in durable social networks with one another and whether or not they are free to escape these networks. This is a question of the social structure of the community and its articulation with the larger society. The Chinese residents' reluctance to use the court resembles the behavior of disputants in bounded, small-scale societies, suggesting that a cohesive and closed social structure may discourage the use of zero-sum courts to settle disputes.

[William] Felstiner's hypothesis that avoidance is a common strategy for dealing with conflicts in American society is well supported in this neighborhood, but ... it is both more costly and less satisfactory than he implies. Moving away may cost too much, and withdrawal from a social relationship with someone who shares one stairwell, porch, balcony, and trash area is difficult. Residents resort to court and self-help strategies first, and avoidance only when other approaches fail. It is the inability of the courts to effectively settle disputes which compels residents to rely on avoidance.... Further, they are often forced to tolerate situations of enduring conflict and hostility....

This study suggests that in some settings legal machinery is accessible to the poor, minorities, and women. American courts are often described as costly, slow, and alienating, yet members of this community use criminal courts and the threat of criminal courts skillfully to further their own interests.... It may be primarily the civil courts which are more available to the more educated parts of the population, while criminal courts are open to all segments of society.

NOTES AND QUESTIONS

1. Merry's study supports earlier findings (reported in a classic article by Richard D. Schwartz) that "disputants turn to formal mechanisms of social control in social settings where informal social controls are ineffective." Schwartz compared two small Israeli communities that differed in the degree to which they used formal as opposed to informal ways of dealing with disputes. Schwartz, "Social Factors in the Development of Legal Control: A Case Study of Two Israeli Settlements," 63 *Yale Law Journal* 471 (1954).

One community, a *kvutza*, was organized as a tight-knit collective, requiring members to be in continuous interaction with each other. Everything from child care to showering and eating was organized communally. In this setting, information about any problems flowed rapidly, and public opinion acted as a powerful sanction. The core economic unit was the community itself, in which a "just society" would be created by giving "from each according to his abilities, to each according to his need."

By contrast, the other community was a *moshav*, which allowed members to have more privacy and also semi-private property. The core unit of production and distribution was the family. Everything from work to meals to showering could be done in private, and lines of communication were more attenuated than in the *kvutza*. Only the *moshav* had a separate Judicial Committee to handle internal disputes, although both settlements used a General Assembly for some aspects of governance. Schwartz posits that a specialized, more formal way of dealing with conflict was necessary for the *moshav* because the community was not tight-knit enough for informal sanctions to work. How does Merry's study fit with Schwartz's findings? How does it differ?

2. A note on control groups and research methods: In his study, Schwartz notes:

> In most of their superficial characteristics, the two settlements are essentially similar. Both were founded at the same time, 1921, by young settlers who had come from Eastern Europe "to build a new life." . . . Both are located on a slope of the Jezreel Valley where they have to deal with the same climate and similar topography. Both have about two thousand acres of land, which supports a mixed farming economy. Both populations have rejected many of the East–European Jewish customs, including traditional religious practices. Though many other Israeli collectives are left-wing socialist, the members of the kvutza [in this study] resemble those of the moshav in adhering to the social-democratic political philosophy represented by the *Mapai* party.

At the time of this study, the two settlements were very close in size, with just under 500 inhabitants each.

In order to test the impact of particular factors, a social scientist will often "hold constant" certain other factors. This is the function of a *control group*. For example, to test whether a certain drug was effective in eliminating allergic reactions, a scientist would look for a group of people who suffered from allergies. This group would ideally be composed of people who were otherwise similar in all relevant characteristics. Half of the group would take the drug being tested, while the other half would not. If the treatment group suffered fewer allergic reactions than the control group, the scientist could ascribe the difference to the effect of the drug. However, suppose that during the experiment, most people in the treatment group also installed newly-invented dust and mold filters in their homes—while the people in the control group did not. Then the scientist could not be sure whether the drug or the filters produced the observed differences in allergic reactions. The new filters could be said to introduce a confounding factor.

What differences do Merry and Schwartz "hold constant" in their study? What other, potentially confounding, factors might exist in these two situations? In a "true" scientific experiment, subjects are randomly assigned to one or another group. This kind of research, however, cannot examine real social life in its full complexity. Researchers generally have to choose between different kinds of precision. Higher "internal validity" in an experiment means that we can be more certain that the conclusions reached are true of this particular experimental situation, where everything has been tightly controlled. Higher "external validity" means that we can generalize what we find with more certainty to other, more real-life situations. Often a trade-off is required:

> Often a research strategy that yields results high in internal validity does so at the cost of leaving external validity questions unanswered, and vice versa. A study randomly assigning collegiate "jurors" [i.e., college students pretending to be jurors] to deliberate in groups of either 6 or 12 would have high internal validity as a test of the effects of jury size, but would be open to the external validity issue of generalization across persons (college students versus real jurors). A study of "naturally" occurring instances in which real juries have consisted of 6 as compared with 12 jurors would have high external validity, but would leave many internal validity questions (e.g., how were the cases tried . . .?) The choice of which type of validity to maximize and which to sacrifice is a hotly debated issue in the social sciences. Usually, researchers reach some sort of pragmatic compromise. They trade-off a bit of internal validity to achieve a higher level of external validity, and vice versa.[4]

One such compromise is a kind of "quasi experiment" in which researchers analyze and compare real-life situations that are very similar in most respects, but that differ in terms of the factor being tested. Of course, researchers must be careful to specify any other potentially confounding differences, and to consider how those differences might influence the results.

3. Merry offers some important additions to the picture painted by Schwartz—although both scholars would say that people turn to formal law when personal connections and informal sanctions fail. Both studies also indicate that informal sanctions are more effective in more tightly-knit communities. Schwartz's story, however, stops here, assuming that if informal sanctions fail, formal sanctions will take care of the problem. Merry takes us further, examining what happens when people do attempt to use formal law to solve their problems. Does she share Schwartz's optimism? What role does formal law play in the community she studies? Are there factors aside from close relationship ties that might affect whether someone decides to go to court?

4. John Monahan & Laurens Walker, *Social Science in Law: Cases and Materials* [6th ed.] 66 (2006).

4.   Idealist (or cultural) versus materialist (or structural) approaches: Since Schwartz's study, numerous changes have occurred in the Israeli settlements he studied. Contrary to his theory, declining face-to-face contact in some communities that were formerly tightly-knit has not led to more formalized legal regulation. Allen E. Shapiro, "Law in the Kibbutz: A Reappraisal," 10 *Law & Society Review* 415 (1976). Shapiro also noted that specialized judicial committees had fallen into disuse even in some communities that had them. Some writers have stressed the importance of a shared utopian ideology in these communities, arguing that ideology was the key reason for continued reliance on informal rather than formal legal approaches: "By now it is clear that kibbutzim's internal organization and external relations can only be understood in the context of their utopian ideology. There is no other way to understand why, for example, they chose not to employ outside labor when it was profitable...." Tal Simons and Paul Ingram, "The Kibbutz for Organizational Behavior," in B.M. Staw and R.L. Sutton, eds., *Research in Organizational Behavior*, at 283–344 (2000); see also Michael Saltman, "Legality and Ideology in the Kibbutz Movement," 9 *International Journal of the Sociology of Law* 279 (1981).

This debate reflects a long-standing controversy in social theory and social science. How much do people's ideas and ideals matter in shaping social life? Does a shared ideology focused on egalitarian communal living have the power to keep people living and working together effectively? Some social theorists reject this approach, pointing instead to the importance of social structure—for example, whether people live in close-knit communities or not, whether their society has marked divisions between rich and poor, how work is divided between women and men, whether there is racial segregation, and so forth. From this more "materialist" perspective, it is more important to study how people *act*—how they live, work, eat, survive in the world. A crude materialist approach views cultural ideas, religion, philosophy, etc., as mere secondary rationalizations. Since the 1970s, fields such as anthropology and sociology have largely moved beyond this division between crudely "idealist" and "materialist" approaches. Instead, many scholars in these disciplines seek to understand how both material conditions and cultural ideas interact to shape human experiences—including the operation of legal systems.

5.   A postscript on Israeli settlements: Simons and Ingram acknowledge that although communal Israeli settlements (*kibbutzim*) resisted hiring outside labor for some time, recent years have brought big changes. As of 1996, 55% of the kibbutzim report using hired laborers rather than members of the community to perform community work, and there are numerous other indications of increasing incursions on the old communal ways of living. Shlomo Getz, "Winds of Change," in U. Leviatan, H. Oliver, and J. Quarter, eds., *Crisis in the Israeli Kibbutz: Meeting the Challenge of Changing Times*, at 13–26 (1998). The communities are beginning to charge members for services that were once free, and privatization is replacing communal aspirations as well as organization. Although it seems clear that these changes are partially driven by shifts in the Israeli and global economy, scholars still

emphasize that there is an ideological component as well: "The roots of the change are economic, but Professor Getz says they also reflect a shift away from socialist values and toward greater materialism and individualism in Israeli society." Karby Leggett, "Pay–As–You–Go Kibbutzim," *Wall Street Journal*, May 26, 2005, B.1.

Even though more communal values are on the wane, we do not see a rise in formal legal bodies within these communities; instead, a mixed picture emerges that is more reminiscent of the complex one painted by Merry:

> The control system of the kibbutz appears to be in transition. There is a distinct loss of legitimacy on the part of the traditional kibbutz adjudicative process operating through multi-functional institutions such as the General Assembly and the various committees.... The development of a court-like institution, however, is only one of the options available and does not appear to be the dominant line of development. Rather, there appears to be a tendency to circumvent adjudication by the adoption of mechanistic rules that minimize the role of discretion and by a considerable bureaucratization of the kibbutz control system. There appears to be an increase in the resort to external sanctions [i.e., the Israeli legal system].... More often, however, the use of external controls is manipulative, strengthening internal bureaucratic control mechanisms.... The evidence suggests that analysis focused on the question of court or no-court, or social control inside or outside the law, may be dealing with a false dichotomy.

Allan Shapiro, "Law in the Kibbutz: The Search Continues," in L. Sebba, ed., *Social Control and Justice: Inside or Outside the Law?* at 343–356 (1996). How do Shapiro's conclusions fit with Merry's findings? Can you use Merry's study to support Shapiro's comment that asking about social control "inside or outside the law" may be focusing on a false dichotomy?

6. <u>Law versus custom</u>: When anthropologists first started studying social control across cultures, they spent a great deal of time arguing over the proper definition of "law"—what is formal "law" as opposed to mere informal "custom"? One early debate asked whether we should define law based on function or form. Bronislaw Malinowski, a famous figure in early anthropology, argued that we should focus on **function**: when comparing law across cultures, we should look at the different ways that societies achieve social order and control—whatever the mechanisms. Alfred Radcliffe–Brown, another anthropological pioneer, urged that when we study law we should examine **formal institutions** that can enforce sanctions (e.g., courts). See Mark Goodale and Elizabeth Mertz, "Anthropology of Law," in David Clark, ed., *Encyclopedia of Law and Society: American and Global Perspectives* (2007). Although Malinowski has been criticized for defining "law" too broadly, it is generally agreed that he "foreshadow[ed] a generation of anthropological research on how order could be maintained in societies lacking central authority, codes, and constables." Laura Nader, *The Life of the Law* 85 (2002).

Suppose a uniformed police officer employed by a city walks a beat in a neighborhood. She has the power to arrest those whom she sees violating city ordinances or state laws. However, suppose this officer also works with youth groups in a basketball league and comes to know both the parents and children in her area. Instead of arresting young teenagers for minor violations of public law, she tells their mothers about their conduct. The chance that she will tell mothers itself becomes an important sanction within the neighborhood. Is this an example of formal legal control, or of an informal "custom"? Is a clear-cut division between formal and informal control useful or even possible? What are its advantages and disadvantages?

7. <u>Legal pluralism and private, non-state governments</u>: As scholars became aware of the many levels of social control at work in societies, they began to talk about "legal pluralism," meaning that there could be a number of different legal systems at work in the same society. The classic situation of legal pluralism involves a colonial government that is operating alongside more indigenous and customary legal systems in a colonized country. However, a leading legal anthropologist, Sally Falk Moore, notes that legal pluralism "can allude to such things as the international context where there are different national legal systems operating in the same arena, it can refer to state law and federal law in a federal system, to colonial law and customary law in a colonial situation, to religious law where there are a multiplicity of officially recognized religions," etc. Sally Falk Moore, *Law and Anthropology* 247 (2005). For example, Native Americans living in the state of Wisconsin are subject both to the laws of Wisconsin and to tribal laws. Students at Stanford University are controlled not only by the laws of California, but also by many university regulation and sanction systems. In theory, there are ways of harmonizing these multiple levels of rule-making and sanctioning—but reality tends to be much more messy.

Many legal professionals in the United States seem to think that it would be good to minimize the levels of legal pluralism in operation: Why else would they spend time trying to "harmonize" laws or to produce uniform and model laws. On the other side of the argument, some scholars have attacked the attempt "to create national, integrated and homogeneous societies out of multicultural, multiethnic and highly differentiated human landscapes." Armando Guevara–Gill and Joseph Thome, "Notes on Legal Pluralism," 2 *Beyond Law* 75 (1992). They argue, for example, that nation-states in Latin America pursued repressive and even genocidal policies in their efforts to reduce legal pluralism. Instead, they urge acceptance of legal pluralism as a tool toward achieving "multi-cultural and democratic political arrangements."

While other scholars have criticized the somewhat blurry way legal pluralism is often conceptualized, it continues to provide a useful reminder of the many messy levels at which formal and informal controls operate. Moore warns that we must be careful to distinguish rules that emanate from the state (that is, from the official government) from other rules: "To deny that the state can and should be distinguished from other rule-making entities . . . is to turn away from the obvious." (p. 357). Notice, however, that Moore is not arguing that we should confine our definition of "law" to state-made rules. Instead, she urges a "subtle, complex, historically and ethnographically grounded, picture of the struggles implied when one talks about legal pluralism." (p. 358). This does not mean that we ignore the different sources of authority and varieties of law or norms. But it does mean that we acknowledge the substantial gray and messy areas.

Macaulay similarly argues that "messy" models of law will be more accurate than unrealistically neat ones: "we cannot divide the world between public and private or formal and informal legal systems." Stewart Macaulay, "Crime and Custom in Business Society," 22 *Journal of Law and Society* 248, 255 (1995). Like Moore, though, he notes that the fact that "corporate police are not public legal officers makes a difference. We may risk obscuring this if we fail to distinguish public from private, formal from informal." (p. 253).[5] Here Macaulay addresses another vexed distinction—the distinction between the public government, and the many private systems that perform the same functions. For example, shopping malls may hire security guards to perform many of the functions that police do. Private groups such as merchants' or homeowners' associations can function to set ground-rules or resolve disputes. See, e.g., Lisa Bernstein, "Opting Out of the Legal System: Extra–Legal Contractual Relations in the Diamond Industry," 21 *Journal of Legal Studies* 115 (1992); Robert Ellickson, "Cities and Homeowners Associations," 130 *U. Pa. L. Rev.* 1519 (1982); Eric Feldman, "The Tuna Court: Law and Norms in the World's Premier Fish Market," 94 *California Law Rev.* 313 (2006).

Courts have upheld the rights of homeowners associations to evict residents, either for bad behavior or non-payment of fines (which the associations may collect when residents violate the associations' rules). Mokoto Rich, "Homeowner Boards Blur Line of Just Who Rules the Roost," *New York Times*, July 27, 2003, at 1. Can you use the concept of legal pluralism to describe what is happening in these cases? Is this a private or public form of government?

For a classification of types of "legal pluralism," see Lawrence M. Friedman, *The Legal System: A Social Science Perspective*, at 196–199 (1975). Friedman distinguishes between horizontal pluralism—the legal subcultures have equal status or legitimacy—and vertical pluralism, where they are hierarchically arranged, "with a 'higher' and a 'lower' legal system or culture." He also distinguishes between cultural pluralism, in which the various systems divide along cultural lines, political pluralism (a federal system is a good example) and socio-economic pluralism (for example, medieval systems, in which there were different rules and laws for nobles and for commoners).

8. In later work, Merry compared how courts were used by people from three different neighborhoods. Sally Merry, *Getting Justice and Getting Even: Legal Consciousness among Working–Class Americans* (1990). Two of the

---

5. Macaulay cites Brian Tamanaha here, who argues strongly for maintaining the distinction.

neighborhoods were less affluent than the third one, although residents of all three areas had very similar occupations and were of similar ethnic backgrounds. By contrast with the two less affluent neighborhoods, which were in densely-populated city areas, the affluent neighborhood ("Riverdale") was a newly-built, attractive suburb. Merry found that residents of Riverdale were less likely to turn to courts when they were experiencing conflict:

> ... court use constitutes a complex marker of social class. Settled-living people aspiring to a middle-class status condemn going to court for family and marital problems; they consider it to be embarrassing, humiliating, and typical of lower groups.... For hard-living people, however, going to court is a more refined alternative to violence, a better way of doing things. (p. 82–83)

One marker of higher social class is a better ability to "escape from community," as Merry puts it—to live a more private, individualized life. How does this finding fit with Merry's earlier study excerpted above? And, how does this account compare with the recent developments in Israeli settlements (described in #5 above)?

Adding another factor to the picture, anthropologist Carol Greenhouse focused on the interaction of religion with law in her fieldwork during the 1970s. She reported that Baptists in a southern U.S. community avoided using the courts, similarly understanding court use as an embarrassment. However, rather than viewing court users as lower class, these Baptists would view them as "unsaved" or less religious: "All conflict is said to flow from the interest of non-Baptists ... Furthermore, it is known that non-Baptists have none of the spiritual faith that would prevent them from going to great lengths in their own self-interest." *Praying for Justice: Faith, Order and Community in an American Town* 117 (1986). This can be viewed as a particular feature of Baptist ideology, or it can be understood as one religious variant of a more general U.S. ideology that views court avoidance as morally superior: "Conflict stigmatizes an individual or a group. Self-restraint, on the other hand, signals mastery over nature (even one's own). Self-restraint is central to the [American] vision of a self-regulating society.... Accordingly, conflict is imagined to pool at the lower end of the social scale ... indeed, [Lloyd] Warner suggests that socialization to self-restraint is one key to the American Dream." Carol Greenhouse, "Signs of Quality: Individualism and Hierarchy in American Culture," 19 *American Ethnologist* 233–254, 246 (1992).[6] Does this generalization seem accurate in today's society? Can you think of examples and counter-examples? Do you think that people who use courts are stigmatized?

III. A Note on Legal Evolution and Rationality

Scholars have also debated another set of questions surrounding the definition of law in its relationship to society. Do particular kinds of societies

---

6. Originally trained in anthropology, Lloyd Warner taught sociology and anthropology at the University of Chicago. He conducted a number of famous studies of communities in the United States during the decades of the 1930s, –40s and –50s. One particular focus of his work was the influence of class on American culture.

institutionalize specific types of legal systems? How does the shape of a particular society influence the pattern of its legal system (if at all)? And—an old controversy—do societies and their legal systems evolve over time toward higher levels of rationality? What is the relationship between wider social issues and forms of rationality found in the law?

Any discussion of these issues would have to begin with the justly famous work of Max Weber. Weber was a political economist who became a foundational scholar in modern sociological thought. He also received legal training early in his career, and later went on to author some very influential writings on the sociology of law. However, these writings were in piecemeal draft form at the time of his death, and wound up being cobbled together by scholars who wanted to see Weber's thought disseminated and published. As a result, the published work of Weber on law contains older work that flirted with "stage models," presenting the development of society and law as a series of distinct stages. Weber later abandoned this approach, but didn't have an opportunity to reverse this in his writings before his death.

(3.2) Max Weber on Law in Economy and Society

Max Rheinstein ed.

(1954).

[Weber discusses legal thought in Germany, where, at the end of the nineteenth century, legal scholarship was highly conceptual. Jurists analyzed typical forms of business transactions—between buyers and sellers, for example—and defined them as legal relationships, that is, as relationships that could be discussed in legal terms (not Mr. Schmidt and Mrs. Schiller, but "bailor" and "bailee"). These "legal relationships" could be further arranged, analyzed, and classified logically, giving rise to what Weber calls "systematization." This never appears, he says, except in "late stages of legal modes of thought. To a youthful law, it is unknown." "Systematization" represents an integration of all analytically derived legal propositions in such a way that they constitute a logically clear, internally consistent, and, at least in theory, gapless system of rules, under which, it is implied, all conceivable fact situations must be capable of being locally subsumed.... Even today not every body of law (e.g., English law) claims that it possesses the features of a system.

Legal systems can differ, then, in the degree to which they are "systematized." There are other differences in the "technical apparatus of legal practice." Weber analyzes the following four "possible type situations:"]

Both law-making and law-finding may be either rational or irrational. They are "formally irrational" when one applies in law-making or law-finding means which cannot be controlled by the intellect, for instance when recourse is had to oracles or substitutes therefor. Law-making and law-finding are "substantively irrational" on the other hand to the extent that decision is influenced by concrete factors of the particular case as evaluated upon an ethical, emotional, or political basis rather than by general norms. "Rational" law-making and law-finding may be of either a formal or a substantive kind. All formal law is, formally at least, relatively rational. Law, however, is "formal" to the extent that, in both substantive and procedural matters, only unambiguous general characteristics of the facts of the case are taken into account. This formalism can, again, be of two different kinds. It is possible that the legally relevant characteristics are of a tangible nature, i.e., that they are perceptible as sense data. This adherence to external characteristics of the facts, for instance, the utterance of certain words, the execution of a signature or the performance of a certain symbolic act with a fixed meaning, represents the most rigorous type of legal formalism. The other type of formalistic law is found where the legally relevant characteristics of the facts are disclosed through the logical analysis of meaning and where, accordingly, definitely fixed legal concepts in the form of highly abstract rules are formulated and applied. This process of "logical rationality" diminishes the significance of extrinsic elements and thus softens the rigidity of concrete formalism. But the contrast to "substantive rationality" is sharpened, because the latter means that the decision of legal problems is influenced by norms different from those obtained through logical generalization of abstract interpretations of meaning. The norms to which substantive rationality accords predominance include ethical imperatives, utilitarian and other expediential rules, and political maxims, all of which diverge from the formalism of the "external characteristics" variety as well as from that which uses logical abstraction. However, the peculiarly professional, legalistic, and abstract approach to law in the modern sense is possible only in the measure that the law is formal in character. In so far as the absolute formalism of classification according to "sense-data characteristics" prevails, it exhausts itself in casuistry.[7] Only that abstract method which employs the logical interpretation of meaning allows the execution of the specifically systematic task, i.e., the collection and rationalization by logical means of all the several rules recognized as legally valid into an internally consistent complex of abstract legal propositions. . . .

Present-day legal science, at least in those forms which have achieved the highest measure of methodological and logical rationality, . . . proceeds from the following five postulates: viz., first, that every concrete legal decision be the "application" of an abstract legal proposition to a concrete "fact situation"; second, that it must be possible in every concrete case to derive the decision from abstract legal propositions by means of legal logic; third, that the law must actually or virtually constitute a "gapless" system of legal propositions, or must, at least, be treated as if it were such a gapless system; fourth, that whatever cannot be "construed" legally in rational terms is also

---

7. Casuistry = a quibbling or evasive way of dealing with difficult cases of duty; sophistry. [Eds. note].

legally irrelevant; and fifth, that every social action of human beings must always be visualized as either an "application" or "execution" of legal propositions, or as an "infringement" thereof. . . .

The Anti Formalistic Tendencies of Modern Legal Development. From a theoretical point of view, the general development of law and procedure may be viewed as passing through the following stages: first, charismatic legal revelation through "law prophets"; second, empirical creation and finding of law by legal honoratiores, i.e., law creation through cautelary jurisprudence[8] and adherence to precedent; third, imposition of law by secular or theocratic powers; fourth and finally, systematic elaboration of law and professionalized administration of justice by persons who have received their legal training in a learned and formally logical manner. From this perspective, the formal qualities of the law emerge as follows: arising in primitive legal procedure from a combination of magically conditioned formalism and irrationality conditioned by revelation, they proceed to increasingly specialized juridical and logical rationality and systematization, passing through a stage of theocratically or patrimonially conditioned substantive and informal expediency. Finally, they assume, at least from an external viewpoint, an increasingly logical sublimation and deductive rigor and develop an increasingly rational technique in procedure.

Since we are here only concerned with the most general lines of development, we shall ignore the fact that in historical reality the theoretically constructed stages of rationalization have not everywhere followed in the sequence which we have just outlined, even if we ignore the world outside the Occident. We shall not be troubled either by the multiplicity of causes of the particular type and degree of rationalization that a given law has actually assumed. As our brief sketch has already shown, we shall only recall that the great differences in the line of development have been essentially influenced, first, by the diversity of political power relationships, which . . . have resulted in very different degrees of power of the imperium vis-a-vis the powers of the kinship groups, the folk community, and the estates; second, by the relations between the theocratic and the secular powers; and, third, by the differences in the structure of these legal honoratiores who were significant for the development of a given law and which, too, were largely dependent upon political factors.

Only the Occident has witnessed the fully developed administration of justice of the folk-community . . . and the status group stereotyped form of patrimonialism; and only the Occident has witnessed the rise of the [national][9] economic system, whose agents first allied themselves with princely

---

8. In "cautelary jurisprudence," lawyers reason by analogy with almost no attempt at inductive or deductive reasoning. Concepts are extended as needed, but lawyers do not attempt to move from particular situations to general propositions which will govern future cases. This is a long way from Weber's "formal rationality."

9. Here we adopt Roth's correction of Rheinstein's translation. Max Weber, *Economy and Society: An Outline of Interpretive Sociology,* ed. Guenther Roth and Claus Wittich (1978).

powers to overcome the estates and then turned against them in revolution; and only the West has known "Natural Law," and with it the complete elimination of the system of personal laws and of the ancient maxim that special law prevails over general law. Nowhere else, finally, has there occurred any phenomenon resembling Roman law and anything like its reception. All these events have to a very large extent been caused by concrete political factors, which have only the remotest analogies elsewhere in the world. For this reason, the stage of decisively shaping law by trained legal specialists has not been fully reached anywhere outside of the Occident. Economic conditions have, as we have seen, everywhere played an important role, but they have nowhere been decisive alone and by themselves. To the extent that they contributed to the formation of the specifically modern features of present-day Occidental law, the direction in which they worked has been by and large the following: To those who had interests in the commodity market, the rationalization and systematization of the law in general and, with certain reservations to be stated later, the increasing calculability of the functioning of the legal process in particular, constituted one of the most important conditions for the existence of economic enterprise intended to function with stability and, especially, of capitalistic enterprise, which cannot do without legal security. Special forms of transactions and special procedures, like the bill of exchange and the special procedure for its speedy collection, serve this need for the purely formal certainty of the guaranty of legal enforcement. . . .

[T]he expectations of parties will often be disappointed by the results of a strictly professional legal logic. Such disappointments are inevitable indeed where the facts of life are juridically "construed" in order to make them fit the abstract propositions of law and in accordance with the maxim that nothing can exist in the realm of law unless it can be "conceived" by the jurist in conformity with those "principles" which are revealed to him by juristic science. The expectations of the parties are oriented towards the economic and utilitarian meaning of a legal proposition. However, from the point of view of legal logic, this meaning is an "irrational" one. For example, the layman will never understand why it should be impossible under the traditional definition of larceny to commit a larceny of electric power. It is by no means the peculiar foolishness of modern jurisprudence which leads to such conflicts. To a large extent such conflicts rather are the inevitable consequence of the incompatibility that exists between the intrinsic necessities of logically consistent formal legal thinking and the fact that the legally relevant agreements and activities of private parties are aimed at economic results and oriented towards economically determined expectations. It is for this reason that we find the ever-recurrent protests against the professional legal method of thought. . . .

Contemporary Anglo–American Law. The differences between continental and common law methods of legal thought have been produced mostly by factors which are respectively connected with the internal structure and the modes of existence of the legal profession as well as by factors related to differences in political development. The economic elements, however, have been determinative only in connection with these elements. What we are concerned with here is the fact that, once everything is said and done about these differences in historical developments, modern capitalism prospers equally and manifests essentially identical economic traits under legal systems containing rules and institutions which considerably differ from each other at least from the juridical point of view. . . .

Indeed, we may say that the legal systems under which modern capitalism has been prospering differ profoundly from each other even in their ultimate principles of formal structure.

Even today, and in spite of all influences by the ever more rigorous demands for academic training, English legal thought is essentially an empirical art. Precedent still fully retains its old significance, except that it is regarded as unfair to invoke a case from too remote a past, which means older than about a century. One can also still observe the charismatic character of law-finding, especially, although not exclusively, in the new countries, and quite particularly the United States. In practice, varying significance is given to a decided case not only, as happens everywhere, in accordance with the hierarchical position of the court by which it was decided but also in accordance with the very personal authority of an individual judge. This is true for the entire common-law sphere, as illustrated, for instance, by the prestige of Lord Mansfield. But in the American view, the judgment is the very personal creation of the concrete individual judge, to whom one is accustomed to refer by name, in contrast to the impersonal "District Court" of Continental–European officialese. The English judge, too, lays claim to such a position. All these circumstances are tied up with the fact that the degree of legal rationality is essentially lower than, and of a type different from, that of continental Europe. Up to the recent past, and at any rate up to the time of Austin, there was practically no English legal science which would have merited the name of "learning" in the continental sense. This fact alone would have sufficed to render any such codification as was desired by Bentham practically impossible. But it is also this feature which has been responsible for the "practical" adaptability of English law and its "practical" character from the standpoint of the public.

The legal thinking of the layman is, on the one hand, literalistic. He tends to be a definition-monger when he believes he is arguing "legally." Closely connected with this trait is the tendency to draw conclusions from individual case to individual case: the abstractionism of the "professional" lawyer is far from the layman's mind. In both respects, however, the art of empirical jurisprudence is cognate to him, although he may not like it. No country, indeed, has produced more bitter complaints and satires about the legal profession than England. The formularies of the conveyancers, too, may be quite unintelligible to the layman, as again is the case in England. Yet, he can understand the basic character of the English way of legal thinking, he can identify himself with it and, above all, he can make his peace with it by retaining once and for all a solicitor as his legal father confessor for all contingencies of life, as is indeed done by practically every English businessman. He simply neither demands nor expects of the law anything which could be frustrated by "logical" legal construction.

Safety valves are also provided against legal formalism. As a matter of fact, in the sphere of private law, both common law and equity are "formalistic" to a considerable extent in their practical treatment. It would hardly be otherwise under a system of stare decisis and the traditionalist spirit of the legal profession. But the institution of the civil jury imposes on rationality limits which are not merely accepted as inevitable but are actually prized because of the binding force of precedent and the fear that a precedent might thus create "bad law" in a sphere which one wishes to keep open for a concrete balancing of interests. We must forego the analysis of the way in which this division of the two spheres of stare decisis and concrete balancing of interests is actually functioning in practice. It does in any case represent a softening of rationality in the administration of justice. Alongside all this we find the still quite patriarchal, summary and highly irrational jurisdiction of the justices of the peace. They deal with the petty causes of everyday life and ... they represent a kind of Khadi[10] justice which is quite unknown in Germany. All in all, the Common Law thus presents a picture of an administration of justice which in the most fundamental formal features of both substantive law and procedure differs from the structure of continental law as much as is possible within a secular system of justice, that is, a system that is free from theocratic and patrimonial powers. Quite definitely, English law-finding is not, like that of the Continent, "application" of "legal propositions" logically derived from statutory texts.

These differences have had some tangible consequences both economically and socially; but these consequences have all been isolated single phenomena rather than differences touching upon the total structure of the economic system. For the development of capitalism two features have been relevant and both have helped to support the capitalistic system. Legal training has primarily been in the hands of the lawyers from among whom also the judges are recruited, i.e., in the hands of a group which is active in the service of the propertied, and particularly capitalistic, private interests and which has to gain its livelihood from them. Furthermore and in close connection with this, the concentration of the administration of justice at the central courts in London and its extreme costliness have amounted almost to a denial of access to the courts for those with inadequate means. At any rate, the essential similarity of the capitalistic development on the Continent and in England has not been able to eliminate the sharp contrasts between the two types of legal systems. Nor is there any visible tendency towards a transformation of the English legal system in the direction of the continental under the impetus of the capitalist economy. On the contrary, wherever the two kinds of administration of justice and of legal training have had the opportunity to compete

---

10. Khadi, Kadhi or qadi: the "Moslem judge who sits in the market place and, at least seemingly, renders his decisions without any reference to rules or norms but in what appears to be a completely free evaluation of the particular merits of every single case." Rheinstein, Preface, at xiviii. [Eds. note]

with one another, as for instance in Canada, the Common Law way has come out on top and has overcome the continental alternative rather quickly. We may thus conclude that capitalism has not been a decisive factor in the promotion of that form of rationalization of the law which has been peculiar to the continental West ever since the rise of Romanist studies in the medieval universities. . . .

Whatever form law and legal practice may come to assume under the impact of [the] various influences [of modern society], it will be inevitable that, as a result of technical and economic developments, the legal ignorance of the layman will increase. The use of jurors and similar lay judges will not suffice to stop the continuous growth of the technical element in the law and hence of its character as a specialists' domain. Inevitably the notion must expand that the law is a rational technical apparatus, which is continually transformable in the light of expediential considerations and devoid of all sacredness of content. This fate may be obscured by the tendency of acquiescence in the existing law, which is growing in many ways for several reasons, but it cannot really be stayed. All of the modern sociological and philosophical analyses, many of which are of a high scholarly value, can only contribute to strengthen this impression, regardless of the content of their theories concerning the nature of law and the judicial process. . . .

The decisive reason for the success of bureaucratic organization has always been its purely technical superiority over every other form. A fully developed bureaucratic administration stands in the same relationship to nonbureaucratic forms as machinery to nonmechanical modes of production. Precision, speed, consistency, availability of records, continuity, possibility of secrecy, unity, rigorous coordination, and minimization of friction and of expense for materials and personnel are achieved in a strictly bureaucratized, especially in a monocratically organized, administration conducted by trained officials to an extent incomparably greater than in any collegial form of administration. . . .

The utmost possible speed, precision, definiteness, and continuity in the execution of official business are demanded of the administration particularly in the modern capitalistic economy. The great modern capitalist enterprises are themselves normally unrivaled models of thoroughgoing bureaucratic organization. Their handling of business rests entirely on increasing precision, continuity, and especially speed of operation. . . .

In the place of the old-type ruler who is moved by sympathy, favor, grace, and gratitude, modern culture requires for its sustaining external apparatus the emotionally detached, and hence rigorously "professional," expert; and the more complicated and the more specialized it is, the more it needs him. All these elements are provided by the bureaucratic structure. Bureaucracy provides the administration of justice with a foundation for the realization of a conceptually systematized rational body of law on the basis of "laws," as it was achieved for the first time to a high degree of technical perfection in the late Roman Empire. In the Middle Ages the reception of this law proceeded hand in hand with the bureaucratization of the administration of justice. Adjudication by rationally trained specialists had to take the place of the older type of adjudication on the basis of tradition or irrational presuppositions.

Rational adjudication on the basis of rigorously formal legal concepts is to be contrasted with a type of adjudication which is guided primarily by sacred traditions without finding therein a clear basis for the decision of concrete cases. It thus decides cases either as charismatic justice, i.e., by the concrete "revelations" of an oracle, a prophet's doom, or an ordeal; or as khadi justice non-formalistically and in accordance with concrete ethical or other practical value-judgments; or as empirical justice, formalistically, but not by subsumption of the case under rational concepts but by the use of "analogies" and the reference to and interpretation of "precedents." The last two cases are particularly interesting for us here. In khadi justice, there are no "rational" bases of "judgment" at all, and in the pure form of empirical justice we do not find such rational bases, at least in that sense in which we are using the term. The concrete value-judgment aspect of khadi justice can be intensified until it leads to a prophetic break with all tradition, while empirical justice can be sublimated and rationalized into a veritable technique. Since the non-bureaucratic forms of authority exhibit a peculiar juxtaposition of a sphere of rigorous subordination to tradition on the one hand and a sphere of free discretion and grace of the ruler on the other, combinations and marginal manifestations of both principles are frequent. In contemporary England, for instance, we still find a broad substratum of the legal system which is in substance khadi justice to an extent which cannot be easily visualized on the Continent.... The first country of modern times to reach a high level of capitalistic development, i.e., England, thus preserved a less rational and less bureaucratic legal system. That capitalism could nevertheless make its way so well in England was largely because the court system and trial procedure amounted until well in the modern age to a denial of justice to the economically weaker groups. This fact and the cost in time and money of transfers of landed property, which was also influenced by the economic interests of the lawyers, influenced the structure of agrarian England in the direction of the accumulation and immobilization of landed property....

The demands for "legal equality" and of guaranties against arbitrariness require formal rational objectivity in administration in contrast to personal free choice on the basis of grace, as characterized the older type of patrimonial authority. The democratic ethos, where it pervades the masses in connection with a concrete question, based as it is on the postulate of substantive justice in concrete cases for concrete individuals, inevitably comes into conflict with the formalism and the rule-bound, detached objectivity of bureaucratic administration. For this reason it must emotionally reject what is rationally demanded. The propertyless classes in particular are not served, in the way in which bourgeois are, by formal "legal equality" and "calculable" adjudication and administration. The propertyless demand that law and administration serve the equalization of economic and social opportunities vis-a-vis the propertied classes, and judges or administrators cannot perform this function unless they assume the substantively ethical and hence nonformalistic character of the Khadi. The rational course of justice and administration is interfered with not only by every form of "popular justice," which is little concerned with rational norms and reasons, but also by every type of intensive influencing of the course of administration by "public opinion," that is, in a mass democracy, that communal activity which is born of irrational "feelings" and which is normally instigated or guided by party leaders or the press. As a matter of fact, these interferences can be as disturbing as, or, under circumstances, even more disturbing than, those of the star chamber practices of an "absolute" monarch.

NOTES AND QUESTIONS

1. What are examples, in modern law, of formal rationality, substantive rationality, formal irrationality, substantive irrationality? See Stephen Kalberg, "Max Weber's Types of Rationality: Cornerstones for the Analysis of Rationalization Processes in History," 85 *American Journal of Sociology* 1145 (1980). How would you classify the following:

a. Congress passes a law requiring all buildings above a certain size to have ramps so that people in wheelchairs have access to them.

b. Two friends are on their way to the movies, and cannot decide which of two movies to go to; they toss a coin to decide.

c. The Supreme Court, in *Roe v. Wade*, decided that restrictions on abortion in the early months of pregnancy violated a woman's right to privacy—a right not expressly stated in the Constitution.

d. In the early years of the Chinese Revolution, "tribunals" were empowered to roam about the country and do "revolutionary justice;" they punished landlords and other "class enemies." There was no right of appeal from the decisions of these tribunals.

e. Statutory guidelines enacted by the state legislature direct judges in family court to award custody according to the "best interests" of the child; the statute includes a list of factors to be considered such as the wishes of the child, the wishes of the parent, the child's age, evidence of abuse of the child, etc. The judge hears arguments from the parents' attorneys, reviews reports on the child and parents prepared by psychologists, and makes her decision.

f. Suppose instead, in the family court case above, the judge appoints a "guardian ad litem" (GAL) to represent the child's interests and investigate the family's situation; the GAL interviews all parties, orders psychological tests done, conducts home and school observations, and reaches a decision. While formal law mandates that the judge make an independent decision, in fact the judge completely defers to the GAL's decision.

g. In a criminal case, a jury may decide on guilt or innocence; the jury deliberates in secret, and does not give any reasons for its decision, which—if the jury acquits—is absolutely final.

h.   A state in the U.S. requires a license to hunt deer; to get a license, an applicant must pay $10 and be a resident of the state who is over 21 years old; a 43 year old woman fills out the application form, pays the clerk $10, and shows him her driver's license; the clerk issue her a license.

i.   A statute forbids "divorced persons" from marrying again "within a year" of their divorce decree. Legislative history reveals that the purpose of this provision is to encourage reconciliation and discourage rapid remarriage to other parties. Susan and Henry get a divorce on June 1st, but they reconcile and remarry two months later. A court holds that this re-marriage is not valid, because it took place within one year, although Susan and Henry argue that the statute was not supposed to apply to cases where the divorced couple re-marries each other.

2.   Legal evolution—Weber's "ideal types": We move now to consider the question of legal evolution. As we will see, Weber's categories for different kinds of rationality can be useful even if they do not neatly map an evolutionary development from charismatic, irrational "primitive legal procedure" based in "magic" through to modern law characterized by rigorous logic and rationality. Simplistic evolutionary schemes of this kind have been controversial, and have been seriously undermined by the empirical evidence. But many scholars think that Weber himself would not have endorsed this kind of oversimplified picture of reality himself. Notice that Weber introduces this discussion by saying, "From a theoretical point of view, the general development of law and procedure may be viewed as passing through the following stages. . . ." What do you think he means by "a theoretical point of view"?

One key feature of Weber's approach to social analysis was his use of the "ideal type" to analyze society:

> . . . sociology seeks to formulate type concepts and generalized uniformities of empirical process. . . . An important consideration in the formulation of sociological concepts and generalizations is the contribution that sociology can make toward the causal explanation of some historically and culturally important phenomenon. As in the case of every generalizing science, the abstract character of the concepts of sociology is responsible for the fact that, compared with actual historical reality, they are relatively lacking in fullness of concrete content. To compensate for this disadvantage, sociological analysis can offer a greater precision of concepts. . . . In all cases, . . . sociological analysis both abstracts from reality and at the same time helps us to understand it in that it shows with what degree of approximation a concrete historical phenomenon can be subsumed under one or more of these concepts. For example, the same historical phenomenon may be in one aspect "feudal," in another "patrimonial," in another "bureaucratic," and in still another "charismatic." *In order to give a precise meaning to these terms, it is necessary for the sociologist to formulate pure ideal types of the corresponding forms of action. . . . But precisely because this is true, it is probably seldom if ever that a real*

171

phenomenon can be found which corresponds exactly to one of these ideally constructed pure types.

Max Weber, *Economy and Society*, at 19–29 (ed. Guenther Roth & Claus Wittich, 1978).

Here Weber is in part reacting against the then-current "historical school," which tried to explain social developments through a process of induction from the details of historical events. This process required scholars to mire themselves in very particularistic and individualist examinations of specific happenings. On the opposite side of the spectrum were "neoclassical" scholars who focused on abstract and formal theories with far less grounding in empirical reality (but more analytic precision). Weber's "ideal type" seeks a middle road:

> The Weberian ideal type may thus be seen as a methodological device for negotiating the conflicting demands of historical accuracy and theoretical precision.... Among other things, ideal types focus attention on one aspect of social reality and thereby help to illuminate one set of causal connections; this is their strength. In doing so, they necessarily leave other sides of reality and other chains of causation in the dark; this is their limitation.

Charles Camic et al., "Introduction," in Charles Camic et al., eds., *Max Weber's Economy and Society: A Critical Companion*, at 1–28, 17–18 (2005). These authors go on to stress that Weber did not believe that a "complete and universal theory" of human social life is possible, because society is always in flux, and because any researchers' perspective is necessarily limited. Ideal types permit the sociologist to move back and forth between the details of empirical evidence and more abstract analytical categories. This puts a more stringent requirement on theory than was found in neoclassical theory— concepts have to be continually assessed vis-à-vis social reality. Weber felt that there is an inevitable trade-off between "empirical completeness and theoretical precision." (Id.) Notice that this position is quite similar to that articulated by Monahan and Walker in the "Note on control groups" above. Quantitative methods make similar trade-offs, and offer only partial views of social reality. We can ask whether this partial character of social science explanation is more hidden by quantitative or qualitative analysis.

In any case, Weber himself explicitly disavowed the idea that any of his ideal types of legal authority actually captured actual historical situations:

> The fact that none of these ... ideal types ... is usually to be found in historical cases in "pure" form, is naturally not a valid objection to attempting their conceptual formation in the sharpest possible form.... The idea that the whole of concrete historical reality can be exhausted in [my] conceptual scheme ... is as far from the author's thoughts as anything could be.

Max Weber, *Economy and Society*. These ideal typical categories provide a very useful framework for assessing characteristics of law. Some would argue that these categories also give us analytical tools for examining the particular shape of law in capitalist society (and perhaps also the historical trajectory that led to it).

But critics of Weber's approach would also caution us against taking the categories too literally as empirical descriptions of actual legal systems:

> From an analytical point of view, Weber's distinctions between four types of authority, with their four types of law, are brilliant. . . . Weber defines them so narrowly, however, that on the surface they appear to be mutually exclusive. In fact the western legal tradition, as it has developed since the late eleventh century, has combined, and therefore transformed, all four of these "ideal" types.
>
> Perhaps Weber would agree with this criticism. . . . But if so, it remains obscured by his failure to develop a theory of the interaction of these four dimensions of the Western legal tradition. That failure may have been due to the very concept of an ideal-type, which by definition does not correspond to historical reality. It may have also been due to Weber's conflicting belief that the ideal type of formal-rational law had in fact become a historical reality and had triumphed in the West and was doomed by its identification with capitalism.

Harold Berman and Charles Reid, Jr., "Max Weber as Legal Historian," in Stephen Turner, ed., *The Cambridge Companion to Weber*, at 223–239, 239 (2000). Berman and Reid detail a number of examples of the ways that Weber's account of legal history is "distorted by his attempt to demonstrate the operation of certain pre-existing models by reference to historical sources." (p. 229). They characterize a unidirectional evolutionary model that progresses through distinct phases as an "oversimplified historiography"— one that generated "serious distortions at the same time that it led to some important insights." (p. 223). They note that it has only been toward the end of the 20th century that scholars have identified the ideological character of such an evolutionary scheme. What assumptions do evolutionary models make about non-Western societies? Can you think of a way that Weber's ideal types can be useful in analyzing law even if they do not neatly map actual historical developments?

3. <u>Legal evolution—Oversimplifying other cultures</u>: In fact, well before the end of the 20th century, anthropologists took the lead in questioning evolutionary models of society and law—models that often understood modern society as the inevitable "telos" or end of an evolutionary process. These models also frequently viewed each successive evolutionary phase as a form of "progress." In what way, for example, would an evolution from "formally irrational" law to "formally rational" law be progressive? How about from "substantively irrational" law to "formally rational" law?

Weber associates earlier stages of legal evolution with "primitive legal procedures," "magic," and "khadi justice." Scholars have pointed out that this approach underestimates the regularities of legal procedures in other cultures, at the same time as it overestimates the rationality of "law on the ground" in Western societies. For example, legal anthropologist Lawrence Rosen studied the role of the Islamic law judge (Weber's "khadi") in Morocco. He reports that "far from being arbitrary or unsystematic, *qadi* justice partakes of regularities which reveal not only Islamic legal history but also the interplay between Islamic law and the society in which it is rooted":

> ... it may be argued that Islamic law is ... based on a logic of consequence rather than a logic of antecedent. Instead of considering prior cases or similar examples, the *qadi* focuses on the consequence of actions as the index of validated assertions and as the criterion for judging social implications....
>
> Justice, then, lies not in the simple invocation of rights and duties but in their contextual assessment and the mode of analysis. Procedure and reasoning are central.

Lawrence Rosen, Equity and Discretion in a Modern Islamic Legal System, 15 *Law & Society Review* 217, 218, 242 (1980–1981).

A recent account of the current status of Khadi's Courts in Kenya by anthropologist Susan Hirsch similarly paints a picture of a complicated and highly rule-governed process. Hirsch's ethnography was based on research conducted from 1985 through 1993. She describes Khadi's Courts as sites of resistance to British-modeled secular rules of evidence and procedure, as well as to secular substantive law:

> Statutes proposed in the Kenyan Parliament that would reform the laws of marriage, divorce, and inheritance constitute blatant attempts to alter Muslim substantive law.... When the act became law in 1972, Muslims, including the kadhis, vowed to ignore it and to continue to apply Muslim laws of succession ...
>
> By turning opposition to the Succession Act into a political project for coastal Muslims, the Chief Kadhi also transforms the Kadhi's Courts into a rallying symbol for the community.

Susan Hirsch, *Pronouncing and Persevering: Gender and the Discourses of Disputing in an African Islamic Court*, at 134, 135 (1998). Rather than representing two different points on an evolutionary scale, here we see the Khadi Courts and westernized secular law as two simultaneous and competing systems. Khadis may be operating following a different kind of logic, but that does not mean that they are operating in an unsystematic or haphazard way.

Thus we see the potential distortions of relying too heavily on evolutionary models of law: "Today, legal anthropologists are no longer fixated with defining 'law' in other cultural settings. Gone is the need to either reinforce or belie a social evolutionary scale mapping the most sophisticated legal cultures through to those who have no identifiable legal system at all." Eve Darian–Smith, "Ethnographies of Law," in Austin Sarat, ed., *The Blackwell Companion to Law and Society*, at 545, 547 (2004). Instead, a great deal of attention has turned to examining the global dynamics involved in the spread of the westernized form of law which Weber identified in its infancy, and to studying the broad variety of indigenous legal systems and cultures that we find around the world. In doing this, some would argue that anthropology has honored a tradition associated with Weber, of turning away from "evolutionary and positivistic versions of sociology ... that sought to discover 'universal laws' of social development." Camic et al., eds., p. 6. What could Weber mean when he said that he was interested in studying the cause of change in legal systems, but not interested in discovering "universal laws"? Is there a difference between "evolution" and "history"? Could a system like capitalism, or formal-rational law, become almost universal across the globe without it being the result of an inevitable evolutionary process?

4.   Different forms of rationality—Sterling and Moore: Interestingly, the kind of logic that Rosen identifies in *qadi* justice is similar to a form of rationality that some scholars argue is missing from Weber's scheme. Joyce Sterling and Wilbert Moore explain the overall theory:

> Although Weber denied that he was posing a unilineal process of rationalization, he did tend to view legal systems as moving from irrational to rational and from substantive to formal rationality. However, he saw a chronic tension between the formal and substantive rationalization of law ... a tension that revolves around the issue of autonomy or predictability. From Weber's perspective, the need to resort to outside ethical or political systems for decision-making lessens the predictability and therefore formal rationality of the system ...; the attainment of formal-rational law would be inhibited by demands for substantive justice.
>
> What is unique about Weber's sociology of law is that he links his typology of legal thought to his typology of political structure.... [H]e identified three pure forms of legitimation: traditional, charismatic, and legal "domination" (rational authority). As law becomes rationalized it becomes its own legitimizing principle.... In logically formal-rational law, the universal principles derived from the legal system itself create the basis for legitimate domination. Weber suggested that there was a direct correlation between the rationalization of law and evolution toward legal domination....

Joyce Sterling and Wilbert Moore, "Weber's Analysis of Legal Rationalization: A Critique and Constructive Modification," 2 *Sociological Forum* 67, 75 (1987).

They go on to argue that Weber neglected an important formative aspect of legal systems: the "goals" of the system.[11] For example, a "culture may place ultimate value" on "economic prosperity." This, or some other goal, would be a "precondition" to "defining the forms of legal rules." They propose a category of "instrumental rationality" to account for this feature of legal development. If we accept this category, how might it affect our characterization of the *qadi* system of justice described by Rosen?

---

11. Weber might have countered that he would not attribute goals to a system, because of his focus on "methodological individualism." Camic et al., "Introduction."

5. <u>Legal evolution versus culture contact</u>: Sally Engle Merry notes that often change in legal systems results not from an internal evolutionary process, but through the imposition of colonial law:

> Colonial law was used to create a wage labor force available to the plantation, mine, and factory out of peasant and subsistence producers.... Much early regulation of colonized peoples forced them to become a capitalistic work force by requiring regular hours, punishing failure to work, outlawing festivals and other entertainments ... prohibiting alcoholic beverages, controlling vagabondage, and defining criminality....

Sally Engle Merry, "Anthropology, Law, and Transnational Processes," 21 *Annual Review of Anthropology* 357, 363–364 (1992). The colonial powers tended to consider traditional law, tribal law, or custom as if it were something fixed, unchanging, and inert. But in fact, the legal codes of colonized peoples were subtle and supple, both before and after the coming of the Europeans.

Merry and Mari Matsuda have each examined the transformation of law and culture in Hawaii. Mari Matsuda, "Law and Culture in the District Court of Honolulu, 1844–1845: A Case Study of the Rise of Legal Consciousness," 32 *American Journal of Legal History* 16 (1988); Sally Engle Merry, *Colonizing Hawai'i: The Cultural Power of Law* (2000). Matsuda examined the records of the basic courts that operated during the period of the Hawaiian monarchy. She found that Hawaiians "flocked to the new courts to resolve disputes and to punish crimes," although the courts were highly "Westernized."

As Matsuda notes, before the period of Western contact, there was a rich, vital Polynesian culture on the islands. Hawaiians lived "in villages tied by kinship." The social system was strongly hierarchical, ranging from commoners to great chiefs. There was a complex agricultural system. Cooperation, obedience, and collective effort were pillars of the economy. There "was no cash economy.... It was considered shameful to drive a hard bargain, or to fail to share with others in need."

The arrival of Western traders and missionaries had a profound effect on the polity, on religion, and on the economy. The Hawaiian monarchy established a system of courts. The judges were lay people, and the proceedings were conducted in the Hawaiian language. These courts decided a whole range of civil and criminal cases. On the criminal side, there were many cases of theft—a crime that once had been rare in the islands. But the "introduction of Western living" brought about much social change: Hawaiians moved to the port towns, "drawn by the promises of wealth and adventure that the traders brought." When Hawaiians became urbanized, they "left their constant source of food and shelter," and entered into the world of the "cash economy." The "social and cultural restraints against theft," such as "shame" and "ostracism," had been "effective in the communal villages," but these restraints worked much less well in the harbor-towns. Also, "Westerners introduced a whole new range of coveted goods," and many Hawaiians were caught in the "trap of rising expectations."

On the civil side, many of the cases in the courts indicate a changing conception of property. Matsuda reports:

Confusion over ownership and use is evident in the cases of theft or contract that follow this general pattern:

Party A: B has my horse and will not give it to me.

Party B: It is not his horse; it is my horse, A gave it to me.

Party A: I did not give it to him; I let him use it because he was my friend.

This paraphrased version of a story that is repeated in the Minute Books indicates the confusion that the concept of property engendered with Native Hawaiians. In pre-contact Hawaii, ownership of important goods, land, and resources was communal and was understood in terms of use rights rather than unitary absolute dominion. An individual or group may have had the right to gather thatch, for example, only from a particular section of land, and only during a particular time. Property was fragmented among various uses, various times, and various people. Families and groups of individuals could share components of property, and all were subject to the claims of others, such as the chiefs, that would take precedence. This sophisticated conception of ownership conflicted with the rather unsophisticated, unitary and physicalist conception of ownership introduced by nineteenth-century Westerners.

The Hawaiian conception of ownership was further complicated by the Hawaiian practice of giving away goods in exchange as part of the bonds of reciprocity and community. In the Hawaiian universe, the purpose of material wealth was to give it away and to thereby achieve a sense of self-worth and status, and to bind others to aid one in the future. In the Western universe, the purpose of material wealth was to hoard as much as possible so as to obtain more, to impress others, and to accumulate an abundance. The Hawaiians in Honolulu were becoming more and more attuned to the Western understanding of the purpose of property. This transition is also indicated in the many theft and contract cases that involve the pattern described above.

In the case of Kapule and Naihe, for example, Naihe reports how the trouble began:

The reason for this is my wife rode to Moanalua and the horse fell down. There is a piece of property Kapule and I enjoy. He was very hospitable and gave medical attention. Kapule gave my wife and me things to make our difficulty there more bearable. Afterwards we gave Kapule money and some clothes. Kapule even gave Keaka, my wife, a horse. Then Keaka said to me "I am embarrassed by Kapule, your punalua [2 men sharing the same woman], because he gave me a horse. I am thinking of giving our canoe to your punalua." I said no. My wife returned to Ewa. After that, Keaka spoke again to me and asked to give the canoe. I agreed to give the canoe because he gave that very valuable horse. That horse which was given to my wife, Kapule and another gave to Kaanaana, their daughter in Kahuku.

The exchange of property Naihe described is not Western-style, tit-for-tat barter. Rather, it is consistent with Hawaiian use of exchange to enhance mutual obligation and to achieve self-worth. As relations between the parties deteriorated, Naihe reported an entangled dispute that takes on a more Western conception of property:

> Kapule did not agree to this saying "these gourds were sold to Naihe. I sold them for $17.00." Then Kapule called for the money. [Naihe said] "I don't have it." That is what I said. Kapule said "I want to sail on our canoe." [I] gave it as [I] was done [with it]. Later Kapule came on that canoe. When I heard, I told my punalua to keep the canoe which he did. We three fought and I got the canoe. This is why I am keeping [it] because Kapule refused to give us [Naihe and Keaka] the horse.

The dispute then became a legal one, with each party claiming an enforceable right to the exchanged properties. The judges resolved the dispute by awarding Kapule the horse and Naihe the canoe. The Western conception of property—absolute dominion, individual ownership, legally enforceable title—prevailed and, more importantly, was promoted by the Native Hawaiians in their act of bringing this dispute to court.

The court records in general, says Matsuda, "suggest three ways in which law altered Hawaiian consciousness." First, the new "state-sponsored formal mechanism for dispute resolution" displaced "existing customary mechanisms." Moreover, the adoption of the new system "carried with it implicit assumptions about power. The power to decide disputes was the power to distribute land, goods, and wealth with finality." This power had once resided in the "hierarchy of the kinship community," but now the power had passed to the courts, thus further undermining traditional authority structures.

Second, the new legal system "promoted an ideology of property that competed with native ideology." Hawaiians came gradually to "accept the legitimacy of absolute, individual dominion over property." The new-fangled courts ignored the old system of "communal ownership and generous exchange." The new concept of property proved to be a concept of "irresistible force." Indeed, "the emergence of the concept of private property in lay discourse so early in the development of the system of statutes and courts suggests that the concept was transferred in part from lay Westerner to lay Hawaiian before the full-fledged, formal reception of Western law."

Third, the "system of legal rules and judicial enforcement provided a welcome mat" for foreigners interested in economic development and the introduction of capitalism. The law "welcomed business and the new business interests brought more people, things, and ideas that were non-Hawaiian."

Matsuda concludes with this point: "The ordinary Hawaiian, sometimes viewed as the passive victim of outside forces, was in fact an active and creative participant in the changing culture of the islands. Hawaiians used the courts and the law, adjusting quickly to a radically different social order." Unfortunately, the end result was arguable "harmful to Hawaiians," because it paved the way for the destruction of their culture and for the loss of their independence.

Merry's account, which accords with Matsuda's, examines the dynamics of this cultural shift. She divides the history of legal transformation in Hawaii into "two major transitions: first from Hawaiian law to a theocratic Hawaiian and Christian law and second to a secular law based on American models." She notes that in each transition, "there were complementarities and contradictions in the underlying cultural logics of the systems in play. Apparent similarities induced acceptance while differences pushed social change into new and unanticipated directions." (p. 45). For example, in the shift to Christian law, Hawaiian elites adopted legal regulations for which a deity (God) was the ultimate authority, just as had been the case in the traditional legal system. But there were key differences between traditional Hawaiian and the new Christian systems: the objective of Christian law was "the creation of a self charged with making itself through discipline and self-control" rather than the maintenance of the ties of community. This cultural change in how people thought about themselves and their communities was coupled with economic changes toward privately-owned property and contract labor. This permitted outsiders to gain possession of land, while use of courts for settling disputes replaced kin and community. Merry's analysis combines materialist and idealist factors in analyzing law's role in a major historical transition.

Both Matsuda and Merry agree that, although the overall process of transition was ultimately detrimental to Hawaiians, they were not mere passive receptacles of colonialism. Of course, the Hawaiian people did not freely choose the changes they made either, but Matsuda and Merry would argue that the Hawaiians did maneuver within the constraints that were imposed on them by the encroaching Western economic and political systems. What would be an example of that kind of maneuvering? Does it really make a difference?

6. <u>Confusing culture contact with legal evolution</u>: A classic article in the law and economics tradition demonstrates the potential distortion that arises when Western theorists use evolutionary models to explain legal change. Harold Demsetz, "Toward a Theory of Property Rights," 57 *American Economic Review* 347 (1967). Demsetz's article tracks the emergence of conceptions of property from the "primitive" communal world of "aboriginals" or Robinson Crusoe (where such concepts are supposed to be unnecessary), through a progression to modern "civilization" with its emphasis on private property. One key example in the article comes from a study of the Montagnais (a Native American group in Canada) by anthropologist Eleanor Leacock. Demsetz uses Leacock's research to argue that the evolution of private

property rights in this group was a natural response to the overhunting of game. (p. 351). He does actually acknowledge that this overhunting of game resulted from the introduction (by French colonists) of the fur trade into the region. However, the fact of culture contact itself does not figure in his account of the subsequent shift to private property, despite the fact that the colonists brought the concept of private property (and an accompanying notion of legal claims) to the area, along with the fur trade. As support for his thesis, Demsetz notes that "the geographical or distributional evidence collected by Leacock indicates an unmistakable correlation between early centers of fur trade and the oldest and most complete development of the private hunting territory." (p. 352). Of course, these were also the geographical arenas in which the most culture contact occurred.

Demsetz's article became widely cited, particularly by scholars in the law-and-economics tradition. To the degree that Demsetz's original theory did acknowledge some complexity, it was certainly lost in many subsequent translations, which have discussed the transition to private property among the Montagnais as if it were part of a positive and inevitable evolution rather than as the result of pressure from an encroaching colonialist and capitalist power. Commentators citing Demsetz have gone so far as to assert that the communal systems of "primitive man" were actually inherently more damaging to wildlife and the environment than capitalist systems based in private property. Robert J. Smith, "Resolving the Tragedy of the Commons by Creating Private Property Rights in Wildlife," 1 *Cato Journal* 439 (1981). One doubts that Eleanor Leacock, the author of the study on which Demsetz relied, would agree with this conclusion. Her work traced the deleterious effects of encroaching capitalism on everything from indigenous communities generally to gender relationships in particular. Eleanor Leacock, *The Montagnais "Hunting Territory" and the Fur Trade* (1954); Eleanor Leacock, "Montagnais Women and the Jesuit Program for Colonization," in M. Etienne and E. Leacock, eds., *Women and Colonization* 25 (1980).

7. <u>Does law in capitalist systems have to be highly "formal rational"?</u> Weber distinguishes between continental (that is, European) "methods of legal thought" and common law methods (found in England). He notes that the English system departs significantly from his ideal type of formal rationality: "English law-finding is not, like that of the Continent, 'application' of 'legal propositions' logically derived from statutory texts." Remember that Weber thinks of the English system as more like "qadi justice," or more "empirical"—that is, as more based on individual factual determinations than on application of abstract principles. However, as Weber points out, England was a center for the development of capitalism. If in Weber's model, formal rationality in law is necessary to capitalist economic systems—then England seems to pose a problem. See David Trubek, "Max Weber on Law and the Rise of Capitalism," 1972 *Wisconsin Law Review* 720.

Weber goes on to name two features of law that support the development of capitalism, in England as well as in other places: (1) the legal profession is financially dependent on and tied to "capitalistic, private interests," and (2) the cost of going to court means that "those with inadequate means" are unlikely to have access to justice. One could argue that Weber actually viewed these two factors as the most important aspects of law in capitalist systems, since he clearly recognized (citing the examples of England and Canada) that a high level of formal rationality in law was not necessarily associated with the spread of capitalist economic systems.

Scholars have also suggested that Weber viewed "calculability" as different from (and more important than) a high degree of formal rationality in capitalist legal systems. Richard Swedberg, *Max Weber and the Idea of Economic Sociology*, 106 (1998). Under this view, law must produce predictable resolutions to disputes in order for capitalist enterprises to flourish—but that doesn't mean that it has to be very formal-rational. Can you explain how a legal system that is low in formal rationality could still be very predictable?

Other scholars have criticized Weber's characterization of English law, pointing out that Weber

> misses the "formal-rational" element in the English emphasis on analogy of cases, preferring to see at work in the common-law courts not the close analysis of comparable judicial decisions in order to extract the principles and rules implicit in them, but the personal, charismatic authority of judges. . . .

Harold Berman and Charles Reid, Jr., "Max Weber as Legal Historian," in Stephen Turner, ed., *The Cambridge Companion to Weber*, at p. 230 (2000). In fact, the common law method does not remain only at the "empirical" level of facts, as Berman and Reid point out, but moves continuously back and forth between abstract and particular levels, further developing in law the capacity to adapt to new situations while maintaining continuity with the past. Elizabeth Mertz argues that this use of analogy (and accompanying forms of reasoning) in fact fits very well with the basic orientation of capitalist societies. Elizabeth Mertz, *Law School Language: Learning to "Think Like a Lawyer"* (2007). She uses a linguistic analysis of the way analogy is taught to first-year law students to demonstrate the way legal language systematizes the concrete details of disputes at a more abstract level.

8.   Western Law and Economic Development: Is a legal system modeled on modern Western legal systems necessary for economic development? Pointing to the example of Taiwan's economic success, Jane Kaufman Winn expresses skepticism. Jane Kaufman Winn, "Relational Practices and the Marginalization of Law: Informal Financial Practices of Small Businesses in Taiwan," 28 *Law & Society Review* 193 (1994). She finds that the "relational structure of traditional rural Chinese society has survived in a modified form in modern Taiwan, and this modern form selectively blends elements of the modern legal system, networks of relationships, and the enforcement services of organized crime." Taiwan's legal system indirectly supports relational practices rather than working through the kind of universal normative order often associated with the idea of a modern legal system. See also Frank K. Upham, "Speculations on Legal Informality: On Winn's 'Relational Practices

and the Marginalization of Law' ", 28 *Law & Society Review* 233 (1994). Could we say that the United States' legal system indirectly supports relational practices rather than working through the kind of universal normative order often associated with the idea of a modern legal system? See the picture painted by Macaulay in his article reproduced in Chapter 2. Wolf Heydebrand, "Process Rationality as Legal Governance," 18 *International Sociology* 325 (2003), argues that while scholars today persist in debating Max Weber's formal and substantive rationality of legal rules, the reality of most Western legal systems is something that Heydebrand calls "negotiated process rationality." This is a mode of governance based on the "logic of informal, negotiated processes within social and sociolegal networks." These networks are not accountable to elected or appointed officials. Negotiated process rationality tolerates diversity and indeterminacy, and it does not yield transparent highly predictable law. To the degree that it affects the outcome of disputes, we lose constitutional safeguards, and we lose both substantive and procedural rights. Moreover, some individuals and interests will be able to play the game of informal, negotiated processes better than others.

John Ohnesorge has reviewed the publications of international organizations such as the World Bank and USAID which actively promote a Western model of the "rule of law" in non-Western nations—as well as commentaries by political leaders and scholars who deal with the concept. John Ohnesorge, "The Rule of Law, Economic Development, and the Developmental States of Northeast Asia" in *Law and Development in East and Southeast Asia* 91 (Christoph Antons ed., 2003). Ohnesorge finds that the non-lawyers tend to assume that presence of the "rule of law" implies that a society is governed by a totally complete and functioning legal system. A society either is characterized by the rule of law or it is not. These writers assume that legal rules are "not subject to significant indeterminacy, and that these are sufficient to provide single correct solutions without resorting to principles, policies or purposes." (Id. at fn. 9.) They also assume that the rule of law is useful because the more the future can be made predictable, the easier it is to plan and take risks in a capitalist society.

By contrast, Ohnesorge notes that legal scholars tend to see the rule of law only as an aspiration. A society honors the rule of law when a high number of its characteristics are met a high percentage of the time. These scholars have read many cases where the rules and their application to the facts were debatable. They are skeptical about whether single correct solutions exist for the kinds of cases that are filtered into appellate courts. Legal realism and experience have taught lawyers that the outcome of particular cases can never be perfectly certain. Under this view, even Westernized capitalist legal systems are unlikely to achieve the level of complete rationalization imagined by non-lawyers.

Ohnesorge points to examples from Asia to demonstrate that it is possible to reach high levels of economic development with legal systems that are, at best, substantively rational. In other words, modern Asian developments pose another "England problem" for those who think that capitalist economies and strictly formal rationality must go hand-in-hand.

9. Formal and Substantive Rationality in Today's Legal System: How does Weber's theory work out when we try to map the current legal system in the United States? Ronen Shamir argues that we can track a continuous cycling between formal and substantive rationality through the history of legal changes in the United States:

> [A]t least in the United States, formally-rational law was developed from within a court-centered system which relied on analogies and precedents, rather than statutory rules, as a basis for its "rationalization". In this configuration, codified law was considered as the ultimate embodiment of substantive-rational law. The enemies of statutory legislation viewed it as a manifestation of arbitrary considerations, as the invasion and corruption of autonomous law, as the enemy of formal rationality. The advocates of the transition from a court-centered system to a system that relied more heavily on statutory legislation, on the other hand, advanced the consciously articulated claim that an enlightened law should be more responsive to social and political considerations and less self-protective by an illusion of an autonomous system of logical rules.
>
> In short, I try to show that the legal realists led a movement in the direction of a "German" legal system: one that relied on statutory rules, enacted by a strong federal state, and developed by academic experts at the direct and indirect service of the state. Unlike Weber's model, this movement was conceived by its carriers as a shift away from, rather than towards, formally-rational law. (p. 46)

> * * *

> [T]he interplay between ideally formal and ideally substantive law corresponds to the interplay between periods of stability and reform in the political arena . . . (p. 63)

> Autonomous law is discarded when its internal tensions and inconsistencies can no longer be sustained. But in order to institutionalize and permanently root desired reforms, a reawakening of formal rationality, as a means of ensuring stability, security and predictability, is again called for. In the sphere of the economic market, this means that the same old capitalists may dominate again after such "radical" changes as, say, the Wagner Relations Act. In the legal sphere, this means that legalistic orientations and strict formal procedures regain their power, albeit under new conditions. It is by invoking Weber's analysis that we may grasp the cycle of *formal rationality—internal contradictions—substantive rationality—substantive irrationality—routinization—formal rationality.* Social change and progress appear, when they do, in the form of a spiral ascent: important and radical changes are introduced through substantive rationality; once in place, formal rationality, albeit on a new "progressive" level, reappears. (p. 64–65)

Ronen Shamir, "Formal and Substantive Rationality in American Law: A Weberian Perspective," 2 *Social & Legal Studies* 45 (1993). Jennings et al. examined the way rules within a single regional water law changed over a 90 year period. P. Devereaux Jennings, et al., "Weber and Legal Rule Evolution: The Closing of the Iron Cage?" 26 *Organization Studies* 621 (2005). They describe finding a cycle between periods of expansion of rules, on the one hand, and periods of refinement or contraction, on the other. Thus they do not find a relentless proliferation of formal-rational rules over time—although they raise the possibility that periodic revision and cutting-down of rules may be rational in a different sense.

Duncan Kennedy shares Shamir's conclusion that logically formal rationality cannot be sustained without interruption, because it inevitably leads to contradictions or gaps. Duncan Kennedy, "The Disenchantment of Logically Formal Rationality," in Charles Camic et al., eds., *Max Weber's "Economy and Society": A Critical Companion* 322 (2005). According to Kennedy, law repeatedly has to adapt to new external conditions. But a model of logically formal rationality [or LFR] fails to take account of this kind of change, because it presupposes a "gap-less" system of internal logic, based on enacted legal norms. Proponents of LFR thus have to engage in what Kennedy calls "abuse of deduction": "They had to make decisions reached on other grounds look like the operation of deductive work premised on the coherence of the system." (p. 338). Kennedy views LFR as becoming increasingly implausible even during Weber's lifetime (which was from 1864–1920). This was true not only because of the ongoing "abuse of deduction" that was occurring, but also because "the dynamism of the capitalist economy generated, constantly, increasingly, legal gaps or conflicts involving large economic and political stakes." (p. 352–353). Thus Kennedy does not view LFR as a good way of ensuring predictability or certainty in law at all, stressing that conforming to LFR is not a way to " 'guarantee certainty' for reasons of economic functionality, or to 'guarantee respect for the separation of powers' between judge and legislator". Frequently, judges in high-stakes cases are confronted with a choice between different plausibly-applicable rules—rules derived from contradictory principles. Logically formal rationality is of no help because

> it is LFR itself that has presented us with the choice in question. LFR has proved internally indeterminate. We can't just "stick to LFR".... With respect to the particular, high-stakes problem that the judge is asked to decide by choosing among alternative-candidate, valid rules, *there is no LFR to "stick to."* Denying this, and proceeding merrily along in full "fidelity to law," or some other such nonsense, is exactly what we mean by the abuse of deduction. (p. 353–354)

In Kennedy's view, then, LFR has been discredited for a long time now. He examines what legal thinkers have done in the wake of a credible theory of LFR, and concludes that a core solution in Europe and the U.S. has been the move to "policy analysis." Policy analysis openly admits that the legal system has to continually deal with conflicting norms, as well as with gaps in deductive law. It requires that we find ways to balance or compromise between these norms, constructing a new norm that will maximize the overall value achieved through the decision (value as determined vis-à-vis "universal" principles such as efficiency, or rights). Kennedy thus characterizes the policy analysis common in U.S. legal reasoning today as a form of "formalized substantive rationality." Kennedy argues that it is "substantive" because "the content of policy analysis is derived from the general political, moral, religious, and expediential goals that drive government in the society as a whole." (p. 358). At the same time, he characterizes policy analysis as "formal," even though it openly acknowledges that it operates in a system where there are normative conflicts and gaps:

> That means that "value judgments" are also inevitable. All that can be hoped for is to make them as rationally as possible—that is, in a way that poses the least danger ... of incalculability and/or politicization of the adjudicative process. This is accomplished within the contemporary mode of policy analysis by incorporating the question of the calculability of the chosen rule, and the question of the appropriate division of lawmaking power between judge and legislature, into the policy analysis itself. (p. 360)

Thus the rules produced by policy analysis are supposed to provide a means of calculation as well as a way of safeguarding the separation between law and politics (or judge and legislator).

How do Shamir and Kennedy differ in their models of the relationship between formal and substantive rationality in today's U.S. legal system?

10. <u>Incommensurability and the Limits of Western Law</u>: There is growing interest in sociology in the issue of "commensurability," defined as "the transformation of different qualities into a common metric." Wendy Espeland and Mitchell Stevens, "Commensuration as a Social Process," 24 *Annual Review of Sociology* 313 (1998). If a key goal of law in capitalist societies is to provide calculable solutions to economic problems, then commensuration is a predictably useful legal tool—it allows lawyers and judges to take all kinds of different problems, settings, and people, and to convert them into a common metric. In her work on the legal struggle for water rights among the Yavapai, Espeland traces an eventual confrontation between the rational decision framework used by the U.S. Bureau of Reclamation (a framework heavily steeped in techniques of commensuration) and the way the Yavapai themselves understood the significance of their land and history. Wendy Espeland, *The Struggle for Water: Politics, Rationality, and Identity in the American Southwest* (1998); Wendy Espeland, "Legally Mediated Identity: The National Environmental Policy Act and the Bureaucratic Construction of Interests," 28 *Law & Society Review* 1149 (1994). As one Yavapai teenager explained, "The land is our mother. You don't sell your mother." (p. 1149). Not only did the Bureau assume that land could be translated into money, it also assumed that the non-monetary costs and benefits of building a dam (that would flood Yavapai lands) could be rendered in a common metric and weighed against each other. As Espeland notes, concepts such as "intrinsic" value, or "price-

lessness" do not make sense in this scheme. To the Yavapai, however, their land, culture, shared history, and ability to survive "as a people" were at stake—and these values were indeed incommensurable. U.S. legal approaches failed at multiple levels to translate this perspective, from the categories used by the administrative agency charged with measuring the costs and benefits of this action, through the law's assumption that formal procedural mechanisms could solve problems of this kind:

> In treating universalistically all those who were designated as having "a stake" in the outcome of this decision, the law, as it was implemented by the bureau, transformed all relationships to the proposed policy into some common standard: qualities became quantities, difference became magnitude. . . . What was presumed to be a neutral and fair way of categorizing and sorting information turned out to be a framework that many Yavapai felt misrepresented not only their interests but them. Law also required that culture be transformed into a category called an "impact" and that culture be interpreted as an entity about which predictions can be made, sustained, and documented. (p. 1172)

In weighing all the possible benefits and costs of the dam, the Bureau came up with a set of measures that included the preferences of a variety of people possibly affected by the plan, described as a "Social Well Being Account" and expressed numerically. Espeland reports: "As one elder expressed it: 'White men like to count things that aren't there.' " (p. 1166). How would Weber analyze this situation? On the one hand, our ability to translate vastly different situations into a common metric through law can be a useful tool in a large-scale society. On the other hand, we can see that there are dangers and limitations to this approach as well. (Mertz 2007 discusses this at length; see note 8 above, and Chapter 6.)

IV. How Does Social Change Affect Legal Change?

(A) Core Models: The Effects of Elites, Class Domination, Culture, Structure, and Process

(1) The Social Context of Legal Change: General Theories

In this section we examine models of the relationship between social change and changes in the law. We begin by describing five basic approaches: "great man," conflict, cultural, structural, and process models. These can overlap, or be combined to produce a complicated picture of how a number of social factors interact to influence law. We also discuss the postulated mechanisms by which changes in society and culture might drive legal change. One such mechanism, discussed throughout this chapter, is public opinion (which is itself analyzed in a number of different ways by scholars from different schools of thought).

(a) "Great man" models and the question of "lag": (Conceptualizing history and law): Albert V. Dicey, an English legal scholar, offered what has become a classic theory of the influence of what he called "public opinion" on social and legal change. In his lectures given at the Harvard Law School in 1898, Dicey locates the beginning of these changes in a new idea that "presents itself to some one man *[sic]* of originality or genius."[12] Dicey is thinking of people such as Adam Smith, Bentham, or Darwin; the list could be augmented in many ways, of course (some might want to add Marx, for example, or Simone de Beauvoir, or W.E.B. DuBois).

Then, according to Dicey, the great man's friends adopt the idea and "preach" it to others. Gradually a whole school "accept[s] the creed." As time passes, "the preachers of truth make an impression, either directly upon the general public or upon some person of eminence, say a leading statesman, who stands in a position to impress ordinary people and thus to win the support of the nation" (p. 23). However, something must happen so that people will listen to a truly new idea and change their values. Dicey talks of "accidental conditions" which enable popular leaders to seize the opportunity. His example is the Irish famine, which enabled political leaders to gain public acceptance of Adam Smith's doctrine of free trade. Professor Marc Galanter has diagrammed Dicey's theory as follows:

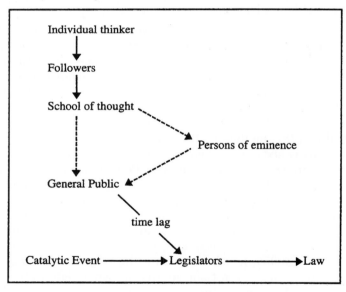

There are a number of difficulties with this approach. First, the picture of a single line flowing from one "great man" is overly simplistic. At any one

12. Dicey, *Lectures on the Relation Between Law and Public Opinion in England During* *the Nineteenth Century*, 2d ed. (1914).

time, a number of schools of thought flowing from different "great men" may be in contention. In Dicey's day, arguably, both Adam Smith and Karl Marx were producing novel, important ideas. Obviously, some schools of thought will be more appealing than others to influential statesmen of the day; ideas may gain currency not because of their merit, but because of their relative political appeal. Second, as Dicey himself recognized, laws will sometimes be introduced in response to crises, and then the fact of the new law itself can influence public opinion: "Laws of emergency often surreptitiously introduce or reintroduce into legislation, ideas which would not be accepted [otherwise] ..." (p. 45). Dicey notes that "A principle derives prestige from its mere recognition by Parliament" (pp. 41–42).

How, then, does an idea move from being accepted by the leading statesmen in Dicey's theory into general public opinion? Dicey talks of a "gradual, or slow, or continuous" (p. 27) process by which tides of public opinion developed in England. He defines public opinion as the opinion of "the majority of those citizens who have at a given moment taken an effective part in public life" (p. 10). On the one hand, Dicey's approach seems to rest on a theory of almost religious conversion, where people are moved by the sheer power of an idea to adopt it. But the history of change that he traces proceeds quite slowly; there are few abrupt changes. This leads Dicey to talk about a process of lag in legal change:

> Thus it may well happen that an innovation is carried through at a time when the teachers who supplied the arguments in its favour are in their graves, or even—and this is well worth noting—when in the world of speculation a movement has already set in against ideas which are exerting their full effect in the world of action and of legislation. Bentham's Defence of Usury supplied every argument which is available against laws which check freedom of trade in money-lending. It was published in 1787; he died in 1832. The usury rules were wholly repealed in 1854, that is sixty-seven years after Bentham had demonstrated their futility; but in 1854 the opponents of Benthamism were slowly gaining the ear of the public, and the Money-lenders' Act, 1900, has shown that the almost irrebuttable presumption against the usury laws which was created by the reasoning of Bentham has lost its hold over men who have never taken the pains or shown the ability to confute Bentham's arguments.... Law-making in England is the work of men well advanced in their life.... English legislators retain the prejudices or modes of thinking which they acquired in their youth; and when, late in life, they take a share in actual legislation, they legislate in accordance with the doctrines which were current, either generally or in the society to which the law-givers belonged, in the days of their early manhood....

> We need not therefore be surprised to find that a current of opinion may exert its greatest legislative influence just when its force is beginning to decline.... among men of a younger generation who are not yet able to influence legislation.

Dicey sees judges as even more likely to lag behind public opinion than legislators, because although somewhat swayed by then-current trends of thought, "they are also guided by professional opinions and ways of thinking which are, to a certain extent, independent of and possibly opposed to the general tone of public opinion.... They are men advanced in life. They are for the most part persons of a conservative disposition." (p. 363–364). Notice all the empirical and cultural assumptions (including many about age and aging) that are embedded in Dicey. Friedman and Ladinsky will have more to say on the question of legal change through history, the role of "great men," and the issue of "lag."

(b) Conflict models (*Law and power*): There is a sharp contrast between the model proposed by Dicey and the views of theorists proposing what have been labeled "conflict models." Scholars writing from a conflict perspective challenge the idea that law reflects a neutral public consensus about values. Law represents, instead, an exercise of power, no matter how the power-holders rationalize what they are doing. In the struggle over resources in society, some will come to dominate others. Law legitimates the use of violence, or the threat of violence, against those who disagree with the dominant view. See, e.g., Emilio Lamo de Espinosa, "Social and Legal Order in Sociological Functionalism," 4 *Contemporary Crisis* 43 (1980).

The work of Marxist theorist Antonio Gramsci (1891–1937) provides an example. Gramsci was a leader of the Italian Communist Party who was imprisoned by Mussolini. Unlike many Marxists, Gramsci rejected the idea that political developments can be explained as an expression of economic structure. He wrote instead about the cultural ascendancy of the dominant class, which occurred through a process of hegemony or cultural control. Hegemonic ideas persuade people to cooperate with legal and social systems that are unfair to them, operating against their interests. This makes physical coercion unnecessary except in the most extreme instances. Under Gramsci's theory, the ruling class controls the ideas that people find acceptable because it controls political parties, schools, universities, the mass media, churches, and the like:

> Except in times of acute stress, the dominant class preserves its hegemony over others because all the classes accept a world view in which the existing order is seen as natural and proper. This general consciousness underlies legal rules, literature, economic behavior, and indeed everything that people do.... Power explains the persistence of some interpretations of shared values; it does not ... explain innovation ... To use it we must explain how all people came to share a world view which advanced the interests of only some of them.

Gramsci points to the work of "traditional intellectuals" as the mechanism for achieving consensus. In the American context, the people who articulate systems of values have included lawyers, ministers, and journalists. These intellectuals, often having roots in the dominant class, translate the values and habits of that class into an ideology which becomes "common sense." Sometimes, especially in democracies, this happens in mobilizing political support.... One aspect of this mobilization of popular support is that intellectuals must develop new concepts of the proper world order in response to changes in the material basis of the dominant class' power. Thus, as the economic focus of the dominant class changed from land to industry, industrialism was changed in the intellectual and then popular view from a monster which would destroy the American Eden into a benevolent donor of material well-being. When power relations between different groups in society change, the ideological system which once adequately justified the relation of one group to another will have to adjust.[13]

Notice that changes in economic and power relations are still driving forces in this theory, but the key operating mechanism that holds the system in place involves ideas rather than raw force or economic exigency.

When we compare Dicey and Gramsci, we see that Dicey generally approves of the system that he describes while Gramsci views it as a system of exploitation. However, apart from this divergence in assessments, how much difference do you see between Dicey's and Gramsci's descriptions of the role of public opinion in legal change?

It is also possible to stress the role of conflict in society and law without positing law as a straightforward tool of the ruling classes. Austin Turk, "Law as a Weapon in Social Conflict," 23 *Social Problems* 276 (1976), points out that, even when it is not corrupted (for example, as in Gramsci's model, by class interests), the legal system may promote conflict rather than social integration. Control of the system itself, for example, is a prize about which groups can fight—the power to appoint judges and administrators is one of the things gained by winning elections. Moreover, the chance to mobilize whatever power the courts possess can be an incentive to abandon acceptance of the status quo. The chance of victories before the courts and legislature may undercut compromise, generating more conflict rather than stabilizing the society. Unpopular statutes or court decisions may provoke great dissensus. The abortion decisions of the United States Supreme Court, for example, were not the product of consensus nor did they produce consensus about how the society should deal with abortion.

(c) Cultural models (Law as culture): Anthropologists have for many years explored the relationship that exists between culture and law. As Sally Falk Moore explains, the fact of this relationship does not mean "that law is tradition-driven," but it simply means that law is part of a package of "durable customs, ideas, values, habits, and practices."[14] Sally Falk Moore,

13. Mark Tushnet, "Lumber and the Legal Process," 1972 *Wisconsin Law Review* 114, 130–131.

14. Moore's definition incorporates both "ideas" and "practices." Some would argue for a definition of "culture" that only includes beliefs and ideas, opposing it to material aspects of social life (such as economic structure). It is fair to say that over recent decades, there is a tendency toward integration of these diverse strands in cultural anthropology as a whole, and legal anthropology in particular.

"Certainties Undone: Fifty Turbulent Years of Legal Anthropology, 1949–1999", in Sally Moore, ed., *Law and Anthropology: A Reader* (2005). Clifford Geertz made a strong argument for this point of view in his Storrs Lectures given in 1981 at the Yale Law School. Clifford Geertz, *Local Knowledge: Further Essays in Interpretive Anthropology* (1983). Like Paul Bohannon before him, Geertz focused on the particular shape of cultural understandings in each society. Different cultures will have divergent, characteristic ideas about law or rules or justice, for example—and this will affect the way legal problems are resolved. Geertz stressed that "the world is a various place, various between lawyers and anthropologists, various between Muslims and Hindus, . . . and much is to be gained, scientifically and otherwise, by confronting that grand actuality rather than wishing it away in a haze of forceless generalities and false comforts." (p. 234). How does this fit with Espeland's conception of incommensurability?

Under this approach, we would ask if legal change is shaped by changes in cultural ideas shared by the people in a society. However, one criticism of some forms of cultural analysis is precisely that they do not lend themselves to examinations of change; rather, they tend to focus on enduring systems of meaning.[15] Critics have also argued that the culture concept reifies the complex diversity that actually exists among people, beliefs, and practices in any given society—converting them into a statically-conceived unit ("a culture") with deceptively clear boundaries. These deceptive boundaries permit anthropologists and others to conceptualize people as "other" or as "exotic"— as if everyone in a particular (usually non-Western) society could be summed up through a listing of cultural stereotypes ("they" believe x, or approach emotion in one "typical" way, etc.).

On the other hand, the culture concept may well be one of those ideas that social scientists "can't live with, but can't live without." It continues to appear in many analyses whose focus is on how one set of people's shared beliefs and worldviews make a difference in their lives, or perhaps how they diverge from another peoples' beliefs. Today, however, most anthropologists would approach this analysis with much more care, acknowledging divergences within supposedly shared cultures, as well as the fuzzy nature of the boundaries (if any) that separate people with supposedly different cultures.

Thus cultural analysis includes an examination of how ideas are integrated with lived experience, while analysis of economic structure also incorporates the role of cultural ideas. Mark Goodale and Elizabeth Mertz, "Anthropology of Law," in David Clark, ed., *Encyclopedia of Law and Society: American and Global Perspectives* (2007). This is a theme that can be found in a number of kinds of anthropological and sociological theories—one example is sociologist Pierre Bourdieu's concept of "habitus," which combines both cognitive and physical orientations to cultural and social experi-

ence. Pierre Bourdieu, *Outline of a Theory of Practice* (1977).

15. Even early theories of "culture" in anthropology did incorporate mechanisms for change—whether through response to changes in environment, contact with other cultures (cultural diffusion), useful internal innovations or inventions, or processes of "acculturation" (often actually through colonization). However, when anthropologists began to analyze the effects of colonialism in earnest, they tended to move beyond the culture concept into models that also included issues of power, force, and domination.

There is also increased attention to the way global connections are affecting the multiple layers of "culture" within any given society; for example, teenagers in very different parts of the world may listen to the same music or absorb ads for the same products—and along with the music and ads they may take in new ideas about their identity as "teenagers," consumers, etc.

We will explore a related idea—the concept of "legal culture"—below. As we will see, legal culture can be understood as an intervening step between general social/cultural change and changes in the law.

(d) Social structural models (Law as a result of social structure): Some other models stress the impact of basic social structure on law. The study by Richard Schwartz of Israeli settlements, for example, focused on the structure of the settlements in asking about the effects of society on law. Sally Merry also examined the structure of social networks and living spaces in asking why some people resort to the formal legal system while others do not. This kind of approach would look at social structural change as an important input to legal changes. Different living arrangements and economic structures will tend to produce divergent legal systems, because different laws are needed to support and police each distinctive system. Notice that there is a close connection here between social structure and social function: the structure of society causes law to have a particular shape, but in many models this is because of functional needs. For example, societies need to resolve disputes if they are to function well. But suppose that a society cannot resolve disputes through gossip and informal negotiation because its members don't see each other enough, or don't know each other well enough. Because of the way that society is structured (i.e., a loosely integrated structure), it will need to have this function (resolving disputes) performed in a different way. This is often referred to as a "structural-functional" model.

The structural-functionalist approach emerged from a tradition in sociology that explains society and law as the product of social consensus. It leans heavily on an analogy between society and the organism of the human body (the so-called "organic analogy").[16] The human body is conceptualized as structured into parts, each of which performs a function that keeps the whole organism going, in a state of equilibrium. This is obviously not a model that emphasizes change. But if change occurs—say, because one part of the system is altered from the outside, thereby knocking all the other parts out of equilibrium—then, the assumption is that the system will soon move back

---

16. Key figures in the development of structural-functionalist theory included French sociologist Emile Durkheim and U.S. sociologist Talcott Parsons. Emile Durkheim, *The Division of Labor in Society* (1984); Talcott Parsons, *Structure of Social Action*, Vol. I (1968), as well as anthropologists A.R. Radcliffe–Brown and E. E. Evans–Pritchard, who used this approach in their ethnographic work on African societies. A.R. Radcliffe–Brown, *Structure and Function in Primitive Society* (1965);

E.E. Evans–Pritchard, *Kinship and Marriage Among the Nuer* (1965). By contrast, anthropologist Bronislaw Malinowski advocated a "functionalist" approach focused on the way societies function to meet individuals' basic needs (i.e., for food, social exchange, etc.). This kind of individual-focused functionalism is different from "structural functionalism," which examines how parts of a social structure function to keep the whole of society working.

into ordered functioning at a new level. The modal form of social existence is not conflictual; societies function because of a high degree of consensus.

One criticism of this approach is that it over-emphasizes consensus and equilibrium, thereby missing the way societies are often characterized by fundamental conflicts. Furthermore, just because society "functions" for some people does not mean that it is working for everyone. And it is easy, using this model, to assume that everything in the status quo is a necessary part of maintaining the system; whereas some parts of the structure may not be functional at all. Conflict theorists, as we've seen, contend that society is not harmonious and stable but is held together by the use or threats of force. Law on the ground, they remind us, can consist of police officers with clubs, or a SWAT team with automatic weapons attacking any group that threatens the stability of the existing order. Instead of normative consensus, conflict theorists say that those at the bottom of the distribution of wealth and status see cheating, manipulation or simple resignation as the ways to cope with an unjust system which cannot be confronted directly.

Interestingly, social structural models can point in very different political and theoretical directions. For example, some Marxist models view the law as a response to economic structure: indeed, they talk about law as part of a "superstructure" that rests upon the foundation of an economic base. Exploitive economic systems are policed by legal systems, which may clothe themselves in contrary rhetoric but in fact simply serve the interests of the dominant class. Law is a mere reflex of the economy, and the government is in no way independent of class interests. This is obviously a kind of "conflict" model; it is also a "materialist" model, because it prioritizes economic needs over ideas and culture. (As we saw with Gramsci, not all Marxist theorists use crude materialist models. Some incorporate the power of ideas and thought to a greater extent in their models of how society operates, and in analyzing the development of law. Indeed, some would argue that although it does help the powerful in many instances, the government or state has some degree of autonomy from class interests—that the legal system can in some cases deliver victories for the working class.)

On the other hand, more conservative economic models also prioritize the economic foundation of society over ideas. They understand the drive for economic efficiency as a core organizing force in society, and view the aim of law as to help in maximizing efficiency. People are characterized as "rational actors," an approach that basically eliminates from the model the effects of emotion, or of intellectual and cultural ideas that exist outside of a rational calculus. This is also a materialist model; it simply differs from the Marxist model in its normative assessment of the situation—Marxists think that the overpowering effects of economic factors on everything else in capitalist systems are detrimental, while conservative economists tend to think that they are positive.

Structural, and structural-functionalist approaches to law do not generally focus on change as an issue. When change does occur, they tend to approach it as a temporary disruption that will be resolved as all the parts of the system realign themselves—whether simply in the service of continued consensual functioning, or to reinforce class distinctions and inequalities, or to return to efficiency.

(e) Processual models (Dispute resolution and problem solving): Finally, a model derived from cross-cultural anthropological research begins by asking how problems or disputes are resolved. Law is a studied as a process. Some scholars using this perspective would stress law's role as an important mechanism for dealing with conflict in society. Indeed, the model can fit well with structural-functionalist approaches, if it analyzes law as performing a function that is useful in keeping an organic, consensual society going. (Of course, you could also analyze law as a process for resolving disputes without assuming that this process keeps an overarching social structure functioning.) Note that, for anthropologists, the processual approach has the advantage of not requiring hierarchical or teleological assessments of the "evolution" of law—instead, all societies and legal systems can be viewed as being at the same level. They face a similar functional problem (resolving disputes) and they do it in a variety of ways. When dispute resolution models focus on the many ways diverse cultures think about problems and disputes, they can also be drawing on cultural approaches to law. Legal anthropologists have combined analyses of the cultural logic of legal processes with studies of how law affects social practices on the ground. John Comaroff and Simon Roberts, *Rules and Processes: The Cultural Logic of Dispute in an African Context* (1986).

Interest in the variety of ways in which societies solve problems led to scholarly research on many kinds of alternatives to formal Western litigation. This paralleled growing interest among U.S. legal professionals in forms of alternative dispute resolution (ADR) like mediation and arbitration. Anthropologists who wrote in this area stressed the importance of looking at law as a process on the ground, as it works out in people's lives. At the same time, legal theorists began to explore the benefits of ADR over formal legal proceedings, and U.S. courts turned increasingly to mediation and other alternatives in realms like family law. Despite the fact that dispute resolution models are arguably less biased or ethnocentric than some others, they have nonetheless been criticized as overly focused on consensus or harmony—as assuming that continuing conflict is a problem to be resolved, rather than a necessary response to social inequalities and injustices. For example, if the legal system puts pressure on battered wives to "be nice" and cooperate in mediation during divorce, they may wind up in informal settings where they can be more easily coerced and bullied. Anthropologist Laura Nader and others have also written about the dangers of exporting Western-formulated "harmony models" such as mediation to non-Western countries—especially without adequate understanding of the specific sociocultural situations in which they are being used. Laura Nader, *The Life of the Law: Anthropological Projects* (2002). This critique stresses the idea that process cannot be simply extracted from, or imported into, social contexts: that dispute resolution processes must themselves be embedded in sociocultural settings if they are to have any effect. Thus a full understanding of their effects requires comprehensive analysis of the context in which they are used.

———

What sort of model(s) of legal change do you see in the following article. What position does it take on "great men," lags, conflict, culture, structure, and the resolution of disputes? Compare its conclusions on the role of public opinion with those of Dicey and Gramsci.

(3.3) Social Change and the Law of Industrial Accidents

Lawrence M. Friedman and Jack Ladinsky

67 *Columbia Law Review* 50 (1967).

Sociologists recognize, in a general way, the essential role of legal institutions in the social order. They concede, as well, the responsiveness of law to social change and have made important explorations of the interrelations involved. Nevertheless, the role law plays in initiating—or reflecting—social change has never been fully explicated, either in theory or through research. The evolution of American industrial accident law from tort principles to compensation systems is an appropriate subject for a case-study on this subject....

II.   DEVELOPMENT OF THE LAW OF INDUSTRIAL ACCIDENTS

A.   Background of the Fellow–Servant Rule

At the dawn of the industrial revolution, the common law of torts afforded a remedy, as it still does, for those who had suffered injuries at the hands of others. If a man injured another by direct action—by striking him, or slandering him, or by trespassing on his property—the victim could sue for his damages. Similarly, the victim of certain kinds of negligent behavior had a remedy at law. But tort law was not highly developed. Negligence in particular did not loom large in the reports and it was not prominently discussed in books of theory or practice. Indeed, no treatise on tort law appeared in America until Francis Hilliard's in 1859; the first English treatise came out in 1860....

In theory, at least, recovery for industrial accidents might have been assimilated into the existing system of tort law. The fundamental principles were broad and simple. If a factory worker was injured through the negligence of another person—including his employer—an action for damages would lie. Although as a practical matter, servants did not usually sue their master nor workers their employers, in principle they had the right to do so.

In principle, too, a worker might have had an action against his employer for any injury caused by the negligence of any other employee. The doctrine of respondeat superior was familiar and fundamental law. A principal was liable for all negligent acts of his agent.... Conceivably, then, one member of an industrial work force might sue his employer for injuries caused by the negligence of a fellow worker. A definitive body of doctrine was slow to develop, however. When it did, it rejected the broad principle of respondeat superior and took instead the form of the so-called fellow-servant rule. Under this rule, a servant (employee) could not sue his master (employer) for injuries caused by the negligence of another employee. The consequences of this doctrine were far reaching. An employee retained the right to sue the employer for injuries, provided they were caused by the employer's personal misconduct. But the factory system and corporate ownership of industry made this right virtually meaningless. The factory owner was likely to be a "soulless" legal entity; even if the owner was an individual entrepreneur, he was unlikely to concern himself physically with factory operations. In work accidents, then, legal fault would be ascribed to fellow employees, if anyone. But fellow employees were men without wealth or insurance. The fellow-servant rule was an instrument capable of relieving employers from almost all the legal consequences of industrial injuries. Moreover, the doctrine left an injured worker without any effective recourse but an empty action against his co-worker.

When labor developed a collective voice, it was bound to decry the rule as infamous, as a deliberate instrument of oppression—a sign that law served the interests of the rich and propertied, and denied the legitimate claims of the poor and the weak.... Conventionally, then, the fellow-servant rule is explained as a deliberate or half-deliberate rejection of a well-settled principle of law in order to encourage enterprise by forcing workmen to bear the costs of industrial injury. And the overthrow of the rule is taken as a sign of a conquest by progressive forces.... [But] from the stand point of social change, good and evil are social labels based on perceptions of conditions, not terms referring to conditions in themselves. Social change comes about when people decide that a situation is evil and must be altered, even if they were satisfied or unaware of the problem before. In order, then, to understand the legal reaction to the problem of industrial accidents, one must understand how the problem was perceived within the legal system and by that portion of society whose views influenced the law.

B.   Birth and Acceptance of the Rule

The origin of the fellow-servant rule is usually ascribed to Lord Abinger's opinion in *Priestley v. Fowler*,[17] decided in 1837. Yet the case on its facts did not pose the question of the industrial accident, as later generations would understand it; rather, it concerned the employment relationships of tradesmen. The defendant, a butcher, instructed the plaintiff, his servant, to deliver goods which had been loaded on a van by another employee. The van, which had been overloaded, broke down, and plaintiff fractured his thigh in the

---

17.   150 Eng. R. 1030 (Ex. 1837).

accident. Lord Abinger, in his rather diffuse and unperceptive opinion, reached his holding that the servant had no cause of action by arguing from analogies drawn neither from industry nor from trade:

> If the master be liable to the servant in this action, the principle of that liability will . . . carry us to an alarming extent. . . . The footman . . . may have an action against his master for a defect in the carriage owing to the negligence of the coach maker. . . . The master . . . would be liable to the servant for the negligence of the chambermaid, for putting him into a damp bed; . . . for the negligence of the cook in not properly cleaning the copper vessels used in the kitchen.

These and similar passages in the opinion suggest that Abinger as worried about the disruptive effects of a master's liability upon his household staff. These considerations were perhaps irrelevant to the case at hand, the facts of which did not deal with the household of a nobleman, great landowner, or rich merchant; a fortiori the decision itself did not concern relationships within an industrial establishment. Certainly the opinion made extension of the rule to the factory setting somewhat easier to enunciate and formulate technically. But it did not justify the existence of an industrial fellow-servant rule. The case might have been totally forgotten—or overruled—had not the on rush of the industrial revolution put the question again and again to courts, each time more forcefully. *Priestley v. Fowler* and the doctrine of respondeat superior each stood for a broad principle. Whether the one or the other (or neither) would find a place in the law relative to industrial accidents depended upon needs felt and expressed by legal institutions in response to societal demands. Had there been no *Priestley v. Fowler*, it would have been necessary—and hardly difficult—to invent one.

In the United States, the leading case on the fellow-servant situation was *Farwell v. Boston Worcester Railroad Corp.*,[18] decided by Massachusetts' highest court in 1842. The case arose out of a true industrial accident in a rapidly developing industrial state. *Farwell* as an engineer had lost a hand when his train ran off the track due to a switchman's negligence. As Chief Justice Shaw, writing for the court, saw it, the problem of *Farwell* was how best to apportion the risks of railroad accidents. In his view, it was superficial to analyze the problem according to the tort concepts of fault and negligence. His opinion spoke the language of contract, and employed the stern logic of nineteenth century economic thought. Some occupations are more dangerous than others. Other things being equal, a worker will choose the least dangerous occupation available. Hence, to get workers an employer will have to pay an additional wage for dangerous work. The market, therefore, has already made an adjustment in the wage rate to compensate for the possibility of accident, and a cost somewhat similar to an insurance cost has been allocated to the company. As Shaw put it, "he who engages in the employment of another for the performance of specified duties and services, for compensation, takes upon himself the natural and ordinary risks and perils incident to

18.   45 Mass. (4 Met.) 49 (1842).

the performance of such services, and in legal presumption, the compensation is adjusted accordingly.'' The worker, therefore, has assumed the risk of injury—for a price. The "implied contract of employment" between the worker and employer did not require the employer to bear any additional costs of injury (except for those caused by the employer's personal negligence).... Shaw and his generation placed their hopes of salvation on rapid economic growth. Perhaps they were anxious to see that the tort system of accident compensation did not add to the problems of new industry. Few people imagined that accidents would become so numerous as to create severe economic and social dislocations. On the contrary, rash extension of certain principles of tort law to industrial accidents might upset social progress by imposing extreme costs on business in its economic infancy. The 1840's and 1850's were a period of massive economic development in New England and the Midwest.... Textiles, and then iron, spearheaded the industrial revolution; westward expansion and the railroads created new markets. Communities and states made a social contribution to the construction of railroads through cash subsidies, stock subscriptions, and tax exemptions. The courts, using the fellow-servant doctrine and the concepts of assumption of risk and contributory negligence, socialized the accident costs of building the roads. That these solutions represented the collective, if uneasy, consensus of those with authority and responsibility is supported by the fact that every court of the country, with but one transient exception, reached the same conclusion in the years immediately following *Farwell*. Moreover, the fellow-servant rule was not abolished by any legislature in these early years. Although legislative inaction is not a necessary sign of acquiescence, it at least indicates lack of a major feeling of revulsion.

C.   Weakening the Rule

A general pattern may be discerned which is common to the judicial history of many rules of law. The courts enunciate a rule, intending to "solve" a social problem—that is, they seek to lay down a stable and clear cut principle by which men can govern their conduct, or, alternatively, by which the legal system can govern men. If the rule comports with some kind of social consensus, it will in fact work a solution—that is, it will go unchallenged, or, if challenged, will prevail. Challenges will not usually continue, since the small chance of overturning the rule is not worth the cost of litigation. If, however, the rule is weakened—if courts engraft exceptions to it, for example—then fresh challenges probing new weaknesses will be encouraged. Even if the rule retains some support, it will no longer be efficient and clear cut. Ultimately, the rule may no longer serve anybody's purposes. At this point, a fresh (perhaps wholly new) "solution" will be attempted.

The history of the fellow-servant rule rather neatly fits this scheme. Shaw wrote his *Farwell* opinion in 1842. During the latter part of the century, judges began to reject his reasoning. The "tendency in nearly all jurisdictions," said a Connecticut court in 1885, was to "limit rather than enlarge" the range of the fellow-servant rule. The rule was strong medicine, and it depended for its efficacy upon continued, relatively certain, and unswerving legal loyalty. Ideally, if the rule were strong and commanded nearly total respect from the various agencies of law, it would eliminate much of the mass of litigation that might otherwise arise. Undoubtedly, it did prevent countless thousands of lawsuits; but it did not succeed in choking off industrial accident litigation. For example, industrial accident litigation dominated the docket of the Wisconsin Supreme Court at the beginning of the age of workmen's compensation; far more cases arose under that heading than under any other single field of law. Undoubtedly, this appellate case-load was merely the visible portion of a vast iceberg of litigation. Thus, the rule did not command the respect required for efficient operation and hence, in the long run, survival.

One reason for the continued litigation may have been simply the great number of accidents that occurred. At the dawn of the industrial revolution, when Shaw wrote, the human consequences of that technological change were unforeseeable. In particular, the toll it would take of human life was unknown. But by the last quarter of the nineteenth century, the number of industrial accidents had grown enormously. After 1900, it is estimated, 35,000 deaths and 2,000,000 injuries occurred every year in the United States. One quarter of the injuries produced disabilities lasting more than one week. The railway injury rate doubled in the seventeen years between 1889 and 1906.

In addition to the sheer number of accidents, other reasons for the increasing number of challenges to the rule in the later nineteenth century are apparent. If the injury resulted in death or permanent disability, it broke off the employment relationship; the plaintiff or his family thereafter had nothing to lose except the costs of suit. The development of the contingent fee system provided the poor man with the means to hire a lawyer. . . .

The contingent fee system was no more than a mechanism, however. A losing plaintiff's lawyer receives no fee; that is the essence of the system. The fact is that plaintiffs won many of their lawsuits; in so doing, they not only weakened the fellow-servant rule, but they encouraged still more plaintiffs to try their hand, still more attorneys to make a living from personal injury work. In trial courts, the pressure of particular cases—the "hard" cases in which the plight of the plaintiff was pitiful or dramatic—tempted judges and juries to find for the little man and against the corporate defendant. In Shaw's generation, many leading appellate judges shared his view of the role of the judge; they took it as their duty to lay down grand legal principles to govern whole segments of the economic order. Thus, individual hardship cases had to be ignored for the sale of higher duty. But this was not the exclusive judicial style, even in the appellate courts. And in personal injury cases, lower court judges and juries were especially prone to tailor justice to the case at hand. For example, in Wisconsin, of 307 personal injury cases involving workers that appeared before the state supreme court up to 1907, nearly two-thirds had been decided in favor of the worker in the lower courts. In the state supreme court, however, only two-fifths were decided for the worker. Other states undoubtedly had similar experiences; whether for reasons of sympathy with individual plaintiffs, or with the working class in general, courts and juries often circumvented the formal dictates of the doctrines of the common law.

Some weakening of the doctrine took place by means of the control exercised by trial court judge and jury over findings of fact. But sympathy for injured workers manifested itself also in changes in doctrine. On the appellate court level, a number of mitigations of the fellow-servant rule developed near the end of the nineteenth century. For example, it had always been conceded that the employer was liable if he was personally responsible (through his own negligence) for his worker's injury. Thus, in a Massachusetts case, a stable owner gave directions to his employee, who was driving a wagon, that caused an accident and injury to the driver (or so the jury found). The employer was held liable. Out of this simple proposition grew the so-called vice-principal rule, which allowed an employee to sue his employer where the negligent employee occupied a supervisory position such that he could more properly be said to be an alter ego of the principal than a mere fellow-servant. This was a substantial weakening of the fellow-servant doctrine. Yet some states never accepted the vice-principal rule; in those that did, it too spawned a bewildering multiplicity of decisions, sub-rules, and sub-sub-rules. . . .

There were scores of other "exceptions" to the fellow-servant rule, enunciated in one or more states. Some of them were of great importance. In general, an employer was said to have certain duties that were not "delegable"; these he must do or have done, and a failure to perform them laid him open to liability for personal injuries. Among these was the duty to furnish a safe place to work, safe tools, and safe appliances. . . . Had the courts been so inclined, they might have eliminated the fellow-servant rule without admitting it, simply by expanding the safe place and safe tool rules. They were never quite willing to go that far, and the safe tool doctrine was itself subject to numerous exceptions. In some jurisdictions, for example, the so-called "simple tool" rule applied:

> Tools of ordinary and every day use, which are simple in structure and requiring no skill in handling—such as hammers and axes—not obviously defective, do not impose a liability upon employer[s] for injuries resulting from such defects.

Doctrinal complexity and vacillation in the upper courts, coupled with jury freedom in the lower courts, meant that by the end of the century the fellow-servant rule had lost much of its reason for existence: it was no longer an efficient cost-allocating doctrine. Even though the exceptions did not go the length of obliterating the rule, and even though many (perhaps most) injured workers who had a possible cause of action did not or could not recover, the instability and unpredictability of operation of the common law rule was a significant fact.

The numerous judge-made exceptions reflected a good deal of uncertainty about underlying social policy. The same uncertainty was reflected in another sphere of legal activity—the legislature. Though the rule was not formally abrogated, it was weakened by statute in a number of jurisdictions.... [By the 1850's] the railroads replaced the banks as popular bogeymen.... Some of the fear of excessive economic power was transferred to them. Disregard for safety was one more black mark against the railroads; farmers, small businessmen, and the emerging railroad unions might use the safety argument to enlist widespread support for general regulation of railroads, but the essential thrust of the movement was economic. The railroads were feared and hated because of their power over access to the market. They became "monopolistic" as the small local lines were gradually amalgamated into large groupings controlled by "robber barons." Interstate railroad nets were no longer subject to local political control—if anything, they controlled local politics, or so it plausibly appeared to much of the public. Farmers organized and fought back against what they identified as their economic enemy. It is not coincidental that the earliest derogations from the strictness of the fellow-servant rule applied only to railroads. For example, the first statutory modification, passed in Georgia in 1850, allowed railroad employees to recover for injuries caused by the acts of fellow-servants, provided they themselves were free from negligence. A similar act was passed in Iowa in 1856. Other statutes were passed in Wyoming (1869) and Kansas (1874). The chronology suggests—though direct evidence is lacking—that some of these statutes were connected with the general revolt of farmers against the power of the railroad companies, a revolt associated with the Granger movement, which achieved its maximum power in the 1870's....

The Granger revolt, and similar movements, were not without lessons for the railroad companies. Despite the fall of Granger legislatures, the legal and economic position of the railroads was permanently altered. Great masses of people had come to accept the notion that the power of the railroads was a threat to farmers and a threat to the independence and stability of democratic institutions. Out of the ashes of ineffective and impermanent state regulation of railroads arose what ultimately became a stronger and more systematic program of regulation, grounded in federal power over the national economy.

The Interstate Commerce Commission was created in 1887, chiefly to outlaw discrimination in freight rates and other practices deemed harmful to railroad users. The original legislation had nothing to say about railroad accidents and safety. But this did not long remain the case.... In 1893, Congress required interstate railroads to equip themselves with safety appliances, and provided that any employee injured "by any locomotive, car, or train in use" without such appliances could not "be deemed ... to have assumed the risk thereby occasioned."

The Federal Employers' Liability Act of 1908 went much further; it abolished the fellow-servant rule for railroads and greatly reduced the strength of contributory negligence and assumption of risk as defenses. Once the employers had been stripped of these potent weapons, the relative probability of recovery by injured railroad employees was high enough so that workmen's compensation never seemed as essential for the railroads as for industry generally. The highly modified FELA tort system survives (in amended form) to this day for the railroads. It is an anachronism, but one which apparently grants some modest satisfaction to both sides. Labor and management both express discontent with FELA, but neither side has been so firmly in favor of a change to workmen's compensation as to make it a major issue.

FELA shows one of many possible outcomes of the decline in efficacy of the fellow-servant rule. Under it, the rule was eliminated, and the law turned to a "pure" tort system—pure in the sense that the proclivities of juries were not interfered with by doctrines designed to limit the chances of a worker's recovery. But the railroads were a special case. Aside from the special history of regulation, the interstate character of the major railroads made them subject to national safety standards and control by a single national authority. For other industrial employers, the FELA route was not taken; instead, workmen's compensation acts were passed. In either case, however, the fellow-servant rule was abolished, or virtually so. Either course reflects, we can assume, some kind of general agreement that the costs of the rule outweighed its benefits.

D.   Rising Pressures for Change

The common law doctrines were designed to preserve a certain economic balance in the community. When the courts and legislatures created numerous exceptions, the rules lost much of their efficiency as a limitation on the liability of businessmen. The rules prevented many plaintiffs from recovering, but not all; a few plaintiffs recovered large [awards of damages]. There were costs of settlements, costs of liability insurance, costs of administration, legal fees and the salaries of staff lawyers. These costs rose steadily, at the very time when American business, especially big business, was striving to rationalize and bureaucratize its operations. It was desirable to be able to predict costs and insure against fluctuating, unpredictable risks. The costs of industrial accident liability were not easily predictable, partly because legal consequences of accidents were not predictable. Insurance, though available, was expensive.

In addition, industry faced a serious problem of labor unrest. Workers and their unions were dissatisfied with many aspects of factory life. The lack of compensation for industrial accidents was one obvious weakness. Relatively few injured workers received compensation. Under primitive state employers' liability statutes, the issue of liability and the amount awarded still depended upon court rulings and jury verdicts. Furthermore, the employer and the insurance carrier might contest a claim or otherwise delay settlement in hopes of bringing the employee to terms. The New York Employers' Liability Commission, in 1910, reported that delay ran from six months to six years.

When an employee did recover, the amount was usually small. The New York Commission found that of forty-eight fatal cases studied in Manhattan, eighteen families received no compensation; only four received over $2,000; most received less than $500. The deceased workers had averaged $15.22 a week in wages; only eight families recovered as much as three times their average yearly earnings. The same inadequacies turned up in Wisconsin in 1901. Of fifty-one fatal injuries studied, thirty-four received settlements under $500; only eight received over $1,000.

Litigation costs consumed much of whatever was recovered. It was estimated that, in 1907, "of every $100 paid out by [employers in New York] on account of work accidents but $56 reached the injured workmen and their dependents." And even this figure was unrepresentative because it included voluntary payments by employers.... A large fraction of the disbursed payments, about one-third, went to attorneys who accepted the cases on a contingent basis.

These figures on the inadequacy of recoveries are usually cited to show how little the workers received for their pains. But what did these figures mean to employers? Assuming that employers, as rational men, were anxious to pay as little compensation as was necessary to preserve industrial peace and maintain a healthy workforce, the better course might be to pay a higher net amount direct to employees. Employers had little or nothing to gain from their big payments to insurance companies, lawyers, and court officials. Perhaps at some unmeasurable point of time, the existing tort system crossed an invisible line and thereafter, purely in economic terms, represented on balance a net loss to the industrial establishment. From that point on, the success of a movement for change in the system was certain, provided that businessmen could be convinced that indeed their self-interest lay in the direction of reform and that a change in compensation systems did not drag with it other unknowable and harmful consequences....

When considerations of politics were added to those of business economics and industrial peace, it was not surprising to find that businessmen gradually withdrew their veto against workmen's compensation statutes. They began to say that a reformed system was inevitable—and even desirable. A guaranteed, insurable cost—one which could be computed in advance on the basis of accident experience—would, in the long run, cost business less than the existing system. In 1910, the president of the National Association of Manufacturers (NAM) appointed a committee to study the possibility of compensating injured workmen without time-consuming and expensive litigation, and the convention that year heard a speaker tell them that no one was satisfied with the present state of the law—that the employers' liability system was "antagonistic to harmonious relations between employers and wage workers." By 1911 the NAM appeared convinced that a compensation system was inevitable and that prudence dictated that business play a positive role in shaping the design of the law—otherwise the law would be "settled for us by the demagogue, and agitator and the socialist with a vengeance." Business would benefit economically and politically from a compensation system, but only if certain conditions were present. Business, therefore, had an interest in pressing for a specific kind of program, and turned its attention to the details of the new system. For example, it was imperative that the new system be in fact as actuarially predictable as business demanded; it was important that the costs of the program be fair and equal in their impact upon particular industries, so that no competitive advantage or disadvantage flowed from the scheme. Consequently the old tort actions had to be eliminated, along with the old defenses of the company. In exchange for certainty of recovery by the worker, the companies were prepared to demand certainty and predictability of loss—that is, limitation of recovery. The jury's caprice had to be dispensed with. In short, when workmen's compensation became law, as a solution to the industrial accident problem, it did so on terms acceptable to industry. Other pressures were there to be sure, but when workmen's compensation was enacted, businessmen had come to look on it as a positive benefit rather than as a threat to their sector of the economy.

E.   The Emergence of Workmen's Compensation Statutes

The change of the businessmen's, the judge's, and the general public's attitudes toward industrial injuries was accelerated by the availability of fresh information on the extent of accidents and their cost to both management and workers. By 1900, industrial accidents and the shortcomings of the fellow-servant rule were widely perceived as problems that had to be solved. After 1900, state legislatures began to look for a "solution" by setting up commissions to gather statistics, to investigate possible new systems, and to recommend legislation. The commissions held public hearings and called upon employers, labor, insurance companies, and lawyers to express their opinions and propose changes. A number of commissions collected statistics on industrial accidents, costs of insurance, and amounts disbursed to injured workmen. By 1916, many states and the federal government had received more-or-less extensive public reports from these investigating bodies. The reports included studies of industrial accident cases in the major industries, traced the legal history of the cases, and looked into the plight of the injured workmen and their families.

From the information collected, the commissions were able to calculate the costs of workmen's compensation systems and compare them with costs under employers' liability. Most of the commissions concluded that a compensation system would be no more expensive than the existing method, and most of them recommended adoption, in one form or another, of workmen's compensation. In spite of wide variations in the systems proposed, there was agreement on one point: workmen's compensation must fix liability upon the employer regardless of fault.

Between 1910 and 1920 the method of compensating employees injured on the job was fundamentally altered in the United States. In brief, workmen's compensation statutes eliminated (or tried to eliminate) the process of fixing civil liability for industrial accidents through litigation in common law courts. Under the statutes, compensation was based on statutory schedules, and the responsibility for initial determination of employee claims was taken from the courts and given to an administrative agency. Finally, the statutes abolished the fellow-servant rule and the defenses of assumption of risk and contributory negligence. Wisconsin's law, passed in 1911, was the first general compensation act to survive a court test. Mississippi, the last state in the Union to adopt a compensation law, did so in 1948....

In essence, then, workmen's compensation was designed to replace a highly unsatisfactory system with a rational, actuarial one. It should not be viewed as the replacement of a fault-oriented compensation system with one unconcerned with fault. It should not be viewed as a victory of employees over employers. In its initial stages, the fellow-servant rule was not concerned with fault, either, but with establishing a clear-cut, workable, and predictable rule, one which substantively placed much of the risk (if not all) on the worker. Industrial accidents were not seen as a social problem—at most as an economic problem. As value perceptions changed, the rule weakened; it developed exceptions and lost its efficiency. The exceptions and counter-exceptions can be looked at as a series of brief, ad hoc, and unstable compromises between the clashing interests of labor and management. When both sides became convinced that the game was mutually unprofitable, a compensation system became possible. But this system was itself a compromise: an attempt at a new, workable, and predictable mode of handling accident liability which neatly balanced the interests of labor and management.

III. The Law of Industrial Accidents and Social Theory: Three Aspects of Social Change

This case study, devoted to the rise and fall of the fellow-servant rule, utilizes and supports a view of social change as a complex chain of group bargains—-economic in the sense of a continuous exchange of perceived equivalents, though not economic in the sense of crude money bargains. It also provides a useful setting for evaluating three additional popular explanations of the origin or rate of social change....

A. The Concept of Cultural Lag

... In a famous book written in 1922, the sociologist William Fielding Ogburn used the example of workmen's compensation ... to verify his "hypothesis of cultural lag." "Where one part of culture changes first," said Ogburn, "through some discovery or invention, and occasions changes in some part of culture dependent upon it, there frequently is a delay.... The extent of this lag will vary ... but may exist for ... years, during which time there may be said to be a maladjustment." In the case of workmen's compensation, the lag period was from the time when industrial accidents became numerous until the time when workmen's compensation laws were passed, "about a half century, from 1850–70 to 1915." During this period, "the old adaptive culture, the common law of employers' liability, hung over after the material conditions had changed."

The concept of cultural lag is still widely used, ... and the notion that law fails to adjust promptly to the call for change is commonly voiced. In popular parlance, this or that aspect of the law is often said to "lag behind the times." This idea is so pervasive that it deserves comment quite apart from its present status in sociological thought.

The lesson of industrial accident law, as here described, may be quite the opposite of the lesson that Ogburn drew. In a purely objective (nonteleological) sense, social processes—and the legal system—cannot aptly be described through use of the idea of lag. When, in the face of changed technology and new problems, a social arrangement stubbornly persists, there are social reasons why this is so; there are explanations why no change or slow change occurs. The legal system is a part of the total culture; it is not a self-operating machine. The rate of response to a call for change is slow or fast in the law depending upon who issues the call and who (if anybody) resists it. "Progress" or "catching up" is not inevitable or predictable. Legal change, like social change, is a change in behavior of individuals and groups in interaction. The rate of change depends upon the kind of interaction. To say that institutions lag is usually to say no more than that they are slow to make changes of a particular type. But why are they slow? Often the answer rests on the fact that these institutions are controlled by or respond to groups or individuals who are opposed to the specific change. This is lag only if we feel we can confidently state that these groups or individuals are wrong as to their own self-interest as well as that of society. Of course, people are often wrong about their own self-interest; they can be and are short-sighted, ignorant, maladroit. But ignorance of this kind exists among progressives as well as among conservatives—among those who want change as well as among those who oppose it. Resistance to change is "lag" only if there is only one "true" definition of a problem—and one "true" solution.

There were important reasons why fifty years elapsed before workmen's compensation became part of the law. Under the impact of industrial conditions Americans were changing their views about individual security and social welfare. Dean Pound has remarked that the twentieth century accepts the idea of insuring those unable to bear economic loss, at the expense of the nearest person at hand who can bear the loss. This conception was relatively unknown and unacceptable to judges of the nineteenth century. The fellow-servant rule could not be replaced until economic affluence, business conditions, and the state of safety technology made feasible a more social solution. Labor unions of the mid-nineteenth century did not call for a compensation plan; they were concerned with more basic (and practical) issues such as wages and hours. Social insurance, as much as private insurance, requires standardization and rationalization of business, predictability of risk, and reliability and financial responsibility of economic institutions. These were present in 1909, but not in 1850.

Prior to workmen's compensation, the legal system reflected existing conflicts of value quite clearly; the manifold exceptions to the fellow-servant rule and the primitive liability statutes bear witness to this fact. These were not symptoms of "lag"; rather, they were a measure of the constant adjustments that inevitably take place within a legal system that is not insulated from the larger society but an integral part of it. To be sure, the courts frequently reflected values of the business community and so did the legislatures, but populist expressions can easily be found in the work of judges, legislatures, and juries. In the absence of a sophisticated measuring-rod of past public opinion—and sophisticated concepts of the role of public opinion in nineteenth century society—who is to say that the legal system "lagged" behind some hypothetical general will of the public or some hypothetically correct solution?

The concept of lag may also be employed in the criticism of the courts' use of judicial review to retard the efficacy of social welfare legislation. In 1911, the New York Court of Appeals declared the state's compulsory workmen's compensation act unconstitutional. As a result of this holding, the state constitution had to be amended—two years later—before workmen's compensation was legally possible in New York. Because of the New York experience, six states also amended their constitutions and others enacted voluntary plans. The issue was not finally settled until 1917, when the United States Supreme Court held both compulsory and elective plans to be constitutional. But it adds little to an understanding of social process to describe this delay in terms of the concept of cultural lag. Courts do not act on their own initiative. Each case of judicial review was instigated by a litigant who represented a group in society which was fighting for its interests as it perceived them; these were current, real interests, not interests of sentiment or inertia. This is completely apart from consideration of what social interests the courts thought they were serving in deciding these cases—interests which hindsight condemns as futile or wrong, but which were living issues and interests of the day.

Conflicts of value also arose in the legislatures when they began to consider compensation laws. The Massachusetts investigating commission of 1903 reported a workmen's compensation bill to the legislature, but the bill was killed in committee on the ground that Massachusetts could not afford to increase the production costs of commodities manufactured in the state. Once more, the emergence of compensation depended upon a perception of inevitability—which could cancel the business detriment to particular states which enacted compensation laws—and of general economic gain from the new system. It is not enough to sense that a social problem exists. Rational corrective action demands relatively precise and detailed information about the problem, and clear placement of responsibility for proposing and implementing a solution. For many years legislatures simply did not consider it their responsibility to do anything about industrial injuries. Since they did not view accidents as a major social problem, and since state legislatures were weak political structures, they were content at first to leave accidents to tort law and the courts. Moreover, state agencies were not delegated the task of collecting information on the nature and extent of industrial accidents until relatively late. The Wisconsin legislature created a Bureau of Labor and Industrial Statistics in 1883, but did not provide for the collection of data on industrial accidents until 1905. When a need for accident legislation was perceived, individual legislators, under pressure of constituencies, began to introduce work accident indemnity bills. Some were inadequately drafted; most were poorly understood. In order to appraise potential legislation, investigating commissions were created to collect information, weigh the costs and report back alternative solutions.

What appears to some as an era of "lag" was actually a period in which issues were collectively defined and alternative solutions posed, and during which interest groups bargained for favorable formulations of law. It was a period of "false starts"—unstable compromise formulations by decision makers armed with few facts, lacking organizational machinery, and facing great, often contradictory, demands from many publics. There was no easy and suitable solution, in the light of the problem and the alignment of powers. Indeed, workmen's compensation—which today appears to be a stable solution—was only a compromise, an answer acceptable to enough people and interest groups to endure over a reasonably long period of time.

Part of what is later called "lag," then, is this period of false starts—the inadequate compromises by decision makers faced with contradictory interest groups pressing inconsistent solutions. There may not be a "solution" in light of the alignment of interests and powers with respect to the problem at any given point in time. Perhaps only a compromise "solution" is possible. What later appears to be the final answer is in fact itself a compromise—one which is stable over some significant period of time. Sociologically, that is what a "solution" to a problem is: nothing more than a stable compromise acceptable to enough people and interest groups to maintain itself over a significant period of time. Theoretically, of course, total victory by one competing interest and total defeat of another is possible. But in a functioning democratic society, total victories and defeats are uncommon. Total defeat would mean that a losing group was so utterly powerless that it could exert no bargaining pressure whatsoever; total victory similarly would imply unlimited power. In the struggle over industrial accident legislation, none of the interests could be so described. Different perceptions of the problem, based at least in part on different economic and social stakes, led to different views of existing and potential law. When these views collided, compromises were hammered out. Workmen's compensation took form not because it was (or is) perfect, but because it represented a solution acceptable enough to enough interests to outweigh the costs of additional struggle and bargaining. If there was "lag" in the process, it consisted of acquiescence in presently acceptable solutions which turned out not to be adequate or stable in the long run. "Lag" therefore at most means present-minded pragmatism rather than long-term rational planning.

B.   Cross–Cultural Borrowing

. . . Workmen's compensation was not an American innovation; there were numerous European antecedents. Switzerland passed a workmen's compensation act in 1881; Germany followed in 1884 with a more inclusive scheme. By 1900 compensation laws had spread to most European countries. In 1891 the United States Bureau of Labor commissioned John Graham

Brooks to study and appraise the German system. His report, published in 1893, was widely distributed and successfully exposed some American opinion-leaders to the existence of the European programs. Most of the state investigating commissions also inquired into the European experience, and a number of early bills were modeled after the German and British systems.

Though workmen's compensation can therefore be viewed as an example of cross-cultural borrowing, care must be exercised in employing the concept. Successful legal solutions to social problems are often borrowed across state and national lines but this borrowing must not be confused with the actual "influence" of one legal system over another. "Influence" carries with it an implication of power or, at the least, of cultural dominance. The forces that led to a demand for workmen's compensation were entirely domestic, as this study has argued. The fact that European solutions to similar problems were studied and, to an extent, adopted here shows not dominance but an attempt to economize time, skill, and effort by borrowing an appropriate model. It would be quite wrong to detect European legal "influence" in this process. The existence of the European compensation plans was not a cause of similar American statutes. Rather, the interest shown in the foreign experiences was a response to American dissatisfaction with existing industrial accident law. Similarly, the current drive for an American ombudsman is not an example of the "influence" of Scandinavian law. A foreign model here sharpens discussion and provides a ready-made plan. Yet the felt need for such an officer has domestic origins.

C.   Great Men and Social Change

Sociologists are fond of pointing out the inaccuracy of the "great-man theory of history," which holds that particular persons play irreplaceably decisive roles in determining the path of social change. The influence of single individuals, they say, is hardly as critical as historians would have us believe. The role of outstanding persons in bringing about workmen's compensation acts seems on one level quite clear. . . . Reformers and academicians served as important middlemen in mediating between interest groups and working out compromises. Their arguments legitimated the act; their zeal enlisted support of middle-class neutrals. They were willing to do the spade work of research, drafting, and propagandizing necessary for a viable law. In the passage of many other welfare and reform laws, outstanding personalities can be found who played dominant roles in creating and leading public opinion—for example, Lawrence Veiller for the New York tenement housing law of 1901, Harvey Wiley for the Federal Food and Drug Act.

The great-man hypothesis is not susceptible of proof or disproof. But the course of events underlying workmen's compensation at least suggests that social scientists are properly suspicious of placing too much reliance on a great-man view. If the view here expressed is correct, then economic, social, political and legal forces made workmen's compensation (or some alternative such as FELA) virtually inevitable by the end of the nineteenth century. Outstanding men may be necessary in general for the implementation of social change: someone must take the lead in creating the intellectual basis for a change in perception. Nonetheless, when a certain pattern of demand exists in society, more than one person may be capable of filling that role. Particular individuals are normally not indispensable. The need is for talent—men with extraordinary ability, perseverance, and personal influence, men who can surmount barriers and accomplish significant results. Obviously, the absence of outstanding persons interested in a particular cause can delay problem solving or lead to inept, shoddy administration. The appearance of truly exceptional persons at the proper moment in history is undoubtedly not automatic. But talent, if not genius, may well be a constant in society; and the social order determines whether and in what direction existing talent will be exerted.

Thus, it would be foolish to deny that specific individuals exert great influence upon the development of social events, and equally foolish to conclude that other persons could not have done the job as well (or better) if given the opportunity. "Great men," however, must be in the right place, which means that society must have properly provided for the training and initiative of outstanding persons and for their recruitment into critical offices when needed. In difficult times, great businessmen, political leaders, musicians, or physicists will emerge. "Great men" appear "when the time is ripe"—but only insofar as society has created the conditions for a pool of creative manpower dedicated to the particular line of endeavor in which their greatness lies.

NOTES AND QUESTIONS

1. In his "The Economic Interpretation and the Law of Torts," 53 *Harvard Law Review* 365 (1940), Roscoe Pound wrote:

> What stands out in the history of Anglo–American law is the resistance of the taught tradition in the hands of judges drawn from any class you like, . . . against all manner of economically or politically powerful interests.

Pound then discusses *Priestley v. Fowler* and the rise of the fellow-servant rule. He argues that the rule was not the product of "a tribunal consciously expressing in legal doctrine the self interest of a dominant social or economic class." Rather, it was the result of the "conception of liability" entertained by courts and lawyers generally in the early 19th century. No court, however composed, would have decided otherwise.

> An exclusively economic interpretation of single decisions and single items of judicial action leaves out of account the tenacity of the taught tradition. It takes no account of the instinctive tendency of the lawyer to refer every case back to some general principle. It ignores the prevailing mode of thought of the time which often reflects an economic situation of the past when the taught ideal was formulated.

Is Pound consistent with Dicey? with Gramsci? Do Friedman and Ladinsky ignore "the taught tradition?" Do they leave out of their reckoning the training, habits and inherited modes of thought of the legal profession? How might they respond to Pound's critique? Is their position a materialist one that downplays the force of ideas and values in explaining major legal change?

2.   In their discussion of "lag," Friedman and Ladinsky state:

> Theoretically ... total victory by one competing interest and total defeat of another is possible. But in a functioning democratic society, total victories and defeats are uncommon. Total defeat would mean that a losing group was so utterly powerless that it could exert no bargaining pressure whatsoever; total victory similarly would imply unlimited power.

Elliott Currie, "Sociology of Law: The Unasked Questions," 81 *Yale Law Journal* 134, 139–40 (1971), took exception to this passage. He said:

> ... The implication is not only that the decline of the "fellow-servant rule" and the rise of workmen's compensation represented such a pluralistic bargaining process, but that the United States, on the basis of this and other evidence, is "a functioning democratic society."
>
> Does the empirical evidence presented by Ladinsky and Friedman support these contentions? A close reading suggests otherwise. Their own evidence, in fact, indicates quite strongly that it was in the interest of the business community to promote workmen's compensation laws, and that without the recognition of that interest on the part of business the laws would not have come into existence. This does not necessarily mean that workmen's compensation was a "total victory" for business, but neither does it suggest a process of bargaining and compromise among competing social interests. What it most clearly suggests is that in capitalist society business holds what amounts to a veto power over legal change.... Nowhere is it suggested that labor (or anyone else) possess a similar power over the adoption or rejection of social reform measures. Fitting this analysis into the "bargaining" model of social change seems a rather Procrustean exercise. The theory seems tacked on to the data, an article of faith more than anything else.

Is Currie's criticism well-taken? Does true bargaining, as he seems to imply, necessarily require something approximating an equality of bargaining power?

3.   William Chambliss, "The Criminalization of Conduct," in Ross (ed.), *Law and Deviance* (1981), says that Friedman and Ladinsky express an "eclectic radical pluralist view of the relationship between ideology and economic structures." However, the "emphasis in the end is on the importance of consensually held values rather than economic relations as the determinant of law." Is this an accurate reading of Friedman and Ladinsky?

4.   Law's legitimacy: One possible incentive for legal change is people's perception of a significant gap between what the law promises and what it delivers. For example, suppose a government receives public support because it promotes full employment and some upward mobility. When government fails to do this, people may support new legislative programs or new political

leaders and parties. In extreme cases, people may support a dictator's rise to power. However, we know that people often expect little from government or view the legal system with cynicism and do nothing beyond complaining or making jokes.

Robin Stryker, "Rules, Resources, and Legitimacy Processes: Some Implications for Social Conflict, Order, and Change," 99 *American Journal of Sociology* 847 (1994), attempts to cope with the difficult and disorderly concept of "legitimacy." Stryker sees at least three meanings of the term. At one extreme, legitimacy refers to deep approval of the rules—attachment, loyalty, allegiance and a favorable view of the legal system or some of its institutions. At the other extreme, the term simply refers to a kind of consent; consent can mean active participation, passive acquiescence or even sullen obedience. All we know, however, in a consent situation is that the rules are not sufficiently illegitimate to provoke resistance. A third meaning is cognitive; people recognize rules as binding, although they may not consciously support them. "Valid rules are part of a meaningful and natural order defining the way things are." We get and renew drivers licenses; we drive on the right side of the road (or the left, in some countries); we expect others to do the same. Most people simply accept these rules and practices, and give little or no thought to the sanctions, formal or informal, that would be used in case of violation.

Stryker notes that principles of legitimacy may conflict. The legitimacy of law, traditionally, rests on its procedures and on the claims of legal reasoning. But in this century, science and technology also pose powerful claims to act as the source of legal legitimacy—for example, when a child psychologist offers her expert opinion in court about "the best interests of the child." Effectiveness, rather than legal logic, becomes the basis of interpreting law.

If there are multiple sources of legitimacy, people may come to question the authority of law—especially if the outcome does not meet their wishes or expectations. Some scholars think they see something they call a "legitimacy crisis." What follows from such a crisis, if one in fact exists? Perhaps resistance and revolution; perhaps mobilization and participation in the political process. But if the parties to social conflict simply make use of "institutionalized legal and political rules," any such "legitimacy crisis" would be "contained and ... limited to playing itself out within the rules of representative democracy." (p. 903).

5.   Individuals' "agency" and structure: A recurring tension in sociological and anthropological theory is the question of how much "agency"—that is, how much autonomy and power—individuals and groups have within the constraints of larger social structures and forces. According to models that view social structure as highly constraining, people have very little agency or power. For example, if class structure is the core determinant of law, it is very hard to imagine that any individual or group could use the law to contest the status quo. On the other hand, some Marxists argue that law cannot be reduced to being a mere reflex of what the powerful (the dominant class)

212

want. The powerful can lose a particular battle. It may be more important to uphold values fundamental to the capitalist order than to gain a particular victory. Law, thus, can become the ground for struggle. Sometimes different factions within the dominant class engage in bargaining. The manufacturers of textiles may want a tariff while the manufacturers of jet aircraft may fear retaliation by other nations and thus advocate free trade. Sometimes the use of law may yield social change—or at least the appearance of it. The dominant class may have to buy off parts of the working class in times of economic crisis. Hirsch and Lazarus–Black and their colleagues discuss the way law can serve as a location in which individuals and groups actually resist the status quo, so that it is not merely a reflex of class relations. Susan Hirsch and Mindie Lazarus–Black, "Performance and Paradox: Exploring Law's Role in Hegemony and Resistance," in Mindie Lazarus–Black and Susan Hirsch, eds., *Contested States: Law, Hegemony, and Resistance* (1994); on the question of conceptualizing structure and agency, see also Carol Greenhouse, "Introduction: Altered States, Altered Lives," in Carol Greenhouse, Elizabeth Mertz, and Kay Warren, eds., *Ethnography in Unstable Places* (2002).

The same issue arises when theorists try to assess the relative autonomy of state actors, because those who run the state have their own interest in preserving their place and position. A more complex view looks at the way bureaucrats and professionals may have multiple pressures on them, so that they are not mere pawns of power interests. What kind of agency does an IRS agent have? On the other hand, some theorists argue, overall we see the dominant class using the state to legitimate its privileges and their defense by the exercise of power. There may be occasional victories through law for the "little guy," they would say, but overall the legal system continues to predominantly serve the interests of the wealthy class. This class justifies the legal system and laws by claiming that they rest on custom, natural law and right reason—or on consensus and bargaining among interests. The individual rights approach, typical of capitalist legal systems, can obscure real power relationships. All are declared equal before the law despite gross inequalities which make assertions of those rights by the dominated difficult or impossible. For example, the largest corporation and the poorest citizen both have the same right to due process of law. However, one is far better able to make use of that right than the other. What do Friedman and Ladinsky think of the way law worked, in their example, to help the working class?

(2) Scandals and Crises: Manufacturing Public Opinion

(3.4) NOTE: Upton Sinclair, *The Jungle*, and the Background of the First Food and Drug Act (1906)

About 1900, there was considerable agitation in the country for some form of government regulation of the quality of food products. In particular, people were shocked when they learned about the quality of meat products.

During the Spanish–American war, it was alleged that American soldiers were forced to eat cans of "embalmed beef." (Theodore Roosevelt testified before the Senate that he would just as soon eat his old hat as the canned food shipped to the men in Cuba). Some states passed laws about food quality. Within the government, Dr. Harvey W. Wiley worked tirelessly to expose adulteration of food products and to get Congress to pass legislation that would ensure the sale of only safe and wholesome food and drugs. Wiley revealed many horrible practices of manufacturers—practices which cheated the public, and, in some cases, poisoned them. Still, Congress had not passed a food and drug law when, in 1906, Upton Sinclair published *The Jungle*, a novel about life in Chicago, centering around the stockyards.

Sinclair was an ardent Socialist. He believed that capitalism was the source of the evil that he saw about him, and he became convinced, as he wrote in his autobiography, that "the heart and center of the evil lay in leaving the social treasure, which nature had created, and which every man has to have in order to live, to become the object of a scramble in the marketplace, a delirium of speculation."[19] The turn of the century was a period in which socialism had considerable appeal to some American intellectuals. It was also a period in which "muckrakers" were educating the reading public about corruption, vice and degradation in American society and about the destruction of American ideals and myths. Or so it looked to Sinclair.

Sinclair's early novels came to the attention of the editor of a radical magazine, *The Appeal to Reason*. The editor offered Sinclair $500 for serial rights to a new novel. Sinclair selected the Chicago stockyards as the scene for his book. In 1904, Sinclair went to Chicago, and for seven weeks he "lived among the wage slaves of the Beef Trust."[20] Then he went home, and he wrote a novel based on his experiences.

The Jungle tells the story of a Lithuanian immigrant named Jurgis Rudkus. He came to the United States, full of naive faith in America. He settled in "Packingtown," the stockyard area of Chicago. The American dream turns into a nightmare for Rudkus, his family and his friends. Every possible horror and tragedy is inflicted on Rudkus and his circle. He is exploited at work, in his rented home, and on the streets. His wife dies in childbirth. His son drowns. Women dear to him are driven into prostitution. He is injured on the job, laid off, and eventually blacklisted. He becomes a wanderer, but he becomes a socialist, convinced that only through this means can the world be saved.

In the first half of the book, there are passages that vividly describe conditions in the packing plants. Tubercular pork was sold for human consumption. Old sausage, rejected in Europe and shipped back "mouldy and white," would be "dosed with borax and glycerin, and dumped into the hoppers, and made over again for home consumption." Meat was stored in rooms where "water from leaky roofs would drip over it, and thousands of

---

19. Upton Sinclair, *American Outpost, A Book of Reminiscences* 143 (1932).

20. Id. at 154.

rats would race about on it." The packers would put out poisoned bread to kill the rats; then the rats would die, and "rats, bread, and meat would go into the hoppers together." Most horrifying of all was the description of the men in the "cooking rooms." They "worked in tank-rooms full of steam," in some of which there were "open vats near the level of the floor." Sometimes they fell into the vats "and when they were fished out, there was never enough of them left to be worth exhibiting—sometimes they would be overlooked for days, till all but the bones of them had gone out to the world as Durham's Pure Leaf Lard."

The book became notorious while *The Appeal to Reason* was still printing it as a serial. George P. Brett, for Macmillan & Co., offered to publish the book if Sinclair would remove the "objectionable passages." Sinclair refused. Other publishers turned it down. Sinclair appealed to the readers of the magazine for support, and they sent in enough money to finance an edition of the novel. Then Doubleday, Page & Co. became interested in publishing the book. Worried about its accuracy, they investigated the situation in Chicago. They became convinced that Sinclair was telling the truth about conditions in "Packingtown," and they published an edition of the book, early in 1906. *The Jungle* created a furor when it appeared. A copy was sent to President Theodore Roosevelt, and letters from the public poured in to the President.

The meat-packers fought back with propaganda of their own, and they did their best to block legislation in Congress. But this time they were not successful. Roosevelt appointed two investigators, and their report confirmed Sinclair's findings. At first, Roosevelt did not release their report. Senator Albert Beveridge had "hammered out the draft of a meat-inspection law," which he attached as a rider to the agricultural appropriation bill. It called for postmortem examination of meat, inspection of meat products, control of sanitation, and exclusion of "harmful chemicals and preservatives." The packers refused to cooperate. The President then released the report.

He also applied pressure for the passage of the pure food law, which had been bottled up in Congress. In this he was greatly helped by the great public uproar over *The Jungle*. The packers and good manufacturers fought a rear-guard action. But one executive admitted that "the sale of meat and meat products has been more than cut in two." State food and drug officials and Dr. Wiley also lobbied for passage. In 1906, Congress passed and the President signed both a pure food and a meat inspection law.

What was Sinclair's reaction to all this? *The Jungle* made him famous. But to him, there was an element of disappointment—or irony—in the outcome. He said: "I aimed at the public's heart, and by accident I hit it in the stomach." Socialism was not advanced by *The Jungle*, although that was Sinclair's real purpose in writing the book.

NOTES AND QUESTIONS

1. Can you think of other examples of the influence of scandal on the formation of law? Both the press and television offer a constant diet of exposé journalism. Are there examples where it has had a major impact? Or is the impact of this kind of journalism likely to be a general distrust of government and large business organizations?

2. When will attempts to create scandal work to provoke legislation? For example, Ralph Nader, *Unsafe at Any Speed* (1965) attacked General Motor's Corvair automobile. The book was a major factor in prompting Congress to pass legislation regulating automobile safety. A few years later, Fred McClement, an Eastern Airlines pilot, wrote *It Doesn't Matter Where You Sit* (1969). This was an attack on the original Boeing 727, an aircraft on which some readers of these materials have flown. Several 727's crashed, and McClement charged that the plane was defectively designed. As far as we can tell, McClement's book had no impact. The plane was redesigned and renamed and later became one of the best selling passenger jet planes. Can you think of reasons why the threat of defective automobiles provoked legislation while the threat of defective passenger jet planes did not? Alternatively, is it fair to conclude that scandal has no impact on airline safety in general? Should we view the McClement book as but a small part of the total public concern about airline safety, fueled by detailed television and newspaper accounts of crashes?

(3.5) Java Jive: Genealogy of a Juridical Icon

Michael McCann, William Haltom, and Anne Bloom

56 *University of Miami Law Review* 113 (2001).

... Given its extensive and enduring presence in our popular media, the *McDonald's Coffee Case* probably supplies more common knowledge about the United States civil justice system than any other single lawsuit. This article dissects that lawsuit as a heuristic case study to illustrate how a dispute over hot coffee evolved into a cultural icon and staple of shared knowledge about the inefficiency, inequity, and irrationality of the American legal system. We document the complex ways in which this story entered into the public mainstream, analyze the social context and actors that made this seemingly trivial event into a powerful cultural icon, and suggest some important ways in which this phenomenon matters for legal practice and politics in the contemporary United States.

The Analytical Framework for the Study

The analysis offered here derives from a larger project on the politics of tort reform and the social construction of legal knowledge. Our general argument in the study identifies three dimensions of power at work in the production of knowledge about the civil legal system in contemporary American society. The *first* dimension concerns *instrumental tactics* that advocates employ to support their claims in legislatures, courts, and popular media. The key actors in tort-reform contests include:

Tort reformers—corporate-sponsored policy elites, intellectuals, public relations specialists, lobbyists, and their elected allies who disseminate simplistic, often fictional anecdotes or "tort tales" to warn the masses and elites about a litigation explosion by greedy, rights-obsessed plaintiffs and lawyers ripping off innocent business corporations and undermining communal norms of civility.

Personal injury lawyers—who regularly represent injured victims in court and contribute huge amounts of money to fight tort reform in legislatures and before judges, but who offer at best feeble efforts to challenge damning anecdotes circulated by the reformers in popular culture.

Academic social scientists—who employ sociolegal studies of civil litigation disputing patterns to challenge tort reformers' simplistic claims in intellectual forums but remain mostly unknown to the mass public and even its political representatives.

Of greatest relevance to this particular paper are the ways in which tort reformers' strategically savvy and largely uncontested efforts to saturate American popular culture with images of greedy plaintiffs and a legal system gone awry have contributed to the general social context in which the *McDonald's Coffee Case* acquired great symbolic significance. We will address this aspect of the story toward the end of our analysis.

The *second* dimension of our study, which is more centrally emphasized in this paper, addresses the *institutional practices* of the mass media, especially newspaper reporting of civil litigation activity. Our approach draws heavily on respected social science analyses regarding how journalists select and represent events for public consumption. In particular, analysts emphasize how the media dramatize, personalize, fragmentize, and normalize narratives of events and relationships, thus reconstructing complex social relations and policy issues in simplistic, systematically skewed ways. Our own aggregate content analysis (not reported herein) shows how news coverage of tort litigation by reporters relying on these routine institutional conventions produces a consistent portrait of legal action that parallels in form and substance the selective, simplistic anecdotal portrayals of civil legal practice disseminated by tort reformers. When one adds to such patterns in coverage evidence that tort reformers actively work to spin events for reporters and are over-represented as sources in news reports, it is not surprising that media coverage generally has echoed tort reform advocates' accounts of the legal system and made them a staple of conventional wisdom in American legal culture.

The *third* dimension of our study looks at the *ideological propensities* in American society that constitute the terrains of shared meaning in which the above-noted instrumental contests and institutional practices have developed. Specifically, we are interested in how powerful, if indeterminate, norms of individual responsibility and suspicion toward formal state intervention in socio-economic life figure into the dominant social constructions of tort law practice. In particular, we refer to the "ethic of individualism" that "emphasizes self-reliance, toughness, and autonomy—qualities that are posed as being central to progress and 'getting along' in a market economy." Indeed, we shall show in coming pages how both popular news accounts and conservative pundits together have reinforced inherited inclinations to focus on individual irresponsibility, negligence, and greed of plaintiffs rather than on corporate accountability, state obligations to secure citizen welfare, or the limits of our regulatory/social insurance systems as the key issues at stake in civil legal contests. As such, the emphasis on individual choices and volitional contracts that are sewn into American law are confirmed and reinforced by the stories that we, as Americans, tell ourselves *about* the law and the law's promises. This will be illustrated not only by the individualized, decontextualized, morally simplistic representations of the McDonald's scalding coffee dispute in popular culture, but even further by the triumph of accounts that essentially reversed the official legal findings of responsibility and blamed the victim for her severe injuries, not to mention her excessive greed.

. . . [W]e recognize that our study has potentially important implications for critically evaluating recent political contests over tort reform proposals. Specifically, our account suggests that the cartoonish construction of the legal dispute over spilled coffee that raced throughout American culture during the late 1990s rendered virtually impossible any intelligent deliberation about the case's inherent reasonableness or justice, much less its larger policy significance for legal reform. Our argument, however, neither depends on nor seeks to demonstrate the proposition that the alleged "litigation explosion" or "legal lottery" system and triumph of irresponsible rights-claiming that the *McDonald's Coffee Case* came to symbolize lacks empirical confirmation, although we generally are convinced by social science scholarship that it does. Rather, our inquiry looks beyond specific policy matters to much broader concerns about the dynamics of legal culture. . . .

The Development of a Legal Dispute

A Grievant Becomes a Claimant: Ms. Liebeck Seeks Recompense

On February 27, 1992, Stella Liebeck purchased a cup of coffee from a drive-through window at an Albuquerque McDonald's. At the time, the seventy-nine year-old Ms. Liebeck had recently retired as a department store salesclerk in Tucson and moved to Santa Fe to live with her daughter, Nancy Tiano. Ms. Liebeck was sitting in the passenger seat of a Ford Probe driven by her grandson, Chris Tiano, a college graduate and assistant golf pro. They had traveled to Albuquerque to drop off Ms. Liebeck's son, Jim (uncle of Chris Tiano), at the airport for an early flight. Mr. Tiano pulled into McDonald's for breakfast shortly after 8:00 am, where Ms. Liebeck ordered an Egg McMuffin value meal and the coffee. After her grandson pulled the car away from the window and fully stopped by a curb in the parking lot, Ms. Liebeck tried to remove the cup's lid to add sugar and cream. Lacking a flat surface inside the small car, she placed the coffee between her legs to free up both her hands for prying off the lid. As the lid came off, the Styrofoam cup tipped, spilling all the coffee into her lap, where it was rapidly soaked up by her sweatpants. Ms. Liebeck screamed in pain, but Mr. Tiano did not understand, later relating that it at first seemed to be "no big deal." "When it happened, I thought, well, you know, we spilled a cup of coffee; it's basically our fault. You know it was our clumsiness that spilled the coffee." After all, spilling coffee or some other hot liquid on oneself is a common occurrence; "It was just a scald," he said repeatedly in his deposition.

The grandson then proceeded to drive out of the parking lot, until a minute later when his grandmother became quite nauseous, and he suspected she was in shock. Now realizing that the incident was serious, he pulled over to the side of the road, helped her out of the car, aided her in removing the sweatpants, and covered her with a sheet from the car's trunk. Mr. Tiano then headed for the nearest hospital, which was full, and then made his way to a second hospital, where Ms. Liebeck was admitted. Doctors determined that the hot coffee had caused third degree burns on her thighs, buttocks, genitals, and groin area—about 6% of her body—and lesser burns over 16% of her body. Third degree burns are extreme injuries in that they penetrate through the full thickness of the skin to the subcutaneous fat, muscle, and bone. Ms. Liebeck stayed in the hospital for over a week, where she underwent treatment by a vascular surgeon and eventually was subjected to a regimen of very painful skin grafts. The surgeon, Dr. Arredondo, reported that her injuries added up to one of the worst burn cases from hot liquids he had ever treated. Due to considerable medical costs, Ms. Liebeck left the hospital earlier than recommended and had to be driven back to the doctor for medical treatment many days by her daughter, who was forced to take time off from work. Ms. Liebeck suffered great discomfort, lost over twenty pounds, was permanently disfigured, and was partially disabled for up to two years following the accident.

A member of a long-time Republican family, Ms. Liebeck had never filed a lawsuit in her life and did not immediately seek relief with the aid of a lawyer, judge, or jury. But she also was aware that a simple coffee spill should not have caused such extensive injuries. Ms. Liebeck explained her *grievance* in a letter sent to McDonald's Restaurants on March 13, 1992, two weeks after the incident:

It seems to me that no person would find it reasonable to have been given coffee so hot that it would do the severe damage it did to my skin. Obviously, it was undrinkable in that it would have burnt my mouth. It seems that the reasonable expectation for a spilling accident would be a mess and a reddening of the skin at worst. Although I did the spilling, I had no warning that the coffee was that hot. It should never have been given to a customer at that temperature.

In short, while acknowledging that she was responsible for the accident, Ms. Liebeck's initial grievance was translated into a claim about a dangerously defective product that caused severe injuries for which the McDonald's corporation was liable. If routine coffee spills cause such damage and disability as experienced in this episode, after all, most people would also be partially disabled, subjected to considerable pain, and permanently disfigured during their lifetime. Still, Liebeck's initial letter made it clear that she had "no intention of suing or asking for unreasonable recompense." She asked for three responses from the corporation: (1) to check the coffee machine and coffee-making process to see if it was faulty; (2) to reevaluate the temperature standards for coffee served to customers, for others must have been severely injured as well; and (3) to cover medical, recuperation, and incidental costs related to her injuries, which initially were left unspecified because the medical treatment was far from over at that time. Later estimates for incurred costs have varied in different accounts, but they hovered around $10,000–15,000 for medical bills, plus other directly related expenditures, for a total of around $20,000. After six months of her grievance without the counsel of a lawyer, however, McDonald's refused her requests for a change of policy and offered only $800 for personal compensation.

A Claimant Becomes a Litigant: Lawyers Attempt to Settle the Dispute

Frustrated by her inability to secure compensation for the physical and financial harm wrought by the scalding accident, Liebeck retained Kenneth R. Wagner and Associates, an Albuquerque law firm, in the fall of 1992. Through a legal assistant at the firm, Wagner learned of S. Reed Morgan, a Houston attorney who had settled a similar case against McDonald's involving scalding coffee (for $27,500) in the late 1980s. Morgan was contacted and agreed to take on Liebeck's cause, in large part because he had been angered by what he saw as callous indifference displayed by the mega-corporation in the previous dispute. Morgan quickly issued a formal request for $90,000 to cover Liebeck's medical expenses as well as pain and suffering. His amended claim fared no better than Ms. Liebeck's original claim, however, and was dismissed by McDonald's.

Mr. Morgan filed a formal complaint on behalf of Ms. Liebeck in the Second Judicial District Court, County of Bernalillo, New Mexico. The complaint alleged that the coffee that Liebeck purchased from McDonald's in 1992 was defective in two regards: First, it was excessively, dangerously hot; Second, inadequate warnings were provided regarding the risks posed by the hot coffee. The key legal claim was that the coffee breached warranties of fitness for its intended purpose of consumption under the Uniform Commercial Code. Along with the claim for compensatory damages, punitive damages were requested on the reasoning that McDonald's sold the coffee with reckless indifference to the safety and welfare of its customers. Once the trial date was set, Mr. Morgan offered to settle the case for $300,000, with no success. . . .

Just a few days before the trial, Judge Robert H. Scott ordered the disputing parties to participate in a mediation session. Based on earlier cases and a projection of what a jury would likely award, the mediator recommended a settlement of $225,000. Once again, however, McDonald's refused the opportunity to negotiate a settlement. The trial commenced in the second week of August 1994.

A Litigant Becomes a Plaintiff: Adversaries Frame the Accident in Legal Terms

The trial produced relatively few important disagreements regarding the facts of the case.... Ms. Liebeck did not contest that she spilled the coffee on herself or that she was responsible for the accident.... Rather, the case turned on contending interpretive arguments, or narratives, devised by each side to select, support, and make sense of the evidence in a coherent, compelling way....

The Defective Products Liability Narrative—Attorneys for Ms. Liebeck systematically labored to present the jury with a coherent and compelling interpretation of the scalding accident that focused on the inordinately hot coffee produced and sold by McDonald's. This *Defective Products Liability Narrative* combined basics of products liability law with supporting themes that suited the circumstances of the accident to legal categories. The relevant products liability law came straight from the Uniform Commercial Code's implied warranties of merchantability and fitness.... Media coverage would consistently state that Ms. Liebeck believed that the spill was McDonald's fault. Technically speaking, she claimed instead that McDonald's had failed to abide by standards that many or most businesses must meet.

To complement the implied warranties, Plaintiff Liebeck marshaled supporting themes. The *first* theme acknowledged that coffee spills were routine events but insisted that Liebeck's injuries were extremely atypical due to McDonald's dangerously hot coffee.... A *second* theme in the products liability frame was that most customers are not aware of this danger posed by coffee served at these temperatures.... The *third* critical theme was that McDonald's knew what their customers did not know about these dangers from its hot coffee. Critical facts offered in evidence for this position included that McDonald's had received over 700 complaints about hot coffee in the previous decade and had paid out nearly three quarters of a million dollars to settle such claims, including some payments of up to $66,000.... *Finally*, Liebeck's attorneys alleged that McDonald's displayed reckless indifference to customers' safety by doing nothing either to reduce the heat of coffee known to be dangerous or to provide adequate warning to customers.... What is more, the plaintiffs urged, the motive that trumped the corporation's concerns for safety was well documented: the desire to lure more customers, to sell more coffee, and to earn greater profits. By emphasizing this pecuniary motive, the plaintiffs attempted to strip the mega-corporation of its family-friendly marketing mask and to expose the fearsome Goliath that the David-like plaintiff was challenging.

All four of these themes were framed as key elements in the legal claim that, under the Uniform Commercial Code, McDonald's coffee represented an unreasonably dangerous product sold in breach of the implied warranty of fitness, and that the corporation thus was liable for injuries suffered by Ms.

Liebeck.... McDonald's quality assurance supervisor conceded that Mc-Donald's coffee was not fit for human consumption when poured. He further acknowledged that the McDonald's corporation did not have a systematic mechanism for informing itself about the severity of injuries caused by its products or for determining how many injuries would justify adjusting the heat of the coffee served.... Mr. Appleton unabashedly acknowledged that "there are more serious dangers in restaurants" than hot coffee and "there is no current plan to change the procedure [for coffee making] that we're using in that regard now."

Reed Morgan presented all such testimony to support his call for punitive damages to punish the callous indifference of the family restaurant chain toward its customers. The closing argument by the plaintiff's lawyers noted that McDonald's sells over a billion cups of coffee a year, generating revenues of $1.35 million each day from such coffee, and that payment of two days' revenue from coffee might constitute a reasonable basis for punitive damages....

The Individual Responsibility Narrative—Defendant McDonald's had conceded many facts at the core of the plaintiff's products liability frame, but countered by emphasizing different facts framed in an alternative interpretive story about the incident. The defendants advanced what we label the *Individual Responsibility Narrative* to state their case. The basic logic of this story line is that people spill coffee on themselves all the time but do not expect others to take responsibility for the outcomes, however terrible. In short, a commonplace event like a coffee spill merited a commonsense response, the same one Mr. Tiano immediately had: The spill was Grandmother's fault, not McDonald's.

The defense advanced specific themes that organized evidence to support this approach. *First*, the defense appealed to the ethic of individual responsibility deeply rooted in American culture. Ms. Liebeck, not McDonald's, spilled the coffee that resulted in injuries; she must accept the blame.... A *second* theme was directly aimed at challenging the plaintiff's key scientific point regarding proximate cause of the injury. McDonald's presented an affidavit from Turner M. Osler, a burn specialist, contending that Ms. Liebeck might have received the same burns if the coffee had been less hot, as low as 130 [degrees] F. Major reasons for the bad burns in this case, the expert testified, included Ms. Liebeck's advanced age and her failure to remove her clothing soaked with the coffee in a timely fashion.

A *third* theme turned on the question of "Why pick on us?" The attorneys for McDonald's argued that systematic marketing studies, presented as evidence, showed that customers prefer their coffee very hot. In fact, this was one of the most appealing traits of McCoffee. One leading reason is that most customers do not drink the coffee immediately after purchase at drive-through windows, but typically wait until they arrive at the office or home. At the same time, it was shown that some other restaurants, and especially those leading in coffee sales, tend to serve their coffee at nearly the same high temperature as McDonald's. Indeed, McDonald's provided evidence that their specifications followed industry standards.... *Finally*, the defense attorneys played on a theme at the heart of the tort reform campaign, implying that Ms. Liebeck's claim was an example of litigious plaintiff seeking damages for harms that she, however unfortunate, caused to herself.... [T]he themes of the defense supported individual responsibility with notions of fairness and common sense, as opposed to the strict letter of business law.

A Plaintiff Becomes a Victor: Jurors Adopt Most of Ms. Liebeck's Account

After a tedious trial over seven days, the jurors took but four hours to reach their verdict: McDonald's Restaurants owed Ms. Liebeck $160,000 in compensatory damages and about $2,700,000 in punitive damages. In calculating compensatory damages, the jury synthesized the contrasting claims and frames into a slightly mixed verdict. The jury agreed with the defense that Ms. Liebeck was responsible for her own accident to a degree. However, the jury fixed the degree of the plaintiff's contribution to the accident at 20%. Assessing the expenses, pain and suffering, disfigurement, and disability consequent to the accident, jurors awarded compensatory damages of $200,000 for the accident. Since they held Ms. Liebeck to be one-fifth responsible for her accident, the jury then discounted the compensatory award by $40,000 (one-fifth of $200,000), which left the plaintiff $160,000 in compensatory damages. Jurors had come to see McDonald's coffee as a product made hazardous by extreme heat, a dangerous brew for which the corporation had to bear primary liability even if Ms. Liebeck was partly responsible for her own injuries.

... To dissuade McDonald's and others from continuing their willful indifference, the jury granted the punitive award—damages designed to deter a wrong-doer from continued bad conduct—recommended by Ms. Liebeck's lawyers: $2.7 million, the number based on an estimate of two days' revenues from coffee at McDonald's restaurants nationwide....

As always, public indications of the logic behind the jurors' judgment were sparse. Still, remarks on the record, along with the award, confirm that jurors were convinced by the key themes of the plaintiff's narrative about corporate liability for a defective product. Jurors who spoke to interviewers frankly admitted that they initially thought the case was a waste of their time.... In contrast, the plaintiff's attorneys' construction of the case changed their minds. Several jurors commented on the strength of the scientific evidence regarding how quickly coffee burns skin at 180 degrees as well as the graphic photos of Liebeck's injuries.... [One juror] concluded from testimony by a McDonald's quality assurance executive that McDonald's was profoundly indifferent to burns and suffering. Juror Betty Farnham was so unimpressed by the claim that 700 complaints were trivial relative to the millions of cups that McDonald's served that she began to doubt that the corporation could see the human suffering underlying the statistics....

Not surprisingly, attorneys for McDonald's promised to appeal the case. However, there is some evidence that some corporate insiders took the verdict to heart, at least initially. An Albuquerque news investigator reported that the temperature of coffee at a local McDonald's shortly after the trial fell to 158 degrees. Moreover, the lids of coffee cups began to carry the clear warning "HOT! HOT! HOT"....

A Victory Becomes Less Spectacular: Judge Scott Remits the Punitive Damages

Trial judge Robert H. Scott on September 14, 1994 reduced the punitive damages from nearly $2.7 million to $480,000, somewhat ironically using the tort reformers' own preferred formula of "three times the awarded compensatory damages" as the upper limit. He did not set aside the verdict or adjust compensatory damages, however. Instead, he agreed with the jurors on key findings. He concurred with them that testimony and evidence showed that McDonald's knew or should have known that its coffee was too hot and unfit for consumption, that McDonald's and its employees were indifferent to consumer safety, and that McDonald's undertook inadequate efforts to warn its customers. He stated that the punitive damage award was appropriate to deter, punish, and warn McDonald's....

The Print Media Construct a Legal Legend

[McCann, Haltom, and Bloom performed a study of the media coverage of this case, building from previous work by themselves and political scientist Lance Bennett. Bennett found that the media favors stories as "newsworthy" based on four features: **Personalization** (focusing on individual characters rather than social or institutional contexts), **Dramatization** (sensationalizing), **Fragmentation** (divorcing particulars from general patterns), and **Normalization** (fitting the news into common norms and expectations). McCann et al. confirmed Bennett's findings in another study that they were conducting, examining news coverage of tort cases over a period of nineteen years.

Based on this, they began with three hypotheses regarding newspaper coverage of the McDonald's Coffee Case: (1) It would give much more coverage to "easy-to-understand specifics, personalized conflict, and sensationalized results" than to "challenging contentions about the complexities of events, of disputing case history, of multi-causal relations, or of the legal process"; (2) It would give little attention to novel story lines (e.g., one explaining the complexities of products liability law), while favoring well-known narratives like the popular Individual Responsibility Narrative; and (3) Its use of fragments and misleading statements would help tort reform activists "to spin the case as another instance of frivolous litigation in which the victim was blameworthy." The study that they describe in the rest of this article wound up largely supporting these hypotheses.]

Articles

The first point to note about the hot coffee case is that it was widely covered in the print media; the jury award was immediately reported in at least twenty-six leading newspapers, and many scores of articles followed in subsequent years. As we shall show below, the case was widely covered because of its easy fit into prevailing newsworthiness conventions. Moreover, the *McDonald's Coffee Case* affords the close observer valuable insights because it generated multiple waves of coverage....[21] [W]e separate *Liebeck* news coverage, gathered through a systematic search of "Academic Universe," into five discrete phases. The *initial* and largest spate of spot coverage followed the announcement of the jury verdict on August 18, 1994. After the first two days, the *Liebeck* case was in both the public and the pundit domain, as we shall show. Two subsequent events might have elicited corrective coverage of the case around September 1, 1994, so we treated these events and their spotty coverage together as a *second* phase. When Judge Scott cut the jury's punitive award by over eighty percent to three times the compensatory award, he inaugurated a *third* phase of coverage. This phase stretched from September 14, 1994, until December 1, 1994, when final case settlement piqued a brief *fourth* phase of coverage. These developments in the dispute occasioned spot coverage and commentaries throughout the final months of 1994. [Media coverage] in Stages 1–4 reveal the process by which legally successful narratives and constructions of fact yielded to factoids[22] and default "common sense" frames, transforming Litigant Liebeck into Symbolic Stella. After spot reports of the settlement ended around December 2–3, 1994, an ongoing *fifth* phase reinforced dissemination of the iconic case to the detriment of the case that plaintiffs argued and jurors decided.

Phase Zero: Omission of Coverage Prior to the Verdict—While much of our account turns on omissions from coverage during five phases, we first note a virtual complete omission of coverage before the first phase.... The failure of reporters to attend the trial or scrutinize the trial record greatly increased the chances that a substantial judgment would generate sensational but incomplete, misleading, and even erroneous coverage shaped by media conventions and prevailing cultural norms....

Newspapers Relay the Verdict: Elision and Imprecision in Phase One

Despite under-development of the story prior to the verdict and concomitant omissions from coverage, Phase One print reports covered the verdict in a predictable, professional manner, repeating the standard emphases of mainstream media.... At the same time, consistent with our general findings, the most dramatic and personalized elements were emphasized in simplistic, familiar renderings, while subtle and complex dimensions of the trial record that did not fit prevailing formulas were left out. This reconstruction and

21. Here we omit a graph from the original article that showed the division of coverage by phases (p. 133). The authors explain that they used Lexis–Nexis "Academic Universe" to search for news coverage of the case during 1994, when the news of the verdict hit (p. 134, note 68).

22. The authors define factoids as: "statements that are taken for facts by virtue of publication and dissemination but, upon inspection, turn out to be at best problematic," borrowing from Norman Mailer.

fragmentation to suit newspapers' standards became accentuated when editorialists and commentators filled the gaps in reporting to yield spin and factoids.

Wire Reports: Routine Concision Leads to Telling Elision—We begin with the Associated Press morning wire-service report for three related reasons: it represented the longest and most detailed national account; it became a basis for coverage by most newspapers in our sample; and the Associated Press reported major developments in later phases as well. The initial news account on August 18, 1994 is reprinted below . . . :

Woman Burned By Hot McDonald's Coffee Gets $2.9 Million

A woman who was scalded when her McDonald's coffee spilled was awarded nearly $2.9 million—or about two days' coffee sales for the fast-food chain—by a jury. Lawyers for Stella Liebeck, who suffered third-degree burns in the 1992 incident, contended that McDonald's coffee was too hot. A state district court jury imposed $2.7 million in punitive damages and $160,000 in compensatory damages Wednesday. Ken Wagner, Liebeck's attorney, said that he had asked the jury for punitive damages equal to two days' worth of McDonald's coffee sales, which he estimated at $1.34 million a day. Testimony indicated McDonald's coffee is served at 180–190 degrees, based on advice from a coffee consultant who has said it tastes best that hot, Wagner said Thursday. The lawsuit contended Liebreck's (sic) coffee was 165–170 degrees when it spilled. In contrast, he said, coffee brewed at home is generally 135–140 degrees. He said McDonald's expressed no willingness during the trial to turn down the heat or print a warning. Defense attorney Tracy McGee already has said the company will appeal. McGee also said the jury was "concerned about an industry-wide practice" of selling hot coffee. Juror Richard Anglada confirmed the jury was trying to deliver a message to the industry. "The coffee's too hot out there (in the industry). This happened to be McDonald's," Anglada said Wednesday. Liebeck's lead counsel, Reed Morgan of Houston, said there have been several lawsuits nationally over the temperature of McDonald's coffee but that he believes the Liebeck case was the first to reach the verdict stage. A California case was settled out of court for $235,000, he said.

Morgan said Wednesday the woman's medical bills totaled nearly $10,000.

According to testimony, Liebeck was a passenger in a car driven by her grandson outside a McDonald's in southeast Albuquerque when she was burned by a cup of coffee purchased at a drive-through window. The jury found, among other things, that the coffee was defective and that McDonald's engaged in conduct justifying the punitive damages.[23]

---

23. Associated Press, "Woman Burned By Hot McDonald's Coffee Gets $2.9 Million," Aug. 18, 1994 [hereinafter AP, "Woman Burned"].

The astute reader should notice two characteristics of the account immediately. For one thing, it is very short, simple, and thin—already well fitted to become an anecdote. Moreover, the characteristically fragmented, disjointed presentation of information is familiar. Virtually no signs of carefully constructed legal arguments presented by the disputing parties, of debate over fundamental legal issues at stake or of contrasting evidentiary claims in the trial survive the Associated Press's reconstruction....

Beneath its surface randomness, the selection and prioritization of information in the Associated Press story exhibits a logic....

The first and most extensively noted information in the article—i.e., identifying the burn injury and the award—*dramatizes* the case. By far, most prominent in the wire report are the monetary figures. The bold headline and the first, third, and fourth sentences each highlight either the $2.7 million punitive damages award or the cumulative $2.9 million award. The fourth mention (fourth sentence) disaggregates the total into two figures, followed by the calculus of two times $1.34 million in coffee sales to determine the punitive damages. This is important, for journalistic norms privilege placing the most important information first, after which repetition highlights the message. Near the end of the report, other lesser but still large sums—an earlier settlement of $234,000 and medical bills of $10,000—are mentioned.... Conversely, the wire account somewhat surprisingly underplays the gory details of the scalding injury that were prominent at trial....

The news account also is highly *personalized*. Indeed, it is filled with mentions of individual actors: Stella Liebeck [and others] ..., but *personalization* deprived client newspapers and readers of contextual elements. For one thing, recognition that the dispute was between a seventy-nine year old retired working-class woman with inadequate Medicare benefits and a huge multi-national corporation and that the legal duel was between a personal-injury attorney and a battalion of corporate lawyers is almost entirely obscured ... [T]he Associated Press failed to remind readers of the vast size and wealth of the McDonald's corporation; it is at most a "fast-food chain," one player in a larger "industry." Indeed, some readers might be uncertain that the corporation, rather than the Albuquerque franchise, was the defendant. Moreover, the attention to the spill accident—although generally incomplete and misleading (and later often flatly erroneous)—further tended to reconstruct the case to suit interpretations based on individual responsibility far more than the plaintiff's case or the jury's rationale. Specifically, no mention is made that: (a) the car was parked motionless to the side rather than at the window or moving; (b) there was little recklessness about the action leading to the accident; or (c) the injuries involved extreme pain, skin grafts, and sustained disability. That the accident was indeed ordinary but the injury extraordinary—Stella Liebeck's fundamental claim—is difficult, at best, to discern from the news account. In sum, *personalization* in this wire story favored McDonald's and disadvantaged Ms. Liebeck.

Important items implicating the corporation in the accident were included in the report, but selective *dramatization* and *personalization* pared details essential to the plaintiff's arguments and the jury's verdict. . . . Conspicuously absent are the most important elements of the plaintiff's defective products narrative that influenced the jury and judge: (1) the scientific evidence from two noted experts about the celerity at which skin burns at 170–180 degrees, without which mere mention of coffee temperatures means little; (2) the details about the plaintiff's immense pain and disability; (3) the fact that a documented 700 complaints had been filed against McDonald's in recent years; (4) the fact that McDonald's administrators admitted the company knew about and ignored the palpable dangers of extremely hot coffee; and (5) the facts about the early stages of the dispute, including Liebeck's initial request for meager compensation, the plaintiff's multiple efforts over two years to settle spurned by McDonald's, the mediator's recommended award, and the like.

. . . [T]he inclusion of some key facts and exclusion of others emphasized the large award to the plaintiff for a seemingly inconsequential mishap—a key contention in the narratives of individual greed disseminated by tort reformers—while obscuring essential elements of the *legal argument* (the *Defective Products Liability Narrative*) that led jurors to find the corporation responsible for the painful injury in question. Failure to mention the legal grounding for that judgment in the Uniform Commercial Code as well as the plaintiff's multiple, amply-evidenced arguments leaves readers to question whether the jury acted on either law or reason, much less both. The enigmatic final statement of the report underlined this question. Albeit "the jury found . . . that the coffee was defective" and "punitive damages" were justified, readers cannot be certain why jurors decided as they did.

On balance, the concise spot-news offered by the Associated Press thus conveyed much relevant information about the case, but it de-contextualized the accident in ways that analysts of the news have led us to expect. The omissions and under-emphases of the wire report repeated in many newspapers tended to discount the plaintiff's defective product narrative far more than the commonsensical individual responsibility frame of McDonald's, which readers and journalists arguably had long been primed to presume in making sense of public events. . . .

Initial Print Reports: More Concision; Less Precision—Reports in the twenty-four newspapers in our Lexis–Nexis "Academic Universe" sample emulated the Associated Press report. . . . [Newspaper coverage was generally less detailed than the AP story. We omit Table 1, in which the authors reported quantitative results of their analysis of these newspaper reports, which revealed three patterns.]

The first pattern consists in elements uniformly included ... the severity of the injuries, the stupendous award, the claim that McDonald's coffee was too hot, and description of the coffee spill.

A second pattern consists in elements regularly excluded altogether. Scientific testimony about the swiftness with which very hot liquids inflict severe burns surfaced only in the tenth sentence of the *Bergen (NJ) Record* and neither in the Associated Press stories nor in stories in larger, "national" papers. Details about the extent and severity of the burns or the infirmity they caused were almost completely absent from the accounts. The *Houston Chronicle* commented on routine civil justice cases in its thirty-seventh and thirty-ninth sentences; no other source in Table One so contextualized the Albuquerque anomaly. Not even one source mentioned the Uniform Commercial Code or the initial inclination of the plaintiff to settle without filing suit or, later, to settle without trial. All sources avoided characterizing the plaintiff as litigious or either party as sympathetic.

[A third pattern showed very little coverage of issues of adequacy of warnings or the jurors' reasoning. There was slightly more coverage indicating that Liebeck wasn't actually driving the car at the time of the accident, and that McDonald's had been intransigent in responding to prior complaints and lawsuits.]

... The four elements invariably covered—the burns, the awards, the temperature of McDonald's coffee, and the spill—... offered a succinct, simple sequence: a woman spills coffee in her lap, sues McDonald's for making coffee so hot that it severely burned her, and gets millions. This sequence preserved the perceived irrationality, if not absurdity, of an extravagant award generated by an everyday occurrence and novel claim.

... [The] newspapers' reports were not merely fragmentary, as wire stories were, but reductionist.... Each element that, by itself, would have made the story less bizarre—the science of burns; Ms. Liebeck's initial request for $20,000 in expenses; and the Uniform Commercial Code—eluded almost all reports.

In sum, ... newspapers constructed the story of the *McDonald's Coffee Case* to suit newsworthiness at considerable cost to precision and comprehensiveness. That the initial reports suited the defense's *Individual Responsibility Narrative* far better than the plaintiff's *Defective Products Liability Narrative* or the jury's decision was an unintended boon for McDonald's and, we shall see, tort reform in the public relations battle that followed the case.

Phase One Features and Commentaries: Enter the Factoids—To be sure, wags and pundits might have distorted the coffee case for partisan, ideological, policy, or satirical purposes no matter how well spot reports had conveyed the facts. Fragmentary or reductionist reportage, however, left editorialists and commentators free to fill in omissions with helpful, if incorrect, information....

Features on reactions to the *Liebeck* verdict, editorials, and letters to the editor tended to shortchange the most technical information on which the plaintiff's case depended, thereby divorcing commentators' views ever further from the case the jurors actually heard.... [The authors then present Table 2, showing patterns of emphasis in articles that appeared soon after the verdict, but which were not spot reports on the verdict.]

As with the spot reports, burns and monetary awards drew widespread comment [in feature articles and commentaries], albeit averaging only about two and one-half sentences per category. The heat of McDonald's coffee, Ms. Liebeck's allegation that its temperature was "too hot," and the specifics of the spill elicited even more sentences than information about the injury and award. The position and immobility of the automobile were still merely a matter for passing comment.... *Most important, information pertaining to the litigiousness of the plaintiff drew the most sentences of any category, despite that category's having elicited not a single mention in spot coverage ... and despite the defense's having presented no evidence that an octogenarian who had never before sued anyone was trifling with McDonald's or trying to pull a fast one.*

Spotty coverage left authors free to adopt differing perspectives on the case's justifiability and significance and to marshal information to suit their presuppositions. Two staff writers for the *Denver Rocky Mountain News* attempted to allay fears that purchased coffee would become tepid or that scalding suits would proliferate, two perils predicted far more often than realized. They noted the severity of the burns and other factors that made the case a poor predictor of things to come. In addition, these two lavished four sentences on past difficulties with hot liquids at McDonald's and two sentences on whether warnings were adequate. The *Chicago Sun–Times* ignored facts about warnings, burn science, or the scaldings that marred the record of the fast-food chain headquartered nearby, although they did not put Ms. Liebeck in the driver's seat or in a moving car. The *Sun–Times* apparently needed no factoids to support its call for jurors to take greater account of individual responsibility and common sense.

Far more commentators fell back on stereotypes and shibboleths to accentuate apparent absurdities that had made the case newsworthy. A brief comment in the *San Diego Union–Tribune* sounded the tort reform refrain immediately via the headline "Java Hijack" and gave short shrift to Ms. Liebeck's injuries, to her repeatedly spurned efforts to settle for modest compensation, to the litany of complaints and lawsuits against McDonald's, or to inadequate warnings about the dangers of hot liquids. The editorial said in its entirety:

> When Stella Liebeck fumbled her coffee cup as she rode in the car with her grandson, she might as well have bought a winning lottery ticket. The spilled coffee netted her $2.9 million in the form of a jury award. Liebeck had sued McDonald's for serving take-out coffee that her lawyer claimed was too hot. This absurd judgment is a stunning illustration of what is

wrong with America's civil justice system. Ironically, it also may become a powerful spur to the cause of tort reform. Our guess is that other greedy copycats in restaurants throughout America soon will be happily dumping coffee into their laps in a bid to make a similar killing in the courtroom.[24]

Amid hyperbole and misstatements, the *Union-Tribune* mischaracterized the events of the accident. It is untrue that Ms. Liebeck fumbled her cup "as she rode." Jurors learned she was a passenger in a parked car.... Editorial writers for the *Arizona Republic* veered into a statement that contradicted their own coverage of the spot news: Ms. Liebeck "... tried to open the cup in a moving car...." Just days after the verdict, in sum, misinformation began to alter the story in a manner that inaccurately highlighted the plaintiff's recklessness. The fact that commentators filled in often inaccurate details about the "reckless" nature of the accident underscores the inclination to focus on matters of individual responsibility and the opening left by fragmentary initial reports that emphasized the incongruities between coffee spilled and millions awarded.

Diana Griego Erwin's editorial for the *San Diego Union–Tribune* recounted the case accurately and without unfair spin, but still imputed litigiousness to Ms. Liebeck and unfairness to jurors. [She omitted] the fact that the Uniform Commercial Code and other state and national legislation long ago made dangerous products a matter for courts....

Other commentaries were festooned with misleading factoids....

The champion at misstating the case and, to some extent, harbinger of conventional beliefs to come was Dave Rossie.... Mr. Rossie's August 28, 1994 column in the *Denver Post* passed over lawsuits and complaints about McDonald's coffee, the science of burns, and warnings, all of which were integral to the products-liability case advanced by the plaintiff. He then compounded these sins of omission with sins of commission. He began his commentary with the hackneyed non sequitur that the *Liebeck* decision proved that the United States was the most litigious society on the planet, and then accused the Associated Press of having excluded inconvenient details. Mr. Rossie supplemented those details with convenient factoids. He noted that the Associated Press report set Ms. Liebeck's hospital bills at nearly $10,000, "which suggests she may have been seen by more than one physician in the emergency room." Although the Associated Press story on which Mr. Rossie relied stated that Ms. Liebeck had endured third-degree burns, it did not state how much of her body was burned so severely. Nor did the Associated Press mention her skin grafts or week in the hospital, during each of which more than one physician undoubtedly saw her. What the quoted language is supposed to insinuate is not clear to us, but Mr. Rossie may have understated the injuries and rehabilitation due to the Associated Press's abbreviated coverage.

24. Editorial, "Java Hijack", *San Diego Union Tribune*, Aug. 20, 1994, at B6.

Mr. Rossie then careened into outright error: "It was brought out in the trial that McDonald's heats its coffee to between 165 and 170 degrees." Actually, both Associated Press stories noted that the McDonald's deliberately served its coffee at 180 degrees or more, a standard that, jurors had learned, was explicitly demanded in McDonald's manuals. The lower range was the plaintiff's estimate of the temperature when Ms. Liebeck opened the lid about four minutes after buying the coffee.... Mr. Rossie then explained the award as follows:

> Ms. Liebeck's lawyers figured out that McDonald's sells $1.34 million worth of coffee a day, and decided that their client was entitled to two days' worth of coffee sales revenues to compensate for her pain and suffering and hospital [sic] bills, not to mention their fees.

[The authors point out that Mr. Rossie here fails to mention that the award was intended to deter McDonalds, although this was included in the original AP report.]

Having misstated matters to slander the lawyers, Mr. Rossie then slandered civil jurors in general "... more often than not, when confronted by a giant, [sic] corporation of uncounted wealth on the one hand and the lone individual, especially a little old lady, on the other, the jury is going to come down on the side of the individual." Leaving to the side the absence of authority for Mr. Rossie's "calculation"—pundits' license, let us agree—and presuming that Mr. Rossie was unaware that scholarly investigations of jurors' sentiments and reasoning refuted his generalization, he adduced exactly no evidence ... [that this was the Albuquerque jurors' motive]. Mr. Rossie concluded that the *Liebeck* case "... should never have gone to trial. The judge should have tossed it before the first 'May it please the court. [sic]'" Had the Associated Press provided a more complete account or had Mr. Rossie researched the case, he might have discovered the latent truth of his first sentiment: the case should never have gone to trial because McDonald's had multiple opportunities to settle. His second sentence is based on profound ignorance of the facts and law that constituted the case but encouraged by selective news coverage.

To summarize: spot coverage of Phase One featured few outright errors, but commentators compensated for omitted information by faulty inference and invention. In such a manner concise, fragmentary coverage fostered a flood of factoids and derisive spin about the accident, which quickly morphed into a fashionable fable about a civil legal system gone awry and the triumph of a predatory plaintiff and litigious lawyer.

Phase Two Coverage in Newspapers: Second Chances for Litigants and Journalists

On September 1, 1994, two developments might have changed the evolving story of Stella Liebeck. First, trial judge Robert Scott directed the parties towards a mediator. Second, a front-page article in the *Wall Street Journal* revealed much about *Liebeck v. McDonald's Restaurants* that had been obscured in or omitted from early coverage. These two events define a second stage in the *Liebeck* litigation.

Mediation: A Non–Story—The directed mediation made little difference to knowledge about the *Liebeck* case because . . . only the Associated Press and the *Chicago Sun–Times* carried the story. . . . [T]his pair of stories provides only the sketchiest indication of how coverage of the Liebeck story might have evolved between August 18, 1994 and September 1, 1994. . . . [Here the authors include Table 3, which shows patterns of references to particular elements in the spot coverage during the first four phases of coverage.] If this pair of spot reports tells us little about reportage of post-trial developments, it nonetheless makes the point that omissions undermined dissemination of the case that the jurors witnessed. . . . Skimpier reports made for an even more fragmented story.

Perhaps the omission of greater moment was the lack of any coverage whatsoever in any of the other twenty-five papers that covered the verdict. . . .

Remediation: The Rest of the Story Reaches Few Readers—Another stimulus, Andrea Gerlin's investigation of the *Liebeck* case as jurors saw it, had enormous potential for broadening and deepening understanding of the *Liebeck* case and verdict. Ms. Gerlin explained in the *Wall Street Journal* how jurors could have reached judgments that pundits and wags had ridiculed and editorialists had pronounced absurd or stupid. She found it easier to understand, if not agree with, the jury once she learned about major facts and legal arguments that had shaped their reasoning. Gerlin recounted McDonald's longstanding and extensive record of scalding its customers. She reviewed testimony from McDonald's officials and experts that made the corporation appear nonchalant and even callous. She reported on the severity of the burns, on the impact that photographs of Ms. Liebeck's injuries had had on jurors, and on some scientific evidence regarding the celerity of burns. Ms. Gerlin discovered reasons for sympathizing with Ms. Liebeck, reasons that had hitherto received but the shortest shrift.

To be sure, Ms. Gerlin's piece shortchanged some aspects of the case. Nowhere did she inform readers that the grandson was driving or that the car was parked away from the window. She also skimped on how the science of burns suggested the urgency of reducing the temperature of hot liquids, on the legal basis for the judgment, and on the long history of the dispute prior to trial. But, overall, the account was complex, rich, and well researched.

Despite the excellence of Ms. Gerlin's report, any potential for at least some increased understanding about the case was not impressively realized. Only seven additional news sources produced articles that wholly or largely reprinted Gerlin's *Wall Street Journal* report. Ms. Gerlin's follow-up and articles based on it complemented Phase One coverage. As in the earlier phase, facts about burns, monetary awards, the heat and defects of McDonald's coffee, and the nature of the spill were amply highlighted. In addition to these staples of spot-coverage, though, the follow-ups to Gerlin did devote attention to the record of McDonald's: past scaldings, complaints, and litigation; resistance and recalcitrance; and flaunting and flouting of standards for coffee in the fast-food industry. These facts cast the defendant in a less flattering light and made the awarding of punitive damages more understandable than it had been when first covered. Relatively sympathetic attention to the case as understood by jurors and plaintiff made this second phase of coverage quite different from the first.

[The authors note that even papers that did pick up on Ms. Gerlin's more complete account could re-frame what they reported in a way that undermined any corrective effect of her reporting. The *Cincinnati Enquirer*, for example, did relay much of Ms. Gerlin's information, but in its editorial interjected many comments about the dangers of increased litigiousness in the United States, and of windfall but ill-founded jury awards.]

Why does Gerlin's correction appear to have made so little difference? Cynics might generalize Pundit Rossie's contention that the Associated Press dislikes to be reminded of its omissions; dailies choose not to emphasize shortcomings and superficiality in their coverage. Having missed crucial details in the first place, most papers seem to have been averse to revisit a matter no longer timely.... When journalistic omissions and commissions meet in a mutually reinforcing peak, erroneous factoids result and familiar story lines (here echoing tort reformers) find implicit support.

Phase Three Coverage in Newspapers: More Omissions and More Factoids

Whatever the explanation of press reticence about Ms. Gerlin's investigations in Phase Two, in Phase Three the press compounded its indifference to key points that proved pivotal to the plaintiff's successful story before the jury. When Judge Scott inaugurated Phase Three by reducing the punitive damages by over eighty percent to three times the compensatory damages, the press had an opportunity to correct details and educate the public about how the civil legal system routinely works.... [W]e have been able to document few reports that took advantage of that opportunity. Crucial omissions persisted and errors of commission proliferated.

Spot Omissions Continue and a Spot Factoid Erupts—We were not surprised that 37.5% fewer newspapers covered the reduction of punitive damages than covered the original award.... The verdict having become nearly month-old news, this waning of interest was predictable. Nonetheless, reduction of coverage exacerbated the original holler of the dollar. If even diligent readers ran across no story of the reduction in punitive damages, they became more likely to remember the outlandish award. Therefore, it is little wonder that even well-informed commentators apparently missed the reduction. This understandable omission conformed the story to news framing but deformed the legal frame that the jury had accepted....

[Coverage in the third phase contained still less information, while repeating inaccuracies about the location and mobility of the car and plaintiff; it framed information in terms of the dangers of litigiousness and failed to balance this with any sympathy for the plaintiff's point of view.]

Phase Four: The Case Settles and the Legend Is Set

On November 30, 1994, McDonald's settled with Ms. Liebeck for an undisclosed sum. Spot coverage about the end of the formal dispute marked a fourth phase and completed the story for most reporters. . . .

In Phase Four, omissions increased again as spot coverage crystallized for a last time. . . . [E]ditorialists and commentators continue to use wildly inflated figures for Ms. Liebeck's award.

Selected information pertaining to the accident itself persisted as a common reference, as did descriptions about the placement and mobility of the automobile, sustaining focus on the accident rather than the product. Beyond those four sorts of information, reporting was skimpy. . . . Again, the four evidentiary claims central to the plaintiff's winning legal construction at trial did not surface at all. The history and current posture of McDonald's corporation graced only the article in the *Wall Street Journal*, which alone recalled an aspect of the dispute trumpeted by the Gerlin investigation. . . . [Erroneous claims persisted.]

Phase Five Begins: McDonald's Lost the Battle but Liebeck Lost the War

The end of 1994 defines a cusp between the first four phases of the Liebeck story and the extended fifth stage that began with the settlement and continues today. . . .

As was the case in commentaries during the third phase, the Liebeck matter had been distilled in editorials, features, and comments to a very shallow account. This account related briefly elements indispensable for identifying the case: hollering dollars, painful burned skin, spilt coffee, and reaction from McDonald's corporation or counsel. The overwhelming focus of the treatment, however, was on Ms. Liebeck's failure to take personal responsibility for her clumsiness and her litigious inclinations towards blaming her misfortune on a well-heeled corporation. In short, by the start of Phase Five, the *Individual Responsibility Narrative* favored by defendant McDonald's had obliterated the *Defective Products Liability Narrative* that had motivated the plaintiff and persuaded the jury. . . .

Indeed, throughout subsequent years, newspaper references to the incident were common if widely variable in type (editorial, letter to editor, advice column, humor column, etc.) and location. Not only was the *Liebeck* case often recalled, but disputes over hot liquids in other settings increasingly received attention in the news. Moreover, invocations of Stella's saga proliferated in commentaries, with inaccuracies increasing in proportion to self-righteous moralizing. Closing out the year, Jeff Pelline wrote in the *San Francisco Chronicle* that "America has a victim complex," as witnessed by "such surreal cases as the woman who recently won a $2.7 million verdict after spilling coffee on her leg in a McDonald's restaurant." . . .

Humorist Dave Barry included inaccurate references to the hot coffee judgment on his list of major reasons for wonder about American society at the start of 1995; the former labeled his retrospective essay "A Great Year for Victims." Columnist Joseph Perkins of the San Diego Union–Tribune even named an annual award "The Stellas." "The award is named for Stella Liebeck, the Albuquerque, N.M. woman who became an instant millionaire and American icon after spilling a cup of McDonald's coffee in her lap and winning a judgment against the fast-food chain...."

The legend of Stella has lived on in newspapers until the present. Spot news coverage of lawsuits for excessively hot liquids or pickles on hamburgers and a chicken head among the new fried chicken wings at McDonald's provide one form of enduring reference keeping memory of the original case and what it represented alive....

One feature of Phase Five coverage is especially notable if, by this point, unsurprising. Whereas quoted reactions regarding the judgment in the first four phases were dominated by those sympathetic to the winning plaintiff (Liebeck's attorney, juror, etc.), by Phase Five, cited authorities and experts were critical of the judgment and/or Ms. Liebeck by more than a two-to-one margin.

Blaming the Victim: Ms. Liebeck in Popular Culture

The transformation of the scalding coffee case into a classic tort tale and Stella Liebeck into the poster lady for the tort reform movement burgeoned outside newspapers. Indeed, the diffusion of the inverted, factoid-riddled morality tale throughout the electronic media, popular culture, and political discourse was so rapid, dramatic, and sustained that every reader of this sentence must be familiar with some invocation of the icon that Stella Liebeck has become. We briefly catalogue just some of the venues in which the story was replicated, usually in derisively cartoonish terms. In doing so, we not only elaborate on the dissemination of the McDonald's coffee chronicle, but we demonstrate through the case study the ways that representations by print media and other media of popular culture are continuously interrelated in constructing the spectacle and lore of law.

TV News Coverage

We found thirty-eight spot news broadcasts mentioning the verdict on TV (fourteen national, twenty-four local) in the two days after the jury award was announced. For the most part, this coverage was similar to the newspaper coverage in what it did and did not provide for public consumption, although it was even less substantial and accurate than the print versions. Accounts were riddled with the same errors and, more important, omissions of critical elements heard at the trial, thus again emphasizing the recklessness of the accident over the dangerous product. One important difference from spot coverage in newspapers was that local TV broadcasts often openly ridiculed the decision that they reported as news. One report joked with a pun about "burned buns" at McDonald's. Another sardonically reported that Liebeck (after "she spilled scalding coffee on herself in a McDonald's restaurant") said, "hot coffee is terrible on the groin and buttocks." Yet another report quoted a customer and an attorney who both said they thought "the suit was stupid," offered no parallel defenses of the suit, and ended by pointing to Liebeck "explaining how to get rich after spilling a hot beverage on their crotch (sic)...."

News Magazines and Newsletters

... [A] quick search of "Academic Universe" identified numerous mentions for "McDonald's and coffee and burn or scald" in *Newsweek*, *Time*, *Business Week*, *US News & World Report*, and *Forbes* between August, 1994 and January 1, 2000. Most such accounts echoed the critical editorials in the newspapers—full of misleading errors, focused on the accident rather than the product, and again openly disdainful of the irresponsible plaintiff and the capricious legal system.

TV News Features and Talk Shows

Ms. Liebeck's saga played widely on television feature news and interview shows.... Perhaps the most incendiary treatment was on an ABC special, *The Blame Game: Are We a Country of Victims?*, hosted by the controversial John Stossel. Like his later attack on the civil legal system, *The Trouble with Lawyers*, Stossel's show mixed selected anecdotes, assorted facts, and a barrage of leading rhetorical questions into a mix of caustic commentary and amusing entertainment. The show began provocatively by citing the *McDonald's Coffee Case* as one of several examples of business owner's complaints about "what's wrong with America...." The show later used a highly selective, simplified cartoon version of the story to illustrate what Stossel posed as a fundamental breakdown in Americans' individual responsibility, civil law, and culture. Roger Conner, of the American Alliance for Rights and Responsibilities, was asked to cap the sermon.... A host of other shows on virtually every major channel offered up similar rituals for responsibility that ripped the hot coffee case, the plaintiff, and the judgment.

Late Night TV

Given the ridicule that permeated supposedly serious news coverage, it is not surprising that late night talk show hosts appropriated Ms. Liebeck's saga for their own comic routines. The best-known episode involved Jay Leno, who several times told jokes referring to the case. Attorney Morgan told us that he wrote Leno in protest, and Leno actually called him in response. However, Leno continued to make jokes about scalding spills of McDonald's coffee at least through February 9, 2001. David Letterman also made reference to the hot coffee liability issue a number of times over several years.

Prime Time TV Comedy

Viewers who do not stay up to watch late night television could catch a longer comic play on the dispute over spilled coffee on the wildly popular

Seinfeld show. The specific episode, titled "The Maestro," initially ran October 5, 1995, and has been rerun many times. The show focuses on the aftermath of an incident in which the zany and socially inept Kramer spills coffee on himself when stuffing a Styrofoam cup into his pants to sneak a latte into a movie theater. After filing a lawsuit, he confronts his friend Jerry who expresses surprise at Kramer's litigiousness. That prompts Kramer to reply "Oh, I can be quite litigious"....

Corporate Advertisements

It took a while, it seems, but eventually the advertising industry appropriated references and images of the case for humorous promotions as well. We found national magazine advertisements for a major hot chocolate product and television commercials for both a major phone company and several automobile manufacturers making explicit references to the hot coffee case. In a like advertisement, a little girl says, "Here's a scalding hot cup of tea, Grandma" in the back seat of Mercedes–Benz careening over rough roads. The fact that corporations could so blithely appropriate the image to promote their products reflects both the dominant story line attached to the coffee case in mass mediated culture and the privileged position of corporate producers in that culture.

[The authors found one movie that also mentioned and mocked the verdict in this case.]

Congressional Hearings

As the Liebeck story was mocked in popular entertainment, it was mostly scorned by public officials as well, which of course found its way back into many newspaper and TV accounts. As such, serious news and popular entertainment, official politics and political comedy, fused together into a complex stream of anecdotal references to Liebeck's litigation as leading symbol of a legal system and civil society gone wrong. "Everybody in America is fed up with being sued by everybody for everything. I just have to refer to the case of the lady that sued and won for having been scalded by a cup of coffee she bought in McDonald's 5 minutes earlier," proclaimed Representative Kasich as Republicans geared up to take action to limit frivolous lawsuits in 1994. Indeed, an electronic subject search of the congressional hearings in 1995 confirmed that the *McDonald's Coffee Case* was a staple of political discourse. Just as the mass media had reconstructed a successful claim of legal right into a cartoon, so did politicians use that cartoon to justify reconstructing and righting the law itself.

The Tort Tale Endures

We have just sampled here the many forums in which the *McDonald's Coffee Case* has become a prominent part of the prevailing legal lore in America. In fact, as one of us sat writing a draft of this very study on July 13, 2000, he heard a story on National Public Radio about a man who had sued after being scalded by coffee in a restaurant. The man insisted that ceramic cups have warning labels on them. The judge denied the claim, saying "What next? Warnings on steak knives?" Such a report obviously was intended as humorous fluff on a serious broadcast. But our point is that it would not be considered funny without the lingering legacy of Liebeck in the public space.

Analysis: How a Court Case Became a Tort Tale

Having seen how an understandable if not unassailable judgment was transformed from a legal outcome to a politically charged cultural icon, we now assess implications of our case study for our contentions in our larger project.

The Mass Media

The *McDonald's Coffee Case* demonstrates in great detail how ordinary news reporting practices both select particular types of events and construct them for the reading public in highly subjective, limited, and problematic ways. But why did this atypical legal case become so typically newsworthy? While many factors were involved, the juxtaposition of a familiar accident with a seemingly astounding award provided a perfect mix of the personal, dramatic, and normal that the press loves, all bound together in a discrete incident. Aspects of the case almost perfectly fit the standard conventions of newsworthiness for "infotainment" coverage. For one thing, the disputing parties fit very familiar images: an elderly woman and the most familiar, ubiquitous family restaurant chain in the world. That nearly everyone has taken out food and drinks from a McDonald's drive-through no doubt mattered also. Moreover, the fact that nearly all persons have spilled hot coffee or hot chocolate or tea on themselves likewise highlights the routine character of the case. What "infotainment" could not handle well—those aspects of the *Defective Products Liability Narrative* that persuaded jurors, to cite the most telling example—could be omitted from coverage without readers' or viewers' notice.

As a result of both newsworthiness conventions and routine exposure to parallel tort tale narratives, widespread coverage of this case: (1) privileged certain facts that fit the predilections for personalized and dramatized stories while omitting other information, issues, and story lines in ways that left the account highly fragmented and routinized; (2) provided little attention to the key facts and narrative logic that proved successful in the official trial phase; (3) failed to provide perspective for this particular, atypical case relative to broader patterns in civil litigation; and, as such, (4) re-presented an event in ways that were open to, and even invited, interpretations consistent with the tort reform agenda by elite news spinners and the mass audience. . . .

This case study also reveals parallels and interconnections between newspaper coverage and other media of cultural knowledge production—especially television daily news, news features, talk shows, and comedy shows, as well as radio, movies, and public forums of official politics—in our "infotainment"-oriented society. Evidence in this article suggests that this broader complex of technologically mediated information production today may be even more conducive to legend production than that of newspapers alone. Moreover, attention to multiple media manifestations of the hot coffee story distinguishes its impact from familiar "big" stories in the news. The infamous story of Stella Liebeck did not hit the public over the head in one huge attack of front-page headlines. Rather, the steady parade of small, thin accounts and brief allusions in multiple media over a sustained period of time quietly supplanted a real victim (McDonald's or herself or both) with a caricature familiar across the American legal and political culture.

Our case study of Ms. Liebeck's saga thus demonstrates a more fundamental general theme of our larger project—that mass media have played a relatively independent institutional role in the specific social construction of legality. By legality, we refer to Ewick and Silbey's provocative, expansive concept regarding the " 'ideas, problems, or situations of interest' to unofficial actors as they take account of, anticipate, or imagine 'legal acts and behaviors.' "[25] Legality thus operates "as both an interpretative framework and a set of resources with which and through which the social world (including that part known as law) is constituted." This role of the media in constructing popular legal meaning is most simply shown by the fact that the story of scalded Ms. Liebeck broke quickly after the jury verdict with little foreknowledge even among tort reform specialists about the lawsuit. It is worth noting in this regard that McDonald's attorneys and representatives said very little immediately after the judgment and experts or other sources cited in the initial articles were weighted to the side of the plaintiff. In other words, the mold for problematic public construction of the *McDonald's Coffee Case* was initially set by journalists relatively free of direct instrumental input from tort reformers and other media-attentive elites. Within two weeks after the event, copious information that would have provided a fuller, more complex account was available to newspapers at very small cost in money or time, but those sources were rarely accessed in the interest of informing readers. In short, newsworthy routines largely defeated legal constructions of the case that won in trial and constructed new legal images for the citizenry to consume, appropriate, and variously integrate into their reserve of "common sense."

At the same time, however, this claim of institutional independence must be qualified with regard to both instrumental actions of elites who routinely "feed" the press and the broader ideological and organizational forces in American society that shape the press as an institution. We take up the former matter in the next section. With regard to the latter, we again stress the propensity for individualistic interpretations that focus on personal responsibility, suspicion toward government intervention, respect for corporate forms of ownership, fascination with large sums of money, etc.—all expressing and reproducing dominant ideological currents in American society—demonstrated by coverage of the *McDonald's Coffee Case* and other disputes. These tendencies in turn are similarly reinforced by the pressures of corporate

25. Patricia Ewick and Susan Silbey, *The Common Place of Law: Stories from Everyday Life* (1998).

organization privileging rapid news generation for easy consumption to maximize sales to customers and advertisers, thus further shaping the context in which the routines of reporting legal events takes place.

Tort Reformers

The argument in the previous section is not intended to suggest that the legions of sophisticated tort reformers contributed little to the rapid rise of Stella Liebeck as a symbol for a legal system gone awry. Most important, the preceding fifteen or so years of concerted tort reform advocacy assaulting the legal system and personal injury lawyers contributed greatly to the context of media reporting, elite discourse, and public understanding that quickly elevated the *McDonald's Coffee Case* to great symbolic significance. The tort reform movement and corporate campaign to impugn the legal system and celebrate norms of individual responsibility provided a public appetite and familiar menu that the *McDonald's Coffee Case* served very well. That the movement's standard charges against the legal system found or generated many allies among newspaper editors and columnists is clear from previous evidence.

Moreover, tort reformers contributed directly to accelerating and sustaining the continuing familiarity of the story in the ongoing phase of the story's public life (since 1995). While the appointed spokespersons and spinners for tort reform did not influence the initial phases of the public interpretation, they had a field day with the *McDonald's Coffee Case* once they mobilized in subsequent months.... The incident became a staple on the list of Horror Stories maintained by the American Tort Reform Association (ATRA) and others, press releases, and other stories. Reporters have told us in interviews that the *McDonald's Coffee Case* quickly became a routine component in the standard tort reform literature regularly fed to the press. For example, Robert Ash, a senior fellow at the Discovery Institute, made the case a lead item in a published and widely distributed address, "Is It Time to Reform the Adversarial Civil Justice System?" in late 1996 ...:

> In sum: when a plaintiff can win a million dollar settlement from McDonald's because its coffee is too hot, when suing and being sued become normal ways of doing business or pursuing political and social agendas, when procedure triumphs over substance.... It's time for fundamental reform to make the legal system accord with new realities.

An ATRA press release decrying a lawsuit against toothbrush manufacturers as late as April, 1999, listed the *McDonald's Coffee Case* as the leading honoree in the "Crazy Lawsuit and Warning Label Hall of Fame."

Corporations were also quick to get into the act of exploiting the high profile case. Mobil Oil took out a substantial advertisement in the New York Times that cited the case, noting that "nearly $3 million was awarded to a customer who spilled hot coffee on herself." Echoing ATRA press releases and paid ads, the Chamber of Commerce sponsored its own ad on the radio: "Is it fair to get a couple of million dollars from a restaurant just because you spilled your hot coffee on yourself? Of course not. It's ridiculous. But it happened."

It is important to underline that the McDonald's Coffee Case was not just another anecdotal tort tale manipulated by the reform troops, however. By 1994, the national tort reform movement was flagging in its energy. A decade of failure to pass major national legislation in Congress had sapped energies and nurtured frustration. The "easy" victories at the state level had been exhausted, and even these were being undone or undercut through effective litigation campaigns by trial lawyers. Moreover, while social science studies refuting the tort reform message had not widely penetrated the public space, challenges to the accuracy of oft-told tort tales and the reformers' grand grievances were becoming more familiar to political elites and leading journalists. The empirically informed retorts on torts by crusading law professors such as Marc Galanter (University of Wisconsin) and Theodore Eisenberg (Cornell University) were regularly finding their way into top national news stories. In short, the tort reform movement was on its heels, locked into an increasingly defensive battle.

Then, along came the *McDonald's Coffee Case*—the perfect anecdotal antidote to the movement's maladies. No better case could have been fabricated by the movement to provide an effective "We told you so" to skeptics in the media, the political establishment, and the general public. Ms. Liebeck's saga, reduced to factoids by ordinary news reporting routines and repeatedly re-spun by reformers, quickly hot-wired the currents of concern about our failing civil legal system and flagging ethos of individual discipline. It seems hardly a coincidence that the next year the story circulated widely in hearings that led to the first major national tort reform legislation passed by Congress. Although President Clinton vetoed that bill, it was clear that the movement had found new life in the aftermath of the scalding coffee story. Indeed, Clinton's successor in the White House made his name as a Texas governor successfully leading the tort reform charge; both of the leading party presidential and vice-presidential candidates were open supporters, in varying degrees, of national tort reform.

Attorney Reed Morgan and the Plaintiffs' Bar

Our larger study of tort reform politics has found that the plaintiff's bar has not actively or aggressively challenged the reformers' charges against the tort system in the court of public opinion. Moreover, we were somewhat surprised to find that Ms. Liebeck's lead attorney, S. Reed Morgan, did not actively attempt to shape initial media constructions of this specific case. Unlike many politically experienced attorneys in public litigation and the stereotype of a publicity-seeking ambulance chaser, Mr. Morgan offered no immediate press release feeding reporters important information framing the logic of the winning case. While he frequently commented on the case, his published answers were mostly responses to specific reporters' questions rather than efforts to amplify why he thought Ms. Liebeck won or the case's connection to larger public issues. Indeed, Morgan clearly indicated in interviews with us that he had no way of anticipating the caricature of the case that would emerge from the press or its rapid transformation into a symbol for the tort reform crusade.

Once negative reaction developed, Morgan did write a letter clarifying ignored aspects of the case he presented and defending the verdict for the public. Exemplary was the letter published in the *National Law Journal* on October 24, 1994. Morgan told us that he wanted to offset the harm of the negative publicity "because it was hurting the system badly ... people that were trying to do something to protect people through the justice system." But it was too little too late to make a difference.

The wider community of trial lawyers also was relatively slow and mostly reactive in its efforts to frame the story in positive ways. An excellent account by Gordon E. Tabor, former President of the Indiana Trial Lawyers Association, was written just weeks after the jury verdict. However, his *McFacts, McMedia, and McCoffee* had little visibility to the mainstream press and general public. As noted above, Ralph Nader attempted to present the overlooked facts and key issues to legislators in 1995, and he later wrote an excellent account of the case with Wesley Smith in their 1996 book *No Contest*. Likewise, the Association of Trial Lawyers of America website carried a defense of the case in the late 1990s, but that also came rather late and was aimed at specialized audiences. Again, this relatively tepid and delayed defense of the case illustrates some of the general political limitations of the plaintiff's bar as an advocacy group. Moreover, these facts confirm the point that the press was relatively free to frame the case of the scalding coffee according to their usual routines and familiar cues, inadvertently doing much of the tort reformers' work for them.

One of the most interesting and important manifestations of the legal lore surrounding the *McDonald's Coffee Case* was among jurors. It is worth noting that the legendary coffee case cultivated skepticism among jurors that was widely recognized by attorneys on both sides of tort cases. "It comes up all the time ... The McDonald's case has entered into American folklore. It has become the poster child for tort reform," summarizes James Burgund, a jury consultant with Jury Selection Sciences in Dallas, Texas. Reed Morgan confirmed this point based on his own experience. Because of the negative stigma attached to the *McDonald's Coffee Case*, Morgan quickly witnessed the prejudice that subsequent jurors brought to his cases. In fact, Morgan has routinely filed motions requesting that no one link him or his law firm to the earlier case to obviate guilt by association with the legend....

Morgan himself was deeply hurt emotionally, professionally, and financially by the legacy of the *Liebeck* case. While the immediate settlement of case generated a decent return, his small practice and its modest income declined after the case. He represented several more victims of hot liquids, but then resolved to take no more such cases. Most important was the sense that he and his humble campaign against dangerous products had been wrongly charged and convicted by the press.

The one emotional thing that came out of this for me was, I kind of had the sense that if you really worked something real, real hard and get to the truth and win, that's the right thing to do. And I was just—there was this tremendous irony, that here's this lawyer who is not really a high profile lawyer, who tries to do quality work and does exactly what he's supposed to do and then this whole tort reform slam comes out of the case. It's like, why don't you pick on a guy that's got a hundred million dollars on a benzene case or an asbestos case? And the obvious answer is because they can make this one look ridiculous, but the nature of the facts.... I still feel to this day like it [the *Liebeck* case] is just escalated somewhere where it shouldn't be.

In our interview, Morgan was unwavering about the justice of the verdict for Ms. Liebeck and the campaign against dangerous products like excessively hot liquids.... In Morgan's perspective, the McDonald's coffee legend did offer a case study about greed, manipulation, and amoral institutional practices. The problem is that the legend itself focused on the wrong parties. This is what he told us about why the coffee case became a media phenomenon:

If you think it through what is going on, the mass media is controlled by big money. It's owned by big corporations. And they are much more interested in selling news and selling papers than selling the truth. So, and then they have the tort reformers feeding it. You have a certain bent of editors for a lot of national newspapers that are conservative. They see a lot of lawsuit news, high verdicts, because people call in high verdicts, they don't call in the 60 percent or so of jury verdicts that are zero verdicts. So they get a perception that here's another out-of-control lawsuit so they write it up. Because they know people want to read that and buy papers....

Conclusion: The Implications of Law's Lore

This essay has aimed to show how an unlikely lawsuit over spilt coffee was constructed by the mass media and tort reformers into a powerful symbol of runaway litigiousness, a legal system gone awry, and the erosion of traditional norms regarding individual self-restraint. We conclude by briefly pondering the broader implications of this legend's legacy for American legal culture.

Most generally, prevailing popular constructions of the hot coffee case have at once reflected and reinforced cultural tendencies to view relationships and events in terms of individual responsibility and blame. As such, the moralistic, individualizing, disciplinary logics of law are underwritten by popular representations about law. The *McDonald's Coffee Case* also, however, illustrates the very social costs and constraining implications of these logics.

We consider first the consequences for political debate about the rationality of the existing tort law system. The construction of the McDonald's case as a lightning rod for concern about the alleged litigation crisis inhibited the emergence of alternative constructions that complicated issues of individual blame with attention to other integrally related public concerns. For example, the injuries suffered by Ms. Liebeck and her frustrated resort to litigation could instead have highlighted the need for better consumer protection standards, better regulatory oversight, the need for expanded medical benefits for the elderly, the inadequate medical insurance options for most citizens in the United States, or the lack of workplace leave compensation policies to deal with family emergencies. After all, the high costs of medical treatment and the loss of wages by her daughter who had to take care of Ms. Liebeck prompted the reluctant plaintiff to sue. But virtually nowhere—in the media, among any of the major players on either side of the dispute, or among the politicians and policy advocates who appropriated the symbolic case for policy reasons—were any of these policy concerns raised in connection to the incident. This is particularly striking, because just a short time before the incident, President Clinton had unveiled proposals for radical transformation of health care and medical insurance in the United States.

Moreover, the core challenge to the enormous discretionary power, pecuniary motives, and unaccountable practices of corporate producers identified by Liebeck's lawyers barely saw the light of media attention. Indeed, what media coverage, popular legend, and political debate all obscured was just how anomalous was Stella Liebeck's victory in court against a multinational megacorporation. The motives of corporate-sponsored tort reformers in assailing this and many other cases are clear enough, of course. Plaintiffs of small means and low status who win substantial awards for challenging corporate recklessness destabilize the prevailing legal logic of distributing economic costs widely and generally supporting the unequal structure of capitalist society. Nevertheless, political activists, lawyers, scholars—including those on the ostensible political Left—were drawn into defending the existing inadequate, inegalitarian, inaccessible tort law system and contesting the case's significance in the moralistic terms of "individual responsibility" and reckless rapacity defined by tort reformers. The social construction of the *McDonald's Coffee Case* thus illustrates the ways in which prevailing hegemonic norms, institutional arrangements, and power relations reproduce themselves in politics.... However, the fact that virtually all parties have assessed the McDonald's case almost solely for what it did or did not reveal about an epidemic of predatory plaintiffs and their greedy attorneys dramatically evinces the narrowly moralistic and undemocratic public discourse characteristic of the contemporary neo-liberal era.

Finally, we note yet one other way in which the hot coffee legend is indirectly, subtly, and generally significant in contemporary American culture. We call attention again to how popular constructions of the hot coffee case have tended to reverse the very attributions of liability found in the official court of law. As is often the case in other legal domains such as criminal justice or welfare law, prevailing narratives tended toward blaming the victim for the painful injuries she suffered and thus stigmatized her efforts to claim rights as a means of redress. Left with little recourse but appeal to a legal system that protects profit, individualizes claims of harm, and commodifies relief, the seriously burned plaintiff was pilloried as selfish, greedy, and irresponsible in the court of public opinion.... [W]e suggest [that] the tort tales that are told and that we retell among ourselves impose a disciplinary force of restraint on the perceptions and practices of citizens as legal actors throughout contemporary American society. We have already noted examples of how the *McDonald's Coffee Case* reinforced concerns about plaintiff greed among jurors in subsequent cases around the nation that personal injury lawyers must address. Other scholarship confirms the anti-plaintiff, anti-rights, and pro-corporate predispositions that jurors typically bring into the courtroom. And yet other studies have similarly demonstrated how local legal officials—clerks, judges, police, etc.—routinely discourage and dismiss legal action on basic rights claims among citizens, and, especially among those "undeserving," many who are least privileged by inherited relations. We thus suggest that the legacy of the *McDonald's Coffee Case* illustrates the subtle ways in which prevailing hegemonic norms, institutional arrangements, and power relations reproduce themselves in ordinary life. The extensive, if unwitting, complicity of the American mass media in contributing to both the reproduction of such legal lore and its centrality in our shared national culture is no small part of this process by which the prevailing hierarchical, unaccountable order is sustained.

NOTES AND QUESTIONS

1. What is McCann, Haltom, and Bloom's view of the role of public opinion in legal change? To what extent do they stress the role of economic pressures in market economies? What, then, is the connection between law, culture, and social structure in this account? Notice that the authors pay special attention to the way the media as an institution has its effect on public opinion. What sorts of factors do they mention as influences on how the media reports on legal issues?

2. In an early article on the issue of culturally-shaped "crises," anthropologist Robert Hayden analyzed how the media handled rising rates and scarcity of liability insurance during the 1980s. Robert Hayden, "The Cultural Logic of a Political Crisis: Common Sense, Hegemony and the Great American Liability Insurance Famine of 1986," 11 *Studies in Law, Politics, and Society* 95 (1991). He traced the media coverage of a so-called "insurance crisis" that began to be widely publicized around 1986. Available research suggests that the insurance industry goes through boom and bust cycles, driven by "larger economic factors affecting insurance markets" such as the competitive practices of the insurance companies themselves. However, this explanation never received much public attention. Instead, the media focused on the purported role of the legal system in creating this insurance "crisis," charging that litigious Americans and outrageous jury awards forced the insurance companies to raise prices.

Hayden draws on anthropological research to explain how this approach could have been persuasive to the American public. He notes that, quite frequently, arguments succeed because they fit with "common sense"—that is, "underlying cultural assumptions of the way the world works, an unreflective form of practical knowledge." This kind of knowledge is powerfully conveyed through anecdotes and shared stories, and is not easily contested through data or research results. Hayden adds that common-sense cultural assumptions "may be shared by the common man or woman, but it is generated by elites"—and thus often serves hegemonic goals. Like McCann and his colleagues, Hayden demonstrates the important place of news coverage, magazines, advertisements, television, and other media in building the one-sided and misleading picture that became publicly accepted. Not coincidentally, Hayden argued, this picture aided the powerful insurance lobby by closing legal forms of recourse against them.

In his article, Hayden lists a number of "outrageous stories"—anecdotes that, however atypical or misleading, played a powerful role in shaping a new public outcry against the legal system (rather than the insurance companies). For example, in one case the AP, UPI and a number of newspapers announced that a woman "was awarded close to $1–million by Philadelphia jury ... after she said that a CAT scan ... made her lose her psychic abilities." In fact, the jury had been directed to disregard the issue of psychic powers. The case turned on evidence that the woman had suffered an allergic reaction to contrast dye administered in spite of the fact that she had informed the doctor of the allergy. The media not only skipped over this important "detail," they also did not widely disseminate the information that the judge in this case eventually threw out the verdict. The average reader, however, was left with the impression that the woman had received a great deal of money, and that it was given her in compensation for a loss of psychic powers.

In another case detailed by Hayden, the media reported that a man was awarded $300,000 for injuries from a fall he suffered when the ladder he had set up in a pile of manure slipped. The media coverage characterized the decision as based on the failure of the manufacturer to warn the buyer "about the danger of setting the ladder up in something as slippery as manure." In fact, the jury award was based on the fact that the ladder, "which had a safety rating that indicated it could support 1,000 pounds at midpoint, broke with less than 450 pounds on it."

Why do these horror stories make such intuitive sense to the American public? Hayden points to a focus on individual responsibility in American culture as one key factor, along with an aversion to using the courts for redistribution of wealth. This general cultural foundation gave insurance companies fertile ground for their concerted public relations campaign to divert blame away from their own practices and onto the legal system. How does Hayden's analysis of the events in 1986 fit with McCann et al.'s research on the *McDonald's Coffee Case*? Although contract cases can also have a redistributive effect, public anger has been focused on tort cases. A number of studies of U.S. attitudes toward the law at the time of Hayden's article were showing that Americans tended to view use of courts with some suspicion. Carol Greenhouse, Barbara Yngvesson, and David Engel, *Law and Community in Three American Towns* (1994). Ethnographic studies conducted in a variety of locations in the U.S. converged on a number of shared cultural themes—an emphasis on individual resourcefulness, restraint, and avoidance.

Hayden points to American culture as a fertile source of ideas that reinforced the common sense understanding that people had become too litigious and that runaway juries were the source of the problem. He says that the horror stories shock people because they offend certain root cultural notions—especially a preference for individualism and self-reliance. McCann et al. also point to a cultural bias in favor of individualism as one factor in public receptiveness to the McDonald's spilt coffee horror story. But is this correct? In *Total Justice* (1981), Lawrence Friedman tried to explain the rise of high liability in terms of American culture. Friedman's argument is that in the 19th century people did not expect "justice" in the sense of recovery of damages in compensation for injuries. Nobody had insurance, medicine was incapable of curing people, the welfare state did not exist, and plagues, calamities, and depressions occurred at random intervals. All of this made life a colossal drama of uncertainty. But the rise of insurance, the welfare state, modern medicine, and like produced a culture in which there is a "general expectation of justice." In the event of calamity, Americans now assume somebody will pay. See also Michele Landis Dauber, "Fate, Responsibility, and 'Natural' Disaster Relief: Narrating the American Welfare State," 33 Law & Society Review 257 (1999).

If Friedman is right, how do his ideas square with Hayden's?

4. In an article published in 2004, Laura Beth Nielsen and Aaron Beim analyzed national and local coverage of employment discrimination suits. Laura Beth Nielsen and Aaron Beim, "Media Misrepresentation: Title VII, Print Media, and Public Perceptions of Discrimination Litigation," 15 *Stanford Law and Policy Review* 237 (2004). They document that the media coverage report a plaintiff win-rate that is almost three times greater than the actual rate; the awards in the cases covered by the media have a median value of almost six times the actual median value of awards in these kinds of suits.

5. Since the 1970s, numerous states have enacted legislation in response to a perceived epidemic of lawsuits: for example, as of 2005 over 30 states had put statutory caps on either general noneconomic compensatory damages, or similar limits specific to medical malpractice cases. Catherine Sharkey, "Unintended Consequences of Medical Malpractice Damages Caps," 80 *New York University Law Review* 391, 412 (2005). Sharkey's article argues that damages caps have had several unintended effects, including encouraging attorneys to ask for more in economic (as opposed to noneconomic) damages, and "knocking out cases of people with potentially serious injuries who do not fare well in the labor market." (p. 492). Stephen Daniels and Joanne Martin recently examined the effects of tort reform in Texas. Stephen Daniels and Joanne Martin, "The Texas Two–Step: Evidence on the Link Between Damage Caps

and Access to the Civil Justice System," 55 *DePaul Law Review* 635 (2006). Their interviews with plaintiffs' lawyers lends support to Sharkey's last claim; as one lawyer interviewed for the study explained:

> "However, we had House Bill 4 and Proposition 12 passed in Texas, which virtually gutted anyone's ability to go in and stand up for the rights of the elderly in the nursing home setting. The biggest problem is the cap on damages; the $250,000 cap does nothing more than hurt the children and the housewives and the elderly the most, because they don't have any economic damages, they don't have any earning capacity and they don't have any lost wages. . . ." (p. 668)

6.   The team of Daniels and Martin has been studying the plaintiff's bar in Texas for a number of years. Stephen Daniels and Joanne Martin, " 'The Impact That It Has Had Is Between People's Ears:' Tort Reform, Mass Culture, and Plaintiffs' Lawyers," 50 *DePaul Law Review* 453 (2000). Long before any legislation was introduced, tort reformers had begun to try to influence legal outcomes through media campaigns. These campaigns were not based on "systematic empirical investigation of the civil justice system," but were instead based on sophisticated marketing techniques, and aimed at conveying a fundamentally political message about the courts to the public and key elites. The goal of this marketing effort was to discourage the use of courts by individuals who sought damages from large companies—often insurance companies. It sounded an alarmist tone, announcing that there was a "litigation crisis," and that "lawsuit abuse" threatened to close down hospitals and ruin businesses. The villains of the piece are of course, the lawyers—followed closely by greedy plaintiffs in search of unfair windfalls, and runaway juries who were out to punish those with "deep pockets" regardless of the merits of individual cases. (Empirical research, incidentally, does not support this "deep pockets" hypothesis. See Neil Vidmar, "Empirical Evidence on the Deep Pockets Hypothesis: Jury Awards for Pain and Suffering in Medical Malpractice Cases," 43 *Duke Law Journal* 217 (1993); Valerie Hans, "The Illusions and Realities of Jurors' Treatment of Corporate Defendants," 48 *DePaul Law Review* 327 (1998).) Some studies have seemed to suggest that exposure to these kinds of ads could negatively affect people's willingness to award high damages, to the extent that it influences their general beliefs about whether plaintiffs generally reap unfair rewards from the civil justice system. See, e.g., Shari Diamond et al., "Juror Judgments About Liability and Damages: Sources of Validity and Ways to Increase Consistency," 48 *DePaul Law Review* 301 (1998); Elizabeth Loftus, "Insurance Advertising and Jury Awards," 65 *American Bar Association Journal* 69 (1979); Philip G. Peters, Jr., "Doctors and Juries," 105 *Michigan Law Review* 1453 (2007) ("This article synthezes three decades of jury research. Contrary to popular belief, the data show that juries consistently sympathize more with doctors who are sued than with patients who sue them.")

Daniels and Martin trace a fascinating link between shifts in public opinion (in reaction to tort reform advertising) and access to justice. In this case, plaintiffs' lawyers perceived a drop in the amount of damages juries were willing to award following the ad campaign. Whether those changes are real or not (and the authors find some evidence to support the attorneys' perceptions), just the belief that juries have changed actually affects legal practice and access to justice—because attorneys, acting on that belief, change the kinds of cases they are willing to take (and how hard they are willing to fight before settling). On the other side, defense lawyers and insurance adjusters

> also adjust their practices to what they believe juries are saying. For instance, [one] defense lawyer . . . said that the insurance companies who hire him are now taking the position that "we ain't paying nothing . . . they are real tight with money . . . because juries are real tight now." (p. 475)

What is the relationship here between public opinion, social change, and legal change?

Daniels and Martin distinguish between "popular culture" and "mass culture," which they see as differing depending on "where particular ideas about the world around us originate, how they are disseminated, and for what purpose." (p. 458). They view the ideas in popular culture as variable and local, emerging "from below as a part of everyday life"—whereas mass culture is consciously imposed from above to broad audiences, and conveys standardized messages. What is the difference between Daniels and Martin's conception of "mass culture" and hegemony? How would McCann's view compare to the view expressed by Daniels and Martin?

7. Despite mounting empirical evidence to the contrary, the fight against the "litigation explosion" continues. Why does it continue to be so successful? Part of the explanation may be the unpopularity of lawyers. Lawyers bear the blame; they make money from lawsuits, and therefore they have a selfish reason for whipping up claims. Susan Daicoff, in her book *Lawyer, Know Thyself: A Psychological Analysis of Personality Strengths and Weaknesses* (2004), argues that lawyers also differ from "normal people" in terms of personal characteristics. Summarizing available empirical research, she concludes that not only does the average law student differ from others in terms of these traits, but then law training and practice encourage or amplify tendencies such as: greater than normal emphasis on logic and thought as opposed to feelings; authoritarianism; increased ambitiousness and aggressiveness when tense or anxious; a decrease in altruism and an increase in cynicism (particularly following law school). Daicoff hypothesizes that this gap in core orientations also contributes to public alienation from lawyers. Conflict theorists might also point to the role of the legal system in protecting the wealthy and powerful in society; anthropologists who have performed ethnography in U.S. courts note as well that the average person frequently encounters the legal system as ignoring their core complaints while besieging them with annoying bureaucratic requirements. Sally Merry, *Getting Justice and Getting Even: Legal Consciousness among Working–Class Americans* (1990); John Conley and William O'Barr, *Rules versus Relationships: The Ethnography of Legal Discourse* (1990).

Whatever the cause, attacks on lawyers are an old theme in popular culture. We can point to Carl Sandburg's poem, "The Lawyers Know Too

Much," in *Smoke and Steel* (1920), where he asks "Why does a hearse horse snicker hauling a lawyer away?" Anti-lawyer jokes are common. The image is that lawyers create trouble among people who would otherwise be peaceful. For a discussion of the public's negative perception of lawyers, see Marc Galanter, *Lowering the Bar: Lawyer Jokes and Legal Culture* (2005). Galanter tracks changes in the numbers and nastiness of lawyer jokes, which he sees as increasing markedly since 1980. He analyzes this resentment as a reaction against the domination of law in our society. Galanter has also traced other sources of criticism aimed at the legal system; in the 1970s, President Carter and others criticized lawyers for not providing better access to justice for lower income Americans, while in the 1980s, a different group of critics began to argue that lawyers were actually bringing too many cases to court. Marc Galanter, "Predators and Parasites: Lawyer–Bashing and Civil Justice," 28 *Georgia Law Review* 633 (1994).

(3) Doubts and Qualifications About Law as the Product of Public Opinion

(3.6) Parental Authority: The Community and the Law

Julius Cohen, Reginald A. Robson and Alan P. Bates

(1958).

[This classic study, a rare example of close collaboration between legal scholars and social scientists, attempted to measure "the moral sense of the community," and compare this "moral sense" with "legal norms". The study was conducted in Nebraska. A trained staff of interviewers administered questions to a carefully selected sample of residents of the state. The total sample population was 860.

The questions concerned various aspects of social and legal norms relating to the authority of parents over children. A sample section of the study follows. First the question is given, as administered to the subjects, then the position of the law is stated, then the "view of the community," then a comparison of the two.]

The Issue: Parental authority to disinherit the child completely. Question 23 deals with this.

QUESTION 23A: "Suppose that either the husband or wife is dead, and the survivor willed all of his or her property to persons or groups outside the family, and left nothing at all for the children. If the parent is legally allowed to do this, it could mean that the child might have to depend on some outside source for the necessities of life. On the other hand, if the parent is prevented by law from doing this, he would not be able to will his property as he sees fit. In these circumstances, do you think that the parent should legally be allowed to will all of his or her property to persons or groups outside the family and leave nothing at all for the children, or should the law prevent this?"

Position of the law: It would seem that the parent would be permitted to disinherit his offspring, except for an amount that would be required to support parentless children under 14. Beyond this exception, the privilege of testamentary disposition would not be affected by the age or economic status of the children, or by the intrinsic worth of the object of the disposition; nor would the privilege be affected if exercise of it resulted in benefit to one child and not to another.

Views of the community: In responding to the situation presented in Question 23A the members of the sample were asked to indicate whether their opinion would be affected by the fact that the child was under or over 21 years of age (23Bi and 23Bii). Following this, in Questions 23Ci and 23Cii, the factor of the economic status of the child was introduced into the picture. Next, in Questions 23Di and 23Dii, respondents were asked to take into consideration with respect to the basic issue the question of the worthiness of the recipients of the parental estate. In the final sub-question (23E), people were asked to suppose that the parent left all his assets to only one of several children, all of whom were in about the same financial circumstances. The way in which community opinion is distributed and its degree of stability in these changing contexts are recorded in Table 12.

TABLE 12
SHOULD THE LAW ALLOW PARENTS TO DISINHERIT CHILDREN?
(Expressed in Percentages of Total Population)

Question	Allow	Prevent	Don't Know
23A (See above.)			
23Bi and Bii			
Child is under 21 years of age	5.5	93.4	1.2
Child is over 21 years of age	35.5	63.4	1.2
23Ci and Cii			
Child is poor	7.0	92.0	1.0
Child is well-off financially	40.8	57.3	1.9
23Di and Dii			
Parents leave assets to unworthy group	5.1	93.8	1.0
Parents leave assets to worthy group	18.6	79.2	2.2
23E Discrimination between children exists	19.4	78.5	2.1

A quick comparison of "Allow" and "Prevent" responses for all parts of this question shows that in all cases a clear majority (and in several instances a very large majority) is of the opinion that the law should not allow a parent to disinherit a child completely. We find an extremely high congruence of views where the child is under 21 years of age, where the child is poor and where the parent leaves his assets to some beneficiary unworthy to receive them.

If the child is over 21 years of age, more than a third of the population would agree that parents should be legally entitled to omit the child from the will. Likewise, where the child is well-off financially in his own right, 40.8% would support a parent's right to make no provision for the child. A much less notable, but still considerable effect is produced by the assumption that the parent wishes to leave all his assets to a worthy cause; 18.6% would agree that the law should support the parent with such a purpose in mind. By and large, however, there appears to be an impressively high degree of agreement in the population that parents do have an obligation to their children which extends beyond their own death.

So far as the relation between community opinion and law on this issue is concerned, it is plain that most persons in the population disagree with the law, except in the case where a parentless child under 14 would be left without support. As indicated earlier, the law in this instance would require the parent's estate to provide support for the child.

[At the end of the study, the authors summed up their findings. They found wide disharmony between social and legal norms in Nebraska. "Of the 17 issues examined, the community and the existing law would disagree as to ten, agree as to five, and perhaps evenly divide as to one.... The majority in the community would favor greater legal restrictions on parental authority over the child than the law presently requires." (pp. 193–94)

These findings, somewhat to the authors' surprise, reflected general community feelings and did not vary as between "social groupings." "By and large, there are no substantial differences between the views of the members of various social groupings within the community toward the issues we studied, based on such factors as sex, residential area, religion, age, income, parenthood, schooling and occupation." (p. 195).

Why the great variance between community and legal norms? The authors saw three major factors: the "built-in professional conservatism" of lawyers and judges; the lack of "pressure" from the public for change; and the "inadequacy of prevailing techniques utilized by law-makers for ascertaining the moral sense of the community." (p. 195).]

(3.7) Review of Cohen, Robson & Bates

Luke Cooperrider

57 *Michigan Law Review* 1119 (1959).

A law professor and two sociologists report herein on a joint attempt to assess the degree of congruence between existing legal doctrine, in a defined area of application, and a factor which the authors call "the moral sense of the community." The justification for the study is provided by the law member of the team, and proceeds from the observation that legal scholars, groping for standards of criticism external to the law, seem to gravitate toward a "sense of justice," or of "injustice"—toward a view of morality, at least, which is shared, to some degree, by the people in the community wherein the law is applicable. The authors vigorously and repeatedly disclaim a position on whether or to what extent such a common moral sense should by the law be taken into account. They assert, however, that law-makers, both legislative and judicial, do in fact frequently refer to it, and the argument is that if the moral sense of the community is relevant at all, then it makes sense to consider how that datum may be ascertained more scientifically than by the divination or intuition of the individual judge or legislator. Their study is offered as an example of how this may be done by making use of the developed techniques of public opinion research. They do not suggest, of course, the canvassing of the community's moral sense in order to establish premises for the adjudication of individual cases. It is argued, rather, that within a given area of law it would be possible to establish community reactions to a selected battery of propositions, and that these reactions could then be used as analogical bases for prediction of community reaction to other situations in a way which, to lawyers, would be quite familiar. Their project is an experimental survey of this type in the general area of parent-child relations. . . .

It is, perhaps, unresponsive to argue the merits of the questions which were propounded to the public, for, as I have said, the authors carefully disclaim any position on the extent to which the law should seek to effectuate the community moral sense which they were investigating. They set out to establish a method, not a matrix for the remaking of the law in the area of family relations. They were, nevertheless, unable completely to conceal their feeling that their study could be used by "lawmakers whose juristic philosophy stakes out as an objective a high degree of harmony between the existing law and the moral sense of the community" as a ready-made set of specifications for law revision in the area of family law. Furthermore, as it seems to me, their failure to consider the basic question—what bearing should community moral attitudes have with reference to the specific problems propounded—has led them into a fallacy which is fundamental, and which would be very difficult to avoid in any similar project. . . .

On . . . six issues where disagreement between law and morals was found, the law, at the present time, occupies a position of laissez faire. The questions relate to parental "authority" (1) to determine whether a child may have a college education, (2) to determine the child's religious affiliation, (3) to prevent the child from entering a career of his own choosing, (4) to transfer custody of a child to another person without legal supervision, (5) to disinherit the child, and (6) to treat the child's earnings as the parent's own property. In all six cases it is assumed that the law bestows upon the parent the "authority" indicated, and in all six cases the community view, according to the survey, was that the law should "prevent" the parents from exercising such authority. It is on these six issues that an unequivocal discrepancy is found between the law and the moral standards of the community, and it must be principally in connection with these issues that we judge the authors' assertions that there is a serious lag between law and public opinion, a lag which they suggest is to be attributed to imperfections in the political process, and to the "dissenting acquiescence" of a population too inert to resist.

Considering these six issues, it will be noted that the parental "authority" referred to in the first three instances is nothing more than the de facto compulsion which the parent, by the very existence of the family relation, is enabled to exert. The extent of its legal recognition is that the state has not established procedures for supervising it, and the probability is that if an issue between parent and child were in some manner raised in court, the court would refuse to interfere unless the acts by which the compulsion was exerted were criminal, or so abusive as to place in legal jeopardy the parent's custody of the child. In assessing the reasons mentioned by the respondents for their indicated views, the authors thought that there was a noteworthy absence of feeling that the law should not intrude itself into the parent-child relationship. The percentage of those who took the "allow" position and who adverted to this point was relatively small, throughout. The authors' interpretation of this fact is exemplified by the following comment: "Although where the choice of a child's religious affiliation is concerned, there is greater expressed sentiment in the community against the role of government than when the issue relates to the availability of a college education, the predominant sentiment, nevertheless, would still recognize the need to respect the child's independent choice of religious affiliation, and, if required, to employ legal sanctions against the parent to effectuate it." (p. 171). A bit farther on the authors indicate that "Those who favored some legal control of parental authority ... were not asked just what specific type of legal controls should be imposed: this would have been far too involved and complicated for our undertaking. It is fairly safe to assume that they favored some government-sanctioned means—the exercise of authority outside the realm of parental control for the achievement of the given ends." (p. 186; emphasis added, in part).

I agree that it would probably have been both impracticable and useless to have raised the "how" question with the average member of the public. But is it not of the essence? I submit that these answers cannot be taken to be, in any practical sense, a true representation of community desires, for it is apparent that the respondents had not the slightest awareness of the practical implications of their answers. Some of the questions incorporated a caveat, "if the law prevented the parents from keeping the child out of college, it would reduce parental control and increase the amount of outside authority over the family to that extent." But how much meaning does this carry to one who is not familiar with the workings of the political-legal machinery of the state? If the questions had been formulated not in the denatured "should the law allow or prevent?" form, but in the terms in which they would be faced by the legislator or the judge—"Should a statute be enacted establishing a Family Liberties Commission with power to conduct investigations into invasions by parents of certain enumerated liberties of their children, to issue subpoenas and compel testimony, and to issue cease and desist orders against parents found to have committed such invasions, and to maintain actions in court to compel obedience to such orders, etc."—or—"Should a child who feels himself aggrieved by the act of his parent refusing to him his right of free religious association be permitted to maintain in the courts an action for injunctive relief, etc."—is it likely that the citizenry would have exhibited the same enthusiasm for the Big Brother approach that this survey seems to have revealed?

The other three of the six instances of disagreement between law and morals are somewhat different, involving situations (transfer of custody, disinheritance, parental ownership of child's earnings) which can, by a lawyer, be more easily conceived of as subjects of legal regulation. As the descent of property is already regulated by law, there would be no great derangement if the applicable law excluded complete disinheritance of a child. It might be doubted that the respondents have envisioned all the implications, but at least the probabilities are greater here that an implementation of their views would not produce practical consequences which would shock the majority of people affected. Administrative difficulties are certainly very substantial with reference to the custody and ownership of earnings issues, however. It is easy to pass a law—"Any person who, without prior approval of the probate court, gives his child into the custody of another person (permanently? for a period in excess of ___ days? with the intent to abandon custody himself?) shall be guilty of a misdemeanor." Enforcement would be another matter, family connections being as casual as, regrettably, they sometimes are. And with reference to the child's earnings, how should the law attend to their protection? It would be possible, I suppose, to require all parents to account as fiduciaries, periodically or upon the attainment by their children of majority, but I would imagine that compliance would be secured only to the accompaniment of a considerable amount of kicking and screaming.

... To me [the study] furnishes strong evidence of the necessity for continuing close attention to the factors which make it practicable and desirable to seek some social objectives through legal standards and sanctions, while making it equally apparent that other objectives must be left to other forms of social control. I have no doubt that the moral views indicated by the survey are effective in assuring that few parents actually exercise the full extent of the "authority" over their children which the law would probably tolerate. I am equally certain that to attempt to bring the law into alignment with these views would be rank folly. Law does not consist solely of norms of conduct. The official sanction through which the norm is enforced is an inescapable concomitant. A personal conviction as to what, in the abstract, ought to be, may serve very well as a moral standard, operating through the conscience and will of the individual, but it cannot be assumed that the same conviction would survive a marriage to official compulsion. Many of the norms which were approved by the respondents in the Nebraska survey are such that they could be brought to bear upon the community only through legal sanctions which, according to this reader's intuition, would be found, by the same persons who approved the norms, to be quite intolerable, and by the agents of the law to be incapable of administration. I would submit, therefore, that an inquiry into popular views of "what the law should be" can be most misleading if it does not raise, with the persons interviewed, the legislative question in all its complexity. If that question were raised, I would doubt the ability of the great majority of all citizens to respond to it in an informed and intelligent way. Query, then, whether the law-maker can expect as much help from the opinion surveyor as these authors suggest.

NOTES AND QUESTIONS

1. Did Cohen, Robson, and Bates really measure the moral sense of the "community" or that of individuals in isolation? Is there a difference? Should they have separately tried to ascertain what "leaders" in the community felt about these questions? Was it incorrect to give equal weight to the opinions of people who had had to make policy decisions (and who had greater experience and information) and those who had never even considered the problems involved? See Herbert Marcuse, "Repressive Tolerance," in Robert Wolff et al., *A Critique of Pure Tolerance* 81–117 (1965).

2. To what extent, if at all, should a legislator, administrator, or judge consult the moral sense of the community? Consider the following:

> Many things that are immoral are, nevertheless, not proper subjects for criminal punishment. And some things that unthinking public opinion has put in criminal codes ought to be taken out. . . .
>
> Quantification of public opinion will be useful, for example, to persuade legislators that the voters are not as benighted as some suppose. . . . But, as respects law reform, precise knowledge of prevailing public attitudes can hardly do more than indicate the limit of mass tolerance for immediate changes.[26]

Is this general viewpoint the same as Cooperrider's? What are the similarities and differences?

3. In her research on attitudes toward contract law among merchants, Lisa Bernstein argues against the approach of Article 2 of the UCC, based on her contention that it doesn't fit well with current prevailing opinions in that community. Lisa Bernstein, "Merchant Law in a Merchant Court: Rethinking the Code's Search for Immanent Business Norms," 144 *University of Pennsylvania Law Review* 1765 (1996), Lisa Bernstein, "The Questionable Basis of Article 2's Incorporation Strategy: A Preliminary Study," 66 *University of Chicago Law Review* 710 (1999). Bernstein contends that the merchant community would prefer more hard-and-fast formal rules to the UCC's approach, which looks to the customs and practices of the industries, and the actual understandings that developed in particular relationships, for guidelines in resolving disputes. Accepting Bernstein's description of prevailing opinion at the time of her interviews, is the opinion of the merchant community a valid basis for altering the UCC? How long does a consensus of a community last? If one decided to change the law to conform with community

---

26. Louis B. Schwartz, "Ascertaining the Moral Sense of the Community: A Comment," 8 *Journal of Legal Education* 319, 320 (1955).

sentiment (assuming that were possible), at what point would one have to seek a fresh reading of the community's pulse? What if you could prove that an opinion had been stable over a long period of time, as opposed to being an immediate reaction to an event?

4. <u>Public opinion and civil liberties</u>: Cohen, Robson, and Bates concluded that the community wanted more controls than the law afforded them. At different times in U.S. history, a sophisticated survey might have shown that the general public believed in stifling unpopular views, or in perpetuating racial segregation. Perhaps it might find a substantial difference between the general public and their political leaders—or between political elites and the courts—in their willingness to interpret the Constitution in ways that protect minority rights. This point was made in Samuel A. Stouffer, *Communism, Conformity, and Civil Liberties* (1955).

In addition, studies have shown that the public's commitment to civil liberties varies according to external factors such as a heightened sense of danger from terrorism or war. In their article in the *American Journal of Political Science*, Davis and Silver report on a national survey of Americans that was conducted after the September 11, 2001 attack. Darren Davis and Brian Silver, "Civil Liberties vs. Security: Public Opinion in the Context of the Terrorist Attacks on America," 48 *American Journal of Political Science* 28 (2004). They found that as people's sense of threat from terrorism reached higher levels, they became more willing to accept curtailments on civil liberties. However, those who had lower trust in government were less likely to allow the level of threat to affect their opinions on civil liberties. African–Americans were least likely to favor a lowering of civil liberties in times of heightened security concerns.

Geoffrey Stone traced the history of American responses to war from the 1700s through the present day. Geoffrey Stone, *Perilous Times: Free Speech in Wartime from the Sedition Act of 1798 to the War on Terrorism* (2004). He concluded that civil liberties have always been at risk during these unstable times, but that in each instance appeals to law eventually helped to restore balance. Stone's overall picture is optimistic: that over time the United States has learned from past mistakes, so that in the post 9–11 climate there was no internment of Arab–Americans as there was of Japanese–Americans during World War II. Do you agree with Stone's overall conclusion? Nonetheless, Stone warns that the U.S. system of justice is never more at peril than during times of war and national crisis. Think back over the various discussions in this chapter of the impact of crises on law—from Dicey to McCann. How does Stone's view fit with these approaches?

Interestingly, Stone urges greater reliance on the formal structure of legal provisions as a protection against these incursions on civil liberties. Thus he proposes that stronger formal rules be put in place to protect civil liberties during wartime; a rule, for example that would prohibit Congress "from enacting wartime legislation that limits dissent without full and fair deliberation." Stone hopes that a formal rule requiring careful deliberation will remind legislators not to cave under the pressures of a perceived "crisis." How well do you think such formal rules would work? Stone himself, in his historical narrative, credits lower-level officials in the Justice Department officials with reigning in the Bureau of Investigation during World War I, for example, and War department attorneys during World War II with objecting to the idea of Japanese internment. (We will return to issues of institutions and institutional actors in subsequent parts of this chapter.)

5.   Is the legal model of Cohen, Robson, and Bates accurate? That is, have they really measured the law with the same care that they lavished on "public opinion"? Alan Milner, in a review of the study,[27] makes this remark:

> In a study which sets out to contrast the "moral sense" with the "law," the latter gets an unjustifiably static treatment. "Law" to Messrs. Cohen, Robson, and Bates consists of norms "in the more traditional sense ... law ready to be applied if and when the occasion calls". This apparently means an application of statutes and judicial precedent without insight or imagination—a condition of immobility which hardly matches up to the decisions of which we know the courts are capable. Into all the questions of their study, for instance, the authors introduced "significant factual variations" to gauge the moral sense more accurately. They naturally found answers to their questions varying just as significantly. But nowhere is there the slightest suggestion that if a judge were faced with a similar variation, he might find a legal way to label it significant and so come up with a decision to suit his own moral sense.

6.   If the moral sense of the community should be consulted, how should it be done?

     a.   What are the advantages and disadvantages of using modern survey research methods?

     b.   What if a lawmaker wanted to use her own hunch or intuition about the moral sense of the community, in making policy choices? Is this a defensible move from a sociological point of view? Is the lawmaker entitled to consider herself as an adequate sample of the community's moral sense? What influences her behavior and hunches, and what influences her perception of her role? Are judges any differently situated than legislators in this regard?

7.   What are the limitations of using surveys? Even on the authors' own terms, is Cohen, Robson, and Bates' study valid only for Nebraska? Does it capture the mood of a particular time, and therefore need constant updating?

Does it matter that the general public often lacks up-to-date knowledge about specific laws? Studies in both the United States and Europe have shown that people know surprisingly little about specific provisions of laws that affect them. Hearst Corporation, *The American Public, the Media, and the Judicial System: A National Survey on Public Awareness and Personal Experience* (1983). Berl Kutchinsky, "The Legal Consciousness: A Survey of

---

27.   Alan Milner, "Book Review," 21 *University of Pittsburgh Law Review* 147 (1959).

Research on Knowledge and Opinion about Law," in Adam Podgorecki et al., *Knowledge and Opinion About Law*, at 101, 103–105 (1973).

(4) Law as the Product of Legal Culture

(3.8) Legal Culture and the Welfare State

Lawrence M. Friedman[28]

... The legal system, in short, is a ship that sails the seas of social force. And the concept of legal culture is crucial to an understanding of legal development. By legal culture, we mean the ideas, attitudes, values, and beliefs that people hold about the legal system.... Not that any particular country has a single, unified legal culture. Usually there are many cultures in a country, because societies are complex, and are made up of all sorts of groups, classes and strata. One should also distinguish between internal legal culture (the legal culture of lawyers and judges) and external (the legal culture of the population at large). We can, if we wish, also speak about the legal culture of taxi drivers, or rich people, or businessmen, or black people. Presumably, no two men or women have exactly the same attitudes toward law, but there are no doubt tendencies that correlate systematically with age, sex, income, nationality, race and so on. At least this is plausible....

Social scientists, approaching the legal system, begin with a master hypothesis: that social change will lead, inexorably, to legal change. This of course puts the matter far too simply. If one asks, how social change leads to legal change, the first answer is: by means of legal culture. That is, social change leads to changes in people's values and attitudes, and this sets up chains of demands (or withdrawals), which in turn push law and government in some particular direction....

... [T]he increase in scope and power [of government] has been in response to demands from society itself. The state did what people wanted it to do ("people" here meaning whoever had influence or power)....

Technological and social changes in society, of course, lie behind rising demands.... All societies are interdependent, but in modern industrial society there is a new, peculiar form of interdependence. Strangers are in charge of important parts of our lives—people we do not know, and cannot control ... Hence we demand norms from the state, from the collectivity, to guarantee the work of those strangers whose work is vital to our lives, which we cannot guarantee by ourselves.

Out of this cycle of demands, the modern state builds up a body of health and safety law. The rules become denser, more formal. Informal norms are

28. In Teubner (ed.) *Dilemmas of Law in the Welfare State*, at 13, 17, 18–19, 20, 22, 23 (1985).

effective in regulating relationships, for small groups, families, people in face to face contact, in villages, in tribal life. They are not good enough for relationships among strangers, who "meet" only in the form of a product that one group makes and the other consumes; or who "meet" in an auto accident. Informal norms do not work for many problems and relationships in large, complex, mobile societies, when the villages have shattered into thousands of pieces, only to form again into the great ant-hills of our cities. For such societies, and such relationships, people demand active intervention from the generalized third party, or, in other words, the law. . . .

Yet the more the state undertakes, the more it creates a climate that leads to still further increases in demand. This is because of a fundamental— and very natural—change in the legal culture. State action creates expectations. It redefines what seems to be the possible human limits of law; it extends the boundaries. After a while, what is possible comes to be taken for granted, and then treated as if it were part of the natural order. Taxes creep forward slowly, benefit programs are added on one at a time, programs of regulation evolve step by step. Each move redefines the scope of the system. The next generation accepts what its parents argued about, as easily as it accepts sunshine and rain. Expectations, then, have been constantly rising. . . .

. . . Obviously, especially in hard times, the state has trouble keeping its promises; and population trends (too many old people on pensions) make things worse. . . .

. . . Demands on government in the 19th century were restrained by the feeling, in area after area, that there was nothing that could be done. . . . The uncertainty of life must have had a profound effect on legal culture. People expected misfortune, and they expected "injustice"—not necessarily human injustice, but the injustice of an unjust world, a world so arranged as to strike out in capricious and unfair ways, or at any event, mysterious, unfathomable ways. . . .

In the contemporary world, the situation has turned upside down. A great revolution in expectations has taken place, of two sorts: first, a general expectation that the state will guarantee total justice, and second (and for our purposes more important), a general expectation that the state will protect us from catastrophe. It will also make good all losses that are not our "fault." The modern state is a welfare state, which is also an insurance state—a state that knows how to spread the risks . . .

(3.9) American Legal Culture: The Last Thirty–Five Years

Lawrence M. Friedman

35 *St. Louis Law Journal* 529 (1991).

... Legal institutions are reflections of social institutions; and they ... have been thoroughly revised and revamped and remolded over the years.

In the last thirty-five years, there have been dizzying changes in every area of life.... And, corresponding to the dramatic changes in technology, and in social arrangements, there have been major changes too, in legal culture—by which I mean the attitudes and expectations of the public with regard to law—and through these changes, in the very fabric of the law itself....

The very fact of change—constant, ceaseless change—is of prime importance in the legal culture. Change is so obvious, so palpable, that it comes to be accepted; it comes to be taken as normal. At one time, law was treated as timeless, immemorial: sacred custom, encrusted with tradition. Stasis was normal; change was exceptional, unexpected, unwanted. A more instrumental concept of law took hold roughly two centuries ago; and each time the pace of social change ratchets upward, the law itself changes, and, more significantly, the idea of a fixed, settled law receives a further blow. What was once inscribed on tablets, and supposed to last an eternity, now comes in loose leaf binders, with pocket-parts for instantaneous change; and new editions every year.... [I]n the computer age, people grow accustomed to the fact of rapid change, rapid manipulation of facts and principles, rapid storage, rapid unstorage; people are therefore less likely to accept the status quo, more apt to demand change that works in their favor. At least this is a working hypothesis.

No field of law has remained static over the last 35 years; many fields have been thoroughly transformed. Constitutional law, and the related field of civil rights, have perhaps changed most of all. (Paradoxically, the keystone text, the 14th Amendment, is exactly the same as it was in 1868; in this branch of law, of course, "interpretation" is all....)

The civil rights revolution, of course, was enormously important in its own right. No problem in American law, and in American life, has been more important, more deep-seated, than the relationship between the black and the white populations; and the relationship between women and men is if anything even more fundamental and pervasive. Changes in that relationship dig very deep into the social fabric. Thirty-five years have brought about dramatic reordering. But the civil rights revolution and the feminist movement are also indicators or outcroppings of an even broader, wider transformation in law and in life. The movements are signs of the tremendous, growing strength of a radical form of individualism, an aspect of general and legal culture which has, more than anything else, contributed to there making of American life and law.

It may seem peculiar to treat the struggle for the rights of (say) blacks and Hispanics as illustrations of radical individualism; a case could be made that the civil rights movement, and the various liberation movements that followed after it, show the power of claims for group rights, rather than for individual rights. But this proposition, I believe, is misleading. The essence of each liberation movement is the demand that society treat each individual as an individual, a unique person; and not as a member of a race, class, religion, gender, or group. "Discrimination" means throwing all blacks, or women, or gays, or handicapped people, into a single basket, making judgments on the basis of group stereotypes or prejudices. Even the arguments for affirmative action are, at bottom, individualistic: past discrimination has put individuals at a disadvantage, and it takes special measures to bring them to the starting line.

Individualism, especially in the form which Robert Bellah and his associates have called "expressive individualism,"[29] is, in general, a feature of character-formation in modern, Western society. But it seems particularly strong, even virulent, in the United States.... At least for white males, the United States from the outset was a country of amazing mobility-geographic, social, cultural. Compared to the United States, even the democracies of Europe seemed stagnant, hide-bound, traditional.

The technological changes of the last thirty-five years have only strengthened American individualism. They have further weakened traditional authority—including the authority of the family. Indeed, the classic patriarchal family hardly exists anymore in the United States. But neither does the matriarchal family. Families may be "headed" by men or (increasingly) by women; but to be "head" of a family is no longer what it used to be; it no longer means some sort of absolute authority.

In traditional societies, authority was vertical, hierarchical. The primary group—those who were in face-to-face contact—exerted the most decisive influence on members of society. The family was in control of the personality and character of the child, and the family, along with village notables—local priests, elders, chiefs, squires—transmitted values and ideas to the child. No other influences could even reach the child in its isolated hut or home. In the television age, on the other hand, authority and power have become much more horizontal. The child is no longer isolated. The parents no longer have the first and last word; their authority is no longer exclusive. From almost day one, images and messages flow in from outside—from television most notably—messages from a larger world. This is one of the major reasons for the emergence of a new kind of person: the expressive individual, oriented

---

29. I have explored this theme in more detail in Lawrence Friedman, *The Republic of Choice: Law, Authority, and Culture* (1990). Robert Bellah, et al., *Habits of the Heart: Individualism and Commitment in American Life* (1985). Expressive individualism is the view that each person "has a unique core of feeling and intuition that should unfold or be expressed if individuality is to be realized." Id. at 334.

toward fads, and fashions, toward the values of television rather than the values of tradition, toward the authority of peers rather than the authority of parents.

The media allow information to reach "huge audiences" in an instant; they increase "opportunities for individuals to obtain information and organize it according to their needs;" the media have a vast "linking power," an ability to "locate persons with certain qualities or interests and communicate with them." This power permits and fosters the formation of horizontal interest groups—groups that are geographically distant, made up of separate individuals, bound together in a "community" formed by mail, radio, or TV. These groups—for or against handgun control; concerned with women's rights or conversely with the traditional family; for environmental protection, or preservation of rare animals; for more or better taxes; for control of poverty—these are the dynamos that turn the engine of public policy today.

Individualism, I believe, underlies the civil rights revolution and its satellites; but it also crops up in every corner of the legal system. It pervades family law, for example. The no-fault divorce, which swept the country from 1970 on, legitimized, in effect, the idea of divorce on demand. Whatever else no-fault divorce means, it represents the triumph of expressive individualism. It strips marriage of the aura of sacredness, of permanence; it denies a public or state interest in the continuation of marriage. Marriage becomes, instead, simply a matter of individual choice. The parties decide when to begin it and when to end it. When marriage fails to bring fulfillment, to either partner, that partner has the absolute right to break the marriage off—and start again, with someone else. That this conception has been so successful in the last two decades, that it spread from West to East so rapidly; that it dealt so cavalierly with traditional scruples against divorce-at-will only demonstrates how strong, how deep-seated, were the changes in legal culture that reached their climax in this period.

The decline of authority is also a decline in trust. Fewer people today seem willing to believe what authorities tell them, including authorities they themselves elected to office. Governments have always lied to their subjects; but the subjects seem less and less inclined to believe what they hear. Of course, to a large extent this skepticism is healthy; and it is a good thing to have such laws as the Freedom of Information Act on the books. But skepticism makes it much harder for leaders to lead; the followers show too much disinclination to follow. It was once possible for government to announce plans for an airport, a highway, a shopping center, and then follow through on the plans. Now there are many more steps in the process, no one accepts the plans as final, the only certainties are controversy, lawsuits, delay.

Most ... are likely to approve of many of the developments of the last 35 years—surely they applaud most of the aims and results of the civil rights revolution. They are also likely to approve of environmental militance; certainly of laws about clean air and clean water, and preservation of wilderness. (Developments in family law are likely to be more controversial.) But not everything that has happened over the last thirty-five years wins high ratings. It seems undeniable that there has been a surge in social pathology in the last thirty-five years. The experts haggle over crime statistics; but there is little doubt that serious, violent crime has exploded in number since the second World War. The poor have always been with us; but the rock bottom welfare poor seem in a more hopeless state than the "respectable" poor of the nineteenth century. Juvenile delinquency, gang wars, the drug culture, homelessness—all of these appear to be symptoms of deep social illness. The cities are in decay. The ghettos seethe with rage.

The causes of social disorganization run deep, of course. But in one sense social illness may be only the flip side of expressive individualism—the fall-out, the detritus, the side-effects. The culture does not encourage people to submerge themselves in some larger cause or entity. The main job of life, as most people see it, is the job of crafting a meaningful self. A certain number—a fairly large number—fail at this job; and failure sometimes brings radical discontent; radical discontent can lead in turn to pathology and crime. I do not mean to suggest that these are the only or even the main explanations of what is wrong with society; there is plenty of blame to go around, and all the civil rights legislation has certainly not gotten rid of racism or sexism, for example; subordination and oppression are still facts of American life. But surely the legal culture has to bear some of the blame for the sorry state of society: the weakness of authority, the aggrandizement of the naked self.

So far I have spoken about changes in legal culture, as they relate to areas of law that affect individuals—civil rights, family law—as well as criminal law and law with regard to forms of deviance. The technological revolution has also of course affected business law in many large and small ways. Many of these effects are quite obvious. Rapid technological change creates new areas of business law; and gives fresh tasks to old areas, like the law of patents and copyrights. But the communications revolution has affected business and business law in more subtle and more profound ways.

The United States became rich and powerful within the protective walls of its oceans. It developed an enormous domestic market, and it thrived on this market. Distance and cost of transport were much more important than any tariff walls in protecting those markets from foreign competition. Exports and imports, significant as they were, never dominated economic life in the nineteenth century. This remained true well into the twentieth century. All this, of course, has now drastically altered. Business is international; no country is an island. Transport and communications here, too, are largely responsible. And as business internationalizes, the law necessarily follows along in its path. Law firms set up branches in Brussels, Singapore, Riyadh. The premises of field after field—antitrust law; immigration law; intellectual property—have to be reexamined, in the light of the demands of a world economy.

The communications revolution has helped reshape American federalism, or what is left of it. In the nineteenth century, and well into the twentieth century, the states were arguably more important in the legal life of the country than the federal government. Law meant, on the whole, local law. States' rights were taken seriously as a fact and as an ideology. The federal government raised a small army and navy, sold or gave away the public lands, and ran the post office. Almost everything else was done by the states.

What killed states' rights was not the Civil War, not the fourteenth amendment, but the railroad, the telegraph, the telephone; the automobile and the jet; and most decisively, television and the computer. A landmark in legal history was the creation of the Interstate Commerce Commission in 1887. This famous statute regulated (or tried to regulate) the great interstate railroad nets. The states were unable, legally and factually, to get a grip on railroads whose tentacles gripped the entire country. Afterwards, the power of the federal government grew slowly but definitely, always in response to the interstate nature of business. The New Deal was another watershed; the great depression almost destroyed state and local government; national calamity gave the federal government an opening, and Washington expanded its power at the expense of the exhausted and bankrupt states.

But there had been panics and depressions before. What was different was the social context. Trains, cars, and planes bound the country firmly into a single economic unit. The telephone and telegraph made it possible to communicate from coast to coast in seconds or minutes. Also, the New Deal emerged in the age of the radio; and Franklin Delano Roosevelt was a master of the art of the radio broadcast. In the days of Lincoln, or even Teddy Roosevelt, how many people in the country recognized the sound of the President's voice? But FDR could reach over the heads of governors and mayors; his "fireside chats" spoke to the whole country at once. Newsreels and newspaper photographs made him an instantly visible presence.

Roosevelt would have been a master of television too. Television is basically a creature of the last thirty-five years, and it has made the President—any and every President—a familiar figure in the home. We see him every day, on the evening news. He speaks directly to the country—indeed, to the world.

And what we see is the President as a human being as well as a leader; television shows us (or we think it shows us) the inside story, not just of the President, but of the celebrities, the lifestyles of the rich and famous, how they look, dress, act, and behave. In fact, political leadership gets converted by TV into just another kind of celebrity status. Everything is visual; everything is a matter of image, impression, manipulation. National networks blot out the local and the trivial; we see the big picture, the national picture, the Presidential picture. The scheme that the framers of the Constitution so carefully devised was a scheme based on slow motion, on localism, on grass roots democracy. It cannot survive as such, in an age of network broadcasting and satellites.

The states retain, of course, considerable legal power and importance. They run the criminal justice systems, the education systems, they manage tort law, family law, real property. Nonetheless, federalism is only a whisper, a shadow of its former self. The Supreme Court upheld the civil rights law of the 1960s on the basis of a commerce clause argument that the nineteenth century would have laughed off the stage. The most local greasy spoon in the South was within the reach of the federal government. And no doubt this is as it should be—in the late twentieth century. Indeed, today not a single branch of law—not education, crime, sex, or real estate—is immune from some form of federal intervention. Nobody seriously believes that the commerce clause, or any other text of federalism, impedes national policy, in any legal domain, in any significant way. If there is a demand for a national policy, in any field, there is a way to do it; and the borders of the states have melted or withered away.

Television and other forms of communication, moreover, have become crucial to the whole political system. They are, to begin with, fiendishly expensive. They increase enormously the corrosive power of money and money-raising on political life. Corruption and money-grubbing by politicians are of course old American habits. But the gross forms of corruption have been replaced by a more subtle and perhaps more dangerous form. Running for office now means scrambling for millions of dollars to buy time on television stations, and to reach huge audiences by any and all means.

In the last thirty-five years, it has become more and more clear that we live in a world of danger, opportunity, and (above all) change. Change in society at large means change in legal culture, in the way people look at the law, what they want and expect from it. In an open society, what they want more and more is free choice and individual rights. This silent, powerful force, of will and desire, conscious and unconscious, has shaken the tree of justice to its roots.

NOTES AND QUESTIONS

1. Is Friedman's argument about legal culture consistent with Friedman and Ladinsky on law, technology, and social change? What is the relationship between his view of the effect of legal culture and the theory of pluralist bargaining? How do Dicey's and Gramsci's views bear on the concept of legal culture?

2. To what degree, if at all, does Friedman's legal culture approach support the claim that law is the will of the people? How is one to deal with the fact that some people in a society are violently opposed to some laws? Does he ignore conflict? How would he deal with Cohen, Robson and Bates?

3. "Legal culture," as the term is used in Friedman's piece, is one of a family of concepts that includes "legal consciousness" (this term is particularly common in European sociology of law), the "sense of justice," and the like. The terms are not always carefully defined or easily distinguished from each other.

One particularly thought-provoking use of the term "legal consciousness" can be found in Patricia Ewick and Susan S. Silbey, "Conformity, Contestation, and Resistance: An Account of Legal Consciousness," 26 *New England Law Review* 731, 739–41 (1992). Ewick and Silbey first discuss two views of legal consciousness which they then discard in favor of their own formulation. The first is as "ideas and attitudes of individuals which determine the form and texture of social life." They associate this view with the "classical liberal tradition in political and legal theory." It focuses on individuals. Political and social life are seen as aggregations of individuals who shape the world with their interests and wishes.

Other scholars take a quite different approach. For them, consciousness is a result, not a cause. It is derived from "social structures." This view is held by Marxists and "structuralists," who "argue that individuals are only the bearers of social relations, and consequently, social relations, not individuals, are the proper objects of analysis." Some scholars who take this view discount the formative importance of "law and legal consciousness." In other words, whatever people may think, their ideas as well as the law itself are produced by the shape of society—capitalist, communitarian, democratic or authoritarian.

Ewick and Silbey do not subscribe wholeheartedly to either of these conceptualizations. For them, legal consciousness refers to way in which "ordinary people—rather than legal professionals—understand and make sense of law." (p. 731). They explain it further as follows:

> [W]e conceive of consciousness as part of a reciprocal process in which the meanings given by individuals to their world, and law and legal institutions as part of that world, become repeated, patterned and stabilized, and those institutionalized structures become part of the meaning systems employed by individuals. We understand consciousness to be formed within and changed by social action. It is, then, less a matter of disembodied mental attitude than a broader set of practices and repertoires, inventories that are available for empirical investigation.

> Conceptualized in this way, consciousness is neither fixed, stable, unitary, nor consistent. Instead, we see legal consciousness as something local, contextual, pluralistic, filled with conflict and contradiction.

Which of the three views is the most similar to Friedman's concept of "legal culture?" How close is Ewick and Silbey's view to Friedman's? If we substituted this view for "legal culture," what modifications, if any, would we want to make in Friedman's explanation of how social change leads to legal change? We will return to the issue of legal culture in Chapter 6.

4.　In a later book that summarizes their study, Ewick and Silbey report that they found three different pervasive frames for popular understandings of law. Patricia Ewick and Susan Silbey, *The Common Place of Law: Stories from Everyday Life* (1998). They talk about popular understandings of law as "legality"—which is constituted by "the meanings, sources of authority, and cultural practices that are commonly recognized as legal." (p. 22). They characterize the three frameworks as follows: (1) "Before the law"—views law as objective and predictable, as rigidly imposed from above, as apart from ordinary life; (2) "With the law"—here law is situated within ordinary life, a strategic game played with everyday tools such as knowledge, skill, and material resources; and (3) "Against the law"—approaches law as an arbitrary imposition of power, leaving people to either submit or resist in often small, subversive ways (like "foot-dragging, omissions," and so forth). Ewick and Silbey find that the position of "against the law" is more typical of relatively powerless people. They also note that the two positions "before the law" and "with the law," while apparently contradictory, are often held by the same people. Although these people characterize law as manipulable ("with the law"), they also think that it is possible to manipulate the law toward a higher goal of impartiality and abstract justice ("before the law"). This more abstract framework of legal consciousness tends to be invoked more in relation to bureaucratic structures, locations where there are "greater degrees of formal organization."

According to Ewick and Silbey, these frameworks affect how people conceive of themselves vis-à-vis the law, and thus affect how they act. Their own consciousness can create constraints, or rule out certain kinds of choices. Conversely, the framework within which they approach law can also bring people to make choices that actually change the constraints of law, albeit in small or subtle ways. How does Ewick and Silbey's model of legal consciousness fit with Friedman and Ladinsky's approach? Can you combine their approach with that of McCann? What does each contribute to a picture of how people's ideas might interact with legal change?

5. Sally Merry, *Getting Justice and Getting Even: Legal Consciousness among Working–Class Americans* (1990), also examined ideas and attitudes about law. Merry focused on the legal consciousness of working class Americans. More precisely, she studied the way in which working class Americans who turned to courts to resolve disputes thought about law and how they used the legal system. Like Ewick and Silbey, Merry found that some Americans hold apparently contradictory ideas about the law. On the one hand, working class plaintiffs attempt to invoke the law to resolve disputes with family members, romantic partners, and neighbors. When they begin the process, they enter with a sense of "legal entitlement"—with a sense that they have rights that will be protected by the law. Frequently, their experiences in court lead them to experience the U.S. system of justice as "ineffective, unwilling to help in these personal crises, and indifferent to the ordinary person's problems." (p. 170). They come to view the legal system as biased, as subject to personal influence and manipulation.

And yet, these plaintiffs will sometimes return to court again, seeking redress. As Merry explains, they may question the way a particular court or judge deals with them, but "they rarely doubt the legitimacy of the law itself or the value of a legally-ordered society." (p. 11). In continuing to insist that they have rights that should be recognized (although they are not), these plaintiffs resist the "vision of society presented to them by elites." Like the subjects of Ewick and Silbey's study, these plaintiffs understand the law as at once manipulable by people with power, but also capable of delivering objective, fair results. Note that Merry does not accept wholesale Gramsci's concept of the hegemony of the dominant class. Such a hegemony would be, presumably, expressed in a particular dominant ideology. Is there a dominant ideology that controls and constrains "legal" ideologies? If there is, how powerful is it? Merry believes that the question is essentially "empirical." We should not simply assume that "hegemony" is a total fact.

(B) The Ongoing Relationship Between Law and Society

Sometimes we can trace the way change continues to reverberate through society and law, so that a shift in society may influence law to change—but that legal change then has a further effect on society, and on and on. In the following excerpt, Edelman, Fuller and Mara–Drita trace a continuing interaction between institutions regulated by law and the law that is regulating them. Institutional structures and cultures "receive" the message sent by legal change in characteristic ways, altering the import of the message in some ways (while also being altered by the process of responding to law). On the other hand, when courts are asked to assess whether institutions have adequately responded to legal mandates, they incorporate some aspects of institutional logic into their ongoing reframing of the law.

(3.10) Diversity Rhetoric and the Managerialization of Law[30]

Lauren B. Edelman, Sally Riggs Fuller, & Iona Mara–Drita

106 *American Journal of Sociology* 1589 (2001).

INTRODUCTION

Diversity rhetoric is quite common in contemporary organizational management. Talk of diversity pervades management periodicals, human resource networks, and business education. In each of these settings, diversity rhetoric extols the virtues of a diverse workforce and advocates "managing diversity" and "valuing diversity." The message of management professionals is that organizations must embrace diversity in order to thrive in the modern world; this requires a new management style that is respectful of the varying cultural styles and backgrounds and the diverse abilities, aspirations, and attitudes of a modern workforce. In contrast to old management styles, which were developed to deal with a homogenous workforce, new management styles must be flexible, willing to defer to the interests of individuals, able to resolve new types of conflicts that arise from varying cultural backgrounds, supportive of varying lifestyles, able to match different types of people to appropriate jobs, and accommodating of different methods of getting work done and different ways of evaluating people.

30. We refer you to the original article for discussions of methodology and tables reporting more of the results.

Organizations appear to be embracing the message: a 1991 survey of 406 organizations showed that 63% of those organizations provided diversity training for managers; 39% provided diversity training for employees; 50% provided a statement on diversity from top management; and 31% had a diversity task force. Another study found diversity initiatives such as diversity action plans, endorsements of diversity in mission statements, and diversity career development and planning to be quite common. As diversity rhetoric and action become more common in American management, a word that once had connotations of stock portfolios now conjures up pictures of a colorful and varied workforce and of civil rights goals achieved. . . .

There is a curious paradox, however, in *how* diversity rhetoric in management carries forth the civil rights legacy: diversity rhetoric in fact expands the conception of diversity so that it includes a wide array of characteristics not explicitly covered by any law. Diversity of thought, lifestyle, culture, dress, and numerous other attributes appear on a par with diversity of sex and race. Further, key proponents of the new managerial model—managers and management consultants—explicitly disassociate their efforts from civil rights law, arguing that diversity is directly valuable to organizational efficiency and important in its own right rather than because it might promote legal ideals.

This paradox suggests that managerial rhetorics, especially when they concern law or issues central to law, may have the potential to transform how managers think about law and ultimately how law is implemented in organizational settings. Managerial constructions of law may, for example, affect the representation and distribution of women, minorities, and other legally protected groups; thus managerial rhetoric about diversity can have critical implications for the realization of civil rights in the employment context.

This article examines the managerial rhetoric of "diversity" as a means of determining how managerial rhetorics may appropriate and transform legal ideals. Of course, diversity rhetoric represents only a portion of all managerial talk about civil rights; there is, after all, much discussion and writing about civil rights generally, and in particular about affirmative action (AA) and equal employment opportunity (EEO). However, whereas those earlier writings were explicitly about law, compliance, or the problems associated with legal compliance, diversity rhetoric—which begins to appear only in the mid 1980s—portrays itself as quite distinct from civil rights law. Rather, diversity rhetoric envisions a style of management that will promote harmony and productivity in a changing world. We assert, however, that in spite of rhetorical claims to the contrary, both diversity and civil rights concern an important legal principle: the fair treatment of employees with different attributes.

. . . After discussing the rise of diversity rhetoric, the key question we address concerns *how managerial rhetoric about diversity constructs both the notion of diversity itself and its relation to civil rights law*. Specifically, we examine the extent to which—and how—diversity rhetoric conceptualizes diversity as a managerial as opposed to a legal issue. We also examine how constructions of diversity change over time within diversity rhetoric, and we assess what factors predict managerial (as opposed to legal) conceptions of diversity.

We use the example of diversity rhetoric to articulate a theory of the *managerialization of law*, or the process by which conceptions of law may become progressively infused with managerial values as legal ideas move into managerial and organizational arenas. The managerialization of law occurs as management consultants rhetorically refashion legal ideas that challenge traditional managerial prerogatives and suggest new ideas, which they claim are more innovative, more rational, and more progressive. We suggest that the managerialization of law has the potential to undermine legal ideals as managers shift the focus of attention from law to management. But at the same time, the managerialization of law has the potential to legalize organizations by reframing the law in ways that make it appear more consistent with traditional managerial prerogatives. . . .

TWO SOCIOLOGICAL FRAMES

Two diverse sociological literatures inform our analysis of managerial attention to diversity. These literatures offer complementary explanations for change in managerial patterns and rhetoric that, when taken together, suggest a new theoretical perspective on how law may be transformed in organizational settings. First, the literature on managerial models addresses questions about why and under what conditions managers promote new sets of ideas and thus provides a context for understanding the rise of managerial attention to diversity. Second, theories of law and organizations, which derive from neoinstitutional organization theory, more explicitly address the role of the professions in diffusing and institutionalizing responses to law. . . .

Managerial Models

We use the term "managerial models" to refer broadly to both managerial practices and ideas (thus, this term would encompass ideologies, paradigms, fashions, and rhetorics). Following Barley and Kunda,[31] we define "managerial rhetorics" as "a stream of discourse that promulgates, however unwittingly, a set of assumptions about [managerial practices]." Thus, managerial rhetorics would include spoken and written ideas that describe, promote, and rationalize managerial practices. [Theorists disagree over why the business world is developing new managerial models, but there is agreement that particular managerial rhetorics usually arise in response to particular management problems.]

. . . Managerial rhetorics thrive where they offer models that appear to enhance organizational rationality and further organizational progress. . . . Managerial rhetorics, then, are cultural phenomena: they draw their legitima-

---

31. Stephen Barley and Gideon Kunda, "Design and Devotion: Surges of Rational and Normative Ideologies of Control in Managerial Discourse," 37 *Administrative Science Quarterly* 363 (1992).

cy from their cultural environments and at the same time help to shape and to construct their cultural environments. Managerial fashion setters use rhetoric not only to construct the cultural problems that require attention but also the solutions that will solve those problems. Managerial rhetorics make new managerial models seem like the most rational and natural ways to proceed.

Theories of Law and Organizations

Institutional theories of law and organizations emphasize organizational responsiveness to the legal environment. In contrast to earlier rational perspectives on law that emphasize organizational responsiveness to internal technical demands, institutional perspectives suggest that organizations adopt a variety of legal structures in response to "institutionalized rules" or normative ideas or practices that have become widely accepted. These institutionalized rules, in turn, flow freely among "organizational fields." Organizational fields refer to the immediate environments of organizations, or "those organizations that, in the aggregate, constitute a recognized area of institutional life: key suppliers, resource and product consumers, regulatory agencies, and other organizations that produce similar services or products". The connectedness of organizational fields allows for the free flow—and hence the institutionalization—of ideas about law. These fields thus become the key source of ideas about how organizations ought to look, how they ought to behave, and even what elements of the environment are important and which ones constitute threats.

Institutional theory posits that the professions are key carriers of ideas among and across organizational fields and that the personnel, managerial, and legal professions are particularly important carriers of ideas about law.... A number of empirical studies have elaborated the role of the managerial professions in constructing the meaning of law. These studies suggest that legal ambiguity amplifies the opportunities for professionals to identify management problems and to propose new ideas to remedy those problems.... As law is communicated by and among professions, it is filtered through a variety of lenses, and colored by different professional backgrounds, training, and interests.

For example, an analysis of wrongful discharge law (a common law doctrine that allows employees to sue their employers when they are fired, under a limited set of conditions), shows that the personnel and legal professions greatly inflated the threat that the doctrine posed to employers. By repeatedly citing a few extreme jury verdicts in states most favorable to the doctrine, legal and personnel professionals created the impression that virtually all cases were won, with large awards, by employees. In fact, however, employers won the vast majority of these cases. But in part to inflate their own status within organizations and to expand the markets for their services, the professions created the impression of a much greater threat than wrongful discharge doctrine actually posed.

Another study, which analyzed organizational complaint handlers' ideologies about discrimination disputes, showed that complaint handlers tended to recast discrimination complaints as managerial or interpersonal problems, thus deemphasizing the legal aspects of these claims. In a third study, the personnel profession was shown to have promulgated the notion that internal grievance procedures offered organizations substantial protection from discrimination lawsuits. Even though there is little hard evidence to support the idea that grievance procedures offer protection from liability, that idea has become widely accepted in organizational fields and has institutionalized the internal grievance procedure as a form of compliance with civil rights law.

THE MANAGERIALIZATION OF LAW

... Legal rules tend to be filtered through a set of managerial lenses chiefly designed to encourage smooth employment relations and high productivity. Thus, *as legal ideas move into managerial and organizational arenas, law tends to become "managerialized," or progressively infused with managerial values.*

We now formulate four hypotheses about factors that produce a managerialization of law. Based on the managerial models and law and organizations literatures, we identify four factors that are important: the passage of time, the professions of actors who carry rhetorical messages, the emphasis on profit as a rationale for the new model (rationality), and the disassociation of the new model from law (novelty). With respect to the idea of diversity specifically, we will argue that these factors predict a construction of diversity that moves away from the ideas of formal civil rights law and toward a much broader understanding of diversity, which conforms to managerial ways of thinking.

Time: ... We suspect that the managerial rhetorics are simply vehicles that carry new constructions of law. Once those new constructions of law are in place, they are likely to become institutionalized and to have a lasting impact on how managers think about the law. This is especially likely where managerial constructions of legal ideas resonate with the broader political and legal culture. Thus ... we predict that managerialized conceptions of law will become institutionalized; that is, that they will remain stable even as a managerial rhetoric itself declines.

HYPOTHESIS 1. *The managerialization of law will increase over time and will then level off.*

Profession: ... As the key fashion setters and participants in managerial rhetorics generally, managers and management consultants have the opportunity subtly to shape or reshape ideas about the nature of the legal environment and appropriate responses to that environment. When these professionals frame a new managerial model as consistent with the law, as different from the law, as irrelevant to the law, or as better than the law, they shape public understandings not only of how to manage but also about the meaning and requirements of law itself. When professionals frame problems as managerial rather than legal—or when they frame solutions to those problems as therapeutic or pragmatic rather than punitive—they shape understandings of law. Thus, the media of managerial rhetoric, which includes professional periodicals, meetings, workshops, and electronic listserves, become powerful forums for the construction and transformation of ideas about law even when their discussions are not explicitly about law.

HYPOTHESIS 2. *Managers and managerial consultants will contribute to the managerialization of law more than will other professionals.*

Rationality: Managerial rhetoric about the rationality of a new managerial model will contribute to the managerialization of law. As discussed earlier, the managerial models literature suggests that managerial rhetorics seek to establish the rationality of a new managerial model by portraying the model as beneficial to organizational goals.... As the rhetoric focuses on the benefits of the new managerial model for organizational profit, it becomes easier for managers to lose sight of the law and to adopt more managerial constructions of law and legal ideas. The focus on profit as a key reason for adopting a new managerial model tends to shift attention away from legal ideals and, therefore, away from the categories of persons specifically protected by the law. Instead, managers think in terms of broad managerial goals such as consistent treatment of all employees. The law is thus reshaped in ways that fit traditional managerial goals and ways of thinking.

HYPOTHESIS 3. *The greater the occurrence of managerial rhetoric about the rationality of a new model, the greater the managerialization of law.*

Novelty: Managerial rhetoric about the novelty of a new managerial model will contribute to the managerialization of law.... Where previous managerial models are related to law, rhetoric about the novelty of new managerial models may delegitimize the law by suggesting previous models are no longer necessary or are inconsistent with the current political environment. To the extent that managerial rhetoric successfully portrays a law-related managerial model negatively or as outmoded, it will allow managers to appropriate and transform legal ideals in ways that are more compatible with managerial interests.

HYPOTHESIS 4. *The greater the occurrence of managerial rhetoric about the novelty of a new model, the greater the managerialization of law.*

... We now turn to an empirical examination of a particular managerial rhetoric—diversity rhetoric—as a means of exploring these hypotheses. After discussing our methodology for studying diversity rhetoric, we present our results in three sections. First, we describe the rise and progression of diversity rhetoric, showing how it generally fits the pattern of other managerial rhetorics. Second, we provide a qualitative analysis of the content of diversity rhetoric, which illustrates the managerial influence on the construction of diversity as well as how managers construct both the rationality and novelty of diversity. Finally, we turn to a quantitative analysis of factors within diversity rhetoric that engender a managerialization of law....

275

THE RISE AND PROGRESSION OF DIVERSITY RHETORIC

... The managerial models literature suggests that new managerial models—and rhetorics—tend to arise as managerial fashion setters devise novel solutions to apparent market-related crises. As managers jump on the bandwagon, rhetorics may become institutionalized and quickly gain acceptance. But managerial rhetorics tend to be short-lived because the status of managers depends on the production of novel ideas. Thus, new rhetorics and models (deriving from new crises) tend to engender the decline of previous ones.

[Here Edelman and her co-authors note that diversity rhetoric also arose in response to a crisis, but in this case the crisis was not market-driven. Instead, the pressure was largely created by changes in law. The authors then present their quantitative results tracing how discussions of civil rights and diversity appear in the management literature, over time. They found that "attention to diversity in the professional management literature ... began in earnest in 1987, rose sharply through 1993, and then declined somewhat between 1993 and 1996." The initial rise occurred "during a period of relatively low attention to civil rights" in that same literature, when there was "an opening for the evolution of a new managerial rhetoric." By 1993, there was more discussion of diversity than of civil rights on its own.]

The rise of diversity rhetoric, then, appears to have come at a time of considerable legal ambiguity and controversy over affirmative action. The 1980s saw a fair amount of opposition to affirmative action from the Reagan administration and from an increasingly conservative Supreme Court.... [M]anagerial rhetoric about civil rights declined in the early 1980s and had reached new lows by 1987, concurrent with the new legal environment. Personnel managers and affirmative action compliance officers needed a new managerial model to replace the emphasis on civil rights law (and possibly to preserve their jobs, many of which had been organized around civil rights compliance). Against this environment, *Workforce 2000: Work and Workers for the 21st Century* appeared in 1987 and predicted dramatic changes in the composition of the American workforce. This publication seems to have provided the perceived crisis that gave rise to new ideas about "managing diversity" and a rhetoric that supported and rationalized those ideas.

[Workforce 2000 was a publication from the Hudson Institute, which is a conservative think tank. It incorrectly predicted that only 15% of new entrants to the U.S. workforce by 2000 would be American-born white males, and that this would produce an economic crisis because of a severe dearth of highly skilled, educated, and talented workers. Edelman et al. note that, "Despite its inaccuracy, Workforce 2000 appears to have been the catalyst that precipitated diversity rhetoric" in the management literature. This shift came from a "crisis" that was actually "socially constructed by management consultants" using "erroneous statistics."]

THE CONTENT OF DIVERSITY RHETORIC ...

Diversity as Managerialization of Law

The formal legal model. Title VII of the 1964 Civil Rights Act protects employees from discrimination on the basis of race, color, sex, national origin, and religion. Other civil rights statutes protect employees from discrimination on the basis of age, veteran status, pregnancy, and disability status, and a few jurisdictions offer protection against sexual orientation discrimination. The categories that Congress chose to protect in enacting civil rights legislation are generally based on an understanding of the historical discrimination and disenfranchisement experienced by these groups.... This "formal legal model," in which diversity is understood as representation along the categories explicitly designated by statutes, is assumed by many legal actors and is well represented in court cases addressing civil rights issues. The formal legal model is not a random list of attributes; rather, it embraces a moral ideal that groups of citizens who have been subject to past discrimination are now entitled to special protection against any further discrimination and to fair opportunity in employment. For now, we treat the formal legal model as an ideal-type against which to compare the managerial conception of diversity. Later, we show that the legal field in fact shares some elements of the managerial understanding of diversity. Thus, although the formal legal model describes a central conception of diversity in the legal field, it is not the only conception.

The managerial conception. Our examination of the diversity rhetoric shows that managerial conceptions of diversity include, but expand significantly upon, the formal legal model. Virtually all the articles do mention at least one legally protected dimension along which diversity is important (usually race or sex). But in addition, the professional literature emphasizes the importance of diverse attitudes, work styles, communication skills, and cultural competence. And some articles advocate diversity on dimensions that seem even further from the formal legal model such as rank or function in the organization, educational background, and even characteristics that might seem trivial, like chattiness or thinking style. As the following examples illustrate, the managerial conception of diversity significantly expands upon the formal legal model and emphasizes nonlegal dimensions.

> At Hallmark, diversity includes, but is not limited to: ethnic origin, religion, gender, age, sexual orientation, disability, lifestyle, economic background, regional geography, employment status, and thinking style.[32]

> [At Westinghouse we] value diverse opinions, diverse skills, and diverse personalities all working in harmony in a team. Diverse people each bring their special skills and the ability to see problems from a different angle, and that's important. ...We look for people from all different social and academic backgrounds and try to mix quiet with talky people, electrical engineers with software and quality-assurance engineers.[33]

---

32. Here Edelman et al. quote Gillian Flynn, "Hallmark Cares," 75 *Personnel Journal* 50, 52 (1996).

33. From David Althany, F. Suzanne Jenniches, "Sharp Isn't Strong Enough to Describe Her," 41 *Industry Week* 32, 33 (1992).

... Almost all of the articles (91%) explicitly mentioned at least one of the legally protected categories, in particular diversity on the basis of race or ethnicity (85%) or sex (78%). But the construction of diversity goes far beyond legally protected categories. The most commonly mentioned nonlegal construction of diversity is "cultural diversity," which was mentioned by nearly half (43%) of the articles. While this might seem like another word for national origin, ethnic, or even for racial diversity, a close reading of the articles suggests that cultural diversity is meant to include but to be far broader than the legal categories. Further, many of the constructions of diversity have nothing apparent to do with legally protected categories. Articles discuss, for example, diversity on the basis of geography (10%), level or function within the organization (10%), training or educational background (12%), communication style (11%), problem-solving abilities or styles (8%), experience (10%), attitude (23%), employee benefits (13%), customers (8%), and services (1%). And, interestingly, over 10% of the articles offered a construction of diversity that explicitly mentioned inclusion of or attention to whites and males. . . .

Thus, diversity rhetoric is not simply a grafting of a new name onto an old model, as Kelly and Dobbin suggest.[34] Rather diversity rhetoric represents a managerialization of law; that is, it supplants legal categories of thinking about employee differences with a new schema that equates dimensions based on historical disenfranchisement with those based on managerial ideas about how to produce an effective and creative workforce.

Rationality—Diversity as a Resource

One of the most prominent themes in the diversity literature is the idea that diversity management (including the idea of "valuing diversity") is not only necessary given a changing workforce, it is also a profitable resource for organizations. Diversity rhetoric asserts that different types of employees increase productivity and effectiveness because people with different characteristics have different attitudes, work styles, and cultural knowledge, which makes them assets to corporations in a changing world. Blacks, women, and older people differ from whites, males, and younger people because they have different cultural backgrounds, live in different geographical areas, walk in different circles, live different lifestyles, and have different worldviews. But people with different dress styles, tastes, lifestyles, and geographic backgrounds also bring variety in expertise and ideas. For that reason, these people can bring a variety of solutions to organizations that white males alone could not. . . .

Diversity rhetoric, then, encourages managers to view diversity as a resource that could aid in a firm's movement into the "new economy"; that is, an economy based upon globalization and heightened competition. The firm well situated in this new economy is one that exemplifies creativity, multicul-

---

34. The reference is to Erin Kelly and Frank Dobbin, "How Affirmative Action Be- came Diversity Management," 41 *American Behavioral Scientist* 960 (1998).

tural competence, and an internal flexibility that mandates nonhierarchical organization and personal empowerment. Diversity is constructed as integral to both individual and workgroup productivity and to matters of hiring and retention. The message is that firms with environments inhospitable to any particular group of employees in the impending tight labor market (for skilled workers) will lose on all counts. Discrimination and exclusion become problematic under this view, not because they are unjust or illegal, but because they inhibit the firm's ability to profit in a global and more diverse world. Moreover, the focus on creativity and flexibility (as opposed to fairness and morality) appears to engender a managerial conceptualization of diversity that expands upon the formal legal model.

The idea of diversity as a resource looks beyond the essential categories of race, gender, national origin and the like to the *reasons* for valuing those people. . . .

Profit is in fact the most frequently cited reason offered by the articles in support of organizational diversity: nearly 50% of all articles refer to its value for organizational profit. In contrast, only 19% of the articles mention law as a reason for supporting diversity and only 30% mention fairness. The emphasis on profit in the diversity rhetoric, then, appears to be a means of rationalizing the need for management techniques that incorporate workforce diversity.

Novelty—Diversity as Different from Civil Rights

Another prominent theme in the diversity literature is that diversity is novel. One of the ways in which diversity rhetoric establishes the novelty of diversity management is to distinguish it from civil rights, either by omitting any mention of civil rights or by explicitly differentiating the two. Slightly fewer than half the articles that we coded (48%) even mentioned civil rights. Of those that did mention civil rights, most did so in a rather perfunctory manner. . . . [Many articles also described civil rights in negative terms, and presented diversity as newer and better. No articles represented a civil rights approach as preferable to diversity.]

One of the more common forms of comparison was to note the *artificial* (imposed) nature of legal mandates in comparison to the *natural* character of the new diversity. The language of artificiality associated with the law appears to derive from the familiar conservative critique that civil rights law involves quotas and lowered standards and thus produces economic inefficiencies. . . .

Our qualitative analyses of diversity rhetoric, then, show that like other managerial rhetorics, diversity rhetoric emphasizes the rationality and novelty of a new model of management. But, perhaps more important, diversity rhetoric subtly alters formal legal ideas of diversity by advocating diversity on a variety of dimensions that go well beyond those specified by civil rights law. We now turn to an analysis of the factors that predict a managerialized conceptualization of diversity.

FACTORS THAT PREDICT THE MANAGERIALIZATION OF LAW

We argued earlier that the managerialization of law is an institutional process in which legal ideas become infused with managerial values. In the context of diversity rhetoric, the managerialization of law occurs when diversity is conceptualized not simply in terms of the representation of legally protected categories of employees, but more broadly in terms of difference itself. In this section, we model the managerialization of law in the diversity context by examining the effects of time, author's profession, the emphasis on rationality (the focus on profit as the motivation for diversity), and the emphasis on novelty (the lack of references to civil rights law or the negative characterization of civil rights law) on an expanded, nonlegal, construction of diversity.

[In this section, Edelman and her co-authors report the results of ordinary least squares (OLS) regressions that test the hypotheses with which their article began.

Hypothesis 1 predicted an initial increase in the number of "nonlegal constructions of diversity and then a leveling off." The study did indeed find a surge in discussion of managerial approaches to diversity, which was followed by "a sustained institutionalization of that conception through the height of diversity rhetoric, and then a leveling off..."

The findings also confirmed Hypothesis 2, which predicted that managers and management consultants were the most likely professionals to "adopt the managerial conception of diversity."]

In our discussion of the content of diversity rhetoric, we showed how authors emphasized the rationality of the diversity model by claiming that it had value for organizational profit. Hypothesis 3 predicted that authors' emphases on rationality would, in turn, affect the managerialization of law. Model 3, then, adds the reasons that authors cite when supporting diversity to the basic model. The omitted category is specifying no reason for diversity. The profit variable is statistically significant, suggesting that where authors rhetorically construct diversity as good for profit, they are also more likely to adopt managerial (nonlegal) conceptions of diversity.

Similarly, we showed that authors emphasize the novelty of the diversity model by explicitly distinguishing the ideas underlying the diversity model from those underlying civil rights law and by negatively characterizing civil rights law. Model 4 shows two measures of novelty (references to civil rights and negative judgments about civil rights) and thus provides a test of hypothesis 4, which predicts that portrayals of the novelty of diversity will contribute to the nonlegal constructions of diversity. Both measures have statistically significant coefficients, suggesting that where authors do not refer to civil rights and where authors have strongly negative views of civil rights, they are more likely to adopt a managerial conception of diversity....

Summary. Taking our qualitative and quantitative analyses together, our findings are consistent with previous studies of managerial rhetorics in a number of ways. Diversity rhetoric is a form of managerial rhetoric, which appears to have arisen in response to the decline of political support for affirmative action and civil rights law generally, as reflected by the decline in managerial rhetoric on EEO and AA.... *Workforce 2000* apparently served as the catalyst for the inception of diversity rhetoric by suggesting that a dramatic change in the workforce was on the horizon. Diversity rhetoric enjoyed considerable renown during the early 1990s, but like other managerial fashions, appears to have entered a period of decline.

Our study differs from previous work, however, by showing how managerial rhetorics about law have the potential to transform legal ideas. Diversity rhetoric, which tends to equate differences based on geography or taste in sports or dress style with differences based on race or sex, offers a conception of equal employment opportunity that is quite different from that embodied in the statutory language of Title VII or other civil rights laws. Diversity rhetoric replaced the legal vision of diversity, which is grounded in moral efforts to right historical wrongs, with a managerial vision of diversity, which is grounded in the notion that organizations must adapt to their environments in order to profit. More generally, our analyses of diversity rhetoric provide support for the argument that managerial rhetoric that is related to law may produce a managerialization of law, or the infusion of managerial values and understandings into legal ideas.

The impact of managerial rhetorics on constructions of law and legal ideas, moreover, is probably part of a broader story about the blurring of organizational fields. To address that story, we add a twist to the relationship between the formal legal model of diversity and the managerial construction of diversity. As we noted earlier, the legal ideal of diversity is itself not as simple as what might be found on the pages of a statute. While we used statutory language as an ideal-type for the purpose of analyzing the managerialization of law, we now offer some theoretical ideas about the more complicated interplay between managerial and legal ideas.

MANAGERIAL RHETORICS AND BLURRING OF FIELDS

Managerial rhetorics do not evolve in a vacuum. And in particular, law-related managerial rhetorics do not evolve independently of legal environments. We refine our discussion by suggesting that diversity rhetoric had some roots both in judicial doctrine and in preexisting managerial discourse. We discuss these possible origins of managerial thinking about diversity and suggest that they may have implications for theories of organizational fields.

The idea that a heterogeneous workforce can be a resource for organizations is in fact similar to a logic that has appeared in at least three legal arenas: cases dealing with juries, educational institutions, and broadcasting. Moreover, in some of these areas, courts have implied that diversity goes beyond categories such as race, sex, age, and disability status that are explicitly protected by law. In decisions concerning these social institutions, judges construe diversity as valuable for its democracy-enhancing, or difference-valuing, capacities; it brings together people with different attitudes and cultural competencies, thus creating better juries, better educational institutions, and better broadcasting. In the famed *Bakke* case, for example, Justice Powell explicitly distinguished diversity from legally protected categories, stating that race is only one of many factors that should be considered in pursuit of diversity in higher education (428 U.S. 265 at 314 [1978]). In *Metro Broadcasting*, the Supreme Court held that programs increasing minority representation were substantially related to the broader goal of "broadcast diversity" or diversity of viewpoints (110 S.Ct. 2997 at 3008 [1990]). And the Fifth Circuit Court of Appeals in *Hopwood* (78 F.3d 932 at 941–948 [1996]) clearly distinguished racial diversity from a broader conception of diversity when it held that diversity was not a sufficiently compelling rationale to justify race-conscious admissions at the University of Texas Law School. In these and related decisions, diversity is associated with the ideals of justice, community, and democracy. Although this logic is not identical to the notion of diversity as valuable for profit and industrial harmony, it is a *parallel logic*, one that employs similar ways of thinking and values in a different context.

The idea of diversity as a resource is not completely new in management either. The idea that teams or groups in organizations benefit from "diverse" membership has been supported in the management literature for decades, although it was usually called "group member heterogeneity." The logic behind this construct was that most group activities require a variety of abilities, skills, and information and therefore a heterogeneous group will be more effective. Early work examined heterogeneity along a number of dimensions including personality, sex, race, and conceptual systems. The effect of group composition on performance has continued to be an important aspect of group problem solving. Recent work has supported the notion that heterogeneity in groups is generally an advantage and that it may offer opportunities for competitive advantage and increased creativity but suggests that the positive effects may only occur in some situations. Whether a heterogeneous group is better depends, for example, on factors such as time constraints, type of group, type of problem, and stage of group development. The diversity as a resource idea follows from the older ideas about group heterogeneity.

Further, one of the key ideas in diversity rhetoric is that employees will perform better if managers value their diverse backgrounds and styles (referred to through out the management literature as "valuing diversity"). This idea has its roots in the human relations school, which originated in the 1920s. The notion that managers can enhance firms' competitiveness through attentiveness to employees' cultural needs is in fact a form of cultural logic that has resurfaced on numerous occasions in managerial rhetoric; Barley and Kunda suggest that the most recent wave of cultural logic (which includes "total quality management" and "world class engineering") blossomed in the early 1980s. They also suggest that management academia has fed the cultural movement in management by engaging in studies of organizational culture. Although we do not posit a strong link between the diversity rhetoric and other cultural rhetorics, the cultural logic that was prevalent in management in the 1980s may have played a role in the development of diversity rhetoric.

Consciously or not, fashion setters who promulgated diversity rhetoric were probably influenced, at least indirectly, by ideas about diversity that existed previously in both the legal and managerial arenas. Of course, few managers follow legal developments or read law cases closely enough to discover judicial rationales. Nonetheless, professional networks provide ways for flows of (filtered) information from legal fields to enter into managerial consciousness. Lawyers sometimes write manuals or articles that appear in the professional personnel literature and influence managerial thinking. Lawyer-dominated organizations like the Bureau of National Affairs run workshops for managers on law-related issues. Some law firms offer websites with information on human resource practices. Employment lawyers participate in the same market of business ideas as do managerial consultants. When lawyers write for managerial audiences or try to sell their own ideas to employers, they are likely to frame both legal problems and their solutions in ways that make sense to managers. Ideas may flow from legal to managerial arenas in more diffuse ways as well. Since *Bakke*, for example, talk of diversity has become commonplace on university campuses. Virtually all managers have spent a good deal of time on college campuses while getting their bachelor's and master of business administration degrees and have therefore had some exposure to the concept of diversity, even if they did not consider it seriously.

That the roots of diversity rhetoric may be found in law or in older managerial ideas has implications for the way that organization theorists think about the "fields" in which organizations operate. Most organization theorists lump all aspects of organizations' environments into organizational fields: they include not only similar organizations, their suppliers, and their customers but also regulatory organizations that influence the field and professionals that operate within and around organizations. Although the construct of a singular organizational field has had a very useful place in organization theory, we suggest that it may oversimplify the nature of organizational environments. . . .

Thus, it may be useful to consider the *multiple* and *overlapping* fields in which organizations operate. . . . [A]t least for the purposes of understanding how managers shape organizational understandings of law, we suggest that it is useful to distinguish at least two other fields that overlap substantially with organizational fields: legal fields and managerial fields. By legal fields, we mean the environments surrounding courts, including legislatures, administrative agencies, lawyers and litigants as well as legislation and legal logics regarding the form and content of justice that surround these actors. Managerial fields include business schools and their faculty, management consultants, and the management professions within organizations as well as the various logics about good management. Other somewhat more distant fields overlap with organizational fields as well. . . .

CONCLUSION

Our analysis shows that managerial rhetoric may help transform law even when it explicitly seeks to disassociate managerial models from law. Diversity rhetoric replaces the formal legal model (which privileges race, sex, religion, national origin, age, veteran status and disability status) with a managerial model that renders categories that are not legally relevant (such as geographic location, organizational rank, dress style, communication style, and attitudes) equally important. The managerial conception of diversity de-emphasizes the law's focus on discrimination, injustice, and historical disenfranchisement and supplants it with a conception of diversity grounded in organizational success.

The managerialization of law has both costs and benefits for legal ideals. The costs come from the potential of the managerial vision to undermine law's moral commitment to redressing historical wrongs. In elaborating the idea of diversity as a resource for organizational competitiveness, managerial rhetoric about diversity tends to deflect attention from the societal and historical practices that disenfranchised particular groups and instead emphasizes the value of recognizing all forms of difference. If the white farm boy from Idaho is considered as important to firm diversity as the black inner-city kid from Los Angeles on the basis of geographic diversity, then diversity can more easily be used to justify a workforce that is primarily white or male (but is diverse on other dimensions). This broad understanding of diversity is more consistent with older ideas about team heterogeneity and it is less threatening to managerial interests in competitiveness, but it tends to divest law of its moral component. Diversity becomes conditional upon serving corporate interests rather than grounded in social justice.

Nonetheless, the managerialized form of law may have a greater capacity than the legal form to institutionalize legal values *within* organizations. Diversity rhetoric may represent a weakened ideal of civil rights, but it has the potential to have a broad impact on the daily lives of employees. Managers naturally resist law that seeks to constrain traditional managerial prerogatives. And while civil rights law offers the ideal that lawsuits would eradicate discrimination, it in fact never provided a panacea for women, minorities, and other disenfranchised groups. Barriers to mobilization, cooling out by organizational complaint handlers, and conservative interpretations of law all serve as important obstacles to the realization of civil rights. But precisely because diversity rhetoric constructs diversity as consonant with managerial interests and values, it may overcome much of the managerial resistance to nontraditional workers by transforming the notion of "difference" from one of legal imposition to one of business advantage. Thus, the managerialization of law can evoke a legalization of organizations: as legal ideas are recast in managerial terms, they may be weakened but they are nonetheless more easily incorporated into organizational routines. . . .

[The authors note that we can find examples of the "managerialization" of law in other contexts. One example is the way companies deal with discrimination complaints internally, turning them into managerial or interpersonal problems. Another example would be private police forces that worry more about minimizing disruption to the corporation than maximizing public safety.]

... We have suggested that, although diversity rhetoric may undermine the legal rights of women and minorities, it may also promote the institutionalization of legal ideas in organizations. Only empirical studies of organizational practices can reveal whether diversity is ultimately harmful or helpful to previously disenfranchised groups. And since there is likely to be substantial variation in the extent to which diversity programs embrace (or neglect) civil rights law, the sources of that variation ought to be studied.

Our study also calls attention to the blurring of boundaries between legal, managerial, and organizational fields. The import of these overlapping fields is that the potential for organizations to influence the law that regulates them may be substantially greater than previously demonstrated by studies of regulatory capture or organizational compliance. But because ideas flow across field boundaries in multiple directions, law may also influence organizations as managers appropriate and transform legal principles, leading to the institutionalization of (metamorphosed) legal ideas in organizational fields.

NOTES AND QUESTIONS

1. What is the relationship between Edelman et al.'s concept of "diversity rhetoric" and "culture" generally? How does it differ from Ewick and Silbey's concept of "legal consciousness?"

2. We have seen that Lawrence Friedman views legal culture as an intermediary between social change and legal change. How does Edelman et al.'s analysis fit with this picture? What kinds of cultural influences on legal change can you trace in this study? Thinking in terms of social structural, cultural, and conflict models of legal change, how would you explain the way institutions and law interact in this instance?

V.   Case Studies of the Production of Law

We have looked at a number of theories about how society affects law, and we have looked at the process of elections and lobbying to gain various ends. Now we turn to several case studies. Does each one fit one or another larger theory about the influence of society on law? Does the case study teach us something about the process by which classes, interests, specific groups or various elites produce legal change? What do they teach us about the legitimating claim that law is the will of the people?

(A) Expert Reform: Changing America's Divorce Laws

In the following reading, Herbert Jacob begins by noting that since 1965 there have been radical changes in legal expectations about family life. States have passed so-called "no-fault" laws; this means that, in a divorce case, "fault" is not supposed to influence decisions about whether a divorce is to be granted, or to whom. Factors such as adultery, desertion, and other forms of marital misbehavior do not play the decisive role they did under "fault" regimes. Moreover, the formal rules governing child custody have shifted to a more gender-neutral form, abandoning the earlier presumption that mothers should automatically get custody of young children. A family's property is generally regarded as marital property belonging to both husband and wife, to be divided in an equitable or equal manner. Wives' rights to support from husbands became problematic as reformers dismantled the old alimony system.

These laws were not the product of social protest or lobbying by an established interest group. They were accompanied by little political conflict. The major changes in divorce law involved much activity, but most of it took place out of sight. This "silent revolution" took place as part of the routine policy process before one state legislature after another. The proponents advocated their reforms as narrow proposals which would produce little real change and cost little money. They relied on experts who emphasized the incremental character of their suggestions. They avoided media attention by casting their action as technical. They built a consensus through consultation with interested parties before seeking legislation. Thus, when routine policy alterations such as this "surface in the form of legislative proposals, a consensus has already been built around a preferred solution in a manner to minimize controversy." (p.13).

The reform statutes passed because of changes in the social and economic environments of families. Fewer men and women marry. People live longer, and so their life span covers many years after children are grown. Women have fewer children. More women, but fewer children, are in the labor market. Women find it necessary to work if the family is to reach a middle class life style. People saw the breakup of marriage was morally possible. Movie stars and public figures got divorces, and this suggested the possibility to others. Jacob also points out that feminism affected many Americans' picture of the ideal family. It helped change the idea that there should be distinctive gender roles. Many feminists in this era relied on an "equality" model, decrying gender-specific laws like alimony that, in their view, treated ex-wives as incompetents who could not care for themselves.

(3.11) *Silent Revolution*

Herbert Jacob

(1988).

The companionate marriage style has become dominant. The romantic ideal not only rules courtship, but it also governs the criteria for continuing marriages. The life span of most Americans produces a prolonged period during which marriages can persist. For most of that time, as we have already indicated, children are not present to focus affection and activity. But in addition, the life style of urban Americans throws husbands and wives together more than in earlier times. In-laws, siblings, and cousins more often live in different neighborhoods or different cities than that of the husband and wife. Neither can find refuge with a nurturing relative as easily as before. The bar, the movie theater, and even the ball park have been largely replaced by television, so that people spend more of their free time at home than before. Finally, husbands and wives have more free time. The standard work week has become five days so that many have the weekend entirely free from work. The workday is usually only eight hours, leaving evenings free from obligatory activities.

In these circumstances, marriages which are not companionate quickly become intolerable. Intolerable marriages more frequently lead to divorce and alternative life-styles appear viable.

One alternative is to seek the companionship of another man or woman. In the early part of the century, both men and women had few contacts with those of the opposite sex other than their kin. Men mostly worked with other men; women stayed at home and visited with other women. By the 1980s that had changed, so that many men came into contact with women other than their wives at their work, and most women who worked came into contact with men other than their husbands. The increased contact between men and women at their workplace undoubtedly accounts for the increased prominence of sexual harassment incidents. But in addition, the increased contact brought men and women together in situations which could lead to friendship and alternatives to companionship within an existing marriage.

Moreover, the moral imperative of lifetime marriage had become undermined. Divorce in the minds of many was transformed from an act of immorality to a symptom of social illness. The remedy was not to punish or to persist in what religion prescribed. Rather, unhappiness resulting from an unsatisfying marriage was perceived as an infirmity that could be either treated with psychotherapy or excised by divorce. The perception of marital unhappiness as a condition to be assuaged rather than one to be abhorred grew gradually in tandem with the broader redefinition of mental illness and social maladjustments. It contributed to legitimizing divorce because divorce was seen as one of several alternative effective treatments. . . .

California's Bold Step

It remained for California to step into the future and explicitly embrace the no-fault concept in divorce. California illustrates the potential for innovation through a routine policy-making process, for it was the first state to adopt no-fault divorce in the context of a thorough reform of its divorce procedures; yet it did so with minimal controversy.

The Social and Political Context of California's Divorce Reform

No-fault was the sort of innovation that many Americans have come to expect of California. That state has long been viewed as an incubator for novel social ideas. Its population had the reputation of adopting a relaxed life style that included not only suburban living and patio barbecues, but also loose marriages and easy divorces. It was, after all, the home of Hollywood; and while the escapades of movie stars did not typify the average Californian, they established an ambiance of nonchalance and experimentation that sometimes permitted Californians to adopt novel ideas.

California in the mid–1960s differed from New York in many ways. California's population had much shallower roots than New York's. The families of most Californians had moved west from elsewhere in the United States since the Great Depression, leaving behind other relatives. They lived in rapidly growing cities which had been ranches and fruit orchards a few years earlier. California's ethnic composition was quite different from that of eastern states because more of its ethnics were Asian–American and later Chicano as well as Irish, Italian, and black. Its Catholic population was smaller than New York's, and the church had not acquired as open a political role. Even in the 1960s, ethnicity played a different and smaller role in California politics than in New York; it was more important that ballot tickets be balanced along geographic lines that recognized the gulf between southern and northern California than that Irish or Italian candidates be offset with blacks or Jews.

Fluidity marked California's politics as it characterized its people. It had been possible for Earl Warren to run for governor on both the Republican and Democratic tickets. The legislature was organized along partisan lines, but it was possible for Republicans to support a Democrat for presiding officer of the assembly as late as 1980. Nonpartisanship had become much more entrenched in California than in New York, while machine politics based on patronage scarcely existed. The major political organizations centered on ideological issues in state wide elections and recruited volunteer workers to the California Republican Assembly and the California Democratic Council rather than to "regular" party organizations.

The 1960s were marked by many political crosscurrents in California. In 1958, California elected the liberal (and Catholic) Edmund Brown, Sr. to the governorship and kept him in office until the conservative Ronald Reagan defeated his third-term bid in 1966. Racial tension erupted in the Los Angeles Watts neighborhood riot in 1965 and in Oakland in 1968, together with simultaneous riots in other northern cities, causing the nation to recognize that race relations were not just a southern problem. The "free speech movement" at the University of California's Berkeley campus focused attention on the rebellious hippy style of a conspicuous minority of its youth. A sometimes raucous but always tense campaign to liberalize California's abortion law occupied the attention of many during the last years of the decade. That bill reached Governor Reagan's desk only a few months before no-fault divorce.

The intellectual climate surrounding divorce was also somewhat different in California than in New York. Traditional values of family life rooted in religion dominated discussions in New York. Californians more openly espoused the newer clinical and therapeutic conceptions which saw marital failure as a symptom of psychological incompatibility and maladjustment rather than as an indication of sin. Such ideas had won widespread acceptance among mental health professionals by the 1960s throughout the United States, but in California they were publicly articulated with stark clarity in legislative hearings.... The therapeutic view received unexpected support from the religious sector when in June of 1966, just after New York had passed its new divorce law, a committee appointed by the Archbishop of Canterbury of the Church of England issued its report on divorce. That report, *Putting Asunder*, advocated eliminating adultery and other marital offenses as grounds for divorce and replacing them with marital breakdown. The English commission couched its recommendations in conservative language which would permit judges the discretion to "dissolve the marriage if, and only if, having regard to the interests of society as well as of those immediately affected by its decision, it judged it wrong to maintain the legal existence of a relationship that was beyond all probability of existing again." Moreover, if the court were not convinced that the marriage "had in fact broken down irreparably, [it] would have a duty to refuse a decree despite the express agreement of the parties." However, the commission's view that divorce was justified when marriages had broken down and its support for no-fault divorce were unequivocal. The publication of this church report made advocacy of no-fault appear much less radical ... The report arrived just in time to buttress California's no-fault proposal, which itself was published at the end of 1966.

In addition, by the mid–1960s the no-fault concept had gained considerable visibility in other contexts. Workmen's compensation, adopted in the first decades of the twentieth century, explicitly replaced a fault-based system of compensating workers for injuries incurred in industrial accidents. In the 1950s and early 1960s proposals for adopting a no-fault automobile accident insurance plan had evoked considerable discussion and controversy. Those plans, eventually adopted in many states, were intended to eliminate fault-based litigation and replace it with compensation of insured drivers from their own insurance policies. No personal connection existed between advocates of no-fault automobile insurance and no-fault divorce, but discussions of no-fault accident insurance familiarized people with the concept and made it appear less radical when it was proposed for divorce.

One further distinction differentiated California from New York. California's divorce law was in practice among the most lenient in the nation. As Herma Hill Kay, a teacher of family law at the University of California's Boalt Hall School of Law and a leader in the reform movement, put it: "It was impossible to make divorce easier in California than it already was." It was, however, a fault-grounded divorce law. To obtain a divorce, husband or wife had to demonstrate that the other spouse had committed a marital offense, such as adultery, cruelty, or desertion. In most cases, the wife was the plaintiff and her complaint usually alleged cruelty, which encompassed a host of sins ranging from disparaging remarks to spouse abuse. The testimony was often arranged and fake, disguising a mutual or negotiated decision to end the marriage. It was this element of dishonesty that provoked some of the proponents of change to seek a no-fault statute and, as in New York, it provided a technical cover for advocating a revolutionary liberalization. But unlike New York, the production of fraudulent evidence was not a visible industry, and the no-fault concept was openly discussed in California, having even been articulated in a California Supreme Court case as early as 1952 in an opinion by the renowned Chief Justice Roger Traynor.

A high divorce rate paralleled California's easy divorce law. Although California's divorce rate did not approach Nevada's and was indeed only eleventh in the nation, it was perceived as being a divorce-prone state by its natives. However, California's law had one quirk that motivated some people to migrate to Nevada for their divorce: a California divorce was not final until one year had passed. During this interlocutory period, ex-spouses were not permitted to remarry. This provision had been intended to prevent hasty divorces motivated by a passing fancy for another man or woman. In fact, it proved to be a major inconvenience, because in the 1960s extramarital cohabitation had not yet become widespread or socially accepted, but many people getting a divorce wanted to begin a new family soon after ending their first marriage. . . .

Innovation through Routine Policy Making

Innovation is usually thought to involve at least two stages. The first is the identification of a problem that involves a serious performance gap requiring a solution. The second is the formulation of a solution. Thereafter, those responsible for making policy decisions must be convinced that the solution is a viable and attractive response to the problem.

Performance gaps are usually a prerequisite for innovation because people are loath to change adequately working procedures. The character of such gaps, however, varies considerably because they are subjective phenomena. It is rare for everyone to agree that a policy is failing or to concur on the dimensions of the failure. Often the client or objects of a policy have a different perception than its administrators, as when people who must wait for months to receive a government payment complain but the administrators of the agency making the payment think all is proceeding normally. The measurement instrument is frequently at issue, with one group arguing that it indicates failure while another points to a different set of facts which suggests adequate performance from their perspective. Thus, parents may complain that their children are not learning to read well enough while school administrators point with satisfaction to rising test score levels. Even the goals of a policy may become subject to dispute, as when one group of citizens calls on the police to stop speeding drivers on their residential street while another group decries the waste of police on traffic enforcement while drug sales flourish.

Performance gaps may be the result of a gradual decay in the operation of a policy or the consequence of a sudden external shock which dramatically changes the conditions confronting administrators. In the former case, a series of small events pulls a policy's achievements increasingly away from its stated goals, creating a gradual awareness of the policy's inadequacy. The social security crisis of the late 1970s was an example of such a gradual decay, when slowly rising payments were not matched by rising revenues for the system. At other times, performance gaps occur because of a sudden change in the environment which the policy and its administrators cannot accommodate. The discovery of AIDS, for instance, suddenly created a public health crisis which pointed to the inadequacy of existing measures for the prevention of sexually transmitted diseases.

In every case the definition of the performance gap is both subjective and of central importance to the subsequent adoption of innovative solutions. Because it is subjective, it may be manipulated by those seeking to promote or block a change. Both sides, however, recognize its crucial significance for the adoption process, because the manner in which the gap is defined either excites or lulls potential opponents. Defined expansively, a performance gap invites wide group participation and public controversy; defined narrowly, it demarcates a restricted field of groups and makes it unlikely that the media will publicize the push for reform.

The formulation of solutions is often dominated by self-appointed experts. The solutions may be specifically designed to address the performance gap, or they may have been devised for other purposes and simply found available for application to the newly discovered performance gap. In the former case, decision makers embark on a rational search-and-choice process in which experts examine the dimensions of the problem, consider available alternative solutions in terms of their promised costs and benefits, and recommend the one with the greatest potential net benefits. Since many of the costs and benefits are difficult to measure, the process depends much more on informed intuition than on mechanical calculation; consequently, the conclusions drawn by the experts are often subject to conflicting interpretations. In many instances, however, the selection of an innovation may be quite different and involve less rational choice and more coincidence.... [S]olutions are sometimes devised for other purposes and [we look] for problems to which they may be attached. A common example is the personal computer which a businessman may purchase for status reasons and then leave to sit on his desk; he may ultimately use it to make corporate financial calculations for which he had never previously felt a need. In this instance, the computer created both the performance gap and its solution. It is likely that experts identify such a solution because of their familiarity with new ideas. Its adoption, however, very much depends on the constellation of participants who happen to be present when the decision is made. Thus, the innovation process may involve much less rational calculation than the search-and-choose model suggests.

The adoption of no-fault divorce in California illustrates these processes in the context of routine policy making. Its shows how a major alteration of public policy may occur with few of the trappings of public debate and controversy. It involved the manipulation of the definition of a performance gap and the adoption of an innovative solution which was waiting to be matched to the problem of divorce.

The Reformers

A key to the distinctive development of divorce reform in California was the identity of the reformers and the manner in which they defined the performance gap and devised their no-fault solution. As other students of innovation have found, the impetus for reform came from a small band of self-appointed experts who elevated the discrepancies between black-letter law and the law-in-action to the status of a performance gap and formulated the solution.

The experts consisted of a small group of elite matrimonial lawyers in the San Francisco Bay area who had long regretted the bitterness engendered by the adversarial divorce process which they witnessed in their professional lives. They felt that much of the conflict they saw in their offices and in divorce courtrooms was the unnecessary product of statutes which required the fabrication of ugly events that would justify divorce on the grounds of extreme cruelty. Their goal was both to eliminate the perjurious evidence which tainted matrimonial lawyers in the eyes of their colleagues and to humanize the divorce process by decreasing the level of conflict. They had quietly worked for many years to win the support of mental health professionals and the organized bar for such a reform.

It is worth noting that some plausible goals which would have sparked intense opposition were not embraced by the reformers. They did not explicitly advocate making divorce easier because divorce was better than family conflict. They did not formulate their goals in terms of achieving equality for women, nor did they champion divorce reform in order to permit greater individual choice among alternate family forms. Instead, the reformers hewed to objectives which appeared politically innocuous.

At the group's core were Herma Hill Kay, a law professor at Boalt Hall (University of California, Berkeley), Richard Dinkelspiel, a San Francisco attorney who was also prominent in Catholic lay circles, Kathryn Gehrels, a prominent San Francisco attorney who handled many upper-class divorces, and Irving Phillips, a psychiatrist associated with the University of California Medical School. These four, who enjoyed both professional and friendship bonds, were interested in no-fault reform principally because it appealed to them on intellectual grounds. They saw it as a cure for the hypocrisy which permeated divorce proceedings in California as they had in New York, and they saw such a change as worthy of the long tradition of reform leadership which characterized much California law making.

A second group of divorce reformers centered around Los Angeles and consisted of Pearce Young, a prominent assemblyman, Roger Pfaff, a vocal judge who presided over the conciliation court in Los Angeles, and several Beverly Hills matrimonial lawyers. The Los Angeles contingent did not always agree with the San Francisco Bay area proponents of divorce law reform, but they provided the necessary southern leg of interest in divorce reform so that the effort could not be dismissed as a northern California aberration.

Laying the Foundation for Reform

As early as 1962, the legislature's Assembly Interim Committee on the Judiciary considered amending the state's domestic relations law, but that committee concerned itself principally with changing the law's provisions for an interlocutory divorce that forced people to wait a year before remarrying. It never reached more fundamental issues. Two years later, domestic relations law was again targeted by the assembly's interim judiciary committee. That committee conducted a wide-ranging examination of California's marriage and divorce laws. It held hearings from January to October of 1964 in Santa Monica, Sacramento, and twice in Los Angeles. It heard numerous witnesses who ascribed divorce to a variety of causes ranging from the advent of the automobile (where out-of-wedlock pregnancies were conceived in back seats) to the changing role of women; they discussed problems of property distribution and child custody. Among the remedies mentioned were family life education courses in schools, marriage counseling, a family court, mandatory divorce counseling, and gender-neutral provisions for child custody.

Many of the members of the core group of divorce reformers testified. Herma Hill Kay addressed each of the four hearings; Judge Pfaff also appeared at each. Los Angeles attorneys Harry Fain and Stuart Walzer, later members of the governor's commission, presented their views, as did the later executive director of the governor's commission, Aiden Gough. Assemblyman Pearce Young, later co-chair of the governor's commission, also participated in the committee's work.

These hearings provided an opportunity for Kay and others to introduce the no-fault concept and some of the other innovations which later marked the 1969 law. No-fault surfaced at the very beginning, when at the committee's January, 1964 hearing Kay testified:

... as long as we are not going to require any detailed evidence as to the grounds for divorce and as long as we have a large number of default divorces in this State, it seems to me a good idea to permit parties to have at least one ground for divorce in which fault is not made necessary.

By October, Kay was ready to make much more specific and far-reaching proposals. She pointed to a Pennsylvania legislative proposal drafted by New York's divorce expert Henry H. Foster, Jr., which unabashedly favored divorce by mutual consent "which of course is true as a matter of practice now but it is not the way the statutes are drafted." However, not all members of the committee were ready to support her proposal. The chairman on that day, assemblyman Willson, demurred saying: "I recognize the problem that you would have in trying to get such a ground through the Legislature and through the people of the state ..." When Kay became more explicit in her support for no-fault, Willson interrupted: "Well now, Professor Kay, I can't subscribe to that. You will have to exclude me from that. I think it is possible for a woman to be wrong or a man to be wrong and break up a marriage." That did not deter Kay from proceeding to advocate elimination of adversarial-style proceedings in divorce cases and establishment of a new family court system to hear all matters related to divorce and other family problems. Thus, two years before the Archbishop of Canterbury's report made no-fault a widely discussed concept and before New York's divorce reform law, Kay outlined the basic features of a complete reform of American divorce law.

Kay was not the only witness to make wide-ranging proposals, although she was probably the most widely respected witness to do so. Judge Pfaff urged extension of his conciliation procedures to the entire state so that more marriages would be saved. Representatives of the U.S. Divorce Reform League advocated taking divorce cases out of court and giving men more rights with respect to their children.

The committee's report, however, scarcely reflected such proposals. It made few specific recommendations and lamely suggested the need for further study and deliberation. No immediate action came from the year's work.

Formulation of the Divorce Proposals

After a hiatus of sixteen months, divorce reforms suddenly revived. Governor Edmund Brown appointed a commission on the family in May of 1966, just as he was preparing to run for a third term against the movie actor and political novice, Ronald Reagan. The idea for the commission seems to have come from the Bay area group, which had a conduit to the governor's office through a former law student of Kay. The official proclamation of the commission did not reveal its likely outcome; its title was the innocuous "Governor's Commission on the Family." It was charged to "study and suggest revision, where necessary, of the substantive laws of California relating to the family," to examine the feasibility of developing courses in family life for California's schools, to consider the possibility of developing a uniform national standard for marriage and divorce jurisdiction, and to look into the establishment of a system of family courts. In fact, the commission responded only to the first and last elements of this charge.

The commission included many of the core Bay area persons who had pressed for divorce law reform, as well as some key legislators and prominent jurists and lawyers from the Los Angeles area. The spark plugs of the commission, however, were the Bay area members, who formulated many of its recommendations. Potential opposition from some conservative members was averted by the illness of one their key spokesmen, Judge Pfaff, who urged conciliation procedures but resisted more fundamental changes; his dissent was limited to a letter to Dinkelspiel, who was co-chair, but it was not printed in the commission's report.

Unlike the interim commission of the legislature, the governor's commission held no public hearings. Indeed, it seems to have worked entirely in the shadow of the heated gubernatorial campaign that took place during most of its life. It issued no press releases and its work did not reach the attention of the media until it was completed and its report published. Under this cloak of obscurity, the commission forged its radical proposal; but while the commission worked, Governor Brown lost the gubernatorial election. With the much more conservative Ronald Reagan in the wings, the commission rushed to complete its work before inaugural day; it managed to convey its report to Governor Brown just two weeks before he left office and its authority expired.

The governor's commission was careful to veil its proposals in as conservative a guise as possible. It first highlighted its plan to consolidate all family disputes in a newly constituted family court that would be available in every county. That court and the conciliation and counseling services connected with it were to help save families from stress and dissolution. Moreover, the commission clothed its report in pro-family vocabulary. It argued that the goal of the law should be "to further the stability of the family" and that the existing law

> represents by its ineptitude an abdication of the public interest in, and responsibility toward, the family as the basic unit of our society. The direction of the law must be, as we have said, toward family stability— toward preventing divorce where it is not warranted, and toward reducing its harmful effects where it is necessary.

The commission's second thrust was its radical contribution, but it too was described with a conservative vocabulary. Claiming that it simply wished to align the law with the divorce process as it really worked, the commission proposed eliminating all fault grounds for divorce and replacing them with the requirement that irreparable breakdown of the marriage exist. Lest that this be seen as an invitation to easy divorce, the commission wrote:

> We cannot overemphasize that this standard does not permit divorce by consent, wherein marriage is treated as wholly a private contract terminable at the pleasure of the parties without an effective intervention by society. The standard we propose requires the community to assert its interest in the status of the family, and permits dissolution of the

marriage only after it has been subjected to a penetrating scrutiny and the judicial process has provided the parties with all of the resources of social science in aid of conciliation.

Note that the commission invoked not only society's interest in stable families but also the therapeutic potential of science that might be harnessed by its proposal. In addition, the commission quoted at length from the Archbishop of Canterbury's report in support of its no-fault proposal.

In order to reduce the law's contribution to marital conflict, the commission also suggested abandoning the conventional vocabulary of litigation in divorce cases. Instead of styling divorce actions in the usual way, "Jones v. Jones," cases were to be referred to as "In re. the marriage of Jones." Instead of a complaint, a "petition of inquiry" was to initiate the proceedings. Even the term "divorce" was to be replaced with "marital dissolution." Each of these proposals closely followed the suggestions made by Herma Hill Kay two years earlier to the interim study committee of the California legislature. Kay, of course, was a key member of the governor's commission and played a central role in drafting its recommendations.

A third set of proposals concerned the disposition of property at divorce. The existing rules permitted property division to be governed by fault. California was already a community property state in which both spouses had a claim to any property accumulated during their marriage. However, innocent parties in a divorce case were eligible for more than half of the community property. When the commission proposed banishing fault, a new rule had to be devised. Without much discussion of its potential consequences, the commission recommended establishing a presumption of equal distribution of community property, except in circumstances when some other division seemed appropriate. Alimony also was redefined. It too was set loose from a consideration of fault and was instead based on need "for such a period of time as the court may deem just and reasonable."

Finally, some questions of child custody were addressed. The commission took note of the fact that many mothers no longer provided full-time care even for very young children, but rather entrusted them to day care and preschool nurseries. Consequently, the commission recommended ending the practice of automatically favoring mothers in deciding custody and establishing a new standard which required that the court consider the "best interests of the child" in determining which parent (or other person) should have custody of children of broken marriages. The report, however, gave little consideration to the precise meaning of that standard.

Despite the commission's elite membership and radical suggestions, its report produced scarcely a ripple of reaction. It was released in mid-December of 1966, during the last days of the Brown administration, as political reporters were speculating on the intentions of the incoming Reagan team and as the rest of world prepared for the Christmas holidays. Because the commission had operated without any publicity, few persons even knew that such recommendations had been made.

Backstage Negotiations and Legislative Maneuvering

Obscurity probably helped more than hurt the prospects of the commission's recommendations, because it shielded them from potential opponents. At the same time, it reflected the absence of organized opposition to its suggestions, because no lobbyist in Sacramento sounded an alarm.

The lack of hostility from the Catholic church was particularly notable. The Commission's report had tiptoed around the potential conflict between civil divorce and religious norms of family life. The report included a discussion of the matter in the following words:

> Our study has convinced us that ... a "breakdown-of-marriage" standard in no way derogates ecclesiastical doctrines of the indissolubility of marriage. When a Civil Court orders the dissolution of a marriage, it does not reach the canonical bonds of the union; it acts rather on the complex of legal rights and duties that make up the legal status of marriage.

However, the commission did not simply rely on this argument. The absence of Catholic opposition was the result of careful cultivation of the Catholic hierarchy. That was facilitated by staffing decisions which substantially assisted communication with the northern California hierarchy. At the outset Governor Brown shrewdly appointed Richard Dinkelspiel as co-chair of the commission. Dinkelspiel was not only one of the core members of the Bay Area reform group, but more importantly, he was a very prominent Catholic layman with ties to the hierarchy. In addition, he was well known and widely respected in the San Francisco and California bars. Secondly, the governor appointed Aiden Gough to be the commission's executive director. Gough was a young law professor at Santa Clara University and perhaps the most available expert in matrimonial law. But he taught in a Jesuit institution, his university's president (who had encouraged him to take the position) was the brother of the Bishop of Stockton, and his family was friendly with the Archbishop of San Francisco. Those ties were helpful in keeping the bishops of northern California informed about the commission's work. The commission won their timely backing for its proposals in the form of a public statement of support for the commission's recommendations before Cardinal McIntyre of Los Angeles, who had more conservative leanings, discovered the outcome of the commission's work. Given the open support of the northern bishops, it was difficult for McIntyre to oppose recommendations. California did not lack political controversies to occupy the attention of its legislature. Governor Reagan sought to reduce state expenditures; the campaign for abortion reform was nearing its climax; the state, like the remainder of the nation, was riveted on Vietnam and the growing domestic opposition to that war. During these distractions, proponents sought endorsement from the California Bar Association. Although the bar proposed numerous changes to the commission's proposal, it accepted its main thrust and told its lobbyist to support a bill which incorporated the bar's suggestions and the commission's proposals. Further, although the commission's proposals were introduced into the legislature in 1967, they lay fallow for two years. This interlude was used to familiarize legislators with the revolutionary concepts of the bill. When the legislature finally turned its attention to the bill, it seemed less radical and had garnered substantial support. . . .

[S]upporters of no-fault had quietly generated public support in the form of newspaper editorials and constituent letters. Even Catholic groups wrote to legislators in support of the no-fault bill. Thus, legislators like the Los Angeles assemblyman found divorce reform an attractive issue upon which to build their legislative reputations, even when their general policy stance was a conservative one. In the meantime, the liberals who had drafted the commission's proposals remained discretely in the background. The coalition . . . led to legislative approval by June of 1969 with less public maneuvering and attention than had accompanied New York's much more modest legislation three years earlier.

Governor Reagan, himself once divorced, proved no obstacle to the bill and signed it into law with only a mild plea for future fine-tuning. It became effective in 1970 and came to be known as the nation's first no-fault divorce law.

The new law followed the general thrust of the governor's commission with respect to the grounds for divorce. It eliminated all fault grounds and permitted divorce only upon a showing of incurable insanity or "irreconcilable differences which have caused the irremediable breakdown of the marriage." The statute mandated the new style of divorce petitions which avoided the terminology of conventional litigation. It eliminated all consideration of fault with respect to property division. However, it went further than the governor's commission in mandating equal division of property by omitting the commission's recommendation and by narrowing the exceptional circumstances justifying an unequal division. Finally, the new law altered alimony so that it would ordinarily be temporary support for the dependent spouse while he or she became self-sufficient.

The official legislative history of the law claimed that the new law was intended to facilitate gender equality. Kay argues that this was an entirely erroneous assertion. Indeed, the new law was not in any way a feminist product. The alimony provisions as enacted were less favorable to women than those that had been recommended by the commission. The principal change was that the legislature added the provision that the "ability of the supported spouse to engage in gainful employment" be considered in alimony decisions, thereby converting alimony to a transitional payment while the dependent spouse entered the labor market. In addition, the new law did not include the commission's recommendation to end the presumption in favor of mothers of young children in deciding custody. Instead, it reenacted the tender years doctrine. Finally, the new law reenacted several provisions which were soon to become an anathema to feminists. One section stated: "The husband is the head of the family. He may choose any reasonable place or mode of living, and the wife must conform thereto." Another confirmed the husband's right to manage community property during the marriage. Gender equality was neither sought nor achieved by California's no-fault law. Indeed, there is no evidence that feminists were active supporters of the new law or held any expectation that women would be treated better under the new law than the old.

Conclusion

. . . While the California no-fault statute was the product of many years of deliberation, the deliberative process attracted very little public attention. None of the principals claimed fame or fortune as the result of the law's enactment. While the leaders of the abortion struggle climbed to more prominent national office, the proponents of no-fault remained in relative obscurity. Perhaps the most telling evidence of the invisibility of the revision process is the complete absence of its mention in the oral history of the Brown and Reagan administrations. Interviews exist for activists over abortion proposals and many other legal initiatives, but none for those involved in the no-fault law.

However, the proponents of divorce reform almost made a fatal error. Carried by their enthusiasm for the therapeutic model, they advocated establishing a new tier of courts to handle family matters and facilitate conciliation. The expense of that proposal and its challenge to the authority of sitting judges threatened to arouse strong opposition. Those elements of the proposal were, however, dropped during its legislative consideration. Without that concession, it is likely that the issue of divorce reform would have become much more conjectural and would have faced Governor Reagan's fiscal veto. By eliminating the costly elements of their recommendations, no-fault advocates were able to utilize the routine policy process to achieve divorce reform.

Nationalizing No–Fault Divorce: The NCCUSL

Policy making involves not only public but also private arenas. That is particularly true of policy changes which are defined as technical legal matters where specialized groups of legal experts play an exceptionally important role. Two such arenas exist in the United States. One is the American Law Institute, which periodically issues "Restatements of the Law of ..." particular areas of the law, such as torts, that become influential accounts of black letter law in the United States. It was this group that issued the "Restatement of the Law of Torts" in 1965 articulating a rule of strict liability which came to play a prominent role in the litigation over asbestos damages. The second is the National Conference of Commissioners on Uniform State Laws (NCCUSL), which issues uniform state laws to guide state legislatures. The NCCUSL joined the American Law Institute in drafting the Uniform Commercial Code, a widely adopted body of commercial law in the United States. The NCCUSL was also a key actor in recommending no-fault divorce to the states.

The same process of routine policy making occurred in the NCCUSL as in California. The manner in which the divorce reformers in the NCCUSL managed to keep no-fault in the routine policy-making mode goes far in explaining how they succeeded in developing a uniform marriage and divorce an despite the organization's long record of failure in divorce law reform.

The NCCUSL is a unique quasi-public body. It was organized in 1892 to promote, among other reforms, a uniform marriage and divorce act for the states. However, after several unsuccessful attempts it abandoned that task and turned to the development of other uniform state laws on such subjects as wills, securities, and the determination of death. It is composed entirely of legal experts. State governors appoint its members from the ranks of law professors, prestigious attorneys, and well-placed legislators. Its budget comes from state appropriations as well as from such grants as it can procure. It works through drafting committees whose products are then debated at its annual conference and usually adopted with only minor changes. Its proposals then go to the American Bar Association (ABA), which generally endorses them. The double endorsement of the NCCUSL and ABA establishes the so-called "uniform act" as an influential model for state legislatures. Few uniform acts win approval from state legislatures without substantial alteration to suit local conditions, but the fundamental concepts underlying those model laws are given a powerful thrust by the endorsement of the NCCUSL and ABA.

However, unlike state legislatures, the NCCUSL avoids the limelight of publicity and the media seldom report its activities. It does not hold public hearings and is not subject to overt pressure group or partisan politics as are legislatures. Its committees often consult with representatives of diverse groups in order to increase the likelihood that its model statutes will win the approval of state legislatures, but such consultation occurs in a relatively unsystematic way through private rather than public channels. All of these characteristics made the NCCUSL an ideal vehicle for promoting no-fault divorce.

Unlike a legislature such as California's, the NCCUSL operates in the broad national arena rather than in the narrow confines of a single state and must reflect national conditions. It usually is more conservative than venturesome California, a fact that makes its adoption of no-fault particularly significant, for by its endorsement of this new standard, the conference placed the cachet of respectability upon no-fault. But it did not happen without considerable effort.

The National Environment for No-fault Divorce

The Intellectual Environment

. . . [N]o-fault was an idea that was increasingly in vogue in several areas of the law. It had been most prominently discussed with respect to auto accident insurance, where reformers proposed that instead of attempting to assess blame for auto accidents, insurance companies should insure their own drivers, who would be reimbursed for damages and injuries regardless of who was at fault. . . .

Divorce had several parallels to traffic accidents. Like those mishaps, it was often difficult to assess blame in failed marriages. While a single event often precipitated the breakup, hundreds of trivial disputes generally preceded it. Like personal injury suits, divorce cases often took long to conclude and the few which went to trial consumed much court time.

However, the link between no-fault in auto accident cases and divorce law remained a conceptual one; its advocacy in one field did not directly affect the other. . . . [W]hereas the application of no-fault to auto accident cases was hotly disputed by personal injury plaintiff lawyers, in part because it threatened to reduce their caseload by diverting claims to a purely administrative procedure, divorce lawyers were generally not hostile to no-fault because, among other reasons, divorces would still require court action and considerable litigation. . . .

Furthermore, the no-fault idea fit well with the therapeutic conceptions of divorce that had become widespread by the 1950s and 1960s. Family breakdown was seen less frequently as sinful and more often as evidence of social maladjustment that could be remedied through therapy. Some marriages could be saved through counseling; in other cases, men and women could be helped to start new marriages by permitting them to escape relationships that had become hopelessly entangled. Assessing blame, as traditional law required, interfered with this process. However, most of these ideas remained confined to a narrow elite of attorneys and therapists and were not widely diffused in the general legal literature on divorce before the 1970s, as witnessed by the fact that no-fault was scarcely mentioned in law review articles on divorce in the early 1960s.

The Social and Political Context

. . . [D]ivorce became increasingly common in the 1960s. Ordinary people began to notice that their neighbors, friends, and relatives were getting divorces, and the public careers of figures like governors Rockefeller and Reagan survived divorce. Making divorce less adversarial, therefore, was consonant with the increasingly accepted perception that divorce should not be made immensely difficult.

That perception also contributed to keeping divorce reform out of the political limelight. Maintaining the old legal order was not perceived to be an attractive issue among political entrepreneurs. Moreover, the feminist movement—which was reviving just when advocates of no-fault pressed their cause—was distracted by other matters. The dominant feminist organization, the National Organization for Women, was just being organized in 1966; it, and its predecessors, concentrated mostly on advocacy of legalized abortion, on equal legal rights for women, and on issues of direct economic significance to women, such as discrimination in the workplace. The potential consequences of no-fault divorce were scarcely visible to feminists, and they neither supported nor opposed them in their major public statements. The absence of feminist concern also kept anti-feminists away from the divorce issue. Anti-feminists mostly reacted to the agenda of the feminists: feminist advocacy of ERA provoked anti-ERA activity; feminist promotion of abortion aroused anti-abortion agitation. The lack of feminist support, therefore, also helps account for the absence of anti-feminist opposition and of political interest in the issue.

Formulating the Problem

As in California, a key element in channeling divorce reform into the routine policy-making mode was the formulation of the problem in such a manner that it would remain in the domain of technocrats rather than politicos. This was done in much the same manner as in California. A handful of little-known legal experts controlled the formulation of the problem.

The advocates of no-fault divorce were several unconnected groups of practicing lawyers and legal technocrats. Most prominent among the practicing lawyers were two matrimonial attorneys in Newark, New Jersey, Leonard Brown and Bernard Hellring, who had become disenchanted with the fault system of procuring divorces for their clients. They were members of the NCCUSL and thus represented the upper crust of the practicing bar, but they were unknown outside a small circle of elite divorce lawyers. As early as 1966, they prepared a report to the NCCUSL urging the formulation of a committee to draft a new divorce law; they did not use the term no-fault but spoke about it in terms of eliminating cumbersome and misleading "forms of action." They were joined eventually by three law professors who had few prior ties with one another or with the two practicing attorneys. One was NYU's Professor Henry H. Foster, who had built a wide reputation as one of the handful of leading matrimonial law specialists in the United States. Foster was well connected with the New York politicians who had produced the new divorce law in that state, was prominent in the ABA Family Law Section, and knew some of the leaders of the conference. The second law professor was Robert J. Levy of the University of Minnesota, a family law expert who was gaining a reputation for his knowledge of the social science literature on the family, but who had not established a wide reputation outside the scholarly world. The third law professor was Herma Hill Kay, who was a key player in the California reform but who did not know well any of the other core advocates of no-fault. All five were technocrats with no more than weak political affiliations. Moreover, until the conference mobilized to draft a new divorce law, they worked independently; indeed, Levy and Kay, who eventually played key roles in the formulation of the new law, were explicitly recruited into the effort by the conference.

The advocates perceived the problem which required a new divorce law in ways very similar to the California reformers. The problem, as they perceived it, was widespread dissatisfaction with divorce procedures that had become prevalent far beyond New York's and California's boundaries. The complaints had three common themes. First, attorneys throughout the country resented the extensive manufacturing or doctoring of evidence to fit the narrow provisions of existing divorce law. Divorce lawyers were under considerable pressure everywhere to put an acceptable gloss to the domestic discord that accompanied divorce petitions. In most states, the easiest way to do that was to base the divorce action on the mental cruelty provisions of the divorce law, which led attorneys to suggest to clients that they testify that their spouse had been disparaging and that they suffered many sleepless nights as a consequence; alternatively, a fictitious slap to the face evidenced physical cruelty. In truth, adultery may have been a cause for the divorce in some of these cases, while in others there was nothing more than a desire to end the marriage. Another cause for the manufacture of supporting evidence lay in state laws which did not allow as quick a divorce as the client demanded; in response, attorneys arranged phoney out-of-state residences so that the more lenient laws of another state could be used. These practices were no secret. Judges in every state quietly accommodated divorce lawyers by not probing into the truthfulness of the evidence they offered; the judiciary of those states with short residence periods like Nevada's openly participated in what became a substantial trade in divorce, which supported a sizable segment of the state's economy. Thus, perjury became a silent partner of divorce proceedings and cast a pall on the practice of family law.

The second widespread cause for dissatisfaction with divorce law was that it forced family disputes into the adversarial mode of court actions. Most divorce cases already had an uncomfortably high degree of emotional conflict. Many divorce attorneys felt that the requirements of the adversarial system heightened that conflict to unacceptable levels. Legal norms had several consequences. Clients could not share a common attorney but each had to have his or her own. Attorneys were bound by the ethical standards of the profession to seek the best settlement for their clients rather than a common compromise. The interests of children were poorly represented unless they too had a separate attorney. The system seemed designed to promote and exacerbate conflict, rather than to provide a way to find compromises and to get the divorce in as painless a fashion as possible.

A third common complaint about the nation's divorce laws was that they were a patchwork of provisions that differed for each state. This particularly bothered matrimonial lawyers handling high-status clients who had large property interests at stake and were more likely than others to live in different jurisdictions. Divorces in such cases seemed unnecessarily complicated.... Consequently, elite divorce lawyers advocated making divorce law uniform throughout the country.

This definition of the problem emphasized the legalistic concerns of the divorce lawyers and usually eschewed larger social issues. For instance, it avoided discussion of the effect of changing divorce rules on the roles of men and women. It implicitly denied any consequences of change for ongoing marriages by presuming that the proposed changes did little more than ratify existing but not legally sanctioned practices. It did not consider the possibility of reforming divorce rules as part of a more far reaching alteration of family policy in the United States, such as establishing family allowances (which might alter child support obligations) or the institutionalization of child care (which together with a parental leave policy might alter the distribution of child care responsibilities). Instead, the advocates of no-fault divorce framed their proposal in more limited, technical terms and thereby discouraged broader participation in the deliberations over the reforms.

Formulating and Adopting the No-fault Solution

The NCCUSL's embrace of no-fault divorce occurred in even greater obscurity and under more control of experts than had been the case in California. Motivated by their own disenchantment with divorce laws, Hellring and Brown rekindled the conference's interest in divorce reform in the early 1960s. Focusing their considerable energies on mobilizing the NCCUSL, they succeeded in placing marriage and divorce on its agenda in the mid–1960s....

Two points seem clear from the available record. First, the drafting committee made little effort to obtain support from Catholics or to disarm potential Catholic opposition. Rather, it appeared to assume that the stance of the Catholic church was immaterial, a presumption that appeared well founded, given the lack of Catholic hostility in California toward no-fault divorce. Secondly, no evidence exists that the Catholic national hierarchy paid attention to the work of the drafting committee. In part that may be due to the fact that the Catholic church was oriented to represent its position in Washington and in state capitols but did not monitor the activity of organizations operating elsewhere. Whatever the cause, the consequence was that the church had no voice in the formulation of the UMDA.

Feminists had almost as little influence. No formal link existed between the drafting committee and the National Organization for Women nor with any other feminist organization. Some women who were also feminists were members of the advisory board, most notably Jessie Bernard and Alice Rossi. Neither, however, had been selected because of her feminist connections. The only two exceptions addressing feminist concerns recorded in available documents are to be found in Levy's 1968 monograph, which he wrote as a briefing paper for the drafting committee, and in positions taken by Alice Rossi. In the monograph, during a discussion of property distribution Levy quotes extensively from the 1963 report of the Committee on Civil and Political Rights of the President's Commission on the Status of Women and from the 1968 Task Force on Family Law and Policy of the Citizen's Advisory Council on the Status of Women; his conclusion was that "the time is not yet ripe to insist upon a '50–50' formula," a change he labeled a "radical innovation." However, that was precisely what Rossi urged in her capacity as a member of the advisory group, together with equal consideration of both parents for custody and time-limited alimony. However, having proposed these provisions, she had no success in persuading the predominantly conservative members of the drafting committee to take her suggestions seriously. Thus feminists, like the Catholic church, had little input or influence in the formulation of UMDA....

Adoption by the conference came after a long debate in which the commissioners examined each paragraph. As in the original formulation of the problem, the debate over the proposed solution used the language of legal technical terms rather than of social concepts and issues. The debate transcripts rarely display an articulated concern over such matters as the fate of divorced women or the differential impact of the law's provisions on minority groups or the poor. When commissioners had such concerns, they couched them in technical terms. That is well illustrated in the debate over whether judges should possess discretion over the granting of a divorce on the ground of matrimonial breakdown. Both in the drafting committee and during the debate by the conference as a whole, enormous attention was lavished on whether the statute should include the word "may" or "shall." At the manifest level it was an abstract, constitutional debate on judicial discretion and judicial power. However, the discussion reflected several, most unspoken, social issues. The debate over judicial discretion was also an argument over whether marital misbehavior should go unpunished; however, if judges retained discretion to deny divorces to persons who had acted badly in their marriage, fault would reenter through the back door. In addition, this discussion may have reflected disquiet over the possibility that judges might deny divorces to the poor, but it also betrayed a concern over the potential for increased welfare costs as well as a regard for equal treatment under the law. At the manifest level, the debate in the conference did not focus on social issues but rather concentrated on the judicial authority denoted by those two words and on the legal definition of irretrievable breakdown.

The technical character of the conference's debate reflected its structure and composition. It was not a representative body and its members did not have to answer to a constituency. Many were law professors who were comfortable in discussing legal technicalities. Neither interest groups nor reporters intervened to raise questions of social conflict. Furthermore, the technical cast of the debates also helped insulate the deliberations from the media. Media representatives were not routinely invited to conference sessions or to the meetings of the drafting committees. Thus the media were usually unaware of the conference's activities. However, even if they had been aware, conference debates would have provided poor copy and a pale television image because the commissioners did not speak the language of political conflict. . . .

By the time the NCCUSL debated its committee's proposal, California had already acted. When skeptics in the conference debate asked whether no-fault was practical or inquired about the opposition of the Catholic church, supporters were able to point to the California experience, where no-fault had been adopted under a conservative governor without active Catholic opposition.

None of the issues raised during the discussion seriously threatened the proposal, and it easily passed the NCCUSL to become the Uniform Marriage and Divorce Act in the terminology of the conference. . . .

With ABA approval achieved, the Uniform Marriage and Divorce Act became a model for state legislatures to emulate. Newspapers duly noted that no-fault divorce was now advocated by lawyers. The UMDA was published by the NCCUSL and distributed to each of its commissioners and sent to every state legislature. A handful of articles on the UMDA appeared in law journals. It was hardly a great event and ... it had little immediate impact on the widespread adoption of no-fault divorce in the United States. Its most important effect was to legitimate no-fault in a way that California's adoption could not. Whereas California's adoption might be discounted because California often adopted avant-garde ideas belittled elsewhere, the NCCUSL and ABA's endorsement of no-fault divorce indicated that this was a reasonable idea that warranted serious consideration by state legislatures, for the NCCUSL and ABA were middle-of-the-road, conservative organizations little given to extravagant social experimentation.

Conclusion

The routine policy-making process within the NCCUSL and ABA was different from California's in one significant characteristic: their decisions had only the status of recommendations to the states rather than of laws with potentially irreversible effects. However, these groups undertook their tasks with great seriousness, believing that the reputations of their organizations were at stake in adopting model laws that could win the respect of the nation's lawmakers. Thus their actions were not without the risk and uncertainty that California legislators also faced.

What made divorce reform an attractive object for the routine policy process was the ability of its advocates to formulate the problem as a matter which required special expertise more than broad public participation. As in California, the reformers did not portray no-fault as a daring experiment but rather as a logical extension of existing practices. The NCCUSL's procedures guaranteed limited visibility among the general public and confined decision making to inside experts until the proposals were transmitted to the ABA. Ordinarily, the NCCUSL would have coopted the relevant ABA experts as well and its proposals would have been routinely adopted by the association. That did not occur with the Uniform Marriage and Divorce Act ... because of personal and institutional rivalries. Nevertheless, the proponents of reform succeeded in confining conflict to the private arenas of the decision-making processes of the two groups, where a compromise was reached in typically technical terms. They did not allow the issue to become transformed into a social conflict which would have invited other groups and members of the general public to intervene....

NOTES AND QUESTIONS

1. Lawrence M. Friedman, "Law Reform in Historical Perspective," 13 *St. Louis University Law Journal* 351, 363, 364 (1969), states that law reform efforts often ratify what has already been done, reflecting rather than causing changes in behavior or attitudes. He says:

Even more commonly, perhaps, fresh law is a hybrid: half ratification, half real inducement to change. Formal legal change often comes at the middle point in a social process which requires a number of distinct steps already taken, but it forces or hurries society along with regard to the steps not yet taken. It is not easy to know whether or not "innovation" is only anticipation of a process bound to happen in any event....

[A]n attempted legal change, in a non-revolutionary setting, will have most effect and be most meaningful when the change is relatively slight. Obviously, a fresh precept is in trouble if it goes against deep-seated interests or emotions.... A change that conforms to what most of the public already wishes to do or which calls for slight, familiar, acceptable change of behavior is far more palatable and far more likely to succeed. "Reform" that is half ratification and half real change is, therefore, not only typical of the work of Anglo–American courts; it is arguably the most vital and productive kind of change.

To what extent was Jacob's "Silent Revolution" the kind of hybrid Friedman discusses? Was it "half ratification, half real inducement to change?" Should we distinguish between legislation that appears to be only ratification but actually involves the opportunity for significant change as it is applied and that which is truly only ratification?

2.   Before "no-fault," as Jacob points out, divorce was formally hard to get, but, in fact, it was very easy to get. Divorce proceedings often were a sham, resting on perjured testimony. In theory, a collusive divorce was illegal. In practice, 90% of all divorces were collusive.

What social forces brought about the situation before no-fault divorce—where there was a sharp distinction between law on the books and law in action? Under the official "fault" regime, divorce was only available for innocent victims of a spouse's misbehavior. Courts were not supposed to grant a divorce to two people simply because they wanted to get divorced. But in fact, divorce was readily available in that time to any couple that wanted one, if they could agree to collude in allocating fictitious "fault" to one or the other spouse. This led to frequent perjury, of course. Lawrence M. Friedman, "A Dead Language: Divorce Law and Practice Before No–Fault," 86 *Virginia Law Review* 1497, 1512, 1515 (2000), tells us that:

> Collusion, in divorce law, means pretending to have grounds for divorce when in fact you have none, or when you choose (as often happened) not to tell the truth about the ones you do have. It must therefore be molded to the list of statutory grounds for divorce. New York, to take the classic example, basically allowed divorce only for adultery....
>
> In light of this, there developed a most interesting practice, which we might call soft-core adultery. This involved a little drama performed in a hotel. The cast of characters included the husband, a woman (generally a blonde who was hired for the occasion), and a photographer, of course. An article in the *New York Sunday Mirror* magazine section, published in

1934, had the intriguing title: "I was the Unknown Blonde in 100 New York Divorces." The "unknown blonde" usually charged $50 for her work. She was in fact a woman named Dorothy Jarvis, who (according to the Mirror) had "retired as a professional co-respondent in view of her forthcoming marriage to a man she met while performing her role." ...

Friedman goes on to explain that the unknown blonde woman normally did not have sex with the men who were paying her, but "simply played a part in a sordid little drama." Her job entailed going to a hotel room with the man who was seeking a divorce. After "a certain amount of undressing," they would go through a staged drama in which they pretended to be surprised in the act by a photographer who burst in the door. Friedman quotes a judge from Nassau County in New York, who said that a "certain amount of naivete [was] essential adjunct to the judicial office" during this time. After all, the New York courts would "grind out thousands of divorces annually" in response to pictures of the very same woman wearing "the same black silk pajamas." Indeed, even the script of the staged drama was repeated, with "access to the chamber of love quite uniformly obtained by announcing that it is a maid bringing towels or a messenger boy with an urgent telegram." Friedman concludes by noting that when the New York judge "spoke of naivete, he really meant the opposite; he meant a knowing and deliberate refusal to intervene...."

If no-fault was a half-revolution, what brought about the other half, that is, the legal recognition of divorces obtained by perjury?

Grace Ganz Blumberg, "Reworking the Past: Imagining the Future: On Jacob's Silent Revolution," 16 *Law & Social Inquiry* 115 (1991), challenges Jacob's assertion that the movement to no-fault divorce was really a revolution. Blumberg asserts that Jacob is a political scientist who focused on statutory language rather than on what the courts were actually doing, and what lawyers were doing in their practice. In practice, she notes, divorce was already frequently readily obtainable. Blumberg thinks that Jacob makes too much of the relative invisibility of the shift to no-fault, because it really wasn't much of a change in law on the ground: "If ... legal developments effect little substantive change, then the invisibility of their enactment is unexceptional." (p. 117)

She continues, saying that in New York divorce by contract was not novel:

> Most obviously, as long as there was any ground for divorce, the parties might always agree, after settling the terms, that one or the other, usually the husband, would be the nominal defendant but would not in fact defend against the plaintiff's claim. Those who found such a scenario distasteful because the sole ground was adultery might, also by agreement, send one spouse to Nevada for six weeks to falsely allege domicile in Nevada and to obtain an uncontested divorce on the pro forma ground of cruelty. (p. 120–121)

Jacob, "Reply to Blumberg," 16 *Law & Social Inquiry* 155 (1991), took exception to Blumberg's challenge. He said:

> [T]he changes in divorce law clearly legitimate a form of divorce that was previously only possible by committing perjury, and according to many they altered the expectations of those contemplating divorce. Divorce clients no longer can pursue the blaming game; they also have a different understanding of what belongs to each of them. . . .

> [T]o imply, as Blumberg does, that the law did not involve "any substantial change" is nonsense. . . . Blumberg's argument that consensual divorce was already available for those who were willing to go to Nevada, Mexico, the Virgin Islands, the Dominican Republic, or Haiti cavalierly takes an affluent person's approach to the law. For most New Yorkers, none of those alternatives were financial feasible in an era when airplanes had not yet become the functional equivalent of the Greyhound bus.

To what extent, if at all, does Blumberg's challenge qualify Jacob's description of a routine policy process? There were powerful groups—the Roman Catholic Church, for example—that might have been expected to oppose no-fault divorce. Why were these groups unable to block the ideas of a group of academics and practitioners?

3.   The various divorce reform bills were presented to American legislatures as the work of experts. Professors and practitioners of family law were involved in the drafting and advocacy of these statutes. Are they experts about the content of a divorce law? On what basis could they claim this status?

Blumberg thinks that legislators were led astray by the "obsessive focus of family law academics on what is fair as between the parties in view of the particulars of their marriage." (p. 149) She argues that distribution of a couple's resources according to the question, "What is fair as between the parties?" can set up a policy that ignores possible overall economic consequences for the divorcing wife and children. A sociological point of view, for example, might focus instead on the question of how a legal change will affect overall poverty levels for single-mother families. This is not an issue that is even considered when the focus remains on individual disputants. Blumberg argues that if divorce reforms result in fewer resources for children in post-divorce families, then policymakers need to ask, "What mix of private and public responses will appropriately address their needs?" (p. 150).

To what extent do legislators rely on such academic experts to resolve controversial social problems? Were the experts in the no-fault revolution telling the legislators only what they already believed? Carl E. Schneider reviewed Jacob's book in 86 *Michigan Law Review* 1121 (1988), and seems to take this position. He argues:

> The revolution is, I think, sparked and sustained by a set of ideological assumptions which are widely shared among many elite segments of

society, assumptions having to do with egalitarianism and with psychologically derived views of human nature. Professor Jacob tends to neglect such factors. While he is sensitive to the broad social changes that underlay the legislative reforms, he only hints at the process by which particular groups of people perceived those social changes, conceptualized them, brought them into social discourse, and proposed legislative responses to them.

How would you fashion a picture of the process by which the attitudes of legislators and their important constituents changed over time so that they would accept the experts' proposed no-fault reforms? How does this process compare with the views of Dicey and Gramsci?

One proposed solution to the problem of obtaining neutral guidance for legal reform was the creation of supposedly objective institutions such as the American Law Institute (ALI) and the National Conference of Commissioners on Uniform State Laws (NCCUSL). In the imagined ideal, elite lawyers would work together to research and propose model laws, putting aside their clients' interests so they could generate disinterested expert opinion about how the law should develop. However, in recent years, these bodies have become sites for political struggle. Organized interest groups have sought to press their views, hoping to generate model laws that will favor them. See, e.g., Edward J. Janger, "Predicting When the Uniform Law Process Will Fail: Article 9, Capture, and the Race to the Bottom," 83 *Iowa Law Review* 569, 582–94 (1998) (warning against the dangers of special interests capturing the private law-making duties of the ALI and NCCUSL); Alan Schwartz and Robert E. Scott, "The Political Economy of Private Legislatures," 143 *University of Pennsylvania Law Review* 595, 596–600 (1995) (discussing law-making at the ALI and NCCUSL); Richard E. Speidel, "Revising UCC Article 2: A View from the Trenches," 52 *Hastings Law Journal* 607, 610–618 (2001) (the politics that prompted Speidel to resign as reporter for the revision of Article 2 of the UCC).

4. The no-fault movement was not just American; there was a strong trend in that direction in European countries as well. See Mary Ann Glendon, *Abortion and Divorce in Western Law* (1987). Particularly in the Scandinavian countries (and most especially in Sweden), a no-fault system now prevails. This is also true in Canada. Other European countries retain some shadow of the fault system, but "divorce is readily available when the spouses reach an agreement on all issues, as they eventually do everywhere in the great majority of cases." (p. 80). European countries, however, vest far less discretion in the judge on property and child support matters. Child support is usually calculated "according to formulas or tables in a relatively predictable fashion." (p. 82).

What accounts for the differences and similarities, as between American experience and European experience? Among other things, Glendon suggests that the United States is more decentralized, more individualistic, more right-conscious than the countries of Western Europe, and has a less developed welfare state. (pp. 112 ff).

What light does a study like Glendon's shed on Jacob's thesis, and on the issues raised in this section? What kinds of information would we want to know about the dynamics of passage of the European or Canadian laws, in order to test Jacob's hypotheses?

5.   In her 1988 *Harvard Law Review* article, Martha Fineman reports on her research into the rhetoric of divorce, examining how the discourse of law and of the helping professions interacted with each other during the process of divorce reform. Not unlike Edelman et al., she argues that the rhetoric of a non-legal discipline (psychology/social work) was penetrating the law, and altering some of its fundamental tenets:

> Helping professionals and other proponents of joint custody asserted that the win–lose philosophy of naming a sole custodian was inappropriate, because parents had equal rights and responsibilities in relation to their children during marriage.... As this view has become accepted, it has altered the way we articulate and conceive of custody issues. The dominant rhetoric no longer describes divorce as a process that terminates the relationship between spouses, establishing one as the custodial parent with clear responsibilities. Rather, divorce is now described as a process that, through mediation, restructures and reformulates the spouses' relationship, conferring equal or shared parental rights on both parents although one, in practice, usually assumes the primary responsibility for care of the children. This is an important substantive shift.

> The helping professions' ability to suggest and obtain such radical change in substantive policy derives in part from their ability to present the debate over divorce and custody as one involving the treatment of an emotional crisis rather than a solution to a legal problem. Custody was merely a "label"; what was really at issue was the states of mind or attitudes of the family members.

Martha Fineman, "Dominant Discourse, Professional Language, and Legal Change in Child Custody Decisionmaking," 101 *Harvard Law Review* 727, 732–33 (1988). How does Fineman's model of the social components to legal change fit with and differ from Edelman's? Can Fineman's and Jacob's views of divorce reform be made compatible with each other?

6.   As Jacob notes, feminists did not speak with one voice on the subject of divorce reform. Some, like Herma Hill Kay, were adherents to "equality" models that sought to ensure that men and women were treated in the same way, as Jacob details. Others, like Fineman, believed that there were differences between men and women that were not accounted for in equality models, or in divorce reform based on those models. These feminists stressed the ways in which women's lives differed, on average, from those of men. (There are also divisions among "difference" feminists in terms of how they see the source of divergences between men and women.) Difference feminists argued that women would continue to carry disproportionate responsibility

for childrearing, and that they were likely to continue to face difficulties in obtaining equal employment opportunities after divorce (both because they tended to have more demands on their schedules due to childrearing, and because of continuing employment discrimination). Thus feminists like Fineman argued that divorce reform should be more focused on the outcomes produced for children and the women who cared for them, than on equality of process. See Martha Fineman, *The Illusion of Equality: The Rhetoric and Reality of Divorce Reform* (1991).

In a later book, Fineman argues that legal policy in the United States suffers from a myth of autonomy, based in an idea of rugged individualism, and missing the fact of the "inevitable dependencies" that all human societies must face (the dependency on others of the young, the infirm, the elderly, and the people who care for them). She urges that some of the dilemmas created by divorce could be better solved by at the level of society generally rather than at the level of private individuals—by providing added economic support for caretakers. Martha Albertson Fineman, *The Autonomy Myth: A Theory of Dependency* (2005). Given what you have learned about U.S. legal culture, what kind of challenges does Fineman's proposal face?

7.   Concern about the plight of children post divorce has not been the sole province of feminist scholars. Sociologists and psychologists have tracked the changes for children following the massive changes precipitated by divorce reform. These include shifts to preferences for no-fault divorce, joint or shared custody, and use of mediation to create a harmonious setting for divorce negotiations. Some psychologists have argued that the new "divorce culture" encourages couples experiencing even just moderate difficulties to part, and that the splitting-up of families has had a widening negative effect on the children of divorce. Judith Wallerstein et al., *The Unexpected Legacy of Divorce: The Landmark 25 Year Study* (2000). Wallerstein performed a longitudinal study on the children of divorce, but did not add a comparison sample until the final stages of the research. On the other hand, Mavis Hetherington performed a longitudinal study that included a comparison group of nondivorced families from the beginning, and came to far less negative conclusions. E. Mavis Hetherington, *For Better or For Worse: Divorce Reconsidered* (2002). She found that there were some negative effects for some children of coming from a divorced family, but that overall children of divorce did not look much different from the children of intact families. What most researchers in the field to date agree on is the negative effects of high levels of conflict on children, regardless of whether they are in intact or divorced families. Paul Amato, "Children of Divorce in the 1990s: An Update of the Amato and Keith Meta–Analysis," 15 *Journal of Family Psychology* 355 (2001).

This last finding has implications for the "harmony" model perpetuated by divorce reform. While mediation and shared custody are ideal solutions for couples who can collaborate, they may not be the best response to high conflict situations. Eleanor Maccoby and Robert Mnookin studied 1,100 California families during the 1980s, as they developed post-separation child custody and visitation arrangements. Eleanor Maccoby and Robert Mnookin, *Dividing the Child: Social and Legal Dilemmas of Custody* (1992). California initially instituted a preference for joint custody, but then in 1989 backed away from this approach, taking a more neutral position. Some states do have a statutory preference for joint custody, and of course a preference for joint custody can exist on-the-ground in courtrooms even in the absence of formal provisions. In their study, Maccoby and Mnookin express concern about the "cookie cutter" move to joint custody—especially joint physical custody—that has been encouraged by divorce reform:

> we are deeply concerned about the use of joint physical custody in cases where there is substantial parental conflict ... Our study suggests that in a number of cases in which families today adopt joint physical custody, there has been substantial legal conflict. To the extent that this custody arrangement is the result of encouragement by mediators, or judges for that matter, we think it is unwise. (p. 285)

The authors stress that joint custody can work very well when parents cooperate. If Maccoby and Mnookin are correct in their concern—that a new model for divorce emanating from the legal system is negatively affecting some post-divorce children—then what model of social and legal change is suggested by this picture? Taking a step backwards, we can then ask where the legal model originated. How does this multi-layered model of social and legal change fit with Edelman et al.'s approach?

   8. <u>Covenant Marriage</u>: While no fault divorce may have sailed under the radar in the 1960s and early 1970s, it has provoked strong opposition during the past decade or so. Some have advocated returning to various fault-based schemes. Over twenty states considered bills that would do this during the late 1990s, but none passed. In 1997, Louisiana enacted a statute which provided that couples getting married could chose "covenant marriage." In effect, these couples agree that they will not get divorced except in very limited circumstances such as physical abuse, abandonment, felony conviction, or adultery. They are also typically required to undergo premarital counseling, and to commit to seeking counseling should problems arise later in the marriage. Those who make this choice also face limits in how quickly they can remarry after a divorce. If a couple makes no such election, then their marriage is governed by a no-fault divorce system. Arkansas and Arizona have passed similar laws. In 2007, there was a major effort to pass such a statute in Oklahoma. Rick Lyman, "Trying to Strengthen 'I Do' With a More Binding Legal Tie," *N.Y. Times*, Feb. 15, 2005, at A1, reports that over twenty states have considered covenant marriage but failed to pass legislation enacting it. Moreover, in those states with this option under five percent of the couples have opted for it. Many engaged to be married are not sure about the wise choice to make, and few really want to think much about the possibility of divorce at this point in their lives.

(B) Pluralist Bargaining and Power

(3.12) Long–Term Continuing Relations: The American Experience Regulating Dealerships and Franchises

Stewart Macaulay[35]

IV.   The Campaign of the Retail Gasoline Dealers: Law and the Balance of Power

. . . The struggle over franchise laws teaches us much about the reality of regulation in the United States. The process involves battles in a never-ending war, moves in an endless game. Both franchisors and franchisees are well-armed with rhetorical symbols dear to Americans: "the free market" and "efficiency" battle "the virtues of small business," and the claims of expectations created by practice. While both sides bring experts into the contest, the manufacturers' economists more often are pitted against the dealers' victims of atrocities at the hands of franchisors. Dealers have advantages at the state level while franchisors usually are large corporations, well versed at playing in the national arena in Washington, D.C.

This is a story of the efforts of the retailers of branded gasoline to improve their position against the major oil companies. The tale of prolonged legal warfare will illustrate all the difficulties in such battles as well as the uncertain nature of the outcome. First, we will examine the nature of this "franchise" relationship—the norms and sanctions in this semi-autonomous social field, looking at the strains which prompted the dealers to seek outside help. We will then sketch the endless battles they won and lost, and we will try to indicate something of the impact of all these efforts.

Before the energy crisis in the early 1970s, the major oil refiners sought to maximize the amount of gasoline sold. Much of their profit came from products such as petrochemicals, and often gasoline was a by-product to be disposed at the best price available. It was uneconomic, because of the structure of the tax laws, to keep crude oil in the ground. Refining petrochemicals or heating oil also yielded gasoline which, as a practical matter, could not be stored for long. Even when a refinery run was planned to produce gasoline, the nature of the technology called for production in large quantities.

The major oil companies sold gasoline in many ways. Much, of course, was sold through service stations bearing the trademark of a major oil company. The company usually owned some of these stations itself, hiring employees to manage them. Most companies, however, contracted with franchised dealers and leased service station premises to them. Until the 1970s,

---

35. In C. Joerges (ed.) *Franchising and the Law: Theoretical and Comparative Approaches*   *in Europe and the United States*, at 179–237 (1991).

most oil companies worked to increase the number of stations offering their products, and many attempted to build national networks of distribution.

The major oil companies made the franchised dealer the focus of their retailing efforts in the 1930s. For a relatively small investment of capital, the companies told dealers that they could run "their own business." For example, a Shell Oil Company advertisement seeking new dealers said,

Work for a good man—yourself. A Shell Dealership offers:

—Paid training;

—Financing Assistance;

—High Income Potential.

When it suited their purposes, the oil companies characterized the dealers as independent business people. However, the companies managed to retain almost the same degree of control over the dealers as they would have had over employees. The companies drafted standard form contracts and leases which guarded their interests. Dealers assumed many obligations under these contracts, including such things as the hours they stayed open, the products they would sell, and responsibility for handling credit card purchases. The franchise usually was for a relatively short term—sometimes as little as 30 days with an optional renewal feature—and franchises could be canceled at will with no need to show cause. Furthermore, some oil companies frequently refused to allow a dealer to have an attorney review their contracts and leases before they were signed because they would allow no changes.

Dealers were well aware that it was good policy to keep the companies' district managers pleased. Dealers knew that their franchise ran for a term, but most assumed that they would be renewed. This view was reinforced the longer they stayed in business and obtained renewals. District managers often told their dealers that there was nothing to worry about, as long as there were no problems. This both reassured dealers and served as a warning of what might happen if there were problems. If a dealer's performance were questionable, the company also could open another station across the street or a block or two away. Finally, the companies offered training for dealers in management skills and business systems. This not only helped dealers become profitable but also served to channel their operations into the companies' patterns.

The dealer was thus given a strong incentive to pour time and effort into managing the station, building good will in the immediate area, and investing in tools, tow trucks and the like. The companies benefited by characterizing their dealers as independent business people rather than as employees. Oil companies could not have devised a better incentive structure which would prompt most employees to work the long hours and take the responsibility assumed by dealers. Also, "independent" dealers were not subject to minimum wage and maximum hour regulations, and they would not unionize and ask to collectively bargain.

Sometimes everyone was happy. Often the oil company and the dealer shared interests. Successful dealers made money and had a degree of independence. Sometimes successful dealers even had some countervailing power. When major oil companies were expanding into new regions of the country, they might seek to entice experienced and capable dealers away from other companies. Companies probably threatened to cancel, both expressly and impliedly, far more than they actually terminated dealers. Oil companies usually renewed even slightly marginal dealers. There were costs in changing dealers by canceling franchises—the replacement, for example, might not do as well.

However, there often were strains in the relationship. These strains were provoked in part by the contradiction between the reality of the situation and the fiction that the dealer was an independent business person. Until the energy crisis of the 1970s, there were recurring price wars in many areas when one refiner wanted to get rid of surplus gasoline or wanted to establish itself. The oil company would order its dealers to cut prices to increase sales. The other major oil companies would respond by telling their dealers to meet the price cuts or to drop the price even lower in order to bring in new customers. The dealer usually had to bear part of the burden of lower prices. Dealers would be given allowances to enable them to survive a price war, but the major oil companies decided how great an allowance to offer and how long to keep it in effect. Truly independent dealers would have had the power to set their own prices based on their own judgment about long term benefits and their own particular situation. This independence was denied to most franchisees in gasoline price wars. Price competition was a tactic which might help a major oil company get rid of gasoline or bring in a few new people to a station once or twice. However, cuts were met quickly by cuts from the station across the street.

Also, dealers often could make more profit selling tires, batteries and accessories (TBA) and even motor oil which they bought from wholesalers than by offering only products supplied by the major oil companies. Refiners controlled the TBA offered by their dealers in many ways, ranging from requirements contracts to what the Federal Trade Commission and the courts later were to label as coercion.

In the late 1960s, many major oil companies decided to deemphasize neighborhood stations, and the servicing and repairing of automobiles and use marketing techniques which would sell more gasoline at fewer stations. Experts began to say that the United States had far too many gasoline stations for efficient distribution. Jordan described the tensions in the relationship as follows:

> The company sees the station as its means of selling petroleum products, with price competition and high volume as keys to profit. The dealer, in contrast, often sees the station primarily as his repair and maintenance operation. Since the bulk of his income tends to come from automotive services that he, not the oil company, provides, he is less concerned than

316

the company about increasing sales of the relatively low-profit gasoline. Moreover, though some agreements do specify a maximum rent, rental rates are often based on a percentage of gasoline sales, in effect giving the dealer a negative incentive. This disparity between the interests of the company and the operator simply does not exist where both are exclusively interested in selling the same product and splitting the profits.[36]

Dealers were told to close service facilities which had been highly profitable to them and turn to self-service, trading stamps, contests, premiums, and extended hours of operation. Major companies began to withdraw from regions of the country where they did not have a large share of the market, leaving many canceled dealers in their wake. After the Arab Oil Embargo in 1973, many major oil companies worked even harder to close their less profitable stations. Gasoline no longer was merely something to be disposed of. This part of their operation had to maximize profit rather than volume.

The major oil companies rationalized their control of their dealership network by their property, trademark and contract rights. Often they owned the stations which were leased to dealers; they claimed ownership of trademarks such as "Standard," "Shell," and "Texaco" and thus controlled those who displayed them; and they drafted form contracts that gave them the right to cancel dealerships at their discretion. Often the oil companies justified their power and policies in terms of efficiency and benefits to consumers. They pictured canceled dealers as inefficient operators who survived by charging customers high prices and running dirty stations. They argued that consumers expected to find the same high quality of product and service at all stations displaying, for example, the "Shell" trademark. The oil companies also pointed out that they supplied most of the capital involved in the network of gasoline stations, and they said that as conditions changed, any particular dealer had few equities to offset required changes in the entire franchise system.

The dealers, of course, saw matters very differently. They said that they were independent business people who created the value of their service station by their labor and their efforts to build good will. They relied on having their franchise renewed because of representations made to them, expressly and impliedly, by the oil companies. They did not deal with the lawyers and top officials who fashioned the legal paper work. They talked to field representatives who led them to believe that they would keep their stations and their independence as long as they did a good job. The dealers' efforts, in partnership with the oil companies, had created the business at the local level. It was unfair for oil companies to pass back to the dealers a major part of the burdens of economic change brought about by OPEC—which was a response to the conduct of the major oil companies in Third World Countries. Finally, dealers made the classic argument of small business against competi-

---

36. Ellen R. Jordan, "Unconscionability at the Gas Station," 62 *Minnesota Law Review* 813, 817–818 (1978).

tion: price competition in gasoline destroyed service and would end with a few near monopolists able to impose whatever prices they wanted, without offering service to customers.

The tensions in their relationship with the oil companies prompted gasoline dealers to organize. Gasoline dealers, both individually and through their organizations, tried to change the nature of their relationship with the major oil companies for more than thirty years. Trade associations proposed informal dispute resolution panels, but the oil companies were not interested. District managers of the oil companies would not allow a dealers' organization to represent dealers in meetings with the company. The managers said that they would only talk with dealers as individuals, and they pointed out a possible conflict of interest—the organizations represented dealers selling competitive products.

When these efforts at informal dispute resolution failed, the organized dealers turned to the legal system. Their basic strategy was to search for a new legal categorization of the relationship, and to collect atrocity stories to provoke a scandal. And dealers hired lobbyists and lawyers with enough experience and skill to counter the representatives of the major oil companies. They appealed to the Federal Trade Commission, state and federal courts, state legislatures, and the United States Congress with varying success over the years. Every legislative representative has retail gasoline dealers doing business in his or her district, and these retailers are "small business," a symbol dear to both major political parties.

From World War II through the 1960s, a number of antitrust actions attempted to protect the status of retail gasoline dealers as independent business people by lessening the oil companies' control. Victories were won by and for dealers; a notable line of cases in the Supreme Court of the United States developed. The Federal Trade Commission and private suits attacked the oil companies' control over the prices charged by their dealers and the response to price wars as well as various attempts to induce dealers to stock only the companies' TBA. The FTC won consent decrees limiting the use of short-term leases of service stations, which the Commission said made the dealers more vulnerable to the oil companies' coercion.

The FTC also attempted to solve many conflicts informally. President Nixon's Task Force on Productivity and Competition complained:

> The efforts of the Commission to protect small dealers from allegedly unfair and coercive business practices constitute a dark chapter in the Commission's history. Much of this enforcement activity does not eventuate in formal proceedings. What happens is that a dealer who is terminated, for whatever reason, is likely to complain to the Commission, knowing that the relevant Commission staff is well disposed toward "small business." The staff uses the threat of an FTC proceeding to get the supplier to reinstate the dealer, and if threats fail—usually they succeed—the FTC may file a complaint charging the supplier with having cut off the dealer because he was a price cutter, or for some other nefarious reason. Our

impression, in sum, is that the Commission, especially at the informal level, has evolved an effective law of dealer protection that is unrelated and often contrary to the objectives of the anti-trust laws.[37]

While these victories undoubtedly changed day-to-day practices of major oil companies, some companies asserted that they always had honored the status of their dealers as independent business people.... Despite such policy statements, some dealers thought that too much pressure to take orders remained. The General Counsel of the National Congress of Petroleum Retailers appeared before a Congressional committee hearing on problems in gasoline retailing. He explained:

> The district manager comes in and sees that another TBA is in your station. That doesn't happen to be the brand they are selling, and he says, "Good heavens. What is this oil doing here?" And the dealer says, "You know, I thought I could sell it, and the Texaco case, and the Simpson case, and all the others say that I am entitled to sell anything I want to sell."

> The district manager says, "You certainly are, Joe Blow; you are a nice family man; you have six kids. Your lease will be over in 4 months, and I will tell you just a little ahead of time so you can be looking around for a new job...." When the pressure gets hard enough, you go along with them.

The Executive Director of the National Congress thought that the pressure often was more subtle. Dealers would be told that the company expected all aspects of the station to be highly profitable and certain targets would be set. Dealers could not achieve the goal for selling, say, Standard's brand of oil if they sold too much Pennzoil or Quaker State.

Since the 1950s, the retailers sought to limit the power of oil companies to cancel or refuse to renew franchises because this power is the source of much of their leverage over dealers.... Throughout the 1950s and 1960s, both the House and Senate Small Business Committees held hearings where franchised dealers, including those who operated gasoline stations, made the populist appeal against big business again and again....

After the failure ... at the federal level, the legislative battle moved to New York. In 1969, the legislature there passed a statute which would have required all franchisors to act in a fair, equitable and honest manner and in accordance with reasonable standards of fair dealing when granting, modifying, terminating or failing to renew a franchise. However, Governor Rockefeller vetoed the bill because of the "unreasonable injunctive rights it would grant dealers."

Next, individual gasoline dealers who had been canceled or not renewed, went to court. Their lawyers, backed by their trade associations, searched for legal concepts which would override the oil companies' carefully-fashioned positions based on property, trademark and contract. Wall Street very suc-

---

37. BNA *Antitrust and Trade Regulation Reporter*, 1969: X–3.

cessfully warded off Main Street, and the dealers usually lost. For example, two lower New York courts refused to apply the Uniform Commercial Code's provisions concerning "good faith" and "unconscionability" to gasoline dealer franchises. The Code, the courts explained, applies only to transactions in goods, and a franchise involves both goods and a lease of real estate. These courts also refused to consider evidence of a custom to renew station leases absent cause for cancellation. Any such custom would contradict the express terms of the franchise document drafted by the oil company lawyers. Yet even these defeats were to play a role in later developments as indicating the need for legislation.

One of the judges emphasized the vetoed legislation and saw legal change in this area as an appropriate legislative task. He remarked that he was "not unsympathetic to the plaintiff's plight ..." and said he was sending copies of his opinion to the appropriate legislative committees. The other judge made the interesting statement that it is "unconscionable, although legal at present, for the ... [Mobil Oil Company] ... to be allowed, without cause, to terminate this lease after 19 years of annual renewal." He thought Mobil's action "harks back to the early days of our nation's industrial development when corporations were king and the workers were only to be used." He concluded that "the Legislature and the Governor of this State will see fit to enact, again, legislation which will protect this vast number of our citizens."

Still a third New York lower court judge did not think he had to await legislation. He pointed to representations made by the Mobil Oil Company to a canceled dealer, noted that Mobil had not allowed the dealer to have an attorney present when the lease was signed since it "would not tolerate changes in any of the provisions of the printed agreements," and stressed that Mobil's refusal to renew because the dealer had not followed Mobil's price-setting directions violated the antitrust laws. He concluded that there was a "fiduciary relationship" which Mobil had violated.[38] Thus, the court refused to grant Mobil's petition to recover possession of its station. However, this innovative exercise was reversed on appeal.

In the early 1970s, state and local gasoline dealers organizations pressed for legislation in many states. After several failures, a bill offering all franchisees protection was passed in Wisconsin. Both Connecticut and New Jersey passed statutes providing that franchisors could not cancel or fail to renew franchises "without good cause." In addition, the Connecticut law provided that any franchisee could submit the question of "good cause" to arbitration in accordance with the rules of the American Arbitration Association.

In Connecticut, Mobil Oil Company led the attack on the new statute. It told twenty-six of its dealers who ran the most valuable stations in the state

---

38. Fiduciary relationships exist when one purports to act for the benefit of another— lawyers are in such relationships with their clients, for example.

that it would not renew their franchises and would take over their stations. It could adopt this strategy because the statute did not apply retroactively to franchisees which had been created before the law became effective. At a legislative hearing, a representative of Mobil said that it could not leave $300,000 stations in the hands of dealers who had tenure granted by the law. Unless the statute were repealed, Mobil would have to take over all of its stations in the state.[39]

Members of the legislature reacted angrily to what they saw as coercion. Some legislators discovered that Mobil's representative was not registered as a lobbyist, and they demanded prosecution. A story appeared in the New York Times[40] which noted that if "Mobil was going to get in trouble for its efforts on behalf of all the oil companies, Mobil's brass would be embarrassed and many of the company's officers live in Connecticut—including the chairman of the board ..." Mobil's officers may have recognized this. At any rate, they withdrew the heavy attack, apologized, and then joined with the Connecticut Gasoline Retailers Association to offer amendments to the statute. Under these changes, franchisors could cancel or refuse to renew a dealer's lease for failure to perform obligations under a contract or where the franchisor converted its property to a use not covered by the franchise agreement. In addition, the provision for arbitration was deleted as an interference with the franchisor's constitutional right of trial by jury.

In New Jersey, major oil companies canceled or refused to renew franchises in response to that state's franchise law. The Supreme Court of New Jersey, however, decided in *Shell Oil Co. v. Marinello*[41] that franchise agreements entered into before the state's law became effective were subject to an implied covenant that the franchisor would renew as long as dealers had substantially complied with their obligations. The New Jersey court was able to rely on the legislation as a declaration of the state's policy warranting the imposition of an implied term in the contract. Imposing an "implied term" is a well-known move in the contract doctrine game, but this was the first time that it was applied to franchises.

Once again action prompted reaction. At the request of oil companies, a federal district court found invalid the decision which implied a covenant to renew as well as the New Jersey statute because they conflicted with the federal Lanham Act governing trademarks.[42] This decision later was reversed

---

39. A member of Mobil's legal staff explained his firm's position in Connecticut:

Our concern with the 1973 amendments to the Connecticut Franchise Act was that they had the effect of giving a dealer, who had invested approximately $10,000 in inventory and equipment, the same long-term property rights in a service station as an oil company supplier-landlord that had invested $300,000 in ac-

quiring the property and constructing the service station improvements....

Letter of November 14, 1974 to Professor Stewart Macaulay.

40. Mar. 19, 1974, at 47; Mar. 20, 1974, at 53.

41. 63 N.J. 402, 307 A.2d 598 (1973), cert. denied, 415 U.S. 920 (1974).

42. *Mariniello v. Shell Oil Co.*, 368 F.Supp. 1401, 1407 (D.N.J. 1974).

on appeal,[43] but for a time it brought all efforts of gasoline dealers in the state legislatures into question.

Despite the dealers' difficulties in getting courts to protect existing franchises, the dealers' organizations did well before many state legislatures. By the mid–1970s, over thirty states had some kind of franchise protection law applicable to retail gasoline dealers whose franchises were created or renewed after the statutes went into effect. Some of these statutes applied only to gasoline dealers; others applied to all franchises including gasoline dealerships.

The dealers' lobbying organizations tried still another approach. They pressed for statutes that would restrict oil companies' operation of retail outlets. If these statutes were passed, oil companies no longer could threaten to take over stations before the effective date of franchise protection statutes as Mobil had done in Connecticut. They also could no longer open company stations to compete with franchised dealers or threaten to do so for leverage. By 1977, twenty eight states had given some consideration to such bills, and laws to this effect had passed in Maryland, Florida, Delaware, Virginia and the District of Columbia. Several bills to this end were introduced in Congress.

Exxon, Shell, Gulf, Phillips, Ashland, Continental and Commonwealth Oil Companies joined to challenge the constitutionality of the Maryland statute. However, the Supreme Court of the United States upheld it.[44] After this decision, the threat of passing these statutes was used to promote a federal legislative solution. The dealers' trade associations continued to struggle in the 1970s to gain federal legislation that would limit termination and nonrenewals and protect existing dealers....

At the beginning of the decade, the large oil companies were supported by people in the Nixon and Ford administrations who opposed these bills as anticompetitive and promoting inefficiency. In 1974, President Nixon vetoed a comprehensive energy bill which included provisions prohibiting fuel sellers from terminating dealer franchises unless the dealer had failed to comply with reasonable requirements of the franchise. The Senate failed to override the veto, and the dealers suffered still another defeat....

The dealers' lobbyists were undaunted after the veto of the energy bill in 1974, and they began still another major federal campaign. Individual dealers and groups of dealers met with their congressional representatives in district after district. They dramatized their plight by recounting atrocity stories and dwelling on the ideology of small business and traditional American hostility to large multinational corporations. International developments now made the dealers' story even more appealing. As the price of gasoline increased in the early 1970s, many Americans were angered by the major oil companies' extraordinary profits. Many thought that the large oil companies had manufactured the entire "oil crisis" to excuse price increases. Dealers claimed that

43. *Mariniello v. Shell Oil Co.*, 511 F.2d 853 (3d Cir.1975).

44. *Exxon Corp. v. Governor of Maryland*, 437 U.S. 117 (1978).

these companies should not pass on the burdens of disruption in the oil business to their dealers and customers when the companies were making record profits.

During 1977, some of the major oil companies changed their position and supported federal dealer protection legislation. The dealers' lobbyists and the companies' lawyers worked out most of the technical objections to earlier legislative proposals, arriving at a compromise with the help of the staffs of the House and Senate committees considering legislation in this area. . . .

Perhaps a major reason for this change was that many companies now felt that they needed federal legislation to preempt the many varying state statutes and to ward off the threat of divestiture of all retail operations. The dealers' associations had produced enough state law that the companies valued uniformity itself. Furthermore, there was always a threat that the dealers could get states to pass laws less favorable to oil company interests than the compromise worked out at the federal level. Finally, the major oil companies were concerned about congressional reaction to proposals for such things as gasoline rationing and a windfall profits tax. Some officials of the large corporations thought it was time to withdraw from the public role as the villain who pushed around local small business.

Congress passed the Petroleum Marketing Practices Act (PMPA), which became effective in June of 1978. While this statute limits cancellation of a franchise to specified grounds, it also leaves the major oil companies relatively free to not renew dealer franchises. The franchisor need only negotiate in good faith for a renewal; it need not negotiate reasonably in light of the dealer's interests. The federal courts have read the PMPA's provisions on nonrenewal so that a dealer's threat of formal legal action is but a paper tiger. Moreover, the PMPA preempts all state legislation which might otherwise benefit gasoline dealers.

In 1984, The Service Station Dealers of America, Inc. returned to Congress seeking amendments to the PMPA, and it has lobbied for legislation at every session since then. . . .

The dealers and legislators championing their cause proposed a statute which would require changes and additions proposed by a franchisor in renewal negotiations to be "fair and reasonable" in addition to being in good faith. . . .

In 1988, the proposed statute amending the PMPA was passed by the House of Representatives but not by the Senate. It was reintroduced in 1989. The Director of Legislative and Political Affairs for the Petroleum Marketers Association of American stated that he thought there was a "50:50 chance that President Bush would veto" the PMPA Amendments if they were passed.

The retail gasoline dealers also returned to the state legislatures.[45] During the 1980s, they won victories in Massachusetts, Nevada and other states.

---

45. The International Franchise Association's treasurer discussed the success of this franchisor organization in blocking proposed state franchise protection legislation. The

However, their lawyers are now defending these statutes against constitutional challenges and charges that they attempt to regulate in an area taken from state power by the PMPA.

Once again, move prompts countermove. The Federal Trade Commission began rule-making hearings on proposed franchising rules in 1986. This process continued through 1990....

What has been the impact of all this legal warfare? Certainly the organized gasoline dealers gained a federal law which gives them broad protection against cancellation during the term of a franchise.... However, the PMPA offers little protection against nonrenewal of a franchise. Moreover, ... the PMPA preempts state legislation dealing with cancellation and nonrenewal.

The number of franchised dealers of gasoline has continued to decline even after the federal legislation went into effect.[46] The price of fuel remains high, and many motorists drive less and buy cars that get high mileage. This limits gasoline sales. Motorists are less willing to pay a few cents a gallon more at their neighborhood stations which do not discount their prices. Automobile manufacturers have decreased the frequency of needed maintenance, and dealers have lost oil change and lubrication business. Automobiles have become more difficult to repair, requiring specialized tools for each make and trained mechanics. This decreases the opportunity to repair cars at service stations. And the federal legislation came in 1978 rather than in 1968. Many of the dealers who might have benefited when the great wave of terminations and nonrenewals began, lost out long before the law was passed.

Thus, the long struggle to gain federal legislation may have produced a law with more symbolic significance than instrumental impact. Of course, it may have benefited those who managed to survive until it was passed. Some dealers may have won renewals before the oil companies established the judicial interpretations that are so favorable to them. There might have been even a greater decline in the number of service stations had there been no federal law.

As we noted, the gasoline dealers' efforts in some states produced statutes offering protection to most franchisees rather than just those who sold gasoline. These statutes are preempted by the federal Petroleum Marketing Practices Act only insofar as they apply to gasoline dealers. There is an ironic twist here. The gasoline dealers worked to pass these statutes, and they included other franchisees only to broaden the appeal of the proposed legisla-

group works to kill these proposals in committee. This allows legislators to vote against these bills without publicity. He said in 1986, that the IFA defeated 27 bills introduced in 18 states. See Bernstein, "IFA Faces Franchise Law Fracas," 21 *Nation's Restaurant News,* Feb. 9, 1987, at 1.

46. Although nobody knows the total number of retail gas outlets—estimates range from 150,000 to 300,000—government figures show that the number of service stations is now 112,000, less than half the 1972 peak. Hershey, "Fill'er Up and Check the Doughnuts," *N.Y.Times,* July 1, 1989, at 16, col. 1, 3.

tion. Those who just went along for the ride are the major beneficiaries of the retail gasoline dealers' lobbying efforts.

NOTES AND QUESTIONS

1.   How do you explain the passage of federal and state gasoline dealer franchise protection statutes? Does the situation fit the model put forward by Friedman and Ladinsky? What aspects of the story are explained by (a) elements of legal culture; (b) aspects of the structure of American law, for example, federalism; (c) power, class and hegemony; (d) "outside" forces such as the Arab oil shock, technological change, and soon?

2.   Can we generalize from Macaulay's story? Can you think of other attempts at reform that were gutted by the judicial and legal tactics of the powerful? To what extent did American civil rights statutes, regulations, and cases of the 1970s come to a fate in the 1980s and 1990s similar to that of gasoline dealer protective legislation?

3.   Why didn't the judges implement the statutes more vigorously in favor of the dealers? Couldn't, for example, the federal statute have been read to require that judges examine negotiations about renewal of a service station for their fairness, rather than leave a large loophole in the statute? Couldn't the Congress have responded quickly, when the federal act was discovered to overturn all the state regulation while offering little protection to the dealers? How might we explain these failures to carry out the purposes of the reforms?

Consider Robert C. Ellickson, *Order Without Law: How Neighbors Settle Disputes* 152–153 (1991). He explains that interest-group theory in sociology

> holds that members of powerful interest groups manipulate the content of norms to serve their own selfish interests . . .
>
> Interest-group theorists would win more converts if they could identify the mechanisms through which well-placed interest groups might manipulate the norm-making process. One can readily understand how concentrated lobbies are able to influence the legal system. The informal-control system, by contrast, is much more diffuse. Florists undoubtedly have had some success in promoting the tradition of Mother's Day gifts, and diamond merchants, the custom of diamond engagement rings. Nevertheless, norms seem generally resistant to deliberate influence. Totalitarian Communist regimes were not able to produce a "new man," Madison Avenue cannot convince most motorists to buckle their seat belts, and the right-to-life movement has little success in stemming the incidence of abortion. One weakness of the various interest-group theories is that they say little about when and how an interest group can control the content of norms.
>
> A second shortcoming . . . is that [these theories] are seriously incomplete. Many fundamental social norms appear neutral in content. It is hard to see how common norms of honesty, reciprocity, promise keeping, and respect for the bodily integrity of others serve the interests

325

of the strong at the expense of the weak. . . . Interest-group analysis must amplify their theories so as to be able to explain norms that are distributively neutral or progressive.

To what extent can we explain the retail gasoline dealers' only partial success as a failure to control the content of informal norms? To what extent could changing the text in statute books affect the norms of those who represented the major oil companies in their everyday contacts with retail gasoline dealers? To what extent could changing the text in statute books change the informal norms held by judges and jurors who dealt with cases under the statute? Would such informal norms affect their reading of the formal ones found in statutory text?

4. Do the gasoline dealer statutes reflect law as the "will of the people?" Or are they special interest statutes likely to place the costs of changes in the petroleum industry on consumers who are not organized into a special interest group able to bargain before the legislatures? To what degree is this typical of American legislation?

5. Many groups—conservative as well as liberal, business as well as civil rights—use the courts as a tool for political action. See Susan M. Olson, "Interest Group Litigation in Federal District Courts: Beyond the Federal Disadvantage Theory," 52 *Journal of Politics* 854 (1990).

6. The turn of the millennium saw a new push for bankruptcy law reform. In 1998, the *Wall Street Journal* reported that

> the six-year-old National Consumer Bankruptcy Coalition, which includes Visa U.S.A., MasterCard International, Inc., the American Bankers Association and the National Retail Federation, has financed much of the research concluding that the bankruptcy laws are too lax, and then it has spread the results in advertisements decrying "bankruptcies of convenience." It has also underwritten opinion polls designed to show public support for industry proposals.

"Card Games: As Bankruptcies Surge, Creditors Lobby to Get Tougher Law," *The Wall Street Journal,* June 17, 1998, at A1. These lenders were quite open about their efforts to "transform the image of lenders from scrooges to victims," and "even wrote their own suggested legislation: key provisions of that draft are in the House bill." If law is a mere reflex of the dominant classes' power, then why would they need to sink this much effort into influencing public opinion? What kind of model does this piece of news imply about the relationship between society, culture, and legal change?

Now consider the outcome: in 2005, a new federal bankruptcy law passed which made it harder to erase debt through bankruptcy. This law, not surprisingly, was "backed by the credit card industry and opposed by consumer groups." "Tighter Bankruptcy Law Favored," *The Washington Post*, February 11, 2005, at A05. See Teresa A. Sullivan, Elizabeth Warren and Jay Lawrence Westbrook, "Less Stigma or More Financial Distress: An Empirical Analysis of the Extraordinary Increase in Bankruptcy Filings," 59 *Stanford*

Law Review 213, 254 (2006) ("This Article provides strong evidence that the principal argument supporting the legislation was simply wrong. Bankrupt debtors were not able to pay in 1981, and they were even less able to pay twenty years later.")

(C) *The Judicial System in Social Context*

(3.13) **The Routinization of Debt Collection: An Essay on Social Change and Conflict in Courts**

Robert Kagan

18 *Law & Society Review* 323 (1984).

In recent years, there have been a substantial number of historical studies of the dockets of American courts, stimulated in some cases by concerns that our society is becoming more litigious, in others by concerns that important kinds of grievances are left unadjudicated, and in still others by a sense that changes in the business of courts will provide insight into the dynamics of the legal system as a whole. There has been great interest in the apparent increase of certain types of court cases, such as product liability, malpractice, criminal procedure, and public law cases. These upsurges in litigation are sometimes taken as a sign that courts are at last dealing with injustices long neglected and sometimes as a sign that something is amiss in the social system if people and organizations more often resort to the courts to resolve their problems. Less attention has been given, however, to discovering precisely what kinds of social changes encourage or suppress particular kinds of litigation, and exactly how they do so. To stimulate further inquiry into those processes, this essay discusses the social, economic, political, and legal factors that have produced a recent decline in contested litigation in a significant sphere of court business—debt collection suits....

In eighteenth-and nineteenth-century American courts, debt collection cases ... seem to have dominated the judicial process. Bruce Mann reports that in a six-month period in 1154, a Windham, Connecticut, justice of the peace heard 47 actions on promissory notes, 4 debt actions on book accounts, and only 9 other kinds of cases. Wayne McIntosh tells us that debt collection cases accounted for over 80 percent of civil cases filed in the St. Louis, Missouri, Circuit Court in 1820 (a depression year), over 50 percent in the 1820–1850 period, and over one-third (still the largest single type of case) in 1865–1895. Debt collection cases were similarly prominent in California trial courts in 1890 and 1910, in Chippewa County, Wisconsin, between 1865 and 1894, and in the Boston Municipal Court and the Suffolk County Superior Court in 1880 and 1890.

While docketed cases usually reflect individual debtor creditor disputes, the role of the courts in forcible debt collection occasionally boiled up into political conflict. The history of the Constitutional Convention in 1787 and the document it produced reflect fears of populist democracy sown by agrarian debtors' attacks against the courts, as in Shays' Rebellion in Massachusetts,

Figure 1. Business Failure and Number
of State Supreme Court Debt Case Opinions
1870-1970

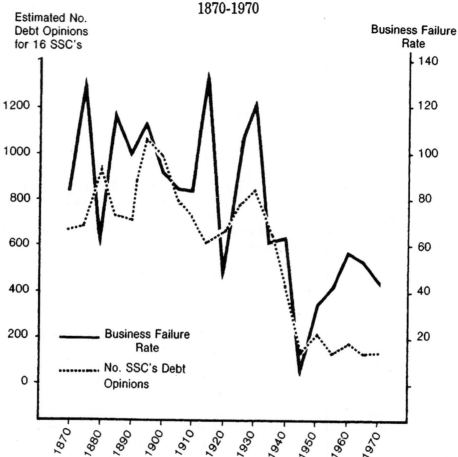

Business Failure Rate: no. failures per 10,000 enterprises listed by
Dun & Bradstreet

Estimated No. Debt Opinions: for 16 state supreme courts (Alabama,
California, Idaho, Illinois, Kansas, Maine, Michigan, Minnesota,
Nevada, New Jersey, North Carolina, Oregon, Rhode Island, South
Dakota, Tennessee, West Virginia)

and occasionally successful attempts by debtors to obtain legislation staying
the collection of debts or making payment easier by obliging creditors to
accept hastily printed (and fast-depreciating) paper money. Similarly, the
plight of agrarian debtors burdened by tight money and unyielding credit

institutions was the fulcrum of widespread grass-roofs political agitation and intense conflict over the gold standard during the Populist movement in the latter part of the nineteenth century. It should not be surprising, then, that even though most debt collection cases in the trial courts were settled or ended in uncontested default judgments, hard-fought debt cases also worked their way with considerable frequency up the judicial ladder to state supreme courts, which in the nineteenth century were often more active than legislatures as policy-making bodies. Debt cases accounted for almost 30 percent of the opinions of 16 representatively selected American state supreme courts in 1870 and about 26 percent of their opinions in the 1870–1900 period. Resolving conflicts and formulating rules of law concerning the debt collection process apparently absorbed more high court attention than any other type of legal or policy issue. In the twentieth century, however, there has been a dramatic decline, both proportionately and in absolute number, in debtor protection/creditors' rights opinions by state supreme courts. . . . The decline was gradual in the 1900–1935 period but has been dramatic since then. In the 1950–1970 period fewer than 7 percent of state supreme court (SSC) opinions involved debt collection matters; the 16 SSCs in the . . . sample decided an estimated 170 debt cases per year, on the average, as contrasted with an estimated 886 per year in 1880–1900 and 717 in 1905–1925.

The gradual disappearance of debt collection cases from state supreme court dockets gives rise to both an historical and a theoretical puzzle. Why has a type of legal dispute so central to socioeconomic relations in a market economy and so often a focus of political conflict all but faded away as a subject for judicial policy-making? In an era in which, as the conventional wisdom has it, an "imperial judiciary" is intruding upon (or is being thrust into) ever-widening areas of economic and social life, why have high courts almost abandoned (or been permitted to neglect) debtor-creditor relations? These questions, in turn, relate to a persistent theoretical issue in the study of law and society: What determines the changing incidence of judicial involvement in a policy area? To address these questions, this essay will examine available data concerning the volume of contested and uncontested cases in trial courts and will discuss five factors or trends that seem likely to affect the incidence of debt litigation: (1) fluctuations in the number or rate of problem-generating events, i.e., debt repayment delinquencies and defaults; (2) litigation costs; (3) legal rationalization, i.e., trends toward the stabilization of legal rules and toward institutionalized contracting and collection processes designed to simplify or forestall litigation; (4) political conflict over existing legal rules and political demands for legal change and (5) trends toward systemic stabilization, i.e., development of regulatory programs, public and private insurance and loss-spreading arrangements, and diversified economic institutions that prevent or deflect debtor-creditor conflict. Examining the limited evidence relevant to each of these factors will lead to an inductively constructed model that suggests how the various factors interact and that helps us understand the changing incidence of litigation in other areas as well. Moreover, the overriding importance of the developments discussed under the heading "Systemic Stabilization" in limiting debt collection litigation emphasizes the powerful role of collective welfare state measures and economic development in shaping modern legal action.

I. PROBLEM–GENERATING EVENTS

One obvious influence on the incidence of certain types of court cases might be the number of transactions or events in the surrounding society that

Data for Figure 1

Sample Year	Average No. Opinions per SSC	Percent Debt Collection	Average No. Debt Opinions per SSC	Estimated Total Debt Opinions, 16 SSC's	Rate of Business Failures @ 10,000 Businesses	Total Business Failures in U.S.
1870	131	32.1	42	672	83	3,546
1875	171	25.4	43	688	128	7,740
1880	208	28.2	59	944	63	4,735
1885	196	23.4	46	736	116	10,637
1890	233	19.4	45	720	99	10,907
1895	242	27.4	66	1056	112	13,197
1900	240	25.3	61	976	92	10,774
1905	213	23.6	50	800	85	11,520
1910	245	18.4	45	720	84	12,652
1915	292	13.2	39	624	133	22,156
1920	228	18.1	41	656	48	8,881
1925	254	19.4	49	784	100	21,214
1930	270	19.8	53	848	122	26,355
1935	215	18.8	40	640	62	12,244
1940	184	14.9	27	432	63	13,619
1945	119	5.9	7	112	4	809
1950	160	9.0	14	224	34	9,162
1955	158	5.6	9	144	42	10,969
1960	172	6.9	12	192	57	15,445
1965	182	4.9	9	144	53	13,514
1970	167	5.2	9	144	44	10,748

can give rise to the kind of legal action in question. This "hypothesis" assumes that, over time, citizens and business organizations are inclined to take a relatively constant (even if small) proportion of their problems and disputes to court and to contest or appeal a relatively constant (even if small) proportion of those court cases. As potentially troublesome social and economic encounters or relationships take new forms or increase in number, one would expect the composition of court dockets to mirror, in a rough way, changes in the numbers of such conflict-producing transactions. In some legal areas, this relationship seems to exist. Thus, the proportion of domestic relations cases on state supreme court dockets has tended to rise and fall with changes in the national divorce rate. State supreme court tort cases involving railroads declined in the twentieth century along with the steady reduction in the number of railroad accidents, while motor vehicle tort appeals rose as death from auto accidents increased. From this perspective, fluctuations in the incidence of nonpayment of debts should produce corresponding changes in debt collection litigation. One available proxy for the incidence of debt delinquency is the recorded data on national business failures. As Figure I and its accompanying data show, between 1870 and 1930, some upswings and some declines in business failures were paralleled by less extreme trends in the number of debt cases in state supreme courts, while at other times the two curves moved in opposite directions. Strikingly, however, the most drastic phase of the decline in debt case appeals, in the mid–1930s and 1940s, matched an equally dramatic drop in the rate and number of business failures. The dockets of some trial courts for which longitudinal data exist also seemed to reflect the business cycle, especially in the 1930s and '40s:

> —In Chippewa County, Wisconsin, debt cases which numbered 407 (40 percent of the civil docket) in 1915–1924, rose to 662 (55 percent of the civil docket) in the 1925–1934 period, which covered the depths of the Depression, only to decline to their earlier level after the holocaust of business failures and mortgage foreclosures of the early 1930s had run its course.

> —In Alameda County, California, my estimates from Friedman and Percival's published data indicate that debt case filings climbed from 236 in 1890 to 929 in 1910 and 1329 in 1930, a path that parallels the rate and absolute number of business failures nationwide for those years, and then declined to 853 cases in 1950 as prosperity returned and the business failure rate went down (Friedman and Percival, 1976).[47]

But the post-World War II data tell a very different story. Between 1940 and 1970 . . . , farm loans, home mortgage loans, and corporate debt increased six fold (far more than the rate of inflation), and consumer loans expanded by a factor of 16. Most of this mushrooming private debt, of course, is repaid on

---

47. The reference is to Lawrence M. Friedman and Robert V. Percival, "A Tale of Two Courts: Litigation in Alameda and San Benito Counties," 10 *Law & Society Review* 267 (1976). [Eds. note].

schedule and does not give rise to potential court cases. But defaulted and delinquent loans have undoubtedly increased in absolute numbers and amounts, probably in rough proportion to the increase in total debt. For example:

—If the delinquency rate for consumer debt held steady at its average level of 1.5 percent of outstanding loans (the bankers' rule of thumb,

Table 1. Private Debt in Billions of Dollars as of End of Year

	1929	1940	1950	1960	1970	1976-78
Corporate Long-Term Loans	$51.1	$43.7	$60.1	$139.1	$360.2	$568.8
Farm Loans	$12.2	9.1	12.3	25.1	58.7	n.a.
Consumer Loans	$ 7.1	8.3	21.5	56.1	127.2	292.7
Estimated* Am't Delinquent	$ .1	.12	.32	.84	2.54	7.61
Mortgage Loans (1-4 family res.)	$18.0	16.5	43.9	137.4	274.6	637.6
Estimated** Am't Delinquent	$n.a.	n.a.	.9	3.65	8.9	28.7

Source: *Historical Statistics of the United States*, 1975; B. Friedman, 1980: 30; Mortgage Bankers Association, 1980.

* Total amount delinquent estimated by using the following percentages: 1929, 1940, 1950, 1960—1.5 percent; 1970—2 percent; 1976-78—2.6 percent.
Source: *Consumer Credit Leader*, 1973.

** Total amount delinquent estimated by using the following percentages: 1956—2.08 percent; 1960—2.66 percent; 1970—3.24 percent; 1977—4.5 percent.
Source: *Historical Statistics*, 1975; Mortgage Bankers Association, 1981.

according to several consumer loan officers I interviewed), delinquencies would have increased in amount from a total of $322 million in 1950 to $2.4 billion in 1973. In fact, the delinquency rate for consumer loans increased by at least 50 percent beginning in the late 1960s, to 2.2 percent in 1973 and 2.6 percent in 1974. The gross dollar volume of new business reported by debt collection agencies to their trade association grew from $40 million in 1965 to $93 million in 1974.

—Home mortgage loans at least 30 days in arrears climbed from 2.08 percent of all loans at the end of 1955 to 3.06 percent in 1965 and 4.3 percent, twice the 1950 rate, in 1975. Nonfarm mortgage foreclosures numbering about 23,000 nationwide in 1950, grew to about 50,000 in 1960, 115,000 in 1965, 95,000 in 1970, and after the inflation and recession of recent years to about 175,000 in 1982.

—The national business failure rate climbed from 4 per 10,000 enterprises in 1945 to 34 in 1950 and to 64 in 1961, averaging 51.4 throughout the 1960s. Absolute numbers of business failures also grew. . . .

In sum, in the 1950s, 1960s, and 1970s, the incidence of individual and business "crises" that one would expect to lead to litigation over debts all increased dramatically. Nevertheless, debt collection cases continued to decline in the 1950s and 1960s in absolute terms and as a proportion of state supreme court cases. Debt litigation in trial courts, too, does not seem to have increased proportionately, although the available data . . . are scattered and far from adequate:

—In rapidly growing Alameda County, California, my estimates, based on Friedman and Percival's published data, indicate that the number of debt cases did grow from 853 in 1950 to 1511 in 1970, but this growth barely exceeded population growth. In 1970, there were 1.4 debt cases per 1000 county residents, compared with 1.2 in 1950 and the much higher rates of 3.8 in 1910 and 2.8 in 1930 (Friedman and Percival, 1976).

—McIntosh's (1980–81)[48] published data on the St. Louis Circuit Court indicate that debt collection cases declined from their nineteenth-century highs to 15 percent of all civil cases filed in 1910, to less than 8 percent in 1940, and further to just under 5 percent in 1955 and 1970. Applying these percentages to the reported total cases yields an estimated 693 debt cases in 1940, 497 in 1955, and 477 in 1970. Thus, at least in this St. Louis court, the absolute number of debt cases filed throughout the 1940–1970 period actually declined.

Not only does the number of debt collection cases filed in trial courts in the post-World War II period seem to have fallen far short of the growth in business failures and loan delinquencies, but the number and rate of contested trial court debt cases declined, both absolutely and proportionately, in two of the three trial courts for which published data exist.

48. The reference is to Wayne V. McIntosh, "150 Years of Litigation and Dispute Settlement: A Court Tale," 15 *Law & Society Review* 823 (1980–81). [Eds. note].

Table 2. Debt Collection Cases Filed in Three Trial Courts

Alameda County Superior Court, California: Source: Friedman and Percival, 1976.

	1890	1910	1930	1950	1970
Estimated number of debt cases	236	929	1329	853	1511
% of all civil cases	33	28	26	12.1	12.8
Debt cases @ 1000 population	2.5	3.8	2.8	1.2	1.4

Chippewa County Circuit Court, Wisconsin: Source: Laurent, 1959.

	1855-64	1865-74	1875-84	1885-94	1895-1904	1905-14	1915-24	1925-34	1935-44	1945-54
Estimated number of debt cases	225	635	1176	956	595	246	407	662	460	422
% of all civil cases	77.3	64.8	59.4	62	52.3	32.8	40.6	54.5	41.4	35.9
Debt cases @ 1000 population	366	76.4	75.9	38.0	18.0	7.7	11.2	17.8	11.3	9.9

St. Louis Circuit Court: Source: McIntosh, 1980-81.

	1820	1835	1850	1865	1880	1895	1910	1925	1940	1955	1970
Estimated number of debt cases	600	234	976	461	800	1016	897	764	693	497	477
% of all civil cases	85.2	64.9	55.4	43.2	28.2	30	15	6.3	7.4	4.8	4.5
Debt cases @ 1000 population	59.7	9.4	9.3	1.7	2.3	2.0	1.3	0.96	0.85	0.62	0.77

—Laurent's (1959)[49] data from the Chippewa County, Wisconsin, Circuit Court indicate that in contract cases (the overwhelming majority of which were debt collection matters) the proportion that apparently was contest-

49. The reference is to Francis W. Laurent, *The Business of a Trial Court: 100 Years of Cases* (1959).

334

ed fluctuated between 17 and 30 percent in the decades between 1865 and 1944, with no clear trend toward lower rates. Yet in 1945–1954, the last decade covered by the study, only 10 percent of debt cases were contested, the lowest rate in the century.

—Another measure of the incidence of strongly asserted legal defenses is the percentage of cases resulting in judgment for defendants. Here, too, the Chippewa County data show no clear trend between 1805 and 1944; defendants hit their peak victory rate in 1905–1914, winning contested judgments in 10.5 percent of contract cases, but then slipped back in the 1915–1944 period to the historically average rate of 4.3 to 6.1 percent. Once again, however, in 1945–1954, at the outset of the post-World War II era, defendant victories in contested contract cases declined to an historical low, a mere 1.5 percent of the cases.

—McIntosh's (1980–81) St. Louis Circuit Court data indicate that the proportion of debt cases resulting in contested hearings and judgments was a steady 25 to 28 percent in 1820–1850, 1865–1895, and 1910–1925. Defendants won contested judgments in only about 5 or 6 percent of cases in each of those periods. In St. Louis, too, the post-World War II period reflects a sharp decline in contested cases, to about 10 percent of debt collection cases in the 1940–1970 period, and a decline in victories for defendants via contested judgments to 2.4 percent of cases.

—In Alameda County, California ... the percentage of contract cases going to trial decreased from 30.3 percent in 1890 to 22.6 percent in 1912 but leapt upward to 57.1 percent in 1930. As in Chippewa County and St. Louis, the percent of cases tried in 1950 declined (to 19 percent) but jumped up to 27 Percent in 1970 apparently counter to the trend in St. Louis.

One possibility ... is that debt collection matters have been diverted to municipal and small claims courts. This suggestion is consistent with studies of contemporary municipal courts and small claims courts which show that their dockets are dominated by debt collection cases. While time series studies of small claims court dockets are lacking, my estimates based on data from California ... indicate substantial growth in the number of debt collection cases in municipal and small claims courts. However, in the municipal courts, at least until 1980, debt cases did not increase more rapidly than the state's population. And in neither the municipal nor the small claims courts did collection cases grow as rapidly as the national debt delinquency totals ... Moreover, the ability of litigants to sue on small debts in small claims courts (the maximum jurisdictional amount in California was increased from $500 to $750 in 1977 and is now $1500) does not explain why debt collection cases arising from the mounting numbers of larger debts (mobile home loans, home

Table 4. Estimated Debt Collection Case Filings in California Municipal and Small Claims Courts

	1955	1960	1965	1970	1975	1980
Municipal Courts						
Total number of civil filings	191,591	213,311	285,217	275,450	302,250	481,663
Estimated number of debt cases*	95,796	106,656	142,609	137,725	151,125	240,832
Debt cases @ 1000 population	7.4	6.7	7.7	6.9	7.0	10.1
Small Claims Courts						
Total number of filings	126,268	189,573	312,283	286,048	409,663	508,434
Estimated number of debt cases*	82,074	123,222	202,984	185,931	266,281	330,482
Debt cases @ 1000 population	6.3	7.8	11.0	9.3	12.4	13.9

Source: State of California, Administrative Office of the Courts

*For method of estimation, see footnote 7.

mortgages, small business loans, corporate loans) have not increased in trial courts of general jurisdiction and have almost disappeared from state supreme courts. Thus, increased litigation in small claims courts accounts, at best, for only a small part of the decline in debt litigation in the general trial courts and courts of appeal.

II. LITIGATION COSTS

In discussing the linkage between problem-generating events (in this case, delinquencies in repayment) and litigation, I assumed that only "some proportion" of delinquencies would lead to declared defaults, and that only some (constant) proportion of defaults would end in collection suits. The "constant proportion" assumption is obviously too simplistic. Consider, for example, the likely impact on litigation volume of changes in the cost of litigation. Creditors are often deterred from bringing suit by the costs of hiring attorneys, enduring court delays, gaining the cooperation of sheriffs in serving process and executing judgments, and so on. Litigation costs, including opportunity costs such as taking time off work to appear in court, undoubtedly lead some debtors not to contest suits they think unfounded. Hence, court dockets might be expected to reflect only that subset of delinquencies or defaults in which the amount at issue exceeds the various costs of litigation, tangible and intangible. If so, court cases could be expected to decline, or to rise more sluggishly than problem-generating events, during periods in which the transaction costs associated with litigation are rising, either absolutely or in relation to the average amount at issue.

For example, one explanation for the post-World War II decline in debt cases in state supreme courts might be that during this period many states created a layer of intermediate appellate courts between trial courts and the supreme court, thus increasing the cost, in time, uncertainty, and attorneys' fees, of pursuing matters to the supreme court. This explanation would predict that the post–1945 fall-off in supreme court debt opinions would be sharper in states with intermediate appellate courts than in those without them. However, the prediction, and hence the explanation, does not hold, for the debt case decline was virtually as great in one group of states as in the others.

The impact of litigation costs on the incidence of debt cases, and especially of contested cases, may be more evident at the trial court level. Because a larger proportion of credit now involves small consumer loans . . ., the average amount at stake in a loan default may be less financially significant to the parties than was the case in earlier eras when proportionately more loans were for the purchase of real estate, farm needs, and commercial goods and facilities, and lenders were less likely to be large financial institutions. In consequence, today's debtors and creditors faced with potential court cases may be more likely to absorb their losses rather than litigate or appeal.

Unfortunately, I have encountered no systematic evidence concerning the average amount of all debts, either in society at large or in the courts, today or in times past. And despite the general impression that court calendars today entail longer delays and that trials and pre-trial discovery proceedings are more expensive, I know of no studies that show that litigation expenses have in fact increased in relation to GNP per capita or some other meaningful baseline. It is undoubtedly true, of course, that credit cards and installment sales have generated vast numbers of smaller debts. In 1972 the average amount of the 1,210,000 "small loans" by California finance companies was $1069, indicating that most were under $1000; the average amount of the defaulted small loan, assuming some pay-back of principal, undoubtedly was even smaller. The average account handed over to debt collection agencies was only $55 in 1965, $90 in 1975, and $130 in 1980. Even given the existence of institutions like small claims courts that are expressly designed to reduce legal transaction costs when little money is at stake, many unpaid debts are probably not worth litigating. In California and other states that preclude debt collection agencies from using small claims courts, the point at which it pays to institute suit or to contest will reflect the fact that collection agencies must employ attorneys and use municipal courts, as must debtors inclined to resist. Hence, one would not expect small claims litigation to rise quite as rapidly as small debt delinquencies.

Nevertheless, the fact that litigation costs may deter lawsuits over small consumer debt delinquencies does not in itself explain the drop in debt collection cases in state supreme courts and in trial courts of general jurisdiction. As noted earlier, there has been a rapid increase in substantial loans—real estate mortgages, commercial and corporate loans—as well as increases in the annual numbers of mortgage defaults and business failures. The average amount of liabilities involved in business failures rose steadily, from $44,700 in 1948 to $175,000 in 1970. Many consumer loans, moreover, are for amounts seemingly worth litigating about. In 1972, the average loan on a new car was $3378. In 1980, debt consolidation loans by California's small loan finance companies (the most common type of finance company loan) averaged almost $2300. Hence, the post-World War II decline in debt litigation and appeals has occurred in the face of an increase in delinquent debts ostensibly large enough, in many cases, to exceed the direct litigation costs, such as attorneys' fees, that would be involved in collecting or contesting them.

It is impossible to reject the notion, however, that increased litigation costs, defined more broadly, have been an important factor in declining litigation rates. The issue is whether all the costs incurred by creditors and debtors in the litigation and appeal process—including the diversion of time and effort from other concerns, delay, the aggravation and anxiety associated with lawsuits and format execution, damage to reputation—have made litigation over delinquent debts increasingly less attractive than alternative courses of action, such as extracting consensual repayment agreements, arranging refinancing, commercial arbitration, or in the case of the debtor simply conceding liability and in the case of the creditor giving in to debtors' excuses or legal defenses, and trying to recoup losses in other ways. Succeeding sections explore such influences on the relative costliness of litigation, first by examining legal changes that may have affected the availability of viable defenses and then by examining, under the head of "Systemic Stabilization," measures that may have made forbearance or "giving up" more feasible.

III. LEGAL RATIONALIZATION

According to one commonly held view of modern life, human and economic affairs are becoming increasingly subjected to rational legal rules and procedures designed to deal with recurrent kinds of problems. If so, the more complete and settled the law, the more one would expect "failed" transactions, accidents, and disputes to be perceived as having clear legal consequences, and the less the likelihood they would lead to contested court cases. Court dockets, then, would be expected to change in response to the social creation of new problems as the law attempts to "catch up." Thus, debt collection cases might well be prevalent in a rapidly growing and changing economy whose credit system was still struggling to achieve stability (as in the latter part of the nineteenth century). However, with the development of a mature commercial society, debt collection cases should become "old problems" covered by a comprehensive set of rules and precedents, and contested cases and appeals should fall from court dockets, except when radically new forms of credit and security arrangements arise.

Legal rationalization of this sort also implies the development of more efficient modes of adjudication. The institution and expansion of federal bankruptcy procedures, beginning with the Act of 1898, can be viewed as an example. At least one-third and probably more than half of the debt collection cases in state supreme courts in the late nineteenth and early twentieth centuries arose from situations in which a debtor's default visited loss or liability on a whole network of individuals or business firms that had dealt with him—creditors who had lent him money, sureties who had vouched for him and innocents who had purchased his property without knowing of liens upon it. As an example of the complexities that follow defaults, consider the not unusual situation of a company that is unable to pay for a new building. Immediately, the question arises of who should have priority in payment from the company's remaining assets—the construction company (pursuant to a mechanic's lien), suppliers of lumber and plumbing fixtures (pursuant to materialmen's liens), or the bank that had financed construction (secured by a mortgage on the real estate). State supreme courts were continually asked to resolve such conflicts among creditors.

Federal bankruptcy procedure, as first established in 1898 and expanded in 1910 to include voluntary filings by corporations, can be seen as an attempt to rationalize the problem of treating competing claimants fairly. State law created incentives for each creditor to rush to the courthouse to win a priority-establishing, winner-take-all judgment, even though such individualistic remedies might lead, as one legal scholar put it, "to a piecemeal dismantling of a debtor's business by the untimely removal of necessary operating assets." Federal bankruptcy sought to establish a collective system that marshals the debtor's assets, allocates them among all creditors according to a set schedule of entitlements and priorities, and thereby "provides a framework for implementing a consensual collective proceeding," either under the supervision of a trustee or outside the bankruptcy process.

The idea of legal rationalization also implies that in dealing with the complexities of modern legal systems, organizations and individuals increasingly will rely on lawyers and other specialists to handle problems and disputes. Legal specialists characteristically process and settle typical cases in law-regarding ways, but they do so informally, without judicial involvement. Thus, the growth of professional police departments, prosecutors' offices, and public defender offices should lower the proportion of criminal arrests that eventuate in trials. Claims adjustment offices in liability insurance companies should keep automobile tort litigation from increasing as rapidly as the number of accidents.

With respect to debt collection, one would expect contemporary sheriffs to be less prone to the legal errors and corruption that in the late nineteenth and early twentieth century often led to cases protesting the judgment collection and execution sale processes. One would also expect modern lending institutions to develop ways of forestalling expensive court contests over unpaid debts. As early as the eighteenth century, merchants began to insist that extensions of credit be memorialized in written promissory notes with clearly stated terms. This tended to foreclose court hearings in which equitable aspects of the underlying transaction would be contested. In his study of Boston courts in 1880 and 1900, Robert Silverman noted:

> The law of debt based on negotiable instruments and other commercial documents was better defined than was tort law in the late nineteenth century. Plaintiffs normally presented documents to substantiate their claims. A properly executed promissory note or other instrument of indebtedness made the calling of many witnesses unnecessary and also made it easier to determine the amount owed. Most debt actions were open and shut affairs in which defendants did not contest plaintiffs' demands.[50]

In the modern economy, as credit becomes dominated to an increasing extent by large, bureaucratized, legally-sophisticated institutions such as banks, multi-state finance companies, and department stores, loan agreements contain standardized language designed to cover virtually every conceivable kind of contingency or dispute, thereby foreclosing possible legal defenses by debtors and competing creditors. Corporate loan agreements now run for pages, articulating the priority of liens to be imposed on the debtor's property or accounts receivable, clarifying the nature and valuation of collateral, and specifying the characteristics of financial reports that are to be submitted by the debtor at periodic intervals. Increasing recourse to bankruptcy by insolvent business firms has encouraged institutional lenders to insist on specific security arrangements that accord secured creditors priority under the law or entitle them to assert their rights before default. Today, a large proportion of loans by financial institutions to small businesses are secured. In consumer credit, as early as the mid-nineteenth century merchants developed conditional sales agreements that in the event of default entitled creditors to repossess and resell consumer durables without first going to court. It was also common to require borrowers to sign "confessions of judgment" or wage assignments that in the event of nonpayment enabled the creditor to obtain a judgment or garnish the debtor's wages without notice and without bringing suit, until this practice was banned about twenty years ago as a violation of due process. To forestall litigation, contracts among

---

50. The reference is to Robert A. Silverman, *Law and Urban Growth: Civil Litigation* *in the Boston Trial Courts, 1880–1900* (1981). [Eds. notes].

business firms for the supply of goods and services now almost routinely include provisions for binding arbitration of disputes concerning the justifiability of nonpayment.

More sophisticated credit information systems also help prevent legal problems and litigation over bad debts. By obtaining independent appraisals, title searches, and audited financial statements, banks evaluate their security interests before lending, thus minimizing the need to sue for deficiency judgments in the event of default and preventing disputes with other creditors. At the turn of the century, credit reference agencies were unreliable. Today, lenders subscribe to interstate services that compile and update credit histories on business and individual borrowers. Some banks now assign numerical credit ratings to individual loan applicants based on the borrower's particular "credit profile," which is calculated by comparing the applicant's financial characteristics with the bank's computerized analysis of the correlates of successful and unsuccessful loans. Consequently, a threat to impair a delinquent debtor's credit rating is often a more credible and effective collection tactic than is a lawsuit.

To the extent that these trends toward legal rationalization are strong and pervasive, one would expect a declining proportion of defaulted loans to result in court cases. A growing proportion of court filings, moreover, would not signify real legal disputes, but would be filed to obtain an uncontested court order authorizing seizure and sale of the debtor's property, or to establish the creditor's legal priority over later filing creditors. From this perspective, one might argue that appeals to state supreme courts in debt cases have become less frequent because the law has become settled, intercreditor conflicts have been drawn into federal bankruptcy proceedings, precedents and carefully drafted agreements cover and resolve most disputes, and, in the growing number of state supreme courts with discretion to select cases on the basis of "importance," the judges are more concerned with new issues than with the complexities of old debtor-creditor law issues.

Some of the available evidence seems to support the legal rationalization hypothesis. In the federal courts, bankruptcy filings increased spectacularly from about 10,000 per year in 1946 to 250,000 in 1975. But the proportion (and perhaps the absolute number) of debt-related "contract" and "business organization" cases in federal Courts of Appeals declined, suggesting that the bankruptcy process was relatively successful in "settling" the claims of competing creditors in a consensual or routine way. Yet it seems unlikely that the marked decline in state supreme court debt cases after the mid–1930s can be explained by the sudden transformation of the law of debtors' and creditors' rights, which had figured in so many appellate cases between 1870 and 1930, into settled doctrine. In fact, as will be shown in the next section, this body of law has, if anything, become more turbulent in recent years.

At the trial court level, as I noted earlier, debt case filings had begun to decline in proportion to population growth by 1900, and this trend continued, with perhaps an interruption at the outset of the Great Depression, through

1970.... This seems consistent with the idea that the legal process became increasingly rationalized as lenders became increasingly adept at devising loan agreements and security arrangements to forestall legal conflict and at routinizing nonjudicial debt collection procedures. On the other hand, from the mid-nineteenth century until after World War II, there was no consistent downward trend in the percentage or number of contested trial court cases or in the already small percentage of judgments for defendants ..., which suggests that in those years the rationalization process was not increasingly effective in suppressing legal conflict. Why would declines in contested debt cases both at the trial court and state supreme court level show up only in the post-World War II period? One possibility, consistent with the legal rationalization hypothesis, is that federal bankruptcy, a primary device for "rationalizing" complex debt collection cases, reached its full jurisdictional and remedial range only after statutory amendments in 1938 and the post-World War II period. Not until the 1950s did annual numbers of business bankruptcy cases grow as rapidly as annual business failures, suggesting that only then did federal bankruptcy become a routine rather than an exceptional forum for resolving the claims of competing creditors. This explanation seems inadequate, however, because bankruptcy filings have not been sufficiently numerous to "absorb" more than a small proportion of state court debt cases and potential appeals. A second possibility, to be discussed in detail later, is that bureaucratized lending institutions did not really dominate a large proportion of the credit market until recent decades. This possibility suggests that the most fundamental causes of declining debt litigation lie not in the law but in fundamental changes in the economic and social system. Before discussing those systemic changes, however, another set of factors that seems to conflict, at least in part, with trends toward legal rationalization should be examined.

IV. POLITICAL CONFLICT

The notion that the law will gradually become "rationalized" and "settled" as potential disputes are short-circuited by carefully drafted legal documents and routinized procedures assumes that the losers in this process accept the existing law and contractual arrangements as the sole and legitimate measure of what they are entitled to complain about. It assumes, too, that the law will inevitably be shaped to reflect the "efficient" ways of doing business favored by large, impersonal, "economically rational" corporate enterprises.

Arguments for economic efficiency and the preferences of business elites certainly carry weight in the legal process. However, American politics has long had a populistic, antimoneyed-interests strain as well. Every legal rule has obvious distributive aspects as well as a relationship to economic efficiency, and every creditor's right may be experienced as a noose around the debtor's neck. Many debtors sense that they are being "ripped off" and some complain about it. Disputes between creditors and debtors are thus more than problems of commercial relations; they reflect politically important social cleavages. Politicians sometimes find it to their advantage to champion the interests of the many debtors in their constituencies against the impersonal practices of banks and merchants, and the well-organized interests that speak in the name of economic rationality or legal certainty do not necessarily prevail in the legislative arena. From this perspective, the law-on-the-books usually is no more than a temporary battle line in a never-ending political struggle between lenders and debtors, and one would expect debt litigation (and/or legislative activity on the subject) to increase whenever debtors or creditors as a politically organized "class" are actively seeking to change or reject the legal status quo.

. . . To help debtors learn about and assert their expanding repertoire of legal rights, creditors have been required to systematically notify consumers and borrowers of their rights in many situations. To prevent needy debtors from signing away statutory protections in return for further extensions of credit legislation has expressly forbidden certain kinds of waivers. To counteract litigation expenses, laws such as the federal Truth in Lending Act (1968) have empowered successful debtors (and their lawyers) to recover attorneys' fees and punitive damages. Government has directly absorbed some of the costs of asserting debtors rights through federally funded neighborhood-based lawyers for the poor and through state and local consumer fraud units that investigate complaints about lending and sales practices. Sometimes the notice and public assistance aspects have been combined, as in a California law that compels licensed debt collection agencies to include in each collection letter a prominent statement giving the debtor the telephone number of the state agency that enforces fair debt collection laws.

Creditors, of course, have not been wholly passive. In reaction to the increased litigation costs threatened by the elimination of pre-judgment remedies, lenders and merchants more often insist on credit agreements obligating debtors to pay the bank or finance company's attorneys' fees in the event of a default. Creditors, too, lobby the legislatures, seeking to carve out exceptions in recently enacted consumer protection statutes, adjust the categories of loans to which different maximum interest rates apply, and so on. To escape ceilings on interest, they invent new kinds of finance or service charges or base their calculations on a truncated 360–day year. Consumer advocates then return to lobby for amendments outlawing or restricting the creditor's adaptations. In recent decades, therefore, debtor and creditor law has constantly been in flux.

Reading this catalogue of legal changes, one might have expected a major explosion of contested debt cases in the courts during the last twenty years rather than the observed decline. A sample of state supreme court debt cases from 1965 and 1970, however, reflects an almost total absence of issues arising out of modern consumer protection law; the cases were hardly different in nature from those of 1900. From the standpoint of the hypothesis that political activism in a policy area will engender increased litigation, these results seem anomalous.

The anomaly can be partially resolved by recognizing that a major effect of new debtors' rights is to increase creditors' litigation costs, reducing the latter's incentive to sue (or to resist debtors' claims). If the law exempts larger amounts of debtors' property from execution, prevents creditors from collecting deficiency judgments, and so on, creditors are encouraged to resort to informal collection efforts rather than to use the courts. Greater debtor access to attorneys reduces creditors' inclinations to bring collection suits against feisty debtors or to pursue contested cases to trial or to higher courts.

... In any case, there is no obvious reason to believe that debtors are in general more acquiescent when they have colorable claims than they were in earlier decades. Therefore, the apparent decline of legal disputes in recent decades might have occurred, as the legal rationalization concept suggests, because creditors quickly adapted to legal changes, so that many cases remain in which debtors quite accurately perceive that they have no legitimate defense. The trend toward legal rationalization may be complemented by a decline (for good economic reasons) in "toughness" on the part of creditors that is manifested in a tendency for lenders to acquiesce in new legal restrictions and to "give in" in the few cases in which debtors make some show of legal resistance. Political conflict over creditors' rights may not lead to more legal conflict if, despite legal change, creditors have become less disposed to enforce the law strictly against debtors and more attentive to other ways of cutting or recouping their losses. To these possibilities we now turn.

V. SYSTEMIC STABILIZATION

... The concept of legal stabilization discussed earlier refers to laws, contractual provisions, and procedures governing discrete transactions and disputes. The underlying hypothesis is that the gradual development of a more comprehensive body of laws and contractual arrangements, routinely applied by legal and bureaucratic specialists, has come to provide out-of-court legal "solutions" to an increasing proportion of individual conflicts. An even more significant litigation-suppressing factor, however, may be systemic stabilization. By this, I mean the development of large-scale economic and social institutions that ameliorate the conditions that cause individual conflicts or that provide collective, administrative remedies (as contrasted to case-by-case legal remedies).

The idea of systemic stabilization does not presume an ineluctable social evolution toward rational collective problem solving or toward stable and effective economic markets. But it does presume that in modern democratic and capitalist societies political demands will often reflect some version of those ideals. The political agenda of the debtor class over the last two centuries, for example, has been dominated less by the quest for specific legal rights, such as the better disclosure of finance charges in individual credit transactions, than by more fundamental (and controversial) demands for systemic solutions to common problems. Judging from Shays' Rebellion, the Populist movement, and New Deal era agitation, debtors' highest priorities have been (1) an "easy money" policy, (2) reliable and flexible sources of credit, and (3) some form of systemic relief—a moratorium, supplementary income, etc.—to help "honest debtors" over those "hard times" that make debt payments unmanageable because of events such as falling crop prices, economic depressions, illness, and lost jobs that are beyond the debtor's control. Modern democratic polities have often responded to demands for "easy money" and income support programs, and they have encouraged the stabilization of private markets through regulation and insurance schemes. To political and economic elites, the development of demand-enhancing, cushioning, and stabilizing measures has been perceived, at least up to a point, as more efficient as well as more politically popular than relying on a system based entirely on free market transactions, tempered and policed only by individually initiated lawsuits that punish individual delicts. Among the primary institutional vehicles for the favored type of systemic problem-solving are (1) governmental regulation and subsidization, designed to stabilize potentially problem-causing economic processes, and (2) loss spreading or absorption via large, diversified economic institutions and insurance systems.

The rise of effective regulatory and insurance mechanisms to deal with certain problems, or the domination of certain markets by large, diversified business units, can reduce the incidence or growth of private-law litigation by eliminating incentives to sue and by reducing the incidence of conflict. For example, the glut of litigation arising from motor vehicle accidents might be dampened both by the creation of comprehensive mandatory "no fault" self-insurance schemes and by governmentally enforced safely standards for highway design, trucking company practices, and the design of motor vehicles. The development of safer vehicles is also facilitated by the growth of large manufacturers with modern research and quality control capacities.

Similarly, the growth of large, diversified financial institutions and of private and governmental insurance against financial hardship may provide the most powerful explanation for the relative diminution, in recent decades, of intense debtor-creditor conflict in the courts. In relation to the factors discussed earlier, such systemic changes create a rich array of possibilities for recouping losses, and thereby: (1) reduce the incentives that creditors have to treat delinquencies as defaults that warrant immediate court action (2) make litigation and appeal for both debtors and creditors a relatively costly way of recouping or avoiding losses, and (3) encourage one aspect of legal rationalization, i.e., more rapid compliance by lending institutions with debtor protection legislation. To understand the impact of these systemic changes, however, we must first look back at the credit market as it was a century ago.

Sources of Instability

Reading the debt collection cases of late nineteenth century state supreme courts creates an overwhelming impression of a far less stable credit system than that which exists today. Many cases involved claims against failed banks or arose in the train of bank failures. In the 1890s, there were an average of more than 100 bank failures per year, out of a nationwide total of about 4000 state-chartered banks (There were also some 3500 federally chartered banks, which were more tightly regulated.) This suggests that there was a significant chance that the bank one trusted with one's money or borrowed from would shut down with little warning. It was even more likely that one's bank would close its doors for a time or suddenly call in or refuse to extend loans, because of the currency shortages that occurred almost every harvest season and periodically resulted in terrifying financial panics.

Late nineteenth-century state supreme court cases also suggest that lending then was far riskier and the security for loans far flimsier than is the case in today's credit markets. Competition for new sources of potential profit in a rapidly changing economy, ... drove retailers, wholesalers, bankers, brokers, landlords or builders to extend credit unwisely. Reliable credit information about would-be borrowers was notably lacking. Many state supreme court cases grew out of situations in which con men (or desperate businessmen) mortgaged the same property to two creditors, or fraudulently acquired goods on credit and then skipped town. Most creditors whose cases reached state supreme courts in the late nineteenth and early twentieth centuries were not large companies or banks, but were individuals—such as small businessman who had extended credit on a sale of merchandise or a farmer who had bought extra land at an execution sale only to encounter the competing claim of an unknown lien holder. Often creditors' only security was that debtors had supplied individual sureties—friends or relatives to back up their promises to pay. Viewed through the lens of SSC cases, credit transactions gave rise to an inordinate amount of litigation over how to distribute obligations among sureties or between sureties and the debtor or creditors.

If problems of insufficient information, inadequate security arrangements, and unstable financial institutions and markets were at the root of creditor-debtor (and inter-creditor) conflicts in the late nineteenth century, the most profound differences between the credit world of that era and the post-World War II period lie neither in changes in the law of creditors' rights nor in the changed incidence of delinquency or default. The crucial changes involve the various ways that today's creditors can insure against debtor delinquency and the greater access debtors now have to sources of emergency funds that can ensure, without recourse to litigation, that payment eventually will be made or that losses will be cushioned and spread. Some of these systemic developments are worth spelling out.

The Stabilization of Banking

In the 1890s, there were over 1300 bank failures in the United States; in the 1920s there were 2900. In 1930–1933, there were 9100 failures, a crisis exacerbated by the Federal Reserve Board's failure to distribute reserves and expand the money supply during 1930. In marked contrast, during the 1947–1960 period there were only 66 bank failures in the nation, and only 62 from 1961 through 1970. The few failures that occurred each year in recent decades were concentrated in banks with less than $100 million in deposits, and nearly three-fourths were among banks with less than $1 million in deposits.

When large banks have failed, the Federal Deposit Insurance Corporation, established in 1933, has usually arranged for a merger; in cases of liquidation, depositors have been paid off immediately.

This stability has been encouraged by a number of factors including: (1) the establishment and comprehensive coverage of federal deposit insurance, which has helped forestall runs on banks, the sudden calling in of loans, and domino-type financial panics; (2) intensified federal regulation of bank reserves and lending practices, along with regulations that (until recently) limited inter-bank competition and prevented banks from engaging in risky nonbanking enterprises; (3) a Federal Reserve Board that has effectively made reserves available to member banks during general "credit crunches" or when particular institutions were suffering from illiquidity; and (4) a great reduction in the number and an increase in the average size of banks, with corresponding increases in the diversification of loan portfolios and sources of income and in the rationalization of banking practices.

Insurance for Individual Debtors

The consumer movement of the late 1960s and 1970s focused on providing new legal rights for individual buyers or debtors faced with unjust treatment or deception. But these victories have far less significance for debtor-creditor relations than the establishment of income security and welfare state protections during the New Deal and during the "Great Society" programs of the mid–1960s. A very large proportion of debtor delinquencies stems from serious illnesses or injuries, layoffs from work, and other sudden decreases in income or increases in expenses. In earlier eras, such events destroyed a debtor's capacity to keep up payments on loans. During the post-World War II period, however, unemployment insurance, disability insurance, more adequate workers' compensation; payments, employer-provided health insurance, Medicade, Social Security, and private pension plans have all become widely available. For debtors, these programs guarantee some continuation of income in hard times and the possibility of maintaining some level of payments to creditors. For creditors, these income-support measures are a reason to prefer reduced payments or refinancing, backed by the debtor's continuing income stream, to a one-time attempt to attach the debtors assets.

In addition, virtually every homeowner, small business, and motor vehicle owner now carries liability insurance, which has transformed the collection of liability judgments, often a source of further dispute and litigation in times past, into the routine drafting and mailing of a check by the corporate treasurer of the judgment-debtor's insurance company. Perhaps the most significant form of debtor insurance in the 1945–1975 period has been a relatively stable economy and an improving set of job opportunities. This is in part attributable to macro-economic policies—Keynesian fiscal policy and more enlightened monetary policy—that can be viewed as aspects of systemic stabilization, and in part attributable to the social insurance schemes mentioned above that limit the negative ripple effects of business failures and plant closings. In the 1940–1975 period, economic downturns were both shorter and shallower, on the average, than those in pre-World War 1I decades. The index of real average weekly earnings of production workers in manufacturing, using 1967 as 100, went from 66 in 1946 to 123 in 1977. Disposable income per capita, controlling for inflation, increased from $2200 to $4500 over that same period. As we have seen, rising income and job security have not prevented an increase in loan delinquencies. But delinquent debtors are likely to have better prospects for regaining solvency and more relatives with savings to bail them out, than did their counterparts in earlier decades. This may make creditors less inclined to sue defaulters immediately.

Insurance for Creditors

For creditors, a universe of debtors with more stable income has made and a radical improvement in security. More and more, a creditor's real security lies not in pledges of individual sureties and cosigners, but in the debtor's job and job skills, which are more likely than in previous decades to generate a steady, and increasing, stream of income which, if default ensues, can be tapped via the garnishment process—lending to a nation of civil servants, salaried managers, and unionized blue collar workers who work for substantial corporations is less risky than lending to a nation of farmers (before crop support payments), small proprietors, and workers in small firms. This enhanced security has been reflected in creditors' willingness to require smaller down payments for consumer loans, and to extend average repayment periods from less than twelve months to more than two and a half years. The smaller monthly payments, in turn, mean that delinquencies can more easily be recouped, presumably reducing the incentive for creditors to rush to court.

Another important source of insurance for lending institutions are the loan guarantees provided by government units. Since the end of World War II, for example, the Federal Housing Authority and the Veterans' Administration have guaranteed millions of home mortgages. Although payments are not available to mortgagees until they foreclose and attempt to collect from their mortgagors, these guarantees should reduce the incentives for contested litigation and appeals. Why fight if the government will pick up the tab? The same would seem to be true of federal guarantees to banks that extend student loans for higher education.

Creditors have also incorporated insurance programs into lending agreements. For example, some lenders now offer purchasers of homes and consumer durables "credit life insurance," which guarantees payment of the unpaid balance of the loan to the creditor in the event of the debtor's demise, and "credit disability insurance" has also become common. Home mortgage lenders are also protected by reinsurance, which the borrower is obliged to provide and pay for in monthly installments. Thus, many adverse events, instead of creating litigation provoking zero-sum conflicts between debtors (or their estates) and their various creditors as to who will bear an entire loss, now result in charges to insurance companies or government welfare funds, which are in turn spread over millions of policy-holders or taxpayers.

Insurance for Business Debtors

Institutional arrangements designed to help precarious businesses maintain their debt payments are not as comprehensive as protections for individuals, but they are surely more significant than in the decades before the New Deal. Most striking is the rich array of federal income maintenance programs for farmers, including below-market rate loans, acreage restriction payments, crop insurance, and price guarantees through crop support payments or governmentally approved marketing agreements. These stabilization measures, together with the drastic decline in the number of smaller, economically less stable farms since the 1930s, have undoubtedly produced a huge reduction in the annual number of farm failures, a major source of debt repayment problems and litigation in the late nineteenth and early twentieth centuries.

Other specific kinds of business borrowers and their creditors benefit from loan guarantees offered by the federal Overseas Investors' Protection Corporation and the Security Investors' Protection Corporation, both loosely modeled on the FDIC. The Small Business Administration has guaranteed billions of dollars of low-interest private loans to small companies, a riskier-than-average set of debtors. When businesses are threatened with income losses or heavy expenses as a result of floods and earthquakes, the government refinances existing debts by offering below-market rate interest loans to firms in the "disaster area." Special federal loan guarantees have been given to creditors who extended existing loans to huge entities, such as Chrysler Corporation and New York City, that were on the verge of default and threatened to pull creditors down with them. The result of these and similar programs is that, by some estimates, the federal government issues, guarantees, or stands as lender of last resort with respect to well over half of the total financial assets of the public. In addition, state governments stand as guarantors for many of the debt obligations of municipalities, housing authorities, irrigation districts, and the like, while federal and state grants enable financially hard-pressed public agencies to acquire money for special projects without having to commit themselves to repayment. These guarantees and direct grants are significant because repayment failures by local public bodies were an important source of litigation in the 1930s and in earlier depression periods.

Diversification in Credit Markets

. . . Since 1950, a smaller proportion of loans has flowed directly between individuals, or between businesses and individuals. By 1970, loans to households and businesses were extended mostly by "financial intermediaries" to which households and businesses commit their funds—commercial banks, savings and loan associations, insurance companies, consumer finance companies, pension trusts, and governmental credit-granting agencies. Economists point out that financial intermediation increases the efficiency of the credit system because it makes for more professional and informed credit decisions and the diversification of risks. I discovered no indicators of how the growth of financial intermediation affects propensities to litigate over delinquent debts, but it is reasonable to suppose that the big bank or insurance company faced with mortgagors behind on payments can afford to be more lenient than a small landlord owed three months' rent by a tenant. Large lending institutions set aside reserves for bad debts and are prepared to live with delinquencies in amounts that don't threaten to exceed the planned reserves. Indeed, they write off bad debts before selling such accounts to collection agencies, which means that any that turn out to be recoverable are just "gravy." Unrecovered losses are treated as additional costs that can be reflected, at least in part, in next year's finance charges and spread over the pool of new borrowers. Losses can also be deducted from federal and state corporate tax obligations, which means not only that they are shared with millions of taxpayers but also that the "real" loss is smaller and more likely to exceed litigation costs. In economic theory, of course, a large lender operates under competitive pressure to limit losses and, like the small landlord or businessman, would litigate if necessary to collect any debt whenever the prospects for recovery exceed litigation costs. But because they have institutionalized mechanisms for routinely accounting for losses and attempting to recoup them, large lenders are, I suspect, less inclined to spend additional money to sue the debtor who fails to pay a judgment or to appeal the case that is lost in the lower courts. The government in its growing role as creditor seems even more inclined to absorb and spread losses rather than litigate to collect delinquent debts.

Diversification in financial markets goes beyond loss-spreading within the loan portfolios of large lenders. Borrowers have seen a remarkable diversification of sources of credit. The licensing of small loan companies to sell and the regulation of maximum interest rates have helped transform a turn-of-the-century industry of small and unscrupulous "loan sharks" into a more stable, lawful industry of consumer finance companies, many of which operate on a scale sufficient to spread their risks over thousands of borrowers and attract stable financing from banks and other lenders. The growth of nonbank lenders, such as pension funds, government agencies, and investment trusts, has also helped provide a more competitive and richer credit environment, thus multiplying opportunities for troubled debtors to forestall litigation by obtaining refinancing agreements, second mortgages on their homes, and additional credit. Under competitive pressure, banks have moved toward more flexible lending arrangements, including long-term loans to business firms and revolving credit. . . .

Bankruptcy

I have noted that federal bankruptcy proceedings are a form of legal rationalization in that they provide an efficient forum for assembling and establishing priorities among competing creditors' claims. However, another feature of bankruptcy, the debtor's discharge from most existing debts, is empirically more important. Stanley and Girth discovered that 70 to 75 percent of bankruptcy cases in the years 1965–68 were "no asset" cases in which creditors recovered nothing, and 10 to 15 percent were "nominal asset cases" in which creditors got little. In the remaining "asset cases," creditors asserted claims totaling $431 million but recovered only $70 million, or 16 cents on the dollar. The growing ratio of individual to business bankruptcy cases in the 1970s probably increased the proportion of no asset—no recovery cases. Therefore, in the vast preponderance of modern bankruptcy matters, competing creditors have little to litigate about. The prominence of the discharge function suggests that bankruptcy as it in fact operates is primarily a form of socially provided "insurance" for debtors, an escape hatch for victims of financial disaster, rather than a means of more efficient adjudication. . . .

[The] "non-stigmatizing" attitude toward bankruptcy, abetted by court rulings forbidding restrictions on lawyer advertising, has been reflected in steeply increasing individual bankruptcy filings—25,040 in 1950, 191,724 in 1967, and an estimated 450,000 in 1982, the equivalent of the population of a large city. Studies indicate that most non-business bankruptcy filings are preceded by a threat of legal action against the debtor (presumably in state court, but very few bankruptcy cases are preceded by an actual state court judgment in favor of creditors). This suggests that legally sophisticated debtors, those whom one might expect to raise possible legal defenses in state trial or appellate courts, are now more inclined to take the "escape hatch" route of bankruptcy. Compared to protracted litigation, the routinized "loss-spreading" bankruptcy mechanism becomes increasingly appealing.

V. CONCLUSION

In sum, despite the marked growth over the last thirty-five years in lending and in the volume of delinquent debts, the number of state supreme court debt cases has declined sharply, and there has been an apparent decrease in contested debt cases in trial courts of general jurisdiction. . . . Although direct evidence is not available, it appears that three factors have contributed to the increased attractiveness of nonlitigation alternatives. One such factor has been legal rationalization, especially the development by lenders of legally "airtight" contractual provisions and security arrangements specifically designed to forestall litigation, and their increasing use of lawyers and other specialists in the routine settlement of debt cases. These measures, presumably, reduce the proportion of debt disputes involving viable defenses and make settlement correspondingly more attractive. The second factor is an increase in the political activity of debtors and their allies. Political action— primarily on behalf of homeowners, farmers, and small businesses in the 1930s and on behalf of consumers in the 1960s—has shifted the locus of demands for reformed debtor-creditor laws away from courts and toward legislatures and regulatory agencies, stimulated the enactment of a multitude of new defenses for consumer-debtors, and enhanced opportunities to learn about and assert these rights. Judging from the fact that the number of contested debt cases has not increased in recent decades, the primary effect of the expansion of debtors' rights and remedies has been to increase the cost of litigation for creditors in cases in which debtors show some inclination toward legal resistance.

The third factor forestalling debt collection litigation, and undoubtedly the most significant one, has been a trend toward systemic stabilization—the development of methods of loss spreading, diversification, insurance, and economic stabilization that prevent financial panics, blunt the edges of individual disputes, and encourage consensual refinancing or absorption of losses rather than protracted litigation. In the 1880s (and even in the 1920s, in the South) the farmer who could not pay off his crop mortgage was threatened simultaneously with the loss of his home and livelihood. The shopkeeper or small manufacturer who could not pay his debts faced similar ruin, as did many a creditor whose debtor could not pay. For them, it made sense to fight for survival in the courts if any plausible legal argument could be made. But this debtor class of small farmers, shopkeepers, and artisans has been replaced by a debtor class composed of incorporated businesses, whose owners and managers usually can find other jobs if their firms face insolvency, and of unionized workers and salaried government employees whose debts are backed by relatively reliable sources of income and various forms of social insurance. For both groups of debtors, bankruptcy has become an increasingly less stigmatizing and more frequently used way of escaping debt and obtaining a fresh start. In parallel fashion, from a creditor class of small banks, merchants and individual speculators, we have evolved a creditor class of large, diversified, insured lending institutions, department stores, and hospitals. Unpaid loans become tax write-offs and increased costs to be reflected in next month's prices or interest rates. The government and insurance companies back up mortgages. New lenders stand ready to refinance the failing and to relend money to the formerly bankrupt.

. . . [T]he institutional stabilization of creditors and collective loss-spreading is not a monolithic, unidirectional trend. The most significant countertrend, perhaps, is the destabilization of households as reliable economic units through family disruption, as reflected in increased rates of divorce, unmarried parenthood, and female-headed homes. Governmental welfare programs represent a partial "collective," social-insurance approach to the resultant growth of financially hard-pressed households. But the splitting and diminution of household income stemming from family disintegration also increase the probability of loan defaults, and have given rise to what has probably been the most rapidly increasing form of debt-collection litigation in the last decade—suits both by abandoned mothers and by governmental units to recover unpaid child-support obligations. . . .

[T]he importance of systemic stabilization in shaping the role of the courts with respect to debt litigation undoubtedly has broader significance for the study of law and society. Social scientists and legal scholars have focused primarily on the mobilization and operation of governmental institutions established specifically for the adjudication or settlement of particular legal disputes, on the patterns of individual-case decisions or outcomes produced by those legal institutions, and on the origins of and justifications for legal rules intended to guide official decisions. While these topics are surely important, study after study tells us that the use of formal decision-making and enforcement processes tends to be extraordinary rather than ordinary. The extent and quality of the justice people experience depends equally, if not primarily, on the operation of nonlegal social and economic institutions that prevent, suppress, or settle most problems and on the broader social, economic, and political factors that affect the incidence and seriousness of harmful acts, accidents, deprivations, and disputes. . . .

NOTES AND QUESTIONS

1.   Studies of the work of courts also show a decline in the number of disputes over title to real estate. In the 19th century, courts decided thousands of cases in which two, or more, parties argued over who owned what piece of land. These lawsuits have become more and more uncommon. Why do you think this is? Are the reasons the same as the reasons Kagan gives for the decline in debt collection litigation?

2.   How would you categorize the reasons Kagan gives for the decline in debt litigation? Which of them are economic, which of them are social, which of them have to do with the structure and habits of legal institutions?

3.   Until recently, modern bankruptcy seemed to favor the debtor far more than the law of bankruptcy as it was in earlier times. Kagan's article discusses the impact of bankruptcy law on the law of debt collection. Bankruptcy is more than an economic matter—social norms about debts and obligations affect how people behave toward creditors. One hears stories about men and women who went bankrupt in the 1930s, during the Great Depression, and who spent much of the rest of their lives trying to pay their debts, even though these debts had been wiped off the books by the bankruptcy court. It is said that this feeling of obligation toward creditors is rare in modern American legal culture. For studies of wage-earner bankruptcy, see Herbert Jacob, *Debtors in Court: The Consumption of Government Services* (1969); Philip Shuchman, "New Jersey Debtors 1982–83: An Empirical Study," 15 *Seton Hall Law Review* 541 (1985). Teresa Sullivan, Elizabeth Warren and Jay Westbrook, *As We Forgive Our Debtors—Bankruptcy and Consumer Credit in America* (1989) is a much discussed larger empirical study of individual bankruptcy. For consideration of this work, see, e.g., Marjorie L. Girth, "The Role of Empirical Data in Developing Bankruptcy Legislation for Individuals," 65 *Indiana Law Journal* 17 (1989); Lisa J. McIntyre, "A Sociological Perspective on Bankruptcy," 65 *Indiana Law Journal* 123 (1989); William C. Whitford, "Has the Time Come to Repeal Chapter 13?" 65 *Indiana Law Journal* 85 (1989).

Large corporations turned to bankruptcy to cope with drastic economic change in the 1980s. For an empirical study, see Lynn M. LoPucki and William C. Whitford, "Venue Choice and Forum Shopping in the Bankruptcy Reorganization of Large, Publicly Held Companies," 1991 *Wisconsin Law*

Review 11. As we saw in Note 6, Reading 3.12, recent bankruptcy law reforms have taken a distinct turn in favor of business and creditors.

Elizabeth Warren, "The Market for Data: The Changing Role of Social Sciences in Shaping the Law," 2002 *Wisconsin Law Review* 1, notes that universities and private research organizations accept funds from interest groups to produce studies that support their positions. Legislators and judges find such studies in conflict with those produced by real social science. They then often decide that they cannot resolve the dispute, and so they feel free to ignore all social science evidence and to base their decisions on "common sense," bias, or the views of those who make the most significant campaign contributions. Warren argues that just this happened in the debates that provoked the changes in the bankruptcy laws that so benefited the credit industry. She says, "When data become a commodity—purchased, packaged, and sold to a willing public under a university imprimatur by those who profit from its distribution—then empirical work becomes little more than cheap ad copy. When that happens, the value of every kind of research academics do declines sharply." (p. 43) See also William R. Freudenburg, "Seeding Science, Courting Conclusions: Reexamining the Intersection of Science, Corporate Conclusions: Reexamining the Intersection of Science, Corporate Cash, and the Law," 20 *Sociological Forum*, Mar. 2005, at 3 ("A large corporation facing a multibillion-dollar court judgment quietly provided generous funding to well-known scientists (including at least one Nobel prize winner) who would submit articles to 'open' peer-reviewed journals, so that their 'unbiased science' could be cited in an appeal to the Supreme Court"); see also Alan Zarembo, "Funding Studies to Suit Need," *L.A. Times*, Dec. 3, 2003, at A1 ("A search of legal databases turned up 10 cases since 1999 in which judges have invoked studies funded by Exxon.").

The Supreme Court of Wisconsin declined to protect a graduate student who blew the whistle and told the *Milwaukee Journal* about research that the University of Wisconsin–Madison was prepared to do for an association of shopping centers. The graduate student's expert, a professor of social psychology, testified that the survey instrument was so bad that he would not have allowed a student to use it for practice in conducting survey research. See *Barnhill v. Board of Regents*, 166 Wis.2d 395, 479 N.W.2d 917 (1992). The graduate student had won a jury verdict that was affirmed by the Court of Appeals. The Supreme Court, however, found that the student's supervisors had "qualified immunity" from this type of suit. Despite its legal victory, the university changed its procedures so that those doing surveys could not sell the university's reputation so easily.

4.   In "Why the 'Haves' Come Out Ahead: Speculations on the Limits of Legal Change," 9 *Law & Society Review* 95 (1974), Marc Galanter distinguishes between "repeat players" and "one-shotters" in litigation. "Repeat players," who are on the whole richer and more powerful than such "one-shotters" as criminal defendants and tort plaintiffs, can adapt their behavior to cope with the threat of litigation. They can structure transactions so that they are likely to win any lawsuit that they bring or that is brought against

them. They can take steps to make litigation unnecessary or less likely. To complete the picture which Kagan has painted, we might want to study to practices of firms such as Sears which sells on credit to consumers or, say, the Boeing Corporation which sells commercial jet aircraft to major airlines. Both are repeat players and both undoubtedly have taken steps to ward off and control litigation. What difference would you expect between the strategies of Sears and Boeing?

5.   Conflict and consensus models of litigation rates: In his 1990 article in the *Law & Society Review*, John Stookey reported on a study of superior court cases filed in Arizona from 1912–1951. John Stookey, "Trials and Tribulations: Crises, Litigation, and Legal Change," 24 *Law & Society Review* 497 (1990). Stookey contrasts the way consensus and conflict models explain changes in litigation rates, and uses his data to examine whether one or the other model does a better job of explaining legal change during times of crisis. He argues that it is important to separate different kinds of cases from each other, rather than presenting aggregates of all kinds of cases (as consensus theorists generally do). Stookey distinguishes four different kinds of cases: cases in which individuals sue each other (Type I), cases in which businesses (or other organizations) sue individuals (Type II), cases in which individuals sue businesses (Type III), and case in which businesses sue each other (Type IV). Stookey points out that conflict theorists generally focus more on Type II and Type III cases—litigation between parties with different social status and power.

Interestingly, Stookey points out that conflict and consensus theorist agree on a basic model of the relationship between crisis, litigation, and policy change. In both models, crisis or turmoil leads to disputes, which lead to litigation and eventually to policy change (and that policy change may itself spark new litigation). Both agree that there will be increased litigation as a result of crises, but they focus on different kinds of cases—consensus theorists looking at intergroup and individual-individual suits equally, while conflict theorists stressing rises in intergroup litigation. In a sense, Stookey argues that the two kinds of theorists are in essence talking past each other—asking fundamentally different questions. Conflict theorists ask—who benefits, who is disadvantaged? Consensus theorists ask whether the overall harmonious functioning of the system is disrupted or restored. Stookey proposes an approach that bridges the divide between the two. He assesses how each might contribute to an understanding of changes in litigation rates in Arizona during a period of time that cycled between good times and crises (two major economic depressions and two World Wars).

Stookey's findings indicate that both approaches can be useful in understanding legal change, and he stresses that it would be important for consensus theorists to include some consideration of the conflict perspective in their model. For example, he did find an overall rise in litigation rates during economic depressions, as predicted by consensus theorists. But he also found that the "effect of depression is most pronounced with regard to [business/organization versus individual] cases"—as would be predicted by conflict theorists. He also found that these cases had the highest rates of plaintiff success, meaning that businesses were most successful in court, and particularly when they sued individuals. Stookey also examined whether policy changes during times of upheaval tended to favor more socially powerful parties. Here he introduces an intriguing wrinkle: there was a victory for the more powerless parties—insolvent farmers—as a result of the Great Depression. This is consistent with consensus theory (the legal system helps to restore social harmony), but not with the crude or instrumental version of conflict theory (only the ruling class ever wins in court; law is simply an instrument of domination).

However, as Stookey points out, there are other forms of conflict theory as well. One alternative is the "structural" Marxist position, which predicts "some concessions to the working class and individual disputants as a way of rationalizing and protecting the system." However, Stookey finds most plausible a third version of conflict theory—the "state manager" approach—which is associated with the work of Fred Block and Theda Skocpol. They

> critique the instrumental and structural approaches as failing to recognize that the state and state managers are not merely pawns of the economically and politically powerful but rather are independent, self-interested actors. From this "state manager" view, we can only predict likely policy changes by considering the goals and motivations of state managers as well as the goals of disputants.

As Stookey explains, this third model predicts that the legal system will generally serve the interests of the dominant class during good times, because business and organizational interests can generally exert more influence over state managers. But state managers also need the support of the "general citizenry," and this may become quite shaky during crises. These are times, then, when state managers are most likely to make concessions to less powerful interests. Stookey concludes that both consensus and "state manager" conflict theories help us to understand why farmers might succeed during a depression: in the face of the instability caused by foreclosures and rising debt, there is pressure from farmers on the legal system to return society to normal functioning (consensus theory), and the actors in charge of the legal system are more likely to respond to that pressure during those times (state manager conflict theory).

Stookey found a different pattern during World War II, but one that also gave support to both consensus and state manager theories. He notes that another issue worth considering is just the effect of an historical sequence of events: World War II followed the Depression, and so this may have affected what sorts of issues were left on the table between people of different classes. The role of state managers in times of war is also different than in times of economic instability. Stookey concludes by urging social scientists to pay more attention to

> the significance of the economic and political characteristics of the disputants and litigants and appreciation of the independent importance of

state managers. Keeping these factors in mind leads to a rich set of questions about the effects of crises on different types of litigation; the ability of losing litigants to obtain policy relief; and the impact of policy change on varying disputants and litigants.

This is a plea for a more complex modeling of the effects of society on law, and on the ongoing feedback loop whereby law and society continue to influence one another. Rather than assuming that a crisis directly impacts law, we have to look at the many mediating factors and circumstances. Can you think of still more factors that might be influencing the shape of litigation and policy changes during times of crisis?

6. Stookey describes consensus models in this way: "To the consensus theorist, law emerges in a passive, evolutionary way to fill the vacuum created by the demise or weakening of informal private or customary means of social control. The role of law is to maintain stability and harmony." (p. 386). By contrast, conflict theory focuses on struggles for power and domination. Compare the consensus, instrumentalist conflict, and "state manager" conflict models with the approach of Kagan, of Friedman and Ladinsky, and of Edelman.

7. John A. Stookey, in "Trying Times: A Sociopolitical History of Litigation during the First Half of the Twentieth Century," 16 *Social Science History* 1 (1992), looks at his data on litigation in Arizona trial courts in another way. He concludes that trial courts have turned from general dispute resolvers to administrative bodies. Moreover, the Arizona trial courts "helped lessen the plight of society's have nots" (p. 55). He concludes:

> ... [T]he trial court can precipitate political change as well as respond to other political institutions. Often the trial courts were a "negative" cause of such change. For example, it was only because they were consistently evicting farmers from their land that a political movement emerged to push for foreclosure relief, and it was partly the failure of trial courts to provide rapid, reliable, and affordable relief for injured workers that led to workers' compensation. Conversely, in the case of rent control, the courts were given new power to wield on behalf of the have-nots.

8. The meaning of litigation rates: Stookey's article is an example of a longitudinal court study: a study of the work of a court over time. One of the first such studies was Lawrence M. Friedman and Robert Percival, "A Tale of Two Courts: Litigation in Alameda and San Benito Counties," 10 *Law & Society Review* 267 (1976). Friedman and Percival studied the work of two trial courts in California—one urban (Alameda) and one rural (San Benito) between 1890 and 1970. They tracked changes in the docket—for example, the percentage of family and tort cases filed rose dramatically in both counties, but property and contract cases fell just as drastically. Uncontested judgments—mostly judgments by default—rose in both counties, and percentage of contested judgments dropped over time.

Friedman and Percival were also interested in the volume of litigation, especially in light of the furor over the so-called "litigation explosion," which posited ever-increasing rates of litigation. Conversely, Spanish scholar José Juan Toharia had found an inverse relationship between economic growth and the volume of formal litigation. José Juan Toharia, *Cambio Social y Vida Juridica en España, 1900–1970* (1974). That is, highly developed legal systems do not show growth in their litigation rates; on the contrary, rates tend to stabilize or decline in the face of rapid economic growth. This hypothesis received initial confirmation from studies of litigation in Sweden and Denmark between 1930 and 1970. Friedman and Percival explain why this hypothesis might seem to make sense: "formal courts processes are slow, expensive, technical"—in other words, inefficient. As economies grow, it would make sense that this inefficiency would be minimized. However, Friedman and Percival's findings do not completely confirm this prediction.

On the one hand, their study did document a higher amount of litigation in 1970 as compared with 1890 in both counties (calculated in terms of cases per 1,000 residents). On the other hand, looking at the pattern in more historical detail, they found that the rate in the urban court (Alameda) was actually higher in 1910 than in current times. Furthermore, these kinds of calculations

> are too crude to be used as indicators of litigation rates. For one thing, they do not take into account either the federal courts or the inferior trial courts. For another thing, they do not take into account the nature of the cases litigated. Before we can speak of "litigation rates" we must define litigation: is an uncontested divorce "litigation?" . . . To test the hypothesis of declining litigation, we would really need some valid measure of dispute settlement, for all courts, in a community. "Litigation" would mean a proceeding containing elements of dispute, that were not resolved before one party filed a complaint, or perhaps not resolved without the intervention of a judge. Perhaps such a "true" rate would show a decline sine 1890; but our figures do not permit us the luxury of a guess. . . .

Quantitative indicators of court performances in these two counties confirm one general hypothesis: the dispute settlement function in the courts is declining. In general, trial courts today perform routine administration; dispute settlement has steadily shrunk as a proportion of their caseload. Most cases today are quite routine. In 1890, a higher percentage of cases involved genuine disputes, and the work of the courts was on the whole less stereotyped. The rate of uncontested judgments has multiplied while the incidence of contested judgments has fallen. A smaller percentage of cases are brought to trial today, and courts issue formal opinions or findings in far fewer cases. Court delays have significantly lengthened.

What factors account for the routinization of the work of modern courts? One possibility is that uncertainty—a prime breeder of litigation—has declined in the law; that rules are more "settled" than in 1890. Some kinds of dispute (over land titles for example) have been largely resolved, or reduced to order by new social arrangements, such as the use of title insurance, and improvement in county record-keeping. But there is no easy way to measure this factor in the aggregate. Our assumption is that some areas of law do become "settled;" but as they do, new uncertainties replace old ones. Land titles were less chaotic in 1930 than 1890; but as this problem faded, the automobile accident more than replaced it, creating a new and complex field of law.

For another possible explanation, one may point to factors associated with urbanization and the particular brand of economic development that had occurred in the United States. The population in 1970 is mobile and rootless. Overwhelmingly, people live in metropolitan areas. They deal primarily with strangers. The ordered social relations of small towns and traditional courts—a world of face to face relations—has vanished.

In this light, we might expect the modern court in San Benito to resemble its 1890 ancestor, and traditional courts, more closely than we would expect of the Alameda court. Surprisingly, however, the data of 1970 do not show much difference between the counties. On the contrary, San Benito's courts play, if anything, a more routinized role than the courts in urban Alameda. In San Benito, more cases involve routine matters, a larger proportion are uncontested, fewer are brought to trial, and courts more rarely issue formal opinions or findings.

There is a general assumption in the literature that "modernization" brings about a general shift from social-harmony litigation to a more formal style of dispute-settlement. Our data suggest a rather different kind of evolution. To be sure, in 1890 it was already true that precious little of the work of the court conformed to the social harmony style. That had perhaps already virtually vanished in the United States, unless one were to find it in the justice courts, which is doubtful. Did it ever exist? The records of colonial courts suggest that at the very dawn of [colonial] American history there were institutions that came closer to the anthropologists' model. But by 1890, the Superior Court of Alameda was already an urban court; and as for San Benito, while it was a small community, it was hardly a tightly-knit, traditional community. On the contrary, it was a raw and new community—a community of recent arrivals, transients, strangers. If anything, it is more of a face-to-face community today; and yet the social harmony style is even more absent.

The evolution, then, does not go from social harmony to legalistic style, and find a resting point. Rather, dispute settlement vanishes completely from the courts; it is replaced by routine administration. Whether the legalistic style was an intermediate phase, or whether the development was directly from social harmony style to routine, our data do not allow us to state with confidence.

Our evidence shows, then, that in the two California courts—one sitting in a bustling urban metropolis, the other not—the dispute settlement function has shriveled to almost nothing; the routine administrative function has become predominant.

This seems on the surface rather curious. Certainly, disputes still arise in society, and they probably must be settled. Yet for some reason, they are not settled in court. Of course, it is theoretically possible that fewer disputes go to court than an earlier period because the number of disputes has fallen. We have no way to measure the number of disputes that might go to court, if courts were costless and freely accessible. Nor do we have any information about the relative number of disputes in San Benito County, compared to Alameda, now or in any other period. It is barely possible that, when genuine disputes do occur in San Benito, a larger proportion of them may actually be taken to court than in Alameda. But there is no obvious reason why the number of actual "disputes" should be so low in the two counties; and the most likely assumption is that the court itself—its style, its mode of operation—discourages its use for dispute settlement, rather than that the number of issues or disputes has declined.

Apparently, litigation is not worthwhile, for the potential litigant; it is too costly, in other words; "Costs" may mean dollar costs. Delays and technicalities are also costly, because of the disruption and expense they may inflict, and uncertainties they introduce into outcomes. All of these costs in fact did rise during the 19th century, although the data are fragmentary. As costs rise, so does the threshold at which litigation becomes worthwhile.

But this pushes our inquiry back one step; it does not answer the basic question. If courts have become too "costly," why has society permitted this to happen? Why have there not been arrangements to keep the dispute settlement function of courts alive, and healthy and productive? . . .

A. Law and Development

Let us, for simplicity, assume economic growth as a goal widely shared in early nineteenth century American society. How could legal process contribute to this end? First of all, it was necessary to dismantle restrictions that restrained the free flow of commerce. Second, new legal arrangements might be instituted or encouraged that would stimulate trade and manufacture. A flourishing economy, a growing economy is an economy of increasing volume. The more of society's goods traded on the market, the better; the higher the turnover, the better.

The economy, then, was to be left as free as possible, not for its own sake, but because free trade would foster prosperity. Business, left to its own devices, would develop tools—forms and techniques—that permitted and encouraged rapid trade. Such forms would be highly standard; they would permit rapid, routine, trouble-free use, as much as was humanly possible. A vigorous market is one in which people absorb losses in the short run, and continue to trade. They do not break off commercial relationships in the midst of a competitive situation, nor do they funnel transactions through courts. Any legal agency which exercises discretion and is careful, slow and individuating, cannot help but interrupt the flow of trade. It is not healthy, then, for the economy, unless parties stay out of court except as a last resort.

Hence, costs are permitted to rise. No invisible cartel raises costs, but costs go up, and they are allowed to; there is little countervailing subsidy. Ordinary disputes, between members of the middle class, slowly drain out of the system. Business also tends to avoid the courts. Business can afford to litigate, but does not welcome the disruptiveness of litigation. For business, too, legal norms (especially procedural ones) disappoint legitimate expectations. This formalization is a cost which society has also allowed to rise, as lawyers professionalize, courts conceptualize, and the law becomes more "scientific."

Hence, too, the relative decline in litigation, although, as we have seen, this is not easy to attest in our two courts. One must remember that the decline in disputed proceedings in court does not mean that "the law" (in a broader sense) is of declining importance in a developing country; quite the contrary. As the economy expands, so does the use of legal instruments: contracts, checks, deeds, articles of incorporation, wills, mortgages. The number of transactions which take legal form increases more rapidly than the population. But this does not mean more "trials" and more use of formal courts to "settle disputes." In modern society, most transactions are private, that is, they take place without the intervention of the state. Thousands of other transactions use the courts, but only in a routine way—to collect debts, legitimize status, and so on.

Routinization, then, accompanies a lowering of the public demand for settlement of disputes in formal courts. Much of the remaining docket hangs on from sheer necessity. One most go to court to win legal freedom to marry, for example. It is a routine but necessary step. For the rest, ordinary people are deterred by the cost, the torpor, the technicality of court proceedings. Businessmen prefer to handle matters themselves, or go to arbitration, which is perhaps less disruptive, and where an arbitrator is more likely than a judge to understand the issues, as businessmen define them. Administrative bodies (zoning boards, workmen's compensation boards) settle many others of society's disputes.

In short, the dispute-settlement trial becomes rarer and rarer. The court system does not expand; the number of judges remains more or less static. The system is rationalized and "improved;" but it remains foreign to the average potential litigant. At the trial level, formal court systems gradually lose their share of dispute settlement cases. Their work becomes, in large part, routine administration.

B.   City and Country

The most surprising result of the study, however, is the striking similarity between the two counties. San Benito is small, and the population is thin. In Oakland, one can talk about "crowded" city courts; but certainly not in Hollister. There is less delay in San Benito, and the court is not rushed or overburdened. Yet little of consequence takes place in court. San Benito is still a small society; yet the main function of a Superior Court is to rubber stamp petitions for dissolution of marriage.

This fact allows us to reject the hypothesis that routinization is to be explained by "industrialization" or "urbanization." There is little industry in San Benito, and no real city. But San Benito is part of an urban, industrial society. It is not isolated from modern influence. It is an hour's drive from the Bay Area megalopolis. The mass media lace all communities together; people in Hollister watch the same programs, eat much the same food, as people elsewhere in the country. They are part of a common culture.

It is a culture in which there seem to be factors in the structure of courts—and, more fundamentally, in social attitudes—which have combined to make "going to court" obsolete, as part of the normal life-cycle of dispute settlement. We cannot identify these factors precisely. But their influence on the work of the courts is far more powerful than the gross demographic differences between "cities" and "small towns."

Whatever the causes, the figures for these two courts show a general movement from dispute resolution to routine administration over the past century.

Friedman and Percival conclude by asking if this movement to routine administration poses a wider social problem. They ask what it means that individuals and businesses alike have turned away from using the courts: "We must ask, what are the institutions that have replaced the courts, and how do they operate? And ... what has society gained and lost, as an ancient structure of decision passes into history?"

9. Compare the findings of Friedman and Percival, and other researchers, about litigation rates, with the widely-held belief that there is a "litigation explosion" which creates a crisis for the system of justice. How would McCann et al., and Hayden, explain the treatment of the so-called "litigation crisis" in the media, and in the popular imagination?

10. Friedman and Percival are also raising the question of whether a decline in litigation rates is necessarily a good thing. What kinds of problems could be involved in a lowered use of the courts? Albert Alschuler has argued that Americans settle too many cases for the wrong reasons—that the way the current legal system is set up puts too much pressure on people to settle. Albert Alschuler, "Mediation with a Mugger: The Shortage of Adjudicative Services and the Need for a Two–Tier Trial System in Civil Cases," 99 *Harvard Law Review* 1808 (1986). In his view, it is preferable if people could "know that they could take their disputes to the courts and that the courts would resolve them. With this assurance people might be less likely to take their disputes to the streets or to the subways." (p. 1859).

11.   To many people, harmony sounds inherently preferable to conflict. But Laura Nader, in *Harmony Ideology: Justice and Control in a Zapotec Mountain Village* 321 (1990), reminds us:

> Conciliation, harmony and resolution have such different uses and consequences as to merit different labels ... Harmony that leads to autonomy is different from harmony that leads to control or oppression or pacification; conciliation may lead to conflict as well as to peace; and resolution may lead to injustice as well as justice. Disputing processes cannot be explained solely as a reflection of some predetermined set of social conditions. Rather, they reflect the processes of an evolving cultural construction, that may be a response to a demand, a product of ruling interests, a result of class conflict or accommodation. Harmony as a general conception for life should be scrutinized in relation to the construction of law, much as conflict and controversy have been examined in relation to the development of law.

Recall Conley and O'Barr's discussion of the possibly deleterious effects of mediation, a seemingly more harmonious form of conflict resolution, on women.

12.   Richard Lempert, in "More Tales of Two Courts: Exploring Changes in the 'Dispute Settlement Function' of Trial Courts," 13 *Law & Society Review* 91 (1978), challenged Friedman and Percival's conclusions about the shift in function of trial courts. Lempert says that data about cases filed cannot tell us conclusively whether courts are playing a less important role in dispute resolution overall. Even if the parties to a dispute never file a case, their predictions about what judges might do could play an important role in how the dispute is settled. The rising costs of litigation can also have an impact on other kinds of dispute resolution. Lempert concludes that Friedman and Percival's data can only tell us that courts are taking on more administrative functions as a percentage of their total activity. These data cannot tell us that the courts' dispute resolution functions have become less socially important.

13.   Lempert also puts added emphasis on a point that Friedman and Percival also raise: we do not, and probably cannot, know how many disputes arose that could have been brought to court but weren't. It is also very difficult to know how perceptions of the legal system might have affected what happened to those disputes. A classic framework for analyzing the phases of a dispute distinguishes between "naming," "blaming," and "claiming." William L. Felstiner, Richard L. Abel, and Austin Sarat, "The Emergence and Transformation of Disputes: Naming, Blaming, Claiming ...," 15 *Law & Society Review* 631 (1980–1981). At the beginning, parties have to identify an emerging problem as an injury (naming), then allocate responsibility to someone else (blaming), and finally frame the solution to their problem as a claim against that person (claiming). Having reached the stage of "claiming," a party may then take the further step of filing a lawsuit, thereby becoming a litigant.

Each step along the way has its problems; the progression does not happen automatically. For example, two people may perceive the same event in different ways; one may decide that it was injurious and offensive while another might brush it off as nothing. Even if someone decides that she has been injured, she may not allocate blame to another ("Oh, it was probably something I did that caused that person to harm me"). Some who do blame others for their injury may make no claim. Many disputes are ended when one party "exits:" an employee may quit (or be fired); a neighbor may move away; former friends may avoid each other. The parties' definitions of the dispute are transformed as it move through these stages—people remember some details and forget others; they inflate some claims and downgrade others; and so on. It is the unusual dispute that travels through the entire process and produces a complaint filed in court. Thus a study of court use can only tell us a small part of the overall story of disputing in any particular time and place.

14.   Laura Beth Nielsen and Robert Nelson are conducting a study that addresses more of this overall story of disputing, using the example of employment discrimination. They compare the data on formal complaints to the EEOC with reports from protected groups of the prevalence of discrimination. Laura Beth Nielsen and Robert Nelson, "Rights Realized? An Empirical Analysis of Employment Discrimination Litigation as a Claiming System," 2005 *Wisconsin Law Review* 663. This comparative exercise leads to the conclusion that only

> a very small percentage of African Americans who feel they are discriminated against in the workplace take a grievance to the EEOC or the courts.... After looking at these numbers, we are inclined to ask not why there are so many discrimination claims, but why there are so few. (p. 706)

Just as in the case of tort cases like the McDonald's Coffee Case, Nielsen and Nelson find that there is a striking contrast between the kinds of employment discrimination awards that are reported in the media, and the average real-life case:

> These data indicate that most discrimination lawsuits have very different outcomes from the image of major plaintiff victories in highly publicized settlements or trial victories, such as those involving Texaco, Mitsubishi, or Home Depot. Most plaintiffs who file federal suit never reach trial. If they do go to trial, they lose more than 60% of the time. If they win, they get relatively modest awards. (p. 701)

The authors conclude by considering the role of the courts in discouraging discrimination. Although they recognize the limitations of litigation as a way of resolving the vast sea of potential discrimination claims that exist, Nielsen and Nelson nonetheless conclude that litigated cases play an important role in setting the scene for other kinds of dispute resolution approaches: "Being exposed to litigation was among the significant predictors to increasing diversity in the managerial ranks of employers." (p. 710, citing Alexandra Kalev et al., "Two to Tango: Affirmative Action, Diversity Programs and

Women and African–Americans in Management," Paper presented at New Legal Realism Conference, Madison Wisconsin, 2004). Thus they recommend a combination of formal and informal legal strategies as a remedy for continued workplace discrimination. Litigated cases, they argue, have power far beyond the immediate remedies for specific parties: they can improve workers' bargaining positions in informal workplace negotiations, and send a signal that alerts workers to the very existence of recognized claims—thereby permitting them to begin the process of "naming" injuries, allocating responsibility to their employers, and setting in motion a claim for justice.

*

CHAPTER 4

The Impact of Law on Society

I. Introduction

In 1990, Congress enacted and the President signed into law two very different statutes, the Americans with Disabilities Act (ADA), 42 U.S.C. § 121 et seq., and the Crime Control Act of 1990. The ADA states as its purpose "to provide a clear and comprehensive national mandate for the elimination of discrimination against individuals with disabilities."[1] The Crime Control Act was a bundle of various anti-crime spending programs and changes in federal criminal law. One provision dealt with the new federal crime of "possession" of child pornography. Among other things, it required producers of pornography to keep a record of the age of people appearing in hard-core pornography (18 U.S.C. §§ 2252, 2275).

The two laws do have at least one thing in common: they seem to be trying to change human behavior. The ADA explicitly outlaws discriminatory behavior against people who have disabilities—the blind, the deaf, people in wheelchair, and so on—whether this discrimination is on the job, or in hotels, motels and restaurants, or on trains, busses and airplanes. The federal statute on child pornography clearly has as its goal stamping out child pornography—preventing people from making it, selling it or possessing it.

A traditional legal scholar would undoubtedly be interested in the way these statutes changed the existing law. From the perspective of a law-and-society scholar, the crucial questions would be different. Such a scholar would surely, among other things, be interested in impact: what difference did these laws actually make in the real world? Did employers actually change their hiring and firing practices with regard to people with disabilities? Did theaters and restaurants become more accessible? Did people produce or use less child pornography? In short, did these laws change behavior?

The "law in action" perspective, discussed and used throughout this book, makes impact a natural concern. In an important sense, the law of disability rights is not the words on the piece of paper that the president signed. Rather, it is the process which the law set off: how employers, grocery store managers, bus companies, airlines, movie theaters, shopping malls—and the disabled themselves—reacted to it. Similarly, the law of child pornography is not the formal language we read in the congressional record, but the behavior of producers, processors and consumers of this material.

Common sense and experience tell us that just because a law is passed, behavior does not necessarily change. For example, providing greater access for persons with disabilities requires employers and merchants to spend

---

1. 1990 *Congressional Quarterly Almanac,* at 452.

money. Doors have to be widened, rest rooms remodeled, elevators added. We would expect that some businesspersons will do all they can to avoid these costs. In fact many business groups lobbied strongly against passage of the ADA for these very reasons. Similarly, child pornography is a multi-million dollar industry, and it caters to the tastes of a small but real segment of the population. This leads us to the first major question to be discussed in this chapter. What makes a law effective? How do we explain "compliance" with the law? Which people will disobey the law? Which ones will evade the law as much as possible? Who will simply ignore the law? And what will motivate these people to obey, disobey, evade, ignore or comply?

Law, of course, is more than statutes. In a broader sense of the word, "law" is any rule, command or order that carries with it authoritative force. In this sense, court decisions and administrative rulings, for example, are just as much types of law as are statutes. And so is advice given in lawyers' offices. And a "law in action" perspective demands that we ask whether and to what extent such advice, decisions and rulings will affect behavior.

While compliance is central to understanding how law affects society, "compliance" does not fully capture the range of ways in which law might have an impact on society. For example, consider the following remark by an attorney, about the impact of the Supreme Court decision in *Bates v. State Bar of Arizona*,[2] which struck down prohibitions against lawyer advertising as unconstitutional: "It is obvious to anyone who practices that lawyer advertising has done more than any single thing to lower the public's opinion of lawyers." The speaker is assuming some degree of compliance with *Bates* and is asking about further implications of that compliance—side-effects, ripple effects, broader and wider consequences. Questions about indirect impact can be asked about any law. Did the ADA drive some employers out of business? Did it make the disabled more or less militant? Did it add to their happiness or their prestige? What did the non-disabled think or do in response to attempts to enforce the statute?

If the police are forced to give criminal suspects constitutional rights, will "the guilty" go free? Will forbidding abortion simply drive it underground and increase the number of women who are injured or die? The impact of law on society includes any consequences which causally follow from a law. This chapter deals first with questions of compliance (direct impact), then goes on to issues associated with more indirect, social consequences of law, and finally turns to the limits of effective legal action.

It is easy for amateurs to speculate about impact, and they do. For example, we hear from politicians that the crime rate is down because of more police work; or it is up because we need more police. However, they rarely marshal evidence to support the claim that police levels actually have the claimed impact on criminal behavior. Similarly, the lawyer who criticized the impact of *Bates* offers no evidence to support his conclusion that advertising "causes" lower opinions of lawyers. We can think of other explanations—if, in

2.   433 U.S. 350 (1977).

fact, people do hold lower opinions of lawyers than they did when lawyers did not advertise. A secondary theme, throughout this chapter, will be how to differentiate between accurate and inaccurate assertions about the impact of law; and how to measure impact; how to tell when impact occurs.

II. Why Do People Obey the Law?

(A) *The Role of Sanctions*

(4.1) Deterrence Theory and Research

Jack Gibbs

in Gary Melton, *The Law as a Behavioral Instrument* (1986).

Deterrence occurs when a potential offender refrains from or curtails ... activity because he or she perceives some threat of a legal punishment for contrary behavior and fears that punishment.

A legal punishment is a legal action by a legal official that is perceived by at least one potential offender as causing pain or discomfort.... Note also that the definition goes beyond statutory penalties and even actual sentences to procedural steps in criminal justice, such as arrest or trial. Those actions presumably are perceived by potential offenders as painful.

TWO CONVENTIONAL TYPES OF DETERRENCE

With few exceptions, ... writers on deterrence distinguish general deterrence and what is called specific, special, or individual deterrence. Full appreciation of the distinction's significance requires explicit definitions.

General deterrence refers to the deterrence of potential offenders who have not been legally punished. To illustrate, suppose that a student with no *arrest history* reads of someone's receiving a six-month sentence for marijuana possession. Insofar as that experience deters the student, each time that he or she refrains from or curtails possession of marijuana constitutes general deterrence. The crucial consideration is not whether the student had possessed marijuana before reading about the punishment, nor is it the nature of that particular experience. All manner of experiences short of actually being punished, even coming to know of statutory penalties, could further general deterrence.

Specific deterrence refers to the deterrence of potential offenders who have been legally punished. The notion does not deny that vicarious experience of punishment can deter; rather, being punished supposedly furthers deterrence beyond any vicarious experience. Reconsider the individual who was sentenced to six months in jail for marijuana possession. If the incarceration prompts that individual to refrain from or curtail marijuana possession, each instance would be specific deterrence. But contemplate this question: To what extent does punishment for one type of crime deter the offender from other types? Researchers have yet to treat the "generalization" question

369

seriously and research is needed to realize a more defensible definition of specific deterrence.

Significance of the distinction. The importance of the general/specific distinction is most obvious when stipulating evidence of deterrence. Assume this finding: ex-convicts commit more crimes per unit of time after incarceration than before. That finding would indicate no specific deterrence, but it would have little bearing on general deterrence.

To appreciate the policy relevance of the general/specific distinction, consider the argument that legislators are preoccupied with general deterrence because it offers cheap crime prevention. What could be cheaper than simply threatening potential offenders? But if recidivists contribute substantially to the crime rate and can be deterred only by serving long prison terms, then crime prevention through deterrence becomes very expensive. Moreover, a strategy for promoting one type of deterrence may not be necessary for the other type. Thus, neither actual punishments nor statutory penalties need be publicized to promote specific deterrence.

A LESS CONVENTIONAL DISTINCTION

The difference between entirely refraining from a criminal act and curtailing commissions is so important that two additional types of deterrence should be distinguished. In the case of *absolute deterrence*, a potential offender has contemplated a crime at least once and has been deterred totally each instance. That an individual has never committed the crime is only a necessary condition for inferring absolute deterrence, because no individual can be deterred without contemplating a crime. To be sure, the term contemplating creates difficulties; but if social and behavioral scientists are unwilling to consider covert behavior, they should leave the deterrence doctrine alone.

The idea of partial crime prevention enters into the notion of *restrictive deterrence*. It occurs when, to diminish the risk or severity of a legal punishment, a potential offender engages in some action that has the effect of reducing his or her commissions of a crime. Briefly illustrating, suppose that a bad-check artist follows this rule: Never hang more than one piece of paper in any town. Such rules are indicative of restrictive deterrence because they have the effect of reducing the number of offenses. Driving behavior often illustrates restrictive deterrence, as when drivers exceed the speed limit by only five miles per hour to reduce the risk or severity of a legal punishment.

Significance of the distinction. Contemplate something improbable—evidence that every professional football player has snorted cocaine at least once. The evidence would fuel allegations that the legal control of narcotics is ineffectual, but it would reveal nothing about restrictive deterrence. Similarly, no crime rate is ever so great as to demonstrate negligible absolute deterrence. So although most writers and researchers ignore the distinction, evidence that bears on either type of deterrence—absolute or restrictive—has little bearing on the other type.

The distinction gives rise to a possible paradox; it may well be that so-called professional criminals are deterred the most. Given such an offender, the most commonly overlooked question is this: How many crimes would the offender have committed had there been no threat of legal punishment? Granted the question is unanswerable, it is relevant in debating penal policy. Critics who assert that legal punishments do not deter may never have thought of restrictive deterrence.

Toward a Theory of General Deterrence

Given the general/specific distinction and the absolute/restrictive distinction, there are four types of deterrence. That number alone precludes stating the deterrence doctrine as a simple proposition such as: Certain, swift, and severe punishments deter crime. Any such proposition would be a gross oversimplification even if types of deterrence could be ignored. It is not clear whether the proposition refers to statutory penalties, to actual punishments, or to both. Even if general deterrence requires some actual punishments, potential offenders may perceive statutory penalties as a threat.

Attempts to reduce the deterrence doctrine to a simple proposition conceal the doctrine's most significant feature; it is first and foremost a perceptual theory. Whether a punishment threat deters depends not on the certainty, celerity, or severity of punishment in any objective sense but on the potential offender's perception. Therefore, in stating the deterrence doctrine as a theory, a theorist should recognize two classes of punishment properties—the objective and the perceptual. The two can be distinguished roughly in terms of procedures for gathering data. The only systematic way to gather data on perceptual properties is to solicit answers from potential offenders to questions about punishments, but objective properties can be studied without such solicitation.

NOTES AND QUESTIONS

1. While Gibbs and most other researchers studying deterrence focus on criminal behavior, deterrence can relate to a wide range of legal attempts to control behavior through the threat of sanctions. For example, non-criminal fines and civil judgments are also sanctions that are designed to deter certain types of behavior. One of the societal justifications often heard for product liability suits is that they serve to deter the further production and distribution of dangerous products. To what extent does the law of contracts also assume a theory of deterrence? A number of contracts scholars have written about what they call "penalty default rules."[3] If a party does not specifically negotiate a term in a contract more favorable to herself, the law will impose one that she probably will not like. Those who make contracts and who know about such penalty default rules are thus given an incentive to consider an issue and do something about it.

3. See, e.g., Eric A. Posner, "There Are No Penalty Default Rules in Contracts Law," 33 *Florida State University Law Review* 563 (2006); Ian Ayres, "Ya–Huh: There Are and Should Be Penalty Default Rules," *id*. at 589.

As Gibbs' article suggests, there is an enormous literature on deterrence—theoretical and empirical. Gibbs himself had earlier written a very thoughtful general account, *Crime, Punishment, and Deterrence* (1975). See, also, Franklin E. Zimring and Gordon J. Hawkins, *Deterrence: The Legal Threat in Crime Control* (1973); Daniel S. Nagen, "Criminal Deterrence Research at the Outset of the Twenty–First Century," 23 *Crime & Justice* 1 (1998); Daniel S. Nagen and Greg Pogarsky, "Integrating Celerity, Impulsivity, and Extralegal Sanction Threats into a Model of General Deterrence: Theory and Evidence," 39 *Criminology* 865 (2001).

2. Gibbs defines two types of studies of deterrence: those looking at objective sanctions and those looking at subjective sanctions. However, he also says that deterrence is "first and foremost a perceptual theory." What does he mean by this comment? What implications does his observation have on the way studies of deterrence should be designed and conducted? Gary Kleck, Brion Sever, Spencer Li, and Marc Gertz, "The Missing Link in General Deterrence Research," 43 *Criminology* 623 (2005), studied whether higher actual punishment levels increased the perceived certainty, severity or swiftness of punishment. They found no detectable impact of actual punishment levels on perceptions of punishment. Criminals are aware of the presence of a police officer, patrol car or a bystander who might intervene. But they seldom are sensitive to the actual risk of arrest where they are or the sanction that might be imposed because they usually lack sufficient information to make such judgments. Assuming that this finding holds true, what does it suggest about theories that say that the law deters crime? Sarah Duguid, "Crime Watch—Drug-dealers, Drunks, Potential Terrorists: These Are Essential Viewing for the Staff at Westminister's CCTV Centre", *Financial Times*, Jan. 28, 2006, at 16, reports: "We have long known we are being watched, but do we know how watched we are? There are four million closed-circuit television cameras in the UK—one for every 14 people. If you live in London you are likely to be on camera 300 times a day." To what extent do closed-circuit television cameras deter crime? To what extent do they only help police determine who committed a crime that was not deterred? Do these two functions work against each other?

3. *A Cost–Benefit Approach to Deterrence:* A large body of work in the law and economics tradition ignores perception, and attempts to look at the "objective" deterrent effect of sanctions on the "rational" actor. For example, see: P. J. Cook, "Research in Criminal Deterrence," in M. Tonry and N. Morris (eds.), *Crime and Justice,* Vol. 2 (1980), at 211–268. Does this imply that economists disagree with Gibbs that deterrence is "perceptual"?

A rational actor, of course, balances the risks of getting caught and the likely penalties against the benefits from the criminal act. See Jan Palmer, "Economic Analysis of the Deterrent Effect of Punishment: A Review," 14 *Journal of Research in Crime and Delinquency* 4 (1977). Scott Decker, Richard Wright and Robert Logie, "Perceptual Deterrence Among Active Residential Burglars: A Research Note," 31 *Criminology* 135 (1993), compared responses of burglars with a control group. Almost all the members of the control group said that they were unwilling to commit burglary regardless of the risk, penalty or reward. The active burglars, however, considered the anticipated gain, the perceived risk of being caught and the likely penalties. Can these findings be explained within a rational actor theory of crime and deterrence? See, also, Bill McCarthy and John Hagan, "When Crime Pays: Capital, Competence, and Criminal Success," 79 *Social Forces* 1035 (2001). They say: "Unfortunately, the structural and personal disadvantages experienced by some youth compromise their formal schooling in spite of their abilities, limit their conventional human capital, narrow their opportunities for licit work and increase their opportunities for offending. Yet, drug dealing and other illegal economic pursuits typically represent short-term solutions that alleviate some problems while exacerbating and initiating others ..." (p. 1054). Many of those who seek to solve their problems by engaging in criminal economic ventures will be caught and sent to jail. Bruce Western and Katherine Beckett, "How Unregulated Is the U.S. Labor Market? The Penal System as a Labor Market Institution," 104 *American Journal of Sociology* 1030 (1999), note that the United States sends large numbers of young men to jail. This takes them out of the labor market and appears to improve the performance of the economy. However, in the long run, jail raises unemployment and may increase the crime rate by reducing legal job opportunities for ex-convicts.

The benefits of crime are not always economic in the narrow sense of that term. See Ralph A. Weisheit, "The Intangible Rewards From Crime: The Case of Domestic Marijuana Cultivation," 37 *Crime & Delinquency* 506 (1991). He interviewed growers and reports that many growers "cultivate marijuana as part of a larger lifestyle, of which marijuana use is often an important part" (p. 512). Patricia A. Adler, *Wheeling and Dealing: An Ethnography of an Upper–Level Drug Dealing and Smuggling Community* (1985), finds that dealers and smugglers engage in frantic hard work focused on short-term maximization of profit so that they can live a hedonistic lifestyle. See John J. Gibbs and Peggy L. Shelly, "Life in the Fast Lane: A Retrospective View by Commercial Thieves," 19 *Journal of Research in Crime and Delinquency* 299 (1982), stressing that commercial thieves enjoy the thrill of crime and the admiration of those who are impressed by their willingness to take chances. Thieves spend money without concern for the future because they expect to be caught and sent to jail sooner or later. They seek only to postpone what they accept as the inevitable. See, also, Jack Katz, "Seductions of Crime: Moral and Sensual Attractions," in Katz (ed.), *Doing Evil* (1988). Ross L. Matsueda, Derek A. Kreager and David Huizinga, "Deterring Delinquents: A Rational Choice Model of Theft and Violence," 71 *American Sociological Review* 95 (2006), use panel data on high risk youth drawn from the Denver Youth Survey. They argue that theft and violence are a function of the perceived risk of arrest, subjective psychic rewards (including excitement and social status) and perceived opportunities. They note studies that show that violence and crime permit inner-city youth to gain respect and honor. They quote one informant as saying: "You do it 'cause you want to be cool.'" Would there be any way to convince young people that crime is not cool? Where are they likely to get the view that it is?

4.   Recall the material on the development of no-fault divorce. Was the prior fault-based law a deterrent to divorce? Was it supposed to be? Does a no-fault system mean the legal system has abandoned any attempt to deter divorce?

(4.2) The Death Penalty Meets Social Science: Deterrence and Jury Behavior Under New Scrutiny

Robert Weisberg

1 *The Annual Review of Law and Social Science* 151 (2005).

INTRODUCTION

The endlessly recycling debates in the United States over whether we should have capital punishment tend to mix two entirely different types of discourse: a retributivist discourse about whether certain criminals morally deserve the death penalty, and a utilitarian discourse about whether the death penalty serves to reduce murder and, occasionally, about whether it has been imposed fairly. On the latter score, social science research has played a persistent, if fitful, role in influencing jurists and occasionally legislators and even the lay public. This review focuses almost entirely on the most visible category of social science research and the death penalty—the question of deterrence. In the final section, I briefly allude to other areas of capital punishment policy and law where social science research has played a role, such as racial issues and jury behavior.

Perhaps no question relevant to law and social science has been so salient in American public opinion in the last few decades, and yet has so vexed social scientists, as, "Does the death penalty deter murder?"

The general hypothesis of the deterrent justification for capital punishment is straightforward: Although many potential murderers may not rationally reflect on the consequences of their actions, a considerable number do weigh negative consequences, consciously or instinctively. Indeed, one reason why homicide detectives sometimes have to struggle to find the right suspect is that many murderers go to great lengths to conceal their acts or escape detection. Conversely, some scholars argue that it is common sense to expect the death penalty to *increase* murders. Such an increase might occur because *(a)* there are suicidal killers out there who will only murder if they think they can then achieve the ultimate penalty, or *(b)* there is a brutalization effect—i.e., executions or the willingness to execute lead some potential killers to act out their intents, either inspired by the role model of the state or because in some way the state's willingness to execute cheapens the value of life.... But data supporting any positive correlation between the death penalty and murders are weak. Moreover, for those who doubt the deterrent effect of the death penalty, it may be self-contradictory to claim that criminals are too impulsive to contemplate the negative consequences of their actions but are still sufficiently sensitive to public signals that they are sometimes motivated to kill by social signals modeling killing.

What about direct evidence of deterrence? Certain seemingly direct measures of the deterrent effect of the death penalty are available. For example, once facing prosecution, almost all criminals seek to avoid punishment, and only in about 1% of cases does a capital defendant actually request the death penalty or waive rights of appeal. And then there is the anecdotal evidence, as in the case of one murderer who said he robbed and killed drug dealers in Washington, DC, where he was conscious that there was no death penalty, but specifically chose not to do so in Virginia because he was frightened by memories of Virginia prisoners in the electric chair.... But such seemingly direct measures are too unsystematic to play an important role in social science research on the death penalty. Thus, the focus of this review is, of course, on more systematic statistical research.

But before examining the undulating history of research on this question, some key qualifications are in order. First, other things being equal, the presence or enforcement of the death penalty obviously will produce fewer homicides than not punishing homicides at all. Thus, the question is one of *marginal* deterrence—i.e., whether the death penalty deters more homicides than the next most severe penalty, which in all jurisdictions is some form of life imprisonment, and in most is the relatively new sentence of life without the possibility of parole. So it is solely for convenience that throughout this review deterrence stands for marginal deterrence.

Second, deterrence is only one way that the death penalty could reduce murders. Another utilitarian justification for punishment is incapacitation, and one might posit that the death penalty reduces the number of murders not by virtue of sending a deterrent message to other potential murderers but simply by preventing the condemned killer from ever killing again. Of course, that issue only arises if, assuming the alternative punishment is always a true life sentence, a convicted murder were able to kill in prison (or perhaps order a killing on the outside). The magnitude of these possibilities lies outside the scope of this review.

Third, the term murder may signify to the lay public any illegal or intentional killing. But of course murder is a complex legal concept covering a number of forms of homicide. Thus, as noted below, statistical analysis of the deterrent effect of capital punishment is somewhat contingent on the question of what type of homicide might be deterred. Most crime data indexes count all homicides explicitly labeled as murder under state law, plus a category called "non-negligent manslaughter".... In this review, murder is the necessarily imprecise term generally used for the types of homicides covered by the research discussed here.

Fourth, whatever measures of statistical significance one uses, social scientists face a couple of blunt facts about death penalty and deterrence.

First, the percentage of people sentenced to death in the United States who actually are executed is minute, so if research is concerned with the actual or perceived likelihood of a death-sentenced murderer suffering the ultimate penalty, the data will always seem insufficient. Second, as discussed below, the executions that do occur are disproportionately centered in a few states—indeed, close to a majority in a single state—so the various effects of skewing hamper sound empirical inference-drawing.

EARLY RESEARCH: THE SELLIN/EHRLICH STANDOFF

Although the issue of the deterrent effect of the death penalty has a long legacy in criminology generally, it began to play a major role in American legal doctrine most notably in *Furman v. Georgia*[4] (1972) and *Gregg v. Georgia*[5] (1976). In *Furman*, the Supreme Court declared all then-operational death penalty laws of the United States unconstitutional. In *Gregg*, it upheld against Eighth Amendment challenges the new type of guided discretion laws that are now used in three fourths of the states and in the federal system. In the years following *Gregg*, important social science evidence of a deterrent effect to which *Gregg* alluded met widespread skepticism and arguably utter refutation in later social science research. And now, 30 years after the restoration of the death penalty in the United States, the state of the research has become roiled again with new claims of proof of that deterrent effect.

Generally, what research existed before 1972 did little to establish any deterrent effect. Most of the early work was done by criminologists or psychologists whose empirical work relied mainly either on comparisons of homicide rates in states with and without capital punishment, or, within a particular jurisdiction, on comparisons of homicide rates before and after executions. But because this research did not employ the statistical technique of multiple regression, it could not meaningfully distinguish the effect of capital punishment on murder from the effects of other factors. One of the oldest studies[6] looked at homicides within 60 days of an execution. Two decades later, another study[7] examined murders eight weeks before and after trials ending in death sentences. Working with sparse data, these studies found no deterrent effect. Another 1950s study[8] compared murder rate changes between states that maintained capital punishment and those that never had capital punishment in the year under study and also measured before-and-after murder rates in states that switched in one direction or another. This study concluded that non-death penalty states have murder rates equal to or lower than those of death penalty states. In a key example, the study noted that South Dakota went from a non-death penalty to a death penalty regime in 1939 and saw in the next decade a modest drop in its murder rate of 16%, but that North Dakota, which was a non-death penalty

---

4. Furman v. Georgia, 408 U.S. 238 (1972).

5. Gregg v. Georgia, 428 U.S. 153 (1976).

6. R. Dann, *The Deterrent Effect of Capital Punishment* (1935).

7. L. Savitz, "A Study in Capital Punishment," 49 *J. Crim. Law Criminol. & Police Sci.* 338–41 (1958).

8. K. Schuessler, "The Deterrent Effect of the Death Penalty," *284 Annals* 54 (1952).

state before and after 1939, enjoyed a drop of 40% for that same decade. This study also attempted to analyze the effects of actual executions and found no evidence of a deterrent effect.

The most notable figure in this early phase of deterrence research was Thorsten Sellin. Sellin, examining the period from 1920 to 1955, found that states retaining the death penalty exhibited murder rates at least as high as those that had abolished it[9]. He also did a rough comparison of contiguous jurisdictions and found that on the whole they exhibited similar murder rates and homicide rate trends even where they differed on capital punishment.

However, Sellin could not explain a few contiguous pairs with dramatic differences—especially Ohio/Michigan and Colorado/Kansas—perhaps because he did not address the possibility that some paired states differ significantly along social, economic, and political dimensions that affect murder rates. Sellin also looked at murder rates in a number of states over time as a way to finesse the initial condition problem. That is, he examined murder rates in particular states when they changed from having the death penalty to abolishing it or from not having it to reinstituting it. And, once again, he found no evidence of deterrence. Sellin acknowledged the problem of recursive effect—the possibility that states abolish capital punishment when and because the murder rate is falling, thus raising a problem of reverse causality—and he performed some tests that yielded results inconsistent with this hypothesis. Finally, Sellin studied killings by life prisoners and discerned that a majority of the small number of prison killers were in death penalty states.

The pivotal moment in the history of death penalty deterrence research came in the mid–1970s with the work of University of Chicago economist Isaac Ehrlich. Indeed, the death penalty deterrence debate might be said to be divisible into two eras: before Ehrlich (BE) and after Ehrlich (AE). Ehrlich was the first to study capital punishment's deterrent effect using multivariate regression analysis.[10] This approach enabled Ehrlich to distinguish the effects on murder of such different factors as the racial and age composition of the population, average income, unemployment, and the execution rate.

Ehrlich's famous 1975 paper examined time series data for the period 1933–1969. He tested the effect on national murder rates of various potential deterrent variables (probabilities of arrest, conviction, and execution), demographic variables (size of population, percentage of minorities in the population, percentage of people ages 14–24 in the population), economic variables (unemployment rate, per capita permanent income, per capita government expenditures, and per capita expenditures on police), and a time variable. Ehrlich concluded that there was a statistically significant negative relationship between the murder rate and execution rate, i.e., a deterrent effect. Specifically, he estimated that each execution resulted in approximately seven or eight fewer murders. This paper was offered to the Supreme Court in draft

---

9. T. Sellin, *The Death Penalty* (1959).

10. I. Ehrlich, "The Deterrent Effect of Capital Punishment: a Question of Life and Death," 65 *Am. Econ. Law Rev.* 347 (1975).

form by the solicitor general when *Gregg* was originally litigated. It was then cited in the plurality decision in the *Gregg* decision itself, in which Justice Stewart cited it as part of a mix of studies that, he inferred, established a scholarly standoff on the question of whether the death penalty deterred murder and so justified treating the deterrence issue as essentially irrelevant to the constitutionality of capital punishment.

Ehrlich's second paper[11] (1977) studied cross-sectional data from the 50 states from 1940 to 1950. That is, whereas the first paper tested how the total U.S. murder rate changed across time as the execution rate changed, Ehrlich now explored the relationship, during a single year, between a state's execution rate and its murder rate. Ehrlich again used multivariate regression analysis, including variables similar to those in the 1975 study (for a deterrent variable he added median time spent in prison as well as a dummy variable to distinguish executing states from nonexecuting states, and, for economic variables, median family income and percentage of families with income below half of the median income). Again, he inferred a significant deterrent effect. Ehrlich himself was publicly cautious about trumpeting his conclusions, but immediately his work received both extravagant public praise and sharp academic criticism. It rapidly entered the political sphere as citable proof that each execution could indeed save at least eight innocent lives. But in the ensuing years, many social scientists tried to replicate Ehrlich's results with differing data and methods, and most were unable to confirm Ehrlich's conclusions. Indeed, in 1978, a National Academy of Sciences scholarly panel publicly criticized Ehrlich's work.[12]

Because Ehrlich's work was, or seemed, so pivotal in the history of research on the death penalty, a fuller description of the problems in his studies may be useful and it is supplied by legal sociologist Richard Lempert.[13] As seen by Lempert, Ehrlich could be credited for deploying multivariate regression analysis to study the deterrence hypothesis, but he could be faulted for not using the technique comprehensively or well. First, as Ehrlich himself recognized, his work failed to measure the length of prison sentences in general or the probability of life sentences in particular. Hence, his work is wanting precisely on the question of marginal deterrence. As Lempert suggests, if murderers who would have been executed or sentenced to life imprisonment during periods when execution rates were high often received sentences of *less* than life when execution rates were low (perhaps reflecting generally more lenient sentences in periods of diminished fear of crime), an association between low homicide rates and high execution rates would not necessarily indicate that executions are a greater deterrent than life sentences. The association might exist because executions and life sentences, or

11. I. Ehrlich, "Capital Punishment and Deterrence: Some Further Thoughts and Additional Evidence," 85 *J. Polit. Econ.* 741–88 (1977).

12. A. Blumstein, J. Cohen, 1978. "Deterrence and Incapacitation: Estimating the Effects of Criminal Sanctions on Crime Rates." Washington, DC: Natl. Acad. Sci. (1978).

13. R. Lempert, "Desert and Deterrence," 79 *Mich. Law Rev.* 1177 (1981).

indeed just life sentences, are greater deterrents than sentences of less than life. The marginal deterrence issue, which is whether executions are a greater deterrent than life sentences, or in today's sentencing schemes sentences of life without parole, is in these circumstances not necessarily addressed by the data.

Second, replication of Ehrlich's data shows that if we eliminate the years 1965 through 1969, the deterrent effect is statistically insignificant or even reverses itself. As Lempert explains this problem, the premise of Ehrlich's approach is not in the first instance empirical, but theoretical. It posits an economic model of why punishment deters, then uses empirical evidence to test the soundness of this deterrence theory, and then finds the theory confirmed. But the theory cannot explain why the economic model yields different results for different periods of years because this model assumes something fairly essential about human nature. The only way to accommodate the issue of time sensitivity to sustain Ehrlich's finding is to take account of other factors, such as the state of racial tension, the rate of gun ownership or use, the Vietnam War and political events of other sorts, and then to see if they explained the model's sensitivity to time period. Not only did Ehrlich not do this, but, Lempert argues, no obvious explanations for the time sensitivity come to mind.

Finally, Lempert suggests a reversal of Ehrlich's technique, treating the results as the statement of a hypothesis and then asking whether that hypothesis jibes with data from various jurisdictions. One researcher did a version of this test on several states and found no support for Ehrlich's hypothesis.[14] Lempert himself takes the approach of borrowing from Sellin's idea that fluctuations in homicide rates over time tend to be similar in contiguous states, so that if one state executes and the other does not, the advantage of the executing state in reducing homicides should increase with each additional execution. Looking back to Sellin through the lens of Ehrlich promises better controls on other relevant variables because each state becomes its own control. Lempert tests Ehrlich's data along these lines and finds no support for the Ehrlich hypothesis.[15]

The newness of Ehrlich's methods, coupled with his striking findings, brought great attention to his research. Justice Stewart's inference in *Gregg* of an empirical standoff on the deterrence issue, prominently citing Ehrlich for the proposition that the death penalty deters, further spurred researchers to examine the deterrent effect of executions. The papers that immediately followed Ehrlich used his data or similar data sets and the same or related statistical methods. Some of this after Ehrlich, or AE, research found a deterrent effect of capital punishment, but others did not, while one study came to mixed conclusions depending on the cross-section year used.

---

14. W. Bailey, "Deterrence and the Death Penalty for Murder in Utah: a Time-series Analysis," 5 *J. Contemp.Laws* 1 (1978).

15. R. Lempert, "The Impact of Executions on Homicide: a New Look in an Old Light," 1983 *Crime & Delinq.* 88 (1983).

A second generation of AE econometric studies in the late 1980s and 1990s extended Ehrlich's national time series data or used more recent cross-sectional data. As before, some papers found deterrence by using, for example, an extension of Ehrlich's national time series data covering up to 1977 ... or national time series data for 1966–1985.... Still, others found no deterrent effect by, for example, using daily data for California during 1960–1963....

Nevertheless, most of these AE studies suffered from their dependence on either national time series or cross-section data. National time series data created a serious aggregation problem. For example, when the murder rate in a state with no executions happens to increase simultaneously with a decrease in the murder rate in a state with a number of executions, the data might mask a true deterrent effect. In contrast, cross-sectional studies, by definition, do not account for changes in criminal behavior and the operations of the criminal justice system over time, nor can they account for cultural factors that might affect the homicide rate in particular regions.

PANEL STUDIES AND THE NEW DETERRENCE CLAIMS

Recently, an impressive new generation of deterrence studies has promised to overcome these difficulties by relying on panel data—that is, data from numerous units (in terms of American criminal justice, the 50 states or all counties in the United States) for numerous time periods. These data sets allow for comparisons across jurisdictions over time; they typically include information on potentially confounding variables; they have enough observations to ensure that analyses based on them will have reasonable statistical power; and they benefit from the increased rate at which executions occurred during the 1980s and 1990s. And, most dramatically, these recent studies, using modern regression techniques, find that executions have not just a significant but a substantial deterrent effect.

For example, one new study by Hashem Dezhbakhsh, Paul H. Rubin, and Joanna Shepherd draws on 20 years of data from 3054 counties nationwide to test the effect of county differences on murder rates.[16] The authors conclude that all types of homicide are deterred by the death penalty, and they infer from their results that each execution prevents as many as 18 murders. Another study by Shepherd[17] uses monthly data from all 50 states over 22 years to test the short-term effect of the death penalty, and also takes the important extra step of examining different gradations of homicide. The gradation factor is important because some might argue that, for example, so-called heat-of-passion killings are impossible to deter or that other types of killings might even be inspired by executions. The Shepherd study finds that the combination of death sentences and executions deters all types of homicide, from impassioned intimate killings to stranger killings and robbery-

---

16. H. Dezhbakhsh, P. Rubin, J. Shepherd, "Does Capital Punishment Have a Deterrent Effect? New Evidence from Post-moratorium Panel Data," *5 Am. Law & Econ. Rev.* 344 (2002).

17. J. Shepherd, "Murder of Passion, Execution Delays, and the Deterrence of Capital Punishment," 33 *J. Leg. Stud.* 283 (2004).

motivated killings, regardless of the race or ethnicity of the killer or victim. It concludes that on the whole each death sentence deters approximately 4.5 homicides and that each execution deters approximately 3 more. Notably, another recent study by Dezhbakhsh and Shepherd focuses on the flipside of deterrence—that is, the effect on the murder rate of delays in or even moratoria on actual executions.[18] Delays between death sentence and execution, of course, depend on the vagaries of the state and federal appellate systems, and moratoria may result from judicial decisions in particular jurisdictions that suspend imposition of death sentences or on executive decisions to suspend actual executions. This study, using state-level panel data from 1960–2000, compares the murder rate for each state immediately before and after the state either suspended or reinstated capital punishment. This approach relies on the fact, or assumption, that many factors that might influence the murder rate, i.e., social or cultural factors or operational changes in criminal justice, change only slightly over a short period of time. In addition, and happily for this study, the various suspensions started and ended in different years in different states and were of widely differing durations. The study finds that 90% of states manifest higher murder rates after suspensions, whereas 70% show murder rate drops after reinstatements. More strikingly, this study concludes that every reduction in the average wait between death sentence and execution of 2.75 years deters an extra murder. The authors pronounce, "The results are boldly clear: executions deter murders and murder rates increase substantially during moratoriums. The results are consistent across before-and-after comparisons and regressions regardless of the data's aggregation level, the time period, or the specific variable to measure executions" (p. 27).

Finally, recent research by a Federal Communications Commission economist, Paul Zimmerman,[19] using state-level panel data from 1978 to 1997, not only finds a deterrent effect but more boldly seeks to distinguish the effects of particular methods of execution (this last effort may be legally moot because virtually all executions now use lethal injection). Using state-level panel data from 1978 to 1997 for all 50 states (excluding Washington, DC), Zimmerman concludes not only that each execution deters an average of 14 murders but that electrocution can push the number closer to the mid–20s.

NEW DETERRENCE STUDIES USING OTHER TECHNIQUES

The new wave of research finding strong evidence of a deterrent effect is not limited to the panel data studies. For example, Cloninger & Marchesini[20] rely on a portfolio analysis in a type of controlled experiment by examining an unofficial moratorium on executions in Texas during most of 1996. They infer

---

18. H. Dezhbakhsh & J. Shepherd, "The Deterrent Effect of Capital Punishment: Evidence from a 'Judicial Experiment,' " Work. Pap. No. 03–14, Dep. Econ., Emory Univ. http://www.economics.emory.edu/WorkingPapers/wp/dezhbakhshpdf03 14 paper.pdf.

19. P. Zimmerman, "State Execution, Deterrence, and the Incidence of Murder.,"7 *J. Appl. Econ.* 163 (2004).

20. D.O. Cloninger & R. Marchesini R., "Executions and Deterrence: a Quasi-controlled Group Experiment," 35 *Appl. Econ.* 569 (2001).

that this hiatus spared few condemned prisoners but caused a significant net increase in lives lost to murder. Another cross-sectional study,[21] covering 58 cities in 1985, sought to measure the influence of criminals' perceived risk of punishment. It concluded that this perceived risk, including the perceived probability of execution, is negatively and significantly correlated with the murder rate. Other studies, including a reentry to the fray by Ehrlich himself,[22] use state-level and cross-section analysis to reconfirm that executions have a significant deterrent effect. And another study, by Ehrlich's coresearcher, Liu,[23] finds that legalizing the death penalty not only adds capital punishment as a deterrent but also increases the marginal productivity of other deterrence measures in reducing murder rates.

Finally, Yunker[24] tests the deterrence hypothesis using two sets of postmoratorium data: state cross-section data from 1976 and 1997 and national time series data from 1930–1997. He finds a strong deterrent effect in the time series data, an effect that disappears when the data are limited to the 1930–1976 period. Therefore, he concludes that postmoratorium data are critical to testing the deterrence hypothesis.

Summarizing this new wave of deterrence research, both the panel-based studies and others, one prolific participant in this research confidently draws even a further conclusion:

> [T]he studies that find a deterrent effect of other criminal sanctions give additional support to the deterrent effect of the death penalty, because, if lesser sanctions deter, then we know that more severe sanctions also deter. The studies that find a deterrent effect of 1. increased police presence, or any other levels of security; 2. arrest rates; 3. criminal sentencing/incarceration terms; and 4. the presence of rules, laws and statutes all provide additional, collateral support for the deterrent effect of the death penalty.[25]

THE NEW STUDIES UNDER SCRUTINY

The apparent power and unanimity of this new round of studies in proving a deterrent effect has, unsurprisingly, provoked a strong response from skeptics. Although the new round of research has not yet been subjected to the depth and breadth of peer review that ultimately undermined confidence in Ehrlich's early studies, some general points of attack and some specific criticism of certain components of the new studies have emerged.

21. H. Brumm & D. Cloninger, "Perceived Risk of Punishment and the Commission of Homicides: a Covariance Structural Analysis," 31 J. *Econ. Behav. Org.* 1 (1996).

22. I. Ehrlich & Z. Liu, "Sensitivity Analysis of the Deterrence Hypothesis: Let's Keep the Econ in Econometrics," 41 *J. Law & Econ.* 455 (1999).

23. Z. Liu, "Capital Punishment and the Deterrence Hypothesis: Some New Insights and Empirical Evidence," 30 *East. Econ. J.* 237 (2004).

24. J. Yunker J., "A New Statistical Analysis of Capital Punishment Incorporating U.S. Postmoratorium Data," 82 *Soc. Sci. Q.* 297 (2002).

25. J. Shepherd, "Statement at the Terrorist Penalties Enhancement Act of 2003 Hearing before House Judiciary Subcommittee on Crime Terrorism and Homeland Security," April 21, 108th Congr., 2nd sess. http://commdocs.house.gov/committees/judiciary/hju 93224.000/hju93224Of.htm (2004).

As summarized by Jeffrey Fagan,[26] two major criticisms stand out. First, all these studies suffer too much from the statistical risk that their overall findings are driven by a few outlier jurisdictions—most notably Texas. Thus, more fine-tuned comparisons between certain states (say, Texas and California) will be needed to retest the results. Next, the studies do not take account of the most important new legal innovation that has arisen in the post-*Gregg* era—namely, the availability of life without the possibility of parole (LWOP) sentences in all death penalty states except two (New Mexico and, ironically, Texas, where a new LWOP law has just been enacted). LWOP sentences are far more numerous than death sentences these days, and beyond their obvious incapacitating effect they may well have a powerful deterrent effect as well. Indeed, LWOP may be the key deterrent even when the potential offender might also somewhat fear a death sentence. The data showing that some death row inmates waive their appeals are at least anecdotal evidence that a criminal code with a maximum sentence of LWOP alone may be more of a deterrent than a code that allows for either LWOP or the death penalty. Other potential lines of criticism that Fagan suggests include the following:

1.   These new studies tend to aggregate several forms of murder, and, as above, the one study that breaks them down purports to find all forms deterrable. This conclusion may be implausible if we believe that heat-of-passion killings are necessarily somewhat harder to deter than other murders. If so, more fine-tuned research will be needed, especially of such specific contextual factors as the availability of guns in certain domestic situations.

2.   The new studies do not control for the phenomenon of autoregression, that is, the influence that trends in certain years may exert over longitudinal or time series data covering succeeding years. This problem is especially serious in the context of very rare events like executions.

3.   The new studies are only sporadically successful, at best, in accounting for controls supplied by the various operations of the criminal justice system, including such essential factors as the success of police in even identifying offenders. It is a virtual cliché of criminal deterrence that the *certainty* of punishment, of any type, is a more effective deterrent than the *possibility* of severe punishment, contingent on apprehension and conviction. If the cliche is true, then initial police success in catching offenders should be a more effective deterrent than the rarer death sentences or still rarer executions. If high-executing states also have higher-than-average homicide clearance or arrest rates, this fact could explain the apparent deterrent effects. Some of the newer studies try to control for murder or homicide arrest rates. . . . But because arrest rates are likely to be particularly high for homicides that are not death-eligible or for which the death penalty is seldom given (e.g., fights between

26. Fagan J., "Deterrence and the Death Penalty: A Critical Review of the New Evidence," Testimony to NY State Assem. Standing Comm. on Codes, Judiciary and Correction, Jan. 21, 2005.http://www.deathpenaltyinfo.org/Fahttp://www.deathpenaltyinfo.org/FaganTestimony.pdf (2005).

friends, crimes of passion), the adequacy of the control is questionable unless arrest rates as well as homicide rates are broken down by the death-eligibility of the crime. Unfortunately, none of the new studies attempts that breakdown.

4. The studies ignore large amounts of missing data in important states such as Florida, thus potentially biasing their conclusions. Fagan suggests that different techniques for restoring missing data should be used to determine whether the lack of available data can explain findings of deterrence.

Finally, to those who tell a deterrence story by using new data and quantitative methods to shore up their findings, Fagan suggests that these researchers look for confirming evidence in actual mechanisms by which deterrence may operate. For example, the deterrence case could find support in evidence that violence prone people are aware of executions and the relative likelihood of executions in their own states. Studies that use only national data improbably assume that violence-prone people are aware of execution rates in faraway states, and this assumption needs scrutiny. Similarly, researchers might offer an explanation of why executions should deter non-death-eligible homicides. Do potential offenders attend to punishments enough to know that murderers may be executed but not enough to know that only certain kinds of murders are death-eligible? Do they know that executions for murder occur but not know how rare they are in many states? Is there any evidence that murderers rationally decide to forego homicide and use less lethal forms of violence? On all these questions about deterrence, argues Fagan, empiricists should consider the contemporary social science research on the generally bounded rationality of human decision making and attempt to apply it to the even more dubiously rational thinking of violent offenders.

One new deterrence study is worth further attention because its findings have been closely examined, and its data reanalyzed, by a leading quantitative sociologist, Richard Berk. Berk's[27] article is a sharp critique of work by H. Naci Mocan and R. Kaj Gittings.[28] Mocan & Gittings use state-level panel data from 1977 to 1997 (including information on all 6143 death sentences in this period) to examine the relationship between executions, commutations, and murder. Their study finds a significant deterrent effect, suggesting that each execution deters an average of five murders. More strikingly, it concludes that each commutation results in approximately five extra murders and that each removal from death row generates an additional murder. Finally, it infers that every set of three additional pardons (i.e., commutations of the death sentence) causes 1 to 1.5 additional murders.

27. R. Berk, "New Claims About Executions and General Deterrence: Déjà Vu All Over Again?" 2 *Journal of Empirical Legal Studies* 303 (2005).

28. N. Mocan N, K. Gittings K., "Getting Off Death Row: Committed Sentences and the Deterrent Effect of Capital Punishment," 46 *Journal of Law & Economics* 453 (2005).

Berk's sharp critique, one with implications beyond the Mocan–Gittings study that is his focus, argues that these new studies show flaws ranging from the "conceptual leap of treating observational data as an experiment to a large number of nuts-and-bolts statistical difficulties." Berk points out that in the Mocan–Gittings study, the mean for the number of executions per state per year is 0.35, implying that each state executes about one prisoner every three years, but he then notes that because the standard deviation is 1.35, skewing is a serious concern. Moreover, Berk notes that in the Mocan–Gittings study, the median is zero, with the mean dominated by a few extreme values (i.e., 29 for Texas in 1997, the last year studied). Thus, statistical leverage becomes a serious problem because extreme values of an explanatory variable are paired with extreme values of the response variable. As Berk says, "The potential impact of leverage on a model's fit becomes a reality," and the problem is especially severe when an extreme value is not just atypical, but also an outlier—that is, located a great distance from the mass of the data. (This is true with respect to the number of homicides per year, for which the mean is 420 but the standard deviation is 607.)

Further, argues Berk, after controlling for potential confounders, we can conclude that once one knows the large number of homicides in a particular state during the 20–year period, knowing the number of executions adds virtually nothing to the analysis. (This phenomenon is especially evident in situations of five executions or fewer.) As for the temporal dimension, when indicator variables for years rather than states are used to account for national trends in the number of homicides and the homicide rate, we gain no new knowledge of any deviance.

Reanalyzing the data, Berk finds that the relationship Mocan & Gittings report seems entirely dependent on the small number of states with more than five executions. If we exclude the 11 observations out of 1000 that involve more than five executions from the analysis, then we find no systematic difference in the average homicide rate between states that have had no executions and those that have had one; we find a slight negative relationship as we move from states executing one individual to states executing three; and we find a slight positive relationship as we move from states with three to those with five.

Berk acknowledges the possible counterargument that states may differ in their inclination and ability to seek the death penalty, so that controlling for state differences is misleading. If so, using just the 1977 homicide rate as a predictor could adjust for that because the factors affecting the homicide rate were hardly stationary over the following 20 years. Nevertheless, Berk concludes that using this factor as a predictor affects the outcome hardly at all. Unsurprisingly, then, if instead of using the number of executions one uses a binary indicator of zero executions versus one or more executions, evidence of a deterrence effect disappears. Equally unsurprisingly, notes Berk, little evidence of deterrence appears when Texas is removed from the analysis. Put another way, if we shuffle the number of executions for all states other than Texas randomly, so that the number is unrelated to any of the other variables for those states, and we then add Texas back into the mix, the result is an apparent deterrent effect similar to the one found in the real data. Still more skeptically, Berk suggests that using monthly time units or county area units cannot solve any of these problems because the number will be zero for the great majority of them. Finally, he questions whether the data from Texas are ample enough to prove a deterrent effect to the death penalty even there.

THE UNCERTAIN FUTURE OF DETERRENCE RESEARCH

Intuitively, the notion that the death penalty deters finds support in some very rough empiricism about recent events in the United States: Murder rates plummeted over the last decade and a half, and some might argue that a steady diet of executions must have played a role. From 1966–1980, the murder rate nearly doubled, from 5.6 to 10.2 per 100,000. During that 1966–1980 period, the United States averaged only one execution every three years, with a maximum of two executions per year, most obviously because that period covers the last national moratorium on executions (June 1967 to January 1976). Conversely, between 1995 and 2000 the national murder rate dropped 46%, from a high of 10.2 per 100,000 to 5.5 per 100,000, while executions for that period averaged 7.1 per year. But of course those figures, however convincing they might look to some, tell us little about the real relationship, if any, between these parallel rates. Similarly, one of the most striking correlations comes in the nation's most active death penalty jurisdiction, Harris County (Houston) Texas, where the murder rate dropped 73% between 1982, when executions were resumed, and 2000. But that correlation may just signal that Texas is too anomalous to tell us much about the nation. More generally, while homicide rates were dropping dramatically across the nation, so were rates for other crimes not punishable by death.

Data from the multiple regression studies already mentioned are less intuitive than the simple statistics given above but are obviously potentially more meaningful. Nevertheless, some have questioned whether the modern econometric approaches, which most of the new research employ, are as powerful or sophisticated as they might appear. As one harsh critic summarized the econometric approaches, "There is simply too little data and too many ways to manipulate it."[29] That is, there are too many ways to select model specifications. As a technical matter, notes another critic, to obtain a significant deterrent effect many new studies take the questionable approach of adding a set of data with no executions to a time series and including an executing/nonexecuting dummy in the cross-sectional analysis.... Thus, we see that the proper specification of econometric approaches is open to controversy, and choices made by researchers, even if defensible, have an inevitable subjective element and could conceivably be more important than the data in determining a study's conclusions.

29. T. Goertzel, "Capital Punishment and Homicide: Sociological Realities and Econometric Illusions," Skept. Inq. July http://www. csicop.org/si/2004–07/capital-punishment. html (2004).

Recall Justice Stewart's remark in *Gregg* that there is an empirical standoff on the matter of the death penalty's deterrent value. That remark may thus now be true even if, when uttered, it distorted the apparent weight of the studies that had been done to that point. It is certainly difficult for the uninvolved observer to be confident of where the truth lies. The claims of the latest round of empirical research appear strong, and the work is not vulnerable to the relatively simple and convincing refutations that followed Ehrlich's initial foray into these matters. Fagan's critique and Berk's close look at the Mocan–Gittings data suggest, however, that the results of even these sophisticated studies will have to be qualified as the analyses of the capital punishment deterrence data become yet more refined. Whether the effects of further scrutiny will be to support the deterrence hypothesis, while perhaps putting it in more precise context, or will be to provide further evidence of the null hypothesis of no effect remains impossible to say. We can, however, conclude with more confidence, now that critics have begun to weigh in on the most recent research, that the relationship between executions and murders still lacks clear proof.

SOCIAL SCIENCE RESEARCH ON OTHER DEATH PENALTY ISSUES

Some of the most incisive and insightful interventions of social science into the operation of the death penalty have addressed issues other than deterrence. I briefly discuss some of these studies here.

Victim–Race Discrimination

When the Supreme Court temporarily suspended the use of the death penalty in the United States in *Furman* in 1972, a major issue was whether capital punishment was being imposed in a racially discriminatory manner. Many noted that the penalty was imposed on minorities, most notably black Americans, in numbers several times greater than their proportion in the population. But because the disproportion was similar in terms of convictions for murder, it was difficult to argue that the death penalty by itself was inflicted disproportionately on black defendants. The belief that the death penalty did indeed discriminate on the basis of the race of the defendant may have influenced the *Furman* outcome, but soon thereafter in *Gregg* the Court held that the new post-*Furman* death penalty statutes were well designed to prevent any such effects.

After the Court reimposed the death penalty in *Gregg,* the focus of the death penalty discrimination research shifted more substantially from the race of the defendant to the race of the victim. A major study, first published in 1983, by David C. Baldus, George Woolworth, and Charles Pulaski[30] examined over 2000 murder cases that occurred in Georgia during the 1970s. It inferred that defendants charged with killing white persons received the death penalty in 11% of the cases, whereas those charged with killing blacks

---

30. D. Baldus, G. Woodworth, C. Pulaski Jr., *Equal Justice and the Death Penalty: A*   *Legal and Empirical Analysis* (1990).

received the death penalty in only 1% of the cases. Ironically but significantly (given that most killings occur between members of the same race or group), the race-of-defendant numbers revealed a reverse disparity—4% of the black defendants but 7% of white defendants received the death penalty.

Baldus et al. also divided the cases according to the combination of the race of the defendant and the race of the victim. They found that capital punishment was imposed in 22% of the cases with black defendants and white victims; 8% of the cases with white defendants and white victims; 1% of the cases with black defendants and black victims; and 3% of the cases with white defendants and black victims. As for prosecutorial penalty-seeking decisions, prosecutors asked for capital punishment in 70% of the black-kills-white cases; 32% of the white-kills-white cases; 15% of the black-kills-black cases; and 19% of the white-kill-black cases.

The Baldus study initially used multiple regression techniques to control for 230 variables; its subsequent regressions included only the theoretically or substantively most important explanatory variables. The study concluded that people killing white victims were more than four times as likely to receive death as those killing black victims. A parallel study using newer data and covering other states[31] came to very similar conclusions. No later research has seriously questioned these results.

The Baldus study was the main evidence used by the defendant in *McCleskey v. Kemp*[32] (1987), a case of a black man charged with killing a white, to argue for a reversal of the death sentence on the basis of racial discrimination. When *McCleskey* went to the Supreme Court, many predicted that the Court would dodge the issue by finding the empirical research unconvincing or not yet sufficient. To the surprise of many, the Court effectively mooted this line of research by its apparent willingness to concede that the Baldus study was accurate. But on McCleskey's claim that his death sentence therefore violated the equal protection clause, the Court followed established doctrine in requiring proof of intentional discrimination. And the statistical evidence in the Baldus study was not designed to show intent, and except in the case of extreme intentional discrimination in which the inference is inescapable, statistical evidence of discrimination will usually be consistent with a variety of causes. Although discriminatory intent cannot be ruled out in some death penalty cases, the discriminatory effects documented by Baldus may well have resulted from a complex mixture of half-conscious or unconscious decisions by various legal system actors, including judges, juries, and prosecutors. And as for McCleskey's alternative Eighth Amendment claim that the effects themselves rendered the death penalty unconstitutional, McCleskey lost because, paradoxically, the Court found that the implications of the Baldus study were too great for the system to bear: The Court assumed the causes of the discriminatory effect Baldus reported probably infected the entire law enforcement system, but the justices feared that if they recognized

---

31. S. Gross, R. Mauro, *Death and Discrimination* (1989).

32. McCleskey v. Kemp, 481 U.S. 279 (1987).

the defense in a capital case, the logic of the decision would effectively require that they put our entire criminal justice system into receivership.

    * * *

But regarding the perceived legitimacy of capital punishment, the increasing number of DNA acquittals during the past decade may be more important than these studies. These DNA acquittals include acquittals of many prisoners on death row and prisoners serving life sentences who would have been on death row had their alleged crimes not been committed during the period of the death penalty moratorium.[33] It is the sheer number of these cases that is so striking. Although death penalty supporters may have acknowledged, in principle, that mistakes can happen in death penalty cases, the general assumption before these DNA acquittals seems to have been that the legal system took its greatest care in cases in which execution was possible, and the chance of error in capital cases was in fact minimal. We now know this is not so, and we can put faces on people who, but for the system's slowness and their own good luck, might well have been executed for murders they did not commit. This human reality may prove to be more important than masses of social science evidence on deterrence and other issues in determining support for the death penalty in the long run.

NOTES AND QUESTIONS

1. Professor Joanna M. Shepherd looked at the studies by economists that found that capital punishment deterred murder and contrasted them with studies by sociologists and others that could not find evidence that this was the case.[34] She attempted to reconcile these findings. She noted that the studies by economists tended to focus on national averages where the results could mask the fact that they were driven by states such as Texas and Florida that use their death penalty aggressively. Those by other scholars dealt with what was happening in individual states that executed far fewer people. During the sample period, Texas condemned 668 people and executed 107. California condemned 560, but executed only 4. Utah condemned 17 and executed but 5.

She turned to the Dezhbakhsh, Rubin and Shepherd data set[35] which is mentioned in the Weisberg article. It is based on all United States counties and covers the years 1977 to 1996. She looked beyond the mere presence or absence of a death penalty statute on the books in a particular state. Instead, she asked whether each state with such a statute had actually used it. She found:

33. B. Scheck, P. Neufeld, J. Dwyer, *Actual Innocence* (2000).

34. Joanna M. Shepherd, "Deterrence Versus Brutalization: Capital Punishment's Differing Impacts Among States," 104 *Michigan Law Review* 203 (2005).

35. See Hashem Dezhbakhsh, Paul H. Rubin and Joanna M. Shepherd, "Does Capital Punishment Have a Deterrent Effect? New Evidence from Postmoratorium Panel Data," 5 *American Law and Economics Review* 344 (2003).

Of the twenty-seven states in which at least one execution occurred during the sample period, capital punishment deters murder in only six states. In contrast, in thirteen states, or more than twice as many, capital punishment actually *increases* murder. In eight states, capital punishment has no effect on the murder rate. . . .[36]

She said that a threshold effect exists. If a state executed less than nine people during the period 1977 to 1996, capital punishment had a net brutalizing effect, inducing more murders. If a state executed more than nine, then capital punishment deterred murder.

This design of this study did not permit Shepherd to explain why capital punishment could prompt more murders. She said that perhaps when the state took life, this suggested that murder was an appropriate solution to problems. In 1890, the French sociologist Gabriel Tarde argued that news of sensational crimes prompted some people to imitate the crimes. Leonard Berkowitz and Jacqueline Macaulay, "The Contagion of Criminal Violence," 34 *Sociometry* 238 (1971), looked at the data on crimes in the United States after the assassination of President John Kennedy, Richard Speck's murder of eight nurses in Chicago, and Charles Whitman's shooting of 45 people from the University of Texas tower. Immediately after these murders, there was a decrease in violent crime. However, soon thereafter the rate began climbing again. There was a substantial increase in the number of violent crimes after these three events. Would a highly publicized execution in a death penalty state deter a potential murder or would the violent death prompt some people to deal with their problems by killing, perhaps working harder to avoid getting caught? We could also note that in a capital punishment state, at least some murderers would have an incentive to kill potential witnesses who might testify against them or kill law enforcement officers seeking their arrest.

2.   Professors John J. Donohue and Justin Wolfers examine many of the death penalty studies very critically.[37] They note that in 1972, the United States Supreme Court found existing capital punishment statutes to be unconstitutional. In 1976, the Court allowed redrafted statutes calling for capital punishment to go into effect. Their conclusion is:

> Our key insight is that the death penalty—at least as it has been implemented in the United States since [the 1976] *Gregg* [case] ended the moratorium on executions—is applied so rarely that the number of homicides it can plausibly have caused or deterred cannot be reliably disentangled from the large year-to-year changes in the homicide rate caused by other factors.[38]

Donohue and Wolfers first look at the homicide and execution rates over the twentieth century. No clear correlation emerges from this long time series. The correlation between executions and homicides varies greatly over

36. Id. at 247.

37. See their "Uses and Abuses of Empirical Evidence in the Death Penalty Debate," 58 *Stanford Law Review* 791 (2005).

38. *Id.* at 794.

time. When the Supreme Court created a moratorium on executions from 1972 to 1976, the homicide rate climbed sharply. Executions began again in the late 1970s, and the number of homicides declined greatly during the 1990s. The decrease could be caused by the deterrent effect of restoring capital punishment. There might be other explanations. The authors note that many of the studies attempt to control for factors other than the death penalty that might affect homicide rates. However, still other factors that have been omitted from these studies may prevent the relationship between the death penalty and homicides from being captured accurately.

Donohue and Wolfers then look at two comparison groups. The results of these two comparisons at least give us reason to wonder whether the death penalty contributes much to the homicide rate. They first compare the United States and Canada from 1950 to 2001. Both nations used the death penalty in the 1950s, and the homicide trends were much the same. However, in 1961, Canada began a process whereby it limited the situations calling for the death penalty more and more. No one has been executed there since 1962. Nonetheless, the homicide rates in the two countries continued to be very similar. The United States Supreme Court decisions that created a moratorium on executions in America from 1972 to 1976, had no direct impact in Canada. Still, there was an increase in the homicide rate during this period in Canada that was roughly the same as that in the United States. In the 1990s, the homicide rate declined sharply in both nations, but Canada was not executing murderers then.

Donohue and Wolfers also consider what has happened in the six American states that did not have the death penalty at any point between 1960 and 2000. They compare the homicide rates in those states with the rates in states that had the death penalty. Both groups of states experienced similar increases in homicide rates from 1972 to 1976, and both had similar declines in the number of homicides in the 1990s.

Next Donohue and Wolfers look at many studies that used regression analysis to attempt to control for the possible effects of things such as national time trends that are common across states and such things as state economic conditions, demographics and trends in law enforcement. They find no coherent picture. From 1976 to 2004, Texas executed 336 people, the largest number of executions in any state with the death penalty. If, however, you omit Texas from your study, the impact of executions becomes statistically insignificant.[39]

39. Carol S. Steiker and Jordan M. Steiker, "A Tale of Two Nations: Implementation of the Death Penalty in 'Executing' Versus 'Symbolic' States in the United States," 84 *Texas Law Review* 1869 (2006), looks at Texas where the state does execute and California where, with some exceptions, the state does not. They offer an explanation: "We suspect that the odd situation of symbolic states—with all of its absurdities, waste of resources, and other serious costs—mediates the ambivalence toward capital punishment that is more prevalent in symbolic states than in executing ones." As the Steikers suggest, many states have the death penalty on the books, but they execute few if any of those convicted of crimes that could have provoked this sanction. However, the federal government has been seeking and obtaining more death sentences during the George W. Bush presidency. The sanction is not just

They consider Shepherd's paper where she finds that the few states that execute many people provoke most of the deterrence found in the econometric studies. She argues for a threshold effect. Donohue and Wolfers are not convinced. They consider several studies that looked at how often states use their death penalty. They say: "the annual number of executions fluctuates very little while the number of homicides varies dramatically." In such cases, it is "a difficult challenge to extract the execution-related signal from the noise in homicide rates."

States vary widely in population. If you compute the number of executions per 100,000 residents in a state, there is no statistically significant relationship between executions and homicides per capita. Dezhbakhsh, Rubin and Shepherd's study is sensitive to many specification effects. They said, for example, that they controlled for partisan influence on the homicide rate by considering the Republican presidential candidate's percentage of the state-wide vote in the most recent election. However, Donohue and Wolfers discovered that Dezhbakhsh and his collaborators actually used the share of Republican votes in six different presidential elections. If you use what they say they were going to measure—the Republican presidential candidate's percentage of the statewide vote in the most recent election—"their data show that each execution leads to 18 lives lost." That is, capital punishment seems to *increase* the homicide rate. Moreover, if you use Dezhbakhsh, Rubin and Shepherd's approach, you discover that executions for murder seem to cause more rape, assault, burglary and larceny but less auto theft and homicide. Increases in police and judicial spending are associated with a higher murder rate. Why would this be so? These hard-to-explain findings give us reason to wonder about the accuracy of the claim that the death penalty deters.

Donohue and Wolfers conclude: "The estimated effects of capital punishment on homicide rates change dramatically even with small changes in econometric specifications. Aggregating over all of our estimates, it is entirely unclear even whether the preponderance of evidence suggests that the death penalty causes more or less murder." How do we know, for example, how many actual killings of people in a city, county, state or the nation were "murders" for which the death penalty could have been imposed if they took place in a jurisdiction that had capital punishment? Do you see the problem? Remember that not all killings are murder, which is a legal category and not a description of a tangible thing. What do the reported data measure? Jeffrey Fagan, Franklin E. Zimring and Amanda Geller, "Capital Punishment and Capital Murder: Market Share and the Deterrent Effects of the Death Penalty," 84 *Texas Law Review* 1803 (2006), say that most studies that find a deterrent effect are based on the total number of nonnegligent homicides in a jurisdiction, despite the fact that only about a quarter of these cases would qualify for the death penalty under any standard. When you limit the study to

symbolic at the federal level. See Christopher Conkey and Gary Fields, "Federal Prosecutors Widen Pursuit of Death Penalty as States Ease Off," *Wall Street Journal*, February 3–4, 2007 at A1, A8.

those cases that under the law might get the death penalty, they find no deterrent effect.

Donohue and Wolfers quote another noted economist, Steven Levitt: "I really think not that the answer is 'yes' or 'no,'" said Levitt, "but that there's not enough information to figure it out. There may never be enough. It may just be a question that can't be answered." Long before Levitt spoke, Ernest van den Haag concluded that it is not possible to make a persuasive statistical case that the death penalty does or does not have a deterrent effect.[40] What are the special problems faced when we try to prove why someone did *not* do something? Suppose Mr. Jones argues with his neighbor Mr. Smith, and Smith's statements and conduct make Mr. Jones extremely angry. However, Mr. Jones does not kill Mr. Smith. Assume that the state in which they live has the death penalty and uses it. Can we say with any confidence that Mr. Jones was deterred by the threat of capital punishment?

3. If the evidence about the deterrent impact of the death penalty is uncertain, why do many legislators so often support it? James M. Galliher and John F. Galliher studied the debate in the New York State Senate and Assembly for nineteen consecutive years beginning in 1977.[41] New York finally passed a death penalty statute in March of 1995. Those legislators who supported a death penalty typically rarely mentioned research showing that it deterred crime. They found that the research showing no evidence of a deterrent effect of capital punishment flew in the face of "common sense." Moreover, the proponents questioned the motives of the social scientists who challenged a deterrent effect. They said that researchers were liberals. The researchers had manipulated data to support their policy preference. One legislator said that these studies "are the work of criminologists, of social scientists; and why they are called scientists, I don't know." Another asserted "[c]apital punishment is a deterrent, there is no question about it, and the findings of any studies notwithstanding." One state senator concluded that "[c]ommon sense and the fact that just about every responsible law enforcement group has come out in favor of the death penalty indicates that it is a deterrent." However, state legislators in other states have refused to enact a death penalty despite the popularity of the idea among many constituents.[42]

4. It is difficult to talk about the death penalty without considering issues related to race. Blume, Eisenberg and Wells looked at data about murder and the death sentence for twenty three years.[43] They found that

---

40. See Ernest van den Haag, "On Deterrence and the Death Penalty," 60 *Journal of Criminal Law, Criminology & Police Science* 141, 146 (1969). Van den Haag advocated the death penalty on grounds other than deterrence.

41. James M. Galliher and John F. Galliher, "A 'Commonsense' Theory of Deterrence and the 'Ideology' of Science: The New York State Death Penalty Debate," 92 *Journal of Criminal Law & Criminology* 307 (2002).

42. See Larry W. Koch and John F. Galliher, "Michigan's Continuing Abolition of the Death Penalty and the Conceptual Components of Symbolic Legislation," 2 *Social & Legal Studies* 323 (1993).

43. John Blume, Theodore Eisenberg, and Martin T. Wells, "Explaining Death Row's Population and Racial Composition," 1 *Journal of Empirical Legal Studies* 165 (2004).

death sentences in black defendant-white victim cases far exceed those in either black defendant-black victim or white defendant-white victim cases. They say, "[t]he disproportion survives because there are many more black defendant-black victim murders, which are underrepresented on death row, than there are black defendant-white victim murders, which are overrepresented on death row." Why might we find that black defendants convicted of killing a white victim are more often sentenced to death than in other kinds of cases?

Franklin Zimring[44] argues that where we once found lynch mobs, now we find people who demand executions of black defendants who have killed whites. The people who support capital punishment usually are also those who distrust government. However, he says, where there is a vigilante tradition, the governmental action now becomes an expression of community will. Steven F. Messner, Eric P. Baumer and Richard Rosenfeld studied the effects of distrust of government and exposure to a vigilante tradition on support for the death penalty.[45] They analyze responses from the General Social Survey of whites and blacks. They find that blacks who are distrustful of government oppose the death penalty. However, for whites extreme distrust of government is associated with a strong likelihood that the same people will favor the death penalty. The authors also find: "White respondents residing in states with a history of frequent lynching are significantly more likely to express support for the death penalty. This effect emerges despite an extensive array of controls for individual attributes and other contextual factors."[46] Soss, Langbein and Metelko report that their study shows that racial prejudice is a strong predictor of white support for capital punishment.[47] Moreover, if blacks live near a white respondent, the respondent is more likely to support the death penalty. However, the authors caution that we cannot dismiss white support for the death penalty as merely an expression of racial prejudice: "The sources of white support are diverse."[48] John K. Cochran and Mitchell B. Chamlin report that many studies show that whites are significantly more likely to support the death penalty than blacks.[49] They examined racial differences in socioeconomic status, religion/religiosity, political ideology, positions on right-to-life and other social issues, fear of crime and victimization experience, experience with the criminal justice system, philosophies of punishment and attribution styles. Controlling for all of these factors, differences in race remain as a key predictor of attitudes on capital punishment.[50]

44. Franklin E. Zimring, *The Cultural Contradictions of American Capital Punishment* (2003).

45. Steven F. Messner, Eric P. Baumer and Richard Rosenfeld, "Distrust of Government, the Vigilante Tradition, and Support for Capital Punishment," 40 *Law & Society Review* 559 (2006).

46. Id. at 582.

47. Joe Soss, Laura Langbein and Alan R. Metelko, "Why Do White Americans Support the Death Penalty?" 65 *Journal of Politics* 397 (2003).

48. Id. at 416.

49. John K. Cochran and Mitchell B. Chamlin, "The Enduring Racial Divide in Death Penalty Support," 34 *Journal of Criminal Justice* 85 (2006).

50. See, also, Baldus, Woodworth, Zuckerman, Weiner and Broffitt, "Racial Discrimination and the Death Penalty in the Post–Furman Era: An Empirical and Legal Overview,

5. James S. Liebman has written "The Overproduction of Death."[51] He describes the system of capital punishment in the United States as follows:

Since *Furman* [1972], an average of about 300 of the approximately 21,000 homicides committed in the United States each year have resulted in a death sentence. Close to 100% of those sentences are reviewed on state direct appeal and, if affirmed, in a state post-conviction proceeding, and, if affirmed again, on federal habeas corpus. Remarkably, during the twenty-three-year period of our statistical study, 1973–1995, the result of this process was the reversal by state direct appeal or state post-conviction courts of at least 47% of the capital judgments they reviewed, and federal habeas corpus reversal of 40% of the capital judgments that survived state review. During the study period, that is, state courts (mainly) and federal courts reversed 68%—i.e., *more than two of every three*—of the capital judgments that were fully reviewed.

This one-in-three figure, however, greatly *overestimates* the likelihood of execution, as is revealed by additional statistical windows on the system. For example, the Justice Department's annual study of the death penalty reports the outcome, as of the study date, of death sentences imposed in each prior year since 1973. Consider the outcomes of death sentences imposed in 1989. The cases of 103 of the 263 people sentenced to die that year had been resolved by the end of 1998 (when the last Justice Department report ends). Among those 103 inmates, 78 (76%) had their capital judgments overturned by a state or federal court; only 13 (<13%) had been executed (compared to 9 who died of other causes). By *this* measure, for every one death row inmate whose case was finally reviewed during that nine-year period and who was executed, exactly *six* inmates had their cases overturned in the courts.

This one-in-seven statistic still overestimates the likelihood of execution. It ignores the fact that there was *no* outcome as of nine years later for 160 (61%) of the 263 people sentenced to die in 1989. That is because the amount of state and federal judicial review needed to uncover the astonishingly high number of reversible legal errors found in capital judgments takes on average about eleven years per capital judgment. No wonder, then, that the approximately 3600 people on death row as of 1999 had been there while their cases underwent review in the courts for an average of 7.4 years. And no wonder that those 3600 death row inmates comprised well more than half of the approximately 6700 individuals sentenced to die in the proceeding *twenty-seven years*. So, not only are a large majority of capital judgments ultimately found to be seriously legally flawed by the courts; worse, *all* of them are suspended for eleven years on average while the massive error-detection operation proceeds. From this perspective, the best description of our capital punishment

with Recent Findings from Philadelphia," 83 *Cornell Law Review* 1638 (1998).

51. James S. Liebman, "The Overproduction of Death," 100 *Columbia Law Review* 2030 (2000).

system is that of the 6700 people sentenced to die between 1973 and 1999, only 598—*less than one in eleven*— were executed. About four times as many had their capital judgments overturned or were granted clemency.

What most condemned men and women do after being sentenced to die is wait—for eleven years, on average. And what most of them, in reality, are waiting *for* is not execution, but reversal of their capital judgments because of serious legal error.

Is this, though, old news? Given that the number of executions has risen dramatically as of late, aren't these one-in-three, one-in-seven and one-in-eleven estimates a thing of the past? Not so. Even in a banner year like 1999, when the number of executions reached a nearly fifty-year high of ninety-eight, only one death row inmate was executed for every three people added to the row in the same year. Thus, ... it is not a dramatic new will to kill, but the monotonous quarter-century drip, drip, drip of men and women accumulating on death row and gradually exhausting their appeals, that has caused executions to rise.[52]

Professor Liebman argues that we should consider the rewards and harms of imposing undeserved death sentences. "[I]f you were a capital prosecutor, it might be in your interest to obtain as many capital sentences as possible— including even undeserved ones—along with the political capital (pun intended) they bring with them, because the onus of any mistakes you make will fall elsewhere."[53] Liebman continues his article, and offers an elaborate proposal for reform.

Professor Liebman paints a picture of the overproduction of flawed death sentences. Are we sure that so many are in fact flawed? Could it be that courts dislike the death penalty and are reversing as many of these cases as they can? On balance, are states paying a heavy price for what may be a small amount of deterrence flowing from the death penalty?

6. The death penalty can serve functions other than deterring murders. For example, consider the case of Christopher Ochoa who served twelve years in prison for a rape and murder he did not commit.[54] In 1988, Ochoa was picked up for questioning after the rape and murder of a 20–year–old Pizza Hut manager in Austin, Texas, who was attacked as she prepared to open the restaurant. Over two 12–hour interrogations, police lied to Ochoa and threatened him. They told him that he would get the death penalty unless he confessed. Ochoa became convinced that he was doomed. His only choice was whether he would get death or prison. He signed a confession. In 1996, the real killer confessed, but the Texas authorities did nothing. In 1999, Ochoa wrote to the University of Wisconsin Law School's Innocence Project. The law

---

52. Id. at 2052–57.
53. Id. at 2072.
54. See Keith A. Findley and John Pray, "Lessons From the Innocent," 47 *Wisconsin*

Academy Review 33 (Fall 2001); Keith A. Findley and Michael S. Scott, "The Multiple Dimensions of Tunnel Vision in Criminal Cases," 2006 *Wisconsin Law Review* 291, 332–33.

students discovered that the physical evidence from the case still existed, and requested DNA tests. Late in 2000, the tests showed that Ochoa had nothing to do with the crime and supported the real killer's confession. In January of 2001, the district attorney's office and the defense filed a joint application to set aside Ochoa's conviction. Ochoa was freed, became a University of Wisconsin Law Student and when he graduated, he was elected by his classmates as one of three student speakers at the ceremony. At least one function of the death penalty is as a tool in plea bargaining. At least, in this case, it proved to be such a coercive threat that it caused a defendant to confess to a crime that he had not committed. Is this an argument against the death penalty or an argument that should be directed to reforms of police interrogation of suspects?

(4.3) The Deterrence Curve

Lawrence M. Friedman, *The Legal System: A Social Science Perspective*
(1975).

In any case, there is no simple, linear relationship between sanctions and sanctioned behavior. Suppose we plotted on a graph the rate of overtime parking at given levels of fine. As fines rose, we would expect the violation rate to fall, but we do not expect a perfect straight line on the graph. Doubling a $5 fine, in other words, will (enforcement staying constant) increase compliance, but compliance will not necessarily double. A threat of twenty years in jail will probably not be twice as effective as a threat of ten years. We expect some sort of curvilinear relationship, a gradual flattening out. At some point, new inputs of fine will produce less and less new compliance, and one may or may not reach a zero effect. This is because, as compliance rises, there are fewer people to affect, and those few are the most difficult cases. One approaches a saturation point, a point of diminishing returns. This is another reason why capital punishment seems to have so little effect in the United States; murder is so heavily sanctioned by peers, conscience, and the state that the pool of potential murderers is small. Also, a person or group may become so saturated with punishment stimuli that nothing worse or more punishing is possible. A man about to be shot will risk anything; he has nothing to lose. His tormenters have lost the power to deter him with additional actions or threats. Totalitarian societies can reach this point. Gestapo tactics, concentration camps, and indiscriminate shooting may produce an atmosphere where many people feel life is intolerable, and nothing could be worse. Hence, more terror will have no effect; it merely drives people to join the resistance. If even the innocent face random, senseless terror, then revolution seems little more fearful than the risks of everyday life.

There are, alas, ample historical examples of such societies of terror. Gresham Sykes has made a similar point about prison life. He studied prisoners in the New Jersey State Prison and found that they misbehaved at what he thought a very high rate. The custodians, "far from being omnipotent rulers," were "engaged in a continuous struggle to maintain order"; in the struggle, they frequently failed. One reason was that officials were "dangerously close to the point where the stock of legitimate punishments has been exhausted and ... the few punishments which are left have lost their potency." In this prison, Sykes felt, the curve had flattened out.[55]

Each legal act will have its own deterrence curve. Perhaps no two curves are exactly the same. That is, any intervention of the legal system—any rule or order communicated to one or more subjects and buttressed by a sanction, positive or negative—will affect behavior more or less, depending on the level of sanction threatened or promised. Many factors affect the slope and the shape of this deterrence curve. The following are some of the basic factors:

I. Characteristics of the threat or promise

   A. The nature of the sanction. Is it a reward or a punishment? Is it light or severe?

   B. The perceived risk of suffering a negative sanction or enjoying a positive one.

   C. The speed at which the sanction is delivered. Is it immediate or far in the future?

II. Characteristics of the persons subject to the sanction

   A. How many people are subject to the sanction? It is easier, for example, to achieve high enforcement of rules that apply only to a few prominent people or entities.

   B. The personality type of the subjects, or the culture in which the subjects live.

III. Characteristics of the behavior to be controlled

   A. How easy or difficult is it to detect and visit punishment on the behavior? For example, it is very hard to stamp out dangerous thoughts, much easier to burn dangerous books.

   B. What is the nature of the demand for the behavior to be controlled? Some behavior is hard to control, because people find it so desirable that they will not readily give it up, or so unpleasant that the law cannot easily stimulate it. For some behavior, there is strong and relatively inelastic demand; sanctions have comparatively little effect; other behavior is quite elastic and responds very quickly to sanctions.

55. Gresham Sykes, *The Society of Captives: A Study of a Maximum Security Prison* 42, 51 (1958). Sykes also felt that "the reward side of the picture has been largely stripped away." The prison gave away all its privileges at the outset—time off for good behavior, for example was subtracted from the prisoner's sentence the day he entered prison. The prisoner therefore found himself "unable to win any significant gains by means of compliance."

NOTES AND QUESTIONS

1.   Some studies, as we have seen, suggest that capital punishment does not in fact deter murder, compared to (say) life imprisonment. Assuming this is true, does the concept of the deterrence curve help explain this finding?

2.   The "deterrence curve" is presumably different for each particular crime or offense. Let us assume that one overtime parking violation out of five is caught. If we have a fine of $1, probably most people will simply park and take their chances. At higher levels of fines, we will get more compliance. If we start towing away cars, we get still more. But at some point, it will be almost impossible to get more "bang" out of more severe punishments.

What would the deterrence curve look like for rape? armed robbery? embezzlement? shooting deer out of season? gambling in a state where gambling is against the law?

3.   It should be clear by now that all studies of deterrence have their difficulties, and in particular all of them are bedeviled by problems of measurement and data. How good are the data on which these studies are based? For expressions of concern about the data upon which much of the statistical study about law is based, see, for example, James A. Inciardi, "The Uniform Crime Reports: Some Considerations on their Shortcomings and Utility," 6 *Public Data Use* 3 (1978); Larry J. Cohen and Mark I. Lichbach, "Alternative Measures of Crime: A Statistical Evaluation," 23 *Sociological Quarterly* 253 (1982); Theodore Eisenberg & Margo Schlanger, "The Reliability of the Administrative Office of the U.S. Courts Database: An Initial Empirical Analysis," 78 *Notre Dame Law Review* 1455 (2003). On the special problems of measurement of crimes committed by juveniles (or by juveniles and adults), see Franklin E. Zimring, "Kids, Groups and Crime: Some Implications of a Well–Known Secret," 72 *Journal of Criminal Law & Criminology* 867 (1981).

4.   Are studies of deterrence too mechanistic? Do they tend too much to treat criminals as rational calculators? Do they treat citizens as if they were constantly and rationally toting up the likelihood of getting caught and what the punishment would be, and carefully measuring this against the amount of benefit or swag they would be likely to get from their crime?

The criticism—that this is too simple a picture or just is plain wrong—has been frequently leveled in particular against economists like Ehrlich who study deterrence. Lempert, "Desert and Deterrence: An Assessment of the Moral Bases of the Case for Capital Punishment," 79 *Michigan Law Review* 1177 (1981), quotes a famous passage from Sir James Fitzjames Stephen, a 19th century British legal historian. Stephen said:

> Some men probably abstain from murder because they fear that if they committed murder they would be hanged. Hundreds of thousands abstain from it because they regard it with horror. One great reason why they regard it with horror is that murderers are hanged.

Lempert remarks:

> The argument is reasonable. It may be that the main benefit of capital punishment is that it teaches people that it is wrong to kill. But the opposite position is also reasonable. It may be that capital punishment teaches people that life is not sacred and that killing is not always a moral wrong (p. 1190).

Which view strikes you as more likely?

For another kind of attack on the general behavioral theories that underlie research on such subjects as sanctions, see the Concluding Word at the end of this chapter.

5. What role does personality play in explaining why people commit crimes? At one time, many people, including scientists, believed there were "born criminals" and even that there were physical signs that gave the game away. The anthropologist E.A. Hooton, in a book published in 1939, noted that criminals seemed to have "low and sloping foreheads," their noses tended to be "higher in the root and in the bridge, and more frequently undulating or concavo-convex" than normal people, and rapists had "narrow foreheads and elongated, pinched noses." E.A. Hooton, *Crime and the Man* 124, 367 (1939). See Lawrence M. Friedman, *Crime and Punishment in American History* 335–339 (1993).

Serious scholars have given up the idea of physical signs of criminal character, but social and personality theories are another question. Many people have used social variables—unemployment rates, poverty, peer group cultures, and the like—to account for crime and deviance. Michael R. Gottfredson and Travis Hirschi, in *A General Theory of Crime* (1990), frame their theory in terms of "low self-control." Criminal acts, they argue, "provide immediate gratification of desires." Criminal acts are quick and exciting, but require little skill or planning. However, they offer "few or meager long-term benefits." They appeal, then, to people with "low self-control," who tend to be "adventuresome, active, and physical. Those with high levels of self-control tend to be cautious, cognitive, and verbal" (p. 89).

How would you go about testing an idea like this? Does the theory strike you as plausible? Would you expect those who participate in various types of crime to be the same kinds of people?

6. The law has more tricks up its sleeves than sanctions (both rewards and punishments). One way of getting compliance is by structuring a situation so that compliance is easier than non-compliance. Karl Llewellyn, the famous legal theorist, who died in 1962, liked to talk about the highway "cloverleaf." This, of course, is a method of structuring entrance to and exit from a major highway or freeway. Legislatures could pass laws regulating or prohibiting left turns across busy lanes of oncoming traffic. However, these laws require police and traffic courts to enforce them. The cloverleaf is more effective. The roadway or ramp sharply turns off the main highway to the right, and then turns to cross over the road on a bridge, or under it through a tunnel. If the lanes of the main highway are separated by a fence or a ditch, it is almost impossible to make an illegal left turn. Also, highway engineers can force

drivers to slow from superhighway speeds by the way they bank the clover-leaf. The socially desired behavior is far easier than deviance.

The legal system is full of devices like the "cloverleaf." There are all sorts of structures, forms and arrangements that force "compliance" along certain lines or make non-compliance difficult. For example, federal income tax is withheld from wages. This makes it much harder to avoid paying what is owed. Compliance is much greater on income from which tax is withheld than on other income. For a brief period automobiles would not start unless seat-belts were fastened. If anything, this "cloverleaf" was too effective and proved to be very unpopular. This law was changed. Some kinds of "cloverleaf" might make a dramatic difference to law enforcement: rather than crack down on drunk drivers, we could build cars that would not start if a driver's breath contains detectable amounts of alcohol. Instead of locking people up in jails, we may order them to be only in certain places and attach an electronic device to their bodies so that they may be monitored wherever they go.

What other kinds of "cloverleaf" can you think of in the criminal justice system? Can you think of examples on the civil side of the legal system? Why don't we see more cloverleaves? Edward K. Cheng, "Structural Laws and the Puzzle of Regulating Behavior," 100 *Northwestern University Law Review* 655 (2006), argues that while many structural means of regulating behavior are possible, there are good reasons why they are not used. For example, he says that automated systems such as speed cameras could cut speeding a great deal. However, these systems expose violations so efficiently that they often provoke resistance. It seems likely that many members of the public do not want speed limits enforced strictly. When the police use radar to determine who is speeding, the response is some decrease in speed but also the purchase of radar detectors. Truckers radio warnings and flash their lights to signal to others that the police are using radar ahead. See, also, Neal Kumar Katyal, "Architecture as Crime Control," 111 *Yale Law Journal* 1039 (2002) ("Design should: (1) create opportunities for natural surveillance by residents, neigh-bors, and bystanders; (2) instill a sense of territoriality so that residents develop proprietary attitudes and outsiders feel deterred from entering a private space; (3) build communities and avoid social isolation; and (4) protect targets of crime.").

(4.4) Interrupted Time Series Studies of Deterrence of Drinking and Driving

H. Laurence Ross

in John Hagan (ed.) *Deterrence Reconsidered: Methodological Innovations* (1982).

... Drinking and driving has been recognized as a cause of traffic crashes for many years, and punitive law has long been regarded as a promising tool in its control. Concern with the problem has increased over time as informa-tion has accumulated concerning the costs of crashes and the role of alcohol in their causation, and dissatisfaction has mounted with regard to the effectiveness of classical control efforts. This situation has led in recent years to a large number of efforts worldwide to redefine and reinforce the laws dealing with drinking and driving, permitting the application of quasi-experimental designs, notably interrupted time series analysis, in evaluating the results obtained.

These efforts occur in a uniquely fortunate research setting for investigating deterrence through law. An important characteristic of drinking-and-driving law in this regard is its relative divorce from other systems of social control. One is less likely to confuse legal effects in this area with those due to custom and morality than in the study of more traditional criminality. Paradoxically, the relative triviality of traffic law in general, which in the past led to its general disregard by criminology, makes its study more enlightening in understanding the effects of legal sanctions.

Another important advantage of drinking-and-driving studies is the availability of relatively good-quality indexes of the target behavior provided by series of fatal crashes, especially when refined according to time of day and number of vehicles involved. Single-vehicle fatal crashes at night overwhelmingly involve the presence of alcohol, and changes in indexes like these reflect well the extent of alcohol-influenced driving. Because fatalities are involved, the "dark figure" problem frequently found in studies of traditional criminality is avoided. Moreover, the gathering of those figures by hospitals and health departments on a regular basis provides data series that are usually insulated from political forces with interests in demonstrating results one way or the other.

A particularly attractive advantage of drinking-and-driving law studies is that innovations in this type of law very often meet the criteria for utilization in interrupted time series analysis. These criteria include an independent variable that changes abruptly at a single point in time, along with dependent variables that are expected to shift sharply and simultaneously and that are reliably measured over an extended time period. In the case at hand the independent variable is a change in the drinking-and-driving law, which usually has its inception at a particular date, and the dependent variables are the crash series along with other series useful in interpreting the mechanism of changes, such as traffic mileage data and sales of alcoholic beverages....

The interrupted time series analytical method is one of the best quasi-experimental methods available for yielding conclusions immune to the plausible rival explanations that frequently threaten conclusions based on field research.

For example the observed change in a dependent variable can be compared with expectation of routine, normal or "chance" variation, by means of newly available tests of statistical significance to determine its likelihood of reflecting merely the "instability" of the curve. The plausibility of the change being explained as a "regression" artifact—a return to more normal levels following unusual and extreme ones—can be ascertained by tracing the course of the curve of the independent variable prior to the legal intervention.

Likewise the possibility that the observed change at the time of the intervention formed part of some longer secular trend in the data can be investigated in the series, providing control for "maturation," "instrumentation," and "testing" effects among others. Finally although the interrupted time series does not control for "history"—the possibility that some simultaneous event rather than the legal intervention produced the change—it is often possible to control for this rival explanation through comparison of series in similar jurisdictions or under different theoretically relevant conditions (such as comparing nighttime with daytime fatalities).

In the following pages I will summarize the evaluative literature concerning three types of legal interventions related to drinking and driving (1) adoptions of "Scandinavian-type" laws in world jurisdictions, (2) enforcement campaigns based on these laws, and (3) formal and informal increments in threatened severity of sanctions for violating drinking-and-driving laws. The bulk of studies cited have used interrupted time series analytical methods, although there are considerable differences in the formality and sophistication of the designs. The more formal and elaborate studies have yielded the more informative and reliable results, but the cumulation of findings based as well on less formal and less adequate investigations supports the generalizability of the findings.

ADOPTIONS OF "SCANDINAVIAN–TYPE" DRINKING–AND–DRIVING LAWS

In the early twentieth century, as the hazards posed by alcohol influenced driving in countries with mass automobile populations became evident, laws restricting this behavior were everywhere adopted. These typically took the form of prohibitions against "drunk driving" or "driving under the influence of alcohol." As further knowledge concerning the problem accumulated, these laws, which I term "classical," were perceived to be ineffective from the viewpoint of deterrence. Among the reasons for this conclusion were the fact that only a tiny fraction of drivers whose skills and abilities were importantly affected by alcohol were apprehended by traditional police patrol, and that the penalties received by those few who were convicted were regarded as trivial.

A new type of law addressing the problem was developed in Norway and Sweden in the years just prior to World War II. This Scandinavian-type law defined the prohibited conduct as driving with blood concentration (BAC) in excess of an arbitrary standard, to be ascertained with the aid of "scientific" tests of breath and blood, and provided for relatively severe punishments. In the Norwegian law of 1936 loss of license and a mandatory prison sentence were prescribed for driving with more than .05 percent BAC (a concentration obtainable by the average male consuming three drinks in one hour); in the Swedish law of 1941, the license was suspended at .08 percent and prison was mandatory at 15 percent BAC. Laws based on similar principles were adopted elsewhere following the war, most notably in Britain in 1967. Favorable reports of the British experience resulted in widespread adoptions of Scandinavian-type laws throughout the world during the following decades. Many of these adoptions have been subject to evaluation, although the quality of the research has not always been adequate. . . .

Great Britain

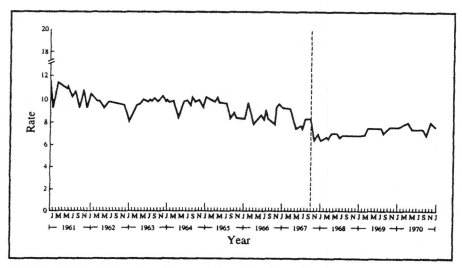

FIGURE 2   U.K. Fatality Rate, Corrected for Month with Seasonal Variations Removed

    Great Britain adopted a Scandinavian-type drinking-and-driving law, The Road Safety Act of 1967, amid great publicity and great controversy, the latter centering on the originally proposed "random stops" permitted to the police to test drivers' breath for BAC levels. This provision was withdrawn in the final version of the law, but British police were empowered to test drivers involved in a traffic violation or an accident, regardless of fault, a provision authorities judged to retain significant elements of random testing. The Road Safety Act prohibited driving or attempting to drive with a BAC in excess of .08 percent. Its most feared penalty was a mandatory one-year license suspension, apparently far less severe than the prison sentences meted out in Scandinavia.

    However, in contrast to the Scandinavian case, the deterrent effectiveness of the Road Safety Act was clearly demonstrable by interrupted time series analysis. Figure 5.4 shows the deseasonalized time series for crash-related fatalities in Britain from 1961 to 1970. The drop in October of 1967 can be seen; it is statistically significant. The most interesting comparison obtained is shown in Figure 5.5, presenting deseasonalized data on serious crashes during weekend nights, when alcohol-influenced driving is relatively common, and Figure 5.6, presenting similar data for the weekday commuting hours when alcohol-influenced driving is quite rare. The effect of the law is clearly seen in the former and, as expected, is absent from the latter. Figure 5.5 also reveals clearly the temporary nature of the Road Safety Act's deterrent effect. Its impact began to decline almost immediately. The existence of an impor-

404

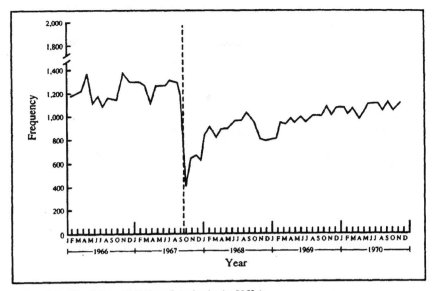

FIGURE 3   Fatalities and Serious Injuries in the U.K.*

*Combined for Friday 10 p.m.–midnight; Saturday midnight–4 a.m.; Saturday 10 p.m.–midnight; Sunday midnight–4 a.m.; corrected for weekend days per month and with seasonal variations removed.

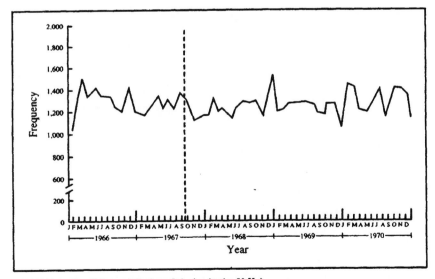

FIGURE 4   Fatalities and Serious Injuries in the U.K.*

*Combined for Monday–Friday 7 a.m.–10 a.m. and 4 p.m.–5 p.m.; corrected for weekdays per month and with seasonal variations removed.

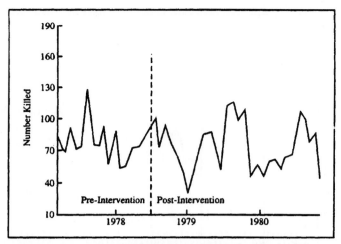

FIGURE 5 Crash-Related Deaths in France. Friday and Saturday, 9 p.m.–3 a.m.

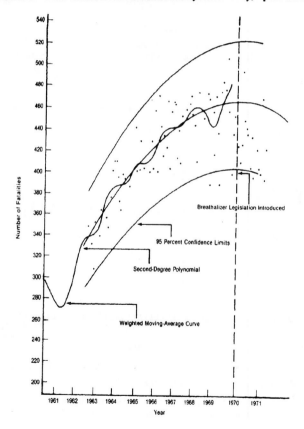

tant effect initially, disappearing over a period of several months, was further noted in independent studies of the proportion of casualties in drinking hours and of the proportion of fatally injured drivers with illegal BACs.

France

Nearly equally controversial in its setting was the French law of July 12, 1978, prohibiting driving with a BAC exceeding .08 percent and providing for mandatory license suspension under certain circumstances. The most remarkable feature of the French law was that, unlike the case in Britain or Scandinavia until 1975, the police were authorized to set up roadblocks to test all drivers for blood alcohol by means of a screening breath test, without the need to show the driver's involvement in an accident or traffic code violation, or any prior suspicion of his or her being influenced by alcohol. This provision was bitterly opposed by civil libertarians but was included in the final legislation nonetheless. A segment of French total fatality data is presented as an interrupted time series in Figure 5.7. The figure shows both an initial decline and a reversion to the status quo ante which are confirmed by statistical analysis. The decline was a statistically significant 173 deaths per month, but 95 percent of the effect had disappeared within 12 months....

. . .

Canada

The Criminal Law Amendment Act embodying the Scandinavian approach to drinking-and-driving law took effect in Canada on December 1, 1969. Although it was inspired by reports of the effectiveness of the British Road Safety Act of 1967, there are important differences between these laws. The Canadian police were empowered to require breath tests only on the basis of "reasonable and proper" grounds to believe a driver is impaired by alcohol. As in Britain, the Canadian legislation set a BAC limit of .08 percent. Penalties for failing the test included fines up to $1000 and/or prison for up to six months, but license suspension was discretionary with the court.

The Canadian legislation has been subjected to two independent evaluations. The first analyzed data for injury involving crashes and fatal crashes for the Province of Ontario separately and for Canada as a whole. ... Their formal analysis follows the interrupted time series analytical model, although the statistical analysis is unorthodox. The analysts' conclusions were positive but guarded: fatalities in Canada following the inception of the law were nine percent below the trend, and the decline was considerably greater than that in the United States, offered as a control jurisdiction. They also noted dissipation of the effect within a year. Their principal reservations had to do with the fact that night time and weekend crashes did not show stronger variations.

The second evaluation by epidemiologists using the same database but different methods was more positive and less guarded ... The writer concluded that the rate of incidence for crash related death and injuries on the basis of population at risk declined by more than 9 deaths and injuries per 100,000 population per quarter, during the first five quarters of the new law and the bulk of the saving was during the nighttime hours.

Inasmuch as observers of the Canadian case concluded that the effect of their law was considerably less than that of the British law, the differences in the situations should be stressed. The level of threat posed by the Canadian law appears to have been lower. Police were not empowered to test a driver's breath without specific suspicion of alcohol influence, and because police cars did not carry testing devices in Canada the demand for a test was more difficult and therefore perhaps less likely to be made. License suspension was not mandatory but at the discretion of the court. Moreover the threat was not as widely publicized in Canada, perhaps because the apparent success of the British law and the more moderate provisions of the proposed Canadian legislation rendered the latter less controversial. . . .

ENFORCEMENT CAMPAIGNS

In addition to occasions for the adoption of laws following the Scandinavian model, the predictions of deterrence theory can be tested by interrupted time series analysis where these laws are reinforced through enforcement campaigns. The campaigns are designed to increase police activity, and with publicity to increase the perception among the relevant population of the certainty of punishment in the event of drinking-and-driving infractions. Notable evaluations have occurred concerning campaigns in Britain, New Zealand and Victoria. The American ASAP experience is also relevant.

The Cheshire "Blitz"

In 1975 it was commonly belief in Great Britain that the Road Safety Act of 1967 had lost its effectiveness. A concerned police chief devised the experiment in the County of Cheshire, of having his men demand breath tests in all situations where this was authorized, between 10 p.m. and 2 a.m. for one week. There resulted 284 tests during the "experimental" period compared with 31 during the previous year, and 38 drivers were found to have illegal BACs compared with 13 in the prior year. Encouraged, the chief expanded his "experiment" to include the hours between 9 p.m. and 4 a.m. during the month of September. He also instructed his men to obtain breath tests whenever possible during a control series of hours, 2 p.m. to 5 p.m. On this occasion the press learned of the measure, and cries of protest rang out in the media that the chief was engaging in "random" testing which had been expressly eliminated from the law by Parliament.

A result was the appearance of a deterrent effect, evident in monthly series of crash-linked serious injuries and fatalities for Cheshire in September of 1975. This is presented in Figure 7. The drop is statistically significant even for the small data base on which the series rests.

The drop was also visible in casualties restricted to night time hours though in that case, with a very small data base the change did not quite reach statistical significance. No comparable change was found for low-alcohol consumption hours of the day.

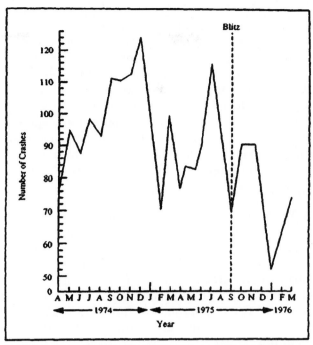

FIGURE 7   Crashes Producing Serious or Fatal Injuries in Cheshire, England

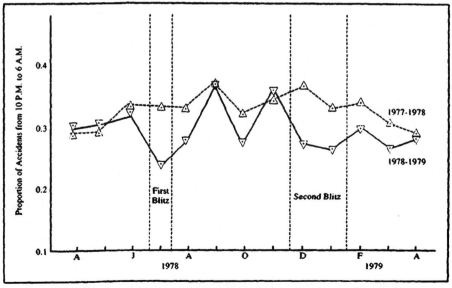

FIGURE 8   Ratio of Nighttime to Total Serious Crashes in New Zealand in the Vicinity of the Enforcement Blitzes

409

The New Zealand "Blitzes"

Although the 1969 New Zealand law was judged by its evaluator not to have produced important deterrent effects, intensified enforcement campaigns during the last part of July and in December of 1978 were found to be effective. Screening tests were quadrupled in the first blitz, and doubled in the second, and both enforcement efforts were supported by official publicity campaigns. Evaluation included studies of liquor consumption in rental ballrooms, road injuries reported to a group of cooperating hospitals, claims filed with the Accident Compensation Commission and serious crashes. Figure 8 presents the ratio of nighttime to total crashes which seems particularly convincing evidence for the deterrent effectiveness of the blitzes.

Enforcement Campaigns in Melbourne Australia

The state of Victoria adopted provisions for random breath testing of drivers in roadblocks in 1976, but use of this technique was initially very limited. However periods of intensified enforcement occurred in Melbourne in 1977 and 1978. The evaluation employed the criteria of reductions in crash fatalities, in serious casualty crashes, and in BACs among driver casualties at night. Changes in the patrolled areas of Melbourne were compared with those in selected control areas. The evaluation was flawed by various methodological deficiencies, but taken at face value the findings led to the conclusion of a substantial deterrent effect.

The American Alcohol Safety Action Projects (ASAPs)

In the early 1970s, 35 projects were funded in various locations throughout the United States embodying, among other things, increases in police patrol for drinking drivers and improvements in the processing of accused offenders in the courts. The typical project increased arrests by a factor of 2.5. Evaluations were planned for each site and for the projects taken together. The site-by-site evaluations were of generally poor quality and are thus not considered dependable. However a formal evaluation by the U.S. Department of Transportation (1979) compared changes in nighttime crashes in the ASAP communities with daytime crashes in the same communities, with experiences in matched control communities, and with national trends. Data from 12 of the 35 sites showed statistically significant diminutions in night time fatal crashes. Although this fraction is not impressive, the authors credibly argued that sites with low initial crash rates and those with growing populations would be less likely to show large reductions. Among those 13 sites with three or more nighttime fatal crashes per month and a growth rate of less than 10 percent, 8 showed significant reductions in nighttime fatal crashes, a more impressive fraction. It was also the case that a correlation between the level of enforcement and the reduction in nighttime fatalities was visible in these 13 selected sites.

SEVERITY

A few evaluations were found or situations in which penalties for alcohol-impaired driving were substantially increased without accompanying increases in enforcement.

The Chicago Crackdown on Drinking Drivers

The supervising judge for Chicago's Traffic Court decreed that during the Christmas holidays in 1970 all convicted drinking drivers would receive seven-day jail sentences. Broad claims were made for the effectiveness of this effort. However, submission of the Chicago crash data to interrupted time series analysis led to the conclusion that the lower rate following December 1970 could not be distinguished from chance variation. Moreover, data from Milwaukee chosen as a comparison city showed a greater decrease though again the decrease was not significant. Official files show that the jail sanction was not frequently applied during the crackdown, and it is possible that the public did not know or believe that penalties had changed. Where drivers were accused of alcohol-impaired driving in the absence of BAC evidence the proportion of convictions declined during the crackdown.

The "Traffictown" Crackdown

A similar experience was reported in a city of 30,000 in New South Wales, Australia, where a local magistrate increased convictions and penalties for drinking drivers. Analysis of this campaign found that serious crashes did not decline perceptibly, but reported crashes decreased and the proportions of crash-involved drivers charged by the police dropped significantly.

The Finnish Law of 1950

Until very recently the Finnish approach to drinking-and-driving law relied on heavy penalties rather than on procedures for BAC testing as in Norway and Sweden. In 1950, Finland increased the maximum penalty for alcohol-impaired driving, set in 1937 at two years in prison, to four years with the possibility of six years in the event of serious bodily injury associated with the violation and seven in the event of death. Typical sentences for alcohol-impaired driving ranged from three to six months in practice, far longer than sentences in Norway and Sweden, and the driver's license was lost for between two and three years on the first offense and permanently on the second.

Interrupted time series analysis was applied to the doubling of the maximum penalty for alcohol-impaired driving in 1950. Although there was a decline in crash-related fatalities in that year, which with certain assumptions could be considered significant, it is unreasonable to attribute it to the change in the drinking-and-driving law. This is because the drop was greater for less serious casualties (where alcohol is a smaller factor) than more serious, and no drop occurred in the series for single-vehicle crashes (in which alcohol is a major factor), whereas multiple-vehicle crashes declined considerably. The

411

conclusion is that greatly increased severity of the drinking-and-driving law in Finland probably did not affect the target behavior.

CONCLUSION

The literature reviewed here finds that adoptions of Scandinavian type laws and campaigns to enforce these laws seem capable of producing important deterrent effects on drinking and driving. However, in all cases in which deterrent effectiveness was noted, it proved to be temporary, disappearing within months of its attainment. My interpretation of this phenomenon is that these legal innovations were successful because they raised drivers' perceptions of the certainty with which they were likely to be punished if they drank.... The deterrence theoretical model is grounded in perception rather than actual levels of threat. Particularly where the new laws and campaigns were most strongly resisted, as in the case of the British Road Safety Act and the Cheshire blitz, public perception of the likelihood of punishment may very well have increased due to the publicity and newsworthiness of the legal changes.

However, in no reported case were the chances of apprehension and conviction raised to very important levels. In Britain, the chances of a driver encountering a breath test in the late 1960s were about one in every two million vehicle miles driven. A Canadian observer writes that according to official estimates there are 26,000 kilometers of impaired driving for every drinking-and-driving charge. In the United States, estimates of the proportion of alcohol-impaired drivers being apprehended run between 1 in 2000 and 1 in 200, the latter concerning driving on patrolled roads during the Kansas City ASAP. In Sweden, ... [a writer] estimates that the real incidence of drinking-and-driving offenses is at least 200 times higher than the reported incidence. In short, it seems a reasonable speculation that notorious and publicized measures directed to drinking-and-driving offenses may increase the perceived probability of punishment, but that the actual level of enforcement has proven to be low. In these circumstances, learning occurs and drivers' perceptions of risk decline toward prior levels. There is not much literature directly reporting empirical data on this matter, but the occasional study dealing with the perceived risk of punishment ... supports this speculation.

The matter is otherwise concerning severity. The three studies evaluating efforts to increase the severity of penalties provide little evidence supporting the effectiveness of these efforts. The doubling of very severe penalties in Finland apparently had no effect on alcohol impaired driving. In Chicago and "Traffictown" the situation of drinking drivers did change, but in unexpected and undesired ways. The proportion of reported violations may have decreased, and the actual punishment of offenders may have diminished, due to efforts of violators and legal personnel to avoid the harsh punishments. In short, the literature concerning drinking-and-driving law supports the theoretical model of deterrence in the specific hypothesis that the extent of the proscribed behavior is a positive function of the perceived certainty of punishment. It does not provide support for the hypothesis that proscribed behavior is reduced as a function of the severity of punishment. However, this finding has to be understood as obtained on the background of very low levels of actual and perceived certainty of punishment. . . . It is likely that the variables in the deterrence model are effective only on reaching a threshold level, and that certainty and severity interact. Thus, severity cannot be expected to have an effect on the background of subthreshold levels of certainty, nor can certainty have an effect on the background or subthreshold levels of severity. Research in the drinking-and-driving law area has not studied increments in marginal severity on the background of meaningful levels of certainty of punishment. It is possible that continued current interest in controlling drinking and driving by legal means may lead to situations in which this question can be studied. . . .

NOTES AND QUESTIONS

1.   Ross finds that severe drunk driving laws have a significant, but only temporary, deterrent effect. What accounts for the brevity of the impact? What, if anything, do these results tell us about the relative deterrent effects of severity and certainty of punishment?

2.   What policy recommendations follow from Ross's research? What would be the best way to deter drunk driving? Do the results he reports support the claim that it is useful to set up occasional roadblocks, and check drivers to see if they are sober? Can we do this constitutionally? If so, would officials who put in place such policies suffer political costs?

Daphne D. Newaz worked with a criminal defense firm, and her husband was an assistant district attorney. Based on this experience, she argues that the following story is commonplace in America:

An individual has only one drink and is not intoxicated. That individual drives home and does not use a signal as he is turning into his home street. He is pulled over by a police officer. That officer notices a smell of alcohol on his breath. The individual tells the officer that he has had only one drink. The official performs field sobriety tests on the individual, and because of the inherent problems with the field sobriety system, notes a number of clues of intoxication. [These field tests involve such things as walking a straight line and turning around in a particular manner] The individual then refuses to provide a chemical sample because he knows that the punishment for refusal is less severe than it is for drunk driving. Furthermore, he feels that giving the police potentially incriminating evidence violates his right against self-incrimination. In short, the individual is arrested and charged with DWI [driving while intoxicated] based on the flimsy evidence of field sobriety tests. The individual is then forced to spend thousands of dollars to get out of jail and hire an attorney. He will probably not spend extra money to go to trial; rather, he will accept probation, a fine, community service, or time already served in jail. The conviction will stay on his record and will not be expunged. All of this results from the individual following the law—believing that he could have one drink and be safe to drive, or rather be safe from breaking the law.

Daphne D. Newaz, "The Impaired Dual System Framework of United States Drunk–Driving Law: How International Perspectives Yield More Sober Results," 28 *Houston Journal of International Law* 531, 571 (2006). Assuming that the situation that she describes is not rare, what might its impact be on deterring drinking and driving?

3. Attempts to reduce drunk driving have received considerable attention since the 1980's. There have also been a number of efforts to evaluate these laws. Almost all studies reach conclusions similar to those presented in this article—stronger laws and enforcement only temporarily reduce drunk driving. See, e.g., H. Laurence Ross, *Deterring The Drinking Driver: Legal Policy and Social Control* (3d ed. 1984); H. Laurence Ross and Robert Voas, "The Philadelphia Story: The Effects of Severe Punishment for Drunk Driving," 12 *Law & Policy* 51 (1990). However, there are some researchers who claim that drunk driving laws actually have a more long lasting deterrent effect. See, e.g., John R. Snortum, "Alcohol–Impaired Driving in Norway and Sweden: Another Look at 'The Scandinavian Myth' ", 6 *Law & Policy* 5 (1984).

Can we say that the answer to effectiveness of the criminal law is high penalties and a real willingness to impose them? Maria Los, *Communist Ideology, Law and Crime* (1988), points out that the former Soviet Union used most of the available techniques of social control. By education, propaganda and rewards it attempted to create good Soviet citizens. Its criminal statutes dealt with familiar crimes such as murder and stealing. It also criminalized much activity left unregulated in most capitalist societies. For example, there were "anti-parasite" laws enforcing the duty to work; there were crimes against the central plan; there were crimes against state property. "Hooliganism" was a catchall crime aimed at "intentional actions which grossly violate public order and express an obvious disrespect towards society."

The Soviet Union exerted great efforts to enforce its laws, at least against those who did not hold privileged positions. There were many different types of police who were not limited by American notions of due process. Citizens were watched by police and networks of informers. Police were aided by such things as laws restricting where people could live and work. People needed permits, authorizations or registrations to engage in most spheres of everyday activity. People carried internal passports, and so it was much harder than in the West to avoid arrest by moving to another city or creating a new identity. Courts seldom acquitted those arrested. Criminal penalties were heavy, and large numbers of people were sent to prison. Prisons were terrible places. The state imposed capital punishment frequently.

Despite all this, Los points out that the Soviet Union had a very high crime rate. "Conventional crime ... appears to be not less wide-spread and diverse, and perhaps even more violent, than that in the countries of the West." (p. 304) Criminal statistics are notoriously hard to gather or to assess.

Nonetheless, assuming that Los' conclusion about the crime rate in the former Soviet Union is generally correct, can you explain why its legal system was not more successful? How would you fit Los' observations into the various theories of deterrence that have been set forth in this chapter? Compare Michael J. Lynch, "Beating a Dead Horse: Is There Any Basic Empirical Evidence for the Deterrent Effect of Imprisonment?" 31 *Crime, Law & Social Change* 347 (1999).

5.   Dan M. Kahan, "Gentle Nudges vs. Hard Shoves: Solving the Sticky Norms Problem," 67 *University of Chicago Law Review* 607 (2000), argues that legislators responding to focused groups lobbying for a new law or new penalties often will enact laws that seem too harsh to police, prosecutors, jurors and judges. These legal officials and groups may use their discretion to bring the laws back to reflect community social norms. Kahan calls this the problem of sticky norms. He suggests that if lawmakers were to apply "gentle nudges" rather than "hard shoves," those who should enforce the law would do so. This enforcement could affect the public judgment about the appropriateness of more severe penalties and open the door for later laws that imposed greater penalties. He says that those who enforce driving under the influence of alcohol laws in the past have tended to treat the offense as if it were the normal behavior of motorists. However, in the 1980s, groups such as Mothers Against Drunk Driving began the attempt to influence public views of the problem. Kahan argues that public attitudes changed. Drunk driving became no longer funny or accepted by many people. Such "privately imposed stigma was the gentle nudge that shook loose the sticky norms that condoned drunk driving." He concedes that this is only one hypothesis, but he suggests that it could be tested empirically. Does his suggestion seem plausible? Of course, people are able to translate the situation to their advantage. They can accept that truly drunk driving is dangerous and unacceptable, but they can convince themselves that they are able to drive safely after consuming enough alcohol to put themselves over the legal limits.

David J. Houston and Lilliard E. Richardson, Jr., "Drinking-and-Driving in America: A Test of Behavioral Assumptions Underlying Public Policy," 57 *Political Research Quarterly* 53 (2004), analyze data from a Gallup Poll based on telephone interviews in 1995. They divided respondents based on their response to questions about the frequency of driving within two hours of drinking any alcohol. Non-drink-drivers never drove within this period. Occasional drink-drivers drove after drinking one to six times in the previous year. Those who had driven within two hours of drinking on more than six occasions were the frequent drink-drivers. Houston and Richardson report:

> [T]hose who drive after drinking often do not see their actions as dangerous or wrong. This result is consistent with studies that find DWI offenders more likely to believe that some people drive better after drinking ..., that many believe they were able to drive safely after their drinking episode ..., that the risks of drinking-driving are overrated, and that it is okay to drink-and-drive as long as one is not caught.... Furthermore, the above results are consistent with conclusions drawn in

other research that frequent drink-drivers are largely indifferent to social norms and cannot easily be deterred through legal sanctions. . . . (p. 60)

Indeed, how often is the problem that people think that they have not had too many drinks to drive safely because their memory of what they have had and their judgment have been affected by the amount of alcohol they have consumed over the course of an evening? After, say, five drinks over an hour or two at a bar, is a person a rational actor able to respond to the certainty and severity of sanctions?

6. *Defining Punishment: The Sanctioning Process.* The essential idea of deterrence, of course, is that people will try to avoid sanctions, that is, they do not want to be punished. But what is a punishment? We assume, no doubt correctly, that jail, fines, whipping and hanging are punishments. But we cannot assume that everybody reacts the same way to every threat of punishment. A $1,000 fine might mean very little to a rich person. A night in jail might be enormously humiliating to some people, routine to others, a badge of pride to others or a source of thrills to others. Also, there are acts which would not be half so attractive if they were not sanctioned—forbidden fruit, where the punishment (or danger of punishment) is part of the thrill, the gain. See Jack Katz, *Seductions of Crime: Moral and Sensual Attractions in Doing Evil* (1983).

All this seems true, but it makes it hard to measure the "severity" of a punishment. Also, in legal theory, if a person is arrested, kept in jail for a while, tried and acquitted, she has not been "punished" at all. But we all know that is not the case; the defendant has been through a terrible ordeal, and may have suffered terribly in the process. Malcolm Feeley's study of the lower criminal courts of New Haven has the suggestive title: *The Process Is the Punishment* (1979). For drunks, for example, a small fine or a brief stay in a cell is not the real punishment; the whole process, from arrest to release, is what delivers the sanction.

Sheldon Ekland–Olson, John Lieb, and Louis Zurcher, "The Paradoxical Impact of Criminal Sanctions: Some Microstructural Findings," 18 *Law & Society Review* 159 (1984), give another example of this kind of "sanction." The article is based on extensive interviews with a group of drug dealers. The dealers were obviously not deterred by the threat of punishment—they were, after all, still carrying on their illegal business. But threat of punishment affected their behavior in many ways. As was true of the people Feeley studied, the process was often the punishment: "an arrest and the accompanying investigation were often perceived to be just as threatening as a prison sentence." Why should this be so? An arrest could ruin their business—it could destroy "a network of relations built over a period of years. . . ." Sources of drugs would dry up, customers would stay away, patterns of dealing with other people in the business could be disrupted, sometimes fatally.

Fear of sanctions also affected the way in which dealers carried on their business. It made them, for example, very careful in dealing with strangers (because of fear of selling to an underground detective, for example). Paradoxically, then, the fear of sanctions increased dealers' "involvement" in the drug business—the depth of their commitment, their "emotional attachment to dealing activities," and to other people in the drug business. The sanction process, in short, produced, or helped produce a distinctive sub-culture, with its own forms of solidarity.

The authors sum up their findings as follows:

1.　The perceived severity of sanctions is in large measure tied to the degree of interpersonal disruption caused by the sanctioning process.

2.　Criminal sanctions are socially complex. The degree of interpersonal disruption is determined in large measure by the organization of the sanctioning process and the tolerance or resilience of the affected network.

3.　Network tolerance, the ability and willingness of a network of actors to withstand the impact of the sanction process, is in large measure a function of the strength of relationships among actors.

4.　Sanctions become more disruptive as they reduce the degree of trust, affect and normative agreement within the deviant target population and as they inhibit or throw out of balance exchange relationships among deviants. Thus, relational tolerance and the sanctioning process are often highly interdependent.

5.　The sanctioning process has an important organizing influence on relationships among those engaged in criminal activities. This is revealed in many ways. For example:

a.　By increasing the constraining nature of activities, the fear of sanctions tends to increase network density and closure.

b.　Network closure and density reduce the chances that bridging ties to alternative networks will form. The structural influence of the hesitancy to form "weak ties" accounts for a substantial reduction in criminal activity not explained directly by the psychological processes of fear and avoidance.

6.　The perceived certainty of punishment depends in large measure on what persons know about particular situations as well as on the degree to which they trust their coactors.

7.　Persons engaged in criminal activities manipulate the perceived and actual certainty of punishment through choices of associates and the structuring of interaction.

What all these generalizations taken together imply is that perceptions of sanction severity and certainty are situational. Deterrence research, especially when restrictive deterrence is at issue, must move beyond official indicators of certainty and severity and beyond scaling procedures that assume stable attitudinal structures. Further understanding requires data that are sensitive to the dynamic relationship between the organization of the sanctioning process and the adaptive strategies of those who are the target of sanctions.

(B) The Role of Peer Groups, Conscience, Moral Appeal, Embarrassment and Shame

In "Conscience, Significant Others and Rational Choice: Extending the Deterrence Model" by Harold G. Grasmick and Robert J. Bursik, Jr., 24 *Law & Society Review* 837 (1990), the authors argue that deterrence theory ought to be integrated with theories that "emphasize sources of compliance with the law other than the threat of legal sanctions," that is, "(1) moral beliefs about right and wrong," and "(2) attachments to peers, family and various significant others."

These variables, to be sure, are hard to measure and manipulate. But Grasmick and Bursik, quite plausibly, argue that they are very important variables in explaining why people obey or disobey laws; they also claim that these variables are not inconsistent with deterrence theory. After all, conscience and peer groups "function as potential sources of punishment which, like state-imposed legal sanctions, vary in both their certainty and their severity." It is, in short, a real punishment to be laughed at—or beaten up— by members of your gang or to be ostracized by your church. And a bad conscience, too, can be very painful.

Hence conscience and peer group factors can fit easily into a "rational choice perspective" on behavior. Embarrassment, for example, can decrease "the expected utility of crime." It is a "physiological discomfort;" it also has or can have long-term consequences: "a loss of valued relationships and perhaps a restriction in opportunities to achieve other valued goals over which significant others have some control." The authors therefore propose to expand the whole notion of deterrence to include these non-state factors.

But how are we to measure potential embarrassment, guilt feelings, and the like? The authors collected data in 1985 from face-to-face interviews with a random sample of adults in an unidentified American city. They asked their subjects whether they were inclined to commit three offenses: tax cheating, petty theft (less than $20) and drunken driving. These offenses were chosen intentionally as offenses whose "consequences" tend to be "somewhat serious, in contrast to more minor offenses such as parking violations, littering, minor forms of illegal gambling, etc." Of the sample, 17% allowed that they would "fail to report certain income or claim an undeserved deduction (tax cheating);" 7.6% said they would "take something from some place worth less than $20;" and 28% (!) said "they would drive an automobile while under the influence of a moderate amount of alcohol."

The authors report:

> One of our objectives is to develop comparable or parallel measures of perceived risks of shame, embarrassment, and legal sanction. At the same time, we need to assess both perceived certainty and perceived severity

for each of the three kinds of costs. For certainty for each of the three offenses, respondents were asked:

SHAME: Would you feel guilty if you . . .

EMBARRASSMENT: Would most of the people whose opinion you value lose respect for you if you . . .

LEGAL SANCTIONS: Do you think you would get caught if you . . .

Responses were given on a four-point scale ranging from "definitely would not" (coded 1) to "definitely would" (coded 4) . . .

Our measure of perceived severity . . . captures the subjective severity of the punishment—the meaning the actor attaches to the punishment. Respondents were asked the following questions for each of the three offenses:

SHAME: If you did feel guilty for doing this, how big of a problem would it create for your life?

EMBARRASSMENT: If most of the people whose opinions you value did lose respect for you, how big a problem would it create for your life?

LEGAL SANCTIONS: If you were caught and the courts had decided what your punishment would be, how big a problem would it create for your life?

The respondent's options were "no problem at all" (1), "hardly any problem" (2), "little problem" (3), "a big problem" (4) and "a very big problem" (5). The means and standard deviations (in parentheses) are reported in Table 1 in the columns labeled "S."

With regard to "certainty," shame tended to score higher than the other types of threat; the "largest certainty" score was 3.67 for "certainty of shame for theft;" the lowest was 2.38 "for the certainty of embarrassment for tax cheating." As far as "severity" was concerned, the highest score was 4.31 for legal sanctions for drunk driving, followed by legal sanctions for theft (4.1) and tax cheating (3.97). The lowest score was severity of embarrassment for tax cheating (3.19). The scores are set out in Table One, which gives means and standard deviations. It also reports a figure in the third column of the table which consists of certainty and severity multiplied together. This figure represents the degree of "threat" which the sanction poses. So, for example, the threat score for shame as a sanction with regard to tax cheating is 10.626—lower than the effect of shame on theft (14.793), but higher than the threat of embarrassment on tax cheating (8.003).

**Table 1. Means (And Standard Deviations) Of Certainty (C), Severi-
ty (S), And The Product Of C and S (C × S) Of Shame, Embarrassment And Legal Sanctions**

	C	S	$C \times S$
Shame			
Tax cheat	3.025	3.307	10.626
	(0.96)	(1.16)	(5.79)
Theft	3.673	3.922	14.793
	(0.71)	(1.02)	(5.15)
Drunk Driving	3.242	3.538	12.165
	(0.92)	(1.21)	(6.12)
Embarrassment			
Tax cheat	2.385	3.130	8.003
	(0.88)	(1.02)	(4.78)
Theft	3.171	3.709	12.209
	(0.81)	(0.99)	(5.26)
Drunk driving	2.891	3.525	10.824
	(0.94)	(1.08)	(5.71)
Legal Sanctions			
Tax cheat	2.874	3.969	11.680
	(0.76)	(0.89)	(4.77)
Theft	2.894	4.103	12.171
	(0.79)	(0.88)	(4.86)
Drunk driving	2.749	4.313	12.050
	(0.81)	(0.79)	(4.70)

Now comes the pay-off: some people admit they intend to cheat on their taxes, drive while drunk, or steal something. But do "present perceptions" of the threats influence "present inclinations to violate the law?" For all three offenses, the authors found "strong evidence of a deterrent effect of shame. For two of the three offenses (tax cheating, drunk driving) shame is the threat which has the greatest direct effect."

Embarrassment was a disappointment. Threat of embarrassment did not have a significant effect on any of the three offenses. The authors say that these findings are "problematic" because past research "suggests that significant others play an important role in generating conformity and nonconformity with legal norms."

This study might not have measured the right thing: its measure "was designed to capture just one mechanism [embarrassment] through which significant others might influence illegal behavior." There might be other mechanisms not studied. Or respondents might feel that they would get away with the offense so that their significant others would not find out what they had done. Or perhaps Grasmick and Bursik's adult respondents were less amenable to peer pressure than the student subjects in most prior studies. In any event, the authors feel that their figures leave plenty of puzzles to be solved. They end with the usual plea for more research.[56]

NOTES AND QUESTIONS

1.   Do you think that this study proved anything? One male colleague who read the article (and who wishes to remain anonymous) commented: "There is a whole line of research based on asking people if X, Y & Z were so, would you commit a serious crime? It is a little like asking me if I were a woman and pregnant, would I have an abortion. How in hell do I know? Of course, I can try to project myself into the situation and guess. But when you know my guesses, what do you know?" Is this a fair criticism?

2.   Shame can be a powerful weapon of deterrence. Some societies make effective use of stigma and shame as mechanisms for controlling deviant behavior. This was true, for example, in colonial Massachusetts Bay; making people sit in the stocks, or the wearing of the scarlet letter made famous in Nathaniel Hawthorne's novel, were only some of the many devices to stigmatize, and shame, people who disobeyed the laws. See Lawrence M. Friedman, *Crime and Punishment in American History* 38–41 (1993).

Some scholars feel that shame is in fact a powerful weapon of deterrence in all societies; that some societies make effective use of shame as a mechanism for controlling deviant behavior; and that all societies might well invoke this tool as a means of social control. See John Braithwaite, *Crime, Shame, and Reintegration* (1989). Braithwaite asserts, however, that there is shame and shame. Social processes that result in shame followed by "reintegration" into society are effective while those that result in stigma and expulsion may be counterproductive.

3.   Grasmick and Bursik talk about "extending" the rational-choice model of deterrence. Have they done so? If you include conscience, fear of disapproval from neighbors or others, embarrassment, and the like, do you have a rational-choice model any more? Is there anything that would not be consistent with a rational-choice model under their reasoning?

---

56.   See Harold G. Grasmick, Robert J. Bursik, Jr., and Bruce J. Arneklev, "Reduction in Drunk Driving as a Response to Increased Threats of Shame, Embarrassment, and Legal Sanctions," 31 *Criminology* 41 (1993). Compare, however, Phillip B. Gonzales, "Shame, Peer, and Oscillating Frames in DWI Conviction: Extending Goffman's Sociological Landscape," 16 *Symbolic Interaction* 257 (1993), stressing that those convicted of driving while intoxicated, their friends, employers and others with whom they interact have ways of coping with the law's attempts to impose shame and embarrassment.

(4.5) Moral Appeal, Sanction Threat, and Deviance: An Experimental Test

Charles R. Tittle and Alan R. Rowe[57]

Three sociology classes were used in the experiment. One class was designated as the control group, while the other two were subjected to the experimental treatment. Each class was organized around a series of eight weekly quizzes worth ten points each. Quizzes were administered during the last 15 minutes of a class period and were collected as the students left. The quizzes were then graded and the scores recorded with no marks being made on the student's paper. At the beginning of the next class period they were returned, and the students were permitted to calculate their own grades.

The difference between the real score as previously determined by the instructor and the score which the student assigned to himself is taken as an indication of cheating. Since the amount that a student could cheat was limited by the maximum score of ten on a given quiz as well as by the actual real score he earned, the index of cheating to be analyzed is based on the proportion of cheating opportunities utilized. If a given student had a total of 21 real points on a series of three quizzes, he had the opportunity to cheat nine points. If he actually cheated three points, he is considered to have cheated 33 percent of the possible.

To minimize moral and ethical dilemmas associated with the research, the authors agreed in advance to keep secret the cheating activity of individual students, even from each other. They further agreed to calculate the course grade on the basis of the scores the students assigned to themselves, and to mark the midterm and final exams in so far as possible without reference to the student's quiz honesty.

In the control group no mention was made during the entire quarter of cheating, the necessity for honesty, or of the possibility of being caught or punished. It was simply explained that taking the quiz at the end of the period was less distracting to the lecture of that day and that this procedure permitted students to leave early if finished or to stay later if more time was needed. Upon return of the quizzes, the instructor devoted about 45 minutes to class discussion of the topic covered on the quiz, during which the correct answers were made clear.

The treatment groups (which were taught in the quarter immediately following) were exposed to the same procedure for three quizzes. Upon return of the fourth quiz, but before self-grading, the class was reminded that they were being trusted to grade their quizzes honestly and that they had a moral obligation to be accurate. No other mention was made of cheating until the seventh quiz was returned. At that point the students were told that complaints about cheating had been lodged, so it was necessary for the instructor to spot check some of the quizzes for accuracy. When the eighth quiz was

---

57. From Charles R. Tittle and Alan R. Rowe, "Moral Appeal, Sanction Threat and Deviance," 20 *Social Problems* 488 (1973).

Copyright © Social Problems Reprinted by permission of Social Problems, The Society for the Study of Social Problems and the authors.

returned, the students were told that the spot check had revealed a case of cheating and that the person was to be penalized (in fact, nobody was penalized).

Hence, comparison of the patterns of cheating between the control group and the treatment groups should reveal the impact of a moral appeal and a sanction threat on the amount of cheating that occurs. First, if a moral appeal is effective, the level of cheating in the treatment groups after the moral appeal should be significantly less than before the moral appeal. Second, if a detection/sanction threat has any additional deterrent effect above and beyond that generated by the moral appeal, the level of cheating after such a threat should be significantly lower than before. Finally, variations from quiz to quiz in the treatment groups should be significantly different than variations in the control group.

Only those individuals who took and graded at least one quiz of the first six and of the last two were included in the analysis and only then if they had some opportunity to cheat on one of the two series. For instance, a student who made perfect scores on the last two quizzes would be excluded, since his inclusion would have contributed to a spurious decline in cheating after the threat. Although the pool of usable subjects was defined with reference to the comparison between quizzes 1–6 and 7–8, the same logic of exclusion was applied when other series of quizzes were compared. As a result, the N for a given series varies depending upon the comparisons being made.

For purposes of analysis, the mean percent of individuals' cheat opportunities utilized was calculated for given series of quizzes and the significance of the difference between series was assessed by a t-test for matched pair differences. Differences between groups were evaluated by a difference of means test. In all cases, tests were one-tailed.

Questionnaire data to enable compositional comparison of the classes and analysis of the differential impact of the threat on various categories of individuals were gathered at the beginning of each of the courses. Students were told that the information requested would make it possible for the instructor to tailor the level of presentation to the needs and capabilities of the students. These data were analyzed using Goodman–Kruskal gamma (1963) and its associated test of significance. For calculation, major field of study was grouped into four categories; age was categorized into three groups—less than 21, 22–25, and 26 or over; motivation for earning a high grade was treated in three categories; expected grade was analyzed in three categories; reason for enrolling was treated in two categories—those indicating high motivation and those indicating low motivation; actual course grade was expressed in three categories; discrepancy between expected grade at the beginning of the quarter and actual grade earned was grouped into three categories—no discrepancy, one grade discrepancy, and two or more grades of discrepancy; and, of course, sex was in two categories.

In examining the impact of the sanction threat on various types of individuals, the percentage decrease in cheating following the sanction threat was used as an indicator. For each individual the difference between the amount of cheating on the two series, 1–6 and 7–8, was divided by the amount of cheating on the first series. The percentage decrease was used rather than the simple difference between the two series because the absolute decrease would have been influenced by the magnitude of cheating on the first series—those who cheated most on the first series would have artificially shown a greater decrease following the sanction threat.

RESULTS

The moral appeal apparently had no effect on the level of cheating (Table 1). In fact, cheating actually increased in both groups, but since there was a corresponding increase for the same series in the control group, it appears that the moral appeal was simply irrelevant to the amount of cheating. In test group A, students cheated an average of 31 percent of the opportunities prior

TABLE 1

MEAN PERCENT OF CHEATING OPPORTUNITIES UTILIZED

	Free (Quiz 1–3)	Moral Appeal (Quiz 4–6)	Spot-check Threat	Sanction Threat	X Individual Difference (1–6)–(7–8)
Test Group A (N = 30)	31% (N = 30)	41% (N = 29)	13% (N = 30)	11% (N = 26)	−22.9
		34% (N = 30)		12% (N = 30)	
Test Group B (N = 51)	41% (N = 47)	43% (N = 47)	32% (N = 46)	22% (N = 29)	−11.5
		42% (N = 51)		31% (N = 51)	
Control Group (N = 26)	27% (N = 26)	33% (N = 24)	24% (N = 26)	28% (N = 12)	−5.9
		30% (N = 26)		24% (N = 26)	

Statistical Tests:
  Q 1–6 group A vs. Q 7–8 group A ($t = 7.50$, df = 29, $p < .0005$)
  Q 1–6 group B vs. Q 7–8 group B ($t = 2.67$, df, 50, $p < .005$)
  Q 1–6 group C vs. Q 7–8 group C ($t = 1.27$, df = 25, $p > .10$)
  Diff. [(Q 1–6)–(Q 7–8)] group A vs. Diff. [(Q 1–6)–(Q 7–8)] group C
    ($t = 6.67$, df = 54, $p < .005$)
  Diff. [(Q 1–6)–(Q 7–8)] group B vs. Diff. [(Q 1–6)–(Q 7–8)] group C
    ($t = 2.68$, df = 75, $p < .005$)
  Diff. [(Q 1–6)–(Q 7–8)] group A vs. Diff. [(Q 1–6)–(Q 7–8)] group B
    ($t = 2.03$, df = 79, $p < .02$)

to the moral appeal and an average of 41 percent of the opportunities after the moral appeal. In test group B, the pre-appeal cheat level was 41 percent and the post-appeal level was 43 percent. Among the control group, cheating on the quizzes corresponding to the pre-appeal condition of the test groups (quizzes 1–3) was 27 percent and in the series corresponding to the moral appeal condition (quizzes 4–6), the cheating level was 33 percent.

The data do seem to show that the threat of being caught and punished did have a significant effect in deterring cheating in both test groups. In test group A the pre-threat cheating average was 34 percent while the post-threat average was only 12 percent, a mean individual difference of –22.9 percent (p <.001). Test group B displayed a decline from 42 percent to 31 percent, a mean individual difference of –11.5 percent p <.005). Although the mean cheating level of the control group also declined from 30 percent for the first six quizzes to 24 percent for the last two quizzes (a non-significant mean individual difference of –5.9 percent p >.10), the difference between the pre- and post-threat conditions for each of the two test groups was significantly greater than the difference for the control group (test group A p <.0005, test group B, p <.005).

The results appear to support the deterrent argument and to demonstrate that fear of sanction is a more important influence than moral appeal in generating conformity to the norm of classroom honesty. However rival interpretations are possible. The findings could be spurious because of weaknesses in the method of data analysis. By using the percent of cheating opportunities utilized by each individual as the basic unit of analysis, we may have permitted considerable idiosyncratic variation because of the low base on which the percents were calculated. For example, a student who on the first four quizzes scored perfectly on four, and an eight and nine respectively on the other two would end up with only three possibilities of cheating on the first series. By "fudging" only two points, he would have a cheating score of 67 percent. This problem is particularly acute, since some of the series encompass only one or two quizzes. Consequently, no individual had more than 50 cheating opportunities on any series considered, and many had only one or two opportunities. Moreover, eliminating from the analysis all individuals who had no opportunity to cheat on either of the main series may have biased the results.

In order to assess the possible effect of these artifacts, the data were recalculated using the percent of all possible cheats utilized by the entire class during any given series of quizzes as the basic unit of analysis. For instance, in test group A, there was a total of 1090 cheating opportunities during the first six quizzes, of which 46 percent were utilized. This alternative type of analysis produced almost exactly the same result as did the analysis using individual data. The difference between the amount of cheating in the pre-threat series for test group A (35 percent) and that in the post-threat series (12 percent) was –23 percent, in comparison with the original figure of –22.9 percent. Similarly, the difference for test group B was –11 percent, a figure very close to the original –11.5 percent. Hence, the results do not seem to be distorted by the method of analysis.

A second possibility is that the test groups differed from control group in some way other than the sanction threat, which may have accounted for the greater decline in the level of cheating on the last two quizzes. After all, the students were not randomly assigned to the three classes, and there was evidence of some decline (although not statistically significant) in the control group. To evaluate this rival interpretation, the classes were compared in terms of the following compositional characteristics: age, sex, reason for enrolling, expected grade, motivation for earning a high grade, discrepancy between the expected grade at the beginning of the quarter and the actual grade earned, and major area of study. No significant differences were found between the control and test groups which could have accounted for the results. Test group B did differ significantly from the control group in motivation for earning a high grade and in discrepancy between the grade expected and the grade actually earned. But the direction of these differences works against the hypothesis. The higher motivation and greater grade discrepancy in the test group should have produced greater incentive to continue cheating during quizzes 7 and 8. The fact that cheating was reduced significantly more in the test group than in the control group therefore strengthens the conclusion that the sanction threat had a causative impact. Thus, it appears that the findings are not due to extraneous differences between the control group and the test groups. Of course, it is possible that other differences not measured could have accounted for the findings, but it seems unlikely since the design was a combination of time series and a control group. If the groups had differed in some way that might have influenced the level of cheating, this should have become evident in the cheating patterns prior to the sanction threat.

Not only did the groups not differ in crucial ways, but there is some "informal" indication that the decline in cheating among the control group was itself attributable to increased fear of sanction near the end of the quarter. A student in another class inquired of one of the authors, point blank, if he were going to check some of the quiz papers. She had heard rumors that students in that class were growing fearful that the "grade-your-own" policy had resulted in so much cheating that the instructor would surely do something before the end of the quarter.

It seems safe to conclude, therefore, that the findings support a deterrent argument. But further questions require some attention. First, the sanction threat had a much greater effect in group A than in group B. Why might this differential effect have occurred? Since the two groups did not differ significantly in the compositional characteristics previously mentioned, only two possibilities suggest themselves, both of which involve credibility. Group B was over twice as large as group A. Hence, a spot check in group A actually implied a greater probability of being caught than it did in group B. Since other research has found the certainty of punishment to be a key variable in predicting whether sanctions will deter, it seems reasonable to imagine that the greater effect of the threat in group A may have been due to the greater certainty of apprehension implied by the threat.

Further, the two instructors/experimenters may have been differentially feared so that the sanction threat was more credible in one case than in the other. In fact, the instructor for group B, which showed the lesser effect, had a reputation among students as lovable and understanding. It is, therefore, quite plausible to postulate that the spot check was a less menacing threat for the students in group B than for those in group A. This interpretation is consistent with the fact that the level of cheating prior to the threat was greater in group B than in group A (42 percent v. 34 percent) and with the apparent additional effect produced in group B by the declaration before quiz eight that a cheater had been discovered and penalized (average cheating declined from 32 percent on quiz seven to 22 percent on quiz eight). It could be that in group B, where credibility was relatively low, the sanction reinforcement made the spot check threat more believable, whereas in group A (a decline from 13 percent to 11 percent), the maximum credibility had already been achieved with the original threat. If this interpretation is correct, the findings lend support to the argument that the certainty of punishment is an essential dimension to be taken into account when dealing with deterrence theory. Moreover, it suggests the applicability to the college teacher (at least in his role as evaluator) of Machiavelli's cogent observation that since it is difficult to be both loved and feared, "it is much safer to be feared, than to be loved, if one must choose."

Second, it is important to determine the type of individual most affected by the sanction threat. Examination of the relationships between measured individual characteristics and the percentage decrease in cheating following the sanction threat reveals three important associations. First, there is a significant relationship between the sex of the person and the effect of the sanction threat (.38, p <.01), which remains when other variables are held constant. Females were influenced far more by the sanction threat than were males. Sixty one percent of all the females registered a 100 percent decrease in cheating after the threat, while only 33 per cent of the males responded so dramatically. Why this should have been true is not clear, although it is consistent with much research in social psychology showing females to be more conforming, more obedient to authorities, and less willing to take chances. Presumably socialization in the female role creates greater consciousness of status and sensitivity to reputation, both of which would intensify fear of exposure for dishonest behavior. At any rate, if this research is a fair indication, we can conclude that females are more likely to be deterred from deviance by fear of sanction than are males.

The data also show significant associations between the influence of the sanction threat and the actual grade the student received in the course (−.42, p <.01), as well as with the discrepancy between the grade he expected at the beginning of the course and the grade he actually received (−.34, p <.05). Those students who had the lowest grades and who were experiencing the greatest discrepancy between the grade they expected and the grade they were actually earning were least affected by the sanction threat. Sixty-seven percent of those who earned a B or higher registered a 100 percent decrease in cheating after being threatened, while only 24 percent of those who earned a D or F reduced their cheating by this much. Similarly, 70 percent of those who were experiencing no discrepancy between the grade they expected and the grade they were earning registered a 100 percent decline in cheating, while only 31 percent of those who were experiencing a two-grade discrepancy reduced cheating by that amount.

These figures are certainly consistent with deterrence theory. Classical criminologists, from whom formal deterrence theory stemmed, argued that the greater the utility of an act, the greater the potential punishment required to deter it. Apparently the students most in need of points were willing to take greater risks and were, therefore, less responsive to the sanction threat. Perhaps they too would have been deterred if the probability of detection had been greater; but it is also possible that increased certainty of detection would have had little additional influence on their behavior, since they were highly motivated and had little to lose anyway.

Interestingly enough, these data are also interpretable within the framework of anomie theory. Those students who lacked the means to achieve the culturally accepted goal of academic success (a goal which they also apparently accepted, if their expected grades are any indication) were most likely to continue cheating in the face of potential detection and punishment. Anomie theory may converge with deterrence theory in directing attention to behavior that is likely to have high utility.

DISCUSSION

Although the evidence does support the deterrent hypothesis, it is not overpowering. Not all cheating was deterred by the threat, and even before the sanction threat was issued many cheating opportunities were not utilized. The failure to deter, just as the differential impact of the threat in the two groups, could have been the result of low credibility. Some students may have believed they would escape detection since the instructor said he was only going to "spot check" the papers. Others may have believed that detection would not really have adverse consequences, since they could plead that it was an honest error or that they misunderstood the real answer. Moreover, a spot check did not pose a threat of detection at all for some types of cheating. A few students merely left questions blank and then filled in the correct answers when they were discussed in class, while others erased a previously wrong answer and put in the correct one. Spot checking such papers would reveal no cheating, although it had occurred in a blatant fashion. For all these reasons, then, it is logical to imagine that if the probability of being caught and punished had been greater, more of the cheating would have been deterred.

Still, it is possible that some of the cheating was simply not deterrable by a sanction threat. For some, fear of sanction may have been irrelevant because they were doing so poorly in the course that the maximum punishment they could imagine would have made no difference anyhow. Others may have been defiant or incapable of comprehending the fact that a threat had been made. And as indicated earlier, some may have been so highly motivated to increase their grade that they were willing to take whatever risk was necessary.

The fact that the moral appeal failed to reduce cheating suggests little commitment to the norm of classroom honesty. But given this apparent lack of commitment, how can we explain why there was not maximum cheating prior to the sanction threat? One reason may have been that the students experienced some fear of being caught and punished even without an actual threat. Being accustomed to instructor evaluation, students probably viewed with some suspicion a sudden reversal that permitted them to grade their own papers. They surely perceived that the instructor was in a position to check the perfect scores beforehand, since he kept them overnight. Moreover, they must have reasoned that perfect scores on all quizzes would create suspicion on the part of the instructor. Thus, although impossible to determine, it seems plausible that much cheating may have been deterred by fear of sanction even before a formal threat was made.

But it would probably be a mistake to attribute all of the conformity to fear of sanction. Moral commitment was no doubt operative to some extent. Some students cheated such a small amount, even when they needed the grade very badly, that one would have to entertain seriously the notion that they had internalized the norm of honesty. Furthermore, a few students actually graded themselves lower than they earned, both in response to a moral appeal and at other points throughout the course. These people may have been super cowards (or there may have been some clerical error); but it seems more likely that they were morally committed or that they were responding out of guilt from having cheated on earlier quizzes.

CONCLUSION

The findings support deterrence theory, and they converge with other recent studies in suggesting that sanctions may play an important role in the maintenance of conformity and social order. But it would be a mistake to draw sweeping conclusions from these results. We were testing the effect of a particular kind of sanction threat—one to be imposed formally by an authority figure. The experiment used a particular type of subject (young adults) and was concerned with obedience to a non-legal norm with little moral or normative support. In addition, the behavior under consideration was instrumental behavior (oriented toward long range goals) and probably episodic; that is, it did not involve deep personal commitments to the deviance as a style of behavior around which one could form an identity. At least three of these conditions are those theoretically most likely to permit formal sanctions to work as deterrents.

It has frequently been suggested that formal sanctions are likely to be effective primarily for those rules that lack general moral support. Presumably if we had been dealing with a norm resting on an internalized moral imperative, there would have been little deviance to deter, and that which was extant would have already resisted informal sanctions from peers, and hence would have been less responsive to formal sanction threats. It has also been argued that sanctions are relevant only to a certain proportion of any population—those who have not thoroughly internalized the norm and are therefore "potential" offenders. The lower the moral support for a norm, the larger is this "marginal" category, and the more likely it is sanction threats will have significant deterrent impact.

NOTES AND QUESTIONS

1. What does this study prove? Look at the various statements in the last two paragraphs in which the authors express cautions about what they learned from their data and how far we can generalize what they found:

Tittle and Rowe are appropriately cautious about some of their variables. They point out, for example, that their subjects were young adults but not everyone falls into this category. They were also Americans who were college students. Indeed, we might want to know more about the background and socio-economic status of their subjects.

The behavior studied, they say, "was instrumental . . . and probably episodic." It did not "involve deep personal commitments to the deviance as a style of behavior around which one could form an identity." Hence, presumably, the study tells us little or nothing about drug addiction or rape, or about the work and mind of career criminals.

2. Note the word "instrumental" in the passage from Tittle and Rowe just quoted. William Chambliss, "Types of Deviance and the Effectiveness of Legal Sanctions," 1967 *Wisconsin Law Review* 703, draws a distinction between "instrumental" crimes and "expressive" crimes—that is, between, roughly, those that are a means to an end and those that come out of emotion, passion or addiction. "Expressive" acts, Chambliss claims, resist deterrence; not so "instrumental" acts. Tittle and Rowe are referring to this kind of distinction in the passage to which we have just referred. Is this an important distinction? If so, why? Can we always distinguish an instrumental from an expressive act? How do we know whether many people experience an emotional urge to kill but do not because they are deterred by the threat of criminal punishment?

3. Moral appeal seemed to make little difference to the students who took part in this experiment. Contrast, in this regard, the findings in Richard D. Schwartz and Sonya Orleans, "On Legal Sanctions," 34 *University of Chicago Law Review* 274 (1967), who claim to find some impact of a moral appeal to pay taxes. For a critical analysis of the methods used and conclusions drawn in the Schwartz and Orleans study, see Lawrence M. Friedman

and Stewart Macaulay, *Law and the Behavioral Sciences* 324–329 (2d ed. 1977).

It is hard to accept the idea that moral appeals have no effect on people's behavior. After all, most of us can think of times (can't we?) when we refrained from doing something because we thought that it was wrong. More objectively, people do respond to requests to recycle paper or save scrap metal during wartime or save water during droughts. Although there may be no external enforcement mechanism, people respond to a moral appeal and do such acts because they think they are right. Why do some moral appeals work while others do not? Consider the lessons the following article would draw from one example of moral appeals reinforced by other-than-legal sanctions:

(4.6) Fear and Norms and Rock & Roll: What Jambands Can Teach Us About Persuading People to Obey Copyright Law

Mark F. Schultz[58]

21 *Berkeley Technological Law Journal* 651 (2006).

I. INTRODUCTION

Among fans of popular music, there is one group that is far more likely than most to respect copyright law. These fans scrupulously observe restrictions bands impose on the copying and distribution of their music. They keep track of these rules and make sure their fellow fans are aware of them. If they find fellow fans stepping out of line, they quickly scold them. They even cooperate with bands' lawyers to enforce the rules. Who are these responsible, rule-loving fans who embrace authority? None other than the fans of the Grateful Dead and their descendants in the jamband community. Notwithstanding their stereotypical image as laid back types with little taste for rules or authority, jamband fans are extremely supportive of the rights of artists to control the copying and distribution of their work. Therein lies a story that is interesting in its own right, but which also tells us a great deal about law, social norms, and persuading people to comply with copyright law.

The jamband community is a vital and growing movement in popular music that includes some of the top-grossing touring bands in the country. The original jamband was the Grateful Dead, but the label now applies to bands from many genres—rock, jazz, country, folk, bluegrass, and even gospel—and includes major acts like Phish, Widespread Panic, and the String Cheese Incident. What defines a jamband more than anything else is its policy regarding intellectual property: jambands allow their fans to record live shows and to copy and distribute the recordings freely. Jambands have enjoyed great commercial success in distributing music via the Internet in forms that other bands have not dared to try. They explicitly attribute their success to the bond of trust they have with their fans.

Jambands can trust their fans because the fan community has developed social norms against copying musical works that jambands have designated as "off limits." These restricted works typically comprise studio recordings or certain live releases sold commercially. The community enforces these norms internally and externally, sometimes even reporting violations to the bands' attorneys. The jamband community has also developed its own file-sharing applications which respect copyright holders' rights.

These social norms certainly make jambands an interesting phenomenon, but one might ask why they are significant. First, they are significant because they defy conventional wisdom, which says that the average individual is unlikely to be persuaded to comply voluntarily with copyright law. As is usually the case, conventional wisdom is conventional for a reason. It finds ample justification in the actions and attitudes of tens of millions of users of peer-to-peer networks. It is widely agreed that a vast divide separates copyright law and social norms. The jamband community, however, provides evidence that this divide is not inevitable.

Second, the social norms of the jamband community are significant because social norms are one of the keys to solving the file-sharing dilemma. File-sharing software has made compliance with copyright law at least partly voluntary for a vast group of people with access to the Internet. The music industry has responded with lawsuits—mostly pursued by the Recording Industry Association of America (RIAA)—calculated to deter file-sharers. The recording industry hopes these lawsuits will change the behavior of file-sharers by instilling fear in potential file-sharers. The problem with a "fear strategy" is that it is very difficult to project threats of detection and legal action credible enough to alter behavior. Some enforcement is useful to demonstrate the moral seriousness of the law and to deter those who are averse to any risk of enforcement, but more enforcement will not necessarily yield significantly more compliance.... While lawsuits are a useful part of an overall strategy for securing compliance, there may not be a great deal more to gain from them. The music industry's most efficient and effective strategy for saving itself is to seek ways to change social norms regarding unauthorized copying.

It thus appears that the jamband community can teach us some useful lessons about persuading people to obey copyright law by fostering pro-copyright norms. These lessons would be particularly helpful if the norms of the jamband community are founded on something beyond the unique circumstances, history, and customs of this particular community. Fortunately, they are. The norms of the jamband community appear to conform to a fundamental norm of human behavior called reciprocity.

In recent years, scholars of law and norms have focused on reciprocity as an explanation for the emergence and endurance of certain social norms. Dan Kahan describes reciprocity as a product of settings that call on people to cooperate with others. In these cooperative settings, individuals adopt not a materially calculating posture but rather a richer, more emotionally nuanced reciprocal one. When they perceive that others are behaving cooperatively, individuals are moved by honor, altruism, and like dispositions to contribute to public goods even without the inducement of material incentives. When, in contrast, they perceive that others are shirking or otherwise taking advantage of them, individuals are moved by resentment and pride to withhold their own cooperation and even to engage in personally costly forms of retaliation....[59]

This Article contributes to the literature on law and reciprocity by adding another detailed case study of how reciprocity makes a community more or less likely to comply with the law. It also reviews in detail the behavioral and experimental economics literature that provides support for, and defines, the phenomenon of reciprocity. This research helps to show how reciprocity explains the social norms of the jamband community. The jamband community has found a way to tap into reciprocity, thus inspiring norms that are unusually supportive of the rights of musicians.[60] ...

II.   SOCIAL NORMS: WHO NEEDS THEM?

Although it is a now tiresome and perhaps discredited cliché that the Internet has changed everything, it really did change music piracy. File-sharing has made unauthorized copying of music a mass consumer phenomenon. This Part discusses how file-sharing has fundamentally changed the nature of the challenge of persuading people to comply with copyright law.... It concludes that the music industry's [litigation] strategy is far better suited to a relatively small number of commercial pirates than to millions of consumers. Research indicates that fostering social norms against unauthorized copying is a key part of an effective strategy for securing compliance with law.

A.   The Changing Nature of Music Piracy

As late as 1994, the music industry expressed optimism that it could beat the problem of piracy. Although it saw piracy as an urgent problem, it contended that increased enforcement efforts and stricter penalties could greatly alleviate the problem. This focus and attendant optimism made sense at the time, because music piracy was still a problem of illicit commercial competition rather than a mass consumer problem. These illicit competitors—commercial pirates—were in it for the money. If one could convince them that

59. Dan M. Kahan, "The Logic of Reciprocity: Trust, Collective Action, and Law," 102 *Michigan Law Review* 71 (2003).

60. Not everyone needs to be so conscientious and involved. Rather, conditions must be right for the most cooperative members of a community—the "conditional cooperators"—to set the tone and conditions of participation for more casual or selfish members. If people can communicate, see others cooperating, and sanction non-cooperators, then reciprocity makes people more inclined to cooperate. Cross-cultural field and laboratory experiments indicate that conditional cooperators exist in all human populations, not just ones that are (arguably) exceptionally kind like the jamband community. The presence of conditional cooperators in all populations makes it more likely that other segments of the music industry can follow its example by tapping into reciprocity....

the risk and consequences of getting caught outweighed the reward from copying, then they were likely dissuaded. With sufficient help from authorities, the music industry might have reasonably hoped to make commercial pirates fear getting caught.

By contrast, the problem of file-sharing has not proven amenable to such straightforward strategies. The music industry first tried to cut off the supply of music by imposing copy-protection technology and suing file-sharing services and software providers. So far, copy-protection technology has proven ineffective both technologically and commercially and may remain so for the foreseeable future. Suits against file-sharing technology providers likely reached their zenith with the recent U.S. Supreme Court decision in *Metro–Goldwyn–Mayer Studios Inc. v. Grokster, Ltd.*[61] In *Grokster*, the Court introduced the doctrine of "inducement," which imposes liability on product and software providers for "distributing a device with the object of promoting its use to infringe copyright, as shown by clear expression or other affirmative steps taken to foster infringement."[62] This is not the result for which the music industry might have hoped, as future developers and distributors of file-sharing technology may be able to avoid liability, provided that they are very careful in their words and actions. In the end, the technology for file-sharing remains available and likely will continue to be available. Indeed, the creators of BitTorrent, the most heavily used file-sharing program for illegal copying, may escape any liability under *Grokster*.

As these supply-side strategies have faltered, the music industry has taken a page from its strategy against commercial pirates by trying to instill fear in file-sharers. Since 2003, the RIAA has sued over ten thousand individuals for uploading files onto file-sharing networks. The purpose of the suits appears to be exemplary rather than compensatory. As an attorney for one defendant put it: "This case had very little to do with [the defendant] and everything to do with the recording industry's attempt to intimidate Internet users around the country and college students in particular, . . . They looked to instill fear. . . ." At this point, the results seem mixed at best. Notwithstanding the RIAA's lawsuits, it is estimated that thirteen million households download files each month. Moreover, in a recent Pew Internet survey, fifty-eight percent of those who download music said they did not care whether it was copyrighted.

B.   The Problem with Deterrence–Based Strategies

The RIAA's experience with its lawsuits has echoed the general experience with such deterrence-based strategies: they are enthusiastically pursued but not necessarily effective. Like the RIAA, lawmakers and other authorities focus almost exclusively on deterrence strategies for securing compliance with law. To many, increasing penalties seems to be the obvious and only way to change behavior. As one commentator put it, "the only way to fend off the non-profit Internet pirate is by increasing prison sentences for Internet

---

61. 125 S.Ct. 2764 (2005).   **62.** Id. at 2780.

pirates." The problem with this strategy is that while having a law and enforcing it has some effect on people's behavior, marginal changes in penalties or enforcement may not change behavior much or at all.

A strategy based on scaring people into complying with copyright law by ratcheting up enforcement and penalties will quickly surpass the point of diminishing returns. Some enforcement is helpful and necessary, because laws do derive a deterrent effect merely from existing and from being credibly enforced. Since consumers were not significant targets of copyright enforcement until recently, the RIAA's suits have the important effect of putting people on notice that infringement is an illicit act that incurs a risk (albeit a vanishingly remote one) of legal sanctions. For some people, this notice alone is enough to change behavior, either because they are unwilling to tolerate any risk of sanctions at all or because illegality represents a symbolic threshold they are unwilling to cross. Nevertheless, increasing penalties or enforcement may not appear to have the direct effect of increased compliance that some lawmakers and music industry advocates seem to assume. Many studies find very little or no deterrent effect at all from increasing the level of enforcement or penalties.

The primary shortcoming of relying solely on increasing the fear of punishment to deter wrongdoing is that it is very difficult to convince people that they are likely to be caught and punished. . . . [P]eople often underestimate their chance of getting caught. The actual risk of getting caught and punished for most crimes is already low, even before filtered through people's perceptions—for example, the likelihood of getting caught for burglary is as low as thirteen percent. Homicide is the rare crime for which society devotes resources sufficient to ensure a deterrent effect—the likelihood of getting caught is about seventy percent. The picture for file-sharing is far bleaker. The RIAA has sued about ten thousand file-sharers, while reports estimate that millions use illegal file-sharing services monthly. The RIAA has a long way to go before it even catches up with the rates for burglary.

Nevertheless, we might consider increasing enforcement and penalties for copyright infringement to the point where people are too scared to not comply. In a free society, however, it is difficult and inefficient to control people's behavior by relying solely on the coercive power of the state. Tom Tyler . . . states: "This type of leadership is impractical because government is obliged to produce benefits or exercise coercion every time it seeks to influence citizens' behavior. These strategies consume large amounts of public resources and such societies would be 'in constant peril of disequilibrium and instability.' "[63] Copyright law already has become controversial enough. Drastically increasing penalties is unlikely to be a politically viable strategy. . . .

C. Normative Strategies

The most efficient and effective way to persuade people to comply with copyright law is to convince them that it is the right thing to do. This strategy

---

63. Tom Tyler, *Why People Obey the Law* 22 (1990).

is not as idealistic as it might at first sound. Authorities rely on the voluntary compliance of most people with most laws, most of the time. In fact, many scholars contend that the legal system in a democracy cannot function without widespread voluntary compliance with the law. If you ask people why they obey the law, they most often cite moral reasons. More important, studies show that people's actions confirm what they say: the most important factor in securing compliance with law is social norms.

People are most likely to comply with law out of a sense of internal obligation or fear of informal sanction from peers for violating community norms....

Normative support for law can come from many places, including enforcement of the law itself. As described above, the very fact that a law makes something illicit is enough to change the behavior of some people. The law can serve as a signal for what is right, and enforcement of the law can serve to educate people about what behavior is acceptable and unacceptable. Nevertheless, enforcement and penalties that get too far out ahead of social norms can have the opposite of their intended effect. If penalties are out of line with expectations about what is just, they can have "crimogenic effects." That is, people may lose respect for the law, and some who would have been inclined to follow it become willing to disobey it or support those who do. Laws can contribute to a social norm—but they cannot compel support for it. If copyright law is to be rescued from non-compliance, it will be because most people choose to obey it voluntarily, like they do most other laws. More thought should be put into increasing normative support for copyright law.

Although the normative strategy sounds like a wonderfully efficient solution, there is a catch. The deterrence strategy may not work as intended, but it has visceral appeal because it offers a very clear prescription: increase consequences, increase compliance. The prescription of the normative strategy, on the other hand, is clear only in the abstract: change social norms to favor compliance. The difficulty, of course, is that changing social norms is, in reality, a very complex challenge. Building norms is not like building a house. Hard work, strong desire, and resources are not enough. Norms likely arise from a variety of sources, including religion, philosophy, culture, education, and biology. There likely is no universal or easy way to establish a social norm.

There are, however, certain behavioral regularities that strongly influence the formation of social norms. This Article's goal, in part, is to contribute to the understanding of how one such human behavioral trait called reciprocity encourages the formation of social norms that support compliance with law....

III. THE JAMBAND COMMUNITY: A CASE STUDY IN VOLUNTARY COMPLIANCE

Although widespread illegal file-sharing appears to be the rule, this Part presents a case study of the social norms of an important exception to this rule. Fans of bands known as "jambands" have developed social norms that encourage voluntary compliance with the restrictions that bands place on the copying of their music. Paradoxically, this community is also remarkably permissive with its intellectual property. Jambands allow their fans to record live concerts and distribute the recordings freely. The recording and distribution of concerts forms the basis of a unique community whose norms are far more respectful of intellectual property than those of mainstream music fans....

A.   A Brief History of Jambands

As the name indicates, most jambands do indeed "jam"—that is, they improvise heavily while playing live music. Many genres, however, share this characteristic. A bit more revealing is the fact that the original and prototypical jamband was the Grateful Dead. Nevertheless, using the Grateful Dead as a reference point for jambands may serve to obscure as much as it does to enlighten. The status of the band as a 1960s counterculture icon carries a certain amount of baggage. When one brings up the Grateful Dead and its fans, known as "Deadheads," some see a uniquely kind and generous community, others see strung-out counterculture dropouts, and still others see a lot of tiresome tie dye kitsch. One must put aside such preconceptions and look past the band's admittedly colorful legacy to understand its true impact....

For thirty years, the Grateful Dead and its zealous fans, known as Deadheads, constituted a unique community. The band toured endlessly, and its fans followed them from show to show, with a core group fashioning their lives and livelihoods around the band. The Grateful Dead's reputation and fortune were largely based on concert performances. The Grateful Dead made each show a unique experience, presenting a unique set list and improvising heavily, often with extended jamming. The band allowed fans to tape these shows openly, and the fans avidly traded the tapes.

Before the Grateful Dead, taping and trading of live concerts was a common but largely underground practice among fans of different bands and musical genres, sometimes tolerated and sometimes not.[64] The Grateful Dead community turned taping and trading into an institution. Grateful Dead taping started out surreptitiously in the late '60s, but grew every year. By the mid-'70s, fans began to tape and trade more openly, and the band and its organization condoned the practice. In the mid-'80s, tapers became so numer-

---

64. See Jackie Loohauis, "Getting an Earful," *Milwaukee Journal–Sentinel*, Apr. 30, 2000, at O1E (describing long history of taping and trading concerts in rock music and other genres). For decades, fans have taped live performances of jazz, see, e.g., id. (noting legendary Charlie Parker bootlegs); Hollie I. West, "The Belated Grammy," *Washington Post*, Feb. 29, 1980, at D1 (discussing Grammy Award winning 1980 release of forty-year-old audience recording made with Duke Ellington's permission); opera, see, e.g., Bill Gowen,"It's All About The Money: Opera Broadcasts Becoming An Endangered Species," *Chicago Daily Herald*, July 11, 2003, at 9 (noting long tradition of bootlegging Metropolitan Opera broadcasts); Stephen Humphries, "Get Your Official 'Bootleg' Here!," *Christian Science Monitor*, Nov. 21, 2003, at 16 (noting that bootlegging of Metropolitan Opera performances goes back to 1901); bluegrass, see [Blair Jackson, *Garcia: An American Life* 277 (1999)] (noting that Grateful Dead guitarist Jerry Garcia taped bluegrass music in the mid-'60s); and rock and roll, see Loohauis, supra.

ous and well-accepted that the band created a tapers' section at concerts, allowing tapers to mail order tickets for this large special section, typically located behind the soundboard....

The Deadhead community was an avid consumer of new recording and communications technology.... They communicated at first through classified ads in magazines such as Relix. Soon after, they were among the early adopters of Internet technology, using Usenet newsgroups and then forming the core of one of the world's very first online communities, the WELL, in 1985. By the time the world wide web became widely available in the mid '90s, and CD burners affordable a few years later, Deadheads were well prepared for the new world of easy digital trading and downloading....

Meanwhile, the phenomenon of tape trading and Deadhead type communities had expanded far beyond the Grateful Dead. By the late '80s, a new generation of musicians began to consciously imitate what the Grateful Dead had made up as it went along. The most prominent among these musicians was the band Phish.... Like the Grateful Dead, they changed their set lists nightly, improvised heavily, and allowed their fans to tape shows....

In August 1995, Jerry Garcia, the guitarist and heart of the Grateful Dead, passed away. The Grateful Dead stopped touring and disbanded, and its many fans sought a new musical home. At this point, the jamband scene truly coalesced. Phish's already large following became larger, and many other bands gained new fans. By 2004, the jamband scene was big enough to support several simultaneous major tours, as well as numerous festivals and smaller bands.

In keeping with the traditions of Deadheads as tech-savvy pioneers, jamband fans embraced the Internet and other new technology. From the early '90s and onward, jamband fans created a vast network of online communities, including countless e-mail discussion lists, websites, databases, and a vast network for digital music trading called e-tree. The jamband community also developed several open-source software applications for use in sharing jamband music, some of which are beginning to have a major impact on the mainstream music community.

These days, the jamband community has expanded far beyond its neo-hippie roots. In fact, jambands now encompass many genres of music including rock, blues, jazz, funk, folk, reggae, bluegrass, and even gospel. Although most jambands still do indeed "jam" and jamband fans still attend multiple shows, the community is defined more by how bands and fans treat one another. At this point, the jamband label indicates that the band belongs to a community with shared norms and follows business practices that depart from the mainstream. Curiously, many of these unique norms and business practices center on the treatment of intellectual property. The next Section sets forth a case study of the jamband community, focusing on the reciprocal relationship between bands and their fans and the unusual treatment of intellectual property.

B.   A Case Study of a Reciprocating Community

Jambands and their fans have forged a unique community based on a mutual passion for music and reciprocal generosity, trust, and respect.... This unique way of doing business begins with an assertion of control—most jambands are far more entrepreneurial than mainstream bands and thus have far more control over their art and business affairs. This control then allows them, paradoxically, to give up some of that control to their most passionate fans, whom they allow to record and distribute live shows. The surrender of control is not complete, however, as the bands set very particular rules regarding the use and distribution of their music, particularly their commercial releases. Perhaps the most extraordinary part of the story is that social norms of the jamband community encourage fans not only to respect these rules, but also to help enforce them. The next subparts recount these facts in detail.

1.   Asserting and Giving Up Control

In many ways that would surprise the casual observer, the Grateful Dead was a paradigm of capitalism. The band ran its own business very effectively, gaining a tremendous amount of freedom and independence from the large amounts of income generated by its endless touring. It supported its own large business organization, Grateful Dead Productions, quite generously. It was able to do things its own way, rarely releasing radio-friendly albums and allowing its fans to tape shows, behaviors that most record companies find alarming. The bands that followed in its wake, like Phish, embraced this spirit of independence. A number of bands have even surpassed the Grateful Dead's model of taking control of their own business affairs. Many have their own labels and promotion companies.... In the world of jambands, the band is often its own business rather than an employee of the music industry.

Jambands use their independence to do things that many other musicians cannot. Among other things, jambands are unique among popular musicians in their generosity toward their fans.... Unlike mainstream concerts, where tapers are considered bootleggers and any taping is surreptitious and secretive, jambands welcome and accommodate tapers.... A jamband show rarely goes unrecorded, and many bands even rely on their fans to keep historical archives of their performances.

2.   A Community Founded on Sharing Music

Taping is not a solitary pursuit, but rather provides the foundation for a vast community that shares concert recordings. The norms of the jamband community encourage more than just generosity from the bands to tapers. The generosity extends from tapers to other fans and then among fans in general. While tapers certainly collect, enjoy, and trade their own tapes, they also create recordings they can distribute free of charge to others. The taper, or another who receives a copy of the initial recording, first formats the recording for distribution by breaking it into individual tracks, compressing the files using lossless music compression software, and creating an information sheet with a set list, source information, and other information. The recording is then "seeded," i.e., released to the community. From there it quickly spreads from one fan to another.

Jamband fans devote large amounts of time and effort to distributing recordings to one another. While some of this activity is in the form of recording-for-recording trades, in no event does money ever change hands. Fans distribute music to other fans at the expense of their own time, efforts, resources, and even money, using technology as simple as the postal service or as complex as cutting edge file-sharing programs created by the jamband community. All of these methods of distribution have an altruistic aspect. A fan who starts with no shows to trade could accumulate a large collection quite quickly just by responding to the frequent free offers on jamband e-mail lists and bulletin boards. The most basic forms of distribution occur via e-mail lists and message boards, typically devoted to specific bands, where fans offer to make copies of a particular recording for a limited number of other fans. Fans also organize "trees," where each recipient of a recording sends copies to a pre-determined group of other recipients, who then make recordings for others. Broadband technology has enabled other ways to distribute jamband recordings, allowing fans to set up computer servers on high speed connections. They fill these computer servers up with copies of shows so that other, anonymous fans may download the shows. In recent years, jamband fans have also collaborated to create open source file-sharing programs for the jamband community.

A large community has formed around this sharing of concert recordings and the bands who allow it. There really is no way to tell how large this community is, since membership is fluid, often anonymous, and requires no membership card. All indications, including the size of various online communities and the scope of various community projects, suggest that the community is substantial. Hundreds of e-mail lists and discussion boards are devoted to jambands and the distribution of their recordings. In the summer of 1998, a community of jamband fans formed an entity called "etree.org," dedicated to the distribution of live recordings. Etree.org has been the springboard for a number of substantial projects, including Furthurnet (an open source software program that facilitates legal file-sharing only), db.etree.org (a huge database that tracks tapes in circulation), the Free Lossless Audio Codec ("FLAC") (an open source lossless compression program), and the Live Music Archive (a huge archive of music available for high speed download on demand). As of spring 2006, the Live Music Archive hosted over 30,000 concert recordings, often in multiple formats.... Jambands' every moments are recorded for posterity, all the stage patter both profound and inane, including the shows where the band caught lightning in a bottle, the flat nights, the inadequately rehearsed new songs, broken guitar strings, and blown amps. If a fan wants to hear a jamband song, he or she need not run out to the music store, as a dozen live versions are available free for the taking.

This all represents, of course, a tremendous surrender of artistic and commercial control. How do the bands make it work? The answer seems to lie in trust: the fans obey the limits set by the bands, they keep paying for commercial recordings, and they remain fiercely loyal.

3.   Setting Rules

Jambands may surrender a great deal of control over their intellectual property to their fans, but they set some very definite rules. Like any other artist, they do not allow their commercial releases to be copied. They also do not allow people to make any commercial gain off their live recordings.

The Grateful Dead's statement on taping and distribution of concerts is an example of a fairly typical taping policy:

> The Grateful Dead and our managing organizations have long encouraged the purely non-commercial exchange of music taped at our concerts and those of our individual members. That a new medium of distribution has arisen—digital audio files being traded over the Internet—does not change our policy in this regard. Our stipulations regarding digital distribution are merely extensions of those long-standing principles and they are as follows:
>
>> No commercial gain may be sought by websites offering digital files of our music, whether through advertising, exploiting databases compiled from their traffic, or any other means.
>>
>> All participants in such digital exchange acknowledge and respect the copyrights of the performers, writers and publishers of the music.
>>
>> This notice should be clearly posted on all sites engaged in this activity.
>>
>> We reserve the ability to withdraw our sanction of non-commercial digital music should circumstances arise that compromise our ability to protect and steward the integrity of our work.

Phish has similar, but even more extensive rules. Their rules detail recording policies, fan site policies, and duplication policies.

Besides these basic rules, many bands add specific wrinkles. For example, some bands insist that fans stop trading all recordings of a show if it is included in a commercially released live album. Other bands require sound-board recordings to be withdrawn if a show is released commercially, but they allow fans to continue to trade audience tapes. "Audience tapes" are made using microphones in the audience, while soundboard tapes are made by patching into the soundboard. Some bands allow distribution through on-demand archives like the Live Audio Archive, while others do not. Some allow only a limited number of releases to be traded, while others restrict only a handful of shows from circulation.

4.   Playing by the Rules

Fans pay attention to the rules set by jambands and work diligently to comply. As a result, a culture of voluntary compliance with intellectual property rules pervades the jamband community. Fans carefully track information about bands' rules, communicate with the bands to clarify them, and publicize them to one another. In addition, jamband fans enforce bands' rules through: (1) informal sanctions such as shaming and banishing; (2) specific rules and policies of fan organizations such as etree; (3) monitoring and reporting illegal activities to band management and attorneys; and (4) software code in file-sharing programs that allow only permitted trading. Fans also appear to base their compliance on a perception that bands' rules are generally legitimate. To the extent that they do not always agree with a band's rules about particular shows, they note that compliance is warranted by the band's continuing generosity.

As noted above, a loose organization called etree.org lies at the heart of the online jamband community, and it exemplifies the community's culture of compliance. Etree is a volunteer effort organized around a set of websites and e-mail lists. Etree describes its mission as follows:

> etree.org is the award-winning leader in lossless digital audio distribution on the Internet! We are a community committed to providing the highest quality live concert recordings in a losslessly-compressed, 155 downloadable format. All of the music on etree.org is free, and 100% legal to download, trade, and burn. We also assist new traders in learning to trade online through our extensive guides[.]

Etree scrupulously plays by the rules. As one etree webpage notes, "The etree.org server team strives to be in strict compliance with the taping policies of every etreed band." It maintains a "zero tolerance" policy against those who violate the rules, stating: "there are performers who are notoriously against taping and trading (Bob Dylan and Live, to name only two). You may not use the etree.org mailing lists to discuss such artists. Solicitations to exchange music by these artists are prohibited and will not be tolerated." In case of doubt as to a band's policies, etree puts the burden on the fan to demonstrate that the band has given permission.

Etree and other jamband community sites maintain detailed information on bands' taping and trading policies. There are sites dedicated exclusively to listing "taper friendly bands," webpages dedicated to publicizing bands' taping and trading policies, and sites that contain lengthy discussions of taping etiquette. There are discussion forums dedicated to listing particular shows designated as off limits by otherwise taper friendly bands. The Live Music Archive has contacted hundreds of bands to receive express permission to add the band to its on-demand archive and has carefully documented those bands (many otherwise friendly to taping and trading) that refused.

The jamband community has several ways of helping to enforce the rules of the community. People who deviate from the norms of the community are chastened on e-mail lists and discussion boards. If their offenses are viewed as grievous enough, they may be labeled "bad traders" and banned from participating in groups or even publicly shamed on "bad trader" websites. Etree declares that its sanctions include "blocking the IP address of known offenders from etree.org web and FTP servers," and "removing and banning known offenders from all etree.org mailing lists."

One of the most remarkable ways in which the jamband community enforces rules is by working directly with authority figures. Etree notes that it monitors the eBay, Amazon.com, and Yahoo! auction sites for illegal sales of bootlegs. To enable its users to report illegal activity, it provides e-mail links to the proper authorities at eBay, Amazon.com, and Yahoo!, and also to the legal teams for several bands. A recent news item on the Jambands.com website (an online jambands magazine) is indicative of how jamband fans work with bands on legal enforcement matters:

Have You Seen The Gregg Allman Anthology?

The Allman Brothers' website is asking for fans' help in tracking down bootleg copies of The Gregg Allman Anthology. It is believed that records were illegally manufactured in Mexico, Singapore or Thailand. If you have purchased a foreign manufactured copy of the album, contact lanam@all manbrothersband.com. The site also states that anyone who turns in an illegal copy of the album, "will be rewarded by Gregg."

One Grateful Dead fan even took it upon himself to hire a lawyer and sue eBay for allowing people to sell bootleg recordings on its site (he lost).

Contrast the image of jamband fans working cheerfully with band management and legal teams to catch bootleggers and rule breakers with the mutual antipathy between mainstream music fans and "the music industry." Jamband fans seem to view band management as people who work for the artists and themselves as part of a community that includes the band. Mainstream music fans, on the other hand, often portray band management as part of a ruthless industry that merely employs musicians and mistreats fans and musicians alike.[65]

The jamband community also helps to enforce rules through software code, building file-sharing programs that are not amenable to illegal copying. These software programs provide a nearly perfect example of what Larry Lessig described in his book *Code and Other Laws of Cyberspace:* software that controls behavior by eliminating the option not to comply. The programs created by the jamband community, however, are an interesting twist on this concept. While Lessig assumes that code will be imposed upon people, the jamband community imposes code upon itself. The most copyright friendly of these programs is a file-sharing application called Furthurnet. Furthurnet is built on an "opt-in" model—only bands that allow taping can be shared on Furthurnet. Furthurnet confronts all users—uploaders and downloaders—with a drop-down menu that contains only bands that permit file-sharing. Uploaders cannot share a file from a band that does not permit taping and

65. Over the last several years, consumers' opinions of record labels and the music industry have grown more and more negative. See, e.g., Fredric Paul, "Why Everyone Hates The Music Industry," http://www.techweb.com/wire/172300219 (last visited Mar. 13, 2006); National Purchase Diary Group, "Consumers Delete Large Numbers of Digital Music Files From PC Hard Drives," Nov. 5, 2003, available at http://www.npd.com/dynamic/releases/press_031105.htm ("Two-thirds of consumers who had recently shared files on P2P networks reported that the lawsuits caused them to have a 'much more' or 'somewhat more' negative opinion of record companies in general.") . . . .

downloaders cannot even search for files from a band other than the "taper friendly" ones on the list. Furthurnet also allows users to report improper files (e.g., commercial releases), keeps track of "off limits" shows from otherwise taper friendly bands, and cooperates with bands in removing improper material. The Live Music Archive also has similar policies, in that it only allows people to upload shows from bands that have granted permission to be included in this on-demand archive.

Another file-sharing program written for the etree community is BitTorrent, currently the hottest new file-sharing program. Intrigued by the problem of limited bandwidth faced by his friends in the jamband community, Bram Cohen created a powerful solution with BitTorrent.... This architecture allows for faster downloads and fits the jamband community's norms of sharing quite well. The jamband community helped test BitTorrent in the summer of 2002 and then quickly adopted it and spread it throughout the jamband community and beyond. Since then, users have widely employed it for other legal purposes, such as distribution of Linux kernel releases and other open source programs, and illegal purposes, including distribution of pirated movies, television shows, and software.

Cohen cites etree in defense of the legality of his work and motives. He claims that BitTorrent is best suited to legal applications, like etree.org, as it is not at all anonymous and its use is easily traceable. As Cohen stated in a *New York Times* interview, " 'it amazes me that sites like Suprnova continue to stay up, because it would be so easy to sue them.' ... Using BitTorrent for illegal trading, he added, is 'patently stupid because it's not anonymous, and it can't be made anonymous because it's fundamentally antithetical to the architecture.' " Etree uses this transparent architecture to its advantage, diligently policing and preventing posting of illegal seeds on its BitTorrent tracker site.

Finally, it should be noted that the jamband community buys into the rules set by artists and their right to set the rules. Fans are willing and active participants in this system. Personal websites frequently refer to the rules, making it clear that any trades must comply. Community members frequently encourage one another to buy jambands' commercial releases. E-mail lists and forums contain careful discussions of the rules and angry flames of those who challenge the community's norms. Unlike the mainstream music world, copyright holders and fans peacefully co-exist in the jamband community.

5. A Reciprocal Relationship

Jambands and their fans have a healthy reciprocal relationship that goes beyond the bands giving away music and the fans respecting and enforcing artists' rights. Jamband fans are incredibly loyal and passionate about the bands they follow. They will travel great distances to attend shows. They will often follow the band on tour, just as Deadheads followed the Grateful Dead. They will proselytize for their favorite bands endlessly, often volunteering to help promote the band by plastering the town with posters.

The bands do a great deal to foster this loyalty and sense of community. They pay attention to the comfort and enjoyment of their fans, holding festivals in pleasant places and setting up travel tour packages for fans traveling to shows. Band management communicates directly with fans on e-mail lists and websites. Fans are offered chances to purchase concert tickets early, and tickets are generally less expensive than mainstream concerts. Many bands also give away music directly—they seed high quality live recordings to the fan community or make them available on their websites.

Fans may also feel more loyal toward jambands because they feel closer to them. As described above, jambands often control their own destinies. In contrast to the mainstream music business, jamband fans are less likely to be separated from bands by a vast industry of middlemen.

6.   New Distribution Models

The trust engendered by this reciprocity between jambands and their fans has allowed jambands to exploit digital distribution channels with unique success. They have used distribution models that most other musicians dare not try. The bands attribute this success to the bond of trust they have with their fans.

The most prominent experiment has been with the sale of high quality live recordings. Phish, the String Cheese Incident, the Dead, and others have all begun to sell fans copies of every show on their recent tours. The bands have made these CDs available through downloads as well as through traditional retail distribution channels. The downloads are in the lossless FLAC compression format created by the jamband community, and contain no copy protection or digital rights management. The bands also allow fans to continue making and trading recordings of these shows. . . .

Other jambands have begun to sell studio albums via downloads as well. These downloads are also in the FLAC format, and contain no copy protection or digital rights management technology. The mainstream music industry has been wary of such wholesale, non-copy protected online distribution. . . .

Why can jambands use such a form of digital distribution where other bands dare not? As Forrester analyst Josh Bernoff noted of Phish, "Phish has the kind of fans who would download these files and pay for them . . . it shows an enormous amount of trust in the fan base to put these recordings out there in MP3 format." The Live Phish website makes it clear that trust is the basis of this venture: "Live Phish Downloads relies on an honor system, and we ask that you do not abuse the unrestricted nature of these files. If you would like to see this type of delivery of shows continue and flourish, please respect our taping policy and don't abuse the system."

Another reason that jambands can experiment with digital distribution is that they control their own destinies far more than most bands. Big labels typically do not let bands determine policies regarding concert recordings or try new methods of distribution. As noted earlier, Phish has always been a special case for its label, Elektra. Elektra has made an exception for taping and trading by Phish fans and also consented to Live Phish (in exchange for a share of the profits). . . .

7. Summary

The jamband community thus offers an intriguing example of how things could be different for the mainstream music industry. . . . The key question to ask, however, is whether this model is transferable. Is it unique to the jamband community, or is it based on principles that can be applied elsewhere? The next Part discusses explanations for the norms of the jamband community that indicate there are some general lessons that the rest of the music industry could draw from the jamband experience.

IV. EXPLAINING THE SOCIAL NORMS OF THE JAMBAND COMMUNITY

The social norms of the jamband community seem to defy expectations. In the view of some, the opportunistic behavior of mainstream file-sharers seems far more natural. Much of the recent legal scholarship that explores social norms would tend to agree. The law and norms literature often explains norms as a product of clearly self-interested behavior, like the satisfaction of pecuniary interests or the desire to advance social or economic status. The norms of the jamband community do not comfortably fit this model, as jambands and their fans cooperate and behave with apparent altruism even where personal gain is uncertain or unlikely.

One might resolve this puzzle by concluding that the jamband community is simply an all-too-rare example of a community that practices what it preaches. . . . This explanation has some superficial appeal, but its dismissal of the jamband phenomenon is too facile. It wrongly assumes that opportunistic behavior is the rule, while the kind of pro-social, cooperative behavior exhibited by the jamband community is a quirky, unpredictable exception. Common experience, confirmed by field studies and laboratory research, says otherwise. Although examples of selfish motivations and behavior abound, people also provide volunteer services, give to charities, and help strangers with no appreciable expectation of any sort of personal gain. . . . This results from a set of behavioral characteristics commonly grouped under the label of "reciprocity."

Reciprocity motivates people to repay the actions of others with like actions—value received repaid with value given, kindness with kindness, cooperation with cooperation, and non-cooperation with retaliation. Under favorable conditions, it takes only a minority of people influenced by reciprocity to push a group to a sustained equilibrium of cooperation. If conditions favor opportunism, however, reciprocity may actually hasten the demise of cooperation by causing people to withhold cooperation. A number of laboratory and field experiments have helped researchers to identify the conditions under which reciprocity is most likely to facilitate cooperation. As discussed below, it appears that the jamband community has happened upon a way of doing things that taps into reciprocity to create norms that encourage fans to

446

respect copyright restrictions. This observation holds promise for the mainstream music community. If it can reproduce some of the conditions that allow reciprocity to encourage pro-copyright norms in the jamband community, it may be able to change mainstream norms that currently favor illegal file-sharing.

This Part begins by briefly reviewing the law and social norms scholarship, explaining why the dominant self-interest based models do not satisfactorily explain the social norms of the jamband community. It then delves into behavioral and experimental economics research that supports and explains the existence of reciprocity in order to better understand how reciprocity generates support for law in the jamband community and elsewhere.

A. Signaling and Esteem as Sources for Social Norms

Beginning with Robert Ellickson's now-classic 1991 study of social norms among cattle ranchers in Shasta County, California,[66] a large body of legal scholarship has examined social norms. Ellickson's study awakened interest in the fact that social norms often regulate human behavior more powerfully than law. Since then, law and social norms scholarship has addressed the origin and evolution of norms, the mechanisms by which they affect behavior, and how law interacts with social norms. Social science has advanced many possible sources for social norms—mutual self-interest, culture, religion, education, psychology, and evolution are all candidates. Recent law and social norms theorists, however, have largely favored rational choice theory, focusing on game theory and rational self-interest to explain how social norms influence behavior.

Many law and social norms scholars thus eschew explanations for social norms that rely on altruism, psychology, or cultural forces. Instead, they contend that people enforce and comply with norms as a result of self-interest expressed through mutually beneficial cooperation. This work owes much to Robert Axelrod's groundbreaking study in game theory, *The Evolution of Cooperation*.[67] Axelrod used computer simulations to show that rational actors were likely to cooperate under conditions where a "tit-for-tat" strategy could produce a stable equilibrium of pro-social, cooperative behavior. The necessary conditions include the possibility for mutually beneficial exchange, repeat interactions among the actors, knowledge of how actors behaved in the past, and the ability to withhold cooperation from actors who had failed to cooperate in the past (i.e., to react "tit-for-tat"). A group of rational actors will thus engage in cooperative, other-regarding behavior when conditions are such that it is in the self-interest of all actors to do so.

A number of law and norms theorists posit that ... norms emerge from and are reinforced by tit-for-tat behavior and self-interest. For example, ... one informs one's peers that one is a "good type" with a "low discount rate," i.e., someone with whom one might want to engage in future transactions.... People want the esteem of their peers. They fear that they will lose the

---

66. Robert C. Ellickson, *Order without Law: How Neighbors Settle Disputes* (1991).

67. Robert Axelrod, *The Evolution of Cooperation* (1985).

esteem of others if they violate norms, and hope to gain esteem by complying with and enforcing norms.

Two important features of these models limit their usefulness for explaining the social norms of the jamband community. First, they tend to look to some form of rational self-interest, narrowly understood, to explain the content of norms. Second, they work best to explain the origin and evolution of social norms within small, close-knit groups where people repeatedly interact with one another. The norms of the jamband community are difficult to explain completely and plausibly in terms of rational self-interest. In any event, the jamband community is not the type of small, close-knit community likely to maintain adherence to norms through the prospect of repeat interaction.

Rational self-interest cannot fully explain the social norms of the jamband community. The seemingly altruistic, other-regarding behavior of jambands and their fans is not easy to reconcile with a narrow understanding of rational self-interest. Nevertheless, ... [these writers] might theorize that jamband community members engage in pro-social behaviors to gain future benefits or avoid sanction. They thus might propose that bands allow taping, tapers distribute recordings, fans abstain from copying commercial releases, and community members promote and enforce rules against unauthorized copying in order to gain and maintain the good opinion of their peers. There are two difficulties with such an explanation. First, it does not tell us why the jamband community values such behavior while the mainstream music community does not. Both groups appear to have the same pecuniary interests: revenue maximization for bands and inexpensive or free music for fans. Self-interest thus cannot account for all of the difference. Second, many of the behaviors encouraged by the norms of the jamband community are relatively costly with an uncertain payoff. While each community member might hope that other members of the community comply with restrictions that bands place on copying and trading lest the bands choose to cut off the supply of free music, there is little incentive for each individual to comply with or enforce rules personally. The community is set up so that it is quite easy to collect free music quietly while leaving the work of building the community and enforcing its norms to others. One's peers are unlikely to know that one has refrained from unauthorized copying or has corrected others who are not complying with the rules, because the jamband community exists largely online.

In a loose-knit, partly anonymous community like the jamband community, self-interest alone is unlikely to maintain compliance with social norms. The jamband community is a large, diverse group that exists across many e-mail lists, online message boards, cooperative efforts like etree and the Internet Archive, and small social groups that meet in person at shows or in particular communities. As with any large, online community, identities are often pseudonymous and people can easily come and go anonymously, with little repeat interaction. In such a large, loose-knit group, it is difficult to establish the conditions for a ... tit-for-tat game. People engage in many interactions with people they may not see again or in situations where no relevant peers can observe their actions. There is great incentive to "cheat" in such situations because of the absence of the signaling or esteem benefits ... For a large, loose-knit group like the jamband community, something more than rational self-interest is thus necessary to explain the emergence and maintenance of social norms.

Recently, law and social norms scholarship has begun to focus on social psychology to explain the norms of large, loose-knit groups. Of particular promise is work that focuses on a human behavioral trait known as reciprocity. These scholars contend that under the right conditions, reciprocity fosters norms that promote pro-social, cooperative behaviors. Although reciprocity is certainly not the only source of social norms, this behavioral trait appears to explain a great deal about how social norms develop in situations calling for collective action and social and economic exchange. A survey of the extensive research on the nature of reciprocity in the next Section confirms that it accounts for many of the differences between the norms of the jamband community and the norms of the mainstream music community.

B.   Reciprocity: What It Is and How It Works

At first glance, the norms of the jamband community seem to defy expectations. The jamband community provides a contrast to the behavior of the mainstream music industry and its fans, as jambands and their fans seem more cooperative and less self-interested than either common experience or some theoretical models would predict. Nevertheless, the norms of the jamband community are not at all extraordinary.

Every day, people cooperate with and behave kindly to strangers, even those they will likely never see again.... Many scholars trace the origin of such cooperative behavior to a deeply held human behavioral trait known as reciprocity. Reciprocity dictates that people's actions should be repaid with like actions—value received repaid with value given, kindness with kindness, cooperation with cooperation, and non-cooperation with retaliation. People are thus conditional cooperators. They are willing to cooperate, but their continuing cooperation depends on what others are doing, the intentions of others, and how well others are doing (for better or worse) relative to themselves....

Social scientists have studied and confirmed reciprocity in laboratory settings through a variety of experimental games. These social dilemma games—including the ultimatum game, the public goods game, and the dictator game—are set up to pose a variety of scenarios where people have the choice of cooperating for mutual benefit, acting opportunistically, and/or acting benevolently. The Sections below examine the research confirming and describing reciprocity in greater detail.

1.   Evidence for Reciprocity

Evidence of reciprocity comes from a number of sources. Scholars tend to cite three categories: common experience, historical evidence and field research, and experimental games. The evidence is strong and widely accepted. Its interpretation is debated, but broad areas of agreement have emerged.

The scholarship on reciprocity often begins by noting common examples of cooperative and benevolent behavior. As noted above, people leave tips and donate money to charity.... Other examples include support for social welfare programs, volunteer service, and care for family members. Some have also noted that cooperation is not always "nice." People will cooperate and incur a cost in order to punish others—for example, socially snubbing somebody who violates community norms or taking a risk to steal from an employer who is perceived as unfair. This common experience is confirmed more rigorously by fieldwork and historical examples from various disciplines such as ethnography, anthropology, and social psychology.

Although common experience and field studies indicate the existence of reciprocity, they do not tell us exactly how it works. We know that people also behave selfishly under many conditions. The "bewildering variety of evidence" calls for controlled study and detailed models....

Researchers have indeed performed hundreds of such experiments, setting up social dilemma games in the laboratory that participants must solve by cooperating or declining to cooperate. The social dilemma games most relevant to this Article's discussion of reciprocity are the public goods game, the ultimatum game, and the dictator game. The following subsections describe these experiments and what they tell us about reciprocity.

a) The Public Goods Game

The public goods game is one of the most important for understanding the nature of reciprocity. In the public goods game, a group of players has the opportunity to benefit from a common resource—i.e., a public good. Its conditions evoke the central problem of cooperation: while we all gain from cooperating, each individual has an incentive to free ride on the efforts of the other players. The game is designed to illuminate such problems as the voluntary payment of taxes and the restriction of one's use of an endangered environmental resource.... These problems have certain parallels to compliance with copyright law. Choosing not to pay taxes is like choosing not to pay for copyrighted works—the consequences of getting caught are undesirable, but unlikely to occur. Similarly, one who downloads free music is in some sense like one who uses an environmental resource—in the aggregate such actions may "deplete" the resource (by undermining incentives to create), but one's individual actions increase one's own welfare without having a tremendous impact on the whole. Each file-sharer free rides on the work of those who create and the willingness of others to compensate that creativity.

In the public goods game, the public good to which players may contribute is typically a pool of shared money. Each player is given money at the start of each round and must decide how much to contribute to the pool. The benefit of contributing is that each contribution is matched by the experimenter, and the increased pool is divided among the players. The catch is that the increased pool of money is shared by all players, without regard to whether they contributed or not.

This is how a typical variant of the public goods game works, with ten players: at the start of each round, each player is given $1, and may anonymously contribute any portion of that $1 to the common pool. The experimenter then divides the amount in the common pool in half, and gives that amount of money to each player. If all 10 players contribute $1 each, the common pool is $10, and they each receive $5. The optimal outcome for the group as a whole occurs when everyone contributes all of their money to the common pool. For example, after 10 rounds each player would have $50 in exchange for a $10 contribution ($1 each round).

The problem that the public goods game presents is the potential for free riding: the selfish player or "rational egoist" can do better by contributing nothing, provided that the other nine players do contribute. In that scenario, the selfish player keeps his $10 plus the $45 that results from the contributions of others, for a total of $55. If everyone does this, however, the common pool is empty and each player ends up with only $10. The worst outcome would occur if a player contributes $1 and nobody else does, in which case the player receives back only $.50. Absent the opportunity to communicate and make enforceable agreements, the expectation is that a rational player will desire the optimal outcome ($55), want to avoid the worst outcome ($.50), will expect other players to see things the same way, and will thus contribute nothing. The predicted outcome is thus "an 'iterated prisoner's dilemma' in which self-regarding players contribute nothing."

This prediction is not borne out when the game is actually played, which tells us some interesting things about human behavior. The experiment has been run often enough with sufficiently consistent results that it is now possible to make generalizations. During the first round, people contribute on average about half of their money to the common pool. This contribution rate occurs even in one round, "one shot" games where there is no potential for future cooperation. If the game is played for several rounds under the standard conditions of anonymity, cooperation deteriorates. Nevertheless, in the last round, where there is no longer a possibility for future cooperation, over 25% of subjects still contribute something. The experimental evidence thus only partly confirms the prediction of an iterated prisoner's dilemma. Some people free ride, but not all do. Free riding may cause cooperation to deteriorate, but never completely eliminates it.

When the rules of the game reduce anonymity, cooperation increases. Simply allowing players to observe each other silently increases cooperation. More important, if players are allowed to communicate, they coordinate their efforts and make agreements; as a result, cooperation increases dramatically and free riding declines. These benefits continue, even into the last round. Communication improves cooperation even in one round games, which contradicts the standard model. These results are surprising, because without enforcement of agreements, it is easy to make and break promises.

When the rules of the game are further refined to allow people to punish others for non-compliance, cooperation increases even more dramatically. People will punish non-cooperators, even at a cost to themselves. In a series of experiments, Ernst Fehr and Simon Gachter introduced the opportunity to punish non-cooperators.[68] There is a cost to the punisher, but the cost to the one punished is even greater. The self-interested model of behavior would predict that such an opportunity for punishment would not change the outcome because a rational actor would not incur a cost to punish others. People might hope that other players would punish bad behavior, but would not voluntarily give up their own income to do so. Rational players would anticipate that motivations would play out this way, so they would not alter their contributions. But people do not behave according to this prediction. The availability of punishment increases and sustains high levels of contribution. In fact, many players incur a cost to punish non-cooperators and 82.5% of the players cooperate fully—contributing all their resources to the common pool. This effect is so strong that even in the final round of the game, where future punishment is no longer a threat, players still contribute 90% on average.

Several models have emerged to explain the behavior of people in public goods games. These models fall into two broad categories—"models of inequality aversion and models of reciprocity. In inequality-aversion [also called inequity aversion] theories, players prefer more money and also prefer that allocations be more equal." Under inequity aversion theories, people have a preference for equitable outcomes and are willing to act on those preferences. Reciprocity theories are a bit more complex, as they posit preferences that focus on the intent and actions of others. If people perceive others to be behaving kindly, they will reciprocate with kind behavior. If they perceive others as behaving unkindly, they will retaliate.

Falk, Fehr, and Fischbacher have proposed an integrated model to fully account for pro-social behavior in social dilemma situations. They contend that people are conditional cooperators. People are willing to cooperate provided that others cooperate and outcomes are equitable. If people are convinced that others will contribute to the public good, they will contribute too. If they expect that some free-riders will hold out, however, their aversion to inequity will cause them to withhold cooperation. They are also willing to punish others, both to achieve more equitable outcomes, as well as to reciprocate unkind behavior.

The conditional cooperator model has been tested further in laboratory and field experiments. Fischbacher, Gachter, and Fehr examined these tendencies in a unique public goods game that specifically measured how much people's willingness to cooperate was based on the cooperation of others. In this game, people were given the opportunity to fill out a table of contributions, indicating their preferred contribution based on increasing levels of average contributions by the group. The experimenters found that most

---

68. See Ernst Fehr & Simon Gachter, "Cooperation and Punishment in Public Goods Experiments," 90 *American Economic Review* 980, 993 (2000).

people were neither free-riders nor pure altruists. About 50% were conditional cooperators, increasing their contributions in proportion to the contributions of others. About 30% of the subjects turned out to be free-riders. In a field experiment designed to test conditional cooperation, experimenters informed students about the contributions of others to a voluntary social fund. People who were informed that contributions were higher than they expected tended to increase their contributions. The data thus supported the conclusion that "people behave pro-socially conditional on the pro-social behavior of other persons."

b) The Ultimatum Game

The ultimatum game is another social dilemma game that focuses specifically on people's propensity for benevolent and vengeful behavior. In this game, the experimenter selects random pairs of people and gives them a sum of money to divide. One player—the Proposer—is given the power to propose how to divide the money. The Proposer can make only one offer and cannot negotiate with the other subject—the Responder. If the Responder accepts, then she may keep the amount offered. If the Responder rejects the offer, however, then both get nothing. Standard assumptions about rational self-interest lead one to expect that the Proposer would offer as little as possible—e.g., one cent—and the Responder would accept, since something is better than nothing.

In this game too, however, people's behavior defies expectations, thus supporting the inequality aversion and reciprocity models. This experiment has been performed many times in different cultures, with different amounts, and with different procedures. While there are almost no offers over 50%, the vast majority of Proposers offer between 40% and 50%, with almost no offers below 20%. Responders often reject low offers (e.g., less than 30%), and the likelihood of rejection decreases with the size of the offer.

The ultimatum game thus demonstrates that people will cooperate at a cost to themselves and will punish others at a cost to themselves. The behavior of Responders particularly supports the existence of reciprocity. They are willing to incur a significant cost in order to punish what they perceive as unkind behavior. People are far more spiteful than most standard economic models predict. The actions of Proposers also support a preference for equity, but they may just be acting strategically. Proposers bring their knowledge of human nature into the laboratory. They know that people are willing to punish behavior perceived to be unfair, so they know they may end up with nothing if their offers are too low.

c) The Dictator Game

The dictator game drastically simplifies the conditions of the ultimatum game to isolate the behavior and motivations of Proposers. The Proposer decides how to split the money provided by the experimenter. The other player is not a Responder in the dictator game because he has no opportunity to respond. Instead, the other player is a Recipient—an anonymous person in another room. It is completely left to the Proposer's discretion whether to give the Recipient any money. "Dictator games are an interesting vehicle for studying the meaning and interpretation of 'fairness'" because they "control[] for strategic behavior in the ultimatum game." At this point, self-interest might be expected to come to the fore because the Proposer can simply walk away with all the money.

Once again, the result defies the predictions of the self-interest model. At least some Proposers still give Recipients money. Perhaps unsurprisingly, the allocations are much lower than in the ultimatum game. On average, Proposers dictate an allocation between 10% and 25% to the Recipient. This result indicates that some of the generosity displayed by Proposers in the ultimatum game is motivated by fear of rejection. On the other hand, since many Proposers offer something in the dictator game, at least some Proposers in the ultimatum game may be motivated by preferences for equitable outcomes.

The generosity of the Proposers also varies based on the degree of social distance between the Proposer and the Recipient or others who know about the Proposer's actions. "Social distance can be defined as the degree of reciprocity that subjects believe exists within a social interaction." In the standard dictator game, the Proposer knows that the experimenter will know whether he allocated any money. One group of experimenters set out to determine how much generosity in the dictator game was influenced by observation of the experimenter. The group created a double-blind procedure that assured the Proposer of anonymity. Nobody else, including the experimenter, could observe or find out what the Proposer chose to do. In the double-blind experiment, 64% of the offers were $0 and only 8% offered 40% or more. The differences between these outcomes and those in standard dictator experiments were statistically significant—in the standard dictator experiment, 18% offered $0 and 32% offered 40% or more. In a later set of experiments, the researchers changed elements of the language and procedures to vary social distance. They found that changing the degree of social distance changed the outcome, with the distributions becoming more generous as social distance decreased. In another experiment where Recipients gave a short description of themselves heard by Proposers, the average allocation rose to 50%. Context can further increase allocations by making the recipient more "deserving" or sympathetic—as in an experiment where the Recipient was the Red Cross.

d) Summary

Research indicates that reciprocity is a powerful, but not inevitable, influence on human behavior. Preferences for cooperation appear to be common, but there are also people who will prefer to behave in a "selfish" manner. If the institutions—or "rules of the game"—tend to allow reciprocity to induce and foster pro-social behavior, then cooperative outcomes are more likely.

2.   How Reciprocity Explains the Behavior of the Jamband Community

Reciprocity appears to explain the most important characteristics of the social norms of the jamband community. The following Sections describe the most salient features of reciprocity, how they can foster cooperative behavior under the right conditions, and how the jamband community taps into reciprocity to foster such behavior.

a) (Some) People Are Pre–Disposed to Play by the Rules

Some people are pre-disposed to cooperate and treat others kindly. The theoretical models that explain reciprocity posit the presence of three different types of people: conditional cooperators, willing punishers, and rational egoists. Conditional cooperators will start out cooperating if they anticipate that others will do so, and will continue to cooperate if others do so and if the outcomes remain fairly distributed. If others do not cooperate, however, they will begin to reduce their cooperation.... The rational egoists or "selfish types" will act opportunistically for their own benefit, unless something constrains them. The willing punishers may supply such a constraint. Their preferences for reciprocity and equitable outcomes are so strong that they are willing to punish those who they perceive as unkind or uncooperative, even at a cost to themselves.

Too many have viewed the file-sharing problem with something akin to pure pessimism. The existence of these three behavioral types indicates that we ought to view people—including music fans—more realistically. "Instead of pure pessimism or pure optimism," one must recognize that people have both the potential to behave well and the potential to behave badly. Neither the rule-breaking of mainstream file-sharers nor the compliance of jamband fans should surprise us, since conditional cooperators and selfish types are present in both populations. Although this point may seem utterly prosaic (some people are cooperative, others are not), it is worth making. The outcomes in both the mainstream music community and the jamband community are both plausible; neither one is inevitable.

The challenge is setting up conditions that encourage compliance. Cooperation is more likely to prevail when conditions allow conditional cooperators and willing punishers to get the upper hand. If conditional cooperators perceive that others are cooperating, they will continue to do so. The jamband community fosters a perception of cooperation, as examples of highly visible compliance abound. Compliance is even more likely if willing punishers are able to exercise their preference to punish opportunistic behavior.

b) Under the Right Conditions, Conditional Cooperators Will Play by the Rules

People are conditional cooperators. In situations that call for cooperating and playing by the rules, people's cooperation depends on whether they perceive a situation as fair. Such perceptions of fairness are based on whether or not others are receiving a windfall from behaving opportunistically. Even if an individual receives some benefit from cooperation, she will judge an outcome to be unfair if others are free-riding or receiving more than their "fair" share. Thus, she will withhold cooperation in a public goods game if others are free-riding and will punish a proposer in an ultimatum game if she believes the proposer is keeping more than a fair share. On the other hand, if she perceives outcomes to be fair, she will cooperate. Unlike the mainstream music industry, jambands create conditions that encourage cooperation. They benefit from conditional cooperation, as fans perceive their behavior as fair and because they perceive that other fans are playing by the rules.

Significantly for copyright owners, preferences for fairness appear to influence market behavior. Daniel Kahneman and others have studied how consumers' perceptions of fairness with respect to factors like pricing, profit margins, wage setting, and rent influence their economic behavior and, in turn, constrain the behavior of other market actors.[69] What is "fair" is a matter of subjective perception: people have some subjectively fair reference transaction in mind against which they measure the fairness of a transaction. Such perceptions of unfairness matter because they strongly influence behavior. People are willing to pay "fair" prices and allow companies "fair" profits. However, if they believe a company is exploiting market power or acting opportunistically, they are willing to punish the company even at a cost to themselves. In a real life example of ultimatum game-type retaliation, Kahneman's research indicated that people would be willing to drive an extra five minutes to avoid patronizing a more convenient store that mistreated its workers or raised its prices to take advantage of the closing of a competitor.

Retaliatory behavior in the marketplace is quite relevant to the problem of file-sharing. Consumers are infamous for their antipathy for the music industry. They assert that the prices for CDs are "too high"; that the industry rips off artists; and that CDs contain only a minority of worthwhile songs. These complaints are all offered as reasons or excuses for file-sharing. Although one may dismiss these assertions as mere rationalizations, the research on reciprocity suggests there may be greater significance to these complaints. Regardless of their validity, perceptions of unfairness are important because people are willing to punish companies for them. When people can choose whether or not to pay for a product, being despised as unfair can have serious economic consequences.

Conversely, being viewed as fair has some economic benefits. People come to the jamband community pre-disposed to cooperate. When they find the bands to be generous—allowing trading and copying and treating fans well in other respects—they reciprocate by treating the band fairly in return. A telling moment occurred recently when the Mermen, a band that tours modestly sized clubs nationally, had its equipment stolen. Fans rallied to raise money for new equipment. As one fan on a message board said in urging others to donate money: "While I have never seen the band, I have heard them many times through this site.... These types of bands are small and not wealthy but let us listen to their music for free." Note the willingness to reciprocate with a band with which the fan had no other connection than free music. Although this example is one of charity for a smaller band, other examples abound. The perception of fair treatment of fans inspires fair

---

69. Daniel Kahneman et al., "Fairness as a Constraint on Profit Seeking: Entitlements in the Market," 76 *American Economic Review* 728, 729 (1986).

treatment in return. Jamband community members often urge one another to play by the rules and buy the bands' commercial releases to show appreciation for all the free music. The perception that jambands behave fairly appears to inspire at least part of the remarkable cooperativeness of the jamband community.

As noted above, conditional cooperators care not only about "fairness" but also about whether other people are playing by the same rules they are. As the results of public goods games show, people will withhold cooperation if they perceive that others are reaping a windfall from free-riding. "Individuals dislike being a so-called 'sucker,' i.e., being the only one who contributes to a public good while the others free ride." On the other hand, "those who believe that others will cooperate in social dilemmas are more likely to cooperate themselves." This is the behavior that charities try to evoke with challenge grants or depictions of busily ringing phones in public television pledge drives. As discussed earlier, people react well to cooperation by others: they will indirectly reciprocate by also cooperating. They are also averse to inequity, however, and in the presence of free-riding will withhold cooperation or punish others if the opportunity is available.

Reciprocity may explain compliance or non-compliance with certain laws. As conditional cooperators, people tend to do what they see others doing. Dan Kahan has thus proposed that reciprocity explains why people voluntarily comply with tax laws.[70] Citing a study sponsored by the Minnesota Department of Revenue, Kahan contends that people are more or less willing to obey tax laws depending on their perceptions as to what other people are doing. If they perceive that others are complying, they are likely to comply; if they perceive that others are not complying, they are less likely to comply.

This phenomenon appears to be at work in both the mainstream music industry and the jamband community. People take cues from the behavior of others. When they are exposed to wide-spread file-sharing, their "propensity to file-share [is] reinforced" notwithstanding legal condemnation. The perception and reality are mutually reinforcing, as ever-increasing amounts of file-sharing trigger increasing awareness of rule-breaking, thus engendering "reciprocity cascades." By contrast, the jamband community has created conditions that encourage compliance with copyright restrictions. Through the etree.org website, on discussion forums and e-mail lists, and on fans' personal websites the message is pounded home: the jamband community is not a place where unauthorized copying is tolerated or common. In the jamband community, reciprocity thus causes compliance to beget compliance.

c) Reduced Social Distance Encourages Cooperation

Decreasing social distance makes reciprocity more likely to influence people's behavior. People are more likely to cooperate and treat others well if they are not isolated and alienated from those who are affected by their

---

70. Dan M. Kahan, "Trust, Collective Action, and Law," 81 *Boston University Law Review* 333, 340–41 (2001).

actions. For example, in the dictator game, people are more likely to act kindly when their acts are known to others or when recipients are made more sympathetic. Similarly, when players were allowed to communicate or even to simply observe one another in the public goods game, they were far more likely to cooperate. Reciprocity is thus related to sociality. The more one is isolated from others, the less likely it is that reciprocity will engender benevolent, cooperative behavior.

Mainstream music fans are not likely to feel much closeness or sympathy for music bands. One fan expressed a common attitude: "I've watched enough MTV to know that most of the rock stars whose songs are being stolen the most live so comfortably that I can't possibly feel sorry for them."[71] Rock stars are distant figures, separated by the many layers of distribution and promotion that comprise the mainstream music industry.

In the jamband community, bands have a closer connection to fans. The fans are more tied to one another and to the bands they follow. Fans communicate using a wide array of online tools and meet up at shows. They collaborate on projects together, working together to distribute shows and build a community. The bands are also less distant from fans: band members and their representatives communicate directly with fans. Business models create both the perception and reality that the band is in business for itself, rather than working for distant, abstract entities like a record label, concert promoters, and Ticketmaster, who take money from fans and give the band a small percentage. While the jamband community is not a close-knit group, many mechanisms draw members closer together and help to reinforce norms based on reciprocity.

d) Punishing Non–Compliance Reinforces Cooperation

Models of reciprocity also account for the existence of free-riders. Like any other community, the jamband community has free-riders. Partial anonymity makes it easy to free ride by breaking the rules—perhaps by selling concert recordings, or by engaging in illegal trading activity, such as the duplication of commercial releases. Such behavior could quickly destroy the community, as bands might be inclined to withdraw permission to tape and trade. One way to counter the harmful effect of free-riding is by setting conditions so that people can punish non-cooperators.

The jamband community enables its members to enforce the rules. There are many individuals who are willing to enforce the rules. They serve as moderators on e-mail lists and discussion boards, etree administrators, and self-appointed guardians of the group norms. On e-mail lists and discussion forums, they appear swiftly to educate naive rule breakers or vehemently scold those who flout the rules willfully. There is also the threat of being banished as a "bad trader" or of having one's Internet protocol (IP) address blocked. Such punishment helps to sustain the norms of the community.

71. David McGuire, "Downloading: The Next Generation," *Washington Post*, Feb. 28, 2005, at 1, available at http://www. washingtonpost.com/wp-dyn/articles/A59632–2005Feb28.html.

e) Conclusion

The jamband community demonstrates that it is possible to encourage norms that support compliance with copyright by tapping into reciprocity. It is necessary, however, to establish the right conditions. In the context of experimental games, this means changing the rules of the game quite literally. The rules need to be set up so that conditional cooperators are not discouraged from behaving pro-socially. The conditions of the game need to be set up so that conditional cooperators do not perceive selfish types as gaining the upper hand. Allowing communication, reducing isolation, and evoking sympathy for the other party are also important. Opportunities to punish also improve outcomes.

The jamband community offers a real life example of how important institutions are to tapping into reciprocity to support compliance with copyright laws. Many of the conditions are the same as those of the mainstream music industry: the laws are the same, the subject matter is the same, and the fans are drawn from the same wide spectrum of American culture, including both selfish and cooperative individuals. What make the difference are the business practices and rules set by the bands, and the social networks they support and encourage. These institutions foster the formation of social norms that support copyright. The next Part discusses how the mainstream music industry might learn some lessons from the jamband community in order to write new rules of the game that allow reciprocity to encourage cooperation.

V.   LESSONS LEARNED

Since the voluntary compliance of jamband fans with copyright law ultimately flows from the deeply rooted, universal behavioral trait of reciprocity, it may be possible to export the success of the jamband community. This Part discusses the lessons to be drawn from the jamband experience and how they might be applied to the mainstream music industry.

A.   Don't Assume the Worst About Music Fans

In light of the millions of people engaged in illegal file-sharing, this statement might be hard to swallow for both the music industry and those who see themselves as realists. Nevertheless, consider that although the music industry appears to have lost sales to file-sharing, it has not lost the majority of its sales. Most people are still buying music legally. It seems likely that at least some of those people could download music illegally if they chose to do so.

Although the focus on massive non-compliance with copyright law is understandable, the phenomenon of massive compliance with copyright law deserves some consideration. Illegal file-sharing is a large problem, but still marginal. The challenge of reducing file-sharing is second in importance to ensuring that most people continue to comply with copyright law most of the time. Most people obey the law because of social norms. Therefore, the music industry should focus on developing and maintaining social norms that encourage widespread voluntary compliance. If most people are persuaded by social norms to comply with copyright law, the music industry and authorities could focus their efforts more efficiently on a handful of people who are not.

The example of the jamband community thus offers reason for copyright owners to consider how they might win people over to their side. If copyright owners pour most of their efforts into enforcement, they will miss the opportunity to encourage voluntary compliance by fostering pro-copyright social norms. In the long term, business practices and rhetoric that encourage voluntary compliance appear to be the most viable solutions to the file-sharing problem.

B. Build Communities Based on Sustained Relationships Between Fans and Bands

As the example of the jamband community shows, people are more likely to cooperate with others when they are in a social context and have reason to find the other party sympathetic. As copyright compliance becomes largely a matter of choice, people need to be treated as more than anonymous consumers. People participating in a loyal fan community are far more likely to perceive themselves as having a reciprocal relationship with the artist.

Quality music, consistently delivered over time, is most likely to generate the sort of loyal following that is found in the jamband community. Fans need a reason to be loyal, and loyalty needs time to develop. Jambands pride themselves on their improvisational prowess, long shows, endless tours, and ever-changing setlists. While this style of music may not be to everyone's taste, a general lesson can be drawn: put the music first and keep giving fans plenty of what they like. One-hit wonders are unlikely to prosper in such a world.

Just as important, jambands build communities by engaging their fans directly. Smaller bands communicate directly on message boards and through e-mail. Bands with larger followings do not engage in as much personal communication, but members of their organizations are active participants in online discussions, providing news and soliciting fan opinions. Perhaps more compellingly to some fans, bands also give fan communities preferred access to free recordings and videos, special limited commercial releases, early ticket sales, and fan appreciation shows. When artists connect so directly and positively with fans, fans are more likely to heed artists' calls to forego illegal downloads.

Increasingly, bands who desire a tighter relationship with fans are using social sites favored by young people, like myspace.com. Myspace.com allows individuals to build webpages containing personal photographs, blogs, and message boards where friends leave messages. Users then designate others as being in their network of friends. Myspace creates a vast online social scene. Bands have stepped into this social scene, building pages that look a lot like those of individual users. They communicate with fans directly through these pages in the apparent hope of being perceived as peers by their fans. Interestingly, fans seem to respond, leaving messages that are personal in nature.

Other bands stay connected by releasing weekly or monthly podcasts. These podcasts typically contain news, updates, and about forty-five to sixty minutes of music, usually taken from a band's live performances. These podcasts keep bands in touch with their fans and provide fans with another legal way to spread the news about their favorite bands.

Fans also may feel more connected with jambands because the artists are often directly involved in all aspects of the music fan's experience. Jambands are often quite entrepreneurial, owning their own record labels and production companies and selling concert tickets directly to fans when possible.

Some of these lessons are among the most difficult to translate to the mainstream music industry. Its current business model centers on discovering a band or musician and turning it into a mass marketed star. Grass roots communication takes much more detail work, and the economies of scale that currently benefit the mainstream music industry are not present. Of course, the music industry can adapt and change its business model. In the end, organizations rewrite the rules of the game to suit new circumstances. Often, new organizations rather than existing ones produce the change necessary to adapt to changed circumstances. If the music industry does not adapt, then it may be organizations like the jamband community that step into the breach.

C.   Improve Perceptions of Fairness

The music industry would benefit greatly from being perceived as fair. One might be tempted to rephrase that statement as "the music industry must behave more fairly," but objective fairness is not what matters.... [P]eople will alter economic behavior when they perceive that the other party is being unfair. "Fairness" may be a soft concept, but it has real economic consequences.

The music industry already has some familiarity with the problem of perceptions of fairness from its experience with pricing concert tickets. The existence of scalpers shows that ticket prices are set "artificially" low. Concert promoters could charge much more for tickets than they do.... [Those] who have examined this seemingly puzzling phenomenon have proposed that the music industry is constrained by consumers' notions of fairness. People might resentfully pay a "scalper" what they consider an unfair price to see their favorite band. But if that favorite band acted with similar unfairness, it probably will not stay a favorite for long. Mistreating fans has long term costs.

The music industry needs to extend this fairness to other aspects of its business model. It cannot afford to dismiss complaints about CD pric~ product quality, and poor treatment as mere rationalizations for file-sha~ These perceptions make a difference in how people behave. Now that essentially have a choice as to whether to pay for music, it is best to avoid provoking the retaliatory spirit of punishing those who are unfair.

To achieve a perception of fairness, the music industry ought to consider both a public relations makeover and a change in attitude. Jambands treat fans with the hyper-sensitive care of the service industry. While the mainstream music industry also cares what fans think, it seems more oriented toward marketing products than ensuring that fans have a good overall experience. This difference in orientation appears to make a difference in how the fans perceive the bands, which in turn appears to make a difference in their willingness to follow rules.

Jamband fans view jambands as motivated, in part, by the interests of fans. The bands work hard to provide fans with a positive experience. String Cheese Incident is perhaps the paradigmatic example. It ensures that fans have a high quality experience through its extensive business organization, which includes a record label, a ticketing agency, a travel agency, and a charitable foundation. Its concerts are described as "an effort to transform the traditional concert environment," with festivals held in beautiful locations, high quality sound, lower ticket prices, and artistic events in which the fans participate. The band has even set itself up as an advocate for fans by making "a commitment to take on the Empire when it filed a lawsuit against Ticketmaster."

A prime example of fairness on the part of jambands is allowing fans to tape and distribute concert music. These recordings serve as the basis of a community, they provide free advertising, they feed the obsession of the most intense fans, and they make fans more favorably inclined to bands overall. Allowing trading of live recordings and older, less profitable material could go a long way toward increasing perceptions of fairness. . . .

Understanding the relationship that bands have with their fans may be an urgent business priority for the music industry. As the industry already understands from the experience of concert ticket pricing, they may have to forego some revenue opportunities to keep fans coming back in the long run. Treating customers right is always important, as they almost always have a choice as to whether to buy one's product. But treating customers well is especially essential when they can choose not to pay and obtain the product for free. To make fans happier, the music industry can start by addressing common complaints about CD pricing, quality, and opportunistic business practices like bundling small amounts of new material with old.

D.   Give People a Chance to Comply and More Will Follow

Our position, from the beginning, was that 80% of the people stealing music online don't really want to be thieves. . . .

It's just wrong to steal. Or, let's put it another way: it is corrosive to one's character to steal. We want to provide a legal alternative. And we want to make it so compelling that all those people out there who really want to be honest, and really don't want to steal, but haven't had a choice if they wanted to get their music online, will now have a choice. And we think over time, most people stealing music will choose not to if a fair and reasonable alternative is presented to them. We are optimists. We always have been.

Steve Jobs

Founder and CEO of Apple, Inc.

December 3, 2003 Interview, Rolling Stone

Is Steve Jobs right? Do people really just need to be given a chance to comply with copyright law? One might predict that very few people would use Apple's iTunes music service if they are at all guided by rational self-interest. If one has the means and knowledge to install and use iTunes software, then one could just as easily do the same with file-sharing software. Given the choice between free music and paying, with an extremely small chance of being sued for infringement, one might predict that potential iTunes customers would opt for free music instead. This prediction is contradicted by a billion paid downloads from iTunes as of February 23, 2006. The success of iTunes shows that mainstream music fans can be persuaded to restrain themselves from infringing behavior. It also represents the music industry's most successful contribution so far to fostering pro-copyright norms.

To create the right conditions for cooperative behavior, people first need a chance to comply. Many people are inclined to cooperate, as shown by the results of experimental games and other instances where people choose not to act opportunistically. For this reason, iTunes and other services are more viable than they might have first appeared. Although it is difficult to compete with a free product, a reasonably priced alternative will dissuade many from breaking the law.

It is also important to give people a prominent example that others are complying. To some extent, people take their cues from the behavior of others. Others will follow the good example of cooperators, if that example exists. People also prefer that outcomes are fair. Not only do they need to feel they are getting a fair deal, but they do not want to be disadvantaged compared to others. People are pre-disposed to obey the law, but nobody wants to be the last sucker who is actually paying for music.

Because people need to know they are not alone in complying, the recording industry needs to reconsider its message to the public. The rhetoric about file-sharing often veers into hyperbole, portraying millions of people breaking the law and the industry's fate hanging in the balance. That rhetoric may be appropriate for litigation and lobbying purposes, but it does not give people the impression that compliance is common. Portraying the music industry as a victim fighting an uphill battle against massive infringement is more likely to encourage non-compliance than engender sympathy. People need to know both that they are not alone in complying and that the music industry is vigorously pursuing infringers. This more confident message would communicate that compliance is the norm, but that those who infringe do not have an unfair advantage over those who comply.

The iTunes example shows that the recording industry can win by serving its customers well. Give people a chance to comply, and some will do so. They will set a good example for others, provided that this example is highlighted rather than undermined by discussions of massive infringement that make one seem foolish for complying with copyright law.

E.   Let the Fans Do Some of the Work

Many have heralded the possibilities of "peer production;" the jamband community demonstrates the potential of "peer consumption." Peer production harnesses networked communications and new forms of social organization to enable groups of volunteers to produce remarkable products, like the Linux operating system. As powerful as peer production can be, it likely is not the best model for the music industry. Amateur production has its limits, and not everyone wants to or can collaborate voluntarily to create music and entertainment. Some, however, are willing to cooperate to help the professionals who create music by distributing music, promoting musicians, paying for their commercial releases, and helping to ensure that others play by the rules by paying for commercial releases. As the jamband community shows, consumer collaboration—or "peer consumption"—can be a powerful addition to strategies employed to persuade people to comply with copyright voluntarily.

Artists should thus find ways to get fans involved in distribution and promotion as much as possible. Ceding control to fans makes them active participants in enforcing copyright restrictions. Some people have such a strong preference for reciprocity that they are willing to incur costs to monitor the behavior of others and punish them. If they are placed in a context where they can monitor and sanction others, they will do so. Such a role for fans helps to push the community equilibrium toward compliance far more deftly than the slow, heavy machinery of legal department review, subpoenas, cease-and-desist demands, and lawsuits. Some ways to accomplish this goal include encouraging fans to start groups that run e-mail lists, fan websites, and online forums. If those groups are then given concert recordings or podcasts to distribute, they might take responsibility for encouraging enforcement.

In sum, focusing on the highest intensity fans is likely a winning strategy. Even if it does not result in widespread copyright compliance, an artist is likely to cement his or her relationship with fans by involving them in distribution and compliance efforts. Such intense fans may be more willing to spend money to support an artist by buying limited run CDs, t-shirts, and other additional items. . . .

NOTES AND QUESTIONS

1.   Schulz draws on several bodies of game theory research as part of his argument for a more cooperative approach to social control. What assump-

tions are we making if we take such research from the laboratory and apply it to "real world" problems? Nonetheless, is this kind of research suggestive and likely helpful in engaging in social engineering? Do you see any dangers if we rely on game theory to "prove" how people will behave in situations related to the legal system?

2.   Matthew Sag, "Piracy: Twelve Year–Olds, Grandmothers, And Other Good Targets for the Recording Industry's File Sharing Litigation," 4 *Northwestern Journal of Technology & Intellectual Property* 133 (2006), points out that the recording industry has filed over 20,000 individual law suits against people it accused of downloading music in violation of its copyright. Many have said that this will alienate the industry's customers and is counterproductive. Sag disagrees. He argues that it is rational for the industry to target the marginal file sharer rather than the consumers who supply large volumes of music for others to download. Everyday people are most likely to be persuaded to switch to buying rather than downloading music. Often those who run the peer-to-peer networks that supply the majority of those who download are off-shore, judgment-proof or protected by layers of anonymity and encryption. Therefore, those who run these networks are unlikely to switch to buying music. Lawsuits against twelve-year-olds and grandmothers are far from a public relations disaster. Instead, they are a public relations coup. They send the message that occasional downloading is consequential. These are the people who are likely to switch from downloading and return to buying CDs. Sag points out:

> The unprompted responses of survey participants who claimed to have stopped file sharing provides further evidence of the effectiveness of end user litigation. According to the most recent Pew survey, 15% of respondents said they had downloaded in the past but no longer do so. Of that 15%, one third cite the recording industry lawsuits as the main reason they stopped. In addition, the Pew survey also indicates that there is a significant crossover between the file sharing population and users of online music services such as iTunes or BuyMusic.com.

From 2003 to early 2007, the recording industry sued 26 people for illegally downloading music in cases brought in the United States District Court for the Western District of Wisconsin. One 72–year–old grandmother who lived in Beloit denied illegally downloading music. She said that she did not know that it was possible to download music online. She turned down an offered settlement of the claim that would have required her to pay $3,000. The case was still pending in early 2007. See Ed Trevelen, "Cracking Down on Music Theft: Recording Industry Gets Very Aggressive," *Wisconsin State Journal*, February 4, 2007, at A–1.

3.   Geoffrey Neri, "Sticky Fingers or Sticky Norms? Unauthorized Music Downloading and Unsettled Social Norms," 93 *Georgetown Law Journal* 733 (2005), disagrees with Sag's conclusion. Neri, relying on Ross' studies of drinking and driving, suggests that when people disagree with a law, they will comply with it only when there is a high probability of being caught. He

argues that the real risk of being sued is small in light of the number of who download. People will come to learn this. Websites exist that are devoted to explaining the true risks. Those who see the present copyright regime as illegitimate will return to downloading, perhaps taking more care to avoid becoming a target of the recording industry.

(C) The Role of Legitimacy and General Respect for Authority

(4.7) Public Mistrust of the Law: A Political Perspective

Tom R. Tyler
66 *University of Cincinnati Law Review* 847 (1998).

I. Introduction

... I would like to ... [describe] what structured interviews with members of the public tell us about the public's perception of the law, legal authorities, and the legal system....

I will argue that legal authorities need to be concerned about public dissatisfaction because public dissatisfaction has political costs. As a political psychologist, I will focus on the findings of studies of the attitudes and behaviors of citizens. These attitudes and behaviors are typically assessed through structured interviews, such as the familiar public-opinion polls conducted by newspapers and academic organizations, or through the in-depth interviews with smaller samples of citizens conducted by legal scholars....

I will address two issues. First, what types of public views should be the focus of our concerns? That is, what types of dissatisfaction have important political implications? Second, what do we know about why such public views are negative?

I am sure that I am not surprising you when I say that the recent results of both public-opinion polls and in-depth interviews with members of the public suggest strongly that the public feels a considerable amount of dissatisfaction with the law and legal authorities. In particular, the public often expresses dissatisfaction with the courts.

II. Public Dissatisfaction
A. *Performance Evaluations*

Let me give just one example. In a study of a representative sample of the citizens of Chicago,[72] I found that a majority of citizens expressed negative views about the local courts. Consider the responses from that study shown in Table 1. Seventy-four percent of those interviewed gave negative overall evaluations of the courts.[73] These questions do not distinguish between civil and criminal cases and, hence, reflect overall evaluations of the courts. Although it is difficult to know the range and depth of public dissatisfaction, these findings suggest that it is fairly broad in scope.

---

72. See Tom R. Tyler, *Why People Obey the Law* 8–15 (1990).

73. See infra Table 1. Negative views mean that those interviewed indicated that court

performance was only "fair," "poor," or "very poor," not "very good" or "good."

I will refer to these evaluations as "performance evaluations" because they reflect public views about how the courts handle everyday problems of the type that they have experienced, or might experience in the future.

The public has had considerable personal experience with the courts. During the year prior to the interview for the study reflected in Table 1, 17% of those interviewed had appeared in court as part of a case, 10% had been a witness or a juror, and 5% had had some other type of personal contact with the courts. Overall, 27% of those interviewed had some type of personal contact with the courts during the year prior to the interview; the primary form of experience was involvement in a legal case. In addition, 51% of those interviewed had some form of contact with the police during the year prior to the interview. Hence, many of those interviewed have some personal basis for making performance evaluations of the courts.

A series of national studies of the American public's general confidence in the "legal system" similarly supports the argument that confidence in the legal system is low.[74] In 1973, 24% of those surveyed expressed a great deal of confidence in the legal system; those numbers dropped to 18% in 1978, to 14% in 1988, and to only 8% in 1993. These percentages suggest that confidence is both low and declining. Recently, less than 10% of the American public expressed "a great deal" of confidence in the American legal system.

The most striking aspect of public dissatisfaction with the courts is found in the public's views about the criminal courts. In particular, there is a widespread belief that the sentences given criminals are too lenient, a criticism of the criminal courts.... As Table 2 indicates, findings drawn from national public-opinion polls suggest that the proportion of adult Americans who believe that the courts are too lenient on criminals is both high and steadily increasing.

I will refer to dissatisfaction with leniency in criminal sentencing as "symbolic evaluation" because most Americans have very little knowledge about criminal sentences, and no personal experience with the criminal sentencing process. In addition, most adult Americans find it difficult to imagine that they would ever be accused of a crime. Therefore, their images about leniency are more symbolic or abstract in nature.

Table 1[75]

Evaluation Of Local Courts (Chicago)

I.   How good a job are the courts doing?

Very good	4%
Good	22%
Fair	47%
Poor	18%
Very poor	9%

74. See Gary A. Hengstler, "The Public Perception of Lawyers: ABA Poll," *American Bar Association Journal*, Sept. 1993, at 60, 63–64.

75. Data are from a sample of the citizens of Chicago (n = 1,575). See Tyler at 51–53.

II.   How often do the courts:

	Resolve cases in a satisfactory way?	Provide citizens with fair outcomes?	Treat citizens fairly?
Always	5%	5%	6%
Usually	29	34	38
Sometimes	49	49	45
Seldom	18	13	11

III.   The courts:

Treat everyone equally	72% disagree
Favor some over others	72% agree
The courts guarantee everyone a fair trial	41% disagree
The courts protect our basic rights	43% disagree
Many innocent people are convicted by the courts	24% agree
Judges are generally honest	43% disagree
Court decisions are almost always fair	44% disagree
The courts are too easy on criminals	80% agree

Table 2
The Percentage Of The American Public Saying The Courts Are Too
Lenient On Criminals

1965	47%	1980	83%
1966	N/A	1981	N/A
1967	N/A	1982	86%
1968	63%	1983	86%
1969	75%	1984	82%
1970	64%	1985	84%
1971	N/A	1986	85%
1972	66%	1987	79%
1973	73%	1988	82%
1974	78%	1989	84%
1975	79%	1990	83%
1976	81%	1991	80%
1977	83%	1992	N/A
1978	85%	1993	81%
1979	N/A	1994	85%

B.   *National–Level Dissatisfaction*

There is also evidence of dissatisfaction with the major, national-level judicial body—the United States Supreme Court—although I think that the evidence is less striking. The combined results of national public-opinion polls concerning the Supreme Court are shown in Table 3.[76] These percentages indicate some dissatisfaction with the Court, yet the level of confidence shown is generally reasonably high (32% have "a great deal" of confidence in the Supreme Court). This finding is consistent with the argument that the Supreme Court has a special place in the minds of the American public and maintains a substantial reservoir of support even when the law and local courts are being criticized.[77] Certainly, the Court fares well in comparison to Congress and the executive branch of government, both of which receive lower confidence ratings.

Further, a separation of these ratings across time does not suggest that lack of confidence in the Supreme Court is increasing. We can juxtapose views about changes in confidence in the general legal system, which have already been reported, with changes in confidence in the Supreme Court. The juxtaposition, outlined in Table 4, makes clear that support for the United States Supreme Court is higher.[78] Further, there is little evidence that confidence in the Supreme Court is declining over time. For this reason, I will focus my attention in this discussion on feelings about the local courts.

Table 3
Public Views About The United States Supreme Court

How much confidence do you have in the United States Supreme Court?	
A great deal	32%
Some	50%
Hardly any	14%
Do not know	4%

Table 4
Confidence In The Legal System And The Supreme Court
(Percentage Who Have "A Great Deal Of Confidence")

	Legal System	Supreme Court
1978	18%	28%
1988	14%	35%
1993	8%	31%

C. *General Dissatisfaction with Government*

Public feelings about the law and the courts may reflect judgments about the legal system, or may simply reflect growing dissatisfaction with all

76. See infra Table 3. These data are for the period 1972–1994. See James Allan Davis, "National Opinion Research Center, General Social Surveys, 1972–1994"(visited Mar. 12, 1998) <http://www.icpsr.umich.edu/GSS/code book/conjudge.htm>.

77. See Tom R. Tyler & Gregory Mitchell, "Legitimacy and the Empowerment of Discretionary Legal Authority: The United States Supreme Court and Abortion Rights," 43 *Duke Law Journal* 703, 755 (1994).

78. See infra Table 4.

government. Robert Putnam, a political scientist, has recently made a broader version of the dissatisfaction argument very salient through his suggestion that the public is becoming disenchanted not just with the law and the courts, but with government in general.[79] His evidence, shown in Table 5, shows dramatic evidence of increasing distrust of government and alienation from government institutions over the past twenty-five years. Therefore, feelings about the legal system must be seen within the context of overall alienation from government: people are not just upset with the legal system.

Table 5
Distrust In Government And Alienation From Government Leaders

	Distrust in government	Alienation from government leaders
1966	28%	31%
1968	37	38
1970	40	46
1972	44	46
1974	58	62
1976	57	63
1978	51	68
1980	60	73
1982	56	64
1984	56	55
1986	60	60
1988	55	58
1990	61	70
1992	65	76

On the other hand, people are not equally upset with all branches of national-level government. Ironically, while the local legal system is viewed quite negatively, at the national level, the Supreme Court is viewed very favorably in comparison to the executive and legislative branches of government. Hence, at the level of national government, which Putnam addresses, the legal system seems to be holding up well in the eyes of the public.

Thus, evidence from public-opinion polls supports the argument that the public expresses considerable dissatisfaction with the courts, especially the local courts. Further, there is evidence that public dissatisfaction with both the courts and the government more generally is increasing. This leads to the obvious question of whether these increases should be of concern to legal authorities.

III.   Inaccuracy in Public Beliefs

One important factor that should influence the degree to which public views are considered by legal authorities when shaping the legal system is the

79. See Robert D. Putnam, "Bowling Alone: America's Declining Social Capital," 6 *Journal of Democracy* 65, 68 (1995) ("The proportion of Americans who reply that they 'trust the government in Washington' only 'some of the time' or 'almost never' has risen steadily from 30 percent in 1966 to 75 percent in 1992.").

quality of those views. Legal authorities have often suggested that the quality of public views should influence the degree to which they are considered.... From this perspective, let me begin by qualifying the findings I have outlined in an important way. There is considerable evidence to suggest that public dissatisfaction with the courts is based upon a variety of misconceptions held by the public about the operation of the courts and of the legal system.

As I mentioned, the criminal courts have been most widely studied, and these studies suggest that the general public knows little about how the courts operate or about the problems of crime with which the courts must deal.[80] People inaccurately estimate the rate of crime, usually thinking that violent crime rates are higher than they actually are, and often misjudge whether violent crime is increasing or declining. Research links these misconceptions to erroneous information given to the public by the mass media, which sensationalizes violent crimes.

Further, the public faults the courts for procedural errors that the courts do not make. It is widely believed that the courts let too many guilty people go free because of legal technicalities. Studies indicate that the public substantially overestimates the proportion of defendants who successfully escape punishment through the insanity defense.[81] Studies also indicate that the public overestimates the proportion of cases that are thrown out of courts due to illegally obtained evidence.[82]

Finally, although studies suggest that the public correctly understands that the sentences given by the courts are less than the public thinks it would give for similar crimes,[83] this finding rests upon public ignorance about the nature of criminal defendants. When members of the public are given information about criminals similar to that available to judges, they do not give more severe sentences than judges give.[84]

Hence, it is important to distinguish public feeling from a knowledgeable critique of the courts and court practices. Nonetheless, I will argue that public views have important implications for the operation of the legal system. The key assumption underlying the political perspective is that we care about how citizens feel about their government, even when those views are poorly formed. Why should we care? In this discussion, I want to ... focus on what I think is a fundamental way in which public feelings influence the operation of law and the courts. This impact occurs because people's views shape the basis of their behavior toward the law....

80. See Julian V. Roberts, "Public Opinion, Crime, and Criminal Justice," in 16 *Crime and Justice: A Review of Research* 99 (Michael Tonry ed., 1992).

81. See Eric Silver et al., "Demythologizing Inaccurate Perceptions of the Insanity Defense," 18 *Law & Human Behavior* 63 (1994).

82. See Eric Silver et al., "Demythologizing Inaccurate Perceptions of the Insanity Defense," 18 *Law & Human Behavior* 63 (1994).

83. See generally Alfred Blumstein & Jacqueline Cohen, "Sentencing of Convicted Offenders: An Analysis of the Public's View," 14 *Law & Society Review* 223 (1980).

84. See Shari Seidman Diamond, "Revising Images of Public Punitiveness: Sentencing by Lay and Professional English Magistrates," 15 *Law & Social Inquiry* 191, 193, 201–04 (1990).

IV.   Compliance with the Law

Past discussions of the effective exercise of legal and political authority have focused on the ability of leaders to shape the behavior of citizens. In particular, the ability to secure compliance with decisions and rules—more broadly labeled the ability to be authoritative—is widely recognized to be a central characteristic of effective organizational authorities. In other words, to be effective, legal rules and decisions must be obeyed. They must influence the actions of those toward whom they are directed. As I argued in *Why People Obey the Law*, "[a] judge's ruling means little if the parties to the dispute feel they can ignore it. Similarly, passing a law prohibiting some behavior is not useful if it does not affect how often the behavior occurs." Hence, "[t]he lawgiver must be able to anticipate that the citizenry as a whole will ... generally observe the body of rules he has promulgated."[85]

It is difficult to gain sufficient compliance to enforce the law using only the threat of punishment. That is, compliance based upon deterrence motivations is a problematic basis for the effective exercise of legal authority. Instead, authorities need the willing, voluntary compliance of most citizens with most laws, most of the time. Research suggests that, in democratic societies such as the United States, the effectiveness of both political and legal authorities is heavily dependent upon the willing, voluntary cooperation of citizens with laws and legal decisions. My argument is that it is inefficient and ineffective to try to manage a democratic society without the ability to secure voluntary compliance with the law. Although some coercion is possible, the legal system relies heavily on the voluntary cooperation of most citizens, most of the time.

A.   Why are Sanctions a Problem?

The problem with sanction-based approaches is that they are costly and inefficient. To make such a system work, it is necessary to develop systems of surveillance that make the likelihood of being caught and punished for rule-breaking high enough to shape people's behavior. This requires both large-scale investments in law enforcement and constant efforts to monitor the behavior of the public.

What makes deterrence strategies especially prohibitive is that their viability depends upon being able to change people's estimates of the likelihood of being caught and punished for wrongdoing. Deterrence research finds that people's behavior is more strongly influenced by the likelihood of being caught and punished than it is by the severity of punishment.[86] Hence, efforts to change behavior have to focus on costly strategies such as increasing the size of the police force or the focus of their enforcement efforts.

Illustrations of the difficulty of deterrence-based strategies include efforts to lessen drug use ... The government has recently made a determined effort

---

85. Lon Fuller, "Human Interaction and the Law", in *The Rule of Law* 171, 201 (Robert Paul Wolff ed., 1971).

86. See Tom R. Tyler, "Procedural Fairness and Compliance with the Law," 133 *Swiss Journal of Economics & Statistics* 219–40 (1997).

to bring the drug-use problem under control through increases in police efforts to apprehend and punish drug dealers and drug users. However, these efforts have had little effect upon drug use. Why? Research suggests that changes in the likelihood of being caught and apprehended, which are influenced by heightened police efforts, influenced only about 5% of drug-related behavior.[87]. . . .

Of course, this is not to say that it is not possible to run a society upon deterrence. However, such a society would look very different than American society, or any other Western democracy. For example, in Eastern Germany, prior to its collapse, over 10% of the population worked for the police. Further, most street corners were under video surveillance so that this large police force could monitor the behavior of citizens. Such systems are costly and inefficient and the societies that seek to govern in this way have tremendous difficulty.

Although it is certainly true of the legal and political systems, the importance of supportive values is not unique to these systems. Studies of work organizations also emphasize the limitations of seeking to manage through control ideologies and emphasize the potential gains associated with supportive organizational values.

B.   *Voluntary Compliance Through Internal Values*

What is needed to avoid the problems associated with seeking to control citizen behavior through sanctions are internal values which lead citizens to want to act in ways that benefit the government. In other words, values must be promoted that lead people to defer to authorities, voluntarily accepting their decisions and voluntarily following rules.

Gaining voluntary cooperation with the law involves creating internalized values that promote compliance. Research suggests two factors are important to gaining voluntary compliance: morality and legitimacy. Morality is concerned with people's personal feelings about what is right or wrong. Legitimacy involves people's feeling that they ought to obey the law. Both of these factors promote voluntary compliance with the law.

In a panel study of American citizens, I have directly compared sanction threats to the influence of morality and legitimacy. I found that morality was the primary factor shaping law-related behavior. A second important factor was views about the legitimacy of the law. In this study, sanction threats had no independent influence on law-related behavior. The strength of each factor is shown in Table 6, which indicates the beta weights when all factors are entered at the same time.

The study outlined suggests the importance of morality and legitimacy as factors shaping people's law-related behavior. In each of the studies considered, these factors independently influence law-related behavior. Further, these factors typically dominate people's behavior and have a greater impact

---

87. See Robert J. MacCoun, "Drugs and the Law: A Psychological Analysis of Drug Prohibition," 113 *Psychological Bulletin* 497, 501 (1993).

than assessments of the likelihood of being caught and punished for wrongdoing. In other words, the way people behave is typically primarily a reflection of their views about what is right and wrong, and their obligations to law and legal authorities.

Although both moral values and feelings of obligation influence behavior, I want to focus on legitimacy—feelings of obligation to the state. I do so because such feelings of obligation are most directly linked to attitudes about the legal system, law, and legal authorities. Hence, from the perspective of the legal system, legitimacy is the key to the effectiveness of legal authorities. The importance of maintaining the feeling among citizens that the legal system has legitimacy has been widely recognized by those who study the effective functioning of organizations. It is supported by the findings just noted. If people feel obligated to obey legal authorities, they obey the law.

Table 6[88]
Why Do People Obey The Law?
Influences On Compliance With The Law

Likelihood of being caught and punished for rule-breaking	.06**
Obligation to obey the law	.16***
Evaluations of the morality of the law	.41***
Proportion of variance explained	25%***

The importance of supportive values such as legitimacy among citizens to the effective functioning of the legal system leads to concerns about the apparent decline in public support for law and legal authorities. If people no longer feel obligated to obey the law, their obedience will decline. Further, it will be difficult to maintain obedience because sanctions have little relationship to obedience.

V.   Performance Evaluations and Obligation

I began this analysis by noting evidence of public dissatisfaction with the performance of legal authorities. I then presented evidence suggesting the importance of perceived obligation to obey the law in shaping public behavior toward law. Because perceived obligation shapes compliance behavior, I argued that it is important to the effective functioning of legal authorities. However, there is a further question, as yet unaddressed: What is the relationship between negative performance evaluations and obedience toward the law? Does public dissatisfaction with the performance of legal authorities lead members of the public to stop obeying the law? These questions are

88. The entries listed are beta weights, which reflect the independent contribution of each factor controlling on the influence of other factors in the equation. Those entries that are starred indicate a statistically significant influence upon the dependent variables, at either the $p < .05$ level (*), the $p < .01$ level (**), or the $p < .001$ level (* * *). The proportion of variance explained is the adjusted R-squared and shows how much all factors explain when considered together.

central to examining the impact of dissatisfaction on legal culture and the viability of legal authorities.

To test this argument, I expanded the analysis of the antecedents of compliance, which was presented in Table 6, to include performance evaluations and symbolic evaluations. The results, shown in Table 7, indicate that performance evaluations have very little impact upon compliance with the law. In particular, dissatisfaction with the performance of legal authorities does not lessen compliance with the law. Dissatisfaction was assessed in two ways. First, dissatisfaction was assessed through performance evaluations based upon questions like those shown in Table 1 (Do authorities provide satisfactory resolution of cases?; Do they provide fair outcomes?; Do they treat citizens fairly?). Second, dissatisfaction was assessed through symbolic evaluations. In this case, symbolic evaluations are indexed by agreement that the courts are too lenient on criminals. As Table 7 indicates, neither type of evaluation shapes compliance with the law. Hence, those expressing performance dissatisfactions do not necessarily feel less obligation to obey the law.

If performance dissatisfactions do not influence behavior, why are they important? Let me provide two explanations. First, they shape whether people seek out legal authorities when they have legally relevant problems. Using the same Chicago dataset, we can examine why people indicate that they would, or would not, go to the courts or the police if they have a legally relevant problem to be solved. Table 8 indicates that performance evaluations shape whether people say they would go to legal authorities with their problems.

Second, performance evaluations shape the public's policy positions. Consider the three-strikes initiative. That initiative was important because it lessened the discretionary authority given to legal officials by restricting flexibility in sentencing. Such constraints upon authorities are not unusual, as is shown in the widespread use of sentencing guidelines. What shapes public views about whether it is desirable to give such discretionary authority? As Table 9 indicates, the public is influenced by both their performance evaluations and their symbolic evaluations when deciding whether or not to give legal officials discretionary authority. Hence, performance evaluations, as well as symbolic evaluations, have an important impact upon other issues which are of concern to the legal system, even if they do not shape feelings of obligation to obey the law.

Table 7

Why Do People Obey The Law? Performance And Compliance

Likelihood of being caught and punished for rule-breaking	.05*
Obligation to obey the law	.16***
Evaluation of the morality of the law	.41***
Performance evaluations of the courts	.02
Symbolic evaluations of the courts	.01
Proportion of variance explained	25%***

Table 8
Why Do People Seek Help From Legal Authorities?

Performance evaluations of legal authorities	.17***
Symbolic evaluations of legal authorities	.07
Obligation to obey the law	.04
Proportion of variance explained	3%***

These findings suggest a reason why legal authorities should care about public opinion. Several years ago I gave a talk to California judges about public dissatisfaction with the courts. When I finished, a senior judge asked why judges should care about public views because the public has many misconceptions about the actual operation of the courts and the true sentences that criminals receive. The discussion revealed that this tendency to dismiss public views was widely shared among the judges present.

Shortly after that meeting, a compelling answer to this question was presented when the three-strikes initiative was proposed and passed in California, despite the opposition of almost all the legal authorities in the state. That initiative removed a considerable amount of discretionary authority from judges. The public supported this initiative because people believed that judicial discretion was being exercised poorly.

In other words, the beliefs of the public had important political consequences for the courts, irrespective of whether those views were thoughtfully conceived, were based upon an accurate understanding of the actions of the courts, or otherwise corresponded to what judges might think were the most relevant issues in evaluating the operation of the courts. As the judges in California learned in this case, public opinion has a political reality which judicial authorities ignore at their own risk.

Table 9
Why Do People Empower Legal Authority

Performance evaluation of legal authorities	.13***
Symbolic evaluations of legal authorities	.14***
Obligation to obey the law	.18***
Proportion of variance explained	7%

However, these findings suggest that we should treat judgments about the obligation to obey legal authorities and performance evaluations as two distinct elements of public opinion. Although most of the public opinion research I have outlined focuses only upon performance and symbolic evaluations, we should actually care about two issues: performance and symbolic evaluations, and feelings of obligation toward the law and legal authorities. Evaluations shape the willingness to seek help from authorities, and to empower them, while feelings of obligation influence obedience toward the law.

The distinction between evaluation and obligation is an important one because much of the discussion about public dissatisfaction with the law has failed to make clear distinctions between various forms of public sentiment. While the increasing public dissatisfaction with the performance of legal authorities and the symbolic dissatisfaction with what the public believes are sentencing practices are clear, what are the implications of this dissatisfaction? The results reported here suggest that this type of dissatisfaction is associated with only some types of behaviors.

The key antecedent of compliance with the law is the perceived obligation to obey the law. Obligation has not been the focus of systematic study in public opinion surveys, so we know little about whether it is declining. However, the results of the Chicago study suggest that perceived obligation remains high. For example, only 9% of those interviewed agreed that "[t]here is little reason for a person like me to obey the law," while only 14% agreed that "[i]t is hard to blame a person for breaking the law if they can get away with it."[89] On the other hand, 84% agree that "[p]eople should obey the law even if it goes against what they think is right," and 84% agree that "I always try to follow the law even if I think that it is wrong." These percentages are interesting because it has already been noted that those within this sample expressed considerable performance and symbolic dissatisfaction with the Chicago courts. Hence, people can feel dissatisfaction about the operation of legal institutions and the actions of legal authorities without losing their feelings of obligation to obey the law.

Why might these two types of public feeling be separate? One possibility is that the development of feelings of obligation to obey the law are basic social and political values that develop during the childhood socialization process. Research suggests that basic social orientations, such as liberalism, conservatism, dogmatism, and authoritarianism are developed during childhood, and persist through adult life. Hence, they may be distinct from the types of evaluations that develop and change in adult life. If so, this suggests the need to better understand the development of people's early feelings about the law.

More broadly, these findings suggest the need to more systematically examine public values and attitudes. The basic argument being made is that the legal system benefits from supportive public values. It is difficult to run the legal system by shaping rewards and the threat of punishment. Therefore, supportive public values are the key to the effective exercise of legal authority within democratic societies such as the United States....

This discussion focuses upon one supportive value—the feeling of obligation to obey the law.... This analysis ... makes clear that the extensive research which has recently been conducted on public evaluations of the legal system has not seriously considered the political importance of dissatisfaction. It is important to more clearly identify desirable public behaviors that might be impacted by dissatisfaction, behaviors such as the willingness to obey the

---

89. Tyler, supra at 46.

law, seeking legal help when legally relevant problems arise, and empowering legal authorities. Having identified such behaviors, the impact of dissatisfaction on these behaviors can then be explored. In other words, dissatisfaction then becomes important because it shapes important public behaviors. In the case of negative evaluations, those evaluations do not shape obedience toward the law. To understand why people fail to obey the law, feelings of obligation must be examined. However, exploring these feelings has not been central to recent studies of public dissatisfaction with the law and with legal authorities.

VI.   What Shapes Legitimacy and Performance Evaluations?

My own research on the topic of discontent examines how people's views about legal authority are shaped by their personal experiences with particular legal authorities such as judges and police officers. Consider the Chicago study that has already been outlined. The Chicago study also explored citizen experiences with legal authorities. It compared the importance of five issues in shaping reactions to experience: the favorability of the outcome (the amount won or lost), voice and participation in decisions, trust in the motives of authorities, quality of interpersonal treatment, and the neutrality of the authorities. Table 10 shows the results of this study as a regression analysis comparing the influence of each element on performance evaluations and the perceived obligation to obey the law. The findings suggest that the most important element in experience that shapes both judgments is trust in the motives of the authority.

A.   Trustworthiness

The key issue in people's reactions to legal procedures is their judgment about the trustworthiness of legal authorities. If people feel that the authorities making legal rules are "trying to be fair" to them, they are much more willing to accept those rules. In fact, research suggests that trust in the motives of authorities is the central factor underlying the willingness to obey legal rules. Further, trust in the motives of authorities influences performance evaluations.

Trust speaks to the quality of the relationship between people and authorities—that is, whether or not people believe that authorities care about them. In other words, it reflects the judgment that the authorities are motivated to solve problems and treat people fairly and that they are trying to act in a professional manner.

Why is trust such a central issue to those dealing with authorities? An important clue is provided by research on people's judgments about the legal system. In the study of citizens in Chicago, citizens recognized the widespread existence of unfair treatment on the part of the police and courts. However, when asked what would happen if they personally dealt with the police or courts, over 90% predicted that they would be treated fairly by the police, and 86% of the people said the courts would treat them fairly. It appears, therefore, that people have an illusion of benevolence—a distorted sense that

478

they are secure. Yet when people actually deal with legal authorities, this illusion is potentially open to question.

Table 10[90]
Aspects Of Experience Which Shape Performance Evaluations
And The Obligation To Obey The Law

	Performance evaluations	Obligation to obey the law
Outcome favorability	.06	.14
Opportunities for voice (participation)	.07	.05
Are the authorities trustworthy?	.33***	.41***
Were you treated with dignity and respect?	.11	.11
Were the authorities neutral?	.06	.01
Proportion of variance explained	18%	13%***

Trust is also important because it speaks to the future. Because intentions develop from a person's character, which people view as generally stable and unchanging, judgments about current intentions allow people to predict the future. People are long-term members of society and, consequently, their loyalty depends on their predictions about what will happen in the long term. For this reason, people's attitudes toward authorities fluctuate as their judgments about the benevolence of authorities change. If they believe that the authorities are trying to be fair and to deal fairly with them, they develop a long-term commitment to society.

The importance of trustworthiness suggests that an important goal for law makers and law-enforcement authorities should be to reestablish the social connection between citizens and legal authorities which underlies feelings of trust in the motives of leaders. If citizens trust that their leaders are trying to do what is best for them, they defer voluntarily to legal rules. This means that people need to believe that the authorities with whom they are dealing care about them and about their problems.

B. *What Shapes Trustworthiness?*

We can examine the question of what shapes trustworthiness in two ways. First, we can use the judgments about whether the authorities provide desired outcomes, allow people to influence the outcome (decision control), allow people to speak and present evidence (voice), behave neutrally, and treat people with dignity and respect to explain judgments that they are trustworthy. The results of a regression analysis using these aspects of what authori-

90. The entries listed are beta weights, which reflect the independent contribution of each factor controlling on the influence of other factors in the equation. Those entries that are starred indicate a statistically significant influence upon the dependent variables, at either the $p < .05$ level (*), the $p < .01$ level (**), or the $p < .001$ level (***). The proportion of variance explained is the adjusted R-squared and shows how much all factors explain when considered together.

ties do to predict inferences about their motives is shown in Table 11. As the table indicates, all five aspects of experience are linked to trustworthiness. These results suggest that the most important antecedent of trustworthiness is participation.

People feel better about authorities following an experience if they are allowed to participate in shaping decisions that affect the resolution of their problems or conflicts. The positive effects of participation have been widely found....

Voice effects have not been found to be dependent on having control over outcomes. Instead, people have been found to value the opportunity to express their views to decision makers in and of itself....

Table 11
Aspects Of Experience Associated With Trustworthiness

Outcome favorability	.14%***
Influence over outcome	.21***
Opportunities for voice (participation)	.39***
Were you treated with dignity and respect?	.17***
Were the authorities neutral?	.17***
Proportion of variance explained	70%

C. Trust in What?

A second approach is to try to understand what type of trust is central to people's evaluations. Trust is a general concept and could potentially reflect concerns about a variety of characteristics or behaviors of legal authority. Consider two possibilities: competence and benevolence. Competence reflects the belief that authorities will solve problems well. Benevolence reflects that feeling that they are motivated to try to be fair and that they care about those with whom they are dealing. When these two characteristics of authorities are considered separately, benevolence is more important than competence.

The findings reflected in Table 12 suggest that people focus most heavily on whether or not they think that the mediator, lawyer, or judge they are dealing with cares about them and their problems and is truly trying to find a solution that is good for those involved. This is ironic because most legal training focuses on issues of competence in understanding and interpreting the law. Gaining deference through making accurate rule-based decisions, not influenced by personal values or biases, is referred to as neutrality.

Table 12[91]
Factors Shaping Evaluations Of The Courts

Competent	.21***	.02
Benevolent	.47***	.14***
Proportion of variance explained	42%***	2%***

91. The entries listed are beta weights, which reflect the independent contribution of each factor controlling on the influence of other factors in the equation. Those entries that

VII.　Implications for What to do About the Problem of Public Discontent

Although I have distinguished between evaluations of performance and feelings of obligation to obey the law, both of these judgments are linked to the same judgment. That judgment is the trustworthiness of authorities. Dissatisfaction flows from assessments that the authorities are not trustworthy. It reflects the assessment that the authorities do not care about those with whom they are dealing, and are not trying to treat them fairly. In other words, it is an evaluation of character, not of competence. Hence, legal authorities need to move away from emphasizing the neutrality of their decision-making procedures as a basis for public support and deference. Such efforts are based upon the belief that competence is the key issue in the public's mind. Instead, legal authorities need to focus on issues of character and benevolence. These issues are central to public evaluations, and to feelings of obligation to obey the law.

Interestingly, there is considerable evidence that the basis of the ability to gain voluntary acceptance from members of the public, as well as the basis of evaluations of authorities, is already changing from neutrality-based to trust-based. Neutrality-based authority gains credibility through signs of professionalism and expertise—for example, the evenhanded application of rules, lack of bias, and the use of facts, rules, and procedures. Such signs of "professionalism" render the particular authority dealt with a minor issue. A person can go to any police officer or judge and receive uniform, consistent treatment. Increasingly, however, there are suggestions that this type of authority is less compelling to the public. Instead, people are focusing on their views about the morality and benevolence of the authority with whom they are dealing.[92] This focus on trustworthiness leads to an interest in knowing the particular authority with whom one is dealing. As a consequence, it encourages personal connections between citizens and authorities and deference based on a knowledge of the authorities' history and values.

An example of the encouragement of trust-based authority can be seen in the recent movement toward community-based policing. In an earlier historical period, police officers walked neighborhood "beats." Consequently, they knew and were known by the members of the community that they policed. Their authority developed from a personal history, which led to trust in their motives and values. That model of policing was then replaced by a model that emphasizes professionalism in policing. Police officers were removed from everyday contact with particular groups of citizens. Instead, they exercised authority over large areas and their authoritativeness was linked to profes-

are starred indicate a statistically significant influence upon the dependent variables, at either the $p < .05$ level (*), the $p < .01$ level (**), or the $p < .001$ level (***). The proportion of variance explained is the adjusted R-squared and shows how much all factors explain when considered together.

92. See Tom R. Tyler & Wayne Kerstetter, "Moral Authority in Law and Criminal Justice," 13 *Criminal Justice Ethics*, Summer/Fall 1994, at 44, 46.

sional training and conduct—that is, to neutrality. Ironically, recent changes toward community-based policing reflect a move back to the earlier trust-based model. Those changes are being encouraged by declining confidence in the professionalism of the police. Hence, individual police officers need to develop personalized connections with people in the community. In essence, authorities need to create their own legitimacy on an individual basis. They cannot rely on the general legitimacy that they may have as a member of the police force.

These results suggest the value of a psychological analysis of public views about the law. For example, psychological theory can explain why mediation is popular (because it provides greater opportunities for participation) and, therefore, can be used to suggest changes in the law and judicial institutions which will increase people's willingness to voluntarily accept judicial decisions. These findings indicate that judicial authorities can, in fact, address problems of citizen discontent and the findings of psychological research suggest ways for judicial authorities to manage this discontent.

NOTES AND QUESTIONS

1. According to Tyler, what are the respective effects on compliance of morality, deterrence, and legitimacy? Is Tyler's position consistent with that of Grasmick and Bursik or Tittle and Rowe? If you see any differences, how might you account for them?

Tyler asserts that "deterrence research" finds "people's behavior is more strongly influenced by the likelihood of being caught and punished than it is by the severity of punishment." Can this be true? Is not deterrence always the product of both severity and certainty—what the punishment is and what the chances are that you will be caught? If there is known to be zero enforcement, naturally, there is no deterrence; however there is also no deterrence if there are no consequences, even if you are detected 100% of the time.

2. Tyler's study of people in Chicago dealt with disorderly conduct, littering, speeding, driving while intoxicated, illegal parking and shoplifting. Suppose that he had questioned these people about serious offenses such as burglary or rape. Would legitimacy likely have become more or less a predictor of compliance then?

3. Tom R. Tyler & Gregory Mitchell, "Legitimacy and the Empowerment of Discretionary Legal Authority: The United States Supreme Court and Abortion Rights," 43 *Duke Law Journal* 703 (1994), reports the results of a 1992 study of a random sample of 502 people in the San Francisco Bay Area. These results are not entirely consistent with Tyler's Chicago study. The subjects were interviewed by telephone about the Supreme Court of the United States and the abortion issue. Those who regard the institutional role of the Supreme Court as legitimate are more likely to defer to the Court's decision on abortion rights. However, only 36% of the respondents said that

power to decide about abortion rights should remain with the Court while 59% thought that the power of the Court to make such decisions should be reduced. Moreover, only 38% of these respondents said that they should accept the decisions made by government leaders when they disagreed with those decisions. 48% said that there were times when it is right to disobey government. Those who viewed abortion as immoral were less willing to allow the Court to make abortion policy. Tyler and Mitchell conclude that institutional legitimacy is generally unrelated to support for particular Court decisions. People evaluate the processes by which the Court makes decisions and not whether they agree or disagree with particular decisions. The key to seeing the Court as legitimate is a belief that it is neutral and not merely the reflection of political concerns. However, dissatisfaction with the outcome of a particular case always leaves the losers unhappy. Tyler and Mitchell say "local legal authorities are supported by much stronger presumptions of obligation to obey than are federal authorities." (p. 762). Does this explain the differences between the two Tyler studies? For a different view of the legitimacy of the United States Supreme Court, see James L. Gibson, *The Legitimacy of the United States Supreme Court in a Polarized Polity* (2006).

4. Kristina Murphy, "Regulating More Effectively: The Relationship between Procedural Justice, Legitimacy, and Tax Non–Compliance," 32 *Journal of Law and Society* 562 (2005), studied Tyler's approach in the context of aggressive tax planning strategies used by Australian taxpayers. Many of them had bought advice from accountants and financial planners that involved compliance with a technical, and often implausible, view of the letter of the law. Her sample consisted of taxpayers who had been accused by the Australian Taxation Office (ATO) of engaging in illegal forms of aggressive tax planning. All had received notice that they owed the ATO significant amounts of unpaid tax, penalties, and interest. The ATO did not have access to individual survey responses. She found in her first study that "taxpayers who felt the ATO treats taxpayers in a procedurally fair manner were more likely to make positive judgements about the ATO's legitimacy and taxpayers who thought their outcome was less favourable were more likely to make negative judgements about the ATO's legitimacy." (p. 574) However, she concluded: "in general, perceptions of unfair treatment appear to have affected taxpayers' judgements of legitimacy more so than having received an unfavourable outcome.... [T]hose who had larger tax debts were not more likely to have made negative legitimacy judgements about the ATO." (p. 575)

Two years after her first study, Murphy ran a follow-up survey of the taxpayers who had participated in Study 1. She found that "procedural justice judgements do predict changes in [the] perceived legitimacy [of the ATO] more so than judgements about gain or loss, and these judgements of legitimacy can go on to influence views about compliance (that is, degree of resistance towards paying tax and the ATO)." (p. 585) However, "[t]hose who felt their outcome had been unfavourable were more likely to engage in tax non-compliance several years later. Using another measure of tax evasion, it was also found that taxpayers' debt level was found to predict subsequent evasion behaviour . . .; those with higher tax debts were significantly more likely to evade taxes in later years." Nonetheless, her data suggested "taxpayers' feelings about the way they felt treated by the ATO appeared to be more important in explaining their views about the ATO's legitimacy than their judgements about gain or loss . . . [V]iews of legitimacy can affect attitudes toward compliance as well as compliance behaviour just as much, if not more so, than judgements about gain and loss." (p. 587) Murphy concludes: "by using a responsive enforcement strategy that adopts the principles underlying procedural justice theory, as well as using discretion in the punishment of first time offenders, regulators may be more likely to prevent widespread resistance toward their decisions, while at the same time nurturing the goodwill of those with a genuine commitment to compliance." (p. 589)

Suppose officials of a tax collecting agency had read Tyler's and Murphy's work. Do you see any concerns that they might have about adopting the approach advocated? If it were adopted, would those accountants and financial planners who sold such schemes be able to say that their customers should feel free to attempt an aggressive strategy because if the taxing authority successfully challenged what they had done, the consequences would not be great?

5.   Austin Sarat reviewed Tyler's *Why People Obey the Law* in an article titled "Authority, Anxiety, and Procedural Justice: Moving from Scientific Detachment to Critical Engagement," 27 *Law & Society Review* 647 (1993). Sarat notes his admiration for the book. The book attempts to rescue thought about the impact of law from a narrow view of rational choice based on "what's in it for me." However, he sees the book "somewhat at war with itself. Detachment is at war with political allegiance, science with policy." (p. 650) Sarat points to the six laws Tyler's respondents were asked to consider—speeding, parking illegally, disturbing the peace, littering, driving while intoxicated, and shoplifting. He notes that between 84% and 100% of the respondents said that it would be "morally wrong" to break these laws. "One wants to know why people think it is morally wrong to obey laws that seem to have such scant moral content or consequence." (p. 652) Sarat is concerned that Tyler is offering advice to authority about how to get people to do what they think that they should not do. "Tyler is, at this point, a modern Machiavelli giving sound advice to the Prince." (p. 658) Yet Tyler writes that he is concerned that authorities may use the appearance of fairness to avoid solving problems. The cultural emphasis is on procedure—that is, form over substance. Sarat asserts "procedural justice cannot be understood as an individual preference for a particular mode of treatment. It is, instead, a set of practices, widespread in our culture, which condition and constrain responses to legal and other cultural institutions." (p. 664) And these practices are not neutral. Tyler shows that white people, for example, are much more likely to be satisfied with police performance than blacks. This might make blacks more cautious than whites when they deal with the police, but is Tyler arguing that blacks have less reason to comply with the law? Or might blacks

still feel a moral obligation to obey the law apart from their evaluations of police practices?

American history, of course, is filled with examples of principled violations of what some people saw as unjust laws—we can point to such examples as the Boston Tea Party or the refusal of people in states such as Wisconsin to obey the fugitive slave acts that called for slaves to be returned to their owners in the South. Tyler just may be suggesting that most Americans have little sympathy with such resistance to authority. Or should we question the answers people gave to Tyler? People do disturb the peace, drink and drive, speed, park illegally and shoplift. Chicago does not have the reputation of being a place where people never violate the law. Perhaps Tyler simply tapped into a cultural norm of not bragging about such violations. Suppose one asked Tyler's questions of a sample of Chicago street drug dealers. Might we expect different answers? Or might they, just as Tyler's sample, think that one should not speed, drink and drive, park illegally, disturb the peace or shop lift? Suppose one asked Tyler's questions to a sample of executives of the largest corporations but instead focused on paying taxes in full, avoiding insider trading, and carefully complying with the Anti–Trust laws. What answers might we expect?

6.　Suppose one of your professors drove to work this morning. She stopped at all stop signs and red lights. She obeyed all speed limits. She parked her car in a legal parking space and stayed no longer than the time allowed. She walked to her office without assaulting anyone. During the day she did not steal money from anyone. Her monthly paycheck will contain deductions that pay all applicable state and federal taxes. How much of this behavior can we explain by her sense that the state and federal government are legitimate or that the particular laws she obeyed were legitimate? Suppose on the way home, the professor drove her car at a speed of ten miles an hour faster than the speed limit. Can we explain her speeding in terms of her belief that the government or the speeding laws are illegitimate? Suppose the professor reproduced several copyrighted articles for her class in a manner that violated the rights of the holder of the copyright. Would you expect her to be able to rationalize her conduct? Might she do this by challenging the legitimacy of the law? How might motivation and rationalization differ? For an attack on the whole concept of legitimacy as an explanation of compliance, see Alan Hyde, "The Concept of Legitimation in the Sociology of Law," 1983 *Wisconsin Law Review* 379.

7.　Niklas Luhmann, *Legitimation durch Verfahren* [Legitimation through Procedure] 2d ed. (1975), presents an important treatment of legitimacy. Luhmann defines the sense of legitimacy as a person's general willingness to "accept decisions, whose content is yet unspecified, within certain limits of tolerance." In modern society legitimacy is essentially procedural. His definition fits, for example, two people who agree to accept the results of a coin toss or a person's willingness to accept the result of a majority vote in an election although his or her candidate might lose. We might not accept the results of an election if, say, an out-and-out Nazi were elected, but this is covered by Luhmann's phrase "within certain limits of tolerance." Suppose that the vote in a presidential election in the United States was very close. Suppose that officials in a particular state said that Candidate A had won their state's vote. However, assume that there were serious allegations of many flaws in the counting of the ballots in that state. Many stated that Candidate B had actually won a majority in the state. Had state officials found that Candidate B had won that state, he would have won the election for president. The Supreme Court of the United States, by a divided vote, overturned an order for a recount in the state in question. Candidate A was declared President of the United States. Would you expect the supporters of Candidate B to accept this decision? Would they support President A's actions? How would people in either group see the Supreme Court? See James L. Gibson, Gregory A. Caldiera and Lester Kenyatta Spence, "The Supreme Court and the US Presidential Election of 2000: Wounds, Self–Inflicted or Otherwise?" 33 *British Journal of Political Science* 535, 555 (2003) ("... *Bush v. Gore* seems to have had a much smaller effect on the attitudes of Americans toward their Supreme Court than many expected. The various analyses presented in this article support the view that the weak effect of the Supreme Court's participation in the election is most likely due to pre-existing attitudes toward the Court that blunted the impact of disapproval of the Court's involvement in the election."). For a related treatment of legitimacy, see Lawrence M. Friedman, *The Legal System: A Social Science Perspective* 112 (1975).

8. If legitimacy leads to compliance, does a feeling that law or the legal order is illegitimate lead to noncompliance? Or to worse? These propositions, of course, seem quite plausible. But under what conditions? And to what extent? Consider the following essay:

(4.8) Flouting the Law

Janice Nadler

83 *Texas Law Review* 1399 (2005).

I. Introduction

Do ordinary citizens flout the law in response to a specific instance of perceived injustice? The idea that general lawbreaking can emerge from one unjust legal doctrine or decision has intuitive appeal. For example, Professor David Cole has argued that constitutional doctrines that allow untrammeled police discretion—such as that which led to the brutal beating of Rodney King in Los Angeles or the tragic police shooting of Amadou Diallo in New York—can undermine the public's perception of the legitimacy of law enforcement generally.[93] This loss of legitimacy and distrust of the fairness of the legal system, Cole argues, can in turn lead to more widespread lawbreaking.

93. See David Cole, "Discretion and Discrimination Reconsidered: A Response to the New Criminal Justice Scholarship," 87 *Georgetown Law Journal* 1059, 1090–91 (1999) (argu-

The Rodney King example is instructive in this regard. In 1992, the acquittal of the four police officers who beat Rodney King touched off the worst civil unrest seen in any American city in nearly thirty years. The streets of Los Angeles became the site of chaos and lawlessness. For four days, city residents looted stores, destroyed property, assaulted and shot one another, and set buildings on fire. When it was over, more than fifty people were dead, nearly 12,000 people were arrested, and over 800 buildings were burned to the ground. Undoubtedly, the causes contributing to the expression of community frustration during this time were numerous and complex. However, there is no doubt that the perceived injustice of the acquittals of the police officers was a "proximate" cause of the 1992 civil unrest in Los Angeles.

The 1992 Los Angeles example is an extreme one to be sure. At the same time, it suggests further, more general questions—questions that are at bottom empirical—about whether, and under what circumstances, citizens' perceptions of injustice lead to diminished deference to the law generally. Does perceived injustice in our legal system—whether in the form of wrongful convictions or acquittals, excessive punitive damage awards, outmoded public morals statutes, sentencing disparities between crack cocaine and powder cocaine, or mandatory minimum sentencing regimes—lead to greater willingness to flout the law in the everyday lives of ordinary people? Further, assuming that this is the case, does flouting typically manifest itself not in mass unrest but in more subtle, lower-level, and harder-to-detect ways, such as littering, tax cheating, theft of services, and jury nullification?

The idea that there is a relationship between perceived injustice of specific laws and diminished general compliance with the law has been either proposed or assumed by many theorists in a variety of contexts. For the purposes of discussion in this Article, I call this idea the Flouting Thesis. Despite its prominence, there is, however, a glaring absence of empirical evidence regarding the Flouting Thesis, which has been widely assumed but never proven. . . . This Article begins to fill this void by presenting the first experimental evidence for the Flouting Thesis and by empirically confirming that perceived legal injustices can have subtle but pervasive influences on a person's deference to the law in his or her everyday life. In this Article, I argue that Americans are culturally attentive to law and feel concerned when they notice injustice in the legal system. When a person evaluates particular legal rules, decisions, or practices as unjust, the diminished respect for the legal system that follows can destabilize otherwise law-abiding behavior. Economic theories of legal compliance uniformly focus on the expected value of outcomes shaped by threatened punishment. But economic theories uniformly ignore the possibility that there are reasons for obeying the law apart from the threat of sanctions.

The broader focus of this Article is on the ways in which law can influence citizen behavior other than through threatened punishment. As

ing that, for people who distrust the legal system, violation of the law is often "romanti-cized, idealized, condoned, or even celebrated") . . .

such, this Article is part of a broader movement emerging in legal scholarship that examines theories of expressive law.... [Some] have argued that, in addition to influencing behavior directly, law also can make a statement that strengthens desirable norms and weakens undesirable norms. For example, antidiscrimination laws may have weakened the norm of racial discrimination; laws that require clean-up after one's pet may strengthen the norm of cleaning up, even in the absence of enforcement. Others ... have focused on the mechanisms through which the values the law expresses can induce compliance, quite independently from the sanctions the law threatens. For example, laws banning smoking signaled to smokers a new societal consensus that exposing others to smoke is offensive and antisocial, triggering smokers to refrain from smoking in certain public places for fear of enduring objections from people nearby. The antismoking values expressed by law induced smokers to comply with minimal state enforcement of antismoking ordinances. More closely related to the topic of this Article, scholars focusing on compliance with criminal law have also noted that the expressive power of law can backfire when a law inadvertently generates disrespect. For example, a well-publicized government crackdown on tax cheating can implicitly send the message that everyone cheats, thereby generating more cheating than would be observed without the crackdown. More generally, these scholars argue that when law is perceived as failing to accurately reflect popular notions of justice, then citizens will be less likely to view the law as a moral authority that guides their own behavior. It is this theory of expressive law that I test empirically in this Article....

II.   Theories of Legal Compliance and Perceived Injustice

As noted earlier, perceived legal injustice can take a variety of forms. The 1992 Los Angeles civil unrest arose as a response to public outrage about acquittals in a widely publicized criminal trial. Decisions of the U.S. Supreme Court that clash with strongly held popular beliefs are another form of perceived injustice.... Perceived injustice can also arise from criminal punishment schemes that do not accurately reflect commonsense notions of desert. A variety of legal scholars and philosophers of law have recognized the possibility that disproportionate punishments can promote lawbreaking among citizens....

Paul Robinson and John Darley[94] have offered the most comprehensive theoretical treatment of the "utility of desert": the notion that by tying criminal liability and punishment to community-based notions of justice and desert, public compliance with the law will increase. Robinson and Darley argue that when the criminal law gains a reputation for assigning liability and punishment in ways that track the intuition of the community as a whole, it is more likely to be viewed as morally authoritative. As a result, people are more likely to defer to the commands of the law generally. Robinson and Darley

94. Paul H. Robinson & John M. Darley, "The Utility of Desert" 91 *Northwestern University Law Review,* 453 (1997).

argue that most people obey the law as a general matter, not so much because they are deterred by the possibility of being caught and punished, but because they either fear disapproval from their social group, or they want to do the morally correct thing—or both. But the norms held by one's social group are themselves influenced and strengthened by the criminal law. Every criminal adjudication offers an opportunity to remind the public of the underlying norm that prohibits the conduct in question. Legislative proposals for new criminal law rules provide an occasion for public debate that strengthens the shared understanding of what conduct is prohibited. Further, if the law has moral credibility, it can guide behavior in situations in which the harm underlying the prohibition is not immediately obvious.

According to Robinson and Darley, then, the moral credibility of the law can strengthen social norms and increase compliance. Because moral credibility plays a key role here, it is important to understand how the law comes to be viewed as a moral authority in the first place. Robinson and Darley contend that the criminal law gains moral credibility from imposing liability and punishment only on conduct that deserves moral condemnation and, conversely, from not imposing liability or punishment for conduct that does not deserve moral condemnation. When a particular criminal rule conflicts with the moral intuitions of the governed community, the power of the criminal law as a whole to induce compliance is in jeopardy because it is no longer viewed as a trustworthy source of information regarding which actions are moral and which are not. In sum, this version of the Flouting Thesis derives from the claim that adopting desert-based (retributive) notions of criminal liability and punishment that closely track community intuitions promotes compliance. . . .

It is worthy to note at this point that all of the variations on the Flouting Thesis reviewed so far share an important feature; they have never been tested. Thirty years ago, Lawrence Friedman noted that there is much yet to be discovered about the Flouting Thesis:

> If a person sees unfairness or illegitimacy or unworthiness of trust in one instance, how far does his disillusionment extend? How much of his attitude spills over into other areas and into his actual behavior? The hypocrisy and unfairness of Prohibition, it is said, brought the whole legal system into disrepute. Legal scholars claim that marijuana laws "hasten the erosion of respect for the law." But how much "erosion of respect"? And where? And what are the consequences?[95]

Yet even today, we do not know much more about the Flouting Thesis than we did when Professor Friedman posed these questions. . . . As an initial investigation, this Article does not (and cannot) aspire to address the important boundary conditions delineated by Professor Friedman; these questions must, of necessity, be left to another day. In the next Part, I present the

95. Lawrence M. Friedman, *The Legal System: A Social Science Perspective* 118–19 (1975).

results of three experiments designed to test the basic claim of the Flouting Thesis.

III.   Experimental Evidence for the Flouting Thesis

A.   *Background: Related Theories and Evidence*

. . . .

A survey study of tax compliance is perhaps the one study that most closely addresses the specific question addressed by this Article: what is the relationship between perceived injustice in the law in a particular instance and more general attitudes about respect for the law and compliance?[96] In the tax survey, people reported on both their own experiences with the IRS, as well as on second-hand information about the experiences of friends, neighbors, and coworkers with the IRS. Especially revealing were the attitudes of people who reported that a friend's, neighbor's, or coworker's contact with the IRS resulted in that person paying more taxes than they supposedly owed. This type of vicarious experience with the IRS was associated with lower perceptions of the fairness of tax laws generally and increased intentions to cheat on taxes in the future.

The results of the tax study suggest that exposure to reports of an unjust legal outcome in a particular situation might lead to lower perceived fairness of the law more generally, which in turn can lead to noncompliance with the law in the future. The conclusions to be drawn from the tax survey results are, however, limited in several important respects. First, all of the data was correlational, so that the causal direction (if causation can be inferred at all) of the connection between exposure to a perceived unjust outcome and lower intentions to comply with the law was ambiguous. It might be, for example, that a person's intention to cheat on her own taxes produced an evaluation that others' experiences with the IRS were unfair.

Second, the tax survey study addressed only the limited question of whether the justice of an outcome relating to one law (or set of laws) is associated with lower future compliance with that same law (or set of laws)— in this case, tax laws. The claim I test in this Article, by contrast, is a stronger one: perceived injustice of a particular law diminishes respect for the law in general, which is manifested in lower levels of compliance with other laws, even those distinct from, and unrelated to, the source of the perceived injustice. The experimental data reported below show empirically that legal injustice can trigger diminished compliance, not only with respect to the unjust law in question, but also with respect to other unrelated laws. In the remainder of this Part, I use original empirical results to show that perceived injustice in a legal rule can generate broader flouting of the law in everyday life.

96. Karyl A. Kinsey, "Deterrence and Alienation Effects of IRS Enforcement: An Analysis of Survey Data," in *Why People Pay Taxes: Tax Compliance and Enforcement* 259, 264–76 (Joel Slemrod ed., 1992) (describing the results of a 1988 telephone survey about tax compliance).

B. *Experiment 1: Testing the Flouting Thesis via Intentions to Comply*

1. Background.—To test the plausibility of the Flouting Thesis, I identified a specific underlying hypothesis and tested it experimentally. According to the Flouting Thesis, the belief that a particular law is unjust increases the likelihood of flouting the law in one's own daily life (even laws that are unrelated to the unjust law in question); conversely, the absence of perceived injustice should not increase flouting behavior. In the experiment, I presented a set of ostensible, proposed legislation designed to be interpreted as either just or unjust. By carefully varying the description of the ostensible legislation, I ensured (through pilot testing) that participants perceived the laws in question as basically unjust (treatment group) or as basically just (control group). According to the Flouting Thesis, the participant's attitude regarding the perceived injustice of laws should diminish his or her willingness to comply with different, unrelated laws.

The predictions of the Flouting Thesis focus essentially on a set of behavioral results: compliance with the law. At the same time, the predictive variable of the Flouting Thesis is a set of attitudes (about the injustice of specific laws). Generally speaking, however, the relationship between attitudes and behavior is not always straightforward.[97] One of the factors upon which the relevant behavioral response depends is the accessibility in memory of the attitude in question. The more easily an attitude is called to mind, the more likely it is to influence the cognitive structure of the behavioral event in question, and thus the more likely a response will follow that is behaviorally congruent with the attitude. In the context of perceptions of the law, the extent to which an attitude about the justice of a particular law affects compliance behavior may depend on the extent to which that attitude is accessible.

Thus, for the purposes of this experiment, it was important to ensure the salience in memory of the attitudes in question, here the perceived justice of the laws presented. For this reason, this study used a priming method in which the attitude is called to mind and is accessible at the time compliance behavior is measured.[98]

2. Experimental Method.—The experiment consisted of two parts. First, participants were exposed to a set of laws (perceived as either just or unjust) in the form of newspaper stories. Participants read six news stories, three that focused on a legal issue, and three that did not. The three news stories describing legal statutes were interspersed with the nonlegal news stories, thus focusing attention away from the purely legal nature of the task. Then,

---

97. Indeed, the conditions under which people exhibit consistency between their attitudes and their behavior is a question that social psychologists continue to debate. See generally, e.g., Icek Ajzen et al., "Explaining the Discrepancy Between Intentions and Actions: The Case of Hypothetical Bias in Contingent Valuation," 30 *Personality & Social Psy-*

chology Bulletin 1108 (2004) (demonstrating that, in the context of a hypothetical donation to charity, people overestimate the likelihood that they will engage in socially desirable behavior); Richard T. LaPiere, "Attitudes vs. Actions," 13 *Social Forces* 230 (1934).

98. A prime is a means of accessing or activating stored thoughts and concepts.

in an ostensibly separate study, the same people indicated their willingness to flout a set of unrelated laws in the future. Willingness to disobey the law (flouting) was measured by using a questionnaire that focused on intentions to engage in fairly common, but legally prohibited, acts.[99]

Newspaper stories were chosen to present the laws of interest in the first part of the experiment for several reasons. First, material presented in a newspaper story format has inherent appeal as a current-event item and is therefore more likely to engage people's interest when compared to the sometimes dense language used in legal statutes. Indeed, other research has demonstrated that reading newspaper stories about current events can increase a person's societal-level concern about the problem at hand. Second, newspaper stories provided a convenient cover story for the first part of the experiment. Participants were told that the researchers were interested in their emotional reactions to the quality of the writing and the style of journalism in the news stories. In the absence of such a cover story, participants may have been left to speculate about the purpose of reading legal statutes.

The participants were 98 undergraduate students.[100] Upon entering the laboratory and signing a consent form, participants were informed that they would be participating in a study on the role of emotions in attitudes about news stories. Participants each read a set of six articles that were ostensibly newspaper stories.[101] Three of these were filler stories (on NASA, oil drilling, and movie ushers) that were identical in content for all participants. Three were stories describing legislation, for which there were two versions—one set of stories was designed to elicit a perception that the laws described therein are just (Just Prime condition), and the other set was designed to elicit a perception that the laws described therein are unjust (Unjust Prime condition). The content of each version varied slightly from its counterpart, depending on the experimental condition. The basic topics of the law-related stories are illustrated in Table 1. Perceived justness was manipulated by varying each story's emphasis, as follows:

99. The law breaking measured here was not intended to represent a fair sample of all behavior that is prohibited by the law. Rather, I sought to measure people's intentions to break laws that they encounter on an everyday basis. I contend that it is these everyday laws that are most vulnerable to flouting following perceived injustice, because of increased opportunity and lower levels of inhibition, compared to laws prohibiting very serious (but more rare) acts such as robbery or murder. Moreover, as a practical matter, it would be exceedingly difficult to measure willingness to engage in these latter, more serious, offenses, precisely because they are less common, and also because people would be less likely to admit to engaging in them.

100. Of these participants, there were 54 females, 44 males, 27 African Americans, 24 Asians or Asian Americans, 23 Hispanics, 22 whites, and 2 self-designated as "other."

101. The length of all stories was kept constant at approximately 500 words.

Table 1.   Content Of Newspaper Stories Containing Primes

News Story	General Emphasis (both versions)	Just Prime Version	Unjust Prime Version
Civil Forfeiture	Purpose and application of (actual) laws permitting the government to seize property under certain circumstances	Emphasized the law enforcement benefits of civil forfeiture laws	Emphasized the civil liberties concerns surrounding civil forfeiture laws
Income Tax	Proposed legislation ostensibly pending before Congress that would affect the amount of income tax paid by middle class taxpayers	Emphasized positive effects of income tax paid by middle class people	Emphasized negative effects of income tax paid by middle class people
Landlord/ Tenant	Proposed Tenant legislation ostensibly pending before the state legislature that would permit landlords to conduct warrantless searches of tenants' apartments under certain circumstances	Emphasized importance of empowering landlords to evict drug-dealing tenants' apartments	Emphasized the civil liberties and privacy concerns in permitting searches of tenants' apartments

A pilot test of the materials using different participants indicated that the legal rules described in the three law-related newspaper stories presented in the Just Prime condition were perceived to be significantly more just, on average, than those presented in the Unjust Prime condition.[102]

Participants were randomly assigned to the Just Prime or Unjust Prime condition. After reading each of the six stories, participants answered a "quiz" question, to ensure they actually read the story. In addition, following each story, participants filled out a questionnaire assessing their opinion of the journalistic quality of the story they just read. The experimenter then collected all materials, thanked the participants, and left the room.

Shortly after the first experimenter left, a different experimenter entered the room and asked participants to sign a different consent form, explaining that they would be asked to participate in a second short experiment. After performing a short filler task, participants completed the Likelihood of Criminal Behavior Questionnaire. In this questionnaire, participants were asked to indicate the likelihood (from 0% to 100%) that they would engage in a variety of illegal behaviors. These items consisted of: drunk driving, parking in a no-parking zone, failing to pay required taxes, making illegal copies of software, eating a small item without paying in the grocery store, exceeding the posted speed limit, drinking alcohol under age 21, and taking home office supplies for personal use.[103]

102. Eighty-eight undergraduate psychology students participated in the pilot study. Each participant read one version of each of the three articles and rated the extent to which the law described in the article was either just or unjust (1—extremely unjust; 9—extremely just). Mean ratings in the Just Prime condition (M = 5.05) were significantly higher than mean ratings in the Unjust Prime condition (M = 2.95); $t(86) = -9.25$; $p < .0001$. Most participants (39 out of 44) in the Just Prime condition assigned ratings of 5 or above to the stories; nearly all participants (43 out of 44) in the Unjust Prime condition assigned ratings of below 5.

103. I chose these particular crimes to maximize variation in responses. Considering the range of acts that are prohibited by the

3. *Experimental Results.*—An analysis of each individual questionnaire item reveals an overall trend: 65 participants exposed to unjust laws indicated a greater likelihood of engaging in each criminal behavior compared to those exposed to just laws. . . .

. . . [C]onsistent with the Flouting Thesis, people exposed to the three newspaper stories describing perceived unjust laws are more willing to park illegally, copy unlicensed software, consume grocery items without paying, and pilfer office supplies, compared to those exposed to perceived just laws. . . .

C. Experiment 2a: Testing the Flouting Thesis via Mock Juror Behavior (Student Sample)

1. *Background.*—The results of Experiment 1 suggest that when people are exposed to unjust laws they are more willing to engage in everyday lawbreaking, such as traffic and software violations. The method used in Experiment 1 relies on self-reports—after being exposed to just or unjust legal rules, participants estimated the likelihood that they would break the law in the future. These self-reports suggest that the prime had differential effects on participants' *attitudes*; yet we cannot definitively predict behavior from such responses. In particular, measuring behavioral compliance with the law is difficult because of the ethical and practical problems inherent in such an inquiry. Ethically, difficulties arise if participants have been induced or encouraged to violate the law.

One alternative method for measuring compliance uses a mock trial paradigm. Participants play the role of jurors, and, after hearing the trial evidence and the judge's instructions on the law, they select an individual verdict preference of Guilty or Not Guilty. The trial materials can be designed so that the evidence is uncontroverted (either in favor of conviction or acquittal). Thus, in this carefully constructed situation, if participants are to follow the law as given to them by the judge, then they must select the decision required by the uncontroverted evidence. Selection of the other verdict indicates that the juror has decided to engage in juror nullification—not complying with the law as explained by the judge. This method of measuring compliance was employed in the present experiment and is described in further detail below.

2. *Experimental Method.*

a. *Participants and Materials.*—Participants were 228 undergraduate students.[104] Participants were exposed to a prime that consisted of a video-taped news story from the television program *60 Minutes.* The focus of the

criminal law, the six that I tested are fairly common among those who consider themselves law-abiding citizens. Had I chosen relatively more serious crimes, such as murder or robbery, the responses would have likely been clustered near 0%, making it difficult to detect any differences attributable to the Unjust Prime.

104. Of these participants 152 were female, 30 were African American, 36 were Asian or Asian American, 26 were Hispanic, and 136 were white. The mean age was 18.6 years.

program was on David Cash, an 18–year–old who watched his friend abduct a 7–year–old girl in the women's bathroom in a Nevada casino. Upon seeing his friend restrain the girl, Cash walked out of the bathroom and did nothing while his friend raped and murdered the girl.[105] Cash and the friend spent the next two days gambling, and Cash bragged about the crime to friends upon their return home to Los Angeles.

The *60 Minutes* videotape was followed by a written story, which appeared to participants to be a newspaper account, but was actually fictional. Participants read one of two versions of the follow-up story. In the Just Outcome story, David Cash is prosecuted for being an accessory to the murder after the fact, and he receives a sentence of one year in prison. In the Unjust Outcome story, David Cash receives no punishment.[106]

In the second part of the experiment, participants served as mock jurors in a case unrelated to the David Cash story. The written materials described a homeless defendant accused of stealing a shopping cart he used to store his personal belongings. Participants were informed that stealing a shopping cart is a felony. The case materials indicated that the defendant had two prior felony convictions, and that the jurisdiction has a "three strikes and you're out" rule. The materials made clear that the defendant, if found guilty, must be sentenced to life in prison with no possibility of parole.

The undisputed facts of the case together with the judge's instructions unambiguously indicated that the law requires a verdict of Guilty. The judge explicitly instructed the jurors that they must follow the law as it is given to them, and must not let sympathy or prejudice bias their decision. Thus, participants who rendered a Not Guilty "verdict" did so despite the judge's explicit instruction that they were required to apply the law to the facts of the case, regardless of how they might feel personally about the law—that is, they engaged in juror nullification.[107] Each subject's verdict preference of Guilty or

105. Cash claimed that he did not know a crime was in progress until after it was too late. He stated, however, that his friend admitted to the crime immediately after emerging from the bathroom.

106. Pilot testing (with different participants) revealed that, on average, participants believed that a sentence of about a year imprisonment was a fair punishment for David Cash. Pilot test participants were also asked to rate the justness of the punishment in the David Cash story for each prime condition, on a scale from 1 (extremely unjust) to 7 (extremely just). Participants rated the Just Prime punishment (one year in jail for David Cash) (M = 4.21) significantly more just than the Unjust Prime (no punishment for David Cash) (M = 2.87), $t(57) = -3.11$, $p < .01$. There were no significant differences based on participant race or gender in the justness ratings of the prime (all F's <1).

107. The evidence presented makes clear that the homeless defendant who stole the shopping cart is undoubtedly guilty. It was nonetheless expected that some participants would be tempted to render a Not Guilty decision in this case because many people would view imposing a punishment of life in prison with no parole for a relatively minor theft offense as disproportionate and excessive. There is room for disagreement here, of course, as evidenced by the popular support for the "three strikes and you're out" sentencing policies that exist in several states.... The possibility of different reactions to the shopping cart theft case makes it particularly useful for these purposes because the variation in responses permits detection of differences that are attributable to the justice prime.

Not Guilty thereby served as the measure of compliance or noncompliance with the law.

b. Procedure.—Participants were randomly assigned to the Just Outcome or Unjust Outcome condition. Upon entering the laboratory, they were presented with the David Cash news story video and were then presented with a follow-up newspaper story in which David Cash either was punished (Just Outcome) or was not punished (Unjust Outcome). A cover story was provided to ensure that the prime was assimilated into the later judgment: the putative purpose of the study was to assess participants' judgments about the quality of the journalism represented in the story. Participants were asked to provide ratings of the *60 Minutes* program, as well as of the follow-up newspaper item reporting the outcome of the case. Questionnaires elicited participants' opinions concerning the extent to which the news item was clear, in-depth, well-organized, and the like. The questionnaires served as filler tasks.

As part of the cover story, participants were then greeted by a different experimenter and taken to a different room to participate in a "second" experiment. After signing a separate consent form, participants were informed that they would act as mock jurors whose task was to render a verdict in a criminal case. Participants read the trial materials and then privately indicated their personal verdict preference of Guilty or Not Guilty.

3. Experimental Results.—For the mock trial data, noncompliance rates were measured by the proportion of all participants who made Not Guilty decisions. The higher the proportion of Not Guilty decisions, the higher the level of noncompliance. According to the Flouting Thesis, observing legal injustice leads to noncompliance. It was expected, therefore, that compared to those primed with a Just Outcome, participants primed with an Unjust Outcome in the David Cash case would exhibit a greater rate of noncompliance, in the form of a higher proportion of Not Guilty decisions in the case of the homeless man. This flouting hypothesis is directly contrary to another plausible effect of the justice prime: it might be that participants told that David Cash was not punished (Unjust Prime) would seek more punishment in the case of the homeless man compared to participants told that David Cash was punished (Just Prime). This is because people who witness an injustice sometimes become more punitive as a result. This experiment, therefore, pits the Flouting Thesis against an alternative hypothesis (the Anger–Blame hypothesis) that predicts the opposite outcome.

Analysis of the data revealed that in fact, and contrary to both the Flouting Thesis and the Anger–Blame hypothesis, there was no statistically significant difference overall between Just and Unjust Prime groups in proportion to Not Guilty decisions.[108] This failure to detect a difference between the two primed groups suggests a boundary condition on the Flout-

108. ... The Total Unjust and Total Just percentages (Exp. 2a) do not differ statistically. $\chi^2 (1) = 0.19$; $p = .66$.

ing Thesis, such that perceptions of injustice might not influence compliance with the law in the context of juror decision making. To explore this possibility further, I separated the participants into two groups based on gender.[109] This generated a total of four groups: males primed with a Just Outcome, males primed with an Unjust Outcome, females primed with a Just Outcome, and females primed with an Unjust Outcome.

Next, the effects of both gender and prime, as well as the interaction between gender and prime, on verdict preference were examined.... The pattern of results ... shows that whereas the responses of female participants are consistent with the Flouting Thesis, the responses of male participants are not.

Note that it is difficult to discern whether the patterns here are attributable to the Unjust Prime encouraging women to choose a Not Guilty verdict, or to the Just Prime encouraging men to choose a Not Guilty verdict, or some combination of both. To further explore this question, I subsequently asked 78 participants drawn from the same population as the current experiment to indicate their verdict preference in the shopping cart theft case. This group did not read the case of David Cash, and they were not exposed to the Unjust Prime or the Just Prime. Therefore, this group provided a baseline measure of the verdict preference regarding the shopping cart theft absent any prior exposure to a just or unjust outcome.

... [T]he proportion of Not Guilty verdicts of female participants in the baseline group fell in between the Unjust Prime group and the Just Prime group.[110] Note that for women, compared to the baseline rate of Not Guilty verdicts, the Unjust Prime appears to increase this rate and the Just Prime appears to decrease this rate, consistent with the Flouting Thesis.[111] For men, the Unjust Prime appears to have no effect on the rate of Not Guilty verdicts, whereas the Just Prime appears to increase this rate. Because none of the tests of simple main effects reach conventional levels of statistical significance, it is difficult to interpret the nature of the effect of each prime.

Especially puzzling are the differential effects of the prime that depended on the gender of the participant. These differences were unexpected and a definitive explanation requires further study. As a preliminary matter, one might posit that these results be explained by differences in attitudes between males and females because of their historical position in the legal system. These attitudinal differences may have been primed by the nature of the

109. The nature of the David Cash case suggested examining whether gender moderates the role of the injustice prime on compliance behavior. This is because the case involved a rape, with a female victim and male perpetrators. The nature of this crime may well have activated gender stereotypes that differentially influence male and female participants. See Sheila T. Murphy, "The Impact of Factual Versus Fictional Media Portrayals on Cultural Stereotypes," 560 Annals of the American Academy of Political & Social Science 165, 165 (1998) (demonstrating that exposure to gender stereotypical portrayals can influence subsequent interpretations of unrelated events).

110. None of the tests of simple main effects discussed here reach conventional levels of statistical significance, but ... are nonetheless suggestive.

111. Again, note the caveat that these patterns are merely suggestive.

materials in the case, because the case involved a crime of violence against a female victim committed by male perpetrators. Consider first the male participants who learned that the legal system imposed on David Cash the punishment he was perceived to have deserved (the Just Prime). A perceived just outcome may have confirmed for male participants that the legal system indeed works to serve and protect all of its citizens, and, in the absence of any threat to the legitimacy of the legal system, male participants subsequently may have felt they had license to bend the rules in the name of justice for the homeless defendant in the second task. This explanation for why male participants were more likely to flout the rules after observing the legal system meting out a just punishment is supported by recent work in experimental social psychology on the phenomenon of "moral credentialing."[112] The theory of moral credentialing holds that people feel licensed to act on questionable motives when they have previously established their credentials as a person of pure motives. For example, a man who credentials himself as nonsexist by hiring a woman might later feel greater license to express a politically incorrect opinion on an unrelated topic. In general, establishing moral credentials serves to liberate people to engage in behavior that they might otherwise avoid for fear of being viewed (by oneself or by others) in a negative light. In the current study, male participants who observed that the legal system meted out a just punishment to David Cash may have subsequently felt licensed to flout the law and pronounce as "Not Guilty" the homeless man who was clearly guilty of stealing the shopping cart. According to moral-credentialing theory, males who observed the legal system justly punish another male who was involved in a crime against a female saw the legal system establishing its credentials as nonsexist and concerned with doing justice. In the subsequent task, failure to follow the judge's instructions is a behavior that might ordinarily be viewed in a negative light, but, given the prior credentialing of the law, male participants who saw David Cash justly punished felt licensed to flout the law and ignore the judge's instructions.

The results are also consistent with prior research that demonstrates that men and women react quite differently when exposed to media portrayals involving female stereotypes. At the same time, it must be acknowledged that without more evidence it is not yet possible to provide a complete explanation for the different responses of men and women observed in Experiment 2a. To further explore the nature of these unexpected effects, I conducted another experiment that used a different sample of participants: adult community members from diverse backgrounds. The next subpart describes in detail the procedure and results of Experiment 2b.

. . . .

112. Benoit Monin & Dale T. Miller, "Moral Credentials and the Expression of Prejudice" 81 *Journal of Personality & Social Psychology* 33 (2001).

D. *Experiment 2b: Testing the Flouting Thesis via Mock Juror Behavior (Community Sample)*

   1. Background.—The Flouting Thesis was confirmed in Experiment 2a but, unexpectedly, only among female participants. To examine whether the absence of the predicted effect among male mock jurors in Experiment 2a extends to other populations, I conducted a similar experiment using a very different sample of participants. Instead of using undergraduate college students from the midwestern United States, I recruited a diverse sample of adults from a wide geographic range. The method of Experiment 2b was very similar to that of the previous experiment; exceptions are noted below.

   2. Experimental Method.

   a. Participants and Materials.—Participants were invited to participate via an email message sent to individuals who had previously registered as a volunteer to participate in web-based research. The email message included a URL to a survey hosted on the Internet. Participants were offered an incentive for participation in the form of a random draw to receive a gift certificate from an online retailer. Participants were assured that their responses would remain anonymous and that identifying information would not be collected.

   An email message was sent to one thousand people, inviting them to participate. One hundred and sixty-five people completed the survey. Of these, 16 people failed to correctly answer two questions designed to test basic understanding of the materials, so their responses were excluded from the results, leaving a final sample size of 149. Of these, 60% were female, and 82% were white. The participants' mean age was 37 years. Two-thirds were U.S. residents. Of non-U.S. residents, the vast majority (about 90%) were residents of common law countries such as Canada, the United Kingdom, Australia, and New Zealand. The responses of U.S. and non-U.S. residents did not differ statistically; the analysis below includes all respondents in the final sample. The materials were identical to those used in Experiment 2a, with one exception in format. The David Cash case was presented in the form of a print newspaper story, rather than a *60 Minutes* TV program.

   b. Procedure.—Participants were randomly assigned to one of three conditions: Just Outcome (David Cash punished), Unjust Outcome (David Cash not punished), or Baseline (no exposure to the David Cash case). Upon agreeing to participate in the survey, participants not assigned to the Baseline condition were presented with the David Cash news story, and were then presented with a follow-up newspaper story in which David Cash either was punished (Just Outcome) or was not punished (Unjust Outcome). Filler questionnaires elicited ratings of the writing quality of the news stories. Participants assigned to the Baseline condition proceeded directly to the next part of the experiment.

   Participants were then informed that they would act as mock jurors whose task was to render a verdict in a criminal case. Participants read the trial materials involving the homeless man accused of stealing a shopping cart (which were identical to the materials used in Experiment 2a), and then privately indicated their personal verdict preference of Guilty or Not Guilty.

They were then asked to rate the likelihood that the defendant was guilty on a seven point scale (1—Definitely Guilty; 7—Definitely Not Guilty).

3. Experimental Results.—As in the prior experiment, noncompliance rates were measured by the proportion of participants who made Not Guilty decisions. Unlike in the prior experiment, in Experiment 2b the prime had a statistically significant effect on compliance rates of both women and men. The results ... are consistent with the Flouting Thesis: compared to those primed with a Just Outcome, participants primed with an Unjust Outcome in the David Cash case exhibited a greater rate of noncompliance, in the form of a higher proportion of Not Guilty decisions in the case of the homeless man.[113]

The Flouting Thesis was therefore confirmed. In light of the gender differences that emerged in Experiment 2a, gender differences were examined in this experiment as well. As illustrated in Table 2, rates of noncompliance for male and female participants were very similar, and this was confirmed in the logistic regression analysis, which revealed no statistically significant effect of gender on rates of Not Guilty decisions.

In addition to indicating their verdict preference, participants also rated the defendant's guilt on a seven point scale (1—Definitely Not Guilty; 7—Definitely Guilty). An analysis of variance revealed that prime had a statistically significant effect on continuous ratings of guilt. The pattern here was similar to the one that emerged from the dichotomous verdict judgments: participants primed with an Unjust outcome rated the defendant as less guilty (Mean = 3.4) compared to participants primed with a Just outcome (Mean = 4.1) and compared to those in the Baseline condition (Mean = 4.2).[114]

Despite the preliminary nature of the inferences to be drawn from the results of these studies, one feature of all three experiments is noteworthy. The duration of exposure to perceived legal injustice was exceedingly brief—in some ways artificially so. In both experiments, participants' exposure to perceived legal injustice lasted no more than 20 minutes. Perceived legal injustice that people observe outside of the laboratory is sometimes longer in duration and more intense in its experienced effects. How could it be the case that brief exposure to unjust legal rules causes people to be less willing to comply with unrelated laws that regulate their everyday behavior? In the next Part, I consider explanations for the influence of perceived injustice on general diminished compliance.

---

113. ... In Model 4, there was an overall effect of the prime on noncompliance, and the rate of noncompliance was greater in the Unjust Prime group compared to the Just Prime group. However, the apparent difference in compliance rates ... between the Baseline and Unjust Prime groups, and between the Baseline and Just Prime groups, did not reach conventional levels of statistical significance. For this reason, it is difficult to determine whether the overall effect of the prime on noncompliance is attributable to an increase in flouting due to the Unjust Prime, a decrease in flouting due to the Just Prime, or both.

114. The Unjust–Just and Unjust–Baseline pairwise comparisons are both statistically significant at $p < .01$.

IV.   Perceived Injustice in the Law and Its Consequences

Can perceived legal injustices result in lower respect for the law generally? The experimental evidence presented here suggests that it can. Real life
events also suggest that this is the case.... In this Part, I suggest several
different possibilities to explain the influence of perceived injustice on willingness to flout the law in everyday life. Because the empirical evidence presented in this Article in many ways represents an initial foray into previously
uncharted territory, the arguments that follow are presented in the spirit of
conjectures designed to generate discussion and debate; more work needs to
be done to demonstrate persuasively the nature and extent of specific factors
contributing to the connection between perceived unjust laws and reduced
compliance generally with the law. Nonetheless, I discuss several potential
explanations which are at least plausible given the experimental evidence.

A.   *The Influence of Popular Culture on Attention to Perceived Legal Injustice*

[Nadler points out that perceptions of injustice "in the laboratory" do not
necessarily tell us "how and why and when people perceive legal injustice in
everyday life." In life, people can perceive injustice "personally," or "vicariously," that is, when it happens to other people.

She also distinguishes between the perception of "unjust legal decisions,
such as jury verdicts," and unjust statutes. In the case of jury verdicts, the
public finds it hard to understand that sometimes a jury verdict that seems
wrong could be correct because of due process problems.

With regard to legislation, Prohibition often is cited as an example of an
unjust law. The laws against liquor during Prohibition were "notoriously
disobeyed." This led civic leaders to worry about the "Flouting Thesis."
Perhaps the drug laws, or some aspects of them, are contemporary examples.

A gap between what ordinary people think is just, and the actual content
of the laws, can be a problem. The question is how to reduce this gap
"between legal rules and citizen attitudes."]

B.   *Expressive Law, Perceived Injustice, and Compliance*

The delicate balance that promotes compliance is assisted enormously by
the fact that, much of the time, the law accurately reflects prevalent mores
about permissible behavior. Thus, criminal law prohibits murder, rape, robbery, larceny, and a host of other acts, the propriety of which almost everyone
agrees. The general convergence of the requirements of the law and commonsense justice means that most people comply with the law most of the time
because they would have refrained from doing the prohibited act, whether it is
murder, rape, or robbery, quite apart from the existence of its legally
prohibited status.

On the other hand, people also refrain from legally prohibited acts in
which they may be genuinely tempted to engage, such as certain traffic
offenses (for example, driving through a red light at an empty intersection) or
offenses against other persons (for example, punching someone who they feel
really deserves it). Democratically produced legislation, for example, can be

perceived as a signal of community norms about behavior. In declaring conduct to be prohibited, the law expresses social disapproval of that conduct, which can itself strengthen people's commitment to acting legally—even when the fear of punishment is absent. Such moral commitments can operate, even on people who have not internalized them, through social pressure to avoid the loss of esteem in others' eyes that would result from engaging in prohibited conduct. In this way, the law itself informs people's ideas about moral and immoral behavior.

To some extent, people also obey the law because they feel they owe a general obligation to legitimate authority. If the law is generally seen as accurately reflecting community norms, it is intuitively plausible that people will be more inclined to defer to it as a moral authority. Under these circumstances, the very labeling of a certain act as criminal might make people more aware of the socially harmful quality of that act. For example, before the existence of severe criminal punishments for drunk driving, many people were unaware of the severity of the risk associated with drunk driving. It may be that drunk driving is increasingly considered in moral terms precisely because it has been labeled criminal.

Thus, laws that plausibly signal community attitudes result in deference and compliance, even if the value expressed had not been previously internalized by all members of the community, as in the drunk driving example. Severe punishment for drunk driving signals the risk of severe harm associated with the act; the previously established moral credibility of the law generally ensures that the signal will be heeded. However, laws that are perceived as completely implausible signals of community attitudes—that is, laws that strike people as so far off the mark that they could not possibly represent what the community believes or values—are likely to have different effects. If the law is seen as imposing unjust or immoral obligations, then rather than signaling community attitudes, the law instead might be perceived as irrelevant, and, intuitively, there would be little reason to defer to it as a moral authority. For example, if the criminal law were to prohibit all sexual intercourse between unmarried couples, most people would view that law as discrepant from their own personal moral views about sexual intercourse; as a result, they would be willing to disobey the law. Further, such a law might have an even broader effect. It might cause people to view the law generally in a different light—as a set of irrelevant and arbitrary rules rather than a coherent expression of community values.

V. Implications and Prescriptions

A. *Sources of Perceived Injustice*

Recognition of initial sources of perceived injustice is a necessary condition for controlling the generally diminished compliance it triggers. In the experiments reported in this Article, justice perceptions were induced by the conditions of the experiment. The primary advantage of this admittedly artificial procedure is that by randomly inducing perceptions of either injustice or justice in participants, we can confidently conclude that the observed mean difference in flouting behavior between the two groups was attributable to the perceptions of injustice of the prime, as opposed to some other cause. At the same time, inducing people to perceive injustice in the laboratory does not advance our understanding of how and why and when people perceive legal injustice in everyday life. Natural sources of perceived injustice in the legal system are varied: A person can experience perceived legal injustice personally, such as when a person feels that he is unfairly targeted by a police officer for a traffic violation because of his race. Alternatively, sources of perceived injustice can be experienced vicariously, such as when a person sympathizes with defendants harshly punished under federal mandatory minimum sentencing provisions.

The sources of perceived injustice that are discussed in this Article generally fall into two categories: perceived unjust legal decisions, such as jury verdicts, and perceived unjust legislation. The problem of perceptions of unjust jury verdicts is perhaps the more difficult problem from a policy perspective. Criminal jury verdicts that are perceived to be unjust oftentimes are indeed unjust from a narrow distributive justice perspective: factually guilty people are sometimes acquitted by juries, and as a result, people who have in fact committed a criminal act sometimes do not receive their just desert. Likewise, factually innocent people are sometimes convicted by juries. Of course, acquittals represent a judgment on the part of the jury or judge that the prosecution has not met its burden of proof, and so many acquittals that appear unjust from a narrow distributive justice perspective are morally defensible when procedural justice considerations are taken into account. Nevertheless, many people find it difficult to give proper weight to procedural justice considerations once they have made an assessment about the "correct" outcome from a distributive perspective.... In sum, because information about jury verdicts is, and should be, available to the public, perceived unjust jury verdicts are bound to occur and to cause general diminished compliance in the ways outlined in this Article.

A second prototype of perceived legal injustice is legislation, or other legal regulation, that conflicts with commonsense notions of what justice requires. Perhaps the most salient historical example is the prohibition on the manufacture, distribution, or sale of alcoholic beverages imposed by the Eighteenth Amendment. During the period when the Eighteenth Amendment was in force, the law prohibiting alcohol was notoriously disobeyed. Toward the end of the prohibition era, prominent leaders worried that such widespread lawlessness had weakened respect for the law generally, leading to widespread diminished compliance with laws unrelated to prohibition—that is, they worried about the Flouting Thesis. Contemporary examples are not always associated with the same extent of widespread disobedience, but these examples provoke controversy and heated discussion nonetheless. These include particular aspects of drug laws (such as the sentencing disparity between crack cocaine and powder cocaine offenses in the Federal Sentencing Guidelines), mandatory minimum sentences of incarceration for certain crimes, sodomy statutes, foster care regulations, and smoking ordinances, to name just a few.

Laws that are enacted with the intention to change social norms and behavior sometimes are met with resistance if the law departs too substantially from the view of ordinary people. Many discrepancies between legal regulation and commonsense attitudes constitute avoidable sources of law-breaking because perceptions of injustice and the diminished respect for the legal system that follow can destabilize the law-abiding behavior of ordinary people. By limiting the incongruities between the condemnation expressed by a particular legal rule and the severity of condemnation implicit in public attitudes, perceived injustice can be diminished. The key question, then, is how to go about reducing discrepancies between legal rules and citizen attitudes.

B. Reducing the Gap Between Legal Rules and Commonsense Justice

In principle, there are several ways to better harmonize legal rules and public attitudes. If there is an existing social norm regarding the issue addressed by the law, one method involves reforming the legal rule in question to better align it with the existing social norm; another method involves altering the social norm to better align it with the existing legal rule. Legal rules sometimes do not directly implicate social norms, but instead implicate what are better described as socially shared attitudes. In these cases, it is possible for the law to conform to public attitudes. I discuss these possibilities in turn.

1. *Modifying Legal Rules.*—Modifying the legal rule to better reflect the existing social norm involves a number of considerations. First, we must make a determination that the existing norm promotes desirable social policies and that the legal rule would be more effective at promoting those policies if it were to better reflect the existing social norm. In other words, we must decide that we want the legal rule to look more like the social norm. Of course, it is not always the case that the social norm is laudable. Historically, there are many instances of prevailing social norms that, in retrospect, many would agree were wrongheaded. These include the norm against the equal participation of women, racial minorities, and gays and lesbians in social and political life; the norm against homosexual sex; the norm against interracial marriage; and the norm permitting harm to the environment (such as littering and polluting the air and water), to name just a few.

Second, assuming the existing norm is desirable, we must make a determination that there is in fact a unified social norm to which we can conform the legal rule. This is often not the case. For example, some of the most contentious issues of the day, such as same-sex marriage, abortion, physician-assisted suicide, and the death penalty involve such deep differences of opinion that we cannot hope to neatly conform the legal rule to existing norms. In these cases, our best strategy is to rely on fair procedures to ensure that the decisions of legal actors are viewed as legitimate and thus likely to be complied with.

Sometimes, the legal rule in question does not really implicate a social norm but instead implicates a socially shared attitude about what justice requires. In these situations, it is possible to measure empirically the socially shared attitude and then conform the law to the consensus (assuming that there is no independent reason to think that the consensus makes for bad legal policy). For example, criminal law rules governing attempted crimes do not really implicate an existing, articulable social norm regarding when and whether it is permissible to attempt to commit crimes. Nevertheless, people are likely to have intuitions about what type of conduct ought to be punished as an attempted crime in specific situations. Moreover, social scientists using the right types of survey instruments and samples ought to be able to measure these popular intuitions.

That this type of endeavor is possible was demonstrated by Paul Robinson and John Darley in their book *Justice, Liability, and Blame*.[115] They tested several different criminal law doctrines (e.g., attempt, justification, excuse, and the like) against the opinions of citizens regarding what the content of these rules should be. But instead of asking questions about criminal law rules in the abstract, the authors asked people to give their opinions about factual scenarios. For example, should a person who cases out a jewelry store with the intention to burglarize it, but then goes no further, be held criminally liable for attempting to commit a crime? From these responses, we can infer what people think the rule ought to be. Robinson and Darley found that, although modern criminal law doctrine imposes liability as soon as a person takes a substantial step toward an offense, most people would impose no punishment when faced with the facts of such a case. Where the legal rule departs from the consensus of the lay public regarding just desert, lawmakers can modify the legal rule to reflect popular consensus, as long as such consensus can be justified in criminal law theory. This assumes, of course, that the theoretical considerations that led to the adoption of the original rule do not overwhelm the reasons for adopting the new, more "popular" rule. In the case of attempt crime standards, there is a proliferation of different approaches, and there seems to be no real consensus among scholars or lawmakers about which approach is superior. In this case, therefore, a sensible approach might be to adopt the rule that best accords with common-sense notions of what justice requires.

Note, however, that we need not limit ourselves to considering only those legal rules about which expert consensus is lacking. There may be other rules that depart from socially shared intuitions that are, on the one hand, widely accepted by legal experts, but on the other hand, amenable to review and revision. Of course, the decision to revise an existing rule in order to better

---

115. See Paul H. Robinson & John M. Darley, *Justice, Liability, and Blame: Community Views and the Criminal Law* 16–20 (1995).

harmonize it with commonsense intuitions must never be taken lightly. This decision process necessarily entails a balancing between theoretical justifications underlying the rule, and justifications for the existing shared intuition. One can imagine situations in which there is a sound reason for the existing rule and a less sound—but still justifiable—reason for an alternate rule; if the alternate rule comports better with socially shared intuitions, this fact weighs in favor of its adoption but is not, in itself, determinative.

2. *Facilitating Understanding of Existing Legal Rules.*—The second main way to reduce the gap between legal rules and commonsense justice is to change the prevailing conception of justice. Education of the public regarding legal rules and procedures is a key method to pursue. Most people are woefully unaware of existing legal requirements. . . .

Given the goal of reducing the gap between legal rules and commonsense justice, the challenge is not only to educate people about the content of existing legal rules, but, in addition, to facilitate a public understanding of the rationale for existing rules. Sometimes, the facts of a well-publicized criminal case will help to make known an existing, but previously little-known legal rule; but if the rationale for the rule is not apparent, that rule might fall into disrepute if it is contrary to commonsense notions of justice, or if it leads to a result widely regarded as unjust. In addition, the perception of an unjust result might arise because of application of procedural rules that most would regard as just and necessary if only they were made aware of the existence of the procedural safeguard and associated rationale.

C. Caveats and Unanswered Questions

It is important at this point to acknowledge several questions that remain unanswered. One important question left open by the experiments reported in this Article is: How stable is the impulse to flout the law in the face of perceived injustice? Measures of how long the perceptions of injustice induced by the procedure were not included in these experiments. Even more uncertain is how long the effects of perceived injustice last outside of the laboratory. These are important yet unanswered questions and are worthy of examination. . . .

Another question left unanswered by the initial set of experiments discussed in this Article is the nature of the psychological mechanism that drives willingness to flout. The experimental results suggest that perceiving an unjust law or outcome increases the likelihood of flouting the law. But it is unclear what it is about perceived injustice that leads to flouting. One possibility is that people explicitly revise their general attitudes toward the legal system upon learning about an unjust legal rule or result, and based on these revised attitudes, make a conscious decision to flout. At the other extreme, it is possible that people's increased willingness to flout does not rise to the level of conscious thought—that is, people who resist legal rules following perceived injustice might not attribute their behavior to the prior perception of injustice. It is also unclear whether increased flouting is constrained to perceptions of injustice, or whether other, more general negative experiences can lead to flouting. For example, it is possible that negative mood is responsible for increased willingness to flout observed in the experiments, rather than perceived injustice per se. These questions can be examined in the future by separating out the effects of mood from injustice and by prompting people to provide an account of their own attributions for their own willingness to flout.

This Article focused on two prototypes: perceived unjust outcomes and perceived unjust legal rules. Of course, there are many other possible sources of perceived legal injustice. . . . Indeed, it may be the case that legal rules and regulations do not often trigger perceptions of injustice in the abstract because ordinary citizens do not often attend to them in the abstract, in the way that participants in Experiment 1 were prompted to do. On the other hand, legal rules certainly are vulnerable to perceptions of injustice when they give rise to an outcome or decision which is itself perceived to be unjust. In these cases, the outcome of individual cases is the mechanism that gives rise to the perception that the rule itself is unjust. As noted earlier, sources of perceived injustice were manipulated in the laboratory in the experiments reported in this Article; future work could examine actual sources of perceived injustice in everyday life. Examination of sources of perceived injustice would help delineate the circumstances under which people are more likely to be prompted to flout the law. . . .

NOTES AND QUESTIONS

1.   Suppose a person thinks that some particular law is seriously wrong or unjust as measured by his or her values or that the actions of law enforcement officials are seriously wrong or unjust by the same standard. What does the Flouting Thesis suggest? Is this person more likely to violate all laws where he or she can get away with it or where the punishment is not great? Or is he or she likely to violate only those laws that have some relationship to the actual perceived injustice? Does the Flouting Thesis suggest that, if I think federal tax officials are acting unjustly, I am more likely to evade taxes? more likely to blow up a federal building? more likely to jaywalk? more likely to shoplift?

2.   To what degree might my ability to rationalize breaking the law affect my willingness and desire to flout it as a response to something that I see as illegitimate?

3.   We have been considering such things as sanction threats, moral appeals and a sense of legitimacy as explanations for why people comply with rules. At least in some part, the answer may be more simple. Most of us are, more or less, socialized to do what those in authority tell us to do. But how far will people go in taking orders without considering what they are being asked to do?

(4.9) Obedience to Authority: An Experimental View

Stanley Milgram[116]

Obedience is as basic an element in the structure of social life as one can point to. Some system of authority is a requirement of all communal living, and it is only the man dwelling in isolation who is not forced to respond, through defiance or submission, to the commands of others. Obedience, as a determinant of behavior, is of particular relevance to our time. It has been reliably established that from 1933 to 1945 millions of innocent people were systematically slaughtered on command. Gas chambers were built, death camps were guarded, daily quotas of corpses were produced with the same efficiency as the manufacture of appliances. These inhumane policies may have originated in the mind of a single person, but they could only have been carried out on a massive scale if a very large number of people obeyed orders.

Obedience is the psychological mechanism that links individual action to political purpose. It is the dispositional cement that binds men to systems of authority....

The legal and philosophic aspects of obedience are of enormous import, but an empirically grounded scientist eventually comes to the point where he wishes to move from abstract discourse to the careful observation of concrete instances. In order to take a close look at the act of obeying, I set up a simple experiment at Yale University. Eventually, the experiment was to involve more than a thousand participants and would be repeated at several universities, but at the beginning, the conception was simple. A person comes to a psychological laboratory and is told to carry out a series of acts that come increasingly into conflict with conscience. The main question is how far the participant will comply with the experimenter's instructions before refusing to carry out the actions required of him.

But the reader needs to know a little more detail about the experiment. Two people come to a psychological laboratory to take part in a study of memory and learning. One of them is designated as "teacher" and the other a "learner." The experimenter explains that the study is concerned with the effects of punishment on learning. The learner is conducted into a room, seated in a chair, his arms strapped to prevent excessive movement, and an electrode attached to his wrist. He is told that he is to learn a list of word pairs; whenever he makes an error, he will receive electric shocks of increasing intensity.

The real focus of the experiment is the teacher. After watching the learner being strapped into place, he is taken into the main experimental

116. Abridged from pp. 1, 2–5, 7–8 in *Obedience to Authority: An Experimental View* by Stanley Milgram. Copyright © 1974 by Stanley Milgram. Reprinted by permission of the author and Harper & Row, Publishers, Inc.

room and seated before an impressive shock generator. Its main, feature is a horizontal line of thirty switches, ranging from 15 volts to 450 volts, in 15–volt increments. There are also verbal designations which range from SLIGHT SHOCK to DANGER—SEVERE SHOCK. The teacher is told that he is to administer the learning test to the man in the other room. When the learner responds correctly, the teacher moves onto the next item; when the other man gives an incorrect answer, the teacher is to give him an electric shock. He is to start at the lowest shock level (15 volts) and to increase the level each time the man makes an error, going through 30 volts, 45 volts, and so on.

The "teacher" is a genuinely naive subject who has come to the laboratory to participate in an experiment. The learner, or victim, is an actor who actually receives no shock at all. The point of the experiment is to see how far a person will proceed in a concrete and measurable situation in which he is ordered to inflict increasing pain on a protesting victim. At what point will the subject refuse to obey the experimenter?

Conflict arises when the man receiving the shock begins to indicate that he is experiencing discomfort. At 75 volts, the "learner" grunts. At 120 volts he complains verbally; at 150 he demands to be released from the experiment. His protests continue as the shocks escalate, growing increasingly vehement and emotional. At 285 volts his response can only be described as an agonized scream.

Observers of the experiment agree that its gripping quality is somewhat obscured in print. For the subject, the situation is not a game; conflict is intense and obvious. On one hand, the manifest suffering of the learning presses him to quit. On the other, the experimenter, a legitimate authority to whom the subject feels some commitment, enjoins him to continue. The aim of this investigation was to find when and how people would defy authority in the face of a clear moral imperative.

There are, of course, enormous differences between carrying out the orders of a commanding officer during times of war and carrying out the orders of an experimenter. Yet the essence of certain relationships remain, for one may ask in a general way: How does a man behave when he is told by a legitimate authority to act against a third individual? If anything, we may expect the experimenter's power to be considerably less than that of the general, since he has no power to enforce his imperatives, and participation in a psychological experiment scarcely evokes the sense of urgency and dedication engendered by participation in war. Despite these limitations, I thought it worthwhile to start careful observation of obedience even in this modest situation, in the hope that it would stimulate insights and yield general propositions applicable to a variety of circumstances.

A reader's initial reaction to the experiment may be to wonder why anyone in his right mind would administer even the first shocks. Would he not simply refuse and walk out of the laboratory? But the fact is that no one ever does. Since the subject has come to the laboratory to aid the experimenter, he is quite willing to start off with the procedure. There is nothing very extraordinary in this, particularly since the person who is to receive the shocks seems initially cooperative, if somewhat apprehensive. What is surprising is how far ordinary individuals go in complying with the experimenter's instructions. Indeed, the results of the experiment are both surprising and dismaying. Despite the fact that many subjects experience stress, despite the fact that many protest to the experimenter, a substantial proportion continue to the last shock on the generator.

Many subjects will obey the experimenter no matter how vehement the pleading of the person being shocked, no matter how painful the shocks seem to be, and no matter how much the victim pleads to be let out. This was seen time and again in our studies and has been observed in several universities where the experiment was repeated. It is the extreme willingness of adults to go to almost any lengths on the command of authority that constitutes the chief finding of the study and a fact most urgently demanding explanation.

A commonly offered explanation is that those who shocked the victim at the most severe level were monsters, the sadistic fringe of society. But if one considers that almost two-thirds of the participants fall into the category of "obedient" subjects, and that they represent ordinary people drawn from working, managerial, and professional classes, the argument becomes very shaky. . . .

[T]he most common adjustment of thought in the obedient subject is for him to see himself as not responsible for his own actions. He divests himself of responsibility by attributing all initiative to the experimenter, a legitimate authority. He sees himself not as a person acting in a morally accountable way but as the agent of external authority. In the post-experimental interview, when subjects were asked why they had gone on, a typical reply was "I wouldn't have done it by myself. I was just doing what I was told." Unable to defy the authority of the experimenter, they attribute all responsibility to him. It is the old story of "just doing one's duty" that was heard time and time again in the defense statements of those accused at Nuremberg. But it would be wrong to think of it as a thin alibi concocted for the occasion. Rather, it is a fundamental mode of thinking for a great many people once they are locked into a subordinate position in a structure of authority. The disappearance of a sense of responsibility is the most far-reaching consequence of submission to authority.

Although a person acting under authority performs actions that seem to violate standards of conscience, it would not be true to say that he loses his moral sense. Instead, it acquires a radically different focus. He does not respond with a moral sentiment to the actions he performs. Rather, his moral concern now shifts to a consideration of how well he is living up to the expectations that the authority has of him. In wartime, a soldier does not ask whether it is good or bad to bomb a hamlet; he does not experience shame or guilt in the destruction of a village; rather he feels pride or shame depending on how well he has performed he mission assigned to him. . . .

[Milgram varied the content of this famous experiment in a number of ways. Further refinements seemed to suggest strongly that what people obeyed was authority; they hated the situation they were in, but they felt they must obey. For example, in one experiment, a "rigged telephone call takes the experimenter away from the laboratory;" before he leaves he asks an accomplice, whom the subject thinks is merely another subject like himself, to conduct the experiment. Here there was a sharp drop in compliance; 16 of 20 subjects refused to go on to the bitter end. (pp. 95–97).

Group effects were also interesting. When the subject was placed between two peers, who defied the experimenter (verbally), only 4 of 40 subjects went on to the bitter end[117] (pp. 116–122)].

NOTES AND QUESTIONS

1. Tyler contends that a society cannot rely solely on deterrence and must find ways to make people comply because they think the authorities are "legitimate." Milgram demonstrates the dangers of uncritical obedience to authority. Are their positions consistent or inconsistent? What advice does each study have for a democratic society? Is their advice consistent or inconsistent? How would you describe the authority of the experimenter in the Milgram study? To what extent, if at all, is that authority analogous to the authority commanded by any government official? Why did Milgram's subjects obey him or his researchers? What do most of us learn about obeying parents, teachers, athletic coaches and police officers? Where, when and how?

2. *Obeying authority in Nazi Germany.* In the background of Milgram's experiments is the terrible, bloody history of the 20th century—and in particular the murder of 6,000,000 Jews and millions of Poles and Gypsies, among others, by the Nazi regime under Adolf Hitler during the World War. The Nazi leaders who planned the Holocaust were undoubtedly monstrously evil men. But what about some of the underlings, people like Adolf Eichmann, the faceless bureaucrat who played such a key role in the process of organized murder but who claimed that he was only following orders? It was an attempt to understand what made an Eichmann tick that drew Milgram to study obedience.

Eichmann, of course, did not personally commit the murders of Jews—the so-called "final solution." These callous murders of men, women and children were carried out by vast legions of "ordinary" Germans as well as citizens of

---

117. Milgram's studies when they were originally reported, evoked a good deal of criticism on ethical grounds. The subjects were all under much tension; three underwent "full-blown uncontrollable seizures" during the experiment. Is this infliction of anxiety in the name of science justifiable? Is this kind of experimentation on human beings acceptable? See Herbert Kelman, "Deception in Social Research," 3 *Transaction* 20 (1966). For Milgram's defense, see *Obedience to Authority*, pp. 193–202. For a criticism of Milgram on methodological grounds, see Wrightman, "The Most Important Social Psychological Research in this Generation," 19 *Contemporary Psychology* 803 (1974). See also, Arthur G. Miller, Barry Gillen, Charles Schenker and Shirley Radlove, "The Prediction and Perception of Obedience to Authority," 42 *Journal of Personality* 23 (1974). [Eds. note].

other countries. What made these actions possible? For a discussion of this question, making explicit reference to the Milgram experiments, see Christopher R. Browning, *Ordinary Men: Reserve Police Battalion 101 and the Final Solution in Poland* (1992). This remarkable book discusses the men of German Reserve Police Battalion 101, a unit which in 1942 carried out orders to kill approximately 1,500 Jewish women, children and elderly men who lived in the Polish village of Jozefow.

Browning explains, on pages 184–85, why the men of Battalion 101 carried out their orders:

> Along with ideological indoctrination, a vital factor touched upon but not fully explored in Milgram's experiments was conformity to the group. The battalion had orders to kill Jews, but each individual did not. Yet 80 to 90 percent of the men proceeded to kill, though almost all of them—at least initially—were horrified and disgusted by what they were doing. To break ranks and step out, to adopt overtly nonconformist behavior, was simply beyond most of the men. It was easier for them to shoot.

> Why? First of all, by breaking ranks, nonshooters were leaving the "dirty work" to their comrades. Since the battalion had to shoot even if individuals did not, refusing to shoot constituted refusing one's share of an unpleasant collective obligation. It was in effect an asocial act vis-a-vis one's comrades. Those who did not shoot risked isolation, rejection, and ostracism—a very uncomfortable prospect within the framework of a tight-knit unit stationed abroad among a hostile population, so that the individual had virtually nowhere else to turn for support and social contact.

> This threat of isolation was intensified by the fact that stepping out could also have been seen as a form of moral reproach of one's comrades: the nonshooter was potentially indicating that he was "too good" to do such things. Most, though not all, nonshooters intuitively tried to diffuse the criticism of their comrades that was inherent in their actions. They pleaded not that they were "too good" but rather that they were "too weak" to kill.

> Such a stance presented no challenge to the esteem of one's comrades; on the contrary, it legitimized and upheld "toughness" as a superior quality. For the anxious individual, it had the added advantage of posing no moral challenge to the murderous policies of the regime, though it did pose another problem, since the difference between being "weak" and being a "coward" was not great. Hence the distinction made by one policeman who did not dare step out at Jozefow for fear of being considered a coward, but who subsequently dropped out of his firing squad. It was one thing to be too cowardly even to try to kill; it was another, after resolutely trying to do one's share, to be too weak to continue.

Daniel Goldhagen criticized Browning's explanation in *Hitler's Willing Executioners: Ordinary Germans and the Holocaust* (1996).[118] Goldhagen also studied the actions of the same Hamburg police battalion in Poland in 1941 and 1942. He said that Browning gave insufficient attention to the cultural and ideological background of the members of the police battalion. He argues that they killed "because, like most Germans, they believed fundamentally in the justice of exterminating Jews." In a debate between the two men, Browning observed that the members of the battalion also murdered Poles with great ferocity. Adam Shatz, Browning's Version, *Lingua Franca*, February 1997, at 48, argues that Browning sees the men of Reserve Police Battalion 101 as "ordinary men," a term that he never defines. Shatz says that Browning means that the members were "like us." Shatz interprets both Browning and Milgram as saying that almost any of us would have become Nazi killers in the same context. Thomas Blass quotes Milgram being interviewed on a television program: "[I]f a system of death camps were set up in the United States of the sort we had seen in Nazi Germany, one would be able to find sufficient personnel for those camps in any medium-sized American town."[119]

Would Goldhagen argue that the Americans would have to develop an ideology that would justify executions or mass murders, similar to the ideology that permitted the extermination of the Jews? Does American culture preclude any such ideology? American soldiers committed atrocities during the Vietnam War and during the Iraq War. From the late 19th century through the first decades of the 20th century, lynch mobs in southern states (and in some northern ones as well) killed and tortured hundreds and hundreds of victims, mostly black, who were thought to be guilty of various crimes. Whole towns turned out eagerly to watch the lynchings, the killers did not wear masks, and they almost never were prosecuted. Who has the best explanation for the history of lynching in the United States: Browning, Goldhagen or Milgram? Would Milgram's view be that one could always find people willing to follow orders to kill or torture, and these people would not necessarily redefine the victims as subhuman or as enemies of the state? The lynch mobs, however, like many Nazis and Nazi sympathizers, were not simply obeying orders. They were ready, willing and eager to do the work.

3. Albert Breton and Ronald Wintrobe, "The Bureaucracy of Murder Revisited," 94 *Journal of Political Economy* 905 (1986), challenge Eichmann's claim to have only followed orders. They say:

118. Goldhagen's book was highly controversial. See, e.g., Fritz Stern, "The Goldhagen Controversy: One Nation, One People, One Theory?" 75 *Foreign Affairs* 128, 136 (1996)("He then moves from specific and harrowing examples to a grotesque extrapolation: having examined the acts of some hundreds or perhaps thousands of people, he insists that almost all Germans were motivated by the same hatred, approved the killing, would have acted in like fashion if change had so decreed."). See, also, Marouf Hasian, Jr. and Robert E. Frank, "Rhetoric, History, and Collective Memory: Decoding the Goldhagen Debates," 63 *Western Journal of Communication* 95 (1999).

119. Thomas Blass, "The Milgram Paradigm After 35 Years: Some Things We Now Know About Obedience to Authority," 29 *Journal of Applied Social Psychology* 955, 955–56 (1999).

[I]t may not be necessary to introduce such concepts as brainwashing, the manipulation of human personality, and others like them that are so often employed to deal with human behavior in totalitarian societies: the unusual amount of loyalty that appears to exist in such regimes could be an entirely rational response to the unusual structure of incentives facing people....

Eichmann did not obey orders any more than a self-employed entrepreneur does when he or she responds to the demands of the marketplace in order to make money. His rewards took the form of promotions, perquisites, and power rather than negotiated contractual sums, but that makes no difference to the question of his guilt or innocence.... Eichmann ... would in all likelihood not even have been sanctioned, let alone executed, if he had pursued the Nazi solution to the Jewish question with less zeal. He would simply have participated less in the informal rewards that would then have gone to the more ardent entrepreneurs ... [S]ubordinates in large organizations ... are placed in a competitive framework in which they are rewarded for entrepreneurial initiatives that promote the interests and objectives of their superiors. The more useful they are to their superiors, the larger the rewards.

To what extent, if at all, is Breton and Wintrobe's explanation of Eichmann's actions inconsistent with that of Milgram?

4. David Luban suggests that the Milgram experiments involved "the corruption of judgment."[120] The teacher "moves up the scale of shocks by 15–volt increments, and reaches the 450–volt level only at the thirtieth shock." Luban points out that the subjects did not confront the question "should I administer a 330–volt shock to the learner?" Rather the question they faced was "should I administer a 330–volt shock to the learner *given that I've just administered a 315–volt shock?*" "By luring us into higher and higher level shocks, one micro-step at a time, the Milgram experiments gradually and subtly disarm our ability to distinguish right from wrong." Do you agree with this interpretation of the Milgram experiments? If so, does it undercut the idea that Milgram has shown that many or most people will obey orders whatever the morality of the order? How often are people in a situation where they will step out on a slippery slope and not see where the incremental steps are taking them? Luban argues that lawyers at least sometimes slip into breaches of ethics by taking a series of micro-steps without seeing where they are going.

5. The articles in this section have suggested a variety of factors that may influence a person's decision to obey the law. These factors have included: legal sanctions, social groups, moral conceptions, and perceived legitimacy. After having read these studies, do you think that it is possible to put the various factors together into a general theory of compliance? Which factors strike you as most important? Which are least important? How does

---

120. David J. Luban, "The Ethics of Wrongful Obedience," in *Ethics in Practice:* *Lawyers' Roles, Responsibilities, and Regulation,* at 94 (Deborah L. Rhode ed. 2000).

the importance of various factors vary across different types of crimes, different times, and different people?

Not only are theories of compliance important in criminal justice but they also are essential to the study of how any agency or bureaucracy works (or does not work). Any complex system of law will try to use a mix of devices to get people to go along: carrots, sticks, and sermons. Often this is done in an ad hoc, seat-of-the-pants way. For a thoughtful discussion of how regulation can be made "responsive" by deliberately putting together a package of "soft" and "hard" incentives, forming a regulatory pyramid in which the toughest measures are reserved for the toughest cases, see Ian Ayres and John Braithwaite, *Responsive Regulation: Transcending the Deregulation Debate* (1992).

It is easy to talk about the people at the other end of a legal rule or order as "subjects," but, of course, they are in fact human beings. Human beings come in a bewildering variety of shapes and sizes, not to mention a bewildering variety of psychological make-ups. A propensity to obey or disobey will depend on who the person is, culturally and psychologically. There is, for example, an enormous literature on what it is that makes a criminal a criminal. There is also a literature on legal socialization—the way in which people are educated or trained into a particular legal culture. See, for example, the essays collected in June L. Tapp and Felice J. Levine (eds.), *Law, Justice, and the Individual in Society* (1977); Ellen S. Cohn and Susan O. White, *Legal Socialization: A Study of Norms and Rules* (1990).

6.   Milgram shows us that people will take orders to do things when we might not expect this. The following article reminds us that many people evade the law and break it when they think they will not be caught.

(4.10) Images of Law in Everyday Life: The Lessons of School, Entertainment, and Spectator Sports

Stewart Macaulay

21 *Law & Society Review* 185, 188, 189–92 (1987).

Our national attitudes about complying with law are complex and sometimes contradictory.... Whatever our attitudes, how compliant are we? Despite our resistance to surveillance and coerced compliance, Americans are relatively law-abiding. Our modern concern with law breaking suggests that while there may be less compliance than we like, we expect a high degree of it. For the most part, our lives and fortunes are not at serious risk in day-to-day living unless we are poor. We do not live under an occupying army enforcing rules at gunpoint. However, most of us do not murder, rape, or rob others. We get licenses, fill out forms, and pay taxes by what we call a voluntary self-assessment system.

Having said this, we could easily compile a long catalogue of Americans breaking the law. Civil disobedience is as American as apple pie. We need mention only the Boston Tea Party, the resistance to the fugitive slave acts, draft riots, and today [1987] the selling of Nicaraguan postage stamps to defy the embargo. . . .

Americans also break the law for less lofty goals. We can laugh when we remember that they call the University of Oklahoma football team the Sooners. Those who reached Oklahoma Territory sooner violated the rules for homesteading on public land and defended what they took by force. . . . We also made treaties with the Native American nations as a ploy that served to trick these people into parting with their land.

There is the whole Prohibition experience as well. American folklore romanticized bootlegging, speakeasies, and the Roaring Twenties. Instead of feeling morally bound to honor the law, many Americans found violating Prohibition a game. . . .

Our inventory of American evasion and shading of the law is long. Probably most of us drive automobiles at speeds greater than those posted. In flight magazines and catalogues carry advertisements for police radar detectors so we can speed without getting caught. Many drive while intoxicated. Large numbers of Americans also participate in the second, or underground, economy. The IRS estimates that only 35 percent of those who are self-employed report their true income. Noncompliance is greatest for independent professionals such as management consultants, CPAs, lawyers, and doctors. Cleaning ladies, handymen, and all kinds of small businesses work to keep income off the books and invisible to tax collectors. . . .

Americans smuggle items across the border and buy stolen goods. There is a large and successful industry importing and distributing illegal drugs that depends on the willingness of many to use controlled substances. . . .

Individuals acting alone are not the only ones who evade the law. Major corporations also break antitrust laws and violate environmental protection and industrial safety regulations. Illegal kickbacks are standard operating procedure in some industries. Other corporate representatives bribe public officials here and abroad. Some of the Fortune 500 also evade the tax laws despite constant audit.

Where do these contradictory attitudes and actions come from? We are socialized to obey authority but also to disobey it on some occasions and in certain ways. Perhaps the message is that we should not "really" violate the law, but the definition of "really" is very vague. For example, [British] mystery writer Dick Francis wrote of one of his character's employees at a wine shop:

> She was honest in all major ways and unscrupulous in minor. She would never cheat me through the till, but . . . spare light bulbs and half-full jars of Nescafe tended to go home with Mrs.P. if she was short. Mrs. Palissey considered such things "perks" but would have regarded taking a bottle of sherry as stealing. I respected the distinction and was grateful for it, and paid her a little over the norm.

NOTES AND QUESTIONS

1. Why do so many Americans violate at least some laws? Newspaper stories suggest the wide variety of noncompliance by many. For example, see Paul Zielbauer, "Highways as Speedways? Drivers Push the Limits—Bigger Cars and Lax Enforcement are Among Factors Cited for 'Speed Creep,'" *N.Y. Times*, Dec. 27, 1999, at A1 ("In New York in 1991, only 14 percent of drivers ticketed on Interstate 87, which runs from New York City to the Canadian border, had been driving over 80 m.p.h., state records show. By 1996, 27 percent were."); Randy Kennedy, "Living Here, but Registered There; New Yorkers Dodge High Fees with Out-of-State License Plates," *N.Y. Times*, Jan. 3, 2003, at B1; David Cay Johnston, "Big Accounting Firm's Tax Plans Help the Wealthy Conceal Income," *N.Y. Times*, June 20, 2002, at A1; John D. McKinnon, "IRS Data Show More Taxpayers Are Using Scams," *Wall Street Journal*, April 15, 2002, at C15; Tom Herman, "Tax Report: Years After Scandal, Millions Continue to Avoid Nanny Tax," *Wall Street Journal*, May 30, 2002, at D2; William M. Bulkeley, "Aftermath: A Changing Society: Hijackers' Passports Highlight Issue of Rampant Fake IDs in U.S.," *Wall Street Journal,* Sept. 26, 2001, at A6; Eduardo Porter, "The Search for Illegal Immigrants Stops at the Workplace," *N.Y. Times*, Mar. 5, 2006, at 3 ("[T]he basic reason illegal immigration hasn't stopped is that the country doesn't want it to."); Katie Hafner, "Wrestling With the Gift of Grab," *N.Y. Times*, July 14, 2005, at G1 ("Even the most upstanding citizens, it seems, can find justifications for a certain amount of petty thievery. Bad service in an expensive restaurant? Slip one of their fancy forks into your purse ... A hotel's prices seem extortionist? You might as well swipe a monogrammed bath mat.").

Why don't their attitudes, sanctions of conscience, and threats of criminal penalties deter Americans? Stewart Macaulay, "Popular Legal Culture: An Introduction," 98 *Yale Law Journal* 1545, 1554–56 (1989), asserts that many school children learn to cheat on exams as part of learning to cope with authority. He continues,

> Americans also learn from sports about breaking rules or honoring them in form but not in substance. Part of the lesson is taught in school and part by sports programs on television.[121] Professional baseball, for example, honors tricking and intimidating umpires. A cynic might speculate that American intercollegiate athletics shows that many universities act as if they honored only the amoral principle: "Don't get caught!" ....

> We can draw an analogy to classic jazz. Composers such as Gershwin, Porter, and Berlin wrote songs which jazz musicians reinvented in many

---

121. See Ken Berger, "Cheating the System: NASCAR crews tweak, bend rules to beat tough inspection," *Newsday*, June 22, 2001, at A82; Viv Bernstein, "Cutting Corners is Out as NASCAR Seeks Clean Start: Eyeing New Fans, Once–Regional Sport Tries to Polish Image," *N.Y. Times*, February 18, 2007, § 8 at 1, 7 ("Nascar suspended five crew chiefs and a team vice president, and assessed fines and subtracted valuable race points from five drivers and teams before Sunday's season-opening Daytona 500.").

ways.... [L]awyers, trial judges, court commissioners, political candidates, office holders, clients, and even people standing at a working class bar are all jazz performers. They play variations on legal themes, and sometimes attempt to put new melodies to the chords....

Individuals in their everyday activities have an amazing variety of ways of bending the seemingly inflexible rules governing these activities....

At least some Americans reason that although a sign announces 65 miles per hour speed limit, almost everyone drives faster, the police are aware of this as are the legislators, and so there is a conventional interpretation of 65 mph to mean "a reasonable speed in excess of 65 mph." In this case, do people really think that they are breaking the law when they drive somewhat faster than the posted speed limit? Or do they feel rather that the law has a certain give or flexibility? If so, does this sense of leeways in the law explain some minor infractions that occur in everyday life?

Can you think of examples of justifications for breaking the law? For example, how do students who cheat on examinations explain doing this? How do those who are below the legal drinking age explain buying alcohol? How do those who use marijuana explain breaking the laws prohibiting its sale? See Andrew D. Hathaway, "Cannabis Users' Informal Rules for Managing Stigma and Risk," 25 *Deviant Behavior* 559 (2004). How do those who violate copyright laws by downloading music rationalize what they have done? See M. B. Scott and S. M. Lyman, "Accounts, Deviance, and Social Order" in Jack Douglas (ed.), *Deviance and Respectability* 89 (1970), a classic work on excuses. See, also, Stephen L. Eliason and Richard A. Dodder, "Techniques of Neutralization Used by Deer Poachers in the Western United States: A Research Note," 20 *Deviant Behavior: An Interdisciplinary Journal* 233 (1999); Astrid Schutz and Roy F. Baumeister, "The Language of Defense: Linguistic Patterns in Narratives of Transgressions,"18 *Journal of Language and Social Psychology* 269 (1999); Mitch Berbrier, "Impression Management for the Thinking Racist: A Case Study of Intellectualization as Stigma Transformation in Contemporary White Supremacist Discourse," 40 *Sociological Quarterly* 411 (1999).

2. One way to avoid the need to justify breaking the law is not to concede that you are breaking it, whatever others might think. Doreen McBarnet has investigated what she calls "whiter than white collar crime," where those with resources can manage the threat of legal sanctions and stigma as they straddle the line between tax evasion and tax avoidance. Those who can afford to hire accountants and lawyers can label their activities as legitimate. She discusses "non-disclosing disclosure" which involves disclosing the relevant facts to taxing authorities but doing so in a way which makes it difficult or impossible for the reader to recognize the presence or extent of a taxable transaction. For example, "[o]ne may bury the salient point on p. 195 of a 300 page document and leave tax inspectors to spot it and its significance if they can.... One may spread salient points which only take on avoidance

significance when read together, between pages 12, 119 and 164, or hide crucial facts in a welter of irrelevancies . . ." She concludes:

> Non-disclosing disclosure plays on the problems of policing complex financial areas, the low risk of being caught, the scope for settlement if one is challenged, and the protection from stigma involved in having disclosed however obscurely. Non-disclosing disclosure minimises the chances of being caught while providing "fraud insurance" if one is.

See McBarnet, "Whiter Than White Collar Crime: Tax, Fraud Insurance and the Management of Stigma," 42 *British Journal of Sociology* 323 (1991). See also McBarnet, "Law, Policy and Legal Avoidance: Can Law Effectively Implement Egalitarian Policies?" 15 *Journal of Law and Society* 113 (1988).

What does McBarnet's description suggest about deterrence and an obligation to comply with the law? To what extent is formal and technical compliance enough? To what extent is a (barely) plausible argument that one has formally and technically complied enough? Or does whiter-than-white-collar-crime suggest that people feel little obligation to comply; only a desire to avoid legal and social penalties for not complying? Marvin Harris, *Cultural Materialism: The Struggle for a Science of Culture* 275 (1980), argues:

> Rules facilitate, motivate, and organize our behavior; they do not govern or cause it. The causes of behavior are to be found in the material conditions of social life. The conclusion to be drawn from the abundance of "unless" and "except" clauses is not that people behave in order to conform to rules, but they select or create rules appropriate for their behavior.

Do you agree? How could we study whether legal rules are only rationalizations or the cause of behavior? What problems do you see in such an endeavor?

3.   We might be tempted to dismiss Americans' views about obeying the law as "Don't really break the law" or "Don't get caught." However, occasionally we are reminded about the power of the norm of law-abidingness. The *Wall Street Journal,* Sept. 8, 1999, at A1 reported: "How much cheating, if any, is acceptable on your tax return? None, according to 87% of the 1,000 adults polled by Roper Starch in late May. But 8% said 'a little here and there,' and 3% said 'as much as possible.' " Could an American political leader still remain in office if she or he were shown to have evaded taxes? The *Toronto Star*, April 12, 2003, at K10, reported that elected officials in Sweden "can get away with extramarital affairs, past drug use, even a career as a porn star. But mishandle anything tax-related and that political career can be history." Would this be true in the United States? See, also, Michael R. Welch, Yili Xu, Thoroddur Bjarnason, Tom Petee, Patricia O'Donnell & Paul Magro, " 'But Everybody Does It . . .' The Effects of Perceptions, Moral Pressures, and Informal Sanctions on Tax Cheating," 25 *Sociological Spectrum* 21 (2005).

4. The Macaulay essay and the notes and questions following suggest that Americans learn to evade rules in school, and many continue afterward to violate at least certain laws. Selena Roberts, "The Road to Success is Paved with Cheating," N.Y.Times, April 8, 2007, § 8 at 3, reports a study that shows that many high school students cheat on examinations but athletes cheat more than their peers. "Suddenly, cheating is the new teenage sex: Everybody is doing it . . . Rules are so yesterday, so uncool." See Raef A. Lawson, "Is Classroom Cheating Related to Business Students' Propensity to Cheat in the Real World' "? 49 *Journal of Business Ethics* 189, 197 (2004) ("[T]he belief among many business students that unethical behavior is widespread in the business world and is necessary in order to advance their careers is a cause for concern. As the next generation of business leaders, students' belief in the need for unethical behavior in the business world could become a self-fulfilling prophecy.") How does this square with Tyler's findings about the obligation to obey laws and Milgram's experiments that showed Americans willing to take orders even when they were told to do something likely to inflict serious harm? Is it likely that some people obey any law without question while others evade what they see as rules without a moral basis? Or would the picture for any individual be more complex? For example, is it possible that Mr. X would not murder or even shoplift because he sees such conduct as wrong, but, as long as he thinks he is unlikely to be caught, would violate copyright by downloading music and fail to pay state use tax on his purchases from Amazon.com.? If there are many people such as our hypothetical Mr. X, what determines which laws they will honor and which they will evade if they think they can get away with it?

III. The Limits of Effective Legal Action

The twentieth century saw a long parade of attempts to change the society through law. Progressive reformers attacked the social problems they saw from the turn of the century until about the First World War. Americans attempted to control alcoholic beverages through the Prohibition Amendment to the Constitution. President Franklin Roosevelt's New Deal attempted to cope with great economic depression of the 1930s, and then his administration used government powers to fight World War II. During the 1950s and 1960s, we attempted to deal with the problems of race through Supreme Court decisions and legislation. For a brief period in the 1960s, the federal government waged "a war on poverty" by focusing law on the problems of the poor. Later federal and state statutes and cases were aimed at gaining women's rights, establishing consumer protection, and defending the environment.

Those who battled for these laws could claim many accomplishments. Nonetheless, the record is decidedly mixed. The picture definitely was not one of authority issuing commands and people and organizations in the society obeying without question. Why? How do we explain the gap between the law on the books and the law in action? Roscoe Pound, then Dean of the Harvard Law School, put a phrase into the vocabulary of those who study law and society in his 1916 speech to the Pennsylvania Bar Association. Pound talked of "the limits of effective legal action."[122] He was reacting to what he saw as the excesses of the Progressive reformers. They tended to approach problems by creating commissions and administrative agencies. They granted these bodies broad discretionary powers so that expert knowledge could be applied to solve social problems. Pound saw this as an attack on the idea of a rule of law. Moreover, he questioned whether we could remake the world as we would like it in this manner. Some would accept Pound's normative position. Others would recast the problem so that instead of the limits of effective legal action, we would learn how better to make laws effective. We also must keep in mind that often those who have power in society will resist legal reforms that might encroach on that power. In an open society, they have many ways to block enactment of reforms that offend them or, once enacted, to evade, limit or overturn them.

The first essay in this section, the one by Suchman and Edelman, offers a survey of what law and society scholars have found when they look at organizations responding to statutes, regulations and cases. They argue that a law and society perspective added to organization theory in sociology might benefit both. However, the picture that they paint of law and organizations such as corporations should suggest some of the limits of effective legal action in the United States where we have a federal system with a separation of powers. After Suchman and Edelman, we will turn to several articles that examine particular limitations on changing society through legal action.

(A) A Law–and–Society View of Organizations Facing Legal Commands

(4.11) Legal Rational Myths: The New Institutionalism and the Law and Society Tradition[123]

Mark C. Suchman and Lauren B. Edelman
21 *Law & Social Inquiry* 903 (1997).

Recent years have witnessed the early stages of a convergence between the sociology of law and the sociology of organizations. Contemporary sociolegal scholarship increasingly recognizes that important aspects of legal life occur within bureaucratic settings, such as law firms, regulatory agencies and corporations. Simultaneously, contemporary organizations theory increasingly acknowledges that important aspects of organizational activity occur within legal environments, such as rights regimes, disputing cultures, and regulatory systems. . . .

---

122. See Roscoe Pound, "The Limits of Effective Legal Action," 3 *American Bar Association Journal* 55 (1917). Compare N.E.H. Hull, "Some Realism about the Llewellyn–Pound Exchange Over Realism: The Newly Uncovered Private Correspondence, 1927–1931," 1987 *Wisconsin Law Review* 921.

123. This a review essay that assesses Walter W. Powell & Paul J. DiMaggio, eds. *The New Institutionalism in Organizational Analysis* (1991).

Sociolegal researchers will find much to like in ... the New Institutionalism in organizational analysis ... [It] takes rule systems seriously; it acknowledges and even exalts the causal force of normative beliefs; and it thoroughly embraces the kinds of cognitive and constitutive effects that play an increasingly large role in sociolegal theory. Moreover, its insights into the behavior of individuals, organizations and societies can deepen and enrich existing treatments of related subjects in the legal realm. In short, the New Institutionalism presents a view of organizational life that fits quite nicely with the central concerns of contemporary sociology of law.

At the same time, however, many who draw their inspiration from the Law and Society tradition may be disconcerted by the image of law itself within organizational institutionalism. In arguing for the importance of rule structures in organizational life, institutional theorists often go a bit too far, embracing a model of the law that verges on naive Legal Formalism. To many organizational theorists, it seems, the law (and, by extension, the state) represents a distinctively explicit, authoritative, and coercive exogenous constraint on organizational behavior. The legal environment depicted by institutional theory is, largely, an environment of "law-on-the-books": Rules are clear, enforcement is firm, and legal effects are substantive. The ambiguity, the politicization, and the symbolism of the "law-in-action" tend to fade from view....

Although institutionalist writings ... contain ... passages expressing ... qualified views of legal constraint, the baseline assumption seems to be that laws are explicit, authoritative, and coercive—at least until proven otherwise.

From the perspective of the Law and Society tradition, this emphasis on the formal dictates of the law has several weaknesses. By treating law as explicit, institutional theory obscures the extent to which law is, in reality, obscure, fragmented and highly ambiguous. Since the earliest days of the Law and Society movement, research has consistently found that law-in-action reflects a crazy-quilt of pluralistic normative orders and overlapping regulatory jurisdictions. Further, by treating law as authoritative, institutional theory obscures the extent to which law is, in reality, malleable, contested, and socially constructed. Not only do organizations occasionally "capture" the law and shape it to fit their own interests, but also organizations often "enact" the meaning of the law through a complex, largely inadvertent cycle of action, mimicry, and interpretation. Finally, by treating law as coercive, institutional theory obscures the extent to which law is, in reality, symbolic, discursive, and constitutive. Although legal environments exert pressure on organizations, they do so primarily by redefining the normative value of old practices or by creating the cognitive building blocks for new ones, rather than by applying substantive penalties in strict accordance with specific sovereign edicts. In short, although *institutional* analysis far surpasses previous organizational theories in its attentiveness to societal rule systems, constitutive definitions, and categorical constraints, its conception of law seems oddly sterile and formalistic....

522

Law as Uncertain and Ambiguous

Law and Society research points to at least three distinct characteristics of law that render it uncertain rather than determinate: legal ignorance, legal pluralism, and legal ambiguity.

Legal Ignorance

When addressing the impact of legal rules on organizational behavior, *institutional* theorists generally assume that organizations know what the law is. Law and Society research, however, suggests that this superficially plausible assumption may be seriously flawed. Legal systems have no automatic mechanism for disseminating information about law, and formal legal publications are accessible only to those with the inclination and skill to find them. People learn lessons about the law from the media, the professions, the educational system, and first-hand experience; however, these lessons are rarely very accurate, detailed, or complete. Although the legal profession may help laypeople to "find the law," lawyers themselves generally remember legal rules primarily as aphorisms and rules-of-thumb, and attorneys' casual legal opinions may be no more reliable than those of their clients. Moreover, studies of corporate criminality report that organizations frequently delegate the task of "knowing the law" to their legal departments—and then intentionally freeze those departments out of corporate decision making. In short, organizations give the law, like other facets of their environments, only selective and imperfect attention, at best.

Legal Pluralism

When "law" does impinge on the perceptions of organizational decision makers, there is no guarantee that it will be the formal, public law of the nation-state. As Macaulay has noted, sociolegal scholars recurrently report: "Many of the functions usually thought of as legal are performed by alternative institutions, and there is a great deal of [interpenetration] between what we call public and private sectors.... Trade associations, sports leagues, church groups, neighborhood organizations and many other 'private' units ... exercise what are, effectively, legal powers."[124] At times, the state will actually grant the full force of law to these local regimes; however, even when the state retains formal authority, local gossip and ostracism generally supplant official legal penalties as the primary sanctions in most communities—including most organizational communities. A corollary to this pervasive legal pluralism is the finding that formal rules are, themselves, transformed by the local communities of regulators and regulateds that must implement them—communities that may differ dramatically from one locale to another.

---

124. Stewart Macaulay, "Law and the Behavioral Sciences: Is There Any There There?" 6 *Law & Policy* 149, 152–53 (1984).

Legal Ambiguity

As telling as these insights may be, however, they only scratch the surface of the critique of Legal Formalism. To talk of "legal ignorance" or "legal pluralism" is to dispute the penetration of law while granting law's existence as an objective reality. Yet, the most problematic aspect of claiming that organizations "know what the law is" may be the embedded assumption that the law "is" a single knowable, determinate thing. Law and society scholarship shows that "the Law" is actually a welter of conflicting principles, imperfect analogies, and ambiguous generalities. Thus, lawyers, judges, enforcers, and target populations negotiate the meaning of law in each application, seeking workable consensus rather than logical certainty. As noted above, institutional processes often generate tacit agreements about the contents of legal mandates and about the standards of legal interpretation; nonetheless, a shared convention is not really the same thing as an objective meaning, and at some level, every application of law remains fundamentally an exercise in social creativity. Contrary to the casual assertions of institutional theorists, it is simply untrue that organizations can only be in compliance or not in compliance with specific regulations.

Given these observations, law may be best conceptualized not as an objective external constraint but rather as a source of uncertainty in organizational life. New laws (and often the processes leading up to new laws) alert organizations to the possibility that the institutional environment may have changed. In itself, however, this alarm does little to clarify the nature or the extent of that change. Rather, the passage of a law provides an occasion for the collective construction of compliance. Legal shifts accelerate sense-making efforts, spawn decision events, spark search activity, and stimulate mimesis. Eventually, these efforts may produce a tentative working agreement on what the law "is" and what it "requires." This meaning, however, is an endogenous product of historical social interactions; it is not an exogenous characteristic of specific words on a piece of paper.

"Law" as Political and Contested

Few institutional theorists would dispute the contention that laws (particularly statutory laws) emerge from a political process. However, a healthy skepticism about the instrumentalism of politics and a predilection for treating the law as exogenous lead institutionalists to see legal rules as neutral and authoritative, once those rules have been formally enacted. In contrast, Law and Society research stresses that the law is thoroughly and unrelentingly political, not only in its enactment but also in its interpretation and application. Courts, enforcement agencies, lawyers, and target populations themselves all act as filtering agents, each possessing the capacity to transform the meaning of the law and the definition of compliance, in accordance with partisan interests and ideologies. Over time, these political constructions become institutionalized in social practice and, often, embraced in judicial opinions. Organizations play a major role in this process, and institutional theorists would do well to consider how organizations *mediate,* not just respond to, law.

The Politics of Legal Enforcement

Perhaps the most obvious locus of postlegislative politics lies in the regulatory agencies chartered to "enforce the law." According to the imagery of Legal Formalism, these agencies act only within the scope of their official charter; but within that limited purview, they use the full force of authorized legal sanctions to pursue universal compliance with clear statutory goals. . . .

In contrast, Law and Society scholarship suggests that legislative ambiguity and administrative politics often result in statutory "mandates" that either provide little regulatory guidance or demand impossible regulatory results, or both. This means that as a practical matter, administrative agencies enjoy a great deal of discretion, and regulators can become politicized both on the basis of their substantive policy preferences and on the basis of internal bureaucratic agendas.[125] Further, faced with constrained budgets and weakly conceptualized compliance measures, enforcement agents look for easily observable symbols of compliance, instead. Regulated organizations, for their part, willingly collaborate in constructing symbolic criteria that meet the needs of regulators without fundamentally disrupting the established routines of the targeted sector.

Each of these departures from the formal model makes regulation look less like top-down coercion and more like bottom-up cooptation. Far from imposing external constraints on passive recipients, regulation often seems to institutionalize the indigenous practices of the regulated population. At the extreme, agencies can become captives of the industries that they oversee— either through direct domination or, more commonly, through a subtle ideological convergence born of repeated contact, regular interaction and pervasive personnel exchange. Thus, the Law and Society tradition suggests that regulation is neither neutral nor exogenous. Rather, the law is made as it is enforced, often with as much input from those who are its targets as from those who are its custodians.

The Politics of Organizational Response

.   .   .   .

[L]egal ambiguity opens the door for political manipulation, selective enactment and self-serving interpretation. To some extent, such activities presumably stem from instrumental calculations on the part of various affected interests. Nonetheless, institutional theory could easily incorporate Law and Society insights on the politics of law while retaining a healthy skepticism about the rationality of organizational action. The primary Law and Society contention is simply that people in different social locations apply and interpret the law differently. At times, these biases may reflect a

---

125. Indeed, one plausible way to understand ambiguous statutes is as devices for overcoming legislative contention by implicitly allowing each side to "make a bet" on the outcome of subsequent interpretation. This technique has the political appeal of permitting the ultimate loser to plead good intentions and to decry the sorry perversion of "legislative intent."

calculated collective strategy; however, at other times, they will simply embody the accumulated impact of facially trivial routines or the framing effects of sincerely held ideologies. Cognitive institutionalists would probably emphasize the extent to which the "political" activities described above involve communities struggling to make sense of their social worlds, rather than the extent to which such activities involve factions scheming to take advantage of one another. In itself, however, this observation does not render the processes of enforcement and interpretation apolitical—or at least it does not render them any less political than the process of legislation itself.

Law as Symbolic and Constitutive

. . . .

Law as Constitutive

Recent Law and Society scholarship—especially in the Critical Legal Studies camp—has increasingly come to see law as operating to constitute social life, rather than to regulate it. Even when actors lack the specific legal knowledge required for effective deterrence, they may nonetheless incorporate general legal categories into their cognitive maps, allowing the law to frame and constrain perceptions of the world. At the most superficial level, law provides a ready-made justification for conformity, helping individuals and organizations to address conflicting cultural demands that their actions be simultaneously rational, moral and predictable. More profoundly, law establishes a taken-for-granted categorical structure for social relations—and provides a set of accepted rituals for manipulating that structure. Law (or, more precisely, the socially constructed interpretation of law) tells us what is and isn't property, who is and isn't an employee, what is and isn't a corporation. Moreover, law establishes procedures for transferring property, hiring employees, and forming corporations, and law makes these procedures efficacious by definition. In keeping with the arguments outlined above, all these categories and procedures remain ambiguous and contested at the margins; however, this does not detract from the fact that their integration into the legal order effectively reifies and "naturalizes" their existence, their relevance, and their core content. While organizations can (and do) dispute whether freelance workers are "employees," they rarely dispute the meaningfulness of the concept of employment or the fact that it has something to do with an exchange of labor for money.

Law as Transformative

Not only does law provide a symbolic framework for *comprehending* social relations, it also provides symbolic resources for *transforming* them. Because the law cultivates an aura of objectivity, universality, and neutrality, the legal system can serve as a potent force for reifying and institutionalizing emerging social conventions. In common law litigation, for example, the legal system produces a series of morality plays that reenact, and thus reinforce, beliefs about goodness, truth, fairness, and equality. Each of these morality plays ceremonially introduces a highly stylized "problem situation" into the public discourse, and each offers up a "just" resolution. The stream of cases may reflect structural biases of the forum, and the stream of resolutions may reflect interpretive biases of the adjudicators. However, by embracing the symbolic trappings of procedural and distributive justice, the legal system makes these biases hard to identify and harder still to articulate.

The legal system provides transformative symbolic resources in the enforcement process as well. Not only do enforcers often accept symbolic conformity in place of substantive compliance, but, more profoundly, the importance of clear categories and bright-line rules in the law actually legitimizes ceremonialism. A standard that might, at first, be nothing more than a convenient regulatory rule-of-thumb becomes, over time, the legal definition of good behavior; formal criteria drive out substantive objectives. More generally, law provides regulators (and their *constituents)* with significant cognitive leverage to reconstitute organizational environments and to reframe environmental demands. By shaping conceptions of the possible and the desirable, law shapes what is expected of organizations and what is required. And by shaping conceptions of the normal and the aberrant, law shapes what is mimicked by organizations and what is ignored.

In short, law is much like other elements of organizations' institutional elements: not an explicit, authoritative and coercive system of material constraints, but an ambiguous, contested, and constitutive system of cultural understandings. The New Institutionalism has taken great strides in bringing law into the organizational picture, but the lessons of sociolegal scholarship call for more careful attention to the law's pervasive informalism and malleability....

NOTES AND QUESTIONS

1.　Sometimes government agencies do enforce laws against corporate officials, and, occasionally, high officers of major corporations are sent to jail. Do Suchman and Edelman adequately take this into account? Or is it such a rare event that it does not effect "day-to-day organizational life?" Does the fact that it might happen affect the story that they tell about how corporations respond to new laws?

2.　What do Suchman and Edelman tell us about the limits of effective legal action? About the indirect social impacts of laws? They tell us that, first, "law is often uncertain, not determinate; second, law is often contested, not authoritative; and third, law is often constitutive, not coercive." Suppose reformers have gained a statute that is supposed to improve the status of women in employment. How will the law's uncertainty affect business corporations' attempt to respond to reform in ways that minimize burdens on them? How will the statute's "constitutive" character affect its ability to improve women's employment status? Is the problem one of legal technique? Are our legislators and judges just bad social engineers? Could we make major improvements if they learned more about how organizations are likely to respond to legislative programs or judicial decisions? Or should we suspect that in some, if not many cases, the system as described by Suchman and Edelman is working just as the lawmakers want it to work?

3. Suchman and Edelman tell us that "law is often constitutive, not coercive." What does this mean? What does law constitute? The authors tell us: "law establishes a taken-for-granted categorical structure for social relations—and provides a set of accepted rituals for manipulating that structure." Does law establish such a categorical structure or does it reflect, often imperfectly, ideas that exist in other institutions of the society? For example, does law create our ideas of property or does it reflect ideas that long have been in the culture of our society? Little children learn early in their lives about the concept of "mine." Their older siblings are usually firm coercive instructors as to this foundation of the concepts of property, and they do not rely on law books in their teaching. That is, is it accurate to say that law is constitutive, or would it be more accurate to say that law is itself "constituted" by something else? Or is it that the influence goes both ways—social norms influence law which then feeds back and influences the social norms? Or would it be better to see law as one of many elements that may constitute our "taken-for-granted" categories that we use to cope with the world?

(B) What Impact is Law Supposed to Have in Society?

(4.12) Moral Passage: The Symbolic Process in Public Designations of Deviance

Joseph R. Gusfield[126]

15 *Social Problems* 175 (1967).

Recent perspectives on deviant behavior have focused attention away from the actor and his acts and placed it on the analysis of public reactions in labeling deviants as "outsiders." This perspective forms the background for the present paper. In it I will analyze the implications which defining behavior as deviant has for the public designators. Several forms of deviance will be distinguished, each of which has a different kind of significance for the designators. The symbolic import of each type, I argue, leads to different public responses toward the deviant and helps account for the historical changes often found in treatment of such delinquents as alcoholics, drug addicts, and other "criminals," changes which involve a passage from one moral status to another.

INSTRUMENTAL AND SYMBOLIC FUNCTIONS OF LAW

Agents of government are the only persons in modern societies who can legitimately claim to represent the total society. In support of their acts, limited and specific group interests are denied while a public and societal interest is claimed. Acts of government "commit the group to action or to perform coordinated acts for general welfare." This representational character of governmental officials and their acts makes it possible for them not only to influence the allocation of resources but also to define the public norms of morality and to designate which acts violate them. In a pluralistic society these defining and designating acts can become matters of political issue because they support or reject one or another of the competing and conflicting cultural groups in the society.

Let us begin with a distinction between instrumental and symbolic functions of legal and governmental acts. We readily perceive that acts of officials, legislative enactments, and court decisions often affect behavior in an instrumental manner through a direct influence on the actions of people. The Wagner Labor Relations Act and the Taft–Hartley Act have had considerable impact on the conditions of collective bargaining in the United States. Tariff legislation directly affects the prices of import commodities. The instrumental function of such laws lies in their enforcement; unenforced they have little effect.

Symbolic aspects of law and government do not depend on enforcement for their effect. They are symbolic in a sense close to that used in literary analysis. The symbolic act "invites consideration rather than overt reaction." There is a dimension of meaning in symbolic behavior which is not given in its immediate and manifest significance but in what the action connotes for the audience that views it. The symbol "has acquired a meaning which is added to its immediate intrinsic significance." . . . The use of the wine and wafer in the Mass or the importance of the national flag cannot be appreciated without knowing their symbolic meaning for the users. In analyzing law as symbolic, we are oriented less to behavioral consequences as a means to a fixed end; more to meaning as an act, a decision, a gesture important in itself.

An action of a governmental agent takes on symbolic import as it affects the designation of public norms. A courtroom decision or a legislative act is a gesture which often glorifies the values of one group and demeans those of another. In their representational character, governmental actions can be seen as ceremonial and ritual performances, designating the content of public morality. They are the statement of what is acceptable in the public interest. Law can thus be seen as symbolizing the public affirmation of social ideals and norms as well as a means of direct social control. This symbolic dimension is given in the statement, promulgation, or announcement of law unrelated to its function in influencing behavior through enforcement.

It has long been evident to students of government and law that these two functions, instrumental and symbolic, may often be separated in more than an analytical sense. Many laws are honored as much in the breach as in performance. Robin Williams has labeled such institutionalized yet illegal and deviant behavior "the patterned evasion of norms." Such evasion occurs when law proscribes behavior which nevertheless occurs in a recurrent socially organized manner and is seldom punished. The kinds of crimes we are concerned with here quite clearly fall into to this category. Gambling, prostitution, abortion, and public drunkenness are all common modes of behavior although laws exist designating them as prohibited. It is possible to see such systematic evasion as functioning to minimize conflicts between cultures by utilizing law to proclaim one set of norms as public morality and to use another set of norms in actually controlling that behavior.

While patterned evasion may perform such harmonizing functions, the passage of legislation, the acts of officials and decisions of judges nevertheless have a significance as gestures of public affirmation. First, the act of public affirmation of a norm often persuades listeners that behavior and norm are consistent. The existence of law quiets and comforts those whose interests and sentiments are embodied in it. Second, public affirmation of a moral norm directs the major institutions or the society to its support. Despite patterned practices of abortion in the United States, obtaining abortions does require access to a subterranean social structure and is much more difficult than obtaining an appendectomy. There are instrumental functions to law even where there is patterned evasion.

A third impact of public affirmation is the one that most interests us here. The fact of affirmation through acts of law and government expresses the public worth of one set of norms, of one sub-culture vis-a-vis those of others. It demonstrates which cultures have legitimacy and public domination and which do not. Accordingly it enhances the social status of groups carrying the affirmed culture and degrades groups carrying that which is condemned as deviant. We have argued elsewhere that the significance of Prohibition in the United States lay less in its enforcement than in the fact that it occurred. Analysis of the enforcement of Prohibition law indicates that it was often limited by the unwillingness of Dry forces to utilize all their political strength for fear of stirring intensive opposition. Great satisfaction was gained from the passage and maintenance of the legislation itself.

Irrespective of its instrumental effects, public designation of morality is itself an issue generative of deep conflict. The designating gestures are dramatistic events since it invites one to consider the matter of motives in a perspective that, developed in the analysis of drama, treats language and thought primarily as modes of action. For this reason the designation of a way of behavior as violating public norms confers status and honor on those groups whose cultures are followed as the standard of conventionality and derogates those whose cultures are considered deviant. My analysis of the American Temperance movement has shown how the issue of drinking and abstinence became a politically significant focus for the conflicts between Protestant and Catholic, rural and urban, native and immigrant, middle class and lower class in American society. The political conflict lay in the efforts of an abstinent Protestant middle class to control the public affirmation of morality in drinking. Victory or defeat were consequently symbolic of the status and power of the cultures opposing each other. Legal affirmation or rejection is thus important in what is symbolizes as well or instead of what it controls. Even if the law was broken, it was clear whose law it was.

DEVIANT NONCONFORMITY AND DESIGNATOR REACTION

In [Emile] Durkheim's analysis of the indignant and hostile response to norm-violation, all proscribed actions are threats to the existence of the norm. Once we separate the instrumental from the symbolic functions of legal and governmental designation of deviants, however, we can question this assumption. We can look at norm-violation from the standpoint of its effects on the symbolic rather than the instrumental character of the norm. Our analysis of patterned evasion of norms has suggested that a law weak in its instrumental functions may nevertheless perform significant symbolic functions. Unlike human limbs, norms do not necessarily atrophy through disuse. Standards of charity, mercy, and justice may be dishonored every day yet remain important statements of what is publicly approved as virtue. The sexual behavior of the human male and the human female need not be a copy of the socially sanctioned rules. Those rules remain as important affirmations of an acceptable code even though they are regularly breached. Their roles as ideals are not threatened by daily behavior. In analyzing the violation of norms we will look at the implications of different forms of deviance on the symbolic character of the norm itself. The point here is that the designators of deviant behavior react differently to different norm-sustaining implications of an act. We can classify deviant behavior from this standpoint.

The Repentant Deviant

The reckless motorist often admits the legitimacy of traffic laws even though he has broken them. The chronic alcoholic may well agree that both he and his society would be better off if he could stay sober. In both cases the norm they have violated is itself unquestioned. Their deviation is a moral lapse, a fall from a grace to which they aspire.... There is a consensus between the designator and the deviant; his repentance confirms the norm.

Repentance and redemption seem to go hand in hand in court and church. [Gresham] Sykes and [David] Matza have described techniques of neutralization which juvenile delinquents often use with enforcement agencies.

> The juvenile delinquent would appear to be at least partially committed to the dominant social order in that he frequently exhibits guilt or shame when he violates its proscriptions, accords approval to certain conforming figures and distinguishes between appropriate and inappropriate targets for his deviance.

A show of repentance is also used ... to soften the indignation of law enforcement agents. A recent study of police behavior lends support to this. Juveniles apprehended by the police received more lenient treatment, including dismissal, if they appeared contrite and remorseful about their violations than if they did not. This difference in the posture of the deviant accounted for much of the differential treatment favoring middle-class "youngsters" as against lower class "delinquents."

The Sick Deviant

Acts which represent an attack upon a norm are neutralized by repentance. The open admission of repentance confirms the sinner's belief in the sin. His threat to the norm is removed and his violation has left the norm intact. Acts which we can perceive as those of sick and diseased people are irrelevant to the norm; they neither attack nor defend it. The use of morphine by hospital patients in severe pain is not designated as deviant behavior. Sentiments of public hostility and the apparatus of enforcement agencies are not mobilized toward the morphine user. His use is not perceived as a violation of the norm against drug use, but as an uncontrolled act not likely to be recurrent.

While designations of action resulting from sickness do not threaten the norm, significant consequences flow from such definitions. Talcott Parsons has pointed out that the designation of a person as ill changes the obligations which others have toward the person and his obligations toward them. Parsons' description sensitizes us to the way in which the sick person is a different social object than the healthy one. He has now become an object of welfare, a person to be helped rather than punished. Hostile sentiments toward sick people are not legitimate. The sick person is not responsible for his acts. He is excused from the consequences which attend the healthy who act the same way.

Deviance designations . . . are not fixed. They may shift from one form to another over time. Defining a behavior pattern as one caused by illness makes a hostile response toward the actor illegitimate and inappropriate. "Illness" is a social designation, by no means given in the nature of medical fact. Even left-handedness is still seen as morally deviant in many countries. Hence the effort to define a practice as a consequence of illness is itself a matter of conflict and a political issue.

The Enemy Deviant

Writing about a Boston slum in the 1930's, William F. Whyte remarks:

The policeman is subject to sharply conflicting pressures. On one side are the "good people" of Eastern City, who have written their moral judgments into law and demand through their newspapers that the law be enforced. On the other side are the people of Cornerville, who have different standards and have built up an organization whose perpetuation depends upon the freedom to violate the law.

Whyte's is one of several studies that have pointed out the discrepancies between middle-class moralities embodied in law and lower class moralities which differ sharply from them. In Cornerville, gambling was seen as a "respectable" crime, just as antitrust behavior may be in other levels of the social structure. In American society, conflicts between social classes are often also cultural conflicts reflecting moral differences. Coincidence of ethnic and religious distinctions with class differences accentuates such conflicts between group values.

In these cases, the validity of the public designation is itself at issue. The publicly-defined deviant is neither repentant nor sick, but is instead an upholder of an opposite norm. He accepts his behavior as proper and derogates the public norm as illegitimate. He refuses to internalize the public norm into his self-definition. This is especially likely to occur in instances of "business crimes." The buyer sees his action as legitimate economic behavior and resists a definition of it as immoral and thus prohibitable. The issue of "off-track" betting illustrates one area in which clashes of culture have been salient.

The designation of culturally legitimate behavior as deviant depends upon the superior power and organization of the designators. The concept of convention in this area, as Thrasymachus defined justice for Socrates, is the will of the stronger. If the deviant is the politically weaker group, then the designation is open to the changes and contingencies of political fortunes. It becomes an issue of political conflict, ranging group against group and culture against culture, in the effort to determine whose morals are to be designated as deserving of public affirmation.

It is when the deviant is also an enemy and his deviance is an aspect of group culture that the conventional norm is most explicitly and energetically attacked. When those once designated as deviant have achieved enough political power they may shift from disobedience to an effort to change the designation itself. This has certainly happened in the civil rights movement. Behavior viewed as deviant in the segregationist society has in many instances been moved into the realm of the problematic, now subject to political processes of conflict and compromise.

When the deviant and the designator perceive each other as enemies, and the designator's power is superior to that of the deviant, we have domination without a corresponding legitimacy. Anything which increases the power of the deviant to organize and attack the norm is thus a threat to the social dominance symbolized in the affirmation of the norm. Under such conditions the need of the designators to strengthen and enforce the norms is great. The struggle over the symbol of social power and status is focused on the question of the maintenance or change of the legal norm. The threat to the middle class in the increased political power of Cornerville is not that the Cornerville resident will gamble more; he already does gamble with great frequency. The threat is that the law will come to accept the morality of gambling and treat it as a legitimate business. If this happens, Boston is no longer a city dominated by middle-class Yankees but becomes one dominated by lower-class immigrants, as many think has actually happened in Boston. The maintenance of a norm which defines gambling as deviant behavior thus symbolizes the maintenance of Yankee social and political superiority. Its disappearance as a public commitment would symbolize the loss of that superiority.

The Cynical Deviant

The professional criminal commits acts whose designation as deviant is supported by wide social consensus. The burglar, the hired murderer, the arsonist, the kidnapper all prey on victims. While they may use repentance or illness as strategies to manage the impressions of enforcers, their basic orientation is self-serving, to get around the rules. It is for this reason that their behavior is not a great threat to the norms although it calls for social management and repression. It does not threaten the legitimacy of the normative order.

DRINKING AS A CHANGING FORM OF DEVIANCE

Analysis of efforts to define drinking as deviant in the United States will demonstrate the process by which designations shift. The legal embodiment of attitudes toward drinking shows how cultural conflicts find their expression in the symbolic functions of law. In the 160 years since 1800, we see all our suggested types of non-conforming behavior and all the forms of reaction among the conventional segments of the society. . . .

The Repentant Drinker

The definition of the drinker as an object of social shame begins in the early nineteenth century and reaches full development in the late 1820's and early 1830's. A wave of growth in Temperance organizations in this period was sparked by the conversion of drinking men to abstinence under the stimulus of evangelical revivalism. Through drinking-men joining together to take the pledge, a norm of abstinence and sobriety emerged as a definition of conventional respectability. They sought to control themselves and their neighbors.

The norm of abstinence and sobriety replaced the accepted patterns of heavy drinking countenanced in the late eighteenth and early nineteenth century. By the 1870's rural and small-town America had defined middle class morals to include the Dry attitude. This definition had little need for legal embodiment. It could be enunciated in attacks on the drunkard which assumed that he shared the normative pattern of those who exhorted him to be better and to do better. He was a repentant deviant, someone to be brought back into the fold by moral persuasion and the techniques of religious revivalism. His error was the sin of lapse from a shared standard of virtue. "The Holy Spirit will not visit much less will He dwell within he who is under the polluting, debasing effects of intoxicating drink. The state of heart and mind which this occasions to him is loathsome and an abomination."

Moral persuasion thus rests on the conviction of a consensus between the deviant and the designators. As long as the object of attack and conversion is isolated in individual terms, rather than perceived as a group, there is no sense of his deviant act as part of a shared culture. What is shared is the norm of conventionality; the appeal to the drinker and the chronic alcoholic is to repent. When the Woman's Anti–Whiskey Crusade of 1874 broke out in

534

Ohio, church women placed their attention on the taverns. In many Ohio towns these respectable ladies set up vigils in front of the tavern and attempted to prevent men from entering just by the fear that they would be observed. In keeping with the evangelical motif in the Temperance Movement, the Washingtonians, founded in 1884, appealed to drinkers and chronic alcoholics with the emotional trappings and oratory of religious meetings, even though devoid of pastors.

Moral persuasion, rather than legislation, has been one persistent theme in the designation of the drinker as deviant and the alcoholic as depraved. Even in the depictions of the miseries and poverty of the chronic alcoholic, there is a decided moral condemnation which has been the hallmark of the American Temperance movement. Moral persuasion was ineffective as a device to wipe out drinking and drunkenness. Heavy drinking persisted through the nineteenth century and the organized attempts to convert the drunkard experienced much backsliding. Nevertheless, defections from the standard did not threaten the standard. The public definition of respectability matched the ideals of the sober and abstaining people who dominated those parts of the society where moral suasion was effective. In the late nineteenth century those areas in which temperance sentiment was strongest were also those in which legislation was most easily enforceable.

The Enemy Drinker

The demand for laws to limit alcoholic consumption appears to arise from situations in which the drinkers possess power as a definitive social and political group and, in their customary habits and beliefs, deny the validity of abstinence norms. The persistence of areas in which Temperance norms were least controlling led to the emergence of attempts to embody control in legal measures. The drinker as enemy seems to be the greatest stimulus to efforts to designate his act as publicly defined deviance.

In its early phase the American Temperance movement was committed chiefly to moral persuasion. Efforts to achieve legislation governing the sale and use of alcohol do not appear until the 1840's. This legislative movement has a close relationship to the immigration of Irish Catholics and German Lutherans into the United States in this period. These non-evangelical and/or non-Protestant peoples made up a large proportion of the urban poor in the 1840's and 1850's. They brought with them a far more accepting evaluation of drinking than had yet existed in the United States. The tavern and the beer parlor had a distinct place in the leisure of the Germans and the Irish. The prominence of this place was intensified by the stark character of the developing American slum. These immigrant cultures did not contain a strong tradition of Temperance norms which might have made an effective appeal to a sense of sin. To be sure, excessive drunkenness was scorned, but neither abstinence nor constant sobriety were supported by the cultural codes.

Between these two groups—the native American middle-class evangelical Protestant and the immigrant European Catholic or Lutheran occupying the urban lower class—there was little room for repentance. By the 1850's the issue of drinking reflected a general clash over cultural values. The Temperance movement found allies in its political efforts among the nativist movements. The force and power of the anti-alcohol movements, however, were limited greatly by the political composition of the urban electorate, with its high proportion of immigrants. Thus the movement to develop legislation emerged in reaction to the appearance of cultural groups least responsive to the norms of abstinence and sobriety. The very effort to turn such informal norms into legal standards polarized the opposing forces and accentuated the symbolic import of the movement. Now that the issue had been joined, defeat or victory was a clear-cut statement of public dominance.

It is a paradox that the most successful move to eradicate alcohol emerged in a period when America was shifting away from a heavy-drinking society, in which whiskey was the leading form of alcohol, to a moderate one, in which beer was replacing whiskey. Prohibition came as the culmination of the movement to reform the immigrant cultures and at the height of the immigrant influx into the United States.

Following the Civil War, moral persuasion and legislative goals were both parts of the movement against alcohol. By the 1880's an appeal was made to the urban, immigrant lower classes to repent and to imitate the habits of the American middle class as a route to economic and social mobility. Norms of abstinence were presented to the non-abstainer both as virtue and as expedience. This effort failed. The new and larger immigration of 1890–1915 increased still further the threat of the urban lower class to the native American.

The symbolic effect of Prohibition legislation must be kept analytically separate from its instrumental, enforcement side. While the urban middle class did provide much of the organizational leadership to the Temperance and Prohibition movements, the political strength of the movement in its legislative drives was in the rural areas of the United States. Here, where the problems of drinking were most under control, where the norm was relatively intact, the appeal to a struggle against foreign invasion was the most potent. In these areas passage of legislation was likely to make small difference in behavior. The continuing polarization of political forces into those of cultural opposition and cultural acceptance during the Prohibition campaigns (1906–1919), and during the drive for Repeal (1926–1933), greatly intensified the symbolic significance of victory and defeat. Even if the Prohibition measures were limited in their enforceability in the metropolis there was no doubt about whose law was public and what way of life was being labeled as opprobrious.

After Repeal, as Dry power in American politics subsided, the designation of the drinker as deviant also receded. Public affirmation of the temperance norm had changed and with it the definition of the deviant had changed. Abstinence was itself less acceptable. In the 1950's the Temperance movement, faced with this change in public norms, even introduced a series of placards with the slogan, "It's smart *Not* to Drink."

Despite this normative change in the public designation of drinking deviance there has not been much change in American drinking patterns. Following the Prohibition period the consumption of alcohol has not returned to its pre–1915 high. Beer has continued to occupy a more important place as a source of alcohol consumption. Hard drinkers are not as common in America today as they were in the nineteenth century. While there has been some increase in moderate drinking, the percentage of adults who are abstainers has remained approximately the same (one-third) for the past 30 years. Similarly Dry sentiment has remained stable as measured by local opinion results. In short, the argument over deviance designation has been largely one of normative dominance, not of instrumental social control. The process of deviance designation in drinking needs to be understood in terms of symbols of cultural dominance rather than in the activities of social control.

The Sick Drinker

For most of the nineteenth century the chronic alcoholic as well as the less compulsive drinker was viewed as a sinner. It was not until after Repeal (1933) that chronic alcoholism became defined as illness in the United States. Earlier actions taken toward promotion of the welfare of drinkers and alcoholics through Temperance measures rested on the moral supremacy of abstinence and the demand for repentance. The user of alcohol could be an object of sympathy, but his social salvation depended on a willingness to embrace the norm of his exhorters. The designation of alcoholism as sickness has a different bearing on the question of normative superiority. It renders the behavior of the deviant indifferent to the status of norms enforcing abstinence.

This realization appears to have made supporters of Temperance and Prohibition hostile to efforts to redefine the deviant character of alcoholism. They deeply opposed the reports of the Committee of Fifty in the late nineteenth century. These volumes of reports by scholars and prominent men took a less moralistic and a more sociological and functional view of the saloon and drinking than did the Temperance movement.

The soundness of these fears is shown by what did happen to the Temperance movement with the rise of the view that alcoholism is illness. It led to new agencies concerned with drinking problems. These excluded Temperance people from the circle of those who now define what is deviant in drinking habits. The National Commission on Alcohol Studies was formed in 1941 and the Yale School of Alcohol Studies formed in 1940. They were manned by medical personnel, social workers, and social scientists, people now alien to the spirit of the abstainer. Problems of drinking were removed from the church and placed in the hands of universities and the medical clinics. The tendency to handle drinkers through protective and welfare agencies rather than through police or clergy has become more frequent.

"The bare statement that 'alcoholism is a disease' is most misleading since ... it conceals what is essential—that a step in public policy is being recommended, not a scientific discovery announced." John Seeley's remark is an apt one. Replacement of the norm of sin and repentance by that of illness and therapy removes the onus of guilt and immorality from the act of drinking and the state of chronic alcoholism. It replaces the image of the sinner with that of the patient, a person to be helped rather than to be exhorted. No wonder that the Temperance movement has found the work of the Yale School, and often even the work of Alcoholics Anonymous, a threat to its own movement. It has been most limited in its cooperation with these organizations and has attempted to set up other organizations which might provide the face of Science in league with the tone of the movement.

The redefinition of the alcoholic as sick thus brought into power both ideas and organizations antithetical to the Temperance movement. The norm protected by law and government was no longer the one held by the people who had supported Temperance and Prohibition. The hostility of Temperance people is readily understandable; their relative political unimportance is crucial to their present inability to make that hostility effective.

MOVEMENTS OF MORAL PASSAGE

In this paper we have called attention to the fact that deviance designations have histories; the public definition of behavior as deviant is itself changeable. It is open to reversals of public opinion and the development of social movements and moral crusades. What is attacked as criminal today may be seen as sick next year and fought over as possibly legitimate by the next generation.

Movements to redefine behavior may eventuate in a moral passage, a transition of the behavior from one moral status to another. In analyzing movements toward the redefinition of alcohol use, we have dealt with moral crusades which were restrictive and others which were permissive toward drinking and toward "drunkards." (We might have also used the word "alcoholics," suggesting a less disapproving and more medical perspective.) In both cases, however, the movements sought to change the public designation. While we are familiar with the restrictive or enforcing movements, the permissive or legitimizing movement must also be seen as a prevalent way in which deviants throw off the onus of their actions and avoid the sanctions associated with immoral activities.

Even where the deviants are a small and politically powerless group they may nevertheless attempt to protect themselves by influence over the process of designation. The effort to define themselves as ill is one plausible means to this end. Drug addiction as well as drunkenness is partially undergoing a change toward such redefinition. This occurs in league with powerful groups in society such as social workers, medical professionals, and university professors. The moral passage achieved here reduces the sanctions imposed by criminal law and the public acceptance of the deviant designation.

538

The "lifting" of a deviant activity to the level of a political public issue is thus a sign that its moral status is at stake, that legitimacy is a possibility. Today the moral acceptance of drinking, marijuana and LSD use, homosexuality, abortion, and other "vices" is being publicly discussed and movements championing them have emerged. Such movements draw into them far more than the deviants themselves. Because they become symbols of general cultural attitudes they call out partisans for both repression and permission. The present debate over drug addiction laws in the United States, for example, is carried out between defenders and opposers of the norm rather than between users and non-users of the drugs involved.

As the movement for redefinition of the addict as sick has grown, the movement to strengthen the definition of addiction as criminal has responded with increased legal severity. To classify drug users as sick and the victims or clients as suffering from "disease" would mean a change in the agencies responsible for reaction from police enforcement to medical authorities. Further, it might diminish the moral disapproval with which drug use, and the reputed euphoric effects connected with it, are viewed by supporters of present legislation. Commenting on the clinic plan to permit medical dispensing of narcotics to licensed addicts, U.S. Commissioner of Narcotics Anslinger wrote:

> This plan would elevate a most despicable trade to the avowed status of an honorable business, nay, to the status of practice of a time-honored profession; and drug addicts would multiply unrestrained, to the irrevocable impairment of the moral fiber and physical welfare of the American people.

In this paper we have seen that redefining moral crusades tends to generate strong counter-movements. The deviant as a cultural opponent is a more potent threat to the norm than is the repentant, or even the sick deviant. The threat to the legitimacy of the norm is a spur to the need for symbolic restatement in legal terms. In these instances of "crimes without victims" the legal norm is not the enunciator of a consensus within the community. On the contrary, it is when consensus is least attainable that the pressure to establish the legal norms appears to be the greatest.

NOTES AND QUESTIONS

1. Does Gusfield convince you that an unenforced law may still be important because of its symbolic functions? Remember his position: "Legal affirmation or rejection is thus important in what it symbolizes as well or instead of what it controls. Even if the law was broken, it was clear whose law it was." See also, Murray Edelman, *The Symbolic Uses of Politics* (1964). What exactly is the symbolic function of law? How does it perform that function? Who is the audience? How do messages about the content of law get to members of that audience? How much must members of the audience know for law to have some symbolic impact?

2. Many states had (and a handful still have) laws which prohibit adultery. These laws were and are rarely enforced. From the perspective of Gusfield, what explanation can be offered for the persistence of these unenforced laws? Are they "symbolic"? If so, of what? Are there other possible explanations why these laws have been kept on the books? Suppose a university professor noted that the laws aimed at the growing, importing, sale and use of marijuana are enforced only in a small percentage of situations and marijuana is widely available throughout the United States. As a result, he argued, the resources invested in the attempt to stop the use of marijuana largely are wasted. The professor concludes that we should repeal all of the anti-marijuana laws and use these resources where they are needed more. What do you think would be the response of governors and legislators? In any event, could someone argue that the repeal of laws against marijuana would be interpreted by many as an endorsement of the use of marijuana? Would repeal then be an example of symbolic legislation in Gusfield's terms?

3. Gusfield has treated the temperance movement in more detail in his book, *Symbolic Crusade: Status Politics and the American Temperance Movement* (1963). He has also written about the symbolic meaning of drunk driving in *The Culture of Public Problems: Drinking, Driving and the Symbolic Order* (1981).

4. A law can be symbolic because the people who proposed it want it to be symbolic only, because a symbolic law is the best they can get under the circumstances or because the proponents are mistaken about what is needed to make the law instrumental. Which one of these explanations fits the history of Prohibition? The history of the sodomy laws?

5. Gusfield describes a pattern in the designation of deviants—from repentant to enemy to sick. He thinks this pattern fits the history of narcotics laws and liquor laws. Can you think of other cases that fit this pattern? Can you think of any situations in which the designation of deviants has gone the other way—from sick to enemy or to repentant? How would you describe the pattern in the way society has treated drunk drivers? People who smoke cigarettes in public places? Companies that dump toxic wastes into rivers? The history of laws against adultery? against marijuana?

6. Jonathan M. Barnett, "The Rational Underenforcement of Vice Laws," 54 *Rutgers Law Review* 423 (2002), questions the idea that morals legislation is only weakly enforced as a clever attempt to satisfy a conflict between those who support the norm and those who would violate it. In at least some instances, "merely symbolic" legislation may be the most effective approach. Barnett divides the public into roughly three types. The mainstream citizens would expect to pay greatly if they were found to violate a widely held moral norm. Citizens on the fringe would not suffer greatly if they were found to violate such a norm because they have little social capital to lose. Moreover, their own subgroup might even applaud such a violation. The marginal citizens have something to lose, but they are not as integrated as the mainstream. They may drift into criminal activities without contemplating

the costs. Government seldom can reach the fringe citizens without an undue investment of resources on police and conduct that violates privacy. There is little reason to devote great efforts to the mainstream; they will honor the norm to protect their position. However, law plus occasional enforcement reminds people on the margin that there is a norm, and that there are risks if it is violated. This keeps violations to an acceptable level.

Barnett draws on psychology and finds that coercive measures to enforce norms can crowd out the moral norms that ordinarily support these norms. Compliance, in some instances, becomes a kind of game—people see what they can get away with; they violate the norm when the police officer turns his or her back. However, there is a risk that substantial levels of successful deviance may undercut the bindingness of the moral norm. If the law is a joke, one is a fool to comply. There are strategies to avoid the general impression that everyone violates the law and that there is no enforcement of the sanctions. Legal authorities often suppress open black markets but tolerate gray markets that are not so blatant. Occasional crackdowns may be effective in reminding people about the norm and the law, but they do not involve all of the costs of a real attempt to enforce the law always everywhere.

Is Barnett's argument inconsistent with Gusfield's story? Would Barnett's argument persuade a person who felt strongly about the moral claim underlying a particular vice law? Is it enough to suppress open black markets, while still tolerating immoral behavior if it is not too open and notorious? If law enforcement is going to allow a level of violation of the law, isn't there a risk that the police will expect to share in the profits of the illegal activity? Moreover, how does society keep the fringe from becoming the new majority?

(C) Can We Depend on Individuals to Implement Rights?

Assume that legislators want to achieve some goal. They could create an administrative agency and charge it with discovering violations of the statutory norms, and then seeking sanctions against those who failed to follow the law. They could assign these duties and powers to an existing administrative agency. However, often legislators create rights and leave their enforcement to individuals who think that their rights have been abridged. This clearly is cheaper than creating an administrative agency or burdening an existing agency with new duties. However, it is one thing to grant rights to individuals and yet still something else for those individuals to enforce those rights. Part of the problem is the cost of lawyers and litigation, but, as the next essay makes clear, much more may be involved.

(4.13) Bargaining in the Shadow of Social Institutions: Competing Discourses and Social Change in Workplace Mobilization of Civil Rights

Catherine R. Albiston

39 Law & Society Review 11 (2005).

Until recently, the United States was virtually the only major industrialized country without a family leave policy. Employers could legally fire workers who needed time off to care for seriously ill children, ill or injured spouses, or aging and dying parents. Employers could also legally fire workers unable to work due to temporary serious illnesses or injuries. And employers could legally fire women who needed time off for pregnancy, childbirth, or related medical conditions so long as they also denied time off to nonpregnant employees who were unable to work. Time off after the birth of a child remained a benefit provided at employers' discretion, a benefit primarily available to well-paid professional or management workers....

Since 1993, however, the Family and Medical Leave Act (FMLA) has provided some workers with a legal right to unpaid, job-protected leave. The FMLA requires covered employers to provide twelve weeks of leave per year to certain workers who need time off for family or medical crises.[127] Workers may use FMLA leave for childbirth or other temporary disabilities, and both men and women may take leave to care for a sick child, parent, or spouse, or a new child in their family.[128] The statute protects workers who use leave from retaliatory harassment, termination, and discrimination.[129] The law also requires employers to provide leave even if they do not allow time off for any other reason. In other words, the statute creates an entitlement because it does not allow employers discretion to deny leave to qualified workers.[130]

New legal rights seem to be an obvious solution to workplace conflict over family and medical leave because they not only create an instrumental tool for enforcement, but also reframe the meaning of leave as a legitimate and important entitlement. Like most civil rights laws, however, the FMLA is primarily enforced through an individual, private right of action that workers must actively claim or "mobilize." Although these formal rights are an important first step, rights mobilization remains embedded within existing practices, deeply held beliefs, and taken-for-granted expectations about work, gender, and disability. This study examines how legal norms and these other institutionalized systems of meaning influence the process of mobilizing FMLA rights in the workplace.

---

127. 29 U.S.C. § 2612. Workers who have worked for their employers for less than one year are not eligible for FMLA leave. In addition, workers who work for companies with less than 50 employees are not covered by the FMLA. 29 U.S.C. § 2611.

128. 29 U.S.C. § 2612.

129. 29 U.S.C. § 2614, 2615.

130. The statute does, however, allow employers to require medical certification of the need for leave and to deny leave if the worker fails to provide this certification. 29 U.S.C. § 2613 ...

This study builds on a long sociolegal tradition that examines how law interacts with other systems of meaning in particular social settings. For example, empirical research has demonstrated how law can be displaced or transformed by alternative normative systems . . . or by organizational practices and goals. . . . Often, however, these studies treat law and other norms as an either/or proposition: either social relationships are ordered according to law, or there is "order without law." Less is known about the complex process through which law interacts with alternative normative systems. . . . Although other systems of meaning matter, actors may still draw upon law as a cultural resource to interpret their social experiences and to influence the behavior of others. In this way, law and other social institutions act in concert to give meaning to social life.

Law may be most likely to interact with other normative systems when new rights attempt to change long-standing social practices. Civil rights laws in particular often challenge social arrangements that evoke strong normative commitments. . . . Actors who mobilize these rights engage not only with legal systems of meaning, but also with the established practices and expectations that rights were intended to change. Consequently, civil rights claims can become a site for contesting, and perhaps changing, the existing cultural frameworks and practices that help construct social life.

The FMLA provides a fertile location to study how law and other social institutions interact because these rights challenge deeply held beliefs about what work and being a good worker mean. For example, the law erodes certain taken-for-granted expectations about work, such as unbroken attendance as the measure of a good worker and employer control over work schedules. It also undermines traditional ideologies about the gendered division of labor in the family by requiring work to accommodate family needs on a gender-neutral basis. And by protecting the jobs of workers who are temporarily too ill to work, it challenges constructions of "disability" and "work" as mutually exclusive categories. By attempting to change these long-standing work practices and implicit assumptions about identity, the FMLA reconceptualizes the relationships among work, gender, and disability, and creates an opportunity for social change.

Although the FMLA attempts to change work, the cultural frameworks that give meaning to work do not disappear overnight. Workers mobilize their rights to leave in workplaces where these cultural frames or schema are likely to persist. Although the law constructs leave-taking as legitimate, implicit norms about work, gender, and disability may construct very different interpretations of the same behavior. The analysis that follows examines how these competing systems of meaning shape workplace rights mobilization and shows how negotiations over FMLA rights can both reinforce and transform deeply entrenched understandings of work, gender, and disability. . . .

Rights Mobilization, Institutions, and Social Change

Most studies of rights mobilization and social change focus on landmark litigation or collective action, rather than the micro-level process of informal workplace negotiations ... Nevertheless, the earlier, more informal stages of mobilization also matter, because most grievants either negotiate their claims informally or simply "lump it".... Accordingly, a complete understanding of mobilization requires attention to the process of mobilizing law in informal as well as formal contexts.

Sociolegal researchers have begun to explore these informal processes in more detail, and they have generally taken a qualitative, interpretive approach to studying informal mobilization.... Like interpretive studies of litigation as a mobilization strategy ..., these micro-level studies examine how rights work as cultural discourses or "schemas," but focus on informal settings and everyday life.... This cultural approach grows out of broader sociological theories about how cultural schemas constrain consciousness and shape action to conform to, and therefore reproduce, existing social structures.... From this perspective, law is part of the cultural " 'tool kit' of symbols, stories, rituals and world views" that people use to make sense of the social world and to solve different kinds of problems.... Of course, law is not determinative; it is only one of many available frames that actors use to construct meaning in social interactions. Nevertheless, actors can mobilize legal rights simply by invoking legal norms to interpret events and to influence behavior in informal interactions....

Viewing rights as cultural or symbolic resources suggests one potential mechanism of social change: Mobilizing rights, even in informal contexts, can undermine taken-for-granted understandings of social organization and delegitimize conduct previously accepted as natural and normal.... In other words, social transformation is possible through the innovative use of cultural schemas to reinterpret, enact in new ways, and therefore transform social structures.... Of course, law is not exclusively a positive force for change; law may also constrain change by narrowly defining the claims that are possible and by obscuring other avenues for action.... In addition, legal rights compete with alternative ideologies that shape how actors understand their experiences.... Although some workplace actors may legitimate taking leave by referencing rights, others may draw on alternative cultural schemas to undermine legal reforms. Accordingly, like formal legal contests, informal rights negotiations can be seen as an interpretive site for both reinforcing and potentially changing social structure.

Alternative Normative Systems and New Institutionalism

. . . .

New institutionalists posit that institutions are the product of a social process over time through which patterns of social behavior come to be taken for granted and expected. Once these patterns become institutionalized, actors experience them as part of reality, just the way things are, rather than as the collective production of meaning. Nevertheless, although institutions appear to be an objective and impersonal reality, they do not exist apart from the patterned social interactions that reinforce and re-create them.... Over time, however, institutions become self-sustaining because these cognitive structures and taken-for-granted expectations tend to constrain what constitutes legitimate action and to channel behavior in ways that reproduce institutionalized practices.

A new institutionalist approach is well-suited to studying the FMLA because this law challenges deeply entrenched work practices and norms. Indeed, long-standing work norms and expectations seem likely to affect how workers think about using their rights to leave. How do these institutionalized practices and expectations enter the process of rights mobilization? "Agents of transformation"—opponents, friends, co-workers, and family members—influence which cultural frames dominate as they draw on cultural discourses, both legal and nonlegal, to interpret workplace experiences.... Agents of transformation who deploy these schemas shape how rights holders evaluate their options for mobilization....

Of course, agents of transformation shape rights holders' perceptions by referencing a range of available interpretive frameworks including not only law, but also other cognitive and normative structures that may undermine law. For this reason, informal rights negotiations can be understood as taking place not only "in the shadow of the law" ..., but also in the shadow of other social institutions.

Power and the Social Institution of Work

In this study, the shadow of social institutions includes two aspects of work that are particularly salient when workers negotiate contested leaves. The first is how power in the employment relation shapes how workers evaluate their options for mobilizing their rights. Employers generally have more power than their employees over the workplace; for example, the at-will employment doctrine gives employers broad powers to fire at will, and employers rather than workers typically control work schedules. These modern workplace arrangements reflect an uneasy truce in a historical struggle over control of the schedule and process of work, a truce that the FMLA potentially disrupts....

Unequal power in the workplace can affect rights mobilization in several ways. First, to the extent that power consists of superior strength or resources, employers who have more resources than their workers may be more likely to prevail in conflicts over rights. Second, power includes employers' ability to prevent grievances from becoming full-blown, public conflicts. For example, employers can create internal procedures to divert grievances from public forums.... Also, workers may not mobilize their rights if they fear demotion or termination in response.... Third, power can be deployed to keep grievances from being recognized at all. For example, employers may withhold information or use persuasion to make workplace practices seem natural and normal, rather than problematic or unfair.... Power also operates through more impersonal cultural forces that shape how actors interpret their experiences. For example, institutionalized meaning systems regarding work are often shared not only by the powerful but also by workers themselves. Consequently, these ideologies can shape how actors understand workplace experiences in ways that legitimate and maintain domination....

Work, Time, and the Construction of Inequality

A second salient aspect of the institution of work—the historical connections among gender, disability, and work—is closely related to this third conception of power. Over time, the interconnected and mutually reinforcing systems of meaning among gender, disability, and work have come to form an invisible cognitive framework that gives meaning to leave for family or medical purposes. In particular, seemingly neutral features of work, such as attendance and time invested in work rather than productivity, have come to define "good workers"....

"Work" is a social institution with relatively standard characteristics that seem natural and normal, many of which focus on time. For example, asked to imagine a typical image or standard of "work," our mental image is likely to include certain features: permanent, uninterrupted year-round work and a standard forty-hour work week on a five-day schedule, and a schedule typically set and controlled by the employer. Of course, many jobs deviate from this standard, but we mark those deviations by referencing (and thus reinforcing) the institutional norm by speaking of "part-time" work, "night shifts," or "working for oneself." Moreover, work that deviates from the institutionalized standard is often devalued. For example, recent research documents how workers who fail to meet a normative standard of forty-hour work week, a regular schedule, and uninterrupted year-round work sacrifice job security, pay, and benefits....

What do institutionalized work standards have to do with gender and disability? Like many social institutions, work reflects and sometimes reinforces existing relations of inequality. For example, feminist and disability scholars have long recognized that standard work schedules are implicitly gendered and able-bodied because they fail to accommodate family responsibilities or disabilities that require temporary absences from work.... Nevertheless, normative work schedules have become so taken for granted that the barriers they create appear to arise from the personal circumstances of women or people with disabilities rather than from the structure of work itself.... For example, caring for family is viewed as a "private" problem, and accommodations for disabilities are labeled as "special treatment." In this way, the role that work's time standards play in re-creating inequality becomes invisible, and penalties for time off become naturalized, just part of the way things are.

Although these aspects of work seem natural and unchanging, work as a social institution is the product and embodiment of history. For example, modern conceptions of work reflect historical struggles to associate work with masculinity and citizenship.... Work's structure reflects early-twentieth-century assumptions that the normative worker is a male breadwinner with a stay-at-home wife, and that women only work for "pin money" until they marry and have children.... Modern work practices also reflect how individuals with disabilities were historically segregated and excluded from civic life.... In addition, our conceptions of work and disability reflect the way that some social welfare laws define "disability" to mean the inability to work, implicitly constructing work and disability as mutually exclusive categories.... Indeed, "work" and "disability" have come to have mutually reinforcing and oppositional cultural meanings that can delegitimate workplace disability claims as "shirking"....[131] Thus, much more is at stake with FMLA rights than simply changing ad hoc work arrangements; these rights disrupt relations of power between employers and workers and undermine deeply entrenched understandings of work, gender, and disability.

This study examines how the institution of work affects the process of mobilizing FMLA rights, and it therefore focuses on institutional, social contextual factors and the construction of meaning, rather than on the individual characteristics of rights holders. It asks: How do workers who need leave but encounter resistance from their employer make sense of their situations? How do they understand conflict over leave and their choices about mobilizing their rights? How do institutionalized expectations and norms about work give meaning to these workplace interactions and shape the process of mobilization? And, more broadly, what are the implications for social change through legal reform?

Method and Data

To answer these questions, this project draws on semi-structured telephone interviews with workers who experienced conflict over leave but did not take their disputes to court. Data such as these are relatively rare because informal disputes generally do not produce court records or other easily obtainable records of the dispute. In addition, employers are rarely enthusiastic about allowing their employees to talk to researchers about conflict over legal rights. To solve these problems, these respondents were located through a statewide telephone information line in California run by a nonprofit organization that gives informal legal assistance to workers. Attempts were made to contact the universe of individuals who called the information line with questions about family and medical leave during a one-year period. Twenty-four of the thirty-five individuals in this group agreed to be interviewed, yielding a response rate of almost 70%.[132] Despite the small size of this

---

131. Several scholars have examined how both public policy and cultural conceptions of disability have moved from a medical model of disability to a rights-based model ... The medical model locates disability in the individual physical or mental characteristics of the individual. In contrast, the rights-based model focuses on removing environmental factors that create barriers for some individuals and there-fore socially construct them as "disabled." This ideological transition has made the ways in which naturalized work practices construct the meaning of disability more visible....

132. Four individuals could not be contacted after multiple attempts, four individuals refused to be interviewed, one number had been disconnected, and two numbers were incorrect.

group of workers, these respondents were fairly diverse in terms of age, race, education, marital status, income, and occupation.... Quotations in this article are identified by numbers that correspond to the appendix information for each respondent.

The interviews, which typically lasted about forty-five minutes, were tape-recorded and transcribed. The data were then analyzed using NUD*IST, a qualitative analysis software program that allows researchers to identify and code themes as they emerge from the transcripts. The analysis identified common themes in workers' experiences, including the factors that influenced their decisions about mobilizing their rights and the problems they experienced taking leave. This analysis involved multiple readings of the interview transcripts to identify themes regarding the mobilization process as they emerged from the transcripts. Through this process, themes such as "gender," "slackers," and the meaning of "time" emerged from the transcripts to shape my analysis of workers' experiences. I then went back to code each instance of these themes systematically and to analyze patterns among those themes. NUD*IST greatly simplifies this process by allowing the researcher to mark interview segments associated with a theme, to sort and index these segments by theme, and to analyze patterns among themes.

Like most qualitative studies, the number of interviews analyzed here is small. Although the small number of subjects requires caution in drawing generalizations, the in-depth approach made possible by small-N studies has the potential to reveal considerable nuance and detail about the mobilization process. Note also that because this study focuses on the experiences of workers who anticipated or experienced some difficulty in obtaining leave, the subjects are not and were not intended to be a random sample of the population of potential leave users. For this reason, I make no claims about how frequently problems with the FMLA arise or about the differences between workers who experience problems and those who do not. Instead, my analysis focuses on how the shadow of social institutions shapes the meaning actors give to leave conflicts and constructs their preferences about mobilizing their rights. More broadly, my analysis details how competing social institutions shape the process of mobilization and construct the meaning of leave, in some instances transforming the meaning of legal rights in the workplace. Accordingly, this inquiry presents a theory-building opportunity to examine how broader social institutions affect informal rights mobilization, as well as the implications of these institutions for inhibiting or facilitating social change....

The Process of Rights Mobilization in the Workplace

. . . .

Power and Workplace Rights Mobilization

Information Control, Agents of Transformation, and Worker Solidarity

One important theme that emerged from these interviews is that unequal power in the workplace can affect how workers think about rights mobilization. Most respondents mentioned at least one power dynamic that influenced how they thought about mobilizing their rights to leave. For example, for some, a threat of termination could silence objections to unfair treatment.

> Um, when I was pregnant, my doctor put in writing that I could not, he didn't want me bending for long periods of time, or looking up for long periods of time because I have a tendency to get dizzy and get off balance when you're pregnant.... So, everything that [my supervisor] wanted me to do was four to six inches from the floor. And there were other courtesy clerks there that could have done the job, but she wanted me to do it. She didn't care if my stomach is showing and everything. There were guys there that were courtesy clerks that could have did the job. And when I told her, "I don't think I'm supposed to be doing this." She'd tell me, "You don't like your job?" You know. And I felt that was pretty cruel, you know for her to treat me that way ... So ... [I did the work and] I ended up losing my baby.... When I returned to work, she started right back up. She told me that she did everything while she was pregnant with no restrictions. That's what she told me.[133]

An explicit threat may not be necessary if workers fear other penalties at work. For example, the following respondent did not pursue her right to return to the same or equivalent job after leave, even though her hours were cut in half when she returned to work.

> I just didn't want to make—cause he's a new manager and I hadn't worked with him. I didn't want to come back with an attitude and then him kind of be negative toward me. It hurt, but I thought well, I still have my job. It's going to be rough because, you know, 20 hours a week.

Some respondents worried that being fired would not only deprive them of a job, but also harm their ability to find future employment. They justified voluntarily quitting rather than pursuing their rights and risking termination by pointing out that no one wants to hire a fired worker, particularly a "troublemaker" who sued a former employer.

Power in the employment relation can operate in more subtle ways to shape how workers come to understand and even know about their workplace rights. Along these lines, one theme that emerged from these interviews is that those who control information about rights have an advantage in workplace negotiations over leave. Information is critical to "naming," or saying to oneself that a particular experience has been injurious, and "blaming," or holding another responsible for the injury.... Indeed, the FMLA recognizes the link between information and enforcement by placing affirma-

---

133. This particular respondent's situation was covered by state law in California, rather than the FMLA. California law requires employers to accommodate pregnancy-related restrictions on the tasks a worker can perform by transferring her to a less strenuous or hazard- ous position where that transfer can be reasonably accommodated (Cal. Gov. Code § 12945). This passage also suggests that the respondent's supervisor applied certain norms about ideal workers. That dynamic is discussed in more detail below.

tive obligations on employers to tell workers about their leave rights.[134] Virtually all respondents mentioned the importance of information about their rights in evaluating their options for mobilization. Arguably, this is to be expected, given that these respondents called a legal information line seeking help; however, some respondents who called already knew about their rights and were seeking legal representation and other forms of assistance. Moreover, despite their diverse work situations, respondents described common patterns through which information about rights was controlled and limited in the workplace. They also described a social process through which they learned about their rights, and the ways in which they informally mobilized this information to their advantage.

Many respondents indicated that their employers attempted to control information in ways that discouraged mobilization and prevented workers from recognizing a legal injury. For example, when workers request leave, employers can stonewall by asserting that the statute does not apply unless the worker can prove otherwise.

> I mean the initial reaction . . . was just sheer, "We're not going to even use this law because we don't know what we can get away with. We don't know . . . if you qualify so until we do, you don't." That was my feeling that's how they treated that law. . . . Their whole attitude is stalwart it or whatever the word is, block it the best you can. Make these folks fight for it . . . . That's the reaction I got.

Employers also can simply remain silent and wait to see whether workers recognize that leave rights might apply.

> The way [R's employer] is, . . . if you don't do your homework they'll let you ride with what you know and if you don't know enough then you shorten yourself. So you had to go in there with as much knowledge as I had, you know, to talk to them.

Informal practices such as these give employers more control over who will take leave, and thus can transform a legal entitlement into a more discretionary benefit. Although information may have been particularly salient for workers who called the legal information line, these findings are consistent with other studies that have found that information about legal rights is both scarce and essential to negotiating successfully with employers. . . . The common patterns among these workers' experiences suggest how control over information can affect the mobilization process. . . .

Although employers could shape respondents' perceptions by controlling information about FMLA rights, most respondents also talked with friends, family, and others to find information about the law and to discuss possible responses to conflict over leave. These social interchanges with others influenced how these respondents thought about mobilization. For example, this respondent indicated that friends encouraged her to see her situation as a legal violation and to pursue her rights.

134. 29 C.F.R. §§ 825.301, 825.302.

> I felt like I was kind of in a situation that nobody had really been in, and so I didn't really know what to do. So people's opinions and their thoughts of what I should do made a big impact because I really had no idea of where to go from here. And I have some friends who were very supportive of this and said, "No, you have to go forward with this. You have to go through with it because they can't get away with this."

Although this respondent's friends encouraged her to mobilize her rights, her stepmother interpreted the situation differently based on her own experience of losing her job before the FMLA was enacted:

> I talked to my stepmother, who had three children, and, um, I guess had had maternity leave for each child, for each birth. And she told me, "That's just the way it is." You know, I shouldn't try to fight it, I shouldn't get myself all upset. That it's what happens.

These conflicting interpretations illustrate how different cultural frameworks—here, acceptance of gender inequality versus empowerment by legal norms—can be deployed by agents of transformation in the mobilization process. For this respondent, legal norms that legitimize job-protected leave facilitated mobilization by undermining the interpretation that losing one's job when one has a baby is "just the way it is." Thus, this respondent's experience suggests how legal discourse can generate alternative interpretive frameworks that challenge established patterns of acquiescence to inequality.

In general, for these respondents mobilization was not a solitary decision based on preexisting, endogenous preferences, but instead a social process in which others' opinions about what they should do shaped their choices. In other words, respondents formed their preferences in part in response to norms and perceptions communicated by others. As I explain in more detail below, those norms and perceptions, in turn, were shaped by actors' experiences within existing systems of inequality in the workplace, and by institutionalized conceptions of work, gender, and disability.

Friends, family, and others can act as agents of transformation in several ways. First, they can encourage workers to mobilize their rights, sometimes by framing a particular experience as unacceptable or illegal.

> I talked to . . . the guy I was co-managing the store with and I talked to another manager [about my situation]. . . . Both of them felt like I had been misled [by the company]. And that [it] had been done purposely.
>
> Interviewer: And did that influence what you did in your situation in any way?
>
> It made me want to talk to somebody in the law.

Exchanges with others can also warn workers about the risks of claiming rights, however.

> You know I've heard horror stories about people taking time off when their baby was born and were getting a lot of flak from their bosses because they took the time. . . . I heard, there was this one guy, he has a

shift that is mid-shift, 12 to 8:30 and when he came back to work they changed it on him.... They changed his shift to a graveyard shift, Monday through Friday when he came back.... I worked graveyard for four years, I didn't want to go back to that.

This last example suggests how actions taken against only one worker can influence how many others think about mobilizing their rights. Stories of retaliation, passed through social networks in the workplace, can discourage workers from requesting leave, even absent any explicit threat directed toward them.

Nevertheless, interactions with agents of transformation do not always discourage mobilization; sometimes social interactions about rights build solidarity among workers. By discussing leave problems with others, workers may uncover a larger pattern of shared grievances....

This last point contradicts the critique that rights undermine collective action by atomizing disputes and isolating grievances from their social context.... This critique may place too much emphasis on how formal rights claims in court atomize grievances by narrowing disputes to legally relevant facts and individualized remedies. This critique also tends to assume that rights mobilization is a solitary, rather than social, process. This assumption overlooks how the informal process of mobilizing rights—finding information about rights and caucusing with other workers about what is appropriate and legal—can help build connections and common interests among grievants. The social process of mobilization may also show workers how rights claims extend beyond their individual interests. Indeed, several respondents said they took steps to pursue their rights to prevent future workers from having a similar experience.

This insight is important because it suggests that individuals who mobilize their rights in informal settings can set in motion a framing process that may lead to eventual collective action.... Just as rights litigation in courts can provide a public rallying point and publicity for a social movement ..., informal rights mobilization through workplace interactions can build solidarity among workers who share common grievances. It can also encourage workers to conceptualize their problems as part of a broader system of power and control. In other words, these data do not seem consistent with the argument that rights are inherently limited as a social change strategy because they frame broader grievances as individual problems. Individual rights do not necessarily create an ideological framework that always causes workers to conceptualize difficulties as individual problems rather than collective concerns. In some instances, the process of sharing information can create a collective framework for interpreting opposition to rights, even if power disparities or coordination problems sometimes prevent formal collective action. Thus, more attention is needed to the context of rights mobilization, particularly social processes within informal contexts, when evaluating the capacity of rights for bringing about social change.

When considering solidarity among workers, one might think that unions would be a key mechanism for helping workers to respond when employers resist FMLA leave. Indeed, two-thirds of the respondents in this study were union members, perhaps reflecting the information line's outreach efforts with unions and other worker organizations. Only about half of the respondents who belonged to unions, however, indicated that the union had been helpful in their negotiations over leave. The primary form of help provided by respondents' unions was to inform them about the information line and the FMLA. Only two respondents indicated that their union advocated for them in their negotiations over leave. Nevertheless, the experiences of these respondents suggest that unions can play an important role in disseminating information about statutory employment rights.[135]

Law as a Symbolic Resource in Leave Negotiations

Even for those workers who negotiate their rights on their own, legal rights can be an important symbolic resource. Most respondents reported that they felt empowered by the legal entitlement to leave as they negotiated with their employers. For example, many respondents said they felt morally justified in pursuing claims to leave once they knew that their employer acted illegally. As one worker put it,

> [Information about FMLA rights] gave me a leg to stand on. And some kind of moral or ethical support knowing that this is what my rights were....

In addition, many respondents described law as a pragmatic resource for confronting employers, even when they did not make a formal legal claim.... Learning about their rights helped these workers frame their experiences in both legal and moral terms and gave them confidence to press for time off. Some workers also drew on law to interpret leave as an entitlement, rather than a personal problem. Thus, these data suggest that even workers who lack financial resources for a court battle can still informally mobilize law to validate their claims to leave....

Rights Mobilization, Social Institutions, and the Social Construction of Leave

Perhaps the most subtle form of power is how the established practices and expectations that make up institutions can shape social action to re-create inequalities embodied in those institutions. Along these lines, the following sections discuss three themes that emerged from these interviews that illustrate how workers' leave negotiations are embedded within the social institution of work. First, I examine how family wage ideology, or the assumption that the normative worker is a male breadwinner with a stay-at-home wife, can shape how workers and others think about the meaning of leave rights.

---

135. Here is an interesting side note about the effect of unions on realizing FMLA rights. Two respondents believed that their employer had denied them FMLA leave because they were active union leaders. In other words, these respondents were convinced that their employers withheld FMLA leave to retaliate against them because they advocated for other union members in workplace matters.

Second, I document how a "slacker" narrative can undermine the FMLA in ways that subtly reinforce the constitutive relationship between disability and work. Finally, I look at how employers can reinterpret leave rights in terms of management objectives, weakening the normative power of the law relative to the institution of work.

Family Wage Ideology

Most respondents who took pregnancy or parental leave discovered that despite the law, family wage discourse framed the meaning of their leave. Indeed, many women found that taking leave changed perceptions of them at work because it seemed to signal that they were no longer committed to their job. For example, one respondent reported that even though her objective performance had been good (as reflected in her performance review), her supervisor's attitude changed after her leave to care for her ill daughter.

> He's like, "Well she's having a problem with her kid...." [Now] he makes me feel like I'm inadequate. Like I can't do the job, like I'm not bright enough.

Virtually all of the female respondents had no difficulty initially taking leave, but when they attempted to return, they encountered resistance and perceptions that they were less reliable and committed to their work.

The experience of a respondent who took pregnancy leave for twins illustrates this phenomenon. This respondent worked as a manager for her employer, a large company, for sixteen years before she needed leave. Nevertheless, her employer assumed she would not return and canceled her health insurance while she was in the hospital. In addition, her boss told coworkers that she did not need her job because her husband could support her.

> They were saying, "Well she doesn't need to get paid," my boss was saying. "She has money—her husband is a doctor."

Despite her years of service, her employer presumed that her husband was the breadwinner, and therefore she did not "need" her job. Her supervisor attempted to justify letting her go by mobilizing a cultural discourse that women (particularly mothers) are and should be economically dependent upon their husbands.

Legal rights also framed her understanding of her situation, however. A friend who was a lawyer told her that she would have a strong legal claim if she tried to return and was fired, and she expressed outrage that her employer ignored her legal entitlement to leave. Nevertheless, she feared that no future employer would hire her once she had been fired. She knew that her employer had fired other long-term employees who needed leave, and she decided to quit.

> Those two got fired first and then I just said, you know, I don't want to get fired. I mean I have a good record and I would hate to have to go and start somewhere at, in your mid-thirties and then your employer that

> you've worked for 16 years fired you? That doesn't look good. And my husband said, "Is it really worth it all?"

However, when she left, to avoid a confrontation with her employer she told her supervisor she could not return to work because she lacked child care....

The male respondents who took family leave had somewhat different experiences. In fact, both male and female respondents reported informal workplace norms that men should not take all the parental leave that is legally available to them. For example, in one respondent's workplace, it was unthinkable that a new father would take more than a week or two of leave.

> There was another guy who was having a baby and I think that they got more pressure to come back to work, OK, "It's OK for you to take a week off and maybe a week and a half off, but let's not go crazy here." And that wasn't, I don't think they would have been open for the FMLA for the men. At least the men I knew just took their vacation and didn't take, didn't use the FMLA when they could've. Because they were pressured to come back to work, like "Hey, you didn't have a baby."

> Interviewer: And there wasn't the same kind of pressure on women?

> No.

While female respondents typically found that they were expected to take leave to care for others, all of the male respondents reported that their employers and coworkers were incredulous and even hostile when they decided to take family leave. Thus, the same family wage discourse constructed different meanings for respondents' leaves depending upon their gender.

These deeply entrenched expectations about work and gender also shape workers' legal consciousness. For example, some male respondents who took unpaid family leave struggled to reconcile leave rights with norms that men should prioritize work over family needs. The experience of the following respondent who took leave to care for his terminally ill wife illustrates this point. This respondent had worked as a laborer for seven years for a public agency in the San Francisco area. When he took leave to care for his wife, he encountered criticism from coworkers for missing work, and also received a disciplinary letter from his employer telling him to keep his leave use to a minimum. When his coworkers, his employer, and even his wife questioned his time away from work, he drew on legal norms to legitimate his leave:

> I always made them understand that I'm under family leave ... and that allows me the right [to take leave].... My wife a lot of times, says "Babe, you can't miss this much work," this and that, and I'd say "Honey, you know, I'm not missing work to miss work. You're sick or whatever and if you need me, I'm here and that's what family leave is, that's why I'm under it, and that's why we fill out the certification papers with your medical provider to protect me in these times of need."

At the same time, however, he believed he should not seek advancement at work while he might need family leave.

There has been plenty of opportunities for me to move up and stuff, but I didn't pursue them because . . . I'm not ready to give 100% responsibility. My responsibility deals with my wife and family at this time. And I've known how sick she is so I didn't pursue any of those advancements for that reason. It was that my priorities are with my family and not moving up at this time. . . . We are pretty middle class. I mean there is nothing we are deprived of. We probably have more things than what most people got, but that has never been a priority to me, like having more or whatever. You know, my priority is my family and that's how I'd like to keep it.

This respondent knew about his legal rights, and he was aware that the FMLA prohibits employers from taking leave into account in promotion decisions.[136] Nevertheless, he understood leave and advancement at work to be an either/or choice—one cannot both pursue a promotion and also care for sick family members. When he justified taking leave by arguing that he passed up opportunities for advancement, he both accepted and reinforced the family wage norm that ideal workers should have no responsibility to care for others. At the same time, his statement that his family is "pretty middle class" despite his choice to put family first implicitly referenced cultural expectations about the male breadwinner role and justified his choice against those norms. . . .

The double bind of meeting expectations about being both a good worker and the family caretaker also affected female respondents, but they struggled with the contradiction between being "good workers" and "good mothers." The following respondent's experience illustrates this conflict. This respondent had worked in the human resources department of a hotel before taking leave for pregnancy disability and childbirth. When she tried to return to work after her leave, she discovered that her employer had filled her position. She was angry, and when friends suggested that she contact a lawyer about pursuing her rights, she did. At the same time, she worried that she was to blame for her situation because she had violated norms about being a good worker.

I was speaking with a lawyer all that time, trying to get back my job and see if they would offer me anything else, but they just wanted to put me in housekeeping. They couldn't find anything for me. At least that's what they were saying. Other situations they were hiring for, other things like sales. And I was like, "Well I can learn sales, anything." A lot of my friends tell me that it's not my fault, that people are just like that. I felt like I was to blame. I even talked to my boss about it. I said, "Didn't I do a good job?"

Although her boss assured her that she had performed well, he also demoted her from human resources assistant to hotel housekeeper. She continued to work as a housekeeper for several months while her lawyer negotiated for her job.

136. 29 C.F.R. § 825.220.

Although she continued to negotiate her rights, she also worried about failing to meet her obligations as a mother, saying, "I just felt that no one else would take care of [my child] like a mother would". She was ambivalent about returning to work because she no longer had the job she loved, and she had to leave her child with another caretaker to work as a housekeeper for less pay.

> I felt bad in my own way and I was very sad. And I think a lot of it was because I knew my child was with this other person. I couldn't do anything about it. My job went to another woman and what was I going to do? All I could do is cry.

Although some of her friends thought she should continue to fight, others suggested a different solution:

> I have one friend, she was always telling me, "If you feel this way why don't you just quit your job and just take care of your son?" Then my husband got a better job offer so that's when I said, I think I will do that.

Eventually, she gave up her negotiations with her employer and quit her job.

This respondent negotiated her rights within three overlapping and contradictory frames: legal entitlements to leave, institutionalized expectations about what it means to be a good worker, and deeply entrenched norms about what it means to be a good mother. The conflict among these frames made claiming her rights psychologically taxing. She hired a lawyer to fight for her job, but she also felt unsure of her claim to being a good worker after missing work for pregnancy leave. At the same time, she worried about not meeting an idealized norm of a mother's intense and personal care.... Her comments reveal the contradictory legal and cultural schemas about the meaning of leave that framed her decision about mobilization....

As these examples illustrate, respondents who took family leave negotiated their rights within a web of meaning made up not only of law, but also of deeply entrenched assumptions about work and gender. Although these respondents negotiated rights within the same web of meaning, the interpretations that flow from those frames varied with gender. As the responses of their employers, friends, and family suggest, culturally, women are expected to quit work to care for new children, whereas men are expected to make work their first priority.... By deploying this cultural frame, agents of transformation help define the meaning of leave and sometimes identify a cognitive path of least resistance for resolving conflict over leave. In this way, institutions can shape workers' preferences and choices about rights mobilization: by providing a graceful explanation for the first respondent to quit, by defining a compromise through which the second respondent justified his decision to take leave, and by suggesting to the third respondent that quitting to care for others was the solution to her dispute. Because they reinforce gendered conceptions of work and family, however, these paths of least resistance help re-create the inequalities that FMLA rights were meant to change.

Slackers and Workers

Respondents who needed leave for their own serious health condition navigated somewhat different informal workplace norms that labeled leave-taking as shirking. Virtually all of these respondents reported that in their workplaces, despite legal entitlements to leave, "committed" workers were expected to come to work even when sick. Conversely, workers who were unwilling or unable to work while sick were perceived as less valuable.

> There seemed to be kind of, I forgot the proper way to word this, the company's attitude towards people working when they're ill and working to the point of causing illness, that was sort of a badge of courage. And I had seen other people in the company pretty much be discounted as valuable employees because they wouldn't or couldn't work when they were sick. And I think that's where my fear came from.

Both employers and co-workers sometimes interpreted taking leave as shirking, as this long-time employee of a public transit company explained.

> Well some people consider that you're a slacker or whatever ... because you're off. They don't consider sick at any point. They know I'm very energetic and hyper and all this stuff, but I should just retire or quit or whatever. I'm in the way.... Some people who are real company-oriented or upward, yuppie types feel like you're not being a good employee if you're off. Even if you do the job efficiently.

Employers communicate this norm through concrete practices such as passing over leave-takers for promotion, transferring (or refusing to transfer) them, cutting their hours, or assigning them undesirable work. These practices mark those who take leave as poor workers, despite legal rights to leave.[137]

Everyday workplace practices can help reinforce perceptions that taking leave for an illness is a form of shirking. For example, not replacing workers who take leave can encourage hostility toward leave-takers, as this employee of a large health maintenance organization described.

> Like for instance the, well the FMLA they have to give you. But what they do is some departments and most of the departments actually, they won't replace you when you get sick, so it causes peer pressure and creates hostility.... amongst your own coworkers.... "Well if this person didn't have so much family leave all the time," you know, that type of situation.... You call in and say, "I'm sick, I'm taking a family leave day." But the end result of that is that it creates hostility in the workplace. They're not supportive because the employer doesn't replace the person.

This particular workplace practice deflects blame for the extra workload away from the employer because it frames workload problems as a conflict among workers, rather than between workers and the employer. Although the law

---

137. Many of these practices are technically illegal. For example, the FMLA prohibits discrimination against workers who use leave rights, including using the taking of leave as a negative factor in employment actions such as hiring, promotions, or disciplinary actions (29 C.F.R. § 825.220). However, these kinds of claims can be very difficult to prove.

has changed, this workplace continued to be structured around the always-ready, always-present worker; the employer lacked any contingency plan or substitute staff to cover workers on leave.

The slacker discourse suggests how systems of meaning other than law can create resistance to rights and discourage workers from using leave. By drawing upon the cultural image of the slacker, employers and co-workers reinterpret mandatory leave rights as a form of shirking. It is important to realize that the slacker judgment is not a spontaneous local norm; its roots lie in the historical construction of work as an institution. The slacker image reflects assumptions that work and disability are mutually exclusive and that therefore one cannot legitimately claim to be both a worker and disabled. In other words, the slacker label references deeply held beliefs that being "really" disabled means not being able to work at all. Accordingly, leave-takers find themselves straddling the cultural line between disability and work and disrupting the mutually constitutive relationship between the two. The slacker discourse both reflects and polices this line by penalizing workers who claim a disability, however temporary that disability may be.

Nevertheless, workers can draw on law as a symbolic discourse to reconstruct the meaning of taking leave, as this respondent discovered.

> What I've done because of this situation and because I've heard all these things, is I've been meeting with groups of employees and telling them that you don't need to go there. People are entitled to this [leave]. If it was you or your family member you would want this leave too. And you sure wouldn't want to come back to work and find out that your own coworkers are being ugly about it. And if they don't replace you, it's not the employee's fault. It actually has to do with the employer. And trying to appease people. I talk to them and explain to them what the rules are and explain to them that the person who is the sick person, is entitled to this time. And you're just making it worse by doing this to them.
>
> Interviewer: And how has this been received?
>
> Actually pretty good. I've been trying to get them not to fuss with each other. . . .

This respondent drew on legal rights to undermine the slacker discourse. First, she explained "what the rules are": that leave is an entitlement, and therefore not subject to qualification or discussion. Second, she referenced legal norms of equal treatment by pointing out that all workers can benefit from the FMLA's protections. She also undercut the employer's slacker interpretation by pointing out that management, not the absent worker, controls workload distribution. This legal counterdiscourse reveals how the slacker label obscures the employer's responsibility for the increased workload. Legal norms also undermine the norm that "good workers" work while sick because legal norms help legitimize time off for temporary illnesses.

This example illustrates how workers can draw on law as a symbolic resource to challenge institutionalized practices and meanings in workplace negotiations over leave. In these micro-interactions, legal discourse can disrupt existing social practices and reveal alternative ways of organizing work life. To the extent that larger social structures are created and re-created through micro-interactions such as these ..., law as a counterdiscourse can be one mechanism for bringing about social change.

Managerial Norms and Needs

FMLA rights also clash with another institutionalized work practice: employers' unilateral control over the schedule of work. Legal reforms can have difficulty penetrating institutionalized practices such as these because they shape how managers respond to the law. For example, organizational conflict managers [can] reinterpret civil rights objectives in terms of managerial norms. Two-thirds of the respondents in this study reported similar patterns in which employers used informal workplace practices to regain control over time off.

Some management strategies for taking back control reflected staffing concerns. For example, one respondent's employer told him about his rights to parental leave, but then asked him not to use them because the employer was short staffed. Another strategy was to limit informally the number of workers who took leave at any one time.... [T]hese employers did not completely ignore the law. They complied at least partially by telling workers about their rights, or by allowing some workers to take leave. Nevertheless, they implemented the law in a way that emphasized managerial norms about work schedules and staffing, rather than the entitlement to leave in the statute. In other words, these informal workplace practices did not produce "order without law," but instead subtly transformed leave rights in the workplace to be consistent with managerial needs.

Managerial practices could affect workers' choices about leave in more subtle ways as well. For example, one respondent described how a management scheme that rewarded workers for meeting production targets undermined leave rights.

> It was bad because we were self-directed, there was a lot of talk about you know, how will [the new law] affect us, as far as covering production numbers and all that when people take and make use of this Act.... They diffuse everything because they get this self-directed, you're your own boss team-oriented thing.... In order of importance it's production, safety and whatever after that. Who knows. Production and safety is all we had to worry about. Fly like a bat out of hell, get it out the door, but don't hurt yourself.

. . . .

By setting goals solely in terms of production and safety, and then rewarding self-directed workers for meeting those goals, employers can create "rules of the game" that undermine collective support for leave. In this workplace, workers enforced time standards against each other to ensure that they met their production goals, and in the process reinforced and legitimated work practices that devalue leave. Other possible and desirable goals, such as balancing production needs against a worker's need for leave, were not considered. In addition, to the extent the workers bought into managerial norms, these norms could diffuse worker resistance by providing ready justifications for resisting leave.

The point here, of course, is not that managerial needs are not pressing or "real" in some sense, any less than workers' needs for leave are pressing and real. The law, however, changes the balance of power between employers and workers by removing employers' unilateral control over scheduling and giving workers an entitlement to leave. Previously, employers could solve their managerial requirements by overriding the needs of workers; now the FMLA requires employers to solve their staffing requirements in other ways. Nevertheless, these data show how rather than developing new organizational strategies to address staffing concerns, employers can subtly reassert their control over the timing and schedule of work in ways that resist and transform legal mandates to the contrary. Although these respondents recognized and resisted this transformation, other workers may have simply accepted their employers' reinterpretation of their rights and not taken leave. Reformulating rights in this way can help employers regain control over work schedules without appearing to refuse to comply with the law.

Conclusion

. . . .

By enacting the FMLA, Congress did not eradicate deeply entrenched beliefs about work that shape perceptions that leave-takers are shirkers, or that women do not need their jobs because they can be supported by their husbands. In addition, cultural ideologies and material practices can work together to resist rights. Workplace structure may determine, for example, which cultural frame is most likely to be deployed, as employers' strategies for controlling information suggest. Conversely, cultural meanings such as the slacker narrative can obscure how employers exercise power over work rules, such as production goals or staffing levels. In the workplaces in this study, these factors combined to reinforce existing conceptions of work that disadvantaged women and people with disabilities.

Thus, rights face resistance from local norms, and these alternative ideologies can arise from the very institutionalized practices and meanings that civil rights attempt to change. Note that this finding contradicts the argument that "rights talk" in our society displaces other cultural norms. . . . Instead, new civil rights become one of many competing cultural frameworks for interpreting social interactions; they do not always dominate in social interactions. In fact, because these rights must be individually mobilized in the context of these entrenched and competing meanings, alternative ideologies may continue to control informal workplace practices despite the formal mandates of the law. . . .

Ironically, formal rights may obscure how institutions and power shape agency because rights appear to provide a legal remedy when employers resist leave. For example, when women quit their jobs without asserting their rights, it may confirm deeply held beliefs that most women prefer caring for children to work because those who prefer to work could sue. But relying on objective behavior alone to interpret preferences ignores how power and legal norms influenced these respondents. It also misses how unequal power can help prevent legal disputes from arising in the first place, even when workers recognize their legal rights. For this reason, qualitative studies that reveal the subjective interplay of these factors are particularly important.

What are the implications of this study for rights and social change? One must exercise caution in answering this question in light of the powerful critique of rights that has been developed by law and society scholars in recent years. Nevertheless, while acknowledging rights' limitations, it is also important to explore in what ways and in what contexts rights might in fact make a difference. And, in a system in which important social values are enforced almost exclusively through private rights of action, the utility of rights must be evaluated in comparison to the alternative—no rights at all. . . .

The data reported here problematize one claim about rights—that they undermine collective action because they inherently create a consciousness among actors that frames grievances as individual problems. Instead, respondents in this study indicated that the existence of legal rights prompted them to talk with others about their experiences in the workplace, to discuss whether their employers' actions were legitimate, and in some instances, to band together to resist their employer's reinterpretation of family and medical leave. In this sense, then, informal rights mobilization can be understood as a social, rather than individual, process of meaning construction as well as action. This process may give rise to symbolic frameworks that delegitimize taken-for-granted practices, such as firing workers who need family or medical leave, and in this way help change deeply entrenched beliefs about work, gender, and disability.

One must be cautious, of course, not to overstate this point, particularly given that this study reveals how social institutions can constrain social change by displacing law or transforming it to be consistent with existing practices and norms. Nevertheless, respondents' experiences also suggest that rights can operate as a powerful cultural discourse in informal negotiations over leave. One cannot dismiss out of hand the symbolic importance of rights claims in the workplace and the instrumental gains that workers sometimes achieve by simply pointing out that an employer's action is illegal. Respondents not only reported feeling empowered by learning about their rights, but also in some instances obtained tangible results by confronting their employer with the law. Thus, rights can still matter even when workers lack the resources to hire an attorney and pursue a formal legal claim. . . .

NOTES AND QUESTIONS

1.   Is Albiston's story one of the success or failure of the Family and Medical Leave Act (FMLA)? Many who have rights do not know about them. Many who know about their rights cannot use them or face real problems when they try to use them. Yet Albiston is not ready to write off FMLA as a total failure. What does she see as the contribution(s) of this law?

2.   How could the FMLA be made more effective? Could a governmental agency provide more information to workers who might need to use it? Could the government provide legal advice to such workers? Could Congress increase the sanctions on employers who failed to follow the demands of the statute? Do you see other steps that could be taken to make the FMLA more effective? Do you see any political problems in getting such steps enacted into law? Might some people prefer the present level of effectiveness of this law?

3.   Phoebe A. Morgan, "Risking Relationships: Understanding the Litigation Choices of Sexually Harassed Women," 33 *Law & Society Review* 67 (1999), reports the stories of thirty one women who reported their sexual harassment to authorities and who considered litigation. At the time of the interviews, ten of the thirty one women had decided not to sue while sixteen were still considering their options. Morgan reports: "the decision to sue rested upon assessments of their abilities to do so while also being good mothers, wives, and daughters. If the filing of the suit threatened the well-being of family members or to strain family ties, then potential plaintiffs were reluctant to embrace such a choice." Those who study law and society have long recognized that there are cost barriers to asserting legal rights. Morgan reminds us that the costs are far more than just the money that must be paid to hire a lawyer. When Congress or a state legislature creates rights, many with arguably good causes of action will not be able to afford to assert their legal claims.

4.   If a lawmaker considers creating individual rights as the solution to a problem, there is always the question of whether those the lawmaker seeks to benefit can use them. Some can afford to hire lawyers, and the type of case may be such that there will develop a pool of lawyers with experience and skill in the area. However, often those the lawmaker seeks to benefit will not be able to turn to lawyers to assert their rights. Stewart Macaulay, "Freedom From Contract: Solutions in Search of a Problem?" 2004 *Wisconsin Law Review* 777, 815–816, notes that those who are familiar with consumer protection laws see "lemon laws" as the most effective legislation in this area. These statutes provide that if a new, or a nearly new, automobile is a "lemon," the manufacturer must replace it free or refund the price. A "lemon" is a car with a serious defect which the manufacturer's dealer cannot fix in a specified number of attempts (often three or four) or one that has defects that prevent the owner from using the car for thirty days or more. Under the Wisconsin statute, a consumer can also sue for damages caused by a violation of the law, and a consumer who prevails will be awarded twice the

amount of any pecuniary loss together with reasonable attorney fees. Many of these statutes also create or recognize arbitration programs to judge lemon law claims. Macaulay says: "Arbitrating a lemon law with a customer usually means that the customer will not buy another car from the manufacturer. Some states publish annually a lemon law index showing the claims and the results [against each manufacturer]—this is not good publicity. As a result, the manufacturers press the dealers to fix the cars or call in help." Sometimes enough is involved to justify hiring a lawyer. Often consumers cannot afford legal representation, and they must go it alone. However, "[l]emon laws favor consumers willing to deal with paperwork, walk into a situation that is totally foreign to them and face a manufacturer's representative who has the advantage of experience." Peter Lewis, "Lemon Law Leaves Sour Taste for Owner," *Seattle Times,* Oct. 14, 2002, at B1.

Joel F. Handler, *The Conditions of Discretion: Autonomy, Community, Bureaucracy* (1986) considers the problem of providing social services to people unlikely to be able to be represented by lawyers. These situations force us to face the limitations of a strategy of giving individuals rights. He points out that the beneficiaries of various types of welfare programs are often in long-term continuing relationships with those who represent an agency. These people may need the good will of those representatives that would be lost if they engaged in litigation. Handler advocates a more cooperative approach, but he does not discount the importance of potential litigation to foster respect for the beneficiaries. He points to examples where voluntary social movement groups, aided in part by the agencies themselves, provide claimants with information, resources, and collective experiences. In this way, they increase each individual's bargaining power and capacity for self-determination. Of course, in order for this to work, legislators and those who run agencies have to want to increase individual bargaining power and autonomy. If those with power see the poor or those in need of special services as undeserving, bargaining power and autonomy will be viewed only as unnecessary costs benefiting people who should be happy to get anything.

5. Joel F. Handler, " 'Constructing the Political Spectacle': Interpretation of Entitlements, Legalization, and Obligations in Social Welfare History," 56 *Brooklyn Law Review* 899 (1990), summarizes one part of Michael W. McCann, *Rights at Work: Pay Equity Reform and the Politics of Legal Mobilization* (1994) as follows:

> According to Michael McCann, . . . [t]he activists in. . . . [the pay equity reform] movement used rights claims and rights consciousness as a mode of political activity, as a tactic for mobilizing social movements and organizing citizens into effective political units. The articulation of legal rights gave rise to rights consciousness, enabling individuals and groups to imagine a new order before rights were formally declared by the state. Rights advocacy not only expanded the awareness of victimization (the construction of problems out of conditions) and generated anger, but also contributed to the development of a sense of legal entitlement, and expectations about possible remedies. Moreover, rights consciousness

developed even though most judicial pronouncements were negative. In the early days of the movement, there were some favorable legal articulations. It was the right historical moment to seize the political initiative, given the changes in legal culture as a result of the civil rights movement, the rise of feminist activism, the changing role of women in the work force, the contribution of key unions, the political power of women in certain strategic locations, and the energy and skills of leaders. What developed was a broad-based movement operating at many levels of government, including court cases, legislative task forces, and administrative hearings. Moreover, the movement spread to the consideration of other women employment issues such as job descriptions, safe working conditions, and child care, and generated more broadly based participatory rights on behalf of women. For example, participation was generated in collective bargaining and in political and administrative activities. In a dialectic process, the definition of concrete rights led to an expansion of horizons. McCann argues, on the basis of extensive interviews, that through organization, people's feelings about themselves changed. Women were now fighting for the recognition of their own worth. A broadened political vision emerged from within a rights-claim campaign.

However, Handler notes: "In some instances, rights seem to 'fail'; in others, they 'succeed.' In some instances, rights seem to result in tangible gains as well as more expressive feelings of self-worth and empowerment. In other instances, rights seem to victimize the victim." If lawmakers passed legislation giving rights to those with relatively little power and status in the society, how might this "victimize the victim?" For example, are lawmakers likely to know whether those rights are being used and for what purposes? Will they be aware whether conditions change for the better or worse?

(D) The Legal Structure and Implementing the Law

(4.14) Rape Law Reform and Instrumental Change in Six Urban Jurisdictions

Julie Horney and Cassia Spohn

25 *Law & Society Review* 117 (1991).

... During the past twenty years there has been a sweeping effort to reform rape laws in this country. Reformers questioned the special status of rape as an offense for which the victim, as well as the defendant, was put on trial. They suggested that the laws and rules of evidence unique to rape were at least partially responsible for the unwillingness of victims to report rapes and for the low rates of arrest, prosecution, and conviction. They cited evidence that these laws and rules of evidence resulted in pervasive skepticism of the victim's claims and allowed criminal justice officials to use legally irrelevant assessments of the victim's status, character, and relationship with the defendant in making decisions regarding the processing and disposition of rape cases. . . .

Concerns such as these sparked a nation wide, grass-roots movement in which women's groups lobbied for rape law reforms. Their efforts resulted in changes in the rape laws of all fifty states. The overall purpose of the reforms was to treat rape like other crimes by focusing not on the behavior or reputation of the victim but on the unlawful acts of the offender. Advocates of the new laws anticipated that by improving the treatment of rape victims the reforms would ultimately lead to an increase in the number of reports of rape. They also expected that the reforms would remove legal barriers to effective prosecution and would make arrest, prosecution, and conviction for rape more likely.

In this study we address these expectations. Using time-series data on more than twenty thousand rape cases in six major urban jurisdictions, we examine the impact of rape reform legislation on reports of rape and the outcome of rape cases.

RAPE LAW REFORM

States enacted reform statutes that vary in comprehensiveness and encompass a broad range of reforms. The most common changes were (1) changes in the definition of rape; (2) elimination of the resistance requirement; (3) elimination of the corroboration requirement; and (4) enactment of a rape shield law. We briefly describe each of these reforms below.

1. Many states replaced the single crime of rape with a series of offenses graded by seriousness and with commensurate penalties. Historically, rape was defined as "carnal knowledge of a woman, not one's wife, by force and against her will." Thus, traditional rape laws did not include attacks on male victims, acts other than sexual intercourse, sexual assaults with an object, or sexual assaults by a spouse. The new crimes typically are gender neutral and include a range of sexual assaults.

2. A number of jurisdictions changed the consent standard by modifying or eliminating the requirement that the victim resist her attacker. Under traditional rape statutes, the victim, to demonstrate her lack of consent, was required to "resist to the utmost" or, at the very least, exhibit "such earnest resistance as might reasonably be expected under the circumstance" (Tex. Penal Code 1980). Reformers challenged these standards, arguing not only that resistance could lead to serious injury but also that the law should focus on the behavior of the offender rather than on that of the victim. In response, states either eliminated resistance of the victim as an element of the crime to be proved by the prosecutor or attempted to lessen the state's burden of proving non-consent by specifying the circumstances that constitute force— using or displaying a weapon, committing another crime at the same time, injuring the victim, and so on.

3. The third type of statutory reform was elimination of the corroboration requirement—the rule prohibiting conviction for forcible rape on the uncorroborated testimony of the victim. Critics cited the difficulty in obtaining evidence concerning an act that typically takes place in a private place

without witnesses. They also objected to rape being singled out as the only crime with such a requirement.

4.   Most states enacted rape shield laws that placed restrictions on the introduction of evidence of the victim's prior sexual conduct. Under common law, evidence of the victim's sexual history was admissible to prove she had consented to intercourse and to impeach her credibility. Reformers were particularly critical of this two-pronged evidentiary rule and insisted that it be eliminated or modified. Critics argued that the rule was archaic in light of changes in attitudes toward sexual relations and women's role in society. They stressed that evidence of the victim's prior sexual behavior was of little, if any, probative worth. Confronted with arguments such as these, state legislatures enacted rape shield laws designed to limit the admissibility of evidence of the victim's past sexual conduct. The laws range from the less restrictive, which permit sexual conduct evidence to be admitted following a showing of relevance, to the more restrictive, which prohibit such evidence except in a few narrowly defined situations. The laws also usually specify procedures for determining the relevance of the evidence; most states require an in camera hearing to determine whether the proffered evidence is admissible.

THE IMPACT OF RAPE LAW REFORM

Proponents of rape law reform predicted that the various statutory changes would produce a number of instrumental results. They expected the reforms, particularly the rape shield laws, to improve the treatment of rape victims and thus to prompt more victims to report the crime to the police. They believed that elimination of resistance and corroboration requirements would remove major barriers to conviction; as a result, prosecutors would be more likely to indict and fully prosecute rape cases, and juries and judges would be more likely to convict in rape trials. They expected that conviction would also be facilitated by the enactment of rape shield laws that restricted admission of evidence of the complainant's sexual history. Finally, reformers believed that definitional changes would make it easier to prosecute cases that did not fit traditional definitions of rape, would prevent jury nullification by having penalties commensurate with the seriousness of the offense, and would lead to more convictions through plea bargaining because appropriate lesser offenses would be available to prosecutors in their negotiations.

Reformers clearly had high hopes for the rape law reforms, but their expectations may have been unrealistic. In fact, the literature on legal impact, which abounds with examples of the remarkable capacity of criminal courts to adjust to and effectively thwart reforms, should lead us to predict that the rape law reforms would have only limited effects on reports of rape and the outcome of rape cases.

The chronic failure of reforms aimed at the court system suggests that reformers have misperceptions about the nature of the judicial process. Most reform proposals assume that we have a hierarchic, centralized, obedient system of courts that will automatically and faithfully adhere to new rules. These misperceptions cause reformers to overestimate the role of legal rules in controlling the behavior of decision makers and to underestimate the role of discretion in modifying the legal rules. Statutory changes like the rape law reform must be interpreted and applied by decision makers who may not share the goals of those who championed their enactment and who therefore may not be committed to their implementation. Numerous studies have demonstrated limited impact of reforms when officials' attitudes were at odds with reformers' goals.

Even if criminal justice officials agree with the legal change in principle, they may resist if it impinges on interests protected by the courtroom work group. Officials may modify or ignore reforms that threaten the status quo by impeding the smooth and efficient flow of cases or that require changes in deeply entrenched and familiar routines. Studies have shown that reforms that interfere with plea bargaining and the production of large numbers of guilty pleas, or that attempt to alter the going rates established by the work group are especially at risk of being undermined . . . .

Other reforms may have limited impact because their passage was primarily symbolic. Faced with a vocal constituency demanding action, decision makers might adopt a policy with little bite to provide symbolic reassurance that needs are being attended to, problems are being solved, help is on the way. Policy makers might, for example, placate constituents by enacting a very weak version of the legal change being sought, by adopting a law that differs very little from other laws on the books or from case law, or by adopting a reform that they know full well will not be enforced.

All the foregoing suggest that the advocates of rape law reform may have been overly optimistic about the effects of the reforms. It also suggests that we should approach the task of interpreting the outcomes of the reforms with great care. It obviously is important to consider not only the specific provisions of the laws themselves but also the comprehensiveness of the reforms, the contexts in which the reforms are to be implemented, and the consequences for decision makers charged with enforcing the reforms. . . .

THE CURRENT STUDY

In this study we assess the impact of rape law reform in six urban jurisdictions. The jurisdictions—Detroit, Michigan; Cook County (Chicago), Illinois; Philadelphia County (Philadelphia), Pennsylvania; Harris County (Houston), Texas; Fulton County (Atlanta), Georgia; and Washington, D.C.— represent states that enacted different kinds of rape law reforms . . . [We selected Detroit, Chicago, and Philadelphia to represent jurisdictions with relatively strong reforms and Atlanta, Washington, D.C., and Houston to represent jurisdictions with weaker reforms. The reforms enacted in the six jurisdictions are summarized below . . .

The Michigan law, considered by many to be the model rape law reform, included all the changes described above. The Michigan statute redefines rape and other forms of sexual assault by establishing four degrees of gender-neutral criminal sexual conduct based on the seriousness of the offense, the amount of force or coercion used, the degree of injury inflicted, and the age and incapacitation of the victim. The law states that the victim need not resist the accused and that the victim's testimony need not be corroborated.

Michigan also enacted a very restrictive rape shield law. Evidence of prior sexual activity with persons other than the defendant is admissible only to show the source of semen, pregnancy, or disease. Evidence of the victim's past sexual conduct with the defendant can be admitted only if a judge determines that it is material to a fact at issue (generally consent) and that its inflammatory or prejudicial nature does not outweigh its probative value.

Although we categorized the reforms adopted in Illinois and Pennsylvania as "strong" reforms, they are neither as broad nor comprehensive as those enacted in Michigan. The Illinois reforms were incremental; in 1978 the state implemented a strong rape shield law very similar to the law enacted in Michigan, but it was six years later before definitional changes were adopted and the resistance requirement was repealed. In 1976 Pennsylvania passed a strong rape shield law and repealed the corroboration and resistance requirements. Although there are significant changes, Pennsylvania retains Model Penal Code definitions of rape and involuntary deviate sexual intercourse, which many reformers believe still place undue focus on the circumstances that define nonconsent.

The reforms adopted in Washington, D.C., Georgia, and Texas are much weaker. Although corroboration requirements have been eliminated or weakened in each jurisdiction, all three jurisdictions continue to require resistance by the victim. Georgia and Texas passed very weak rape shield laws that give judges considerable discretion to admit sexual conduct evidence. Washington, D.C., has not amended its rape statutes since 1901, but case law restricts the introduction of evidence of the victim's prior sexual conduct. Washington, D.C., and Georgia have traditional carnal knowledge definitions of rape, as did Texas until relatively minor definitional changes were made in 1983....

Case Selection

We gathered court records data on rape cases processed from 1970 through 1984 in the six jurisdictions. We collected data on rapes reported to the police during the same time period from the FBI's Uniform Crime Reports (UCR). In each jurisdiction we collected data on forcible rape cases and on other sexual assaults that were not specifically assaults on children. We performed all analyses for both forcible rape and total sexual assaults. Because the pattern of results did not differ with the inclusion of other sexual assaults (and because the types of offenses included varied from jurisdiction to jurisdiction), we present here only the results for forcible rape cases since they are the most comparable. In Michigan, where the reforms included definitional changes, we selected the closest equivalent crimes for the forcible rape analysis (details described below).

Dependent Variables

The dependent variables include the number of reports of forcible rape; the indictment ratio (indictments divided by reports); the percentage convicted (convictions divided by indictments); the percentage convicted on the original charge (convictions for rape divided by indictments); the percentage incarcerated (incarcerations divided by convictions); and the average sentence (average maximum sentence—in months—for defendants incarcerated after a conviction for rape).

Our unit of analysis was the indictment (the term indictment will be used broadly to include informations filed in those jurisdictions in which the grand jury is not used). When we calculate the indictment ratio, we use data from two sources—the UCR and our population of cases from the court files. Thus we do not have the perfect correspondence that we would have if we had been able to follow individual cases from report through court filing. Because most indictments seem to follow the reports fairly closely in time and because there is no good model for making other assumptions, we divided the number of indictments filed in a given month by the number of rapes reported in that same month. In all other analyses the data are based on the indicted cases, and month of indictment is used for the time variable. Thus when we calculate convictions as a percentage of indictments, we are looking at the percentage of cases indicted in a particular month that resulted in conviction.

Time-Series Analysis

We used interrupted time-series analysis to evaluate the impact of the rape law reforms on the dependent variables. We analyzed monthly data over the fifteen-year period to see whether changes in the rape laws produced increases or decreases in the level of the series. In each time-series analysis the interruption was the change in the rape law of the particular jurisdiction. The number of years before and after the reform varied somewhat, depending on when the law was reformed in each state.

Controls

The major weakness of the time-series design is that it does not control for the "history" threat to internal validity. Even when a discontinuity in the series occurs at the time of the intervention, other events occurring at about the same time actually may be responsible for the effects noted. In the case of rape law reforms, increased national attention to the problems surrounding the prosecution of rape cases might have sensitized criminal justice officials and led to any observed changes in processing. We were able to control for history in this research by using a multiple time-series design because the reformed jurisdictions made their legal changes at different times. If national attention to rape issues led to changes in the processing of rape cases, these changes should appear at approximately the same time for all jurisdictions. If, on the other hand, these changes coincided with the legal reforms in each jurisdiction, we have strong evidence that the legal reforms caused the changes.

570

Interviews with Criminal Justice Officials

To more fully evaluate the rape law reforms, in 1985 and 1986 we interviewed criminal justice officials in the six jurisdictions. We conducted lengthy, structured, face-to-face interviews with a sample of 162 judges, prosecutors, and defense attorneys. We selected officials who had experience with rape cases before and after the legal reforms went into effect or who had handled a substantial number of rape cases in the post reform period. We also interviewed police officers and rape crisis center personnel in each jurisdiction.

RESULTS

The results of the time-series analyses are summarized in Table 2. The results of our analyses indicate that, contrary to reformers' expectations, the reforms had little effect on reports of rape or the processing of rape cases. The only clear impact of the laws was in Detroit, and even there the effects were limited. Below we discuss the results for Detroit in detail and then briefly summarize the results for the other five jurisdictions.

The statutory changes adopted by Michigan in 1975 produced some of the results anticipated by reformers. There was an increase in the number of reports of rape and in the ratio of indicted to reported cases. Additionally, the maximum sentence for those incarcerated increased. On the other hand, there was no change in the percentages of indictments resulting in conviction or in conviction on the original charge or in the percentage of convictions resulting in incarceration.

Our analysis of monthly reports of rape revealed that the new law produced a significant increase of about twenty-six reports per month (see Figure 1). Because our measure of reports did not allow us to separate changes in reporting from changes in crime rates, we compared reports of rape with reports of robbery and felony assault for the period 1970 through 1980. If the increase in reported rapes reflected a general trend in violent crimes, we should have seen similar increases for these other crimes. Such increases were not evident. The pattern for felony assault reports was much like that for reported rapes, but the time-series analysis indicated no significant change coincident with changes in the rape laws. The pattern for reported robberies was quite different, and there was no significant change at the time when reporting of rapes increased.

Our results also indicate that the reforms had some effects on case processing in Detroit. The case processing variables are measured for the offenses of rape, sodomy, and gross indecency before the 1975 legal changes and for the offenses of first-and third-degree sexual conduct after the changes. Figure 2 presents the plot of the ratio of indictments to reported rapes. The time-series analysis of these data indicated that the indictment ratio increased by .18. Thus, not only were there more indictments simply because of an increase in the number of cases reported, but prosecution of these cases was more likely following the legislative changes.

Table 2. Summary of the Results of the Time-Series Analysis

Jurisdiction	Reports	Indictment Ratio	% Convicted	% Convicted–Orig. Charge	% Incarcerated	Average Sentence
Detroit	26.53**	.18***	−2.26	0.07	−.15	62.54***
Chicago[a]	0.95	−.42	−0.16	1.03	NA[b]	47.67***
Intervention moved back one year						49.20***
Philadelphia[c]	1.65	.04	−0.01	0.19	.07*	10.35**
Intervention moved back one year					.09***	13.46**
Washington, D.C.						
Shield law	−0.80	.002	0.02	0.01	.06	35.33
Corroboration	−5.07**	−.003	0.04	0.06	.08	70.86
Atlanta[a]						
Shield law	−3.94	−.09	0.01***	−0.05	−.003	29.17
Corroboration	0.02	−.05	0.01	−0.07**	.01	42.74*
Intervention moved back one year			0.01***	−0.07**		42.86*
Houston Num =	1.30***	−.14***	0.12***	0.09***	.06*	73.63***
Den =	0.99***					
First two years after reform	17.25***	−.08*	0.06	0.02	.07	84.94**

NOTE: For each jurisdiction we present the intervention coefficient. Detailed results are available from the authors.

[a] In Chicago the percentage indicted variable was logged.

[b] We did not analyze the percentage incarcerated in Chicago because almost all values were 100 percent.

[c] In Philadelphia the percentage convicted on the original charge variable was logged.

[d] In Atlanta the percentage indicted and the percentage convicted variables were logged.

*$p < .05$ **$p < .01$ ***$p < .001$

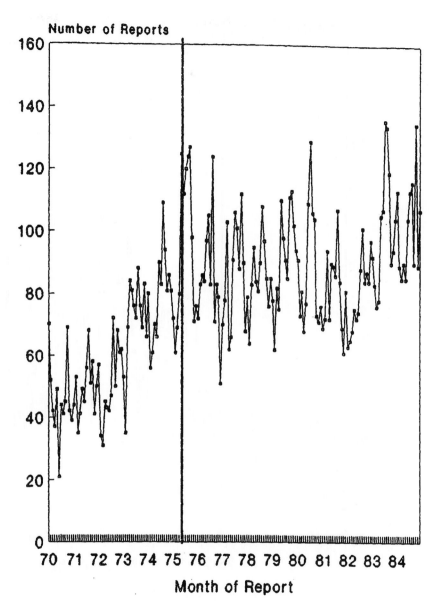

Solid line indicates date of reform

Figure 1. Reports of rape, Detroit, Michigan, 1970–1984

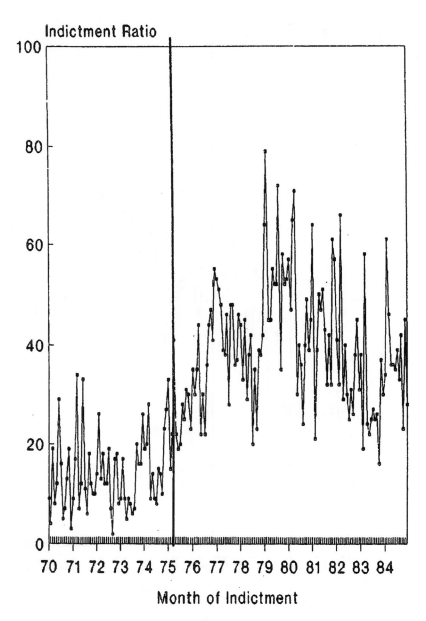

Solid line indicates date of reform

Figure 2. Indictment ratio for rape, Detroit, Michigan, 1970–1984

The likelihood of conviction, on the other hand, did not change as a result of the reforms (Figure 3). With the increase in reports and indictments, however, the steady conviction rate indicates that prosecutors were obtaining more total convictions in the post reform period. This was confirmed by a statistical analysis of the absolute number of convictions. We also found that the reforms did not change the likelihood of incarceration but that the average sentence received by those incarcerated increased by about sixty-three months.

Some reformers predicted that the definitional reforms would lead to an increase in plea bargaining, since the graded criminal sexual conduct offenses would make it possible to reduce original charges to charges still within the sexual offense category. When we examined the percentage of cases convicted on original charges, we found no evidence of a decrease that would correspond to a greater reliance on plea bargaining. In fact, the percentage of cases convicted on the original charge increased after the new laws went into effect, although the increase was not statistically significant . . .

Michigan's strong and comprehensive reforms produced some, but not all, of the effects anticipated by reformers. The strong evidentiary changes enacted in Illinois (1978) and Pennsylvania (1976), in contrast, had no effect on reports of rape or the processing of rape cases in Chicago or Philadelphia. Figures 4–7 present the plots for reports and indictment ratio for those two cities.

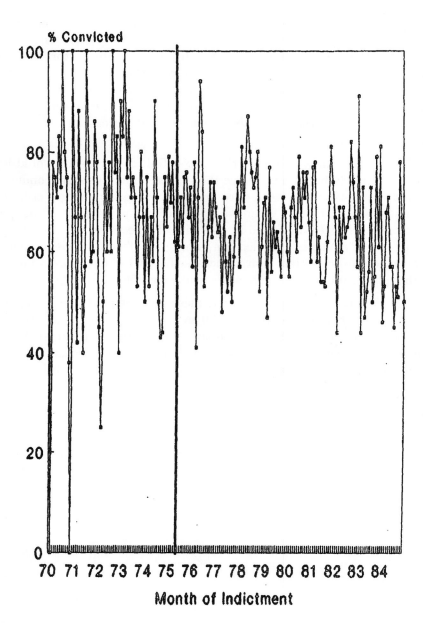

Solid line indicates date of reform

Figure 3. Percentage convicted for rape, Detroit, Michigan, 1970–1984

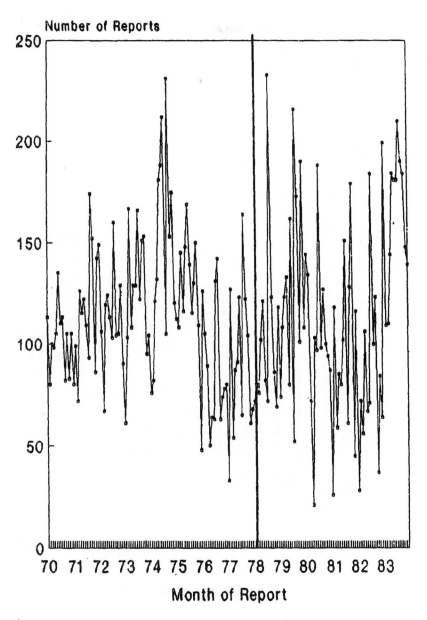

Solid line indicates date of reform

Figure 4. Reports of rape, Chicago, Illinois, 1970–1983

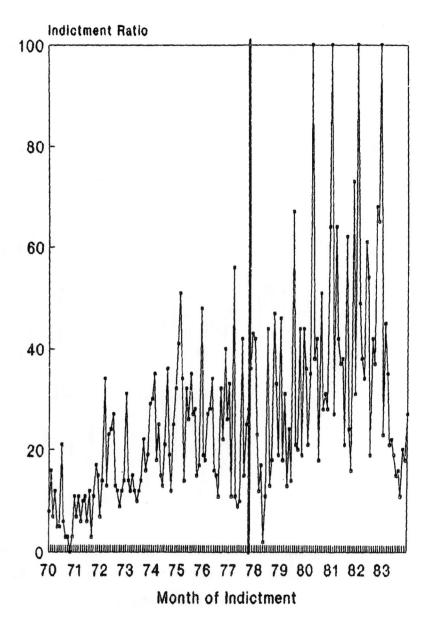

Solid line indicates date of reform

Figure 5. Indictment ratio for Rape, Chicago, Illinois, 1970–1983

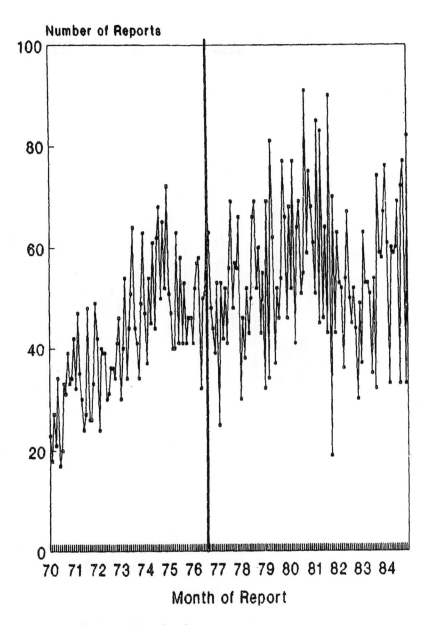

Solid line indicates date of reform

Figure 6. Reports of rape, Philadelphia, Pennsylvania, 1970–1984

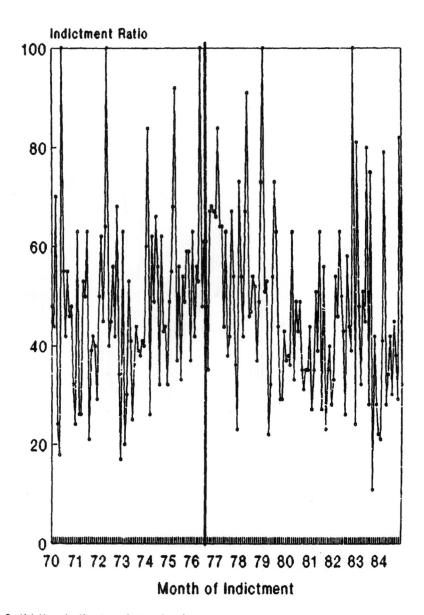

Solid line indicates date of reform

Figure 7. Indictment ratio for rape, Philadelphia, Pennsylvania, 1970–1984

The three cities with weaker reforms also showed almost no evidence of impact for the changes in rape laws. The only significant effect found for Washington, D.C., was a decrease in reported rapes after the elimination of the corroboration requirement. We have no theoretical rationale to explain such a decrease; we suspect that it was merely coincidental with the new law. In Atlanta there were some changes in the processing of rape cases but none that could be attributed to the legal reforms.

We found a number of changes in Houston, but most occurred years after implementation of the new laws, suggesting that they were due to other causes. Still, some charges occurred at the time of the rape law reform. The number of reported rapes increased by an average of 17.25 reports per month, and the indictment ratio decreased by .08. The average sentence for those incarcerated for rape increased by almost eighty-five months.

The graph of reported rapes (Figure 8) shows a long-term increasing trend, and the statistical model that best fit the data was one representing a very gradual increase. Such an effect is quite unlikely to be produced by a legal reform. To test whether the trend might simply be part of a general increase in crime in Houston during those years, we looked at the monthly data for reported robberies and reported assaults for the same period. The plots show long-term trends similar to the trend for reported rapes, but without the increase in level apparent for reported rapes immediately after the law reforms. That slight increase in reported rapes thus might have been produced by the publicity surrounding the reforms.

The significant decrease in the indictment ratio was not what reformers predicted. We suspect that it was a result of the increase in the number of rape reports; as reports of rapes increased in Houston, the number of indictments did not keep pace (Figure 9). Similarly, the impact on sentences probably follows from the decrease in the indictment ratio. As more cases came into the system and as prosecutors became more selective, it is quite likely that the average case being prosecuted was more serious, producing an increase in average sentence length.

DISCUSSION

Our analysis of the impact of rape law reforms in six major urban jurisdictions revealed that legal changes did not produce the dramatic results anticipated by reformers. The reforms had no impact in most of the jurisdictions. While the greatest, albeit limited, impact was found in Detroit, where a single reform dramatically changed all the rape laws, a simple strong reform-weak reform distinction cannot explain the pattern of results. We found no greater impact in two jurisdictions with relatively strong reforms—Chicago and Philadelphia—than in the three jurisdictions with relatively weak reforms.

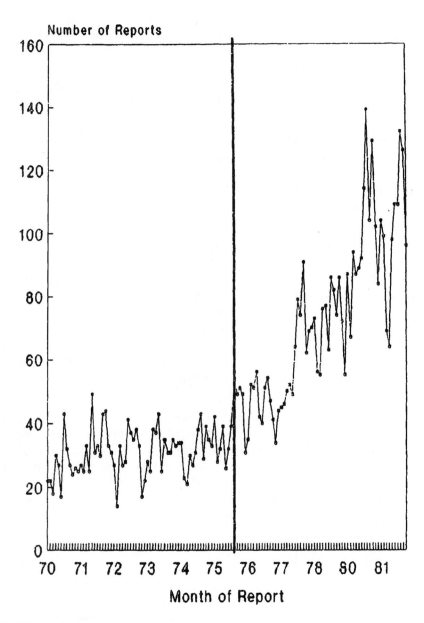

Solid line indicates date of reform

Figure 3. Reports of rape, Houston, Texas, 1970–1981

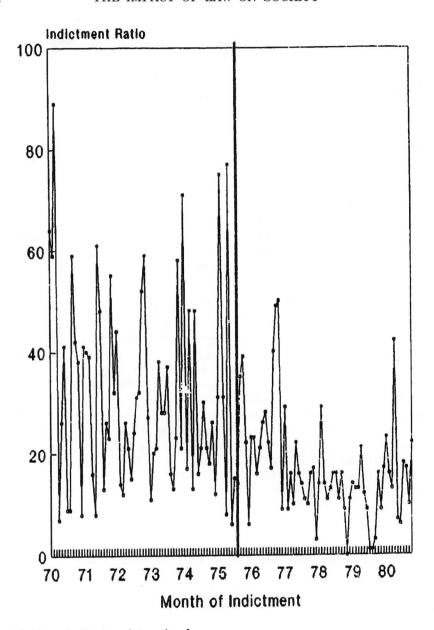

Solid line indicates date of reform

Figure 9. Indictment for rape, Houston, Texas, 1970–1980

As noted earlier, many reforms have failed because reformers assumed that the behavior of decision makers in the criminal justice system is controlled by legal rules. A failure to appreciate the role of discretion in case processing often leads to reforms that do not include adequate incentives for changing behavior. In order to understand our results, we look first at the specific provisions of the rape law reforms, considering how they actually affected decision makers.

Definitional Changes

Reformers anticipated that replacing the single crime of rape with a series of gender-neutral graded offenses with commensurate penalties would lead to an increase in convictions. They predicted that the availability of appropriate lesser charges would enable prosecutors to obtain more convictions through plea bargaining and would discourage jury nullification by providing other options to juries reluctant to convict for forcible rape.

We found no evidence of an increased likelihood of convictions in Detroit, where definitional changes took effect, or in any of the other jurisdictions. The fact that we found no decrease in the proportion of cases resulting in convictions on the original charge indicates that there was no increase in plea bargaining. Our interviews led us to believe that the reforms' implicit focus on the seriousness of the crime of rape may have created an unwillingness to plea bargain that counteracted the facilitative effects of the definitional changes. In Detroit, in fact, the Wayne County Prosecutor's office has an explicit policy restricting plea bargaining. The policy requires the complainant's approval prior to reducing charges. In addition, the policy provides that charges of criminal sexual conduct in the first degree may only, except in unusual circumstances, be negotiated down to criminal sexual conduct in the third degree (CSC3) and that CSC3 charges may not be reduced.

Reformers also expected that the new laws would encourage juries to convict on lesser charges in cases that might otherwise have produced an acquittal for forcible rape. This assumes that prosecutors will ask for instructions on lesser included charges. Prosecutors in Detroit, however, said they were reluctant to ask for these instructions because they feared that jurors would be hopelessly confused if given definitions for criminal sexual conduct in the first, second, third, and fourth degrees. Thus the complexity of the law, considered important for its inclusiveness, may have undermined one of the reformers' goals.

Elimination of Corroboration and Resistance Requirements

Reformers predicted that eliminating the requirements for corroboration and resistance would make it easier to prosecute cases and therefore more likely that prosecutors would file charges and obtain convictions. We believe that reformers were overly optimistic about the effects of these largely symbolic changes. For one thing, court decisions over the years had already considerably loosened both requirements. Officials in every jurisdiction reported that a prompt report or physical evidence of intercourse could corroborate the victim's testimony; thus, it was almost always possible to get past a motion for a judgment of acquittal. As one judge stated, "the case law was so broadly interpreted that a scintilla of corroboration was satisfying." Similarly, courts had ruled that a victim was not required to put her life in jeopardy by resisting an attack, and that evidence of force on the part of the offender was tantamount to proof of nonconsent by the victim. By the mid–1970s the corroboration and resistance requirements could be viewed as minor hurdles if prosecutors wanted to proceed with a case, and formal elimination of the statutory requirements was therefore irrelevant in practice.

More important, elimination of the requirements does nothing to constrain the discretion of decision makers.... [R]eformers often assume that removing alleged legal obstacles will allow decision makers to behave in the "correct" way, when in fact problems are typically not the product of artificial barriers or constraints but of conscious behavioral choices made both individually and as a group by professionals within the system. As one of our respondents explained, the law may no longer require corroboration, but that does not mean that the prosecutor will file charges when the complainant's story is totally uncorroborated.

Prosecutors often make charging decisions based on their estimates of whether cases could be won before a jury; if they believe a jury will look for corroboration and resistance, they will continue to require them for charging. Many prosecutors we interviewed believed, in fact, that jurors are unlikely to convict in the absence of these factors. As one prosecutor noted, "Juries still expect some resistance or some explanation as to why there was none. This is especially true if it was a date gone sour, if we can't show some resistance in this case we're in a lot of trouble." Concerning corroboration, another stated, "If you're talking about consent defenses, jurors are still looking for corroborating evidence—physical injury, a weapon, a hysterical call to the police; old habits and old attitudes die hard, and we can change the law but we can't necessarily change attitudes."

Juries might be influenced if instructed that the victim need not resist her attacker and that her testimony need not be corroborated. Many officials we interviewed believed, in fact, that it could be very important for jurors to hear this, not from the prosecutor, but from the judge. Even when a statute explicitly states the lack of a need for resistance or corroboration, however, such instructions are given at the discretion of the judge and the prosecutor. Some judges routinely give the instruction; others instruct only if requested to do so by the prosecutor. Some judges reported that the prosecutor always asks for the instruction; some said that prosecutors never do. Thus, the potential for impact of the reforms is again diminished by the discretionary nature of the criminal justice system.

Analysis of elimination of corroboration and resistance requirements, then, suggests that reformers had unrealistic expectations concerning their impact. Although these reforms may have sent an important symbolic message, they did not significantly alter the decision making context. Neither requirement was an insurmountable hurdle before the reforms, and the reforms themselves did not constrain the discretion of prosecutors or jurors. In the post reform period, as in the pre reform period, corroboration and resistance evidence may still be important to the successful prosecution of at least some kinds of rape cases.

Rape Shield Laws

Reformers predicted the rape shield laws would have a greater impact on the processing and disposition of sexual assault cases than would the other reforms. They anticipated that the restrictions on evidence damaging to the complainant would prompt more victims to report rapes to the police and would lead directly to an increase in convictions and indirectly to an increase in arrests and prosecutions.

Effects of Weak Shield Laws

We did not expect the weak shield laws of Washington, D.C., Georgia, and Texas to have a significant impact on case processing. The laws adopted in each of these states continue to allow judges considerable discretion in deciding whether to admit sexual history evidence. Case law in Washington, D.C., for example, excludes evidence of the victim's prior sexual conduct with parties other than the defendant but allows evidence of the victim's reputation for chastity if the judge determines that its probative value outweighs its prejudicial effect. The Georgia law allows evidence of the victim's sexual reputation or sexual conduct with third parties if the judge finds it supports an inference that the accused reasonably could have believed the victim consented. And ... Texas does not categorically exclude any sexual conduct evidence; rather, such evidence can be admitted if the judge finds that the evidence is relevant.

By leaving so much to the judge's discretion, the shield laws enacted in these jurisdictions did little to alter the "rules" for handling rape cases.... [T]he Texas shield law in essence made no change. The motion in limine had always been available to prosecutors to exclude irrelevant evidence, and the judge always determined relevance. Prosecutors in Atlanta suggested that Georgia's rape shield law was actually weaker than the case law in effect prior to the law's passage. In both states, much stronger reforms had been presented to legislators. The weak shield laws that were passed can be viewed as symbolic policies designed to placate the interest groups lobbying for change.

Effect of Strong Shield Laws

The rape shield laws enacted in Michigan, Illinois, and Pennsylvania are much stronger. The laws in all three states generally prohibit the introduction of evidence of the victim's past sexual conduct. The prohibition includes evidence of specific instances of sexual activity, reputation evidence, and opinion evidence. There are only very narrow exceptions to the shield. All three jurisdictions permit introduction of the victim's past sexual conduct with the defendant, but only if the judge determines that the evidence is relevant. The shield laws enacted in these states, then, sent a strong message to defense attorneys, prosecutors, and judges. They clearly stated that certain types of sexual history evidence are inadmissible. Unlike the laws adopted in

Texas, Georgia, and the District of Columbia, they also attempted to place meaningful limits on judges' discretion to admit certain kinds of evidence.

One important procedural aspect of the rape shield laws is the requirement of an in camera hearing for determining admissibility of evidence relating to the victim's sexual history. Our interviews with judges, prosecutors and defense attorneys, however, revealed that in camera hearings are rarely if ever held, especially if the evidence concerns sexual conduct between the victim and the defendant. Prosecutors reported that they generally concede the relevance of evidence of a prior sexual relationship between the victim and the defendant and do not challenge defense attorneys who attempt to introduce the evidence without requesting a hearing. Similarly, judges use their discretion to overlook the in camera requirement or to overrule prosecutors' objections to the introduction of the evidence.

It is not surprising that criminal justice officials have found ways to circumvent the formal procedural requirements of the shield laws.... In camera hearings are time consuming and would be a waste of time if judges routinely rule that evidence of a prior relationship between the victim and the defendant is relevant. Rather than going through the motions of challenging the evidence and perhaps alienating other members of the courtroom work group, prosecutors concede the point.

Noncompliance might also be attributed to agreement among prosecutors and judges that evidence of a prior sexual relationship between the victim and the defendant is always relevant to the issue of consent. Reformers believed that the relevance of this kind of evidence would depend on factors such as the nature and duration of the sexual relationship or the separation in time from the alleged rape. We believe decision makers have developed a much simpler rule based on shared norms of relevance and fairness in evidentiary issues. Their "admissibility rule" states that if the sexual conduct was with the defendant, it is relevant. Like "going rates" in sentencing ... or "normal crime" categories in charging ... the rule routinizes and simplifies the decision making process.

The disregard of the requirement for hearings contradicts ... [one writer's] assertion that legal rules are most effective when they specify procedural steps in case processing. The in camera hearings required by rape shield laws, however, differ from other procedural requirements in one important way. While the laws mandate hearings in certain situations and clearly specify the procedures to be followed, they do not provide for review or sanction of judges who fail to follow the law. Moreover, if a defendant is acquitted because the judge violated the law and either admitted potentially relevant evidence without a hearing or allowed the defense attorney to use legally inadmissible evidence, the victim cannot appeal the acquittal or the judge's decisions. If, on the other hand, the judge followed the law and refused to admit seemingly irrelevant sexual history evidence, the defendant can appeal his conviction. All the consequences, in other words, would lead judges to err in favor of the defendant.

The avoidance of in camera hearings clearly undermines the reforms to the extent that issues of relevance are not debated if the sexual conduct was between the victim and the defendant. Their absence does not mean legally prohibited evidence of sexual conduct between the victim and third parties is being admitted. To the contrary, it appears that hearings are avoided on these issues because the members of the work group agree that such evidence cannot be admitted. The other side of the admissibility rule, in other words, is that sexual conduct between the victim and parties other than the defendant is not relevant. Judges in every jurisdiction stated that defense attorneys don't even attempt to introduce the more questionable kinds of sexual history evidence. As one judge in Chicago explained, "Attorneys are warned that I will interpret the law strictly and they don't even try to bring it up unless it concerns the victim and the defendant."

If evidence clearly proscribed by the law is effectively excluded, we must consider other explanations for the lack of impact of the strong rape shield laws. Why is it that even these strong laws did not produce the types of changes envisioned by reformers? For one thing, the shield laws primarily affect cases that go to trial and, particularly, the small percentage of cases tried before a jury. Moreover, sexual history evidence is only relevant in cases where the defense is consent. Since it is unlikely that consent will be the defense when a woman is raped by a total stranger, this means that sexual history evidence will be relevant only when the victim and the defendant are acquainted. The shield laws, then, have the potential to affect directly only the relatively few rape cases in which the victim and the defendant are acquainted, the defendant claims the victim consented, and the defendant insists on a trial.

Unfortunately, no data are available on how often a complainant's sexual history entered into cases before the rape shield laws were enacted. Although reformers cited horror stories regarding harassment of victims in court, most respondents in jurisdictions we studied could recall few, if any, pre-reform cases in which defense attorneys used this tactic. If testimony regarding the victim's sexual history with third parties was rarely introduced, then restricting the use of such evidence would produce little change. Respondents in several jurisdictions reported, in fact, that previous case rulings had accomplished much of what the rape shield laws were designed to do.

We have discussed the weaknesses of the individual reforms and have explained why the reforms did not produce the instrumental results anticipated by reformers. These results might also be due to the fact that the reforms had the potential to affect only certain types of cases.... [There is an important] distinction between aggravated rape and "simple" rape. Aggravated rapes are those that involve strangers, multiple assailants, or armed force; simple rapes are committed by unarmed acquaintances, acting alone.... [M]ost of the rape law reforms have been directed at simple rape cases, and thus the greatest impact should have been seen in these cases. If, as we argue above, the laws fail to place meaningful constraint on the discretion of decision maker, then impact could only be achieved by modifying decision makers' basic distrust of victims of simple rape. Further research should address this issue.

Evidence of Impact

Two sites did show some evidence of impact. In Detroit we found increases in reports of rape, in the ratio of indictments to reports, and in the length of the maximum sentence. In Houston also we found some evidence of increases in reporting and sentence length, but they were accompanied by a decrease in the indictment ratio.

Reports

We were surprised to find increased reports of rape in the jurisdiction with the weakest reforms (Houston) as well as in the jurisdiction with the strongest reforms (Detroit). The appearance of the increase just as the new laws went into effect suggests that the increases may have resulted from the publicity surrounding the reforms. If an increase in reporting resulted from actual improved treatment of victims due to the legal changes, we would expect a more gradual impact on reporting as knowledge of the improved treatment spreads through the community. Unfortunately, the scope of our study limits our ability to interpret these results. Because the legal reforms in Houston and Detroit were among the earliest in the country and because they coincided with extensive national media attention to the crime of rape, we suspect that their implementation may have occasioned more publicity than resulted in the other jurisdictions. However, we have no data to support this speculative explanation.

It is also possible that the increases in reporting we detected actually reflect changes in police behavior rather than in the behavior of victims. We had to rely on Uniform Crime Reports to measure reporting by victims, and these data are a product not only of victim complaints, but also of police decisions on whether to count complaints as valid reports of criminal incidents. Again, however, we do not have data on police department operations that would allow us to test this possibility.

Indictments

The most interesting results are our findings on the impact of reforms on the likelihood of indictment. Our analysis revealed a significant increase in the ratio of indictments to reports in Detroit, but a significant decrease in the likelihood of indictment in Houston. As we noted earlier, it seems very likely that the decrease in Houston represents a failure to keep up with the increase in reported rapes. If prosecutors simply continued to prosecute about the same number of cases, an increase in cases entering the system would result in a decrease in the indictment ratio. In Texas, indictment is by grand jury; the additional burden of taking a case to the grand jury may have affected judgments about how many cases could be prosecuted.

In Detroit we found an increase in the indictment ratio even as the number of reported cases increased. The results could have been produced by changes in police or prosecutor decisions or by both. It seems more likely that prosecutors would be most affected, because the legal changes generally involved evidentiary rules affecting the likelihood of obtaining convictions at trial. Our interviews tended to confirm this. Detroit police reported that prosecutors were refusing fewer warrants in rape cases since passage of the laws, and a victim-witness unit respondent said that more "date rape" cases were getting into the court system.

This increase in the indictment ratio suggests that prosecutors are more willing to file charges in borderline cases. We can speculate that some of the additional cases being reported in the post-reform period were the kinds of cases victims were reluctant to report prior to the police of reform legislation: cases involving acquaintances, cases involving sexually promiscuous men or women, cases with little or no corroborating evidence, and so on. Presumably, some of these additional cases were the simple rape cases that ... were so difficult to prove in the pre reform era. Given this assumption, we might have expected the indictment rate to decline. The fact that it increased even as reports increased is thus an important finding.

The greater willingness to prosecute might be due in part to the fact that the definitions of the various degrees of criminal sexual conduct are much clearer than the old definition of rape. The current Michigan law provides clear guidelines for prosecutors to follow in screening rape cases. It carefully defines the elements of each offense, specifies the circumstances that constitute coercion, and lists the situations in which no showing of force is required. Although the judges, prosecutors, and defense attorneys we interviewed in Detroit thought the new laws might be confusing to jurors, they nevertheless spoke approvingly of the clarity and precision of the new statute. One prosecutor commented that "the elements of force and coercion are clearly spelled out." Another explained that the law "sets out with greater particularity what the elements of the offense are." By spelling out the acts that constitute sexual assault, the circumstances that imply consent and nonconsent, and the types of evidence that are unnecessary or irrelevant, the Michigan laws may have made it easier to recognize acceptable cases.

Although our finding of no increase in the conviction ratio in Detroit represents a failure of reformers' expectations, the stability of that ratio is important. If, as we suggested, the increase in indictments that occurred resulted from more borderline cases entering the system, we might have expected a decline in the overall likelihood of conviction. The fact that the total number of convictions kept pace with the increase in indictments suggests that defendants in these borderline cases are being convicted.

Sentencing

We found an increase in average sentence coinciding with the change in law in Houston and Detroit and increases in sentence length over the time period studied but not attributable specifically to the law reforms in other jurisdictions. We suspect that these widespread increases reflect changes in attitudes toward the crime of rape rather than changes in the laws of rape. The enactment of rape law reforms, while not aimed directly at increasing sentences for rape, reflected public demands that rape be treated as a very serious offense. Judges may have responded by imposing more severe sentences on those convicted for rape. These changes in attitudes toward the crime of rape might also have fostered a reluctance to plea bargain—and a consequent increase in sentence severity—in rape cases.

The Effect of Comprehensive Changes

Although we found some evidence in Houston of increases in reporting and in sentence length, the impact we found in Detroit, although limited, stands out as the only example of the reforms affecting official decision making in the manner predicted by reformers. One interpretation of the finding is that the criminal justice system can only be affected by the kind of dramatic, comprehensive changes enacted in Michigan. Clearly, the Michigan reform was broader than those adopted in the other five jurisdictions we studied. It also was accomplished in one major revision of state codes. Although we have explored the weaknesses of the individual legal changes, it may be that only a comprehensive reform package, by sending a strong and unambiguous message to decision makers, can overcome the resistance to change inherent in the system.

Our findings clearly contradict ... [the] idea that a reform involving drastic change will encounter greater resistance within the system, especially when the behavior affected is perceived as important.... We suspect that if attitudes are to be changed, dramatic, comprehensive changes that demand attention may be required....

We do not have measures of officials' attitudes before and after the law reforms, but we did conduct interviews across our six jurisdictions following the reforms. Although respondents in all jurisdictions expressed attitudes generally favorable toward the legal reforms, Detroit officials took the strongest positions on excluding complainant's sexual history when they were questioned about a series of hypothetical cases. We cannot be sure, of course, that those attitudes were the product of the comprehensive reforms and not a causal factor that led to their enactment....

CONCLUSION

We have shown that the ability of rape reform legislation to produce instrumental change is limited. In most of the jurisdictions we studied, the reforms had no impact. Our results are not surprising in light of the large body of literature detailing the failure of legal reforms. We found, like many others who have studied reforms aimed at the court system, that the rape law reforms placed few constraints on the tremendous discretion exercised by decision makers in the criminal justice system.

591

The results of our study suggest that instrumental change will be especially difficult to achieve when reforms are designed to remove legal barriers to prosecution and conviction. If, for example, work group norms support prosecution and conviction of rape cases in which the victim did not resist or her allegations cannot be corroborated, then officials find ways to circumvent the legal barriers, and as a result the official removal of these barriers will have little effect in practice. If, on the other hand, informal norms oppose prosecution and conviction of these kinds of cases, simply removing the legal barriers will be ineffective unless the discretion that allows informal norms to guide decision making is constrained or meaningful incentives to change the norms are created.

Reforms aimed at improving the treatment of victims may be less likely than other reforms to provide even minimal constraints on discretion or incentives to change. Victim-oriented reforms are unlikely to facilitate the smooth and efficient flow of cases through the system, and they may conflict with values concerning the rights of defendants. In our legal system, the defendant has considerably more "power" than the victim. Not only are the rights of the defendant constitutionally protected, but in defending those rights the defendant has, at least in theory, an advocate in the defense attorney. The prosecutor does not play the same role for the victim, but is instead an advocate for the state, and the interests of the state may often conflict with those of the victim. The protections afforded the defendant are further guaranteed by the process of appellate review. Judicial decisions that negatively affect the defendant can be appealed to a higher court; decisions that impinge on a victim by decreasing the likelihood of conviction are legally unreviewable.

This suggests that the advocates of rape law reform may need to create incentives for change by monitoring implementation of the reforms and by applying public pressure on criminal justice officials who fail to comply. In some jurisdictions the officials we interviewed said that there was intense monitoring at the time of the law reforms but that the public and the media lost interest shortly thereafter. These officials perceived very little continuing attention to their handling of rape cases. Such attention may be necessary to produce and preserve change.

The fact that the rape law reforms did not produce the broad effects anticipated by reformers does not mean, of course, that the reforms had no impact. Most respondents in the six jurisdictions expressed strong support for the reforms, which they felt had resulted in more sensitive treatment of victims of rape. Officials believed that passage of the reforms sent an important symbolic message regarding the treatment of rape cases and rape victims.

In the long run, this symbolic message may be more important than the instrumental change that was anticipated but generally not accomplished. Under the old laws it was assumed that chastity is relevant to consent and credibility; that corroboration is required because women tend to lie about being raped; and that resistance is required to demonstrate nonconsent.

These assumptions clearly were archaic in light of changes in attitudes toward sexual relations and toward the role of women in society. Those who lobbied for rape law reform sought to refute these common law principles and to shift the focus in a rape case from the reputation and behavior of the victim to the unlawful acts of the offender. In doing so, the reforms may have produced long-term attitude change that is difficult to measure in a legal impact study.

We did find more than symbolic impact in Detroit. We speculated that the increase in the indictment ratio there represented a greater willingness to prosecute in "borderline" cases. Because we were not able to examine the impact of the reforms on different kinds of cases, we could not test this hypothesis directly. We also could not test for more subtle kinds of impact that might have been masked when we analyzed case outcomes overall. We have discussed ... the distinction between "aggravated" rape and "simple" rape and ... [the] assertion that these cases have always been dealt with in very different ways. If the proportion of real and simple rapes entering the courts has changed, some effects of the rape law reform could have been masked. Further research should address this issue.

NOTES AND QUESTIONS

1.   A number of studies have found that the various types of rape reform had relatively little instrumental impact. Wallace D. Loh, "The Impact of Common Law and Reform Rape Statutes on Prosecution: An Empirical Study," 55 *Washington Law Review* 543 (1980), for example, studied prosecution records from Seattle from 1972 to 1977. He found that the main impact of the reform laws was only symbolic. Rita Gunn & Rick Linden, "The Impact of Law Reform on the Processing of Sexual Assault Cases," 34 *Canadian Review of Sociology* 155 (1997), find little impact from a reform in Winnipeg that was similar to the Michigan reform laws. They comment:

> The success of rape law reform may also have been limited by the fact that sexual assault cases are inherently difficult to prosecute, as the crime typically takes place in private and there are rarely witnesses other than the victim and the accused. Since the prosecution must establish proof beyond a reasonable doubt when evidence may consist simply of one person's word against another's, factors such as corroboration and recency of complaint are important in presenting a strong case even if they are not legally required. (p. 169)

Gunn and Linden also point out that rape is not treated entirely differently from other crimes. Conviction rates in contested trials for all crimes are low. Police and prosecutors exercise discretion to filter out cases that they fear will not be won at trial and so attrition from complaints to arrests to prosecutions to convictions is present in all offenses. And most convictions come from plea bargaining. Cases that are tried involve something unusual.

2.   Stacey Futter and Walter R. Mebane, Jr., "The Effects of Rape Law Reform on Rape Case Processing," 16 *Berkeley Women's Law Journal* 72, 73–

74 (2001), report: "The results of our study strongly suggest that implementation of more liberal and feminist-oriented legal provisions during the years 1970–1991 did, for the most part, increase the number of rape reports that police / agencies deemed well founded.... [There were also] increases in the number of 'clearances.' " Clearances reflect the number of arrests or other situations where the police deem the crime solved. It does not necessarily measure the number of convictions that sent people to jail.

3. <u>Jury Simulation Studies of Rape Reform.</u> Eugene Borgida, "Legal Reform of Rape Laws," in Leonard Bickman (ed.), 2 *Applied Social Psychology Annual* at 211 (1981), studied rape shield laws by jury simulation methods. These laws limit evidence of the victim's prior sexual history in a rape trial. Borgida tested the common law rule that allowed evidence about the victim's prior sexual experience into evidence, moderate reforms that leave the decision about admissibility to the discretion of the trial judge, and radical reforms that blocks almost all such evidence.

Borgida attempted to answer many of the questions often raised about jury simulation studies. He used qualified adult jurors, including some who were only eligible and some who had just served on a criminal jury. (However, he excluded those who had served on a case involving sexual assault). He used a 2 to 2 ½ hour professionally produced videotape of a trial after consultation with attorneys and those serving at a rape crisis center about its content. All trial variations had the key procedural features of an actual trial—opening statements, victim's testimony and cross-examination, closing arguments, and the judge's charge. (However, apparently, there was no voir dire to select the jurors). He used six person juries which deliberated for a maximum of 50 minutes. Jurors made only a guilty/not-guilty decision. They did not impose the penalty. Still Borgida concedes that there could have been a problem with role-playing: "Role playing must be acknowledged as a threat to the external validity of our findings."

In the first study, Borgida used *6 different versions* of the videotaped trial, where consent as a defense was in issue: (1) In half the cases consent was probable; in half it was not (e.g., victim and defendant were close friends or hardly knew each other; complainant's resistance was varied; the place they met was varied). (2) Then the type of exclusionary rule applied to victim's past sexual history was varied—common law, moderate and radical reform. The results showed that jurors were reluctant to convict defendant when any testimony about the complainant's prior sexual history with third parties other than the defendant was introduced, even when consent was unlikely in the circumstances. When prior sexual history was introduced, jurors readily inferred consent; more carefully and unfavorably scrutinized complainant's rather than defendant's character; attributed more responsibility to complainant; and even downgraded the skill and competence of the prosecutor. (In other words, they found rationalizations for acquitting the defendant). Rather than weigh the facts in the case, jurors seemed to respond primarily to prior sexual history and base a judgment on it alone. Only the radical reform rule in an improbable consent situation led to convictions at a high rate. Even in a conviction-biased case, the admission of prior sexual history testimony—under either the common law or the moderate reform rule—was clearly detrimental to the prosecutor's case. In an acquittal-biased case, even the radical reform rule did not enhance the conviction rate. Rape is a judgment that these jurors did not want to reach. Note that this is a simulated study—even where the subjects know that they are "playing a game," they do not convict for rape except in very clear cases.

In the second study, the judge gave the jurors instructions concerning the use of the victim's prior sexual history. Of course, the control group got no such instruction so Borgida could compare the impact of the instruction on the test groups. One group received the general instruction from the Minnesota rules of Criminal Procedure about deciding the case only on the basis of the evidence. The other group received a special limiting instruction as advocated by some reformers. Jurors were told:

> Some people wrongly assume that a woman who has consented to sexual relations in the past is more likely to have consented to sexual relations on a particular occasion like the one in this case. However, the fact that a woman has engaged in sexual relations with one man, or with several, does not prove that she consented to the act in issue. This is important to keep in mind because such beliefs may unfairly prejudice your assessment of the evidence in this case. Once such impressions of the complainant's moral character are formed, subsequent considerations of the evidence may no longer be as impartial as they should be.

Borgida found that the special limited instruction was not as effective in reducing prejudice as the general one. When they thought about the issue, jurors disagreed with the reformers about the likelihood of consent by a sexually experienced woman. The jury system brings into court (or into an experiment such as this one) the opinions and views of the community, for better or worse.

Borgida's study is more than 25 years old as this text is written. In your opinion, is it likely that if another researcher ran the same study today, she might get different results? Do you think that attitudes about women's sexual experience have changed in that time? That the attitudes of police and prosecutors have changed? That the attitudes of those likely to be found on juries have changed?

4. Bill Lueders, *Cry Rape* (2006) cautions us not to assume that everything about the crime of rape has changed. The book is the story of Patty, a single mother who reported that she had been raped at her home in Madison, Wisconsin in September of 1997. A rookie police detective did not believe her because she did not act as he thought rape victims would act. Under intense questioning by more senior officers, Patty recanted. Then she tried to reassert her claim that she had been raped. In February of 1998, the Madison Police Department charged Patty with obstruction of justice. Patty's lawyer got the state crime laboratory to test her bed sheet, and the lab found semen on the sheet. DNA taken from the semen matched that of a man known to the police.

Patty brought claims before the Madison Police and Fire Commission and then a federal law suit. As part of these claims, she was subjected to cross examination on a deposition by a private lawyer hired by the City. Lueders characterizes the lawyer as tormenting and bullying Patty as she was forced to recount the details of her rape. In October 2004, the man whose DNA had been found on the sheets was convicted of raping Patty and sentenced to 50 years in prison. After Lueders' book was published in 2006, the Madison City Council apologized to Patty, paid her lawyer's fees and expenses, voted not to employ the law firm who had handled the deposition for ten years, and asked the Madison Police Department to create a new policy on interviewing victims of crimes such as rape. The Chief of Police, who had not been Chief when the incidents took place, finally issued an apology late in 2006. Note that none of the various rape reform laws deals directly with what happened to Patty.

5. <u>Linguistic Analysis of Rape Reform.</u> Gregory Matoesian studied the rape shield law as it played out in one of the more famous trials of the past quarter century. Gregory Matoesian, "Language, Law, and Society: Policy Implications of the Kennedy Smith Rape Trial," 29 *Law & Society Review* 669 (1995). See also Gregory M. Matoesian, *Law and the Language of Identity: Discourse in the William Kennedy Smith Rape Trial* (2001). He concluded that rape shield statutes are unlikely to block some of the assumptions that they were designed to screen out. Unfortunately, he says, defense attorneys in rape cases still have ample room to drop subtle hints about rape victims' sexual histories and characters—hints that play on enduring sexist assumptions that many jurors bring with them to the trial. In the case Matoesian analyzed, Patty Bowman (then age 29) accused William Kennedy Smith (then age 30) of raping her at about 4:00 a.m. in March of 1991. Smith was prosecuted for this offense. Bowman was the single mother of a chronically ill infant. Smith was a medical student, and the nephew of Senator Edward Kennedy, the late President John F. Kennedy, and the late Senator Bobby Kennedy. Bowman was the stepdaughter of a wealthy industrialist. The trial was one of the first to be televised nationally, and many followed it closely. On December 11, 1991 the jury found Kennedy Smith not guilty of rape after just 77 minutes of deliberation. There was no question that Smith and Bowman had had sexual relations on the beach near the Kennedy house; the issue was whether she had consented or had been forced into sex without her consent. We must remember that the prosecution had the burden of proving absence of consent beyond a reasonable doubt.

Roy Black, Smith's lawyer, could not question Bowman about her prior sexual activity because of the Florida rape shield law. However, Matoesian analyzed the language of cross examination that he found in the trial record. He argued that Black questioned Bowman in such a way as to draw on the taken-for-granted assumptions about men and women at bars, sexual relations between a man and a woman who have just met that night, and the likely conduct of a woman who has been raped. Black did not have to ask the specific kind of questions blocked by the shield law to prejudice the jury against Bowman; Matoesian details the way that Black could still draw on assumptions when questioning her, without ever crossing the line drawn by rape shield statutes. Matoesian asserts: "jurors possess a stultifying penchant for entertaining traditional stereotypes about the nature of male/female sexual relations and for incorporating this inaccurate extralegal evidence in their deliberations."

Black cross-examined Bowman about meeting Smith in a trendy nightclub:

Black:	You had an engrossing conversation?
Bowman:	Yes sir.
Black:	You didn't have to be involved with the rest of the bar scene?
Bowman:	Yes sir.
Black:	You had found somebody that you had connected with?
Bowman:	Yes sir.
Black:	You were happy to have found that?
Bowman:	It was nice.
Black:	You were no longer—, in fact you were with him almost exclusively?
Bowman:	I don't know.

* * *

Black:	And you were interested in him as a person?
Bowman:	He seemed like a nice person?
Black:	Interested enough to give him a ride home?
Bowman:	I saw no problem with giving him a ride home . . .
Black:	You were interested enough that you were hoping that he would ask you for your phone number?
Bowman:	That was later.
Black:	Interested enough that when he said to come into the house, you went into the house with him?
Bowman:	It wasn't necessarily an interest with William. It was an interest in the house.
Black:	Interested enough that at sometime during that period of time you took off your pantyhose?
Bowman:	I still don't know how my pantyhose came off? . . .
Black:	. . . [W]hen you arrived in the parking lot in the car you kissed Will. Is that correct?
Bowman:	I testified that when we arrived at the estate, he gave me a goodnight peck.
Black:	That's all it was?
Bowman:	Yes sir.
Black:	Nothing of any—, nothing more than that?
Bowman:	No.
Black:	Did you describe this to Detective Rigolo as a sweet little kiss?
Bowman:	I said a short sweet little kiss . . .
Black:	Even though you were concerned, for example, about your child, you still wanted to see the house?
Bowman:	Yes.
Black:	Even though you had to get up early in the next morning to take care of her, you still wanted to see the house?

Bowman: I wasn't planning on spending any extended amount of time in the home.

Matoesian states: "the victim [Bowman] engaged in a myriad of activities with the defendant prior to the incident which, on the face of it, appeared more congruous with a male and female in an incipient relationship or, perhaps at the very least, an 'interest' in an incipient relationship, than with a crime of rape." Black generated skepticism about her story by subtle contrasts in his questioning. There was an underlying ironic structure: "You weren't interested in him, but you went into the house with him?" "It was late in the evening, but you wanted to see the house?" How can you have "a short sweet little kiss" from a man you just met in a bar? How do you have a innocent interest in the Kennedy family house when you take off your pantyhose? If you were with Smith "almost exclusively" at the bar, were you not picking him up for sexual reasons?

Matoesian drew on studies of men's and women's differing ideas about sex and relationship to raise questions about whether these ironic contrasts are as straightforward as they might seem. Perhaps someone might take off her pantyhose because they feel uncomfortable, but this action could be understood by someone else as inviting sex. John Conley and William O'Barr, in their book *Just Words* (1998), report on the responses of male and female students who were asked to read Matoesian's research. Male students responded by interpreting the removal of pantyhose as an invitation to sex. Some of the female students, however, made a distinction between removing pantyhose and removing underwear; they felt that someone who was about to go for a walk on the beach might well remove pantyhose without intending to consent to intercourse.

Other gestures that from one perspective might be taken to indicate an "all-or-nothing, impersonal, and penetration-oriented normative preference" may, from another perspective, be signals of incipient interest in developing a romantic relationship—one which might eventually lead to full-blown sexual intercourse, but not necessarily immediately. Two people with quite different (sometimes gendered) perspectives might disagree as to whether certain actions constitute consent to impersonal sex. Or, someone could be unsure of what she wants at first, but then become clear that she does not want to engage in sex. Under sexist stereotypes, "good" women would never be interested in impersonal sex. If a woman has indicated that she might be interested, then some might unconsciously assume she is not a "virtuous" woman—and therefore cannot claim rape under almost any circumstance. This is exactly the kind of thinking that rape shield laws were designed to prevent. But notice that Matoesian is here dealing with a deep level of culture and language that cannot be regulated simply by prohibiting discussion of a particular topic such as the victim's prior sexual history.

In her testimony, Bowman also described Smith after sexual intercourse as smug, calm, arrogant, cold and indifferent. When Attorney Black directly examined the defendant, Smith testified that after intercourse on the beach, "we chatted for a couple of minutes and I kissed her and I said, 'I gonna go to bed.' " She asked to come into the house, and he said that it was too late. "I was tired. I mean I'd been out late and I really, I guess, I wanted her to leave ... maybe that was not romantic but, you know, that's what happened." Bowman asked for Smith's telephone number, and he claimed not to know the number at the house.

Matoesian says: "After the alleged incident ... the defendant was 'calm,' 'cold,' and 'indifferent' to the victim—'not being very nice' nor 'too romantic' ... [T]he defendant does not invite the victim to spend the night, which might preserve at least a minimal sense of 'romance,' and when the victim is thus put in the unenviable face-threatening position of having to ask permission to come in the house, possibly to spend the night, he refuses her request ... And ... the defendant never asks for the victim's phone number, as she had hoped he would and which would perhaps again restore a minimal sense of 'romance' or even salvage remotely the possibility of a future date and the genesis of a relationship.... Through this motivational nexus of gender relevant norms, the defense attempts to expose the putative purpose of the evening not as 'romance' or even as a prelude to a possible future relationship or an impending date but, at its starkest, as impersonal sex."

Attorney Black also asked Bowman about "your daughter's father" rather than "your ex-husband." Matoesian notes that this comment mobilized the jury's ideas about sexual history. Bowman belonged to the nonmarital category of "unwed mother," which carried "attendant characterological and sexual history inferences such a designation culturally inherits." Implicitly, the jury was being told that Bowman might well be willing to have sex even the first time she met William Kennedy Smith as a step toward a relationship with a member of a celebrity family.

In his opening statement to the jury, Attorney Black also challenged Bowman's version of the events by pointing to her reactions after the alleged rape:

> She goes into the house. She goes to the kitchen area—and makes a call to her friend Ann Mercer, who is an acquaintance. That's the first time they have ever gone out together was that night. She doesn't call anyone in her family, the police, any relative, but she calls Ann Mercer and says, "I've been raped. Come and pick me up."

Then when Black cross-examined Bowman's friend, Ann Mercer, he drew attention to the fact that after Bowman said that she had been raped, she then commented several times that she wanted to find her shoes. Bowman did not leave immediately although she had a car there. Had she done this, she would have expressed a concern for her safety or her distaste for the experience. Instead, she was concerned with finding her shoes. Black worked to paint the situation as one where Bowman consented to sex under the assumption that she was developing a romantic relationship with a medical student who was a member of the Kennedy family ... Black's implication was that Bowman claimed rape when she discovered that Smith wanted only impersonal sex, and he wanted her to go home.

Matoesian says that "the causal efficacy of [the] shield [law] can be ... distinguished from the complex details of covert descriptive inference, legal-cultural inferences superseding the statutory perimeter of [the] shield's operation and thereby eroding its significance." This does not mean that rape shield laws are useless; to the contrary, Matoesian notes that it is quite possible that these laws have been "modestly successful, blocking the derivation of inferences regarding overt sexual history reference." However, this may just begin to address the many levels of complex cultural inferences at play in trials—a level that can only be addressed through more detailed analysis of how language and culture work in these settings. He concludes: "the rape trial, like other adversarial trials, is not necessarily about truth and falsity but about winning and losing in a warlike yet tightly structured game of forensic strategy—a war of words, utterances, and ideas, a war in which the ability to perform knowledge through talk represents the preeminent weapon of domination."

See also the discussion of limitations and advantages of legal intervention in domestic violence cases (and other policy areas) in the notes following Reading 2.2 in Chapter 2.

(4.15) Tilting at Windmills: *Brown II* and the Hopeless Quest to Resolve Deep–Seated Social Conflict Through Litigation

Gerald N. Rosenberg

24 Law and Inequality 31 (2006).

Like the Masters and Apprentices of Jedi Knights and Sith Lords, major Supreme Court cases often come in pairs. But unlike their "Star Wars" counterparts, the second decision seldom receives the same acknowledgment and attention as the first.... [T]he 1954 *Brown*[138] decision is celebrated as one of the Supreme Court's greatest decisions, but the 1955 decision of the same name (*Brown II*)[139] is often overlooked. In 2004, there were numerous commemorations of the fiftieth anniversary of Brown throughout the country, yet the fiftieth anniversary of *Brown II* in 2005 was hardly noted. Focusing on the lead cases ... rather than the follow-up cases ... is understandable because the former set out the constitutional principles while the latter apply them. But for principles to matter, they must be implemented. Thus, it is fitting that the University of Minnesota Law School and *Law & Inequality: A Journal of Theory and Practice* have chosen to focus on the fiftieth anniversary of *Brown II*.

---

138. 347 U.S. 483 (1954).   **139.** 349 U.S. 294 (1955).

I. Introduction

On May 31, 1955, the U.S. Supreme Court announced its decision in *Brown v. Board of Education* (*Brown II*). The issue in *Brown II* was how to implement the Court's decision in the first *Brown* case, decided a year earlier on May 17, 1954, that racial segregation in public elementary and secondary schools was unconstitutional. In its 1954 *Brown* decision, the Court requested further argument on the issue of implementation. At the reargument, the lead plaintiff, the National Association for the Advancement of Colored People ("NAACP"), took a position that they called "generous in the extreme."[140] Although urging immediate desegregation, the NAACP was willing to forego immediate implementation if the Court set a firm deadline for desegregation no later than September 1956. In contrast, the Southern states argued against either immediate desegregation or any firm deadline for doing so. They argued for giving discretion to local district courts and officials with no deadline or timetables. The United States, arguing as an *amicus*, took a middle position, arguing that desegregation should be as "prompt as possible."

The position that some of the Southern states took before the Supreme Court was extraordinary. In essence, they made it clear that they would not conform to any decision requiring desegregation. Consider the colloquy between Chief Justice Warren and a lawyer for South Carolina, S. E. Rogers:

> Warren: "But you are not willing to say here that therewould be an honest attempt to conform to this decree,if we did not leave it to the district court?"
>
> Rogers: "No, I am not. Let us get the word 'honest' out of there."
>
> Warren: "No, leave it in."
>
> Rogers: "No, because I would have to tell you that right nowwe would not conform, we would not send ourwhite children to Negro schools."[141]

Rogers admitted in response to questions that this would result in no desegregation, "perhaps not until 2015 or 2045." Thus, reargument ended with at least one Southern state stating it would not conform to a Court decision requiring desegregation.

In *Brown II,* the Court remanded the cases to the district courts from which they originated and ordered them to take "such proceedings and enter such orders and decrees consistent with this opinion as are necessary and proper to admit to public schools on a racially nondiscriminatory basis with all deliberate speed the parties to these cases."[142] Clearly, the Court didn't accept the NAACP's call for either immediate desegregation or a firm deadline. On the other hand, it did order the lower federal courts to desegregate the public

---

140. Michael Klarman, *From Jim Crow to Civil Rights: The Supreme Court and the Struggle for Racial Equality* 313 (2004).

141. "Argument: The Oral Argument before the Supreme Court in Brown v. Board of Education of Topeka, 1952–1955" at 414 (Leon Friedman, ed., 1969).

142. 349 U.S. at 301.

schools with "all deliberate speed." Although the Supreme Court didn't back away from *Brown*, it didn't press forward either.

Supporters of desegregation have consistently criticized the decision. Calling *Brown II* "misguided," Klarman has recently written that the "justices chose vagueness and gradualism."[143] Charles Ogletree is harsher, understanding *Brown II* as "a critical compromise, which . . . undermined the broad purposes of the campaign to end racial segregation immediately and comprehensively."[144] Ogletree argues that with the "all deliberate speed" standard, the Court's "reluctance to take a more forceful position on ending segregation immediately played into the hands of the integration opponents." The essential argument of *Brown II's* critics is that by not requiring immediate desegregation, nor setting a firm date for desegregation, segregationists were encouraged to evade the decision and resist desegregation. The underlying assumption is that if the Court had acted more forcefully, desegregation would have occurred.

In this Article, I argue that this "legalist" criticism misses the underlying political factors at work. It is overly legalistic because it focuses too narrowly on the Court to the exclusion of the larger society. It unduly privileges the Court and abstracts it from the broader political, social, and economic world in which it operates. To look to the words of the Court as the cause of the lack of desegregation is to look in the wrong place. To sharpen my point: it would not have mattered what the Court ordered in *Brown II* because there was insufficient political support for desegregation. The problem was not in the Court but in the broader society itself. Looking to the courts to overcome racism and racial segregation has a romantic allure but is no more likely to succeed than tilting at windmills is likely to subdue enemies.

Arguments about "what ifs" are suggestive rather than definitive. Exploring a counterfactual—asking what would have happened if the Supreme Court had ordered immediate desegregation—cannot produce unassailable findings. But this is the problem faced by the legalist critics of *Brown II*. To support my argument that the language of *Brown II* was irrelevant to desegregation, I can examine what actually happened in the wake of *Brown II* and highlight the factors involved. I can also explore other decisions involving segregation to see if strength of judicial language produces compliance. Doing so strongly suggests that the language of *Brown II* played little role in accounting for subsequent events.

II. Lack of Implementation

The argument starts by examining the implementation of *Brown* in the eleven Southern and six Border states and the District of Columbia that legally required or allowed racial segregation of public schools. What implementation? By the 1963–64 school year, barely one in one hundred African–American children in the eleven Southern states of the Old Confederacy was

---

143. Klarman, supra, at 320.

144. Charles Ogletree, *All Deliberate Speed* xiii (2004).

in a school with Whites.[145] Excluding Texas and Tennessee, which accounted for most of the desegregation, fewer than one-half of 1% of African–American school children were in school with Whites. That is, almost a decade after *Brown*, nothing had changed for nearly ninety-nine out of every one hundred African–American children in those states. They still attended all Black schools.

There was some implementation in the Border states. The District of Columbia led the way with 97% of its African–American school children in school with Whites in the 1956–57 school year. The six Border states moved more slowly, only reaching the 50% figure in the 1964–65 school year, a full decade after *Brown*.

While the record in the Border states was better, nowhere was *Brown* fully implemented. The decision was widely and openly flouted. To the legalist critics, this can be explained by *Brown II's* vague and loose standard. If only the Court had required immediate desegregation or set a firm date for it, these critics argue, desegregation would have occurred. However, there is a powerful alternative explanation for the lack of desegregation that focuses on the lack of broader support throughout the country for school desegregation. Political and social forces (both local and national) did not support desegregation, providing no pressure for compliance. The Supreme Court, acting alone, lacked the power to implement *Brown*.

III.   Why No Implementation

A closer look at these factors suggests seven reasons why it would not have mattered what the Court said in *Brown II*.

A.   *Congress*

Congress never supported the Court's decision. In fact, a sizable number of its members did just the opposite. In 1956, in a remarkable document entitled "A Declaration of Constitutional Principles" (commonly referred to as the *Southern Manifesto*), 101 members of Congress attacked the *Brown* decision as an exercise of "naked power" with "no legal basis." They pledged themselves to "use all lawful means to bring about a reversal of this decision which is contrary to the Constitution and to prevent the use of force in its implementation." Two House members from North Carolina refused to sign the document. They were rewarded by the voters with early retirement. It was not until 1964 that a majority of Congress committed to ending segregation throughout the country.

B.   *The President*

Presidents did little better. The immensely popular World War II hero Dwight Eisenhower was president in 1954 when *Brown* was decided and remained in office throughout the 1950s. However, he never lent his prestige

145. Gerald N. Rosenberg, *The Hollow Hope: Can Courts Bring About Social Change?* 50 (1991).

to the decision. As Roy Wilkins, the Executive Director of the NAACP at the time put it, "if he had fought World War II the way he fought for civil rights, we would all be speaking German today."[146] Similarly, although President Kennedy is generally considered to have supported desegregation, he took little concrete initiative in school desegregation and other civil rights matters until pressured by events.

C. State Legislation

There was an old saying in the South, "as long as we can legislate, we can segregate."[147] In response to *Brown*, Southern state legislators enacted hundreds of new laws requiring and preserving segregation. By 1957, at least 136 new segregation laws and constitutional amendments had been added to the books. Virginia went the furthest, practicing "massive resistance" which included such steps as closing the public schools and re-opening them as segregated private academies.

D. Local Courts

Another old Southern saying, "litigate and legislate," focused on the judiciary. In the U.S. system, state and local judges are selected locally, meaning they share local beliefs and culture. In the South, this meant that many judges were committed to upholding segregation. They had myriad ways of doing so, ranging from upholding state legislation supporting segregation to interminable foot-dragging to outright prejudice. Indeed, several of the cases litigated with *Brown* in the early 1950s were still being litigated more than a decade later in the 1960s.

E. Southern Governors

Given the position taken by Southern judges and legislators, it is no surprise that Southern governors opposed desegregation as well. Often expressing themselves in strong language, many governors took extraordinary actions to prevent desegregation and made extraordinary statements. Although there is no dearth of examples, consider the action of Arkansas Governor Orval Faubus, who ordered the National Guard to stand at the door of Central High School in Little Rock to prevent the implementation of a federal court order requiring desegregation. Consider also the words of Alabama Governor George Wallace in 1963, nearly a decade after *Brown*: "I draw the line in the dust and toss the gauntlet before the feat of tyranny and I say segregation now, segregation tomorrow, segregation forever." Somewhat less poetically, Mississippi Governor Ross Barnett announced his opposition to desegregation this way: "Ross Barnett will rot in a federal jail before he will let one nigra cross the sacred threshold of our white schools."

F. Private Groups

Elected and appointed officials usually reflect the preferences of the electorate. The deep-seated opposition to ending segregation exemplified by

146. Roy Wilkins, *Standing Fast: The Autobiography of Roy Wilkins* 222 (1984).

147. Harrell R. Rogers, Jr. & Charles S. Bullock III, *Law and Social Change: Civil Rights Laws and Their Consequences* 72 (1972).

the actions and words of many Southern legislators, judges, and governors, was widely supported by White Southerners. Not only did they elect and re-elect vociferous supporters of segregation to public office, but they also took steps to reinforce segregation. These ranged from economic coercion and harassment to explicit refusal to follow federal court decisions to violence.

G. Violence

The final factor that made the Court's language irrelevant was violence. In 1955, when *Brown II* was decided, the Southern states had a fully developed system of apartheid. To many White Southerners, desegregation was a threat to their way of life. Organized White violence against Blacks to reinforce the apartheid system holds a long and tragic history in the South. In the wake of both *Brown* decisions, and later the civil rights movement, White groups arose to enforce segregation through violence. Some, like the White Citizen's Councils, purported to be non-violent. Others, like the Ku Klux Klan, both preached and practiced violence. From the murders of Emmet Till (1955) and Medgar Evers (1963) to the attacks on the Freedom Riders (1961) and the Birmingham church bombing (1963), White violence against Blacks took a heavy toll. In the summer of 1964, Mississippi alone witnessed brutal attacks against African Americans and civil rights workers including thirty-five shootings, sixty-five bombings (including thirty-five churches), six murders, and eighty beatings.

Overall, these seven factors go a long way to explaining why desegregation did not occur in the wake of *Brown II*. They illustrate that political and social forces (local and national) did not support the Court, providing no pressure for compliance. In such a situation, the language of the Court was irrelevant.

IV. Change

The bleak picture painted above does not tell the whole story. By 1972, more than 91% of African–American school children in the eleven Southern states were in integrated schools. Many "legalist" critics of *Brown II* argue that desegregation occurred because the Court finally "tightened its language."[148] In [a series of] cases . . . the Court rejected excuses for maintaining segregation, required the adoption of plans for immediate desegregation, and expanded remedies to include busing. To the legalist critics, this shows that the language of the Court was vitally important to desegregation.

The problem with this analysis is that, once again, it is too Court-centered. Examining the broader picture shows that desegregation occurred principally because Congress acted, supplying incentives for desegregation and imposing costs for maintaining segregation. The court-centered explanation neglects fundamental changes in the political, social, and economic context.

---

148. See Gary Orfield et al., *Dismantling Desegregation: The Quiet Reversal of Brown v. Board of Education* 8 (1996); Gary Orfield, *Must We Bus? Segregated Schools and Nation-* *al Policy* 13–15 (1978); J. Harvie Wilkinson III, *From Brown to Bakke: The Supreme Court and School Integration: 1954–1978*, at 11 (1979).

Title VI of the 1964 Civil Rights Act[149] permitted the U.S. Department of Health, Education, and Welfare ("HEW") to cut off federal funds to programs in which racial discrimination was practiced, and the 1965 Elementary & Secondary Education Act[150] provided a great deal of federal money to generally poor Southern school districts. By the 1971–72 school year, federal funds comprised 12% to 27.8% of Southern state school budgets, up from 4.6% to 11.1% in the 1963–64 school year. This combination of federal funding and Title VI gave the executive branch a tool to induce desegregation when it chose to do so. When HEW began threatening to cut off funds to school districts that refused to desegregate, dramatic change occurred. By the 1972–73 school year, over 91% of African–American school children in the eleven Southern states were in integrated schools, up from 1.2% in the 1963–64 school year. With only the constitutional right in force in the 1963–64 school year, no more than 5.5% of African–American children in any Southern state were in school with Whites. By the 1972–73 school year, when economic incentives were offered for desegregation and costs imposed for failure to desegregate, in no Southern state were fewer than 80% of African–American children in integrated schools.

Federal funding was not the only economic inducement for desegregation in the late 1960s and early 1970s. Another powerful factor at work was the desire of many Southern communities to attract industry and the belief that a peaceful, desegregated school system was an important inducement. Thus, the less industrialized South had a strong economic incentive to desegregate. Also, there had been cultural change in the South. The Civil Rights Movement changed the country, and the South was no exception. By the late 1960s and the early 1970s, rabid support of segregation had weakened. In such a changed cultural context, powerful economic incentives could overcome weakened cultural barriers.

Courts played a role in this process. Once Congress acted, the judicial system was given a set of tools with which it could work. This suggests, however, that it was not the language of the courts but the actions of Congress that played the key role, as well as broader economic and cultural changes. After Congress acted, school districts that violated court orders risked not only the loss of federal funds but also an important competitive advantage in attracting new industries. In contrast, school districts that desegregated maintained eligibility for federal funds, and their communities could make a stronger pitch for new industry. School desegregation occurred in the years 1968–72, then, because a set of conditions provided incentives to desegregate and imposed costs for failing to do so. When those conditions were lacking, as in the first decade after *Brown*, constitutional rights were flouted. The language of judicial decisions was largely irrelevant.

149. 42 U.S.C.A. § 2000d (2003).   **150.** 20 U.S.C. § 2701 et seq. (1994).

V.   Other Cases

The argument that the language of *Brown II* was not responsible for the lack of desegregation is also supported by examining other civil rights cases in the period before Congress passed the 1964 Civil Rights Act. Even when the Court used clear, strong, and unequivocal language, little change occurred. I consider voting rights, transportation, and the Little Rock crisis that led to *Cooper v. Aaron.*[151]

A.   Voting Rights

In the late 1950s and early 1960s, the United States brought dozens of voting rights suits in the South under the 1957 and 1960 civil rights acts alleging that African–Americans were systematically being denied the right to vote. Even though many legal victories were achieved, very little registration occurred. In 1963, the U.S. Civil Rights Commission concluded that five years of litigation under the acts had "not provided a prompt or adequate remedy for wide-spread discriminatory denials of the right to vote." The Commission cited the efforts in one hundred counties in eight states where, despite the filing of thirty-six voting rights suits by the Department of Justice, registration of African–Americans increased a measly 3.3% from approximately 5% in 1956 to 8.3% in 1963. Another study found that eight years of litigation under the two acts in the forty-six most heavily segregated Southern counties resulted in the registration of only 37,146 Blacks out of 548,358 eligible, a mere 6.8%.

The negligible results of these legal victories finally led administration officials to the conclusion that litigation to achieve voting rights for African–Americans in the South was fruitless. The problem was not with lack of legal victories or with weak, compromised, judicial holdings. Rather the problem was that White Southerners were not going to grant African–Americans the right to vote, regardless of what courts said. In congressional testimony, U.S. Attorney General Robert F. Kennedy acknowledged the point, noting that the "problem is deep rooted and of long standing. It demands a solution which cannot be provided by lengthy litigation. . . ."

The solution was to forego litigation and entice Congress to act. It did so in 1965, passing the Voting Rights Act.[152] The crux of the Act by-passed state officials and provided for direct federal action to enable African–Americans to vote. The results were striking. In the first few months after passage of the Act, more than 300,000 African–Americans in the South were registered. There was a 45% increase in the number of Southern African–Americans registered to vote, measured from the period just before passage of the Act to just after it. When Congress acted, change occurred. When courts acted, no matter how forcefully they stated the law, little changed.

B.   Transportation

Judicial attempts to desegregate interstate transportation show the same results. Despite several Supreme Court cases banning segregation in transpor-

151.   358 U.S. 1 (1958).   **152.**   42 U.S.C. § 1973 (1965).

tation and in facilities used by interstate travelers, interstate travel in the South remained segregated.... As one commentator put it, by 1960, if not earlier, the Court "clearly established" that laws requiring segregation in interstate transportation and facilities were unconstitutional.[153]

The Court's holdings and language may have been clear, but segregation was unaltered. The dramatic and courageous Freedom Rides of the spring of 1961 showed that the strength of judicial rulings has little relation to actual behavior. On May 4, 1961, an integrated group of thirteen "Freedom Riders" left Washington, D.C., on regularly scheduled Greyhound and Trailways buses, with a public itinerary through Virginia, North Carolina, South Carolina, Georgia, Alabama, Mississippi, and Louisiana. Their trip was intended to show that segregation in public interstate travel had not ended. On Sunday, May 14, the attack on the Riders in Birmingham, Alabama and firebombing of one of the buses outside of Anniston, Alabama, demonstrated the extreme violence of the Freedom Ride. It is harder to imagine a more vivid illustration that interstate travel remained segregated. It was not until the passage of the 1964 Civil Rights Act that such segregation finally came to an end. As with voting rights, when Congress acted, change occurred. When courts acted without political support, little changed.

C. Little Rock

A final example of the fact that even clear, strong, and unequivocal language from the Supreme Court would not produce change, absent political support, comes from the events at Central High School in Little Rock, Arkansas in 1957. In response to a federal district court decision requiring desegregation of the school, Governor Faubus and the Arkansas legislature took steps to block the desegregation. Dramatically, the governor ordered the National Guard to stand in the doorway and physically prevent nine African–American students from entering the school. The ensuing violence made it impossible for the African–American students either to enter or remain in the school. In response to this explicit defiance of a federal court order, President Eisenhower ordered the 101st Airborne Division to Little Rock to guarantee the safety of those nine courageous young African–Americans. The federal troops stayed for the remainder of the school year.

The lower court decision was appealed to the Supreme Court, which convened in a special session for only the fifth time in thirty-eight years to hear the case. In *Cooper v. Aaron*,[154] the Court upheld the desegregation order in unequivocal terms, writing that the "constitutional rights of respondents [Black students] are not to be sacrificed or yielded to the violence and disorder which was occurring." This was, as the opinion stated, "enough to dispose of the case," but the Court continued for several pages to underline its determination that *Brown* be followed. It reminded the parties that Article VI of the

153. Louis Lusky, "Racial Discrimination and the Federal Law: A Problem in Nullification," 63 *Columbia Law Review* 1163, 1168 (1963).

154. 358 U.S. 1, 16 (1958).

Constitution makes the Constitution the "supreme Law of the Land" and unearthed the 1803 case, *Marbury v. Madison*,[155] and Chief Justice Marshall's words in that case that it is "emphatically the province and duty of the judicial department to say what the law is." Finally, in an unprecedented move, all nine justices individually signed the opinion. It is hard to imagine stronger language or a stronger holding. Indeed, supporters of the role of the Court point to Little Rock and *Cooper v. Aaron* as examples of how clear and unequivocal judicial language produces results.

What were the results? Although the presence of the United States military allowed the nine African–American children to attend Central High School, little desegregation occurred. Once federal troops left, so did any hope of more than token desegregation. Indeed, as of June 1963, six years after Governor Faubus' defiance of the federal court order, only 69 out of 7,700 students (less than 1%) at the supposedly desegregated, "formerly" White, junior and senior high schools of Little Rock were Black. In contrast, Governor Faubus' active defiance of court decisions requiring desegregation brought him national popularity. He was re-elected governor in a landslide in 1958. He was also honored by Americans in December 1958, chosen as one of the ten men they most admired by respondents in a national Gallup poll. As with *Brown II*, the problem was not with the language of the judicial decision. Instead, it lay with the lack of political support for desegregation.

VI.   Conclusion: The Irrelevant Court

I have argued that the language of *Brown II* was irrelevant to desegregation. Because the political support necessary to dismantle the apartheid system was lacking in 1955, it would not have mattered what standard the Court adopted. It was not until the mid–1960s that Congress and the President were willing to make the massive commitments necessary to end apartheid. When those commitments were made, desegregation occurred. Without those commitments, little changed. To focus on judicial holdings is to stick one's head in the sand of law books and judicial decisions and ignore the political world in which law operates.

Given *Brown's* lack of impact, why is it widely held in such high regard? Along the same lines, given the irrelevance of the holding of *Brown II*, why is it so roundly criticized? I suggest there are two reasons. First, since the mid–1960s, the United States has become officially committed to being a non-segregated society. *Brown* stands as a constitutional symbol of that commitment. This is a noble vision, one of which Americans can be proud. To the extent that *Brown II* failed to live up to this vision by failing to require immediate desegregation, it is seen as a blemish on the official commitment.

There is, however, an additional reason which is much less noble. Celebration of *Brown*, and criticism of *Brown II*, privileges lawyers and courts. If *Brown* ended segregation, and if lawyers made *Brown* possible, then lawyers and courts are heroes and we should look to them for social change. *Brown II*

---

155.   5 U.S. (1 Cranch) 137 (1803).

is thus criticized for undercutting this heroic vision. This is a less noble vision because it is wrong. As I have shown, it was the actions of Congress and the President, not the courts, that ended segregation in practice. Without political support, court decisions will not produce social change. To valorize lawyers and courts encourages reformers to litigate for social change. But if political support is lacking, the effect of this vision is to limit change by deflecting claims for reform away from substantive political battles, where success is possible, to harmless legal ones where it is not. In this way, courts play a deeply conservative ideological function in defense of the status quo. When social reformers succumb to the "lure of litigation" they forget that deep-seated social conflicts cannot be resolved through litigation. The legalist criticism of *Brown II* encourages us to look to legal solutions for political and cultural problems. That is no more likely to succeed than tilting at windmills is likely to subdue enemies.

Courts are not all-powerful institutions. They were designed with severe limitations and placed in a political system of divided powers. To adopt a "legalist" critique of *Brown II* abstracts the Court from the political and cultural system in which it operates. Blaming the holding of *Brown II* for the failure of desegregation clouds our vision with a naive and romantic belief in the triumph of rights over politics. And while romance and even naiveté have their charms, they are not best exhibited in courtrooms nor in scholarship.

NOTES AND QUESTIONS

1. Rosenberg's conclusion is "courts are impotent to produce significant social reform." Do his data really demonstrate that this is true? What is his (implicit) definition of "impact?" How does he go about measuring it? Does he leave out any evidence that you would like to see? Michael McCann criticizes Rosenberg's book, *The Hollow Hope: Can Courts Bring About Social Change?* (1991). This book sets forth Rosenberg's general thesis about the impotence of courts, and in particular, the failure of the *Brown* cases to end segregation in the South. McCann notes that Rosenberg considers "defiance of desegregation rulings by white southerners as a sign of ineffective reform litigation." Others, however, have stressed how this resistance helped the process of building a civil rights movement and helped nurture support for the civil rights cause throughout the country and also in the government. McCann says:

> And even more problematic is the standard for assessing change that Rosenberg uses in his analysis. The expectation that courts must unilaterally generate in a short time behavioral changes across the nation that uniformly comply with specific legal mandates to qualify as "significant" impact connotes a standard that is so high as to assure its own negative conclusion.[156]

156. Michael McCann, "Causal versus Constitutive Explanations (or, On the Difficulty of Being so Positive . . .)," 21 *Law & Social Inquiry* 457, 480 (1996).

McCann does say "Rosenberg utilizes his casual model very effectively in *The Hollow Hope* to refute a rival casual hypothesis that court decisions alone can generate significant social change. As a debunking enterprise, his approach is very powerful." (We should note that a study by the Harvard Civil Rights Project found that "black and Latino students are now more isolated from their white counterparts than they were three decades ago." Greg Winter, "Schools Resegregate, Study Finds," *N.Y. Times*, Jan. 21, 2003, at A14). However, McCann says that Rosenberg's model would be "more compelling if joined to a more pluralistic, interactive, constitutive understanding of law in social practice."[157] Is McCann saying that the failure of the *Brown* case to bring about significant desegregation of the schools should be seen as a catalyst for events and attitudes that changed the position of African Americans in contemporary society? If so, how could anyone prove exactly what role the *Brown* decision itself played in influencing the changes that took place after 1954?

Aldon D. Morris, "A Retrospective on the Civil Rights Movement: Political and Intellectual Landmarks," 25 *American Review of Sociology* 517, 524, 527 (1999), argues that "By 1950 the legal method was the dominant weapon of Black protest, and it required skilled lawyers rather than mass action. The legal method depended on the actions of elites external to the Black community whereby Blacks had to hope that white judges and Supreme Court justices would issue favorable rulings in response to well-reasoned and well-argued court cases." The 1955 Montgomery, Alabama, year-long mass-based bus boycott changed the tactics and the balance of power. The Black community then seized the initiative and began exercising its power in order to overthrow Jim Crow in the south. "By overthrowing Jim Crow in a matter of ten years, the civil rights movement taught the nation and the world an important lesson: a mass-based grass roots social movement that is sufficiently organized, sustained, and disruptive is capable of generating fundamental social change."

What part did the *Brown* decision play in creating this mass movement? Can you fashion a plausible account of the contribution of this decision to the success of demonstrations, appeals to religious beliefs, and America's position in the Cold War? But suppose the NAACP had never brought the constitutional challenge to segregated schools. Might the mass-based grass roots social movement have formed anyway? Can we do more than just speculate? Rosenberg is skeptical about the influence of *Brown* on the Civil Rights Movement. Michael J. Klarman, *From Jim Crow to Civil Rights: The Supreme Court and the Struggle for Racial Equality* 385–442 (2004), argues that resistance to *Brown* by southern white political leaders—the backlash against *Brown*—generated its own counter-backlash and helped galvanize the resistance of African–Americans to white supremacy. He also argues: "For the Court to have vindicated their cause, especially when few other important institutions were doing so, provided blacks with 'moral support.' Because a

---

157. Id. at 472.

principal obstacle for any social reform movement is convincing potential participants that success is feasible, *Brown* must have facilitated the mobilization of civil rights protest." (p. 369)

2. Larry D. Kramer, "Popular Constitutionalism, Circa 2004," 92 *California Law Review* 959, 971 (2004), questions Rosenberg's conclusion that decisions by the Supreme Court of the United States were "either inconsequential or ineffective as engines of social change." He says:

> To say the Supreme Court can rarely undertake or sustain bold policy initiatives is not to deny that judicial rulings can nudge matters in one direction or another when public opinion is uncertain or divided. And even apart from directly molding substantive values, judicial decisions can shape the political agenda by addressing issues that elected officials do not or will not face, by offering a means for weak or excluded groups to enter the public debate, by providing one side or another with leverage in ongoing political bargaining, by creating constraints or disincentives that affect how or which parties proceed, by stimulating counter-mobilization, and in a myriad of other, similar ways.

In the late 1940s and early 1950s, when the NAACP was planning its strategy to improve the position of the Negro in American society, what avenue other than a constitutional challenge through the courts was open to them? What would have happened had they appealed to Congress for a statutory remedy? At this time, powerful Democratic Congressmen and Senators from the South dominated the committee structure of Congress, and they succeeded in blocking any measures that might interfere with white supremacy. Practically speaking, did the NAACP have any chance to persuade the white majority—in the north as well as in the south—to change the ideas held by that majority about race and segregation? In short, at that time was there any real alternative to a court-centered strategy? Neil K. Komesar, *Imperfect Alternatives: Choosing Institutions in Law, Economics, and Public Policy* 5 (1994), reminds us: "Institutional choice is difficult as well as essential. The choice is always a choice among highly imperfect alternatives. The strengths and weaknesses of one institution versus another vary from one set of circumstances to another."

Compare also Louis Menand, "Civil Actions: Brown v. Board of Education and the Limits of Law," *The New Yorker*, Feb. 12, 2001, at 91, 96 ("One of the lessons of *Brown* is that most efforts to secure equality in this country sooner or later run into a form of de-facto segregation that no American court is likely to strike down: segregation by wealth. The Supreme Court, in the nineteen-seventies, drew the line at requiring school districts to be equally funded and at obliging states to pursue desegregation by busing students between cities and their suburbs. Those cases . . . mark the end of the *Brown* era.")

3. Malcolm M. Feeley, "Hollow Hopes, Flypaper, and Metaphors," 17 *Law & Social Inquiry* 745, 758, 760 (1992), argues that Rosenberg really was writing about the contrast between a deep belief that the Supreme Court is

all-powerful and what Rosenberg considered the reality—that the Court is, essentially, weak and powerless. Feeley asks what social functions does the myth of a powerful court serve? He suggests: "the myth is functional for the legal profession, particularly the elite of the profession—professors at leading law schools, federal judges, bar association leaders, partners in major firms and the like. By promoting the belief in an extraordinarily powerful court, they enhance their own status. By fostering the myth of extraordinarily powerful judges, they imply extraordinarily powerful lawyers, law professors, and law students." He continues: "This belief of the powerful agent of good is also part of the quintessential American myth, the power of the Lone Ranger who emerges from nowhere to challenge injustice." Feeley concludes, however, "if Rosenberg had lowered his expectations, he would have concluded that the power of the courts relative to other governmental agents is not insubstantial."

Lawrence M. Friedman, "Brown in Context," at 49, 51, 52, 60 in *Race, Law, and Culture: Reflections on Brown v. Board of Education* (Austin Sarat ed. 1997) notes that many law professors criticized the Supreme Court for "violating sacred canons of style and craftsmanship." These academics seem to say that had Chief Justice Warren's opinion in the case been better written, the case would have had more impact. Friedman responds: "But anybody who feels that a more tightly crafted and better reasoned opinion in *Brown* would have had a bigger (or even different) impact on life in rural Mississippi (or Washington, D.C., for that matter) than what Warren actually wrote, can't be living on this planet." He continues: "*Brown*, like other significant cases, did send out a *definite* message; it had a social meaning for its audience. This message, in essence, was unmistakable." What was that message? Friedman says that the Chief Justice wrote in a style of commonsense morality. He was piercing "the veil of lies about the position of blacks in southern society. He was refusing to use the person-from-Pluto approach. The 'commonsense' style of *Brown* is the medium for emphasizing context, reality, for rejecting the dry formalism that made it (stylistically) possible to pretend that all was well in the house of the South." Can we say that if *Brown* did not desegregate schools, it did put the actual position of blacks in southern society (and northern society too) on the agenda of those who influence opinion in the United States? How might one go about studying this particular thesis about the actual impact of the *Brown* opinion?

4.   There are some examples of courts having success in bring about change. See Michael Klarman, "The White Primary Rulings: A Case Study in the Consequences of Supreme Court Decisionmaking," 29 *Florida State University Law Review* 35 (2001) ("The Court's most important white primary decision, *Smith v. Allwright*, inaugurated a political revolution in the urban South"). Edward L. Rubin and Malcolm M. Feeley, "*Velazquez* and Beyond: Judicial Policy Making and Litigation Against the Government," 5 *University of Pennsylvania Constitutional Law Journal* 617 (2003), discusses the impact of federal judicial decisions that issued orders to officials in various states to reform their prison systems. Of course, the authors say that it was

clear to everybody, including the judges involved themselves, that courts were not the optimal institutions for this job. But it was also obvious that nobody else was doing anything much to improve the conditions in these prisons.

(E) Impact—The Importance of Communication Networks

(4.16) Tarasoff, Myth and Reality: An Empirical Study of Private Law in Action

Daniel J. Givelber, William J. Bowers and Carolyn L. Blitch

1984 *Wisconsin Law Review* 443.

When the California Supreme Court ruled in *Tarasoff v. Regents of the University of California*[158] that psychotherapists owe a duty of care to third parties threatened by their patients, it did so in the face of claims from professional organizations that this new duty would interfere seriously with the practice of psychotherapy. The court announced that "[i]n this risk-infested society we can hardly tolerate the further exposure to danger that would result from a concealed knowledge of the therapist that his patient was lethal." The court appeared confident that its ruling would not interfere with psychotherapy, particularly with respect to the potentially violent, but the source of that confidence was not readily apparent. In *Tarasoff*, as in other well known tort decisions, a court announced a rule designed to change private behavior without reliable data regarding the practices it was intending to change, the extent of the problem it was trying to remedy, or the costs which the proposed cure would impose. Moreover, like other appellate courts, the California Supreme Court had insufficient means of securing this information before it ruled, and no mechanism for monitoring the impact of its decision.

Courts often create tort rules in the context of a dispute between a seriously injured party and the putative injurer, and thus are subject to the pressures created by sympathy for the plight of the plaintiff. There may be vivid evidence of the plaintiff's suffering, and possibly testimony dealing with industry practice and the feasibility of precautions and safety measures. Rarely, however, will there be reliable data concerning what is, to a trial court, a legally irrelevant issue—the costs and benefits generated by a new rule applicable to all future conduct. In place of reliable data, the court will be confronted with the exaggerated and conflicting arguments of counsel. Lawyers, those in academia as well as those in practice, are among the most skilled practitioners of "worst case" analysis. Judges, in turn, are among our most practiced skeptics. This combination of circumstances may often lead appellate courts to discount a defendant's prediction of disaster. Whether for this reason or others, the California Supreme Court in *Tarasoff* dismissed as "speculative" the professional claims that the new duty would hamper psy-

158. 17 Cal.3d 425, 551 P.2d 334, 131 Cal. Rptr. 14 (1976).

chotherapy while embracing the equally speculative conclusion that the new rule would enhance public safety.

The court, like other appellate courts, also lacked the means by which to communicate its new rule to the group whose behavior it was designed to govern—California psychotherapists. Once copies of the opinion were mailed to the parties and made available to the public, the court's role was at an end. The court had no control over who learned about the case or what they learned. Nor did the court have any role in initiating enforcement of its rule; that remains the prerogative of the injured. Yet, if the court's ruling was to enhance public safety, someone had to tell the therapists about their new obligation and how to meet it.

Who filled this role? It seems doubtful that psychotherapists, or any other group of dispersed individuals, retain lawyers to advise them of changes in their tort obligations. If so, then other groups such as the media or professional organizations (including the very ones opposed to the duty in the first instance), may have had the primary role in educating therapists as to what they were now supposed to do. The information about *Tarasoff* disseminated by these professional organizations and publications may well have skewed the court's message to reflect the concerns and perspectives of mental health professionals. The message may also have travelled further than anticipated. While *Tarasoff* is a California opinion, it deals with a question which concerns therapists everywhere. Professional discussions may understandably concentrate on the substance of *Tarasoff*, without emphasizing its limited jurisdictional reach.

This Article presents data relevant to the issues before the California Supreme Court in *Tarasoff*, as well as to the broader debate of how tort rules influence behavior. We have investigated a number of the claims concerning psychotherapist understanding of and response to *Tarasoff*. We have two goals in mind with regard to the findings we present. First we propose to substitute data for rhetoric with respect to the *Tarasoff* debate itself. Given the publicity surrounding the *Tarasoff* case and the amount of commentary it has spawned, it is important to evaluate how much the *Tarasoff* duty has in fact contradicted and influenced psychotherapeutic practice. Our second goal is to present empirical data regarding how an appellate decision becomes translated into a rule of conduct. All agree that *Tarasoff* was an important decision—that it would have an impact on psychotherapeutic practice. But how are court decisions disseminated and presented? Our findings raise questions about the accepted wisdom that courts should not attempt to articulate specific rules of conduct. . . .

II. THE *TARASOFF* CONTROVERSY

The *Tarasoff* decision of the California Supreme Court held that a therapist has an obligation to exercise reasonable care to protect those whose physical well-being is threatened by the therapist's patient. To trigger this duty, a mythical, if familiar, figure called the "reasonable therapist" must believe that the patient actually might harm some identified or identifiable person. Once this belief exists, the therapist must exercise care to protect the potential victim. Warning the likely victim of the potential danger, the California Supreme Court has suggested, likely would be a response under many circumstances, but the specification of what care is reasonable "depends upon the circumstances of each case, and should not be governed by any hard and fast rule."

The version of *Tarasoff* requiring therapists to exercise "reasonable care" to protect potential victims is the second, and now official, *Tarasoff* decision. In the first, and subsequently withdrawn, opinion (*Tarasoff I*), the California court imposed an explicit duty on therapists to warn potential victims threatened by their patients.

When *Tarasoff I* was originally published, the Northern California Psychiatric Society spearheaded a drive to persuade the court to reconsider its ruling. In a petition seeking reconsideration, the Society, the American Psychiatric Association, and state and local organizations of psychologists and social workers, all of whom joined together as *amici curiae*, successfully urged the California Supreme Court to rehear the case.

The brief seeking review of *Tarasoff I* argued that the decision severely and negatively impinged upon the work of psychotherapists and upon those in need of psychotherapy. This argument rested on a number of points. First, the duty to warn was ill-advised since it compromised the confidentiality necessary for effective psychotherapy, particularly with regard to potentially violent patients. Furthermore, it contradicted professional ethical standards which both emphasize the need for privacy in therapeutic communications and command therapists to concern themselves solely with the welfare of their patients. Second, the duty to warn would ultimately decrease the public safety as well as the liberty of potentially violent patients, rather than increase both as the court hoped, because awareness of the legal obligation would either complicate the treatment of potentially violent patients or deter therapists altogether. Those therapists who did treat such patients would be left with few realistic options other than involuntary commitment and treatment. Third, since therapists tend to over-predict future violence and share no legitimate criteria for evaluating the likelihood of violence, requiring therapists to warn whenever a "reasonable therapist" would evaluate the patient as imminently dangerous was both ill advised and unfair since it required therapists to act according to a professional standard which did not exist.

In July 1976, eighteen months after the original decision, the California Supreme Court issued a new opinion which modified the therapist's obligation from warning the potential victim to exercising reasonable care to protect potential victims. Warning the threatened third party was still prominently mentioned as an example of reasonable care but was no longer considered the exclusive means by which a therapist could meet his or her legal obligations. . . .

616

III. STUDY METHODOLOGY

We surveyed a sample of 2875 psychiatrists, psychologists and social workers located in Boston, Chicago, Detroit, Los Angeles, New York, Philadelphia, San Francisco and Washington, D.C.—the eight largest standard metropolitan statistical units as of the 1970 census. The sample was drawn from the biographical directories of the American Psychiatric Association, the American Psychological Association, and the National Association of Social Workers. For each professional group in each location, the sample was first stratified by location, profession, experience and apparent setting of practice (private, institutional, or both). Respondents were then randomly selected from within each cell. The survey was mailed early in 1980, and 59.5% of the sample returned questionnaires—48% of the psychiatrists, 62% of the psychologists and 68% of the social workers. The respondents were well distributed in terms of the sample criteria—profession, location, experience, and type.

Since our survey was designed in part to measure legal impact and since the first *Tarasoff* decision was promulgated five years prior to the date of our investigation, we faced the twin difficulties of asking our respondents to recall their behavior, and changes in that behavior, over a five-year period and of relying on our respondents to describe accurately what motivated any behavioral changes which they did report. Moreover, knowing that *Tarasoff* was a highly publicized and politicized case, we were afraid that our respondents might follow a "party line" propagated within their professions in answering the questionnaire.

To deal with the "party line" problem we decided to separate our questions about behavior from our specific questions concerning the *Tarasoff* case and not to mention the decision until the very end of the questionnaire. We originally went even further and prepared two versions of the questionnaire. One version contained all questions, including those about *Tarasoff*. The other version was divided into two parts: the first contained all questions except those dealing with *Tarasoff*; the second contained questions about *Tarasoff* alone and was to be sent to respondents only after they had returned the first part of the questionnaire. We pre-tested both versions on equal samples of 100 therapists in Boston and San Francisco and found no meaningful differences in responses, whether *Tarasoff* was mentioned only at the end of the questionnaire, or not at all. Since there was a lower response rate from the therapists who received the bifurcated questionnaire, we decided to proceed with the single questionnaire with the *Tarasoff* questions placed at the end. . . .

A. Knowledge of *Tarasoff*

1. DO THERAPISTS KNOW ABOUT *TARASOFF*?

The answer to this question, as Table 1 demonstrates, is overwhelmingly yes. The figures pertaining to California therapists are truly striking— virtually every psychiatrist, and nine out of ten psychologists and social workers had heard of the decision by name or had heard of a case "like it" but did not recognize the name. Knowledge of the case among 96% of the California psychiatrists is remarkable; it is a fair guess that there is no other legal decision, with the possible exception of controversial cases such as *Brown v. Board of Education*, which could command this level of recognition among a subgroup of lay persons. Yet psychiatrists from places other than California are not far behind—87% know the case by name and another 7% have heard of a case like it. Indeed, psychiatrists outside California have as great or greater knowledge of the case than California based psychologists and social workers. The strong showing by psychiatrists should not obscure two other facts: nine out of ten California psychologists and social workers also know about the case, while almost three out of four out-of-state psychologists know about it, as do more than half of the non-California social workers. These data demonstrate that the court and its critics were justified in believing that the *Tarasoff* decision would be well known and therefore might have a substantial influence on therapeutic practice.

TABLE I

Knowledge Of The Tarasoff Case By Profession And Location

Knowledge of The Tarasoff Case	Percent each profession/location					
	Psychiatrist		Psychologist		Social Worker	
	California	Other States	California	Other States	California	Other States
Heard of Tarasoff Case	96	87	86	56	76	32
Heard of case like it	1	7	8	18	13	24
Never heard of Tarasoff or a case like it	3	6	6	26	11	44
Total Percent	100%	100%	100%	100%	100%	100%
Total Respondents	(113)	(341)	(146)	(432)	(163)	(472)

2. FROM WHICH SOURCES DID THERAPISTS LEARN THE MOST ABOUT *TARASOFF*

Since therapists, particularly those who practice outside of California, are unlikely readers of California court decisions, it seems safe to assume that information about the case comes from professional rather than legal sources. This is what Table 2 shows.

618

TABLE 2
Knowledge Of The Case By Profession And Location
Among Respondents Knowledgeable About Tarasoff, Primary Source Of

| Source of Knowledge | Percent each profession/location | | | | | |
| | Psychiatrist | | Psychologist | | Social Worker | |
	California	Other States	California	Other States	California	Other States
Attorney	10	6	8	6	7	9
Administrator/ Supervisor	6	1	9	4	15	17
Colleague	14	8	18	17	21	25
Professional Organization/ Literature	65	77	53	62	37	31
Newspaper	4	4	6	7	10	12
Other	1	4	6	4	10	6
Total Percent	100%	100%	100%	100%	100%	100%
Total Respondents	(104)	(287)	(124)	(276)	(123)	(222)

Professional organizations and literature provided our respondents with their primary source of information about *Tarasoff*. The professional contrasts are striking: psychiatrists were more likely to identify professional organizations and literature as their primary source than were psychologists, who in turn were considerably more likely to name these sources than social workers. These figures reflect both *Tarasoff's* controversial history and the extent to which the case was addressed in the literature of the respective professions. If we combine professional sources, i.e., professional organizations and literature, colleagues and administrators, we see that more than eight out of ten psychiatrists and psychologists and more than seven out of ten social workers learned most about *Tarasoff* from professional sources. Very few people, one out of ten or less for every group, learned about the case from lawyers.

Two facts emerge. The first is that the case is extremely well known. The second is that mental health professionals learned about the case from professional organizations and each other, not from lawyers or general circulation newspapers. Given that the message has been delivered by groups which actively intervened in the case and by publications likely to be critical of the decision, we can speculate that our respondents may not have a favorable view, or even an accurate understanding, of the decision. To that question, among others, we now turn.

DO THERAPISTS UNDERSTAND WHEN *TARASOFF* APPLIES?

The *Tarasoff* duty arises whenever a therapist determines, or pursuant to the standards of the profession, should determine, that his or her patient presents a serious danger of violence to another. The court's approach thus shifts the inquiry from what an individual therapist actually believed to what a competent therapist ought to have believed. Courts typically evaluate conduct in this manner, making social judgments about the appropriateness of questioned behavior. Do therapists appreciate the distinction between a subjective and objective test? Table 3 presents our respondents' answers to the trifurcated question of when *Tarasoff* imposes the duty to protect another: whenever the patient makes a threat, whenever a reasonable therapist would assess the patient as dangerous towards another, or whenever the therapist actually makes such an assessment. Nine out of ten thought that the *Tarasoff* obligation applies both when a therapist actually believes someone is dangerous and also when a reasonable therapist would believe this. They understand correctly the court's statement in this regard.

Only about one out of four (slightly more for social workers) believed it applied whenever there was a threat. There are two ways of viewing this figure: with satisfaction that three out of four understand that *Tarasoff* is concerned with danger, not threats, or with distress that one out of four does not. The appropriate view the *Tarasoff* critics might suggest is probably the latter—it is somewhat unsettling to find a substantial number of therapists who believe that threats *per se* should trigger a warning.

TABLE 3

Among Respondents Knowledgeable About Tarasoff, Belief That The Case Applies Under Selected Circumstances By Profession And Location

	Percent each profession/location					
	Psychiatrist		Psychologist		Social Worker	
Circumstance	California	Other States	California	Other States	California	Other States
Whenever a patient/client threatens to harm another person	29	20	22	25	29	35
Whenever a patient/client threatens to harm another person, and the therapist believes there is a serious possibility he might do so	94	89	96	86	93	92
Whenever a patient/client threatens to harm another person and a reasonable therapist would believe that there is a serious possibility that he would do so	89	89	93	90	94	91
Total Number of Respondents*	(107–110)	(293–315)	(123–135)	(299–306)	(136–140)	(225–242)

* due to non-response, number of respondents may vary within the range shown

DO THERAPISTS BELIEVE THAT THEY CAN MAKE MEANINGFUL ASSESSMENTS OF FUTURE VIOLENCE?

The amicus brief asserted that therapists cannot predict future violence, citing studies tending to show that therapists over-predict violence and are more often wrong than correct in such predictions. The studies cited were studies of people who had been committed because of alleged violent tendencies and later released. There are, however, no comparable studies demonstrating the same level of unreliability regarding predictions made about people who are in the community or have ready access to it. Without taking a position in this debate, we investigated how therapists viewed their own ability. The results are contained in Table 4.

TABLE 4

Possibility Of Predicting Dangerousness For Outpatients By Profession And Location

| Possibility of Prediction: | Percent each profession/location | | | | | |
| | Psychiatrist | | Psychologist | | Social Worker | |
	California	Other States	California	Other States	California	Other States
Impossible to predict	3	5	7	4	6	6
Patient possibly violent	14	15	16	18	19	24
Patient probably violent	35	28	27	25	20	19
Patient almost certainly violent	35	31	33	33	33	34
Patient certainly violent	13	21	17	20	22	17
Total Percent	100%	100%	100%	100%	100%	100%
Total Respondents	(112)	(333)	(139)	(409)	(146)	(438)

Our respondents proved to be rather more confident about their ability to predict future violence than the arguments of the *Tarasoff* critics suggested. When asked to indicate the firmest prediction they would be willing to make about the possibility that an outpatient of theirs might physically harm another, only 5% of our respondents felt that there was "no way to predict" such behavior, and over three-quarters felt that they could make a prediction ranging from "probable" to "certain."

WHAT DO THERAPISTS BELIEVE THAT *TARASOFF* REQUIRES: WARNING, REASONABLE CARE, BOTH OR NEITHER?

We present our findings in Table 5, which has two parts. Table 5–A indicates the percentage of our respondents who believed that *Tarasoff* requires particular interventions. Table 5–B has a narrower focus; it presents data on two formulations, warning and reasonable care, and shows the percentage who believe the case requires one of these interventions but not the other, the percentage who believe it requires both, and the percentage who believe it requires neither.

Table 5–A shows that more than three out of four respondents believe *Tarasoff* requires warning the victim, while only slightly more than one-third believe that it mandates the exercise of reasonable care. Californians—again over 90% for each group—are more likely than non-Californians to believe it requires warning, and less likely than non-Californians to believe it requires reasonable care. Perhaps even more striking are the relative percentages of therapists who believe that it requires only warning as against those who believe that it demands only reasonable care. As Table 5–B indicates, Californians tend to believe the decision requires warning but not reasonable care, with psychiatrists (68%) leading the parade. In contrast, only about 5% believe the care requires reasonable care but not warning. The remainder tend to believe that it requires both reasonable care and warning. The majority of California respondents misstate the formal holding of *Tarasoff*.

The figures are somewhat better for non-Californians. Yet this difference is slight; by and large, the case appears to be misunderstood as involving and requiring the warning of potential victims.

Again, therapists may be reacting very practically to a genuine uncertainty when they conclude that the decision requires warning. Warning, after all, is an intervention specifically identified by the California Supreme Court as a sometimes appropriate means of satisfying the *Tarasoff* duty. Faced with possible legal liability and the anxiety of dealing with a potentially violent patient, therapists may take refuge in the certainty of concrete rules. Warning a victim is very specific behavior, readily explainable to the patient as being legally required. Moreover, it may seem to the therapist to be the one sure way of avoiding liability. Unfortunately, this perception may not be entirely accurate; it will depend on what a "reasonable" therapist would do under the circumstances.

Other misinterpretations of the case by our respondents demonstrate their desire for concrete rules to guide behavior. Thus, as Table 5–A shows, "notifying superiors" rather than exercising reasonable care is the second most frequently identified behavior thought to be required by *Tarasoff*. This is extremely specific behavior which is not required by the *Tarasoff* decision, but it may represent exactly what administrative personnel in a mental health setting would want a therapist to do. We see that social workers who are less likely than psychiatrists to have ultimate administrative responsibility are much more likely than psychiatrists to identify this as being required by *Tarasoff*. Therapists who are troubled by how to respond to a particular violent patient may also find notifying a superior to be a congenial response; it transfers, or at least shares, the responsibility for what may be a very difficult decision. Here again, our respondents may be grasping for certainty to minimize the risk of liability rather than responding to the actual requisites of the *Tarasoff* ruling.

TABLE 5–A

Among Respondents Knowledgeable About Tarasoff, Belief That Case Requires Certain Interventions By Profession And Location

| | Percent each profession/location | | | | | |
| Belief Tarasoff Requires | Psychiatrist | | Psychologist | | Social Worker | |
	California	Other States	California	Other States	California	Other States
Warn potential victim	92	84	91	76	94	72
Notify superiors or administrators if in an institutional setting	17	37	36	44	50	53
Warn guardian, family, friends	21	33	42	41	39	38
Use reasonable care to protect victim	30	33	31	43	38	40
Inform police	25	33	41	26	43	29
Deal with potential violence in therapy	13	20	21	30	30	33
Seek professional consultation	6	14	11	17	22	24
Seek emergency involuntary commitment	10	20	8	11	13	15
Total Number of Respondents	(112)	(326)	(140)	(321)	(146)	(257)

TABLE 5–B

Among Respondents Knowledgeable About Tarasoff, Belief That Case Requires Warning Potential Victim, Reasonable Care, Neither Or Both, By Profession And Location

| | Percent each profession/location | | | | | |
| Belief Tarasoff Requires | Psychiatrist | | Psychologist | | Social Worker | |
	California	Other States	California	Other States	California	Other States
Warning the victim only	68	57	66	46	59	46
Using reasonable care to protect the victim only	5	6	5	13	3	14
Warning the victim and using reasonable care	24	27	25	30	34	26
Neither warning the victim nor using reasonable care	3	10	4	11	4	14
Total Percent	100%	100%	100%	100%	100%	100%
Total Respondents	(112)	(326)	(140)	(321)	(146)	(257)

Given that therapists believe *Tarasoff* requires warning, how does this requirement change clinical behavior? The amicus brief characterized the duty to warn as a breach of confidentiality, and argued that confidentiality is central to the therapeutic process and zealously guarded by therapists. To determine whether this is so we asked the next question.

623

WHAT ARE THE PRACTICES OF PSYCHOTHERAPISTS REGARDING COMMUNICATING INFORMATION CONCERNING A PATIENT TO THIRD PARTIES?

Table 6 presents data showing the percentage of our respondents who have made various extratherapeutic communications within the twelve months prior to responding to the survey. The pattern is remarkably consistent. The overwhelming majority have communicated about patients to other health professionals and insurers, and a substantial majority have done so to family, friends and public authorities. Very few have communicated to potential victims. Psychiatrists are most likely to have made extratherapeutic communications, social workers the next most likely, and psychologists the least likely. For four of the five forms of communication, California psychiatrists lead the other five groups in percentage making the communication. Thus, while confidentiality may well represent an important ethical and therapeutic value, it is apparently a value which therapists, in their work, will frequently be forced to compromise.

The infrequency of warnings deserves comment. It is hardly surprising that fewer therapists warned than communicated with other health professionals, or insurance companies, or family and friends, but it is striking that so many more therapists communicated with public authorities than with potential victims. These differences may reflect either the relative difficulty of locating warnable victims, or a therapist's preference to discharge his or her obligation for the welfare of others by dealing with public authorities.

TABLE 6
Communication of Information About A Patient/Client To Third Parties During Last Twelve Months By Location And Profession

| | Percent each profession/location | | | | | |
| | Psychiatrist | | Psychologist | | Social Worker | |
	California	Other States	California	Other States	California	Other States
Communication To:						
Governmental or private health insurers	90	91	76	77	82	69
Patient's/client's family or friends	74	69	62	65	69	70
Other health professionals	96	93	81	86	89	90
Persons threatened by patient/client	17	14	5	5	9	14
Public authorities (e.g., police, child welfare, correctional personnel)	70	66	55	61	67	67
Total Number Of Respondents*	(106–116)	(303–342)	(122–135)	(362–408)	(149–151)	(400–465)

* due to non-response, number of respondents may vary within the range shown

Some of the communications noted in Table 6 may require greater breaches of confidentiality than others. Patient and therapist may agree, for example, about the need for the therapist to communicate with third party

624

insurers and little may be lost from the relationship as a result. Communications to other health professionals may stand on the same footing. Indeed, so may any communication if it is sensitively handled within the therapeutic relationship. Nonetheless, there may be communications which the therapist feels constrained to make even though making them contradicts the therapist's best clinical judgment. To determine whether warnings have this quality, we investigated the next question.

TO THE EXTENT THAT THERAPISTS DO WARN THIRD PARTIES, ARE SUCH WARNINGS MADE CONTRARY TO THE THERAPIST'S CLINICAL JUDGMENT?

Table 7 shows the percentage of our respondents who have made a given type of extra therapeutic communication and who have, at some time in their careers, done so contrary to their best clinical judgment. We see that 45% of those who have communicated with potential victims feel that they have had to violate their own clinical judgment in making an extra therapeutic communication, as against between 30% and 32% of those who have made other communications. This Table suggests that the therapists who warn victims are those most likely to feel that they have at one time acted contrary to their best clinical judgment. . . .

TABLE 7

Disclosure Of Information To Third Parties In Last Year By Belief That Respondent Has Compromised Clinical Judgment At Some Point In His Or Her Career

Disclosure To	Percent Compromised Clinical Judgment	Total Number of Respondents
Governmental or private health insurers	32	(1245)
Patient's/client's family or friends	31	(1081)
Other health professionals	30	(1406)
Persons threatened by patient/client	45	(144)
Public authorities (e.g., police, child welfare, correctional personnel)	32	(982)

The tension between warning and sound clinical judgment may simply be inherent in the *Tarasoff* requirement that therapists protect victims. The California Supreme Court, after all, never suggested that it was adopting the *Tarasoff* duty because it made clinical sense. Rather, it adopted the duty out of a view that the increase in public safety compensated for whatever was being taken from professional autonomy. Whatever the public safety gains, our data suggest that therapists feel they pay a higher clinical price by warning than by making other forms of third party disclosures. . . .

625

HAS *TARASOFF* INFLUENCED THERAPIST ATTITUDES REGARDING APPROPRIATE INTERVENTIONS IN THE TREATMENT OF POTEN- TIALLY VIOLENT PATIENTS?

To answer this question, we asked therapists to indicate changes between 1975 and 1980 in their willingness to employ certain interventions in the treatment of potentially violent patients. This period runs from the date of the first *Tarasoff* opinion (December 1974) to the date of the survey and should reflect *Tarasoff's* influence. To further insure that we are measuring *Tarasoff's* impact, we divided our respondents into three groups: those who believed themselves legally bound by the *Tarasoff* principle, (2) those who believed themselves ethically, but not legally, bound, and (3) those who either had not heard of the decision or did not believe themselves legally or ethically bound by it. We reasoned that if *Tarasoff* has influenced psychotherapeutic practice, it would be most evident among those respondents who have heard of the case and believe that they are legally bound by it.

Table 8 presents the data. The most dramatic effect of *Tarasoff* can be seen exactly where one would expect it: in increased willingness to notify potential victims (line 5), public authorities (line 4), and police (line 6). Those who feel legally bound have become more willing since *Tarasoff* to employ warning interventions than those who believe themselves only ethically bound, and clearly more willing than those who don't consider themselves bound by *Tarasoff* at all.

Tarasoff appears to have influenced willingness to take notes (line 3), and to initiate involuntary hospitalization (line 9). Here, however, the ethically bound psychiatrists prove slightly more willing than those legally bound, although the differences are neither great nor entirely consistent. These findings provide support for the view that *Tarasoff* may encourage efforts to document patient treatment and some slight support for the claim that *Tarasoff* will lead to an increased use of involuntary commitment. Such conclusions must be viewed with caution: these findings could reflect general changes in views over time regarding the treatment of the potentially danger- ous patient. It is also possible that changes in therapeutic practice reflect differences in the patient populations seen by our respondents. We return to this issue below.

Interestingly, those who view themselves as bound by *Tarasoff* do not indicate either less willingness to treat dangerous patients than the others (line 1) or more willingness to terminate treatment (line 2). To explore this issue further, we asked the following question:

HAS *TARASOFF* DISCOURAGED THERAPISTS FROM TREATING PO- TENTIALLY DANGEROUS PATIENTS?

Table 9 presents data regarding whether and when our respondents treated patients they assessed as likely to be harmful to others. The amicus position suggests that awareness of the decision will discourage therapists from treating dangerous patients. Furthermore, traditional notions of deter- rence suggest that the aversion should be greatest among those who believe

TABLE 8 PERCENT OF RESPONDENTS IN EACH PROFESSION WITH VARYING BELIEFS ABOUT TARASOFF WHOSE WILLINGNESS TO EMPLOY CERTAIN INTERVENTIONS WITH DANGEROUS PATIENTS CHANGED BETWEEN 1975–1980

Change in Willingness to Employ:	Psychiatrist			Psychologist			Social Worker		
Intervention	Legal	Ethical	Neither	Legal	Ethical	Neither	Legal	Ethical	Neither
1) Less willing to treat	32	42	45	32	31	32	28	28	26
2) More willing to terminate	30	29	34	24	24	27	27	23	24
3) More willing to take notes	36	43	23	45	34	25	42	41	30
4) More willing to notify public authorities	59	54	36	51	36	25	47	49	42
5) More willing to notify victims	75	60	35	70	52	31	56	57	28
6) More willing to notify police	48	33	25	50	34	23	39	28	25
7) More willing to consult lawyers	37	48	31	30	30	28	30	24	28
8) More willing to consult administrator	39	35	37	33	23	23	36	30	36
9) More willing to initiate involuntary hospitalization	32	30	20	39	23	28	37	38	30
10) More willing to initiate voluntary hospitalization	34	32	31	50	39	41	43	39	46
Total Number of Respondents*	(217–224)	(89–91)	(59–61)	(246–254)	(94–99)	(109–115)	(226–236)	(68–71)	(195–207)

* Due to non-response, numbers of respondents may vary within the range shown.

627

themselves legally obligated. As the Table indicates, this is clearly not the case. If the proposition were valid, people believing themselves legally bound would be more likely than others to have stopped treating such patients. Therefore, those legally bound by *Tarasoff* would be more likely than others to have treated such patients in the past, but not currently, or less likely to have treated such patients in both the current year and in prior years. The data (lines 2 and 4) show the opposite. Therapists bound by *Tarasoff* are more likely, not less, to have treated such patients during the current year and earlier and are less likely, not more, to have last treated such a patient prior to the current year. These data on professional practices are consistent with our findings regarding changes in willingness to treat.

The clear majority of all therapists have treated a dangerous patient, and a reasonably high percentage have treated them in the past and were continuing to do so in 1980, when the survey was conducted. Among those who do treat such patients, has *Tarasoff* actually influenced interventions?

HAS *TARASOFF* INFLUENCED THERAPISTS TO WARN POTENTIAL VICTIMS, INVOLUNTARILY HOSPITALIZE POTENTIALLY VIOLENT PATIENTS, OR OTHERWISE ATTEMPT TO RESPOND TO THE LEGAL OBLIGATION TO PROTECT POTENTIAL VICTIMS?

We examined this question by asking our respondents to provide details concerning their interventions in the most recent case in which they treated a patient they assessed as dangerous. We also asked for information about another situation: the most recent case in which the patient uttered an explicit threat. The results are presented in Tables 10 and 11.

Turning first to the data on the last dangerous case presented in Table 10, we see that awareness of *Tarasoff* and the belief that it is legally or ethically binding has a consistent and noticeable influence across professions in one situation: warning the potential victim. Beliefs also seem to have a positive influence in two other areas: including notes about the patient and recommending voluntary hospitalization. There is a very small difference with regard to initiating involuntary hospitalization.

There are two points about these differences in hospitalization and note taking practices. First, the hospitalization and note interventions are not uniform: with regard to hospitalizations, ethically bound social workers and psychologists are more likely than legally bound ones to have initiated involuntary hospitalization, and ethically bound therapists in each profession were at least as likely as legally bound ones to recommend voluntary hospitalization. With regard to making notes, social workers show no patterns of influence. Second, and most importantly, most of the differences that do exist are quite small. The largest difference is in terms of warning practices between legally bound psychiatrists and those who reject or are ignorant of *Tarasoff*: a difference of sixteen percentage points. However, comparable differences for psychologists and social workers are seven points in each case.

TABLE 9 PERCENT OF RESPONDENTS IN EACH PROFESSION WITH VARYING BELIEFS ABOUT TARASOFF PRINCIPLE WHO HAVE OR HAVE NOT TREATED DANGEROUS PATIENTS DURING VARIOUS TIME PERIODS

	Psychiatrist			Psychologist			Social Worker		
	Legal	Ethical	Neither	Legal	Ethical	Neither	Legal	Ethical	Neither
1) Never treated a dangerous patient	15	14	27	25	27	39	23	25	29
2) Treated dangerous patients before 1979–80	16	20	19	20	17	26	14	19	25
3) Treated dangerous patients only during 1979–80	9	6	8	6	9	6	9	11	8
4) Treated dangerous patients both prior to and during 1979–80	60	60	46	49	47	29	53	45	39
Total Percent	100%	100%	100%	100%	100%	100%	100%	100%	100%
Total Respondents	(271)	(111)	(67)	(310)	(115)	(141)	(28)	(89)	(246)

TABLE 10 Percent Of Respondents In Each Profession With Varying Beliefs About Tarasoff Who Employed Certain Interventions In Most Recent Case (1975–1980) Involving Dangerous Patient

Intervention Employed:	Psychiatrist			Psychologist			Social Worker		
	Legal	Ethical	Neither	Legal	Ethical	Neither	Legal	Ethical	Neither
1) Declined or terminated treatment	5	4	5	2	8	3	11	6	8
2) Included note	67	61	51	50	42	47	59	58	50
3) Notified public authorities	11	9	14	10	9	5	15	20	17
4) Notified potential victim	21	16	5	19	18	9	19	15	11
5) Notified police	10	12	11	6	12	7	9	2	3
6) Consulted lawyer	10	7	5	6	10	3	6	9	6
7) Consulted administrator	12	7	11	9	12	10	12	20	17
8) Initiated involuntary hospitalization	32	29	27	12	12	7	21	18	15
9) Recommended voluntary hospitalization	26	32	22	27	25	19	30	36	26
Total Number of Respondents	(197)	(75)	(37)	(188)	(67)	(58)	(188)	(55)	(145)

To understand more clearly how *Tarasoff* has influenced actual behavior, however, we must examine the final Table (11) dealing with interventions in cases involving threats. The *Tarasoff* case involved a patient who threatened

TABLE 11 Percent of Respondents in Each Profession with Varying Beliefs About Tarasoff Who Employed Certain Interventions in Most Recent Case (1975–1980) Involving a Threat

Intervention Employed	Psychiatrist			Psychologist			Social Worker		
	Legal	Ethical	Neither	Legal	Ethical	Neither	Legal	Ethical	Neither
1) Declined or terminated treatment	5	5	16	3	12	0	8	14	6
2) Included note	61	51	47	56	62	25	58	57	57
3) Notified public authorities	11	13	5	3	12	0	15	21	12
4) Notified potential victim	33	23	5	37	31	25	31	21	14
5) Notified police	24	10	11	7	15	6	18	21	8
6) Initiated involuntary hospitalization	30	36	0	13	19	0	25	14	8
7) Initiated voluntary hospitalization	22	26	16	22	39	19	16	7	26
Total Number Of Respondents	(110)	(39)	(19)	(76)	(26)	(16)	(87)	(14)	(51)

an identified person. Therapists may therefore view *Tarasoff* as dealing with threatening patients specifically rather than dangerous patients generally. Indeed, this view is the emerging judicial interpretation: therapists have not been liable to victims of their patients when the victim could not have been identified beforehand. When we look to cases involving threats, beliefs about *Tarasoff* do have consistent patterns of influence with respect to warning and, more importantly, the differences between the groups are greater. With regard to warning, there is a twenty-eight point difference among psychiatrists, a fourteen point difference among psychologists, and a nineteen point difference among social workers, between those believing themselves legally bound by *Tarasoff* and those who reject or have not heard of it. Differences in note taking and involuntary hospitalization also exists between polar groups.

These data suggest that *Tarasoff* has influenced therapists' behavior most markedly in situations which gave rise to the case in the first instance, threatening behavior. This conforms to our earlier findings that therapists believed that the case required warning. It also suggests that our respondents tend to read the case narrowly; that is, that *Tarasoff* requires particular interventions with regard to the threatening patients specifically, rather than the dangerous patient generally.

V. CONCLUSION

... As we have shown, many therapists misstate the [*Tarasoff*] case in two major respects: they believe that it demands warning rather than reasonable care, and they believe that it is legally binding upon them when technically this may not be true. Yet, given the sources of information upon which the therapists relied, these views are readily understandable. In their rush to condemn the *Tarasoff* decision, the professional critics may have disseminated information leading to the very misperceptions which they sought to avoid.

Ultimately, however, the decisions themselves, rather than the criticisms, have been the likely source of confusion among therapists concerning their legal obligations. Rules designed to facilitate ad hoc and post hoc resolutions of disputes between an injured and his injurer do not provide very much guidance to those who attempt to behave in a way that avoids liability. The "reasonableness" standard may give courts and juries the discretion necessary to achieve situational justice; what it clearly does not do, however, is tell psychotherapists, any more than it tells police, "public servants" or insurance adjusters, how to behave in a concrete situation. "Warn the victim," on the other hand, does provide a clear, if rather simplistic, guide for the risk averse.

Moreover, therapists may be entirely reasonable in viewing *Tarasoff* as requiring warning. First, the court told them that they had to warn. The court then took eighteen months to reconsider and shift to a reasonable care standard. Having been alerted to their new obligation, therapists may not have felt free to suspend action with potentially violent patients while awaiting word from the court. Rather, they may have moved to incorporate the new rule into their practice.

Whatever their source, these legal misapprehensions have had consequences. The belief that the case requires warning influences therapists to do just that, particularly when the patient utters a threat, even though therapists are most likely to identify warning as the kind of third party communication which compromises their clinical judgment. Clearer understanding of the final ruling in the case would not eliminate all, or even a large percentage, of warnings, but it might encourage at least some therapists to respond with more clinically appropriate interventions in at least some cases....

Our findings also suggest a somewhat heretical point about tort doctrine and its influence on behavior. They suggest that if an appellate court desires to change behavior, it should use judicially established standards of behavior, not jury determined standards. The judicially determined rule of *Tarasoff I*, protect through warning, appears to have affected therapist attitudes, knowledge and behavior to a far greater degree than *Tarasoff II*....

... [T]he prevailing view that courts should not attempt to set specific standards of conduct needs reexamination. To the extent that it is based on the notion that courts are impotent when it comes to changing behavior, the anti-court argument does not comport with reality. To the extent that it is based on the proposition that compensation should be the primary goal of tort law, it is unnecessary. It may be justified on the grounds that courts cannot develop sound behavioral rules, but that case has yet to be made.

NOTES AND QUESTIONS

1. Another impact study of a tort decision is Jerry Wiley, "The Impact of Judicial Decisions on Professional Conduct," 55 *Southern California Law Review* 345 (1981). In *Helling v. Carey*, 83 Wash.2d 514, 519 P.2d 981 (1974), the defendant was an eye doctor. Plaintiff sued the doctor because the doctor had not detected plaintiff's glaucoma; other eye doctors testified that routine glaucoma tests were not given to young patients. The jury found for defendant, but the appellate court reversed, and opened the way to liability. Eye doctors were required to give tests for glaucoma, or face tort suits if a patient contracted this condition.

Wiley's study of the impact of the case came up with a surprising result: there was little impact, because most eye doctors were already testing for glaucoma. The expert testimony, in other words, was simply wrong.

What factual assumptions were at issue in the debate over the *Tarasoff* case? One, which was prominently mentioned, was whether psychiatrists could in fact predict if a patient was liable to become violent or dangerous. There is considerable dispute on this point. See Alexander D. Brooks, "The Constitutionality and Morality of Civilly Committing Violent Sexual Predators," 15 *University of Puget Sound Law Review* 709 (1992).

2. There are many other situations in which a rule or doctrine is communicated through professional channels. For example, officials at state departments of education tell school teachers whether they can hold prayers

in classes or decorate Christmas trees in their classrooms. Officials in the state attorney generals' offices and local district attorneys' offices tell police officers about the latest interpretations of Supreme Court decisions concerning the proper procedures for arrest. Obviously, there is room for differences of opinion if not distortion in the process.

Officials of large corporations must somehow learn about legal requirements and how to comply with them. Lauren B. Edelman, Steven E. Abraham and Howard S. Erlanger, "Professional Construction of Law: The Inflated Threat of Wrongful Discharge," 26 *Law & Society Review* 47, 77–78 (1992), studied how corporate lawyers and officials in personnel departments interpreted legal rules fashioned in the 1970s and 1980s that seemed to limit the rights of employers to fire employees when the employers did not have a legally recognized reason to do so. Courts in many states, particularly California, seemed to grant new rights to employees, and limits on the rights of employers to fire at will became news in the business press. Enterprising entrepreneurs sold elaborate programs designed to train employers about how to deal with these new cases. However, Edelman, Abraham and Erlanger point out that many of these people exaggerated the real threat posed by the new rules. They argue:

> [P]ersonnel professionals and practicing lawyers have a shared interest in constructing the threat of wrongful discharge in such a way that employers perceive the law as a threat and rely upon those professions to curb the threat. That threat—and the proffered solution—would help both professions to gain a symbiotic jurisdiction over corporate response to the legal environment....

See also Lauren B. Edelman, "Legal Environments and Organizational Governance: The Expansion of Due Process in the American Workplace," 95 *American Journal of Sociology* 1401 (1990).

3.   In a classic study, Vilhelm Aubert, the late Norwegian sociologist of law, investigated the impact of a Norwegian law about the work conditions of housemaids. The maids were poor women, mostly uneducated; they were not unionized, and they worked in people's homes. The message embodied in the law never got through to them. See Vilhelm Aubert, "Some Social Functions of Legislation," 10 *Acta Sociologica* 98 (1967). How big a role does wealth and class play in the communication process? Is it possible that the poor, at least in some situations, have a more accurate perception of the law in action—for example, with regard to law concerning welfare, immigration and crime—than the middle class and the wealthy?

4.   The psychologists and psychiatrists who knew (or thought they know) about *Tarasoff* were (technically) incorrect in their understanding of the case. What exactly was their misunderstanding? How did it come about?

5.   There have been a number of other studies of the impact of the *Tarasoff* case. D. L. Rosenhan, Terri Wolff Teitelbaum, Kathi Weiss Teitelbaum, and Martin Davidson, "Warning Third Parties: The Ripple Effects of *Tarasoff*," 24 *Pacific Law Journal* 1165 (1993), report on a survey conducted

in 1987. A questionnaire about *Tarasoff* was filled out by 872 psychiatrists and clinical psychologists in California. The overwhelming majority of the respondents had heard of the case.

The results of the survey suggested to the authors that the case "seems to have changed the nature of clinical practice." Some 37% of the respondents said that the case "has led them to focus more frequently on dangerousness with their patients. In addition, 32% of therapists reported that they concentrate more often on patients' less serious threats" (p. 1210). The survey results also suggest that the case has altered therapists' views of confidentiality. They are more willing than before at least to consider disclosing confidences because of the case. The therapists are also more likely to consult other professionals if they feel a patient is potentially dangerous.

Peter H. Schuck and Daniel J. Givelber, "Tarasoff v. Regents of the University of California: The Therapist's Dilemma," in Robert L. Rabin & Stephen D. Sugarman, eds., *Torts Stories,* at 99, 113–114, 117 (2003), review various studies about the impact of the decision. They conclude:

> The profession ... initially responded to *Tarasoff* with alarm. A quarter of a century later, we know that the alarmists were wrong. *Tarasoff* has been woven into clinical practice and has become a professional standard of practice among providers. We know of no evidence that it has adversely affected the practice of psychotherapy, led to a diminution in the availability of treatment for the potentially dangerous, caused an increase in the rate of involuntary commitments, or generated an increase in violence among those who do not seek treatment because of concerns about confidentiality. . . .

> In the end, whether *Tarasoff* has had a salutary impact on mental health practice turns upon an assessment of the importance of responding to potentially violent out-patients. Whatever else may be said about the *Tarasoff* decision, it focused attention on this problem and has generated apparently sound clinical approaches to it.

Compare Alan A. Stone, *Law, Psychiatry, and Morality* 187 (1984): "The reality is that the present mental health system lacks the wisdom to predict, the ability to treat, and the security to protect society against violence. *Tarasoff* and its progeny will not change this reality."

See also Peter C. Carstensen, "The Evolving Duty of Mental Health Professionals to Third Parties: A Doctrinal and Institutional Examination," 17 *International Journal of Law and Psychiatry* 1 (1994). Carstensen notes another impact of the *Tarasoff* decision far beyond the borders of California. The mental health professions in many states have lobbied successfully for statutes that limit the potential liability of therapists in the *Tarasoff* situation. Often the statutes narrowly limit the kind of threat by a patient that can give rise to liability. Some statutes also define responses to a threat that the therapist may make that will discharge the duty to rescue the threatened third party. Is it likely that these statutes will undercut the ripple effects of the *Tarasoff* decision that Rosenhan and his colleagues discovered?

6.   Lawyers play an important role in the legal system as middlemen, or information brokers. They know the law, and they convey that knowledge to clients, when the clients need it. A couple that plans to get a divorce probably knows only a little about the divorce laws (some of it no doubt wrong); but they rely on the lawyer for more precise information. However, most people most of the time do not consult lawyers. People without legal training communicate to others who lack such training about what they can and cannot do. Superiors in organizations often tell their subordinates what to do and what to avoid doing. How do ordinary people learn about rules and doctrines? Since a rule that nobody knows obviously can have no impact whatsoever, what institutions and roles in the legal system are designed to teach or tell people about rules and doctrines? How do people learn that murder, rape and robbery are against the law? How do people learn the requirements of the federal and state laws imposing income taxes? How do people learn about the traffic laws and changes in those laws? How do people learn about laws required that their dogs and cats be licensed and not roam uncontrolled by a person (the so-called "leash laws")? The *Tarasoff* case was disseminated through professional groups. A decision that applies to the public at large gets whatever communication it gets through newspapers, radio, and TV. *Roe v. Wade* and *Brown v. Board of Education* are two of the most famous Supreme Court decisions of the twentieth century. Very many, if not most, people have heard of them, but very few have ever read the Supreme Court's opinions in those cases. How accurately do you think they are understood by most people? Through what channels did they learn about these cases? Are these channels likely to be different for whites and blacks, men and women, people in different regions of the country, or those with different levels of formal education?

7.   At least some of the impact of decisions of the Supreme Court of the United States may turn on the public's acceptance of them as a legitimate resolution of a social and legal problem. Those in the news media face great difficulties in covering the Supreme Court. Few reporters have the legal background and the historical knowledge to understand the significance of the Court's decisions. There are about thirty accredited Supreme Court correspondents, but the commitment of newspapers, wire services and television news departments to full-time coverage has been declining for some time. The Court does not itself explain what it has done beyond issuing orders and judicial opinions. A reporter cannot interview justices as she might interview representatives in Congress or administration officials, up to and including the President of the United States. News reports can be very misleading. The Supreme Court often issues four to six major decisions on a single day toward the end of a term, and the press has to decide how to report them. Decisions that are immediately newsworthy often are not the most important ones in the long term. Linda Greenhouse, the *New York Times'* Supreme Court reporter concludes in her "Telling the Court's Story: Justice and Journalism at the Supreme Court," 105 *Yale Law Journal* 1537, 1559 (1996): "I see a Court that is quite blithely oblivious to the needs of those who convey its

work to the outside world, and a press corps that is often groping along in the dark, trying to make sense out of the shadows on the cave wall."

Elliot E. Slotnick, "Media Coverage of Supreme Court Decision–Making: Problems and Prospects," 75 *Judicature* 128 (1991), points out that most people get their news from television, and there is a tendency for television to report reactions of officials of government and of interest groups to the Court's decisions rather than what the Court actually did or said. These reactions are more dramatic and entertaining, but they tend to be overstated and are often misleading. Television can blur the message, and may influence the impact of the case. Ethan Katsh, "The Supreme Court Beat: How Television Covers the U.S. Supreme Court," 67 *Judicature* 8 (1983), analyzed coverage of Supreme Court decisions during the period 1976 to 1981. Television news reported only about one case out of five, and it was less likely to say anything about business and economic decisions. Abortion and civil liberties cases were much more likely to gain some coverage. The public got a distorted picture of the actual work of the Court.

The public gets even less information about the lower federal courts and the state courts. Again, coverage tends to reflect the entertainment value of particular cases. Such things as a very large verdict or a woman suing McDonald's restaurants, alleging that its food caused her to be obese, get their thirty seconds or a minute. Television largely ignores the day to day patterns of activity in the courts. There are programs like *Law and Order* on TV, and countless stories about crime, trials, police and detective work, not to mention straight dramatic stories that include some message about law or the legal system. There is very little research on the way such messages influence public attitudes and behaviors.

If few people in a society know much about the detail of most laws, how do they make judgments about the legitimacy of the Supreme Court of the United States or the Supreme Court of California? As we saw, in a few notable instances—notoriously, the affair of McDonald's and the scalding hot coffee—there is all too much attention to atypical cases, lasting far longer than thirty seconds or a minute. Moreover, there is too much misinformation. Still, on the whole television largely ignores the information people would need to make judgments about whether their governor, senators, assembly persons or police are acting in an acceptable manner or how do to behave so as to avoid legal sanctions. How do people learn what they can and cannot do?

(4.17) The Ex Ante Function of the Criminal Law

John M. Darley, Paul H. Robinson and Kevin M. Carlsmith

35 *Law & Society Review* 165 (2001).

A legal code in a complex society is designed to have several functions. First, it is designed to announce beforehand the rules by which citizens must conduct themselves, on pain of criminal punishment. Second, if a person

637

violates one of these rules of conduct, the criminal law must determine whether the violator is to be held criminally liable. Third, another part of its adjudicatory function, where liability is imposed the law must determine the general range, or "grade," of punishment to be imposed.

It is the first function that is of interest to us here, the so-called ex ante function of the criminal law. The code announces in advance what actions count as criminal; thus the citizenry can use the announcement to guide their actions to avoid criminal conduct. The law, in other words, draws "bright lines" between allowable and unallowable conduct, and those lines enable the citizens to regulate their conduct so they do not break the laws. To use a familiar metaphor, the criminal law specifies what sorts of actions are "out of bounds," and the penalties for those actions, so the players will "stay in bounds." The criminal justice system relies on people knowing the law and knowing where the boundaries for their conduct lie. Ignorance does not excuse unlawful conduct, a fact summarized in the phrase "ignorance of the law is no excuse." Such a rule is defended as a useful means of creating an incentive for citizens to learn the law.

Citizens need to know these codes if these laws are to function successfully in an ex ante mode. If, for instance, the code requires that a person who is aware of the location of a felon report that location to the police, people need to know that the code requires such conduct. If the code requires that a person help another person whose life is in danger, then for the code to guide the behavior of the potential rescuer, he or she has to be aware that the code requires that helping action....

The purpose of this study is primarily to ... determine whether people are aware of the lines drawn by legal codes in the United States. Do people know what the law says?

Obviously, it is important to specify what kinds of laws we are talking about.... [E]veryone is usually aware that the codes criminalize murder, not because they are aware of the specific statute that criminalizes murder but because they cannot conceive of a criminal code that would not criminalize such an action. So as not to turn the question of whether people are aware of the content of laws into a straw man issue, we decided to test whether people are aware of the content of laws that are genuinely important and not simply derivations from consensually-held moral intuitions.

For our research, we chose to see whether people are aware of the laws about such issues as being required to assist a stranger in distress, report a known felon, or retreat before using deadly force in defense of self or property. These laws struck us as being about important conduct, about situations in which many of us may find ourselves and in which the guidance of the legal code would be invaluable. More important, however, is that they struck criminal code drafters as important.

In the United States, the bulk of the criminal codes are set by the states rather than the federal government. Prior to the 1960s, the criminal codes of many states were a somewhat disorganized and internally inconsistent amalgamation of survivals from English Common Law. Laws were passed to deal with the circumstances that confronted the states as they became settled, and other idiosyncratic determinants. In the 1950s, having recognized the legal complexities and the moral disproportions created by these discrepancies, the influential American Law Institute set a committee of distinguished scholars to the task of creating a unified criminal code that had consistent doctrinal underpinnings, one that could be a model for adoption by the various states. The results of this work, the Model Penal Code, was published in 1962 and has since been adopted, in whole or in part, by more than 36 states. This shared reliance on the Model Penal Code ... has created some uniformity among American criminal codes; nonetheless, many states have adopted minority positions on one or another aspect of criminal law.

The fact that some states have deviated from the majority concerning certain laws has created the possibility of a natural experiment about the ex ante function of the legal code. Do the citizens of states holding majoritarian legal views and the citizens of states holding deviant legal views know the different "bright lines" drawn by their legal codes? If the laws are successful in their ex ante function, the citizens of both the deviant and the majoritarian states will be able to correctly say what is and is not criminalized by their state of residence. This is a test of what we have called the "ex ante function." They may or may not agree with what the law does and does not criminalize, but they are aware of it.

Our hypothesis is that people do not have a clue about what the laws of their states hold on these important legal issues. This hypothesis stems from various sources and from our own experiences; in doing our research ... we learned some of the laws that define criminal conduct, and they are not always or even often what we thought they would be.... If we were to have guessed what lines the laws draw between criminal and noncriminal conduct, we nonlaw professors would often have guessed entirely wrong. Also, in a previous study[159] ... we asked citizens to report what they understood their state laws to be, and we were struck by how wrong their guesses were.

Why is it that people often think they know their state's laws? We suggest a several step process: First, general attitudes determine whether a person thinks a particular action is morally acceptable or unacceptable. Second, when people are asked their personal view on the criminality of the action, their own moral attitudes determine whether they perceive the action as criminal, and if so, they decide the liability appropriately assigned to that action. Finally, when people are asked whether the state in which they reside criminalizes that action, they answer yes or no not because they know what the code says but because they assume that the state, in its moral wisdom, shares their personal moral views. We believe citizens follow this process consistently when asked to respond to questions about their state's laws.

159. John M. Darley, C. A. Sanderson & P. S. LaMantia, "Community Standards for Defining Attempt: Inconsistencies with the Model Penal Code," 39 *American Behavioral Scientist* 405 (1996).

Why do citizens assume that the legal code corresponds to their moral intuitions? Psychologists have frequently found what they call a "false consensus effect"; thus, a person tends to overestimate the prevalence in others of his or her own opinions and preferences ... We suggest that this overestimation is particularly likely to occur when value-laden beliefs are at issue. In such an instance, people may simply feel that "others agree with me about this law, and so that is what the law says." The premise a person requires for this inference is that the legislators agree with the majority or will go along with the majority opinion, and this is what produces such a correspondence.

Nevertheless, we suspect that it is unlikely that the person goes through this inference chain. The inference is more likely to be spontaneous and automatic.... [C]itizens should not be accurate about state laws; instead, their answers about their own state's laws should correlate with their personal views about the criminal or noncriminal nature of the action, which in turn should be predicted by the relevant attitudes. We thus have gathered evidence about this assertion and present our results herein.

Method Overview

Our research concerns whether various elements of the criminal code are fulfilling their ex ante function—whether they provide the bright lines that set off criminal conduct from allowable conduct. We translated this idea into the following questions: Are citizens of a state aware of the criminal laws of that state? More specifically, does the presence of a particular law in a state cause those citizens to report that their state law is anything close to what the law actually holds? Do they deviate at all from what people in other states think the governing law is? We also provided an initial test of the second version of the ex ante hypothesis: that the presence of a state law comes to affect how people view the behavior in question and thus influences their attitudes and personal beliefs.

We selected four states, each with a somewhat deviant law about what counts as criminal conduct. We asked selected residents of these states to read a series of scenarios.... One scenario described an offense that is criminal in most states, but not in the deviant state, or an action that is criminal in the deviant state but not in the other states. Respondents assigned liability or no liability ratings. If they assigned liability, they were also asked to assign punishment ratings to the actor in the different scenarios. Each state served as an experimental group for one scenario, and as a control group for the other three.

Our first question is whether the citizens of a state with a deviant law knew the content of that state's law; therefore, the residents were asked to report what liability and punishment would be assigned by the law of the state in which they lived. To test our hypothesis, they also reported their own opinions on what liability and punishment was appropriate for the actor, and their attitudes on issues directly relevant to the law in question.

Participants

The 203 participants (37% female) resided in one of four states and were employed by their state university system.[160] We selected individuals from state universities because they represent a relatively diverse population in terms of occupation, income, and education. There were 49 respondents from the University of Texas at Austin, 50 from the University of Wisconsin at Madison, 46 from the University of South Dakota at Sioux Falls, and 58 from the University of North Dakota at Grand Forks.

We primarily targeted staff members from each university, although faculty and student-employees were not removed from our study. Eighteen percent of our participants held doctorates or professional degrees, 30% held master's degrees, 28% held bachelor's degrees, 13% held associate's degrees, and 10% held high school degrees. The mean age was 42, with a range of ages from 18 to 64.

We excluded respondents who had lived in their current state of residence for less than one year (N = 6). Those retained in the sample had lived in their home states, on average, 28 years. Our sample was somewhat racially homogeneous, reflecting the fact that the institutions sampled were in small Midwestern towns: Eighty-six percent described themselves as Caucasian, 3% Asian, 3% Hispanic, and the remainder self-described as "other" or declined to state. Thirty-seven percent identified their political affiliation as Democrat, 17% as Republican, 25% as independent, and the remainder identified themselves with smaller groups (e.g., Libertarian, Green/Environmental).

Materials

Participants read four short vignettes that described potentially illegal behaviors. As we mentioned previously, for each participant one of the vignettes corresponded to a law that was particular to his or her state. The descriptions averaged 143 words. What follows are the particular issues used in the vignettes.

Duty to assist.

Following English Common Law tradition, most legal codes do not impose a duty to assist a person in trouble, even if that assistance can be given without much risk or inconvenience to the potential assister. Wisconsin, however, has a state law (Wis. Stat. Ann. § 940.34[1], [2]) that requires its citizens to provide aid, assuming that doing so does not constitute a reasonable threat to the rescuer's own safety. Our vignette describes a person who comes across a victim of a recent mugging who is lying unconscious in the street. Although there is a telephone nearby, the bystander chooses to continue on his way.

160. Although it is possible to quarrel with the representativeness of the sample, in a sample consisting of university employees, respondents are, on average, better educated than other citizens of the state. Moreover, people working at an institution in which discussions of legal questions are likely to be more frequent are likely to be better informed about legal codes than are other citizens of the state.

Duty to retreat.

All states permit the use of force, up to and including deadly force, in self-defense. North Dakota and Wisconsin, however, require that a person attempt to retreat prior to the use of deadly force (N.D. Cent. Code § 12.1–05–07; Wis. Stat. Ann. § 939.48). To capture views concerning this law, our scenario describes a person whose life is clearly being threatened and who opts to employ deadly force rather than to retreat by driving away from the scene. He knows he could safely retreat.

Misprision of a felony.

In South Dakota, there is a legal obligation to report a known felon (S.D. Codified Laws Ann. § 22–11–12), whereas in the rest of the country one need not report such knowledge. Our vignette describes a character who fails to report the whereabouts of an old friend who had recently committed a felony.

Deadly force against property.

All states permit the use of deadly force to protect oneself from mortal danger, and all states permit the use of force to protect one's property. With the exception of Texas (Tex. Penal Code Ann. § 9.42), however, there must at a minimum be a reasonable belief of a possibility of death or unlawful force before one can employ deadly force in retaliation. In other words, the mere taking of property does not suffice as a defense in the use of deadly force, except in the state of Texas. Our scenario describes an individual who shoots and kills a retreating burglar in order to reclaim stolen property.

Attitude scales.

At the conclusion of the study, participants completed a short attitude scale related to each of the ex ante laws we were testing. . . . Each subscale consisted of three items that tapped opinions close to the underlying principle of the ex ante laws. Using a 7–point attitude scale, we asked participants to agree or disagree with a series of opinion statements. . . .

Survey.

The opening page of our survey consisted of an informed consent statement, with links to more-detailed descriptions of the study and the researchers. Anonymity was assured. After giving their consent, participants were shown the four vignettes and were asked to indicate whether the perpetrator was guilty of any crime, and if so, what they believed was an appropriate punishment. Respondents replied to the question "What do you think is an appropriate punishment?" using a 13–point scale, which began with "no liability" then progressed to "liable, no punishment," "1 day," "2 weeks," etc., and finally to "life in prison" and "death penalty" (see Figure 1).

No   Liable, no   1 day 2 wks. 2 mos. 6 mos. 1 yr. 3 yrs. 7 yrs. 15 yrs. 30 yrs. Life in Death
liability punishment   prison penalty

Figure 1.   Punishment Scale

It was important to us that the respondents separate their own views about liability from the liabilities they thought the authorities would impose. We therefore told them that we would ask both questions, but on the first question, we made clear that we were interested in their personal opinions, and not what they thought the law stated.

We asked participants, after responding to the four vignettes, to repeat the process a second time, but this time in accordance with what they believed their state law said. We explicitly stated that if they did not know their state's law, guessing was perfectly appropriate, and told them their responses may be quite similar to their personal sentence recommendations or they may be quite different. We asked, "What does your State consider an appropriate punishment?" and we used the same 13–point scale for the participants' responses.

The survey concluded with the attitude scales and a variety of demographic questions, such as age, race, political affiliation, education, and residence history.

Results Preliminary Analyses

. . . .

A chi-square analysis revealed a similar pattern of results across three of the four vignettes (see Table 1). A similar proportion of respondents from both deviant and majoritarian states predicted punishment regardless of their state's law. E.g., 36% of Wisconsinites believed their state would punish someone for failing to assist a person in need, whereas 39% of all other respondents believed this would be criminalized.

Table 1.   Percentage Of Respondents Predicting State Punishment

Case	Majority States	Actual (Expected)	Deviant States	Actual (Expected)	Deviant State	Chi-Square
Duty to assist	39	(0)	36	(100)	WI	0.16
Deadly force	77	(100)	49	(0)	TX	13.16*
Duty to retreat	71	(0)	79	(100)	ND & WI	1.85
Misprison of a felon	76	(0)	80	(100)	SD	0.30

Note: *indicates $p < 0.001$

In other words, in three cases, state law does not appear to be a factor in how people come to "know" their state law. The exception to this pattern comes from the Texas law that permits the use of deadly force in defense of property. It is clear that Texans do, in fact, know or guess that their state law does not punish a person for this behavior. For now, simply note this possible exception to the generalization that people do not seem to be aware of the laws of their state.

ANOVA of Predicted State Sentence by Case and State Law

In the preceding analysis we took a dichotomous approach to the data by coding all of the responses as either punishing or not punishing. In the next analysis we employed a more sensitive test by utilizing the full range of responses.... [161]

As before, state law seems to make little difference in people's predictions of their state's sentence: With respect to "duty to assist," respondents from Wisconsin (the deviant state in this case) predicted a sentence of 3.2 (corresponding to slightly more than one day in jail), whereas all of the other respondents predicted 3.4 ($t(86) = 0.51$, ns).[162] 7 Similarly, the difference was negligible for the "misprision of a felon" case (5.7 versus 5.6, $t(64) = -0.14$, ns) and was marginally different for the "duty to retreat" (7.9 versus 7.0, $t(167) = -1.63$, $p = 0.11$). Finally, as expected from the chi-square analysis, the residents of Texas predicted that their state government would respond more leniently toward the use of "deadly force." The average Texas sentence was 5.0 (corresponding to two months in jail), whereas residents of the other three states averaged 7.1 (approximately one year in jail). This difference was significant ($t(63) = 3.35$, $p = 0.001$), and it continues to suggest that Texans might know their state's rules on the use of deadly force....

ANOVA of Personal Sentence Recommendation by Case and State Law

As we have mentioned, a possible function of the legal codes is to morally educate the citizens who are governed by these codes. Even though citizens may be unaware of the exact laws of their states, it is a possibility that they were, nonetheless, educated by the debates surrounding the passage of these laws, which is reflected in their views of the appropriate punishments. This is the "strong" version of the ex ante hypothesis. This fact directs our attention to the liability ratings made by respondents reporting their personal views.

We determined whether respondents from the states with deviant laws reported personal punishment preferences differently from all of our other respondents....

We observed large differences for the different vignettes ($F (3,540) = 68$, $p < 0.001$), but relatively small differences according to the presence or absence of the particular ex ante law ($F (3,180) = 2.39$, $p = 0.07$). E.g., residents of Wisconsin are required by law to render assistance to a person in need, but Wisconsin respondents were no more likely to impose jail time for

161. For this analysis, we treated our scale as a continuous interval scale, although it does not meet this assumption. The differences between "no liability," "liable but no punishment," "one day," and "one week" are clearly not equivalent; similarly, the differences between "30 years in jail," "life in jail," and "capital punishment" are not the same. We conducted the same analyses without the endpoints and with true interval scaling (according to actual sentence length) and obtained essentially identical results under both conditions.

162. All tests in this analysis assume unequal variances to control for our often-disparate sample sizes.

an actor who failed to do so than were nonresidents (3.64 versus 3.34, t (78) = –0.84 *ns*).

Similarly, although residents of South Dakota are obliged to report felonious activity, their ratings of criminal liability were indistinguishable from that of the respondents from the other three states (3.57 versus 3.31, t (74) = – 0.82, *ns*). In North Dakota and Wisconsin there is a duty to retreat and to use only the minimum force necessary for self-protection. However, residents of these states were actually more forgiving of violators of this code than were residents of states with no duty to retreat (6.87 versus 7.21, t (200) = 0.57, *ns*). Finally, with regard to the use of deadly force in the protection of property, Texans were found to be slightly more permissive in assigning criminal liability (4.42 versus 5.78, t (82) = 2.24, p = 0.03).

The simple conclusion is that the presence of a law that might have changed personal views about what the law should be appears to have little effect on ordinary citizens for three of the four actions we studied. In the case of Texans and killing in defense of property, we found an interpretative ambiguity. They, more than the citizens of the other states, reported that their state law permitted deadly force in defense of property, which was true. They also reported personal punishment preferences that were more permissive, and thus directionally in accord with their state law. . . .

[In the next section, the authors use various statistical tests to choose between two models of the "relationship among state laws, individual attitudes, and individual behavior." One model assumes that when the state makes an act criminal, this influences peoples' attitudes, and, in turn, their beliefs about appropriate punishments. Then the law influences their actual behavior. The other model assumes that peoples' attitudes are shaped by their past experiences, and that these attitudes influence their "individual sentencing recommendations." The "actual state code," in other words, does not influence what people think is in the code. Generally, the authors find that the data confirm this second model rather than the first.]

Discussion

We have demonstrated that, for a number of laws, the citizens of states that hold deviant versions of these laws are unaware of their content. The laws we chose to study, we again argue, are not the trivial ones that no citizen will bother to know; they are important laws, concerning whether one has a duty to help a person in distress, report a known felon, or retreat rather than respond with deadly force when threatened.

In our study (holding Texas aside), the citizens showed no particular knowledge of the laws of their states. But when we asked them to tell us about their state laws, they were able to tell us what they thought those laws were. What source did they draw on to answer this question if it was not their knowledge of the actual laws? We suggest that, consistent with the concept of the consensus bias, they decided what they believed to be the lines between criminal and noncriminal actions—essentially a moral judgment—by assuming that their state had "gotten it right"; they guessed that the law of the state was what their personal opinion thought it should be. This result is demonstrated by the moderately high and consistently reliable correlations between respondents' personal opinion about what the law should assign in the way of punishments and their reports about the punishments the state laws in fact assigned.

Before we suggest some conclusions that might be drawn from our study, we should clarify the limitations of our findings. First, there is the interesting case of Texas. We cannot conclusively rule out the idea that the citizens know the laws of the state and, because they are the duly pronounced laws, are authoritatively influenced to agree with them and thus assign personally preferred sentences accordingly. We favor the alternate view, that the lenient opinions of the Texans were there first and influenced the passage of the correspondingly lenient laws. Which of these views is true requires further research. Researchers doing field experiments using geographically contiguous states that have differing laws may help to sort out the possible alternative explanations of our results, such as a culture-of-honor explanation.

We were struck by the difference in our results between the variant Texas law and the variant laws of the other three states. In each of the other cases, the legislature is imposing an extra obligation on its citizens to act: to retreat rather than to retaliate, to assist a person in distress, or to inform the police if the location of a criminal is known. We presume that the Texas legislature, in promulgating its law concerning the use of deadly force in defense of property, was not attempting to impose on its citizens the obligation to shoot people who are stealing their property; instead, it was allowing them the choice to do so without fear of criminal prosecution. The Texas legislature, therefore, decriminalized something that is considered criminal in other states, while the legislatures in the other states deviated and criminalized something that is not considered criminal in most states.

It may be that the proper interpretation here is that citizens' lack of knowledge of the nature of the laws of their states generally arises when their legislatures attempt to impose extra obligations on their citizens. In these instances, we suspect, the legislatures believe that these extra obligations are morally required ones, and that many of the citizens believe this as well. Nevertheless, when a legislature decriminalizes an act, or resists adopting, for instance, the *Model Penal Code's* recommendation to criminalize that act, it does so because it is convinced that the citizens of its state do not regard the act as criminal (and it is likely that the legislators do not regard it as criminal either). One way of expressing this asymmetry is that, on some occasions, one passes laws "in order to make the citizens morally better"—and this effort might be primarily a symbolic rather than a practical one.

Our samples of citizens in each of the four states are not large, and they were not drawn by careful, formally structured, sampling procedures. Our sample of the laws on which to test our hypothesis about knowledge of those laws was also not formally specified. We chose laws that we thought met the criterion of being important in guiding citizen behavior in instances that citizens might confront, and in which differences among states existed. We are thus heir to a number of the criticisms that can be leveled against field experiments in general, and ours in particular. Further, because we chose not to inflict a longer series of questions on respondents, we were not able to do a complete job of tracing paths from demographics to punishment-relevant attitudes to punishments assigned.

Based on past research, . . . we do not believe that demographic variables are strongly linked to people's attitudes about just punishments, so the low and occasional correlations we found between demographic variables and the proximate attitude measures are about what we would expect to find in larger-scale studies. We might, however, suggest what we would expect from studies more oriented toward tracing the paths between a broader sample of attitudes and views on just punishments. General attitudes—such as opinions toward the degree to which crime was rampant, or the low success rate of the police in catching criminals—may predict what we have called the more-proximal attitudes (e.g., allowing deadly force in defense of property), which would in turn predict leniency of sentence assigned to a person who does use force in defense of property. General attitudes would only occasionally be predicted by demographics, and rarely strongly predicted by them. Whether these expectations are true awaits further research.

Nonetheless, having acknowledged these limitations, we now suggest what will follow if our findings, tested in other studies, continue to hold true. First, a psychological point: People do report what they take the laws of their state to be. . . . [P]eople often generate their perceptions of what the law of the state must be from what they think is the morally appropriate form for that law to take. That is, people use their moral intuitions about whether various actions are permissible or proscribed to generate what they believe the laws must be. Given that people's moral intuitions vary considerably, many people are often wrong about what the actual law of their state holds. They are, in other words, ignorant about the content of the law.

We . . . argue . . . that support for the criminal justice system depends on it being perceived as delivering just punishments to individuals who intentionally commit actions that they know are criminal. . . . If the legal system contains many laws—the contents of which are not known and not intuited correctly by the citizens—and it punishes certain actions with criminal sanctions, and the citizens become aware of this practice, then the moral credibility of the law is sacrificed. This is not only our argument. . . . Our current research suggests . . . that perhaps respect for the system is preserved by the fact that one of the predicates of our argument is not always, or even often, fulfilled: People do not normally become aware that the laws are at variance with their moral intuitions. What might make them aware of these differences, and what the consequences of that awareness might be, remains a topic for further investigation. . . .

We were led to wonder how it was that the citizens of a state were meant to learn the laws of their particular corner of the land. But if we examine the ways in which the transmission of knowledge from the halls of the legislature to the heads of the citizens is supposed to take place, we find a puzzling silence. Not much is written about how this should specifically come about. Do legislatures assume that every citizen memorizes the state code and consults it when necessary (e.g., at the instant of seeing an individual in distress)? Do the drafters count on the debates of the legislatures penetrating the popular consciousness? Do they expect newspapers to hasten the news of drafting controversies to the waiting multitudes?

We did have a very preliminary look at newspapers as a transmission system; we did a search (via Lexis–Nexis) on newspapers in the capital cities of the states in our study for periods before and after the state codes were passed. For instance, the Wisconsin Code was enacted in 1983 and went into effect in 1984, and we searched 1980 to 1990. We used key phrases and words such as "duty to assist," "good Samaritan," "assist," and, finally, simply "duty" and turned up no leads. We also did similar searches, using the relevant key words we could think of, for the other states and found nothing. If we can use newspaper coverage as a proxy for attention paid by public media, then this is not the medium to count on for transmission of knowledge about criminalization rules to citizens.... A second point can be made here. Our search of the newspapers extended far enough past the date of the adoption of the relevant laws so that we should have found reports of trials of persons accused of violating those laws, but we did not find any such reports. This result may be another indicator that the passing of these "be a better person" laws is a symbolic activity, which does not have much effect on what actions prosecutors actually choose to prosecute. We are then left with the odd thought that those who got the written code of their state "wrong" are in some sense right about how the law is administered in reality, while those who got it "right" are wrong about who actually will be prosecuted. This seems an undesirable state of affairs.

By contrast, it is interesting to note that we were able to find numerous articles from Texas papers on a case in which a citizen chased a burglar (who had given up the unsuccessful burglary attempt) for three blocks before shooting him in the back and killing him with a concealed handgun.[163] The defendant, who declined to mount any defense, was acquitted by a jury. Even in this instance, though, it appears that the "story" was more about the defendant's use of the concealed weapon than about the defense of property statute.

As this example suggests, it is difficult to claim that the code drafters of the states are taking the steps necessary to make the laws known. We suspect

---

163. As one of the reviewers points out, this shooting came too late to come under Texas statute § 9.42. That is, the actor was not entitled to shoot the fleeing felon after the long pursuit; and yet the jury acquitted him. This verdict does suggest that the legislature might have correctly perceived public sentiment regarding the use of deadly force in defense of property as legitimate!

that making them known is a problem that never even occurred to code drafters. Perhaps the reason for their obliviousness is that legislators believe that the codes they draft simply reflect the moral norms of the community. (They ignore the fact of the drafter debates on these issues, which they should have realized signaled disagreement, rather than consensus, among even sophisticated citizens.) Given that "everyone would agree that" the entire content of the criminal code is exactly what is held as the morally right system by any right-thinking person, there is no need to make citizens aware of the code. They are already aware of it via the mechanism of their own moral intuitions. But as we, and others, have shown in a variety of studies ... people's moral intuitions often differ sharply from the *Model Penal Code* in particular and criminal codes in general. Thus, when ordinary people intuit what the code holds from their opinion of what it should hold, they often get the code wrong, and the ex ante function of the law suffers accordingly.

We suggest that wise code drafters take on the burden of educating the community on the lines that the code draws between allowable and criminal conduct. Even wiser code drafters should take on the burden of explaining to the community why it is that that subset of laws, which the legislature chooses to adopt and which violate the moral intuitions of the community, are nonetheless morally appropriate or otherwise justified.

NOTES AND QUESTIONS

1. We run our legal system with the idea that everyone is presumed to know the law, and ignorance of the law is no excuse. One look at the collected statutes of any state plus the United States Code that collects the work of Congress tells us that this must be a presumption against fact in most instances. There is simply too much law for anyone, including lawyers, to know it all. Many statutes are highly specialized, and they have no application or relevance to ordinary citizens. But what about laws that are less specialized and that might apply to anybody—like the laws discussed by Darley and his collaborators? How can they be effective if there is such widespread ignorance of the law? Do the findings of this article shed any light on this question?

2. Suppose you agree with Darley and company that it would be a good idea for many reasons if people knew more of what was against the law and the penalties for violating various provisions of it. How would you try to communicate the rules to ordinary people? If we want a license to drive a car, we must show our knowledge of the traffic laws. Most states publish booklets designed to convey this knowledge, and many schools teach driver education. Most of us know that we have to pay taxes, and, again, the federal and state governments publish booklets that attempt to teach us what is required. Could a state use this approach with other bodies of law? Do you think that requiring schools to teach the various criminal laws would be effective?

A Concluding Word

The materials in this section make one thing very clear: the impact or effectiveness of law is not to be taken for granted. Even deciding whether a law is effective is often debatable. How, for example, should we label a law that achieves about 60% of its goals? Is it effective or ineffective? The answer may depend on which law we are talking about. We do not expect laws against speeding to be totally effective, and perhaps this hardly matters. But laws and rules which are meant to deter or prevent the hijacking of airplanes, terrorist attacks or the collapse of a major dam require a much higher level of effectiveness. What is the socially optimal level of effectiveness, for example, of laws against child molestation or the killing of endangered species? Or, on the other hand, of laws against jaywalking or parking overtime? Moreover, measurement of effectiveness often is difficult. Every scholar who works in this area would agree that the question of impact is important but that scholarship has just scratched the surface. It is troubling that there is no general agreement about some basic theoretical issues.

In addition, we can always ask: effective from whose standpoint? "Impact" is both direct and indirect. Every rule, regulation, decision or statute, if it has any behavioral consequences at all, sets off ripples of consequences. It may affect in subtle and complex ways the individuals, groups and institutions that react to the acts and symbols of the legal order. For one imaginative exploration of the subject of impact and effectiveness, see Gunther Teubner, in "Regulatory Law: Chronicle of a Death Foretold," in 1 *Social and Legal Studies* 451 (1992). Teubner's essay is subtle and difficult. However, the central point seems to be that the orthodox view of impact fails because it is too wooden, too narrow and ignores the way social systems are actually structured. Social life is made up of a whole series of codes or realms ("discourses"), which are little worlds in themselves. "Impact" studies should really be studies of how such little worlds are coupled or fail to couple. Each little world may be "immune" to the other, may ignore the others totally, or may be "structurally coupled." The study of effectiveness should really be dissolved into a study of how various "discourses" collide, harmonize or interfere with each other. Teubner's article is a response to Hubert Rottleutner, "The Limits of Law: The Myth of a Regulatory Crisis," 17 *International Journal of the Sociology of Law* 273 (1989), a very thoughtful critique of Teubner's approach.

CHAPTER 5

The Legal System as a Social System: Structure, Rules and Roles

I. Introduction

We have used the term "legal system" many times, but we have not yet defined it. Basically, what we mean when we speak of the legal system is a set of sub-systems which, for one reason or another, people choose to call "legal." There is room for dispute about which sub-systems fit most comfortably within the definition of law. But it is clear that some of them fit very well; for example, the judicial system, made up of courts and their supporting personnel. By common consent, this is a sub-system which is part of the legal system.

When we call the judicial system a system, we mean nothing more than that it is a network of people, institutions, and relationships, which have a recognizable boundary; that is, we can either see where it begins and ends, or define it in such away as to make that point clear. This doesn't mean that boundaries don't blur sometimes. We can, however, talk about the judicial system, and define it so that no one could reasonably confuse the judicial system with the army, the educational system, the Bureau of Standards, or a circus.

A system, then, is some bounded part of that gigantic reality we call society. Unless it is wholly insulated from society—which is impossible—a system must adapt to its social environment and to its externally generated needs. In other words, it must coordinate the activity of those people who are part of the system, so that they work together (more or less) to attain its goals.

In much of the material considered up to this point, we have ignored or postponed considering the legal system as a system. We have assumed a simple arrangement in which "the law" gives out orders to the public, that is, people outside in society. We have considered how the legal system gets its orders from society. Mostly, we treated the legal system as if it were a single person or entity, or a kind of undifferentiated mass. We know, however, that the legal system is quite complex. Even the court system is complicated. There are high courts and low courts. Lines of force and communication move up and down. Appeals go up; orders come down. In an administrative agency, the top must get feedback from the bottom; the bottom must get and obey orders from the top. These processes, however, never work perfectly—any more than in the outside world.

What we have learned so far applies to the internal workings of the legal system too. If level A of a system promulgates rules to be obeyed by level B, when will there be compliance? What was considered in Chapter 4 is relevant

651

to this question also. That is, we must think about sanctions, about the value system at level B, about the pressure of peers.

Nevertheless, it is useful to focus, as this chapter does, on the special problems that arise within the legal system. The chapter is divided into two major parts. The first part deals with the consequences of the way legal systems are structured. Some legal systems, particularly those in continental Europe and Latin America, rely more on action by legal officials while others, particularly Anglo–American ones, rely on the parties' lawyers to gather and present evidence. Then there are problems of coordination and control; here we look at many of the devices legal systems use to coordinate activity—rules and surveillance among others. Second, certain specialized roles—notably the lawyer and the judge—are particular to legal systems; in the final part of the chapter we deal with these roles.

II.   The Structure of the Legal System

(A) Adversary v. Inquisitorial Structures: Anglo–American Contrasted With Continental European Approaches

The Anglo–American "adversary" system of conducting trials is often contrasted with the approach taken in continental Europe that is sometimes called "inquisitorial." How do these legal processes affect the outcome of trials? Which approach is better? John H. Langbein, in "The German Advantage in Civil Procedure," 52 *University of Chicago Law Review* 823 (1985), as the title suggests, comes out strongly in favor of the continental system.

Under German practice, the court, not the lawyers, bears the "main responsibility for gathering and sifting evidence." Also, the system, unlike the American system, does not draw a sharp distinction between "pretrial and trial, between discovering evidence and presenting it. Trial is not a single continuous event. Rather, the court gathers and evaluates evidence over a series of hearings, as many as the circumstances require."

In Germany, a case begins with a complaint. However, the plaintiff's lawyer in his complaint will talk not only about the facts of his case but also about the kind of proofs to be presented. He may append actual documents or records. The judge will read the pleadings and start work on an "official dossier, the court file." The judge, when she is ready, may schedule a hearing. At the hearing, she "serves as the examiner-in-chief." Lawyers, according to Langbein, do not coach witnesses, and the elaborate rhythm of examination and cross-examination familiar in an American court is largely absent. At the end of a witness' testimony, the judge prepares a summary. Compared to the "longwinded narrative of American pretrial depositions and trial transcripts," the German system is concise and economical. Also, there are virtually no rules of evidence mainly because there is no jury in civil cases. If experts are needed to deal with an "issue of technical difficulty," the court will choose the experts and define their role. The battle of experts that is so common in

American courts—the partisan nature of expert testimony—is largely, if not entirely, avoided.

The German system also "lessens tensions and theatrics" and "encourages settlement." German proceedings "have the tone not of the theatre, but of a routine business meeting—serious rather than tense." Most of the advantages that Langbein sees in the German system depend on the centrality of the judge, who does not have to share power with a jury and who is stronger vis-à-vis the lawyers than an American judge.

But doesn't this position of strength pose a danger to efficiency or fairness? The Anglo–American system "of partisan fact-gathering has the virtue of its vices: It combines responsibility with incentive. Each side gathers and presents proofs according to its own calculation of self-interest." What is the system of incentives in Germany? It rests, according to Langbein, on the professionalism of the judges. Judging is a separate career line. Unlike in America, experienced lawyers are not named by political officials to be judges. And judging is, Langbein claims, a career "that creates incentives for diligence and excellence." Thus, one does not find the party hacks—lawyers rewarded with judgeships by political leaders—who so disfigure local justice in the United States.

NOTES AND QUESTIONS

1. Samuel R. Gross, "The American Advantage: The Value of Inefficient Litigation," 85 *Michigan Law Review* 734, 740–41, 753, 756 (1987), responds to Langbein's article. Gross argues: "efficiency is a poor measure of the quality of a procedural system . . ." He contends:

> The main measure of the social value of a judgment [from a court], however, is not speed but accuracy. . . . Langbein believes that the German system is more likely than ours to reach factually correct results. While this is a plausible consequence of his description of the superior rationality of German procedure, I am unconvinced. I do not think that there is enough evidence for a useful comparison, for two reasons: First, while the cost and duration of a legal proceeding are (at least in principle) directly observable, its accuracy is almost always unknown since we rarely have any external evidence by which to judge it. . . .

> Second, the important question is not how these two fact-finding systems might perform in the abstract, but how many errors they produce in practice. In practice, however, most cases are not litigated. As a result the answer to the question depends in part on the composition of the set of cases that are presented for adjudication, and in part on the resolution of those that are not. This makes cross-national comparisons extraordinarily difficult. In the civil context it would be necessary to consider: (1) the effect of the method of adjudication in each system on the composition of that small subset of disputes that are channeled to litigation in each country, and (2) the "accuracy" of the dispositions of

those disputes that are not pursued at all, or settled short of litigation.... The data for these comparisons do not exist and would be
exceedingly difficult (perhaps impossible) to gather, and the systems
involved are so complex that I am skeptical of arguments on either side
made without data, especially arguments based solely on the nature of the
processes of formal adjudication....

The more substantial benefits of procedural inefficiency have to do
with its effects on conduct outside of court. Every legal system leaves
some "zone of immunity" around individuals, a sphere of actions that
because of their nature or magnitude are not as a practical matter subject
to governmental control.... In other words, inefficiency limits the effectiveness, the "penetration" of formal legal rules, and creates room for
divergent results and for patterns of behavior based on nonlegal
norms.... Often, however, [we cannot bring] formal rules into line with
developing operational norms. Informal norms of behavior suffer from the
limitations of their advantages: their relative flexibility and their responsiveness to interests that legal systems are hard pressed to regulate—
trust, reputation, civility, etc. Because of these features, such norms may
operate very well in practice, and yet be too vague, too complex, too
changeable, or too personal to enact as laws, or even fully to articulate.

2. Marc Galanter, "Adjudication, Litigation, and Related Phenomena"
in L. Lipson and S. Wheeler (eds.) *Law and the Social Sciences* at 151, 177
(1986), makes the following comment:

One durable stereotype depicts the common-law judge as a passive
umpire, in contrast to the civil-law judge who actively manages the case
before him.... The contrast is a serviceable one, although contemporary
common law and civil law courts hardly represent polar opposites. The
spectrum of forum passivity and activity runs from the sort of complete
disputant control found in many mediative processes to the total control
by the forum familiar in commissions of inquiry....

Common-law judging lies at some distance from the passive end of
the spectrum.... What is more striking about the common-law judges
than their purported passivity is their tendency to delegate and supervise
rather than to engage in continuous and detailed work on the case....
This tendency for common-law judges to be management rather than
production workers is connected with the lower ratio of judges to lawyers
... [in common law than civil law systems], the higher status enjoyed by
common-law judges, and their relative freedom from hierarchic control.

On the actual, as contrasted with the ideal, role of the civil law judge,
Galanter refers to John Henry Merryman, *The Civil Law Tradition: an
Introduction to the Legal Systems of Western Europe and Latin America* (2d
ed., 1985). Merryman recognizes the differences between judges in the two
systems, but he cautions us not to put undue stress on these differences. He
writes:

People talk about an "inquisitorial" system of proof-taking as contrasted with the "adversary" system of the common law. The characterization is quite misleading. In fact, the prevailing system in both the civil law and the common law world is the "dispositive" system, according to which the determination of what issues to raise, what evidence to introduce, and what arguments to make is left almost entirely to the parties. Judges in both traditions have some power to undertake inquiries on their own, and in Germany the law and the judicial tradition encourage the judge to play an active role in the proceedings. Elsewhere, however, civil law judges are more passive. (pp. 114–115).

3.   Professor Langbein has also written about the merits of German criminal procedure. See Langbein, "Land Without Plea Bargaining: How the Germans Do It," 78 *Michigan Law Review* 204 (1979). A thoughtful essay on the difference between the two types of systems is Mirjan Damaska, *The Faces of Justice and State Authority: A Comparative Approach to the Legal Process* 186–200 (1986). There are fewer studies of the law-in-action in the civil law systems of Europe, Latin America or Asia than studies of American or British police, lawyers and courts—at least fewer studies available in English. This is understandable. Something of the flavor of these systems in action can be gleaned from popular literature. For example, Nicholas Freeling's Inspector Henri Castang novels or George Simenon's mysteries which feature Maigret try to show us the French criminal justice system in action. Of course, in the United States too there are thousands of books, plays, movies and TV shows that pivot their action about police, trials and other aspects of criminal justice. Such literature is a lot more fun than reading scholarly studies. However, we can question these stories' accuracy and whether the world they portray is typical.

There are at least two important studies of French criminal law in action that were written in English. Professor Hodgson's research focuses on claims that police practices in the United Kingdom could be improved if its legal system were changed to be more like those in Continental Europe. You should be aware that, unlike most of the other continental legal systems, the French do use a jury in certain cases.

(5.1) The Police, the Prosecutor and the *Juge D'instruction*: Judicial Supervision in France, Theory and Practice

Jacqueline Hodgson

41 *British Journal of Criminology* 342–361 (2001).

Investigation: The Legal Framework

In Anglo–American systems, the judiciary is quite separate from the lawyers who prosecute and defend, and their role is largely limited to adjudicating in the trial process.

In France, however, in common with many other European countries, there is a career judiciary, collectively known as the *magistrature*, whose members exercise the functions of *procureur*[1], *juge d'instruction* and trial *juge*. They enjoy a common training and it is possible to move between the three functions. As *magistrats*, the *procureur* and *juge d'instruction* exercise a judicial role in the pre-trial supervision of investigations—even though the *procureur* is also responsible for the prosecution of offenses. The separation of these three functions acts as a series of checks, a guarantee ensuring the protection of the rights of the accused and the careful scrutiny of the dossier of evidence at each stage of the case.

The French *Code de procédure pénale* (CPP) sets out the powers, duties and responsibilities of the police, and those responsible for the supervision of criminal investigations. The police are responsible for recording crime, gathering evidence and seeking out those who have committed offences (Article 14 CPP) and they must inform the *procureur* of all *crimes*[2] or *flagrant*[3] offences (Article 54 CPP). In more serious or complex cases, an *information*[4] is opened on the authority of the *procureur* and the *juge d'instruction* takes responsibility for the investigation. In other instances, the police are under the direction of the *procureur* (Article 12 CPP).

The nature of this direction is set out in Article 41 CPP. The *procureur* is responsible for the investigation and prosecution of offences, and in carrying out this task, she directs the activity of the police (whose powers she shares) and supervises the detention of suspects in police custody (the *garde à vue*). The initial decision to detain a suspect is made by a senior police officer, but the *procureur* must be informed as soon as possible, and her express authority is required for detention beyond 24 hours (Articles 63, 77 CPP).

Since 1993, the *garde à vue* period has been closely regulated and a number of safeguards are now provided for those detained. A formal record of detention must be kept detailing interrogation times, rest periods and the duration of the *garde à vue* (Articles 64, 65 CPP). As soon as the suspect is placed in detention she must be informed of her rights which include having a member of her family or her employer informed of her detention (Article 63–2); to see a doctor (Article 63–3); and to see a lawyer for 30 minutes, 20 hours after the start of the detention period (Article 63–4). The lawyer must be told of the nature of the offence investigated, but not the reason why the suspect has been detained.[5] She is allowed to consult with her client in private, but is

---

1. The *procureur* and her *substituts* (deputies) are public prosecutors collectively known as the *parquet*.

2. Offences are classed as *crimes* (the most serious, such as murder); *délits* (such as assault or burglary) and *contraventions* (the least serious). These classifications represent a hierarchy of gravity and will determine the mode of trial for the offence.

3. Around 85 per cent of offences are *flagrant*. This ... in general, refers to offences

which are being, or have recently been committed. The distinction is important in determining the powers of the police and the length of time the suspect may be detained in custody.

4. This is the process of passing the case to the *juge d'instruction*. An *information* is opened and the process of *instruction* begins.

5. This will change under the June 2000 reform: from January 2001 lawyers will have to be informed by the police of the date and the nature of the offence in connection with which their client is being held.

not permitted to be present during any interrogation. She may also make written observations on the custody record.

At the close of detention, the *procureur* decides whether to charge or release the suspect, or send the case to the *juge d'instruction* for further investigation. Originals and certified copies of all evidence gathered by the police must be sent to the *procureur* (Article 19 CPP). Everything is recorded as a signed statement, a *procès verbal*, and placed in the *dossier*, or case file. The dossier attaches to the case through until trial and it is reviewed by the *juge d'instruction* if appointed, as well as the *juges* at trial. . . .

The *juge d'instruction* supervises the investigation in around 8 per cent of the cases. This is done by the *procureur* opening an *information*, which is mandatory for *crimes*, the most serious offences, and at the discretion of the *procureur* for *délits* and *contraventions* (Article 79 CPP). The *juge d'instruction* is empowered to undertake any lawful investigations which she considers useful in the search for the truth (Article 81 CPP). These may include telephone taps or staging a confrontation between witnesses and the accused, as well as interviewing witnesses and gathering expert evidence. These may be done on the *juge's* own initiative, or at the request of the *procureur*, the accused or the victim (Article 82 CPP). Other than the questioning of the *mise en examen* and preparation of the report on her background (the *enquête de personalité*) investigations may be delegated to police officers through the *commission rogatoire* (Article 151 CPP), granting them the same powers as the *juge d'instruction* herself (Article 152 CPP).

The *mise en examen* may have a lawyer present whenever she is brought before the *juge* for questioning or for a confrontation with another witness, and, through her defence lawyer, she may make written submissions at any point in the investigation which are then placed on the case file (Article 199 CPP), The lawyers for both the accused and the victim have access to the dossier of evidence and may make copies for their own use (Article 114 CPP). As well as an investigative role, the *juge* also exercises a purely judicial function in deciding whether to keep the suspect in custody during the period of investigation. This has been widely criticized in France (see e.g. *Commission de justice pénale et droits de l'homme* 1991; *Commission de réflexion* 1997), as a confusion of investigative and judicial functions and the recent reform in June 2000 creates a *juge des libertés et de la détention* who will determine the issue of pre-trial detention.

The judicial character with which investigations are imbued also influences the structure of the trial process and the probative value afforded evidence gathered during the investigation. The *dossier* of evidence (even where no *information* has been opened) is regarded not as a police file, but the fruit of a judicially supervised enquiry and written statements may therefore be accepted without the need for oral testimony and cross-examination. In the lowest court, the *Tribunal de Police*, police statements are considered proof of the *contravention* unless the contrary is proved (Article 537 CPP). Where cases are investigated by the *juge d'instruction*, any application to exclude evidence because of a procedural irregularity is made, not during the trial itself, but within a month of the close of the investigation....

The Centrality of the *Procureur*

Just as jury trial and vigorous cross-examination are often regarded as the hallmarks of an adversarial system, so the *juge d'instruction* takes on an almost iconic status to common law commentators. But the process of *instruction* in France is almost as exceptional as jury trials in Britain. The law permits, and indeed anticipates that the vast majority of cases will be investigated by the police under the supervision of the *procureur*, qua *magistrat*. The absence of direct judicial investigation in most cases is in exact conformity with the law, and a number of mechanisms (described above) are provided which avoid judicial supervision in its purest form: the appointment of the *juge d'instruction* is mandatory only in cases of *crimes* and provision is made for virtually all tasks to be delegated to the police through a *commission rogatoire*. Furthermore, even where cases are investigated under the supervision of the *juge d'instruction*, the all important preliminary enquiries, including interrogation of the suspect, will have already been carried out by the police under the responsibility of the *procureur*.

Within the structure of the law itself, it is the *procureur* who occupies the central position of judicial supervision in the criminal process. She must be notified of all *crimes* and *délits* and is responsible for their investigation and prosecution. She supervises the *garde à vue*, deciding whether to authorize and later to prolong detention. She possesses broad discretion over both charge (so being able to avoid the mandatory opening of an *information* for *crimes*, by proceeding on the basis of a *délit*) and the precise point at which the case is passed on to the *juge d'instruction*....

However, whilst the practice of *procureur* supervised investigations is not a deviation from the law, it does represent a model of judicial supervision which is different from that provided by the *juge d'instruction*. First, supervision is characterized by the law in different ways.... [Several writers] focus upon the word "*contrôle*" which, they say, is used most often and signifies oversight and accountability, rather than minute direction. This is true of the *garde à vue*, but in the investigation and prosecution of crime the *procureur* is required to direct (*dirige*) police activity (Article 41 CPP). However, the nature of this "oversight" and "direction" is left open. There is nothing in the text of the law which anticipates that the *procureur* should be present at the police station for the interviewing of witnesses or the suspect. The police retain the initiative in arresting and detaining a suspect and then reporting to the *procureur*. This practice was reflected in the modification of the requirement to inform the *procureur* of detentions in *garde à vue* "without delay" to "as soon as possible" (Article 63 CPP). According to the explanatory document accompanying the change, this was in recognition that it was not always possible to inform the *procureur* immediately and to allow the *parquet* in each area the freedom to specify how they wished to be notified—for example, by fax.

The *juge d'instruction* is characterized as being more directly involved in the investigation. She is personally required to conduct (*procéder à*) the investigation and police involvement is by active delegation through the use of *commissions rogatoires,* which represents a significant transfer of power from the *juge* to the police, rather than the regulation or supervision of an existing power. And once an *information* has been opened, the police are no longer permitted to question the *mise en examen*—only the *juge d'instruction* may do this. The level of control and direct supervision suggested by the legal text in the two instances is not the same—indeed if it were, there would be no logic in having two separate procedures and two different *magistrats.*

Secondly, the *procureur* and the *juge d'instruction* occupy different parts of the institutional structure of the criminal process. On account of France's political history, the role of the state is a constant background feature in all discussions of law ... and in the area of criminal justice this focus is on the relationship between the *magistrature* and the elected government. Under the republican model of government (brought about in France by the 1789 Revolution), the state is said to represent the will of the people and guarantees the rights and freedoms of the individual, The law is a legitimate expression of this political power and the unelected judiciary must give effect to it, whilst at the same time remaining subordinate to it. The *procurer* represents the public interest and is part of the *ministère public* which is under the direction of the Minister of Justice. The minister may issue national circulars addressing general issues of prosecution policy, may give direct instructions concerning a specific case and may remove a case from one *procureur* to another. She is also a powerful influence in the process of appointment and promotion of *procureurs*. This creates a tension between the accountability of the *procureur* as part of the *ministère public* representing the public interest and her independent status as a *magistrat*. In contrast to the *procureur*, the *juge d'instruction* is not answerable to a government minister and is free from hierarchical control of this nature. Furthermore, the *juge d'instruction* does not prosecute the case and her role in investigations is cast in more neutral terms than that of the *procureur*: she is charged with searching for the truth, she investigates the offence rather than the accused and looks not simply for evidence on which to prosecute, but to *charge* or *décharge.* ...

Judicial Supervision in Practice

... In my own study of the investigation and prosecution of crime in France, fieldwork was carried out in Paris, two large urban centres, a medium size town and one small area of 170,000 inhabitants during the period 1993–94 and 1997–98. Researchers spent between one and four months at each site, located in the offices of *procureurs, juge d'instruction*, police and *gendarmes*, where we were able to observe the ways in which criminal investigations are directed and supervised on a daily basis, as well as the conduct of pre-trial hearings and the questioning of suspects and witnesses. By being placed in the office of the group being observed, we were able to follow cases through the process and to supplement our observations with discussion of particular cases or decisions and the wider issues which arose out of them. We were also allowed access to case dossiers at each stage of the process. This method (or blend of methods) produced a rich stream of data, allowing for the collection of formally determined categories of information whilst at the same time remaining sufficiently flexible to respond to new issues which emerged once in the field. At the end of the observation period we conducted 20 interviews (primarily with *magistrats*) and received 37 questionnaire responses from *procureurs* and 12 from police. Based upon some of the data from this empirical study, I will examine the legal culture in which judicial supervision is understood and the ways in which it is put into practice.

The Relationship between *Magistrat* and Police

The appeal of judicial supervision to foreign commentators is its potential to ensure a wider investigation, where the police might also follow leads which exculpate, as well as incriminate, the suspect. And although the law does not expressly require it, this is implicit in the wider structure of the criminal process: the status accorded the dossier as the product of a judicial enquiry; the relatively minor role afforded the defence lawyer. But in contrast, the work of both the *procureur* and the *juge d'instruction* is perhaps best characterized as being concerned with the *outcome* and the *form* of the police investigation, rather than the method: neither is concerned to monitor closely the work of the police. This is done quite literally by monitoring the output of the investigation and ensuring that procedural safeguards have been complied with: that statements are signed and in triplicate; that *garde à vue* documentation records times, medical visits and the communication to the suspect of her rights; that the *procureur* has been informed of the suspect's detention and any extension authorized; or that the *commission rogatoire* has been carried out within the time requested. The *magistrat* performs a kind of (necessarily retrospective) bureaucratic review of the investigation carried out by the police. Great reliance is placed upon written evidence and authenticity of form is equated with a wider guarantee of legitimacy in relation to how the evidence was obtained. As one *substitut* we observed warned an accused who wished to correct something in his statement taken by the police: "I am paid to read the dossier of evidence. I believe what I read ... This is written and signed."

This characterization is also true of more direct forms of supervision undertaken by the *magistrat*. Although required to direct or carry out the investigation, it was extremely rare for *magistrats* to intervene directly in the police enquiry. The *juge d'instruction's* heavy reliance upon *commissions rogatoires* has been well documented and her caseload is such that whilst she may discuss the progress and outcomes of investigations with officers, the initiative and direction of the case remains with the police. Even the opening of an *information* itself was often at the request of the police in order that they could progress their investigation by employing wider powers (typically a phone tap) which only the *juge d'instruction* could authorize. Similarly, *procureurs* were often responsible for the detention of suspects in *garde à vue* across a wide area and had too many cases in progress at anyone time to allow for anything more than minimal involvement via telephone or fax. As one *substitut* . . . told us: ". . . at times it feels as though you are working on a production line." The new *temps réel* procedure requiring officers to report even minor cases to the *procureur* has the advantage that a decision about the disposition of the case can be taken immediately, but in an environment of stretched resources, it has increased the workload yet further.

However, the disengagement of *magistrats* from the case investigation is not purely a resource issue. It is part of the legal cultural expectations of what constitutes supervision and direction, the context in which these broadly defined legal duties are interpreted by *magistrats* in practice. The legal text is framed such that the *procureur* or the *juge d'instruction* could undertake personally large parts of the investigation, but for a number of reasons, there is no expectation that this will take place. In part, it is a function of the paradoxical structural relationship between the *magistrat* and the police, in which the *magistrat* is an authority over the police, yet at the same time is dependent upon them. In our questionnaire survey, although most *procureurs* (85 per cent) said that they would never see the police, whatever their rank, as colleagues and 79 per cent described officers as subordinates, there is a recognition that cooperation and trust are more likely to foster a good working relationship than assertions of authority. One *substitut* . . . told us, "I think that, really, I direct [the investigation], but equally, so do the police . . . Fine, you can assert your authority, but that is not an effective way to get things done." Another *substitut* . . . also explained the importance of trust given the dependence of *magistrats* upon the police: "I think you need to be aware that you cannot work without the police. Then if you want to do a good job, there needs to be a relationship of trust and mutual respect. Legally, hierarchically, we give them orders, but anyone who thinks that it just needs to be written in the law to work like that is mistaken."

The importance of trust in the police-*procureur* relationship was particularly apparent in the approach of the *parquet* to visits to the police station. On the rare occasions when these were made, they were announced in advance and more likely to be for practical reasons or to enhance relations with the police, than to assert authority or to check on those detained in police custody. This was borne out by the police themselves who, far from seeing visits as a form of regulation or monitoring, complained that the *procureur* "never had time to come to the station these days." The consequence of a more surveillance-based approach was explained to us by a *substitut*: "There used to be a woman in the *permanence* who did go down to the police station and it caused a terrible rumpus. The police were furious that she just turned up. You have to be careful when you go down—so that the police don't think it's because you're suspicious of them." Similarly, the relationship between *juge d'instruction* and police was consistently characterized to us (both by the *juges* themselves and the police) as being based upon trust, though of a different kind. One group of officers explained their approach to working with the *juge d'instruction* in this way: "We propose the way forward ... we find the leads to follow up.... the *juge* directs the investigation, but we carry it out and keep him informed.... you need to gain his trust and persuade him ... it's not a question of permission, it's a question of trust." The nature of the process of *instruction* is such that the police may be left for weeks or even months before reporting to the *juge*, unlike the initial enquiry which takes place over a matter of days. As a result, the police may feel more, rather than less, freedom when acting under *commission rogatoire*. One *juge d'instruction* ... contrasted her role with that of the *procureur*: "[The police] probably see the *juge d'instruction* as a director, someone they have to report to. The *procureur* is seen as someone who keeps a closer eye on them."

But while resources and dependence upon the police dictate the approach of the *magistrat* to some extent, the wide discretion afforded to the police is also part of the ideology of the *juge* that the functions of *magistrat* and of police should be kept separate. There is a distance between the two which cannot be bridged. As one *procureur* ... put it: "There is a part of [the police's] work that I cannot evaluate. I can only talk of their role in the legal procedure, how they report on the telephone. We inhabit different worlds. They do not know the world of judges and I do not know the world of nightclubs." This comment was echoed by a senior police officer ..., who said, when asked about relations with the *parquet*: "Our work is different. They are in their offices and we are outside on the ground." Levy ... explains, "... there is a professional ideology which opposes the magistrate, incarnation of the law whose hands must remain clean, to the policeman, who inevitably soils himself by contact with the underworld and who must as a result be kept at a distance."

This professional distance between *magistrat* and police has clear functional benefits to the *magistrature*. Whilst the *magistrat* deals with the relative "moral certainties" of legal procedure, distant from the realities of investigation and interrogation, the police are left to do what is necessary to get the evidence the *magistrat* requires to do her job. The *magistrat* is not concerned to look too closely at the methods employed, provided her dossier is complete at the end of the day, but in the event of a major police transgression she remains free to condemn the offending officers and to emerge unscathed.

Two contrasting examples illustrate this point. In the first case, the accused appeared before the *substitut* with cuts to his face and nose. He did not contest any of the charges made against him, but protested at the rough treatment he suffered when arrested and claimed that the police had stolen something from him. The *substitut* ignored these complaints without further enquiry and simply told him to "Stop talking rubbish" and to "Tell it to the court." It was left to the defence lawyer to raise an official complaint before the court that day. When asked about his approach to the suspect, the *substitut*'s lack of commitment to due process rights was clear: "You have to bear in mind that he has several convictions and does not respect the law, so his word counts for less than that of the police." In the second case, the suspect, a juvenile, was held on suspicion of assaulting a police officer. In the dossier, there was a medical certificate relating to the injuries of the suspect, but not the police. This clear documentary evidence prompted an immediate response from the *substitut* who instructed the police to ask the suspect's father if he wished to lodge a formal complaint, before then instigating an official enquiry into the affair. Although responsible for supervising the police investigation, there is a sense in which the *magistrat* does not want to delve too deeply into "police work" unless compelled to do so. The detention and interrogation of suspects is perhaps the paradigm example of this.

Interrogation and the Search for the Truth

In keeping separate the functions of *magistrat* and police, interrogation is regarded by *magistrats* as "dirty" work best left to the police. It might be argued that although the *procureur* is responsible only to *contrôle* the *garde à vue*, this relates to the conditions of detention; the actual interrogation of suspects or witnesses is part of the investigation, which she is required to *dirige* or direct. Yet, most *procureurs* never leave their offices. Despite being conscious of the limitations of the kind of supervision which they can provide, such as the risk of being manipulated by the limited accounts given by the police over the telephone, or the fact that things might be left out of written statements (there is no tape recording), 87 per cent of our questionnaire respondents said that they rarely or never visited the police station. When asked if she had ever been present during the questioning of a suspect or a witness, one *substitut* ... told us: "That would make me ill at ease. If I realize that there are questions that should have been asked, I ask the police to put them to the suspect, but I am not actually present. I can go to the scene and make sure all the evidence is seized after a search, yes. But I do not sit in on interviews." For her, this was strictly police work. It fulfilled a necessary function, but one in which she declined to take part: "The *garde à vue* is a constraint which can last 48 hours, or four days for drugs cases. It is to put the pressure on ... With people who resist, it breaks them down." The reluctance of the *procureur* to visit the police station is all the more interesting given the relatively high number of questionnaire respondents (40 per cent) who reported suspecting that violence or excessive pressure had sometimes been used against the suspect during *garde à vue*. In one area observed there was concern that suspects were being brought to court bloodstained and untidy. The police were instructed by the *procureur* that this was not acceptable and that it did not look good before the court. No enquiry was made, however, into why suspects arrived in this state. The French police have had the reputation of being violent towards suspects and although both police and *magistrats* claim that this is a relic of the past, part of the "old ways", serious cases of violence continue to occur and the 1990s have witnessed the police shooting of a number of suspects both in and outside the police station. Recently, five officers were imprisoned for seriously assaulting two suspected drugs traffickers whilst they were held in *garde à vue* in 1991. The victims were beaten about the face, head, body and genitals with fists and truncheons, threatened with a syringe and a blow torch, sexually assaulted and urinated on.

While such cases of violence are extreme and will be condemned publicly, there is a general tolerance among *magistrats* of the kinds of pressure that the police might need to exert to make the suspect tell "the truth". And the crime control ideology of the *procureur* means that in most instances, "the truth" is a confession. Suspects in police detention who say little when questioned, or deny the offence, are repeatedly interviewed on the instructions of the *procureur* in order to get "the full story" or "a satisfactory explanation". It is also a common reason for prolonging detention or remanding the person in custody during the *instruction*. As one *procureur* told the police on the telephone: "I let the *garde à vue* do its job. We can always prolong it. Keep interviewing him from time to time to refresh his memory." Another *substitut* from the juvenile section of the *parquet* explained that, "the 48 hours can be used to get him [the suspect] to crack. I systematically prolong the *guard à vue* to ensure this. Frequently, it's the first interview in the morning after they've spent the night in custody that they crack, because they're tired and vulnerable and realize that we will keep them in custody ... It's not an environment where the police hit them—it's more psychological."

Even questioning which might be classed as overbearing or oppressive by a British court is considered acceptable, and at times necessary to get at "the truth." One *substitut* ... told us that when he spent some time at the police station as part of his training, he saw a suspect slapped across the face: "It's not shocking, it was just to move things on. It was a drugs case and the officer wanted to know the truth ... I wouldn't call that violence". Another, very experienced *substitut* ... explained: "It's true that the *garde à vue* exerts a certain psychological pressure and for some people that pressure may lead to slightly ill-considered admissions.... But that is not the point of view of a *procureur*—there are no innocents in *garde à vue*." This, he explained, was why cases were frequently kept for up to five days before opening an *information*: "The reason it's five days is because that is the limit for *flagrance*. That way, the police still enjoy wide powers and we can carry out the investigation ... we want to get the culprit ... The *juge d'instruction* is not going to interview the suspect three or four times, sit across the table from him and say 'Are you going to admit this?' The police station is a hostile environment. It's unpleasant and the police will use more pressure. And that does not make it unlawful—sometimes you need some pressure."

The *juge d'instruction* also reaps the benefits of the relatively invisible and unregulated conditions of police interrogation. For example, the suspect, once *mise en examen*, may only be interviewed by the *juge d'instruction*, her lawyer is present and has access to the dossier of evidence and the statement made is meticulously recorded. However, where a suspect emerges once the *information* has been opened and is not yet *mise en examen*, it was common for the *juge* to direct the police to interview her as a witness, avoiding the safeguards of the process of instruction, and so leaving the police free to prepare the ground. Interviewing a suspect in the relative invisibility of the police station is seen as a valuable and legitimate investigative tool. As one *juge d'instruction* explained when asked why he opposed the safeguard of tape recording of police interrogations, "It's unbelievable! And to think that we might end up doing that here ... You should just leave the police to do their job. When you're dealing with difficult people like drug addicts and hooligans, you need to put the pressure on. I don't mean hitting them, but you have to make them talk."

Although leaving the hard work of interrogation to the police, the *juge d'instruction* had her own ways of putting pressure upon suspects. Typically, evidence against the suspect will be temporarily withheld from the dossier so that the lawyer is denied access to it and the suspect is unaware of it and may "trip up" and contradict it. But perhaps the most important trump card held by the *juge d'instruction* is her power to detain suspects in custody. As with so many things, detention is justified in the eyes of *magistrats* as a necessary tool in the search for the truth. We were frequently told that only "guilty" people were detained.... The reform in June 2000 will remove this power from the *juge d'instruction* and transfer it to the newly created *juge des libertés et del la détention*. This has been received warmly by lawyers, who hope that this will end the practice of bargaining [for] liberty with confessions

Unsurprisingly, given the distance from police interrogation which the *parquet* and *juge d'instruction* prefer to keep, a greater role for the defence pre-trial is widely opposed by *magistrats* as likely to hamstring the police in their ability to question the suspect (and obtain admissions) and so to interfere with the effectiveness of the investigation. In contrast to those whose professional standards and ideology are considered beyond reproach as *magistrats* searching out the truth, lawyers as paid partisan representatives of the suspect's interests are considered ill-suited to act in this capacity. Of our questionnaire respondents, 97 per cent considered the current arrangement of up to 30 minutes consultation with a lawyer after 20 hours of detention to be appropriate both to the needs of the accused and of justice. Eighty-four per cent thought that the lawyer should not have access to the suspect at the start of the *garde à vue* (as will soon be the case after the June 2000 reform takes effect) and 89 percent thought they should not have access to the dossier. The reasons offered for this were that it would undermine the confidentiality and effectiveness of the investigation in searching out the truth, as well as the "spontaneity" of the suspect's remarks. The suspect may collude with her lawyer in giving an account or, worse still, refuse to speak altogether. The presence of an outsider is viewed negatively, it risks interfering with the psychological pressure that detention in *garde à vue* necessarily exerts. For the *magistrats* in an inquisitorial process, the defence lawyer acts not as a participant but as a guarantee of procedural fairness and one which ultimately legitimates the judicial enquiry: "In France, the lawyer is not there to advise the person, but to signal any problems in the conditions of the *garde à vue*; not so much to provide legal advice as moral support" ... When asked what the defence brought to the process of instruction one *juge d'instruction* told us: "They do not bring anything to the case—it is not their job to. I investigate the affair and their job is primarily to ensure that the correct procedure has been followed and to challenge any irregularities." A greater role for the defence pre-trial would undermine the structure of judicial supervision, where the supervisor can be trusted to guarantee the respect of due process rights because of her status as *magistrat*.

The *Magistrat*: Society's Trusted Representative

Rooted in their own adversarial legal culture, many foreign commentators imagine the judicial supervisor in adversarial terms, investigating a case that has two sides, representing defense interests which are in opposition to those of the police and prosecution, as well as investigating the guilt of the suspect. But in the French system, there is only one side to the case investigation which the *magistrat* undertakes—that of seeking out the truth—and all other interests, including those of the accused, are subordinated to this. Searching out the truth is not achieved through opposition and conflict, checks and balances: to the French *magistrat* these may stand in the way of obtaining crucial evidence. Instead, it is achieved through a concentration of power in the hands of one person, who represents neither the narrow interests of the defence or prosecution, but what are claimed to be the wider interests of society. *Magistrats*, as administrators of the law enacted by the state, give effect to the will of the people. This gives them an authority and a legitimacy which is quite different from the defence lawyer in particular, who is seen as representing the partisan interests of the accused, working for money rather than for justice. The defence lawyer is less trusted than even the police. A *juge d'instruction* explained that a defence witness statement in court: "has less validity than if the statement was taken by a police officer because we do not know the circumstances. It could have been taken with a gun to the witness's head. If taken by the police, we know that it was taken under proper conditions."

Acting in the public interest, it is the *magistrat* who is trusted to define what is in the interests of the investigation and so, in the interests of justice, including decisions which affect the rights and liberties of the individual—whether it be the detention of the suspect, denying her the right to a lawyer, doctor or contact with a family member whilst in *garde à vue*, or placing her in pre-trial custody. Her status as *magistrat* overrides her function as investigator or prosecutor. This is especially true of the *juge d'instruction* whose role is almost one of prejudgment. In contrast to the adversarial model which carries the conflict through to trial, the French model disposes of issues during the period of investigation. One *juge d'instruction* commented: "In away, our job is to prepare the case for trial. We establish a dossier of evidence ... In England [rape or incest cases] take a long time to try at court because all the witnesses are heard. We [the *juges d'instruction*] do all that beforehand. The court is not going to start over again when the evidence has already been taken ... what you do at court, we do in my office. It is not done in public.'' The low acquittal rate of cases after *instruction* is taken as proof of their success and one *juge d'instruction* told us proudly that in ten years, only two of the cases he had sent to trial had resulted in acquittals.

The extent of the *magistrat's* power in the investigation in contrast to the relatively diminished role of the defence, is justified on the basis of the former's independence as a judicial inquirer, her status as a *magistrat*. Yet, we have seen that in practice independence does not guarantee neutrality and in particular, the stance of the *procureur* in representing the public interest is predominantly one of crime control. One former *juge d'instruction* entering the *parquet* reflected on her changing role: "For the *parquet*, the question, the aim, is always to charge. They are acting for the public. That will be uppermost in their mind." The rights and interests of the accused are not protected, but redefined with the "interests of the investigation." The guilt of the suspect is presumed and denials are rejected. Evidence of violence committed on the suspect by the police was ignored and left for the defence to raise at court; the word of the victim or of the police was consistently preferred over that of the suspect; serious cases meant an almost automatic request for a remand in custody, even where the evidence was thin. At trial, the most serious charge which the evidence might support was preferred: the public interest demanded that nothing should risk going unpunished.

The *magistrat* as a neutral agent applying the law, someone above personal or partisan interests is a powerful image within the rhetoric of judicial supervision and one which is internalized by the *magistrats* themselves. It permeates all contact between *magistrat* and accused. Explanations of charges, remands in custody, the opening of an *information* or the sentence at court are consistently prefaced with the phrase "I am obliged by the law to . . ." or "I am required to . . ." The accused is admonished by the state and by the law, not by the individual *magistrat*. As one *substitut* explained: "[Suspects] ask me to take pity on them, but I cannot. I have no other solution but to apply the law . . . I have no choice." Decisions are impersonal and non-negotiable, uniform and not discretionary. The fragility of this claim was revealed as the *substitut* qualified her remarks in the following way: "Even so, there is a great deal of latitude . . . we are all different. Each *magistrat* has their own way of doing things, of applying the law, of being severe or not. The differences are individual, personal." In making judgments about the gravity of the offence or the disposition of the offender, or deciding whether to issue a summons or take a more serious view and send the case to trial that day, appeals to legality allow the *magistrat* to hand out tough decisions behind the veil of the "requirements of the law".

The law allocates quite separate functions to the *procureur*, the *juge d'instruction* and the trial juges in order that each may act as a brake upon the power exercised by the others, but their status as *magistrats* binds them together in significant ways. There is a great deal of formal and informal communication between the three. They are generally housed in the same building, the *Palais de Justice*, they may lunch together and they frequently appear before one another at court or hearings during instruction. This contact has many advantages, in that they are not isolated from the conse-quences of their decisions and they have a global view of the criminal process. But their sense of working together also leads them to discuss cases with their colleagues in a way which goes beyond, for example the *juge d'instruction* obtaining a better insight into a case from the *procureur* involved in the original investigation, and risks compromising the independence of the deci-sion made. *Juges d'instruction* (or even *juges delegués*) frequently discussed with the *procureur* whether someone should be placed in pre-trial custody, for example; and the vice-president of the court frequently sat down and dis-cussed the afternoon's cases with the *procureur* to make sure that there were no problems.

Although instruction is a legally separate phase, the practical fact that the *procureur* has followed the case from the outset means that in many instances, opening an *information* is not a fresh investigation, but the continuation of an ongoing one, passed to the *juge* because time has run out or additional powers are required. In some instances the *procureur* and *juge d'instruction* (and even the police) discussed what charge the information was to be opened under and the necessary *commission rogatoires*. The *procureur* and *juge d'instruction* are in close contact and strategies are often discussed between the two: whether holding the suspect's wife will make him talk; whether placing the suspect in detention will precipitate more information from other witnesses; and in some cases, the suspect is primed by the *procureur* before being passed to the *juge*. One *juge d'instruction* ... ex-plained that he felt closer to the *parquet* than to the trial judges: "The *parquet* works on the case before and after me. Our jobs are complementary. When I get a dossier, I always bear in mind that I am working for the *parquet*. The two roles are very complementary. We're on the same wave length." The *instruction* builds upon what has gone before. Often the same officers will continue the investigation; the evidence collected so far becomes part of the file; and the views of the *parquet* are actively sought out. Aware of this, some police commented to us that they thought fresh officers should be brought to the case once an information is opened, to avoid initial case theories prevail-ing and to allow new perspectives to emerge.

Most *magistrats* saw these close working relationships as unproblematic. Discussion beforehand did not prevent them from playing out their role at the appropriate time: the pre-trial hearing or the trial. It did not undermine the system of checks and balances which the separation of functions is designed to achieve. Others were less sure. One *juge delegué* explained the conflict she felt: "It can be difficult to release somebody if the *juge d'instruction* has worked hard on a case. There is a pressure from being part of the same institution. You want to satisfy your colleagues." Another *juge d'instruction* ... questioned whether such discussions undermined their independence and the principle that their functions should be kept separate: "There is a solidarity. We are the same, we come out of the same college, we know each other. It takes a certain strength of character. I have managed to make a distinction between my friendship with a person and their job function ...

Sometimes I'm shocked by the way some people talk about cases before and after trial. It encroaches on one's independence ... It's shocking sometimes ... I once heard a trial judge saying 'but we have to defend the police.' '' But for most *magistrats*, this culture of cooperation was unproblematic. In contrast to the defence lawyer who is regarded with suspicion, *magistrats* continually point to their status as *juges* as a guarantor of their independence and objectivity. The *juge d'instruction* feels no conflict of interest in her power to place in custody those she is investigating; cases can be discussed freely without the fear of compromising independence. As one *juge d'instruction* ... said: "The issue of independence does not mean that you cannot communicate."

* * *

[The following article reports a detailed case study of a murder investigation in France and then points to how this process differs from that found in common law systems. We have cut the case study and reproduce only the author's conclusions about the French criminal justice system.]

(5.2) Anatomy of a French Murder Case

Bron McKillop

45 *American Journal of Comparative Law* 527 (1997).

* * *

9. Comments on the Case from a Common Law Perspective

(a) The relative importance of the investigation

The investigation in this case, was by any standard, comprehensive, thorough and well recorded. The dossier produced from the investigation, including the summarizing requisition by the prosecutor, formed the basis for the committal decision and, more importantly, the basis for the hearing. The judges, the prosecutor and the lawyers for the accused and the civil parties were all familiar with the dossier and referred to it during the hearing. The presiding judge interrogated the accused and the witnesses from their depositions in the dossier and generally sought to have their oral evidence conform to those depositions. Some witnesses simply confirmed their depositions as read out by the presiding judge. The expert witnesses generally gave oral summaries of their often quite lengthy written reports. The hearing thus became essentially a public review and confirmation of the contents of the dossier, and hence of the conclusions that were reached in the investigation. It could be said that the investigation was the crucial and determinative phase of the whole process and that the hearing simply added a public dimension to the investigation.

If the investigation in France, as evidenced by this case, is primary and the hearing secondary, then the reverse could be said to characterize the adversarial system. What happens at the hearing, or rather the trial, in that system is crucial in determining guilt or its absence in that it is only on the evidence adduced at the trial before a court that is meant to know nothing of that evidence beforehand that the determination is made. The investigation does no more than collect material that will be presented, selectively, by the prosecution at the trial and within the limits of examination-in-chief.

One consequence of this difference in relative importance of the investigation and the trial is that outcomes are more predictable in the French than in the adversarial system. The French investigation that results in a committal for trial will generally result in a conviction at the hearing. Only those cases in which the investigation reveals strong evidence of guilt are sent to a hearing so that hearings should normally result in convictions. The acquittal rate in the *cours d'assises* throughout France for the five years 1988–92 in fact averaged 5% of all cases heard. In the adversarial system the trial is something of a lottery. Outcomes are dependent upon many variables— witnesses depart from their proofs of evidence or their prior testimony or are unexpectedly damaged in cross-examination, the defense produces some surprises, the judge rules on the admissibility of evidence in ways that may not have been predicted, counsel perform well or badly, the jury is capricious, to mention a few such variables. These variables may make for good theatre but they are not conducive to predictability in the criminal justice system.

(b) The centrality of the dossier

The investigation in this case was recorded on documents which constituted the dossier. There were 270 such documents, many (such as expert reports and files of photographs) having multiple pages. The documents were generated by the *gendarmerie*, the prosecutor, the investigating judge, the police, experts, counsel for the accused and the civil parties, the accused and his wife. When the investigation had been completed the dossier was sent to the *procureur-general* at Angers. It was then placed before the *chambre d'accusation* there and, after the committal, was returned to the prosecutor at Le Mans. It was subsequently made available to the judges of the *cour d'assises* who sat on the case in Le Mans. It then went on to the *cour de cassation* for the appeal. It was finally returned to the prosecutor in Le Mans. The dossier generated by the investigation thus served as the foundation for subsequent phases of the total process and as the integrating link between the successive phases.

If it is accepted that the investigation is the most important phase of the French criminal justice system then the fact that the dossier generated by the investigation is documentary means that the French system is essentially a written one. The written record of the investigation controls the subsequent phases of the process. Knowledge about the offense and the offender is to be found, and generally only to be found, in the written record. Witnesses called at the hearing are expected to confirm their depositions and reports as in the dossier and not disturb the pre-existing written record. In fact no transcript is made of the oral evidence of the witnesses at the hearing so should the case go on appeal to the *cour de cassation* that court will be confined to the depositions and reports of the witnesses obtained during the investigation for its knowledge of the evidence. If the trial is accepted as the most important phase of the adversarial system and the trial is based on oral evidence then that system can be characterized as an oral one.

There is an important comparative advantage in having the written record of the investigation central to the criminal justice process. This lies in having the testimony of the witnesses, particularly the witnesses to the events comprising and surrounding the offense, collected relatively soon after the occurrence of those events, when memories are fresh. Evidence given many months and often years after such events as generally happens in trials under the adversary system can hardly be as reliable. The maximization of this advantage requires, of course, that the testimony be collected as thoroughly and probingly as practicable.

One qualification to the centrality of the dossier is exemplified in this case. The jury, it will be remembered, were not allowed access to the dossier either during the hearing or when deliberating with the judges prior to the decision. The jury was confined to the oral evidence at the hearing and some photographs in the dossier that the presiding judge allowed them to see. This deprivation seems to be explicable in terms of the reluctance of the legal professionalism of the system to allow too great an intrusion by lay people. The extent of the deprivation will depend on how fully the witnesses at the hearing are able to recount orally what is in their depositions.

(c) Control of the investigation by legal professionals

The gendarmerie notified the prosecutor's office of the shooting in this case soon after they had been informed of it. The prosecutor on duty notified the investigating judge on duty soon after that. They both attended the scene of the shooting that night.

The initial investigation, however, was carried out by the local *gendarmerie*. This lasted for some 45 hours, during 43 of which the accused was held under a *garde à vue*. Statements were taken during this period from all the witnesses to the events in question and the accused was interrogated. There was some involvement by the prosecutor during this period (e.g., authorizing the sealing of the victim's house, extending the *garde à vue*) but none by the investigating judge.

The second phase of the investigation was carried out, instigated or controlled by the investigating judge, although the prosecutor was kept informed and had the right to be heard. This second phase included numerous interrogations of the accused, commissioning the various experts to report, and arranging for and officiating at the re-enactment and the confrontation. The investigating judge also commissioned the *gendarmerie* to carry out "the fullest investigation" but the *gendarmerie* replied that they had already done so and had already transmitted the results. The investigating judge would have been aware of this so the commission would seem to have been something of a formality, for the purposes of a proper record. The investigating judge also issued a commission to the police to inquire into matters relating to the accused's *personnalité*. Many interviews were conducted by police and gendarmes pursuant to this commission. The results were forwarded to the investigating judge who put them into the dossier.

The investigating judge, it will be seen, in fact, carried out, instigated or controlled most of the investigation in this case. He has done most of the interrogation of the accused, has commissioned all the expert reports and the *personnalité* inquiries, and has arranged for and officiated at the re-enactment and confrontation. Statements from the witnesses to the crucial events were also sought by the investigating judge although they were already in the dossier. These statements, and they were important ones for the purposes of the investigation, were the only ones generated by the *gendarmerie* and not by the investigating judge.[6]

The subordinate role of the *gendarmerie* and the police in this investigation contrasts with the role of the police in criminal investigations in common law jurisdictions. The police in those jurisdictions generally have discretion to investigate as they see fit without control from prosecutors or the judiciary. For particularly intrusive investigative measures such as the search of premises or the interception of telecommunications the warrant of a magistrate or judge will normally be required, but decisions to pursue such measures and plans for their pursuit will be those of the police. Prosecutors are generally presented with the results of the police investigation for the purposes of prosecution in court and have little or no say in how those results are achieved.

(d) The *garde à vue*

The *garde à vue*, which in this case lasted for about 43 hours, is a crucial but contentious feature of French criminal procedure. The *garde à vue* is available to the judicial police in cases of flagrant offenses (which the present one was) and in non-flagrant cases not requiring an investigating judge. The provisions regulating the *garde à vue* in cases of flagrant offenses authorize the judicial police to hold in custody a suspect and any persons at the scene of the offense for a period of 24 hours. This period may be extended on the authority of the prosecutor or the investigating judge by another 24 hours in the case of a suspect. All that transpires under a *garde à vue* is to be recorded by the judicial police, including the periods of interrogation and of rest. A person held under a *garde à vue* has a right to a medical examination after 24 hours of being so held. At the time of the present case there was no provision for the presence of a lawyer or for legal advice during the *garde à vue*. Nor was there provision for a detainee to inform relatives or friends. The judicial

---

6. It should be noted as regards the investigating judge that that officer's relative importance in French criminal investigations has been declining steadily over the years in comparison with the activities of the judicial police and prosecutor.... [T]he proportion of cases involving an investigating judge to total cases investigated has fallen between 1960 and 1988 from 20% to less than 10%.... It should also be noted that the investigating judge has been abolished in most Continental jurisdictions, including Germany in 1975 and Italy in 1989.

police were thus able to keep the suspect isolated and to themselves for a period up to 48 hours, and the witnesses for up to 24 hours.

The *garde à vue* had often been criticized in France as allowing the police too much power over a suspect likely to be particularly vulnerable immediately after arrest. The socialist government in power until May 1993 enacted legislation with effect from March 1993 which allowed a suspect detained under a *garde à vue* access to a lawyer from the twentieth hour of the *garde à vue*, with provision from January 1994 for such access from the beginning of the *garde à vue*. The conservative government in power from May 1993 repealed this latter provision but allowed access to a lawyer from the twentieth hour to continue. The socialists had also provided that suspects under a *garde à vue* were to have the right to inform their families by telephone of their whereabouts, and that witnesses were no longer to be held under a *garde à vue* except in special circumstances. The conservatives in fact extended the right of suspects to inform their families of their whereabouts to include the right to inform parents, siblings, co-habitees and employers.

The *garde à vue* gives to the French judicial police at the beginning of an investigation powers generally greater than those legally available to the police in adversarial systems. The exercise of these powers has become significant in the totality of the French criminal investigation, to an extent apparently never intended by the framers of the Criminal Procedure Code. Given that the judicial police are also commissioned by investigating judges and prosecutors to do much of the remaining investigative work, it could be maintained that most criminal investigation is actually done by the police. As already demonstrated, however, there is significant control of that work by the investigating judge or the prosecutor.

(e) Re-enactment and confrontation

Re-enactment and confrontation as exemplified in the investigation in this case are generally not a part of criminal investigations in common law jurisdictions. The main purpose of the re-enactment seems to have been the re-creation for the benefit of the investigating judge of the behavior of all concerned in the events associated with the shootings. The players in those events would be able to make manifest what they believed had happened and the investigating judge would thus arrive at a better understanding of the events. Another purpose would seem to have been to provide a photographic record of the re-creation for the benefit of those involved in subsequent stages of the proceedings, particularly the judges and jurors at the hearing. Although the photographic record was seen by the jurors as well as the judges in the present case, it seems clear that the re-enactment is essentially an investigative device carried out for the benefit of the chief investigator, in this case the investigating judge. The record is available to the participants at the hearing to allow them to confirm (or perhaps question) the thoroughness of the investigation rather than as evidence of the events in question. . . .

There were two confrontations between the accused and the accusing witnesses in the present case—one arranged by the *gendarmerie* during the *garde à vue* and the other arranged by the investigating judge. Confrontation is more integral to the French system than is re-enactment. Confrontation, unlike re-enactment, is specifically dealt with in the Criminal Procedure Code. Article 118 requires that the accused's lawyer be present at any confrontation unless such presence is waived by the accused. Article 119 allows the prosecution to be present at any confrontation. Under article 120 the prosecutor and the accused's lawyer can only ask questions at the confrontation by leave of the investigating judge. Article 121 regulates the form of the record (*procès-verbal*) of any confrontation. Under article 152 the powers accorded the judicial police under a commission to make inquiries (*commission rogatoire*) from an investigating judge do not include a power to conduct a confrontation with the accused. There is no provision for any confrontation at the hearing although the allegations of the accusing witnesses will be put to the accused at the hearing by the presiding judge.

Confrontation of the accused with the accusing witnesses is, of course, an integral part of the adversarial system, but this happens at the trial rather than during the investigation. This again highlights the primacy of the trial for the adversarial system and of the investigation for the French system. . . .

(f) Official experts

The experts used in the present case were inscribed on lists maintained by the courts. Except in exceptional circumstances, only such experts can be used for the purposes of any investigation. As indicated above there is a national list of experts maintained by the *cour de cassation* in Paris and there are regional lists maintained by the *cours d'appel* in the jurisdictional regions into which France is divided. (The *cour d'appel* for the region which included Le Mans was located in Angers.). . . . Experts under this system are expected to be neutral and impartial, to serve science rather than the parties, but they are used in the process of law enforcement and would be likely to share the values of the agencies of law enforcement. . . . The conclusions of those experts were uncontested by other experts and they were not seriously challenged by the defense lawyer. If there is a conflict between experts resolution of that conflict can and should be sought by reference to other experts on the lists, normally during the investigation but also, if necessary, at the hearing.

All this differs significantly from the use of experts in adversarial procedures. There the prosecution and the defense seek out their respective experts and those experts are used to support competing positions. . . .

(h) The position of the accused

(i) The accused as a source of information

The accused in this case, from the time of his arrest as the suspect through to the hearing, was treated as someone in possession of knowledge important to the disposition of the case. He was held by the local *gendarmerie* for 43 hours in a *garde à vue* and interrogated on and off over that period, including being confronted by the three main witnesses to the shootings. He made no admissions during this period, which led the *gendarmerie* to note that it was "impossible to obtain a coherent reply" from the accused and that he remained "imperturbable before the seriousness of the facts". The Commander of the *gendarmerie* at Le Mans who gave evidence at the hearing referred to the exceptional "defiance" of the accused during the *garde à vue*. The accused was clearly regarded by the *gendarmerie* as unusually uncooperative in their pursuit of the truth.

It was not until the accused was brought before the investigating judge that he admitted being at the scene and shooting with his shotgun (four shots through the door) and his revolver (two shots into the air to frighten his wife). When the ballistics expert later reported that a shot had been fired at point blank range into the left side of the deceased, the accused was brought before the investigating judge for his response, which was that he had fired no such shot and that he did not even see the deceased when he entered the house or any person at all in the hallway where the deceased was. When interrogated further about the revolver shots, the accused admitted that he had fired a third shot, not into the air, which had hit his wife in the back of the head, but that he had no intention of killing her.

At the hearing the accused was closely interrogated by the President about the inconsistencies between the accused's version of events and the version taken to be established by the eye-witnesses and the experts. The improbabilities of the accused's version (regarding the shots fired with the shotgun and the failure of the accused to have seen the deceased in the hallway, for example) were pointed out in an endeavor to have the accused confirm the established version.

It is apparent that the accused was expected, both during the investigation and at the hearing, to divulge what he knew about the relevant events to complement the version otherwise established. This would have allowed the full truth about those events to be made manifest. The failure at the beginning to divulge anything and later to divulge fully was treated as an avoidance by the accused of an obligation to contribute information within his knowledge to the common endeavor of establishing the truth.

It would hardly be accurate to describe an adversarial accused as an information source. The adversarial system is posited upon the prosecution having to prove the guilt of the accused without the accused having to assist. The accused has a right to silence, incorporating a privilege against self-incrimination, and is to be presumed innocent until proved guilty by the prosecution. Investigating police will generally seek a statement if not a confession from a suspect but the suspect need not say anything and should be so informed by the police. . . .

(ii) A right to silence?

The accused in this case was interrogated by the *gendarmerie*, the investigating judge and the President of the *cour d'assises*. He responded to all of them though he made no admissions to the *gendarmerie*. He was not told by the *gendarmerie* or the President that he did not have to answer their questions or to say anything. The law does not require that he be so told. The investigating judge at the "first appearance interrogation" did so warn the accused, as the law required, but does not appear to have so warned the accused at subsequent interrogations, the law not expressly so requiring. The warning at the first interrogation failed to have any effect as then for the first time some admissions were made.

The accused, of course, could have declined to answer any questions, both during the investigation and at the hearing. This did not happen and apparently it happens very rarely in France. Why is this?

One explanation is in terms of the "centuries-old tradition of inquisitorial proceedings" in consequence of which an accused "almost never would conceive it possible not to submit" to interrogation. A related explanation might be that the accused feels obliged to cooperate with officials in the manifestation of the truth of events in which he or she was involved.

Another explanation may flow from the fact that an accused, both during the investigation and at a hearing, is obliged to submit to interrogation. An accused under a garde à vue is available to the *gendarmerie* or the police for up to 48 hours for the purposes of interrogation, an accused must attend at the office of the investigating judge for questioning when required to do so, and an accused must submit to the interrogation of the presiding judge at any hearing. It is much more difficult to maintain silence under such conditions than it is under the adversarial system where powers of detention by the police for interrogation are generally more restricted and where an accused is not obliged to give evidence and so be subjected to interrogation.

A more fruitful explanation, in my view, has to do with the inferences that may be drawn from the silence of an accused. The law prescribes that the judges and jurors ask themselves, when deliberating upon their verdict, "what impression the means of defense have made upon their reason." If an accused does not respond, or responds partially or implausibly, to incriminating evidence, the effect upon the minds of the judges and jurors is very likely to be adverse to the accused. Where the legal culture encourages responses to officials and where responses are thus expected, it is not difficult for courts to draw adverse inferences from the silence of accused persons, or more particularly the failure to respond to official questioning. The legal culture in France would not support a rule, as in some common law jurisdictions, prohibiting comment by a judge or a prosecutor to a jury on the failure of an accused to answer questions from the police or to give evidence. Certainly at hearings in France it is not uncommon to hear the presiding judge inform an accused who is silent or prevaricating under interrogation that the court will draw its own conclusions from such behavior.

To what extent, then, does an accused in France have a right to silence, or a privilege against self-incrimination? It is generally asserted that there is such a right or privilege. It is based, somewhat tenuously, on two articles of the CPP—article 62 allowing the police (to do no more than) to bring a person who refuses to answer their questions about a flagrant offense before a prosecutor, and article 114 requiring the investigating judge to notify a defendant at the first interrogation that he or she is free not to make any statement. These provisions are not likely to subvert the culture of response rather than silence nor impede the drawing of adverse inferences from silence.

(iii) Presumption of innocence

The accused at an adversarial trial is said to benefit from the presumption of innocence. This means no more than if the prosecution fail to adduce sufficient evidence to prove the guilt of the accused then the accused is entitled to an acquittal. In other words, the prosecution bears the burden of proving the guilt of the accused. The presumption does not operate in such a case to establish the accused's innocence, the result is simply that the accused has not been proved guilty. The presumption of innocence has, however, acquired an emotive and symbolic value for critics of legal regimes that do not boast such a presumption.

It is sometimes suggested that there is no presumption of innocence in the French legal system. In so far as the presumption requires the prosecution to adduce sufficient evidence to prove guilt, the presumption cannot in those terms be properly applied to the French system. The prosecution does not adduce evidence at a French hearing. Such evidence as is adduced is adduced by the presiding judge, either by interrogating the witnesses or by reading from the dossier. In that sense any burden of proof is on the court.

In an extended sense it is possible to speak of a burden of proof on the prosecution in France in that a prosecutor has overall charge of and responsibility for any criminal investigation and the consequent production of a dossier that goes to the court for the purposes of the proof, or the manifestation, of the guilt of the accused. All of which means that the notion of the presumption of innocence peculiar to the adversarial system has to be recast to point up corresponding processes in the French system. This again involves a shift in focus from the adversarial trial to the French investigation.

One aspect said to characterize the adversarial presumption of innocence is the requirement of proof of guilt beyond reasonable doubt. A similar standard of proof is required in the French system. It is expressed as a subjective (personal) conviction (*"intime conviction"*) of guilt based on the evidence. However the evidence is put before the court, there should be no finding of guilt in either system unless that evidence convinces the court to the exclusion of any reasonable doubt.

(iv) The *personnalité* of the accused

At the beginning of the hearing in this case the accused was interrogated about his *personnalité* and witnesses were called on those matters. There was evidence, for example, that the accused was often violent towards his wife, but there was also evidence that he was a hard-worker. There was evidence that eight years before the subject shootings the accused "had taken a shotgun" to his wife and was only prevented from firing at her by the intervention of their elder son. The accused had no previous convictions, but if he had had they would have been read out by the presiding judge as part of the material on the accused's *personnalité*. The facts of the case were not broached until after these matters had been dealt with.

The "behaviour, morals, associates, family background and means of existence" of the accused had been explored during the investigation under a *commission rogatoire* (curriculum vitae) issue by the investigating judge to the Commissioner of Police at Le Mans. The records of this exploration were in Part B of the dossier, entitled *Renseignements et Personnalité*.

There is a legislative requirement that an investigating judge conduct an inquiry into the *personnalité* of an accused although no express requirement that evidence of *personnalité* be adduced at the hearing. There is a French legal adage that: on *juge l'homme, pas les faits* (one judges the man, not the facts), which expresses the philosophy underlying the attention given to the accused's *personnalité* as well as to the facts of a case. A further explanation for the attention given to both facts and *personnalité* during the investigation and at the hearing may be found in the practice at the hearing of dealing with the questions of guilt and punishment together. Whatever the explanation for treating the accused's *personnalité* along with the facts of the case, such treatment has become standard procedure in the French criminal justice system. The procedure has its critics in France and it has been the subject of some reconsideration recently. The socialist government in the reforms to the Criminal Procedure Code prior to losing power in May 1993 sought to have *personnalité* matters dealt with after the facts at hearings. This reform was, however, one of those countermanded by the conservatives on their return to power.

What is a common lawyer to make of this procedure whereby material on the accused's *personnalité* is revealed to the court at the beginning of the hearing? As to matters of personal history such as family background, education and employment record, these are matters relevant to sentencing rather than liability for the common lawyer and would be canvassed only after any conviction. Though regarded as irrelevant to liability they would not normally be prejudicial to an accused on that question. As to evidence of bad character (e.g., that the accused was often violent towards his wife), such evidence could not, subject to certain exceptions, be given at a common law trial on charges similar to those in the present case. Such evidence, categorized as evidence of disposition or propensity, is variously said to be unreliable or insufficiently probative as regards the facts in issue, or disproportionately prejudicial. Evidence of the accused's good character, on the other hand without apparent consistency, is generally admissible in common law systems on the question of the accused's guilt. The French system allows evidence of both good and bad character in the accused to go before the court at the hearing....

[One reason is] ... the common law's skepticism about the capabilities of the jury. This skepticism is to the effect that juries may not be able to draw the proper inferences from some types of evidence, such as evidence of bad character, and may be unduly prejudiced against the accused by that evidence. This view of the jury is not without irony in that the jury is championed by common lawyers as bringing the experience and capabilities of a cross-section of society to the task of judging accused persons. This view also presupposes that judges can determine when juries are likely to be unduly prejudiced by probative material.

While there can clearly be prejudice to an accused under the French system when prior convictions and other material evincing bad character are indiscriminately aired at the outset of a hearing, the arrangements at common law to protect an accused from evidence of bad character that is of some probative value but prejudicial in other respects can hardly claim to be more rational or justifiable....

Perhaps the most significant conclusion to be drawn by an anglophone from the study is that the investigation is of determinative importance in the French criminal justice system and that the hearing or trial does little more than present the results of the investigation in public. This means, further, that the characteristics of the investigation become the characteristics of the whole system. Thus the dossier produced by the investigation contains the material on which all the subsequent decisions in a case are made and provides the link between the stages through which a case passes. The dossier being written (or documentary) means that the system is essentially a written one. Those who are instrumental in compiling the dossier—the investigating judge, the prosecutor, the judicial police, official experts—are professionals within the system who, within their respective areas of competence, work together to realize the objectives of the system. The system is thus ultimately a bureaucratic one in that it is characterized by trained and interdependent official operatives the results of whose activities are to be found in written records.

It could also be concluded that, partly as a result of the bureaucratic character of the investigation and hence of the whole criminal justice system, and partly as a result of the pursuit of the objective that the truth of a matter be manifested, the suspect/accused is pressured to be responsive to the needs of the investigation and the system as a whole. There is pressure, in other words, to "assist the officials with their inquiries", to provide all information relevant to the manifestation of the truth, to participate in the realization of the objectives of the system. Without this participation it is difficult for the officials to close the file. A non-cooperative or an adversarial position is thus counterindicated by the system. This combination of bureaucratic endeavor and pursuit of the truth could also help to explain why the system concerns itself with the whole person of the suspect/accused, with his or her *personnalité* as well as with the allegation of a particular offense.

NOTES AND QUESTIONS

1. We might expect that many American lawyers would be very critical of the French criminal justice system as described by Hodgson and McKillop. Suppose an "innocence project" in France looked at those in prison, seeking cases where innocent people had been found guilty. Would you predict that such a project would find any or many such people? Such projects in the United States do find situations where the legal system failed and the wrong person was convicted. Does the French or American system seem better suited to avoiding such mistakes? However, looked at from the bottom up from the perspective of an accused who is poor, how different are the French and American criminal justice systems? What is different? What is similar?

2. Almost all criminal justice systems face the problem of dealing with large numbers of people if not substantial overload. Should we expect that all criminal justice systems might be very different in practice from their officially announced forms, which tend to reflect their strongest claims to legitimacy? To what extent do factors other than mass processing influence the way things are done, whatever constitutions and formal traditions say?

3. In *A Sociological Theory of Law* 150–151 (1991), Adam Podgorecki draws a distinction between "legal systems based mainly on statute law and legal systems based mainly on precedent." The "statute" systems tend to be "hierarchical" and to stress legal logic. A "statute" system "provides specific directives on how to create new norms and how to incorporate them, into the already existing normative body." The system "alienates both the state officials and average citizens from the real social problems and from each other." Still, this "gap" may be "functional in the long run for officialdom since it gains more authority over the population." But "access of the average member of the society to the law" is limited.

Legal systems based on "precedent" have a different character. They "correspond to the more pluralistically structured societies. Their binding messages come from many scattered sources which are often contradictory." They tend to be flexible, adaptive. The legal profession has a sort of "inductive ability" to find relevant cases. In these systems, professionals build a highly technical world, but they are less "servile" than the lawyers in statute systems. "Statute law systems" may flourish in totalitarian societies "due to their manageability." Precedent-based systems "invite and utilize the participation of heterogeneous social groups while being in this way vulnerable to potential disruptions. Statute legal systems, on the contrary, when they are challenged become even more closed."

Obviously, Podgorecki is thinking of differences between the legal systems of, say, his native Poland particularly in the period before the end of Communist rule, and that of, say, Canada, where he was living when his book appeared. Do the differences he points to between the two systems really flow from the form of the systems? Are there other reasons that account for these differences? Even if we suspect that there is more to it than the form of the legal systems involved, does such a conclusion suggest that the form plays no part in explaining these differences?

4.   Is there some way to test differences between procedural systems? One possibility is to mount mock trials, differing only in one or another aspect of procedure that corresponds to differences between civil and common law. See John W. Thibaut and Laurens Walker, *Procedural Justice* (1975). See, further, on the contrast between "adversary procedure" and "non-adversary or inquisitorial procedure," Blair H. Sheppard and Neil Vidmar, "Adversary Pretrial Procedures and Testimonial Evidence: Effects of Lawyer's Role and Machiavellianism," 39 *Journal of Personality and Social Psychology* 320 (1980). The problem with this line of research is to go from what is found in the world of the experiment to the world of the law in action in common and civil law countries.

(B) *The Arrangement of Legal Institutions*

(5.3) **Kagan, Cartwright, Friedman and Wheeler**

Kagan, Cartwright, Friedman and Wheeler[7] studied the evolution of state supreme courts. They looked at experiences in sixteen states from 1870 to 1970. They drew a sample of 6,000 cases. Many, but not all, of these states took steps to deal with an increasing docket as the population of the various states continued to grow. The authors offer a typology of state supreme courts. Type 1 states have low populations, do not have intermediate appellate courts and do not give the supreme court discretion as to what cases to hear. These courts are likely to take formal approaches as hard pressed judges adopt a mechanical approach to turn out the required opinions. Type 2 states have medium or large populations, but give their supreme court little discretion in case selection. As a result, the highest court has a relatively heavy caseload and also is likely to take more formal approaches in opinion writing. Type 3 states have medium or large populations, but they have substantial controls over the caseloads of their supreme court. These states created intermediate appellate courts and gave the state supreme court discretion as to whether to hear a particular case. As a result, caseloads are relatively light.

They find that Type 1 courts reversed lower courts less than the other types. Type 3 supreme courts reversed more than other types. Type 3 courts are more likely to declare laws to be unconstitutional, and they are more likely to decide in favor of defendants in criminal cases who are bringing appeals. The authors argue that these Type 3 courts are more likely to concentrate on significant cases in new areas of law. This has weakened institutional restraints on judicial activism. These courts produce more con-

7. "The Evolution of State Supreme Courts," 76 *Michigan Law Review* 961 (1978).

curring and dissenting opinions which suggests that their cases were more often controversial. Their opinions are longer than those from the other types of courts, and they cited more cases and law review articles. Of course, the authors have no independent measure as to whether control over the docket and lighter caseloads produce "better" opinions and decisions. The authors state: "At most we can say, rather timidly, that the reduction of caseload in courts with high-discretion may increase our *chances* of getting better judicial opinions."

NOTES AND QUESTIONS

1. Kagan and his associates present evidence suggesting that the structure of a court system affects how the system works. What effect does this have on the actual results of the cases? The authors have only indirect evidence of an effect of structure on the results of cases. If a state supreme court can select its cases and control the demands on its time, it can write longer and better footnoted opinions. It may reverse more decisions from the courts below than a court that cannot select what to hear. Nonetheless, we cannot be sure that a court that can control its docket reaches better results than courts that cannot. For a comparative study of three American state supreme courts (Alabama, Ohio and New Jersey), see G. Allan Tarr and Mary Cornelia Aldis Porter, *State Supreme Courts in State and Nation* (1988).

2. W. T. Austin, "Portrait of a Courtroom: Social and Ecological Impressions of the Adversary Process," 9 *Criminal Justice and Behavior* 286 (1982), looked at the layout of a North Carolina courtroom where criminal cases were tried. The judge sat on a raised bench placed against the back wall of the courtroom. The jurors sat in seats along a side wall to the judge's left. The witness, court reporter and prosecutor all were located within an area—a triangle—bounded by the judge's bench and the jury box. The defense sat to the judge's right outside of this area. Bailiffs sat behind the defense table, close enough to control a defendant if necessary. Information flowed from the witnesses and the judge to the jury. The prosecutor could face the jurors while the defense looked on from behind the prosecutor. The prosecutor could look directly at witnesses and stare, smile, frown and otherwise communicate by body language to the jurors. Austin concedes that this study cannot tell us about the impact of this arrangement on the outcome of cases. Is it possible that furniture arrangements might affect the outcome of cases? How could you find out?

3. There is a theatrical element to judicial process. Judges wear costumes (robes) and we can see law books, depositions and official documents as stage props. Moreover, the stage setting—courtrooms, legislative chambers and the like—may affect what happens there. Consider Murray Edelman, "Space and the Social Order," 32 *Journal of Architectural Education* 2 (1978):

> The scale of the structure reminds the mass of political spectators that they enter the precincts of power as clients or as supplicants, susceptible to arbitrary rebuffs and favors, and that they are subject to

remote authorities they only dimly know or understand. And the same monumentality carries a reciprocal meaning for the functionaries who enter these buildings regularly to exercise power. For them, the grand scale of the setting in which they make decisions emphasizes their authority and their distinction as a class from those who are subject to their decisions. Such spaces legitimize the power of elites and of officials in exactly the same way that they highlight the vulnerability of non-elites.... Spaces affirm the established social roles by encouraging those who act and those who look on to respond to socially sanctioned cues and to ignore incompatible empirical ones.

What message is given out by the theatrical aspects of courtroom behavior? By the "costumes" of judges and lawyers? By the use of the term, "Your Honor," and phrases such as "May it please the court ..." By the requirement that everybody rise when the judge enters? By the judge being seated on a platform above everyone else in the room? By bookshelves displaying important law books that are seldom opened by anyone? Would justice be better served in a more relaxed and less formal setting? Or do such things as the costumes, architecture, vocabulary and customs of deference serve to take the situation out of the ordinary and point all who are involved toward a search for justice?

4. Stewart Macaulay, Access to the Legal Systems of the Americas: Informal Processes, unpublished paper (1974), notes:

The structure of the legal system itself tends to discourage these citizens from using it. Factors of distance and convenience are important. Some agencies are found only in the large towns in a region, and others are located in the capital of the country. The time and cost of transportation becomes a barrier because the citizen must go to the agency in most instances; few agencies come to the citizen. Even office hours are important. High status people can leave their employment at a relatively low cost, but lower status people may lose a day's wages or even their job if they go to a government office or courtroom [during working hours]....

The citizen seeking some government service faces delay and what appears to be an utterly unreasonable and irrational process. He or she must get in line and wait, only to be sent to yet another line where he or she is told to come back next week. Any transaction seems to require multiple copies of several documents, and each must bear the documentary tax stamps. One must produce documentary evidence of birth, payment of taxes and entitlement to the service. In Chile, at least, these were part of what was called *"trámites,"* a term that often struck an English speaker as far too close to "trauma" in his or her language....

Those without influence can wait, rebel, or just give up and not seek the service supposedly offered to all by the legal system.... Many just stay away, making a calculation, the economists tell us, that the value of the service does not outweigh the cost of waiting to get it. Part of those costs may be frustration and a sense of powerlessness in the face of such a process. Others wait, fill out forms (if they are literate), buy tax stamps, go from office to office and finally emerge with the desired documents entitling them to the service. Sometimes it's worth the trouble, sometimes not.

Macaulay points out that those with influence do not stand in lines. In many countries they can hire people who are experts at coping with the bureaucracies. On the functions of lines and delay, see Barry Schwartz, "Waiting, Exchange and Power: The Distribution of Time in Social Systems," 79 *American Journal of Sociology* 841 (1974); Yoram Barzel, "A Theory of Rationing by Waiting," 17 *Journal of Law and Economics* 73 (1974).

Do factors such as the location of courts and administrative agencies, the cost of transportation, or problems involved in lines, forms, delays and missing work affect American and European legal systems or is this only a Third World problem?

5. The "Haves" in the Structure of the Legal System. One of the most widely cited articles in the law and society field is Marc Galanter, "Why the Haves Come Out Ahead: Speculations on the Limits of Legal Change," 9 *Law & Society Review* 95 (1974). In this piece, Galanter tries to explain the outcomes of cases in trial courts in essentially structural terms. He discusses "the way in which the basic architecture of the legal system creates and limits the possibilities of using the system as a means of redistributive (that is, systematically equalizing) change."

Galanter divides parties into "one-shotters" and "repeat players." A one-shotter is a person or business that seldom deals with the legal system. Its claims are too large (relative to its size) or too small (relative to the cost of remedies) to be managed routinely and rationally. A repeat player has had, and anticipates having, repeated litigation, it has low stakes in the outcome of any one case, and it has the resources to pursue its long-run interests.

Repeat players, such as large corporations, cope with litigation: they have advance intelligence, and so they are able to structure the next transaction and build a record to justify their actions. They develop expertise and have access to specialists—both lawyers and expert witnesses skilled in dealing with particular types of transactions. They enjoy economies of scale and have low start-up costs for any particular case. For example, an auto manufacturer may be challenged by many buyers about the safety of the gas tanks on its vehicles. It can afford to have a basic legal strategy planned and invest in the needed engineering studies to defend itself. Repeat players can develop informal relations with institutional incumbents such as judges, hearing examiners and clerks of court. These officials may learn, for example, that they can trust the repeat player's assertions and claims.

Repeat players may not settle a particular case when a one-shotter would do this. Repeat players must establish and maintain credibility as a combatant. If they give in too easily in one case, it may affect the demands made in the next one. They can play the odds and maximize gain over a series of cases, even suffering maximum loss in some cases. Seldom will they find any one case critically important. As a result, they can play for rules as well as immediate gains. They are interested in anything that will favorably influence the outcomes of future cases. Repeat players may settle cases where they expect unfavorable rule outcomes. They are likely to discern which rules may penetrate and which are symbolic, and they can trade off symbolic defeats for tangible gains. Finally, repeat players can invest the resources necessary to secure the penetration of rules favorable to them.

Galanter considers litigation patterns. One-shotters may sue one-shotters. Often such cases are between parties who have some intimate tie, who are fighting over some unsharable good. Such disputes may have overtones of spite and irrationality. Cost barriers ration access to the legal system for many of these cases. Repeat players may sue repeat players. However, the sanctions of long-term continuing relations minimize such cases; disputes here usually are settled without going to court. A few of these cases occur frequently: for example, an organization such as the American Civil Liberties Union may push a case to trial and appeal to vindicate what it sees as a fundamental right. Governmental units may find it hard to settle cases because of the unfavorable publicity likely to be generated. Occasionally, both parties are repeat players but they do not deal with each other often or they lack mutually advantageous long-term continuing relations. For example, two computer software firms may battle over intellectual property rights to features of competing computer programs.

Perhaps the remaining two litigation patterns are more interesting. Repeat players may sue one-shotters. Often cases here take the form of stereotyped mass processing with little of the individuated attention of full-dress adjudication. Lenders seek default judgments, attachments of wages, confirmation of their title to property sold under conditional sales and so on. The court serves almost as an administrative agency rather than a place where bargaining takes place in the shadow of the law. The great bulk of litigation falls in this category. No particular case raises major policy concerns; taken together all of these cases reflect the conditions of a mass society in the face of an ideology of individualism.

Finally, one-shotters may sue repeat players. The one-shotter seeks outside help to create leverage against an organization with which he or she has been having dealings. Now the one-shotter is at the point of divorce. For example, a consumer is unhappy with the failure of repairs to his or her car; an employee wants to dispute his or her firing by an employer; a tenant wants to force a landlord to make repairs to an apartment. Here all of the advantages of repeat players play out in full. While some one-shotters do win such suits, the configuration of the parties suggests that we should expect repeat players to defeat their claims in most of such cases.

Galanter also talks about how the nature of American legal institutions increases the advantages of repeat players. Our claim handling facilities are largely passive and reactive; the client must mobilize them and so faces cost barriers to access. However, parties are treated as if they were equally endowed with economic resources, investigative opportunities, and legal skills. Most American legal institutions are characterized by overload which also affects the balance of advantages and protects the possessor of money or goods against a claimant: for example, overload means that decisions will be delayed. Delay discounts the value of recovery. Overload requires that a litigant raise money to pay the costs of keeping a case alive. Overload induces institutional incumbents to place a high value on clearing dockets, discouraging full-dress adjudication in favor of bargaining, stereotyping situations and routine processing. Moreover, it serves to induce judges and administrators to adopt restrictive rules to discourage litigation.

Galanter looks at the implications of the system that he has described:

> Structurally, (by cost and institutional overload) and culturally (by ambiguity and normative overload) the [American legal] system effects a massive covert delegation from the most authoritative rule-makers to field level officials (and their constituencies) responsive to other norms and priorities than are contained in the "higher law." ... It permits unification and universalism at the symbolic level and diversity and particularism at the operating level. (p. 148)

(C) Systems for Controlling Behavior within Legal Institutions

(1) Rules and Their Rivals

(5.4) Legal Rules and the Process of Social Change

Lawrence M. Friedman

19 *Stanford Law Review* 786 (1967).

I. RULES OF LAW

A. General Introduction

The common word "rule" has a variety of meanings. We speak of rules of law and also of rules of the game of checkers and rules of personal behavior (as when a person says, "I go to bed at midnight as a rule" or "I make it a rule to avoid fried foods"). In general, the word "rule" is used in law to describe a proposition containing two parts: first, a statement of fact (often in conditional form) and, second, a statement of the consequences that will or may follow upon the existence of that fact, within some normative order or system of governmental control. Or, as Roscoe Pound has put it, a rule is a "legal precept attaching a definite detailed legal consequence to a definite detailed statement of fact." Pound's definition is accurate enough for present purposes. It is broad enough to include statements of common-law doctrine as well as statutory provisions, administrative regulations, ordinances, decrees of dictators, and other general propositions promulgated by legitimate authorities which are intended to govern or guide some aspect of social or individual conduct. All of these propositions may be called legal "rules" in that they all append legal consequences to given facts.

It is very clear that some of the propositions enunciated in appellate cases are (or purport to be) rules.... Statutory phrases or sentences are also rules. The heart of the federal patent law—"[w]hoever invents or discovers any new and useful process ... may obtain a patent"—is a rule. The consequences of a rule may sometimes be omitted from the verbal formulation but if the rule is to be operational, the consequences must be there, even if not expressed. "Thou shalt not kill" is a rule of law under the definition used here if (and only if) there is an implication that he who kills will or may be visited with consequences imposed upon him by some authority sanctioned by law. Most of the consequences mentioned so far have been punishments, but they just as easily may be rewards, as in the case of the patent rule quoted.... All rules are directed toward conduct, and the kind of conduct they are concerned with can be called the substantive aspect of the rule.

In addition, however, rules have what might be called a formal aspect. Rules differ from each other in more than their subject matter. There are certain highly abstract categories into which rules can be sorted and classified. These correspond to the most basic and abstract categories of legal relationships. Thus, some rules grant rights, some grant privileges, some permit, some forbid, and some give positive commands. Some rules say "may" and some say "shall." Some rules of evidence set up (in legal jargon) rebuttable presumptions; others, conclusive presumptions. Differences among rules in regard to these dimensions are differences in form.

In addition, all rules have a jurisdictional aspect, or an aspect of distribution of power. This is an aspect of legal rules that is sometimes overlooked. A legal rule, as we use the term here, attaches consequences to facts. But consequences do not attach to conduct by themselves; someone must manipulate the strings. Each rule, to be a meaningful rule, must carry with it a ticket to some person, agency, or institution, authorizing, permitting, forbidding, or allowing some action to take place. Each rule has its institutional and distributive side as well as its formal and substantive side. It distributes, or redistributes, power within the legal system or within the social order. Without this aspect, a rule would be a mere exhortation, essentially empty or rhetorical, like the preamble to a statute.

The distributive aspect of a rule is often implicit. An ordinary criminal statute, for example, contains no explicit jurisdictional statement; it merely defines certain conduct as criminal and assesses punishment for commission of that crime. The jurisdictional aspects of the ordinary criminal law rule are implicit and, in actuality, quite complex. They can be understood only by understanding the institutional context and the history of the common-law system. This tells us that appellate courts will have some responsibility for administration of the law—for example, by deciding its outer limits of applicability. Primarily, however, the law will be carried out by policemen, district attorneys, trial judges, and other operational arms of the criminal process.

Other statutes or rules are addressed in the first instance to lawyers, or to judges, or to administrative officials. In many, but by no means all, cases the rule explicitly grants power or authority. Still other rules may be addressed to doctors, plumbers, or private citizens generally, authorizing, preferring, or forbidding certain behavior. Here too, however, there is ultimately in the background an explicit or implicit grant of jurisdiction to some governmental authority to take the steps necessary to implement the provisions of the rule.

The three aspects of a rule just discussed are interrelated. Substantive, formal, and distributive aspects of a rule cannot really be understood in isolation and cannot be sharply distinguished from each other. Nonetheless, it is useful to analyze rules according to these aspects in order to see more clearly the way aspects of rules respond to specific social and institutional conditions.

B. A Note on Rule Skepticism

One reason why more jurisprudential and sociological attention in the last generation has not been paid to rules is because rules no longer enjoy quite the favor they once did. Indeed, it is fashionable in the academic world to decry them. Many legal realists described themselves as "rule skeptics," and legal education is heavily influenced by rule skepticism. Many students begin, naively, with the notion that rules of law are always precise and that these rules can be easily and mechanically applied to clear-cut situations. Much professional energy is directed toward dispelling these notions and toward demonstrating that certainty in the law is an illusion, since life is far too complex to be summed up in little maxims. As a result, legal scholarship is strongly influenced by the attitudes of rule skepticism, and the bulk of scholarly writing today is rule skeptical, in one way or another.

Rule skepticism, reduced to the extreme, means either (1) that some pretended rules are not the true operating rules; or (2) that some rules are unreal in the sense that they are varied, misused, or ignored as they are applied and that those who apply rules actually govern in their discretion, using the rules as mere handles or shams. The first of these two possible meanings is not an objection to the study of rules, but only a call for more sophistication in the study. Indeed, many of the realists were rule skeptics only in a limited sense; they recognized that their job was not to destroy rules, but to gain more precision in understanding the true operational rules....

The second meaning of rule skepticism is a more fundamental objection to the reality of legal rules, because it goes to the heart of the problem of government. Laws on paper are meaningless; they must be enforced or applied. At the cutting edge of law, rules devolve upon human operators, not machines. In their hands rules may become a mockery. Thus, for example, a criminal statute may say that he who commits assault suffers such-and-such a penalty. No exceptions or mitigations are mentioned. But the policeman who finds two men brawling in a bar may close his eyes and ignore the fight, break up the fight and say nothing further, or arrest the two men and throw them in jail. The district attorney may decide to let both of them go or book them for trial. At trial the judge may dismiss the case if he wishes. Therefore, the statutory rule is (so the argument goes) in part or in whole unreal. The policeman, the district attorney, the judge—these govern, not the rule.

To examine the problem more closely let us go back to a consideration of the nature of a rule. A rule is a direction; it is a tool for carrying out some task of government. Government can be effectuated either through personal surveillance or through formal directives to other persons (rules). Control exclusively through personal surveillance would be possible only for very simple societies. As society and government become more complicated, specific functions are allocated to this agency or that person, and bureaucratic organization necessarily replaces personal rule. At this point, rules enter into the structure of government. There is always, however, an operating level—a level at which laws are personally administered—by a policeman, for example. Yet, if it is true that administration at this level is never governed by rules, then government is not merely difficult, it is impossible—and no country, state, city, hospital, army, or large corporation can be run with any semblance of plan.

What is meant, then, is not that the policeman and other operating units of a system disregard formal rules altogether, but that they sometimes completely disregard them, and other times displace them a little. They may in some cases not disregard them at all. One of the major accomplishments of behavioral scientists—and of the legal realists—has been to highlight the gap between living law and book law. But this gap is not constant; it varies from region to region, from field of law to field of law, from time to time. However, the extent to which discretion is allowed and the extent to which it is actually exercised are social facts which, if we knew enough, could be explained by general laws of behavior.

Moreover, as an empirical proposition, it is probably not true that most legal rules are "unreal" in the sense that they are not or cannot be translated into behavior or enforcement. Most legal rules are in fact obeyed by those to whom they are addressed. Violations of the rules are promptly and efficiently punished. The general meaning of rules is in many—probably most—cases clear enough to form the basis of behavior. Nevertheless, there is a view among some students of the legal process that most rules are inherently uncertain and that most legal concepts are flexible and variable in meaning.... In fact, however, if one views impartially the whole of the legal system, it can be differentiated into three major areas. Some of the substantive content of the legal system consists of rules which are dormant—that is, there is no attempt at conscious, consistent enforcement. Other parts raise classic problems of uncertainty. These are the unsettled, but living, problems of law—such as the question of what constitutes due process of law. A third—and vital—part of the legal system consists of rules which are well settled in the special sense that they are acted upon by many persons in a particular manner and their applicability to given situations is not challenged. "Well settled" may mean, then, not that a dubious situation cannot be imagined or that the application of a rule is inherently free of doubt, but that it is actually free of doubt as a matter of ordinary, patterned human behavior. If most of the operating (as opposed to the dormant) rules of the legal system were not well settled in this sense, many of the normal processes and activities of life that people carry on with reference to legal rules would be profoundly altered. In a complex social and economic system, a legal system on the model of law school appellate cases would be insupportable. There are strong needs to know what is lawful and unlawful in our common, everyday actions. We need to know, for example, whether we are validly married if we go through certain forms (valid in the sense that our claim to validity will be either unchallenged or highly likely to survive any possible challenge). We need to know the permissible ranges of speed. Moreover, in business affairs, we need to know that a deed in a certain form executed in a standard manner truly passes title to a piece of land. If every such transaction had to be channeled through a discretionary agency, the economic system could not survive in its present form. A market economy and a free society both impose upon the legal system a high demand for operational certainty in parts of the law which regulate important aspects of the conduct of everyday life and everyday business.

The legal system must therefore limit operating rules which do not govern—that is, which do not in themselves provide a clear cut guide to action on the part of those persons to whom the rule is addressed. Some rules do provide the possibility of a clear-cut mandate; others do not. There is a significant difference between a rule which provides that no will is valid unless it is signed by two witnesses and a rule which provides that wills need or do not need witnesses, depending upon the circumstances and the demands of equity and good faith. Rules of the latter sort (discretionary rules) are tolerable as operational realities only in those areas of law where the social order or the economy can afford the luxury of slow, individuated justice. If there is a social interest in mass handling of transactions, a clear-cut framework of nondiscretionary rules is vital.

Of course, it has to be emphasized once more that when one speaks of the needs of the social order and the economy, one is speaking of operational realities, rather than of the way rules look on paper.... Some rules which appear discretionary on paper may not be truly discretionary in their manner of application, and vice versa. Some formally discretionary rules do not imply discretionary practice because the discretionary feature of those rules is jurisdictional only; it is a delegation to some lower agency, which in turn may adopt nondiscretionary rules. Suppose, for example, a rule of law purports to impose a punishment upon any person who sells "unwholesome" and "diseased" food. "Unwholesome" and "diseased" are critical items in this rule, but they obviously have no single objective meaning. Who shall decide what they mean? If the rule is statutory and if it is silent as to mode of enforcement, we may assume that the usual processes of criminal justice will provide whatever enforcement is needed or wanted. If policemen, district attorneys, and private citizens feel the law is being violated, they may invoke the criminal process. Ultimately, an appellate judge may put some additional meaning into the terms, though it is not likely that the problem will be litigated often enough for him to do so in a very precise way or that he will have the means at his command to frame intelligent regulations. He might, however, hold that some specific practice is a purveying of "unwholesome" food as a matter of law. On the other hand, the task of enforcing these provisions may be handed over to an officer of the executive branch and his staff or to an administrative agency. In Wisconsin, for example, at the end of the nineteenth century it became the "duty" of the dairy and food commissioner "to enforce the laws regarding ... the adulteration of any article of food or drink." The statutes defined "adulteration" in broad language. For example, food was adulterated if "any substance or substances have been mixed with it, so as to lower or depreciate or injuriously affect its strength, quality or purity." Under these statutes the commissioner and his staff might assume the task of laying down further rules capable of clear obedience; or they might delegate rulemaking power further down the administrative hierarchy....

As a general proposition, we may guess that there is a strong tendency within the legal system toward the framing of nondiscretionary rules at some level and that it is strongest where it is socially important to have mass, routine handling of transactions, which are channeled through some agency of the legal system, or where relative certainty of legal expectation is important. A rule can be nondiscretionary in operation so long as it is formally nondiscretionary at any one rulemaking level of the legal system (which has many, many such levels) or if it is nondiscretionary at the point of application. Consequently, the legal system may have many more discretionary rules formally speaking than operationally speaking ...

III. JUDICIAL RULEMAKING

Courts, as we have stressed, are equipped to handle a normal flow of trouble cases (which for them are routine). They must also be equipped to assimilate and bring about change, at least in a gradual manner. Finally, they must be able to deal with "crises." A "crisis" in the nonquantitative sense is a sudden demand upon the court, different from past demands, which puts the smooth, normal functioning of the court in jeopardy. A crisis is not simply a difficult case in the usual sense—that is, a case which lies within a gray area of law and evokes sharply different responses.... In a "crisis case," sharp, widespread impact can be foreseen as the result of decision. In such a case, demands are made on the court, which, however met, might so alienate or disappoint one important segment of society that social support of the court might be endangered. This kind of crisis case is never common, and is particularly rare on the trial court level.

The response of high courts to what they sense as a potential source of crisis has been a frequent subject of study. Most of the study concerns, quite naturally, the United States Supreme Court. The arts by means of which the Supreme Court delays, equivocates, and avoids some extraordinary issues are therefore well known and have been frequently catalogued. The Court has at its disposal an enormous arsenal of tools of defense. It can temporize and compromise. It can split a case down the middle. It can balance results against ideology by deciding a case on grounds so narrow that those grounds evade some burning issue. The Court also can simply refuse to hear certain cases. Others it can accept but delay from term to term. Some matters, if delayed long enough, will vanish or be diverted into another forum. Finally, some issues can be decided in such a way as to limit the notoriety of the result. The Court cannot hide the precise outcome of its cases, but it may issue brief, unsigned, per curiam decisions. Newspapers and trade journals are unlikely to note or notice these low-key opinions . . .

[A]ctivism contains potentially grave dangers for the Court. Any highly charged issue is likely to be costly. In most of its work, the Court is protected from harm by the general support it enjoys in the country (and as to which it does not essentially differ from other legitimate institutions the Presidency, the Congress, officers of state). . . . [T]he legitimacy of the Court is an outstanding bulwark of protection against harmful criticism.

. . . Since the Court itself has no instruments for measuring public reaction, and certainly no mode of predicting impact other than common sense, it must rely on its own judgment as to the best course to follow, and, in appropriate cases, fall back upon a firm body of principle. Strictly as a matter of political expediency, the Court can be dangerously wrong. . . .

[However,] . . . most crisis-like crises are not crisis producing for the Court as an institution. Though the underlying issues are highly controversial, they can be efficiently decided by the Court since society welcomes a once-and-for-all resolution by a legitimate, impartial tribunal. When the precise event or the person at issue is the source of the crisis, then the crisis is nonrecurring in the sense used here, and it poses (in our society) few or no long-term difficulties for the Court.

Institutionally more serious is a crisis which is made up of recurrent cases and which does not vanish with a single resolution, but which heralds a new situation for the courts. Either a new social problem emerges out of the social background (as in the segregation cases) or a demand on the courts is met by a judicial response which in turn creates additional demand for fresh definitions of the rights and duties of the parties and the forces that they represent (as in the obscenity cases).

A rational court will attempt to reduce such a situation to institutionally manageable proportions. In the face of recurrent events, the court is therefore likely to develop a rule that can be delegated to other authorities for administration. From the standpoint of the court, this is an important element of a solution to the problem. Of course, the solution must be substantively "correct" as well; it must be in accordance with principle as the Court defines principle. But the form of resolution of such problems (as distinct from substance) is likely to be dictated by institutional needs. The kind of rule which emerges from a recurrent crisis of substance will be a rule which serves the formal requirements of the system and answers the substantive social demands.

What sort of solution will meet this requirement? From the formal standpoint, it is likely to be a rule which perhaps can end the constant probing by litigants for definition and the constant search for the boundaries of the rule. Such a rule will be as objective, as quantitative as possible. An objective, quantitative rule minimizes the risk of further litigation and maximizes the extent to which other private or public agencies can apply the rule, thus taking pressure for decision away from the courts. Such a rule, in form, will be either a rule of refusal or a rule expressed or expressible in quantitative form. A rule of refusal is not usually a rule which accepts and satisfies a fresh demand for social reform, but on occasion it can serve this function. For example, a court might conceivably rule that no power existed in any branch of government to censor any book on the grounds of obscenity. This would be a rule which refused to litigate the question of obscenity at all, not for jurisdictional reasons, but by obliterating the concept of obscenity as a basis for judicial exercise of discretion. Notice that such a rule is hard-and-fast and therefore expressible in quantitative terms—rules of refusal are rules whose quantitative term is zero. In essence, then, crisis situations will tend to generate in a court a movement of doctrine toward quantitative expression. . . .

[As an example of this process, the author uses the so-called reapportionment cases. The Supreme Court of the United States had long refused to hear cases in which citizens complained that electoral districts, in state legislatures for example, were unfairly apportioned. A later case overturned a racially motivated gerrymander of a town in Alabama. All this encouraged fresh attacks on the rule of refusal.

In *Baker v. Carr*, (369 U.S. 186 (1962) the Supreme Court reversed itself, and held that a complaint about the apportionment of the General Assembly of Tennessee did "present a justiciable constitutional cause of action." But the court said nothing about the standards that would or should govern apportionment; they merely sent the case back for trial. The court, in other words, made only a minimum decision—conceivably the problem would then go away; or the legislatures would rouse themselves and do the work of reapportionment themselves.

When this did not happen, the court was faced with a continuing problem; within a year, a flock of lawsuits had been filed on the strength of *Baker v. Carr*, and the legality of virtually every legislature was under a cloud. Finally, in 1964, the court decided a group of six cases, . . . which reached a more quantitative solution.]

In essence, these cases enunciated a rule that both houses of a bicameral legislature must be apportioned substantially on a population basis. Anything short of this offends the Constitution. . . . [T]he rule laid down by the Court was as logical, as quantitative, and hence as workable as the situation permitted. A more discretionary rule would have invited constant litigation; it would have lacked even the bare formal prerequisites of stable solution. The actual formulation—"one man, one vote"—met these formal prerequisites. It contained in itself, by virtue of its relatively clear-cut contours, at least the possibility of a stable solution—a relatively permanent and operational delegation of authority to the lower courts and, hopefully, to the state legislatures.

Of course, a hard-and-fast rule is only an attempt to provide a solution; it was yet possible for the Court to be submerged in a storm of protest. To serve as a stable solution, the new rule must be generally accepted, or the costs of challenge, measured against the likelihood of change, must successfully deter challenges. If the new rule is unacceptable, it will be followed by more and more challenges, and the Court may either have to retreat from its rule or (even more serious) suffer losses in power or prestige. There is often, then, a period of anxious waiting. In the case of the reapportionment rule, there now seems little doubt that the rule will prevail. . . .

When a rule can be stated in "yes-no" terms, it satisfies the conditions of quantitative certainty, and it is formally capable of stable delegation. Not all rules, however, are susceptible of statement in such terms. The . . . doctrine [before *Baker v. Carr*] was a rule of refusal, capable of statement as a simple "no"; once it was abandoned, no simple "yes" rule was possible. It was necessary, then, for the Court to work its way toward a rule capable of quantitative statement in a more literal sense. As we have seen, the Court did so. But it is not always easy for appellate courts to work out quantitative rules, even when, sociologically speaking, circumstances impel the Court toward such rules and when societal patterns or the Court's great reservoir of prestige would allow any solution to be stable. . . .

[T]he ultimate application of a rule to a fact situation must be concrete or precise, or it is not an application at all. Similarly, appellate decisions take a simple "yes-no" form, they reverse or affirm. But in formulating general rules to govern whole classes of cases, courts do not find it easy to lay down obviously precise, quantitative rules. In Anglo–American law it would be completely unthinkable that a court could decree or even evolve a workmen's compensation system or a social security law. Those programs rest on statutes with elaborate quantitative tables, schedules of rates, dollars, and ages. They require a taxing system and a large administrative staff. They presuppose some means of gathering information, of evaluating it, and of devising technical instruments for carrying policy into effect. All this is beyond the customary power, as well as the customary role, of the courts. Laws of this form in our legal system are promulgated only by legislative bodies.

. . . There is nothing inherent in a "court" to prevent it from devising new programs and, specifically, from promulgating rules in precise, quantitative terms. There is nothing inherent in a "legislature" that prevents it from deciding concrete cases. Historically, the institutional ancestors of American courts and legislatures performed many tasks which, to the modern eye, seem curious reversals of their roles. Legislatures long exercised appellate jurisdiction; the name of the highest English court (the House of Lords) preserves the memory of this period. In the United States, too, appellate decision-making in state legislative bodies persisted well into the nineteenth century, and county courts in the American colonies were important administrative agencies— levying taxes and overseeing construction of roads, for example....

The legitimacy of an institution is not unchanging, and, with respect to the courts, does not rest on a single ideal core of meaning. Legitimacy is culturally defined; its effect on the power and style of courts is specific to a given time and place. In the recent history of the common-law system, it was conventionally stated that judges could not legitimately "make law." ...

In the main, courts still deny their power to make new law. This denial is itself no small limitation on their power. It helps ensure that judge-made law results in only small, incremental changes in the existing fabric of doctrine. A great leap forward is rare. Even constitutional law—where a major change can be legitimated through appeal to the higher mandate of the Constitu- tion—shuns sudden advances. The reapportionment cases, for instance, exem- plify a cautious, step-by-step movement. In general, judge-made law inches forward in a glacial kind of creep. When a court overrules a past decision, it often claims to be redressing an error rather than changing the law. Cases make small changes in law and call them no change; big changes are called small changes....

In the twentieth century, partly because of the effect of legal realism upon the style of judicial opinions, judicial creativity is somewhat less verbally restrained than it was in the late nineteenth century.... New theories legitimate particular kinds of bold creativity—the duty of courts to expound the Bill of Rights to protect the individual against government or the duty of courts to keep law in touch with what is deemed to be the temper of the times. Yet changes in judicial behavior, all in all, are not deep; they are style rather than substance. Change in the law, through the medium of courts, remains incremental and gradual, rather than sudden or revolutionary. There is still a commitment to the common-law approach, to evolutionary move- ment, and to constant recourse to grand principles of law, established prece- dent, or constitutional phrases as the major premises of judicial reasoning. Legal realism has not freed the courts from an obligation to society, only from an obligation to a certain style of legal logic; the pull of social responsibility, coupled with an awareness of the limits of judicial knowledge and the limits of judicial capacity to effect social change, may lead to greater, not lesser, caution in action and to greater, not lesser, accountability in principle and reasoning.

But past and present disabilities on the kind of rules that can be legitimately enunciated are an embarrassment to courts when problem situa- tions call for rules of stable delegation, since these, as we have seen, will tend to be quantitative rules. The evolutionary, incremental character of judicial behavior in rulemaking implies (on the contrary) slow, inductive movement along a continuum, and clandestine changes in law—qualitative rules, rules expressed in terms of reasonableness, rules empty of content except as courts fill them with content, rules capable of expansion by small degrees, discretionary rules concealing the reality of change. Thus, the history of judicial systems harbors a considerable dilemma: How can the legitimate limits of judicial rulemaking be reconciled with the institutional need for quantitative rules?

One solution, frequently adopted, is to enunciate rules of a flat "yes-no" nature—rules of refusal, for example. But such rules are not always appropriate. Still another technique is to ratify or absorb into judge-made law quantitative measures whose legitimacy derives from other branches of the legal system or from elsewhere in society. One example of this technique can be seen in the course of the evolution of the Rule against Perpetuities. The rule, in essence, puts a limit on the length of time property can be "tied up" in a family or held in a family trust. Originally phrased in terms of "reasonableness," the rule could not in the long run remain in that form, just as the rule in *Baker v. Carr* had to move in the direction of more certainty. In sharp contrast to the swiftness of *Baker v. Carr*, the evolution of the Rule against Perpetuities from a rule of reason to a stable quantitative rule took more than a century. The process was much the same, however. A rule of "reasonableness" in perpetuities law would have precluded any stable delegation to conveyancers, lower courts, and the general public. Rational calculations in the dynastic planning of estates would have been much more difficult without a hard-and-fast rule to ensure safe predictability. Perhaps the simplest solution might have been a flat quantitative limit on the duration of trusts containing contingent interests—perhaps fifty or one hundred years; or fifty years following the duration of a life estate. A legislature might choose such a method, but it is not the style of a court. Hence the evolutionary character of the rule. The original formulation was characteristically vague; the final formulation, "lives in being plus twenty-one years," for all its irrationalities, is in theory capable of "mathematical" accuracy in application. The twenty-one-year period is not measured by anybody's minority, although the choice was not entirely accidental. It has some rational relationship to the period of minority, but it was powerfully influenced by the fact that twenty-one years was an available number with preexisting legal significance, so that it could be adopted and embodied within a rule of law without transgressing the bounds of judicial legitimacy. The history of the Rule Against Perpetuities, then, illustrates not only the tendency of courts to evolve rules that are mathematical in the broadest sense, but also one technique for solving the dilemma of how to achieve quantitative results without the legitimate means available to a legislative body....[8]

For courts the most embarrassing area of conflict is one lacking the possibility of quantitative rule making, stable delegation, agreement upon policy, or any signs of a non-judicial solution. In such areas of law the courts

---

8. The evolution of a formally stable rule does not ensure its survival for any period. No sooner had the Rule Against Perpetuities reached its "mathematical" form than it began to decay—that is, it began to lose some of its mathematical properties.... A formally stable rule may indeed be all the more vulnerable to pressure in that its results are "harsh"—that is, universalistic. As we have noted, *Baker v. Carr* began a process of evolution by overturning a formally stable rule of refusal....

are continually plagued by pressure from litigation for constant redefinition and refinement. In these areas, public awareness of the problem is high, but no consensus is visible, and no solution to the substantive problem seems feasible. In such an area, the law will show a considerable degree of uncertainty and flux, prediction will be difficult, and "trends" will be ambiguous. Indeed, the very term "trend" implies a high degree of policy agreement on the part of the courts. A trend means substantive movement in one policy line toward some absolute limit. As we have seen, courts prefer making changes by degrees when they can. Many areas of law have characteristics which rule out any current formal solution. How far the Constitution permits suppression or control of "obscene" literature and art is one such question.... The law is now in a period of constant testing of boundaries. The courts are the forum for dispute between those who wish to push literature further toward graphic sexuality (out of conviction or, in the case of some publishers, for gain) and those who see grave social dangers in unbridled literary sexuality. There is no obvious solution. Rules that might satisfy the formal requirements of stability are unacceptable—that is, either a rule allowing all censorship or all censorship of such-and-such a type, or a rule so formulated as to bar once and for all any control by the state over the limits of sexual frankness in literature and art....

Ultimately, if the Court cannot solve the problem and if the problem does not vanish of its own accord (through a radical change in popular tastes or levels of toleration), some extrajudicial solution will have to be reached. This is so because the very definition of a problem implies a social impulse toward solving it. No "issue" or "problem" lasts more than two or three generations. There are, to be sure, eternal issues or problems, but these are not problems in the sense used here; rather they are formulations of human dilemmas on so high a level of abstraction that they cannot ever really be resolved. Problems such as poverty, crime, or the ugliness of cities can exist through all time, but such specific issues as whether slavery shall exist in Missouri Territory, whether fair-housing ordinances can constitutionally be enacted, whether fetishistic literature can be sold in drug stores, and whether hospitals shall be immune from tort actions must be resolved; they cannot drag on forever. If an issue is sharply enough defined to be perceived as a "problem" by the public or some significant segment of the public, there is a strong movement toward resolution, by definition. Society has a whole battery of institutions and mechanisms for resolving current problems. Otherwise society could not survive. If the first agency to which the issue is referred cannot resolve it, those raising the issue will seek a more authoritative agency (or a more efficient one). If worst comes to worst, the issue will not find its agency, and society might even be destroyed by the ensuing struggle.

NOTES AND QUESTIONS

1. Friedman makes the point that you need quantitative rules to mass process transactions. It is easy to register voters who can show that they are

18 years old, but it would be very hard to make the right to vote depend on whether the voter "is mature enough reasonably to understand the American system and able to cast an informed vote." Who would make the determination? On what basis? How could we keep bias from affecting the decision? Even if we could solve these problems, could we afford the cost of making such a determination in every case?

Formalism, however, has many uses (and abuses). A hard and fast rule, as enunciated, is not necessarily carried out in a hard-and-fast way. Keith Hawkins, "The Use of Legal Discretion: Perspectives from Law and Social Science," in Keith Hawkins (ed.) *The Uses of Discretion* 13, 36–37 (1992), pointed out:

> where the form of a rule or set of rules is devised to circumscribe or channel discretion, the objective may not actually be achieved. Sometimes the opposite effect will happen. ["Discretion" is slippery and "adaptive."] Rules may serve to displace discretion to other sites for decision-making within a legal system, and thereby possibly to enlarge it, or create the conditions for its exercise in more private, less accountable settings.... Rules are valuable to legal actors, not simply because they can offer secure guidance, but because any ambiguity, factual or normative, surrounding them gives leeway for the exercise of discretion, which grants flexibility in their application.

Doreen McBarnet and Christopher Whelan, "The Elusive Spirit of the Law: Formalism and the Struggle for Legal Control," 54 *The Modern Law Review* 848, 871 (1991), discuss what they call "creative compliance"—that is, "using the law to escape legal control without actually violating the law." People who are supposed to be subject to legal rules manipulate these rules legalistically and literally, to rationalize their own purposes. The authors comment:

> The irony is that if the rule of law may be used as a weapon to limit rulers and further the interests of underdogs, it is much more readily available for use by those who already have the resources, expertise and power to use the rhetoric, and the mechanisms of law, effectively.
>
> This is not, however, to say that formalism is inevitable in law. The drift to form we describe here in the context of law and finance is the product of a complex and dynamic interplay of structures, situations, ideologies and motivations. The repertoire of formalist mechanisms and ideologies is available but only brought into play when there is motivation to do so, and when those with such motivations have adequate resources, organisation or political muscle to use the system in this way. Rules are not always "privileged" in practice. Broad standards may be tolerated, even by sophisticated subjects, in other situations with other motivations in play. There need not always be a perceived interest in clear rules. There may also be countervailing interests in vague open regulation. Creative compliance is just one of several strategies in dealing with law. Negotiation may be preferred by regulatees and may be seen to be

enhanced by vague laws. Negotiation may also be preferred by regulators. Parties may settle out of court to avoid establishing rules. Law may be perceived as symbolic and ineffective anyway so that there is a preference for simply keeping quiet and letting policies of anti-avoidance and anti-formalism prevail, but only as empty words. In short, demand for formalism is not inevitable. Nevertheless, where formalism is wanted and pressed for, it may be hard to resist within the current structures and ideologies of law.

2.   Can you think of examples of the movement of vague, open-ended rules toward a more objective or numerical form? How about examples of the opposite movement?

In the abortion decision, *Roe v. Wade*, 410 U.S. 113 (1973), the United States Supreme Court decided that states could not regulate abortion at all, except to require that it be performed by a doctor, during the first three months of pregnancy; until viability (roughly three more months), the states could regulate only to protect the health of the mother; after the fetus becomes viable—the last three months of pregnancy—states may prohibit abortion altogether, and take any other steps it deems proper to protect the interests of the unborn child.

Does this case illustrate the movement of rules toward the quantitative? How would Friedman analyze the rule enunciated in this decision? Do you agree with Friedman's position? To what extent, if at all, can we say that the attempt at a quantitative rule worked to solve the abortion problem? The problem certainly has not gone away. Indeed, there has been persistent attack on the "trimester" rule. How would Friedman explain these attacks?

(2) Communication and Control

This section will consider some of the general problems in designing a system for controlling the behavior of persons within a large organization. Our main focus in the chapter is on legal and governmental institutions, but in this section we will be dealing with the problem more generally.

There are many ways to set up a system of control. In some sense every company, hospital, or organization of any sort devises its own particular method. Nevertheless, the methods reduce to a few basic types. In *Politics, Economics and Welfare*, by Robert A. Dahl and Charles E. Lindblom (1953), four "central socio-political processes" are mentioned; that is, four means of "control and calculation." The first is the price system or, in other words, the market. The other three they call hierarchy, polyarchy, and bargaining. Hierarchy is a "process in which leaders control nonleaders. One of its most familiar forms is bureaucracy." Polyarchy is a "process, sometimes called democracy, in which nonleaders control leaders." Bargaining is a "process in which leaders control each other. The American system of checks and balances is a bargaining process; so also is political control through the great pressure groups—business, labor, and agriculture." (p. 23)

The process of control which we discuss in this chapter is mostly hierarchy—at least in theory. That is, it is a process in which there is a clearly defined top and bottom—leaders and followers, superiors and inferiors—and in which orders are given from the top. Within an organization, there is only limited scope for democracy, and the marketing system hardly operates at all. Bargaining, however, is another matter. Dahl and Lindblom define it as a process in which leaders control each other; but within an organization it is the process whereby rulers and the ruled interact with each other and control each other. We have seen bargaining at work at many points in this volume.

We start, then, with a simple idea. Most organizations are supposed to be organized on a hierarchical basis. In fact, however, hierarchy is much modified by bargaining. How does the top control the bottom? How does it see to it that policy is carried out? Any reader can, off the top of his/her head, state some of the techniques that are used: rules, inspections, reports, and so on. The readings will examine these techniques in more detail.

One of the basic requirements for a legal system is that rules, directives, doctrines, or standards must be communicated to those people who are supposed to act on the basis of the rules. It is possible that some laws are intended only to be symbolic and that these are an exception. But usually, a rule is useless unless it reaches its audience.

Many legal rules and practices control or facilitate communication from outside to inside. Law students become familiar with the need to file papers, give notices, enter formal complaints in court, make petitions to the legislature, and so on. Other rules and practices concern communication within the system. Modern legal systems are so large and so complex that they must constantly face and meet problems of information and control within the system. When a system is large and complex surveillance and spot checks alone will not do. These must be supplemented with formal rules. How are these rules to be articulated? How are they to be communicated to other people within the system, and to the public?

The methods are enormously varied. Forms of communication range all the way from direct personal contact, to formal, published regulations. There is a great difference, too, between a huge sign on an interstate highway which states simply that the speed limit is 65 miles per hour, and the complicated regulations of the Internal Revenue Service, which fill volume upon volume upon volume, and which basically only lawyers and tax accountants can read.

(5.5) The Regulatory Process in OPA Rationing (1950)

Victor A. Thompson

The problem of highly formal rule systems is one which becomes more acute in large societies, and particularly in areas where there is an attempt to control complicated activities in detail. Victor A. Thompson has described such a process. The Office of Price Administration (OPA) was the agency which, during the Second World War, fixed prices on all commodities, and administered the rationing of scarce commodities. Naturally, this required an enormous body of rules and regulations. Everything from shoes to sealing wax to cabbages, had to have a ceiling price, and the volume of regulations was immense.

By law, regulations of "general applicability and legal effects" must be filed and published in the Federal Register. The Federal Register is the official collection of federal regulations. It is not very interesting reading. Even most attorneys do not regularly read the Register. Publication in the Register is "obviously communication with intermediaries or interpreters" rather than with people supposed to follow the rules. Publication is, however, also a "means of communicating instructions to judges"—a way of making a regulation valid and official.

Not all regulations are legally required to be published in the Federal Register—only those which are to be enforced with sanctions. Yet officials of OPA regularly published great quantities of other material in the Federal Register. For instance, applicants were "told where to pick up application forms, how to fill them out, where to mail them. They were told the number of the forms they were to use.... They were told what kind of pencils to use ... in filling out the form." What was the source of this peculiar behavior? Thompson thinks that attorneys who drafted regulations thought the public had a "right" to be informed; that this right was satisfied by publication in the Federal Register; and hence they published much material beyond what was strictly required.

Yet, at the same time, some important items were excluded from the regulations published in the Federal Register. For example, official interpretations and field instructions were materials of great importance, but they were not put in the Federal Register. (Some were reproduced in mimeographed form and distributed to field attorneys). For example, if people could not get along with the amount of fuel oil that they were allocated, it was possible to get a "hardship" ration. The regulations did not say how one could tell if his situation amounted to a hardship. A field instruction, however, laid down a rather precise standard. A person who had less than half the fuel oil he should have, at a given point in the year, faced a "hardship." The public was never told about this rule of thumb.

It is no wonder that legal documents and nonlegal instructions became so scrambled that members of the public and local officials had trouble telling them apart. In 1943, OPA adopted a loose-leaf system. It distributed the loose-leaf binders and pages which could be replaced to local boards. Legal documents, together with annotations which explained the legal documents, were kept in the loose-leafs. The annotations were not found anywhere except in the loose-leafs that were sent to the board, and they were not printed in the Federal Register. Also important statements of enforcement policy were not communicated to the public.

Rationing legal documents were drafted by attorneys. They made heavy use of cross-references. There were few sections of the regulations which could be read, without many references to other sections of the regulations; these referred to still other sections; meanwhile the reader no doubt became completely lost.

Why was this elaborate system of cross-references used? In part, Thompson thinks it was simple laziness. Drafting attorneys did not want to repeat what they said. But another reason was a "strong reluctance ... to rephrase something already in the regulations. The attorney learns that the best way to get a consistent reaction from a court is to use words which a court has already interpreted. Synonyms for those words will not do." The attorneys carried this attitude over into their drafting of regulations, even though no court would ever interpret the vast majority of these. There were other strange drafting practices: Sometimes drafting attorneys would make a major change by changing a key word or two in some part of the regulations. Unfortunately, changes of this sort "were completely uninformative to anyone but the legal researcher." For example, in 1942 OPA decided to change the rules about eligibility to buy recapped and second grade tires. At first, only the driver of an automobile which regularly carried passengers to work had been eligible. OPA decided to make all members of the car club who had cars eligible. The original provision stated that the driver had to present to the board a certificate "that other practicable means of transportation are not available." The amendment changed this to read "that other practicable means of transportation, exclusive of the automobiles of other workers, are not available." This does the trick, but in a devious and uninformative way. In fact, the real message about the change was carried by newspapers, instructions, meetings, and so on. Thompson also recounts how the drafting attorneys sometimes terminated provisions, not by repealing them, but by inserting a date after which the regulation was ineffective. If the date was the same as the date of the amendment, this got rid of the provision without saying so.

One fuel-oil hardship provision was amended by changing the phrase "may apply" to read "may before September 13, 1943 apply." The amendment was issued September 10, effective September 13. Thus, "after September 13, a person would be informed by the legal document that he could apply for a hardship ration if he did so before September 13, a date already passed. He would be instructed fully how to apply, etc. Such a person must have thought Washington was full of practical jokers."

Another drafting tool was the attorney's use of the amendment as a kind of printer's instructions. Attorneys drafted amendments which were simply instructions to someone "to make certain changes in words and phrases in various pages of a mythical document called the regulations." Thompson gives an example of a rather simple change in the fuel-oil rationing system which took the form of the following amendment, a printer's instruction of one sentence:

Subparagraph (1) of paragraph (a) of 1394.5001 is amended, a new subparagraph (16a) is added to such paragraph (a) and in subparagraph (23) of such paragraph (a), the phrase "structure, including a house trailer," is substituted for the word "structure"; in subdivision (iii) of subparagraph (1) of paragraph (a) of 1394.5151, the word "or" is added after the phrase "its use"; and a new subdivision (iv) is added to subparagraph (1) of such paragraph (a); in paragraph (a) of 1394.5253 the phrase "other than a house trailer," is inserted between the phrase "in any premises," and the phrase "or for hot water"; in paragraph (a) of 1394.5256 the phrase "other than a house trailer" is inserted between the words "private dwelling premises" and the words "during the heating year"; in paragraph (b) of such section, the phrase "private dwelling premises other than a house trailer" is substituted for the phrase "the premises"; in paragraph (c) of such section the phrase "other than a house trailer," is inserted between the words "private dwelling premises" and the words "and the amount"; a new paragraph (d) is added to such section; in 1394.5259, the phrase "paragraphs (c) and (d)" is substituted for the phrase "paragraph (c)"; in paragraph (a) of 1394.5403, the phrase "(other than those which are house trailers)" is inserted between the word "cars" and the word "may"; and a new paragraph (k) is added to 1394.5902; as set forth below.

The attorneys were the "defenders of complete accuracy in all documents. Every written document was 'cleared' by the attorneys for accuracy. They insisted upon completely refined and qualified statements, both in the legal document they drafted and in non-legal documents which they cleared. The result was often a document or statement so qualified as to be almost unreadable. The attorneys appeared not to be concerned at all with ease in reading, but only with the accuracy of the statement." They were therefore tremendously preoccupied with definitions. Every ration order contained a long list of words, all of them carefully defined. The result was great complication—and poor communication.

Thompson describes a system which operated at three quite distinct levels. Attorneys wrote documents to satisfy what they imagined to be the needs of "the law," not to mention their own professional urge. The loose-leaf system, among others, was devised to do the real job of communicating with the local boards and other officials. And still other techniques had to be used to take care of the general public. These included news stories, industry letters or bulletins mailed out to all interested members of a particular industry, and so on. OPA had a whole information department, charged with the duty of keeping the public informed about OPA programs.

The loose-leaf system did not work perfectly by any means. It was hard to follow changes in the regulations and instructions. Changes appeared in the form of page replacements. To make the amendment process more communicative, the practice arose of sending along a newsletter which would explain what it was that the amendments were all about. But the newsletter itself tended to become rather uninformative.

The loose-leafs had other disadvantages. It was hard to keep them up-to-date and accurate. Once a loose-leaf became inaccurate because of some mistake in insertion of pages, it was almost impossible to correct it. Spot checks of loose-leafs in 1945 indicated that most of them were not accurate or up-to-date. The only way to solve this problem was to educate carefully the people who had the job of making the page replacements. But apparently very little of this was done; hence, "probably few of the Board loose leafs were accurate." In short, OPA, with a task of great complexity, seemed at times almost deliberately anxious to complicate its own life and the life of the public.

There is obviously a tremendous difference between the simplicity and directness of a posted speed limit, and the highly involute documents of OPA. Some of the problems obviously stemmed from the fact that the legal documents were designed for so mixed an audience: actual users of OPA rulings, that is, merchants and the public, the field offices of the OPA, and the audience of lawyers. This last audience, whether or not it made actual use of legal documents, was thought to judge them for accuracy and craftsmanship, and would presumably think worse of the draftsmen if they fell short. You might think that it was foolish to consider this audience at all, but Thompson brings in considerable evidence of its invisible presence.

How do you explain the conduct of the OPA lawyers, who were, one imagines, reasonably competent people, anxious to help OPA do its job, aware of the country's wartime needs, and probably aware too of the complexities of the problems they faced? Why did they act in the fashion that Thompson describes? Why were they so neglectful of the need to communicate with the public part of their audience?

Was all the lawyering in OPA dysfunctional? Consider the general performance of the agency as described by John Kenneth Galbraith, in a book review (*N.Y. Times*, May 18, 1975, Section VII, p. 4, col. 1):

> The Office of Price Administration, with which I was associated in World War II, had a heavy complement of lawyers ... by some it was said to be overlawyered. It was an excellent fault. Few agencies have ever had a higher potential for corruption. A minor decision on the price of oil could mean millions which sundry predators would gladly have shared. The agency went through the war without a scandal. The lawyers, combining professional suspicion with a high sense of rectitude, were a principal reason. (We also ensured that enough people participated in every decision so that any predation would have to be a conspiracy).

Consider the standard American appellate decision as a communication device. It too has multiple audiences. For example, the Supreme Court decisions on the admissibility of confessions in criminal cases could have the following audiences: (a) the immediate parties; (b) the lower court whose ruling has been affirmed, reversed, or to which the case is remanded; (c) other lower courts which will have cases in the future; (d) police officials, prosecutors, and other enforcement officers; (e) lawyers, especially criminal lawyers, who serve as "brokers" of information for the general public; (f) actual and potential criminals and their families; (g) the general public which does not commit crime, but which grants or withholds prestige to the Court, and which assesses the political meaning of acts of government; and (h) the academic community, mostly in law schools or political science departments, which will judge the merits of the case from the standpoint of policy, craftsmanship, and soundness as law. Obviously the appellate opinion will not reach all of these audiences with equal force and effect, and it will affect behavior in each sphere rather differently. Which audiences will best understand the message? Which ones will be most likely to alter their behavior? To which audiences is the court really addressing itself? Which audience does it most try to please? Are there still other audiences?

What audiences were the lawyers in Thompson's study trying to reach? Which ones did they reach? Considering the nature of the regulations, and the communication flowing from OPA offices in Washington to the local rationing boards, how much discretion did the local boards have? What can we assume were the limits on that discretion?

How does the bureaucratic organization of an agency affect its success in operating? During World War II, there were very many violations of OPA rules and orders. See Marshall B. Clinard, *The Black Market: A Study of White Collar Crime* (1952).

The following excerpt from Herbert Kaufman's book is from a study of the way in which the national forests were administered. Like a number of other agencies, the Forest Service has jurisdiction over a big domain, geographically scattered. There is need for some control from the center; field officers need guidance. Some of their decisions, in other words, have to be specified in advance, or, as Kaufman puts it, "preformed."

There are various degrees of "preforming." The central administration may "spell out several series of steps among which the employee shall choose. It may allow the option of acting or not acting, but define the steps . . . to be followed if the decision is to act." This Kaufman calls an "authorization." An authorization says, in effect, that if you do such and such in such and such a way, you will not be punished. Indeed, you will in fact be backed or supported; hence an authorization is, in a way, a grant of power. It is, of course, also a limit on behavior.

A direction ordinarily leaves no options; directions "constitute notice that if cases of a given class arise, failure to take the prescribed steps will result in the imposition of penalties. They are descriptions of what must be done in particular circumstances." Still more restrictive is the prohibition, "promulgated to prevent designated actions by establishing penalties for those who commit them."

(5.6) The Forest Ranger: A Study in Administrative Behavior

Herbert Kaufman[9]

Although authorizations, directions, and prohibitions (and, indeed, goals) may accurately be described in the formal sense in terms of penalties and immunities from punishment, it is quite clear that they do not depend for their effect entirely, or even mostly, on fear of organizational sanctions. Far more importantly, their effectiveness turns on the desire of organization members to observe official requirements, on the feelings of guilt—the pangs of conscience, or, in a manner of speaking, the intra psychic sanctions—aroused in members who violate official requirements, established by the leaders of the organization. In every conversation with field men in the Forest Service, it quickly becomes evident that anxieties about sanctions are by no means absent; it also becomes apparent, however, that other factors play a major part in producing adherence to requirements.

By issuing authorizations, directions, and prohibitions, it is therefore possible to influence the behavior of the members of organizations. An extensive, elaborate network of such issuances envelopes every district Ranger. The network is anchored in more than eighty Federal statutes providing explicitly for the establishment, protection, and management of the national forests; in scores of Presidential proclamations and executive orders on the same subject; in hundreds of rules, regulations, and orders of the Secretary of Agriculture; in many court decisions. It is also rooted in uncounted statutes, Presidential orders, departmental rulings, and regulations of staff agencies (the Civil Service Commission, the Bureau of the Budget, the General Services Administration, and others) governing the federal service over-all. But it is not to them directly that the Rangers look to find out what they are authorized, directed, and forbidden to do; for the Rangers, the "bible" is the Forest Service Manual put out by the Washington office of the Forest Service, which incorporates, explicates, and interprets the relevant legal documents applicable to the agency, and which contains also additional provisions promulgated by the Washington office under the authorizations in those documents.

The Manual in force [in 1960] . . . [consisted] of seven volumes. . . .

The volumes of the Manual are loose-leaf binders. Additions are inserted at appropriate points; rescinded portions are removed; amended portions are

9. Copyright © 1960 John Hopkins Press, Baltimore, published for Resources For the Fu- ture, Inc. Reprinted from pp. 91–99, 101–07, 126–40, 142–45, 149–53, by permission.

inserted after the changes in the original sections have been posted. In the course of a year, hundreds of additions, rescissions, and modifications are issued from Washington; just getting them filed and posted takes many hours every month. But, in this fashion, the categories of authorization, direction, and prohibition, are constantly defined, made more precise, and kept up to date as errors, omissions, uncertainties, and conflicts are corrected....

Each region, in addition, puts out its own authorizations, directions, and prohibitions controlling field personnel. They take the form of supplements to the Service-wide Manual, interpreting and clarifying and rendering more specific the materials emanating from Washington so as to fit them to the needs of each Region. Printed on paper of a different color, but using the same system of classification, they are inserted in the volumes of the Manual beside the sections to which they refer; like the Washington office, the regional offices issue additions, changes, and rescissions, and scarcely a day goes by without at least one arriving in each Ranger's mail....

Over and above these administrative manuals are technical handbooks describing minutely the conduct of technical operations. Some are published by the Washington office, most by the regional offices. They set forth in detail the standards and procedures for timber surveys and valuation; construction and maintenance of recreation areas; location and construction and maintenance of roads; automotive and equipment maintenance; design and procurement and erection of signs; siting and building permanent improvements (warehouses, lookout towers, etc.); planting trees; fire reporting and damage appraisal. In different regions, depending on the character of their workloads, one finds different books, but none of the Ranger districts visited in the course of this study had fewer than a half dozen on hand. They add hundreds of pages of instruction for field personnel.

Some regions issue "Guides" for field personnel. These pull together the essence of existing regulations and assemble them, with explanations and additional requirements, in handbooks that are somewhat easier to read and follow and consult than the formal rules....

Finally, when most of the functions that make up resource management attain a level of activity higher than can be handled by cursory, rule-of-thumb methods, formal district plans for them are drawn up. Indeed, for two functions, the Washington office requires every Ranger district to have a plan; there is none without a fire plan and a timber plan. For the others, Regional offices establish requirements....

Plans, at least as they are treated in the Forest Service, are preformed decisions. They set long-range (eighty to a hundred or more years for a function like timber management; five, ten, or twenty years for others) quantitative and qualitative goals, break these down into shorter-range objectives, and sometimes reduce these to annual targets. They spell out the steps and stages by which the goals are to be achieved, including methods of operation, and priorities by geographical area, in each district. Out of these functional plans grow the substantive targets and quotas of the Service as a whole. At the same time, once adopted, the field plans govern the actions of the field officers and their work crews; if they depart from the procedures, or fail to fulfill their quotas, and the departures are detected, they may be called to account just as if they had violated authorizations or directions or prohibitions in the Forest Service Manual. . . .

All functional plans of this formal kind, combined with the guides and handbooks and the Manual with all its supplements, constitute an impressive network of standing orders influencing Ranger behavior. They are not the whole network, though. For there is a steady flow of ad hoc instructions from higher headquarters to the Ranger districts—memoranda, letters, circulars. And there are inspectors (described later) and visitors from above who issue informal, oral directives in the course of their sojourns in the field. Intermittent, irregular, unpredictable, these are usually directed to very limited aspects of district management, and are of temporary duration. All the same, in the aggregate, added to the other types of preformed decisions, they provide the finishing touches to a remarkably complete means of administrative control touching every facet of official Ranger activity.

Yet authorization, direction, and prohibition are only one category of preformed decisions. Equally important in the day-to-day functioning of a district is the process of channeling decisions proposed by Rangers through higher headquarters before permitting them to take effect—that is to say, before investing them with the immunities and guarantees implicit in formal authorizations. This enables supervisors and regional foresters and their respective staffs to reshape such proposed decisions, and thereby to determine in advance what will actually take place on the Ranger districts.

The formal mechanism for ensuring review is limitation of authorization. Much of the business on a Ranger district involves transactions that can be legally completed only by higher headquarters; a sale of timber worth more than two thousand dollars, for example, can legitimately be consummated only by a forest supervisor (or by a regional forester if the volume exceeds 10 million board feet, or by the Chief if it is 50 million board feet or more), and only very small sales are below these limits . . . While the Rangers and their subordinates do most of the physical and paper work of preparing items for higher action, the actions are not binding until the approval is obtained. Sometimes it comes almost automatically; sometimes proposals are radically modified or even rejected. The decision rests with the higher officers.

Clearance is complemented by dispute settlement as a means of bringing policy questions to the attention of higher officials for resolution. From time to time, a supervisor's staff assistant specializing in a particular function (or group of functions on the smaller forests) takes issue with the way a given Ranger manages the function that is the staff man's specialty. Staff assistants concentrating on recreation, for example, are wont to complain that this function is not given due attention, or that some activities charged to recreation management accounts would be more appropriately charged to the control of something else. . . . In fact, each staff officer at every level, since his energies and attention are concentrated on one segment of the total spectrum of Forest Service policy, displays an inclination to feel more can be done in his function than is actually done by the men in the field. Some of them gradually, and probably inadvertently, edge over from exerting pressure to see that their work is adequately done to commanding line officers as to precisely what ought to be done. . . .

If a Ranger gives in to a staff officer, or if a staff officer does nothing about a Ranger's resistance to his actions or recommendations, such clashes subside. If a staff man attempts to pressure a Ranger into compliance, the Ranger will ordinarily protest to the forest supervisor. If a Ranger objects to staff interference or ignores staff suggestions, the staff officer may carry his case to the forest supervisor. In either event, the supervisor convenes the disputants, hears their arguments, and adjudicates the conflict. Almost without exception, this settles the matter.

The net effect of this procedure is to call to the attention of the forest supervisors (and higher line officers) policy alternatives in the management of Ranger districts that might otherwise go unnoticed. It thus gives them additional opportunities to clear the air of uncertainty, to eliminate ambiguities in standing orders, to say what will be done in particular instances. It suspends the force of decisions until they have been reviewed and approved, modified, or rejected at higher levels. It is a method of preforming decisions in the field that would otherwise not rise for clearance. It employs conflict for purposes of organizational integration.

That is not to say the Forest Service is constantly beset by internal wrangling. Indeed, it is a classic illustration of the process of multiple oversight of administration; although the Rangers, like all line officers below the Chief, are at the focal point of many converging lines of communication from many sources in the administrative levels above them, they find reason to object to only a fraction of the suggestions of the staff men, frequently call upon them for advice and assistance, and manage to work out many differences of opinion without resort to formal adjudicatory proceedings. But the lines of appeal are clear and available to administrative officials, and they are not unused.

The consequences of clearance and dispute settlement, however, cannot be measured by the actual frequency of their employment alone. For almost every Ranger, knowing that works he undertakes and agreements he negotiates and plans he proposes (particularly if these are offensive to one of the agency's clientele) are subject to review and possible change or veto, screens out projects and requests to which the reactions of the reviewers are difficult to anticipate or likely to be negative, and concentrates instead on those more apt to win approval. If a project seems particularly desirable or necessary, or an applicant for the purchase of timber or the use or exchange of national forest property is especially insistent, and a Ranger therefore feels under pressure to proceed along a doubtful line, he normally queries his supervisor or his supervisor's staff assistants before acting. Sometimes, unwilling to risk the embarrassment of having an applicant go over his head and possibly win approval for what he denied, or of commencing negotiations only to be overruled, a Ranger refers the applicants to higher headquarters in the first instance. Thus, over and above what is required by explicit regulations, there is considerable informal clearance. This avoids some clashes with staff assistants that might otherwise arise, and eliminates some rejections and vetoes and criticisms by higher headquarters. But it also gives officers at higher levels additional opportunities to preform decisions about what goes on in Ranger districts.

Of course, the absence of disputes may just as well be evidence that staff officers are failing to influence the Rangers as that the Rangers are fully compliant. So the anticipation of reactions cut both ways—but more toward Ranger compliance with staff officers' recommendations than toward staff officers' hesitation to offer advice and suggestions. For staff officers and staff assistants are ordinarily in closer and more continual touch with supervisors than are the Rangers, and they share the supervisor's broader territorial perspectives. While the Rangers will not brook what they regard as interference in their administration of their districts, they also recognize that the shared contact and vantage points of the line and staff officers at the higher level mean those officers are likely to see many things the same way—and for valid reasons. So the Rangers are not apt to protest vigorously unless the provocation seems to them particularly great.

Then, too, if no disputes arise a supervisor cannot be sure that excessively compliant Rangers or unduly timid staff officers are not permitting the work in the field to proceed further and further from the objectives proclaimed by Forest Service leaders. Anticipation of reactions simplifies the influence of dispute settlement as an influence on Ranger behavior because there are occasional reactions, they are resolved at higher levels, and more often than not are resolved in favor of the staff officers.

Clearance and dispute settlement, as a result, reach far beyond what the formal mechanisms per se imply. They are for this reason among the major techniques by which Ranger behavior in the field is molded by the organization.

DETECTING AND DISCOURAGING DEVIATION

Reporting

To determine whether behavior of men in the field conform to the requirements of preformed decisions promulgated by organization leaders, the leaders must obviously keep themselves informed about what actually goes on in the field. The easiest way for them to do so is to ask the field men what they are doing. Hence, reporting is a common characteristic of all large-scale organizations....

Data on individual actions are primarily for financial and bookkeeping purposes rather than for program and policy control; they permit administrators in the forest and regional offices to maintain surveillance of receipts and expenditures. But they also keep the higher administrative echelons informed about what their subordinates are doing. The payrolls, requisitions, and vouchers sent from the field to be charged against the functional accounts and sub-accounts established for a district constitute a running record of what goes on in the district. By consulting the record from time to time, the Rangers' superiors can keep abreast of the Rangers' activities, and they are able to assemble from such reports the statistics embodied in their own summaries.

Moreover, as noted earlier, many transactions—large timber sales, for example, and special-use permits—must be signed by supervisors and regional foresters before they take effect. As a result, these officers do not have to ask for special reports on many functions in order to compile their own reports; the information is readily at hand. . . .

Over and above regular, periodic reports of both the tabular and individual-action types, there are frequent calls for special reports on an ad hoc basis. In addition, the written documents are supplemented by uncounted informal reports; every time the Rangers get in touch with higher headquarters for guidance or advice or preliminary clearance of a proposed field action or to settle a dispute with a staff man, and every time a visitor from a higher level appears on a district, the Rangers' superiors get new insights into what is happening in the field.

All in all, then, the flow of information from the districts to the forests, the regions, and to Washington is steady, massive, detailed, and comprehensive. In one way or another, the Rangers themselves furnish facts revealing how closely they are adhering to the preformed decisions of the Service leaders, facts that disclose any deviations from the promulgated standards. It is doubtless true, as members of the Forest Service at every level aver, that the system of reporting has not been set up to expose deviations so much as to provide the leaders with the knowledge they need realistically to plan and guide the destinies of the agency. Distrust is not the driving force behind the system. Just the same, whatever the intentions of those who established and maintain the upward flow of reports, one result is to bring to their attention any continued departures from announced behavioral norms.

Theoretically, a field officer who does depart from announced policies, as a result of the tendencies toward fragmentation that pull at all Rangers, could falsify his reports to conceal his digression. In practice, this is seldom feasible, for misrepresentation in one report would soon produce contradictions with so many others that it would require almost all a man's time and energy as well as the most extraordinary ingenuity to tamper with all of them so as to make them consistent. What is more, many people—employees, users of national forest products and facilities—would eventually have to be drawn into the conspiracy. And even if all the reports were successfully altered, the information in the reports would then conflict with that obtained by higher levels through the other channels described in this chapter. It is almost inconceivable that manipulations of the records could long escape detection.

In any case, the incentives to falsify reports are not very strong. In the first place, the penalties for occasionally inadequate performance are far less severe than those for misrepresentation: the risks of dishonesty are infinitely greater than those of honesty. Secondly, . . . the whole ethos of the Service discourages falsification. The observer of the organization quickly gets the feeling such behavior would be regarded as not only immoral, but cowardly, unmanly, degrading to the individual and to the Service (whose members have a fierce pride in it), and that any man who practices it must end with contempt for himself for not having the courage to fight for those departures from policy that he believes right or to admit his errors when he is wrong.

Official Diaries

Rangers, assistant Rangers, and their principal aides are required to keep official diaries throughout the year. The diaries show to the nearest half-hour how each workday is spent. On standard Service-wide forms, the field officers and employees record each thing they do, describing the activity in enough detail for any inspector to identify it, the functions to which the activity is chargeable, the time at which it began and was completed, and the amount of office, travel, and field time it entailed. They thus compile a full running record of the way they employ their time. . . .

Forest Service officials do not designate disclosure of deviation as the chief function of the diaries. Rather, they contend the information in the diaries is needed to enable the leaders to formulate and adjust policies and objectives to what the record shows is practicable on the ground; it puts the leaders in touch with reality, and tells them as much about the shortcomings of their own programs and goals as it does about the men in the field. The diaries, they say, are designed for the guidance of the top echelons rather than to force field officers to testify against themselves. And there is no denying the diaries are used for this purpose.

But the fact remains that the diaries also expose deviations from decisions issued at higher levels to regulate the behavior of men in the field. The practice of keeping diaries may have been instituted for other reasons, and it may be employed in other connections. Nevertheless, exposure of deviation is one of the consequences, and few members of the organization are unaware of this.

The diaries are kept accurately for the same reasons that reports are not "doctored." In the first place, falsifying them is far too difficult. If inconsistencies between the diaries and work reports were not quickly discovered, then contradictions between what the diaries recorded and what was actually accomplished in the woods would soon come to light. Furthermore, discrepancies between the entries in the diary of one forest officer and those of his colleagues, subordinates, and superiors could not be long concealed. In any event, the entries are made throughout the year, so manipulating them for purposes of hiding the truth would take elaborate, long-range planning, and great investments of effort. . . .

Secondly, there is apparently a feeling of ethical, professional, and organizational obligation to keep the records straight. Members of the Service speak with obvious repugnance of tampering; it is regarded as petty and contemptible conduct, contrary to the traditions and the welfare of the agency. To be sure, few diaries are actually current, as regulations require; except for what one Ranger called "streaks of religion," during which he enters his activities faithfully at the end of each day, most men rely on their memories, aided by brief notes and consultations with co-workers, to fill out the forms for days— or even weeks—during which more urgent business was given precedence. And there is by no means unanimous enthusiasm for the diaries; some men argue that other reports supply all the information that can be gleaned from them. Still, even one Ranger who objected strongly to keeping one admitted that he is conscientious about its accuracy and completeness even though it has disclosed occasional failings for which he was reprimanded. Unquestionably, they are not precise to the minute, but they could reflect fairly closely what actually happens in the field.

The diaries are collected by higher headquarters and analyzed periodically. Current pages, kept in the field for the use of field administrators, are available to visiting inspectors. And they are studied by representatives of higher levels.

Along with diaries of their own activities, officers in the field are also required to maintain equipment-use records that are in effect diaries of their equipment. Each piece of apparatus and each vehicle is covered by a log in which an entry must be made every time it is employed. The ostensible objectives are to furnish cost data, and to provide information from which it can be determined whether the equipment is used enough to justify it; in the language of the Forest Service, equipment must "earn" its purchase. But discrepancies between reported use of equipment and technical and financial plans, travel allowances, travel entries in personnel diaries, and work accomplished in the woods are occasionally discovered by comparing equipment records with other documents and inspection reports. Within limits, property records and other reports must tally. They send up warning flags when what happens in the field diverges from what is enunciated as policy at the center.

District Rangers and their subordinates thus leave behind them in time a wake of paper that is a highly visible chronicle of their operations. If they stray from the designated channels, they do not ordinarily get very far before their divagations are disclosed. . . .

Inspection

In the end, however, regardless of how much of their field behavior is described in what the field men tell about their achievements, and in their inadvertent disclosures when they employ staff services, the only sure way to find out what goes on at the level where the physical work of the organization is done is to visit the field and see. This practice has been highly developed and carefully systematized in the Forest Service. . . .

TYPES OF INSPECTION

The broadest type of inspection—that is, the type that covers the broadest range of activities—is the General Integrating Inspection.... [A] General Integrating Inspection is designed to find out how good a job a line officer is doing when his total responsibilities are considered. Taking the whole gamut of national forest administration tasks as its subject, it reveals whether an organizational unit is administered in accord with policy, and whether everything that could be done is done.

Functional Inspections are narrower in scope but greater in depth than General Integrating Inspections. They normally concentrate on individual functions—timber management, wildlife management, recreation management, information and education, engineering, etc.—and explore in detail the way they are administered. A General Integrating Inspection takes up the balance among functions; a Functional Inspection turns to the balance among tasks within a function. A General Integrating Inspection relies on samples and general impressions; a Functional Inspection rests on minute examination and analysis of figures and methods. General Integrating Inspectors strive for "horizontal" sweep; Functional Inspectors aim at "vertical" comprehensiveness....

Fiscal–Administrative Inspections—essentially, audits of fiscal operations and administrative housekeeping functions—do for office management, including accounting and record-keeping and reporting, what General Functional Inspections do for field operations. Books, files, and records are examined for maintenance according to standard. Manuals and work plans are reviewed to see if they are up-to-date and accessible. Procedures for handling paper work are studied. Diaries are checked for currency and completeness. Reporting promptness and accuracy are evaluated. Thus, not only is behavior compared with preformed decisions by means of reports and records; in addition, reports and records are themselves inspected to ensure the reliability of the data they provide, and to make sure field officers are familiar with the decisions to which they are expected to conform.

Two additional types of inspection are ad hoc in character rather than recurrent. They are substantially hearings on major failures of one kind or another, although they are sometimes employed to see what can be learned from unusual accomplishments as well. Boards of review look into the causes and consequences of large-scale, unexpected reverses, such as huge fires; investigations are inspections of alleged misconduct on the part of forest officers. Unlike the other kinds of inspection, these occur only when something extraordinary happens; they focus on the exceedingly unusual....

When a region is inspected by Washington, or a national forest by a regional office, the inspectors ordinarily visit randomly chosen Ranger districts, for every inspection involves study of field work. Every Ranger interviewed has had the experience of being visited by people from Washington and region offices as well as being checked by their own respective supervisors. Since the number of inspections of one kind or another by supervisors' offices average three or more a year over and above the reviews by higher levels, every Ranger can count on at least several inspections every year; inspectors and functional specialists thus come through with high frequency, and the chances of defections from preformed decisions going undetected are correspondingly reduced....

[Yet] the more experienced Rangers are quite casual about inspection, for they know that only the most grievous mismanagement is likely to get them into serious trouble. The atmosphere of inspection is not one of a trial or even a competitive examination. In the evenings, when the work is done and notes written up, the inspectors and the inspected gather socially to discuss personal and organizational affairs—such things as shifts of personnel, promotions, retirements, additions to staff, organization policies and strategies and problems—meeting professional equals rather than as superiors and subordinates, inquisitors and as defendants. The practice of rotation and transfer of foresters, ... combined with the travels of inspectors, acquaints members of the Service in each region with their workers; inspection is a mode of communication and of face-to-face contact that helps bind the agency into a unity. Men in the field, rather than fearing inspection, tend to welcome the opportunities it affords them to keep abreast of developments in the organization, to learn the latest rumors and gossip, and to give their own ideas to their superiors at first hand.

The fact remains, however, that the written reports follow every inspection are blunt and hard-hitting; criticisms are not softened, punches are not pulled....

Inspectors summarize their principal findings for the officers they investigate, and the inspected officers are thus both forewarned of what is to be reported and given a chance to answer the criticisms and thus possibly to have some of them explained or eliminated. If a report nevertheless contains material to which they object, they may submit a written protest; several of the Rangers interviewed have done so on occasion. One Ranger expressed mild annoyance at the appearance in reports of findings not actually discussed with him in advance, and another was somewhat irritated by intimations that he was unaware of deficiencies that any good forester would recognize—deficiencies, in some instances, that he himself called to the attention of the visitors. On the whole, however, the Rangers indicate they believe inspection reports are accurate and fair despite their sometimes painful candor.

But inspections are not only a mode of detection. They are also a method of communicating preformed decisions to the men in the field, of reducing the ambiguities of previously issued policy statements, and of finding out whether such policy statements require revision in the light of field experience. That is, they are all additional techniques of preforming Ranger decisions; they help determine the contents of such decisions.

For inspectors do not merely note violations of policy pronouncements and suggest in general terms that the field men look up the appropriate provisions and figure out how to conform. Rather, they indicate quite precisely what is to be done—what neglected projects should be undertaken, what activities should be reduced or halted or expanded or intensified, what procedures should be improved or corrected. They direct and prohibit action. They interpret authorizations and plans and budgets. They clarify ambiguous statements. In so doing, they claim merely to explain what policy statements and rules and regulations mean; this, in fact, is why they are said to be engaged primarily in training. Yet it is clear that they fill in whatever interstices may remain in the fabric of preformed decisions; they tighten the weave.

Not every such elaboration of the body of administrative issuances is initiated by the inspectors. To be sure, in the written documents, in the conversations during tours of the physical facilities, in the discussions of tentative findings and recommendations, and even in the informal social evenings, the visitors volunteer their ideas on a great many matters even in the course of a couple of days. But some of their advice and suggestions are requested by field men unable to interpret an instruction, or uncertain about how to resolve apparent contradictions between various provisions, or anxious to find impressive support for an interpretation on which they have been overruled by someone else. The inspectors do not simply impose themselves on the field officers; the field officers take whatever advantage they can of the presence of representatives of higher levels by inviting interpretations and elaborations of the rules. In a sense, this is a form of clearance. In any event, the Rangers elicit by their queries some of what is told them by their superiors.

At the same time that inspections increase the volume and specificity of decisions flowing to the field, they afford the Rangers opportunities to influence the formation of some of the decisions they will be expected to abide by. For the Rangers take advantage of the personal contacts with the inspectors to voice their complaints, their needs, their preferences, and their aspirations. If objectives are unattainable with the funds available, they point this out. If a prescribed procedure is excessively burdensome, they let the inspectors know. If they see potentialities in the management of their districts that call for amendments or additions to existing orders, they do not hesitate to urge them.... There is a flow of communication upwards as well as downwards within the inspection process, and it may be presumed to guide and limit to a small degree the contents of the rules and orders Rangers are called upon to observe.

Yet while inspections generate elaborations of authorizations, directions, prohibitions, and other preformed decisions, and contribute to the substance of those decisions, their distinctive function is to uncover deviation by field men from the behavior prescribed by the organization. Even if there were no inspectors, orders would flow out to the field, and reports and reactions would flow back to the center. But leaders would then be dependent entirely on evaluations of field accomplishments by the very men who did the physical work, men with heavy stakes in making their performance look as good as possible. Inspectors from higher levels, checking the fieldwork, furnish more disinterested judgments as to whether or not the work conforms to policy pronouncements. In the last analysis, this is the rationale of inspection.

NOTES AND QUESTIONS

1.   Kaufman describes a system of communication and control that is, in some ways, quite complicated. Yet it does not seem to be as dysfunctional as the OPA system described by Thompson. Are there important differences between the two situations?

2.   Kaufman mentions the strong *esprit de corps* of the Rangers. It is possible, of course, that this spirit—and the devotion to duty that flows from it—exists in spite of, rather than because of, the elaborate rules and regulations that hedge about the work environment of the Rangers. Is there any evidence in the piece which enables one to judge one way or the other? How could we test the impact of the network of regulation on the performance of the Rangers?

(5.7) Connie A. Bullis and Phillip K. Tompkins

Connie A. Bullis and Phillip K. Tompkins, "The Forest Ranger Revisited: A Study of Control Practices and Identification," 56 *Communication Monographs* 287 (1989), studied the Forest Service some twenty years after Kaufman's research. They approached the Forest Service as an example of what they call "concertive control" of large organizations. They tell us:

> Concertive control operates through the process of identification.... As contributors cooperate and communicate in a natural effort to overcome division, an overlap between the individual and group develops. As members identify more strongly with the organization and its values, the organization becomes as much a part of the member as the member is a part of the organization. Members then allow organizational decision premises to be inculcated into them. When the identity of the contributor is merged with the perceived corporate interest, this process is easier and more effective. Members think in organizational terms and act as agents of these juristic persons, experiencing autonomy while making organizationally preferred decisions. Beliefs, values, and symbols direct behavior indirectly.
>
>   This concertive form of control is simultaneously unobtrusive and a source of high morale. Rather than focusing on more obvious compliance with commands or rules, the focus is on less obvious compliance in decision making. The theory posits that this process of identification results in a profound internalization of the preferred decisional premises of two kinds: First, the factual and value premises valued by the organization are internalized. Second, consideration of the organization's interests above other parties' interests becomes a natural and preferred premise....

[R]esearch has not addressed the core claims of the theory: (1) the relationship posited between organizations' use of concertive control and members' identification and (2) the claim that members who identify more highly with the organization (a) place organizational value premises as most important in their decision making and (b) consider the organization's interests first in making decisions.

The exception is Kaufman's (1960) descriptive study of the U.S. Forest Service ... [However] [s]ince 1970, several environmental factors have had strong impacts on the [Forest Service] organization. The most relevant of these was that the relationship between the organization and the public was clearly redefined. During the 1970s, two prominent court decisions brought about this change. The Forest Service was indicted for clear cutting; clear cutting is the practice of harvesting all the trees on a tract before replanting and stands in contrast with methods which leave some trees while others are harvested. While clear cutting is still held by many to be an ecologically sound method, a public political movement made a "sustained and intense" effort to stop the practice. Not only did the Forest Service lose on this issue, it also saw the end of the era in which the agency could act as if it alone knew what was best for the public. The court decisions contributed to a series of environmentalist laws, most notably the Renewable Resource Planning Act of 1974 and the National Forest Management Act of 1976 which required integrated, continuous, long-term planning for the management of resources and for public participation in that planning. The diverse relevant publics have become consistently active in establishing national forest management priorities. Expert management (based on values) gave way to managing based on the (political) public will.

In other words, the relationship between this organization and its relevant environment changed. Previously, decisions were made based on shared values, or decision premises, among members. Currently, diverse, powerful, and active outside audiences constantly participate in decisions. Rather than accepting Forest Service decisions as expert decisions, public groups and individuals regularly work to have them reversed. The shared values which provide the basis for concertive control are no longer able to operate in relative isolation from the multiple, competing external values and external laws. Scholarship has questioned whether centralization is workable or desirable in more complex environments such as this. Yet, culture control has been offered as an alternative in some cases. The Forest Service example represents an opportunity to examine this relationship ...

[W]e conducted fifty-five interviews with key professional employees such as personnel and training officers, staff officers, line officers, and resource specialists [of the Forest Service].... The results indicate that there have been several changes in the system of control since Kaufman wrote. We present our findings as they compare with Kaufman's.

Bureaucratic Control

In the first loop of the double-interact system, the Manual continues to hold a primary position. It explains "what to do, who is to do it, how, when, where and why to do it" (Kaufman, 1960, p. 96) as it did in the past. At the time of this study, it had tripled in size since Kaufman wrote. The agency continues to devote considerable human resources to the maintenance and updating of the Manual. A regional officer in charge of public appeals reported that there is now a more rigid criterion for judging whether the lower officer made the "right" decision. The appeals officers first determine whether the Manual was followed. In the past, this determination was far less rigid and formal than it is today. Sixty-five percent of the decisions discussed were reportedly based partially on the Manual. Fifty percent echoed the regional officer's report that the Manual had increased in importance while the others reported that it had always been consulted.

Kaufman identified planning as another method of preforming decisions in situations which were less routine than those covered in the Manual. Due to laws enacted during the 1970s, planning has increased since Kaufman wrote. Plans are comprehensive, detailed, and take a long-range view. Some rangers believe that planning has cost fifty cents per acre, an investment that takes the place of "getting things done on the ground." Plans are now generated for larger areas of land and involve more balancing of multiple resources and uses. Rather than relying on individual functional plans at the district level, the Forest Service relies on fully integrated plans at the forest level. Moreover, according to three planners (a full-time position which was new since Kaufman's time), national practices, and the Washington office, a computer system functions to integrate these comprehensive plans fully with the budgets. Interviewees referred to plans in their accounts of fifteen percent of decisions. One hundred percent reported that planning had increased in importance.

Kaufman identified ad hoc instructions, letters, memos, and oral communication as useful in situations which are not covered through standing orders. The ongoing written and verbal communication further directs those implementing policy. Seventy-eight percent of decision accounts included this type of communication. Eighty-eight percent reported that this ongoing communication is more strongly emphasized now due to better communication technology and more people concentrated together in larger offices. In Kaufman's time, many offices relied on radio contact because telephones were not universally available. Many ranger district offices were more remote, making physical contact difficult. In contrast, over 100 ranger districts had been eliminated during the interim; most of these were combined into adjacent district offices, making contact far more routine.

Clearances and dispute resolutions also are more important today. As Kaufman noted, authority is limited such that higher officers must clear lower officers' decisions. Forest supervisors and regional specialists reported that they are now required to review and approve of lower officers' "problem formulation" statements. In other words, rather than "rubber stamping" decisions post hoc as was done in the past, higher officers are now involved in the formulation of the decisions. One forest supervisor, in reprimanding a ranger who acted without approval, admonished, "you're not running your own private ranch anymore. I WILL be involved earlier in the process." The "onslaught of the public" as well as the better communication technology changed decision making so that the regional office and the public have more decision power than the ranger. Forty-five percent of interviewees reported early clearance or concern with warding off later disputes as part of their decision making process. One hundred percent reported that this is more prevalent than in the past.

Kaufman pointed out the value of financial and work-load planning in preforming decisions. The detailed records of budget allocations and expenditures are now integrated with the forest-level planning discussed earlier. Previously, rangers could occasionally make small adaptations by using funds from one account to complete a project supposedly funded from another account. With the current integration, the monitoring of funding as integrated with the work actually carried out on the ground is very thorough, allowing for little deviation. Twenty-eight percent of the discussed decisions involved financial considerations. One hundred percent reported this channel to be stronger than in the past.

Overall, this system by which decisions are preformed by higher officers has become stronger since Kaufman wrote. There is even less leeway for deviance in the 1980s than in 1960.

Like the practices functioning to preform decisions, the deviation detection loop is multi-channeled. Should organizationally incorrect decisions be made, the deviation would most likely be detected by the channels of this loop. How have feedback practices changed?

First, many reports are demanded. All of our interviewees agreed that reports are more frequent and more comprehensive than they were. Together, they provide a running record of all that happens on the ground. In one staff officer's words, "We know what's going on as well as they do." With more complexity in the reports, a more aware and involved public, and more communication between administrative units, there is a stronger disincentive to falsify reports now than in the past. Twenty-three percent of decisions involved direct considerations of reports to be made to higher offices. One hundred percent reported that there are more reports and more lengthy or complex reports now than in the past.

720

One channel in the feedback loop, the daily diaries maintained by rangers, has been discontinued. Rangers found them to be cumbersome to maintain.

As in the past, overhead services are provided from the higher offices in the interest of helping those on the ground and relieving them of paper work. More diverse resource expertise is available now than in the past. For example, archaeologists and economists are employed. However, with a strong focus on efficiency, one policy reported by the Washington office, and practiced in several cases we observed, is to concentrate this expertise at higher offices rather than lower offices. For example, bridge designing specialists had been frequently assigned to forest level offices. There were not enough bridge needs at the forest level to occupy them full-time so they spent a portion of their time in less specialized work. By moving such employees to the regional level, they could serve a number of forests and work in their specialty area full-time. Similarly, forests are encouraged by higher offices to concentrate specialists in the forest office for use on a number of districts. Some specialists such as an historian, are available only at the national office. Higher office staff, then, are more likely to be directly involved "on the ground" in providing recommendations and decisions. Ten percent of decisions involved considerations of such available resources. Thirty-eight percent reported that this practice is more prevalent than in the past.

Inspections were used as higher officers regularly visited ranger districts with the goal of detecting and correcting any problems or deviations. These visits are no longer termed "inspections" but rather, "reviews." Reviews carry a more positive connotation. Official policy dictates that reviews occur in specified time periods. However, some of officers conduct more reviews than required, depending on problems and preferences. Three regional officers reported conducting surprise reviews. Thus Kaufman's comment could be made today just as well as in the past: "Whether going along quietly and routinely or beset by catastrophe, members of the Forest Service can be as certain of inspections (or reviews) as they are of death and taxes" (p.140). Eighteen percent reported decisions involved considerations of reviews. Forty percent reported them to be more prevalent than in the past. Sixty percent reported them to be as prevalent as in the past.

Every interviewee reported that appeals by the public have increased due to the public's increased involvement. An information office reported that the number of appeals increased more than five times between 1960 and 1980. The public has changed from a primarily friendly or neutral one (with the exception of those who abused the resources) to a multi-faceted, often hostile one. Rangers are concerned about maintaining superiors' support when the appeals occur rather than if the appeals occur. Thirty percent of decisions included considerations of possible appeals.

Frequent transfer of employees also discouraged deviation. If an employee moved, the replacement would likely discover and report any deviations which were evident. Although no one indicated an official change in policy, the regional and forest level officers we interviewed indicated that in practice, moves are less frequent now than in the past. Both regional personnel officers estimated that rather than moving every two to three years, employees may stay in one place for more than five years. However, transfers do occur and do continue to provide an impetus to keep one's house in order, so that one's successor will find no dirty laundry. Five percent reported decisions involved considerations of leaving appropriate records for one's successor. Ten percent reported that transfers had increased while sixty percent reported that they had decreased. The remainder did not perceive a change.

Sanctions continue to serve as a threat to potential deviations. Demotions, suspensions, and reprimands are all clearly delineated in policy. The regional personnel officers and appeals officer indicated that they are used, and are potent in an organization which prides itself on its scandal-free history. The appeals officer reported needing to use official sanctions more than in the past although use continues to be rare. Subtle sanctions are used as well. In reporting on difficult decisions, fourteen interviewees reported that those who disagree with the organization eventually must leave. Eighteen percent reported directly considering sanctions in their decision examples. Sixty percent reported that this practice is more prevalent than in the past. Twenty-five percent reported that it was similar to the past. Sanctions were mentioned as threats on four occasions during meetings.

Overall, the network of communication practices which discourages and detects deviations has become stronger since Kaufman wrote. While the tone of the field visits has changed and the diary has been deleted, the increase in reports and public appeals as well as generally closer communication ties between hierarchical levels have created a far more powerful deviation-detection system. . . .

The use of symbols noted by Kaufman has also declined. Offices are more frequently located in federal buildings with other federal offices, rather than the distinctive log cabins they once were. Policy has changed so that fewer employees are given uniform allowances, and consequently cannot be formally expected to wear uniforms. Forest Service employees might never be identified by community members as such; this was once unavoidable. One employee wished uniforms were required because "if you run into people in the woods, you don't know if they are or are not Forest Service people anymore." Eighty-five percent reported this decrease.

The overwhelming trend has been a decline in these unobtrusive control practices which encourage the strong identification of members with the organization.

The single exception is in the practice of participation in policy setting from the field officers. Their "input" into policy changes is solicited as it has been through the years; field officers continue to feel as though they do in fact exercise some power in this process by providing valuable knowledge about specific situations. Washington officers agree that they could not/would not revise policies without this consultation. This practice continues to provide a participative climate. Participation in policy setting, is, however, consultative rather than delegative.

Conclusions

Unlike the networks which serve to communicate preformed decisions and detect and discourage deviations, concertive control practices have weakened dramatically. Control, while continuing to be strong, has been transformed by placing more emphasis on external, bureaucratic control and less emphasis on internal, concertive control through identification. . . .

[T]his research has supported the theory's crucial connection between identification and implementation. It answers the question: How, at the concrete level, does organizational identification serve the organization? The answer: It is associated with more than a feeling of good will among members. It is associated with the premises perceived as most important by members in day-to-day decision making, the point most important to organizational activity.

These results have supported the theorized connection between concertive control practices and member identification. . . . [I]n this organization, identification was stronger when concertive control practices were stronger. These results emphasize the distinction between bureaucratic and concertive control. The bureaucratic control practices serve to communicate decision premises explicitly. The organization must exert more communicative "energy" in controlling employees. Concertive control engenders identification more implicitly. Adapting the individual so that s/he actively seeks to internalize the premises is a less obvious practice.

. . . [I]nterviewees led us to a serendipitous finding. They consistently expressed a yearning for the past when employees made "correct" decisions "autonomously." They continue to feel a strong urge to identify with the organization. Employees seem less satisfied with bureaucratic than concertive control. This active desire should not be ignored in future research. It is part of the identification process.

Finally, concertive control, or strong culture, should be approached with caution. While we are sympathetic to the nostalgia expressed by employees for the identities and identification of the past, the homogeneity of that "strong" culture made the organization less flexible and adaptive to the changes in its environment. During the 1970 legal cases . . ., some of the people on the ground recognized the organizational threat at early stages of the Monongahela and Bitterroot controversies. They were unable to communicate their concerns up the line successfully in the face of the strong homogeneous culture which emphasized concertive action. Opposition was not "heard." The heterogeneity of the current "weak" culture is no doubt more flexible, more adaptive in relation to its environment—including the political climate and its inevitable fluctuations. Strong culture, then, may create inflexibility as members think in concert.

Michael J. Mortimer, "The Delegation of Law–Making Authority to the United States Forest Service: Implications in the Struggle for National Forest Management," 54 *Administrative Law Review* 907 (2002), argues that the United States Forest Service has been involved in heated and protracted controversies because Congress has delegated power to it in vague terms. Environmentalists fight those who would harvest timber in the national forests; both groups are organized and have the resources necessary to fight. Mortimer says that the "Sierra Club alone has annual revenues exceeding $40 million . . ." (p. 932). Congress avoids taking responsibility for making decisions by delegating power to the USFS. Battles then are fought before courts about the USFS use of this power. Mortimer asserts:

> [A]ny management paradigm the agency adopts will never adequately satisfy the various multiple-users. That dissatisfaction, expressed particularly in lawsuits, forces the agency to alter its positions, and seek new paradigms to temper the dissatisfied. In doing so, the agency merely replaces one group of critics with another group of critics. The result is an agency staggering like a drunk down a dark alley, reeling from one side to the other, never able to regain its balance. (p. 955)

To what extent can we explain the changes in the practices of the Forest Service over the twenty years between Kaufman's study and that of Bullis and Tompkins as a response to the challenges of the various interest groups ready to fight the USFS? Can we expect a tendency to limit the discretion of the field level officials when an administrative agency is subject to repeated litigation?

3. Lief H. Carter, *The Limits of Order* (1974), is a study of a prosecuting attorney's office in a California county with a population of about 600,000. It is modeled on studies such as Kaufman's investigation of the forest ranger, but Carter found a different pattern of operation. Great discretion was given to the deputy prosecutors. Almost all important decisions relating to the prosecution of a particular case were made by those at the bottom of the chain of command with little effective guidance from the supervisors. Attempts to use rules and surveillance as means of supervisory control tended to fail.

Carter explains the tendency toward a case specific approach in terms of organizational technology and environment. The techniques for deciding whether a deputy prosecutor had done a good or a proper job were underdeveloped. The superior officials disagreed among themselves about the goals of the prosecutor's office, the weight to give each goal, and the appropriateness of the means that might be used to achieve these differing goals. Moreover, deputy prosecutors had no career commitment to the office—most of them served for a few years to gain experience and contacts and then left for the greater financial rewards of private practice. The young lawyers recruited to be deputies saw themselves as independent professionals and not as subordinates carrying out orders. The job itself was one in which prosecutors dealt with situations of uncertainty and unpredictability. Information comes both from the arresting officer and from defense attorneys. One never knows the whole truth. The deputies must accommodate conflicting requests and expectations from the police, the judges and the defense attorneys. The police want the person they arrested punished; the judges want efficient processing of cases; the defense attorneys want all mitigating factors to be given weight. Because the prosecutors have continuing relationships with court personnel and defense attorneys they must reach some sort of accommodation.

Other sources of uncertainty and diversity can also undercut efforts by supervisors to exercise control. Cases are infinitely various. Sometimes the law is unclear; sometimes the evidence is shaky; sometimes it is hard to tell how the judge will react on procedural matters or in sentencing. Carter remarks that the situation is something like an assembly line, where those in charge cannot agree whether they are producing Cadillacs or Chevrolets, and where the supervisors cannot predict what materials will be at the plant at any given time. (p. 42)

Carter does not condemn this discretionary system. He comments:

When we assess the performance of the criminal justice system, we should not limit ourselves to using only the criteria of order and regularity. . . . Bureaucratic controls can interfere with the alternative conception of justice as learning. This alternative conception requires that those who do justice maintain the capacity to learn new information about the cases they handle, about social preferences concerning crime, and about the consequences of punishment. . . . Such a strategy does, of course, increase the degree of idiosyncratic behavior—people in similar organizational positions will operate differently—but in conditions of technological and informational ambiguity and uncertainty, diverse behavior is rational, not only because it avoids wasteful segmentation and duplication of effort but because diverse behavior is a wise strategy for seeking ways of improving technology itself. (p. 162)

There are other studies of prosecutors' offices and other aspects of the criminal justice system that contain information about systems of control or lack of control. See, for example, Roy B. Fleming, Peter F. Nardulli, and James Eisenstein, *The Craft of Justice: Politics and Work in Criminal Court Communities* (1992). An earlier and quite important study of the criminal courts as organizations is James Eisenstein and Herbert Jacob, *Felony Justice: An Organizational Analysis of Criminal Courts* (1977).

4. An organization exercises control the same way a state exercises control: it can use force and incentives, but it can also try to get compliance through other means. If there is solidarity inside the organization, then peer pressure may do the trick. Also there may be internalized norms: just as some

people, as Tyler suggested, are disposed to obey the law, so some employees are disposed to follow company or agency rules, do their best for the organization and so on.

A special kind of "peer group" orientation is professionalism. A company doctor will presumably follow medical ethics and medical norms—will act as a "professional"—whether or not there are company rules that say she must. The same may be true of a company lawyer. These are not the only examples. Every occupation has its "professional" norms, and these exert a more or less powerful effect on job-holders. But, as Carter noted, "professionalism" is not always a factor that pushes toward compliance with organizational goals. It may well pull in the opposite direction.

Elizabeth W. Morrison, "Doing the Job Well: An Investigation of Pro–Social Rule Breaking, 32 *Journal of Management*" 5, 7 (2006), studied intentional violation of known organizational rules that is "motivated by the desire to do one's job better or to do what one believes to be appropriate in a given situation." For example, speed might be very important, and procedures could get in the way of doing the job quickly. A supervisor might give an employee some time to seek a new job rather than just fire the employee. Those who deal with other organizations might do favors that break internal rules in order to keep beneficial relationships going. A majority of her respondents offered examples of their pro-social rule breaking. While Morrison concedes that lower level employees might misperceive the best interests of their organizations, she argues that "organizational leaders may want to consider places where they should allow some latitude around rules in order to encourage and enable appropriate forms of extra-role behavior." (p. 24)

5.   The word "bureaucracy" sometimes conjures up an image of a system where top level people make decisions and give orders which bottom level people follow mindlessly. Jeffrey M. Prottas, *People Processing: The Street–Level Bureaucrat in Public Service Bureaucracies* (1979), points out, however, that the lowest ranking nonclerical workers often have a great deal of power. This power rests on their complex relationship with clients and supervisors. A bureaucracy often has the job of categorizing and processing people, as a condition of their receiving benefits, treatment or services. Superiors control the rules and the procedures. The targets of regulation—the clients—control information about themselves, subject to what has been stored in the computer. Street-level bureaucrats create "the file." They can exercise discretion and rationalize it by what they put in the file. They can highlight some facts and ignore others. The way in which decisions get made, and power exercised, in bureaucratic systems, is extremely variable and complex.

A classic article, David Mechanic, "Sources of Power of Lower Participants in Complex Organizations," 7 *Administrative Science Quarterly* 349 (1962), stresses the power of clerks, secretaries, those who run duplication rooms and the like. They have access to information. They learn how to circumvent rules and directions that they see as illegitimate. Those who have held their jobs for a long time often know how to go around ordinary procedures and get things done. (They may, for example, know other secretaries and clerks who owe them favors). They have many ways to reward supervisors they like and punish those they dislike. Young lawyers in law firms learn to cultivate the secretaries in their office and the people they deal with in the office of the Clerk of Court. Often, they find to their surprise, that such people know more about the law in certain areas and how things are done than experienced lawyers and judges.

Mark Bovens and Stavros Zouridis, "From Street–Level to System–Level Bureaucracies: How Information and Communication Technology is Transforming Administrative Discretion and Constitutional Control," 62 *Public Administration Review* 174, 177 (2002), tell us:

> A number of large executive organizations have undergone a process of gradual but fundamental change over the past few decades. Key in change was information and communication technology (ICT). The sheer dynamism caused by the introduction of computers affected both the organization of the street-level bureaucracy and the underlying legal setup. In a relatively short period of time, the street-level bureaucracy has changed into what we could call a *screen-level bureaucracy*. The decision-making process has been routinized ... Insofar as the implementing officials are directly in contact with the citizens, these contacts always run through or in the presence of a computer screen. Public servants can no longer freely take to the streets, they are always connected to the organization by the computer. Client data must be filled in with the help of fixed templates in electronic forms. Knowledge-management systems and digital decision trees have strongly reduced the scope of administrative discretion. Many decisions are no longer made at the street level by the worker handling the case; rather, they have been programmed into the computer in the design of the software.

Bovens and Zourides also note: "Computerization, taken too far, makes insufficient allowance for special circumstances and can lead to absurd or downright hazardous situations." (p. 182) Can we expect street-level bureaucrats facing absurd situations to find ways around the fixed templates in electronic forms?

Perhaps the most important street-level bureaucrats who play a role in the legal system are the police, although we do not usually think of them this way. Their role in the operation of criminal justice is crucial. There is a rich and growing literature on the police, their functions and dysfunctions. Two classic studies are James Q. Wilson, *Varieties of Police Behavior* (1968) and Jerome H. Skolnick, *Justice Without Trial: Law Enforcement in Democratic Society* (1966). Other important articles are Donald Black, "The Social Organization of Arrest," 28 *Stanford Law Review* 1087 (1971); Herman Goldstein, *Policing a Free Society* (1977); Jerome H. Skolnick, *The New Blue Line: Police Innovation in Six American Cities* (1986); and Samuel Walker, *The Police in America: An Introduction* (2d ed. 1992). On the history of the police, see Samuel Walker, *A Critical History of Police Reform: The Emergence of*

Professionalism (1977); and Erik Monkkonen, *Police in Urban America* (1981).

Lawrence M. Friedman, in *Crime and Punishment in American History* 461 (1993), comments on the structure of criminal justice in America:

> Indeed, the criminal justice "system" is not a system at all. This particular mirror of society is a jigsaw puzzle with a thousand tiny pieces. No one is really in charge. Legislatures make rules; police and detectives carry them out (more or less). Prosecutors prosecute; defense attorneys defend; judges and juries go their own way. So do prison officials. Everybody seems to have veto power over everybody else. Juries can frustrate judges and the police; the police can make nonsense out of the legislature; prison officials can undo the work of judges; prosecutors can ignore the police and the judges. The system is like a leaky garden hose: you can try to turn up the pressure at one end, but more water does not come out at the other. All you get is more water squirting out of the holes.

How far, if at all, can we expect templates and decision trees in computerized systems to patch the leaky garden hose sufficiently to keep one group from successfully subverting the efforts of reformers to change the system?

It is illuminating, of course, to compare policing in the United States with policing in other countries. For a fascinating comparison with Japan, see Setsuo Miyazawa, *Policing in Japan: A Study on Making Crime* (1992). There is a growing literature on the Japanese police. See Patricia G. Steinhoff, "Pursuing the Japanese Police," 27 *Law & Society Review* 827 (1993).

6.   Every bureaucracy and every administrative agency has an organizational structure that can be analyzed in two ways: first, as an internal skeleton, a way of controlling itself, of managing its staff, workers and the like; and second, as an external force—a way of doing (or trying to do) what it has been mandated to do in the outside world.

There are innumerable studies of administrative agencies and each one can be analyzed in these terms. The task of the agency determines, in part, its structure. An agency that the public goes to voluntarily probably will behave differently than an agency which "regulates" in some hostile way or that tries to control behavior. Contrast the Forest Service, for example, with the activities of the Securities and Exchange Commission, which regulates the stock markets and which tries to ferret out and punish stock fraud. On this agency, see Susan P. Shapiro, *Wayward Capitalists: Target of the Securities and Exchange Commission* (1984). Nancy Reichman, "Regulating Risky Business: Dilemmas in Security Regulation,"13 *Law & Policy* 263 (1991), argues that to understand the activities of agencies that regulate such matters as the market in corporate securities, we must consider both the structure of the federal and state agencies involved as well as the structure of the targets of regulation. Privileged players with knowledge, skill and resources can play the regulatory system in ways that undercut its protections for those lacking these resources.

III. The Roles of Actors in the Legal System: Job Descriptions, Who Gets the Jobs, and Rewards and Punishments

(A) Judges

The judge is a more ubiquitous figure in legal history than the lawyer or any other legal professional. There are many societies that do not have lawyers, but few that do not have courts and judges. A judge is a third person who has authority to resolve disputes between two or more disputants. A judge can make his or her decisions "stick," that is, judges have power to implement their decisions, unlike a mediator who can only persuade and facilitate.

Societies do not grant the power to apply their laws to just anyone. How does society make sure that judges will do their job in a satisfactory manner? In part, society relies on formal rules and sanctions. Judges who take bribes can be prosecuted as criminals. There are judicial codes of ethics. Statutes may state formal qualifications for the position. In extreme situations, judges can be impeached and thrown out of office.

However, formal rules and sanctions concerning judging probably are not very important to the day-to-day functioning of the judiciary. Less formal practices, rules and sanctions probably do most of the work most of the time in most societies. A society is likely to exercise care in selecting people for this position. Whether by appointment or election, the process should keep the wrong people from gaining positions as judges. The legal culture has norms about judges and judging. Political officials, leaders of the legal profession, and those who watch television programs about lawyers and trials hold more or less well-formed ideas about what a good judge should do. In the United States, judicial appointments interest few people, apart from those seeking the position and their relatives, and a few politicians and members of the bar. Occasionally judicial confirmation hearings can be national news and provoke intense feelings.

The work of most judges in this society goes on without a great deal of publicity. The Supreme Court gets massive media coverage of some of its work, but much of its work never reaches the general public. Other judges, for the most part, operate in the shadows. Occasionally, what a judge does may be controversial and get some play in the newspapers, but most judges, most of the time, work far below the threshold of public notice. Other judges and lawyers, of course, pay more attention. They may applaud good judging or criticize bad judging. Judges naturally wish to satisfy their peers. This has an impact on behavior. Moreover, men and women with unconventional views are not likely to be nominated, appointed or elected to the bench in the first place.

In other societies, the work of judges is even more obscure and anonymous than in the United States. High court judges in France, for example, do not sign their opinions, which are dull, dry and didactic. These opinions convey a message that decision-making is a purely technical task. The personality of a judge writing an opinion in an American high court is more likely to shine through. On the other hand, lower-level investigative judges in civil law countries play a role that American judges do not. For example, the Mafia in 1992 assassinated two Italian judges whose investigations threatened its power. In South Africa, a judge, Richard Goldstone, uncovered police scandals in the same year. In 1999, Baltasar Garzon, a Spanish investigative magistrate, issued a criminal indictment against General Augusto Pinochet, the former Chilean dictator, charging him with murder, genocide and terrorism related to the killing of 94 Spanish citizens, among the many tortured and killed by Pinochet's government during his time in power. Pinochet was in Great Britain, getting medical treatment. The British police arrested him as a result of the Spanish warrant. After a long battle, the courts found that the General could be extradited to Spain, but the British Foreign Secretary allowed Pinochet to return to Chile because his age and health would preclude him from participating meaningfully in a trial. See, e.g., Craig S. Smith, "Aiming at Judicial Targets All Over the World," *N.Y. Times*, Oct. 18, 2003, at A4.

We must remember, too, that there are judges and judges. In American society, "judges" include justices of the Supreme Court, local justices of the peace, traffic and police court judges, administrative law judges and so on. There are also "arbitrators" who decide labor and commercial disputes, and they, like judges, have the authority to impose a solution on the parties. We do not usually call arbitrators "judges" because they do not sit in a court. "Mediators" are something less than judges because they do not have formal authority to impose their will on the parties. They can only try to guide parties to a settlement; often, of course, they are very influential.

What type of decision-maker is best suited to resolve a particular type of conflict or deal with a particular type of problem? As noted, business people and labor unions often use arbitrators. Mediators are common in family disputes. See Vilhelm Aubert, Competition and Dissensus: Two Types of Conflict and of Conflict Resolution, 7 Journal of Conflict Resolution 26 (1963), which draws a distinction between conflicts over "values" and those over "interests." Aubert argues that the type of conflict affects the appropriate type of person or body to resolve it. It is, for example, very difficult to mediate a conflict of value because most people do not think it proper to sell out their values. Something is either right or wrong. Of course, conflicts of value can be transformed into conflicts of interest which can be compromised, but this is not easy to do. Volkmar Gessner draws a somewhat similar distinction. He says that there are "people" conflicts, "role" conflicts, and "norms" conflicts. These are best resolved, respectively, by "advisers" (or mediators), "arbitrators," and "judges." *Recht und Konflikt* [Law and Conflict] 179 (1976). On the "ideology" of mediation and its disadvantages, see Karla Fischer, Neil Vidmar, and Rene Ellis, "The Culture of Battering and the Role of Mediation in Domestic Violence Cases," 46 *Southern Methodist University Law Review* 2117 (1993).

We can accept that judges may have important powers in American society. This raises the question: who gets to be a judge and how does the process work? Once we have some ideas about this, the next question is whether the nature of the process matters to the society at large. Does it matter who gets appointed to the bench in the United States? Should we care whether judges are Republicans or Democrats, men or women, white or African–American, young or old, rich or poor? Do judges who are former prosecutors treat defendants differently than judges who were former defense lawyers? Have we reason to think that decisions differ systematically from category to category? How important is it to have "diversity" on the bench? Exactly how much creativity does a judge have? How important is it to have judges who are really expert in the law?

(5.8) W. Bush's Judiciary: The First Term Record

Sheldon Goldman, Elliot Slotnick, Gerard Gryski and Sara Schiavoni

88 *Judicature* 244 (May–June 2005).[10]

American politics intensified during the 2004 presidential election year. Although the appointment of judges was not a major issue in the campaign, both parties addressed it in their party platforms and on occasion the issue was publicly raised, particularly with regard to the Supreme Court. When the hoopla was over, George W. Bush won reelection by a narrow electoral college victory and he and his administration returned to the business of government—including staffing the judiciary, which has been a major concern of the Bush presidency and his core constituency.

This article, a continuation of a series published biennially in *Judicature* for more than a quarter of a century, examines judicial selection and confirmation politics, focusing on the last half of W. Bush's first term. We also offer comparisons of the demographic portrait of W. Bush's entire first term appointees with his four immediate predecessors in the White House.

Our narrative of appointment and confirmation processes and politics is based primarily on personal interviews with key participants and observers both inside and outside government. The statistics on judicial backgrounds and attributes are based on data from the questionnaires completed by all judicial nominees and submitted to the Senate Judiciary Committee. Other sources of data include home-state newspaper articles, standard biographical reference works, and, in some instances for information about political party affiliation, the Registrar of Voters or Boards of Elections for the counties in which the judges resided. Some missing biographical information was generously provided by appointees themselves.

A key to understanding the high level of tension and confrontation, particularly concerning appointments to the courts of appeals, is the recognition that W. Bush was elected president in 2000 after losing the popular vote but winning a Supreme Court decision in *Bush v. Gore*. Democrats, still stewing from Republican obstruction and delay of Clinton nominees during the last six years of the Clinton presidency when Republicans controlled the Senate, were outraged when, from their perspective, the Bush administration, instead of seeking compromise and consultation with Democratic senators in the appointment of judges, particularly to the appeals courts, acted as if the President had won a national mandate.

When in June of the first year of W. Bush's presidency the Democrats gained control of the Senate, the administration continued to deny the legitimacy of the Democrats' grievances surrounding judicial selection and the Democrats brought obstruction and delay of appeals court nominees to an unprecedented level. In the congressional elections of 2002 the Republicans regained control of the Senate, leaving the Democrats only the filibuster as a way to demonstrate opposition to particularly objectionable nominees specifically and the administration's approach to judicial selection in general. Against this backdrop we turn to an accounting of the selection and confirmation processes and politics during the last half of W. Bush's first term.

The Selection Process

[The authors describe the selection process which the Bush administration followed. There was a "Judicial Selection Committee" which met weekly. Lawyers from the Justice Department took part, and so did White House Counsel, Alberto Gonzales.

In the past, "identification of potential district court nominees" was largely in the hands of senators from the state in which the district was located, if they were members of the President's party. But during the Bush administration, the "White House's role in designating nominees has increased dramatically," especially so with regard to appointments to the court of appeals. There remained, however, at least some degree of consultation with Republican senators.

What about senators from the other party? The Democrats claim that they have been largely shut out of the process; the Republicans tend to differ on this point.]

The role of diversity

Attention to pursuing diversity in judicial appointments can be traced historically to the Carter administration, whose behavior with regard to seating nontraditional judges, those who were not white males, was unprecedented. The two-term Clinton presidency took diversity to historic highs with virtually half of his district court judges (47.6 percent) and his appeals court judges (50.8 percent) characterized as "nontraditional." It is in this context that the record of the present administration can best be viewed.

In addressing this issue, members of the administration were quick to acknowledge the importance of seating a diverse bench. Dabney Friedrich [Associate White House Counsel] volunteered that this is "something the President cares about very much, and he makes an effort to find qualified minorities and women for the federal bench.... His record is impressive on this front.... He has had a number of firsts." These have included the first African American woman to sit on the Fourth Circuit Court of Appeals....

... Commenting on the "gaps" in the Bush diversity record, an aide to a Democratic senator noted that, "with respect to different demographics ... we do know ... that the number of African American nominees is significantly less than [the number appointed by] former President Clinton and particularly in the south."

Making an additional observation on the diversity front, an aide to a senior Democratic senator suggested, "It appears that diversity of views is ... not valued so much. Loyalty along ideological lines is more valued than ethnic or racial diversity."

The Federalist Society's role

We turn now to exploring the role of the Federalist Society, a group whose adherents have been characterized as generally successful in obtaining judicial seats. Historically, of course, the group that has played the most prominent role in judicial selection processes has been the American Bar Association through its Standing Committee on Federal Judiciary. As discussed below, the removal of the ABA's input in the pre-nomination stages of the selection process has altered the group's most favored status. Some would argue that the Federalist Society has stepped into that breach, albeit in a non-institutionalized informal way, and that they are playing an even more central judge making role than had ever been attributed to the ABA.

The Society's purpose, succinctly stated on its website, underscores its direct interest in the outcomes of judicial selection:

"Law schools and the legal profession are currently strongly dominated by a form of orthodox liberal ideology which advocates a centralized and uniform society.... The Federalist Society is a group of conservatives and libertarians interested in the current state of the legal order. It is founded on the principle that the state exists to preserve freedom, that the separation of governmental powers is central to our Constitution, and that it is emphatically the province and duty of the judiciary to say what the law is, not what it should be...."

When asked about the Society's place in judicial selection, Dabney Friedrich noted that, "the Federalist Society has no official role in the judicial nominations process. Obviously, we receive recommendations and input from many interested individuals and organizations."

Recognizing that some critics of the Society have suggested that membership in the organization, per se, should be a red flag against receiving a federal judgeship, an aide to a Republican senator on the Judiciary Committee observed that it is "unfair to say that a certain membership disqualifies you.... You know the ACLU is not a group that many Republicans look upon with great favor, and yet that was not used to bludgeon [Clinton appointees]. I have no idea how many of Bush's nominees were ACLU members, nor do I particularly care. They're good lawyers and they understand the difference between law and politics and that's got to be the standard."

In a similar vein, Friedrich noted that, "a lot has been made of the fact that some of the President's judicial nominees are members of the Federalist Society, but the criteria that we consider in evaluating judicial candidates are experience, temperament, character, and judicial philosophy." ...

While it appears that the Society does not play a direct or formal role in the Bush selection process, few would suggest that the symmetry between the Society's purpose and the administration's recruitment goals is without consequence....

Ultimately, it was pointed out by an aide to a Democratic senator on the Judiciary Committee, the most important question is not really one of the nature of the role of the Federalist Society in judicial selection or the number of its members nominated to the appellate bench. Rather, the broader concern as this aide sees it is one of a president

> indicating that he doesn't have a litmus test. [Yet] what you see in the files of nominees is that they have distinguished themselves in various areas, whether they're in the Federalist Society and have their conception of federalism and the commerce clause, or perhaps in anti-choice activities, or perhaps in anti-environmental efforts, but there's a kind of a matrix. Some people hit all three or four of them, some people only hit a few. And one of those factors appears to be the Federalist Society and some of the others that don't have the Federalist Society have something else.

The ABA's role

If the role of the Federalist Society has been prominent in federal judicial selection during George Bush's first term, it is equally apparent that the historic role of the American Bar Association has been altered dramatically through its removal from the pre-nomination stage. Since the presidency of Dwight Eisenhower, the ABA, through its Standing Committee on Federal Judiciary, had been given an opportunity to evaluate candidates for the federal bench before their names were announced publicly. The present administration viewed such a most favored status in judicial selection as both unwarranted and unjustifiable. While the ABA could make its views about prospects for the bench known like any other group or individual, they could only do so once a name had formally emerged as a nominee, and such input would have no special status. The ABA does continue to conduct its evaluations of candidates and, indeed, while the Judiciary Committee under Orrin

Hatch's direction had also eliminated the ABA's special status in his Committee's hearings processes, the Committee Democrats continue to insist on receiving the ABA evaluations before proceeding with a nomination hearing on a candidate. . . .

An electoral issue?

The final issue to be assessed regarding the selection process of the Bush administration for choosing federal judges is what role, if any, did the President's choices play as an electoral issue. Nan Aron suggested that this concern has historical relevance, particularly for the Republicans, but now has taken on more of a Democratic flavor:

> We've always known, particularly since the '50s, how engaged the right wing in this country is in judicial nominations. The Earl Warren bumper stickers were prevalent in the South back then. . . . Now this has become, thanks to George Bush, a much larger base issue for the Democrats. And one reflection of this is the 170 organizations that came together to oppose [the nomination of] William Myers. So I think as far as the Democrats are concerned this issue, particularly if and when there is a Supreme Court vacancy, will be a principal issue of concern for the base. I mean, who would have thought that even four years of just courts of appeals nominees would have engendered this much opposition and interest among the [core] constituency of the Democratic party?

Aron recognized, of course, that the electoral sway of the judgeship issue went well beyond the Democrats. Indeed, she noted, President Bush "used the issue of judgeships to effectively reach out to his right wing base and motivate them to vote." The mechanism for doing so, however, was not necessarily overt. "While the issue of judgeships was not widely discussed during this recent election, certainly gay rights and abortion rights were frequently mentioned topics, and one could see that Bush used the issue quite effectively to mobilize his base." . . .

The view that the issue of judgeships was perceived to "matter" electorally and that specific proxy issues were surrogates for it was shared by a Republican Senate leadership aide, who said, "They believe it is a winning issue for them. . . . I certainly know that it's a base issue, it is a proxy vote on abortion for a certain percentage of the base. They hear the word 'judges' and they hear 'abortion.' . . . And to some extent it's a proxy vote for this [gay] marriage issue."

While the view that the judgeships issue had an impact on the outcome of the presidential election was not articulated in any of our interviews, the perception that the issue played to the parties' core base voters and helped to bring out the vote was widely shared. At the same time there was some sense that the issue may have had a more direct impact on specific senatorial races, particularly the defeat of Democratic Senator Thomas Daschle, the sitting minority leader.

Confirmation politics

Our consideration of the judicial selection process of the Bush administration to this point represents, of course, only one-half of the advice and consent processes outlined in our Constitution. We now turn our focus to the critical and highly contentious politics of confirmation during George Bush's first term. The starting point for any understanding of the playing out of the confirmation process for federal judicial nominees must focus on the divisive atmosphere in the Senate. In the words of one Republican Senate leadership aide, "It's nasty." An aide to a Republican senator on the Judiciary Committee underscored that the partisan acrimony in the confirmation process has both procedural and substantive roots. Procedurally, when the focus is on filibusters,

> both sides feel that they have been not only aggrieved but badly aggrieved. Then, substantively there is a lot of concern from the Republican side that some of these nominees [were] not just denied certain processes ... but were personally attacked, their names destroyed.... I think even if I tried to be an objective observer, I would say certain things really were beyond the pale, some of which were only said by groups, but a few things which were actually said by senators. I think when you make it personal, when you attack people's integrity, intelligence, ability, it's hard not to take that personally.

Elaborating on the role of advocacy groups in feeding Senate divisiveness, this aide continued:

> Groups on both sides always want more than what their senators typically want to give or pursue. They feel passionate about their issues, and that's good in some respects, but when the passion turns to venom it is certainly not helpful to bipartisanship and it's usually destructive.
>
> . . .

In this challenging atmosphere, how can one characterize the President's success in confirming his judgeship nominees? While it is often said that numbers do not lie, it is clear that, in the judicial selection arena, numbers can mean very different things in the hands of different observers. Several of our sources characterized George Bush's success in seating his nominees in quite glowing terms. In a statement issued on November 20, 2004, approaching the end of Bush's first term, the ranking minority member of the Senate Judiciary Committee, Patrick Leahy, attempted to place the first-term performance in historical context:

> Democrats and Republicans in the Senate have confirmed ... more federal judges than were confirmed for President Reagan during his first term, more than in President George H.W. Bush's presidency, and more than in either of President Clinton's terms.... With this historic number of confirmations, we are at the lowest number of vacant seats on the federal courts in 16 years.

This record of achievement did not go unnoticed by an aide to a Republican senator on the Judiciary Committee:

> For all of the frustration that I know some Republicans and some conservative groups have felt, [the] Democrats are right. Two hundred plus nominees is a lot of people to get confirmed. The courts of appeals record is quite solid. A number of individuals who, shall we say, hold different positions than a lot of Senate Democrats are now serving on the bench. There's no question that a lot of people who could easily not have been confirmed were, in fact, confirmed.

Indeed, this record of accomplishment led some of our sources to feel compelled to comment on why so many judges had been confirmed and so relatively few have been blocked. According to an aide to a senior Democratic senator on the Judiciary Committee,

> I know that senators thought long and hard about opposing nominees and which nominees to oppose. I know they made decisions based on priorities and thinking they did not want to be obstructionist and oppose many many nominees and [they] didn't. . . .

[The confirmation process has been full of conflict and controversy. Some senators even talk about a "crisis." There is a widespread perception that "a good deal is amiss in the process through which federal judges get confirmed." Both parties claim the other party was too aggressive and divisive. One problem is that "the current state of affairs represents a no-way-out, win-win situation for the combatants." The "confrontational and divisive confirmation battles" result in the "seating of some quite conservative nominees, on the one hand, or a potential political issue that appeals to the conservative electoral base if there is obstruction and delay." This helps the Republicans. For Democrats, there is the "occasional victory of derailing a controversial nomination," and "the development of [an] . . . important electoral issue."]

The blue slip

Historically, the blue slip system is an internal Senate process through which home state senators are given the opportunity to object to a nomination by withholding a return of a blue slip, seeking the senator's comments, to the Judiciary Committee chair. Ostensibly, this procedure helps to ensure consultation across party lines since, historically, and for the most part, hearings would not be held on a nominee absent the returned blue slip. While there are a few points in time, specifically during the committee chairmanships of Senators Kennedy and Biden, where the senators asserted that, under some circumstances, adherence to the blue slip system would not be absolute, there is no universally acknowledged precedent of its violation. And, during the Clinton years, there is ample evidence that the withholding of the blue slip by a single Republican home state senator was sufficient to stall a nomination.

During the W. Bush presidency, during the tenure of Orrin Hatch as Judiciary Committee chair, however, the possibility was first raised that it took both home state senators withholding the blue slip to stop a hearing from going forward and, in addition, a distinction was drawn regarding the applicability of the blue slip process in appeals as opposed to district court nominations.

This distinction in the blue slips' meaning under Orrin Hatch's chairmanship was acknowledged by Judiciary Committee Majority Counsel Bruce Artim, who said, "The rule Senator Hatch has lived by, blue slips are dispositive for district court nominees. For the appellate courts, blue slips are a significant factor. He doesn't believe [with courts of appeals] that a single home state senator should have veto power, particularly if there has been meaningful consultation with the White House and the opposing senator."

This distinction was embraced by C. Boyden Gray, who claimed that it even existed during his service as White House Counsel during the presidency of the first George Bush. Gray accentuated the differences between district and appeals court confirmation processes with considerable senatorial deference at the district level and the assertion that the blue slip system simply did not apply to the circuits—"at the appellate level those nominations are the president's."

Such a characterization flies in the face of the charges made by Senator Leahy in his end-of-term statement on judicial nominations:

> When Republicans were being asked to consider the nominations of a Democratic President, one negative blue slip from just one home state Senator was enough to doom a nomination and prevent a hearing on that nomination. This included all nominations, including those to the circuit courts.

This notion that the present approach to the blue slip both rewrites and reinvents history was also reiterated in our interview with two Democratic Senate aides. According to one, "it certainly applied when Clinton was in the White House to the circuit courts. It has, in my experience, always applied to both district and circuit court nominees. Were blue slips sent out for circuit court nominees? Yes. Well, why would you send them out if they weren't required, they weren't followed?"

For the record, the second aide noted that in Clinton's second term 25 circuit court nominees didn't get a hearing or vote in committee. "It's just fiction to claim that the blue slips don't matter for circuit court nominees. They clearly matter."

Violating rules and norms ...

[There has also been sharp controversy over other rules and norms. For example, the Democrats claimed that there was a norm, that to force a vote on a nomination and end debate, there had to be consent from a minority member, but the Republicans had ended debates without such consent. The Republicans, in turn, defended their actions by accusing the Democrats of abusing the rule.

Particularly controversial was the fact that the Democrats blocked a few nominees—those that they considered particularly extreme in their view or otherwise undesirable—through the device of a filibuster. (A filibuster involves gaining the floor of the Senate to debate and continuing to talk until the majority gives up; the device was perfected by Southern senators through the 1960s when they fought desegregation of the races). The Republicans claimed that this was an "unprecedented abuse of process;" and threatened to use what came to be called the "nuclear option," that is, eliminating the filibuster entirely.]

Recess appointments

Before turning our attention to considerations of the so-called nuclear option, two additional phenomena in judicial confirmation processes during Bush's first term are worthy of mention. These are the President's use of recess appointments to seat two judicial nominees who had been highly controversial and, relatedly, the May 18, 2004, deal that allowed for the confirmation of a slate of judicial nominees very late in the congressional session in exchange for a promise to make no more additional recess appointments.

Recess appointments are a constitutionally provided mechanism through which judges can be seated while the Senate is out of session, and they can remain in office through the end of the following congressional session. In order to remain in office, they have to be renominated and confirmed. While not everyday occurrences, there is certainly precedent for recess appointments being the mechanism through which judges first ascend to the bench when Congress is in extended recess. Perhaps the two most famous instances are at the Supreme Court level, with Chief Justice Earl Warren and Justice William Brennan each receiving such appointments. At the end of the Clinton Administration, Roger Gregory, an African American nominee, was given a recess appointment to the U.S. Court of Appeals for the Fourth Circuit—becoming the first African American to be seated on that southern circuit. This was a bold move that overcame Senator Jesse Helms's obstructionist behavior, which had derailed several potential nominees, including Gregory, during Clinton's presidency.

For its part, the [Bush] administration was quite comfortable utilizing recess appointments to fill vacancies. . . .

While 10 nominees had been filibustered by the Democrats, only two, Charles Pickering and William Pryor, received recess appointments. . . .

In the wake of the recess appointments of Judges Pickering and Pryor, as the calendar continued its inexorable march toward the fall election, a somewhat surprising pre-Memorial Day deal was struck between the White House and the Senate leadership wherein a list of 25 additional judicial nominees would be confirmed without opposition, in exchange for which the White House promised to make no additional recess appointments through the end of the presidential term. Our interviews on both sides of the aisle made it clear that both Senate Majority Leader Frist and Senate Minority

Leader Daschle were involved in forging the agreement with the White House. . . .

At the end of George W. Bush's first term in office, it was clear that relationships in the advice and consent arena were highly divisive and tension ridden. While the May 18, 2004, agreement resulted in the seating of a large cohort of judges, it did little to lessen the partisan divide and, indeed, Republicans continued to focus their energies and their rhetoric on the 10 filibustered candidates. One matter that would clearly set the tone at the beginning of Bush's second term would be the administration's behavior with regard to these nominees. In one of the first acts of his second term, George Bush renominated seven filibustered nominees whose confirmations were stalled during the President's first term. . . .

None of the changes in the judicial selection landscape at the outset of the President's second term offers unusual hope for dramatic improvements in the relationships we have explored. For one, the Republican hold on the Senate majority has grown and become more solidified. Second, Arlen Specter has risen to the chair position of the Senate Judiciary Committee, replacing Orrin Hatch. Our interviews did not reveal any likelihood of great changes being pursued by Senator Specter. Indeed, Senator Specter became the center of controversy before ascending the chair when he suggested that the President would run into difficulty with nominations of extreme opponents of abortion. The subsequent uproar from the Republican base and the necessity for the Senator to underscore his loyalty to the President seemed to suggest that the Senator would be less likely to act independently and buck the leadership.

The nuclear option

Perhaps the biggest area in which the Republican senate leadership has become engaged at the outset of George Bush's second term in office has been the threat to employ the so-called "nuclear option" as a mechanism to break the Democratic filibusters. At bottom, the nuclear option would proceed as an effort to change the Senate's filibuster rules, which presently require 60 votes to end debate, to a simple majority vote for obtaining cloture. If, indeed, the Republicans can change the rule by a bare majority vote then, it follows, they would surely have the same majority to invoke cloture and end the filibusters. While there was a good deal of talk about resort to the nuclear option in the latter half of Bush's first term, focused consideration on going that route mushroomed in the first months of Bush's second term. . . .

Clearly, the resolution of that debate will have enormous consequences for the politics of judicial selection in George Bush's second term and, perhaps more broadly, the institution of the Senate as a whole. The May 23, 2005, compromise seems to have put the nuclear option on hold, with great uncertainty as to the circumstances under which it would be revived.

Returning to our concern with W. Bush's record, it is well to keep in mind that despite the high-profile filibusters and delays, the 108th Congress confirmed 85 individuals to lifetime positions to the federal district courts and 18 to appeals courts of general jurisdiction.... For the first term as a whole, there were a total of 168 district court and 34 appeals court confirmations. Nine district court and 17 appeals court nominees went unconfirmed. We turn now to a consideration of the demographic portrait of those who were confirmed during the President's first term and how they compare to W. Bush's four immediate predecessors in office.

District court appointees

Gender and ethnic diversity have characterized George W. Bush's presidential appointments, including those to the judiciary. For the district courts, about one-third went to nontraditional candidates, that is, those who were not white males, a record surpassed only by President Bill Clinton, as seen in Table 2. The demographic portrait of W. Bush's nontraditional appointees during his first term compared to his traditional appointees is presented in Table 1.

Table 1: How the Bush nontraditional appointees compared to his traditional appointees to the federal district courts during his first term

	Nontraditional appointees		Traditional appointees	
Occupation	%	(N)	%	(N)
Politics/government	7.3%	(4)	8.9%	(10)
Judiciary	65.5%	(36)	43.4%	(49)
Large law firm				
100 + members	9.1%	(5)	11.5%	(13)
50–99	—	—	8.0%	(9)
25–49	1.8%	(1)	7.1%	(8)
Medium size firm				
10–24 members	3.6%	(2)	6.2%	(7)
5–9	1.8%	(1)	6.2%	(7)
Small firm				
2–4	5.5%	(3)	4.4%	(5)
solo	—	—	2.7%	(3)
Professor of law	1.8%	(1)	0.9%	(1)
Other	3.6%	(2)	0.9%	(1)
Experience				
Judicial	74.6%	(41)	47.8%	(54)
Prosecutorial	49.1%	(27)	41.6%	(47)
Neither	12.7%	(7)	30.1%	(34)

	Nontraditional appointees		Traditional appointees	
Undergraduate education				
Public	50.9%	(28)	46.0%	(52)
Private	40.0%	(22)	48.7%	(55)
Ivy League	9.1%	(5)	5.3%	(6)
Law school education				
Public	45.5%	(25)	51.3%	(58)
Private	40.0%	(22)	37.2%	(42)
Ivy League	14.6%	(8)	11.5%	(13)
Gender				
Male	36.4%	(20)	100%	(113)
Female	63.6%	(35)	—	—
Ethnicity/race				
White	45.4%	(25)	100%	(113)
African American	20.0%	(11)	—	—
Hispanic	32.7%	(18)	—	—
Asian	1.8%	(1)	—	—
ABA rating				
Well Qualified	72.7%	(40)	69.9%	(79)
Qualified	23.6%	(13)	29.2%	(33)
Not Qualified	3.6%	(2)	0.9%	(1)
Political identification				
Democrat	9.1%	(5)	5.3%	(6)
Republican	76.4%	(42)	88.5%	(100)
None	14.5%	(8)	6.2%	(7)
Past party activism	34.6%	(19)	55.8%	(63)
Net worth				
Under $200,000	9.1%	(5)	4.4%	(5)
$200–499,999	27.3%	(15)	15.9%	(18)
$500–999,999	18.2%	(10)	23.0%	(26)
$1+ million	45.4%	(25)	56.6%	(64)
Average age at nomination	46.6		50.2	
Total number of appointees	55		113	

Table 2:   U.S district court appointees compared by administration

	W. Bush		Clinton		Bush		Reagan		Carter	
	%	(N)	%	(N)	%	(N)	%	(N)	%	(N)
Occupation										
Politics/ government	8.3%	(14)	11.5%	(35)	10.8%	(16)	13.4%	(39)	5.0%	(10)

	W. Bush		Clinton		Bush		Reagan		Carter	
	%	(N)	%	(N)	%	(N)	%	(N)	%	(N)
Judiciary	50.6%	(85)	48.2%	(147)	41.9%	(62)	36.9	(107)	44.6%	(90)
Large law firm										
100+ members	10.7%	(18)	6.6%	(20)	10.8%	(16)	6.2%	(18)	2.0%	(4)
50–99	5.4%	(9)	5.2%	(16)	7.4%	(11)	4.8%	(14)	5.9%	(12)
25–49	5.4%	(9)	4.3%	(13)	7.4%	(11)	6.9%	(20)	5.9%	(12)
Medium size firm										
10–24 members	5.4%	(9)	7.2%	(22)	8.8%	(13)	10.0%	(29)	9.4%	(19)
5–9	4.8%	(8)	6.2%	(19)	6.1%	(9)	9.0%	(26)	9.9%	(20)
Small firm										
2–4	4.8%	(8)	4.6%	(14)	3.4%	(5)	7.2%	(21)	11.4%	(23)
solo	1.8%	(3)	3.6%	(11)	1.4%	(2)	2.8%	(8)	2.5%	(5)
Professor of law	1.2%	(2)	1.6%	(5)	0.7%	(1)	2.1%	(6)	3.0%	(6)
Other	1.8%	(3)	1.0%	(3)	1.4%	(2)	0.7%	(2)	0.5%	(1)
Experience										
Judicial	56.6%	(95)	52.1%	(159)	46.6%	(69)	46.2%	(134)	54.0%	(109)
Prosecutorial	44.0%	(74)	41.3%	(126)	39.2%	(58)	44.1%	(128)	38.1%	(77)
Neither	24.4%	(41)	28.9%	(88)	31.8%	(47)	28.6%	(83)	31.2%	(63)
Undergraduate education										
Public	47.6%	(80)	44.3%	(135)	46.0%	(68)	37.9%	(110)	55.9%	(113)
Private	45.8%	(77)	42.0%	(128)	39.9%	(59)	48.6%	(141)	34.2%	(69)
Ivy League	6.6%	(11)	13.8%	(42)	14.2%	(21)	13.4	(39)	9.9%	(20)
Law school education										
Public	49.4%	(83)	39.7%	(121)	52.7%	(78)	44.8%	(130)	52.0%	(105)
Private	38.1%	(64)	40.7%	(124)	33.1%	(49)	43.4%	(126)	31.2%	(63)
Ivy League	12.5%	(21)	19.7%	(60)	14.2%	(21)	11.7%	(34)	16.8%	(34)
Gender										
Male	79.2%	(133)	71.5%	(218)	80.4%	(119)	91.7%	(266)	85.6%	(173)
Female	20.8%	(35)	28.5%	(87)	19.6%	(29)	8.3%	(24)	14.4%	(29)
Ethnicity/race										
White	82.1%	(138)	75.1%	(229)	89.2%	(132)	92.4%	(268)	78.2%	(158)
African American	6.6%	(11)	17.4%	(53)	6.8%	(10)	2.1%	(6)	13.9%	(28)
Hispanic	10.7%	(18)	5.9%	(18)	4.0%	(6)	4.8%	(14)	6.9%	(14)
Asian	0.6%	(1)	1.3%	(4)	—	—	0.7%	(2)	0.5%	(1)
Native American	—	—	0.3%	(1)	—	—	—	—	0.5%	(1)
Percentage white male	67.3%	(113)	52.4%	(160)	73.0%	(108)	84.8%	(246)	67.8%	(137)
ABA rating										
EWQ/WQ	70.8%	(119)	59.0%	(180)	57.4%	(85)	53.5%	(155)	51.0%	(103)
Qualified	27.4%	(46)	40.0%	(122)	42.6%	(63)	46.6%	(135)	47.5%	(96)
Not Qualified	1.8%	(3)	1.0%	(3)	—	—	—	—	1.5%	(3)
Political identification										
Democrat	6.6%	(11)	87.5%	(267)	6.1%	(9)	4.8%	(14)	91.1%	(184)
Republican	84.5%	(142)	6.2%	(19)	88.5%	(131)	91.7%	(266)	4.5%	(9)
Other	—	—			0.3%	(1)	—	—	—	—
None	8.9%	(15)	5.9%	(18)	5.4%	(8)	3.4%	(10)	4.5%	(9)
Past party activism	48.8%	(82)	50.2%	(153)	64.2%	(95)	60.3%	(175)	61.4%	(124)

	W. Bush		Clinton		Bush		Reagan		Carter	
	%	(N)	%	(N)	%	(N)	%	(N)	%	(N)
Net worth										
Under $200,000	6.0%	(10)	13.4%	(41)	10.1%	(15)	17.9%	(52)	35.8%*	(53)
$200–499,999	19.6%	(33)	21.6%	(66)	31.1%	(46)	37.6%	(109)	41.2%	(61)
$500–999,999	21.4%	(36)	26.9%	(82)	26.4%	(39)	21.7%	(63)	18.9%	(28)
$1 + million	53.–	(89)	38.0%	(116)	32.4%	(48)	22.8%	(66)	$4.0%	(6)
Average age at nomination	49.0		49.5		48.2		48.6		49.6	
Total number of appointees	168		305		148		290		202	

* These figures are for appointees confirmed by the 96th Congress for all but six Carter district court appointees (for whom no data were available).

In terms of occupation at time of appointment, one statistic clearly stands out: almost two-thirds of the nontraditional appointees were serving on the bench compared to less then 45 percent of the traditional appointees. In terms of judicial experience, three-fourths of the nontraditional appointments had judicial track records compared to less then half of the traditional appointments. Clearly the bench was the major path to a judgeship for a nontraditional candidate while for traditional appointees the route to the bench was about equally divided between a career in private practice and the judiciary.

A larger proportion of nontraditional than traditional appointees had prosecutorial experience. Indeed, only less than 13 percent of nontraditional appointees had neither judicial nor prosecutorial experience. More than twice the proportion of traditional appointees had neither judicial nor prosecutorial experience. For nontraditional appointees, a stellar record of professional experience clearly helped their ascent to the bench and in some instances may have overcome their relative lack of partisan activism.

Looking at undergraduate and law school education, there were few major differences, although nontraditional appointees had a slightly greater tendency to have had an Ivy League education. There were only slight differences in the ABA ratings of nontraditional as compared to traditional appointees. However, two of the three Bush appointees rated "not qualified" were nontraditional.

Appeals court appointees

Thirty-four W. Bush nominees to appeals courts of general jurisdiction were confirmed during his first term. Of these, 12 were nontraditional and 22 were traditional (white males). These relatively small numbers alert us that comparisons of proportions of Bush's nontraditional to traditional appeals court appointees in Table 3 must be interpreted very cautiously. This is also true for Table 4, which compares all of W. Bush's appointees with those of his four immediate predecessors.

744

Table 3: Bush's nontraditional appointees compared to his traditional appointees to the federal appeals courts during his first term

	Nontraditional appointees		Traditional appointees	
Occupation	%	(N)	%	(N)
Politics/ government	8.3%	(1)	27.3%	(6)
Judiciary	83.3%	(10)	27.3%	(6)
Large law firm 100+ members	8.3%	(1)	4.5%	(1)
50–99	—	—	9.1%	(2)
Medium size firm 10–24 members	—	—	13.6%	(3)
Small firm solo	—	—	4.5%	(1)
Professor of law	—	—	9.1%	(2)
Other	—	—	4.5%	(1)
Experience				
Judicial	100%	(12)	40.9%	(9)
Prosecutorial	25.0%	(3)	40.9%	(9)
Neither	0.0%	(0)	36.4%	(8)
Undergraduate education				
Public	41.7%	(5)	31.8%	(7)
Private	50.0%	(6)	45.4%	(10)
Ivy League	8.3%	(1)	22.7%	(5)
Law school education				
Public	41.7%	(5)	36.4%	(8)
Private	41.7%	(5)	27.3%	(6)
Ivy League	16.7%	(2)	36.4%	(8)
Gender				
Male	41.7%	(5)	100%	(22)
Female	58.3%	(7)	—	—
Ethnicity/race				
White	41.7%	(5)	100%	(22)
African American	33.3%	(4)	—	—
Hispanic	25.0%	(3)	—	—
ABA rating				
Well Qualified	66.7%	(8)	68.2%	(15)
Qualified	33.3%	(4)	31.8%	(7)

	Nontraditional appointees		Traditional appointees	
Political identification				
Democrat	16.7%	(2)	—	—
Republican	75.0%	(9)	100%	(22)
None	8.3%	(1)	—	—
Past party activism	33.3%	(4)	86.4%	(19)
Net worth				
Under $200,000	16.7%	(2)	0.0%	—
$200–499,999	16.7%	(2)	22.7%	(5)
$500–999,999	16.7%	(2)	22.7%	(5)
$1+ million	50.0%	(6)	54.5%	(12)
Average age at nomination	51.7		49.9	
Total number of appointees	12		22	

Table 4: U.S. appeals court appointees compared by administration

	W. Bush		Clinton		Bush		Reagan		Carter	
	%	(N)	%	(N)	%	(N)	%	(N)	%	(N)
Occupation										
Politics/government	20.6%	(7)	6.6%	(4)	10.8%	(4)	6.4%	(5)	5.4%	(3)
Judiciary	47.1%	(16)	52.5%	(32)	59.5%	(22)	55.1%	(43)	46.4%	(26)
Large law firm										
100+ members	5.9%	(2)	11.5%	(7)	8.1%	(3)	5.1%	(4)	1.8%	(1)
50–99	5.9%	(2)	3.3%	(2)	8.1%	(3)	2.6%	(2)	5.4%	(3)
25–49	—	—	3.3%	(2)	—	—	6.4%	(5)	3.6%	(2)
Medium size firm										
10–24 members	8.8%	(3)	9.8%	(6)	8.1%	(3)	3.9%	(3)	14.3%	(8)
5–9	—	—	3.3%	(2)	2.7%	(1)	5.1%	(4)	1.8%	(1)
Small firm										
2–4	—	—	1.6%	(1)	—	—	1.3%	(1)	3.6%	(2)
solo	2.9%	(1)	—	—	—	—	—	—	1.8%	(1)
Professor	5.9%	(2)	8.2%	(5)	2.7%	(1)	12.8%	(10)	14.3%	(8)
Other	2.9%	(1)	—	—	—	—	1.3%	(1)	1.8%	(1)
Experience										
Judicial	61.8%	(21)	59.0%	(36)	62.2%	(23)	60.3%	(47)	53.6	(30)
Prosecutorial	35.3%	(12)	37.7%	(23)	29.7%	(11)	28.2%	(22)	30.4	(17)
Neither	23.5%	(8)	29.5%	(18)	32.4%	(12)	34.6%	(27)	39.3	(22)
Undergraduate education										
Public	35.3%	(12)	44.3%	(27)	29.7%	(11)	24.4%	(19)	30.4	(17)
Private	47.1%	(16)	34.4%	(21)	59.5%	(22)	51.3%	(40)	51.8	(29)
Ivy League	17.6%	(6)	21.3%	(13)	10.8%	(4)	24.4%	(19)	17.9	(10)

	W. Bush		Clinton		Bush		Reagan		Carter	
	%	(N)	%	(N)	%	(N)	%	(N)	%	(N)
Law school education										
Public	38.2%	(13)	39.3%	(24)	32.4%	(12)	41.0%	(32)	39.3%	(22)
Private	32.4%	(11)	31.1%	(19)	37.8%	(14)	35.9%	(28)	19.6	(11)
Ivy League	29.4%	(10)	29.5%	(18)	29.7%	(11)	23.1%	(18)	41.1	(23)
Gender										
Male	79.4%	(27)	67.2%	(41)	81.1%	(30)	94.9%	(74)	80.4	(45)
Female	20.6%	(7)	32.8%	(20)	18.9%	(7)	5.1%	(4)	19.6%	(11)
Ethnicity/race										
White	79.4%	(27)	73.8%	(45)	89.2%	(33)	97.4%	(76)	78.6%	(44)
African Amer.	11.8%	(4)	13.1%	(8)	5.4%	(2)	1.3%	(1)	16.1%	(9)
Hispanic	8.8%	(3)	11.5%	(7)	5.4%	(2)	1.3%	(1)	3.6%	(2)
Asian	—	—	1.6%	(1)	—	—	—	—	1.8%	(1)
Percentage white male	64.7%	(22)	49.2%	(30)	70.3%	(26)	92.3%	(72)	60.7%	(34)
ABA Rating										
EWQ/WQ	67.7%	(23)	78.7%	(48)	64.9%	(24)	59.0%	(46)	75.0%	(42)
Qualified	32.4%	(11)	21.3%	(13)	35.1%	(13)	41.0%	(32)	25.0%	(14)
Political identification										
Democrat	5.9%	(2)	85.2%	(52)	2.7%	(1)	—	—	82.1%	(46)
Republican	91.2%	(31)	6.6%	(4)	89.2%	(33)	96.2%	(75)	7.1%	(4)
Other	—	—	—	—	—	—	1.3%	(1)	—	—
None	2.9%	(1)	8.2%	(5)	8.1%	(3)	2.6%	(2)	10.7%	(6)
Past party activism	67.7%	(23)	54.1%	(33)	70.3%	(26)	66.7%	(52)	73.2%	(41)
Net worth										
Under $200,000	5.9%	(2)	4.9%	(3)	5.4%	(2)	15.6%	(12)*	33.3%**	(13)
$200–499,999	20.6%	(7)	14.8%	(9)	29.7%	(11)	32.5%	(25)	38.5%	(15)
$500–999,999	20.6%	(7)	29.5%	(18)	21.6%	(8)	35.1%	(27)	17.9%	(7)
$1+ million	52.9%	(18)	50.8%	(31)	43.2%	(16)	16.9%	(13)	10.3%	(4)
Total number of appointees	34		61		37		78		56	
Average age at nomination	50.5		51.2		487		50.0		51.8	

• Net worth was unavailable for one appointee.

** Net worth only for Carter appointees confirmed by the 96th Congress with the exception of five appointees for whom net worth was unavailable.

Note that the two recess appointments by President W. Bush and the one by President Clinton are not included in the statistics.

A striking finding in Table 3, much like the finding in Table 1, is that nontraditional appointees were drawn principally from the ranks of the judiciary. Ten of the 12 nontraditional appointees were sitting judges at the time of their nominations to the appeals bench. And all had judicial experience. Only about a fourth of the traditional appointees were serving as judges when nominated and less than half had judicial experience. Five of the 12 nontraditional judges were promoted from the federal district bench and one, Roger Gregory, was serving a recess appointment on the U.S. Court of Appeals for the Fourth Circuit at the time of his nomination to a lifetime position on that court. Only four traditional judges of the 22 appointed during Bush's first term were promoted from the district courts. Two of the traditional appointees were law professors at the time of their nominations.

Table 3 shows that somewhat more traditional than nontraditional appointees had prosecutorial experience in their professional profiles. About one third of the traditional appointees had neither judicial nor prosecutorial experience. In terms of legal education, the traditional appointees had the edge when it came to an Ivy League law school education. The ethnic/gender breakdown included five women who were white, one who was African American, and another who was Hispanic American. Among the nontraditional men were two Hispanic Americans and three African Americans. The ABA ratings of the nontraditional and traditional appointees were essentially the same. . . .

Summing up

George W. Bush's first term record of judicial appointments, not surprisingly, suggests that the administration was intensely focused on placing on the bench highly professionally qualified men and women and those with diverse ethnicity who shared the President's judicial philosophy. Although this article did not consider judicial decisional behavior and thus we cannot provide empirical evidence of the extent to which the President was successful in appointing like-minded jurists, the evidence we have presented suggests that the W. Bush cohort of appointees was highly qualified, with the second-highest proportion of nontraditional judges in American history. To this extent, George W. Bush's first term judicial record is a successful one.

Was the Bush administration successful in muting the controversy over judicial appointments? The answer is clearly no, even though ultimately two-thirds of appeals court nominees (34 of 51) and 94.9 percent of district court nominees (168 of 177) were confirmed. The Democratic filibusters of certain appeals court nominees during the 108th Congress and continuing into the 109th gave a very public face to the contentiousness over nominations that previously had occurred behind the scenes. Threats to change the Senate rules that would end a filibuster by a simple majority vote, dubbed the "nuclear option" because of anticipated explosive political fallout, only deepened the divide between Republicans and Democrats.

Clearly the Democrats were sending a message to the President that if he wants his judicial nominees confirmed, including to the Supreme Court, he must aim for more moderate conservatives for whom there would be confidence that they would administer justice fairly and impartially and in fact be neutral arbiters of the law. The President, on the other hand, seemed to be sending a message that he will continue to be resolute in his determination to appoint to the courts those who share his constitutional vision. The outcome of the senatorial elections in 2006 may affect the resolution of this impasse if both sides do not display a willingness to compromise and defuse the tensions.

Nevertheless, on the basis of the statistical portrait of those confirmed during President George W. Bush's first term, we can note that the third branch of government continues to be staffed by an increasingly professionalized judiciary and by those with diverse backgrounds. The tilt, however, is also toward a Republican-appointed bench . . .

To what extent the contentiousness over judicial selection and confirmation and the more recent attacks on the judiciary by some conservative politicians and interest groups will erode the confidence Americans have in the judicial branch of government remains to be seen. Whether the independence of the judiciary likewise will be compromised is a question to be answered by unfolding events. . . .

NOTES AND QUESTIONS

1. Federal judicial selection obviously is a political process. Technical legal skill is but one factor considered by the President and the Senate Judiciary Committee. Political leaders have long considered religious and ethnic background, race and gender important. Why? In part, their concern is symbolic. Appointing Jews, African–Americans or women says something positive about their place in American society. In part, the reasons are political: these appointments satisfy groups from which they come, or repay the work of the people who supported the Administration.

Is there an instrumental significance as well? Did the Supreme Court of the United States decide cases differently than it otherwise would have decided them because Thurgood Marshall, an African–American, or Sandra Day O'Connor, a woman, were Associate Justices, participating in the deliberations and voting? Of course, it would be difficult to prove the influence of any one Justice on the outcome of particular cases. It would be even more difficult to prove what part of their influence turned on their race or gender as opposed to, say, their experience as a civil rights lawyer or as a state political leader. Justice O'Connor said that the Supreme Court was influenced in many ways by Justice Marshall's experiences. See Sandra Day O'Connor, "Thurgood Marshall: The Influence of a Raconteur," 44 *Stanford Law Review* 1217 (1992).

Elaine Martin, "Men and Women on the Bench: Vive la Difference?," 73 *Judicature* 204, 208 (1990), surveyed men and women federal judges appointed by President Carter. She says:

> This study examined the sex role conflicts, sex role attitudes and personality characteristics of men and women federal judges appointed by President Carter in an effort to determine if women brought a perspective

to the federal bench not otherwise represented. In all respects, the findings suggest that women have certain expectations and attitudes that are not the same as men's.

Despite their high status as judicial elites, women federal judges continue to carry a heavier burden at home and experience more conflict between their parental and career roles than their men colleagues. The majority of women had to overcome sex discrimination, as well as sex-role conflict, in order to purse their legal careers. Women judges remain attuned to the difficulties that other women face in combining family and career as evidenced by their advice to young women lawyers.

Women judges in this study, perhaps as a consequence of these personal experiences, evidence greater attitudinal feminism than men. Women are also stronger in their support of increased political, judicial and social roles for women than men judges.

There are a variety of ways in which the different perspectives represented by the women studied here could have an impact on their behavior as judges. Their differences might influence such things as decisional output, especially in cases involving sex discrimination; conduct of courtroom business, especially as regards sexist behavior by litigators; influence on sex-role attitudes held by their male colleagues, especially on appellate courts where decisions are collegial; administrative behavior, for example, in hiring women law clerks; and . . . collective actions, through formal organizations, undertaken to heighten the judicial system's response to gender bias problems in both law and process. . . .

[A]ny gender differences among judges in voting and sentencing behavior may be limited to a narrow category of cases. . . . All women are not alike any more than all men are alike. As the numbers of women judges increase, more sophisticated analysis can include such variables as judicial role orientations, feminist ideology and political partisanship . . .

See also Peter McCormick and Twyla Job, "Do Women Judges Make a Difference? An Analysis by Appeal Court Data," 8 *Canadian Journal of Law and Society* 135 (1993). The authors found no evidence from a large sample of cases that women judges responded to legal issues in ways that distinguished them from men judges. The authors felt that "the class and character preferences built into the triple hurdles of university entrance, law school admission, and judicial recruitment," combined with the traditions and prejudices of the profession, "may seriously limit the immediate impact of women on the bench" (p. 147). For a critique of this article, suggesting that the differences are too subtle to be captured by the kind of research employed, see Joan Brockman, A Difference without a Distinction (id at 149). Compare Claire L'Heureux–Dubé, "Outsiders on the Bench: The Continuing Struggle for Equality," 16 *Wisconsin Women's Law Journal* 15, 21 (2001). The author is a justice on the Supreme Court of Canada. She says: "women and members of minority groups who beat the odds and attain an appointment to the bench in our countries are still very much treated as 'outsiders,' interlopers in a white, male-dominated judiciary.''

In an interesting study, Joyce Sterling in 1990–1991 surveyed the attitudes of practicing lawyers in Colorado toward women judges. Joyce S. Sterling, ''The Impact of Gender Bias on Judging: Survey of Attitudes Toward Women Judges,'' 22 *Colorado Lawyer* 257 (1993). Sterling found that women judges ranked significantly lower than male judges, as appraised by lawyers. The lawyers also, somewhat surprisingly, ranked women judges much lower than men on items that dealt with courtesy, compassion, and satisfactory performance in settling cases. Were these rankings just gender bias? Perhaps, but women lawyers were just as negative, or more so, with regard to these attributes. Were women judges too tough? If so, was it because they were trying not to appear ''feminine'' and weak?

It is fair to say that questions about the impact of race, ethnicity and gender on the judging process are still open. Certainly, the existing small amount of research does not give definitive answers. What would you expect to be the result if the bench came to ''look like America?'' Suppose the proportion of women and minority judges was about what it was in the general population. What changes, if any, might come about in style or substance? Why? What is there in the experiences of women and minority group members that might affect their behavior? What factors in the ideology and structures of the legal system might, to some extent, offset the gender or race of the judges? See Donald R. Songer, Sue Davis and Susan Haire, ''A Reappraisal of Diversification in the Federal Courts: Gender Effects in the Courts of Appeals,'' 56 *Journal of Politics* 425 (1994). In this study of obscenity, search and seizure and employment discrimination cases, female judges differed from their male colleagues only in employment discrimination decisions. See, also, Elaine Martin, ''Differences in Men and Women Judges: Perspectives on Gender,'' 27 *Journal of Political Science* 74 (1989); John Gruhl, Cassia Spohn and Susan Welch, ''Women as Policy Makers: The Case of Trial Judges,'' 25 *American Journal of Political Science* 308 (1981).

Carol T. Kulik, Elissa L. Perry and Molly B. Pepper, ''Here Comes the Judge: The Influence of Judge Personal Characteristics on Federal Sexual Harassment Case Outcomes,'' 27 *Law and Human Behavior* 69 (2003), looked at 143 cases dealing with sexual harassment. These cases involved the behavior of federal district judges who sit alone trying these cases. They found that plaintiffs were more likely to win their cases if the judge was younger than 50 or had been appointed by a Democratic president.

> When the case was heard by an older judge, the probability that the decision would favor the plaintiff was only 16%. However, the probability of a decision favoring the plaintiff when the case was heard by a younger judge was 45%. When the case was heard by a judge who had been appointed by a Republican president, the probability that the decision would favor the plaintiff was only 18%. However, the probability of a

decision favoring the plaintiff when the judge had been appointed by a Democrat president was 46%. (p. 80)

The results indicated that there were no effects of judge gender or race.

Jennifer L. Peresie, "Female Judges Matter: Gender and Collegial Decisionmaking in the Federal Appellate Courts," 114 *Yale Law Journal* 1759, 1778 (2005), conducted an empirical analysis of 556 federal appellate cases dealing with sexual harassment or sex discrimination that were decided in 1999, 2000 and 2001. Unlike the Kulik, Perry and Pepper study that dealt with trial judges, these cases were decided by appellate judges sitting in panels of three. Peresie found:

> Male judges were more likely to find for plaintiffs when at least one female judge was on the panel. Because the regressions controlled for ideology, the results indicate that regardless of the ideology of the male judge, sitting on a panel with a female judge increased the likelihood that he found for the plaintiff.... [A]dding a female judge to the panel more than doubled the probability that a male judge ruled for the plaintiff in sexual harassment cases (increasing the probability from 16% to 35%) and nearly tripled this probability in sex discrimination cases (increasing it from 11% to 30%). Further, conservative male judges were affected as much as liberal male judges were by the presence of a female judge.

Why might gender matter at the appellate but not at the trial level?

(5.9) Ideological Voting on Federal Courts of Appeals: A Preliminary Investigation

Cass R. Sunstein, David Schkade, & Lisa Michelle Ellman

90 *Virginia Law Review* 301 (2004).

Introduction

Over many decades, the United States has been conducting an extraordinary natural experiment with respect to the performance of federal judges. The experiment involves the relationship between political ideology and judicial decisions. Many people believe that political ideology should not and generally does not affect legal judgments, and this belief contains some truth. Frequently the law is clear, and judges should and will simply implement it, whatever their political commitments. But what happens when the law is unclear? What role does ideology play then? We can easily imagine two quite different positions. It might be predicted that even when the law is unclear, ideology does not matter; the legal culture imposes a discipline on judges, so that judges vote as judges, rather than as ideologues. Or it might be predicted that in hard cases, the judges' "attitudes" end up predicting their votes, so that liberal judges show systematically different votes from those of conservative judges.

It is extremely difficult to investigate these questions directly. It is possible, however, to identify a proxy for political ideology: the political affiliation of the appointing president. Presidents are frequently interested in ensuring that judicial appointees are of a certain stripe. A Democratic president is unlikely to want to appoint judges who will seek to overrule *Roe v. Wade* and strike down affirmative action programs. A Republican president is unlikely to want to appoint judges who will interpret the Constitution to require states to recognize same-sex marriages. It is reasonable to hypothesize that as a statistical regularity, judges appointed by Republican presidents (hereinafter described, for ease of exposition, as Republican appointees) will be more conservative than judges appointed by Democratic presidents (Democratic appointees, as we shall henceforth call them). But is this hypothesis true? When is it true, and to what degree is it true?

More subtly, we might speculate that federal judges are subject to "panel effects"—that on a three-judge panel, a judge's likely vote is influenced by the other two judges assigned to the same panel. In particular, does a judge vote differently depending on whether she is sitting with zero, one, or two judges appointed by a president of the same political party? On one view, a Republican appointee, sitting with two Democratic appointees, should be more likely to vote as Democratic appointees typically do, whereas a Democratic appointee, sitting with two Republican appointees, should be more likely to vote as Republican appointees typically do. But is this in fact the usual pattern? Is it an invariable one? Since judges in a given circuit are assigned to panels (and, therefore, to cases) randomly, the existence of a large data set allows these issues to be investigated empirically.

In this Essay, we will examine a subset of possible case types, focusing on a number of controversial issues that seem especially likely to reveal divisions between Republican and Democratic appointees. In brief, we will explore cases involving abortion, affirmative action, campaign finance, capital punishment, Commerce Clause challenges to congressional enactments, the Contracts Clause, criminal appeals, disability discrimination, industry challenges to environmental regulation, piercing the corporate veil, race discrimination, sex discrimination, and claimed takings of private property without just compensation. We will offer a more detailed description of our subjects and methods below.

The central purpose of this Essay is to examine three hypotheses:

1. Ideological voting. In ideologically contested cases, a judge's ideological tendency can be predicted by the party of the appointing president; Republican appointees vote very differently from Democratic appointees. Ideologically contested cases involve many of the issues just mentioned, such as affirmative action, campaign finance, federalism, the rights of criminal defendants, sex discrimination, piercing the corporate veil, racial discrimination, property rights, capital punishment, disability discrimination, sexual harassment, and abortion.

2. Ideological dampening. A judge's ideological tendency, in such cases, is likely to be dampened if she is sitting with two judges of a different political party. For example, a Democratic appointee should be less likely to vote in a stereotypically liberal fashion if accompanied by two Republican appointees, and a Republican appointee should be less likely to vote in a stereotypically conservative fashion if accompanied by two Democratic appointees.

3. *Ideological amplification.* A judge's ideological tendency, in such cases, is likely to be amplified if she is sitting with two judges from the same political party. A Democratic appointee should show an increased tendency to vote in a stereotypically liberal fashion if accompanied by two Democratic appointees, and a Republican appointee should be more likely to vote in a stereotypically conservative fashion if accompanied by two Republican appointees.

We find that in numerous areas of the law, all three hypotheses are strongly confirmed. Each finds support in federal cases involving campaign finance, affirmative action, sex discrimination, sexual harassment, piercing the corporate veil, racial discrimination, disability discrimination, Contracts Clause violations, and review of environmental regulations. In such cases, our aggregate data strongly confirm all three hypotheses. Indeed, we find many extreme cases of ideological dampening, which we might call "leveling effects," in which party differences are wiped out by the influence of panel composition. With leveling effects, Democratic appointees, when sitting with two Republican appointees, are as likely to vote in the stereotypically conservative fashion as are Republican appointees when sitting with two Democratic appointees. We also find strong amplification effects, such that if the data set in the relevant cases is taken as a whole, Democratic appointees, sitting with two Democratic appointees, are about twice as likely to vote in the stereotypically liberal fashion as are Republican appointees, sitting with two Republican appointees—a far larger disparity than the disparity between Democratic and Republican votes when either is sitting with one Democratic appointee and one Republican appointee.

In most of the areas investigated here, the political party of the appointing president is a fairly good predictor of how individual judges will vote. But in those same areas, the political party of the president who appointed the other two judges on the panel is at least as good a predictor of how individual judges will vote. All in all, Democratic appointees show somewhat greater susceptibility to panel effects than do Republican appointees.

But there are noteworthy counterexamples to our general findings. In three important areas, ideology does not predict judicial votes, and hence all three hypotheses are refuted. This is the pattern in criminal appeals, takings claims, and Commerce Clause challenges to congressional enactments. In two other areas, the first hypothesis is supported, but the second and third hypotheses are refuted. These two areas are abortion and capital punishment. In each of these areas, judges apparently vote their convictions and are not affected by panel composition.

We offer a number of other findings. We show that variations in panel composition lead to dramatically different outcomes, in a way that creates serious problems for the rule of law. In the cases we analyze, a panel composed of three Democratic appointees issues a liberal ruling 61% of the time, whereas a panel composed of three Republican appointees issues a liberal ruling only 34% of the time. A panel composed of two Republican appointees and one Democrat issues a liberal ruling 39% of the time; a panel composed of two Democratic appointees and one Republican does so 50% of the time. These differences certainly do not show that the likely result is foreordained by the composition of the panel; there is a substantial overlap between the votes of Republican appointees and those of Democratic appointees. Ideology is hardly everything. But the litigant's chances, in the cases we examine, are significantly affected by the luck of the draw.

To understand the importance of group dynamics on judicial panels, it is important to emphasize that a Democratic majority, or a Republican majority, has enough votes to do what it wishes. Apparently a large disciplining effect comes from the presence of a single panelist from another party. Hence all-Republican panels show far more conservative patterns than majority Republican panels, and all-Democratic panels show far more liberal patterns than majority Democratic panels.

Our tale is largely one of effects from ideology on individual voting and panel outcomes. But it is important not to overstate those effects. The pool of cases studied here is limited to domains where ideology would be expected to play a large role. Outside of such domains, Republican and Democratic appointees are far less likely to differ. The absence of party effects in important and contested areas (criminal law, takings, and federalism) testifies to the possibility of commonalities across partisan lines, even when differences might be expected. And even where party differences are statistically significant, they are not huge. In the entire sample, Democratic appointees issue a liberal vote 51% of the time, whereas Republicans do so 38% of the time. The full story emphasizes the significant effects of ideology and also the limited nature of those effects. We shall spend considerable time on the complexities here....

Our main goal in this Essay is simply to present and analyze the data—to show the extent to which the three hypotheses find vindication. But we also aim to give some explanation for our findings and to relate them to some continuing debates about the role of ideology on federal panels. Our data do not reveal whether ideological dampening is a product of persuasion or a form of collegiality. If Republican appointees show a liberal pattern of votes when accompanied by two Democratic appointees, it might be because they are convinced by their colleagues. Alternatively, they might suppress their private doubts and accept the majority's view. It is also possible that they are able to affect the reasoning in the majority opinion, trading their vote for a more moderate statement of the law. In any case, it is reasonable to say that the data show the pervasiveness of the "collegial concurrence": a concurrence by a judge who signs the panel's opinion either because he is persuaded by the shared opinion of the two other judges on the panel or because it is not worthwhile, all things considered, to dissent. The collegial concurrence can be taken as an example, in the unlikely setting of judicial panels, of responsiveness to conformity pressures. These pressures make it more likely that people will end up silencing themselves, or even publicly agreeing with a majority position, simply because they would otherwise be isolated in their disagreement. We will discuss these issues at greater length after presenting the data.

We also find evidence within the federal judiciary of "group polarization," by which like-minded people move toward a more extreme position in the same direction as their predeliberation views. If all-Republican panels are overwhelmingly likely to strike down campaign finance regulation, and if all-Democratic panels are overwhelmingly likely to uphold affirmative action programs, group polarization is likely to be a reason. Finally, we offer indirect evidence of a "whistleblower effect": A single judge of another party, while likely to be affected by the fact that he is isolated, might also influence other judges on the panel, at least where the panel would otherwise fail to follow existing law.

We believe that our findings are of considerable interest in themselves. They also reveal much about human behavior in many contexts. A great deal of social science evidence shows conformity effects: When people are confronted with the views of unanimous others, they tend to yield. Sometimes they yield because they believe that unanimous others cannot be wrong; sometimes they yield because it is not worthwhile to dissent in public. In addition, a great deal of social science evidence shows that like-minded people tend to go to extremes. In the real world, this hypothesis is extremely hard to test in light of the range of confounding variables. But our data provide strong evidence that like-minded judges also go to extremes: The probability that a judge will vote in one or another direction is increased by the presence of judges appointed by the president of the same political party. In short, we claim to show both strong conformity effects and group polarization within federal courts of appeals. If these effects can be shown there, then they are also likely to be found in many other diverse contexts.

In fact, the presence of such effects raises doubts about what is probably the most influential method for explaining judicial voting: the "attitudinal model." According to the attitudinal model, judges have certain "attitudes" toward areas of the law, and these attitudes are good predictors of judicial votes in difficult cases. Insofar as party effects are present, our findings are broadly supportive of this idea. But the attitudinal model does not come to terms with panel effects, which can both dampen and amplify the tendencies to which judicial "attitudes" give rise. Since panel effects are generally as large as party effects, and sometimes even larger, the attitudinal model misses a crucial factor behind judicial votes.

A disclaimer: We have collected a great deal of data, but our subtitle—a preliminary investigation—should be taken very seriously. The federal reporters offer an astonishingly large data set for judicial votes, including over two hundred years of votes ranging over countless substantive areas. Our own investigation is limited to several areas that, by general agreement, are ideologically contested, enough to produce possible disagreements in the cases that find their way to the courts of appeals. Of course it would be extremely interesting to know much more. Might ideological voting and panel effects be found in apparently nonideological cases involving, for example, bankruptcy, torts, and civil procedure? What about the important areas of antitrust and labor law? How do the three hypotheses fare in the early part of the twentieth century, when federal courts were confronting the regulatory state for the first time? In cases involving minimum wage and maximum hour laws, did Republican appointees differ from Democratic appointees, and were panel effects also significant? Do the hypotheses hold in the segregation cases of the 1960s and 1970s? In the future, it should be possible to use the techniques discussed here to test a wide range of hypotheses about judicial voting patterns. One of our central goals is to provide a method for future analysis, a method that can be used in countless contexts.

This Essay will be organized as follows. Part I will offer the basic data, testing the three hypotheses in a number of areas. Part II will disaggregate the data by exploring circuit results. Part III will speculate about the reasons for the various findings, with special attention to collegial concurrences, group polarization, and whistleblower effects. Part IV will investigate some normative issues.

I. The Three Hypotheses

A. *Aggregate Data*

We examined a total of 4958 published majority three-judge panel decisions, and the 14,874 associated individual judge's votes, in areas involving abortion, capital punishment, the Americans with Disabilities Act, criminal appeals, takings, the Contracts Clause, affirmative action, Title VII race discrimination cases brought by African–American plaintiffs, sex discrimination, campaign finance, sexual harassment, cases in which plaintiffs sought to pierce the corporate veil, industry challenges to environmental regulations, and federalism challenges to congressional enactments under the Commerce Clause. Our methods for finding and assessing these cases . . . leave room for errors and for a degree of discretion. We are confident, however, that the basic pattern of our results is sound. To keep the inquiry manageable, our investigation is limited to recent time periods (sometimes from 1995 to the present, though sometimes longer, certainly when necessary to produce a sufficient number of cases in a particular category). We believe that limited though the evidence is, our results are sufficient to show the range of likely patterns and also to establish the claim that the three principal hypotheses are often vindicated.

Our sample is limited to published opinions. This limitation obviously simplifies research, but it also follows from our basic goal, which is to test the role of ideology in difficult cases rather than easy ones. As a general rule, unpublished opinions are widely agreed to be simple and straightforward and to involve no difficult or complex issues of law. To be sure, publication practices are not uniform across circuits, and hence the decision to focus on published cases complicates cross-circuit comparisons. But that decision enables us to test our hypotheses in the cases that most interest us (and the public), while also producing at least considerable information about the role of party and panel effects across circuits.

Table 1. Summary of Votes by Individual Judges and Majority Decisions of Three-Judge Panels
(proportion voting for the liberal position on the given issue)

Case Type	Individual Judges' Votes							Panel Majority Decisions				
	Party			Panel Colleagues				Panel Composition				
	R	D	D - R	RR	RD	DD	DD - RR	RRR	RRD	RDD	DDD	DDD - RRR
Campaign finance (vote to uphold)	.28	.46	.18	.29	.34	.53	.24	.23	.30	.35	.80	.57
Affirmative action (vote for)	.48	.74	.26	.47	.62	.73	.26	.37	.50	.83	.85	.48
EPA (vote against industry)	.46	.64	.18	.48	.54	.66	.19	.27	.55	.62	.72	.45
Sex discrimination (vote for Plaintiff)	.35	.51	.16	.36	.41	.57	.21	.31	.38	.49	.75	.44
Contracts (reject const challenge)	.24	.30	.06	.19	.26	.45	.26	.16	.26	.32	.50	.34
Pierce corp veil (vote to pierce)	.27	.41	.14	.25	.31	.51	.26	.23	.29	.37	.56	.33
ADA (vote for Plaintiff)	.26	.43	.17	.24	.35	.45	.21	.18	.27	.47	.50	.32
Abortion (vote pro-choice)	.49	.70	.21	.58	.55	.65	.07	.53	.51	.62	.78	.25
Capital punishment (vote against)	.20	.42	.22	.29	.29	.30	.01	.18	.22	.38	.33	.15
Title VII cases (vote for Plaintiff)	.35	.41	.06	.39	.35	.42	.04	.43	.31	.45	.56	.13
Federalism (vote to uphold)	.95	.99	.04	.96	.97	.97	.01	.97	1.00	.98	1.00	.03
Criminal (vote for Defendant)	.33	.36	.03	.33	.33	.33	.00	.31	.31	.40	.34	.02
Takings clause (find no taking)	.23	.20	-.03	.23	.20	.23	.00	.26	.17	.24	.25	-.01
Average across all case types	.38	.51	.13	.39	.43	.52	.14	.34	.39	.50	.61	.27
Case types with a panel difference	.34	.50	.16	.35	.40	.53	.17	.29	.36	.49	.64	.35

Table 1 shows the percentage of stereotypically liberal votes in a variety of areas. It reveals both individual votes and majority decisions of three-judge panels. Note first that in a number of areas, there is strong evidence of ideological voting in the sense that Democratic appointees are more likely to vote in the stereotypically liberal direction than are Republican appointees. We measure ideological voting by subtracting the percentage of liberal Republican votes from the percentage of liberal Democratic votes; the larger the number, the larger the party effect. The overall difference is 13%—not huge, but substantial. The extent of this effect, and even its existence, is variable across areas. We shall discuss these variations shortly.

We can also see that the votes of judges are influenced by the party affiliation of the other two judges on the same panel. As a first approximation, we measure this influence by subtracting the overall percentage of liberal votes by a judge of either party when sitting with two Democratic appointees from the percentage when he or she sits with two Republican appointees. Surprisingly, this overall difference, 14%, is as large as the basic difference between parties. This is our simple measure of panel effects, though it is part of a more complex story. As we shall see, there are multiple ways to assess the influence of the other judges on the panel.

Finally, it is clear that these two influences result in actual decisions that are very much affected by the composition of the panel. The clearest point is a sharp spread between the average outcome in an all-Republican panel and that in an all-Democratic panel. Indeed, the likelihood of a liberal outcome is roughly twice as high with the latter as with the former. For litigants in highly controversial areas, a great deal depends on the luck of the draw—the outcome of a random assignment of judges.

Figure 1. Party and Panel Influences on Votes of Individual Judges
(on average for ideological case types)

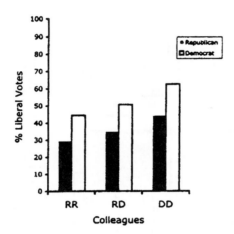

Figure 1 captures the aggregate party and panel effects across those areas in which there is ideological voting. The most striking lessons of this figure are our principal themes here. For both Democratic appointees and Republican appointees, the likelihood of a liberal vote jumps when the two other panel members are Democratic appointees, and it drops when the two other panel members are Republican appointees. For purposes of discussion, we might take, as the baseline, cases in which a judge is sitting with one Democrat and one Republican, and compare how voting patterns shift when a judge is sitting instead with two Democratic appointees or two Republican appointees. We can readily see that a Democrat, in the baseline condition, casts a liberal vote 51% of the time, whereas a Republican does so 35% of the time. Sitting with two Democratic appointees, Democratic appointees cast liberal votes 63% of the time, whereas Republican appointees do so 44% of the time. Sitting with two Republican appointees, Democratic appointees cast liberal votes 45% of the time, whereas Republican appointees do so only 30% of the time. Thus, Republican appointees sitting with two Democratic appointees show the same basic pattern of votes as do Democratic appointees sitting with two Republican appointees.

The aggregate figures conceal some significant differences across case categories. We begin with cases in which all three hypotheses are supported and then turn to cases in which they are not.

Figure 2. Voting Patterns for Case Types with Both Party and Panel Effects

(■ (black) = Republican appointees, □ (white) = Democratic appointees)

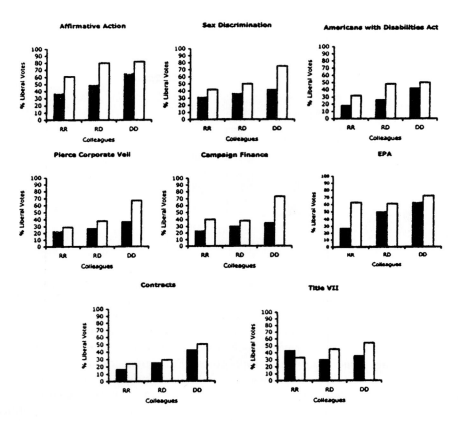

B.   *All Hypotheses Supported*

1.   Affirmative Action

Let us start with affirmative action, which shows the basic pattern of results as in the aggregate data (Figure 2). From 1978 through 2002, Republican appointees cast 267 total votes, with 127, or 48%, in favor of upholding an affirmative action policy. By contrast, Democratic appointees cast 198 votes, with 147, or 74%, in favor of upholding an affirmative action policy. Here we find striking evidence of ideological voting. We also find significant evidence of panel effects. An isolated Democrat sitting with two Republican appointees votes for affirmative action only 61% of the time—halfway between the aggregate numbers for Democratic appointees and Republican appointees. More remarkably, isolated Democratic appointees are actually slightly less likely to vote for affirmative action programs than are isolated Republican appointees, who vote in favor 65% of the time. Thus, we see strong evidence of ideological dampening.

The third hypothesis is also confirmed. On all-Republican panels, individual Republican appointees vote for affirmative action programs only 37% of the time—but 49% of the time when Republican appointees hold a two-to-one majority. On all-Democratic panels, individual Democratic appointees vote in favor of the plan 82% of the time, compared to 80% with a two-judge Democratic majority. An institution defending an affirmative action program has about a one-in-three chance of success before an all-Republican panel— but more than a four-in-five chance before an all-Democratic panel! In a pattern that pervades many of the doctrinal areas, the rate of pro-affirmative action votes on all-Democratic panels is almost triple the corresponding rate of Republican votes on all-Republican panels.

2. *Sex Discrimination*

In sex discrimination cases from 1995 to the present, Republican appointees voted in favor of plaintiffs 35% of the time, whereas Democratic appointees voted for plaintiffs 51% of the time. Hence we find strong evidence of ideological voting, though not as strong as in the affirmative action context. When in the minority, Republican appointees vote in favor of sex discrimination plaintiffs 42% of the time, identical to the 42% rate of Democratic appointees when they are in the minority. The most striking number here is the percentage of pro-plaintiff votes when three Democratic appointees are sitting together. Here 75% of Democratic votes favor plaintiffs, far higher than the rates of 50% or less when Democratic appointees sit with one or more Republican appointees. On all-Republican panels, Republican appointees vote at a strongly anti-plaintiff rate, with only 31% favoring plaintiffs; this rate increases steadily with each Democrat on a panel.

3. *Sexual Harassment*

Sexual harassment cases are a subset of sex discrimination cases; for that reason, they have not been included as a separate entry in our aggregate figures. But because the area is of considerable independent interest, we have conducted a separate analysis of sexual harassment cases. Republican appointees vote in favor of plaintiffs at a rate of 37%, whereas Democratic appointees vote for plaintiffs at a rate of 52%. Sitting with two Democratic appointees, Republican appointees are more likely to vote for plaintiffs than Democratic appointees sitting with two Republican appointees by a margin of 44% to 41%. On all-Democratic panels, Democratic appointees vote for plaintiffs at a 76% rate, more than double the 32% rate of Republican appointees on all-Republican panels. It might be expected that gender would be relevant to rulings in sexual harassment cases, and for this reason we did a separate analysis of whether gender predicts likely votes. The answer is that gender does not matter. Female judges are not more likely than male judges to vote in favor of plaintiffs in our sample of these cases, and judges who sit with one or more female judges are not more likely to vote for plaintiffs than those who sit only with male judges. The party of the appointing president, not gender, is the important variable.

4. Disability

Under the Americans with Disabilities Act, judges of both parties are influenced by the colleagues with whom they sit on a panel. In data collected for the period from 1998 to 2002, 45 Republican appointees vote 26% of the time in favor of plaintiffs; sitting with one Republican and one Democrat, the rate is 25%, about the same as the aggregate figure. When sitting with two Republican appointees, however, the rate drops to 18%, and when sitting with two Democratic appointees, it jumps to 42%. Democratic percentages move in the same directions, though with a slightly different pattern. The overall pro-plaintiff vote is 43%, but it is 32% when a Democratic appointee sits with two Republican appointees (significantly lower than the 42% rate for Republican appointees sitting with two Democratic appointees), and it rises to 48% with one other Democrat and to 50% on all-Democratic panels.

5. Piercing the Corporate Veil

Cases in which plaintiffs attempt to pierce the corporate veil follow a very similar pattern to sex discrimination cases, with all three hypotheses confirmed. Republican appointees accept such claims at a significantly lower rate than Democratic appointees: 27% as opposed to 41%. But here as elsewhere, Republicans sitting with two Democratic appointees, voting 37% in favor of veil-piercing, are more liberal than Democrats sitting with two Republican appointees, voting in favor of piercing only 29% of the time. The most extreme figures in the data involve unified panels. Here, too, the pro-plaintiff voting percentage of Democratic appointees on all-Democratic panels is almost triple the corresponding number for Republican appointees on all-Republican panels: 67% as opposed to 23%.

6. Campaign Finance

In cases since 1976, Republican appointees cast only 28% of their votes in favor of upholding campaign finance laws, substantially lower than the 46% rate for Democratic appointees. Hence the first hypothesis—ideological voting—is tentatively supported. With respect to the second hypothesis, involving ideological dampening, the results are suggestive as well. When sitting with two Democratic appointees, Republican appointees vote to uphold campaign finance laws 35% of the time. When sitting with two Republican appointees, Democratic appointees vote for such programs 40% of the time.

Now we turn to the third hypothesis, involving ideological amplification. On all-Republican panels, Republican appointees vote to uphold 23% of the time, while on all-Democratic panels, Democratic appointees vote to uphold 73% of the time. The corresponding numbers on two-judge majority panels are 30% and 38% respectively. Thus, there is evidence of a substantial difference between the behavior of all-Democratic panels and Democratic majority panels—but Republican judges tend to vote the same regardless of whether they are on unified panels or Republican majority panels.

7. *Environmental Regulation*

. . . [W]e limit our investigation to the D.C. Circuit, which hears the vast majority of environmental cases. From 1970 through 2002, Democratic appointees voted against agency challenges 64% of the time, whereas Republican appointees did so 46% of the time. There are also significant findings of group influence. Republican appointees show ideological amplification. On all-Republican panels, Republican appointees vote against industry challenges just 27% of the time, but for members of two-Republican majorities this figure rises rapidly to 50%, and finally to 63% for a single minority Republican.

Interestingly, Democratic appointees do not show ideological amplification in this domain. A single Democratic appointee accompanied by two Republican appointees votes against industry challenges 63% of the time, but when joined by two Democratic appointees, the rate rises only to 72%. Their invalidation votes are largely impervious to panel effects.... [H]owever, ideological amplification can be found among Democratic appointees when an environmental group is challenging agency action. A panel of three Democratic appointees is more likely to accept the challenge than a panel of two Democratic appointees and one Republican. The likelihood that a Democrat will vote in favor of an environmentalist challenge is highest when three Democratic appointees are on the panel—and lowest when the panel has two Republican appointees.

8. *Contracts Clause Violations*

We examined Contracts Clause cases with the thought that Republican appointees would be more sympathetic than Democratic appointees to Contracts Clause claims. Our speculation to this effect was rooted in the fact that conservative academics have argued for stronger judicial protection of contractual rights through constitutional rulings. But our speculation turned out to be wrong. There is mild evidence of ideological voting with respect to the Contracts Clause, but it runs in the opposite direction from what we predicted, apparently because those who make Contracts Clause objections are more sympathetic to Democratic than to Republican appointees.

In cases from 1977 to the present, Republican appointees vote on behalf of plaintiffs 24% of the time, whereas Democratic appointees do so 30% of the time. More striking in this context are the panel effects, which are large for both parties. On all-Democratic panels, Democratic appointees vote in favor of plaintiffs 50% of the time; on all-Republican panels, Republican appointees vote in favor of plaintiffs only 16% of the time. Moreover, the dampening effects are large and in the predicted direction. Sitting with two Democratic appointees, Republican appointees vote in favor of plaintiffs in 42% of the cases, whereas a Democrat sitting with two Republican appointees does so just 24% of the time.

9.   *Title VII*

In cases brought under Title VII by African–American plaintiffs, we find small but nearly statistically significant evidence of ideological voting: Democratic appointees vote for plaintiffs 41% of the time, whereas Republican appointees do so 35% of the time. The small size of the difference is noteworthy, and we are not entirely sure how to explain it. Democratic appointees show ideological dampening, with a 33% pro-plaintiff vote when sitting with two Republican appointees, and ideological amplification, with a 54% pro-plaintiff vote when sitting with two Democratic appointees. The pattern for Republican appointees is a puzzle. When sitting with two Republican appointees, Republican appointees actually vote for plaintiffs at a higher rate—43%—than when sitting with one or more Democratic appointees. When sitting with two Democratic appointees, Republican appointees vote for plaintiffs at a 35% rate, slightly higher than the 30% rate shown when sitting with one Democrat and one Republican. Overall, this pattern is similar to others with both party and colleague effects, except for the apparently anomalous voting of all-Republican panels, for which we have no good explanation.

C.   *All Hypotheses Rebutted*

In three areas, all of our hypotheses were rebutted (Figure 3). The simple reason is that in these areas there is no significant difference between the votes of Republican appointees and those of Democratic appointees. Contrary to expectations, the political affiliation of the appointing president does not matter in the contexts of criminal appeals, federalism, and takings.

Figure 3. Voting Patterns for Case Types with Neither Party nor Panel Effects
(■ (black) = Republican appointees, □ (white) = Democratic appointees)

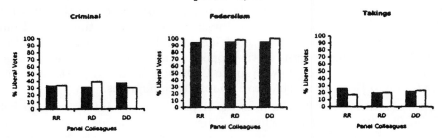

1. Criminal Appeals

It might be anticipated that Democratic appointees would be especially sympathetic to criminal defendants and that Republican appointees would be relatively unsympathetic. At least this is a popular platitude about judicial behavior. Hence the three hypotheses might be anticipated to receive strong support. But all of them are rejected, at least in three courts of appeals from 1995 to the present. We selected the courts of appeals for the D.C. Circuit and for the Third and Fourth Circuits on the theory that we would be highly likely to find ideological voting in criminal cases in those circuits. (We follow widespread but informal lore here, which suggests that ideological splits are especially severe on these circuits.) But we found no such effects. The overall rate of votes for defendants is between 30% and 39%, with no significant differences between Republican appointees and Democratic appointees and without significant panel effects. We conclude that Republican appointees and Democratic appointees do not much differ in this domain; we attempt to explain this finding below.

2. Federalism and the Commerce Clause

Since 1995, the overwhelming majority of federal judicial votes have been in favor of the constitutionality of programs challenged under the Commerce Clause. Indeed, Democratic appointees vote to validate the challenged program over 99% of the time! The numbers are not materially different for Republican appointees, for whom the overall validation rate is 95%. No panel effects are observed. A possible reason for the agreement is that for many decades, the United States Supreme Court gave a clear signal that courts should be reluctant to invalidate congressional enactments under the Commerce Clause. To be sure, the Court has provided important recent signs of willingness to invoke that clause against Congress. But neither Republican nor Democratic appointees seem to believe that those signals should be taken very seriously. Perhaps things will change in this regard as the lower courts internalize the Court's messages. One qualification about our findings should be noted here: The difference between Republican and Democratic appointees is statistically significant. But this apparent difference is only of technical interest, since both groups of judges vote to uphold nearly 100% of the time, and panels vote to uphold at least 97% of the time regardless of which combination of judges sits on a panel (see Table 1).

3. Takings

When plaintiffs challenge a governmental decision as violative of property rights, Democratic appointees and Republican appointees again show no significant differences in voting. Only 23% of Republican votes are in favor of such challenges. It might be expected that Democratic appointees would show a substantially lower level of invalidation rates, but the percentage of Democratic votes to invalidate is nearly identical: 20%. No panel effects can be found. Note in this connection that our investigation did not include the

Court of Claims, where, according to informal lore, ideological divisions are common. It would be valuable to know whether a study of that court would uncover party and panel effects.

D. Ideological Voting Without Amplification or Dampening: The Unique Cases of Abortion and Capital Punishment

It is possible to imagine areas dominated by ideological voting. In such areas, judges would be expected to vote in a way that reflects the political affiliation of the appointing president—but panel effects would be minimal. This is the pattern of outcomes in only two areas that we investigated: abortion and capital punishment (Figure 4).

Figure 4. Voting Patterns for Case Types with Only a Party Effect
(■ (black) = Republican appointees, □ (white) = Democratic appointees)

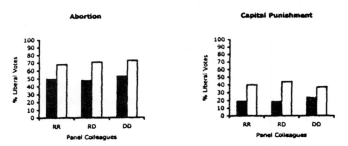

Democratic appointees cast pro-choice votes 70% of the time, compared to 49% for Republican appointees. Here again we find evidence of ideological voting. But panel effects are absent. Sitting with two Democratic appointees, Republican appointees vote in favor of invalidation 53% of the time, not appreciably different from the 48% rate when sitting with one or more Republican appointees and the 50% invalidation rate in all-Republican panels. Similarly, sitting with two Republican appointees, Democratic appointees vote in favor of abortion rights 68% of the time, not much less than the 71% and 73% rates when sitting with one or two other Democratic appointees, respectively. The failure of the third hypothesis is even more striking. A Republican vote on an all-Republican panel is essentially the same as on a panel of two Republican appointees and one Democrat. A Democratic vote on an all-Democratic panel is essentially the same as on a panel of two Democratic appointees and one Republican.

Capital punishment shows a similar pattern: a large party difference but no other significant effects. Republican appointees vote for defendants 19% of the time on all-Republican panels, 19% of the time on majority Republican panels, and 24% of the time on majority Democratic panels. Democratic appointees vote for defendants 37% of the time on all-Democratic panels, 44%

of the time on majority Democratic panels, and 40% of the time on majority Republican panels.

E. *Panel Decisions*

Thus far we have focused on the votes of individual judges. For litigants and the law, of course, it is not the votes of individual judges, but the decisions of three-judge panels, that are of real interest. Let us now turn to panel outcomes.

In terms of the political affiliation of the appointing president, there are four possible combinations of judges on a three-judge panel: RRR, RRD, RDD, and DDD. Variations in panel composition can have two important effects, which should now be distinguished. The first involves the sheer number of people leaning in a certain direction. Suppose, for example, that Republican appointees are likely to rule in favor of a particular type of program only 40% of the time, whereas Democratic appointees are likely to rule in favor of such programs 70% of the time. As a simple statistical matter, and putting to one side the possibility that judges are influenced by one another, it follows that the likely majority outcome of a panel will be affected by its composition. Under the stated assumption, a panel of all-Democratic appointees is far more likely (78%) to uphold the program than a panel of two Democratic appointees and one Republican (66%), while an all-Republican panel would be much less likely to do so (35%).

This is an important and substantial difference. As noted, however, this statistical effect assumes that judicial votes are not influenced by judicial colleagues. Suppose that an individual judge's likely vote is in fact influenced by the composition of the panel. If so, then the mere majority force of predispositions, just described, will not tell the full story of the difference between all-Republican panels and all-Democratic panels. In fact, the statistical account will understate the difference, possibly substantially. To illustrate with our own data, let us assume for the moment that the average percentages reported in the bottom row of Table 1 do accurately represent individual voting tendencies for case types that show differences in panel decisions. Figure 5 compares the predicted percentages, based on 34% for Republican appointees and 50% for Democratic appointees and using the calculation above, to the observed averages from the same row of the Table. The predicted panel effect (DDD%—RRR%) is 23%, but the observed effect is 35%. It is clear that to explain these results, something must be at work other than majority voting with different ideological predictions.

* * * *

III. Explanations

* * * *

[Sunstein and his colleagues next discuss possible explanations for their findings. First of all, they look at those situations where the hypotheses are rejected—criminal appeals, takings, and federalism cases. Perhaps the law here is especially clear. Another possibility is that the judges simply do not disagree on points in these areas. There may not be a conservative or liberal position here.

Figure 5. Predicted vs. Actual Panel Decisions
(for case types with a panel difference)

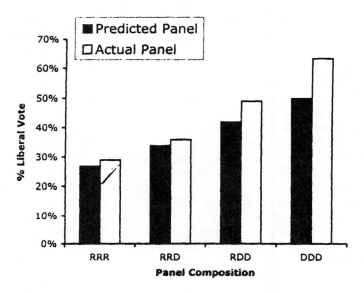

Second, there are situations where "party affiliation is what matters," and the judges vote their convictions "regardless of the composition of the panel." This is the case with abortion and capital punishment. Perhaps the judges' convictions here are simply so strong that they outweigh any panel effects.]

C.   Why Aren't the Effects Larger?

We have been emphasizing the existence of strong party and panel effects. But this is only part of the story. It would be possible to see our data as suggesting that most of the time, the law is what matters, not ideology. Note here that even when party effects are significant, they are not overwhelmingly large. Recall that Republican appointees cast stereotypically liberal votes 38% of the time, whereas Democratic appointees do so 51% of the time. Half of the votes of Democratic appointees are stereotypically conservative, and over one-third of the votes of Republican appointees are stereotypically liberal. More often than not, Republican and Democratic appointees agree with one another, even in the most controversial cases. Why is this?

We think that the answer has three parts. The first consists of panel effects. Republican appointees often sit with one or more Democratic appointees, and the same is true for Democratic appointees. If judges are influenced by one another, the random assignment of judges will inevitably produce some dampening of differences. The second factor involves the disciplining effect of precedent and law—a factor that might be labeled "professionalism." In the context of Commerce Clause challenges to legislation, we have explained judicial agreement across party lines partly on the ground that precedent is seen to dispose of most current disputes. Sometimes precedent will allow some, but not a great deal of, space for ideological differences to emerge. Undoubtedly the large measure of agreement is partly a product of the constraints of law itself. In some areas, those constraints will ensure that Republican and Democratic appointees do not disagree. In other areas, they will permit disagreement, but they will discipline its magnitude.

The third factor involves legal and political culture. For all of their differences, Democratic and Republican judicial appointees are almost never ideologues or extremists. If a sex discrimination plaintiff presents a strong claim, Republican appointees will agree with her, even if the law allows judges to exercise discretion; if industry shows that an environmental regulation is plainly arbitrary, Democratic appointees will strike it down as arbitrary, even if the law would allow them to uphold it. The process of legal training imposes strong limits on what judges seek to do. In any case, the political culture constrains presidential appointments, ensuring a kind of filtering that will, for the most part, prevent presidents from nominating (and the Senate from confirming) people whose views are perceived as extreme. The high levels of agreement between Republican and Democratic appointees are undoubtedly affected by this fact. The most general point is that insofar as our evidence shows less in the way of party effects than some people might expect, professional discipline and legal consensus help explain the level of agreement.

D.   Why Panel Effects?

* * * *

[The authors next discuss why their data show panel effects. Why is there a difference between, say, a three Democrat panel and a two Democrat and one Republican panel? First of all, the disagreeing judge might contribute "some information about what is right." Also, a dissent on a three-judge panel is likely "to be both futile and burdensome." Furthermore, it is possible that the Democrat who is outvoted by two Republicans has been nonetheless able to move the opinion "in the direction of greater moderation." This is something that their figures cannot capture.

They also note the social science research that shows "if people are confronted with the unanimous views of others, they tend to yield."

Social science research also helps explain the behavior of all D or all R panels. This research shows that groups of "like-minded people tend to go to extremes." Since this study focused on votes, not <u>opinions</u>, it is possible that research on opinions would show that "a unified panel is less likely to be moderate than a divided one."

What explains group polarization? Several reasons have been advanced. If all three agree, then the discussion is likely to "move people further in the direction of their initial inclinations." They are just not going to hear the other side. Also, people, as they gain "confidence" about a point, "become more extreme in their beliefs." In the case of an all D or all R panel, the judges might become more extreme "simply because their view has been corroborated and ... they have become more confident after learning of the shared views of others."]

3. The Whistleblower Effect

Imagine that existing law is not entirely clear, but that fairly applied, it requires one or another outcome. It is easily imaginable that like-minded judges, unaccompanied by a potential dissenter, will fail to apply the law fairly. This is not because they are essentially lawless. It is because when the law is unclear, fallible human beings might well be inclined to understand the law in a way that fits with their predilections.

These points provide a possible explanation for some of the differences between panels with two-to-one majorities and panels in which all judges were appointed by a president of the same political party. Consider affirmative action cases. In some of these cases, three Democratic appointees might well be inclined to vote in favor of validation even if existing doctrine argues the other way. If no Republican appointee is on the panel, there is a risk that the panel will unanimously support validation despite existing law. The effect of the Republican is to call the panel's attention to the tension between its inclination and the decided cases. Of course, her effort may fail. Her co-panelists might persist in their views, perhaps with the claim that those cases can be distinguished. But when existing law does create serious problems for the panel, the presence of a judge with a different inclination will have a large effect. We speculate that in the areas in which there is a large difference between two-to-one majorities and three judges from the same party, this effect—the whistleblower effect—is playing a role.

Our data do not allow this speculation to be tested directly, but a separate study shows the importance of a potential dissenter, or whistleblower, in ensuring that courts follow the law. More particularly, a Democratic appointee on a majority Republican court of appeals panel turns out to be extremely important in ensuring that such a panel does what the law asks it to do. The basic point is that diversity of view can help to correct errors—not that judges of one or another party are more likely to be correct.

To understand this study, some background is in order. Under the Supreme Court's decision in *Chevron U.S.A. v. Natural Resources Defense Council*, courts should uphold agency interpretations of law so long as the interpretations do not clearly violate congressional instructions and are "reasonable." But when do courts actually uphold such interpretations? Existing law allows judges considerable room to maneuver, so that courts inclined to invalidate agency interpretations usually can find a plausible basis for doing so. The real question is when they will claim to have found that plausible basis. The relevant study, extending well beyond environmental protection to regulation in general, confirms the idea that party affiliation has an exceedingly large influence on outcomes within the D.C. Circuit. If observers were to code cases very crudely by taking account of whether industry or a public interest group is bringing the challenge, they would find that a panel with a majority of Republican appointees reaches a conservative judgment 54% of the time, whereas a panel with a majority of Democratic appointees reaches such a judgment merely 32% of the time.

For present purposes, the most important finding is the dramatic difference between politically diverse panels, with judges appointed by presidents of more than one party, and politically unified panels, with judges appointed by presidents of only one party. On divided panels in which a Republican majority of the court might be expected to be hostile to the agency, the court nonetheless upholds the agency's interpretation 62% of the time. But on unified all-Republican panels, which might be expected to be hostile to the agency, the court upholds the agency's interpretation only 33% of the time. Note that this was the only unusual finding in the data. When Democratic majority courts are expected to uphold the agency's decision on political grounds, they do so over 70% of the time, whether unified (71% of the time) or divided (84% of the time). Consider the results in tabular form:

	RRR panel	RRD panel	RDD panel	DDD panel
Invalidate agency action	67%	38%	16%	29%

It is reasonable to speculate that the only seemingly bizarre result—a 67% invalidation rate when Republican appointees are unified!—reflects group influences and, in particular, group polarization. A group of all-Republican appointees might well take the relatively unusual step of rejecting an agency's interpretation. By contrast, a divided panel, with a built-in check on any tendency toward the unusual or extreme outcome, is more likely to take the conventional route of simply upholding the agency's action. An important reason is that the single Democratic appointee acts as a "whistle-blower," discouraging the other judges from making a decision that is inconsistent with the Supreme Court's command that courts of appeals should uphold agency interpretations of ambiguous statutes.

E.   A Preliminary Investigation—and Future Directions

We have emphasized that this is a preliminary investigation. It should be possible before terribly long to do what we have done here for multiple domains of the law, extending over time. The data are readily available, and most of the work involves mere counting. As we have suggested, it would be exceedingly interesting to know whether the three hypotheses hold in the pre-New Deal era of tensions between courts and the regulatory state, and also in the struggle over school segregation. So, too, it would be valuable to know whether similar patterns can be found in the legal disputes over slavery, in judicial review of decisions by the National Labor Relations Board and the Federal Communications Commission, in cases brought under the Federal Tort Claims Act, and in cases involving foreign affairs and war.

We could easily imagine that ideological disagreements between judges appointed by presidents of different parties would be greater or weaker in certain historical periods. It might be hypothesized, for example, that such disagreements were weakened in the 1940s, when the nation seemed to form a consensus against an aggressive role for the federal judiciary. It might also be hypothesized that such disagreements would be especially strong since 1980, with powerful partisan divisions about the appropriate role of the federal judiciary. Are these hypotheses correct? Ultimately, it would be desirable to compile an extensive data set about votes on federal courts of appeals, showing the diverse patterns into which those votes fall.

IV.   What Should Be Done?

It remains to investigate the normative issues. Is it troubling to find a large effect from party or panel composition? Should we be concerned if like-minded judges go to extremes? Is there reason to attempt to ensure diversity on the federal courts, or to promote a degree of diversity on panels? There is a widespread view that judges appointed by presidents of different political parties are not fundamentally different and that, once on the bench, judges frequently surprise those who nominated them. The view is not entirely baseless, but it is misleading. Some appointees do disappoint the presidents who nominated them, but those examples are not typical. Judges appointed by Republican presidents are quite different from judges appointed by Democratic presidents. To take evidence from just one area, "partisanship clearly affects how appellate courts review agency discretion." We have acknowledged that the effects that we find are large but not massive. Because of the disciplining effect of precedent, and because judges do not radically disagree with one another, there is significant commonality across political parties. But in the most difficult areas, the ones where the law is unclear or in flux, both party and panel effects are large enough to be a source of serious concern.

It is difficult to evaluate the underlying issues without taking a stand on the merits—without knowing what we want judges to do. Suppose that three Republican appointees are especially likely to strike down affirmative action programs and that three Democratic appointees are especially likely to uphold those programs. At first glance, one or the other inclination is troubling only if we know whether we disapprove of one or another set of results. And if a view about what judges should do is the only possible basis for evaluation, we might conclude that those who prefer judges of a particular party should seek judges of that party and that group influences are essentially beside the point.

But this conclusion is too strong. In some cases, the law, properly interpreted, does point toward one or another view. The existence of diversity on a panel is likely to bring that fact to light and perhaps to move the panel's decision in the direction of what the law requires. The existence of politically diverse judges and a potential dissent increases the probability that the law will be followed.... The presence of a potential dissenter—in the form of a judge appointed by a president from another political party—creates a possible whistleblower who can reduce the likelihood of an incorrect or lawless decision. Through an appreciation of the nature of group influences, we can see the wisdom in an old idea: A decision is more likely to be right, and less likely to be political in a pejorative sense, if it is supported by judges with different predilections.

There is a further point. Suppose that in many areas it is not clear in advance whether the appointees of Democratic or Republican presidents are correct. Suppose that we are genuinely uncertain. If so, then there is reason to favor a situation in which the legal system has diverse judges, simply on the ground that through that route, more reasonable opinions are likely to be heard. If we are genuinely uncertain, then there is reason to favor a mix of views merely by virtue of its moderating effect. In the face of uncertainty, many people choose between the poles.

Consider an analogy. Independent regulatory commissions, such as the Federal Trade Commission, the Securities and Exchange Commission, the National Labor Relations Board, and the Federal Communications Commission, often make modern law and policy. Much of the time, such agencies act through adjudication. They function in the same fashion as federal courts. Under federal statutes, Congress has attempted to ensure that these agencies are not monopolized by either Democratic appointees or Republican appointees. The law requires that no more than a bare majority of agency members may be from a single party.

An understanding of group influences helps to justify this requirement. An independent agency that is all-Democratic or all-Republican might move toward an extreme position—indeed, toward a position that is more extreme than that of the median Democrat or Republican, and possibly more extreme than that of any agency official standing alone. A requirement of bipartisan membership can operate as a check against movements of this kind. Congress was apparently aware of this general point. Closely attuned to the policy making functions of the relevant institutions, Congress was careful to provide a safeguard against extreme movements.

Why do we fail to create similar safeguards for courts? Part of the answer must lie in a belief that, unlike heads of independent regulatory commissions, judges are not policy makers. Their duty is to follow the law, not to make policy. An attempt to ensure bipartisan composition would seem inconsistent with a commitment to this belief. But the evidence we have discussed shows that judges are policy makers of an important kind and that, in some contexts, their political commitments very much influence their votes. In principle, there is good reason to attempt to ensure a mix of perspectives within courts of appeals.

Of course the idea of diversity, or of a mix of perspectives, is hardly self-defining. It would not be appropriate to say that the federal judiciary should include people who refuse to obey the Constitution, or who refuse to exercise the power of judicial review, or who think that the Constitution allows suppression of political dissent and does not forbid racial segregation. Here, as elsewhere, the domain of appropriate diversity is limited. What is necessary is reasonable diversity, or diversity of reasonable views, and not diversity as such. People can certainly disagree about what reasonable diversity entails in this context. We are suggesting here that there is such a thing as reasonable diversity and that it is important to ensure that judges, no less than anyone else, are exposed to it, and not merely through the arguments of advocates.

A competing argument would stress a possible purpose of the lower federal courts: to produce a wide range of positions, so that Supreme Court review will ultimately follow an exploration of a number of possible interpretations. For those who emphasize the value of diverse decisions, what we have treated as a vice might instead be a virtue. On this view, it is desirable to have unified panels of ideologically similar judges, simply in order to produce a wide band of arguments for the Supreme Court to assess. We do not believe that this is an irrelevant concern; it weighs in the balance. More (reasonable) positions are better than fewer. We would respond only that Supreme Court review is exceedingly rare and that most of the time, court of appeals decisions are effectively final. In these circumstances, it is not clear that the gain in the range of ideas outweighs the competing considerations to which we have pointed. . . .

NOTES AND QUESTIONS

1. To what extent do the patterns found by Sunstein, Schkade and Ellman undercut the values of the rule of law? Can citizens (including those running large corporations) predict the outcome of cases so that they can pattern their behavior? Would not those interested in the boundaries set by the law have to know which judges would sit on the three judge panel hearing their case? However, do you think that the findings of the three authors would be news to lawyers practicing before particular United States Courts of Appeal?

2. Sunstein, Schkade and Ellman's work also suggests that we might like to discover how the three judges out of the seven or nine that sit on a particular circuit court are selected for a particular case. Suppose that the clerk of the court together with the chief judge of the circuit select the panels for the various cases. Would they have some power to affect outcomes by giving certain cases to judges appointed by Republican presidents, others to judges appointed by Democratic presidents, and still others to mixed panels? J. Robert Brown, Jr. and Allison Herren Lee, "The Neutral Assignment of Judges at the Court of Appeals," 78 *Texas Law Review* 1037 (2000), look at

the procedures for assigning judges to panels used by the various circuits. They say that there is enough discretion in the process so that judges could be assigned to particular cases so as to influence outcomes.

3.   Would you expect that the effect of being appointed by a Republican or a Democratic president would wear off over time? Federal judges serve for life and the world changes. Might judges appointed by Presidents Carter and Reagan be less influenced by the selection process that put them on the bench than those appointed by Presidents Clinton and George W. Bush?

4.   <u>Electing State Court Judges.</u> Unlike federal judges, many American state judges are elected. The systems differ: sometimes the voters choose between two or more candidates; sometimes they vote only to approve or disapprove a candidate nominated by the Governor. Many people wonder whether voters know enough about the judges and about the requirements of the position to make an intelligent choice. A distinguished Justice of the Supreme Court of Wisconsin, for example, was defeated in his race for reelection after he wrote an unremarkable opinion affirming a decision allowing the Milwaukee Braves baseball team to move and become the Atlanta Braves.

Nicholas P. Lovrich, Jr., John C. Pierce and Charles H. Sheldon, "Citizen Knowledge and Voting in Judicial Elections," 73 *Judicature* 28 (1989), studied "what kind of person votes in the low-salience [judicial] elections." Their study was part of a survey in the Spokane, Washington metropolitan area. They determined that people who think that they are well-informed about the courts are likely to be well-informed. Moreover, those who are well-informed are more likely to vote than those who are unsure of their knowledge. Knowledge is an important element in deciding whether or not to vote. Those who actually voted do not differ markedly in their socio-economic or neighborhood status. See, also, Nicholas P. Lovrich, Jr. and Charles H. Sheldon, "Voters in Contested, Nonpartisan Judicial Elections: A Responsible Electorate or a Problematic Public?" 36 *Western Political Quarterly* 241 (1983).

Melinda Gann Hall and Chris W. Bonneau, "Does Quality Matter? Challengers in State Supreme Court Elections," 50 *American Journal of Political Science* 20 (2006), examined 208 elections to states' highest courts from 1990 through 2000 in the 21 states using elections to staff their courts. They find: "challengers appear to enter state supreme court races when they might have a reasonable chance of winning, and voters in the aggregate cast ballots for incumbents after considering whether opponents may, or may not, be qualified." They also find that differences in campaign spending between incumbents and challengers are important in determining incumbents' success. "[A] 1% increase in spending by the incumbent over the challenger can add about 1.6% to the incumbent's vote share." Many worry that judicial elections have become increasing more expensive, and candidates must accept contributions to finance campaigns. See Owen G. Abbe and Paul S. Herrnson, "How Judicial Election Campaigns Have Changed," 85 *Judicature* 286 (2002). This may create at least the appearance that judges' votes have been bought. See Adam Liptak and Janet Roberts, "Campaign Cash Mirrors a High Court's

Rulings," *N.Y. Times*, Oct. 1, 2006, at 1 (reporting that in a class action suit before the Supreme Court of Ohio in 2004, every justice in the 4 to 3 majority had taken money from affiliates of the companies being sued while every justice in the minority had taken money from the lawyers for the plaintiffs).

Judges who run for re-election have to raise money for their campaigns. Judges probably have less leeway to make explicit promises than candidates for Congress. Presumably, however, big contributors expect something from a judge they support, even if that something is left fairly implicit. See Anthony Champagne, "Campaign Contributions in Texas Supreme Court Races," 17 *Crime, Law and Social Change* 91 (1992). Champagne points out that judicial campaign finance can be an aspect of interest group politics. For example, physicians, outraged over "what they perceived as the pro-plaintiff tone of the Supreme Court's malpractice decisions" in Texas, mounted "a major funding effort for their slate of Supreme Court candidates in the 1988 election" (p. 104).

Joel Goldstein, "The Impact of the Louisville Courier–Journal's Editorial Endorsements on the Outcome of Local Judicial Elections," 73 *Judicature* 108, 112 (1989), found that voters who used the newspaper's endorsements in voting for candidates for the local district court were better educated, more ideological and had a greater sense of political efficacy. However, the study "found that the newspaper endorsements had a large gross impact upon the vote, but that its influence on electoral outcomes was muted by the fact that about half of the voters used it as a positive referent, while the other half used it as a negative referent."

5. Do elections influence the way judges behave? In theory, they do— and should (to a point). A judge facing election, we would think, would be sensitive to what the electorate wants. Of course, this sensitivity would apply only to a few relatively controversial or highly publicized cases. On this subject, see Melinda Gann Hall, "Electoral Politics and Strategic Voting in State Supreme Courts," 54 *Journal of Politics* 427 (1992). Hall looked at the behavior of elected state judges in death penalty cases. Liberal judges dislike the death penalty, but white Americans across sociodemographic categories seem to favor capital punishment. See M. Dwayne Smith and James Wright, "Capital Punishment and Public Opinion in the Post–Furman Era: Trends and Analysis," 12 *Sociological Spectrum* 127 (1992). Hall found evidence that liberal state judges, facing reelection campaigns, had some tendency to "join conservative majorities in death penalty cases" in the four states that she studied. These results, though limited to this one situation, suggested to Hall that it "may well be the case that justices behave much more strategically than originally believed. Instead of public policy goals driving judicial deci-sions, basic self-interest may also be an important consideration to the state supreme court justice when rendering decisions" (p. 443).

Hall notes, quite properly, that her results do not in anyway suggest "a general model of judicial decision making." In many states, judicial elections are not contested in any meaningful sense. And, as we pointed out, only a few cases are likely to have much meaning for the constituency.

John Blume and Theodore Eisenberg, "Judicial Politics, Death Penalty Appeals, and Case Selection: An Empirical Study," 72 *Southern California Law Review* 465, 488, 502 (1999), find almost no correlation between how a state selects its appellate judges and reversals in death penalty cases. They do find an effect in Ohio. Officially, Ohio has nonpartisan judicial elections, but in fact its elections are partisan. There a significant relation between partisan election status and reversal rates emerges. However, they tell us:

> In the appellate data, the hypothesis that partisan election of judges correlates with death penalty affirmance holds up for North Carolina, Pennsylvania and Texas. All have partisan elections and low reversal rates.... Alabama, Mississippi, and Illinois, which have partisan elections, have high capital sentence reversal rates. Therefore, partisan elections, standing alone, cannot explain the pattern of appellate results. States without partisan elections also show varying reversal rates. Oklahoma and Florida have high reversal rates. Indiana has a low reversal rate. Overall, we did not find a statistically significant relation between judicial selection method and reversal rate....

> Taken together, the state-specific stories suggest that judicial selection methods can neither insulate judges from political pressure nor always lead to quantifiable manifestations of such pressure. California lacked partisan judicial elections, yet justices were voted out of office on the death penalty issue. California continued to have a fairly low reversal rate in capital cases. Tennessee and South Carolina also supported the belief that political pressure affects judges in capital cases. But judicial behavior in capital cases had been politicized in Mississippi and Texas, without noticeable changes in their treatment of capital cases.

6.   What is the role of a judge? How should she or he go about business? How much creativity is there in the very nature of the job?

(5.10) The Case Against Strict Constructionism: What am I? A Potted Plant?

Richard A. Posner

The New Republic, September 18, 1987, at 23.

Many people, not all of conservative bent, believe that modern American courts are too aggressive, too "activist," too prone to substitute their own policy preferences for those of the elected branches of government. This may well be true. But some who complain of judicial activism espouse a view of law that is too narrow. And a good cause will not hallow a bad argument. This point of view often is called "strict constructionism." A more precise term would be "legal formalism." A forceful polemic by Walter Berns in the June 1987 issue of *Commentary*—"Government by Lawyers and Judges"—summarizes the formalist view well. Issues of the "public good" can "be decided legitimately only with the consent of the governed." Judges have no legitimate say about these issues. Their business is to address issues of private rights, that is, "to decide whether the right exists—in the Constitution or in a statute—and, if so, what it is; but at that point inquiry ceases." The judge may not use "discretion and the weighing of consequences" to arrive at his decisions and he may not create new rights. The Constitution is a source of rights, but only to the extent that it embodies "fundamental and clearly articulated principles of government." There must be no judicial creativity or "policy-making."

In short, there is a political sphere, where the people rule, and there is a domain of fixed rights, administered but not created or altered by judges. The first is the sphere of discretion, the second of application. Legislators make the law; judges find and apply it.

There has never been a time when the courts of the United States, state or federal, behaved consistently in accordance with this idea. Nor could they, for reasons rooted in the nature of law and legal institutions, in the limitations of human knowledge, and in the character of a political system.

"Questions about the public good" and "questions about private rights" are inseparable. The private right is conferred in order to promote the public good. So in deciding how broadly the right shall be interpreted, the court must consider the implications of its interpretation for the public good. For example, should an heir who murders his benefactor have a right to inherit from his victim? The answer depends, in part anyway, on the public good that results from discouraging murders.

Furthermore, most private law is common law—that is, law made by judges rather than by legislators or by constitution-framers. Judges have been entrusted with making policy from the start.

Often when deciding difficult questions of private rights courts have to weigh policy considerations. If a locomotive spews sparks that set a farmer's crops afire, has the railroad invaded the farmer's property right or does the railroad's ownership of its right of way implicitly include the right to emit sparks? If the railroad has such a right, shall it be conditioned on the railroad's taking reasonable precautions to minimize the danger of fire? If, instead, the farmer has the right, shall it be conditioned on his taking reasonable precautions? Such questions cannot be answered sensibly without considering the social consequences of alternative answers.

A second problem is that when a constitutional convention, a legislature, or a court promulgates a rule of law, it necessarily does so without full knowledge of the circumstances in which the rule might be invoked in the future. When the unforeseen circumstance arises—it might be the advent of the motor vehicle or of electronic surveillance, or a change in attitudes toward religion, race, and sexual propriety—a court asked to apply the rule must decide, in light of information not available to the promulgators of the rule, what the rule should mean in its new setting. That is a creative decision, involving discretion, the weighing of consequences, and, in short, a kind of legislative judgment—though, properly, one more confined than if the decision were being made by a real legislature. A court that decides, say, that copyright protection extends to the coloring of old black-and-white movies is making a creative decision, because the copyright laws do not mention colorization. It is not being lawless or usurpative merely because it is weighing consequences and exercising discretion.

Or if a court decides (as the Supreme Court has done in one of its less controversial modern rulings) that the Fourth Amendment's prohibition against unreasonable searches and seizures shall apply to wiretapping, even though no trespass is committed by wiretapping and hence no property right is invaded, the court is creating a new right and making policy. But in a situation not foreseen and expressly provided for by the Framers of the Constitution, a simple reading out of a policy judgment made by the Framers is impossible.

Even the most carefully drafted legislation has gaps. The Constitution, for example, does not say that the federal government has sovereign immunity—the right, traditionally enjoyed by all sovereign governments, not to be sued without its consent. Nevertheless the Supreme Court held that the federal government has sovereign immunity. Is this interpolation usurpative? The Federal Tort Claims Act, a law waiving sovereign immunity so citizens can sue the government, makes no exception for suits by members of the armed services who are injured through the negligence of their superiors. Nevertheless the Supreme Court has held that the act was not intended to provide soldiers with a remedy. The decision may be right or wrong, but it is not wrong just because it is creative. The 11th Amendment to the Constitution forbids a citizen of one state to sue "another" state in federal court without the consent of the defendant state. Does this mean that you can sue your own state in federal court without the state's consent? That's what the words seem to imply, but the Supreme Court has held that the 11th Amendment was intended to preserve the sovereign immunity of the states more broadly. The Court thought this was implied by the federalist system that the Constitution created. Again the Court may have been right or wrong, but it was not wrong just because it was creative.

Opposite the unrealistic picture of judges who apply law but never make it, Walter Berns hangs an unrealistic picture of a populist legislature that acts only "with the consent of the governed." Speaking for myself, I find that many of the political candidates whom I have voted for have failed to be elected and that those who have been elected have then proceeded to enact much legislation that did not have my consent. Given the effectiveness of interest groups in the political process, much of this legislation probably didn't have the consent of a majority of citizens. Politically, I feel more governed than self-governing. In considering whether to reduce constitutional safeguards to slight dimensions, we should be sure to have a realistic, not an idealized, picture of the legislative and executive branches of government, which would thereby be made more powerful than they are today.

To banish all discretion from the judicial process would indeed reduce the scope of constitutional rights. The framers of a constitution who want to make it a charter of liberties and not just a set of constitutive rules face a difficult choice. They can write specific provisions, and thereby doom their work to rapid obsolescence or irrelevance; or they can write general provisions, thereby delegating substantial discretion to the authoritative interpreters, who in our system are the judges. The U.S. Constitution is a mixture of specific and general provisions. Many of the specific provisions have stood the test of time amazingly well or have been amended without any great fuss. This is especially true of the rules establishing the structure and procedures of Congress. Most of the specific provisions creating rights, however, have fared poorly. Some have proved irksomely anachronistic—for example, the right to a jury trial in federal court in all cases at law if the stakes exceed $20. Others have become dangerously anachronistic, such as the right to bear arms. Some have even turned topsy-turvy, such as the provision for indictment by grand jury. The grand jury has become an instrument of prosecutorial investigation rather than a protection for the criminal suspect. If the Bill of Rights had consisted entirely of specific provisions, it would have aged very rapidly and would no longer be a significant constraint on the behavior of government officials.

Many provisions of the Constitution, however, are drafted in general terms. This creates flexibility in the face of unforeseen changes, but it also creates the possibility of multiple interpretations, and this possibility is an embarrassment for a theory of judicial legitimacy that denies that judges have any right to exercise discretion. A choice among semantically plausible interpretations of a text, in circumstances remote from those contemplated by its drafters, requires the exercise of discretion and the weighing of consequences. Reading is not a form of deduction; understanding requires a consideration of consequences. If I say, "I'll eat my hat," one reason that my listeners will "decode" this in non-literal fashion is that I couldn't eat a hat if I tried. The broader principle, which applies to the Constitution as much as to a spoken utterance, is that if one possible interpretation of an ambiguous statement would entail absurd or terrible results, that is a good reason to adopt an alternative interpretation.

Even the decision to read the Constitution narrowly, and thereby "restrain" judicial interpretation, is not a decision that can be read directly from the text. The Constitution does not say, "Read me broadly," or, "Read me narrowly." That decision must be made as a matter of political theory, and will depend on such things as one's view of the springs of judicial legitimacy and of the relative competence of courts and legislatures in dealing with particular types of issues.

Consider the provision in the Sixth Amendment that "in all criminal prosecutions, the accused shall enjoy the right ... to have the Assistance of Counsel for his defense." Read narrowly, this just means that the defendant can't be forbidden to retain counsel; if he can't afford counsel, or competent counsel, he is out of luck. Read broadly, it guarantees even the indigent the effective assistance of counsel; it becomes not just a negative right to be allowed to hire a lawyer but a positive right to demand the help of the government in financing one's defense. Either reading is compatible with the semantics of the provision, but the first better captures the specific intent of the Framers. At the time the Sixth Amendment was written, English law forbade a criminal defendant to have the assistance of counsel unless abstruse questions of law arose in his case. The Framers wanted to do away with this prohibition. But, more broadly, they wanted to give criminal defendants protection against being railroaded. When they wrote, government could not afford, or at least did not think it could afford, to hire lawyers for indigent criminal defendants. Moreover, criminal trials were short and simple, so it was not ridiculous to expect a person to defend himself without a lawyer if he couldn't afford to hire one. Today the situation is different. Not only can the society easily afford to supply lawyers to poor people charged with crimes, but modern criminal law and procedure are so complicated that an unrepresented defendant will usually be at a great disadvantage.

I do not know whether Professor Berns thinks the Supreme Court was usurping legislative power when it held in the *Gideon* case that a poor person has a right to the assistance of counsel at the state's expense. But his article does make clear his view that the Supreme Court should not have invalidated racial segregation in public schools. Reading the words of the 14th Amendment in the narrowest possible manner in order to minimize judicial discretion, and noting the absence of evidence that the Framers wanted to eliminate segregation, Berns argues that "equal protection of the laws" just means non-discriminatory enforcement of whatever laws are enacted, even if the laws themselves are discriminatory. He calls the plausible empirical proposition that "separate educational facilities are inherently unequal" "a logical absurdity."

On Berns's reading, the promulgation of the equal protection clause was a trivial gesture at giving the recently freed slaves (and other blacks, whose status at the time was little better than that of serfs) political equality with whites, since the clause in his view forbids the denial of that equality only by executive officers. The state may not withdraw police protection from blacks (unless by legislation?) but it may forbid them to sit next to whites on buses. This is a possible reading of the 14th Amendment but not an inevitable one, unless judges must always interpret the Constitution as denying them the power to exercise judgment.

No one really believes this. Everyone professionally connected with law knows that, in Oliver Wendell Holmes's famous expression, judges legislate "interstitially," which is to say they make law, only more cautiously, more slowly, and in more principled, less partisan, fashion than legislators. The attempt to deny this truism entangles "strict constructionists" in contradictions. Berns says both that judges can enforce only "clearly articulated principles" and that they may invalidate unconstitutional laws. But the power to do this is not "articulated" in the Constitution; it is merely implicit in it. He believes that the courts have been wrong to interpret the First Amendment as protecting the publication of foul language in school newspapers, yet the words "freedom of speech, or of the press" do not appear to exclude foul language in school newspapers. Berns says he deduces his conclusion from the principle that expression, to be within the scope of the First Amendment, must be related to representative government. Where did he get that principle from? He didn't read it in the Constitution.

The First Amendment also forbids Congress to make laws "respecting an establishment of religion." Berns says this doesn't mean that Congress "must be neutral between religion and irreligion." But the words will bear that meaning, so how does he decide they should be given a different meaning? By appealing to Tocqueville's opinion of the importance of religion in a democratic society. In short, the correct basis for decision is the consequence of the decision for democracy. Yet consequences are not—in the strict construction-ist view—a fit thing for courts to consider. Berns even expresses regret that the modern Supreme Court is oblivious to Tocqueville's opinion "of the importance of the woman ... whose chastity as a young girl is protected not only by religion but by an education that limits her 'imagination.'" A court that took such opinions into account would be engaged in aggressively consequentialist thinking rather than in strict construction.

The liberal judicial activists may be imprudent and misguided in their efforts to enact the liberal political agenda into constitutional law, but it is no use pretending that what they are doing is not interpretation but "decon-struction," not law but politics, because it involves the exercise of discretion and a concern with consequences and because it reaches results not foreseen 200 years ago. It may be bad law because it lacks firm moorings in constitu-tional text, or structure, or history, or consensus, or other legitimate sources of constitutional law, or because it is reckless of consequences, or because it oversimplifies difficult moral and political questions. But it is not bad law, or no law, just because it violates the tenets of strict construction.

NOTES AND QUESTIONS

1. Many elected officials and political commentators have objected to what they call "activist judges." The term came into modern popular usage in the 1967 nomination of Thurgood Marshall, an African American, to the Supreme Court. See Trevor Parry–Giles, "Character, the Constitution, and the Ideological Embodiment of 'Civil Rights' in the 1967 Nomination of Thurgood Marshall to the Supreme Court," 82 *Quarterly Journal of Speech* 364 (1996). Marshall was opposed by a group of senators from the South. They thought that they could not assert that no black was qualified for the Supreme Court or that a man who had been so involved in arguing *Brown v. Board of Education* should not be appointed to the court. Instead, Senator Sam Ervin said: "Judge Marshall is by practice and philosophy a legal and judicial activist, and if he is elevated to the Supreme Court, he will join other activist Justices in rendering decisions which will substantially impair, if not destroy, the rights of Americans for years to come to have the Government of

the United States and the several States conducted in accordance with the Constitution.''

2. Judge Ralph Winter argues that those who are judicial activists or who champion this approach are impatient with pluralist compromises produced by the political process in legislatures. He says:

> Activist judges also are quite confident about the superiority of judicial processes. The urge to take over a school system, welfare program, prison, or mental hospital is based not only on righteous indignation over governmental inertia and inefficiency but on an abiding belief that courts, unlike other agencies of government, can exclude from consideration "irrational" factors such as public reaction or problems in raising revenue while taking into account the latest teaching of the social sciences. Only courts can concentrate fully on reaching the right solution by taking into account all of the "relevant" considerations. Only they can engage in really successful social engineering.

Winter also asserts that a "political conservative may be a different kind of judge than a political liberal, therefore, but not necessarily less activist." See Ralph K. Winter, "The Activist Judicial Mind" in Mark W. Cannon and David M. O'Brien, *Views from the Bench: The Judiciary and Constitutional Politics*, at 290, 300, 301 (1985). To what extent does Winter's argument apply to the case made by Judge Posner? Does Judge Winter seem to disapprove of the Supreme Court's decision in *Brown v. Board of Education*, the school desegregation case? Would you characterize segregation of the races as a pluralist compromise?

Professor Lori A. Ringhand examined the voting record of United States Supreme Court justices from 1994 to 2005, in "Judicial Activism: An Empirical Examination of Voting Behavior on the Rehnquist Natural Court" (forthcoming 2007). Conservative justices voted to overturn federal laws more often than liberals. Liberals voted to strike down state laws more often than conservatives. Conservatives were more likely to vote to reverse the courts own precedents. By Ringhand's standards, Justices Scalia and Thomas were the most activist. See Activism Is in the Eye of the Ideologist, N.Y. Times, Sept. 11, 2000, at A18.

3. J. Woodford Howard, Jr., "Role Perceptions and Behavior in Three U.S. Courts of Appeal," 39 *Journal of Politics* 916 (1977), reports the results of interviews with thirty five judges serving on the Second, Fifth and District of Columbia United States Circuit Courts. Five were innovators who would make law whenever the opportunity occurred. Nine thought that lawmaking should be held to a minimum. Only one said that judges should merely interpret the law. Twenty judges took middle positions, stressing the limits on judicial lawmaking but acknowledging that there were appropriate occasions to act. James L. Gibson, "The Role Concept in Judicial Research," 3 *Law & Policy Quarterly* 291 (1981), reports on a study of California and Iowa judges responding to six questions. The responses are remarkably similar but for the statement: "It is just as legitimate to make a decision and then find the

precedent as it is to find the precedent and then make the decision." 40% of California judges agreed or agreed strongly while only 22% of the Iowa judges agreed or agreed strongly.

Lawrence M. Friedman notes that many judges deny any creative role for themselves. They say that they just apply the law. He asks a number of questions:

> But what about the way the judges describe themselves; what about their vigorous denials that they pay attention to anything but "law." Are they simply fooling themselves? Or are they fooling us—hiding behind a screen, like the Wizard of Oz? Are they naive? Or disingenuous? All of these are possible. Are they mouthing sentiments about autonomy because they feel they are supposed to? Possibly. But maybe, if you recite pious platitudes long enough, you may come to believe them. These are, after all, the safest sentiments to have. If you have been nominated for a federal judgeship, and are about to be grilled by hostile Senators, you had better espouse the most naive positions imaginable—that is, if you want to be confirmed.

See Lawrence M. Friedman, "Judging the Judges: Some Remarks on the Way Judges Think and the Way Judges Act," in John N. Drobak (ed.) *Norms and the Law*, at 139, 151 (2006).

4.   There has been a great deal of research on the role perceptions of judges. John T. Wold, "Going Through the Motions: The Monotony of Appellate Court Decision Making," 62 *Judicature* 59, 62, 64, 65 (1978), suggests that we may be placing too much emphasis on judicial creativity. He interviewed 34 justices on the intermediate courts of appeal in California. He reports:

> They [the judges] perceive their job as primarily one of "processing" a largely repetitive caseload. Specifically, the judges felt their basic mission to be the tasks of reviewing for correctness the records of trial courts and applying the law as enunciated by the state supreme court.
>
> "We have chances for creativity a couple of times a year, maybe," asserted one justice. "But we're too busy to think that much. We give each case full consideration, but this is essentially an assembly line." ... [M]any jurists stressed that they also had had to develop methods for coping in psychological terms with the less intriguing aspects of their job. . . .
>
> "Liberal" and "conservative" political ideologies, as well as notions of judicial "activism" and "restraint," appear to have very limited relevance to the work of the California intermediate courts. Any attempts to base judicial appointments to the courts of appeal on ideological considerations may thus fail to accomplish their intended purpose. Apparently, whatever the ideological stripe of newly-appointed justices, they quickly become cogs in a system of case processing and routine dispositions.

Lenore Alpert, Burton M. Atkins and Robert C. Ziller, "Becoming a Judge: the Transition from Advocate to Arbiter," 62 *Judicature* 325 (1979), suggest that many judges leave the bench because the job is not what they expected. Judges find that they are isolated socially and politically by the demands of their role. They find that they do not make as much money as they made as lawyers because judicial salaries do not keep up with inflation. Those who remain judges tend to conform to organizational expectations and rewards.

5.   Is the role of the American—or British—judge radically different from the role of the civil law judge? In theory, yes. The common-law judge has a more "active" role in law-making than is conceded to the civil-law judge. But there may not be so great a difference in practice. José Juan Toharia, in a study of Spain's judiciary, divided judges into "active" and "passive" ones, depending on how they conceived their function. An "active" judge stresses the judge's creativity, and his or her role as a defender of rights and liberties. Such a judge values flexibility and is concerned with the social consequences of decisions. The "passive" judge is more attuned to formalism and judicial autonomy. See *El Juez Español: un Análisis Sociológico* [The Spanish Judge: A Sociological Analysis] (1975). See, also, Martin Shapiro, *Courts: A Comparative and Political Analysis* (1981). Shapiro offers a chapter on "judging and mediating in Imperial China" and a chapter on Islamic courts.

6.   American judges, and judges in the Western world in general, have a great deal of independence. Even elected judges do not fear reprisals if they decide, say, against the government. But in many totalitarian countries that may not be the case. How much freedom did judges have in Nazi Germany or in the Soviet Union under Stalin? How much freedom did judges have in China or Cuba in the early 1990s?

There is a particularly rich and interesting literature on the German judiciary under Adolf Hitler between 1933 and 1945. See, for example, Ingo Mueller, *Hitler's Justice: The Courts of the Third Reich* (Deborah L. Schneider, trans.) (1991). For a thoughtful essay on cultural differences in the reaction to this book, see Walter Weyrauch, "Limits of Perception: Reader Response to Hitler's Justice," 40 *American Journal of Comparative Law* 237 (1992). On the behavior of the judges in the former German Democratic Republic ("East Germany") under the Communist regime and their fate when German reunification did away with their jobs and their station in life, see Inga Markovits, "Last Days," 80 *California Law Review* 55 (1992). Contrast the post-World War II largely favorable treatment of the Nazi judges, as Mueller describes it, with the treatment of the Communist judges, as Markovits recounts.

In the Philippines, a period of martial law ended when an authoritarian leader lost power, and a more democratic period followed. How did all of this affect the work of the Supreme Court of that country? For an attempt to answer this question rigorously, see C. Neal Tate and Stacia L. Haynie, "Authoritarianism and the Functions of Courts: A Time Series Analysis of the Philippine Supreme Court, 1961–1987", 27 *Law & Society Review* 707 (1993).

7. The role of the trial judge differs from that of the appellate judge. In the lower criminal courts, for example, due process is at a minimum and large numbers of people are processed for relatively minor crimes. Here "the process itself is the primary punishment," that is, the stigma, detention and the whole cluster of the costs of pretrial process, may loom larger than the actual sentence that the judge hands out. See Malcolm M. Feeley, *The Process Is the Punishment: Handling Cases in a Lower Criminal Court* (1979).

In an important study, *Felony Justice: An Organizational Analysis of Criminal Courts* (1977), James Eisenstein and Herbert Jacob argue that court studies have focused too much attention on judges. Eisenstein and Jacob argue that courts are "organizations;" that what goes on in a courtroom is most profitably analyzed "as a group activity." Their book is a study of courtroom "workgroups," made up of all the personnel in the courtroom— prosecutors, defense counsel, clerks, bailiffs, as well as the judge. It is the interaction between the members of the work groups that "determines the outcome of criminal cases." [p. 10] See also Jeffery T. Ulmer, "Trial Judges in a Rural Court Community: Contexts, Organizational Relations, and Interaction Strategies," 23 *Journal of Contemporary Ethnography* 79 (1994).

Austin Sarat, "Judging in Trial Courts: An Exploratory Study," 39 *Journal of Politics* 291 (1977), suggests that trial judges can be divided into four types: (1) The *game type* enjoys the activities of judging and likes the rituals and rules of the court; (2) the *status type* is motivated to prove that they are in charge, and this type of judge often demeans others to elevate him or herself; (3) the *obligation type* sees being a judge a chance to do good and a duty; (4) the *program type* enjoys working on problems and pushes compromises or acceptable solutions rather than trying cases and letting the chips fall where they may. While these categories point to particular behaviors, Sarat's research failed to find that the type of judge made significant differences in the sentences given those convicted of crimes.

Marc Galanter, Frank S. Palen and John M. Thomas, "The Crusading Judge: Judicial Activism in Trial Courts," 52 *Southern California Law Review* 699 (1979), offers a slightly different set of categories: (1) The legalist judge who is oriented to the application of general rules in individual cases; (2) the mission-oriented judge who perceives his or her responsibility as using the law and judicial power to advance substantive goals such as cracking down on drunken driving; (3) the programmatic judge who responds to patterns of cases coming to the court; and (4) the entrepreneurial judge who steps outside the court and uses the press and politics to get results. The authors claim that local legal culture establishes the roles of trial judges. Active judges can move up to higher courts if their activity pleases those who influence judicial selection. Lawyers have many ways informally to sanction judges who step out of appropriate roles. For example, lawyers gossip about judges among themselves and with newspaper reporters. This may create a reputation which becomes more widely known. This reputation, in turn, may affect other rewards and punishments from the larger community.

8.　Marc Galanter, "Judicial Mediation in the United States," 12 *Journal of Law and Society* 1 (1985), discusses a new emphasis and openness about part of the role of trial judges in civil (non-criminal) cases. Trial judges more and more accept promoting settlements as part of their task and exchange information about how to succeed in getting parties to settle. Judges, for example, call conferences for reasons related to preparation for trial, but they use the opportunity to push for settlement. Galanter reports:

> Judges will often attempt to define "the present value of this case" or otherwise suggest the terms of settlement. A number of judges proudly sketch what some call the "Lloyds of London method": lawyers are asked to estimate what they think the case is worth and the probability that they will prevail; by combining these calculations the judges produces a figure that is "the synthesis of the probabilities of liability and the possibilities of damages." This is, of course, a fancy version of splitting the difference—a prospect which some find undisturbing since "All [that equally competent lawyers] ... need from the court is an indication that a figure somewhere between their two figures is fair." Other judges pursue the search for agreement by asking the parties to reveal their best offer: each hands the judge a slip of paper and the judge, comparing them, can tell whether there is a possibility of agreement....
>
> Judges are advised to give the lawyer something to "take back" to his client—often a calculation or estimate that has the judge's imprimatur on it. Some judges warn against attempts to influence litigants, but others include clients in settlement conferences and even hold private discussions with parties....

Why have trial judges turned into settling judges? Galanter offers a strategic explanation:

> There is more law—more legislation, more administrative regulation, more published judicial decisions. This proliferation of legal controls responds to and stimulates higher expectations of protection and redress among wider sections of the public. As the body of authoritative material becomes more massive, more complex and more refined, decision-makers (and other actors) are both constrained and supplied with resources and opportunities for legal innovation.
>
> Adjudication has become more complex, more expensive, more protracted, more rational—and more indeterminate. It is freer of arbitrary formalities, more open to evidence of complicated states of fact, and responsive to a wider range of argument. As the cost and complexity of litigation increases, both the potential inputs as well as the possible outcome of the trial became a source of bargaining counters that can be used at other phases of the process.... As the process became more costly and complex, it creates new strategic options for litigants while subjecting them to new contingencies....
>
> Demand for brokers who can help secure this information at low cost and risk converges with changes in judicial ideology. Judges share the

widespread elevated expectations of a beneficent result at the same time that they have less faith that legal doctrine provides a single right answer; or that full-blown adjudication will produce the most appropriate outcome. Concern with outcomes is juxtaposed with the realization that outcomes are affected by the contingencies of the process—by cost, delay, uncertainty, bargaining power and so forth. . . . Judicial promotion of settlements, along with interest in arbitration, mediation, and various alternatives, is a response to these concerns.

See, also, Ronald Bacigal, "An Empirical Case Study of Informal Alternative Dispute Resolution," 4 *Ohio State Journal on Dispute Resolution* 1 (1988). This a study of Federal District Judge Robert R. Merhige's handling of the Westinghouse uranium cases of the 1970s: "Addressing the merits of the case, Merhige offered a qualified ruling which he used to maneuver the parties toward a settlement on damages. His settlement efforts varied from hosting negotiation cocktail parties in his own home to requiring counsel to work on 'Saturdays, Sundays, and some days that aren't even on the calendar.' " See, further, Peter Schuck, "The Role of Judges in Settling Complex Cases: The Agent Orange Example," 53 *University of Chicago Law Review* 337 (1986).

9. There are many studies of sentencing by trial judges in criminal cases. The key question in most of this research concerns the degree to which factors other than the law and evidence affects sentences imposed on those convicted of crime. See Lawrence E. Cohen and James R. Kluegel, "Determinants of Juvenile Court Dispositions: Ascriptive and Achieved Factors in Two Metropolitan Courts," 43 *American Sociological Review* 162 (1978). Several studies suggest that girls and women are given harsher punishment than boys and men, particularly when sexual delinquency is involved. See Meda Chesney–Lind, "Judicial Enforcement of the Female Sex Roles: The Family Court and the Female Delinquent," 8 *Issues in Criminology* 51 (No. 2, 1973); Steven Schlossman and Stephanie Wallach, "The Crime of Precocious Sexuality: Female Juvenile Delinquency in the Progressive Era," 48 *Harvard Educational Review* 65 (1978).

What kind of judge would be more likely to be severe toward juvenile delinquents—a well-read young judge who kept up with professional literature, did not wear robes to court and was knowledgeable about delinquency; or a judge with the opposite traits? Somewhat surprisingly, a team of social scientists studying juvenile justice in the Boston area found that the more "progressive" judge was the more severe; that is, he more often recommended procedures that ended up with commitment of the juvenile. They were the judges who were most concerned with delinquency as a social problem, who were most trusting of the institutions to which juveniles were sent and most open to a "social welfare ideology." See Stanton Wheeler, Edna Bonacich, M. Richard Cramer & Irving K. Zola, "Agents of Delinquency Control: A Comparative Analysis," in *Controlling Delinquents*, at 31, 54 (Stanton Wheeler ed., 1968).

An intriguing article, which can be compared with the Wheeler study, is Martin A. Levin's, "Urban Politics and Judicial Behavior," 1 *Journal of Legal Studies* 193 (1972). Levin compared criminal court judges in two cities, Pittsburgh and Minneapolis. In Pittsburgh, old-time machine politics was still vigorous at the time of the study. Judges, nominated by the political parties and elected in partisan elections, tended to be lawyer-politicians. In Minneapolis, city elections were nonpartisan, political parties were weak, and judges were selected through a process heavily influenced by the organized bar. Judges tended to be lawyers without a history of political activity.

The Minneapolis judges were much harsher toward people accused of crime. They were "more oriented toward 'society' and its needs and protection, and towards the goals of their professional peers." Pittsburgh judges were "oriented towards the defendant rather than towards punishment or deterrence." They were "particularistic and pragmatic." Proceedings in Pittsburgh were more informal than in Minneapolis; judges seemed to understand and sympathize more with young ethnics who got in trouble; they were ethnics themselves. The style of the Minneapolis judges (typically white Protestants) was formal, the outcomes considerably more severe.

What is particularly interesting is that no one intended these differences in outcome, as such. Certainly, the political bosses in Pittsburgh, who made up slates of judges, were not interested in lighter sentences for those who stole cars or held up gas stations. The difference in output would seem to come from the structural difference in the process of selection and recruitment of judges in the two cities. The structural difference was reflected in a cultural difference—a difference in the attitudes and work habits of the judges. The attitude of the judges was, in turn, reflected in how they handled their cases.

(B) Lawyers

(1) Major Changes in the Profession: Conditions of Practice in Different Settings

(5.11) Review Essay: Fall from Grace or Business as Usual? A Retrospective Look at Lawyers on Wall Street and Main Street

John M. Conley and Scott Baker
30 *Law & Social Inquiry* 783 (2005).

[The following is a review essay, based on several classic studies of the legal profession and later work. The classic studies are:

Jerome E. Carlin. Lawyers on Their Own: The Solo Practitioner in an Urban Setting. San Francisco: Austin and Winfield Publishers, [1962] 1994. Pp. xxxii + 234.

Jerome E. Carlin. Lawyers' Ethics: A Survey of the New York City Bar. New York: Russell Sage Foundation, 1966. Pp. xxix + 267.

Erwin O. Smigel. The Wall Street Lawyer: Professional Organization Man? New York: Free Press of Glencoe, 1964 Pp. ix + 369.]

"The individual practitioner of law in Chicago is a self-made man who came up the hard way from poor, immigrant surroundings." So began the serious empirical study of American law practice. The year was 1962 and the book was Lawyers on Their Own: The Solo Practitioner in an Urban Setting, by Jerome Carlin (p. 1). Carlin's book reported on a qualitative, interview-based study of 83 Chicago lawyers who practiced on their own. Two years later, Erwin Smigel (1964) came out with a comparable study of the country's largest firms, The Wall Street Lawyer: Professional Organization Man? Then, in 1966, Carlin published Lawyers' Ethics: A Survey of the New York City Bar, based on more than 800 interviews, which examined the ethical beliefs and practices of a cross section of New York lawyers.

The picture that emerges from these three groundbreaking studies of law practice is straightforward. On Wall Street, in the biggest and most prestigious firms, things were good, at least for those who could get past the discriminatory entry barriers. Lawyers worked hard, but not too hard; did interesting legal work; were financially satisfied; competed for partnership, but prospered even if they lost; and enjoyed the benefits of practicing in a coherent, supportive, and ostensibly stable cultural environment. At the other end of the spectrum, among solo practitioners on "Main Street," things were very bad. It was a constant struggle to survive, and everyone was on his own. Survival was day to day and brought neither security nor satisfaction. Ethics was a frequent casualty of this Darwinian contest. When they thought of them at all, Main Street lawyers saw Wall Street lawyers not as colleagues but as an entirely foreign and hostile "other."

Somewhere between then and now the situation changed dramatically, almost to the point of role reversal. The recent literature about the realities of law practice tends to be relentlessly negative ...: ethical standards are abysmal, lawyers are workaholics, and the demands of practice ruin their personal and family lives. Purportedly empirical studies show epidemic dissatisfaction among lawyers, and rates of alcoholism, mental illness, and suicide that far exceed those in the general population. In contrast to what Carlin and Smigel reported 40 years ago, however, things are now said to be worst in the biggest firms. While big-firm practice is often depicted as an economic pressure cooker and an ethical cesspool, more recent studies of small-firm and solo lawyers reflect professional lives that, while stressful, are considerably more appealing in most respects except compensation.

In this essay, we examine more than 40 years of empirical studies of law practice in an effort to understand exactly what changes have occurred in lawyers' lives, and why. In part I we review in greater detail the state of the profession in the 1960s as reported by Carlin and Smigel, and contrast that with the picture presented in a number of more recent books and articles. We are particularly attentive to the big firm-small firm divide that seemed so significant to Carlin and Smigel, and that has continued to be a dominant theme in the literature. In part II we examine the reasons for the changes that have been observed, exploring economic and other factors external to law firms, as well as those—which we loosely label "cultural"—that seem to work from within. In part III we focus on the empirical evidence that bears on the concept of the lawyer as a "professional" as opposed to a worker or entrepreneur. While the normative writing on the topic has tended to decry a decline from a golden age, or to deconstruct that claim, the empirical literature tells a more complex story of contested ideals and practices.

In fact, much of the debate surrounding the changes of the last 40 years seems to come together under the heading of professionalism. Confounding the predictions that would have been made in the 1960s, Wall Street lawyers emerge as the pawns of market forces, their professionalism a casualty of their desperate and sometimes puzzling responses to those forces. Small practice lawyers, by contrast, have found new ways to create professional communities as they cling to survival in what has always been a difficult economic environment.

I. HOW HAS LAW PRACTICE CHANGED?

Comparing Smigel's account of Wall Street practice and Carlin's parallel study of Main Street lawyers with more recent empirical research, several themes emerge. Among the biggest firms, brutal economic forces have reportedly ended life as Smigel knew it. Competition is fierce and unending, with such consequences as corporate-style mergers and acquisitions; the loss of security among partners who were formerly set for life; even longer odds for associates, with the reward for success often nothing more than an oxymoronic "nonequity partnership"; intolerable working hours for everyone; and a catastrophic decline in ethical standards. One of the few things on the plus side is much greater representation of women, though not necessarily at the partnership level; racial diversification has moved much more slowly. In small firms and solo offices, things seem to have improved. While the problems that Carlin reported in 1962 persist—or have been exacerbated by the huge growth in the lawyer population—no recent study shares the dismal tone of Carlin's original. Small-firm and solo lawyers survive and some prosper; while they continue to attack ethical regulation as the work of an elite cartel, they maintain their own vision of professionalism.

A. Large Firms

A useful way to track the changes in large-firm practice is to begin with Smigel and progress through Michael Kelly's (1996) *Lives of Lawyers* to Milton Regan's (2004) *Eat What You Kill*, with intermediate stops at several other sources. As noted above, Smigel's *Wall Street Lawyers* paints a picture of prosperity, general satisfaction, and stability, although change was clearly on the horizon. Smigel described the day-to-day work as routine, though remuneratively so. His Wall Street lawyers followed an orderly progression from task-oriented associate to junior partner who managed projects in a specialized area to senior partner, a generalist who exercised strategic control over a broad range of matters. Looking through the eyes of both partners and associates, Smigel analyzed the combination of legal ability, hard work, business getting, and social background that governed a competition for partnership in which only about 10 percent of associates succeeded. In spite of this high fatality rate, the competition will strike contemporary readers as remarkably genteel, perhaps because of the firms' near-perfect success in placing the losers in attractive and well-paying positions with clients and smaller firms.

The stability that Smigel observed is not at all surprising given the firms' homogeneity. More than half of the partners in the Wall Street firms he studied came from private high schools, more than 70 percent had gone to law school at Harvard, Yale, or Columbia, and 30 percent were listed in the Social Register. As for religion, ethnicity, and race, he found (pp. 44–45) that "while most large law firms are now employing Jewish lawyers, they probably limit the number of Jews they will accept"; and that Catholics were discriminated against not as Catholics per se, but because of "their 'lower-class' origins, their foreign-born parents, and their lack of 'proper' education." During his 18 months of research he "heard of only three Negroes who had been hired by large law firms," two of whom were "women who did not meet the client." Women of all races were virtually nonexistent, excluded because of "(1) objections from the client, and (2) the expectation that the girls would get married and leave" (p. 47).

But Smigel foresaw change, and outlined it with remarkable prescience. The rapid expansion of economic activity that followed World War II was leading big firms to get even bigger. At the time, "Wall Street" was almost synonymous with "big," as Smigel's 1959 survey found only 17 American firms outside Manhattan with more than 50 lawyers. This "trend toward bigness" was already producing "mammoth" firms of more than 100 lawyers (p. 351). Although most of his informants believed that such firms had "reached or passed their optimum size," he predicted continued growth in cities throughout the country (pp. 350–51).

He further predicted that all firms, even those that did not grow, would become more specialized and more bureaucratic. The managerial demands on partners would intensify and firms would be organized and governed more like businesses and "less in the tradition of the profession" (p. 351). . . . At a more detailed level, Smigel's (p. 351) specific predictions about the changes that would come to pass were stunningly accurate, and are therefore worth quoting at length:

> Given the need for the specialist and the related need to coordinate them, even those firms that do not grow will become more like today's large firms, especially if new legal specialties continue to develop. For the large firms it may mean that the scope will become increasingly narrow. If the number and scope of specialties increases, it should be expected that the

amount of dissensus in an organization should also increase. To offset this, the tendency of the organization then will be to extend its bureaucratic hold over its workers. This tendency, plus the predicted growth of firms considered large at this stage of their development, should make them more bureaucratic. We have in fact seen that this is already happening as a consequence of associates' demands and the increasing difficulty involved in recruitment. The people who control the firms will find themselves further and further away from the lawyers they employ. Time spent on managerial duties will increase, and the number of managerial positions will multiply. Office mechanization of employment records, billing procedures, or cost accounting systems will increase and so will office regulations and an increasing need for discipline on lower level aspects of the job. Even the practice of the law will change (as it is changing in medicine), for machines will be able to "Shepardize" a matter (research it) faster and perhaps more thoroughly than a lawyer.

Finally, he took note—in a single paragraph—of the emerging conflict between the lawyer's professional and personal lives. "Some of these men value family over firm and leave the large law office"; one of his informants "knew a lot of men who lost their partnerships on the New Haven Railroad" (p. 75). But at this point in history it was not yet a major problem for the firms, since "default" by lawyers who wanted to spend more time at home simply "eliminated a type of lawyer they cannot use" (p. 75).

The quality of Smigel's foresight becomes clear if one jumps ahead thirty years to Marc Galanter and Thomas Palay's (1992) "The Transformation of the Big Law Firm" ... Whereas Smigel had found only 38 law firms in the United States with more than 50 lawyers (21 of them in New York City), by 1985 there were 508. The large firms were also growing much more quickly. Consistent with Smigel's prediction of more businesslike behavior, multicity branch offices, mergers, performance-based compensation systems, marketing, the lateral hiring of partners from other firms, and the use of nonlawyer firm managers were all becoming common features of the legal landscape.

These changes had a particularly strong impact on associates. On the one hand, they were being recruited more aggressively and paid a lot more (Wall Street starting salaries rose from $10,000 in 1967 to $65,000 in 1986, driven largely by two controversial increases by New York's Cravath, Swain & Moore). Moreover, Galanter and Palay (p. 53) reported that meritocracy ruled in hiring: "Religious, racial, and gender barriers have been swept away. The social exclusiveness that was still a feature of the world of elite law practice in 1960 has receded into insignificance." On the other hand, associates were working much longer hours, and the big firms had decreased the percentage of associates making partner and stretched out the time to partnership.

The day-to-day correlates of these structural changes are vividly depicted in Michael Kelly's (1996) ethnographic *Lives of Lawyers: Journeys in the Organizations of Practice*.... The project ... [was] a lengthy, open-ended, interview-based ethnography of five practice organizations: a large, recently merged private firm; a medium-sized "quality of life" private firm; a corporate in-house counsel department; the law department of a public agency; and a small partnership of "cause" lawyers who focused on criminal defense and civil rights work.

In examining a generation of change in the legal profession, Kelly discovered that "two different reactions or stories, one accepting, one critical, have emerged as explanations of these changes" (2). Both stories focused on big firms. One version, rooted in "the new legal journalism" pioneered by the *American Lawyer*, was an "upbeat, even breathless and celebratory" economic story of "the emergence of top-tier firms, great leaders, brash young lawyers who are magnets for business, and the general excitement of it all" (2). The other was "a story told with some emotion about a decline in values, the triumph of greed, the transformation of law from a public good to a marketplace commodity, and a 'profession' degenerating into a mere 'business' " (p. 2).

In a chapter entitled "Playing in the Big Leagues at McKinnon, Moreland and Fox" (p. 25), Kelly picked up Smigel's Wall Street story in the late 1980s. Big firms had pushed well past the 100–lawyer barrier that Smigel's informants foresaw. Kelly also documented the further erosion of the line between professional and business organizations. The pseudonymous McKinnon firm had grown in a way probably unthinkable to Smigel's informants: "through skillful acquisitions and mergers—the 'rape and pillage' method, as one associate laughingly puts it" (p. 27). McKinnon was one of a new breed of entrepreneurial firms, with a reputation and self-image as "young . . . aggressive, hard-working, talented business advisors and transactional lawyers, with an expanding client base of entrepreneurs" (p. 27).

McKinnon's internal norms and day-to-day practices were undergoing radical change in the wake of its "raping and pillaging." By the mid–1990s mergers and acquisitions had become commonplace in the profession, justified by claims about "synergy," "cross-marketing opportunities," economies of scale, and client demand for full-service firms . . . But this merger mania has had a dark side. Law firm break-ups have also become commonplace, and the 1990s and the early years of this century have seen the spectacular failures of such respected legal institutions as San Francisco's Brobeck, Phleger & Harrison and Boston's Hill & Barlow. . . . Examining this aspect of the merger phenomenon, Kelly used the McKinnon case to highlight the idiosyncratic cultures of law firms and the inherent difficulty of melding them. . . .

Although Kelly presented but a single big-firm case, there is abundant reason to believe that he accurately identified some of the most important trends in big-firm practice. As noted earlier, a much-discussed survey literature . . . suggests that lawyers work harder than ever before, feel more pressure, and consequently suffer from abysmal levels of satisfaction, epidemic mental health problems, and constant temptation to cut ethical corners. While . . . these apocalyptic inferences may be overblown, it is hard to find any vestiges of Smigel's Golden Age in contemporary accounts of large-firm practice.

Another body of evidence that complements the work of Galanter and Palay and Kelly comes from a nine-year teaching project in which one of us ... [Conley] has conducted over 100 interviews with lawyers in a variety of practice settings. The large-firm informants have confirmed that the trends prophesied by Smigel and first identified in the 1990s are still with us, and more problematic than ever. These lawyers have emphasized the growth in firm size; the merger of large firms into even larger multinational entities; the growing and sometimes extreme specialization in individual lawyers' practices; the threatened extinction of the medium-sized, single-city firm; the ever-widening base of the associate-partner pyramid in large firms, coupled with the ever-lengthening odds of making partner; the demise of some prominent large firms; the increasing pressure to bill hours felt by both partners and associates; frequent job switching by lawyers at all levels; and a decline in client loyalty. They have ascribed it all to an economic climate that grows harsher and more competitive every year.

Most of Conley's large-firm informants rated a declining quality of life as the single biggest challenge facing the profession. Some of them admitted to constant tension between the personal and professional, with the latter usually prevailing. Others claimed success in managing the conflict. Even here, however, follow-up questioning revealed details that seemed not to add up; one informant, for example, described long days, work on a majority of weekends, and travel on an almost weekly basis, and then characterized her work-family balance as healthy.

In a partial refutation of Galanter and Palay's claim about the disappearance of gender bias in large firms, Conley's informants stressed the disproportionate impact that these pressures may have on women. They emphasized that the time demands are greatest during the very years when women would like to have children and spend the most time with them. In one particularly riveting interview, a litigator in a national firm who is the mother of three young children said that, because of a trial, she had had only two days (days, not weekdays) off during the last quarter of 2003. A couple of women volunteered that their careers have been manageable only because of their decision not to have children. A fortunate few reported that a happy combination of an enlightened husband with a more flexible job and exceptional childcare helpers has enabled them to meet their family obligations without sacrificing their careers. For most, though, the conflict is intractable and something must give way.

Other sources, beginning with Cynthia Fuchs Epstein's ... ground breaking *Women in Law*, have also painted an improved but still troubling picture of both gender and racial progress in large firms. While women now comprise at least 50 percent of the class at most law schools and are well represented in the junior associate ranks, a number of studies demonstrate that relatively few achieve partnership and even fewer advance to leadership positions in their firms. . . . The explanation usually advanced is the inability to reconcile the tyranny of billable hours with the reality of women's lives. On the racial front, the story is qualitatively similar—entry-level opportunities have improved and overt, intentional discrimination is rarely alleged—but quantitatively worse, with the number of minority partners being barely measurable. . . . Explanations range from subtle racism . . . to the lack of mentors and role models to the public service burdens borne by minority lawyers in high-visibility firms. . . .

To conclude this story of change, the most recent study of big-firm practice is also the most negative. In *Eat What You Kill: The Fall of a Wall Street Lawyer,* by Milton Regan (2004), the Wall Street elite now occupy that circle of hell that Carlin had reserved for the most desperate of solo practitioners. The book chronicles the rise, fall from grace, and eventual conviction and imprisonment of John Gellene, a star bankruptcy lawyer at the old, rich, and influential Wall Street firm of Milbank, Tweed, Hadley & McCloy. Regan based the book on court transcripts, financial documents, and other public records, and, most importantly, interviews with a wide range of participants in and observers of the Gellene case. While representing a large company in a corporate bankruptcy—a lucrative assignment for the firm—Gellene failed to disclose that he and other Milbank lawyers had represented parties that were potentially adverse to the company in some unrelated matters. He never corrected this omission on multiple occasions when it might have been relatively easy to do so.

Approaching the Gellene story as a legal ethicist, Regan's major aims are to figure out why Gellene risked "all he had . . . by failing to make a simple disclosure" (p. 4), and how to prevent such things from happening in the future. His explanation focuses heavily on Gellene's individual psychology, but also situates the protagonist in the context of contemporary Wall Street practice. Regan sees an interaction between Gellene's personal insecurities and the law firm environment in which he worked. Regan observes that at several points in Gellene's career, the pressure of law-firm competition led him to brush aside as trivial the completion of tasks that were in fact quite significant. When he first went to work at Milbank, for example, he failed to complete his bar application paperwork and then hid for years the fact that he was not actually licensed to practice law. Gellene refused to take advantage of subsequent opportunities to fix the various problems, not because of any rational fear of the consequences, but because he was pathologically afraid of looking stupid. These same forces were at work in the bankruptcy case, compounded by the desire not to cost Milbank its fee by disclosing a potential conflict of interest. In a nutshell,

> Gellene wanted to avoid disclosure because it would lead to disqualification [of Milbank]. He wanted to avoid disqualification because he was anxious about his future in a competitive law firm, and he wanted to cultivate a relationship with an important partner who he anticipated would prefer that he not disclose the connection. (p. 349).

So Gellene's story becomes an epitome of all that has changed for the worse in Wall Street practice. The story, Regan writes, "offers a window to the dramatic forces that have irrevocably transformed elite law firm practice over the past quarter century" (p. 4). In general, radical economic changes appear to have forced the genteel Wall Street of the 1960s to become the "eat what you kill" Wall Street of the 1990s. Regan's analysis goes beyond simple economic determinism, however, and we will revisit it in part II when we consider the question of why practice has changed as it has.

B. Small Firms

As depicted by Carlin ..., the life of a small-firm lawyer was nasty and brutish, if not necessarily short. According to a contemporary newspaper review of Lawyers on Their Own, the book was "a look at the other side of the legal tracks.... Bar associations should do something about this unpretty picture if they are to justify the existence of individual lawyers" (p. xi).

By Carlin's account, the fundamental problem that solo lawyers faced was the obvious one of isolation: from other lawyers, from both the support and the ethical discipline of the organized bar, and from the more lucrative and "respectable" kinds of clients and business. The isolation began at the outset of the typical solo career (p. 3):

> The individual practitioner of law in Chicago is a self-made man who came up the hard way from poor, immigrant surroundings. His father, generally an immigrant from Eastern Europe with little or no formal education, was in most cases the proprietor of a small business. The one burning ambition of the son was to escape from the ghetto, to rise above his father, to become a professional man.

Most of these lawyers told Carlin they had had no specific intention to become a lawyer, but found the law easier to get into than medicine or the other professions. Most went to night law school, required multiple tries to pass the bar exam, and began an apprenticeship of space-for-services arrangements with established lawyers, trying to subsist on the crumbs of business that the latter left behind. Those who succeeded performed a mix of real estate, business, tax, personal injury, divorce, probate, collection, and criminal work for individuals and small businesses. Carlin (pp. 17–18) characterized their work as

> those residual matters (and clients) that the large firms have not preempted: (1) matters not large enough or remunerative for the large firms to handle ... [and] (2) the undesirable cases, the dirty work, those areas of practice that have associated with them an aura of influencing and fixing and that involve arrangements with clients and others that are felt by the large firms to be professionally damaging.

Moreover, the nature of such steady work as was available—title searching, bookkeeping for business clients, "fixing" things with local authorities— meant that the solo lawyers were "only rarely called upon to practice law in the traditional sense" (p. 208), and were subject to constant poaching from nonlawyers.

Even relative success with such work did not end the isolation, however, as solo practitioners rarely joined firms, but instead were condemned by "the rigidity of the class structure of the metropolitan bar" to constitute a permanent professional underclass (p. 18). The pursuit of business led many to join religious, ethnic, or civic organizations, but this participation was viewed as a competitive rather than a social endeavor, and often an unrewarding one; as one lawyer put it (p. 128), "You're not the only lawyer in the Elks or the Legion." Not surprisingly, the fate of solo lawyers produced both disaffection and ethical problems. Surviving as an independent professional produced little satisfaction; on the contrary,

> Finding himself on the lowest rung of the status ladder of the profession, with little or no chance of rising, his practice restricted to the least desirable and least remunerative matters—to the dirty work of the profession, and beset by competition from lawyers and laymen alike, the individual practitioner is frequently a dissatisfied, disappointed, resentful, angry man. (p. 168)

Doing this "dirty work" often produced "sharp conflict" between the rules of professional conduct and "the practical demands of individual practice" (p. 155). Conflicts were brought about by the need to engage in the then-forbidden practice of solicitation, the pressure to make payoffs and buy political influence on behalf of clients, and the difficulty of maintaining an appropriate relationship with clients who also became business partners. Solo practitioners saw ethics rules as ivory-tower pronouncements written and enforced by elitist big-firm lawyers who never had to worry about making a living.

So daunting were these problems that Carlin devoted his next project to the ethics of solo practitioners in New York. The news was comparably grim (p. xxii): "The lawyer most prone to ethical deviation is the lawyer who is on his own or in a small firm, representing 'ordinary' clients." The explanation was again isolation, as such a lawyer had "no coterie of colleagues to sustain him in stresses and strains of his practice."

The Chicago story was picked up in the 1970s by John Heinz and Edward Laumann. Their study of the Chicago bar ... was based on structured, quantitatively analyzed interviews with more than 700 lawyers. They observed a "great divide ... between the kinds of law practices that serve primarily corporate clients and those that serve primarily individual persons or small businesses" (p. 91). Confirming Carlin's basic insight, they described the bar as being divided into "two separate professions" that differed in prestige and social background and whose members had little personal contact with each other. Ironically, though, the more prestigious of these "hemispheres," the one whose members represented corporate clients rather than individuals, enjoyed less independence. Heinz and Laumann (p. 171) found that "corporate clients to a large degree dictate the nature of the work done," whereas lawyers representing individuals "dominate their clients and the decisions that are made about the work."

Two decades later, when Carroll Seron ... published *The Business of Practicing Law: The Work Lives of Solo and Small–Firm Attorneys*, the structure of small-firm practice seemed generally similar, but the grimness that characterized Carlin's portrait was gone. Seron conducted 102 90–minute interviews of a random sample of solo and small-firm lawyers in New York City and the surrounding metropolitan area. The Business of Practicing Law is organized around such themes as "Negotiating Time," "Getting Clients," and "Serving Clients and Consumers" (pp. 31, 48, 106). The effect of reading Seron's book is to listen in on a group of lawyers having a series of roundtable discussions about the principal issues in their professional and personal lives.

Seron's focus was on individuals dealing with the demands of being a practicing lawyer. She emphasized such "structural" factors as economic forces, including the changing needs and demands of clients, and the tensions of managing both a law practice and a family (p. 143). Not surprisingly, the lawyers she studied found it hard to respond to those pressures. While many derived satisfaction from at least some of their work and from a sense of professionalism, most were, above all, small business people striving for a slice of an ever more competitive pie. In common with all small business people, when work simply had to be done, these lawyers had to do it themselves. Such pressures were most acutely felt by women lawyers, the vast majority of whom reported having principal or sole responsibility for the management of their households.

Despite all these difficulties, the small-firm world that Seron depicted was nowhere near as dismal as the one that Carlin had described more than thirty years earlier. Unlike Carlin's informants, most of Seron's subjects came to law as a matter of choice rather than desperation. Like Carlin's lawyers, they found professional responsibility a challenge, although the problem was more subtle than fixing cases. Their major concern was delivering a professional service in an economic environment where clients are also "empowered consumers" who are "more interested in price than quality" (p. 107).

But Seron's lawyers reported coping, if barely, with the demands of "responding to the emotional-legal demands of clients, carrying a large enough caseload to pay the bills, charging enough to earn a living, and yet feeling that they are able to provide 'quality' service" (p. 110). They valued " 'being patient, being kind' " to clients, and "the need to be truthful and honest" (p. 112). And while they decried the organized bar's call for pro bono service to the poor as "an elitist claim to good works" (p. 129), they believed that they were performing a significant public service by making representation available and affordable to ordinary people. Above all, they carried on, if not wholly satisfied, then at least not on the edge of despair.

Other recent studies offer additional reasons to conclude that Carlin's depiction of the small office is no longer accurate or, perhaps, was limited by the theoretical perspective of its author or the localized nature of its sample.

The best of these newer works challenges the theme of isolation that pervades Carlin's work.... A study by Lynn Mather, Craig McEwen, and Richard Maiman, is based on 163 interviews with divorce lawyers in Maine and New Hampshire in 1990 and 1991. Mather and her colleagues shared Seron's focus on the influence of structural factors on individual lawyers. At the same time, however, they saw their lawyer-informants as participating in multiple "communities of practice," including their local legal communities, "communities of divorce lawyers" (p. 41, 47), and the legal community more generally. As we discuss in more detail in part II.C, these communities help to provide a set of shared professional resources that is nowhere in evidence in Carlin's portrayal.

Leslie Levin ... has revisited Carlin's specific claims about the ethical shortcomings of small-firm and solo lawyers in an interview study of 41 New York City-area practitioners. Levin reported that, just as in Carlin's day, the majority of disciplinary cases still involve small-office lawyers, but suggested that the underlying reality is complex. The lawyers themselves continue to believe that the elite segment of the bar fails to understand the environment in which they must compete and unfairly proscribes business practices that they view as legitimate, such as paying referral fees or cutting corners in notarizing documents. On the other hand, these lawyers reported knowing (and caring) little about the formal rules of professional responsibility and admitted that serious misconduct can come about when lawyers trying to survive on their own "simply are overwhelmed by their circumstances" (p. 385).

But in spite of these difficulties, Levin's informants, like Seron's subjects, worry a great deal about providing an appropriately professional level of service. Most of them work hard at updating their legal knowledge, while many also limit the areas in which they practice. And like the divorce lawyers that Mather and her colleagues studied, Levin's informants seek to overcome the inherent isolation of their practices by forming and participating in ad hoc professional networks. We return to this theme in parts II.C and III.B.

C. The Rise of the Employee–Lawyer

One final trend that has been widely chronicled over the last 40 years is the growth in the number and percentage of lawyers who work for someone else. Richard Abel ... documented the trend statistically in his 1989 classic, *American Lawyers*. Between 1948 and 1989 the proportion of all American lawyers who were partners in private firms stayed constant at about 25 percent. Over the same period, lawyers in solo practice declined from over 60 percent to just one-third of the total. Employed lawyers—principally associates in private firms, in-house corporate counsel, and government lawyers—took up much of the slack. These trends have continued.

Associates in large law firms account for a good deal of the growth among the "employed": big firms are bigger and more highly leveraged, so they have many more associates, in both absolute and relative terms ... Associates, though, are employees who hope to become partners, however unrealistic that dream may be. More interesting is the growth in the in-house counsel segment (from just over 3 to almost 11 percent of all lawyers, according to Abel), since these lawyers are corporate employees who aspire to stay that way.

Conley's . . . interview subjects have provided a detailed and consistent picture of the change in in-house practice. A generation ago, the stereotype of the in-house counsel was a lawyer who had left private practice, often after being passed over for partner, and was relegated to doing routine, repetitive corporate work, while everything interesting was farmed out to private firms. The current picture represents an almost total reversal. Now, cost-control concerns dictate that as much work as possible be done in-house. Corporate counsel see themselves as fully capable of handling anything other than litigation, which they now manage much more closely than in the past, and very large transactions that require the short-term application of extraordinary resources. Significantly, in-house counsel also perceive a dramatic shift in the power relationships they have with their outside lawyers. Twenty-five years ago, a corporate counsel might have seen himself or herself as dependent on a single outside law firm that the company had relied on for years. Now, in-house counsel believe that they call the shots, using outside lawyers on an as-needed basis, forcing firms to compete for individual pieces of business, and taking an assertive role in monitoring fees.

Because they are now doing much more, in-house counsel report, their staffs have more and better lawyers than a generation ago. They believe themselves to be every bit as able as their outside counterparts, and describe their in-house career path as a matter of choice rather than relegation. They typically ascribe their choice to quality-of-life concerns, although not in the simple sense of hours worked. On the contrary, they believe that they work hours that are at least as long as their private-firm counterparts. Rather, they talk of the benefits of having a single client. On the professional side, this reduces the need to perform triage among the conflicting, nonnegotiable demands of multiple clients, with some getting your best work, some getting work that is just good enough, and some getting ignored. This, they believe, leads to a more rational and, consequently, less stressful day-to-day work environment. On the personal side, periods of peak work tend to be more predictable than in law firms. Although unexpected crises can and do occur, they know what is going on inside the company and can anticipate many problems. In a private law firm, by contrast, the lawyer may not hear from the client until the crisis is at hand.

Early in this evolution, Eve Spangler raised the question of what these changes meant for the professional standing of the lawyers involved. Her study . . . was based on structured interviews with lawyer-employees in large private law firms, corporations, government agencies, and legal services offices. Spangler repeatedly stressed that the employed lawyers she studied, regardless of where they worked, were in economic and structural terms much more like corporate employees than independent professionals. Ultimately, she concluded, "the fate of staff attorneys seems to move somewhat closer to the fate of every man, that of relatively powerless individuals being absorbed by very powerful organizations" (p. 195) . . .

II. WHY HAVE THINGS CHANGED?

In this part we consider the reasons for the changes in law practice that have been observed over the last 40 years. The explanations that have been advanced fall into two general categories. The first consists of "hard," largely economic forces that are external to law firms. Small and solo practices have faced severe economic pressure since the beginning, while for large, elite firms worrying about money is a relatively recent phenomenon. In what has become the standard account of big-firm change, economic forces are said to exert a strong deterministic effect, or at a minimum are treated as the most influential contributors to a more complex causal picture. In the second category are "soft" factors—norms, attitudes, beliefs, and values—that are internal to individual lawyers, practice organizations, and practice communities. These influences are subtle and difficult to measure, but they have been argued to be no less real than economic forces in their impact on the profession, among both large and small firms. Although some of these factors are psychological, we will group them under the shorthand heading of "culture" because, as will become evident, their essential contribution is to shape shared understandings in social contexts.

In this part we consider evidence for both the hard and soft explanations. We begin by setting out the standard economic story. We next review some research from the law and economics tradition that tests the critical premise of that story: that lawyers are rational economic actors. We then take up cultural explanations. Some of the relevant research argues that economics has served as rationalization rather than reason for some of the dramatic changes in large-firm practice, while other studies focus on the cultural means that small-firm and solo lawyers have evolved to combat the isolation that so troubled Carlin.

A. Economics: The Standard Account

Regan's . . . depiction of Milbank, Tweed and the fall of John Gellene presents a vivid instance of the standard economic account of change in large law firms. By the late 1960s client companies were increasingly buffeted by the competitive pressures of globalization and a technology-driven decline in the life cycles of their products. As they looked for ways to cut costs, legal services were not exempt. Clients began to shop, in the process realizing that large firms were generally fungible and that work could be divided up among competing firms. As a consequence, whereas large firms had once sent one-line bills "for services rendered" that were paid without question, they were now forced to act like retailers, cutting prices to match the competition and even offering loss leaders. Firm profit margins fell as big-firm lawyers were suddenly thrust into the cutthroat global economy. Large corporate firms that had prospered for generations went out of business without warning.

By Regan's account, the impact of these economic forces on the professional lives of Wall Street lawyers and the cultures of their firms was direct and dramatic. For the first time, law firm partners were forced to think like business managers. Smigel had been right, though not in precisely the ways he had envisioned. Stability and predictability were immediate casualties. Lawyers quickly realized that the key to profitability was attracting " 'high end' legal work, which involves more customized services for which the firm can charge a premium" over ordinary hourly rates. In biological terms, firms now needed to identify and move into ecological niches in which they could claim a competitive advantage. The most-valued partners would be those who could provide the customized services that would command premium fees, and the most-valued clients would be those needing such services and able to pay for them.

Driven by these new economic forces, firm decision makers now routinely did the formerly unthinkable. Lifetime tenure and lockstep compensation vanished. Partners who could not add value in the new economic climate had their compensation cut or were forced out. As in Regan's title phrase, if you didn't kill, you didn't eat. The long-standing reluctance to steal lawyers from other firms also became a thing of the past as firms engaged in bidding wars over lawyers with a demonstrated ability to generate "high end" work. And just as clients now changed law firms without hesitation, the firms began to "fire" clients whose work was not sufficiently profitable.

Within the firms, the partnership competition—what Marc Galanter and Thomas Palay ... had famously called the "tournament of lawyers"—turned into a lifetime ordeal. Associates striving to make partner still work sweatshop hours, nurture relationships with powerful partners, seek to develop unique skills, and struggle to become known to major clients. But now it never ends. Many firms have gone to two-tiered partnerships. Successful associates graduate initially to a nominal "nonequity" partnership, whose members are merely associates with an honorific title. Only a small fraction of those ever become revenue-sharing or "equity" partners. Even equity partners must keep looking over their shoulders. A common retort is that Wall Street partners "must" do these things only if they insist on maintaining an income far beyond the dreams of avarice—couldn't they work and worry less if they would accept a salary that was merely exorbitant? The current reality, however, is that cutting back is not an option for those who want to stay in the firm. Those who drop out of the perpetual tournament will find themselves on the street.

Regan presents the evolution of Milbank and the tragedy of Gellene as a case study in the money-driven transformation of Wall Street practice. Confronted by economic pressure for the first time in its long history, Milbank responded as others had. The particular move that ultimately begat the Gellene scandal was an effort to specialize in the representation of large corporate debtors in the bankruptcy reorganization process. Milbank had bankruptcy experience, but did most of its work on behalf of individual creditors: steady piecework, but not highly profitable. Directing a reorganization on behalf of a large debtor, on the other hand, was a major project that could yield huge fees, ordered by the bankruptcy court and payable off the top of the estate. To move into this niche, it hired Larry Lederman, a "rainmaker" from the mergers and acquisitions powerhouse Wachtell, Lipton, Rosen & Katz, and gave him a free hand to wheel and deal. Gellene, now a bankruptcy partner but never secure in the new dispensation, saw Lederman as his ticket to continued success in the tournament. Economic pressures worked in grotesque synergy with his own psychological problems as Gellene committed his bizarre crime. Since even rainmakers are only a bad year away from unemployment, Lederman felt the same pressures. Consequently, when Gellene obliquely raised the possibility of a conflict on at least one occasion, Lederman either missed the point or chose to ignore it.

It should be pointed out that in spite of the strong economic theme that dominates the Gellene story, Regan's own analysis is not deterministic. In addition to economics, he also makes persuasive cases for the respective contributions of Gellene's psychological problems, pure greed, and the ethical environment in the big-time bankruptcy bar, and ultimately declines to accord primacy to any single factor. Instead, all are seen as part of an indivisible whole, all having attributes of both chicken and egg.

B.   Testing the Premise of Economic Rationality

The key to the conventional economic story of change in the legal profession is the premise that lawyers are rational and knowledgeable economic actors. However, law and economics research on this point has been inclusive. We begin with the dominant theoretical account of the structure of large law firms, the tournament model. Research on this model appears to confirm the power of economic determinants and the rationality of lawyers' responses to them, although other, case-specific evidence indicates that the model does not apply in all conditions. We then review research on the setting of associates' salaries, which tends to show that when confronted with new economic realities, law firms take a follow-the-leader approach, which may or may not make economic sense.

1.   Tournament Theory and Exponential Growth

For at least the past 50 years, large law firms have hired associates from elite schools and put them through the grueling seven to ten-year "tournament" analyzed by Galanter and Palay. At the end of the tournament, a fraction of the associates make partner. Those who do not are fired, a fate that until recently has been quite tolerable, because the firms have been able to "outplace" almost all the losers with clients or top-notch smaller firms. Since it consumes a significant part of the career of every lawyer who passes through the firm, the tournament is a defining element of big-firm life.

To understand the economic explanation for the tournament, consider first why lawyers hire associates. Lawyers can, and often do, work as solo practitioners. What motivates some lawyers to hire associates to join them in a common enterprise? The economic answer is investment in human capital.

Over time, lawyers invest in the acquisition of skills. They learn how to manage transactions, try cases, and handle clients, along the way developing a reputation for sound legal work. In other words, they create their own human capital. No matter how much human capital a lawyer has, however, she has only so many hours in a day to use it. As a result, many lawyers, especially senior practitioners, will have excess human capital. They will attract more legal work than they can do by themselves. Rather than let this work go to a competitor, the senior lawyer (the partner) shares her human capital with a junior lawyer, or associate.

But as the partner-associate relationship solves the problem of excess human capital, it invites others. After a time, the two lawyers become mutually dependent. The associate finds it costly to leave because, in a new job, he will have to learn the habits and desires of another partner and another set of clients. On the other hand, the partner cannot easily fire and replace the associate because of the cost of bringing a replacement up to speed. Yet even as this interdependence gives both partner and associate a measure of security, it also gives both of them incentives to act opportunistically. The associate, knowing that the partner will be reluctant to fire him, has an incentive to shirk. The partner, knowing that associate will be reluctant to quit and start over in a new firm, has an incentive never to increase the associate's wages.

The tournament system mitigates these incentive problems. By holding out the lucrative, if distant, partnership prize, the tournament defers some of the associate's compensation. If the associate shirks, quits, and/or steals clients, she forfeits her chance for the prize. The tournament thus replaces an intrusive and maybe ineffective way to control associate misbehavior—direct monitoring—with a less costly and more efficient alternative. At the same time, it disciplines the temptation to hold associates in perpetual wage servitude. If the partnership fails to promote a certain percentage of associates each year, associates will lose faith; many will quit and few will agree to work for the firm in the future. The tournament system thus appears to be a rational response to the distinguishing characteristics of the legal business, a way to leverage human capital without exposing it to theft.

Galanter and Palay argued that firms using the tournament system would be forced to grow at an ever-increasing rate. The growth argument is elegant in its simplicity. Each year the firm promotes a fixed number of associates. Each of these associates needs to be replaced by a new one. In addition, however, all the newly minted partners need associates to whom they can assign work. By the time the associate becomes a partner, she will have accumulated her own human capital, her own clients, and her own reputation. If the partnership promotes wisely, the new partner will have more work coming in than she can do herself. She will be forced to delegate and share her human capital with associates. To maintain the associate-to-partner ratio, the firm will have to hire even more associates. Testing this theory against the data, Galanter and Palay ... found that the largest firms have in fact grown at an exponential rate since 1922, with an unexplained spurt around 1970.

But while the tournament demands that law firms grow exponentially, revenue can constrain growth: without sufficient clients and paying work, firms cannot grow. Since demand for legal services is not infinite, growth pressure leads to revenue pressure. This tension between growth and revenue can be used to explain many of the structural and behavioral changes in large firms that Regan and others have documented, including multitiered partnerships, eat-what-you-kill compensation systems, client stealing, and ethical lapses.

The impact of revenue pressure on associates is especially profound. For the tournament to work well, firms must promote associates who will make profitable partners. To do this, the firm needs to be able to distinguish between "good" and "bad" associates. Billable hours provide one mechanism for sorting associates. Through hours billed, each associate reveals her relative preferences for work and leisure. The firm can then identify and promote those associates who attach great value to work and little value to leisure. The end result is a rat race: each associate bills frenetically, trying to show that she is the "good" associate. Over time, the consequence is continued growth in associates' billable hours.

Can it be so simple? Galanter and Palay's model has been criticized as an inaccurate account of what actually happens in the promotion process. David Wilkins and Mitu Gulati have argued that the tournament model pays insufficient attention to "the internalization of professional norms relating to competence, client loyalty, and collegiality," and that associates' diligence depends in large part on "what they are taught from law school forward that doing so is an important part of being a professional." Others have made the point that monitoring associates' work product is not that difficult, since associates bill hours and produce documents ... If so, the tournament becomes unnecessary: the firm can discipline opportunism based directly on the associate's observed output. Finally, Richard Sander and Douglass Williams have argued that Galanter and Palay make too much of the data. They found that "[firm] growth is more irregular than tournament theory predicts, that its geometric form is unsurprising, and that the partnership promotion rates are often less consistent than the tournament theory implies."

Above all, the tournament system can work only if associates are willing to play by the rules. There is mixed evidence on associate reaction to the tournament. One survey at two major law firms in a northeastern city found that associates, if given the choice, preferred more leisure time to more money.... A survey of Texas associates indicated that half would be unwilling to take less money in exchange for less work, although a quarter would make the trade if they were certain that it would not affect their advancement. The most direct evidence ... [contradicting] these surveys, is that elite firms have no shortage of highly marketable law students and young lawyers who are eager to enter the tournament.

In one instance, however, associates actually opted out. Bruce Price studied law firms in Silicon Valley during the dot-com bubble. These firms had more work than they could handle in a very tight legal labor market. According to one partner, the only criterion for hiring a junior associate was whether the applicant "had a 'butt to put in the chair' " (p. 745). These same associates lacked commitment to the firm. Instead of pursuing partnership, most planned to move to a dot-com company in a year or so, earning their law-firm salary plus a large equity stake in the emerging company. Because the associates believed that they had far more attractive options than law-firm partnership, they refused to adopt the assumptions of the tournament model. Instead, Price found, they acted opportunistically. . . .

One small Silicon Valley firm responded to the tournament's failure by raising salaries dramatically. As reported by Price in a later paper, in 1999 the firm of Gunderson Dettmer lost five out of 12 first-year associates. The firm had to turn away start-up clients because it could not staff the deals. Because of the shrinking pool of associates, those who remained at the firm had to work longer hours. Morale was low.

To counter these developments, Gunderson raised first-year salaries from $90,000 to $125,000 with a $20,000 guaranteed bonus—a boost in compensation of more than 60 percent. The firm instituted the pay raise to accomplish two goals. First, partners thought the salary increase would enable the firm to attract and retain associates. Second, partners wanted associates remaining at the firm to know that more help was on the way. This strategy would work, of course, only if other firms did not match the raise and capture the associates that Gunderson was trying to recruit. As is discussed in more detail in the next section, however, that is just what happened: law firms throughout the country unexpectedly responded to the pay increase with massive increases of their own.

The tournament literature sends a mixed message about the power of economic forces. The tournament model, with its assumptions about the pursuit of economic efficiency, plausibly accounts for the general trend toward exponential growth. The fact that the tournament failed under a specific set of market conditions does not undermine this conclusion; on the contrary, the Silicon Valley associates refused to play because of an economic calculation of their own. The Gunderson firm responded to the failure of its tournament with a move that appeared rationally conceived at first, but was confounded by the unexpected and perhaps irrational reaction of the national market. We turn next to that development.

2.   Associates' Salaries

When Gunderson Dettmer dramatically raised associates' starting salaries, the increase spread rapidly through the national legal market. A little more than a month after Gunderson moved, the increase was matched by

Cooley Godward, a Silicon Valley competitor of Gunderson. But Cooley also increased the salary for its associates at its Reston, Virginia office. This move was not necessary to compete in Silicon Valley, but might have been viewed as essential to internal firm morale. Within three weeks after Cooley's move, four other California firms and one national firm, Shearman and Sterling, matched the Gunderson increase, raising the salaries of associates in all their offices, including those in Washington, D.C., and New York. Within a few months, all the other major firms in New York and Washington moved to substantially higher salaries. From there, the salary increase spread through the rest of the national market.

In the South, for example, firms responded to the Gunderson shock wave by increasing their associates' salaries by an average of 34 percent—not quite a Gunderson increase, but a very healthy raise nonetheless. And they did it even though southern firms did not face competition for associates from dot-com clients, the trigger for Gunderson's original move, nor were they competing with New York and Washington law firms.

The firms' follow-the-leader behavior on salaries may have been driven by the fear of a loss of prestige if they did not keep pace. As one partner interviewed by Price described his firm's thinking:

> [M]y firm paid huge bonuses in New York last year, $40,000 or something like that, to every associate in the New York office, because [another firm] did. We don't compete with them, but they did it anyway because of how they wanted to be perceived in the New York market. And so we all followed Gunderson. I don't know why. I have no idea. It was stupid, in my view.

As this lawyer acknowledges, firms that did not face the special economic conditions of Silicon Valley acted as if they did. It is not clear why Shearman and Sterling felt compelled to respond to a couple of small California firms. Once Shearman and Sterling moved, though, the other biggest firms in New York and Washington apparently concluded that they had to match. But there is no reason to believe that firms in Chicago or Dallas, let alone those in Charlotte, North Carolina, or Birmingham, Alabama, had to match salaries initially determined by the odd market conditions of Silicon Valley in order to attract satisfactory associates. Nonetheless, more than half the original raise filtered all the way down to firms in midsized southern cities. For firms not in direct competition with the leaders, following them makes economic sense only if their own clients might view a failure to follow with suspicion. But this is a big if. Do clients really track associate salaries or even think about associates as long as the quality of the work is satisfactory? Perhaps the better explanation is that large law firms were simply pursuing that ego-gratifying intangible called "prestige."

The pursuit of prestige is not necessarily irrational, as prestige and profit are not mutually exclusive goals. In fact, prestige becomes a useful proxy for profit if clients hire or fire law firms based on perceptions of prestige. To maximize prestige, the rational firm simply follows the practices of firms it views as having a higher pedigree, independent of the actual value of a specific practice for that firm. That seems to be what happened to associate salaries: a few firms decided to do something that made economic sense in their particular circumstances, and the trend propagated, with firms at every level mimicking the behavior of their "betters."

What emerges is an explanation that mixes the "hard" and the "soft." Economic factors account for a new development. In order for the innovation to become a trend, the appropriate psychological and cultural factors must come into play. At first glance, the propagation of the trend may seem economically inefficient. But in the end, if clients want service from the most "prestigious" law firms, the economists might have been right all along. We turn next to a more detailed analysis of the "soft" factors.

C. Cultural Factors

The law and economics literature thus provides inconsistent responses to the question of whether the changes over the last 40 years can be attributed to lawyers' rational responses to economic forces. In this section we review another perspective on the causes of change that has emerged from research in the ethnographic tradition. This work has illuminated the role of such "soft" factors as the norms, attitudes, and behaviors that operate within practice organizations and practice communities. We label such factors "cultural," a nontechnical use of the word that is nonetheless consistent with its more formal meaning for the anthropologists and other social scientists who use it as a term of art. . . .

1. Large–Firm Culture

The study of large firm culture dates back at least to Smigel. Although he was one of those who never mentioned culture explicitly, many of the issues he discussed were cultural in nature. Analyzing the organization and management of the Wall Street firm, for example, he found that formal structure was minimal and highly variable from firm to firm, leading him to ask "why [the] organization worked even though it seemed to be loosely organized". According to those he interviewed, culture substituted for structure. They attributed their firms' success to the intelligence of the personnel, their strong sense of professional responsibility, their similar ethnic and socioeconomic backgrounds, and their espirit de corps. Smigel also highlighted the salutary effect of "controlled competition" (pp. 256–57), which included lockstep raises; the remarkably positive self-images possessed by the lawyers; and the strength of the informal rules—what we would now call cultural norms—that guided minute-to-minute judgments about such things as when to ask for help and how to deal with clients.

As we noted earlier, Smigel predicted change with remarkable accuracy, and much of the change he predicted was in the cultural realm. In terms of cause and effect, Smigel was an economic determinist, believing that changes in the external business climate drove changes in the norms, values, and behavior of lawyers and firms. Two decades later, Spangler's study of employed lawyers captured some of these changes in process. In a chapter about partners and associates in five large New England firms, Spangler documented a transitional stage between Smigel's idyllic picture of Wall Street firms and the darker portrait that dominates the contemporary literature. She acknowledged Smigel's work as a starting point, referring to his depiction of the big firms' earliest efforts at "systematic attention to administrative rationalization and coordination." Writing after twenty additional years of big-firm expansion, she found that "the distinction between a professional organization of men and a bureaucratic organization of offices" had become "more apparent than real".

Like Smigel, Spangler said nothing explicit about culture and she, too, seemed to be an economic determinist. Firm structures and practices, including the hiring and nurturing of associates and the criteria for making partner, were explained as rational responses to the economic needs of the firm. Spangler's focus on economics is epitomized by the fact that her book is the earliest publication in which we have seen the phrase "eat what you kill" applied to law firm compensation.

But the power of culture still manifests itself in significant ways. One example is Spangler's brief but intriguing analysis of governance styles. Here, her explanation is more historical than economic; the implication is that a variety of styles can come about for internal, idiosyncratic reasons, and that any of them can prove economically adaptive. One of her five firms was "patriarchal," "with a powerful senior partner who dominates the partnership group, delegates little power, and generally maintains control over the firm, firing off memoranda on even such minutiae as Friday afternoon office attire". Two others operated in a "collegium" mode: "the large law practice in which policy-making and administrative duties, more or less systematized, are widely shared among the partners". This form arose when a founding or otherwise dominant partner retires and there is no obvious successor as patriarch. Collegia tended to be less formal, more democratic, and, consequently, less disciplined in their decision making. She described the other two firms as "entrepreneurial": "partnerships in which personal relationships remain the chief connection between lawyers and their personal clients". These were newer, often ad hoc firms organized around a limited number of lawyers who controlled large clients; thus, "the finder [as opposed to the 'minder' or the 'grinder'] is still king".

The interplay of culture and economics is further complicated by Spangler's discussion of the relationship between the various firms and their city (presumably Boston). The patriarchal and collegial firms shared a market niche, representing clients such as "Harvard, the Mass General [Hospital] and the estates of the Pilgrims who died three hundred years ago"—old Boston, in other words. The two newer, entrepreneurial firms aggressively pursued other kinds of business, apparently the real estate and technology companies in and around Boston that were beginning to boom when Spangler did her research. In fact, one of the two firms promoted its "up to-the-minute technology," including "computers compatible with those of its major clients". Although

810

Spangler did not pursue this angle, those familiar with Boston's twentieth-century history will suspect that the entrepreneurial firms and their clients had an ethnic mix that differed sharply from the overwhelming WASP (or Yankee, as the locals would put it) predominance in the established firms.

Spangler's data support a variety of conclusions about culture and economics. It is clear that the "old Boston" clientele and their law firms shared a business culture, as did the "new Boston" clients and their lawyers. But what was the direction of causation? Perhaps the old Boston clientele sought out the two traditional styles of firms (patriarchal and collegial), and thus effectively determined their governance structures, whereas the demands of "new Boston" high-tech clients imposed selection pressures that favored entrepreneurial law firms. If so, could a firm seeking to enter a new economic niche simply adopt the cultural trappings favored by the relevant clientele, reducing culture to a marketing strategy? Alternatively, perhaps old Boston clients gravitated toward old Boston firms because of the shared cultural backgrounds and styles of the personnel, with the same happening on the entrepreneurial side. In this view, law firm governance style was a symptom of other, deeper sensibilities that brought lawyers and clients together, making it difficult if not impossible for law firms to perform quick cultural changes in pursuit of business opportunities.

Spangler's analysis leaves these questions open, and the ambiguities persist in the more recent literature. One thing that is clear is that law firms have moved en masse toward Spangler's entrepreneurial model; nothing illustrates this better than Regan's study of the formerly stodgy Milbank, Tweed. But the role that cultural factors may have played as both causes and effects of change remains enigmatic.

The ethnographic interviews of both Kelly and Conley have highlighted many of these complexities. In the single case of Kelly's "McKinnon, Moreland and Fox" (discussed in part I.A), cultural factors seem both to have contributed to the firm's drive to expand and to have been a determinant of the success or failure of individual mergers and acquisitions. The firm's managers justified the various moves on general economic grounds, but it was equally clear that growth for growth's sake was viewed as an essential part of the culture of "playing in the big leagues" (p. 25)—another variation on the pursuit of prestige that we discussed in part II.B. It is impossible to say whether culture was the egg to economics' chicken or vice versa. But regardless of what set the moves in motion, Kelly's informants agreed that whether individual acquisitions would work out or not depended on the cultural fit between the merging entities.

The McKinnon firm's most successful expansion move was its acquisition of the entire environmental department of another firm—precisely because the new group was largely left alone and not required to renegotiate its day-to-day beliefs and practices. Kelly found that the jury was still out on McKinnon's merger with a midsized litigation boutique that had taken place a couple of years before he began his research. Among the cultural problems were the "aggressive 'ego beating' tactics" typical of McKinnon litigators; the smaller firm's discomfort with "the impersonality, the overspecialization, and the unfriendly 'company' atmosphere" of the larger firm (according to one lawyer, "you have to sign a statement if you want to go to the bathroom"); and the poor fit between the two firms' associates (lunchtime reminded one associate "of high school, where one calculates who is sitting with whom, who carries the conversation, who goes out with whom") (p. 35–37).

Conley's informants expressed similarly mixed views on the relationship of culture and economics. In discussing large-firm firm growth, lawyers typically presented narratives of economic determinism. They began with the proposition that nationwide and even international mergers are essential to maintaining the biggest and most lucrative corporate clients. Such clients, the story goes, demand a physical presence everywhere and huge manpower reserves to meet crises. The narratives that Conley heard were also peppered with references to "synergy" and "economies of scale." Growth through merger was said to be a good thing because lawyers in the larger, merged entity would be able to interact synergistically, making the combined output of the new firm greater than the sum of the parts. But the only concrete example of synergy that any respondent offered was to point out that when you have a question about an area of law in which you do not practice yourself, you can almost always get an answer inside the firm. The references to economies of scale were similarly vague. The principle is obvious when, for example, two manufacturers can share a single factory for less than the cost of maintaining two separate ones. Its applicability to large law firms—groups of lawyers who sell time—is less apparent. The large-firm lawyers that Conley interviewed cited centralized billing and purchasing operations, but, when questioned, did not believe that these economies had material effects on their bottom lines.

Conley's big-firm informants also talked about "cross-marketing" opportunities within a larger firm: lawyer A, who is doing a client's securities work, attempts to persuade that client to take its environmental work away from the current environmental counsel and give it to A's partner, B. At some point, the theory goes, a "tipping effect" occurs, and all of the client's legal work flows into the firm. The same lawyers acknowledged, however, that cross-marketing is slow and difficult in practice. Does the firm merge in order to set itself up for cross-marketing opportunities? If it does, it may find itself with massive excess capacity, at least in the short term. On the other hand, how does it compete for more of the client's business unless it already has the capacity?

All of Conley's informants believed that law firms have distinct cultures; that even if their work is nearly identical, different firms approach it in different ways, use widely varying systems of governance and compensation, and have, for lack of a better term, widely divergent "atmospheres." When pressed, big-firm lawyers uniformly agreed that firm cultures are extremely difficult to blend. In practice, they acknowledged, the more likely outcome of a merger is that one predecessor firm will "win" and the other will "lose," with its members forced to choose between changing their ways and leaving. This is hardly a formula for synergy.

Conley ultimately came to question whether economics is a rationale or a rationalization for big-firm growth and mergers. No big-firm lawyer he interviewed was able to give an economic explanation for growth and merger activity that went any deeper than the mere recitation of such formulas as "the clients demand it," "we have no choice," and the aforementioned synergy and economies of scale. Quite to the contrary, his informants uniformly acknowledged that there were sound reasons to believe that their growth strategies were likely to fail. Conley suspected that large-firm lawyers were using the language of economics to justify what was in reality herd behavior and the pursuit of status and prestige. Since expansion is now "the game," Conley concluded, everyone wants to play it, and everyone seems to be able to put a patina of economics over behavior whose motivations may be fundamentally noneconomic. As we discussed in connection with associate salaries, the pursuit of prestige is not necessarily inefficient. But if these lawyers were actually achieving efficiency, it would appear to have been in spite of themselves.

Economics and culture come together vividly in Regan's portrait of Gellene and Milbank. In spite of the strong economic theme that dominates the story, Regan's analysis is not strictly deterministic. In addition to economics, he also makes persuasive cases for the respective contributions of Gellene's psychological problems, pure greed, and the ethical environment in the big-time bankruptcy bar, and ultimately declines to accord primacy to any single factor. Instead, all are seen as part of an indivisible whole, all having attributes of both chicken and egg.

Regan's concept of culture is sophisticated and contemporary: a flexible, changeable tool kit of shared resources, a set of beliefs, values, and understandings that individuals draw on in making sense of reality. Economics and other external forces can affect culture, but at the same time culture influences the way in which its members interpret such forces. The relationship between culture and the individual is complex, working in both directions. While culture does not dictate the behavior of individual members, it does frame their options and structure the processes through which they make decisions. By the same token, individuals can shape their culture through acts of compliance or resistance.

Economic changes appear to have set in motion the changes that culminated in the "eat what you kill" culture of Milbank of the 1990s. But is the economic account a "just so" story, concocted after the fact as a too perfect explanation for the current state of affairs? Did economic change really dictate the cultural change? Or did the members of Milbank and similar firms, their values already changing for other reasons, construct economic stimuli in a way that reinforced a process that was already under way?

So also with the relationship between Gellene, as individual member, and the Milbank culture. From the start of his career, in the odd bar application episode, Gellene displayed the traits that would be his downfall: ignoring everything but billable hours, and then hiding his sins of omission. Did he propagate those traits within the Milbank culture, or did it reinforce them in him, or both? Did people like Lederman and their values change Milbank, or were he and others attracted to it because of what they already saw there? Regan does not purport to resolve such questions definitively in the Milbank case, nor has anyone else with respect to large law firms generally.

2.   Is There Such A Thing As Small–Firm Culture?

In the literature on small-firm practice, the trend has been has been to pay increasing attention to the influence of cultural factors in lawyers' daily lives. Looking back over 40–plus years, it is difficult to determine whether this trend is more reflective of actual changes in law practice, shifts in the perspective of those who study it, or the localized samples that all of the principal studies have employed.

Carlin's work might be read as a denial of the existence of culture among small-practice lawyers. Carlin did not write about culture as such; indeed, his primary theme was the isolation of solo practitioners, their very separation from any kind of supportive cultural environment. To the extent that culture is latent in the book, it is the culture of solo practice, not of solo practices. And an odd culture it was. Although its members shared such "values" as a willingness to cut corners and a disdain for large firms and their elitist concept of "ethics," it is not apparent how the sharing came about in a professional world devoid of the sort of rituals and practices through which culture is usually transmitted. On the contrary, the clear implication is that the "sharing" was a statistical illusion, simply the sum of many individual reactions to the same set of problems. Some readers may be reminded, as we were, more of the ethnology of some reclusive predator like the wolverine than the ethnography of a human society.

A generation later, the lawyers that Seron studied continued to be solitary in finding and serving their clients. They also tended to approach the problems of getting business, meeting client demands, running an office, reacting to the organized bar, and balancing personal and professional lives in remarkably similar ways, a theme that is present if undeveloped in Carlin's work. Seron's individualists differed from Carlin's in two respects, however. First, their shared beliefs and values tended to be more positive, in several senses of that word: seeing the practice of law as a worthwhile enterprise rather than the only way of earning a living open to them, feeling that they could perform a valuable service for clients instead of merely doing their dirty work, and having a sense of doing things "right." Second, the sense of Seron's account—and it is little more than that—is that the sharing among these lawyers was somehow real, more than a statistical generalization about individual responses. But the mechanism through which beliefs and values were transmitted remained elusive.

Conley's interviews have suggested specific ways in which solo lawyers overcome the isolation described by Carlin and create culture. He was told that their practices can be lonely in a professional sense. He heard many times that, however congenial the office staff may be, practitioners feel a strong and regular need to talk things over with another lawyer. This need can sometimes be satisfied by a single partner, a lawyer with whom one shares office space, or an occasional lunch companion from across town. Nonetheless, it is never as easy as it is for the big-firm lawyer who has a dozen colleagues on his or her hallway. Thus, his informants concluded, the isolation described by Carlin is a real and constant threat, but it can be mitigated if not overcome by the formation of small, local-level, often transient communities based on shared needs and interests.

The idea that even small-practice lawyers can constitute themselves as cultural communities with strong norms has been most fully developed by [Lynn] Mather and her colleagues in their study of divorce lawyers in Maine and New Hampshire. At the outset, they posed the question of how individual lawyers "think about and actually make" the decisions that arise in their daily practices.... Reflecting on their data, they focused on "lawyers' individual values and identities in making day-to-day decisions". These values are shaped by the "collegial norms and conceptions of roles" that emanate in informal ways from the multiple "communities of practice" in which individual lawyers participate. The authors do not routinely use the term "culture," but communities of practice are clearly presented as cultural entities that play a critical role in determining the nature and character of individual lawyers' practice.

Mather and her colleagues found that these communities reinforced a set of norms and values that they characterized as "collegial control of work", and that we would describe as professional culture. It includes "shared languages, knowledge, and identities," "internalized norms of conduct learned in life, in law school, and during socialization into practice," "pressure from peers to behave in particular ways," and "formal norms of conduct and the threat of sanction for violating those norms". Lawyers call on these shared resources in responding to such difficult day-to-day challenges as dealing with clients who reject their advice, "responsibly doing their jobs with limited resources" when representing clients of modest means, and relating to other lawyers in settlement negotiations.

Levin ... has reported an identical phenomenon in her study of small-practice ethics, although she uses the term "networks" rather than communities of practice. Lawyers use networks to help resolve both difficult legal questions and ethical quandaries. Levin was struck by the ability of these networks to "develop their own identifiable ethical cultures even when lawyers are not formally affiliated."

There was no evidence in Carlin's work of the existence of such local-level communities. Perhaps they did not exist; it may be that, at least in some places and practice specialties, lawyers have only recently learned how to mitigate structural isolation. Or it may just be that social scientists have only recently become interested in subtler forms of cultural affiliation, or at least better at identifying them.

III.   THE QUEST FOR "PROFESSIONALISM"

A final major theme in the literature of the last 40–plus years is the question of whether the practice of law continues to be—if it ever was—a "profession." The meaning of "profession" has been debated by sociologists for more than a hundred years ... All of the various approaches share the minimal idea that a profession is an occupation or calling whose practitioners must have extensive training and specialized expertise. By persuading the public of their expertise, the members gain the privilege of controlling entry and regulating each other's conduct. Some theorists have treated professions as economic cartels, "distinguished by the strategies of social closure they use to enhance their market chances". Those who take this position often stress that the claimed expertise can be more a matter of mystification than real accomplishment; premodern medicine is a frequently cited example. Others have taken a more idealistic view, stressing that professionals assume a duty to their clients that transcends economic self-interest; the client, in other words, is more than a mere customer. As Eliot [Freidson] ... has put it, professionals share "an ideology serving some transcendent value and asserting greater devotion to doing good work than to economic reward."

Both approaches to professionalism share the core concept of autonomy, from the state as well as from the client. The state grants autonomy by conferring the privilege of self-regulation, while clients who depend on professionals' specialized knowledge have no practical standing to challenge their judgment. As a result, professionals have historically been able "to make a living while controlling their own work" (p. 17). In the two sections that follow we consider the development of the concept of autonomy since Carlin and Smigel. The first section reviews the reported decline of the autonomy of the big-firm lawyer, while the second asks whether small-firm and solo lawyers have gained any since Carlin depicted them as virtual slaves to their clients.

A.   Large Firms and the Reversal of the Smigel/Carlin Hierarchy

The early 1960s Wall Street lawyers depicted by Smigel seem to have been autonomous professionals by any definition. In their secure economic environment, they saw themselves as giving their best independent advice to clients without fear of economic consequences to themselves—perhaps because there wouldn't be any. Smigel gave no indication that clients ever fought their lawyers' advice—there was no "pushback," to use the contemporary business jargon—or asked them to do shady things. That same secure environment allowed them to practice "strategies of social closure," including discrimination, that, in turn, reinforced their security. Carlin's solo practitioners, by contrast, were barely recognizable as members of the same profession.

There is abundant evidence that all this has changed. In their study of the Chicago bar in the 1970s, Heinz and Laumann ... found that "corporate clients to a large degree dictate the nature of the work done." Regan's ... chronicling of the travails of Milbank, Tweed makes the point with riveting clarity. By the late 1990s, Milbank and their Wall Street peers had lost their secure relationships with cash-cow clients. Facing their own pressures, client companies had come to view lawyers as just another class of vendors, their services fungible. Large legal matters were now put out to bid, with the bidders required to lay out precisely how they would meet the client's requirements and at what price. The days of big-firm lawyers deciding what work needed to be done, how it should be done, and what it was worth were over.

Just as they were losing their independence in their dealings with clients, lawyers were also losing their professional autonomy within their firms. The never-ending partnership tournament imposes lifelong pressure to produce. As the Gellene case illustrates, a partner who is seen to do excellent work still requires a rainmaker patron, and even that patron is never free from the duty to bring on the next batch of rain. Big-firm lawyers have joined the real world.

B.　Small Firms and the Struggle for Survival

By Carlin's account, small-firm and solo lawyers never had any professionalism to lose. The struggle to survive precluded it. Subsisting on marginal business, these lawyers did not have the luxury of refusing work or telling clients that there were some things they just would not do. And, by Carlin's account, they did not seem to care, looking on professional responsibility and bar discipline as economic cartel activity directed against them by elite firms.

This seems to have changed, too, however. Only a decade after Carlin, Heinz and Laumann ... reported that even as large firms had become the creatures of their corporate clients, small-firm lawyers who represented individuals tended to "dominate their clients and the decisions that are made about the work." More recent research by Seron and Levin confirms that small and solo practices continue to face great economic pressures, and that bar regulation is still looked upon as something of a big-firm plot. But the cynical, almost nihilistic attitude toward professionalism that appalled Carlin is absent. On the contrary, as Levin emphasized in her analysis of local-level networks, promoting professionalism is an important value in the informal culture of solo and small-firm lawyers.

It is hard to say whether Carlin had an unusual sample or whether small-practice lawyers have evolved a new professionalism. Or perhaps they have simply created and internalized a professional myth that they now pass off to researchers, wittingly or unwittingly. In any event, there seems to be no lack of demand for entry into the small-firm and solo end of the profession. In fact, Hofstra University School of Law on Long Island has just decided to open a night school that will educate even more of the sorts of lawyers that Seron studied, while in North Carolina, Elon University has announced the opening of a new law school in Greensboro that will add to the state's supply of small-practice lawyers.

The unmitigated negativity of Carlin's books has always troubled us. Was it portrait or caricature? In the late 1950s, didn't a lot of graduates of "good" schools go into solo practice by choice? What about successful plaintiffs' lawyers and soloists whose practices grew with the small businesses they represented? Why didn't more of these lawyers turn up in Carlin's random sample? One of us (Conley) was reminded of his father (in Boston) and father-in-law (in Baltimore). Both were Catholic ethnics, the sons of poor immigrants, who worked their way through working-class law schools in the 1930s and started solo practices. By the late 1950s, both had stable practices that supported a comfortable middle-class life for their families. Both seemed to enjoy their work so much that five children from the two families went to law school. And both seemed to have many peers who were similarly situated. Maybe Chicago was different.

C. Lawyers as Workers?

As we noted in part I.C, Spangler observed in 1986 that large numbers of lawyers were becoming functionally indistinguishable from corporate workers. But she also found that most of them resisted this proletarian characterization:

> With the exception of poverty lawyers ... few attorneys seem concerned about the intrinsic difficulties of being employees. They show little inclination to act in keeping with their common interests and experiences as staff people. Indeed, focused as most of them are on the content of their work rather than its organization, they fail to perceive their commonalities.

Somehow, a shared sense of professional status prevented these lawyers from constituting themselves as a "new class" of high-end wage laborers. Even as they lost control of their professional lives, they perpetuated a self image of professional independence. Only legal aid lawyers—"overworked, underpaid, and harried", as well as far to the left of most other lawyers on the political spectrum—had begun to dabble in unionization and other forms of collective action. For the rest, "common experiences [had] not yet given rise to common consciousness or joint politics".

Subsequent research has continued to confirm the point. In his study of the in-house legal department of a large real estate development company, Kelly examined the theory that corporate employment is destructive of professional identity. He found the opposite, that "the reality of autonomy may be strongest in [the corporate legal department], in which the lawyers are literally the employees of the client they serve". He saw in that department the highest expression of such "professional" values and behaviors as collegiality, the client's respect for the independent judgment of the lawyer, and the lawyer's readiness to provide far-reaching counsel that goes beyond legal technicalities. The same was true in the legal department of the Maine Public Utilities commission. Thus, in a continuation of what Spangler had observed, employed lawyers showed no evidence of becoming a "new class" of workers. Perhaps they are simply victims of false consciousness. Or perhaps, for all their potential sources of professional dissatisfaction, they may take comfort in their single greatest advantage: not having to find clients.

IV. CONCLUSION

After more than 40 years of the empirical study of law firms, what do we know? As a descriptive matter, large-firm life is reported to be harder than it was in the 1960s. Clients demand more, treating legal services as a commodity to be bought in the marketplace. Firms compete ruthlessly with each other for clients, associates, and rainmaking partners. Within the firm, the partnership tournament never ends. Racking up astronomical billable hours has become a lifelong quest, and no one is indispensable anymore. As the story of John Gellene illustrates, ostensibly secure lawyers may commit stunning ethical lapses in the drive to maintain a competitive edge.

Large-firm associates also say that they are unhappy, despite compensation in excess of most federal judges. Yet even as many associates decry the destructive impact that their work has on their personal lives, there is no shortage of highly credentialed law students willing to work 80–hour weeks for a lot of money and a very long shot at an equity partnership in a big-city corporate firm. These aspiring associates no longer face the overt discrimination that closed the Wall Street firms of Smigel's day to all but white Anglo–Saxon Protestant gentlemen of impeccable pedigree. But even as women and—to a lesser extent—minorities find it easier to get a foot in the door, they still do not succeed in proportionate numbers.

The small-firm lawyers and solo practitioners of Main Street never had a Golden Age, real or mythical. For these lawyers, life has always been a struggle to survive. They continue to hunt for work. They draft wills, advise small businesses, and help people navigate the civil and criminal legal systems. They rail against professional rules promulgated by elite-firm lawyers. But in spite of all these obstacles, and as big-firm lawyers spend more of their time watching their backs, contemporary solo and small-firm lawyers—the ones who have been studied, in any event—derive community and support from lawyers down the hall or across town. And as big-firm lawyers come increasingly under the control of their corporate clients, the small-practice lawyer remains his or her own boss.

Somewhat surprisingly, the in-house lawyer is widely reported to inhabit the best of all professional worlds. These lawyers do interesting work, get paid well, and avoid the unpredictable workloads associated with the large firm. Perhaps most importantly, in-house lawyers do not have to pound the pavement of either Wall Street or Main Street in search of clients.

As we have noted before, in assessing all of this reported change it is difficult to sort out the respective effects of actual change on the ground, the shifting interests and theoretical perspectives of the researchers, and the localized samples on which all of the major research projects have been based. But if the reported changes in lawyers' lives are real and widespread, the literature that began with Carlin and Smigel does not provide a simple answer to the question of why they have come about. Economic forces can be tangible and powerful. In the case of large firms, there can be no doubt that global economic competition has placed them under pressures of a sort they have never faced before. But even here, it would be a gross oversimplification to say that "economics did it." Certain trends can be characterized as a rational response to economic forces, but others cannot. Lawyers explain change by references to such vague financial concepts as "synergy" and "economies of scale." Moreover, there is considerable variation in the way that big firms have responded to allegedly deterministic economic stimuli. The best reading of the literature respects the power of culture, and concludes that economic pressures have interacted with such "soft" factors as the house norms of particular firms to produce individual outcomes that may or may not advance economic efficiency.

At the smaller-practice end of the profession, the major development in the literature from Carlin to the present has been the repeated finding that ostensibly isolated lawyers—Carlin's "wolverines," as we characterized them earlier—form robust and useful cultural communities. Even as the cultural environment has deteriorated on Wall Street, it is strengthening on Main Street. As Wall Street eats its young, Main Street has found ways to identify and pass along values that a number of researchers have identified as "professional."

Defining the legal profession as a cartel or a calling is well beyond the scope of this essay. Those on both sides of the question agree on the fact of autonomy, however: autonomy in dealing with the state, autonomy in relationships with clients, and the occupational autonomy that flows from the first two. Perhaps the most surprising finding in our review of 40 years of research has been the relative loss of autonomy in every sense among Wall Street lawyers, and the concomitant gain on Main Street. We are not ready to predict that the editors of elite law reviews will start migrating to small towns to hang out their shingles. But change is apparent, the word is getting out, and some kind of market correction is not beyond the realm of possibility.

NOTES AND QUESTIONS

1. The legal profession has changed in a number of ways over the past half century. There were, for example, about 286,000 lawyers in 1960, or 1 for every 627 people in the country. There were about 1,660,000 lawyers in 2000, or 1 for every 264 people. The big jump came between 1970 and 1980, when the number of lawyers increased from about 355,000 to 542,000, or from 1 for every 572 people to 1 for every 418 people. There are more big firms today than in the past, and they keep getting bigger. In 1980, 17% of the bar worked as solo practitioners or with one other lawyer. 7% worked in firms of 101 or more lawyers. In 2000, 11% worked as solos or with another lawyer. 28% were in firms of 101 or more lawyers. See Clara N. Carson, *The Lawyer Statistical Report: The U.S. Legal Profession in 2000*, at 1, 8 (American Bar Foundation 2004).

However, perhaps the most noticeable change over this period is that women start becoming lawyers in large numbers. There were only about 5,500 women lawyers in America in 1951, or 3% of the total number. The 1970s saw women enter the profession in great numbers. The number had climbed to 44,185 in 1980, or 8% of the total. There was a steady increase from 1980 to 2000 when women were 27% of the lawyers in the country. In academic year 1963–64, 4% of the first year enrollment in the nation's law schools were women. In academic year 1998–1999, women made up 47% of the first-year enrollment. Carson, at 3. In 2000, 43% of the lawyers under 30 and 38% of those between age 30 and 35 were women. Only 11% of those between 55 and 65 and 5% of those 65 and over were women. Carson, at 11. Carson reports:

> Differences between the employment distributions of the male and female lawyer populations in 2000, although narrower than in 1980 and 1991, remained significant ... Female lawyers were more likely than male lawyers to be employed in government, legal aid, public defender programs, education, or private industry. On the other hand, a somewhat higher proportion of male lawyers (75%) were engaged in private practice than were females (71%). Males were also more likely to practice in law firm settings rather than solo while females were more likely to practice in solo settings than in firms. (Id. at 9)

As the data shows, there has been a striking increase in the number of lawyers over the past 25 to 50 years. This raises the question of why the organized bar did not act to limit the number of lawyers in order to limit the supply and drive up the price of lawyers' services. At one time the bar tried to do this. Lawrence M. Friedman, *A History of American Law* 495–498 (3d ed. 2005), tells us about lawyers organizing in the late 19th century to control the number of lawyers and who could practice law. The work was carried out by "the 'decent part' of the profession, that is, primarily well-to-do business lawyers, predominantly of old-American stock." Friedman continues:

> Nothing so dissatisfied the "decent part" of the bar as the fact that it was easy to set up as a lawyer. They felt that the country was flooded with lawyers, and that many of these lawyers were mediocre or worse ... After the Civil War, the trend toward laxity was reversed.... In 1890, twenty-three jurisdictions asked for some formal period of study, or apprenticeship. A written bar exam became increasingly the norm. In much of this development, the bar lobbied hard for more rigor. The motives were, as usual, mixed. Many lawyers sincerely wanted to upgrade the profession. This mingled with a more selfish desire to control the supply of lawyers, and keep out price cutters and undesirables. (Ibid., pp. 498, 500).

Jerold S. Auerbach, *Unequal Justice: Lawyers and Social Change in Modern America* (1976), argues that the "decent part" of the bar was motivated by anti-Semitic and anti-immigrant prejudice. They sought to defend their professional status and income from a flood of immigrants into the profession. They advocated high educational requirements, bar examinations and character and fitness committees. Over time, they were successful in most states. In the 1920s, many law schools began aptitude testing as part of the admissions process, and many schools regularly failed about a third of their entering classes. Nonetheless, many proprietary law schools served the demand of working class people for a legal education, and many of their graduates found ways to pass bar examinations. While the organized bar may have succeeded in limiting the number of people allowed to practice law to some extent, the demand for legal education in the 1970s found many who were not from elite families able to jump the hurdles standing in the way of admission to law school and then to the bar. See, also, Daria Roithmayr, "Deconstructing the Distinction Between Bias and Merit," 85 *California Law Review* 1449 (1997).

2. Professor Richard Abel has been a pioneer in the comparative study of the legal profession. He has published a book on the legal profession in the United Kingdom, *The Legal Profession in England and Wales* (1987). Perhaps the most notable comparative work on lawyers is the three volume collection edited by Abel and Philip S.C. Lewis, *Lawyers in Society* (1988 and 1989). The genesis of this book was the formation of a Working Group for the Comparative Study of Legal Professions, created by the Research Committee on Sociology of Law of the International Sociological Association. Under the leadership of Abel and Lewis, national reporters collected information about the legal profession in 19 nations. The first volume of Lawyers and Society, The Common Law World, contained essays on the United States, Canada, Great Britain, Australia, New Zealand and India. Volume 2, on the Civil Law World, contained essays on Norway, Germany, Japan, the Netherlands, Belgium, France, Geneva (Switzerland), Italy, Spain, Venezuela, and Brazil. The third volume contained more general and interpretive essays.

A valuable overview, in the third volume, is Philip S.C. Lewis, "Comparison and Change in the Study of Legal Professions," at 27. For a critical review of the entire three-volume effort, see Miek Berends, "An Elusive Profession? Lawyers in Society," 26 *Law & Society Review* 161, 177 (1992).

There are, of course, many other books and articles in English on the comparative study of legal professions. See, for example, John Morison and Philip Leith, *The Barrister's World and the Nature of Law* (1992) (English barristers); Dietrich Rueschemeyer, *Lawyers and their Society: A Comparative Study of the Legal Professions in Germany and the United States* (1973); see also Rogelio Perez–Perdomo, *Latin American Lawyers: A Historical Introduction* (2006).

It often is said that the American legal profession is the largest in the world, in terms of lawyers per 100,000 population. However, the legal professions of many other countries are also growing quite rapidly. The Japanese legal profession, on the other hand, was notoriously small. As of 1980, there were some 11,466 "registered practicing attorneys" in Japan. One reason was the severe difficulty of passing the Japanese Legal Examination. Less than 2% of those who take this exam actually passed! See Kahei Rokumoto, "The

Present State of Japanese Practicing Attorneys: On the Way to Full Professionalization?," in Volume 2 of Abel and Lewis, at 160, 163, 165.

The situation in Japan may change drastically. Ichiko Fuyuno, "Japan Grooms New Lawyers: Slew of Law Schools Open Up, as Deregulation Spurs Litigation," *Wall Street Journal*, April 13, 2004, reports:

> For decades, Japan has worked hard to mass-produce everything from Toyota Corollas to Sony Walkmans. Now, it is gearing up to pump out a more contentious product: lawyers. This month, 68 new law schools opened within Japanese universities. The schools—the first U.S.-style law schools in Japan—started classes this month with 5,600 students enrolled. They are part of the Japanese government's ambitious plan to boost the number of lawyers to 50,000 by 2018, from 23,000 now ...

> Still, some legal experts question whether the new law schools will help foster more, better lawyers in Japan. For one thing, the government is so rigid in its lawyer-expansion program that it is setting a quota on how many students will pass the new bar exam—fewer than 3,000 a year until 2010. A Bar Association official says the quota was established in part because of pressure from existing attorneys, who worry they will suddenly see competition soar.

Martin Fackler and Ichiko Fuyuno, "Japan Lawyers See Seismic Shift: Influx of British, U.S. Firms Jockey for Position Ahead of New Rules," *Wall Street Journal*, Sept. 16, 2004, report that Japanese law was changed, effective in April of 2005, so that American and British lawyers and law firms would be able to practice in Japan and offer advice on Japanese law for the first time. They note:

> One big attraction in Japan for the foreign firms is the rising demand for legal services, brought about by the country's slow transformation into a more litigious society. Until the 1990s, Japan was known as a place where Western legal rules didn't seem to apply, where courts were shunned as overly confrontational and deals and disputes were settled with a handshake and a bow. But a decade of globalization and deregulation has broken down old, informal business alliances and clubby industry cartels, unleashing a fiercer brand of competition.

Tom Ginsburg and Glenn Hoetker, "The Unreluctant Litigant? An Empirical Analysis of Japan's Turn to Litigation," 35 *Journal of Legal Studies* 31, 56–57 (2006), reports:

> From 1986 to 2001, the Japanese civil litigation rate increased by 29 percent.... We find no support for the hypothesis that cultural factors play a major role. Among legal reforms, the expansion of the bar and civil procedure reform had the largest cumulative impact.

We must be careful when we compare lawyers in various countries. Nations differ as to which people they will allow to call themselves lawyers. Nonetheless, if we look closely, we may find members of various occupations doing the same work in different countries. In Japan, for example, much of the work that is done by corporate lawyers and in-house counsel in the United States is done by people who have graduated from a undergraduate law course at a university but have not passed the bar examination. Does it make any difference whether a person can call himself or herself a "lawyer" or is it enough to ask what work he or she does?

3. Does it matter who becomes a lawyer any more than it matters who becomes a dry cleaner, television repair-person or accountant? A classic statement that it does is: David Riesman, "Law and Sociology: Recruitment, Training, and Colleagueship" in William Evan (ed.) *Law and Sociology* (1962).[11] Reisman argues:

> Precisely because the commitment of going to law school and the socialization that it ensures for those who do go is less thorough-going than medical education imposes, and because, moreover, no . . . [official policy] has limited the numbers who can get a legal education, the law remains par excellence the career open to talent. Librarian of Congress, President of Chrysler, Secretary of State, and at less exalted levels insurance executive, realtor, publisher—almost any managerial, commercial, or nonspecialized intellectual job you can think of—are within the reach of the law-trained . . . [person]. It is arguable that this escalator that the law provides is at least as important as a function of legal training as the functions more frequently discussed; arguable that the criminal law, or the sanctioning, legitimation, and interpreting functions, . . . have no greater impact on the social order than this function of keeping open the channels of mobility for the boy [or girl] who can talk, who is not too narrowly self-defined—who is a kind of roving fullback of American society and can and does go anywhere. (pp. 17–18) . . .

> I have . . . described the so-called legal mind, as selected and turned out by the best national law schools, as the nonlegalistic mind: the mind that has learned skepticism of abstractions and yet at-homeness with them.

4. While upward mobility might be a social good, why are there so many lawyers in America? And what are the social consequences of having so many people in this profession? We could argue that the United States is a nation of individual rights, and Americans need legal representation to preserve their freedoms from infringement by individuals, corporations and the government. We could hypothesize that the powerful need many talented lawyers to blunt the force of all of the government regulation from the New Deal period to the 1960s. For many smart and verbal people who are not particularly good at mathematics, law is the default career choice. From the outside at least, the work looks interesting and the profession offers both status and good pay.

Many people are alarmed at the sheer size of the American legal profession. They have worried aloud about the impact of this "horde of lawyers" on the economy and the polity. There is a lively debate over the question of whether lawyers are a drag on the economy. See Charles R. Epp, "Do Lawyers

11. A version of the essay also appears at 9 *Stanford Law Review* 643 (1957).

Impair Economic Growth?" 17 *Law & Social Inquiry* 585 (1992); Frank B. Cross, "The First Thing We Do, Let's Kill All the Economists: An Empirical Evaluation of the Effect of Lawyers on the United States Economy and Political System," 70 *Texas Law Review* 645 (1992). Derek C. Bok, then President of Harvard University (and a lawyer himself), thought that the United States might have too many lawyers. In his "A Flawed System of Law Practice and Training," 33 *Journal of Legal Education* 571, 573 (1983), he wrote:

> Not only does the law absorb many more young people in America than in any other industrialized nation; it attracts an unusually large proportion of the exceptionally gifted. The average College Board scores of the top 2,000 or 3,000 law students easily exceed those of their counterparts entering other graduate schools and occupations, with the possible exception of medicine. The share of all Rhodes scholars who go on to law school has approximated 40 percent in recent years, dwarfing the figures for any other occupational group. Some readers may dismiss these statistics on the ground that lawyers often move to careers in business or public life. But the facts fail to support this rationalization, for roughly three-quarters of all law school graduates are currently practicing their profession. . . .

> The net result of these trends is a massive diversion of exceptional talent into pursuits that often add little to the growth of the economy, the pursuit of culture, or the enhancement of the human spirit. I cannot press this point too strongly. As I travel around the country looking at different professions and institutions, I am constantly struck by how complicated many jobs have become, how difficult many institutions are to administer, how pressing are the demands for more creativity and intelligence. However aggressive our schools and colleges are in searching out able young people and giving them a good education, the supply of exceptional people is limited. Yet far too many of these rare individuals are becoming lawyers at a time when the country cries out for more talented business executives, more enlightened public servants, more inventive engineers, more able high school principals and teachers.

For a response, see Robert McKay, "Too Many Bright Law Students?" *Id.* at 596, 599. (Rather than limiting the number of law students, "a better approach would be to make other professions more attractive than they now appear to be, in terms of educational challenge and long-range career attractions.")

Is Bok correct? What sorts of evidence would you need in order to check if he is right or wrong? Does his statement assume that lawyers are essentially parasites? What is the counter-argument?

5. Many lawyers are paid very well, and this probably is a factor in attracting people to the profession. Ellen Rosen, "For New Lawyers, The Going Rate Has Gone Up," *N.Y. Times*, September 1, 2006, C7, reported: "The going rate [for beginning lawyers] at large firms in New York has

reached $145,000—apart from starting and year-end bonuses—while the base salary in cities other than New York is approximately $10,000 lower, according to an annual study released Aug. 1 by the National Association for Law Placement." These jobs in the largest firms are reserved for recent law school graduates with the best credentials. Cameron Stracher, "Cut My Salary, Please!" *Wall Street Journal*, April 1, 2006, A7, argues:

> [M]ost associates know their chances of making partner at the big firms is less than 5%; thus, firms are paying them essentially to forgo the opportunity at partnership, in much the same way that professional football teams pay astronomical salaries to players whose careers last only four or five years. Once they depart for smaller firms or in-house jobs, they will not see their former salaries for years, if ever.
>
> But what makes economic sense to the firms makes less sense for young lawyers. For one thing, each salary increase has been accompanied with a corresponding increase in billable minimums. When I started practicing, lawyers were expected to bill around 1,800 hours a year. These days, it's about 2,200. Those 400 extra billable hours translate to about 600 more hours at work, or approximately two to three more hours in the office each day. Even at 1,800 hours I worked until nine at night, and most weekends. At 2,200 hours, a lawyer might as well move a cot into his office.
>
> Bonuses, salary increases and partnership chances are all tied to billable hours. Many law firms will not even grant a bonus unless an associate reaches a certain minimum, which used to be unheard of. Associates are paid more for their work, but not in proportion to the toll it has taken on their lives. In effect, the increase in billable hours has simply covered the rise in salaries. Even though most lawyers say they would prefer to work less and be paid less, associates are working longer to pay for their own raises. With the recent salary hike, they will be paying even more.
>
> Meanwhile, the work itself has actually grown more dreary, if that is possible. Higher salaries have forced firms to look for new ways to increase revenues. One obvious solution is to throw more lawyers on a case, and to be more aggressive about litigating and challenging small matters that might otherwise go uncontested. The result is that the youngest lawyers get the most trivial and unnecessary work. Law firms claim they staff matters "leanly," but that doesn't justify the huge increases in the costs of litigation (and deal-making), which can only partly be explained by increases in fees. Instead, firms are lawyering matters to death, and killing their associates in the process.

The folklore of second- and third-year law students suggests that they know of the long hours, the small chance of making partner and the salaries. Why do so many of the best students take these unsatisfying jobs? Leigh Jones, "As Salaries Rise, So Does the Debt," *National Law Journal*, February 1, 2006, reports that students who were in-state residents and attending public law schools were paying up to 267 percent more for their legal education in 2005 than those who went to law school in 1990. Beginning lawyers have much more debt when they graduate than did their predecessors. Those in smaller firms earn much less than those in the largest ones. In 2004, the median salary for first-year associates in firms of 26 to 50 lawyers was $65,000. The median salary in those firms in 1990 was $45,000. The median salary in firms of two to 10 lawyers was $48,000 in 2004 and $30,000 in 1990. Thus, the price of legal education has gone up much faster than even what beginning lawyers in large prestigious firms are paid. In the last 25 years, the number of lawyers entering public interest practice has declined from 5.4 percent to 2.9 percent.

6. Conley and Baker question Carlin's highly negative picture of solo and small firm practice. Joel F. Handler, *The Lawyer and His Community* (1967), found "The aggression, tensions, discontent, and economic insecurities of the big city were almost nonexistent in Prairie City; the Prairie City lawyers liked their community, their work, and their way of life." Why might the size of the community make a difference to solo and small firm lawyers?

(2) Major Changes in the Profession: Women and Minority Group Lawyers

(5.12) Gender Penalties Revisited

Nancy Reichman and Joyce S. Sterling

© 2004.

Reports of cracks in the glass ceiling of the legal profession have been around for nearly two decades. Many speculate that since women now comprise the new majority of students in U.S. law schools it is only a matter of time until women control the practice of law....

Certainly the status of women in the profession has improved since the 1970s when women began to enter the profession in substantial numbers. But, unfortunately, recent data on the profession suggest that neither changes in the number of female law students nor changes in the number of female associates has substantially changed the profile of the profession. While it may be wrong to continue to say that the glass is half empty, the glass is certainly not yet half full.

This report examines three dimensions of gender disparity: compensation, promotion, and retention/attrition. They are inter-related; inequity in one dimension can produce inequities in the others. Compensation disparity is clearly the foundation of gender disparity. When compensation disparity and promotion disparity are combined, they result in problems of "retention." The disparities that occur in these 3 components result in "sticky floors" on which women get stuck and "glass ceilings" against which women's advancement rebounds.

The data that form the basis of this report include the results of the 1993 CWBA [Colorado Women's Bar Association] analysis of the 1993 CBA [Colorado Bar Association] Economic Survey and 2000 CBA Economic Surveys as well as 100 in-depth interviews with Colorado attorneys. Where appropriate, national data are introduced for comparative purposes.

STUDY BACKGROUND

GENDER PENALTIES, c. 1993

In 1993 the Colorado Bar Association and the Colorado Women's Bar Association created a survey to assess and compare the economic status of male and female attorneys in Colorado. Using the Colorado Supreme Court's list of licensed, active attorneys, questionnaires were mailed to a random sample of 3100 attorneys. Confidential responses were received from 55.8% of the sample. 73.2% of those responding were male and 26.8% female, proportions that closely approximated the proportion of male and female attorneys in Colorado at that time.

A significant area of difference between men and women was in the average earned income reported in the 1993 survey. The average net income (after expenses but before taxes) for full-time women lawyers was only 59% of the average income for full-time male practitioners ($53,893 compared to $90,953). Some of the overall disparity between men and women attorneys was explained by men's longer tenure in the profession. However, when years of practice were correlated with income, the significant gap between men and women remained. While income for male and female practitioners beginning their careers was fairly equal, female practitioners with 1 to 3 years experience averaged only 82% of the income of their male counterparts. At the 4 to 9 years of experience level, female attorneys reported making 86% of the average income of male attorneys of comparable experience, and at the 10 to 20 years of experience level, female attorneys made only 76% of the average income of their male counterparts. There were too few women who had practiced more than 20 years to make a statistically meaningful comparison with men at this level of experience.

When income reported in the 1993 survey was correlated with firm size, female attorneys across all firm sizes made substantially less than male attorneys. The pattern of economic disparity continued when types of employment (sole practitioner, partner, associate, etc.) and areas of practice (criminal, litigation, family law, etc.) were compared. The data analysis also compared the number of hours billed, hourly rates, and collection rates for male and female attorneys and concluded that these factors did not explain the economic disparity.

The CBA/CWBA Economic Survey results were disturbing to a number of Colorado lawyers. The CWBA took the lead and formed a study group to consider possible explanations for these economic disparities. These discussions led to the first study of career histories of male and female attorneys in the Denver metropolitan area. Our goal was to collect career narratives that could reveal patterns of constraint and choice in the formation of legal careers and the determination of compensation. We conducted in-depth interviews with 100 attorneys (52 women and 48 men) in the Denver Metropolitan area. The sample was restricted to lawyers currently working in law firms of more than ten lawyers at the time of those interviews, although a number of those attorneys worked in other sectors at various points in their careers. The sample was purposefully selected to insure sufficient numbers of well matched men and women who could develop a picture of private law practice that was deep enough to offer insights into firm culture and broad enough to cover a range of practice types. Only attorneys with a minimum of five years practice experience were included to insure that our interviewees had sufficient experience to reflect on factors that influenced their careers. We attempted to select equal numbers of men and women in similar positions including managing partners, senior partners, mid-level partners, new partners and senior associates. This sampling plan presented a number of challenges. We found that women had not been practicing in the larger firms long enough to be found in comparable numbers to men in the highest positions of these firms. We were surprised to find that it was equally difficult to find similarly situated male associates in the small firms.

In addition to the sampling approach described above, we sampled a category of lawyers that we designated as "migrants." These lawyers were individuals who had made a minimum of three career moves between firms. Many of these individuals had, in fact, made more than three moves. The individuals in this final part of the sample turned out to be extremely valuable informants. Not only could they add to the breadth of practice contexts we explored, they often helped to round out our in-depth exploration of a few firms.

The first wave of interviews was conducted over two years (1996–1998). The interviews were taped and transcribed. We began interviews by asking when and why people decided to go to law school, where they received their undergraduate education and legal education, and the nature of their parents' occupations. Then the interviews proceeded in an unstructured format to collect information on all the career choices that our respondents had made— including initial job choices (clerkships for example) and then decisions they made along their career paths. We wanted information on decisions to change jobs, work part-time, have families, etc. We asked for their perceptions of what was important (people and events) to a legal career. All respondents were guaranteed individual as well as law firm anonymity. This guaranty was essential since the Denver legal community is small enough that individuals could be identified by giving only a few personal or professional characteristics. Pseudonyms are used throughout this report. We modified the quotes from lawyers to disguise identities and to maintain the flow of the conversation.

GENDER PENALTIES c. 2000

In 2000, the CBA again surveyed a random sample of Colorado lawyers, including both members and non-members of the CBA. Respondents were again asked to report their earned income, in this case earned income in 1999. We expected to observe a narrowing, if not the disappearance, of the income gap between men and women attorneys in Colorado. We were stunned to discover that the gap had not disappeared, but had actually increased in some sectors of legal practice.

The perpetuation of the income discrepancies motivated us to revisit our original sample of Denver lawyers. We attempted to find the original 100 respondents and to re-interview them to determine career changes that had occurred since our initial interviews—5 to 7 years earlier. Only 3 of the original 100 respondents were not locatable. Many of the respondents had moved since we last talked to them, almost 60% of the sample had moved from their previous jobs. During the second wave of interviews, we wanted to pick up the career histories where we left off in what we now called "Time One." We started the interviews by going back to the Time One interview and reminding people what they were doing when we last talked to them. We then asked them to bring us up to date on their career moves. In addition, we asked people to fill out a short web-based survey.

The Imperative for Gender Equity

It is important to distinguish the concepts of equality and equity as they are often confused. Equality is defined in terms of sameness, the same number, degree, value, or intensity; or the same rights, privileges, ability, rank, etc. ... Equity, on the other hand, is defined as "justice, impartiality; the giving or desiring to give each person his due; anything that is fair." To pursue equity can mean to treat people differently in order to treat them fairly. It is the imperative for fairness that motivates this report....

The Persistence of Gender Penalties In Compensation, Promotion and Retention

Compensation

All full-time lawyers

A comparison of 1993 and 1999 mean net income of Colorado lawyers indicates that overall the gap between the earned income of men and women lawyers remained stable. In 1993, the average full-time woman lawyer earned only 59 cents for every dollar earned by her male counterpart. In 1999, the gap narrowed by one percent; the average full-time female attorney earned 60 cents of that earned by the average man....

Colorado is not alone. A recent study of Michigan's lawyers conducted by the State Bar of Michigan found that the average female attorney earned only 71 cents for every dollar earned by her male counterpart. *After the JD*, a national study of lawyers admitted to the bar in 2000, reveals gender differences in nearly all areas of practice with the largest difference between men's and women's salaries in the largest firms, i.e., in firms with more than

251 lawyers and in corporate law departments. Overall, the median salary for women admitted to the bar was $66,000 compared to a $80,000 median salary for similarly situated men, a female to male ratio of 0.83.

The compensation gap between men and women is not unique to the legal profession either. Studies of full-time workers conducted by the US Department of Labor show a persistent, albeit narrowing, gap in men and women's earnings....

Years in Practice

The Colorado data allowed us to investigate whether the gap narrowed for full-time lawyers with different tenure in the profession. Given the attention focused on compensation disparity after the first CBA study we expected the gap between men and women to narrow, particularly in the case of newer lawyers....

As expected, we find some improvement for women lawyers with 1–3 years experience (82% of men's income in 1993 and 92% in 1999) and those with 4–9 years experience (86% of men's income in 1993 and 96% in 1999). However, the differential between the earned income of men and women lawyers widened slightly for lawyers with less than 1 year's experience in the practice of law (women made 96% of men's income in 1993 and 92% of their income in 1999). The gap for those with 10–20 years actually increased slightly (76% of men's income in 1993 and 74% in 1999) as well.

A study of two groups of University of Michigan graduates shows similar patterns in the differentials between the earnings of male and female attorneys with 15 years experience. At their fifteenth year of practice, the ratio of female-to-male average earnings for lawyers who graduated between 1972 and 1978 was 0.63. Study authors expected the gap between men and women to narrow for later years of graduates who had the benefit of increased numbers of women entering the profession. This was not the case. The female-to-male 15th year earnings ratio for graduates between 1979 and 1985 dropped slightly to 0.61.

Type of Position

Controlling for the type of position, the promise for women's advancement remains mixed. Women partners in 1999 narrowed the differential in earnings from 69% in 1993 to 78% in 1999. Surprisingly, the differential for associates grew in the six years between surveys. In 1993, the average female associate earned 94 cents to the dollar earned by her male counterpart; unexplainably in 1999 she earned only 65 cents to the dollar earned by the average man....

The CBA Economic Survey allowed for other comparisons not developed in this report. Women's earnings have declined for solo practitioners/space sharers (60% in 1993 and 52% in 1999), and in-house counsel (79% in 1993 and 71% in 1999). The income gap has remained the same for government attorneys (83% in 1993 compared to 83% in 1999).

Promotion

The partnership rate, defined as the percentage of partners who are women, has remained relatively flat nationally, ranging from almost 11% in 1991 to 16% in 2002. The Denver data on partnership (reported by NALP [National Association of Law Placement]) are more promising; however, only 18–21 firms reported to NALP in the period . . .

As points of comparison, consider the following data from the business world. According to the Catalyst Census of Women Corporate Officers, overall, women made up 15.7 percent of senior officers of Fortune 500 companies in 2002, up from 12.5 percent in 2000 and 8.7% in 1995, when the census began. In 2002, women comprised 7.1 percent of the 496 Chief Financial Officers (CFO) and 16.1 percent of the 453 General Counsels (GC) up from 5.6 percent of the CFO positions and 13.7 percent of the GC positions in 2000.

The EEOC recently released a study analyzing disparity in law firms of 100 or more employees that demonstrates that it may be more than a matter of time until women's representation in the ranks of partners is equal to their representation as law graduates. They conclude that women are less likely to be promoted. Using a combination of NALP and EEOC 2002 data about the number of partners and associates, they calculated an odds ratio that a woman would be promoted to a partner in a firm. When two groups have the same odds, the odds ratio equals one. In this case, the odds ratio was 5.330, "not even odds for the two groups;" men have significantly greater odds of becoming partners than women. Given these 2002 data, a man was five times more likely than a woman to become a partner. Note that this analysis does not take into account different qualifications such as years in practice.

Our in-depth study of 100 lawyers illustrates a similar pattern of promotion disparity. Consider the 29 associates we interviewed, all of whom had at least 5 years of experience when we first interviewed them, and who, all things being equal, should have become partners seven years later when we interviewed them again. 67% of the men were promoted to partnership, while only 46% of the women were promoted during the same time period. Considering movement to in-house as a different, yet still upward, career move one notices that nearly all the men moved up in status either in their firm or through a move; only slightly more than half of the women demonstrate that kind of upward career trajectory. (Of course the numbers are small.) Only women are represented among those who stayed at a firm without promotion or became inactive in the legal field—a clear indication of sticky floors.

Table 1: WHAT HAPPENED TO ASSOCIATES BETWEEN TIME 1 and TIME 2

	Women	Men
Became a partner at their firm	18%	25%
	(n = 3)	(n = 3)
Moved & became partner elsewhere	24%	42%
	(n = 4)	(n = 5)

Moved in-house	12%	25%
	(n = 2)	(n = 3)
Moved but not a partner	12%	8%
	(n = 2)	(n = 1)
Stayed at firm, not promoted	18%	0
	(n = 3)	
Left Law or Inactive	18%	0
	(n = 3)	
TOTAL	n = 17	n = 12

. . .

Retention

Much of the national attention on issues of retention has focused on the issue of associate retention; however, our research shows that the pipeline of women lawyers leaks at all levels.

Considering our oldest group of women, women who graduated from law school in the 1970s, we found that 31% of them had retired by the time we interviewed them in 2003; not one of the men who graduated from law school in that same period had done so when we scheduled our second round of interviews. This finding is reinforced by the results of the Catalyst study of 6300 graduates from selected law schools. They found that of those graduating in the 1970s, only 30% of the women law graduates, compared to 51% of the men, are still working in law firms.

A stunning finding about women we interviewed who graduated from law school in the early part of the 1980's was that 40% left law practice to pursue other career opportunities. These are women in their late forties and early fifties, presumably at the peak of the legal careers and with substantial wisdom to offer their legal organizations. Interestingly, none of the younger women we interviewed had "opted out" of law practice to take care of their children as a recent New York Times article would suggest.

Because we interviewed men and women with at least 5 years experience, we missed the very young lawyers who are the subject of much of the news on lawyer attrition. As demonstrated by national data the gap between men's and women's attrition is persistent over the last decade. Women are more likely than men to leave their first law firm within 3 years. Notice as well the effect of changing market conditions in the first years of the 21st century. Associate departures from first law firm employment dropped below 40% for the first time since 1989 and by 2001 were at their lowest levels since these data were collected. . . .

Persistent Impact of Professional Trends on Gender Penalties

While the fortunes of many individual lawyers improved since their first interview, many of the key concerns raised in *Gender Penalties* remained concerns in the second round.

Centralized management of law firms continues to dominate law practice; decisions within firms remain hidden and individually negotiated. Most importantly, according to some, the complexion of law firm management has changed. Lawyers use words like "dictatorship" or "young Turks" to describe firm governance.

> When I first became a partner you voted compensation to all of your partners. You did what everyone used to call the beauty contest book. You would write these pages and pages about how incredibly wonderful you were and why you deserve more money then anyone else. And then the management committee I think would assign certain points to each person or there was a base that everybody had to get so that it wasn't possible to make no money. But then there were discretionary points that all of your partners spent time distributing among you. And I think that had worked very well for a very long time but it started breaking down. I'm not sure if it was the size of the firm or if it was women coming into the partnership. I'm not sure which it was. But it started breaking down and so you started seeing people who were really kind of getting screwed over big time. And they changed the system [so that compensation was set by the management committee]. One of the reasons that they said they changed the system was because they were afraid it would sort of disintegrate or fall into old boy-ism where it was the women who were going to be hit every time. Because you would see groups of people who would sort of pool their points and throw them somewhere. [Under the new system], the management committee had a great deal of say and control and at the same time you knew who was responsible and could hold them accountable. And to that end you always knew what everyone made [Paula Richards, Time 1].

In the late 80s, Richards began to notice gender inequities and brought them to the attention of the management committee who were "... appalled. They had never thought about it [gender bias] ... they were not threatened by it." They decided to introduce diversity training. She goes on to explain,

> Did it get better in terms of compensation? For those of us at the top maybe but not for the newer female partners. It really didn't get better. I cannot tell you the answer. I think that the reason it did not get better for some of the younger people is because the complexion or the makeup of the management committee started to change and it started to change with the addition of younger people, people who tended to be about my age who in some ways were more threatened by the women being there than the older partners had been. And who in some ways were more competitive with everybody including the women and in some ways who saw success by a woman as somehow diminishing them. So that may have been why it didn't get fixed for everybody [Paula Richards, Time 1].

Two-tier partnerships and other "innovative" positions have become an accepted part of law firm structure in many of the medium and large firms. These "innovations" have not necessarily worked to the advantage of women.

Rather, they have produced increased stratification within firms, creating a new form of "employee" lawyer without change in the traditional professional model that informs most firm cultures and compensation structures.

> I love to get on my soapbox about this, so the only language I have is inflammatory. I feel like being a non-equity member is like being a serf. There is this mysterious, quote, formula for setting your compensation, but no matter how hard you work in any given year you never share in the upside of that year. You may be rewarded in the next year, and you may not. You share all the downsides. You have all the liability, you have all of the responsibilities for keeping track of your own stuff, supervising others, bringing in practice development. On the other hand you are a member of a firm that consistently under-budgets revenues by twenty percent a year, who consistently over-budgets overhead by twenty percent a year. So you're taking it in the shorts at both ends. You are always paying the higher overhead number which helps determine your compensation and you are never sharing in the extra twenty percent at the end of the year. So I just hate it. I think that smart people should never do that, it's a bad deal. But it's just one of the steps along the way, and by the time you get there, you've worked so hard. [Mary Reever, Time 2]

While both men and women occupy these positions, they are more likely to become traps for women. Despite the fact that most large firms offer "part-time" programs, very few lawyers take advantage of them.

Time to partnership is still 7–9 years in most firms, but some firms now have stretched partnership decisions to 8–10 years. Many attorneys are starting families at the critical moments in their careers when partnership decisions are looming. Given traditional gender roles, this is likely to have a greater impact on women's careers than on the careers of their male counterparts.

Changes in the market for legal services continue some of the gender penalties revealed in our earlier report and have brought new challenges to regional law firms as routes of opportunity for women. In the period between the first and second interviews, the economy went from the peak of a record-long boom to what many define as a recession. Several trends are noteworthy.

As a result of competition from the dot.com businesses and lawyers who serviced them, the salaries of law firm associates increased dramatically, arguably way ahead of the market. This put increased pressure on the leverage systems of large and medium sized firms, particularly regional firms. More senior lawyers in these firms report finding themselves working more hours and spending even more time on client development at a point in their careers when many expected they would be able to ease up on or at least control the pace of their practice. While men often responded to this inconsistency between personal expectations and changing firm demands by moving to new practice settings that required little or no leveraging, many women opted to retire early or move out of law to start a new career.

Lawyers report that the number of associates hired directly out of law school in large and medium firms has declined significantly, again with potentially different impact on men and women. Lateral hires who can bring a book of business or law specialty with them have become more prevalent in larger firms. Although quantitative data are not yet available, several lawyers have observed that women are not well represented among lateral hires. Barbara Kray, an emerging career lawyer, describes a situation where the firm brought in two male laterals. She was surprised to learn that they did not come into the firm with their own books of business, as she thought that this was a necessary requirement.

> I have a bone to pick with that right now. We have hired some laterals who actually have more experience than I do but they are from out of state and they don't have any of their own work. And they are men. My bone is that the head of the department is giving work to them because they wouldn't have work on their own as opposed to giving it to me because he figures oh she'll get her work—one of her clients will need something or she has other means of getting it. I do think that's going on or that's my perception [Barbara Kray, Time 1].

She notes that she could have used the work.

If women continue to have less access to client development either because they do not have access to business generating networks or because they are perceived to have more difficulty generating business and are not elevated to positions and networks that allow them to realize their potential, they will have trouble making lateral moves.

Finally, law firms have not been immune to the changing nature of careers generally. "Non-performance based" means of career advancement, including movements like lateral transfers and changing companies, as well as instrumental uses of social relationships with coworkers, supervisors, or other organizational mentors have become acceptable and routine. Young lawyers perceive and operate under "new realities" in terms of professional advancement.

> When I went to law school people tried to get clerkships with judges, and then they tried to go into the biggest named firm they could. There were always a few people who did other things but that was the whole focus, and I'm not sure that gets you where you want to go anymore or you need to do it. I mean I think there are different ways to get ahead.

> When I went to work we really couldn't switch among big firms. It was not accepted. I suppose somebody could come up with some example but basically you left and you went to something different. It would be like raiding, it would be inappropriate ... It was one thing to compete for clients and what not, but you didn't steal. Whereas now you can go from one firm to another and nobody thinks about it, and partners do it. So when I came out of school I think you were more making a choice and eliminating others. Your decision was more important because you were closing off certain doorways [Connie Newton, Time 1].

Choices and Constraints

Although men and women report the same high level of overall job satisfaction, women tend to be more dissatisfied with particular aspects of their work such as compensation and job opportunities. The survey distributed to each lawyer interviewed included questions that tapped the multiple dimensions of professional practice.

Seventeen questions about lawyers' satisfaction, including satisfaction with the tasks they perform, the intellectual challenge of their work, opportunities for advancement, and control over work, to name just a few, were asked. Men and women reported statistically similar levels of satisfaction in all but two areas: opportunities for advancement and compensation (including salary, benefits, and bonus, if applicable).... [W]omen are significantly less satisfied with compensation; 14% of the women and none of the men responded at the bottom of the seven point scale.... Fewer women were satisfied with the opportunities for advancement and compensation.... [O]nly 41.7% of the women compared to 77.4% of the men expressed high levels of satisfaction with career opportunities....

Although the difference between men and women in other dimensions of satisfaction did not reach statistical significance, the trend was towards less satisfaction by women. Most notably, ... women expressed less satisfaction with relationships at work....

To get a better sense of how satisfaction might relate to career trajectory and compensation, the reasons for each career change reported in the interviews was analyzed.... Our study found that women tend to report career changes as a result of their dissatisfaction with compensation, a ''dysfunctional'' firm, or their interest in an alternative lifestyle. Men tend to characterize changes in their careers as the result of ''opportunities.'' ...

Systematic differences in why men and women move both reflect and reinforce their different gender status inside and outside the practice of law. It is perfectly [gender] appropriate for women to cite ''family'' or ''lifestyle'' as the reason they are leaving their firms. Indeed, some women reported that they did just that rather than express their dissatisfaction and risk closed doors in their future. Similarly, men may find it [gender] inappropriate to cite family or lifestyle as the reason they leave, preferring instead to focus on their new opportunities. Both responses, appropriate from their gender perspective, tend to reinforce the stereotypes of women's commitment to the practice of law.

Both women and men described tension between work and personal life. Both spoke about their need to ''get a life'' and the personal costs of overwork. But the push/pull of career and family was experienced quite differently; the constraints they faced and thus the ''choices'' they made were embedded in the gendered nature of both work and home. Women and men resolved these painful dilemmas quite differently [in ways] that pushed women (and not men) away from traditional private practice and [led] ... to disparate impact on compensation. Faced with both conflict within the work organization and life changes outside the organization, women partners, not just young women lawyers with young families, took on new career opportunities away from private legal practice or in some cases chose to retire. Men facing work-personal life dilemmas, tended to reconstitute their practices in ways that enabled them to get more control over their work, but they remained in the practice of law. To what extent these decisions reflected gendered choices (e.g. a woman's willingness to give up higher incomes to engage in something worthwhile) or gendered opportunities (a man's professional network) is hard to determine precisely. Whatever the reason, the impact is to move women away from more lucrative compensation and reinforce gendered expectations about commitment and competence.

Equally interesting and with some consequence for compensation are differences between men and women in how they make their moves. Men's stories are replete with examples of how they were thinking about making a move when coincidentally a friend called and asked them if they might be interested in a change. They appear willing and able to capitalize on friendship networks. . . .

Women's stories of career movement, by way of contrast, frequently mention clients' repeatedly offering them in-house positions or other lawyers leaving and taking them along. Unlike the men, women in our study relied more heavily on those with whom they worked to provide them with new opportunities. These were people who know and appreciated their performance record, rather than friends who might only know their potential. . . .

The Career Trajectories of Men and Women

The in-depth interviews we conducted with 100 attorneys over the two phases of our project enabled us to develop extensive career histories within the context of individual life histories, in particular the interweaving of career and family, as well as within broader historical events, i.e., legal and social changes that influence work structures and opportunities. Few studies of the profession examine how careers unfold over time. Instead, they develop "snapshots" of legal careers, analyzing short segments. Moreover, most studies of women's careers focus on how they depart from the masculine norm rather than considering women's careers on their own terms.

Looking at women's careers we noticed distinct "generations" according to when women entered legal practice. Using the generational differences of women lawyers as our point of reference, we grouped the lawyers we interviewed accordingly. A reminder here: When we picked our sample to interview, we picked them to allow comparison by their position: senior partner, associate, of-counsel. The idea of using generations as a point of comparison developed out of our analysis that revealed important differences that were masked using firm position as a point of reference for our comparison of men and women.

Several general trends are noteworthy.

The careers of women lawyers "map" differently than those of men and in ways that may continue to produce overall pay disparities between them. Women moved more than men, women moved earlier than men, women were more likely to move downward than men. 46% of the women we interviewed made their first firm move by the second year of practice. Only 14% of men moved at such an early point in their career. Instead, we find that men were likely to make their first move around the fourth or fifth year of practice. This difference suggests that women made decisions to leave jobs long before firms made decisions about potential partnership, while men's first move appears to correlate more closely to the partnership decision. Indeed, it appears that women made decisions about their law firm job sometimes even before our analysis of law firm practice suggests they would have received meaningful feedback on their future potential within the firm. By the fifth year of practice, 71% of the men made moves and 74% of the women had made a move. By this point in a lawyer's career, he/she can assess their "fit" within the firm and should have received at least informal cueing about their progress on the track to partnership. There was no evidence that movement was associated with age cohort or time spent in practice. That is, these patterns appear to be equally true of lawyers who entered the profession 15 years ago or today.

Table 2:   Generations

	Women	Men
Grand Old Men		7
		(14.6%)
Mature Career	16	21
	(32.7%)	(43.8%)
Peak Career	10	6
	(20.4%)	(12.5%)
Emerging Career	23	14
	(46.9%)	(29.2%)
Total	49	48
missing		3

Not only did women move earlier than men, they show slightly higher rates of movement than men. We classified 53% of the women in our sample as having high rates of movement—movement that exceeds the sample median rate of 1.11 moves per 10 years—compared to 41% of the men. . . .

Important generational differences among women (not as obvious in the career histories of men) make it difficult to create and sustain a "critical mass" or momentum for change. The women who were the pioneers in law define their early careers in terms of being one of the boys. They believed that for women to succeed, their gender/sex needed to be invisible. In contrast to the younger woman who brought her children to the office to "show them off" (Elizabeth McConnell), more senior women, if they had children at all, tended to hide them from their co-workers (Connie Newton). The new realities for women are recognized and appreciated in this commentary from one senior woman about another senior woman who doesn't "get it."

> She came to work a year ago and has been assigned to work with him. She's really really kiss ass and I'm not at all. But she is much more concerned with being one of the guys than I think I ever was and the other women in the firm really resent it because at the time when I started there was no alternative, you were either one of the guys or you weren't there. You don't have to do that now and yet that's how she is. So, a lot of the other women really resent her behavior and her actions [Sher Sherwood, Time 1].

Despite some generational differences, the similarities in the career histories of women lawyers challenge popular perceptions that a woman's successes (or failure) is the result of something "unusual" or unique. One mature woman lawyer who has retired notes that many senior women "don't think their story is retraceable." This is not their fault, she says. They have been told, "you got to do what you want because you're so special." This fuels women's perception that their success is a matter of luck. "It just happened for me, so I can't do that for someone else." (Connie Newton) . . .

Mature Career Lawyers

We define the lawyers who graduated from law school between 1969 and 1979 as "Mature Lawyers." The mean age of the women in this group was 56 compared to 54 for the men. The median years in practice for this group were 27 for the women and 31 for the men. A significant number of lawyers in this cohort began their careers in some type of government work. This was not true for any other cohort in our study. It is not surprising that so many of the mature career women found their first job in government as it was one of the few options available. One mature woman suggests that she landed her first job in government after striking out with private law firms because the government sector was more "into trying to have some sort of affirmative action plan."

> I went around to probably 15 plaintiffs firms armed with this letter from these great plaintiffs lawyers. You know what? Only one of them offered me a job. I have thought about that ever since. I bet if I had been a male with those kinds of letters and that much experience somebody would have hired me at a much better salary [Jana Castle].

We cannot explain why a government start was not found to be the case for the careers of any of the other cohorts of men.

The retirement of several women is a noticeable feature of this cohort. Women offered different reasons for their decision to stop practicing law, but in each narrative we hear the woman's desire to "cut back" or change the dimensions of her practice. Retirement, rather than some new arrangement within a law firm is their "choice" in part because avenues within law are closed to them and, in part, because they have "lives outside of law." Interestingly, many of these women continue to do law work as volunteers, or on contract for some specified project. When he heard about this group of incredibly talented pool of women, one thoughtful lawyer pondered whether they were a pool of talented lawyers who could be called in to cover when more junior lawyers, typically but not necessarily women, took time off for their families.

Several men in this cohort have made moves away from practices that required them to keep other [more junior] lawyers busy, Like women, they too are frustrated and burned out. What is different from the similarly tired and burned out women is that on the one hand, they are able to imagine and implement new possibilities for their careers. They do see "happy, wonderful, professional families down the street that welcome them with open arms." On the other hand, they cannot easily imagine their lives outside of law . . . .

Women who had trouble finding "fit" earlier in their careers continued to do so. Consider this, perhaps extreme, example of searching for fit. Sally O'Hare began practicing in a legal aid office, moved to a high level government position, then to a large regional firm, and then to a national practice, and from there to a small local firm, back to a large regional firm and finally is of-counsel to a budding new practice.

While a few of the mature women reported having held leadership positions within their firms; more than half of the men had been managing or founding partners of their firms. To the extent that women assumed leadership positions, they did so often as the "token woman," champions of gender neutrality typical of this generation of pioneer women lawyers. [They were] encouraged to fit in rather than make waves. Although she never served on a management committee, one senior woman recognized that administrative work might have value in furthering one's career . . . .

Both the career value and the tendency to become "one of them," was cited by another senior woman who did serve on her firm's executive committee.

> I went from being kind of this unhappy partner feeling a little bit ignored and other things, and then all of a sudden you're on the executive committee. And it's so funny, it's kind of, I always call it the Patty Hearst syndrome. But it doesn't take long before you start to kind of identify, with the group you're now with [Sue Grafton, Time 2].

Women who take on these roles particularly as the first and/or token woman resist being categorized as "women's voice."

> My role is much broader than [being the woman's voice]. I think that anyone has got to be concerned about the finances of the firm, how the firm runs, women's issues, I mean all issues. So, you know you're a woman and presumably you have a sensitivity to women's issues but on the other hand the role is simply not to provide input on issues related to women. It's just having a woman on the Executive Committee. It's been great. The wonderful things about it are that you find what everyone is

doing which is great because people are doing fascinating [Joan Gabel, Time 2].

Peak Career Lawyers

The third cohort of lawyers, "Peak Career Lawyers," graduated from law school between 1980 and 1984. The average age of women in this group was 51, the average age of men was 48. Peak career women practiced an average of 21.5 years, peak career men 22 years. Women in this cohort who pursued a traditional career path have hit glass ceilings—they have either gone as far as they want to go given the structure of work or they have been blocked from further advancement. Some have responded to their frustrations at work by moving out of legal practice, others, like some of the mature men, have set up as solo practitioners.

Joy Drew was an extraordinarily successful lawyer in a large firm who no longer practices law. She explained her "choice" to us

> In an environment where you've got coastal firms moving in and a lot less loyalty from clients, I kind of looked at that and said, "Life's too short." Because it was never about the money for me . . . I mean the money was nice, don't get me wrong. It's certainly not something I think you would do for much less money, you know, I would not practice law for what I'm making now. So, I don't want to say it's not at all about the money, but the money wasn't worth it any more. It just wasn't worth it any more. Despite the fact that my compensation had been growing tremendously [Joy Drew, Time 2].

Sandra Boxwell began her legal career as assistant general counsel for a Fortune 500 company. She stayed in this job for more than ten years. As the company began downsizing and she turned 40, she began to think about going into private practice. She joined a national law firm with an office in Denver. She negotiated to enter the firm as a partner. Unfortunately the firm imploded after 1 year. She left with a number of lawyers from the firm for another national law firm with a Denver office. She entered the national firm as "of counsel," since the firm was only willing to take in 2 of the group as lateral partners; both were men. Two years later she became a partner. By the time we interviewed her a second time, Sandra had been practicing law for 20 years. Given her career progression and savvy during the first interview, we would have predicted that she would be a successful senior partner in the firm she joined. However, shortly before we interviewed her the second time, she quit the firm and opened a solo office. She described her choice to leave as motivated, in part, by her inability to get the resources she needed to get her work done.

> I certainly was one of the higher billing partners that period of my time there. But it was still hard to attract associates to work with me because I was never one of the partners who was yelling at them that they had to do my work. I was never willing to say, "you have got to work, you've got to get this done and you've got to get this done now. And no, you cannot work on his work. You've got to work on my work." It was very hard for

me, and it got to be not worth the effort to try to put out what I needed to put out to get the associates to stay on my work. They would tend to put my work down and pick up somebody else's work. Take up my work again. My clients were getting pissed off. It got to be frustrating. I think the associates liked me. It certainly wasn't a popularity contest. It's just that that's the way their bread is buttered. I'm not complaining. I mean, it was my turn. I got to be the head of the hiring committee, which meant that I had to interview all these same people who wouldn't work for me later and to persuade my partners to have interviews with them so that they could ultimately go and work for them. These kinds of things began to happen to me [Boxwell, Time 2].

This cohort is noteworthy as well for examples of women who took a less traditional path and are now finding success at their firms. Judy Findley's career story represents this trend. She began her career at a large regional firm. After six years practicing at a firm during which time she had two children, she decided that she needed more flexibility. She began working "part-time," set hours each day. She subsequently decided that she wanted to be closer to home and moved twice, both times to small firms. Although she was happy at these firms, they proved to be less financially stable than she needed. She returned to the large regional firm on a part time arrangement.

> I proposed that I would come back on a non-partnership track and this time it was called senior counsel. By this time my girls were [old enough] so I didn't really care about a scheduled part time like 11:00 to 5:00. I just wanted less pressure to bill hours.

She quickly found she was billing lots of hours. After two years, at which point she was billing a full-time load, she decided it was silly not to go back on partnership track, an opportunity that had been discussed with her ever since she returned. She became a partner and shortly thereafter joined the firm's upper management.

We had very few "Career" men. Thus, it was hard to identify a career trajectory pattern for them, other than to note that they were more likely to remain in private practice and to look like the mature men who preceded them.

Emerging Career Lawyers

The fourth cohort, "Emerging Career Lawyers," includes attorneys who graduated from law school after 1985. The median age of women in this group was 45. The median age of emerging career men was 40. While there was some movement out of law by women, what distinguished this cohort was the entrepreneurship of some of the women who spun off from larger firm practice to create or join their own small firms. This was not without some financial risk to them. Emerging Career Men moved into different practice organizations as well, but unlike the women their movement tended to be from large to medium size or national law firms with promising new, sometimes entrepreneurial, opportunities. The career stories of Susan Fry and

Bradley Harris illustrate the gender difference we saw between the career trajectories of Emerging Career lawyers. She saw opportunities in striking out on her own; he saw opportunities in starting a new practice group at a large national firm.

Bradley Harris began his career at a large regional firm. On an upward trajectory throughout his tenure as an associate, Harris became a partner during his eighth year at the firm. Shortly thereafter he went through what he defined as his "malaise" questioning whether he wanted to practice law anymore. Pondering his future as a lawyer didn't seem to be the consequence of any particular event, just something that happens from time to time. He hadn't resolved his career issues when a friend from a national firm called to recruit him to start up a new practice group at that firm. It didn't take him long to recognize that that "short, medium, and long-term opportunities for me would all be better at this shop." He made the "difficult" decision to leave and join the national firm.

Susan Fry began her career at a large out of state firm. She worked there for two years and then moved to another state "for a guy." She landed in a smaller local firm. She was there for less than a year because her husband got a job in Colorado. She joined a large regional firm in Colorado, the same one where Harris started, but for her it was "the most unfriendly firm I had ever worked at. By the time I left, there were partners who didn't know if my job was to work in that firm as an attorney or clean the toilets." She was "pigeonholed" into a practice she came to hate and which did not offer her great assignments. She left the large firm and moved to a boutique. She also was divorced. She stayed at the boutique firm for 8 years during which time she remarried and started a family. The boutique firm began to disintegrate. She left after she finally ran a big case on her own.

> For the first time in my entire career I was the lead attorney. The ball finally rolled my way. Thirteen years, but finally I was the one who had to make the decisions on a daily basis. Go to the court hearings, talk to the client. It was me. And after I developed that for a year, I said that's it. Now's the time.

With a colleague, she established her own firm. Her practice is no longer "pigeonholed." She has a great variety of cases and the time to market for more. Her own firm offers less pressure and more time for her family. As for money, she reports "we're making what a first year associate in one of the big firms downtown is probably making, but I'm much happier."

Explaining Difference

Many, if not most, law firms have moved toward compensation systems that reward productivity and performance. Many have taken great pains to introduce objective measures of productivity designed to reduce the subjectivity of compensation and to value performance.... Lock-step models that valued tenure and experience have been superseded by criteria about performance and productivity—billables, collectibles, etc. Interestingly, the compensation schemes changed just as women were entering the profession.

Gender intervenes in two ways that challenge the objectivity of "productivity" models and the fairness associated with "objective" measures of performance. The first way is captured in models of income disparity like the recent GAO study that suggests that half of the 40% of the gap between men and women's earnings can be explained by barriers to women's investment in human capital (specifically hours worked and training), depreciation of human capital due to career interruptions, and by women's concentration in occupations or segments of occupations that are lower paying and less desirable, largely so, it seems, because women occupy them. The second way gender matters is that largely "unexplained" consequence of simply being a woman in a work world that tends to be organized around men's lives.

... In a radical statement of this general hypothesis, Catherine McKinnon notes that,

> "... virtually every quality that distinguishes men from women is already affirmatively compensated in this society. Men's physiology defines most sports, their needs define auto and health insurance coverage, their socially designed biographies define workplace expectations and successful career patterns, their perspectives and concerns define quality in scholarship, their experiences and obsessions define merit, their objectification of life defines art, their military defines citizenship, their presence defines family, their inability to get along with each other—their wars and rulerships—defines history, their image defines God, and their genitals define sex."

Gendered organizations silently create job descriptions, evaluate work performance, and define work rules around the "cult of domesticity"—men as ideal workers; women as caregivers.

Gender Constructs Opportunities for Productivity

Opportunities to be productive lawyers are often the result of the assignments that are given and relationships forged among lawyers and potential clients. Certainly, individual initiative is a factor when considering a young lawyer's efforts. But so is the distribution of assignments. The distribution of assignments is socially constructed in a world where gender stereotypes still operate. Thus, when an assignment is not given to a woman because someone thinks she won't want to travel, or because someone thinks the client is too tough or too sexist for her to handle, or simply because she is pregnant, that woman is not given equal opportunity to be productive.

Susan Fry described a situation when a senior (woman) partner assumed that her male colleague would be available for travel and didn't even think to ask her, even though she was the one working the case.

> We did a lot of work for BIG CLIENT and on a typical Friday afternoon at 4:00 p.m., BIG client had an operational accident. I got this assignment

to analyze every potential aspect of liability. I worked all Friday night, all day Saturday, Saturday night pumping out this memo and the senior partner flew to the scene. On Saturday night she called me at the office and asked me for the phone number of a junior guy associate in our section who was one of the good old boys. She wanted him to fly out to the site of the accident, to drive to the work with the government guys and try to figure out what was going on. I just didn't say anything at the time. I remember giving her the number and calling this guy and telling him basically get your bags packed and go out to the site. I hung up the phone and I just started crying. I was working all weekend on this and yet when it came time to do the fun stuff, I wasn't thought of to go out there. I could do it all and I was not called. The next day I decided I had to complain ... She called me and basically apologized and said, "well, you know I just knew this other guy's availability and I wasn't sure." It was really like I'm sorry, but you know she is not. She wanted to do this great mentor women thing but then she never really pulled it off when it came time to hand out the work and do all that kind of thing [Susan Fry, Time 1].

Subtle bias in the way cases are assigned may make it difficult for women to perform in ways that get them noticed by their more senior colleagues.

We have a couple of just monster cases in the office that have been broken up into kind of discreet segments and there are teams working on different pieces. Another woman partner isn't too busy right now. She's the woman who has a young child and they do not approach her to staff cases. She has to go in and say "I hear you're looking for someone to do this work" and they all stare at her "oh do you want to do that." I don't know why exactly .... She's been actively working her whole life and then all of a sudden she has a child and people don't get it. They think, she's a single mom, she might not be there when the going gets tough even though she's always been there in the past. I mean I heard a conversation where two of the male partners in her department were wondering aloud to each other what was her child going to do to her and to them [Mary Reever, Time 1].

Women report that gender is a factor in the distribution of firm resources which hampers their ability to get their work done. This can occur when associates give preference to the work assigned by senior male colleagues because they know who has the power in the firm. One mature career woman described how senior men get [more] "work product" from associates than do women. Although women do much of the associate training, she suggested they tend to lose the benefits of training new lawyers when male partners "hog" the talent....

And from another senior lawyer we learned how she was unable to maintain a good book of business given the difficulty she had keeping associates on her work. She believed that the associates were making good political choices when they attached to more powerful male partners. Nevertheless,

> To invest that kind of time and then have your associate just move on and take all of that effort on your part somewhere else is very disheartening and very difficult. It's actually one of the reasons I left private practice cause I had grown my book to a point where I couldn't service it myself any longer or I was going to go nuts. I finally got to a point where I hired a new associate dedicated to my work and she was very, very good and that got recognized very quickly and people started to take her away—little by little, bit by bit. What can you do? She needs to get out there and work with other partners if she wants to move up the ladder internally in the firm. I saw the handwriting on the wall that I wasn't going to keep her captive to me very much longer. Then I was back to servicing a book that was about to kill me [Joan Hunt, Time 2]

Success is social and the bottom line is that boys clubs still exist. Women continue to report facing barriers when attempting to build relationships that further their training or provide access to clients and cases that are opportunities for greater productivity.... In sum, women have a harder time reaching the big clients that offer more opportunities "to be productive."

In several interviews, women described instances where they would show up for meetings and find that the issues [had been] resolved without their input or consultation.

> I was elected to an important committee at my firm. I was the only woman. Well I found out that these guys were holding impromptu meetings over lunch and stuff and I wasn't being invited. So I thought, I'm not going to be their token so they could say they have a woman on management.
>
> Q: How did you find out about the impromptu meetings?
>
> A: Just slip of tongue, you know things were being decided and I wasn't part of it [Patricia Snow, Time 2].

. . .

> Women have trouble finding the time to build productive networks because women work a second shift at home. Women tend to face a more compounded set of career choices and problems than most men. Differences in how men and women describe work-life balance illustrate this phenomenon. For men work-life balance was regret that they could not see more of their children. For women, it was exhaustion from trying to maintain two roles.... Although arguably the "second shift" is not something law firms can control, if firms truly want women in firm leadership then they must understand the conditions under which many women operate.

Gender Constructs Perceptions of Productivity

Women report that the work they do "disappears." In her book *"Disappearing Acts,"* Joyce Fletcher describes how certain behaviors "disappeared"—not because they are ineffective, but because they get associated with the feminine, relational, or so called softer side of organizational practice—not real work. In our study, women report that they are over represented in the time intensive support work of law firms (associate and recruitment committees, etc.) that is not highly rewarded, despite the fact that it is truly investment in the future of the firm. Paula Kramer, a peak career lawyer, was a department head in a medium size firm when we first interviewed her. She was the "go to" person for cases in a new practice area that she developed. She also was head of the recruitment committee and the associates' committee. All were essential to the smooth operation of the firm, but she was rarely given credit for the work she did on them. She told us that at "every compensation meeting I have ... been really miserable." She finally got so angry about the firm's low valuation of her work that she decided to write the executive committee a memo.

> I felt that I was a good contributor and there were a lot of things that I did besides bring in business that were important to keeping the people happy and clients and also people who work here. So, I wrote this memo and I said "that if we were this far apart in our views of what they thought I was worth, then I would never be happy." I wouldn't have gone on as before and I would sort of resign and then it was like one more year of having just you know really a minimal increase when other people were shooting up. So, I think they just hadn't thought about it. I don't think it was necessarily intentional. Although, I have a husband who makes a good living and I'm not "head of the household" [Paula Kramer, Time 1].

When we inquired about the reaction of the executive committee to her memo, Paula said that the committee was shocked and suddenly worried that she would quit the firm. They did raise her salary significantly, but still not as high as the partner above her.

In a different kind of disappearance, Kramer also described a situation where her hard work was assumed to be just "luck." As she told us: "I think they really thought that my settling this big case was just luck and it would probably never happen again" [Paula Kramer, Time 1].

Or women's work is taken for granted as in the case of several women who were told that they were to become partners but the partnership agreement never materializes.

> There is a big discrepancy in what partner means to different people, and in that firm the male partners were the real partners. I was supposed to become what they called equity partner, but I never got the written agreement. Every time I raised the question it was brought up again and rewritten. And that went on, seriously for many years. My husband kept saying, "You're not getting it. He's hiring all female associates but women never really become partners. It took me a long, long time to really wake up and realize I did not have to take the kind of, I will now call it, abuse. I would never have called it abuse while I was doing it.

While I was doing it, it was just suck it up and do the job, and that "just, that's it." It also took me a while because as an older student it had been so ingrained that it was going to be really tough to get a job and to make it that I was scared to death, not to, you know, rock the boat at all. But when it came to the point where he was going to hire in an associate for more than I was making, I said, "that's it. I am done." "Oh no, you have to do this for the good of the firm." I said, "I don't, I really don't" [Donna Hart–Emerging Career, Interview 2].

For their part, many women who have grievances do not speak up. One of a growing number of quietly successful part-time lawyers, this senior woman underscores two dimensions of the problem of "voice." Women lawyers, like women generally, have a difficult time with self-promotion. Even when they are ready to address their grievance, women don't have access to the very information they need to "document" and "legitimate" their grievance.

Maybe I'm not promoting myself or I'm not promoting women but at the same time I think well I'm doing a good job, I'm doing, I'm creating part time as an acceptable career path. But I really have not confronted my employer on what I ought to be paid, and I guess it's because I judge that it was satisfactory to me and I really didn't have any hard facts [Jana Castle, Time 2].

When we asked this woman whether she might consider seeking partnership, she responds with worry that drawing attention to her needs might make matters worse.

I would have to assert myself about that, and it would be a change. Because I don't know that anyone has ever been a partner here who hadn't worked full time. For my own preservation, I have a situation that I like, that works well for me professionally, personally, and I kind of don't want them to have to address my status, because it might be worse for me than better [Jana Castle, Time 2].

Women quite rightfully worry about being labeled "Bitch" if they become the squeaky wheel about compensation or if she "grand stands" about her accomplishments. When she is silenced in this way, her productivity becomes less visible. After describing a situation where a woman friend and colleague complained about inequity and found her compensation frozen as a result, Patricia Snow, an emerging career lawyer discusses the dilemmas she faces when she considers whether or not to complain. She concludes that if things get so bad, leaving is a rational "choice," otherwise you keep on doing your work.

We've had this discussion numerous times. We make a very decent salary. We work on really interesting things. The level of our practice is higher than most. The question is what do you want to do? [when you see inequity]? Do you want to go out and start out all over? The kinds of things we work on, you need a big firm behind you. We always come out to the same place. If you are going to practice law, yeah there's the side that is absolutely awful. But there's also a great upside as well. You know if you get to the point where you just can't take it anymore, you should leave if that's what really is bothering you. I went through our roster, and women have left [Patricia Snow, Time 2].

Women face a double bind in law firm culture that on one hand demands that they "fit in" and on the other hand demands that they get noticed. Women tend to hide, particularly when they need an accommodation. Epstein reports on a woman who worked part-time and who always worked with her door closed so that her colleagues would never know exactly when she was or was not at the office. This invisible strategy adopted by many women for hiding part-time status, ultimately undermines the "face time" often described as an important part of a lawyers professional capital. And it is the opposite of strategies adopted by men who told us they want senior partners to believe that they are always at the office. Several men in our study said that they always left their door open and lights on and a coat jacket hanging in the office in order to convey the impression that they have stepped out of their office and will return.

Commitment is the soft side, the subjective dimension of compensation, that often separates men and women. Hard to define, commitment is often measured (and we use that term loosely) by the display of availability and conformity with the heroic worker whose business card indicates how to contact him 24/7. Lawyers are expected to bill considerable amounts of hours, to spend time marketing and developing business, and to participate in career-enhancing organizational activities (usually some sort of civic activity). But beyond billing in excess of 2000 hours a year and the business generating extra-curricular activities, many lawyers include putting in long hours, always being available, and visibility as important measures of their commitment to law. This might include appearing at the office on Saturday, whether they had work to complete or not, consistent and continual availability for "around-the-clock" work in trials or for transactional closings of one kind or another. Law is a greedy institution, organized around the expectation that a lawyer will have "someone at home" to take care of the non-work part of his life....

Men with families are often assumed to be committed out of necessity even when there is no evidence to support that. Women's dissatisfaction with their work environment must be understood in the context of legal practice that continues to organize according to masculine gendered norms.

Gender Stereotypes Become Self–Fulfilling

Most troubling is that unintentional gender bias can be self-fulfilling. When people assess others on the basis of gendered assumptions, the behavior that results often re-affirms the stereotype. This hypothetical, ... illustrates the point. A senior partner gets a big case and asks a junior partner, Craig, to put together a team. It is a plum assignment for a new associate. Two associates, Jim and Sue, seem appropriate based on their experience and workload. Recognizing that the case may take several years to develop and that the client is a little picky, Craig worries about continuity. He has heard that there is national data that women turn over more rapidly than men. Craig thinks, "I put a woman on this case, she may leave and I may end up in trouble with the case and with the senior partner." He gives this plum assignment to Jim. Sue works on other things. After a while, Sue says I'm not getting any good assignments with this firm and she leaves. Craig says, "knew it!" (Epilogue: One year into the case Jim leaves the firm for a "better opportunity").

Or, Jane announces she is pregnant. Immediately she notices that both the quantity and quality of work dries up. Six months later she has her baby and takes maternity leave. Somewhere around four weeks into her leave, she starts to think about work and, in particular the last six months or so of work at the firm. She wonders whether she will ever get back on track and thinking that she might not, she decides she might want to stay home for a while—those diapers look pretty good compared to twiddling her thumbs in the office. The partners say, as we have heard, "told you so. We have bad luck with pregnancy."

Bringing About Change

Over the last decade, many law firms have taken steps to address issues of diversity. And many have tried to accommodate different kinds of work arrangements. Nevertheless, there is still much that can be done and needs to be done. The subtle and not so subtle forms of gender bias that are often taken for granted and unintentional cannot be changed without sustained attention to them. To change a system as steeped in tradition as the legal profession requires a bold, thoughtful, approach.

The complexity and scope of change necessary to address gender inequity calls for strategies that organizational development specialists call small wins, incremental change that delivers cumulative change over the long run. Breaking the cycle of gender bias is a marathon, not a sprint. Anyone who has trained for endurance recognizes the importance of setting intermediate goals....

NOTES AND QUESTIONS

1. Reichman and Sterling note that women face problems finding appropriate mentors within law firms and in making long-term continuing relationships with clients. In their article "Investing in Relationships: Social Capital and Your Personal Development Portfolio," *American Bar Association. Commission on Women in the Profession*, Winter/Spring 2002, at 12–13, they point to the importance for lawyers of social capital—the "productive relationships that become available by virtue of a person's position in a social network." They drew on their interviews with 100 male and female lawyers in their original Colorado study, and note that women face constraints on their ability to gain social capital:

> Traditional gender roles also interfere with amassing capital. When men take their male clients to baseball games, they introduce friend-

ship—however superficial and strategic—to the attorney-client relationship; this often results in repeat business. When women take male clients to baseball games, "strategic friendships" might develop, but the cross-gender aspect can keep it "strictly business"—partly to ensure it isn't perceived as a "date." . . .

Interestingly, some female lawyers report that they bring along husbands or male friends to avoid the appearance of a date. But developing a "business" friendship can be made even more complex by introducing dual roles of wife-lawyer into the business interaction . . .

Many men we interviewed admitted feeling less comfortable mentoring women. Yet our interviews also suggest that women are not mentoring other women in significant numbers. Younger women described more senior women as too busy . . . One woman described a very helpful session with a male mentor who walked her through an analysis that had been giving her trouble. She said that she tried very hard not to impose on him or make the interaction "personal." But it is precisely making it personal—developing a sense of friendship—that men find most helpful.

Why might what Reichman and Sterling call a "mature career lawyer" or a "peak career lawyer" who was male and in his 40s or 50s, hesitate to mentor a younger woman associate in his firm? Why might a female lawyer in one of these categories hesitate to mentor a younger woman associate? In their *Capital University Law Review*[12] article, the authors assert:

Despite the more than 15 years that women have been entering the legal profession in numbers equal to men, men and women are still uncertain how to develop these relationships outside traditional gender roles, either family roles such as that of father-daughter or dating roles. These traditional gender roles interfere with mentoring relationships and with the development of professional relationships with other lawyers and clients. The message from our informants was that women must take enormous steps to neutralize the power imbalance rooted in gender (they cannot let down their guard—an essential component of trust) that they identify as "mistakes." These are the very components of behavior that are most rewarding for one's career. (pp. 960–961)

Reichman and Sterling do not suggest that no women lawyers succeed in gaining mentoring and achieving positions where they hold the trust and respect of clients. For example, David Wighton, "Wall Street's Woman of Influence: Rosemary Berkery of Merrill Lynch," *Financial Times,* May 5, 2005 at 12, reports that Ms Berkery is "one of the most influential lawyers on Wall Street."

[T]he 52–year–old's real influence comes from what she describes as her role as consigliere to Stan O'Neal, Merrill's chairman and chief

---

12. "Recasting the Brass Ring: Deconstructing and Reconstructing Workplace Opportunities for Women Lawyers", 29 *Capital U.L.Rev.* 923 (2002); see also, Nancy J. Reichman and Joyce Sterling, "Sticky Floors, Broken Steps and Concrete Ceilings in Legal Careers", 14 *Texas J. Women and the Law* 101 (2005).

executive. "He looks to me for business advice and judgment on a wide range of issues even if they don't call for a legal opinion." ...

"In the past, a CEO might have looked to the senior partner of a law firm as his trusted adviser," says Ms Berkery. The general counsel increasingly fills that role. "In part, it is because so much of what we do has a regulatory impact and a reputational impact ..." She is in a stronger position to give general business advice because, unlike most general counsels, she has worked in general management.

Berkery worked for O'Neal when she was head of investment products and marketing in the private client part of the firm. When he became president of Merill, he appointed her as general counsel. John P. Heinz, Robert L. Nelson, Rebecca L. Sandefur, and Edward O. Laumann, *Urban Lawyers: The New Social Structure of the Bar* 271–72 (2005), point out that in their survey in Chicago in 1995, women lawyers were overall just as satisfied with the practice as men. Women were less satisfied than men with specific parts of their employment situation, such as prospects to advance and salary. Moreover, the authors caution that they interviewed men and women who still were lawyers; they did not interview those who had dropped out of the profession.

Reichman and Sterling's findings are largely supported by other studies of women lawyers. See, e.g., Kathleen E. Hull and Robert L. Nelson, "Assimilation, Choice, or Constraint? Testing Theories of Gender Differences in the Careers of Lawyers," 79 *Social Forces* 229, 252 (2000).("We found that work-family tension had a significant negative effect on the odds of making partner, but only for women. We also found that having children significantly increases the odds of being a partner in a law firm, but separate models for men and women reveal that this is significant and positive only for men. Women intent on partnership appear to consciously avoid or postpone parenthood."); Kathleen E. Hull and Robert Nelson, "Gender Inequality in Law: Problems of Structure and Agency in Recent Studies of Gender in Anglo–American Legal Professions," 23 *Law & Social Inquiry* 681, 702–703 (1998) ("Women appear to have achieved a level of formal equality within the world of law practice, only to discover that formal equality does not translate into substantive equality when the taken-for-granted structures of the profession and the legal system do not mesh well with the needs, concerns, and everyday realities of women's lives.... And change may come on the domestic front as well as in the professional domain. These studies generally treat women's greater family responsibilities as a given, without adequately acknowledging that more equitable domestic arrangements may matter as much as (if not more than) unilateral reforms on the employer side."); Robert Granfield, "Lawyers and Power: Reproduction and Resistance in the Legal Profession," 30 *Law & Society Review* 205, 217 (1996)("[I]t is impossible to speak about inequality in the legal profession independent of inequality in society.")

Women corporate lawyers may require more women executives to rise to positions of power and leadership in corporations before these lawyers will advance. There are relatively few women at the top of business organizations. See, e.g., Julie Creswell, "How Suite It Isn't: A Dearth of Female Bosses," *N.Y. Times*, Dec. 17, 2006, § 3, at 1, 9–10 ("If a C.E.O. declares through his actions that men and women are important to the performance of the company, the rest of the company takes notice and changes the paradigm."); Brooke Masters, "Women Pay Price of Wall Street Bias," *Financial Times*, Dec. 18, 2006, at 14 (Louise Marie Roth's *Gender and Money on Wall Street* (2006) "offers a worm's eye view of how boys-will-be-boys culture undermines banks' efforts to retain and promote women and, instead, steers them into the least rewarding and respected parts of the industry."); Karen S. Lyness and Christine A. Schrader, "Moving Ahead or Just Moving? An Examination of Gender Differences in Senior Corporate Management Appointments," 31 *Group & Organization Management* 651 (2006). However, is it clear that if more women become chief executive officers of businesses, this will benefit women corporate attorneys?

2. John Hagan, Marjorie Zatz, Bruce Arnold and Fiona Kay, "Cultural Capital, Gender, and the Structural Transformation of Legal Practice," 25 *Law & Society Review* 239 (1991), studied large law firms in Toronto, Canada. They argue that the arrival of women in the profession helped the large law firms deal with what Galanter and Palay labeled the tournament of lawyers. Law firms sell the work of their young associates for more than they pay the associates. The associates accept this situation because some of their number will be promoted to partnership and gain a share of the firm's wealth. As long as the law firms keep gaining more work from old clients and work from new clients, they can afford to add new partners and the additional associates needed to support these partners' work. However, firms cannot continually expand because work comes and goes. Young women lawyers help solve the problem. They are smart and willing to work hard. However, the years that associates compete for the few partnerships available are the years that women typically have children. Moreover, many women prefer a more cooperative than competitive environment, and many women resent the subtle and not-so-subtle forms of discrimination they face in large law firms. As a result, many women associates drop out from the tournament. The firm does not have to consider them for partnership, and it can blame the young women for making the choice of family over career. And for every woman who drops out, there is another younger woman who just graduated from law school waiting to take her place. See, also, John Hagan and Fiona Kay, *Gender and Practice: A Study of Lawyers' Lives* (1995); Fiona M. Kay, "Flight from Law: A Competing Risks Model of Departures from Law Firms," 31 *Law & Society Review* 301 (1997) (the article notes that women leave law firms at a much higher rate than men, and it describes factors pushing women out of firms as well as those pulling them toward other more attractive options).

3. <u>Racial Diversity in the Legal Profession.</u> The other group of people who, in increasing numbers, have come to law schools in the past two or three decades are members of minority groups. Jonathan D. Glater, "Law Firms are Slow in Promoting Minority Lawyers to Partnerships," *N.Y. Times*, Aug. 7,

2001, at A1, reports a survey by the *Times* of the 12 highest grossing law firms in the United States. It showed that minority partners accounted for about 5 percent of the new partners at the seven firms that supplied data. The numbers at famous firms such as Sullivan & Cromwell, Shearman & Sterling and Jones, Day, Reavis & Pogue were much lower. See also a story about a report of the Equal Employment Opportunity Commission, in *U.S. Law Week*, October 28, 2003: "In 2002, 5.3 percent of legal professionals were Asian, 4.4 percent African American, 2.9 percent Hispanic, and 0.2 percent Native American." The Chair of the EEOC said that 85 percent of minority women associates leave their law firms after seven years. "This, in turn, causes law firms to be more reluctant to hire minority women ... Minority women attorneys in private law firms report a sense of isolation in their profession, she added."

David B. Wilkins and G. Mitu Gulati, "Why Are There So Few Black Lawyers in Corporate Law Firms? An Institutional Analysis," 84 *California Law Review* 493 (1996), note that virtually all Blacks who start at a given elite law firm leave before becoming partner. The authors focus on training and development of associates within the firms. It is not efficient for firms to attempt to train everyone who joins a firm because so many associates will leave. Moreover, while it is in the firm's interest to offer training and mentoring to associates, many partners and senior associates do not see it in their personal interest. They want to deal with associates they trust and who can work with only limited supervision. Wilkins and Gulati cite studies showing a tendency for senior members of groups to mentor those with whom they can identify and understand. Moreover, some senior members fear making a mistake and offending a member of a minority group. However, in many large law firms, associates are not monitored closely, and there are no objective indicators of their skills and talent. An associate must become known to enough partners to gain the right reputation. Blacks are often channeled into litigation, but in many firms this is not the prime road to partnership because not enough partners will learn what those involved in a particular case have done and are doing.

Jonathan Birchall, "Wal–Mart Lays Down the Law: The US Retailer is Pushing for Greater Diversity at the Upper Levels of its Top Law Firms," *Financial Times*, February 21, 2007, at 11, reports that the general counsel of Wal–Mart sent a letter to 100 law firms that it had used in the past. It said, "Wal–Mart will end or limit our relationships with law firms who fail to demonstrate a meaningful interest in the importance of diversity." The general counsel found that while a law firm might look good in terms of broad statistics, the "relationship partners" who handled dealings with Wal–Mart tended to be white males. Often they would not assign the most desirable work to blacks and women. Wal–Mart made 40 changes and moved $60 million of its business from white male to minority and female relationship partners. It also stopped doing business with two law firms. The general counsel at Sara Lee, an African American, took similar steps. A lawyer who was a fellow at the American Enterprise Institute called the action "socially acceptable racism." Sara Lee's General Counsel said "if there had been suitable progress within the profession, efforts like ours and Wal–Mart's would not have been necessary." Is client demand for diversity likely to change the practices of major law firms? How many clients such as Sara Lee and Wal–Mart would have to move in this direction to influence major law firms?

Richard O. Lempert, David L. Chambers and Terry K. Adams, "Michigan's Minority Graduates in Practice: The River Runs Through the Law School," 25 *Law & Social Inquiry* 395 (2000), surveyed the University of Michigan Law School's minority graduates from the classes of 1970 through 1996. They found: "By any of our study's measures Michigan's minority alumni are, as a group, highly successful in their careers." (p. 401). "They are well represented in all sectors of the legal profession. They are successful financially, leaders in their communities, and generous donors of their time to pro bono work and nonprofit organizations." Importantly, "Minority graduates of the 1990s look the most like their white counterparts with respect to the size of the firms they practice in, and they are considerably less likely than minority graduates of prior years to be currently practicing in firms of 10 or fewer lawyers" (pp. 431–32).

4. Paralegal workers are found in many law firms. They often are college educated but do not have law degrees. They learn to do some of the legal research and more routine document drafting. Jennifer L. Pierce, *Gender Trials: Emotional Lives in Contemporary Law Firms* (1995), reports a participant observation study of a large law firm and the legal staff of a large corporation. Pierce had worked as a paralegal in a law firm before she went to graduate school. She studied lawyers and paralegals working on litigation. Most, but not all, lawyers were male. Most, but not all, paralegals were female. She summarized her findings in her introductory chapter:

> In contemporary law firms, emotional labor takes the form of care taking and deference for female paralegals. When trial attorneys lose their tempers, blow hot and cold, and yell or scream, their paralegals are expected to stay calm, and be comforting and deferential in the face of such outbursts. By playing this emotional role, women paralegals unwittingly reproduce their subordinate position in the law firm hierarchy. On the other hand, women who violate these emotional norms are harshly criticized for their "unprofessional behavior," sanctioned through a reduction in the annual raise or in the most extreme case, faced with termination ... Male paralegals ... are not held to the same norms as women ... Many women paralegals I interviewed reported that they hated "playing mom" to trial lawyers for whom they worked, yet found themselves compelled to so.

Pierce describes the male trial lawyers she studied as rude, arbitrary, confrontational and willing to win by any means as long as they do not get caught. Pierce says that such self-centered adolescents need long-suffering mothers who are willing to excuse anything. She notes that women litigators cannot play this role, and they are sanctioned when they try.

In "Reflections on Fieldwork in a Complex Organization: Lawyers, Ethnographic Authority, and Lethal Weapons," in Rosanna Hertz and Jonathan B. Imber (eds.), *Studying Elites Using Qualitative Methods*, at 94 (1995), Pierce describes her field methods. Pierce refused to play the role that the lawyers expected, and this exposed the informal take-for-granted norms in this law firm. "Through male lawyer's reactions to my outlaw position, I uncovered the operations of power and privilege that were never formally stated. (p. 106)" For example, one male lawyer challenged her by saying, "You don't like me, do you Jennifer?" She responded, "That's right, Todd, I don't like you." She comments: "[H]e not only expected me to apologize for not being friendlier to his overtures, but also to tell him that I liked him. In this light, my response can be read as a disruption of social norms" (p. 99).

Pierce, of course, studied only two firms, and in the mid–1990s. How far can we generalize from a study of this type? What does it tell us, if anything, about the position of women at all levels in law firms and legal departments of corporations? Do you think there are law practice settings where women do not face the role expectations she describes, or face them to a much smaller degree?

In general, how could you study the positions of men, women and members of minority groups in law firm settings and in corporate legal departments? What methods could you attempt to use with any chance of getting the cooperation needed to implement them? What would be the advantages and disadvantages of each method?

(3) *What Do Various Kinds of Lawyers Do and Does it Matter?*

In the material that follows, we will look at lawyers in various settings. One question is what do lawyers in each setting do and for whom? Also, why does the particular task fall to lawyers and does legal training and experience affect how it is done? Another normative question is whether what is being done is good or bad. At least, part of this judgment may turn on an empirical question: what are the consequences of what lawyers are doing in each of these settings?

(a) *GOVERNMENT LAWYERS*

Large numbers of lawyers work for governments. We would expect the federal Department of Justice and the various state attorneys general offices to be staffed largely by lawyers. However, large numbers of lawyers will be found in almost every state and federal administrative agency. Presidents of the United States such as William Howard Taft, Franklin D. Roosevelt, Richard M. Nixon, and Bill Clinton had legal educations and had been admitted to practice, although we might debate how much real legal experience these men had before they went into politics. Governors of states large and small often are lawyers. Traditionally, lawyers are often elected both to the Congress of the United States and the legislatures of the states. However, the proportion of members of the various legislatures who are lawyers has been declining over the last quarter of the 20th century. See Andrew Blum,"Losing Its Allure: Lawyer/Legislators Are a Dying Breed. It Just Doesn't Pay," *National Law Journal*, Sept. 7, 1992, at 1; Richard Perez–Pena, "Making Law vs. Making Money: Lawyers Abandon Legislatures for Greener Pastures," *N.Y. Times*, Feb. 21, 1999, Sec. 4, at 3 ("In 1969, 61 percent of New York's state legislators were lawyers; today, 34 percent are. In California, the figure has fallen to 22 percent from 48 percent 30 years ago.").

Many reasons have been offered to explain this decline in the number of lawyer-legislators. Serving as an elected representative in past times was only a part time job, and a lawyer could continue his or her practice while he or she served. Increasingly, legislative service has become a full time job, and a lawyer who would seek election would have to give up much of his or her practice. The pay for serving as a legislator is far less than many lawyers make in practice. Moreover, we now have many more conflict of interest statutes that seek to limit a lawyer-legislator's ability to use his or her office to benefit clients. Before lawyers were allowed to advertise, even a losing campaign for office at least might serve to make the candidate's name known to potential clients. Today, there is no need to work so indirectly. Lawyers can seek attention in the yellow pages of telephone directories or even put on television commercials.

Both Congress and the state legislatures do hire armies of lawyers as members of the staff of committees. See, e.g., Victoria F. Nourse and Jane S. Schacter, "The Politics of Legislative Drafting: A Congressional Case Study," 77 *N.Y.U. Law Review* 575, 608, 609 (2002). One of their findings is summarized by a staff person they interviewed: "Senators don't read the bill, don't read the conference report. Most work—bills and reports—[is] totally staff driven." However, another respondent observed: "A lot of things are staff driven and the staffer sells it to the senator, but that's not freelancing. It's a member's power, not the staffer's." If a staff member were not to be supported by a senator, the staff member might not be fired, but she or he certainly would lose reputation and probably would find it hard to work with other staff members in the future.

Does the legal background of those who hold these many positions in the various levels of government in the United States matter? Some government lawyers' jobs call for them to appear before courts or administrative agencies and use the traditional skills of the profession. At the very least, government lawyers should do better reading statutes and regulations than those who lack a legal education. Lawyers may share a culture so that there will be many taken-for-granted assumptions that they have in common. This may aid in dealing with other lawyers who are opposed to what a particular lawyer wants. See, e.g., Terence C. Halliday, "The Idiom of Legalism in Bar Politics: Lawyers, McCarthyism, and the Civil Rights Era," 1982 *American Bar Foun-*

dation Research Journal 911, 984–985; Terence C. Halliday, "Knowledge Mandates: Collective Influence by Scientific, Normative and Syncretic Professions," 36 *British Journal of Sociology* 421, 439–440 (1985). We can wonder how far the common experience of being a lawyer will outweigh strongly held normative positions. If there is a sharp division on a normative issue, lawyers may not be able to talk to each other. Their common profession may not be enough to outweigh issues of right and wrong.

The number of lawyer-legislators may be declining, but it is still substantial. Does it make a difference to legislatures whether they have many or few lawyers? Dick Dahl, "A Natural Marriage," *Massachusetts Lawyers Weekly*, September 28, 1992, at 29, says:

> In "Democracy in America," which was written more than 150 years ago, Alexis de Tocqueville commented at length about the remarkable preponderance of lawyers in American legislative life, and he did so in a manner that would not please those who say there are too many lawyers. To de Tocqueville, lawyers were a critically necessary component of democracy, comprising a class "of the people," yet with aristocratic inclinations.
>
> "Lawyers, forming the only enlightened class not distrusted by the people, are naturally called on to fill most public functions," he wrote. . . . [L]awyers tended to serve the status quo, operating as "an almost invisible brake" when "the American people let themselves get intoxicated by their passions. . . ."

In the 21st century, is it likely that lawyers are "a class of the people, yet with aristocratic inclinations?" Are they likely to serve as "an almost invisible brake?" If they represent their constituents, will they fail to consider the general interest beyond their district? Are lawyers likely to fight for principle or are they likely to get along by going along and negotiating compromises? How might we answer any or all of these questions?

We might assume that lawyers would be more legalistic, less willing to compromise, more insistent on following procedures and the like than those trained in other fields who are elected or run agencies. Kenneth E. Boulding, an economist, in "Truth or Power," 190 *Science* 423 (1975) asserts:

> The lawyer's "problem" is not to produce testable propositions, but to win the case. For politicians, likewise, the problem is to win elections and to please the majority of their constituents. The "scientific" problem-solving which is involved in getting the best legislation or the best decisions is incidental to the larger problem of political survival. We should not necessarily blame lawyers and politicians for behaving like lawyers and politicians. It is, in fact, what we hire them and elect them to do. The legal and political subculture is not the result of pure chicanery and foolishness. It has evolved over many generations for some very good reasons. The main reason is that where decisions involve distributional changes, that is, where they make some people better off and some people worse off, problem-solving in the scientific sense would not come up with any answers. Legal and political procedures, such as trials and elections,

are essentially social rituals designed to minimize the costs of conflict. The price of cheap conflict, however, may be bad problem-solving in terms of the actual consequences of decisions. So far, the social invention that will resolve this dilemma does not yet seem to have been made.

Mark Miller, *The High Priests of American Politics: The Role of Lawyers in American Political Institutions* (1995) reports that there are three types of lawyer-legislators. First, there are nominal legislators. They practice law as their primary career, and politics is an outside interest. Second, there are nominal lawyers. They hold a law degree but either never have practiced law or have largely abandoned it. Politics is their career. Third, there are real lawyers. They have practiced law for more than five years before they became full-time legislators. They are fully socialized into both the world of law practice and politics. Miller suggests that the nominal lawyers will not act differently than nonlawyers as they play their role as legislators. He also found that lawyers in Congress are more hesitant than other members to challenge actions of the federal courts. Miller conducted his survey in 1989. We might ask whether conditions changed during the Clinton and Bush presidencies so that the lawyer members would be less likely to respect the courts.

John P. Plumlee, "Lawyers as Bureaucrats: The Impact of Legal Training in the Higher Civil Service," 41 *Public Administration Review* 220 (1981), found that government executives who had legal training tended to be more liberal and less cynical than those without such training. However, the differences were not great enough to be statistically significant. Generally, he found, those who rise to the top of administrative agencies tend to act in a similar fashion whatever their education or professional credentials. There is relatively little published material on the work of lawyers inside government, but see Donald L. Horowitz, *The Jurocracy* (1977). An interesting historical account of an important period in which lawyers played a crucial role in government is Peter H. Irons, *The New Deal Lawyers* (1982).

Lawyers also are lobbyists, pressing client interests before Congress and state legislatures. Robert L. Nelson, John P. Heinz, Edward O. Laumann and Robert H. Salisbury, "Private Representation in Washington: Surveying the Structure of Influence," 1987 *American Bar Foundation Research Journal* 141, interviewed 776 people who represented private interests. They found that lawyers are a significant group among such representatives, but they are not as numerous nor as active in policy making as generally assumed. Representatives, lawyers and others, are not likely to exercise influence in the policy-making process beyond that exerted by their client organizations. Laumann and Heinz, "Washington Lawyers and Others: The Structure of Washington Representation," 37 *Stanford Law Review* 465, 501 (1985), conclude:

> [E]ven the formal occupational distinctions between lawyer and nonlawyer representatives may be breaking down. If it is true not only that lawyer and nonlawyer representatives do similar work, serve much the

same clients, are recruited from similar social backgrounds, and maintain relationships with substantially overlapping networks of government officials and industry contacts, but also that they work side-by-side in the same firms and are hired in common by clients, then one would be hard pressed to identify the functional distinctions between lawyers and non-lawyers. As we noted ... the distance between the lawyer and client may also be narrowing. That some Washington lawyers are creating, housing, and maintaining trade association clients is an example of how tenuous the distinction between lawyer and client has become.

The authors end their article by asserting: "for many purposes we might safely ignore the fact that the Washington lawyer is a lawyer." (p. 502). The work of this research team has been published as a book, John P. Heinz et al., *The Hollow Core: Private Interests in National Policy–Making* (1993). There are a few influential people in Washington who happen to be legally trained. For example, Vernon Jordan was a close friend of President Clinton and a Washington insider. Stephen Hess, a senior fellow at the Brookings Institution, said:

> Mr. Jordan long ago stopped practicing law and became a trusted adviser to politicians and corporate leaders. He fell into "an old tradition in Washington of people who can carry messages because they have built respect for their word ..."
>
> "They build trust in what they do by getting the message straight and being good negotiators. In the sort of interactions he has, it probably doesn't make much difference whether he's a partner in a law firm or an investment banker."

Patrick McGeehan, "A Clinton Adviser to Join Lazard Frères," *N.Y. Times*, Dec. 1, 1999, at C1.

(b) CORPORATE LAWYERS

(5.13) The Hired Gun as Facilitator: Lawyers and the Suppression of Business Disputes in Silicon Valley

Mark C. Suchman and Mia L. Cahill
21 *Law & Social Inquiry* 679 (1996).

Lay discourse often criticizes the legal profession for generating disputes and for introducing adversarial bias into "naturally cooperative" social relations. Many academic observers, too, suggest that attorneys foster an inflated "rights consciousness" that disrupts more flexible and consensual extralegal relationships. Often, lay discussions and scientific analyses alike move from initial observations regarding lawyers' disputatious impact on bilateral relationships to more speculative assertions regarding lawyers' chilling effects on larger systems of economic activity. The underlying assumption seems to be that self-interested attorneys goad their clients into an excessively punctilious awareness of legal rights and that such an awareness, in turn, drains the reservoir of trust and good faith that would otherwise lubricate the wheels of commerce.

Despite the pervasiveness of this jaundiced view, recent years have witnessed a persistent trickle of evidence that the lawyer's economic role may be somewhat more positive than the prevailing imagery would suggest. This alternative perspective is particularly visible in the growing social, scientific literature on corporate legal practice. As researchers have turned their attentions to the high-priced business attorney, they have had to confront the vexing question of why apparently rational executives would be willing to pay such large sums of money for the services of an unproductive troublemaker. While one could perhaps explain the demand for legal counsel entirely in terms of corporate self-defense, the empirical evidence suggests that lawyers may be earning their keep as more than simply hired guns.

In this regard, at least two general themes seem to be emerging: First, several researchers have highlighted lawyers' potentially significant contributions to the "engineering" of complex transactions. By designing and implementing innovative legal devices, attorneys assist their clients in minimizing transaction costs, circumventing regulatory constraints, escaping encumbering liabilities, and pursuing various strategic objectives. As Powell notes, these devices range from publicly developed statutes and regulations, to privately developed case law, contracts, corporate charters, and the like. Whatever their form, however, such legal innovations provide governing frameworks for economic tasks that might otherwise prove unfeasible.

A second, less well-developed theme in the recent literature addresses the contributions that lawyers make by deploying evocative symbols rather than by providing concrete technical services. In this view, clients face a complex, turbulent, and unpredictable social environment, and they seek legal counsel primarily as a way of fending off cognitive chaos. Thus, lawyers are rewarded for performing rituals that persuasively symbolize certainty and order, even when those rituals produce few material benefits. Hints of this orientation can be seen in Abbott's claim that society values professionals primarily for their ability to "manage sources of disorder" and in Flood's assertion that "the central role business lawyers play is in managing uncertainty." While many authors include both the reduction of actual unpredictability and the reduction of perceived unpredictability under the rubric of "uncertainty management," the two aspects of the lawyer's role are conceptually distinct. Not all substantive legal engineering involves uncertainty reduction, and not all uncertainty reduction involves substantive legal engineering. Consequently, it is important to distinguish the technical task of designing effective legal devices from the presentational task of conveying reassuring symbolic messages—and to recognize that recent research finds corporate lawyers doing a significant amount of both.

The present essay adds to this emerging body of evidence on corporate lawyers' positive contributions to commerce; however, it should not be read as an unconditional assault on earlier, more critical assessments. Our analysis does not dispute the claim that lawyers occasionally inject elements of rights consciousness into arenas previously governed by informal norms of reciprocity and good faith. Nor does it question the assertion that such a transformation, were it to occur, might well disrupt preexisting extralegal business practices. Rather, the following pages advance the more limited contention that neither an elevation of rights consciousness nor a disruption of commercial conviviality are inevitable consequences of an assertive legal profession. The argument, here, takes the form of a detailed empirical counterexample, constructed from qualitative interview data on the role of lawyers and law firms in California's Silicon Valley.

Contrary to the popular image of lawyers as purveyors of discord, Silicon Valley attorneys see themselves (and are seen by others) as key players in an informal apparatus of socialization, coordination, and normalization that serves to avert potential disputes between members of the local business community. This integrative role becomes most notable in interactions between Silicon Valley lawyers and the region's high-technology entrepreneurs and venture capitalists, and it is on this central aspect of Silicon Valley legal practice that the present essay focuses. By virtue of their distinctive location within the Silicon Valley community, lawyers quite literally produce and reproduce the social structures underpinning the local high-risk capital market. Through their relations with both entrepreneurs and investors, they identify, create, transmit, and enforce the emerging norms of the community. In so doing, Silicon Valley lawyers absorb and control some of the central uncertainties of encounters between venture capitalists and entrepreneurs, facilitating what might otherwise be prohibitively costly, complex, and unpredictable transactions. They accomplish this in at least three distinct ways, at three distinct levels of analysis: (1) Silicon Valley lawyers directly absorb some of the uncertainties of individual transactions through their day-to-day professional activities; (2) Silicon Valley lawyers help to define the informal norms of the local business community through their overall pattern of relations with their clienteles; and (3) Silicon Valley lawyers work to formally incorporate these local norms into the national legal regime through their activities in courtrooms, in professional education projects and in regulatory arenas. After briefly outlining the distinctive challenges of high-technology financing, this paper will examine each of these three legal contributions, in turn.

THE UNCERTAINTIES OF VENTURE CAPITAL

Running along the southern third of California's San Francisco peninsula, "Silicon Valley" encompasses roughly 16 municipalities, most of them in Santa Clara County ... In 1990, the region's population stood at slightly under 1.5 million, having approximately quintupled in the preceding four decades. Further, with a 1990 median family income of almost $54,000, Santa Clara County is among the wealthiest communities in the nation. Despite these distinctive demographics, the sociological significance of the region lies as much in its organizational population as in its human population. As the nickname suggests, Silicon Valley is home to a substantial portion of America's microelectronics industry. Over 60% of the American Electronics Association's 1,800 members have their corporate headquarters in California, and the majority of these are located in Santa Clara County. Somewhat more broadly, one study has estimated that in 1990 more than 3,000 high-technology establishments of one kind or another were operating in the region, employing roughly 267,000 people. With annual sales of well over $40 billion, the region is the nation's ninth largest manufacturing center; and with a job-creation rate of roughly 40,000 positions per year through much of the 1980s, the local economy has been among the nation's fastest growing.

In a very real sense, Silicon Valley is an industrial community built on venture capital. In the past 20 years, the San Francisco Bay Area has become the primary locus of venture capital activity in the United States, with over a third of the nation's largest high-risk investors maintaining offices in the region. Indeed, according to one of the most comprehensive studies of venture capital finance to date, California-based funds manage roughly a quarter of the US venture capital pool, with over 10% of the nationwide total being controlled by firms headquartered in a single Silicon Valley office complex— 3000 Sand Hill Road in Menlo Park.... This concentration of venture capital has clearly facilitated the proliferation of new high, technology ventures in the region. Historically, Silicon Valley start-ups have enjoyed both lower mortality and faster growth than equivalent companies in other regions—an achievement due, in large part, to the availability of start-up financing. Thus, the history of venture finance is an integral part of the history of the Silicon Valley organizational community, and vice versa.

Taken broadly, the terms "venture capital" and "venture finance" refer to the external funding of a wide range of high-risk business activities. In the context of Silicon Valley, the most important of these high-risk activities is the formation of new technology-based corporations. The difficulty of funding such start-ups through bank loans or other conventional financial vehicles becomes clear when one considers a few "vital statistics" on these enterprises: According to one Silicon Valley consultant, over 60% of the start-up companies in an average venture capital portfolio will enter bankruptcy before the investors can recoup their original stake; less than 10% will ever reach the most desirable "liquidity event," an initial public offering (IPO). Further, even the most successful new companies often take several years to show a profit and substantially longer to offer positive returns on investment....

... Given these considerations, new technology-based companies are often unable to secure commercial loans at any price. Moreover, even when such backing is available, most start-ups find themselves poorly positioned to assume the burdens of regular debt service or to accept the strictures of heavily covenanted borrowing agreements.

In contrast to conventional lending institutions, venture capital funds address these risks through specialized intra-and interorganizational social structures rather than through the elaborately crafted protective provisions of individual financial instruments. In particular, venture capitalists attempt to manage the risks inherent in high-tech start-ups by (1) emphasizing long-term equity investment, (2) adopting a patient capital-gains-oriented financial strategy, and (3) replacing inflexible covenants with direct oversight of corporate operations.

The organizational structure of the venture capital fund facilitates such efforts: The typical fund is a limited partnership. The general partners (usually individuals) organize the fund, contribute a small share of its financial reserves, and take responsibility for its investment decisions. The limited partners (a mixture of institutional investors and wealthy individuals) provide the bulk of the fund's capital (often over 95%) but otherwise stand aloof from its daily operations and from its legal and financial liabilities. As the fund realizes gains from its portfolio, limited and general partners share the returns in roughly an 80:20 ratio; however, if no gains materialize, the fund has no ongoing obligation to repay investors with either dividends or interest. Generally, such venture capital partnerships are established with a 10–year term. This limited life span preserves both (1) the short-run freedom for general partners to incur losses during a portfolio company's initial capital-burn phase, and also (2) the long-run incentive for general partners to produce satisfactory returns in time to attract reinvestment in a follow-on fund.

Despite these specialized organizational structures, however, the financial market in Silicon Valley faces substantial challenges that are absent even from venture capital investing in many other settings. In particular, *high-technology* start-ups confront investors not only with high failure rates and dramatically variable returns but also with large elements of sheer guesswork. Markets for new technologies are notoriously difficult to predict, with the performance of any given start-up often depending on technological developments that postdate the firm's founding. These market-shaping developments, themselves, often pivot on essentially random elements of timing and serendipity—both within the start-up's own R & D, production and marketing efforts, and within the R & D, production and marketing efforts of its actual and potential competitors. Consequently, the commercialization of new technologies is highly "path-dependent," and even the most knowledgeable analysts cannot forecast long-run outcomes with any degree of certainty. Further, when the rate of new innovation is rapid and when the mix of commercially available technologies in the future will reflect the mix of investment decisions in the present, high-technology investors may have difficulty even identifying a relevant universe of technologies from which to construct a balanced portfolio.

Equally formidable cognitive hurdles plague high-technology entrepreneurs, as well. Lacking recourse to conventional lenders, innovators face the challenge of raising start-up funding at a reasonable cost in a time-sensitive environment where even small delays may (or may not) prove commercially disastrous. The average venture capital fund finances only 6 out of every 1000 business plans that it receives each year, and founders must invest substantial time and effort into a start-up long before they know whether their search for capital will ultimately pay off. Further, with no solid base-line for judging company valuations, entrepreneurs are often hard-put to evaluate the fairness of those few funding offers that they do receive. Moreover, since most venture capitalists demand a relinquishment of corporate control, founders may have difficulty predicting whether the "post-money" corporation will make effective use of their intellectual property and "sweat equity"—particularly since a majority of board seats are likely to be held by investors with substantial stakes in various competitors, buyers, and suppliers. Finally, all these problems are further compounded by the fact that many high-technology entrepreneurs come from engineering, hobbyist and academic backgrounds and thus lack either independent financial resources or relevant business experience. As one attorney puts it:

> A lot of people who start companies have spent their careers as engineers—or, even less sophisticated, in academia. It's all new. People who have been through this a few times may have very set ideas about what kind of valuation they want, how they want the corporation structured. But somebody who has never done it, they generally have no clue what's going on.

On the whole, then, high-technology start-up financing poses challenges not only of risk but also of uncertainty. Although lay parlance often employs these terms interchangeably, the organizational decision-making literature uses them to describe two distinct conditions. Under conditions of "risk," decision-makers may not be able to predict the future deterministically, but at least they can describe it probabilistically: With a little effort, individuals can identify the full range of options and outcomes, and they can determine roughly how likely it is that any given option will produce any particular outcome. Consequently, despite the presence of risk, decision-makers can still make rational choices based on expected-value calculations, and markets can still produce efficient coordination based on contingent-claims contracts.

Uncertainty, on the other hand, arises when decision-makers cannot determine either (1) the full menu of alternative behavioral options or (2) the relative probability of alternative possible outcomes. Unlike risk, uncertainty is deeply incompatible with the neoclassical model of fully rational decision-making. Instead of producing a careful expected-utility analysis of all lines of action, conditions of uncertainty tend to produce "boundedly rational" decision strategies, involving "good enough" choices, gut feelings, and rules of thumb. At a more macroscopic level, uncertainty elevates transaction costs and exacerbates intra-organizational strains and power struggles. Consequently, unresolved uncertainty poses a fundamental cognitive and organizational obstacle to the formation and maintenance of stable markets for high-technology start-up capital.

In a turbulent environment such as this, large-scale economic activity depends heavily on the emergence of social structures capable of managing relevant uncertainties. Significantly, organization theory speaks of "managing" uncertainty (rather than of "eliminating" uncertainty) in order to allow for the fact that uncertainty can be resolved in at least three distinct ways: Most obviously, social structures may develop that reduce the actual level of environmental turbulence—by, for example, formulating industry standards, establishing barriers to entry, or regulating competitive activities. Somewhat more restrictively, social structures may evolve that localize uncertainty within certain parts of the environment or that allow the costs of uncertainty to be absorbed by certain specialized organizations or subunits—by, for example, establishing stockpiles and other structural buffers, creating insurance schemes, or chartering brokers and arbitrageurs. Finally, social structures may arise that moderate the cognitive challenges of uncertainty without eliminating environmental turbulence, itself—by, for example, propounding "normalizing" cultural accounts, enacting simplified representations of reality, or institutionalizing ritualized practices whose efficacy is assumed rather man tested. All these responses are visible to a greater or lesser extent in the activities of Silicon Valley lawyers.

THE ROLE OF LAW FIRMS IN MANAGING UNCERTAINTY

For the reasons outlined above, the uncertainties of high-technology finance persistently threaten to render transactions between entrepreneurs and venture capitalists costly, unstable, and cognitively intractable, even when such exchanges might, in the abstract, seem mutually beneficial. In Silicon Valley (and perhaps in other regions as well), the local legal community shoulders a substantial share of the responsibility for managing such challenges. In contrast to the conventional image of lawyers as sources of disruptive litigiousness, Silicon Valley law firms seem to be active facilitators of local economic development—both through their efforts to absorb some uncertainties and to subject these to collective control, and through their parallel efforts to symbolically downplay other uncertainties and to render these less paralyzing. Indeed, by reducing both perceived and actual levels of cognitive disorder, the local bar may substantially moderate pressures toward disputatiousness in the community as a whole.

Specifically, Silicon Valley's legal practitioners appear to foster market development and to suppress business disputes in three distinct but interrelated ways: First, and most simply, Silicon Valley lawyers often interpose themselves as third-party buffers in particular transactions. While such active intervention may be ethically problematic from the standpoint of the larger legal profession, it allows attorneys to directly absorb transactional uncertainties, facilitating agreements that might otherwise prove unattainable. Second, Silicon Valley lawyers also stabilize the local capital market in general, by transmitting community norms to their clients and by embodying those norms within standardized contractual structures and practices. In so doing, attorneys reduce the transaction costs of negotiating agreements, creating a cooperative climate in which the dangers of opportunism and uncertainty fade from view: Tutored in community norms, contracting parties know which demands are (or are not) "legitimate" and "reasonable"—which concessions they may expect of others, and which concessions others may expect of them in return. Third, Silicon Valley lawyers increasingly act to insulate the local community against exogenous regulatory shocks and competitive challenges, by transforming parochial norms into national legal standards. This "double-institutionalization" of local expectations further reduces the uncertainty of high-technology start-up finance, once again facilitating economic expansion. The following pages will examine each of these market-building activities, in turn.

Absorbing Uncertainty in Individual Transactions

At the simplest level, Silicon Valley law firms reduce the uncertainties of new-company finance by directly interposing themselves into otherwise-problematic corporate transactions. Rather than standing aloof from their clients' operations, as prescribed by conventional legal ethics, many law firms in Silicon Valley display a striking willingness to absorb elements of transactional uncertainty into the law firm's own operations if this will facilitate an endangered deal. This practice appears most vividly in the selection of fee structures and in the drafting of "opinion letters." Each of these activities serves to mitigate some of the uncertainty inherent in the founding and funding of high-technology start-ups.

Fee Structure

Long before a new venture secures financial backing, the founders must engage in a number of relatively hazardous and costly activities, such as leaving jobs with former employers, developing a business plan, and approaching potential investors. Consequently, one of the primary sources of uncertainty for the potential high-technology entrepreneur is the possibility that these efforts may never pay off—either in funding commitments from investors or in a successful enterprise. In this context, Silicon Valley lawyers can facilitate new-company formation by assuming a portion of the risk that financial backing will fail to materialize. In particular, since one of the start-up's primary pre-financing costs is the cost of hiring legal counsel, law firms can absorb a portion of the founders' entrepreneurial uncertainty by foregoing conventional billing and by substituting a payment scheme conditioned on the start-up's subsequent success. Historically, two such contingent-payment schemes predominate: deferred billing and equity compensation.

Often, Silicon Valley law firms offer their corporate clients a deferred-billing structure that amounts, essentially, to a "contingency fee" for business transactions. As a partner in one of the core Silicon Valley law firms explains:

> Normally, we will take on start-up companies and make an effort to keep the billable hours down, without compromising the legal issues involved. Frequently we will hold, delay or suspend billing until financing can be obtained. In effect, we become partners with the start-up client. With

most of our start-up companies, either by express agreement or by some tacit understanding, there is an attempt made to either completely suspend billing or to go forward on the billing on a very limited basis.

By delaying or waiving billing, a law firm assumes the risk that if its client fails to secure financing, the law firm will, in effect, have provided free legal work. Most unfunded start-ups are essentially judgment-proof, and most successful Silicon Valley attorneys "realize that if a company doesn't get funded, we're not going to look to the founders, personally, to pay." This downside is balanced, of course, against the possibility that a client will successfully locate financing and will then pay the law firm's premium fees out of the newly obtained capital reserves.

Another common payment structure among lawyers with start-up clients is the acceptance of corporate stock in lieu of monetary compensation. Like deferred billing, this strategy, too, involves a gamble on the law firm's part: The corporation could fail, leaving the stock virtually worthless, or the corporation could eventually go public, dramatically increasing the value of the law firm's holdings. Since the cost of pre-financing legal services is, in effect, pegged to the company's stock price, the uncertainty of the funding search is shared (in part) between the start-up and its outside counsel.

Significantly, stock compensation provides entrepreneurs with important symbolic reassurance, as well as with economic risk spreading: Equity compensation schemes (particularly employee stock options) are an important element of Silicon Valley culture, and by accepting payment in stock, a law firm can express confidence in its entrepreneurial clients and in their products. Indeed, in addition to accumulating common stock as equity compensation during the funding search, local law firms often augment their holdings by purchasing preferred stock alongside the venture capital investors in the first-round financing. . . .

Clearly, contingent fee structures—including both deferred payment and equity compensation—can fulfill a number of interrelated purposes. In addition to reducing entrepreneurial uncertainty and serving as important cultural symbols, creative fee arrangements accomplish the far more mundane task of increasing access to (and demand for) legal services within the community. Since small garage-based enterprises can rarely afford traditional hourly legal bills, charges tailored to the start-up life cycle may substantially increase the pool of potential clients. Even if some of the clients thus acquired are not, in themselves, "worth the risk," an expanded client base may have substantial appeal for law firms operating in a rapidly developing, network-oriented community such as Silicon Valley. Among other things, Silicon Valley lawyers are selling their practical start-up experience and their community connections, and these attributes are enhanced by every additional client that comes through the law firm's doors—even those clients that eventually fail.

Before moving on, it is perhaps worth noting that Silicon Valley's favored payment schemes are not entirely unproblematic. In particular, both deferred payment and equity compensation tread near the boundaries of professional ethics, as defined by the California Business and Professions Code and the California Rules of Professional Conduct. When lawyers are to be paid from the proceeds of a financing, their own interests in prompt payment may conflict with their client's interest in securing the best overall funding package. More significantly, when lawyers accept stock in a client, they may be compromising their professional detachment and objectivity. In particular, attorneys who receive equity compensation run the risk of developing interests (as shareholders) that are adverse to the interests of the corporation or to the interests of other stakeholders, including the founders. This problem becomes particularly severe when company counsel participates as a stock purchaser in a financing, alongside the investor syndicate. Technically, all of these issues can be remedied by the informed consent of the various affected parties. Nonetheless, it seems clear that Silicon Valley law firms tend to read the profession's ethical strictures somewhat less restrictively than would their counterparts in other settings.

Together, then, the billing practices and ethical interpretations of Silicon Valley law firms encourage attorneys to take on financial risks and to absorb entrepreneurial uncertainties that lawyers in many more established communities would generally avoid. One local attorney, for example, recounts an instance in which the Silicon Valley branch of a prominent San Francisco firm had accepted a "funky," "fast-paced" start-up client, pending approval from the firm's New Business Committee in the city:

> In the middle of the afternoon the Valley office got a call from San Francisco saying, "Hey, we can't approve this client that you sent us, because what you guys are saying here is you'll discount your time by 50%, and you're going to let them pay it over six months on installments: Installments? We don't believe in installments. And you'd be taking stock in the company? The implications! We haven't even thought about the tax issues, the conflict of interest issues.... And then the statement at the bottom of the memo that the law firm may never get paid back at all— We're not in the business of extending credit."

> So what exactly are they supposed to do now? They're apoplectic because they've been trying to explain to the people back in San Francisco, which is isn't very far away, how you go into Silicon Valley practice. And here, in 1991, the guys in San Francisco still don't understand how a business deal is struck in the Valley. They're dying to get involved in it, but they don't understand how you build a relationship.

Opinion Letters

In addition to absorbing some of the uncertainties facing entrepreneurs, Silicon Valley law firms also absorb some of the uncertainties facing investors. Just as Silicon Valley lawyers contrast their "entrepreneurial" fee arrangements against the more restrictive practices of big-city lawyers, many local attorneys also pride themselves on a willingness to assume investor-side risks in order to bridge the gap in imperiled financing transactions.

This facilitative orientation becomes most visible in the distinctive attitude of Silicon Valley lawyers toward the "opinion letters" that they write in support of their clients' representations in venture capital financing agreements. Technically, opinion letters report a law firm's assessment of the veracity and validity of claims contained in contractual documents, and in this sense, these letters would appear to be primarily informational in purpose. Yet, since the vast majority of Silicon Valley opinion letters merely restate the client's pre-negotiated representations and warranties, their actual informational value would seem to be slight—particularly given the fact that venture capital investors are hardly naive buyers. Thus, a more plausible framework for understanding these informationally superfluous writings would be to see them as devices for managing the uncertainties inherent in financing untested, judgment-proof start-ups: Since a law firm is legally responsible for the veracity of its opinion letters, even a simple reiteration of the client's representations would place the law firm's resources on the line as a kind of insurance against deception.

This aspect of the opinion letter is well illustrated by the following anecdote. The narrator, a Palo Alto lawyer, describes an instance in which a rival firm had failed to draft "standard" representations regarding their client's intellectual property rights:

> The representation was drafted with an unusual number of hedges, and it raised a flag. So I call up the company counsel, and I say, you know, "Please deliver the skeleton."
>
> After a couple of days, I get a long letter. It's not about the state of their intellectual property rights; it's about how the ABA subcommittee on intellectual property rights has published a report saying that when you write intellectual property reps, you should qualify them in all of the following ways.
>
> So the lead venture capitalist has the typical VC reaction to that, which was to fly off the handle. He calls up the entrepreneurs, and they call up their lawyer, and the lawyer says, "Well, I've got to write my opinion letter, and there have to be all these qualifications." And now the entrepreneurs are really getting upset, because they're sensing that this guy may be overly cautious. He may not be willing to go out on a legal limb for them.
>
> So they ended up dumping him and coming here, because we'd been saying, "Gosh, we deliver that opinion all the time. Yes, we understand the risk involved in giving an opinion that might not be totally 100% right; but weighing the costs and the benefits, we'd be willing to give you that opinion."

Traditional legal ethics, of course, would look askance at the idea of knowingly drafting representations and opinion letters that "might not be totally 100% right"; however, by exposing itself to liability for misrepresentation (or for lack of due diligence), the Silicon Valley law firm is able to lift some of the hazards of a failed investment off the shoulders of the venture capital fund.

Essentially, the law firm interposes its own deep pockets between the concerned investor and the judgment-proof client, facilitating completion of what might otherwise be a prohibitively uncertain transaction. . . .

On the whole, then, Silicon Valley attorneys see themselves as facilitators rather than as voices of caution in the venture financing process. Admittedly, from an external perspective, the facilitative effects of local legal norms might not necessarily outweigh the ethical and professional considerations underlying more traditional models of law-firm behavior. Nonetheless, it is easy to understand how, in a close-knit and dynamic interorganizational environment, conventional professional strictures might come to be seen as deal-killing catechisms rather than as useful components of a smoothly functioning capital market. Indeed, metaphorically, many venture capital financings in Silicon Valley look less like careful apportionments of legal rights than like a collection of parties—founders, investors, attorneys, etc.—standing in a circle, with each agreeing to indemnify the party on his or her left against any damage caused by the party on his or her right, as the entire circle slowly edges its way over a cliff. The desirability of such a social structure depends, of course, on the desirability of encouraging people to jump off cliffs. But it seems clear that, in the absence of such arrangements, high-technology entrepreneurship would be substantially less common.

Suppressing Uncertainty through Community Norms

In addition to accompanying their clients over the cliffs of new-company finance, Silicon Valley law firms also seem to be working to make the drop a bit less precipitous. In particular, the region's attorneys employ their distinctive interorganizational position to create, transmit, sustain, and enforce a normative and cognitive order that increases both the stability and the predictability of the local venture capital market. Years of vicarious experience with the start-up process give Silicon Valley lawyers unusual credibility as business advisors; and years of close contact with the local financial community give Silicon Valley lawyers unusual power as venture capital deal makers. Together, these roles place the region's law firms in an excellent position to shape client behaviors and to set client expectations. This influence emerges most strongly in three major activities: gatekeeping, proselytizing, and sorting.

Gatekeeping

As a result of their status as repeat players and reputational brokers in the venture capital financing process, Silicon Valley law firms play a substantial role in determining which clients gain access to which investors, and vice versa. Local attorneys both accept and refer clients selectively, and as a result, they can use their capacity as "deal makers" to screen out entities that challenge the community's taken-for-granted assumptions or that threaten the community's social cohesion. One senior partner, commenting on changes in his firm's practice over the past 15 years, touches on an example of such exclusionary power:

We have a better sense of when these things end up going forward and when they don't—in part based on what the financial expectations are and in part based on our assessment about how capable and/or sophisticated an individual is. If an idea is too outlandish, we will frequently advise the entrepreneur that we just don't think we can be of help.

Historically, attorneys in this firm were very much encouraged to go out and take on any and all business. But clients are coming through more and more on the basis of the perception that somehow we can enable transactions where transactions might not otherwise be possible. So, as a result, we are encouraging attorneys to be more selective. For example, if a client comes in, we want to know whether they're litigious. Frequently, the lawyer carries the ball for the client, in terms of opening up connections and introducing the client to the business world. We want to make sure that we're not making an introduction that will ultimately backfire on us.

Gatekeeping activities such as these help to establish normative boundaries around the Silicon Valley community, albeit perhaps at the risk of stifling structural innovation. The resulting increase in community cohesion reduces the costs associated with choosing business partners and assures that all parties to a transaction will share a common framework of basic values and assumptions. In essence, gatekeeping moderates the uncertainty of anonymous market relations, protecting the cultural underpinnings of the local economy.

Proselytizing

In addition to screening out potential deviants, Silicon Valley lawyers can also reduce uncertainty in the venture capital market by affirmatively encouraging clients to adopt the community's preferred models for action. In contrast to the traditional image of detached professionalism, local start-ups often turn to their attorneys not only for legal advice but also for general business guidance. In this expanded counseling capacity, lawyers have the ability to foster and reinforce community norms by promoting certain types of financing transactions over others. Thus, beyond evaluating the legal implications of proposed contracts, a robust Silicon Valley legal practice often involves educating inexperienced entrepreneurs in the less formal aspects of Silicon Valley's venture capital market. As one prominent attorney put it:

The lawyers in Silicon Valley who are experienced in venture financing provide a very important service. If it's the entrepreneurs' first company, experienced lawyers make them very comfortable with venture financing and, in a very professional way, provide them with the guidance that may need. After all, the venture capitalist on the other side of the table has been through it many, many times. One of the major contributions, then, that experienced lawyers make is to level the playing field and to provide supplements for the entrepreneur with a lack of experience in this process.

873

Significantly, these "supplements" appear to consist primarily of reassurance and tutelage in community norms, rather than of conventional adversarial representation. Silicon Valley law firms participate in a culture that depicts venture capital transactions as being natural and desirable rather man as being "evil" (in the words of one entrepreneur-turned-venture capitalist) and oppositional. Consequently, a nonadversarial orientation toward venture finance represents an essential element of the outlook that local attorneys seek to inculcate in their clients. In the words of one senior attorney:

> It is not an adversarial process. People who view it properly, who have a lot of experience in venture financing, realize that they are creating a very long-term partnership between the venture capitalists on the one hand and the entrepreneurs on the other. So it's important that it be very fair, that parties can live with each other for a long time. . . .

Anti-adversarialism, however, is not the only lesson imparted by Silicon Valley's lawyer-evangelists. In addition to preaching cooperation, local business attorneys also promote the sorts of clear and stable expectations that make such cooperation possible. Thus, for example, when entrepreneurs are relatively inexperienced or when a particular type of deal is relatively new, lawyers may serve as a crucial source of information about the range of "reasonable" terms and valuations. As an attorney who specializes in "corporate partnerships" states:

> The markets for these deals are very inefficient and people don't have a good idea of what kind of payments are involved. So as lawyers who see a lot of these deals, we're sort of a repository of information about how these deals get done. Even though we don't, obviously, tell clients what others are charging, we can influence what they might ask for.

More generally, Silicon Valley lawyers facilitate smoothly functioning capital markets by socializing entrepreneurs in the conventions of the local investor community and by assisting entrepreneurs in translating that community's occasionally cryptic responses:

> We're one of the forces that makes the fundraising market more efficient by saying to clients: "What you do is you have a business plan. You refine that to the point where it meets the standards and the criteria that venture capitalists expect in business plans. It shouldn't be 800 pages long, and so forth and so on."
>
> Then you get that out and get feedback, and we'll read those tea leaves. That's an area where we're very active. There is, in fact, a lexicon that you have to understand: What are the venture capitalists saying to you? What does this mean? What should I expect? How long will this take? How much will it cost? How much of the company can I keep? What valuation should I look for? All those sorts of things.

Thus, as proselytizers, Silicon Valley lawyers work to "civilize" their clienteles, indoctrinating new entrants into the routines and vocabularies of the local business community. In a setting where the rapid influx of companies and technologies threatens to undermine social coherence, law firms help to define and communicate the socially constructed boundaries of "reasonable" behavior. In contrast to the traditional "hired-gun" stereotype, such ministrations increase the likelihood that financial transactions will reflect the cultural norms of the community rather than the individual interests of the client. Once again, this treads near the boundaries of conventional legal ethics. Yet, such social regulation may be the price for a viable market: In spreading the venture capital gospel, Silicon Valley lawyers suppress both the appearance and the reality of decision-making uncertainty, permitting the routinization of what would otherwise be prohibitively complex and costly transactions. As one senior partner notes:

> I think that venture capital practice is a specialty which is practiced very well in Silicon Valley, yet it is not even understood in a lot of other places. When I deal with lawyers in other parts of the country, they don't think like a Silicon Valley lawyer would think. You will find that they will go crazy over a lot of stuff that would just draw a yawn from a Silicon Valley law firm. Without the evangelical activities of Silicon Valley's local attorneys, venture capital investing would be much more difficult and, presumably, much less common.

Sorting

Both gatekeeping and proselytizing call on law firms to standardize their clients' activities by enforcing the norms of the Silicon Valley business community; yet such regulatory efforts are not the only routes to reduced uncertainty. Uncertainty is fundamentally a cognitive condition, and in addition to constraining the overall range of behavioral variation, law firms can also manage uncertainty by developing conceptual schemata that make sense of whatever variability remains. Thus, in a third set of community-building activities, lawyers formulate and apply simplifying cultural typologies, both to steer start-ups to "appropriate" investors and also to select "appropriate" contractual structures for specific transactions.

Both varieties of sorting are fairly well recognized within the Silicon Valley community. At least one law firm, for example, has formed a standing committee to handle the task of categorizing clients and matching them with venture capitalists:

> When a partner has a new company that needs financing, committee members will brainstorm on who would be the best firms to send it to. Based on our knowledge of venture funds, and based on our knowledge of people in those funds, we can make introductions to people who we think would be good people to look at a particular proposal.

Analogously, once financings are actually under negotiation, attorneys will often recommend particular contractual structures, on the basis of relatively stylized assessments of various transactional profiles. As one senior lawyer observes:

> There are a lot of folks out there who have three cookie cutters and they just ask: "Is it A, B or C?" They are going to force these things into one of those cookie cutters and then say, "I got this. We'll just ignore the fact that you don't fit these profiles for the following reasons. We'll just pretend you do and we'll just cram you into this structure."

Despite this somewhat pejorative description, typology-building serves an important function in facilitating interorganizational relations, particularly in settings characterized by high levels of underlying uncertainty: With industries, start-ups, funders, and contractual provisions all sorted into a limited number of neat, cognitively tractable pigeon-holes, the search for suitable partners and the negotiation of satisfactory agreements becomes substantially easier. Rather than engaging in a hyperrational exploration of all conceivable alternatives, lawyers, entrepreneurs, and venture capitalists can overcome their cognitive limitations by focusing on just a handful of highly typified options. In the words of one junior partner at a large Palo Alto law firm:

> San Francisco firms don't know the ropes as well. Form documents and other stuff all really institutionalize efficiency and allow us to do the work cost-effectively.

Despite (or, more accurately, because of) the inherent uncertainty of high-technology finance, such ready made deals flourish in Silicon Valley—created and sustained at the hands of the local legal community.

Averting Uncertainty through Legal Standards

In addition to establishing community boundaries, promoting normative transactions, and categorizing recurrent situations, Silicon Valley law firms also reduce the uncertainty of local capital markets by translating the region's informal norms into the currency of the larger legal system. As gatekeepers, proselytizers, and sorters, attorneys build and transmit common understandings within the surrounding organizational community. However, the routinizing influence of Silicon Valley lawyers does not end there. In their professional capacities, the region's attorneys shape both the interpretation and the regulation of their preferred financing instruments, both locally and nationally. Increasingly, the Silicon Valley bar appears to be embedding the community's distinctive business practices not only in individual contracts but also in the local and national legal discourse, through standardized trade practices, professional form books, judicial doctrines, and administrative regulations.

Local Legal Standards

Locally, lawyers' adherence to community norms has the effect of homogenizing financing structures, making contracts increasingly similar across transactions. Such isomorphism both limits the range of plausible models and restrains debate over specific provisions. As one Palo Alto attorney observes:

> If there's a transaction with one of the other Silicon Valley law firms, the transaction costs tend to be minimal. Very often, they've adopted our forms or vice versa. Usually, the forms that are used representing the

investor are the same as were used representing the company, because they follow well-defined molds. There's no negotiating on it really. I remember one attorney at another firm saying that a couple of years ago, he had this whole set of negotiating responses to my firm's forms. But in the last few deals that I did with them, their forms were virtually identical to ours, and there wasn't anything to argue over.

The consequences of this transition are twofold: First, as the preceding quotation suggests, standardization reduces the cost of individual transactions, since parties need not expend resources arguing over issues that have already been "worked out." Thus. simple economics would predict that both the overall number of transactions and also the ratio of standard to nonstandard terms will rise. Second, the emergence of standard forms may have normative and cognitive effects that further reinforce the trend toward institutionalization. In particular, as contracts come to routinely incorporate clauses that have been "decided" years before, lawyers may hesitate to rock the boat by overzealously promoting client interests on specific issues. Indeed, excessively partisan advocacy can itself come to be seen as a mark of bad citizenship:

> It's very hard to argue against a provision that you, yourself, insisted on in some other transaction. During the early days, negotiation was much more contentious. But the lawyers who were contentious—who lost sight of the fact that the goal was to achieve a long-term harmonious relationship between the investors and the entrepreneur—really dropped out. There were a number of lawyers who over-negotiated agreements and created their own work as part of the process. Sooner or later, those lawyers stopped getting business.

The more pervasive the standard, the more normatively and cognitively difficult will be the task of enunciating an opposing perspective. And the more often attorneys must "cool out" their clients by justifying dominant conventions, the more likely these attorneys are to perceive such conventions as not only "common," but also "right," "fair," "effective" and ultimately "legal." In this sense, by homogenizing and routinizing venture capital transactions, Silicon Valley lawyers help to construct a de facto "local law."

Initially, the binding character of these emergent contractual standards rests primarily on the extralegal pressures that attorneys encounter in establishing and protecting positions within the local community. Under certain circumstances, however, local norms can take on the force of official law: In the unlikely event that a financing agreement were to actually end up in court, the "trade practices" of the community could be invoked to guide the judicial interpretation of ambiguous contractual terms. Thus, by standardizing contracts and by categorizing transactions, Silicon Valley attorneys help the community to construct a "law of its own"—facilitating the region's favored practices by selectively modifying the strictures of the larger legal regime.

National Legal Standards

As well as developing local trade practices that partially substitute for external laws, Silicon Valley attorneys have recently become increasingly proactive in shaping the larger legal regime, itself. The dramatic economic growth of Silicon Valley in the 1970s and 1980s brought the region's distinctive capital market to national attention, and by virtue of practicing in this novel setting, Silicon Valley lawyers often find themselves well situated to influence relevant laws throughout the rest of the country.... [V]enture capital legal work has historically been concentrated in the hands of a relatively limited number of law firms, and these few firms have exercised a substantial leadership role in bringing the "venture capital gospel" to the nation at large. As one leading Bay Area attorney notes:

> If you look at the number of law firms that are actually involved in venture capital, it is quite small. I chair an annual institute on venture capital, and I would say that the five firms or six firms that have people on the program are the firms that are doing 95% of the professional venture capital in the United States. And they are all either here or in the Boston area.

To a large extent, the same experience base that allows Silicon Valley lawyers to play a proselytizing and standardizing role within the local community lies at the root of their national influence as well. Thus, for example, a prominent Palo Alto attorney (and a founding member of the American Bar Association's Subcommittee on Emerging Growth Ventures) comments:

> Most of the other people on the Emerging Growth committee, from other parts of the country, just don't have deals like the venture capital financings that we have had. It is just a difference of scale. When you have so many financings, you focus on regularizing pieces of them.

Silicon Valley lawyers "regularize" the national regime both by example and by fiat. As exemplars, several local attorneys have become active disseminators of the Silicon Valley model. In addition to organizing various national conferences and seminars (such as the offerings of the Practicing Law Institute), these prominent practitioners have taken a leading role in producing form books, outlines, and treatises that spread the region's indigenous practices beyond the community's borders. A tabulation of Library of Congress listings indicates the extent of this influence: 42% of all lawyer-authored publications falling under the heading "Venture Capital–Law & Legislation—United States" have at least one co-author from a Silicon Valley firm; and in the subset of these works dealing with "Small Business–Finance," the level of Silicon Valley authorship rises to fully 67%. Although the overall number of publications is small (12 in the broader category, 6 in the subset), the ubiquitousness of authors from this single legal community is quite striking.

As well as providing examples, however, local attorneys also occasionally assume a more direct role in shaping the nation's venture capital laws. In particular, Silicon Valley lawyers enjoy a disproportionate presence on various government and professional panels charged with reviewing and revising the rules of new-company finance....

Presumably, the stability of the Silicon Valley regime greatly benefits from the prominence of indigenous attorneys on the national stage. With local luminaries writing (or rewriting) global regulatory structures to comport with Silicon Valley's own trade practices, local organizations can largely escape the dislocations that often accompany outside legal mandates. Rather than suffering the uncertainties inherent in new externally generated governance structures, Silicon Valley is able to impose those uncertainties on other, potentially competitive industrial communities.

CONCLUSION

The preceding pages suggest that Silicon Valley lawyers facilitate the operation of local markets for high-technology start-up capital by eliminating or moderating crucial uncertainties that might otherwise elevate transaction costs and foster interorganizational discord.... If this analysis is correct, the role of lawyers in managing uncertainty may have been a significant factor in allowing Silicon Valley to succeed at the difficult business of high-technology entrepreneurship, where many other communities have failed.

In closing, however, several modest cautionary notes may be in order. First, ... it would probably be a mistake to see the Silicon Valley experience as entirely premeditated and intentional. A senior partner at one of Palo Alto's largest law firms hardly stands alone in offering a somewhat more haphazard image:

> Developing formats for big deals was a challenge, because we were developing things that nobody had done before. Being on the frontier is exciting to talk about, but it is very scary when you're out there. A client asks you a question and you just don't know what to do. The venture capital business was enormously unexpected. When I came here, I thought it was a cheesy little stupid business. We didn't see it coming, and we didn't have any support.

Given the enormous uncertainties that Silicon Valley law firms encountered in their own activities during the community's early years, many of the region's legal innovations seem to occupy an uneasy middle ground between Powell's "legal devices" and Flood's "snow jobs." One Palo Alto associate, for example, reports the following piece of firm mythology:

> If you go back to the early 1980s, this firm was justifiably criticized for glad-handing clients and saying, "We're experts. We know everything you guys are going through. What you need to do is to find *a path to liquidity by accessing the capital markets* through an *initial public offering* of stock." Being able to say that made them sound very sophisticated and knowledgeable to the client. I don't think they necessarily knew how to do that, but they figured they'd be able to learn it pretty damn quickly. And, by and large, they got pretty lucky.

For the most part, Silicon Valley's legal improvisations "worked"—sometimes by virtue of skillful design, often by virtue of luck, and occasionally by virtue of the young industrial community's ability to accommodate, incorporate, and exploit solutions that more established communities would never have tolerated. Thus, while the region's lawyers, entrepreneurs, and financiers clearly prospered in tandem, on the whole they appear to have done so as much by unforeseen coevolution as by careful long-range planning.

This skepticism about human prescience entails, as a second caveat, a modicum of caution about treating the current situation in Silicon Valley as final and permanent. Many organizational theorists have argued that industrial development is an inherently dynamic process, with early periods of turmoil-and-uncertainty—often being followed by long spells of placidity and routine. If this is true, then it is entirely possible that the Silicon Valley depicted in the preceding pages is but a transitory phenomenon, and that as entrepreneurial ardor cools and uncertainty abates, lawyers will retreat to the profession's more conventional bounds. Indeed, the comments of one local attorney suggest that this transition may already be underway:

> This isn't the Wild West any more; people came out and institutionalized it. The more ways in which you take away the risk, the more detailed the deals get. Now at some point the other side says, "Well, I was giving you certain rights because you were taking chances right next to me. Now that you've cut out all those chances, I want the best price." So it is just a process of maturation.

While such maturation does not negate the importance of law firms in laying the community's historical foundations, it does serve as a reminder that the facilitative posture of the local bar may not be a stable attribute, fixed for all time.

Perhaps more important still, a recognition of the dynamic character of community structure argues against any facile assumption that Silicon Valley represents a uniquely optimal set of social arrangements. The regime described above is but one of many possible endpoints (or, more correctly, temporary equilibria) in a long and intensely path-dependent process of social and economic change. While Silicon Valley's legal, industrial and financial institutions have clearly coevolved to a state of high mutual adaptation, there is little a priori reason to believe that this particular local equilibrium is better than any other: As valuable as uncertainty management may be, law firms are hardly the only organizational actors capable of performing such services, and it would be extremely difficult to determine whether the prevailing arrangement is, in some abstract sense, the "best possible."

In short, the preceding account of Silicon Valley legal practice represents a description and an explanation but not necessarily a recommendation. Silicon Valley illustrates the importance of cognitive uncertainty as a source of both transaction costs and interorganizational conflicts, and it demonstrates the potential contribution of corporate lawyers in managing this uncertainty and thereby reducing the volume of disputes. Thus, the development of this distinctive community teaches quite a bit about the ways in which law firms interact with the organizational environments around them. At the same time, however, these lessons have their limits. However felicitous Silicon Valley's trajectory may have been, it has hardly been inevitable. While local law firms have clearly played an important role in the region's growth and persistence, Silicon Valley's development—like much economic history—has been a path-dependent tumble of mutual adaptation, rather than a relentless march toward perfection. The resulting community is undeniably secure and resilient; but whether it is "efficient" or "optimal" in any universal sense remains fundamentally uncertain and open to dispute.

NOTES AND QUESTIONS

1. The Problem–Solving Lawyer. Much of the literature on the legal profession focuses on things other than what lawyers actually do: we learn about their background, training, ethics, the structure of the profession, status within the profession and so on. This is because, for one thing, it is not easy to study what large firm lawyers do. All lawyers are elusive creatures. They are concerned about the attorney-client privilege. High-prestige lawyers may be particularly difficult to study. Their time is very valuable, and they may be unwilling to give it to a researcher. They go to great lengths to avoid offending clients that pay huge retainers. Hence, it is not easy to know exactly what tasks corporate lawyers accomplish. John Flood, "Doing Business: The Management of Uncertainty in Lawyers' Work," 25 *Law & Society Review* 41 (1991), did his research as an associate in a large law firm. He tells us that corporate lawyers put together business deals in ways that limit their clients' concerns about uncertainty. They draft the necessary documents in ways that usually avoid trouble with regulatory agencies. Sometimes they give formal opinions about legal aspects of transactions; often they offer informal reassurance. Often clients assume that lawyers know far more than they do about the law governing an area, how it would be interpreted, what the language of a contract means, what risks are important enough to deal with and the like. Lawyers admire an ability to improvise and convince the client that everything is under control when they are unsure. He concludes that lawyers manage uncertainty rather than solve problems. Often their skill is putting aside problems and hoping that they will not have to deal with them later.

Consider, in addition, the following:

A. In his classic work, *The Growth of American Law: The Law Makers* (1950), J. Willard Hurst discussed the role of lawyers as "social inventors." Lawyers "contrived or adapted institutions (the corporation), tools (the railroad equipment trust certificate), and patterns of action (the reorganization of corporate financial structure or the fashioning of a price structure for a national market)" (p. 337). Lawyers, in other words, made a contribution to the growth of the economy and to the development of the American polity by inventing legal devices and putting them to use—presumably in ways that facilitated business or economic growth or (more neutrally) in ways that had an impact on society.

What type of law firm is more likely to be the source of innovation and develop new business practices or legal devices? Will this role be played by general corporate firms or those that specialize in some line of practice such as mergers and acquisitions? On this point, see Michael J. Powell, "Professional Innovation: Corporate Lawyers and Private Lawmaking," 18 *Law & Social Inquiry* 423 (1993), an account of a modern instance of social invention by lawyers to cope with unwanted corporate take-overs during the merger-mania of the 1980s. See also Ronald Gilson, "Value Creation by Business Lawyers: Legal Skills and Asset Pricing," 94 *Yale Law Journal* 239 (1984); Ian M. Ramsay, "What Do Lawyers Do? Reflections on the Market for Lawyers," 21 *International Journal of the Sociology of Law* 355 (1993). See, also, Lisa Bernstein, "The Silicon Valley Lawyer as Transaction Cost Engineer," 74 *Oregon Law Review* 239 (1995); Mark C. Suchman, "Translation Costs: a Comment on Sociology and Economics," 74 *Oregon Law Review* 257 (1995).

B. Kenneth Lipartito, "What Have Lawyers Done for American Business? The Case of Baker and Botts of Houston," 64 *Business History Review* 490 (1990), studied a law firm formed in the last part of the 19th century. It solved various legal problems created by the growth of the corporate form and the expansion of business in Texas. It dealt with relations between the state government and its corporate clients. It served, much as Silicon Valley lawyers served almost a hundred years later, as a link between entrepreneurs and investors. For example, in the late 19th and early 20th centuries, there were many fluctuations in both the economy of Texas and the country as a whole. Lawyers found ways to deal with various creditor interests through the equity receivership. Corporations provoked strong and hostile reactions from workers and farmers during this period. Firms such as Baker and Botts dealt with state governments that tried to regulate. Sometimes the firms invented new structures and established their legitimacy; sometimes they negotiated definitions of the key terms in statutes and standards; sometimes they sought and gained new statutes and amendments of existing ones. These corporate lawyers moved from the boardroom to the courtroom and then to legislative halls and sought compromises that benefited their corporate clients. Baker and Botts also served to bridge the differences between New York bankers and Texas business people. The firm had many members who had cosmopolitan educations from the large eastern universities, but still had connections with those who counted in Texas.

Yves Dezalay and Bryant Garth, "Law, Lawyers and Social Capital: 'Rule of Law' versus Relational Capitalism," 6 *Social & Legal Studies* 109 (1997), suggests that the American model of lawyers as social brokers is being exported around the world. Business is transnational, and thus there is an increasing amount of transnational legal practice. Many American firms, for example, have branches in foreign countries. This American model rests on organizing practice in large international law firms in such a way that lawyers can mobilize social capital thereby gaining privileged positions of power. Lawyers become legitimate intermediaries between business power and the state because they function at the crossroads of different places of power. See, also, Yves Dezalay and Bryant Garth, *The Internationalization of Palace Wars: Lawyers, Economists, and the Contest to Transform Latin American States* (2002), which looks at the contest between lawyers and economists to influence governmental policy in these nations. One important change in the work and structure of the legal profession is the increasing trend toward a more "globalized" practice.

Most transnational lawyers probably do not think of their practice as "ideological" or as based on an "ideology." However, Bryant Garth has pointed out that there is an international ideology of "free trade, minimal governmental regulation, and a common understanding of how conflicts ought to be normally resolved." Or, as Susan Silbey, ... " 'Let Them Eat Cake,' Globalization, Postmodern Colonialism, and the Possibilities of Justice," 31 *Law & Society Review* 207 (1997), puts it:

> Law is relegated to ... [a] ... subordinate role as a background figure providing context but little determinative action ... [T]he market narrative is a parable about lowering expectations about what collectivities can or should do. It thus asks us to limit our conceptions of justice to a contentless efficiency.

Transnational legal practice rests on this ideology and presupposes it. On this and other aspects of the practice, see the thoughtful article by Garth, "Transitional Legal Practice and Professional Ideology, Issues of Transitional Legal Practice," *1985 Michigan Year Book of International Studies* 3 (1985). See, also, Debora L. Spar, "Lawyers Abroad: The Internationalization of Legal Practice," 39 *California Management Review* 8, 22 (1997)(The key to success is talented people with great local knowledge. However, "once they become part of this system, the firm's 'walking assets' are highly valuable and difficult to replace. Retention is thus key, particularly in foreign markets where local knowledge is liable to be concentrated in just a handful of people.").

C. Robert S. Strauss played several key roles in the Carter Administration, such as Chairman of the Democratic National Committee, and he returned to government from private practice to serve as President Bush's Ambassador to Russia. In an article describing what happened to lawyers who held top positions in the Carter Administration, Ruth Marcus, "What Price Fame—and Who Pays It?", *National Law Journal*, August 12, 1981, p. 1, col. 2, p. 54, cols. 2–3, writes:

> He doesn't pretend to be the typical lawyer, buried in the minutiae of cases and versed in arcane points of tax or securities law. It's been years since he was in the firm library....
>
> But ... Mr. Strauss knows people across the country and abroad, so that when a client in Chicago wants to open a factory in Canada, say, Mr. Strauss can pick up his phone, talk to the Canadian businessman who

might be interested in sharing such a venture, and arrange a meeting—all in five minutes of work and five of small talk.

"If you're around people and make a good impression, they think of you favorably and look you up when they need somebody...."

It's not so much a matter of knowing the law as of having common-sense knowledge of people. "I've never been a great intellectual, never a great academic, but I've been a great performer," Mr. Strauss explains, "And clients come to people who get things done."

Mr. Strauss can put together the ingredients for the factory deal and leave it to the contract lawyers to work out the details. He can negotiate takeover tactics for a corporate client; [his firm's] antitrust, securities and contract lawyers worry about the technicalities....

"I just had a man here in my office this morning talking about his estate," Mr. Strauss says in explanation of his sort of practice. "He didn't want my legal advice. He wanted my judgment."

2.   Corporate lawyers, then, solve problems, drawing on all of the resources that they command. To what extent is this a positive thing? To what extent do corporate lawyers sabotage the rule of law and planned regulation? Consider the following:

A.   A former corporate lawyer argued in the *Wall Street Journal,* February 23, 1984, at 26, col. 3, that large-firm lawyers engage in "public-interest work" in their everyday practice by suggesting ways for major businesses to accomplish what they desire safely within legal restraints:

Because ... [business lawyers] advise powerful public and private entities, these lawyers have a more consistent impact on the lives of American citizens than other types of counsel. The typical company seeks their advice to avoid future costly legal battles. Yet, by advising a company of the legal parameters within which it must operate, the business attorney necessarily serves as guardian of the public interest. He has the daily responsibility of ferreting out and making certain that his client honors the myriad of pollution, pension, occupational safety, securities and other laws that protect the public....

Tediously stitching and restitching boundaries and spaces, decade after decade, hoping the design someday will show itself, does not, of course, make for exciting copy.... But most of the real progress toward evolving a system of laws that will allow more people to act as they choose takes place largely through day-to-day wrangling of attorneys daily confirming laws that protect others, while protecting the aspirations of their client.

B.   Ben White, "Profile: Rodgin Cohen", *Financial Times,* July 11, 2006, at 28, describes the work of the Chairman of the Wall Street law firm Sullivan & Cromwell. Among many other actions, he has broken down barriers to creating modern financial institutions. White reports:

Mr. Cohen joined the banking law department at Sullivan & Cromwell in 1970, after attending Harvard and Harvard Law School and spending two years in the army.

At the time, restrictive federal law meant banks operated exclusively in local markets. Mr. Cohen started studying federal statutes and spotted a legal loophole saying banks could move their headquarters within 50 miles, regardless of whether or not they cross state lines.

"So we took the head office of First Fidelity in New Jersey and moved it into Pennsylvania" to be able to open branches there, Mr. Cohen said. "And the Comptroller of the Currency approved it. And I think at that point people began to see the handwriting on the wall. Very soon thereafter they took down most of the barriers on geographic expansion."

C.　Professor Robert Gordon, in "Bargaining with the Devil," 105 *Harvard Law Review* 2041 (1992), discusses "the ideology of the corporate lawyer as the responsible counsellor who does not simply tell clients what they can get away with, but rather tries to persuade them to adopt corporate policies that will comply with the general norms and purposes of the legal system and that will benefit society as a whole" (p. 2052). He notes, however:

> It is quite unclear whether corporate lawyers have ever lived up to this ideal of the counsellor-in-legal-and-social responsibility. It is clear, however, that this ideal was, until recently, a standard part of the self-image and general belief system of the corporate bar, and therefore probably had some effect on practice.... It is also clear, unfortunately, that in the last decade most traces of this admirable ideology have vanished, except among retiring lawyers (pp. 2052–2053).

Assume that the counsellor-in-legal-and-social responsibility ideology has all but died. Does this undercut the point of the corporate lawyer quoted above who argues that corporate lawyers actually help in the enforcement and effectiveness of the country's regulatory laws? See, also, Marc Galanter, "Lawyers in the Mist: The Golden Age of Legal Nostalgia," 100 *Dickinson Law Review* 549 (1996).

D.　James Gould Cozzens, *Guard of Honor* (1948), a controversial novel, dramatizes what some lawyers in positions of power do. The action in the book takes place at a World War II United States Army Air Force base in the Deep South. The United States Army had always been heavily segregated. African–Americans were given only menial jobs, and officers were always white. As a result of various pressures, the Army ordered desegregation. The Air Force formed a squadron of "Negro" pilots who later went into battle over Germany.

In the novel, Bus, the General in charge of an air base in Florida, was a great leader of fighter pilots but ill suited to running a large training base. Several of the officers who served under him were old Army and Army Air Force types who also had little experience coping with the demands of running a large base. Colonel Ross had served in the Air Force in World War I and then held a Reserve Officer's Commission. He was a lawyer and judge in civilian life. He serves as the General's chief adviser and trouble shooter. The novel tells how Ross handled several crises in such a way as to protect the General. All of these crises involved the problems of race in American society in the early 1940s.

The General's best friend, Benny, an Air Force colonel, pilots the General's plane. Benny approaches the airfield for a night landing, and discovers a B–26 bomber landing immediately in front of him. Benny narrowly avoids a crash by outstanding flying. After landing, Benny confronts the B–26 pilot, hits him in the face, and this sends him to the hospital. The B–26 pilot is black—part of a newly formed squadron of black bomber pilots from Tuskegee Institute. A radical young white lieutenant brings a black newspaperman and the injured pilot's father to the base, thus threatening publicity about the incident. The General does not want his friend Benny charged in a disciplinary proceeding. In such a proceeding, Benny would be subject to strong sanctions. The Judge manipulates the situation. Benny is not charged but apologizes. The injured pilot is awarded a medal as a result of his actions before coming to the base, and the Judge uses the award ceremony to defuse the conflict.

One of the General's administrative officers created a segregated Officers' Club at the base for the black pilots, and they are quartered in segregated barracks. This violates explicit Air Force regulations. Some of the black pilots attempt to enter the white officers' club, and one takes a Military Policeman's gun from him. Two black leaders are arrested by the MPs. The Judge also manipulates this situation to keep the blacks from being formally charged, but the Air Force General Staff learns what happened. It writes an order for the General's signature requiring the black squadron to stay together during their training "in order to promote the close integration essential in a self-sustaining combat unit." The Judge modifies the order to make it less burdensome on the black pilots and crew. He then explains it at a meeting with the black officers, and their resentment is directed at him rather than at the General. He persuades them that it is more important for them to show that black pilots can be successful in combat than to desegregate this base's officers' club.

Colonel Ross is sympathetic to the black squadron, and he does not believe in segregation. He thinks that the black pilots have been treated badly. However, he knows that the General's skills are needed in the war effort. An officer from the Air Staff in Washington tells Colonel Ross that the General "was the best man we had to command large scale fighter operations." Colonel Ross knows that if there are formal legal proceedings, the General would be in serious trouble. He would be disciplined, and he probably would not be given a command when Allied forces invaded Europe and Japan.

Cozzens' story involves the Colonel's use of evasion, legalism, cover-up and compromises, all in the service of what the Colonel sees as the priorities

886

of the situation. As a result of the Colonel's efforts, the black pilots are treated much better than the career Army officers at the base would have treated them. Nonetheless, their rights are not vindicated. It is the Colonel who decides that the General is essential to defeating Germany and Japan, and that this goal outweighs desegregation, civil rights and following the letter of Air Force directives. Cozzens portrays the Colonel as a wise lawyer making difficult but important judgments. He portrays the radical white lieutenant who championed the black pilots' rights as young and foolish.

Colonel Ross, of course, is a fictional character. But there are probably many "Colonel Rosses" in the legal profession managing affairs in large organizations. On balance, do you think they do more harm than good? Why? Can you defend those who play such roles? Some lawyers, of course, help their clients break the law and minimize the chance of getting caught. See, e.g., Michael Levi, Hans Nelen and Francien Lankhorst, "Lawyers as Crime Facilitators in Europe: An Introduction and Overview," 42 *Crime, Law and Social Change* 117 (2004).

4. One of the major developments since the 1970s, is the increase in status and power of lawyers who work in the legal departments of large corporations. See John P. Heinz, Robert L. Nelson, Rebecca L. Sandefur, and Edward O. Laumann, *Urban Lawyers: The New Social Structure of the Bar* 297–98 (2005). Consider the following:

A. Robert L. Nelson and Laura Beth Nielsen, "Cops, Counsel, and Entrepreneurs: Constructing the Role of Inside Counsel in Large Corporations," 34 *Law & Society Review* 457 (2000), constructed ideal typical roles that such lawyers might play. First, there are the cops. These lawyers give rule-based legal-risk advice. They approve contracts, respond to legal questions that executives pose, and implement programs to insure compliance with legal regulations. They are lawyers who happen to work in a corporate setting. Second, there are the counsel. They give mixed law and business ethics advice. They give advice based not only on legal knowledge but on business, ethical and situational concerns. One such lawyer in the sample said he was willing to deceive executives about the law to get them to make what he sees as correct decisions. Others use the gray areas in the law as ways to exercise influence. Third, there are the entrepreneurs. They go beyond avoiding trouble. These lawyers claim expert knowledge in law, management and economic ideas. They identify with the corporation and seek to make money and advance the interests of their corporation. In a sample of inside counsel, Nelson and Neilsen found 17% were cops, 33% entrepreneurs and 50% counsel.

All of these lawyers face problems in trying to stop a business decision. If they are known as cops, the business people will seek ways around them. Business people view in-house lawyers with a mixture of suspicion and appreciation. Often engineers and sales people have to submit proposed contracts to the legal department for review, and often they do not welcome this step in company procedures. This is captured in a Dilbert cartoon.

Dilbert, an engineer, asks the company lawyer to review the contract and says, "I need it today." The company lawyer says that he cannot approve it because "somebody might sue us for no good reason." Scott Adams, Dilbert, Sept. 24, 1995, available at http://www.comics,com/comics/dilbert/archives/. In another Dilbert cartoon, Dilbert complains to the representative of a vendor that his contract document is in "incomprehensible weaseleze." Dilbert says: "My only choice is to sign something I don't understand or get my lawyer involved and miss my deadline." Adams, supra, Sept. 15, 2001. Interestingly, after reading Suchman and Cahill, Ashby Jones, "Silicon Valley's Outsiders: In–House Lawyers?—General Counsel Often Seen as Impediments to Plans or Secondary 'Cost Centers'" *Wall Street Journal*, October 2, 2006, at B3, suggests that in Silicon Valley in-house lawyers lack respect and power. This reflects a relatively new industry that worships technical innovation. " 'No'— the message in-house lawyers often have to deliver—isn't the message some driven entrepreneurs want to hear."

B.   Deborah A. DeMott, "The Discrete Roles of General Counsel," 74 *Fordham Law Review* 955, 980 (2005), suggests that corporate scandals such as the Enron case and the federal regulation that followed them, might decrease the power of inside counsel: "One likely source of weakening in relationships among general counsel and the corporation's directors is the use of independent outside counsel who are chosen and retained by audit committees comprised of independent directors to facilitate compliance with new requirements imposed by Sarbanes–Oxley legislation, the SEC, and stock exchange listing rules. Once advised by independent counsel, independent directors may prefer to establish an ongoing relationship with outside counsel."

6.   Most lawyers, of course, do not work for big law firms representing major corporations. On "solo" practitioners outside a big city, see Joel Handler, *The Lawyer and His Community: The Practicing Bar in a Middle-Sized City* (1967).

(c) LAWYERS FOR INDIVIDUALS

(5.14) Lawyers and Consumer Protection Laws

Stewart Macaulay

14 *Law & Society Review* 115 (1979).

The conventional model of the practice of law views lawyers as those who apply legal rules in the service of client interests, checked only by the constraints of the adversary system. A study of the impact of consumer protection laws on the practice of Wisconsin lawyers shows this to be an oversimplification. Lawyers for individuals tend to know little of the precise contours of consumer protection law. They most often serve as mediators between buyer and seller, relying on general norms of fairness and good faith. Lawyers for businesses are more likely to make use of the law, but they are seldom called on to deal with particular disputes. Lawyers' own values and interests are reflected in the way in which they represent clients. As a result, reform laws which create individual rights are likely to have only symbolic effect unless incentives are devised to make their vindication in the long-range interest of members of the bar. Moreover, an understanding of the many roles played by lawyers also requires a more expanded picture of practice. The picture of the lawyer as litigator in the adversary system may itself serve largely symbolic functions.

I. INTRODUCTION

Towards a New Model of the Practice of Law

In Western culture the lawyer has been regarded with both admiration and suspicion for centuries. Both judgments seem to rest on a widely held image of what it is that lawyers do or ought to do. On one hand, the profession paints a picture of itself defending individual liberties by advocacy and facilitating progress by creative social engineering. Novels, plays, motion pictures, and television programs have reinforced this view. On the other hand, a debunking tradition ... shows lawyers as people who profit from the misfortunes of others, as manipulators who produce results for a price without regard to justice, and as word magicians who mislead people into accepting what is wrong. Fiction supports this view too. Yet much of this writing may cost us understanding because the debunkers accept the classic stereotype of good lawyering as a yardstick, measured against which actual practice falls short.

In this classical model of practice, lawyers apply the law. They try cases and argue appeals guided by their command of legal norms. They negotiate settlements and advise clients largely in light of what they believe would happen if matters were brought before legal agencies. Of course, it is this mastery of a special body of knowledge, certified by success in law school and passing a bar examination which gives one the status of being a lawyer and justifies the privileges which come with being a member of the profession. In the common law version of the model, lawyers represent clients in an adversary system. They take stock of a client's situation and desires and seek to further the client's interests as far as is possible legally. The lawyer is a "hired gun" who does not judge the client but vigorously asserts all of the client's claims of right, limited only by legal ethics. Lawyers place the interests of clients ahead of their own. A high place in the legends of the profession, for example, is awarded to the heroic and lonely advocate for an unpopular client, who battles for justice in the face of threats to person and pocketbook. However, even these aggressive lawyers cannot go too far because of the operation of the adversary system. An aggressive lawyer on one side will be matched on the other, and from this kind of advocacy a proper outcome will emerge. As a result, lawyers need not, and should not, be influenced by their own ethical judgment of the client's cause.

Only the most innocent could think that this classical model describes professional practice. The model may reflect some of what goes on, but it is, at best, a distortion. Both Wall Street and Main Street lawyers often operate in situations where they do not know much about the relevant legal norms or where those norms play an insignificant part in influencing what is done. Lawyers regularly engage in the politics of bargaining, seeking to work out solutions to problems which are acceptable to the various interests. Rather than playing hired gun for one side, lawyers often mediate between their client and those not represented by lawyers. They seek to educate, persuade and coerce both sides to adopt the best available compromise rather than to engage in legal warfare. Moreover, in playing all of their roles, ranging from arguing a case before the Supreme Court of the United States to listening to an angry client, lawyers are influenced by their own values and self interest. They will be more eager to do things which they find satisfying and not distasteful and which will contribute to their income both today and in the future.

The legal profession may find the classical model valuable in justifying its activities and status. The public may benefit too insofar as this conventional view of practice is a normative indicator of what a lawyer ought to do and what influences behavior. Nonetheless, the classical model has costs: it may serve to mislead clients about what lawyers can, should, or will do. It may obstruct serious thought about the techniques and ethics of counseling, mediation and negotiation. And it may undermine effective efforts at reforms through law. Over the past twenty years when reformers have won victories in such areas as civil rights, sex and racial discrimination, and consumer protection, their successes have come in the form of cases, statutes, and regulations which, along with other things, have granted rights to individuals or groups. But the actual nature of law practice may leave these rights as little more than symbolic words on paper with only marginal life as resources in the process of negotiation.

This case study will develop some ideas about an expanded picture of the practice of law. I will consider the roles played by lawyers in connection with a number of consumer protection laws which create individual rights. . . .

A. Description of the Research

The research on which this article is based began as a study of the impact of the Magnuson–Moss Warranty Act, 15 U.S.C. § 2301–12 (Supp. V 1975) in Wisconsin. This statute, which became effective on July 4, 1975, was heralded as an important victory for the consumer protection movement, and was given national news coverage and prompted an outpouring of law review articles.

As our research developed, it quickly became apparent that the focus of the study was too narrow. We found that most lawyers in Wisconsin knew next to nothing about the Magnuson–Moss Warranty Act; many had never heard of it. When asked about the statute, they tended to respond with comments on consumer protection in general. It was extremely difficult to find lawyers who knew much about any specific consumer protection law other than the Wisconsin Consumer Act [WCA], Wis. Stat. 421–427 (1975), a law largely concerned with procedures for financing consumer transactions and collecting debts. A few lawyers were well informed about the WCA, but most knew only of "atrocity stories" about debtors who had used the statute to evade honest debts. However, we also found that, in spite of this ignorance of the specific contours of consumer protection regulation, most lawyers had techniques for dealing with complaints voiced by clients, or potential clients, who were dissatisfied with the quality of products or services or could not pay for what they had bought. These techniques will be the major focus of this article.

What follows is based on in-person and telephone interviews conducted by a research assistant and me during the summer of 1977. We talked with about 100 lawyers in five Wisconsin counties and with representatives from each of the state's ten largest law firms, from the legal services programs in Milwaukee and Madison, from Wisconsin Judicare, a program for paying private lawyers to handle cases for the poor in the northern and western parts of the state and from all the group legal service plans registered with the State Bar of Wisconsin. In addition, a questionnaire concerning experiences with the Magnuson–Moss Warranty Act was sent to all lawyers who had attended an Advanced Training Seminar dealing with that statute, sponsored by the State Bar of Wisconsin. While in no sense is this study based on a representative sample of all lawyers in Wisconsin, there was an attempt to seek out lawyers whose experiences might differ. The great consistency in the stories that this very diverse group of lawyers had to tell suggests that almost any sample would have served for the study. Even at points where very divergent interpretations were offered by the lawyers interviewed, their description of practice was consistent. Moreover, the information I gathered was consistent with, and helps explain, the findings about lawyers and consumer problems of the American Bar Association–American Bar Foundation study of the legal needs of the public. This ABA–ABF study was based on a random sample of the adult population of the United States, excluding Alaska and Hawaii.

However, my study has some obvious limitations. I cannot offer percentages of the lawyers who have had certain experiences or who hold particular opinions. Often the lawyers themselves could say no more than they get a certain kind of case "all of the time," or that they "almost never" litigate. Since lawyers have no reason to compile statistics, usually they offered only general estimates of their caseload. Many informal contacts and telephone calls never appear in lawyers' records, and lawyers are unlikely to have a very precise memory of them. Moreover, many of the attorneys interviewed were former students of mine, and others seemed glad to aid a University of Wisconsin law professor's research. This effort to be helpful, while appreciated, may have introduced some distortion. On one hand, these lawyers may have been willing to go along with the interviewer's definition of the situation, which was implicit in the questions asked, rather than challenge the entire basis of the inquiry. On the other hand, a few may have modified a fact here and there to present a good story to entertain their old professor or to make themselves look good. While I cannot be sure that this did not happen, again the consistency of the stories across 100 lawyers suggests that this was not a major problem.

Finally, it should be noted that this article reports the author's interpretations of what he was told. Not all of the attorneys were asked exactly the same questions since, as the study progressed, the responses dictated a change in the focus from the Magnuson–Moss Warranty Act to consumer protection laws and then finally to the practice of law itself. This article, then, is an empirical description of a corner of the legal world that my assistant and I explored in some depth rather than a report of quantifiable data from a survey of a random sample of the bar. It should be read as a report from a preliminary study, offering suggestions the author thinks are true enough to warrant reliance until someone is willing to invest enough to produce better data and lucky enough to find a way to get them.

II. THE IMPACT OF CONSUMER PROTECTION STATUTES ON THE PRACTICE OF LAW

Heinz and Laumann ...[13] tell us that "the tendency of lawyers' work to address congeries of problems associated with particular types of clients organizes the profession into types of lawyers: those serving corporations, and those serving individuals and individuals' small businesses." They point out that corporate work is likely to involve "symbol manipulation," while work for individuals will carry a heavy component of "people persuasion." My study offers additional confirmation of these observations. Certain members of the Wisconsin bar were much more likely to see an individual with a consumer complaint, while others were much more likely to be asked to lobby against consumer protection legislation, to draft contracts to cope with such laws, and to plan defensive strategies for dealing with consumer complaints. We will deal with these two types of lawyers separately.

Lawyers for Consumers

Lawyers see but a small percentage of all of the situations where someone might assert a claim under the many consumer protection laws. Some claims are never asserted because consumers fail to recognize that the product they receive is defective, that the forms used in financing the transaction fail to make the required disclosures, or that the debt collection tactics used by a creditor are prohibited. Other claims are recognized but resolved in ways not involving lawyers. Some consumers see the cost of any attempt to resolve a minor consumer problem as not worth the effort. Resolving never to buy from the offending merchant or manufacturer again, they just "lump it." Some fix a defective item themselves, while others complain to the seller or the creditor and receive an adjustment which satisfies them. It is likely that most

---

13. The reference is to John P. Heinz and Edward O. Laumann, "The Legal Profession: Client Interests, Professional Roles, and Social Hierarchies," 76 *Michigan Law Review* 1111 (1978).

potential claims under consumer protection statutes are resolved in one of these ways.

Some consumers go directly to remedy agents without consulting lawyers. For example, they may turn to the Better Business Bureau in Milwaukee or to one or more of several state agencies which mediate consumer complaints. A few may go directly to a small claims court. Others contact the local district attorney who, at least in the smaller counties in Wisconsin, often offers a great deal of legal advice or even a rather coercive mediation service to consumers who are potential supporters in the next election.

Many lawyers in private practice reported to us that they never saw a case involving an individual consumer. Those who represented businesses and practice in the larger firms were likely to say this, but some business lawyers reported that they answered questions about consumer matters from clients and friends. Other lawyers talked about encountering consumer cases only now and then. Lawyers did see what they called "products liability" cases where a defective item had caused personal injury. However, these cases typically do not fall under consumer protection statutes, and the fact of personal injury opens the door to the chance of a substantial recovery. A specialized group of attorneys is expert in the techniques of asserting or defending products liability cases. Most lawyers knew these specialists and many referred cases to them. No similar network of access to specialists in consumer protection law seemed to exist. Several attorneys mentioned one lawyer whom they thought was an expert in consumer protection, but when I interviewed him, he said that he now tried to avoid such cases.

Those few dissatisfied consumers who survive the screening process and come to lawyers may have special characteristics or kinds of problems. First, some people will bring cases to lawyers that others would see as trivial but which they see as a matter of principle. Second, when regular clients appear with minor consumer problems, a lawyer may attempt to handle them in order to keep a client's good will; one lawyer called this a kind of "loss-leader" service. For example, a lawyer in a small county had drafted a wealthy farmer's estate plan and set up a corporation to handle some of his dealings in land development. The farmer, dissatisfied with a Chevrolet dealer's attempts to make a new car run satisfactorily, called his lawyer and told him to straighten out matters. The lawyer successfully negotiated with the dealer and sent the farmer a bill for only a nominal amount. Third, debtors who cannot pay are sometimes pushed into a lawyer's office by the actions of a creditor. The debtor or the lawyer may see consumer protection law as offering a way to lift some or all of the burden of indebtedness for an expensive item such as a car, a recreational vehicle, or a mobile home. Problems which the consumer might have been willing to overlook may now become the basis for a legal attempt to rescind the sale.

Consumer cases also are brought to the attention of lawyers through informal social channels. . . . Many lawyers pointed out that they had friends, relatives, and neighbors who asked for advice informally. People who might not make a visit to a lawyer's office about a consumer matter will raise their problem with a lawyer they see at a church supper, a PTA meeting, or a cocktail party. One lawyer noted that it was hard to have a drink at a bar in Madison on a football weekend without being called on for free legal advice....

Decisions about whether or not to contact a lawyer are affected by personal factors. One lawyer remarked that many people seem to need reassurance that it is legitimate to complain and make trouble for others. Many people are hesitant about admitting that they were cheated by a retailer or manufacturer when they think they should have known better. Some lawyers said that most of their clients, both those who come to their office and those who ask for advice during informal contacts, come to them through friendship networks. A former client may talk with a friend at work or at a bar and end up sending the friend to see the lawyer. Some people seem to need the encouragement of friends before they can take the plunge. There seems to be a "folk culture" that defines, among other things, which kinds of cases one should take to a lawyer, which call for solutions not involving lawyers, and which should be just forgotten. Those facing aggressive debt collection procedures are likely to be told to see lawyers; those with complaints about the quality of products are usually advised just to forget it.

Many lawyers seek to avoid taking clients with consumer protection problems. Firms that specialize in representing businesses discourage individuals from bringing their personal problems to the firm by the expensive elegance of their offices and often by the location of those offices. Everything about these firms tends to tell potential clients that these are expensive professionals who deal only with important people on important matters. One who is not to the manor born would hesitate to waste the time of this professional establishment with a mere personal matter.

Even lawyers who look more approachable have techniques for avoiding cases they do not want to take. Receptionists try to screen cases so that minor personal matters will not waste their bosses' time. Lawyers engage in techniques of conversion or transformation of attitudes. Some try to brush off individuals by talking to them briefly on the telephone in order to keep them from coming to the office. Some listen to people who come to the office for only a few minutes and then interrupt to spell out the cost of legal services. These attorneys see their role as that of educating would-be clients to see that they cannot afford to pursue the matter. The lawyer serves as a gatekeeper, keeping people from burdening the legal system.

If the potential client with a consumer matter is not rejected out of hand, lawyers may still limit their response to nonadversary roles. One part played fairly often might be that of the therapist or knowledgeable friend. The client is allowed to blow off steam and vent anger to a competent-seeming professional sitting in an office surrounded by law books and the other stage props of the profession. By body language and discussion, the lawyer can lead the client to redefine the situation so that he or she can accept it. What appeared to the client to be a clear case of fraud or bad faith comes on close examination to be seen as no more than a misunderstanding.

The lawyer may then "help" the client consider the practical options open in the situation. It may be against the client's interests to pursue the matter: legal action may cost more than it is worth, either directly or indirectly in terms of the client's long-run interests. The client may also have adopted too narrow, perhaps too legalistic, view of the case. The client's grievance may be one which the lawyer could translate into a perfectly legitimate indeed compelling legal argument, but the "law" may not be the only standard by which the merits of each party will be judged. Such arguments, needless to say, may anger the potential client; or they may make the client feel foolish for being upset and bothering a lawyer. On the other hand, by helping the client see the case in a new light, the lawyer may be indulging in a kind of therapy.

Perhaps the lawyer will take a further step and combine the therapist role with that of an information broker or a coach, hearing the complaint and then referring the client elsewhere for a remedy. This gets the would-be client out of the office less unhappy than had the lawyer just rejected the case and offered nothing. People can be sent to state agencies which mediate consumer claims or to private organizations such as the Better Business Bureau. Some lawyers go further and try to coach clients on how to complain effectively to a seller or creditor or how to handle a case in a small claims court without a lawyer. Sometimes this information and coaching may be of more help than formal legal advice. Consumers may need to be reassured that they have a legitimate complaint, to be given the courage to complain, to learn where to go and whom to see, and to be given a few good rhetorical ploys to use in the process of solving their problems. Sometimes the coaching does not help the client. The referral only prompts the client to give up. Few lawyers know what happens when they tell a client to complain to the seller or go to a state agency. Clients rarely report back to the lawyer unless they are friends or neighbors. On the other hand, such referrals may serve to help lawyers see themselves as helpful people.

Attorneys who become more involved in a case may find themselves playing the part of go-between or informal mediator. They may telephone or write the seller or creditor to state the consumer's complaint. The very restatement of that complaint by a professional is likely to make it a complex communication. On one level, the attorney is reporting a version of the situation which may be unknown to the seller or creditor even in cases where consumers have complained before seeing a lawyer. The lawyer may be able to organize a presentation so that the basis of the complaint is more understandable, and transform it so that it is more persuasive. The fact that the report comes from a lawyer is likely to give the complaint at least some minimal legitimacy. The lawyer is saying that he or she has reviewed the buyer or debtor's story, that the assertions of fact are at least plausible, and that the buyer or debtor has reason to complain if these are the facts.

The lawyer is more likely than the consumer to get to talk to someone who has authority to do something about a problem. For example, the consumer may have gotten no farther than the sales person, while the lawyer may gain access to the manager or owner of the business. The lawyer is likely to speak as a social equal of the representative of the seller or debtor, though such may not be the case for the consumer. This may be important. A retailer, for example, may care little about the opinions of a factory worker complainant, but wish to avoid having a professional judge him or her as foolish or unreasonable. Finally, the attorney's professional identification conveys a tacit threat that an unsatisfactory response could be followed by something the seller or creditor might find unpleasant. Indeed the unstated and vague threat of further action may be coercive precisely because it is vague. If sellers and creditors were aware of the cost barriers to litigation, and if they knew, or appreciated, just how much of a paper tiger most attorneys are in consumer matters, they would be less easily intimidated.

At this point, a seller or creditor may assert that the client has just misunderstood the situation or has told the lawyer only part of the story. At this stage lawyers often discover that a client's case is not as clear-cut as the client claimed. However, sellers and creditors still are more likely to make conciliatory responses to lawyers than to buyers or debtors, as long as the lawyers do not ask for too much. And it is part of a lawyer's stock in trade to know how much is too much. One lawyer told us:

> I enjoy negotiation. Of course, what happens is not determined by the merits ... One has a discussion about what is best for everyone. You do not make an adversary matter out of it. It is a game, and it is funny or sad, depending on how you look at it. You call the other side and tell him that you understand that he has a problem satisfying customers but that you have a client who is really hot and wants to sue for the principle of the thing. Then you say, "Maybe I can help you and talk my client into accepting something that is reasonable." The other side knows what you are doing. It is a game. You never want to get to the merits of the case.

The seller or creditor is likely to make some kind of gesture so that the lawyer will not have to return to the client empty-handed. The simplest gesture the seller or creditor can make is a letter of apology, explaining how the problem occurred and accepting some or all of the blame. A supervisor may attempt to blame an employee with whom the consumer dealt, perhaps remarking that it is difficult to find good sales people or mechanics. Manufacturers often blame dealers, and dealers, in turn, seem eager to pass the blame on to manufacturers. In addition to an apology, the merchant may also offer token reparations such as minor repairs or free samples of its products.

More rarely, the lawyer may be able to persuade a seller or manufacturer to offer the consumer a refund or replacement for a defective product. Sometimes a lawyer can gain a refund or replacement even where the flaw in the thing purchased was not so material as to warrant "revocation of acceptance" under Section 2–608 of the Uniform Commercial Code. New car dealers or fly-by-night merchants are unlikely to do this; new car dealers are tightly controlled by manufacturers, who seem to value cost control more than consumer goodwill; fly-by-night operators seldom worry about repeat business. But Sears, Montgomery Ward, J.C. Penney, and many other large department stores, have an announced policy of consumer satisfaction. One can get his or her money back without having to establish that there is something materially wrong with the product. Other retailers and manufacturers do not announce this as their policy, but will grant refunds or replacements selectively when their officials think that the customer has reason to complain or if repeat business is valued. In such cases, a telephone call from a lawyer may be enough to swing the balance in favor of the complainant—it probably seems easier to make a refund than to argue with a lawyer. Occasionally, a lawyer may be able to persuade a new car dealer who has sold a client a used car to pay some percentage of the cost of repairs of a major item such as a transmission, provided the work is done in the dealer's shop. A lawyer may be able to persuade a creditor to give a client more time in which to pay rather than repossessing the item in dispute. But lawyers are seldom able to persuade a seller or creditor to pay a large sum as damages to an aggrieved buyer or debtor.

The lawyer's view of the adequacy of the remedy offered by the merchant or lender will necessarily turn on a reappraisal of the client's case in light of the other side's story, the ease of taking further action, the likelihood of success of such action, and the client's probable reaction to what has been offered. The lawyer may have to persuade the client to see the situation in a new light. The response of the merchant or lender must also be considered. The axiom that "there are two sides to every story" now becomes a reality for the client. An important part of the lawyer's task now is to persuade the client to see the problem as an adjustment between competing claims and interests, rather than as one warranting a fight for principle. From the lawyer's perspective, the client must now be guided to the view that what the merchant or lender has offered is probably the best that could be expected. Anything more may require legal services more costly than the client can afford or is prepared to pay.

In this context, lawyers are often pushed into a role Justice Brandeis described as "counsel for the situation." ... [S]uch a lawyer must be advocate, mediator, entrepreneur, and judge all rolled into one. He or she is called on to be expert in problem solving and asked to produce a solution which will be acceptable over time rather than only an immediate victory for the client. This often means persuading or coercing both the other party and the client to reach what the lawyer sees as a proper solution, often "translating inarticulate or exaggerated claims ... into temperate and mutually intelligible terms of communication." At all levels of law practice, this is a difficult task. The client tends to want vindication, while the lawyer is talking about costs balanced against benefits. It is an especially difficult task when the client is angry but has what the lawyer sees as a questionable case that involves too little money to warrant even drafting a complaint let alone litigating. Clients in consumer protection cases often find it hard to believe that they cannot do better than the lawyer says they can. . . .

Only in rare instances will lawyers go further than conciliatory negotiation in a consumer matter. If the antagonist fails to offer a satisfactory settlement, the lawyer may counter with more explicit threats of unpleasant consequences. But some lawyers report that once overt threats are made, one is likely to have to draft and file a complaint before any offer of settlement will be made by the other side. One reason is that serious threats from a lawyer are likely to prompt sellers or creditors to send the matter to their lawyers. But even at this point, the lawyers for both sides have every reason to settle rather than litigate. . . .

There are a number of reasons why lawyers either refuse to take consumer protection cases or tend to play only nonadversarial roles when they try to help a client with such a complaint. The most obvious explanation is that the costs of handling these cases in a more adversarial style would be more than most clients would be willing to pay. Few consumers can afford many hours of lawyers' time billed at from \$35 to \$75 an hour just to argue about a \$400 repair to their car or even a repossession of a \$5,000 used car. Few lawyers can afford to spend time on cases that will not pay. . . .

Consumer product quality cases are very similar to products liability litigation except for the factor of personal injury. But this factor in products liability offers the chance for recovering very large damages and prompts lawyers to work for contingent fees.

Not only are consumer protection cases unlikely to warrant substantial fees, but they usually require a major investment of professional time if litigation is to be considered seriously. Those most expert about consumer laws tend to be the lawyers who counsel businesses and draft documents in light of these laws. Yet these are the lawyers least likely to see an individual consumer's case—except, perhaps, as a favor to a friend. Most other lawyers in Wisconsin know very little about any of the many consumer protection laws, and it is difficult for most attorneys to master all of the relevant statutes, regulations, and cases in this area. Most of them did not study consumer law in law school. Either they graduated before most of it was passed or they did not take elective courses in this area when they were in law school. Moreover, since consumer protection cases worth an investment of time come up so infrequently, a lawyer is not even likely to know whom to call for help. Most lawyers in Wisconsin lack easy access to the text of consumer protection law. Most are unlikely to own the necessary law books themselves. The folk wisdom of private practice dictates that one should buy only those law books that are likely to pay for themselves. Most lawyers have access to the Wisconsin statutes, the decisions of the state courts, and at least some of the state administrative regulations. Fewer have access to federal materials dealing with statutes such as Truth in Lending (15 U.S.C. § 1601, et seq. [1970]) or the Magnuson–Moss Warranty Act; and only a very few have ready access to loose-leaf services dealing with trade regulation. Many lawyers rely heavily on practice manuals and on continuing legal education handbooks for most of their legal research. However, there are not many of these in the area of consumer protection. Lawyers in Milwaukee and Madison have access to relatively complete law libraries. Lawyers in other areas could travel to these cities to do research or hire a lawyer who practices there to do the work. But this is not practical if the potential recovery in a case is small. Even those in Milwaukee or Madison would have to leave their offices to use the libraries located there, and the time invested in doing this might be too much for a client who can pay only a modest fee.

Furthermore, consumer protection law is complex and involves many qualitative concepts, such as "reasonable" or "unconscionable." This uncertainty makes the law hard to apply; even an expert cannot be sure how a court would decide a particular case....

Apart from the nature of the law itself, consumers often face difficult burdens of proof under these laws. The buyer who wants to return the car, in our example, would have to establish that the car was defective when it was delivered or that the seller or manufacturer was in some way responsible for a defect that appeared later. This kind of evidentiary problem is faced often in products liability litigation where personal injury puts several hundred thousand dollars at issue, and there the matter usually is established by expert testimony.... However, experts are expensive, and one cannot afford to use them in the typical action arising under a consumer protection statute or regulation. One office offering legal services to the poor was able to use expert testimony in cases involving complaints about automobiles because it could call on a program which trained poor people to be automobile mechanics, but this kind of access to experts is rare.

We were told about a case where all of these difficulties were surmounted, and it can serve as an example of how rarely one might expect a consumer case to be taken as far as the complaint stage on the way toward litigation. A wealthy doctor ordered a $500,000 custom-made yacht from a boat yard. He refused to accept delivery, asserting that the boat was defective in many respects. He sued to recover his down payment, and also asked for a large sum as damages. His complaint reflected a high degree of creativity in the blending of traditional and newly developing contract and consumer protection theories. Only the wealthy can afford to pay for such creativity as well as the expert testimony that was called for. The example suggests that consumer protection law may most benefit an unintended population: the wealthy who can afford to pursue individual rights in dealing with the purchase of yachts and other luxury goods. The reformers may have aimed an inadequate weapon at the wrong target.

Problems of cost and difficulty in litigation have not gone completely unnoticed by those who draft consumer protection legislation. Some of these statutes seem based on the assumption that the individual rights they create will be reinforced by provisions for lawyers at low or no cost either as part of an antipoverty program or as a benefit of membership in a particular group.

Other statutes award attorneys' fees to consumers who win, and many of these newly created rights open the way for class action suits. Magnuson–Moss even makes a bow toward encouraging suppliers of consumer goods to set up informal arbitration schemes. All of these approaches may have had some effect, but neither singly or all together do they offer an adequate solution to the problems of cost and difficulty in consumer litigation. There are a number of reasons why this is so.

Low-cost or free legal service plans employ lawyers who are willing to deal with consumer problems. Legal Action for Wisconsin (LAW), a program to supply legal services to people with low incomes in Milwaukee and Madison, probably sees as many consumers as any group of nongovernmental lawyers in the state. However, LAW's services are limited and must be rationed carefully. LAW's attorneys may make a telephone call or write a letter seeking relief if either strategy looks appropriate but most often its lawyers refer clients to the consumer mediation service of the Department of Justice or to the Concerned Consumers' League, a private organization which trains low-income consumers to complain effectively or to use the Small Claims Court. Occasionally, LAW lawyers will make an appearance in the Small Claims Court on a consumer matter, but they try to avoid this so that they can devote their time to what they see as more important matters. Sometimes, the LAW lawyers will attempt to work out a complicated consumer financing problem that looms large in the life of a poor client, and they frequently attempt to use the federal Truth-in-Lending law or the Wisconsin Consumer Act to strike down a transaction. Sometimes they assert a highly technical defense based on these statutes as a surrogate for bankruptcy or to fight a breach-of-warranty claim. For example, it may be easier to find a clause in a form contract which violates statutory requirements than to prove that the goods were defective and that the seller is responsible for the defects. . . .

Members of a number of labor unions, condominiums, cooperatives, and student organizations are entitled to the benefit of legal services under various plans. However, under almost all plans the amount of service is limited and carefully defined. Usually a member is entitled to a specified number of telephone calls or office visits. If a legal problem warranting more service is discovered, the member can retain a plan lawyer at a reduced rate. The use of these plans by members with consumer disputes varies, but few lawyers working for plans see many of these matters.

Members of cooperatives and of primary and secondary school teachers' unions almost never bring consumer matters to the lawyers who serve those plans. Lawyers employed by these plans believe that members face few consumer disputes which they cannot resolve by their own actions. One lawyer reports that members of his plan tend to read *Consumer Reports*, to shop carefully both for price and the cost of financing, to be able to borrow from a credit union rather than paying high rates to a loan company or an automobile dealer, and to buy goods that would need servicing only from businesses likely to be able to provide it. In short, they are model consumers who need little legal advice. Another lawyer suggests that they are the type of people who are unwilling to admit it when they do make a bad purchase or allow themselves to be fooled or cheated. Those who deny they have problems also have little need for legal advice.

The members of the condominium group plans also bring few consumer protection problems directly to their lawyers. However, these lawyers attend condominium association meetings and often make presentations on how to avoid common consumer frauds and what to look for in consumer contracts. Before or after these meetings, individual members often ask for informal advice about consumer matters, and this may be the extent of the legal service needed by these condominium owners.

When we turn to student plans we see a very different picture. Students at several campuses of the University of Wisconsin are entitled to legal service, and many of them use these benefits. Typically, plan employees train the students to handle their own case before a small claims court or tell them how to invoke the complaint procedure of the state agency that mediates consumer complaints in the area in question. Students often prefer to assert their rights rather than compromise. Some students seem to delight in battling local landlords and merchants in whatever forum they can find. But students tend to have the time to devote to such battles, and landlords and retailers tend not to value student patronage enough to remedy complaints voluntarily. When a pattern of unfair practice by a particular retailer or landlord is discovered, the plan's lawyers attempt to find a general remedy for the students to prevent future abuses.

Members of plans that benefit industrial unions fall somewhere between cooperative members and the students in terms of using their services in the consumer area. Industrial union plans usually are framed so that the lawyers cannot get rich off them, and often have problems of overload. As a result, their services are strictly rationed. One firm which provides legal services to many union locals' plans will write letters to merchants or refer members with consumer complaints to a small claims court or the mediation service of a state agency, but little more. One of their attorneys says that he only writes letters and will not telephone sellers, because if he telephoned, he would have to listen to the seller's side of the story and there is never time to do this. This lawyer sees consumer matters as less important than the many other kinds of cases that plan members regularly bring to him. . . .

Some consumer protection statutes have followed the pattern set by civil rights acts and allowed successful consumers to recover reasonable attorneys' fees. One might expect this to be an incentive for lawyers to handle these matters. However, few lawyers know about the attorney's fee provisions in consumer protection statutes, and those who do know about them point out that these really are contingent fees because one must win the case in order to benefit. As a result, these statutes are unlikely to be very attractive in close cases, since they do not give lawyers the opportunity to win very large fees in some cases to offset the cases they lose, where they will have invested their time for no return. Furthermore, most statutes leave the amount of recovery to the discretion of the trial judge. Many trial judges do not like awarding bounties to lawyers who bring certain types of cases. These judges often will award fees at a rate far below that usually paid in the community for attorney's services. . . .

The economic barriers to claims made under consumer statutes might be overcome to some extent if many small claims could be aggregated into a class action. . . . However, this is not a technique suited to most consumer problems, which turn on the facts of individual cases and present no common problem to aggregate. Moreover, class actions are hard to manage successfully. . . .

There may be other important factors besides the economic ones we have discussed that make Wisconsin lawyers reluctant to take consumer cases, and that affect the way they handle the ones they do take. Some of the information gained in our interviews suggests that problems with an individual rights strategy in the consumer area would not be solved if these cases were made only a little more attractive economically. Many of the attorneys interviewed represent banks, lenders, local car dealers, or even the major automobile manufacturers when they are sued in local courts. These lawyers would face a pure conflict of interest if they were to take a consumer protection case against one of their regular clients.[14] Other lawyers have less direct but nonetheless important ties to the business community. Although these ties to a segment of that community may enable a lawyer to be more effective in working out reasonable settlements or at least gaining a gesture, an over-aggressive pursuit of a consumer claim might risk the goodwill of existing and potential clients or endanger a whole network of contacts. Even lawyers who would face no direct conflict of interest think it important to avoid offending business people unnecessarily. One lawyer in northern Wisconsin stressed that, "you can always get a merchant's name in the newspaper just by filing a complaint. However, this will make him bitter, and you will pay for it in the future." Lawyers' contacts are part of their stock in trade. They know, for example, where to get financing or who might want to invest in a business deal their client is interested in. Lawyers also often get clients through referrals and recommendations, and bankers and retailers frequently serve as experts who can tell others where to find a good lawyer. In short, most lawyers in private practice must work hard to become and stay members in good standing of the local business and political community if they are to prosper.

We cannot expect lawyers concerned with the reaction of business people to take a tough approach to solving consumer problems; they have too much to lose and little to gain. It is safer to refuse these cases or refer them to a

---

14. A conflict of interest problem does not always stop a lawyer from acting as a mediator. One lawyer told us that "in one case a customer came to the office, and he had a complaint against a store we represent. Clearly, the store should have made good on the matter, and so I called the store and told them to fix things up. They did without question, and the man left my office happy."

governmental agency which mediates consumer complaints against business. It is safer to call an influential business person to try to work out matters in a low-key conciliatory manner than to file complaints. If the lawyer handles the situation skillfully, a conciliatory approach can even gain the appreciation of the business person against whom the consumer is complaining. A dissatisfied customer can be transformed into a person with much less sense of grievance. Whether or not the consumer is persuaded that a conciliatory approach is the best one, considering the whole picture, the consumer's lawyer serves at least the short-run interest of the business complained against if the client is persuaded to drop the matter and go away.

The local legal community recognizes legitimate and not so legitimate ways of resolving problems. For example, most lawyers feel strongly that one should not escalate a simple dispute into full-scale warfare which will benefit neither the parties nor the lawyers. Lawyers interested in the good opinion of other members of the bar and bench will follow accepted, routine, and simple ways of dealing with consumer problems. Only when one is doing a public service by going after a fly-by-night company or some other disreputable firm is a tough adversary stance seen as appropriate. There is also a segment of the legal community that is hostile to consumer protection law and to those who assert their rights under them. They view business people at least local business people as honest and reasonable. While misunderstandings are always possible, these lawyers doubt that serious wrongs are ever committed by the local bank, automobile dealer, or appliance store. Consumers who complain often are seen as dead beats trying to escape honest debts or as cranks who are unwilling to accept a business' honest efforts to make things right. For example, one lawyer who practices in a large city states:

> Most of the fraud now is against the lenders. Debtors, especially the young kids, are wise to the tricks. They know that it costs money and takes time to get the wheels in motion, and it isn't worth the trouble if there isn't too much money involved. Recently a young woman bought a brand new car and financed it through a bank. She got a job delivering photographic film and put over 100,000 miles on that car within a year. Then when she was tired of making payments, she just left the car in the bank's parking lot and put the keys and all the papers into the night deposit slot with a note saying, "Here's your car back." What can the bank do realistically? They may be entitled to a deficiency judgment, but it is not worth the trouble to get it under the new laws. . . .

> The hallways outside small claims courts are crowded with little old people, crying because of the way young kids have screwed them out of several month's rent. . . . A judgment is just a piece of paper and the Wisconsin Consumer Act has made collection procedures so difficult that a judgment is almost worthless.

. . . [M]ost lawyers serve business interests or relatively well-off individuals who run businesses. Undoubtedly the quotations are accurate descriptions of some consumers whom lawyers encounter. On the other hand, some lawyers view the average consumer-client more positively. Another lawyer in the same small town as the two interviewed together says, "local people are being ripped off by local merchants every day.... Attorneys in town can't believe that these guys whose fathers went to the country club with their fathers could be dishonest. They consider these rip-offs just 'tough dealing.' But the local merchants have absolute power—people have to deal with them, and merchants just can't resist the temptation to use this power for all they're worth."

Many lawyers also have personal reasons for hostility to consumers and consumer protection laws. Lawyers are engaged in small businesses themselves. They may face problems when they try to collect fees from clients. They see and read about dissatisfied clients who have been bringing enough malpractice suits to drive up the malpractice insurance rates for all lawyers. Moreover, they themselves are unlikely to face serious consumer problems. Attorneys tend to be affluent enough and sufficiently well connected that the businesses they have personal dealings with will make efforts to keep them happy. Some lawyers make many major purchases from or through clients. Lawyers generally understand the consumer contracts that they sign....

As I have suggested, a lawyer who holds such a negative view of consumer laws and consumers who complain is likely to find wholly inappropriate an aggressive pursuit of the remedies granted by these laws. A number of attorneys suggested that a lawyer has an obligation to judge the true merit of a client's case and to use only reasonable means to solve problems. These lawyers seemed to be saying that an attorney should not aggressively assert good cases under ill-advised or unjust statutes, but no one went so far as to say this explicitly. A reasonable approach in the consumer area was seen as a compromise. For example, several attorneys were very critical of other members of the bar who had used the Wisconsin Consumer Act so that a lender who had violated what they saw as a "technical" requirement of the statute would not be paid for a car which the consumer would keep. While this might be the letter of the law, apparently a responsible lawyer would negotiate a settlement whereby the consumer would pay for the car but would pay less as a result of the lender's error. Several lawyers said that if a lawyer for a consumer offered an honest complaint about the quality of a product or service, it would be resolved in a manner that ought to satisfy anyone who was reasonable. A lawyer who sued in such a matter would be only trying to help a client illegitimately wiggle out of a contract after he or she had a change of heart about a purchase, particularly if the case was one a manufacturer or retailer could not afford to defend on the merits. A lawyer who represents Ford in actions brought in certain areas of Wisconsin commented, "The economics are not only a problem for consumers. How many $200 transmission cases can Ford defend in Small Claims Court? Lots of suits are bought out only because it is easier to buy them off than defend them. A lot of people forget that there are cost barriers to defending cases too. Ford cannot bring an expert from Detroit and pay me to defend product quality cases, and a lot of lawyers for plaintiffs know this and count on it when they file a complaint."

Those attorneys who often press consumer rights are called such things as members of the "rag-tag bar" who have no rating in Martindale–Hubbel and who ignore the economic realities of practice. An older lawyer comments that many younger lawyers are very consumer minded and seem to be "involved emotionally with clients when the word consumer comes up." One attorney who characterizes himself as an "establishment lawyer" explains that in Madison and Milwaukee there now are many lawyers who do not depend on practice for their total income or who live life styles in which they need far less than most people. He is particularly concerned about women lawyers who, he believes, live off their husbands' income and thus are freed to play games and crusade without recognizing the economic realities of practice. Still another attorney points out that consumer cases are often brought by young lawyers just beginning practice. Since they have few cases and want to gain experience, these beginners often refuse to accept reasonable settlements and file complaints. Similar objections are made to some legal services program lawyers who fail to go along with the customs of the bar about the range of reasonable settlements, and who are seen as far too aggressive in asserting questionable claims against established businesses. Some older "establishment" lawyers are annoyed by the mavericks, while others view the younger lawyers with amusement, predicting that they would learn what to do with such cases as they grew up.

Not all lawyers are tied to the local business and legal establishments. Yet even those lawyers who are not in the club face disincentives to using consumer lawyers. Of course, these lawyers are not free to treat every potential client who walks in from the street as the bearer of a major cause. They must ration their time among the worthwhile cases that come to them and balance their good works with enough paying clients so that they can meet payrolls and pay the rent and utility bills. Many who call themselves "movement" lawyers and who are engaged in representing various causes do not honor consumerism any more than do establishment lawyers. Consumer protection is viewed by many of these "progressive" lawyers as only a middle-class concern. It just is not as important as criminal defense of unpopular clients or battling local government authorities on behalf of migrant laborers. Even some who see themselves as radicals seem to have internalized many of the norms of capitalist society about paying debts and avoiding trouble by being careful at the outset of transactions. This attitude is reflected in the following comments of a person who regards himself as a progressive lawyer and who has represented a number of unpopular clients:

> You want to avoid filing complaints and trying consumer lawsuits. Partly this is economic, but we cannot overlook another important reason. What have you done when you win one of these cases? You have saved a guy a couple of bucks in a minor rip-off. It just isn't fun. It would be a boring hassle. If you win, the client gets only a marginal benefit, and he won't be grateful. So this kind of case will fall to the bottom of the pile

of things to do. There are many cases that are far more satisfying. We take consumer cases sometimes, but they are not the things we really enjoy.

You may feel funny about even negotiating consumer cases. A lawyer often can get his client something he is not really entitled to. For example, one client had a contract with a health club. There was nothing really wrong with it. The client was just tired of the club. We wrote a letter on our letterhead, and the club folded and let him out of the deal. This isn't the way the case should have come out, but it is the way it works. You do not get a great deal of satisfaction out of such a case, and you will try to avoid doing this sort of thing when you can.

... A number of lawyers report that many Wisconsin judges and their clerks are not sympathetic to an adversary handling of consumer protection laws. One lawyer explained that the local judges are all experienced lawyers who understand how such cases should be handled, and so he could end consumer cases without much difficulty by simple motions; the judges just were not going to let these cases go to juries or even to trial. Judges and clerks will see that their time is not wasted by cases which they think never should have been brought to them. Many judges will help consumers handling their own cases in a small claims court reach some kind of settlement, but if a consumer wants to try the case, some judges respond by applying the rules of procedure and evidence very technically so that they will not have to reach the merits. These lawyers tell stories about trial judges who refuse to enforce individual claims based on Wisconsin administrative regulations designed to protect consumers. The judges, it is said, seem to view these regulations as illegitimate enactments by liberal reformers in Madison who are out of touch with conditions in the rest of the state.

Judges are also likely to be unfamiliar with these regulations and with federal materials, and they may lack ready access to copies of these laws or to articles in law reviews explaining various provisions. A lawyer for a local retailer, it was reported, successfully defended a consumer case, in which his client had violated a state regulation, on the ground that the Wisconsin Administrative Code lacked a good index; the lawyer for the consumer had not played fairly when he raised a law with which lawyers in the community and the judge were not familiar. Another lawyer remarked that he would not use the Magnuson–Moss Warranty Act in a case brought in a state court, although this is just what the drafters of that act planned, because "as soon as you throw federal law at a state judge, they freak out since they have no familiarity with federal law. You would have to spend an hour and half convincing them that they had jurisdiction." Still another attorney commented "judges hate consumer cases because they simply do not understand the new law. The courts are just now getting used to the Uniform Commercial Code [the UCC became effective in Wisconsin in 1965]. If you try to use consumer laws, you are letting yourself in for a lot of briefing to educate the judges." One trial judge gained some measure of local fame among the bar by threatening to declare the Uniform Commercial Code's provisions on unconscionable contracts void for vagueness. Other trial judges, or their clerks, flatly tell lawyers that consumer cases just will not be tried in their courts. Of course, a lawyer who wanted the formal state or federal law to penetrate into a county in which such a judge sat would always be free to appeal, but the cost barriers placed before this route assure trial judges a large degree of freedom to do what they see as justice in the teeth of consumer protection laws which displease them.

Perhaps "atrocity stories" about judges are exaggerated, but insofar as they are repeated among lawyers, they are likely to affect the strategy any attorney will pursue. For example, few lawyers would look forward to arguing that a contract was "unconscionable" under Section 2–302 of the Uniform Commercial Code before the trial judge who was so unhappy about the open texture of this provision of the UCC. Young lawyers who have mastered the administrative regulations designed to protect consumers will learn to hesitate to display their wisdom before a trial judge who has never heard of such laws and who is unlikely to sympathize with their goals. Reformers and law professors often assume that laws published in the state capital automatically go into effect in all the county courthouses in the state. Experienced lawyers know better.

Lawyers for Business

In contrast to lawyers for individuals, attorneys for business play fairly traditional lawyer's roles when they deal with consumer law: they lobby, draft documents, plan procedures, and respond to particular disputes by negotiating and litigating. Indeed, our idea of what is a traditional lawyer's job may flow largely from what this part of the bar does for clients who can afford to pay for these services. . . . But even when we turn to business practice, the classical model of lawyering is only a rough approximation of what happens. This suggests that the amount of the potential fee is not the only factor prompting problems with the classical view. I will consider each of these traditional kinds of lawyer's work in the business setting, looking at what is done for clients, which lawyers do what kinds of work, and the degree of independent control exercised by lawyers in each instance.

Lawyers working for manufacturers, distributors, retailers and financial institutions are likely to be present at the creation of any law that purports to aid the consumer. . . .

Not surprisingly, the role of the lobbyist for business is a specialized one, usually played by a small number of lawyers from the larger firms in Milwaukee or Madison, or by lawyers employed by industry trade associations. Smaller businesses seldom hire lobbyists. They rely on being represented by larger businesses or trade associations, or they contact their representatives in the legislature directly. Often legislators who are lawyers find themselves representing home-town businesses before state agencies as a matter of constituent service. . . .

In order to gain concessions from those pushing consumer protection, business has to give something. These lawyer-lobbyists make judgments about which regulations are reasonable, acceptable or inevitable, and then try to sell this view to their clients. Only a few lawyer-lobbyists have the power to make decisions without consulting their clients, and some clients will not accept their lawyers' opinions about what is reasonable and what is not. Nonetheless, the lawyers generally have great influence on the decisions about which laws must be accepted and which ones can be fought. One reason for this is that often they control much of the information necessary for making such judgments. For example, to a great extent they are the experts both about the political situation facing the agencies and legislators and about the intensity of commitment to a particular proposal of those who speak for consumers.

After consumer laws and regulations are passed, business lawyers help their clients cope with them. Much of the work involves drafting documents and setting up procedures for using these forms. For example, both the federal Truth-in-Lending Law and the Wisconsin Consumer Act required a complete reworking of most of the form contracts used to lend money and sell on credit. The Magnuson–Moss Warranty Act demanded that almost every manufacturer, distributor and retailer selling consumer products rewrite any warranty given with the product and create new procedures to make information about these warranties available to consumers. This is traditional lawyers' work, requiring a command of the needs of the business, a detailed understanding of the law, and drafting skills. Moreover, the uncertainties and complexities of many consumer protection laws call for talented lawyering if the job is to be done right.

Counseling business clients about consumer protection laws and drafting the required contracts and forms is the stock-in-trade of the largest firms in the state and a small group of lawyers with a predominantly business practice; some of this work is also done by the inside legal staff of some large corporations. Some of this work can be mass-produced by lawyers for trade associations. Many lenders, retailers, and suppliers of services in smaller cities rely on standard forms supplied by these trade associations. Small manufacturers and financial institutions may send problems concerning consumer protection laws to lawyers in Milwaukee or Madison, either directly or through a referral by their local attorney. There is also a "trickle-down" effect: lawyers who are not expert in consumer law often collect copies of the work product of the more expert, receiving them from clients who get them from trade associations or through friends who work for the larger law firms. They may simply copy these forms or they may produce variations on them but with little or no independent research.

Several lawyers commented that the flood of regulation of the past ten years has made it hard for a smaller law firm or a solo lawyer to keep up with all the new law and to maintain the resources needed to advise business. Some do very well for their business clients, but it is difficult for younger lawyers to gain all the needed knowledge quickly. Lawyers who represent business must be ready to alert their clients to changes in the law which require review of the way business is done. These lawyers usually have their own copies of the federal and state administrative regulations as well as the expensive loose-leaf services necessary to keep up to date. Large law firms and corporations with house counsel can afford to have someone in their office specialize in the various consumer laws. They can send them to continuing legal education programs put on at the state or national level. Indeed, many of these law firms face the problem of coordinating their large staff so that all of their lawyers will recognize a problem of, say, the Truth-in-Lending Act and then call on the resident expert in the area. A consumer law specialist in a large law firm often can call on people working for the various agencies for informal advice about how the agency is likely to respond to particular procedures or provisions in form contracts. Of course, any lawyer can call on the agency, but often these specialists from the large firms will know the administrative officials from previous contacts or from participating in continuing legal education programs.

Some of the lawyers who have been involved in this redrafting of forms and fashioning of new procedures saw the task as one of making the least real change possible in traditional practices while complying with the new laws or regulations. They designed new forms to ward off both what they saw as the unreasonable governmental official and the unreasonable consumer in the unlikely event that the matter ever came close to going to formal proceedings before agencies or courts. Other business lawyers, however, used the redrafting exercise as a means to press their clients to review procedures and teach their employees about dispute avoidance and its importance. In some cases the lawyer's views significantly influenced the client's response to a new law. For example, many business people are proud of their product and service and want to give broad warranties, but their lawyers usually convince them that this is too risky. The Magnuson–Moss Warranty Act attempts to induce manufacturers of consumer products to create informal private processes for mediating disputes. At least some business people have expressed interest in taking such steps to avoid litigation and in experimenting with new procedures for dealing with complaints by consumers. However, lawyers, in at least two of the largest firms in Wisconsin strongly advise their clients to avoid creating private dispute resolution processes. These lawyers see the benefits as unlikely to be worth the risks, and they are in the position to have the final word with many clients about such matters. This is an area about which lawyers are supposed to be expert; a business person who has paid for an expert opinion is likely to listen to it.

Finally, business lawyers do become directly involved in the process of settling particular disputes when attempts to avoid or otherwise deal with them have failed; lawyers in the largest firms seldom have to help ward off individual consumers, but some lawyers for business regularly are involved in particular cases. For example, lawyers represent banks and other creditors in collections work. At one time this was a routine procedure that yielded a default judgment and made clear the creditor's right to any property involved. However, many of the traditional tactics of debt collection have been ruled out of bounds or are now closely regulated by state and federal laws. Lawyers who do collections work describe what seems to them to be a new legal ritual to be followed whenever a debtor who is armed with legal advice resists a collection effort. The lender first attempts to collect by its own efforts, and then it files suit, often in a small claims court. The debtor responds, asserting that something was wrong with the credit transaction under the Truth-in-Lending Act or the Wisconsin Consumer Act, or by asserting that the creditor engaged in "conduct which can reasonably be expected to threaten or harass the customer ..." or used "threatening language in communication with the customer ..." as is prohibited and sanctioned by the Wisconsin Consumer Act (Wis. Stat. 427.104[g], [h] [1975]). The lender then has to respond, either by offering to settle or by claiming to be ready to litigate the legal issues. Then the lawyers on both sides negotiate and, occasionally, battle before a judge.

Large retailers who sell relatively expensive products or services face a regular flow of consumer complaints. Almost all of them are resolved without the participation of lawyers, but an attorney may have to enter the picture occasionally. This may not happen until the consumer files a complaint in court. Often the business lawyer will be facing an unrepresented consumer in a small claims court. Several of these lawyers commented that the consumer was only formally unrepresented since the judge often seemed to serve both as judge and attorney for the plaintiff, particularly in pre-trial settlement negotiations. These are expensive cases for a business to defend if the consumer gets a chance to present the merits of the claim to the court. One law firm in Madison represents one of the largest automobile manufacturers in such matters, but it sees only three of four such cases a year. Interestingly, these cases almost never involve an application of the many consumer protection laws or even the Uniform Commercial Code; the real issue is almost always one of fact concerning whether the product or service was defective. The law firm's recommendation about whether to settle is almost always final. Their recommendation will be rejected only where the manufacturer wants to defend a particular model of its automobiles against a series of charges that the model has a particular defect; the manufacturer may be far more worried about a government order to recall that model than a particular buyer's claim.

Another situation that brings out lawyers is the consumer complaint that prompts a state agency to begin a regulatory enforcement action. Typically, a business lawyer will try to settle rather than litigate this kind of case, but, of course, the possibility of formal action affects the bargaining by both sides. Here, too, the lawyer has great influence on the client's decision about whether to settle or fight. The lawyer's advice is likely to involve a mixture of predictions about the practical consequences of the proposed settlement, the outcome of a formal enforcement proceeding, and the risks of adverse publicity if the matter goes to a public forum.

It should be stressed that most of these lawyers for business do not see themselves as hired guns doing only their clients' bidding. However, most of our sample viewed their clients as responsible people trying to do the right thing. Members of the elite of the bar seldom see any "but the most reasonable business people," at least when it comes to consumer problems. Of course, it is not surprising that these lawyers tend to see their clients as reasonable people, since the lawyers are likely to hold the same values as the clients. Business lawyers concede that consumer protection laws make more work for them, and thus increase their billings, but they also see their clients as being swamped by governmental regulation and paperwork which serves little purpose. They are unhappy because they cannot explain these laws to their clients in common sense terms. Some business lawyers are concerned about easy credit practices and how simple it is for consumers to evade debts when they become burdensome. They worry that the importance of keeping promises and paying one's debts is being undermined by reforms directed at problems which politicians invented. Several remarked that when they left law school, they were strongly in favor of consumer protection, but after a few years in practice, they see matters differently. In short, as we might expect, Wisconsin business lawyers are not radicals and are comfortable representing business interests.

At the same time, some business lawyers concede that occasionally they must persuade their clients to change practices or to respond to a particular dispute in what the lawyers see as a reasonable manner. For example, these lawyers may tell their clients that they must appear to be fair when they are before an agency in order to have any chance of winning in this era of consumer protection. In this way, they may be able to legitimate sitting in judgment on the behavior of their clients and occasionally manipulating the situation to influence clients' choices.

A few of the lawyers we interviewed reported having to act to protect their own self-interest when dealing with a business client. One prominent lawyer, for example, described a case where he represented an out-of-state book club in a proceeding before one of the state regulatory agencies; he took the case only as a favor to a friend who had some indirect connection with the club's officers. As the case unfolded, the lawyer discovered that the book club had failed to send books to many people who had paid for them. It was not clear whether the situation involved fraud or merely bad business practices. The lawyer insisted that the book club immediately get books or refunds to all of its Wisconsin customers and sign a settlement agreement with the agency which bound the club to strict requirements for future behavior. The attorney explained that the business had been trading on his reputation as a lawyer when it got him to enter the case on its behalf. Once it became clear that the administrative agency had a good case against the client involving conduct at least on the borders of fraud, the lawyer felt that the client was obligated to help him maintain his reputation as an attorney who represented only the most ethical businesses.

III. DISCUSSION

In this section I will try to integrate the findings of this study into a broader picture of the practice of law, with some special attention to a question central to other recent research on the legal profession: are lawyers agents of social control or are they so tied to their clients as to lack the professional autonomy so often ascribed to them?

A descriptive model of practice would accept much of the classical view as a starting point. Traditionally, we have emphasized lawyers being involved in certain transformations: clients bring problems to lawyers who, in Cain's terms,[15] "translate [issues] into a meta-language in terms of which a binding solution can be found." For example, lawyers translate client desires to transfer property to others into such legal forms as declarations of trust, deeds, and wills. Lawyers try to convert some of the many factors involved in an automobile accident into a winning cause of action for negligence. Indeed, ... it is the lawyer's authority over this meta-language which gives the profession much of its status and market control; one goes to law school to master it in order to enter the profession, and entry usually is gained by passing a bar examination where that mastery can be displayed.

However, even when clients come to lawyers for relatively defined services such as drafting a will or a contract, the lawyers' work may involve often overlooked interactions whereby lawyers influence the outcome, and these interactions also must be part of our sketch of practice. For example, some may hesitate to ask for certain provisions in their will if they fear even implicit disapproval by a lawyer who, with his gray hair, three-piece suit, and symbols of membership in the legal profession, may be seen to represent conventional morality. The lawyer, also, may ask questions necessary for counseling or drafting which force the client to consider possible consequences and make choices that he or she has not foreseen or has avoided thinking about. The lawyer may tell a client that the law blocks taking certain action, but sometimes an attorney can suggest other ways of achieving at least some of the client's purposes. Just by explaining the requirement for a cause of action in negligence, the lawyer can affect the client's memory, or willingness to lie, and thus affect the outcome.

If our model is to have a wider focus, we will have to recognize other translations and transformations which only indirectly involve legal rules but which often take place in interactions between attorneys, clients, opponents, and legal officials. As I have pointed out in this article, lawyers play many roles in these interactions, including the gatekeeper who teaches clients about the costs of using the legal system, the knowledgeable friend or therapist, the broker of information or coach, the go-between or informal mediator, the legal technician, and the adversary bargainer-litigator. In playing these roles, lawyers often have to transform their clients' perception of the problem and their goals. Sometimes clients do come to lawyers seeking fairly specific services—a client may want to make a will, to convey property, or gain a license to run a television station. However, the lawyer is often involved in transforming both the client's perception of the problem and the goals.

15. The reference is to Maureen Cain, "The General Practice Lawyer and the Client: Towards a Radical Conception," 7 *Internation-* *al Journal of the Sociology of Law* 331 (1979). [Eds. note].

Sometimes the lawyer will turn away a client, saying that (1) the client has no case legally, (2) it is against the client's best interest to pursue the matter as the costs will exceed the likely benefits, (3) the client is unreasonable to complain or seek certain ends as judged by standards other than the law, or (4) some mixture of these arguments. On the other hand, the lawyer may seek . . . to redefine a conflict of value into a conflict of interest which can be settled by payment of a reasonable amount of money rather than by a public declaration of right and wrong.

And the lawyer may be involved in transforming the views of the opponent about both the client and the situation so that an acceptable settlement will be forthcoming. Sometimes lawyers use their status as experts in the law, legal arguments, and express or implied threats of legal action in this process of persuasion. Often, however, a legal style of argument fades into the background. The attorney may not be too sure about the precise legal situation or may worry about seeming to coerce the other party. In such situations lawyers are likely to appeal to some mixture of the interest of the opponent and to standards of reasonableness apart from claims of legal right. Then, as I have stressed, if there is a settlement offer, the lawyer must sell it to the client, and here again appeals are likely to be made primarily in terms of reasonableness or interest rather than right.

The research reported here shows lawyers for individuals playing these nonadversary roles without great knowledge of the contours of consumer law, while the lawyers for corporations act more traditional parts—lobbying, counseling, drafting documents, and defending cases after complaints are filed. However, lawyers for corporations are at least occasionally pushed out of the character of legal technician. For example, a lawyer for one of the nation's largest law firms, who has an extensive corporate practice, sees himself as engaged in "the lay practice of psychiatry." He explains that a manager of a large corporation often is worried about making a decision, but he or she has few people with whom to talk openly. Others in the corporation tend to be rivals; psychiatric help is unthinkable as it would indicate weakness. However, it is legitimate to see an attorney seeking legal advice. Often this lawyer finds himself asking questions which lead the manager to see the options and their likely costs and benefits. The questions are justified as necessary in the process of giving legal advice; their actual function, the lawyer says, is a very directive short-term therapy. Sometimes he does not need to ask many questions, because it is enough to serve as an audience while the manager thinks aloud. Another lawyer engaged in corporate commercial litigation sees lawyers as curbing the influence of ego and pride on the part of business executives in dispute resolution. . . .

An evaluation of what I have discovered about lawyers in the consumer protection area suggests a number of things about the strategy of creating individual rights to bring about social change. On the positive side, one might view the practices of the lawyers I studied as yielding a kind of rough justice. Lawyers for business, prompted by federal and state statutes and regulations, work hard to help their clients comply with the disclosure requirements that have been demanded. . . .

Lawyers for individuals have guarded an expensive social institution—the legal system—from overload by relatively minor complaints. Consumers who are dissatisfied with such things as warped phonograph records, defective hair dryers, or inoperative instant cameras can return them to the seller. Almost always, the seller will replace them or offer a refund if they cannot be fixed. If the seller refuses, the buyer can shop elsewhere next time, and the buyer has an "atrocity story" with which to entertain friends which, in turn, may affect the seller's reputation. In short, many problems can be left to the market. At the other extreme, consumers who have suffered serious personal injuries as the result of defective products usually can find a lawyer to pursue their case aggressively, since the growing law of products liability offers generous remedies which will support contingent fees. Moreover, products liability and government-ordered product recalls together give manufacturers a great incentive to pay attention to quality control and avoid problems.

It is necessary to sort out claims falling between these poles. Defects in new automobiles and mobile homes, for example, often warrant buying at least a little of a lawyer's time, especially when manufacturers and sellers fail to remedy the problem after a customer makes a complaint. But a full-scale war using elaborate legal research and expert testimony usually would be a waste of resources. A telephone call or a letter from a lawyer may be all the effort the claim is worth. If all clients with cases supporting substantial fees had to subsidize cases involving only small sums, then lawyers might buy all of the necessary law books and learn all the details of consumer law, but this might price legal services out of the reach of some who now can afford them. Alternatively, lawyers could be subsidized by governments to master consumer laws and litigate, but many citizens would see better uses for tax revenues.

Also on the positive side, those lawyers who are willing to do something for clients with a consumer case may be defending the values of social integration and harmony. In Laura Nader's[16] phrase, they are seeking "to make the balance" by restoring personal relations to equilibrium through compromise. They do this by clearing up misunderstandings and promoting reasonableness on both sides, avoiding vendettas aimed at hurting the opponent. They offer their clients their status and contacts but rarely an expensive-to-acquire legal knowledge which allow them to reach the person who has power to apologize, to offer a token gesture, or to make a real offer of settlement. The fact that a manager or owner accepts the blame and apologizes may be as effective in placating the client as a recovery of money. The real grievance may rest on a sense of being taken, insulted, or treated impersonally. Lawyers can help their clients see themselves not as victims but as people with minor complaints; they can help them get on with the business

16. The reference is to Laura Nader, "Styles of Court Procedure: To Make the Bal- ance," in L. Nader (ed.), *Law in Culture and Society* (1969). [Eds. note].

of living rather than allowing a $200 to $300 problem to become the focus of their lives. . . .

Rather than pour gasoline on the fire of indignation in members of a "self-centered, demanding, dissatisfied population which has grudges," almost all of the lawyers interviewed in this study seem far more likely to use some type of fire extinguisher. Even lawyers who see themselves as progressive and those who work for group legal service plans try to push aside potential clients whom they judge to be "crazy," to want something for nothing, or to be acting in bad faith.

It would be difficult deliberately to plan and create a system such as the one I have described. Perhaps it could only have arisen in response to laws that created a number of individual rights which could not be fully exercised. By relying on lawyers as gatekeepers, we get enough threat of trouble to prompt apologies, gestures, and settlements which are acceptable, but not enough litigation to burden legal or commercial institutions. We avoid having to reach complete agreement on the precise boundaries of the appropriate norms governing a manufacturer's and seller's responsibility for quality defects and for misleading buyers short of absolute deliberate fraud. We avoid having to live with inappropriate norms which might result from the confrontation of interest groups in the legislative and administrative processes. We avoid having to resolve difficult questions of fact concerning the seller's responsibility for the buyer's expectations and for the condition of the goods— questions which often cannot be resolved in a satisfactory manner. Finally, we offer some deterrence to consumers who want to defraud sellers or creditors or to those who are eager to get something for nothing.

On the negative side, one could highlight the unequal access consumers have to remedies, despite the merits of their cases. Some do not see lawyers at all, but we cannot be sure that their complaints lack merit or are trivial or that they are resolved in some other manner. Those few who do seek legal services will get only what the lawyer sees as appropriate, some will get turned away with little more than token gestures, while a very few will recover their full statutory remedies through legal action. . . .

Arguably, whether or not a claim is trivial or significant does not turn on whether there is enough at stake to support a substantial legal fee. For example, in this era of inflation, perhaps, the $400 many spent to replace four defective "Firestone 500" steel-belted radial tires would have seemed trivial to successful lawyers, or many consumers would have thought that to be the case. Nonetheless, the amount was not trivial to many of those faced with this problem. . . .

Conciliatory settlements may subvert the purposes of consumer protection law because they can shield socially harmful practices from effective scrutiny by the public or some legal agency. . . . The conciliatory tactics favored by lawyers may block the market correction called for by consumer protection legislation and prevent public awareness that the markets are not being corrected.

We can ask whether we should be satisfied to delegate the power of deciding which claims will be asserted, and to what extent, to individual lawyers who are typically white, middle-class males well integrated into their communities. . . .

Lawyers who play "counsel for the situation" may leave the rest of us a little uneasy. What qualifies these lawyers as experts in problem solving? Certainly this was not the approach of their law school training, and we can wonder if their professional experiences have produced wisdom in finding good solutions to such problems as are involved in women's rights, consumer protection, racial discrimination, or environmental protection. In short, there is a problem of legitimacy. As is true in the case of so many empirical studies related to law, once again we have stumbled on the problem of discretion and the expert whose skill rests on experience rather than on training and science. And a counsel for the situation has little accountability to much beyond his or her own conscience.

The mystification involved in the gap between the classical picture of the lawyer's role and the portrait painted here also may be objectionable. Clients may find themselves manipulated and fooled. Few clients probably go to lawyers seeking to have their situations redefined or their problems solved by apologies and token gestures. At least some clients do not want a "counsel for the situation" but a lawyer who will take their side. The settlement worked out after a five-minute telephone call may be the best possible in light of the lawyer's and the business' interest, and an objective observer might be able to defend it as serving some social interest. But do clients know how their interests regularly are offset by all of the others involved? If they knew, would they accept the situation?

Conciliatory strategies require little investment of professional time as compared to more adversarial ones. Mediation does not require much knowledge of consumer law, and a lawyer can negotiate a settlement based on rules of thumb rather than hard legal research. However, lawyers get an exclusive license to practice because they are supposed to be expert in the law. . . . Many who have never seen the inside of a law school might be better conciliators than lawyers, since legal education does little to train students for this part of practice, but non-lawyers are not given the privilege of representing clients. In theory, lawyers are qualified to negotiate and mediate because they assess the legal position and work from this as a baseline. Lawyers who know almost nothing about consumer law are operating from a different baseline. . . . [A]n official of the Federal Trade Commission who was concerned about the failure of the Magnuson–Moss Warranty Act, condemned Wisconsin lawyers who were not fully acquainted with that statute two years after it had become effective as being guilty of serious malpractice. He thought that perhaps a malpractice action or two might wake up the Wisconsin bar. Several lawyers interviewed in this study commented that many lawyers do not know enough consumer law to recognize that it offers a good legal theory and that if they did see this, it might change the course of their negotiations.

But it seems unfair to blame lawyers who almost never see a consumer case involving more than a few hundred dollars for not mastering a complicated and extensive body of law and for not purchasing expensive loose-leaf services to keep up to date. While, perhaps, we can ask lawyers to do some charity work, they cannot provide reasonably priced services for every case that comes in the door. There is no way that any lawyer can know much about all branches of the law; lawyers naturally become expert in the areas they see regularly.

The lawyers studied seem to be responding predictably to the social and economic structures in which the practice of law is embedded. Liberal reforms such as consumer protection laws create individual rights without providing the means to carry them out. Grand declarations of rights may be personally rewarding to those who struggle for legislative and appellate victories, but, in practice, justice is rationed by cost barriers and the lawyer's long-range interests. Even lawyers working for lower-income clients must pick and choose how much of their time and stock of goodwill to risk investing in a particular case.

We could see most of the individual rights created by consumer protection laws, as well as many other reforms of recent times, as primarily exercises in symbolism. The reformers gained the pretty words in the statute books and some indirect impact, but the practice of those to be regulated was affected only marginally.... Of course, it is possible that as time passes, lawyers will become more and more aware of at least some reform laws. It may take a generation or two for some of them to penetrate into day-to-day practice. Perhaps as new forms of delivering legal services develop and old areas of practice are reformed out of existence, lawyers will turn to some of these new reforms as an unmined resource and find ways to make exploitation commercially feasible. Nonetheless, if awareness of a more empirically accurate view of legal practice is not developed, reformers are likely to go on creating individual rights which have little chance of being vindicated, and, as a result, they may fail to achieve their ends repeatedly. And a gap between the promise of the law and its implementation may have consequences for the society.

A kind of classic response to the empirical picture of professional practice that I have drawn is to call for a return to the adversary model with, perhaps, some additional legal services supported as a government or group benefit and with new institutions for dispute resolution, such as neighborhood justice centers. Whatever the merit of any of these new measures and the philosophically comforting virtues of such proposals, the issues raised by the empirical sketch I have drawn are not likely to go away so easily....

Apart from mediating and acting as counsel for the situation, this study seeks to add to the classical model of practice the idea that the lawyer's own interests and values play an important role whatever the ideal of service asserted in professional theory....

It is probably the case that if a new reform law can be seen as likely to yield substantial fees, some lawyers will gear their practice toward clients who want to bring such cases.... [P]ersonal injury practice has relatively low prestige among the attorneys ... Nonetheless, the development of the doctrines of products liability during the 1960s prompted many lawyers to become specialists in the area—contingent fees, a good chance to win high verdicts and settlements, and real advantages from specialization have produced a recognizable segment of the bar. Moreover, causes such as civil rights may draw the attention of organizations such as the NAACP which will provide the lawyers. But if one has neither an organized cause nor the chance of a real monetary payoff, reforms resting on individual rights are likely to produce no more than the conciliatory gestures reported by this study. In such situations, the inability to mobilize needed legal services may be a form of social control blunting the impact of efforts at reform through law....

Undercutting the conventional picture of practice may have costs. Law, as is the case with many professions, justifies its position by the mastery of a special body of knowledge, and this mastery is produced by training and certified by examinations. Law school and bar examinations deal with the rule of law and not deals reflecting cost-benefit calculations and the emotions of clients. This view may help give or defend a measure of status and wealth for those who learn the law so that some will be induced to try to master it. And it may be useful in our kind of society to have a group of people capable of calling governmental, corporate and private power to account by legal standards. The theory of the adversary system may offer unpopular or powerless people some degree of protection from bias or a politically expedient solution to the problem they present to the powerful. This theory is a major part of the reason why our government provides some amount of legal service to those accused of a crime when they cannot afford their own lawyer. It is a major part of the rationalization that a lawyer for an unpopular client can offer in an attempt to ward off pressures against causing difficulties by vigorous advocacy. The ideal of disinterested service to clients may draw some people into the profession and offer nonpecuniary rewards to lawyers so that more of this kind of service exists than it would in a system where the single-minded pursuit of self-interest was recognized as fully legitimate.

Of course, this argument rests on untested empirical assumptions. We do not know whether these normative ideals have enough influence on behavior to be worthy of concern. It may be that the classical view has had little importance beyond making lawyers who do little public service feel bad on occasion. However, the empirical assumptions are only untested. They have not been disproved, and the argument is plausible enough for attention. Nonetheless, many of the nonadversary roles played by lawyers also seem to have some social value—experts in coping with the claims of other individuals, corporations or the government by using all available tools including, but not limited to, legal rules can offer useful help to citizens. Perhaps the classical position does serve as a golden lie (Plato, *The Republic*, Book III), misleading both lawyers and the public for a good purpose. Yet it has costs, particularly as more and more people discover that lawyers' behavior so often fails to conform to the model. There seems, moreover, no reason to assume without even making an attempt that we cannot rationalize when a lawyer can be expected to refuse a case, to mediate and play counsel for the situation and when to vindicate rights. Perhaps no ideological statement ever can be without flaw, but the classical picture of the practice seems to fit the legal profession of the 1980s so poorly as to be embarrassing.

NOTES AND QUESTIONS

1. Macaulay describes several strategies a lawyer might following when faced with a consumer protection case. How far can you generalize his findings? Are there analogies in family law practice? torts practice? criminal practice? Would many corporate lawyers serve as gatekeepers or coaches to their clients, as Macaulay uses these terms? If not, why not? When would what kinds of lawyers be most free to reject a potential client or refuse to carry out the wishes of an existing client?

Individuals who have suffered personal injuries today often seek help from a member of the personal injury bar. Frequently, the client pays nothing or a relatively small amount unless the lawyer produces a victory. For a study of the growth of this specialized part of the profession, see Sara Parikh and Bryant Garth, "Philip Corboy and the Construction of the Plaintiffs' Personal Injury Bar," 30 *Law & Social Inquiry* 269 (2005)("Mr. Corboy and his peers constructed a thriving subprofession that is characterized by a unique blend of working-class ideology, trial craft, professional bar leadership, Democratic politics, local philanthropy, and a market referral system—all of which reinforce the dominance and prestige of its own elite"). Herbert M. Kritzer, "Contingent–Fee Lawyers and Their Clients: Settlement Expectations, Settlement Realities, and the Issues of Control in the Lawyer–Client Relationship," 28 *Law & Social Inquiry* 795 (1998), argues that contingent fee lawyers have constant concern about the impact of what they do on future clients, and this may conflict with the interests of a present client. Herbert M. Kritzer, William L.F. Felstiner, Austin Sarat and David M. Trubek, "The Impact of Fee Arrangement on Lawyer Effort," 19 *Law & Society Review* 251 (1985), report that lawyers working on a contingent fee spend less time than hourly fee lawyers on cases with stakes of $6,000 or less. However, contingent fee lawyers may spend more time than hourly fee lawyers on larger cases where the potential payoff to them is very large. Herbert M. Kritzer, *The Justice Broker* 90, 168, 168–176 (1990), argues that rather than acting as a professional, lawyers in ordinary civil matters typically act more as brokers. A professional uses the kind of knowledge associated with a formal academic program; a broker uses insider knowledge associated with working in a setting day-in and day-out. He says:

> Some kinds of cases, particularly in the federal courts, draw very heavily on the formal legal skills (e.g., legal research and analysis) around which legal education is centered, and it is clear that for those areas the lawyer as portrayed by the professional image makes the most sense. However, in the most typical areas of ordinary litigation, torts and contracts, the

lawyer must draw much more heavily on the informal, insider kinds of legal skills than on the formal skills.

Kritzer argues that people other than lawyers could handle much of the ordinary disputes. There is little in a lawyer's training that gives her an advantage in developing contacts with insiders, bargaining and convincing clients to accept solutions to their problems which their broker has worked out with the other party. Would you expect most lawyers in small towns and medium-size cities to agree? What might they say in response to Kritzer? See, generally, Herbert M. Kritzer, *Risks, Reputations, and Rewards: Contingency Fee Legal Practice in the United States* (2004). Gillian K. Hadfield, "The Price of Law: How the Market for Lawyers Distorts the Justice System," 98 *Michigan Law Review* 953 (2000), questions the price of all legal services because of barriers to entry, limits on the unauthorized practice of law and the like. Jennifer B. Lee, "Dot–Com, Esq.: Legal Guidance, Lawyer Optional," *N.Y. Times*, February 22, 2001, at G1, reports that several web sites have offered legal services. "On the Internet, consumers can bury themselves in research, search for lawyers, chat with lawyers and get the papers to initiate a simple legal proceeding like a divorce, often at little or no cost." See, also, Michael Orey, "Seeking Clients, Lawyers Find Them on the Net," *Wall Street Journal*, June 16, 2000, at B1 ("Skeptics of the plaintiffs' bar might call this development online ambulance chasing.").

2. Macaulay stresses that we must avoid the assumption that the interests of lawyer and client are identical. Lawyers are not simply agents of their clients. To what extent would you expect lawyers, in transactions involving major corporate clients, to act in self-interested ways that are not necessarily what the clients might want or need? Contrariwise, to what extent would you expect a major corporate client to be able to bend a large law firm to its will, and bring about behavior that is not necessarily in the firm's self-interest? And what motives and incentives do you think would influence the work of in-house counsel?

Roman Tomasic, an Australian sociologist of law, considers similar issues in his "Defining Acceptable Tax Conduct: The Role of Professional Advisers in Tax Compliance," *Centre for National Corporate Law Research, Discussion Paper No 2/1990.* Tax practitioners—both lawyers and accountants—in Australia protect their firms. They note that they are in business for the long-run. When clients appear with unrealistic expectations about avoiding taxes, the practitioner must teach the client to be realistic. Advisors talk about being unpaid agents for the Australian Tax Office (ATO).

However, Tomasic notes:

In the hard light of practice reality the temptation and pressure to cut corners can be very great for the smaller practitioner. Many small to medium firms have little desire to come to the attention of the ATO even though they are probably less able to resist client pressure than are the larger firms. The smaller firms tend to deal directly with the owners of small businesses and they are likely to be placed under greater pressure than are the larger firms. The corporate clients of larger firms tend to be represented by an employee who, inevitably, has less financial stake in the result of the tax advice given by the larger firm than will the owner of the smaller business. (p. 18).

3. Macaulay's essay reminds us that the problem of communicating the law is one which the legal system constantly faces. Often lawyers perform the function of communicating the law to clients. A lawyer who is an expert on personal injuries, divorce or tax law, may be able to perform this function quite well with regard to her special field. But beyond this, these lawyers might lack practical knowledge of other branches of law, and they may not have access to the relevant legal materials. Thus, they may fail to serve as efficient channels of communication.

4. Austin Sarat and Susan Silbey, "The Pull of the Policy Audience," 10 *Law & Policy* 97 (1988), criticize Macaulay's article. Their article attacks much of the work of the law and society movement. They consider this work too respectful of the status quo, too geared to the audience of policy-makers, and too meekly reformist. They use Macaulay's article as an example of an essay animated by ideas of "liberal reform," which does not go far enough to penetrate to the roots of problems in American society.

They concede that the article does expose the ways in which law practice maintains a "facade of responsiveness despite the systematic denial of remedy." But they say that, for Macaulay, the essential problem is "[a]wareness, or lack of awareness," rather than "the fundamental contradictions" of the social situation. According to Macaulay, they say, law reform failed because of a "problem of perception not intention ... consumer protection is no longer seen as a rationalization of fundamentally inequitable market relations ... [which is Sarat and Silbey's view]. They fault Macaulay for thinking that the difficulty lies not in the fundamental goal of the overall system, but simply the "means chosen to achieve consumer protection."

Do you agree with Sarat and Silbey? How might you defend Macaulay's work against Sarat and Silbey's attack? Or is their criticism well taken? Could we explain the conflicting positions by seeing Macaulay as far more pessimistic about the possibilities of major social change while Sarat and Silbey are more romantic and utopian? Consider, particularly, the last two paragraphs of Macaulay's article.

(5.15) Law and Strategy in The Divorce Lawyer's Office

Austin Sarat and William L. F. Felstiner

20 *Law & Society Review* 93 (1986).

I. INTRODUCTION

Traditionally, the sociology of the legal profession has portrayed lawyers as important intermediaries between clients and the legal system ... [M]any more people see lawyers than have direct contact with formal legal institutions. Lawyers serve clients as important sources of information about legal rights, help clients relate legal rules to individual problems, and introduce clients to the way the legal process works. The information provided by lawyers shapes in large measure citizens' views of the legal order and their understanding of the relevance, responsiveness, and reliability of legal institutions. What lawyers say to their clients is not necessarily derived from statutes, rules, and cases and does not involve a literal translation of legal doctrine, nor could the legal system as it is presented in the lawyer's office be understood by clients from untutored observation.

More is at stake, however, in the interaction between lawyers and clients than a unidirectional movement of information and advice from lawyer to client. In addition, this interaction provides one important setting where law and society meet and where legal norms and folk norms come together to shape responses to grievances, injuries, and problems. In some instances those worlds may be complementary; in others there may be little fit between them.

Despite the importance of the discourse between lawyers and their clients, we know very little about what actually goes on in the lawyer's office. Our understanding of lawyer-client interaction has a very shallow basis in systematic empirical research. Legal sociologists are, in this respect, far behind sociologists of medicine, who have over many years conducted numerous studies of doctors and patients. Researchers have been frustrated by norms of confidentiality, the routines of busy professionals, and an inability to convince lawyers of the need for research on lawyer-client communications. Yet without direct knowledge of such communications, it is difficult to pose or answer major questions about the content, form, and effects of legal services, the nature of dispute transformation, and the transmission of legal ideology. Indeed it may be that we have ignored an important means of understanding the law itself . . .

II. THE RESEARCH, THE CASE, AND THE CONFERENCE

In the research from which this paper is derived, we developed an ethnographic account of lawyer-client interaction in divorce cases. We chose to examine divorce because it is a serious and growing social problem in which the involvement of lawyers is particularly salient and controversial. Concern among many divorce lawyers about their role suggested that field research on lawyer-client interaction in this area would encounter less resistance than in other areas of legal practice.

We observed cases over a period of thirty-three months in two sites, one in Massachusetts and one in California. This effort consisted in following one side of forty divorce cases, ideally from the first lawyer-client interview until the divorce was final. We followed these cases by observing and tape-recording lawyer-client sessions, attending court and mediation hearings and trials, and interviewing both lawyers and clients about those events. Approximately 115 lawyer-client conferences were tape-recorded.[17]

17. Neither the lawyers nor the clients that we studied were randomly selected . . . We began the process of securing lawyer participation by asking judges, mediators, and law-

Our major objectives were to describe the ways in which lawyers present the legal system and legal process to their clients, to identify the roles that lawyers adopt in divorce cases, to describe the actual context of legal work, to analyze the language and communication patterns through which lawyers carry out these functions, and to examine the ways that lawyer-client interaction affects the development and transformation of divorce disputes. In this paper we describe the interaction between one lawyer and one client in one conference. Not all of the themes of our research are represented here; rather, the paper is devoted to exploring the ways in which lawyers and clients negotiate their differing views of law and the legal process and how that negotiation influences decisions about preferred paths to disposition.

We have observed several patterns through which such decisions are made. Some result in a contested hearing on the main issues. Most, however, do not. In this paper we describe the most common pattern that we observed, namely an exchange in which the lawyer persuades a somewhat reluctant client to try to reach a negotiated settlement. This pattern involves three steps. First, the legal process itself is discussed and interpreted. Here we ask the following questions: What do lawyer and client say about the process? What information does the client seek? What kind of explanations does the lawyer provide? The description of the legal process prepares the way for a decision about settlement by providing the client with a sense of the values and operations inherent in formal adjudication. Second, there is a discussion of how best to dispose of the case. What issues should be settled? What issues, if any, should be fully litigated? What allocation of work does the client prefer? How does the lawyer respond to this preference? Third, there is a discussion of what the client will have to do and how she will have to behave if a settlement is to be reached. Here we examine what the legal process values in human character and what it wishes to ignore, what the process validates and what it leaves for others to reinforce. This discourse we call the "legal construction of the client."

In this lawyer-client conference these themes are interwoven so that an understanding of each is necessary to the full comprehension of the others. The discussion of the nature of the legal process serves to introduce and then justify the lawyer's argument about the best method of disposing of the case. Having reached agreement on method, he must decide how to produce satisfactory outcomes and encourage the client to think and act in a way appropriate to achieving them. Because each of these elements is developed as part of a dialogue that is shaped by client questions, expectations, and

---

yers to name the lawyers in each community who did a substantial amount of divorce work. In each instance, the list eventually contained about 40 names. We stopped trying to add names to the list when additional inquiries were not providing new names. We asked all lawyers on each list to cooperate in the research. Most agreed, but only slightly more than one-quarter in each site actually produced one or more clients willing to participate in the research. We left the choice of clients to the lawyers, except that we did ask them to focus on cases that promised to involve several lawyer-client meetings. . . .

demands, discussions of these themes are neither linear nor free of contradiction.

In this paper we focus on one lawyer-client conference to provide the reader with the maximum opportunity to follow these themes and see them at work "on location." Only through such concentration are we able to convey the level of detail that we believe is necessary to convey the full social significance of the interplay between the lawyer and client.

This conference is typical of our sample of conferences. . . .

The lawyer involved in this case graduated from one of the country's top-ranked law schools. He was forty years old at the time of the conference and had practiced for fourteen years. His father was a prominent physician in a neighboring city. The lawyer had spent four years as a public defender after law school and had been in private practice for ten years. He considers himself a trial lawyer and states that he was drawn to divorce work because of the opportunity it provides for trial work. He is married and has never been divorced.

The client and her husband were in their late thirties and had no children. Their marriage had been stormy, involving both substantial separations and infidelity by the husband. Both had graduate degrees and worked full-time; financial support was not an issue. They owned a house, bank stocks, several limited partnerships in real estate, his retirement benefits, and personal property. The house was their major asset. It was an unconventional building to which the husband was especially attached. Housing in the area is very expensive. This divorce was the client's second; there were no children in the first marriage either. She had received extensive psychological counseling prior to and during the case which we observed.

The parties in this divorce initially tried to dissolve their marriage by engaging a mediator and did not at that time individually consult lawyers. The mediator was an established divorce lawyer with substantial experience in divorce mediation. At the first substantive session, the mediator stated that he did not think that further progress could be made if both the spouses continued to live in the house. Although she considered it to be a major sacrifice, the wife said that she had moved out of the house to facilitate mediation after her husband absolutely refused to leave. Thereafter, she visited the house occasionally, primarily to check on plants and pets. The client reported that she was careful to warn her husband when she intended to visit.

Over time, however, this arrangement upset her husband. Rather than raise the problem at a mediation session, he hired a lawyer and secured an ex parte order restraining the client from entering the property at any time for any reason. The husband had previously characterized the lawyer that he hired as "the meanest son-of-a-bitch in town." The restraining order ended any prospects for mediation and the client, on the advice of the mediator and another lawyer, hired the lawyer involved in this conference.

Subsequently, a hearing about the propriety of the ex parte order was held by a second judge. The issues at this hearing were whether the order should be governed by a general or a divorce-specific injunction statute, what status quo the order was intended to maintain, and whether the husband's attempt to secure the order violated a moral obligation undertaken when the client agreed to move out of the house. The second judge decided against the client on the first two issues, but left consideration of the bad faith question open to further argument. The client's therapist attended the hearing and the lawyer-client conference that immediately followed. At that conference the therapist stressed that contesting the restraining order further might not be in the client's long-term interest even if it corrected the legal wrong.

The conference analyzed in this paper followed the meeting attended by the therapist and was the seventh of twelve that occurred during the course of the case. It took place in the lawyer's office five weeks after the first meeting between lawyer and client. Its two phases, interrupted for several hours at midday, lasted a total of about two hours.

The people referred to in this conference are:

Lawyer	Peter Edmunds
Client	Jane Carroll
Spouse	Norb
Spouse's lawyer	Paul Foster
First judge	John Hancock
Second judge	Mike Cohen
Therapist	Irene
Financial consultant	Bob Archer

III. THE LEGAL PROCESS OF DIVORCE

Clients look to lawyers to explain how the legal system works and to interpret the actions and decisions of legal officials. Despite their lack of knowledge about and contact with the law, clients are likely to have some general notions that the law works as a formally rational legal order, one that is rule governed, impersonal, impartial, predictable, and relatively error free. How do lawyers respond to this picture? In this conference we are interested in the image of the legal process that the lawyer presents. Does he subscribe to the formalist image or does he present the kind of picture that would be drawn by a legal realist, one in which rules are of limited relevance, impersonality gives way to communities of interest shaped by the needs of ongoing relationships, routinization provides the only predictability, and errors are frequently made but seldom acknowledged? Or does he present some mix of the two images or a set of messages different from both?

In this conference the lawyer presents the legal process of divorce largely in response to questions or remarks by the client. In many conferences clients ask for an explanation of some aspect of the legal system's procedures or rules. In this conference the client repeatedly inquires about both. While most of her questions concern the details of her own case, several are general.

Thus, she invites her lawyer to explain the way that the legal process operates as well as to justify its operation in her case. At no point does the lawyer deliver a monologue on how it works. Instead his comments are interspersed in the discussion of major substantive issues, particularly concerning what to do about the restraining order and how to proceed with settlement negotiations. Throughout the conference the client persists in focusing on the restraining order until finally she asks:

> Client: How often does a case like this come along—a restraining order of this nature?

> Lawyer: Very common.

> Client: It's a very common thing. So how many other people are getting the same kind of treatment I am? With what, I presume, are very sloppily handled orders that are passed out.

> Lawyer: Yeah, you know, I talked, I did talk to someone in the know—I won't go any further than that—who said that this one could have been signed purely by accident. I mean, that the judge could have if he looked at it now—said, I would not sign that, knowing what it was, and it could have been signed by accident, and I said, well, then how does that happen? And he said, well, you've got all this stuff going; you come back to your office, and there's a stack of documents that need signatures. He says, you can do one of two things: you can postpone signing them until you have time, but then it may be the end of the day; the clerk's office is closing, and people who really need this stuff aren't going to get the orders, because there's someone else that needs your attention, so you go through them, and one of the main things you look for is the law firm or lawyer who is proposing them. And you tend to rely on them.

The lawyer thus states that a legal order of immense consequence to this woman may have been handled in a way that in several respects is inconsistent with the formalist image of a rational system: It may have been signed by accident. Moreover, the lawyer claims that he has received this information from "someone in the know," someone he refuses to identify. By this refusal, he implies that the information was given improperly, in breach of confidence. Furthermore, the lawyer's description of how judges handle court orders suggests a high level of inattention and routinization. Judges sign orders without reading them to satisfy "people who really need this stuff." While the judge is said to ignore the substance of the order, he does pay attention to the lawyer or law firm who requests it. The legal process is thereby portrayed as responding more to reputation than to substantive merit. Thus, the client is introduced to a system that is hurried, routinized, personalistic, and accident prone.

Throughout this conference, the theme of the importance of insider status and access within the local legal system is reinforced by references to the lawyer's personal situation. . . .

926

The lawyer later claims that he knows one of the judges involved in this client's case well enough to tell him off in private ("I'll tell you when this is over, I'm going to take it to John Hancock and I don't think he'll ever do it again") and that he supported the other's campaign for office. These references suggest that a lawyer's capacity to protect his client's interests depends in part on his special access to the system's functionaries who will react to who he is rather than what he represents. We found this emphasis on insider status, reputation, and local connections repeatedly in the cases that we observed. The lawyer in this case and the other lawyers we studied generally presented themselves as well-connected insiders, valuable because they are known and respected rather than because they are expert legal technicians.

The kind of familiarity with the way the system works that insiders possess is all the more important in divorce cases because the divorce process is extremely difficult to explain even to acute outsiders.

> Client: Tell me just the mechanics of this, Peter. What exactly is an interlocutory?
>
> Lawyer: You should know. It's your right to know. But whether or not I'm going to be able to explain this to you is questionable.... It's a very ... It's sort of simple in practice, but it's very confusing to explain. I've got an awful lot of really smart people who've—who I haven't represented—who've asked me after the divorce is over, now what the hell was the interlocutory judgment?

The communications that we have been discussing are, for the most part, explicit. The message is in the message. But there is also a way in which the language forms that the lawyer employs to describe the legal process communicate something about that process itself. Although this lawyer is articulate and knowledgeable, his reactions to many of the client's questions are nevertheless circuitous and confusing. Interviews with clients, as well as our observations, suggest that this failing is common. Instead of direct description, lawyers frequently use analogies that seem to obscure more than they reveal. This practice, of course, may be seen as a simple problem of communication. Yet it also suggests that law and legal process are themselves so dense and erratic that they pose a formidable barrier even to well educated and intelligent lay people....

Moving from the restraining order to the question of how a settlement could be reached, the client asks why her lawyer did not acknowledge to the other side what he had shared with her, namely that a court battle might end in defeat. In response the lawyer might simply have said that it is poor strategy in a negotiation to tell the other side that you recognize that you may lose. Instead he says:

> Lawyer: Okay. I'll do it in my usual convoluted way, using lots of analogies and examples. When you write to ... when a lawyer writes to an insurance company, representing a person who's been injured in an automobile accident, usually the first demand is somewhat higher than what we actually expect to get out of the case. I always explain that to

927

clients. I explain it very, very carefully. I don't like to write letters of any substance without my client getting a copy of it, and inevitably, I will send a copy of it to my client with another letter explaining, "This is for settlement purposes. Please do not think that your case, which I evaluate at $10,000, is really worth $35,000." And then months later when I finally get the offer to settle for $10,000, I will convey it to my client, and they'll say, well, I've been thinking about this, and I think that you're right; it really was worth $35,000. I then am in a terrible position of having to talk my own client down from a number that I created in the first place and that I tried to support and convince them—of course, they wanted to be convinced, so it was easy—that's the difference between a letter that you send to your adversary and a letter that you, or than what you communicate to your client. They're two different kinds of communications. I truly, I mean, where I am is that I . . . The way I evaluate the case is the way I did when Irene was here. This is an objective evaluation for your use, and there is this tension and conflict in every representation. You have hired me to represent your interests. I do that in two fashions. One, I tell you the way I truly see the picture, and then I try to advance your cause as aggressively as I can. Sometimes—almost always—those are inconsistent. I mean, the actions, the words, and so forth are inconsistent.

. . . This example is . . . drawn from an area of law unrelated to divorce. The lawyer's point is the hypocrisy of orthodox settlement negotiations. Even if warned, he claims, clients are likely to confuse demands and values. That is their error. In the legal process words and goals, expressed objectives and real objectives, are usually "inconsistent." . . .

To the client, "justice" demands that the error of the restraining order be righted. For the lawyer that kind of justice simply gets in the way of what for him is the real business of divorce: to reach a property settlement, not to right wrongs or vindicate justice. There is, if you will, a particular kind of justice that the law provides, but it is not broad enough to include the kind that the client seeks. For her justice requires some compensation, or at least an acknowledgment that she has "been treated unjustly." When she finally gets the lawyer to speak in terms of justice, he admits that it cannot be secured through the legal process.

Client: But as you say, if you want justice in this society, you look somewhere other than the court. I believe that's what you were saying to Bob.

Lawyer: Yeah, that's what I said. Ultimate justice, that is.

Legal justice is thus juxtaposed to ultimate justice. The person seeking such a final accounting is clearly out of place in a system that focuses much more narrowly. To fit into the system the client must reduce her conception of justice to what the law can provide. But perhaps the language of justice serves, for this client, a purpose that is neither as abstract nor as disinterested as her language suggests. This client identifies justice solely with the vindication of her own position. She never refers to a more general standard. Thus the failure of law to provide justice is, for her, a failure to validate her position. The language of justice also serves to bolster her image of herself as an innocent, rather gracious, victim of an evil husband and his untrustworthy lawyer. Tendencies toward self-exculpation and blaming are quite common in the divorces in our sample, although the use of the language of justice toward such ends is not. This language also serves to exert moral pressure on this lawyer to validate the client's sense of herself even as he attempts to explain the limits of the legal process.

In total, the lawyer's description of the legal process involves an open acknowledgment of human frailties, contradictions between appearance and reality, carelessness, incoherence, accident, and built-in limitations. The picture presented is both cynical and probably considered by the lawyer to be realistic. Whereas others claim that legal actors, particularly appellate judges, present the law in highly formalistic terms and work to curtail inconsistencies and contradictions in legal doctrine, many of the lawyers that we observed engage in no such mystification. If critical scholars are right in arguing that mystification and the presentation of a formalist front are necessary to legitimate the legal order, then what we and others have seen in the legal process as it is experienced at the street level suggests that one tier of the legal system, in this case divorce lawyers, may work to unwind the bases of legitimation that other levels work to create. Of course, it is possible, although unlikely, that the legal order derives its legitimacy from its most remote and least accessible elements or that the legitimacy of law is not much affected by how it is presented by lawyers and perceived by clients in the lawyer's office.

IV. TO FIGHT OR TO SETTLE?

Given such a legal process, how should divorce disputes be managed? This concern is central in most of the cases that we observed, and it is an issue that may recur as lawyer and client discuss each of the major controversies in a divorce case. Generally the question is whether the client should attempt to negotiate a settlement or insist on resolution before a judge. This question is sometimes posed issue by issue and sometimes across many issues.

While many clients think of the legal process as an arena for a full adversarial contest, most divorce disputes are not resolved in this manner. Although not all lawyers are equally dedicated to reaching negotiated agreements, most of those we observed advised their clients to try to settle the full range of issues in the case. This is not to say that these divorces were free of conflict, for the negotiations themselves were often quite contentious. Although some of our lawyers occasionally advised clients to ask for more than the client had originally contemplated or to refuse to concede on a major issue when the client was inclined to do so, most seemed to believe that it is generally better to settle than contest divorce disputes. Thus, we are interested in the ways in which lawyers get their clients to see settlement as the preferred alternative.

The conference we are examining revolves around two major issues: (1) whether to ignore or contest the restraining order; and (2) what position to take concerning disposition of the family residence. Much of the conference is devoted to discussing the restraining order—its origins, morality, and legality; the prospects for dissolving it; the lawyer's stake in contesting it; and the client's emotional reaction to it. Substantively the order is not as important as the house itself, which received much less attention and generated much less controversy. Both issues, however, force the lawyer and client to decide whether they will retain control of the case by engaging in negotiations or cede control to the court for hearing and decision. The lawyer definitely favors negotiations. . . .

The major ingredient of this settlement system is the primacy of the lawyers. They produce the deals while the clients are limited to initial instructions and after-the-fact ratification. The phrase "we would have given it our best shot" is crucial. The "we" seems to refer to the lawyers. Indeed, their efforts could come to nothing if either client backs out at the last minute. The settlement process as described thus has two dimensions—a lawyer to lawyer phase, in which an arrangement is worked out, and a lawyers versus clients phase, in which the opposing lawyers join together to sell the deal to their clients. If the clients do not accept the settlement as a package, the only alternative is to go to trial. Furthermore, if the professionals are content with the agreement they have devised, dissatisfied clients not only have nothing to contribute but also had perhaps better seek psychotherapy:

> Lawyer: And if we have to come down a little bit off the 10 percent to something that is obviously a real good loan—9 percent—a percentage point on a one-year, eighteen-month, $25,000 loan does not make that much difference to you. And that's worth settling the case, and I'll say, Jane, if we're going to court over what turns out to be one percentage point, go talk to Irene some more. So that's the kind of a package that I see putting together.

The client in this case is reluctant to begin settlement negotiations until some attention is paid to the restraining order. While she acknowledges that she wants a reasonable property settlement, she reminds her lawyer that that is not her exclusive concern:

> Client: Yes, there's no question in my mind that that [a property settlement] is my first goal. However, that doesn't mean it's my only goal. It's just my first one. And I have done a lot of thinking about this and so it's all this kind of running around in my head at this point. I've been looking very carefully at the parts of me that want to fight and the parts of me that don't want to fight. And I'm not sure that any of that ought to get messed up in the property settlement.

The lawyer responds by acknowledging that he considers the restraining order to be legally wrong and that he believes it could be litigated. Thus, he confirms his client's position and inclination on legal grounds. Yet he dissents from her position and opposes her inclination to fight on other grounds. First, he states that the restraining order, although legally wrong, is "not necessarily ... completely wrong" because it might prevent violence between spouses. This complicated position is a clear example of a tactic frequently used by lawyers in divorce cases—the rhetorical "yes ... but." The lawyers we observed often appeared to be endorsing the adversarial pursuit of one of the client's objectives only to remind the client of a variety of negative consequences associated with it. In this way lawyers present themselves as both an ally and an adviser embracing the wisdom of a long-term perspective.

Second, the lawyer is worried that an effort to fight the restraining order would interfere with the resolution of the case, that is, of the outstanding property issues. Although the lawyer considers the restraining order to be a legal mistake, its effect would end upon final disposition of the house. In the meantime, the client can either live with the order or pay for additional hearings. He believes that it would be unwise for her to fight further not only because the contest would be costly but also because it would postpone or derail entirely negotiations about the house and other tangible assets. Thus when the client asks whether the issue of the restraining order has been raised with her husband's lawyer, her lawyer says:

> Lawyer: Well, we've talked to him. My feelings are still the same. They're very strong feelings that what has been done is illegal, that I want to take it to the Supreme Court. I told Foster off. I basically told him the contents of the letter. I said that I think that Judge Cohen is dead wrong, and I would very much like to litigate the thing. On the other hand, I have to be mindful of what Irene said, which is absolutely correct, does that move us toward or away from the ultimate goal, which is the resolution of the case and what you told me when we started off now in very certain terms.

The lawyer's position in this case can be interpreted as a preference for negotiations over litigation based on his determination that this client has more to lose than gain by fighting the restraining order and for the house. In this view the lawyer is neutral about settlement in general and is swayed by the cost-benefit calculation of specific cases. Thus there is a conflict between the client's desire for vindication on what the lawyer perceives to be a peripheral issue and the lawyer's interest in reaching a satisfactory disposition on what for him is a much more important issue. Time and again in our study we observed lawyers attempting to focus their client's attention on the issues the lawyers thought to be major while the clients often concentrated on matters that the lawyers considered secondary. While the disposition of the house in this case will have long-term consequences for the client, the restraining order, as unjust as the lawyer understands it to be, is in his view a temporary nuisance. His sense of justice and of the long-term best interests of his client lead him to try to transform this dispute from a battle over the legality and morality of the restraining order to a negotiation over the more narrow and tangible issue of the ultimate disposition of the house and other assets, which he believes can and should be settled.

In attempting this transformation, the lawyer allies himself with the therapist:

> Lawyer: I agree with Irene that that [fighting the restraining order] is not the best way.... It's probably the worst way. This [negotiating] hopefully is the best way.

This reliance on the therapist is noteworthy because it is often assumed that a therapeutic orientation is antithetical to the adversarial inclination of law and the legal profession. Yet in this case the lawyer uses the therapist to validate his own position. The legal ideology and the therapeutic ideology seem to him to be compatible; both stress settlement and disvalue legal struggles.... However we interpret this observation, it is clear that this lawyer, and most of those we observed, construct an image of the appropriate mode of disposition of a case that is at odds with the conventional view in which lawyers are alleged to induce competition and hostility, transform noncontentious clients into combatants, and promulgate a "fight theory of justice."

The client's own ambivalence toward settlement continues throughout the conference....

She may have to live with her ambivalence, but her lawyer needs a resolution of this issue. The lawyer seeks this resolution by allying himself with the "don't fight" side of the struggle. Her advocate, her "knight," has thus become the enemy of adversariness. Through him the legal system becomes the champion of settlement. Ironically, the client's ambivalence serves to validate the lawyer's earlier suggestion that he might be wasting his time and her money trying to settle this case because she might refuse at the last minute to agree to a deal. The conference reaches closure on the fight/settle issue when the lawyer again asks whether he has her authority to negotiate on the terms they had discussed and repeats his earlier warning that this is their last chance for a settlement:

> Lawyer: Well, then I will make a ... my best effort—we are now coming full circle to where we were this morning, which is fine, which is where we should be. I will make my best effort to effect a settlement with Foster along the lines that you and I have discussed and the specific terms of which I can say to you, Jane, I recommend that you sign this. The decision, of course, is yours. If you don't want to sign it, we're going to go ahead with the litigation on the restraining order and probably a trial. Things can change. We can effect a settlement before the restraining order, which is highly unlikely, or between the time the restraining order issue is resolved and the actual time of trial, maybe there will be another settlement. I'm not going to suggest or advise, after this attempt, that either one of us put any substantial energy in another try at settlement. I just think it's a waste of time and money.

The lawyer's reference to "coming full circle" reflects both the centrality of the dispositional question and the amount of time spent talking about issues the lawyer considers to be peripheral. Having invested that time the lawyer secures what he wanted, both an authorization to negotiate and an agreement on the goals that he will pursue. The client, on the other hand, has aired her ambivalence and resolved to try to end this dispute without a legal contest. Both her ambivalence and her eventual acceptance of settlement are typical of the clients we observed.

V. THE LEGAL CONSTRUCTION OF THE CLIENT

To get clients in divorce cases to move toward accepting settlement as well as to carry out the terms of such agreements, lawyers may have to try to cool them out when they are at least partially inclined toward contest. In divorce as in criminal cases, the lawyer must help redefine the client's orientation toward the legal process. In the criminal case this means that lawyers must help the client come to terms with dropping the pretense of innocence; in divorce work this means that lawyers must help their clients view the emotional process of dissolving an intimate relationship in instrumental terms. In both instances, lawyers and clients struggle, although rarely explicitly, with the issue of what part of the client's personality is relevant to the legal process. Thus, the discussion of whether to fight or settle is more than a conversation about the most appropriate way to dispose of the case. Contained within the discourse about negotiation is the construction of a legal picture of the client, a picture through which a self acceptable to the legal process is negotiated and validated. This construction is necessary because the legal process will not or cannot deal with many aspects of the disputes that are brought to it. Legal professionals behave as if it were natural and inevitable that a litigant's problems be divided up in the manner that the legal process prescribes. Lawyers thus legitimate some parts of human experience and deny the relevance of others, but they do not explicitly state what is required of the client. Rather, the approved form of the legal self is built up from a set of oppositions and priorities among these oppositions.

The negotiation of the legal self in this case begins by focusing on the relative importance of emotions engaged by the legal process and the symbolic aspects of the divorce as opposed to its financial and material dimensions. Throughout this conference the lawyer warns his client not to confuse the realms of emotion and finance and instructs her that she can expect the legal process to work well only if emotional material is excluded from her deliberations.

This emotional material is rather complex and difficult for both lawyer and client to sort out. The client is, in the first instance, eager to let her lawyer know that she feels both anger and mistrust toward many participants in the legal process. This combination of feelings is clearly expressed as she talks about the restraining order and the manner in which it was issued:

> Client: So I was a total ass. I moved out of the house and left myself vulnerable to that, which I was certainly not informed of by any attorney in the process of mediation. And I was setting myself up for that.

> Lawyer: In my view, it would have been a rather extraordinary attorney that could have advised you of that, because, in my view, that's not the

law. So I'm hard-pressed to see how a lawyer could have said, don't move out of the house or you may prejudice your situation by moving out of the house.

Client: But obviously, some attorney did, right? We have the case of Paul Foster, who interprets the law in that fashion. Well, I'm angry about all that. However ...

While her lawyer once again validates her sense of the legal error involved in issuing the restraining order, her anger is fueled by the failure of her husband's lawyer to accept this interpretation of the law.

The client continues to express her anger throughout the conference, especially when the conversation turns directly to her husband's lawyer:

Client: The other option I see could have been that Norb would have gotten different legal advice from the beginning. So the thing, I suppose, that I'm concerned about, I'm concerned about Foster. I'm concerned about the kind of person he is. I distrust him as thoroughly as I do Norb, and I think you have been very measured in your statements about him. I think he's a son-of-a-bitch, and there's nothing I've seen that he's done that changed my mind about that. And I think that he has a client that can be manipulated.

The client's mistrust is not reserved exclusively for the opposition. She is, to an extent, wary of her own lawyer as well:

Client: But when I think of myself—you know, this is a very vulnerable time in my life, and one of the things that has happened is a major trust relationship has ended. And then suddenly in the space of what—six weeks or something—I'm supposed to entrust somebody else, not only with the intimate details of my life, but with the responsibility for representing me. And that's not easy for me under any circumstances. I really like to speak for myself.

The predicament in which the client finds herself—needing to trust a stranger when trust has just been betrayed by an intimate is one that faces and perplexes divorce clients generally. . . .

Because she feels betrayed by her husband, the client wants "some gesture from him" as a means of establishing the basis for negotiations. Moreover, she feels that she is already two points down vis-à-vis her husband. First, he has the house and has denied her any access to it, although her departure was an act of generosity done for the good of the marital community. Second, she "knows" that he is going to get the house and that she will at best get half its market value. She repeatedly asks the lawyer about gestures or concessions to even this score:

Client: So I wrote this as a draft to send to Norb. . . . And obviously I'm still waffling. . . . I mean, I don't know exactly how to give up this hearing. Part of me says, it's real clear and I ought to. But I want some gesture from him. . . .

934

Client: Okay. That's not going to be a problem for me, all right? I don't think that one percentage point is going to be a problem for me. This is the problem for me. I feel that, even to get to this point, I have given up a substantial amount. One thing that I've given up is the home in Pacifico-la. . . . I want some attention to be paid to what I have already conceded to even get to this point. . . .

Client: I just think that's a very, very big concession, and I think if I'm to take another kind of settlement, then that is the first thing that ought to be seen. Now, that's a very good faith negotiation thing for me to do, say, okay, Norb has this tremendous emotional investment in the house; I'm willing to let go of mine. . . .

How does the lawyer respond to the client's emotional agenda, to her efforts to define those parts of herself that are legally relevant? With respect to the problem of trust and the need for a gesture, the lawyer once says, "Ouch," once, "I don't blame you," and once he changes the subject. He does tell the client that her husband is unlikely to reestablish trust by giving up the restraining order. In addition, there is a brief exploration of whether she could buy the husband's share of the house, an alternative doomed by earlier recognition that it would involve an expensive and probably fruitless court battle. There is a joke about taking $25,000 to forget the restraining order. Otherwise nothing is said.

Why? Lawyer and client could have discussed the kind of gestures short of unconditional surrender that might have satisfied her and been tolerable to her husband. The lawyer could have explored the possibility that the husband might agree to his client's occasional, scheduled visits to the property or to $5,000 more than a 50/50 split in recognition of giving up the house. Perhaps he feared that further exploration might complicate his efforts to have his client focus on reaching an acceptable division of property. There can be little doubt that this objective governed his thinking. . . .

By playing down the question of trust the lawyer is telling the client that the emotional self must be separated from the legal self. Gestures and symbolic acknowledgment of wrongs suffered belong to some realm other than law. He is, in addition, defending himself against a kind of emotional transference. Much of the emotion talk in this conference involves the lawyer himself, directly or indirectly. In the discussion of trust the client makes the lawyer into a kind of husband substitute ("a major trust relationship has ended. And then ... I'm supposed to entrust somebody else ..."). The client described him as her "knight in shining armor," an image of protection and romance; she acknowledges having sexual fantasies about him and she speaks of her expectation that he would protect her from "judicial abuse." These demands on her lawyer typify the kind of environment in which divorce lawyers work. Moreover, the discussion of trust and its betrayal signals to her lawyer the need for an elevated watchfulness. He may, like her earlier source of protection and romance, not be fully trusted. The gesture implicitly demanded of him is an embrace of her sense of justice and of what that implies in practical terms.

By downplaying emotions and signaling the limited relevance of gestures, the lawyer defends himself against both the transference and the test. He must find a way to be on his client's side (e.g., repeatedly acknowledging the legal error of the restraining order) and, at the same time, to keep some distance from her ... Achieving this precarious balance is a peculiar, although not unique, difficulty of divorce practice.... To maintain this balance the lawyer acknowledges the difficulty of separating emotional and property issues, but continually reminds the client of its necessity if they are going to reach what he calls a "satisfactory disposition" of the case:

> Lawyer: I mean, people have a very, very hard time of separating whatever it is—so I think for shorthand, we call it the emotional aspect of the case from the financial aspect of the case. But if there is going to be a settlement, that's kind of what has to happen, or the emotional aspect of the case gets resolved and then the financial thing becomes a matter of dollars and cents and the client decides, I'm tired and I don't want to fight over the last $500 or the last $100.

The need to exclude emotional issues is thus linked to a warning that emotions can jeopardize satisfactory settlements. The notion of satisfactory disposition, however, is itself problematic. The lawyer's definition of "satisfactory" tends to exclude the part of the client's personality that is angry or frustrated. Satisfactory dispositions are financial. The question of who is satisfied is left unasked. For the client, no definition of the case that ignores her emotions seems right; to the lawyer, this is the only definition that seems acceptable. Moreover, the responsibility for finding ways to keep emotions under control is assigned to the client. The lawyer offers no help in this task even as he acknowledges its relevance for this client and for the practice of divorce law. If no settlement is reached it will, at least as far as their side is concerned, be because of a failure on the part of the client....

As the lawyer sees it, the client will only be able to make an adequate arrangement with her husband when she can contemplate their relationship unemotionally. As the client sees it, the second separation seems impossible if the first is carried out. She cannot become free of her husband if she thinks about legal problems in material terms only—if she fails to take her feelings into account she will continue to be affected by them. Thus, the program the lawyer presents to the client appropriates her marriage to the realm of property and defines her connection to her husband exclusively in those terms. She, on the other hand, sees property issues embedded in a broader context. The client speaks about the separation of the emotional and financial issues as being difficult to effect because it is unnatural. The market does not exhaust her realm of values, and she has difficulty assigning governing priority to it. Yet this is what the lawyer indicates the law requires.

Nevertheless, the separation of emotional and economic matters may benefit the client. While it does exact an emotional toll, concentrating on the instrumental, tangible aspects of the divorce may produce a more satisfactory disposition than focusing on the emotional concerns. The lawyer may be trying to explain to his client that in the long run she is going to be more interested in the economics of the settlement than in the vindication of her immediate emotional needs. In his view, legal justice, although narrow, is justice nonetheless, and his job is to secure for her the best that can be achieved given the legal process as he knows it.

Putting emotional matters aside may also serve the interests of lawyers untrained in dealing with emotional problems and unwilling to find ways to cope with them. It allows lawyers to sidestep what is clearly one of the most difficult and least rewarding aspects of divorce practice. In so doing they are able to avoid assuming a sense of responsibility for the human consequences of being unresponsive to emotion. In this conference, for example, the lawyer suggests that the legal process works best for those who can control their emotions and concentrate on the instrumental, the calculating, the pecuniary. . . .

VI.　CONCLUSION

Lawyer-client interaction involves attempts to negotiate acceptable resolutions of problems in which lawyers and clients usually have different agendas, expectations, and senses of justice. As in any negotiation, the parties possess different information and have different needs to fulfill. Clients know their histories and goals, lawyers must learn about them. Lawyers know the law and the legal process, clients must find out about them. Every conference is thus to some extent competitive: Each of the participants sets out to fulfill their own agenda and generally only provides what the other wants on demand.

Competition and accommodation between lawyer and client shape the course of divorce litigation—when negotiations are initiated, how they are conducted, what is asked for and offered, and whether a case is settled. Moreover, the manner in which the contest over agendas and expectations is resolved may also have a powerful effect on the way clients feel at the end of the process, on their levels of satisfaction, and on their views of the legitimacy of law. Interactions between lawyers and clients also provide one occasion for the construction and transmission of legal ideology. The dialogue between lawyers and clients reveals the sense of rights, actionable injuries, and justice that people bring to the legal process and that the process, through the words and actions of lawyers, is willing to recognize and act upon.

A.　*Lawyer–Client Interaction: The Lawyer's Perspective*

Clients bring to their encounters with lawyers an expectation that the justice system will impartially sort the facts in dispute to provide a deductive reading of the "truth." They expect the legal process to take their problems seriously, and they usually seek vindication of the positions that they have adopted. They expect the legal process to follow its own rules, to proceed in an orderly manner, and to be fair and error free. . . .

To some extent, it is the job of lawyers to bring these expectations and images of law and legal justice closer to the reality that they have experienced. For them legal justice is situational and outcomes are often unpredictable. The legal process provides an arena where compromises are explored, settlements are reached, and, if money is at issue, assets are divided. Lawyers are intimately familiar with the human dimensions of the legal process. They know that in most instances the process is not rule governed, that there is widespread use of discretion, and that decisions are influenced by matters extraneous to legal doctrine. Moreover, they believe that most clients cannot afford or would not want to pay the cost of a full adversarial contest. They may conclude, therefore, based on experience, that the client who demands vindication today will want both a larger financial settlement and a smaller lawyer's bill tomorrow.

Because lawyers' experience is so much more extensive than that of clients, lawyers attempt to "teach" their clients about the requirements of the legal process and to socialize them into the role of the client. Some of the client's problems and needs will be translated into legal categories and many more will have legal labels attached to them. The client in contact with a lawyer and the legal process must frequently be talked into a frame of mind appropriate to the needs of legal business.... In the lawyer's office the client is likely to be introduced to a system of negotiations in which formal hearings are rare, rights are no guarantee of remedies, unfamiliar rules of relevance are asserted, and the nature of their own disputes and objectives are transformed....

In fact, the range of client expectations with which lawyers must come to terms covers almost everything that is involved in a divorce—the distribution of property, the level of support, the rights to custody, the speed with which things are done, the wisdom of the rules and the judges, the roles that lawyers are willing to play, the times at which they are available, and the fees that they charge. Moreover, the clients that we studied expect their lawyers to tell them about their rights and obligations and to predict how they will fare in contests over houses, retirement benefits, visitation rights, support payments, and the like. Whatever their reservations about lawyers as a group and litigation as a means of resolving disputes, they expect their lawyers to navigate them through troubled waters. They want to believe that charts exist, that shoals are marked, and that channels to safe harbors are defined. But lawyers present a different picture: Where clients want predictions and certainty, lawyers introduce them to the frequently unpredictable reality of divorce. While not every client is mistaken about all of these matters, many divorce lawyers understandably feel that they must constantly be on their guard against clients who seek what cannot be delivered. A major professional function therefore is to attempt to limit clients' expectations to realistic levels.

A heavy dose of cynicism helps lawyers accomplish this goal. The cynic chips away at the legal facade until the client realizes that she is enmeshed in a system ridden with hazards, surprises, and people who are out to get her. By focusing on the mistakes, irrationality, or intransigence of the other side, the lawyer creates an inventory of explanations that puts some distance between himself and responsibility for any eventual disappointment. Yet at the same time that he creates doubts about the legal process, the lawyer must give the client some reason to rely on him. The lawyer's emphasis on his insider status is one means of doing this. Nothing is guaranteed, the lawyer acknowledges, but the best chance for success rests with those who are familiar with local practice and who have a working relationship with officials who wield local power. This formula is repeatedly presented to clients by the lawyers in our sample. By stressing the importance of being an insider, the lawyer is not necessarily suggesting that the system is corrupt. He is not promising that he has an illegal way to deal with an illegal system but rather creating an atmosphere in which the client will feel that she is being helped to attain a reachable goal despite being trapped in a system laced with uncertainties. The interests of the legal professional in this instance depart from the interests of the legal system. This lawyer constructs a picture of the legal process that fixes the client's dependency on him as it jeopardizes her trust in any other part of the system. The consequences of this for the client's view of law in general or participation in its legitimation rituals seems quite remote from his concerns. His talk, the image of the legal process that he constructs, is the talk of a cynical realist. The legal process he presents inspires neither respect nor allegiance. . . .

B. *Lawyer–Client Interaction: The Client's Perspective*

Because divorce clients may not direct their litigation does not mean that they play no part in it. Because clients may acquiesce in the end to the lawyer's agenda does not mean that they do not make demands on their lawyer during the process. Clients may insist that lawyers attend to issues beyond those that are technically relevant and with which lawyers do not feel particularly comfortable; they may persist in bringing these matters into the conversation even after lawyers think that they have been settled. Clients may, in addition, resist recommendations that a lawyer believes are obviously in the client's interest. They may press lawyers to explain and justify advice given, actions taken, and results produced. Finally, clients may insist that lawyers interpret and account for the actions of others, particularly their spouse, their spouse's lawyer, and judges, and that lawyers justify these actions in light of the client's sense of what is appropriate and fair. In these ways, clients transform the agendas of lawyers as well as their preferred professional style.

This conference allowed the client to express her frustrations with a legal process that refused to protect her "rights." . . .

In addition, the conference provided the client with an opportunity to work through conflicting goals: She did not want to capitulate to her husband but she did want to put an end to the fighting between them. Like many of the clients we have observed, she is uncertain about what she really wants. The wisdom of a negotiated settlement is clear to the lawyer, but for her it is fraught with ambiguity and difficulty. She insists that her lawyer concede, at least to her, that her need for a symbolic "gesture" is comprehensible and legitimate. In so doing she secures some acknowledgment of her self-conceived victimization and some limited vindication. This drama, in which clients insist that their lawyers validate their partial and biased understandings, is a routine part of the divorce process. Lawyers, especially experienced divorce lawyers, understand this and provide such validation even when, as in this case, they attempt to discourage their clients from seeking it in the courtroom.

C. The Consequences of the Two Perspectives

The competing perspectives of lawyer and client and the manner in which they are articulated establish the boundaries within which the strategy and tactics of divorce litigation develop. When the client feels betrayed and victimized, the lawyer may have to spend a significant amount of time and energy in selling negotiation as the means of resolving the case. This effort may affect the timing as well as the style and success of settlement efforts. Most of the lawyers we observed invest considerable effort in these client management activities. In our sample it is the exceptional lawyer who fans the flames of the client's anger or accepts uncritically the client's version of events without reminding the client of the difficulties and costs of acting out of emotion.

Moreover, when divorce clients demand to know about the legal rules that will be applied, the probabilities of achieving various results, the costs they will incur, the pace at which various things will happen, and the roles that different actors will play, there are no standard answers that lawyers can give. What the client is asking for is a distillation of the lawyer's experience as it is relevant to cases like hers. What the lawyer can provide is not a corpus juris learned in law school or available in any texts but rather a personal view of how the legal system actually works in the community in which he is practicing.

The lawyer's emphasis on the uncertain and personalistic nature of that process may have three effects. First, the extent to which the lawyer's picture of the legal system is at variance with the image that the client brings to her contact with the law may help to explain the common finding that experience with the legal process often results in dissatisfaction and a lower level of respect for law, regardless of substantive outcome. Clients are brought face-to-face with the law's shortcomings by the testimony of their own lawyers as well as by the results that they experience.

Second, this characterization of the legal process may increase the client's dependence on the lawyer. People in the midst of divorce frequently feel a reduced sense of control over their lives. Their former lover and friend has become an enemy. They cannot live where and as they did, they must relate to their children in new ways, they may face new jobs and major economic threats, and their relations with family and friends may be strained, sometimes to the breaking point. When lawyers then introduce clients to an uncontrollable and unpredictable legal system, their sense of reduced control over their lives may become even stronger. They are, in essence, further threatened by a system that they had expected would reintroduce structure and predictability into their lives. In this situation, the lawyer's services become more essential and the lawyer himself more indispensable.

Finally, the lawyer's emphasis on the client's need to separate emotional and instrumental issues may help to construct or reflect a vision of law in which particular parts of the self are valued while others are denied or left for others to validate. In the legal realm, lawyers insist that the rational and instrumental are to govern. While this lawyer clearly recognizes the human consequence of this opposition and hierarchy, he never questions it but instead treats it as both necessary and inevitable. Throughout this conference the lawyer encourages the client to be clear headed and to grant priority to monetary issues. By defining the ultimate goal as the resolution of the case and resolution in terms of the division of property, and by seeking to exclude the emotional focus that the client continues to provide, he expresses the indifference of the law to those parts of the self that might be most salient at the time of the divorce. The legal process of divorce becomes at best a distraction, at worst an additional trauma. By the end of the conference both lawyer and client speak in terms of a divided self, she, if only briefly, to fight against it or at least to express her ambivalence, he to do its bidding in the name of a system that is unchanging and unchangeable. . . .

NOTES AND QUESTIONS

1. In *Lawyer and Client: Who's in Charge?* (1974), Douglas E. Rosenthal studied personal injury claim cases. He was interested in the relationship between lawyers and clients, and the exercise of authority and control over problems that the clients see as important. According to the traditional view of the relationship, the client is "passive, follows instruction, and trusts the professional without criticism, with few questions or requests"; lawyers believe that such clients "will do better than the difficult client who is critical and questioning." (pp. 13–14). Opposed to this is the "participatory" ideal, where the client is active, informed, and shares in responsibility and devices. The "participatory theory" asserts "that it is primarily the client's own responsibility to grapple with the problem. Instead of delegating responsibility to the professional and leaving the decisions to him, while being kept only minimally informed, the participating client seeks information to help him define his problem and what he wants to accomplish, rather than waiting to be told how to proceed." The client reviews and assesses what has been done, and how the professional did it; he questions and appraises the consistency and accuracy of the professional's answers. The client is "aware that there are open choices to be made in solving his problem and expects to have his concerns reflected in the choices made."

Contrary to expectations, Rosenthal found that participating clients "do not get worse results," but rather "they actually get better recoveries from their legal claims." He says: "The single form of client participation which appears to have the greatest influence on successful case outcome is making follow-up demands for attention.... Even the most experienced and skillful [lawyers] make errors of fact as well as judgment. If a client is active in following the details of his case and resourceful in informing himself about the elements of a claim, he may be able to catch something pertinent that the lawyer misses.... [T]he more ... activity the client employs and the more persistently he employs them, the better his chances of protecting his emotional and economic interests in the case outcome. The client who is most likely to suffer is the one who has strongly motivated interests but fails to express or safeguard them.... The participatory model does not diminish the importance of the lawyer's role in problem solving. The benefits of client activity appear to derive only from greater collaboration with the attorney, not from the client's exclusively performing the attorney's functions."

Was the client in Sarat and Felstiner's study an "active" or a "passive" client? Would Rosenthal's conclusions hold up in a study of divorce practice as well as in personal injury?

2.　Under certain circumstances, lawyers may become the great champions of mediation in a divorce setting. See Craig A. McEwen, Richard J. Maiman and Lynn Mather, "Lawyers, Mediation, and the Management of Divorce Practice," 28 *Lawyer & Society Review* 149 (1994). Suppose, in Sarat and Felstiner's story, Jane and Norb as well as their two lawyers had to appear before a mediator who was not a lawyer. How, if at all, might the story have changed? What had Norb to gain by making any concessions to Jane? See also Austin Sarat & William L.F. Felstiner, *Divorce Lawyers and Their Clients—Power and Meaning in the Legal Process* (1995).

3.　David L. Chambers, "Divorce Attorneys and 40 Clients in Two Not So Big but Not So Small Cities in Massachusetts and California: An Appreciation," 22 *Law & Social Inquiry* 209 (1997), looked at the Sarat and Felstiner study and concluded: "Twenty-five lawyers, forty clients: so much learned, so much left to learn." As Sarat and Felstiner acknowledge, the lawyers and clients whom they studied may be atypical. Getting access to these people was a victory that many scholars doubted could be obtained. We know much more than we did before the study. Nonetheless, we cannot over-generalize from Sarat and Felstiner's stories. The lawyers may have wanted the approval of the scholars, and the presence of the researcher may have undercut the absolute power of the lawyers so that the clients may have been emboldened to assert themselves more than they would have without an observer present. It seems likely that Sarat and Felstiner did not study divorce among the working class and the poor, and they did not emphasize whether there might be gender differences in the way lawyers dealt with clients. In a study done in Israel, Bryna Bogoch, "Gendered Lawyering: Difference and Dominance in Lawyer–Client Interaction," 31 *Law & Society Review* 677 (1997), found little difference between men and women lawyers in their interaction with clients. Both men and women clients gave greater deference to male lawyers. Occasionally, some women lawyers were more accepting of their clients' emotional concerns, but many were not. Why might many women lawyers in divorce situations stick even more closely to the lawyer role than men?

Marsha Kline Pruett and Tamara D. Jackson, "The Lawyer's Role During the Divorce Process: Perceptions of Parents, Their Young Children, and Their Attorneys," 33 *Family Law Quarterly* 283 (1999), reports a study of 41 parents, 22 children and 28 attorneys. The clients see the lawyers as disorganized and inefficient. They do not pay attention, and they do not follow through after conferences. The clients thought that lawyers had so many cases that they could not remember the details of the clients' lives. Often the children saw the lawyers as pirates, vampires or wolves who scared children and stole their homes from them. "They did not help mom and dad stay friends." The lawyers saw the system as flawed, but they could not see any alternatives. Few clients had enough money to afford anything better, and one of the big problems was the opposing lawyer who could not control his or her client's unreasonable behavior. On the other hand, William L.F. Felstiner, Ben Pettit, E. Allan Lind & Nils Olsen, "The Effect of Lawyer Gender on Client Perceptions of Lawyer Behavior," in Ulrike Shultz and Gisela Shaw (eds.) *Women in the World's Legal Professions* (2002), conducted a telephone survey of recent clients of American lawyers. They found that the incidence of disrespectful behavior by the lawyers was very low. There were no measurable differences between men and women lawyers as to whether their clients saw them as friendly, confident, organized, polite, trustworthy or fair. William L.F. Felstiner, "Synthesising Socio–Legal Research: Lawyer–Client Relations as an Example," 8 *International Journal of the Legal Profession* 191 (2001), stressed the relationship of lawyer overload and their inattention to clients. "Even if they follow a killing regime, lawyers can do just do much" (p. 195). Most lawyers who handle divorces or personal injury cases take on all work that they can get because they have no assurance that any clients will come in the door tomorrow or next week.

4. <u>A note on divorce attorneys' professional legal culture</u>: From the 1960s to the present time, research on divorce attorneys has tracked an interesting combination of views on law. Hubert O'Gorman described divorce attorneys as taking two different attitudes toward their roles: for some, the core role of law in situations of family conflict was that of the counselor, while others viewed themselves as advocates in more adversarial roles. *Lawyers and Matrimonial Cases* (1983). This finding found substantial support in later research. Kenneth Kressel, Allan Hochberg, and Theodore Meth, "A Provisional Typology of Lawyer Attitudes Towards Divorce Practice," 7 *Law and Human Behavior* 31 (1983). Gilson and Mnookin similarly reported in 1994 that divorce attorneys see their professional job to be that of a "problem solver" mobilizing the law to resolve clients' difficulties. Ronald Gilson and Robert Mnookin, Disputing through Agents: Cooperation and Conflict Between Lawyers in Litigation," 94 *Columbia Law Review* 509 (1994). Although they based this conclusion on a very small, non-random set of interviews, their conclusions fit well with other studies which show that divorce attorneys see their goal in representing clients to be a reasonable or fair settlement.

Lynn Mather, Craig McEwen, and Richard Maiman, *Divorce Lawyers at Work: Varieties of Professionalism in Practice* (2001); Austin Sarat and William Felstiner, *Divorce Lawyers and Their Clients: Power and Meaning in the Legal Process* (1997). Divorce attorneys also frequently mention the emotional character of the work they do, something for which training in formal law does little to prepare them. There seems to be growing interest among divorce attorneys in less adversarial forms of representation, from use of mediation to "collaborative divorce." (See also Chapter 3, Reading 3.11 and notes).

5. John Heinz and Edward Laumann, *Chicago Lawyers: The Social Structure of the Bar* (1982), suggest that the legal profession is made up of distinct strata, and, in particular, of two distinct segments that they call "hemispheres." Stewart Macaulay, "Law Schools and the World Outside Their Doors II: Some Notes on Two Recent Studies of the Chicago Bar," 32 *Journal of Legal Education* 506, 508–510 (1982), has described their study:

> Heinz and Laumann tell us that different kinds of lawyers do very different things and that there is a clear hierarchy in the legal profession. They say that one could posit a great many legal professions, but much of the variation within the profession can be accounted for by one fundamental difference—that between lawyers who represent large organizations and those who represent individuals or the small businesses controlled by those individuals. Corporate work is likely to involve "symbol manipulation," while work for individuals will carry a heavy component of "people persuasion." Corporate lawyers tend to have far fewer clients a year than those who represent individuals, and corporate lawyers are paid to discover unique legal issues and cope with them rather than mass process routine work for many clients.
>
> How do they arrive at these conclusions? They tell us that lawyers tend to specialize and represent limited, identifiable groups or types of clients and to perform as broad or narrow a range of tasks as the clientele demands. There is virtually no likelihood of co-practice across five distinct clusters of legal work: (1) large corporate business work, (2) specialty corporate business practice such as patent law or admiralty, (3) labor affairs, (4) municipal government work, and (5) service to individuals and their businesses. In brief, a patent lawyer is unlikely to be competent to try a first-degree murder case; corporate lawyers know little about divorce practice; and if you want to get something from City Hall in Chicago, you need a lawyer who knows the right people.
>
> The work some lawyers do is likely to be far more highly regarded by the profession than the work done by others. A subsample of the lawyers interviewed by Heinz and Laumann were asked to rate the "general prestige with the legal profession at large" of each of thirty fields. A panel of law professors from Northwestern University and researchers from the American Bar Foundation was asked to rank these same fields as to intellectual challenge, rapidity of change, degree of work done for altruistic motives, ethical conduct, and freedom from client demands. Heinz and

Laumann tell us that the general pattern of prestige ranking is unambiguous: fields serving "big business" clients such as securities, corporate tax, antitrust, and banking are at the top of the prestige ranking while those serving individual clients such as divorce, landlord and tenant, debt collection, and criminal defense are at the bottom. That is, the more a legal specialty serves the core economic values of the society, the higher its prestige within the profession. Moreover, the higher the score of a field on service-based, altruistic, or reformist motives, the lower its prestige. The fields with the highest prestige were seen as having the highest intellectual challenge by the law professors and researchers who rated them. Many attorneys do not consider "people persuasion" to be real lawyer's work. However, the income lawyers received from various types of practice was not significantly associated with the prestige of particular fields.

Heinz and Laumann give us a picture of lawyers and clients in various fields by using a type of correlational analysis. A striking U-shaped pattern emerged from the association of nine variables across the thirty fields of practice examined. The variables were (1) the extent to which a field had business rather than individual clients, (2) the percentage of clients represented by the lawyer for three years or more, (3) the degree to which clients were referred by other lawyers, (4) the freedom lawyers had to select their cases, (5) the degree to which a field involved negotiating and advising clients rather than "highly technical procedures," (6) the amount of governmental employment in a field, (7) the presence of lawyers in a field who attended local rather than national elite law schools, (8) the number of high-status Protestant lawyers in a field, and (9) the number of lawyers of Jewish origin in a field.

One can describe the associations Heinz and Laumann find by imagining a circle which represents the legal profession in Chicago. First, the circle could be divided horizontally. The top half would represent lawyers who primarily go to court; the bottom, lawyers who primarily counsel clients in their offices. Second, the circle could be divided vertically. The side to the left would be occupied by lawyers whose clients were primarily individuals and their businesses; the side to the right would contain lawyers who represent larger corporations. Lawyers in each quarter of the circle are more alike than those in the other quarters, at least when measured on the nine variables used in the research. However, to reflect the profession more accurately, the circle would have to be pushed apart at the top since lawyers who litigate for individuals are very unlike those who litigate for large corporations. On the other hand, those who counsel wealthy individuals are likely to be somewhat similar to those who counsel corporations. Thus, when they look at the thirty fields of practice, Heinz and Laumann get a U-shaped pattern of association.

Fields closer together in the U-shaped pattern tend to be more similar, as measured by Heinz and Laumann's nine variables, than those further apart. Divorce, representing plaintiffs in personal injury work, and criminal defense involve appearances in court for individuals and are clustered together. Other clusters include: probate and personal tax work, which involve a great deal of office practice for individuals; general corporate and banking practice, which tend to involve office work for corporate clients; and business litigation and antitrust defense, which involve court appearances for corporations. If we start in the upper left corner of the U, we find lawyers who specialize in divorce, personal injury work for plaintiffs, and criminal defense. These fields also have the lowest prestige within the profession; those who specialize in them tend to practice alone or in small firms; and these attorneys almost always attended local law schools. As we go around the U, prestige increases, the law firms become larger, and the lawyers tend to have gone to national law schools.

Interestingly, there is substantial support from all lawyers for normative statements asserting the rights of individuals against concentrations of power in large corporations, labor unions, or the state. Also surprising, perhaps, is the finding that lawyers whose fields had the highest prestige ratings tended to support such civil liberties as free speech far more than nonlawyers or lawyers whose fields are in the personal business cluster. General corporate lawyers, not surprisingly, tend to score fairly low on a scale of economic liberalism used by the researchers.

John P. Heinz, Robert L. Nelson, Rebecca L. Sandefur, and Edward O. Laumann, *Urban Lawyers: The New Social Structure of the Bar* 46–47, 83, 85–86 (2005), report a second survey of the Chicago bar. The authors were thus able to compare that bar in 1975 and in 1994–95. They say: "Is the legal profession still divided into hemispheres? *Hemi* means half, and it is now hard to argue that the two parts are approximately equal in size … By our estimate, the amount of Chicago lawyers' time devoted to corporate fields and to fields serving other large organizations is more than twice that devoted to personal client fields." However, there was an even more clear distinction between those who served ordinary individuals and those who served corporations and the wealthy. Nonetheless, the growth in specialization had caused the bar to be differentiated into smaller clusters. The authors also note that "lawyers in 1975 and 1995 had similar views about what legal work is respected and what is derogated … The lowest third of the prestige order contains numerous personal client fields, many of which involve contact with clients who not only lack wealth and social power but suffer stigmatization: divorcing couples, children in trouble with the law, criminals, and people facing financial ruin."

What difference, if any, does the status and prestige of various legal specialties make? There are clearly behavioral differences. Wall Street firms do not, for example, advertise, and they do not make use of grubby ways of getting business such as paying ambulance drivers for referrals. However, many elite law firms publish newsletters on slick paper that purport to keep their clients up to date on the latest legal developments that might affect them. See Carroll Seron, "New Strategies for Getting Clients: Urban and Suburban Lawyers' Views," 27 *Law & Society Review* 399 (1993); Carroll Seron, "The Status of Legal Professionalism at the Close of the Twentieth Century: *Chicago Lawyers* and *Urban Lawyers*," 32 Law & Social Inquiry 581 (2007).

Can we say, for example, that better lawyers tend to work for richer people? See Jack Ladinsky, "Careers of Lawyers, Law Practice, and Legal Institutions," 28 *American Sociological Review* 47 (1963). Would that depend on what we meant by "better?" Heinz and Laumann find that the higher the score of a field with regard to service-based, altruistic, or reformist motives, the lower its prestige. What does that tell us, if anything, about the profession? For a thoughtful discussion of some of the issues raised by Heinz and Laumann, see Howard Erlanger, "The Allocation of Status Within Occupations: The Case of the Legal Profession," 58 *Social Forces* 882 (1980).

6. Roman Tomasic, "Social Organisation Amongst Australian Lawyers," 19 *Australia and New Zealand Journal of Sociology* 445 (1983), reports on a study of the legal profession in Australia. Tomasic asked his sample of lawyers how much time they spent on various activities. He ended up with four "clusters" of activities, corresponding to four types of lawyers: property lawyers, litigation lawyers, commercial lawyers, and generalists. Like Heinz and Laumann, he concluded that the legal profession "is far from being a homogeneous occupational group." It would be "more realistic to speak of a number of legal professions," with a "multiplicity of roles and functions."

7. Some lawyers, often referred to as "public interest" or "cause" lawyers, use their skills for various causes; some attempt to bring legal services to those who need but cannot afford them. The classic study is Richard Kluger, *Simple Justice: The History of Brown v. Board of Education and Black America's Struggle for Equality* (1975), which details the long struggle of the lawyers of the National Association for the Advancement of Colored People that resulted in the Brown decisions. See, also, Austin Sarat and Stuart Scheingold, eds., *Cause Lawyering: Political Commitments and Professional Responsibilities* (1998); Austin Sarat and Stuart Scheingold, eds., *Cause Lawyering and the State in a Global Era* (2001); Terence C. Halliday, "Politics and Civic Professionalism: Legal Elites and Cause Lawyers," 24 *Law & Social Inquiry* 1013 (1999); David Luban, "Taking Out the Adversary: The Assault on Progressive Public–Interest Lawyers," 91 *California Law Review* 209 (2003); Thomas M. Hilbink, "You Know the Type . . . : Categories of Cause Lawyering," 29 *Law & Social Inquiry* 657 (2004). Liberal or left wing goals established cause lawyering, but in the last few decades cause lawyers have represented conservative or right wing ideas as well. See, e.g., Ann Southworth, "Conservative Lawyers and the Contest over the Meaning of 'Public Interest Law' ", 52 *UCLA Law Review* 1223 (2005).

On ideas about providing lawyers for the poor, see Joel F. Handler, *Social Movements and the Legal System: A Theory of Law Reform and Social Change* (1978); Louise G. Trubek, "Lawyering for Poor People: Revisionist Scholarship and Practice," 48 *Miami Law Review* 983 (1994); Louise G. Trubek, "The Worst of Times . . . And the Best of Times: Lawyering for Poor Clients Today," 22 *Fordham Urban Law Journal* 1123 (1995); Ann Southworth, "Collective Representation for the Disadvantaged: Variations in Problems of Accountability," 67 *Fordham Law Review* 2449 (1999); Ann Southworth, "Lawyers and the 'Myth of Rights' in Civil Rights and Poverty Practice," 8 *Boston Public Interest Law Journal* 469 (1999).

*

CHAPTER 6

Law, Culture, and History

I. An Introductory Note

Most of the readings thus far have dealt with American law and the legal system of the United States. But each country has its own legal system. No two are exactly the same. Of course, most of the general concepts and issues we have taken up in this book are relevant to the legal systems of other countries as well. Whether a given law, rule, or decision has an *impact* on society, and if so, what impact, is a question that can be asked about laws, rules, or decisions in China or the Chad Republic or Argentina, as well as about the United States. And one can discuss the deterrent effect of punishment in any of these countries as well.

Nonetheless, each society and each country has its own specific history and traditions; and each has its own specific culture. So, questions about impact and deterrence can indeed be asked about every society; but the answers will not be the same. At some level of abstraction, it may be possible to talk about issues that are either universal or at least apply to whole categories of societies. But the details will, nonetheless, be both interesting and enlightening.

In this collection of readings, all sorts of questions and issues have been raised explicitly; and various hypotheses have been advanced. And the authors of the articles reprinted here have tried to reach conclusions—conclusions which, for the most part, they base (or try to base) on evidence.

But there is always the question, how far can you *generalize* the results? We frequently asked this question ourselves. If there is a study of American college students, published in 1980, let us say, is it valid for middle-aged French women as well? Or for people who lived in the Roman empire? That is almost always a difficult question to answer. The social sciences are not in the happy situation of some of the natural sciences. What is true of the pull of gravity on falling bodies in Wichita, Kansas today, for example, was true of the pull of gravity in Patagonia yesterday, and will be true of falling bodies in Shanghai tomorrow. It may even be true of gravity on Mars. "Social science" is very far from this kind of certainty. It may never achieve it at all.

Experimental science is obviously not an option for most studies of legal systems; but occasionally, as we have noted, there are so-called natural experiments. There may be two neighboring states (Wisconsin and Illinois, for example), which are similar in many ways—contiguous mid-western American states. One has the death penalty. The other one does not. This gives us a (very rough) kind of control group, if we want to know the impact of the death penalty on the murder rate. It is a far more sloppy and treacherous "experiment" than a medical experiment where half the patients get a drug and the other half get a sugar pill, and neither group knows which is which. In law-and-society research, many researchers are constantly looking for something that at least approximates the sugar pill. Once in a while they come close. Mostly, the sugar pill eludes them.

But one of the values of studies of history and culture is that they can provide substitutes for the sugar pill. They can give us a basis for comparison, and thus compensate, at least in a small way, for the missing control group. In historical studies, we can compare the "then" with the "now"; in cross-cultural studies, we can compare the "here" with the "there". The comparisons of course are quite imperfect, but often it is the best we can do.

We have not neglected history or culture totally in the material thus far. In this chapter, however, we will briefly look at these two aspects of legal systems in a somewhat more focused way. But exactly what do we mean by history and culture (at least for purposes of this chapter)?

(A) History

Each country, each society, each community, has its own history. There are great similarities between the legal systems of England and the United States, but there was no slavery, no civil war, no 14th Amendment in the 19th century history of England; no crisis over Ireland, no Queen Victoria, no rotten borough system in American history. Differences in historical events and personalities quite obviously leave a deep imprint on the legal system of a country.

One specific aspect of the *legal* history of countries has given rise to a good deal of discussion. This has to do with historical membership in a particular "family" of legal systems. Legal systems change all the time, but they change against a certain traditional or historical base. Everybody knows that American law (Louisiana excepted) is part of the *common law* family. This is a group of legal systems that trace their origin to the English legal system. All of the members of the common law family are former British colonies, or colonies of colonies. They include the United States, Canada (aside from Quebec), Ireland, Australia and New Zealand, the Bahamas, Trinidad, and the rest of the English-speaking Caribbean nations; and, for the most part, the former British colonies in Asia and Africa—including Singapore, Nigeria, India, and Hong Kong.

This is a big and important family. Even bigger is the so-called *civil law* family. This is a group of legal systems that traces its origin, ultimately, to classical Roman law—at least as this body of law was rediscovered, and expounded, in the middle ages. Virtually all of the European countries are members of the civil law family. Just as the British Empire spread the common law, colonialism spread the civil law. The Spanish and Portuguese brought the civil law to Latin America, and the French brought it to their colonies in Africa, and to Quebec. The civil law has also been borrowed or adopted by a number of countries anxious to "modernize" (as they saw it) their legal systems. Japan and Turkey are well-known examples.

Large parts of the post-colonial world now belong, nominally at least, to these two families, but there are other obviously other major categories as well. Islamic law is important in many countries, from Indonesia to the Middle East and Africa. Indigenous law also remains important across the globe—as we see, for example, in Native American tribal courts in the U.S., or the official recognition of indigenous law in South Africa today.

There are obvious differences between, say, common law and civil law. There are differences in institutions. Most civil law countries do not use juries. Legal educational traditions are quite different in France compared to, for example, the United States. All sorts of concepts and ideas are difficult to translate from one system to another. But how significant are these differences? In Chapter 5, we looked at the French criminal justice system; obviously, it differs greatly from the American system. Is it less fair? Better able to handle crime? The questions we can ask about the criminal justice system—in France, or elsewhere—can be asked about everything else: family law, property, commercial law, patents and copyright, torts.

(B) Culture—and the Role of Language in Culture

As we noted in Chapter 3, it would be hard to find a more slippery concept than "culture." As a rather common English word, it has many different meanings. Here we use it to refer, in the broadest sense, to a people's way of life—their shared beliefs, and customs, the tools they use, the way they see the world, the behavior they learn, the ideas and habits that are transmitted from generation to generation.[1] Some early analysts thought of particular cultures as quite cohesive and general; they would say that a culture tends to be very tough, sticky, and long-lasting. This approach was subsequently challenged by anthropologists and other scholars who pointed out that some aspects of culture change very rapidly, and are extremely volatile. Looking at cultures as necessarily enduring and resistant to change seems to reduce the complexity of cultures to static and simplistic stereotypes. There is both continuity and massive change in the complicated reality of people's lives over time.

Just as scholars have written about culture in general, they have also written about legal culture. It is a commonly used phrase in the literature. Unfortunately, it too is a fairly slippery term; and has been used with all sorts of meanings. It is possible, here too, to look at legal culture as something tough and enduring—in which case, legal culture and legal tradition are overlapping concepts. But others use legal culture to mean ideas, beliefs, and

---

1. See Chapter 3 for further discussion of the controversy in anthropology around the culture concept.

attitudes toward law and the legal system, within some population. In this sense legal culture can be, and often is, as changeable as the wind.

There is a large literature on the subject, although it would be fair to say that there is no real consensus that emerges about the meaning and utility of the concept of legal culture. See for example, David Nelken, ed., *Comparing Legal Cultures* (1997); note, in particular, the essay by Roger Cotterrell, "The Concept of Legal Culture," id., p. 13, which is quite critical of the notion, and the reply by Lawrence M. Friedman, "The Concept of Legal Culture: A Reply," id., p. 33. For an interesting specific study of a national system, see Erhard Blankenburg and Freek Bruinsma, *Dutch Legal Culture* (1996). Anthropological linguists and sociolinguists have also pointed to the multi-layered role of language in legal culture. See, e.g., Susan Hirsch, *Pronouncing and Persevering: Gender and the Discourses of Disputing in an African Islamic Court* (1998). In the second section of this chapter, we will explore this relationship in more depth.

II. Does History Make a Difference? Two Readings

(6.1) William Forbath

"Law and the Shaping of Labor Politics in the United States and England," in Christopher L. Tomlins and Andrew J. King, eds., *Labor Law in America: Historical and Critical Essays* 201

(1992).

In addition to being the nation's portliest president, William Howard Taft was a high court judge. A state, then a federal, judge, and ultimately tenth chief justice of the U.S. Supreme Court, Taft was the leading architect of American judicial activism in labor strife. In the spring of 1894, as the United States circuit judge for the Sixth Circuit, Taft presided over some of the crucial proceedings in the judicial repression of the great Pullman Boycott. He interrupted his court business to deliver the commencement address at the University of Michigan Law School. His subject was "The Right of Private Property," and he warned that that right was "at stake" in "the social conflict now at hand."

By the conflict at hand Judge Taft did not mean merely the Pullman Boycott. He pointed to a broader attack on property, and especially on "corporate capital," in the nation's politics as well as in its industries. The chief aggressors, according to the judge, were "labor organizations ... blinded by the new sense of social and political power which combination and organization have given them." Congressmen, state legislators, and local "peace officers" all encouraged "the workingman to think that property has few rights which, in his organized union, he is bound to respect." With the connivance of such pandering politicians, labor organizations under leaders like Debs were pressing the nation toward socialism.

The present seemed bleak, but Judge Taft remained optimistic about the future. The current drift toward "state socialism" would be reversed. The main "burden of this conflict" was bound to "fall upon the courts," he declared, and the courts would prevail. He contrasted America's situation with England's. There "the assaults of socialism on the existing order" would surely prove more enduring than here. England had bequeathed to her colonies the common law, with its high regard for "security of property and contract." But England lacked our Constitution. In England "parliament has always been omnipotent." In the United States, courts had been able to insulate the rights of contract and property "much further . . . from the gusty and unthinking passions of temporary majorities." In the United States these rights were "buttressed" by a "written Constitution" against "anarchy, socialism and communism." The American judiciary, in other words, had constitutionalized many of the basic common law rules of the industrial game and, by doing so, removed them from the political arena. In time, Judge Taft assured his audience, the American labor movement would come to its senses. "Longer experience" with our "complicated [constitutional] form of government" and with staunch judges like himself would enlighten the unions as to the futility of radical politics.

To our ears the judge's confidence sounds misplaced. Did it not require a nineteenth-century habit of mind to believe that constitutions molded a working class's political outlook? To be sure, what Taft regarded as "socialism"—what we would call social democracy—became the creed of the twentieth-century labor movement in England and not in America. But could that have had much to do with "our written Constitution"? Don't Judge Taft's ideas simply betray his lack of a modern sociological imagination?

I think not, and in this essay I suggest that Judge Taft was largely right. We—particularly those of us who till the fields of legal and social history—now tend to look to deep sociological factors for our theories of causation. But in our readiness to appreciate how social groups and classes mold the law, we tend to overlook how the legal order molds those very groups as they clash and compromise over it. By comparing American and English labor's experiences with their countries' legal orders during the decades around the turn of the century, I aim to show how America's constitutional scheme and the unique powers of courts within that scheme shaped the distinctive character of the nation's labor movement. More broadly, this comparative discussion will suggest how profoundly courts and judge-made law have molded our political culture and identities.

Comparative history is said to work best when it begins with similar contexts and concurrent events in the histories of two societies and proceeds from such sameness to the exploration of revealing differences. A comparative approach seems promising here because of the profound similarities in the contexts—both institutional and cultural—of labor activity in the two countries. First, the two legal systems had much in common. The courts of both countries worked in the same common law tradition. Indeed, the judiciaries of both nations launched an almost simultaneous wave of attacks on strikes and boycotts in the 1880s and 1890s, and they elaborated a common body of rules and precepts to restrain workers' collective action.

Second, the two nations' labor movements also had structures and traditions in common. For example, the two most important labor leaders in turn-of-the-century America, Samuel Gompers and John Mitchell, were English immigrants, as were hundreds of lesser-known union leaders. They brought with them ideas and models from English trade unions. In England, conversely, the pioneers of industrial unionism and "independent labor politics" drew inspiration from their American counterparts.

Third, when confronted with mounting judicial attacks, the labor movements on both sides of the Atlantic responded alike. Each sought legislation that would repeal hostile judge-made law and legalize peaceful industrial protest. They strove for a regime of strict laissez-faire regarding workers' concerted activities. In both countries, moreover, labor met with legislative success. Here, however, the fruits of comparison begin to appear. In England, where, as Judge Taft reminded us, there was no institution of judicial review, the courts grudgingly acquiesced in their own demotion. Parliament had the final word, and labor's political victories were preserved. In the United States, by contrast, the courts swept aside one court-curbing statute after another.

The importance of this relatively subtle constitutional difference, and of the different results it generated in this case, emerges in the subsequent divergences in political strategy and vision on the part of the two movements. During this period—the late nineteenth and early twentieth century—each movement was embroiled in a battle over the political soul of trade unionism. On one side were those who championed "independent labor politics" and wished to pursue broad, class-based social and industrial reforms; on the other were those who held that labor should steer clear of politics as much as possible, other than to reform the ground rules of private ordering. In England those who championed broad reformism prevailed; in the United States they lost. The comparison I am drawing suggests that the two movements' different experiences with courts and legislatures did much to shape these divergent outcomes.

THE INSUFFICIENCY OF THE "DEEPER" FACTORS

The traditional account of American "exceptionalism" is familiar. Both in its general form and in specific comparisons of English and American experience, the account has been roughly this. The unique social context of the United States produced a working class that lacked "class consciousness" and, instead, was individualistic. From the dawn of industrialization, American workers have been wedded to individualistic strategies for bettering their lot and have largely resisted efforts to improve their condition as members of a class. Even American trade unionists have always been "pragmatists," not "class conscious" but "job conscious." Accordingly, socialist and class-based reform politics have been the province of intellectuals and agitators on the margins of political life.

The picture of the American working class on which this traditional account rests was first drawn in scholarly fashion in the 1910s and 1920s by the founders of American labor history, John Commons and the "Wisconsin School," and particularly Commons's brilliant student Selig Perlman. Commons, Perlman, and scores of other scholars after them sought to explain the phenomenon widely known as American "exceptionalism"—American workers' apparent deviance from other countries' working-class history, their supposed lack of class consciousness. Some emphasized the privileged economic condition of American workers in the nineteenth and twentieth centuries, their affluence and mobility. Others singled out the unique ethnic and religious divisions within the American working class. Generally, accounts of American "exceptionalism" have underscored both these factors and also pointed to the unusual pervasiveness of liberalism and individualism in American life, to America's tenacious two-party system and to its distinctively "weak" and fragmented liberal state.

As a result of the work of the "new labor historians," however, the received accounts will no longer do. Launched in the 1960s and by now a venerable tradition itself, the new labor history's detailed reexamination of nineteenth-century working-class life and politics has undermined the classic picture of the American working class as distinctively conservative, cautious, and individualistic. The new labor historians have rediscovered that the history of the workplace in industrializing America is one of recurring militancy and of class-based, as well as shop-and craft-based, collective action. Measured by the scale, frequency, and duration of strikes, workers' disposition toward collective action was greater in the United States than in most European nations, and considerably greater than in England, during the late nineteenth and early twentieth centuries.

The new labor history also shows that the mutualism that American workers displayed at work frequently carried over into their communities and their political and cultural lives. As Sean Wilentz and others have argued, the political ideas, cultural values, and forms of associational life that characterized the nineteenth-century workers' movements in the United States, in England, and on the Continent, were far more similar than the traditional story allows. Broad and radical reform politics characterized the mainstream views of the Gilded Age labor movement. The more cautious "pure and simple" union philosophy of Samuel Gompers was also active, but as a minority perspective in this era of American labor history. Most Gilded Age observers agreed that American unions were *more,* not less, wedded to political radicalism than their English counterparts.

Thus the key question that the work of the new labor historians poses, but has yet to answer, is this: If late nineteenth-century American workers and trade unionists were so radical, then why, by the early twentieth century, did most of them end up supporting unions and political parties that were more conservative than those embraced by their counterparts abroad? If the American labor movement was not born with a comparatively narrow, interest-group outlook or an inveterate bias against broad, positive uses of law and state power, then how did that outlook and bias become dominant in the labor movement by the early 1900s?

Of course, the old sociological explanations still beckon as potential answers to this newer question. But, again, the work of the new labor historians suggests that many of these social factors can no longer bear any great explanatory weight. For example, the view that American workers enjoyed unparalleled opportunities to rise into the middle class figures prominently in most traditional explanations for American "exceptionalism." One can imagine the same view incorporated into an account of the demise of class-based reform politics. However, the mobility story's empirical foundations have proven shaky. Sophisticated recent quantitative histories of the American working class have shown that the bulk of America's working class was no more mobile (into the middle class) than England's. Nor did any significant portion of the nineteenth-century industrial working class actually ever "go west" from urban shops and factories into farming, as traditional accounts have assumed. Even mobility *within* the American working class (from unskilled to skilled work) was far more varied and uneven than was thought. Moreover, it now seems clear that the typical forms of social mobility for nineteenth-century American workers, and, more important, their typical *aspirations* for it, were not incompatible with seeking material gains for themselves *as workers*— rather than as the individualistic incipient entrepreneurs that the mobility story always describes. Thus the mobility story probably must relinquish its place as a key factor accounting for the peculiarities of American labor politics.

Ethnic division is the other principal factor in traditional accounts. In any revised account, ethnic and racial cleavages will surely remain central. However, as Wilentz observes in surveying the field, "the familiar arguments that American exceptionalism arose from some unique divisions within the American working class are no longer as compelling as they once were." Indeed, the new labor history demonstrates that in many contexts "ethnicity could be more of a reinforcement to class solidarity than a distraction from class antagonisms."

Thus, most of the key reasons for the divergence between the political paths of the American and English labor movements must be located elsewhere, not in the character of the working-class or labor movement so much as in the character of the state and polity; less, that is, in labor and more in the arenas in which labor made and remade its visions and strategies. Perhaps, then, we should return to Judge Taft's quaint emphasis on courts and constitutions.

THE TWO FORMS OF GOVERNMENT

The powers it conferred on the courts were a critical—perhaps *the* critical—politics-shaping aspect of the American Constitution. The courts, however, did not operate in a vacuum. As Taft insisted, the American Constitution's safeguards against "socialism" consisted not only in the unique role of the courts but in the entire "complicated form of government." Thus we cannot fully assess Taft's prophecy about the role of the American Constitution in twentieth-century working-class history without considering England's and America's entire forms of government. In addition to the powers of the judiciary, three aspects of the nineteenth-century American state and polity seem central: federalism, the nature and role of political parties, and the absence of an administrative state elite. Along each of these three dimensions the English state and polity differed sharply, with important implications for the interplay of state and class formation. For now I will simply sketch these three other significant differences. I will then turn to comparing labor's experiences with the courts in the two countries. There we will see these other differences in play, complementing and reinforcing the difference between judicial and parliamentary supremacy.

The framers hoped that the far-flung and federal nature of their new republic would help avoid the formation of a class-based political "faction" of have-nots in the national arena. Their hope was realized. By the 1830s the United States had become the world's first nation with a mass franchise: by that decade, virtually all white adult males enjoyed the vote. Thus throughout the era of industrialization propertyless male industrial workers were voters. Yet, as Ira Katznelson has recently reminded us, the "diffuse federal organizational structure of the United States took much of the charge out of the issue of franchise extension, for there was no unitary state to defend or transform." American labor reformers had to contend with multiple and competing tiers of policy-making authority. This structural exigency raised the costs and reduced the efficacy of labor reforms. So doing, it strengthened the case for voluntarism.

The English state, by contrast, was unitary. During the nineteenth century, as England became an industrial nation, the making of public policies toward industrial workers happened increasingly at the center of government, as did the administration of those policies. The structure of government enabled the country's dispersed and localized unions and labor reform associations to meld their political claims.

Just as the United States was the first nation with a mass franchise, so the nineteenth-century American political party was the world's first mass-based party. Yet, the ties it forged with worker-constituents were often intensely local and particularistic. As working people were incorporated into the polity, their party loyalties generally hinged on local patronage and neighborhood, ethnic, or religious bonds—not on the broader bonds of class. Indeed, during the decades when this institutional matrix emerged and was consolidated, the industrial working class had barely been born. While not immutable, these nonclass-based, particularistic, and patronage ties to the two old parties had staying power.

In 1894 the head of the Tailors' Union, John Lennon, argued this way against the prospects of independent labor politics: "We have in this country conditions that do not exist in Great Britain. We have the 'spoils' system which is something almost unknown in Great Britain and on account of it we cannot afford to try at this time to start a political party as an adjunct with their unions.''

"Spoils" or local patronage was not a currency available to England's political parties by the time that country's male workers were fully enfranchised. In the mid–1870s England undertook major civil service reforms. Therefore, the English parties could not adopt local patronage as a means of drawing in the new mass of working-class voters. Accordingly, England's Liberal and Conservative parties relied upon class-based programmatic appeals in competing for workers' votes in a way that the Democrats and Republicans in the United States did not. Like the unitary structure of the English state, this leaning toward programmatic reforms strengthened the hand of the English trade unionists who championed broad reformism.

Late nineteenth-century England's professional civil service did more than cut off the possibility of patronage-based "machine" politics as a way of mobilizing working-class voters. It also supplied the socialists and progressives in the English labor movement with valuable allies in the corridors of state power. The upper tiers of the professional civil service constituted a powerful *nonjudicial* state elite—a substantial group of high-placed policy makers with institutional autonomy, permanence of office, and interests as well as a tradition of their own. This alternative, and often reform-minded, state elite vied with the courts for primacy in governing industrial affairs and provided significant support for the English trade unionists who championed a more statist politics. Indeed, as we shall see, many reform-minded members of this administrative elite worked hard to *persuade* often reluctant English unions to champion their reform proposals, in this respect they did not merely lend credibility to, but actually helped create, a more statist outlook among English trade unionists.

In contrast, institutional space did not exist in the nineteenth-or early twentieth-century American state for an organizationally autonomous administrative state elite. There was, of course, no lack of reform-minded, university-educated professionals in the United States who were ready and eager to do the same policy-making and state building work undertaken by their English counterparts. In a handful of states—and across a narrower range of industrial issues—they managed to do so. But administrative posts with power and influence comparable to England's high officialdom did not exist in the United States. The state and federal constitutions had been designed to frustrate those who would centralize and expand executive policy-making authority and administrative capacities, encouraging instead the emergence of what political scientist Steven Skowronek has called a "state of courts and parties."

Late nineteenth-and early twentieth-century America saw an unholy but highly successful alliance between the judicial elite and party bosses against civil service reformers and would-be welfare state builders. The party pols saw the reformers' efforts to create a professionalized civil service and a centralized welfare state as threats to the localized, patronage forms of government on which their power rested. To the courts the reformers' vision of the modern administrative agency undermined the separation of powers as well as judicial prerogatives. They concluded that it lay outside the constitutional pale.

The victories of this alliance in upholding the old scheme of government deprived the era's labor movement of the kinds of powerful state-based allies enjoyed by their English comrades. The lack of such allies, in turn, made broad reform politics less availing in the United States.

The reformers' defeats also deprived the labor movement of a corps of factory and mine inspectors and labor law administrators comparable to England's. Already in the 1860s England's factory inspectors had earned the admiration of no less a critic than Karl Marx. By the 1890s, England had roughly 140 full-time factory and mine inspectors covering roughly 190,000 workplaces. In sharp contrast to the United States, their jobs were insulated from changes in political administration; their occupation had become a reformist profession, with its own schools and traditions.

At the turn of the century most labor laws in most American states remained in what a classic study calls "the pre-enforcement stage"; they either were hortatory and had no penalty provisions or, at best, required enforcement by private civil actions rather than by state officials. More advanced states relied on the affected employee or his union to try to prevail on the ordinary state attorneys to prosecute their complaints. Seventeen states were in the "enforcement stage" at the turn of the century; they had factory and mine inspectors. Throughout the nation, all of 114 inspectors covered some 513,000 workplaces; many of them were merely policemen on special assignment, and many others were less than full-time inspectors.

Small wonder, then, that in turn-of-the-century America, English immigrant miners and factory workers could be heard bemoaning the paucity and powerlessness of American mine and factory inspectors. Even in the most progressive states, factory and mine inspectors often were scarce in comparison to England and lacked many of their English colleagues' enforcement and rule-making powers; "the courts remained the fundamental agency for securing compliance." Accordingly, courts held greater sway over the interpretation, administration, and enforcement of labor laws, and they tended to nullify by hostile construction many of the reforms that they didn't strike down. This too helped make the "progressive" vision of state-based industrial reform seem unavailing to many American trade unionists.

These, then, were the contrasting state structures and traditions within which judicial supremacy operated upon labor's political choices in America and parliamentary supremacy swayed labor's politics in England. I turn now to those developments.

THE AMERICAN STORY

The mainstream of the American labor movement in the late nineteenth century hewed to the idea that workers could use the ballot to transform the face of industry. Largest of Gilded Age (1880s–90s) labor organizations was the Knights of Labor; the Knights strove to meld trade union and political endeavors, appealing to the "laboring classes" as both producers and citizens. The organization reached out from a base among coal miners and artisans to a constituency that embraced the burgeoning mass of unskilled factory workers. In addition to waging strikes and boycotts, the Knights created labor parties and ran and elected candidates to local and state government. Unifying all these activities was the project of preparing the "toiling classes" for self-rule. Workers read traditional republican principles to mean that in an industrial society the very survival of republican government demanded using governmental power to quell the "tyranny" of corporations and capital. Toppling "corporate tyranny" entailed a host of legislative reforms: hours laws and other workplace regulations, the abolition of private banking, public funding for worker-owned industry, and the nationalization of monopolies.

During the Gilded Age the American Federation of Labor also emerged. Many of its founders were trade union leaders like Samuel Gompers, who shunned the wide-ranging reform ambitions of the Knights; they also diverged from the Knights by insisting that unions were best built on a craft basis rather than by embracing all who toiled in a given industry. Gompers was the preeminent spokesman for this somewhat narrower trade union philosophy. During this era, however, the outlook associated with Gompers was far less distinct from the competing vision embodied in the Knights than it later became. Indeed, a great many AFL unions and union activists in this period shared the Knights' vision of inclusive unionism, their broad reform ambitions, and their faith in lawmaking and the ballot.

By the turn of the century, however, Gompers's outlook had become the predominant one. The Knights of Labor were defunct, and the AFL was the nation's leading labor organization. Government bludgeoning of one major strike after another had left the AFL leadership wary of inclusive unionism and broad-based sympathetic actions. Soon the AFL would also begin to assail many varieties of labor laws and social and industrial "reform by legislation," and the republican rights talk of the Gilded Age movement would give way to a liberal, laissez faire language of protest and reform.

This new antistatist labor outlook did not preclude involvement in national as well as state politics; to the contrary, the early twentieth-century AFL became increasingly involved in electioneering and lobbying. But its initiatives focused on *voluntarist* goals—above all, to halt hostile judicial interventions in labor disputes. Increasingly, the organization's dominant unions set their faces against the broader, class-based reform politics and inclusive unionism that had marked the earlier era.

What part did the courts play in these developments? In spite of the obstacles that we have canvassed—the federated form of American government, the patronage and particularistic cast of political parties, and the absence of a strong administrative state apparatus and elite—the Gilded Age labor movement's successes in electing local and state candidates and passing labor reforms meant that in some late nineteenth-century industrial states, the laws regulating hours and workplace conditions and enlarging workers' freedom of collective action compared favorably with England's. These successes seemed to vindicate the view that politics and legislation were powerful engines of industrial reform.

Once legislative reforms were passed, however, it was the courts that determined how they would fare; and during the 1880s and 1890s the state and federal courts were more likely than not to strike down the very laws that labor sought most avidly. By the turn of the century, judges had voided roughly sixty labor laws. These constitutional cases figured prominently in the battles that raged through the 1890s between the champions of broad and minimalist labor politics. One such debate occurred at the 1894 AFL Convention, concerning whether the AFL would embrace "independent labor politics" and adopt a "political programme," which had been proposed by some of the federation's socialist unions. The program included the goal of a legal eight hour workday. Speaking to that point, Adolph Strasser of the Cigarmakers declared: "There is one fact that can't be overlooked. You can't pass an eight hour day without changing the Constitution of the United States and the Constitution of every state in the Union.... I am opposed to wasting our time declaring for legislation being enacted for a time after we are all dead."

Henry Lloyd, a widely known journalist, a key figure in the Labor Populist alliance, and a champion of broad labor reform responded by describing the depth of support for a legal eight-hour day at a recent labor conference that he had attended in England. Unimpressed, Strasser retorted, "Is it not a fact that in England there is no constitutional provision [to stymie an eight-hour law]?" Then Strasser pointed proudly to the craft unions like his own Cigarmakers, who had gained the eight-hour day "by themselves ... passing and enforcing [their own] law without the government."

Invalidated labor laws were both powerful evidence and a potent symbol of the recalcitrance of the American state. The courts seemed so formidable partly because judicial review of labor laws was bound up with a broader judicial power. We have noted the extent to which courts controlled the interpretation, administration, and enforcement of reform legislation. Not only could judges strike down labor laws; they could also nullify them by hostile construction. And nullify they did. Typically, they treated labor legislation as ill-considered tinkering with a governmental domain that belonged by right to the judiciary and the common law.

Judicial review of reform legislation arose at a key moment of collective decision making in labor's political history. During this moment the courts helped turn minimalist politics from a minority outlook of cautious craft unionists like Strasser and Gompers into what seemed the surest path to most of the labor movement, a movement that would come increasingly to be dominated by craft unionists like themselves.

The thrust of a Gompers's or Strasser's voluntarist outlook was this: Labor should improve its lot through organization and collective bargaining.

The less it relied on the state and the more it attained in the private realm of market relations, the better.

But the courts did not simply leave alone this private realm of market relations. First, of course, it was the common law that defined the metes and bounds of workers' marketplace conduct. In the early nineteenth century, the legal bounds on workers' "combinations" and strikes were more generous in the United States than elsewhere. Nonetheless, the ante bellum American courts set sharp limits on what counted as a legally tolerable strike or as allowable strike activities, limits that changed remarkably little over the course of the nineteenth century. Moreover, the application of these legal restraints grew dramatically harsher and more pervasive. Beginning in the 1880s, the courts vastly enlarged their role in regulating and policing industrial conflict. Also at this time, the characteristic form of legal intervention changed, and the labor injunction was born. By a conservative reckoning, at least forty-three hundred injunctions were issued between 1880 and 1930. This figure represents only a small fraction of the total number of strikes in those decades but a sizable proportion of the larger strikes and a significant percentage of sympathetic and secondary actions. During the 1890s, for example, courts enjoined at least 1 percent of recorded sympathy strikes. That percentage rose to 25 percent in the next decade, and by the 1920s 46 percent of all sympathy strikes were greeted by antistrike decrees. As injunctions multiplied, the language of judge-made law became pervasive in industrial strife. Anti-union employers and state officials constantly spoke a court-minted language of rights and wrongs. Again and again trade unionists attributed the repression of strikes and protest to judge-made law—even when no injunction was in sight.

As the legal repression of labor protest and collective action intensified, the mainstream of the labor movement relinquished positive regulation or reconstruction of industry as its central political project. The prime object of labor's political energies became simply escaping the burdens of semi-outlawry. Thus the AFL strove to legalize all the peaceful forms of collective action that stood under judicial ban. It contested judge-made law everywhere: in the courts, of course, but equally in the legislatures and in the public sphere. In the course of this decades-long campaign, trade unionists began to speak and think more and more in the language of the law, abandoning a republican vocabulary of protest and reform for a liberal, law-inspired language of rights. They no longer proposed to use legislation to quell the "tyranny" of capital. "Labor," they would declare, "asks no favors from the State." It wants to be let alone and to be allowed to exercise its rights.

The protracted nature of this struggle to end legal repression returns us to the significance of the courts' power to hobble labor legislation. From the 1890s through the 1920s, labor prevailed on legislatures to pass many statutes loosening the judge-made restraints on collective action; in all, the states and Congress passed roughly forty court-curbing reforms during these decades—reversing substantive labor law doctrines, instituting procedural changes, and narrowing and, in some instances, flatly repealing equity jurisdiction over labor. At least twenty-five of these statutes were voided on constitutional grounds, and most of those not struck down were vitiated by narrow construction. Until the national emergency of the Great Depression and the constitutional revolution waged by FDR and the New Dealers, courts had both the power and the will to trump these measures. So, during these four formative decades, as the number of antistrike decrees multiplied and the burdens of outlawry persisted, the AFL's political energies were riveted on gaining this indispensable—but negative, laissez-faireist—reform, and the AFL's voluntarist perspective hardened.

To be sure, the debate between minimalists and radicals continued. The anticapitalist republicanism of the Gilded Age labor movement was carried into the twentieth century by the Socialist party and others, and socialist and "progressive" labor leaders were prominent in many important AFL unions throughout the period. Moreover, the relative autonomy of the state federations of labor meant that broad reform politics remained dominant in some industrial states. Nevertheless, from 1900 onward most American trade unionists agreed with Gompers that it was folly to try to remake industry by legislation; legislation was a distressingly unreliable engine of reform, and the only things that labor ought to seek from government was what it could not gain otherwise: above all, repeal of the judge-made restraints on collective action. Even those with a broader reform vision than Gompers's had to concede that this goal was labor's political sine qua non, and for the AFL leadership, it became the defining theme of an increasingly rigid, antistatist politics. Thus the recalcitrance of the American state of courts and parties got labor stuck in this stage of "negative" reform and minimalist politics—a stage that, as we shall now see, the English labor movement in this same era left behind.

THE ENGLISH STORY

The Common Law and the Common Beginning

American and English courts worked within the same common law tradition. They restricted workers' collective action through an almost identical body of rules and precepts. All the key common law doctrines of American labor law hailed from or developed simultaneously in England. But despite this profound similarity in legal systems, English courts played a different role in regulating workers' collective action during the nineteenth and early twentieth centuries. The English judiciary shared policy-making initiative and power with Parliament, and Parliament was the more powerful actor. There were, to be sure, persistent tensions, and as we will see, English courts were no less ill disposed than American ones toward legislative measures that loosened the legal reins on workers. But Parliament held the trumps.

In the first decades of the nineteenth century English labor law was more hostile to unionism than American. It was also more statutory. In contrast to the United States, modern trade unionism and both craft and industrial workers' collective action emerged in England under a legal regime forged chiefly by the legislature. Inspired by events in France and their domestic reverberations, the Combination Acts of 1799 and 1800 criminalized unions along with many other associational activities of the lower classes. Other statutes also prohibited combinations in specific trades. In addition, unions were (under broadly defined circumstances) criminal conspiracies "in restraint of trade."

With the easing of upper-class anxieties, Parliament repealed the Combination Acts in 1824 and thereby ended the English state's efforts flatly to bar combinations among artisans and laborers. For the next half-century English trade unions existed in an often precarious position of semilegality, prone to the vagaries of judicial interpretation of the law of criminal conspiracy. Statutory reforms had increased employers' reliance on conspiracy law. As unionism extended beyond traditional crafts, strikes became an increasingly common aspect of labor organization. The courts greeted these developments by enlarging the bans of conspiracy doctrine to cover more and more kinds of strikes and strike activities.

Ousting the Criminal Law

In the late 1860s, this burgeoning law of labor conspiracies inspired the newly formed Trades Union Congress to turn to politics. Founded in 1868 by the national leaders of such major unions as the engineers, the carpenters, and the bricklayers, the Trades Union Congress (TUC) became England's enduring labor federation. At the time, however, most English trade unionists were wary of centralization. Other efforts at forming national union federations had failed. If they wanted to overcome the workers' ingrained particularism and jealous independence, the ambitious leaders who founded the TUC had to demonstrate the new federation's worth. They did so by successfully lobbying against repressive judge-made and statutory labor law. Led by the new Parliamentary Committee of the Trades Union Congress, the unions in 1871 secured from Parliament the Trade Union and Criminal Law Amendment Acts. Then in 1875 Disraeli's government, prompted by competition for the votes of the newly enfranchised upper layers of the working class, met the unions' demands for greater protection from the courts with the Conspiracy and Protection of Property Act. The 1875 act contained what English labor lawyers ever since have called the "golden formula": acts by two or more persons, done in the context of a "trade dispute," were not liable to prosecution unless the acts were crimes if done by individuals. The 1875 act created a broad immunity indeed; it "marked the end of the significance of criminal law in labour relations" in England.

Broad as these immunities were, the "golden formula," along with the 1871 acts' immunity for labor from restraint of trade prosecutions and legalization of picketing, was virtually identical to provisions of several statutes passed by American state legislatures in the 1880s and 1890s. Courts struck down or sharply vitiated all of these late nineteenth-century American statutes, and the era saw the harshest (and most frequent) labor conspiracy convictions in the nation's history. In contrast, in England criminal prosecutions against labor virtually ceased after the 1875 act. This is what was remarkable from an American perspective: not the legislature's liberality—American legislatures had matched that—but the judiciary's acquiescence in the sharp revision of judge-made law.

Parliament's decision and its judicial aftermath taught English labor that Parliament could rule the courts in the setting of state policy. The 1875 act and its aftermath of judicial restraint would also figure as crucial precedent in the next chapter of Parliament versus the courts, involving civil injunctions and damage suits.

The "Collectivist" Alternative

The legislation of 1875 brought in its wake a full-blown alliance between the TUC leadership and the Liberals. Labor "formed," in Engels's acid phrase, "the tail of the 'Great Liberal Party.'" By 1886 the TUC boasted ten 'Lib–Lab" members of Parliament. Their views on the uses of law and state power were laissez-faire and anti-interventionist, more adamantly so than those of many middle-class MPs in the Liberal party. Born of the self-help ethos of strong craft unions and of the English working class's long exclusion from politics and its mistrust of government paternalism, it was an outlook that closely resembled that of Gompers and his AFL craft union allies across the Atlantic.

In the United States, as we have noted, this laissez-faire creed remained something of a minority viewpoint in the 1880s. In contrast to their English brothers, American workingmen had long enjoyed the ballot, and, as David Montgomery has shown, the Radical Republicans of the Reconstruction era had imparted to most American trade union leaders a strong belief in "reform by legislation." The Radicals, their ideology, and their Reconstruction programs had taught labor's advocates the potentialities of an active democratic state for transforming oppressive social and labor relations.

Thus at the beginning of our period, the more radical and more statist alternative enjoyed stronger support in the United States. But it found adherents in England too. In both countries, it was the trade unionists who led the less skilled who tended to insist that mere laissez-faire was not enough, that positive state support and regulation were necessary. A broad view of the uses of law and state power generally went along with a broader, more inclusive unionism. In the United States this more radical vision belonged to the Knights of Labor and to the socialist and progressive wing of the AFL. In England it was associated with the "new unionism" of the less skilled and unskilled workers, which emerged in the 1880s, led by working-class socialists like John Burns and Tom Mann, who led the great London dock strike of 1889 and founded the Dockworkers' union. These new unions stood outside the pale of the "labor aristocracy" that dominated the TUC.

Just as unionists associated with the inclusive Knights created local labor parties and ran labor candidates for local elections, so Burns and Mann were founders of the Independent Labour Party, the small socialist party of late nineteenth-century England. In retrospect it is ironic that their brightest inspiration lay in the success of the Knights in America.

The Employers' Counteroffensive

In the mid–1890s, English labor leaders of all political stripes began to speak about a threatened "Americanization" of English industry. The phrase rested on a fear that giant American-style trusts and combinations were emerging in England. The specter of "Americanization" also had a more specific set of referents—one suggested by English trade unionists' constant talk of "Homestead" and "Pullman." These American comparisons were used to characterize what English labor historians have called "the employers' counteroffensive" of the 1890s. Prompted by the rise of the "new unionism," particularly by the new unions' tumultuous strikes and radical politics, and also by mounting international competition, the employers' counteroffensive was marked by the renewal of judicial activism against striking unions. This, above all, made "Americanization" an apt description. The courts' renewed involvement in labor strife took a form that was already familiar by virtue of stories from America: stories of injunctions, heavy damage awards, and the use of judicially sanctioned violence against strikers.

As in the United States, a series of antiunion high court decisions encouraged the creation of employers' associations devoted to organized strikebreaking, and the new employers' associations, in turn, encouraged greater resort to the courts for antistrike decrees and damage judgments. *Temperton v. Russell,* decided in 1893, was the first of these hostile decisions. It involved a refusal by plasterers and stoneworkers to work on materials bound for an antiunion construction firm. By ruling for the building firm, *Temperton* announced the applicability of civil conspiracy doctrine in circumstances in which the 1875 act precluded a finding of criminal conspiracy. In so doing, the case introduced a vast new uncertainty about the bounds of concerted action, since it signaled that the "golden formula" did not insulate traditional tactics from civil liability. Other civil cases followed, similarly holding actionable union conduct that was immune from criminal sanctions under the 1875 act. The employers' counteroffensive was marked by grim nationwide lockouts against long-established craft unions like the engineers as well as against the newly organized Dockers. Accompanying these lockouts was the employers' increasingly massive and systematic recruitment of strikebreakers. The picket line was often the striker's only chance to speak to strikebreakers whether to exhort, cajole, or shame, or to menace. Yet the lower courts had begun routinely to enjoin picketing. The most important case upholding the judicial repression of picketing was *Lyons v. Wilkins* (1896). The opinions of both the trial and the various appellate judges suggest that their views on the allowable bounds of labor protest were roughly identical to those that characterized most American federal and state court judges at the time. *Temperton, Lyons,* and the cases that followed inspired alarm over how far the borders of allowable protest and mutual aid would narrow. Americanization seemed to be approaching with a vengeance.

Taff Vale

Then came the 1901 House of Lords decision in *Taff Vale,* which upheld an injunction and damages award against Welsh railway workers and their union. The *Taff Vale* strike was emblematic of the employers' counteroffensive against the new unionism, involving a struggle for recognition waged by the Amalgamated Society of Railway Servants (ASKS), which embraced both skilled and semiskilled workers. In resisting the strike, an obdurate railway management had turned to the services of a recently founded employers' association that operated a national network of "Free Labour Exchanges." When the Free Labour strikebreakers first arrived at the Cardiff station, they were met by a large band of pickets. At the head of the pickets was Richard Bell, the Amalgamated general secretary. Bell distributed to the imported workers a leaflet notifying them of the strike and offering them return fares. At least a third of the workers were browbeaten into accepting the offer and returned to London and Glasgow.

The Law Lords held that Bell's and the picketers' "besetting" of the strikebreakers at the station was illegal under *Temperton.* The Lords also held that not only could strikers and their leaders be held liable for such conduct, but so too could union treasuries. Henceforth, unions might be liable for heavy damages for any of the kinds of boycotts, strikes, and strike activities that were falling under judicial bans.

After *Taff Vale* even the most conservative of the "old guard" were persuaded of the need for vigorous action to repeal the judge-made law of industrial conflicts. But during the years immediately following the decision the Conservative government resisted all talk of restoring the "golden formula." Meanwhile, the Liberals seemed downright indifferent to labor's plight, as the party's leaders temporized, uncertain how far they wanted to redraw the boundaries of allowable collective action. Within a few years, the Liberal party lost the allegiance of hundreds of local unions and trade councils, as these groups turned away from restrained Lib–Lab politics toward supporting independent labor candidacies.

Taff Vale and the courts trebled the number of trade unions that affiliated with the Labour Representation Committee, predecessor of the Labour party. This dramatic growth of the LRC was a triumph for the radicals and socialists, but it did not overnight transform the character of labor politics. Many old guard unions that had affiliated with the LRC were quite unsure where they stood on the question of collectivism. Still wary of broad reform ambitions, they were wedded only to the goal of creating a sufficiently strong bargaining position to force the next Liberal government to undo the effects of the *Taft Vale* decision. The radicals' desire to forge a long-term alternative to liberalism would have to await the outcome of the immediate struggle.

Both desires—the immediate one for repeal of *Taft Vale* and the long-term one for a collectivist alternative—were, however, educated by experiences that made them seem attainable. It was hardly reckless for trade unionists to believe that if pressed, Parliament could swiftly quell the courts. The 1875 act, and the effective immunities from conspiracy and restraint of trade prosecutions that it created, had not only taught labor a lesson in the efficacy of reform by legislation; they also meant that labor could cast "repealing *Taft Vale*" as restoring Parliament's own rule with respect to an issue Parliament had already once decided. Thus Labour MPs spoke constantly of the need for legislation "to restore to the trade unions an immunity which for thirty years they have enjoyed" and "to prevent workmen being placed by judge-made law in a position inferior to that intended by Parliament in 1875." In 1906 the Liberal prime minister, Campbell–Bannerman, would champion the Trade Disputes Act precisely in the language of restoring the "old borders" and Parliament's authority over labor law.

Even with respect to the long-term goal of a collectivist alternative to liberalism, the more radical trade unionists had good reasons to believe that the state was relatively amenable to their new program. Here the role of the high civil service is central and the contrast with the United States becomes marked, for the latter lacked both a central administrative apparatus and a nonjudicial state elite. As I have pointed out, by the 1890s England's high civil service in offices like the Board of Trade contained "new liberals," who keenly supported not only new protective legislation like minimum wages laws, but also the expansion of the state's responsibilities (and administrative capacity) to embrace ambitious "collectivist" welfare measures like old age, health, and unemployment insurance. Indeed, around the turn of the century high-placed progressive administrators were negotiating with labor leaders about the part unions might play in administering various forms of state-based social insurance. The Board of Trade had begun "sending speakers to trade councils and other organizations and appointing trade unionists to the Labour Department." In England, the idea of a national government won over to classwide social "reform by legislation" had none of the utopian quality it bore in the United States.

Enlightened politicians and administrators also had no doubt that they, and not the courts, were the proper policy makers respecting strikes. Even during the grim 1890s and into the early 1900s, while *Taff Vale* remained good law, they stood for a policy of government support for trade unionism. From 1901 through 1905 the Board of Trade's high officials advocated reforming labor law "so as to minimize the scope for judicial involvement."

Thus in weighing whether to invest their political fortunes in independent labor politics, trade unionists knew that significant state actors had already made an investment of their own in the labor movement. The question was whether fielding independent labor candidates would force the Liberals' hand.

The answer turned out to be yes. In the face of Liberal temporizing the LRC put fifty independent candidates in the field in the general election of 1906. And in the face of this showing virtually all Liberal and a significant number of Conservative candidates committed themselves to the TUC's Trade

Disputes Bill. The bill became law that year. Section 1 restored the "golden formula," applying it to civil conspiracy law, so that henceforth any act done in concert, in contemplation or furtherance of a trade dispute, was not actionable unless it was illegal if done by an individual without concert. Section 2 repealed the courts' bar on peaceful picketing, immunizing pickets from civil and criminal prosecution. Section 4, the most controversial, specifically repealed *Taff Vale*. By ruling out tort actions for damages or equitable relief against unions for wrongs committed by either officers or members, section 4 embodied, in Kahn–Freund's words, "the British solution of the problem of the labor injunction." Thus the 1906 act gave English labor an extraordinary freedom from legal restraints. According to Sidney and Beatrice Webb, "most lawyers, as well as all employers, regard[ed the extent of these immunities] as monstrous." Nevertheless, Parliament had spoken, and apart from some minor skirmishes, the courts acquiesced in labor's new freedom of collective action.

CONCLUSION

"The Legislature cannot make evil good," declared the judge who had authored *Taft Vale* in a 1908 opinion construing the monstrous new act, "but it can make it not actionable." Not all the high court judges were as outspoken. Some insisted on greater stoicism in the judicial administration of the disturbing new immunities. However, other Law Lords besides the author of *Tafi Vale* sometimes made plain how they would have treated the act if, like their American counterparts, they had enjoyed the power of judicial review.

By 1906 American judges had struck down four statutes containing provisions similar to those in the 1906 English act and left none standing. The English judges lacked that power. Accordingly, labor gained another dramatic lesson in the efficacy of reform by legislation. The year that the TUC's Trades Disputes Bill became law—1906—marked the official founding of the Labour party. More important, it marked a turning point in the evolution of English labor politics.

Ending the legal repression of trade unionism lent enormous impetus and authority to the radicals and socialists who had led the battle for independent labor politics. Over the next several years, this impetus and authority would enable them to mobilize the ambivalent "old guard" unionists—and, thereby, the TUC—in support of the new party and its "collectivist" program of social reforms. Reading the labor press and the speeches of Labour candidates in the years following 1906, one finds the proponents of a broad reform program appealing again and again to Labour's swift triumph over the courts. The stump speakers and publicists of the new party pointed to this victory and called on their uncertain comrades to look anew at Parliament as a vehicle of working-class aspirations. Now that labor had secured its legal status in the industrial arena by gaining collective laissez-faire, it was no longer treacherous, but timely instead, to focus upon other, positive reforms. And the acquiescence of the Liberals and the administrative elite in adopting labor's own version of labor's rights supplied a balm for the old fears of government-sponsored reforms. Those fears were bred of a dependency on middle-class advocates and representatives; the party vowed to break that dependency and to press forward with the rest of its program—old age pensions, unemployment insurance, an eight-hour day.

The old guard might have responded to these progressive appeals as did their counterparts in early twentieth-century America, resisting any fundamental break with their voluntarist, antistatist outlook. However, the victory over the courts meant that labor's industrial liberties were no longer in jeopardy; the political sina qua non had been gained in England, and the manifest support of the powerful progressive state elite in that battle—and the promise of its support in battles to come—made it seem a wise wager to depart from the voluntarist heritage and embrace a broader and independent labor politics.

Embrace it they did. The party's membership doubled between 1906 and 1911. And during those years Parliament passed an eight hour day for miners; a noncontributory old age pension scheme; provision for the first trade boards, which would administer a minimum wage; and finally sickness and unemployment insurance schemes. Prodded by the unions and the Labour party, and guided by the progressive state-builders in the permanent civil service, "it had laid the foundations of the welfare state."

In the United States achieving a secure legal status for trade unionism consumed several decades. A constitutional revolution had to occur before that sine qua non could be attained. During the Gilded Age the movement's mainstream had been disposed toward broad regulatory and redistributive politics. But its experiences with what Judge Taft called our "complicated" constitutional form of government—a continent-sized, fragmented, federalist state dominated by obdurate constitutional courts and tenacious, multiclass parties—drove it toward a narrow, antistatist outlook. It spurned "socialism," as the judge prophesied it would, and embraced instead a labor variant of the courts' own laissez-faire Constitution.

NOTES AND QUESTIONS

1. <u>Structure versus Culture</u>: Forbath is trying to explain why England and the United States diverged so greatly in the way their labor movements developed, and the way the labor movements interacted with the legal system. Forbath stresses that *structural* elements, rather than *cultural* elements in the history of labor relations and labor law, are the key explanatory variables. Do you find his explanation persuasive? How would you go about proving or disproving it? What method does Forbath use?

2. The structural elements in American history that Forbath stresses include judicial review under a written constitution (lacking in England), a fragmented and federal system, and a weak civil service. Which of these is the most important, according to Forbath?

3. Forbath's subject is labor law. But the structural elements he stresses are quite general. What other fields of law, do you think, would have been decisively shaped by these elements, presumably in ways that differed greatly from the way they were shaped in English legal history.

4. <u>England versus the United States</u>: England and the United States share a common legal tradition; but they have been separated for more than 200 years. The various fields of law have been going their own separate ways as well. In family law, for example, England never had such a thing as a common law marriage; divorce was essentially not possible until 1857; and legal adoption of children did not enter English law until 1926. In the United States, formal adoption entered the legal system in the middle of the 19th century.

Why the difference between the two countries? For one answer, see Lawrence M. Friedman, *A History of American Law* 149 (3rd ed., 2005): he argues that the "point of adoption, as a legal device, was ... land and money.... Most of the statutes stressed the rights of the new son or daughter to inherit ... [T]he landless poor do not need an adoption law." The laws thus reflect "the master fact of American law and life: In this society an enormous mass of ordinary people owned land and other types of property." The situation in England, still dominated by a small group of landed gentry, was quite different.

Is this the same kind of explanation as Forbath's explanation of differences in labor law? If not, how is it different? Are the two types of explanation inconsistent?

5. Forbath's study is historical, but based on persistent structural differences between England and the United States. The United States is still much more decentralized than England. The situation with regard to judicial review is rather complicated. There is still no formal judicial review of legislation in England; but England is a member of the common market, and has signed various treaties on human rights which are enforceable through international courts (see below, *postscript*).

What would you expect to be the situation today, in labor law? How different, would you guess, are English and American labor law? Family law? The law of contracts and torts?

(6.2) Harsh Justice: Criminal Punishment and the Widening Divide Between American and Europe

James Q. Whitman

(2003).

At the beginning of the twenty-first century, criminal punishment is harsh in American, and it has been getting harsher. In the year 2000, the incarcerated population reached the extraordinary level of 2 million, roughly quintupling since the mid–1970s. America's per capita incarceration is now the highest in the world, approaching, and in some regions exceeding, ten times the rate in Western Europe. Large-scale incarceration is only part of the story, though. Juveniles have increasingly been tried "as adults"—something that Western Europeans find little less than shocking. New sorts of punishments have been invented over the last twenty-five years, from boot camps to electronic monitoring devices; and old sorts of punishments, from chain gangs to public shaming, have been revived. Some of the new harshness has involved matters almost everybody regards as momentous: in particular the death penalty, reintroduced in the United States at the very moment that it was definitively abolished in Western Europe. At the same time, some of the new harshness, has involved almost laughably trivial matters: "quality of life" policing has landed people in jail—if only for a night—for offenses like smoking cigarettes in the New York subway; and the Supreme Court has declared that police may jail persons for something as minor as driving without a seat belt. All of these developments, whether trivial or momentous, have been surrounded by a jarringly punitive rhetoric in American politics, perhaps best exemplified by the Phoenix sheriff who proudly declares that he runs "a very bad jail."

None of this is news. Everyone who reads the newspapers knows that we have been in the midst of a kind of national get-tough movement, which has lasted for about the last twenty-five years. Still, Americans may not quite grasp how deeply isolated this period has left us in the Western world. Punishment in America is now, as Michael Tonry observes, "vastly harsher than in any other country to which the United States would ordinarily be compared." There are certainly some parts of the world that have turned harsher over the last twenty-five years. This is true in particular of some Islamic countries. But among Western nations, only England has followed our lead—and even England has followed us only up to certain point. As for the countries of continental Western Europe, the contrast between their practices and ours has become stark indeed. The Western European media regularly runs pieces expressing shock at the extreme severity of American punishment. Meanwhile, continental justice systems have come to treat America as something close to a rogue state, hesitating to extradite offenders to the United States.

To be sure, this era of American harshness will presumably not go on for ever, and it may already have slowed. Nevertheless, it is the disturbing truth that we now find ourselves in a strange place on the international scene. As a result of the last quarter century of deepening harshness, we are no longer clearly classified in the same categories as the other countries of the liberal West. Instead, by the measure of our punishment practices, we have edged into the company of troubled and violent places like Yemen and Nigeria (both of which, like many jurisdictions in the United States, execute people for crimes committed when they were minors—though Yemen has recently renounced the practice); to China and Russia (two societies that come close to rivaling our incarceration rates); pre–2001 Afghanistan (where the Taliban, like American judges, reintroduced public shame sanctions); and even Nazi Germany (which, like the contemporary United States, turned sharply toward retributivism and the permanent incapacitation of habitual offenders). What is going on in our country?

The question I want to approach is the cultural roots of harsh criminal punishment as it has emerged in contemporary America. Most especially, it is about, how harsh criminal punishment can develop in a society that belongs to the Western liberal tradition. America is, after all, a country that belongs to something it is fair to call the Western "liberal" tradition, elusive though the concept of liberalism may be. Certainly there are many aspects of American culture that seem manifestly to belong to a humane strain of liberalism. Ours, of all Western countries, is the one that is most consistently suspicious of state authority. Ours is the country with the inveterate attachment to the values of procedural fairness. Ours is the country that—unlike Germany or France—never succumbed to any variety of fascism or Nazism. Why, then, is ours not the country with the mildest punishment practices? Certainly, in most respects, Americans define their values by opposition to illiberal societies-to the societies of places like China or the Afghanistan of the Taliban or Nazi Germany. How could our patterns of punishment be bringing us closer to them than to the dominant polities of the contemporary European Union?

The answer ... is drawn from history—a comparative history that reaches back to the eighteenth century, to a time before the French and American revolutions. In particular, it is drawn from a close comparative study of the United States, on the one hand, and the two dominant legal cultures of the European continent, France and Germany, on the other. There are good reasons to choose France and Germany for such a study. Of all the continental countries, these are the two that cry out most for close comparison with our own, in this era of American harshness. They are large and powerful industrial nations that have been strongholds of humane and democratic Western values since 1945. They are countries that have set the tone for all of the continent for many generations, and that continue to set much of the tone for the human rights jurisprudence of the European Union. Not least, they are the countries that we have measured ourselves against since the time of the American Revolution, Indeed, they are countries that, once upon a time, seemed precisely to lack the humane and democratic values that *America* stood for, France and Germany, as they exist today, are the descendants of the "despotic," state-heavy, hierarchical societies against which we defined ourselves two and half centuries ago. They are also countries that have had recurrent episodes of authoritarian government, from the nineteenth century through the horrific 1930s and 1940s. Yet at the end of the millennium, they are countries that punish far more mildly than ours does. Why?

[Michael] Foucault, in his famous *Discipline and Punish*, described modern punishment as the product of an ominous shift from disciplining the body to disciplining the soul. This makes for a dramatic, and sometimes fitting, description of continental punishment; and it also makes for a fitting description of some aspects of American punishment. But it tells us nothing about how punishment practices could diverge on the two sides of the Atlantic, with America striking off alone on the road to intensifying harshness. Much the same objection applies even to the most sensitive recent work on "modernity." Of course large industrial countries share some "modern" features, but what they share can hardly explain how they have diverged; and these countries have diverged.... We cannot understand American punishment without understanding America; and the same goes for the rest of the "modern world." Sensible criminologists have always been ready to acknowledge that different cultures produce different forms of punishment....

Like other wise scholars, I will accordingly focus on comparative culture; there is something in the American idiom, something in American culture, that is driving us toward harsh punishment.

Of course, "American culture" is a vast topic, and I should emphasize from the outset that there are important aspects of American culture that I am not going to explore with any care. It is clear, for example, that American harshness has something to do with the strength of its religious tradition, and especially its Christian tradition. Part of what makes us harsher than continental Europeans is the presence of some distinctively fierce American Christian beliefs. It is also the case that American harshness has something to do with American racism—though, as we shall see, continental European race relations are not noticeably better than American, While I will touch on both of these issues repeatedly, I will not discuss either in any detail. Perhaps most important, it is clear that the relative harshness of American punishment has a great deal to do with the prevalence of violence in American society—both because Americans have higher rates of violent crime, and because American patterns of violence also make themselves felt in prisons, policing, and elsewhere. The difference in patterns of violence matters immensely, and it certainly deserves attention....

Instead, leaving race, Christianity, and violence to one side, this book will focus on two quite different aspects of American culture: on American patterns of *egalitarian social status* and on American patterns *of resistance to state power*. American society has a deeply rooted tradition of status egalitarianism: a strong dislike for social hierarchy runs throughout through American history. American society also displays a recurrent suspiciousness in the face of state power. These are both features of American life that are integral to the American style of liberalism. They are also features of American life that differentiate us unmistakably from the countries of continental Europe. Countries like France and Germany show much more tolerance for traditions of social hierarchy than we do, and much more tolerance for state power as well. And, as I am going to try to show, these most characteristically "liberal" features of American culture have contributed to making American punishment uniquely harsh in the West.

To Alexis de Tocqueville, the absence of an "aristocratic element" implied that America would have *mild* criminal punishment. "Societies become milder," he declared in his *Democracy in America,* "as conditions become more equal": after all, people who are equal can be expected to have more reciprocal empathy, and therefore to go easy on each another. America, he thus concluded in 1840, being the most egalitarian country, must inevitably have "the most benign criminal justice system." ... Americans display unmistakably deep-rooted patterns of status egalitarianism; Tocqueville was right about that. Yet our punishment is unmistakably harsh. As for market orientation: it would be hard to point to any society that is more "contractualized," more market-oriented, than ours. Yet ours is the society of harsh punishment.

The explanation I will offer involves a comparative legal history that reaches well back into the eighteenth century. The key to understanding how Tocqueville ... went wrong lies, I am going to argue, in understanding the link between traditions of social hierarchy and the dynamic of *degradation* in punishment. Contemporary American criminal punishment is more *degrading* than punishment in continental Europe. The susceptibility to degradation lies at the core of what makes American punishment harsh. And our susceptibility to degradation has to do precisely with our lack of an "aristocratic element."

The literal meaning of "to degrade" is to reduce another person in status, to treat another person as *inferior;* and it is that literal meaning that I will take as my point of departure. We all know intuitively that degradation, in this sense, often plays a significant role in punishment: part of what makes punishments effective is their power to degrade—their power to make the person punished feel diminished, lessened, lowered. Within the world of criminal punishment, such degradation is achieved in the widest variety of ways, from beatings to mutilation to day-glo orange prison uniforms.

Now, contemporary France and Germany are countries, I am going to show, with a deep commitment to the proposition that criminal offenders must not be degraded—that they must be accorded *respect* and *dignity.* The differences between continental and American practices can be little short of astonishing. Some of the most provocative examples come from continental prisons. Prison is a relatively rare sanction in continental Europe, by sharp contrast with the United States, and sentences are dramatically shorter. Nevertheless, there are continental prisons, and there are continental prisoners. But those comparatively few continental offenders who do wind up in prison are subjected to a regime markedly less degrading than that that prevails in the United States. Thus continental prisons are characterized by a large variety of practices intended to prevent the symbolic degradation of prison inmates. Prison uniforms have generally been abolished. Rules have been promulgated attempting to guarantee that inmates be addressed respectfully-as "Herr So-and-So" or "Monsieur So-and-So." Rules have also been promulgated protecting inmate privacy, through such measures as the elimination of barred doors. Most broadly, these measures include what in Germany is called "the principle of approximation" or "the principle of normalcy": the principle that life in prison should approximate life in the outside world as closely as possible. Like all ideals in the law of punishment, this one is sometimes realized only fitfully: to study norms of dignity in prison is often to study aspirations rather than realities. France in particular lags well behind Germany in implementing these practices, and life in French prisons can be very tough. Nevertheless, the "principle of approximation" does have real meaning, and indeed it has led to some practices that will seem astounding to Americans. German convicts, for example, are supposed to work at jobs that are real jobs, like jobs in the outside world. This means that they enjoy far reaching protection against arbitrary discharge, and even four weeks per year of paid vacation (!). All of this is intended to dramatize a fact about their dignity. The lives of convicts are supposed to be, as far as possible, no different from the lives of ordinary German people. Convicts are not to be thought of as persons of a different and lower status than everybody else....

Prisons are not the only places where this continental commitment to dignity shows itself. There are many examples that take us beyond life within prison walls. Thus in America we are far less bothered by public exposure for criminal offenders than Europeans are—whether those inmates are being kept behind barred prison doors that expose them to the view of all, or being shown on Internet broadcasts, or being subjected to public shame sanctions, or having their records opened for public inspection. There are other examples, involving deprivation of civil and political rights. The oldest legal form of status degradation—automatic deprivation of rights of participation—still survives in America. Convicted American felons are frequently automatically deprived of civic rights-a practice of status degradation that has disenfranchised a substantial proportion of the African–American population in some regions ... French and German prison systems, by contrast, have programs that encourage inmates to exercise their (almost always unimpaired) right to vote. On the deepest level, American criminal justice displays a resistance to considering the very personhood of offenders, This is a resistance that shows in the triumph of determinate sentencing in America, and it is a resistance that is absent in Western Europe.

These are differences of profound significance, I am going to argue, differences that take us a long way toward understanding how American punishment culture has come to differ so much from French and German. Cultures that systematically show respect for offenders are also cultures that are likely to punish with a mild hand; conversely, cultures (like our own) that have no commitment to respect for the offender are likely to show harshness. Where do these differences come from? ...

[T]hese are differences we can only explain it we are grasp some deeply rooted differences in social values and social structure. But the sociology we need is a historical sociology. The continental commitment to "dignity" and "respect" in punishment is something that has grown very slowly since the eighteenth-century, and it is a commitment that offers striking evidence of a fundamental connection between degradation in punishment and traditions of social status. For at its core, as I want to demonstrate ..., it is a commitment to *abolishing historically low-status treatment.*

To understand the differences that divide us from the French and the Germans, we must indeed begin in the eighteenth century. France and Germany are countries in which, two centuries or so ago, there were sharp distinctions between high-status people and low-status people. In particular, there were two classes of punishments: high-status punishments, and low-status punishments. Forms of execution are the most familiar example: nobles were traditionally beheaded; commoners were traditionally hanged. There are many other examples, too: low-status offenders were routinely mutilated, branded, flogged, and subjected to forced labor; all while being displayed before a raucous public, both before and after their deaths. High-status offenders were generally spared such treatment. Forms of imprisonment differed by status as well. Two and a half centuries ago, high-status continental convicts—who included such famous eighteenth-century prisoners as Voltaire or Mirabeau could expect certain kinds of privileged treatment. They were permitted a relatively normal and relatively comfortable existence, serving their time in "fortresses" rather than in prisons. Their "cells" were something like furnished apartments, where they received visitors and were supplied with books and writing materials. They were immune from forced labor and physical beatings. They were accorded easy and regular visitation privileges. They were permitted to wear their own clothing and to provide their own food; they were permitted to provide their own medical care as well. They were shielded from public exposure, and indeed from all forms of shame. Low status prisoners by contrast were subjected to conditions of effective slavery, often resulting in horrifically high mortality.

The subsequent development of punishment in these countries can be captured, in its broadest outline, in a simple sociological formula: over the course of the last two centuries, in both Germany and France, and indeed throughout the continent of Europe, *the high-status punishments have slowly driven the low-status punishments out.* Gradually, over the last two hundred years, Europeans have come to see historically low-status punishments as unacceptable survivals of the inegalitarian status-order of the past. More and more offenders have been subjected to the relatively respectful treatment that was the privilege of a tiny stratum of high-status persons in the eighteenth century. In particular, what used to be the privilege of relatively respectful imprisonment has slowly been extended to every inmate. This is a generalization that can only be made in broad outline: I speak of tendencies that, while always present, are never fully realized. What has happened, has happened only within the limits of the possible. There is no way that every ordinary inmate can really be accorded all the accommodations and comforts that an imprisoned Voltaire or an imprisoned Mirabeau once enjoyed. It has happened, in part, only recently: the full-scale abolition of low-status punishments has occurred only over the last twenty-five years, and is indeed still in the process of occurring. Nevertheless, it has happened. The old "honorable" forms of imprisonment have driven the "dishonorable" forms out: within the limits of the possible, everyone in a continental prison is now treated in the way only aristocrats and the like were once treated, and norms of dignified and respectful treatment have become generalized. This is a development that is, moreover, entirely typical of continental European law: as I have argued elsewhere, in almost every area of the law, we see the same drive toward a kind of high-status egalitarianism—of an egalitarianism that aims to lift everyone up in social standing. These countries are the scene of a leveling-up egalitarianism—an egalitarianism whose aim is to raise every member of society up in social status. . . .

Nothing of the kind has happened in the United States, by contrast; and this reflects the fact that the history of social status in the American world is very different. Our traditions of punishment do not begin the way continental traditions do: with an eighteenth-century practice of making sharp distinctions between high-and low-status punishment. The common-law world does not have the same long history of legally guaranteeing high-status treatment for some. In certain ways, in fact, English status-differentiation had already begun to break down in the later Middle Ages and sixteenth century. Certainly by the mid-eighteenth century the contrast between the continental and Anglo–American worlds was very striking: by around 1750, special high-status treatment had already begun to vanish in both the British colonies and in metropolitan England. Over the course of the nineteenth century, this historic tendency became consistently stronger in the United States, as special high-status treatment was regularly attacked. The consequence is that our large sociological tendency ran in a direction opposite from that of continental Europe. Where nineteenth-century continental Europeans slowly began to generalize high-status treatment, nineteenth-century Americans moved strongly to abolish high-status treatment. From a very early date, American showed instead, at least sporadically, a typical tendency to generalize norms of low-status treatment—to level down. The tale of this American development is, as we shall see, exceedingly complex. Most important, it is bound up with the history of American slavery in ways that have to be carefully traced and carefully weighed. What matters though . . . is principally what did not happen. Americans never displayed the European tendency to maintain and generalize older high-status patterns of treatment.

In this, the law of punishment is, once again, simply typical of the law more broadly: Europeans live with the memory of an age of social hierarchy and feel a corresponding horror at historically low status punishments. To tolerate the infliction of degrading punishments, for Europeans, is to tolerate a return to the bad old world of the ancien regime, when ordinary people had to fear flogging, mutilation, and worse. We do not live with memories of that kind in the United States (despite our history of slavery), and the European urge to replace low-status punishments with high-status ones is an urge that we do not feel. We can revive old-style public shaming, for example, without feeling any European qualms: humiliating and degrading offenders, for us, does not smack of social hierarchy: We have not learned to think of humiliation and degradation, in the way that Europeans do, as inegalitarian practices. . . . At least since Montesquieu, people have believed that harsh punishment is produced by strong states, with relatively unbridled power. . . .

978

Following this idea, one would imagine that the countries that punished harshly were what Montesquieu called the "despotic" ones. In particular, one would predict that America, home of a powerful antistatist tradition, would punish mildly. And indeed, most Americans assume that our traditions of resistance to state power, and especially our traditions of procedural protections against prosecution, make our country uniquely liberal in its criminal justice. Yet, despite our unmistakably libertarian traditions, ours, among Western countries, is the one with distinctively harsh punishment. This too is a puzzle for any of us attached to the values of liberalism. Part of the solution to the puzzle is that Americans overestimate the distinctiveness of their traditions. Europeans have procedural protections too. . . . Indeed, they have been actively extending their procedural protections over the last quarter century.

But the issue goes beyond procedural protections. It is my aim to show that traditions of state power can make for mildness in punishment, in ways that our scholarship has not fully grasped—ways that have to do primarily with two aspects of state power: the exercise of systematic mercy and the tendency toward bureaucratization.

Mercy is the most important of the aspects of state power that I will discuss. "Mercy" is complex concept. In part, it is a concept that assumes, once again, relations of a status hierarchy. Mercy comes de haut en bas: superiors accord it to inferiors. In this, mercy is akin to degradation: when we show a person mercy, we confirm his inferior status—more gently, but just as surely, as when we degrade him. A society with a strong tradition of acknowledging and enforcing status differences will thus often be a society with a tradition of mercy.

There is more to the concept of mercy than that, though. Mercy involves respecting individual differences. A merciful justice looks down on the offender, and asks: what is it that might entitle this offender to milder punishment than others who have committed the same offense? In this sense, mercy involves individualization of justice—a willingness to distinguish between more deserving and less deserving persons. The contrary of mercy, as understood in this sense, is formal equality: a system that operates by the principle of formal equality is a system that aims to treat all persons exactly alike, extending no special mercy to anyone. . . .

The values of mercy have shown themselves to be much stronger in French and German justice, over the last quarter-century, than in American justice. This is partly because practices of mercy that date back to the eighteenth century and beyond, have never died in continental Europe: both France and Germany still dispense general amnesties, just as the royal and princely governments of the eighteenth century did. But it is not just a matter of the literal survival of ancien regime practices of mercy. It is also that a vaguer spirit of mercy pervades continental justice. Individualization of punishment, and a concern for individual deserts, run throughout both French and German law. American law, by contrast, is much more hesitant to individualize. To be sure, there is plenty of mercy in America. Nevertheless, the strong tendency of the last twenty-five years has been toward formal equality.... and there is no doubt that America differs dramatically from continental Europe by this measure. Unlike the French or the Germans, we display a powerful drive to hit every offender equally hard.

Why are the values of mercy so much stronger in continental Europe?

Part of the answer that I will give takes us back once more to the European history of status hierarchy. Mercy does indeed come de haut en bas; and a long continental tradition of condign grace can still be detected in the law of today. Moreover, traditions of status-oriented thinking have conditioned continental jurists to think in terms of distinctions between persons in a way that is relatively alien to American legal thought. Making distinctions between persons has been the stuff of continental law for centuries: French and German jurists have always resisted the idea that everybody is exactly alike. One consequence is that today both French and German justice are much readier than American justice to make individualizing distinctions among offenders. Formal equality is just not at home in continental Europe. Traditions of status are not the only source of the strength of the values of mercy in continental Europe though. Those values have another taproot too, and one that is of fundamental importance for understanding the shape of continental criminal justice: France and Germany are countries with much stronger states than ours.

What we mean by a "strong" state is of course no simple matter; the proposition that France and Germany have stronger states calls for some real care in definition. For my purposes here, I will mean two things when I describe continental states as "strong": Germany and France have state apparatuses that are both relatively powerful and relatively autonomous. They are powerful in the sense that they are relatively free to intervene in civil society without losing political legitimacy. They are autonomous in the sense that they are steered by bureaucracies that are relatively immune to the vagaries of public opinion. The relative power and autonomy of these continental states, I am going to argue, has done a great deal to keep the values of mercy alive in continental society and to promote other forms of mildness in criminal punishment as well.

The connection between state power and mercy is clearest in the survival of amnesties, and in the various ways in which the old practice of pardoning has persisted in modern practices of individualization: The power of the continental states has also produced another, especially important, form of mildness: both Germany and France display a notable tendency to define many acts, not as *mala in se*, but as *mala prohibita*—not as acts evil in themselves, but simply as acts the state may choose to prohibit through the exercise of its sovereign power. This capacity to define forbidden acts as merely forbidden, not evil, has been of great importance for the establishment of relatively mild orders of punishment in contemporary Europe. The contrast with the United States is stark: ... contemporary American law has a strong tendency to define all offenses as inherently evil and consequently to punish them harshly. And as I will suggest, the capacity to define offenses merely as *mala prohibita* is a capacity that European states enjoy largely because the exercise of state power has much more untroubled legitimacy in continental Europe than it does in the United States.

State power, in short, has made for mildness, in continental punishment. This is a claim that will seem exceedingly paradoxical to Americans. We have a very long tradition of resisting state power, and many protections for offenders that involve guarantees of due process. (Indeed, in general Americans tend to have procedural protections where Europeans have substantive ones.) Moreover, it is certainly the case that state power does not always breed mildness in continental Europe. There are undeniably aspects of continental justice in which the application of state power comes down hard-most importantly in investigative custody, the preconviction form of imprisonment that is the focus of the worst problems in continental incarceration. But these differences do not alter the picture of the divergence of the last quarter century. If continental Europeans have a weaker tradition of procedural protections, it is nevertheless the case they have been working to improve their procedural protections over the last twenty-five years. In this too, the continental tale is a tale of a deep structural drive toward increased mildness. Indeed, even with the problems of investigative custody taken into account, the strength of continental states has ... made the application of the power to punish far more sparing than it is here at home. State power has turned out, in northern continental Europe, to make for mild punishment. Much mercy comes, in fact, from the power of continental states. Much mercy comes from their autonomy too. This is partly for a reason that is obvious—indeed, a reason that has captured the attention of every thoughtful commentator on the American punishment scene. American punishment practices are largely driven by a kind of mass politics that has not succeeded in capturing Western European state practices. We have, as many commentators observe, "popular justice:" and indeed populist justice. The harshness of American punishment is made in the volatile and often vicious currents of American democratic electioneering. Calling one's opponent "soft on crime" has become a staple of American campaigning—even in judgeship elections, whose candidates were longtime holdouts for norms of decorum; and this has had a powerful, often a spectacular, impact on the making of harsh criminal legislation in the United States. Even practices that have nothing directly to do with election campaigns are part of a momentous American pattern—a pattern in which public officials use garish punishments as a way of grabbing political publicity. Prosecutors in particular have been making political hay all over the country through actions such as leading Wall Street executives out of their offices in handcuffs or televising the names of the busted clients of prostitutes.

Politicians in continental Europe do sometimes try to play to the same public instincts that American politicians play to. For the most part, though, American-style politics has failed to exert an American-style influence on German or French criminal justice.... Part of explaining why France and

Germany are different involves explaining why this kind of politics has not made any headway in those countries; and that, in turn, involves exploring the relative autonomy of German and French state apparatuses. Manifestly, the weakness of the politics of harsh punishment in Germany and France reflects the autonomy of the state in both countries: what is at work in both countries is a basic tension identified long ago by Max Weber: the tension between democratic politics and bureaucratic control. In both Germany and France, bureaucrats have succeeded in keeping control of the punishment process, without becoming subject to decisive pressure from a stirred-up public. The success of bureaucratic control also has some other consequences for continental punishment, ... consequences such as the careful effort to define and train prison guards as civil servants.

There is, in fact, an intimate nexus between the politics of mass mobilization, unchecked by bureaucracy, and the making of harshness in criminal punishment; and that is a fact that should raise some uncomfortable questions for any of us who like to think of ourselves as committed to the values of democracy....

[A]t the end of the day, my claim will be a simple one, and one that I think ought to have special resonance in America. Criminal punishment is milder in continental Europe today largely because Europeans have been shaped by social and political traditions that we in the United States have vigorously rejected. The continental Europe of today is recognizably descended from the continental Europe of the eighteenth, and even the seventeenth, centuries. It is a world of strong, condescending states, with a close historical connection to norms of social hierarchy.

It is, in short, the world whose values the traditions of the American Revolution condemn. Americans already feared strong states and strong traditions of social hierarchy in the eighteenth century; and most of them undoubtedly still associate strong states and strong traditions of social hierarchy with all that is harsh and nasty in human relations. Yet in the long run, ... the traditions of the continent have developed into the milder traditions, at least in the law of punishment....

Our parting of the ways with Europe, over the last twenty-five years, should force us to confront some fundamental, and hard, questions about the workings of criminal justice. Degradation matters, in ways that our philosophies of criminal punishment have neglected. There are unexpected facets of the exercise of state power that matter in neglected ways as well. Most of all, social and political traditions matter. Criminal punishment is not something that can be analyzed in abstract and general terms. It differs deeply from society to society, and it differs in ways that reflect fundamental divergences in social and political values.... there is one seemingly obvious explanation for the differences between the United States and continental Europe that I ... downplay. This is the explanation that holds that continental justice is milder today because the continental countries experienced fascism and Nazism. German and French lawyers can often be heard making this claim:

their countries, they say, learned the lesson of fascism in the 1930s and 1940s, and that is why they have turned to humane practices today. This, claim is by no means entirely false, ... Nevertheless, it is by no means entirely true either. The place of the fascist period in European development is much more ambiguous than this frequently repeated explanation would suggest. Moreover, the historical roots of the differences are far older than the fascist period, and indeed far older than the twentieth century....

It is precisely the capacity of comparative lawyers to identify relative differences that gives comparative law its special value. No absolute descriptive claim about any legal system is ever true. Human society is much too complex for that; there are always exceptions. If we make the absolute claim, for example, that American law is committed to the values of the free market, we are saying something false: there are many exceptions. On the other hand, if we claim that American law is more committed to the values of the free market than are most comparable legal systems, we are saying something that is both true and extremely important. As this example suggests, relative claims can be a good bit more revealing than absolute ones. Therein lies the unique strength of comparative law. It is precisely because they deal in relative claims that comparative lawyers can walk the high road to the understanding of human legal systems, as they have been trying to do since Montesquieu.

At the same time, comparative lawyers always run the risk of creating false impressions—of seeming to claim more than they should. Let me therefore emphasize that my claims ... are relative ones. I do not mean to argue that American punishment is always and everywhere harsh and degrading; and I certainly do not mean to argue that German or French punishment is never degrading or never harsh. I do not mean to deny that there are regional differences in America—just as there are regional differences in Germany in France. What I mean to say is that American punishment is often more degrading and often harsher—and that where we find these relative differences, we can detect the intermittent strength of some real, if subterranean, differences in fundamental values that are widely shared in each of the three societies that I discuss.

NOTES AND QUESTIONS

1. This is the introductory chapter to a book, which expands on the thesis that Whitman sets out in this introduction, and tries to illustrate it. The key concept is that a long historical tradition gives us insight into the differences between the United States, and continental Europe, with regard to some aspects of criminal justice. What assumptions about culture and institutions is Whitman making, at least implicitly?

2. Whitman does not mention at all the fact that France and Germany are civil law countries; the United States, on the other hand, is a common law country. It would seem, then, that the "history" he thinks is so vital and enduring, is not a *legal* history at all. Why should this be the case?

3. Most American states allow the death penalty; no European country does. Outside the United States, the only wealthy industrial nation that provides for the death penalty is Japan. How do these fact fits in with Whitman's thesis? Why do you think the death penalty has persisted in the United States?

Would your answer be different if, for example, polling data showed that people in Belgium or Denmark had more or less the same view of the death penalty as Americans?

4. When people talk about American culture and society, they frequently invoke history—they talk about the Puritan legacy, as an explanation for modern laws about sexual behavior; or about the influence of the frontier on modern American criminality and violence. Are these arguments consistent with Whitman's approach? In any event, how valid do you think these explanations are? How would you go about proving or disprove them?

III. Note: Convergence and Divergence

We have mentioned the concept of "history" as including membership in one of the major families of legal systems—common law or civil law, for example. At various points, we have noticed the differences between them. Procedural differences are particularly striking (see above, Chapter 5, on French criminal procedure).

What is the fate of these traditions in the contemporary world? Some scholars think the various systems are converging, that is, that they are getting more and more alike. Others deny this.

Among those who deny is a European legal scholar, Pierre Legrand. In fact, one of his articles has the provocative title, "European Legal Systems Are Not Converging," 46 *International and Comparative Law Quarterly* 52 (1996). Legrand feels that the outlook, philosophy, and training of common law lawyers—what he refers to as their "*mentalité*"—is "irreducibly different" from that of the civil law lawyer (p. 64). The common law and the civil law "cannot ever reach perfect understanding between each other" (p. 75). In Europe, even though England is a member of the European Union, the legal systems of England and the continent "have not been converging, are not converging and will not be converging" (pp. 61–62). The training and the mind-set of the two groups of lawyers are simply too different; and indeed the two types of system are so different, that the distance between them cannot be bridged. The common law, for example, "was never systematised nor has it ever aspired to be." Law, in England, "is seen as a technique of dispute resolution." The common law stresses facts: "For the common law lawyer, any construction of an ordered account of the law firmly rests on the disorder of fragmented and dispersed facts.... In the civil law tradition, on the contrary, the aim is rapidly to eliminate any trace of the circumstances and to establish an idea or a concept. Accordingly, the facts are immediately inscribed within a pre-existing theoretical order where they soon vanish. It is that order itself—and certainly not the fact—which is regarded as the fount of legal knowledge; the emphasis is on universals'' (pp. 68–69).

Those who disagree might, first of all, argue that Legrand is not describing either type of legal system accurately. They would also start their argument from an entirely different premise. They would begin with the idea that the social conditions of a given society shape its legal system. If societies become more alike, then it follows that their legal systems will also become more alike. They will, in essence, "converge." Lawrence Friedman has talked about the "tendency of legal systems ... to evolve in parallel directions." See "Borders: On the Emerging Sociology of Transnational Law," 32 *Stanford Journal of International Law* 65, 72 (1996). Why should this be so? Because, he says, of a "basic postulate of the sociology of law," which is that "legal systems are never totally autonomous." Rather, they reflect "what is happening in their ... societies;" and in the long run, "they assume the shape of these societies." We expect the law of medieval France to have the "smell of the middle ages;" while the "law of modern, capitalist France ... must reflect modern capitalism and all that goes with it." Systems, then, of modern societies face similar problems, have similar institutions, and reflect similar realities (at least in general). Modern French law will be much closer, in many ways, to modern English law, than it will be to medieval French law. A French, Australian, and Japanese lawyer can talk about income tax laws, land use planning, corporate governance, air traffic control, computer software protection—these areas of law are certainly not identical in these various countries; but they resemble each other—and in the aggregate, these modern fields of law make, say, French law much more like Australian law, than it is like the French law of the 14th century.

Convergence, according to Friedman, is "a natural process, in societies that are moving along the same general paths." It is a "real process—powerful, massive, and unstoppable." Friedman argues, however, that convergence might be masked by the "bad habits of traditional legal scholarship," which "centers on a narrow range of issues, which or may not have much to do with the living, breathing system of law" (id., at 74).

On this point, see also John Henry Merryman, "On the Convergence (and Divergence) of the Civil Law and the Common Law," 17 *Stanford Journal of International Law* 357 (1981).

IV.   Culture and Language: Macro– and Micro– Levels of Analysis

The previous two readings traced the way differing histories can arguably contribute to divergences in law, even when two legal systems emanate originally from a common source—as with the United States and England. In this section we examine two additional (generally intertwined) influences on law: culture and language. Scholars have looked to both the general cultural backdrop against which law operates, and to the specific impact of *legal* culture, in asking about the trajectories of different legal systems. They have examined these issues at both broader, "macro" levels, and also through studies of the details of interactions at the "micro" level. They have also analyzed the various ways that language can operate as a filter for law. We begin with an excerpt that discusses the different "voice" in which East German judges spoke (at a time that marked the end of their distinctive legal system and culture). Markovits concludes by asking how this might compare with the approach of judges in the U.S.

(6.3) Last Days

Inga Markovits

80 *California Law Review* 55 (1992).

[In this article, Prof. Markovits describes the last days of the East German legal system. The German Democratic Republic (DDR) had been established by the Soviet Union, and propped up and maintained by the Soviet Union. Germany was divided in two—the east was the DDR, the west was the German Federal Republic. Berlin, isolated in the middle of the DDR, was also divided into two parts, separated by a wall. It was a crime for a East Berliner—or an East German in general—to try to get to the West. Those who tried to go—the *Ausreiser*—suffered legal and social consequences.

In 1990, the East German government collapsed; the wall was dismantled, and West Germany in essence swallowed up East Germany. East German law then ceased to exist.

The article is written in the form of a diary, chronicling the final month or so of the East German legal system. Prof. Markovits, German by birth, a professor of law at the University of Texas, was the leading authority in the United States on East German law—a legal system which, after 1990, was solely of historical value. But the end of the regime was also an opportunity for western scholars to learn more about the legal system of the communist regime in East Germany, to do research which had not been possible before.

Prof. Markovits observed court proceedings during the final days, and interviewed lawyers and judges who were soon going to be replaced. In the article, too, she makes some general observations about the nature of East German law.]

Socialist law never liked conflict. It smelled too much of self-assertion and the wish to absent oneself from collective felicity. Although all disputes adjudicated in East German courts involved what were essentially personal matters (conflicts between state-owned enterprises were handled by special economic tribunals, while institutional conflicts and public law disputes were not subject to judicial review), courts were nevertheless expected to downplay the private elements in a dispute and to concentrate instead on its social dimensions. "To generalize a conflict" ("*einen Konflikt verallgemeinern*") the technique was called: to interpret a specific controversy as a symptom of underlying social tensions and to find a solution that would not only right individual wrongs but also address their causes, prevent their recurrence, and thus ensure collective peace in the future.

By definition this feat could only be achieved with the cooperation of all participants. Social harmony is not divisible. Hence the pedagogic leanings of socialist procedure and its dislike for zero-sum solutions. Socialist trials were not supposed to divide a collective into winners and losers, but to unite it in common allegiance to socialist norms of behavior. That explains the East German preference for unanimity and for settlements. Rather than fighting it out, the parties were encouraged to work at what was called an "autonomous solution" (*eigenverantwortliche Lösung*).

But the term is misleading. The purpose of compromises and settlements in GDR law was not to increase the parties' autonomy. Western experiments with alternative dispute resolution often pursue the goal of empowerment: when we replace adversary proceedings with processes that give more voice to the parties themselves, we do so in the belief that people know what is good for them and generally should control their own lives. East German attempts to promote settlements were not motivated by the wish to limit state authority over private affairs. Socialist law did not strive for autonomy but for harmony. If to us settlements are better than judgments, to socialists settlements are better than discord. Our law thrives on conflict. But East German law was meant to prevent conflict, to overcome, or at least to diffuse it. Children, please no fighting! . . .

SEPTEMBER 24, 1990

Back at the *Littenstraße* courthouse. Today I have appointments with two lay assessors. They were part of the army of lay people on which the East German legal system relied. Lay people served as judges of social courts (already abolished) that adjudicated minor civil and criminal law conflicts and most first-instance labor law disputes, and as lay assessors, who still sit, together with a professional judge, in civil, family, and labor law cases. Almost more important than the judicial role of these people was their responsibility to explain and popularize the law within the collectives that elected them.

Herr Habermann, my first interviewee, looks so little like a foot soldier of socialist law that at first I mistake him for a plaintiff or defendant awaiting his case. Long wavy dark hair parted in the middle, mingling at shoulder level with a long dark beard. In the midst of all this hair an earnest and friendly face. To my surprise, Herr Habermann is not only a lay assessor, but a Party member since 1978. I would have thought that the Party required a more conventional appearance. What made him join? He read the Party Program and found it convincing.

We talk about the disappointment of Socialist hopes. Herr Habermann originally was a math and physics teacher. He left teaching for an engineering job when he no longer could take the political indoctrination at school. "The things they made us do!" "They" are the Party functionaries with whom Herr

Habermann shares the same political affiliation. To him, the Party seems divided into a top and a bottom, with the top—"those aged gentlemen"—largely divorced from reality, and the bottom a place where he and people like him "tried to get things moving." Engagement in local politics also led to his work as lay assessor: Herr Habermann himself had some problem with his apartment, became involved with the local housing administration, eventually joined the borough committee of the National Front, and was nominated as lay assessor.

The picture he conveys of the Party is one of local activism and central ossification. I look with some skepticism at this gentle Rasputin. From what I know, much mindless and docile rigidity also exists at local Party levels. But maybe Herr Habermann is one of those innocent and energetic people who forever spot jobs that need to be done and do them. His present work supports this hypothesis. He became unemployed when his engineering firm was privatized, Herr Habermann tells me, but now is an entrepreneur. Entrepreneur? Yes, he discovered a niche in the brand-new market. After the *Wende*, GDR stores no longer want to stock the modest, gray East German school notebooks, which used to sell for ten pfennigs, but only the colorful and glossy West German kind, which sell for up to one mark each. Herr Habermann has gotten hold of a large lot of the old notebooks and sells them, at a few pfennigs apiece, to East German schools, which can use the savings. He reckons his stock will last another month or two. By then he hopes to have found a job. He will in any case no longer be needed as lay assessor.

Herr Daschke, Herr Habermann's colleague, conforms better to my image of a lay assessor: a small, serious, official looking man in a beige Sunday suit. I meet him in Judge Schomburg's office. He was (still is) assigned to Frau Schomburg's court, and as I come into the room, the two just say a tearful good-bye. Today is Herr Daschke's last day in the courthouse, after thirty-seven years as lay assessor.

Herr Daschke, sixty-two, was originally a carpenter. He started his community career as representative of his brigade, then became a job safety inspector, and is now a full-time union functionary. He obviously loves the law; besides his work as lay assessor, he represents employees in labor law cases and participates twice a week in the union's legal consultation service. In the early 1950s, when the East German government replaced all inherited bourgeois judges with so-called people's judges—working-class men and women with some crash-course training in law—Herr Daschke almost joined the judiciary. But his carpentry job paid too well.

What does he like about the law? It is useful for workers, and the workers use it. Many employees consult him during the union's legal-service hours. Because he understands the setting and knows the enterprises' collective agreements, Herr Daschke thinks he does a better job than a lawyer could do when representing a fellow worker in court. Would he take the case of a worker of whose claim he disapproved? Yes; "law is law." A worker has the right to representation. He sees nothing wrong with winning cases that his client should have lost. With respect to the individual worker, the law clearly is perceived as an instrument of protection.

And overall, does he think that socialist law did a good job? Law, for Herr Daschke, is labor law. Yes, for a long time the law kept everyone content. But it could not stem the collapse of labor discipline beginning in the early 1980s. Above all, the rules on "material responsibility" did not work: East Germany's system of penalizing workers for damage caused to their employers through negligence, shoddy work, absenteeism, and the like. Interested more in education than restitution, the law on material responsibility did not define liability in terms of damage done, but operated with penalties measured by reference to the offender's wages. Since most sanctions amounted to no more than a fraction of the culprit's monthly pay, and could be paid in barely noticeable installments, employers were not interested in receiving the money and employees were not burdened by its loss.

Herr Daschke criticizes East German managers for not having taken advantage of the law on material responsibility to stage "confrontations" in the enterprise that could have raised awareness about the need for better discipline. Instead, managers would either forgo sanctions (why bother about a few marks in an economy in which money counted less than labor, then in short supply?) or fire an employee (which was against the law). Who could be surprised? But Herr Daschke does not like an approach to law based on cost-benefit calculations. "If you do not correct a worker's attitudes in his own enterprise, who else would do it?" "The market," I am tempted to reply. But Herr Daschke's labor law was meant to operate in a more personal way than anonymous market forces. It focused on each worker's needs and capabilities (hence the orientation in material responsibility cases on an offender's individual wage) instead of abandoning him to the smacks of some invisible hand. I am reminded of what a judge in this courthouse said to me: "The Labor Code was too good to us."

I ask Herr Daschke why he spent so much time and effort on his community work. "We were all people who did not want to stand aside," he says. He talks about the Party in similar fashion as Herr Habermann: describes the distance between the top and the bottom; how criticism from below would get lost on its way up the hierarchical ladder; how reports would "get more beautiful" with each step closer to those in power. "The Party always has had members and comrades," he says. The comrades, he implies, were people like him: laboring in the vineyard.

A picture too idealistic not to instill suspicion. But I remind myself: Herr Habermann and Herr Daschke cannot be typical lay assessors. In this final week, most lay persons no longer show up for court duty. They have more important things to do, have written off the system, or never felt strongly about it in the first place. Herr Habermann and Herr Daschke must be more committed to socialist law than most of their colleagues. I find indirect support for this presumption when I ask Herr Daschke for his telephone number. It turns out that he has none: he has been on the waiting list for a telephone since 1975. "Now I probably could get one, but it would be too expensive," he says a little apologetically. Surely, as a full-time union functionary, he could have pulled a few strings? The fact that Herr Daschke, after all these years, has no telephone confirms my image of him as the selfless servant of a legal system that expected selflessness to be part of human nature but only rarely found this expectation fulfilled. It is not just that the East German Labor Code was "too good" to the people to whom it applied. Socialist law could only have worked if people also were "too good" to be true: nonmaterialistic, diligent, eager to place the interests of the collective ahead of their own comfort. But how many Habermanns and Daschkes could there be?

Afternoon

An interview with Peter Stodczyk, a civil law judge at the Court of Appeals, thirty-one years old. Unlike most other judges I have met, he does not come from a working-class background. Both his parents are lawyers: his mother a prosecutor, his father a now-retired military judge. Herr Stodczyk has the relaxed grace of someone to whom things have come easily.

How did one become a judge in the GDR? It took good grades and a politically acceptable background. Fulfilling only one of these prerequisites usually was not sufficient. Students had to apply for admission to university a year or two before their high school graduation. At that age, very few youngsters had any realistic image of the law; in fact, several people in this courthouse told me that they chose law out of fascination with American courtroom dramas on West German television. Herr Stodczyk, through his parents, knew a bit better what his choice entailed.

Students who wanted to become judges or attorneys—the so-called "justice students"—were trained at the Humboldt University in Berlin (future prosecutors and economic lawyers were educated elsewhere). But the Ministry of Justice controlled the admissions process. High school students applied to the local district court and eventually were interviewed by an official at the Ministry whose apparent task it was to determine the applicants' political reliability. Nobody I talked to seems to have viewed this part of the application process as anything but a test of one's ability to recognize and plausibly articulate the desired answers. Nobody seems to have been offended by it either.

Before taking up his studies, Herr Stodczyk completed three years of military service. Female students would do production or office work. One had to take part in working-class exertions before being allowed to set off on a more intellectual trail. The four-year study of law was highly structured. Students of the same year attended most lectures together. Classes focused on general and abstract issues, with few practical exercises and case discussions. One-third of a law student's time was spent on Marxism–Leninism and similar pursuits. Teachers tended to avoid embarrassing topics. The ruthlessly repressive use of law during the Stalinist 1950s and 1960s was never mentioned in class. Political criminal law—with the exception of issues relating to so-called border violations—was barely touched upon.

Most law students were Party members by the time they entered law school. Those who were not would join the Party at some point during their university years. In either case, the decision seemed so natural, so inevitable for future judges, that neither Herr Stodczyk nor anyone else remembers noticeable external pressures or internal turmoil accompanying the event. During the third year of their studies, students were "directed" towards their future jobs: judge or attorney. Many students at the Humboldt University would have preferred the latter: attorneys made more money and enjoyed greater professional independence. But in a country with 592 private lawyers, and no noticeable increase in their numbers projected by the government, the Colleges of Advocates, who recruited their new members, could be selective. They tended to choose few women, and only those men with good connections or the very best grades. Peter Stodczyk did not care: he had wanted to be a judge in any case.

Why judge? Because he had been brought up to believe in justice. And what does he mean by justice? "A state in which everything is in legal order" (*"in dem alles seine gesetzliche Ordnung hat"*). Herr Stodczyk pauses for a second. "And in which each individual gets his due. But not at the expense of others," he adds. A mixture of old and new: legal discipline and the balancing and protection of rights. But the sequencing of the answers reveals something about Judge Stodczyk's image of himself: a keeper of order, a guardian of social peace rather than a defender of personal autonomy.

Did he, as a judge, feel burdened by the absence of free speech? No, not really. To Herr Stodczyk, external political constraints mattered less than one might have thought because he could always speak freely among his colleagues. He admits that criticism would rarely produce results (and how could it, I think, since it was kept within safe boundaries.) Instead, the function of critical speech seems to have been therapeutic: it made it easier to respect oneself and others. In fact, conversations among Herr Stodczyk's colleagues were so open that he was shocked to learn, after the *Wende*, that a fellow judge at another court had lost his job for saying things that routinely were said within Herr Stodczyk's own collective. From his perspective, this courthouse—or, rather, the dozen or so judges assigned to his court of appeals—formed a civilized and rational enclave within an oppressive society, allowing withdrawal from the unpleasant political realities on the outside. A simple, narrow, and contented professional life.

Later, thinking back on our conversation, I am struck most by Peter Stodczyk's tone: neither defensive nor aggressive, but artless, unguarded, human. I probably am so surprised because Herr Stodczyk is the first male judge whom I have interviewed at length. I must have expected a more "male" style of expression. But, in fact, talking to him gave me the same impression I gained from talking to other legal professionals in the GDR: they do not sound like lawyers, certainly not like lawyers in the United States. I hear no cutting remarks or quick repartees, encounter no attempts to score points against an opponent, see no restructuring of every conversation into a win-or-lose debating competition. And there is another striking difference: male and female lawyers in the GDR speak in the same voice.

In the United States, men and women seem to argue about the law in different ways. In the faculty lounge of my law school, the talk is fast, sharp, and largely negative when the men dominate the conversation. When they are among themselves, the women's talk is more relaxed, chattier, warmer, less linear, more open to compromise. When men and women discuss an issue together, men are likely to raise "men's" points and women "women's" points. In the legal literature, you often can tell from the mere title of an article whether the author is a man or a woman: men write about legal principles and concepts, women (especially feminists) about human interactions—empathy, sharing, sexual domination.

Here at the *Littenstraße* courthouse, men and women speak the same legal language. At its best, it is simple, concrete, pragmatic, focusing on results. At its worst, it is unintellectual and imprecise. But I can never tell, from the words alone, whether they are spoken by a man or woman. The flavor of a conversation in a group of men or women does not change if someone from the opposite sex joins in the debate. Much more than in Western discussions, speakers disappear behind their arguments; they seem less self-possessed than capitalist lawyers. Here, I notice little vanity among the men and no self-pity among the women. Both seem to find it easier to forget about the impression they make and instead to listen to what the other says.

It is surprising to find such effective human communication in a country in which speech, for forty years, had to take place under such precarious circumstances. Maybe the constraints and distortions of language in the world around them taught people in the GDR to listen closely to what was said ... But I believe that the main factor in Peter Stodczyk's intellectual socialization was not the interaction with his female colleagues but socialist law itself.

American law has often been criticized by feminist writers for being "male": abstract, hierarchical, competitive, coldly rational. Socialist law, one might be tempted to argue, is "female": concrete, cooperative, caring, searching for collective warmth. Hence the "different voice" of East German lawyers: contributive and conciliatory, echoing the voice of women.

But on second thought, an analysis of socialist law in gender terms loses much of its persuasiveness. The male/female dichotomy seems questionable enough if applied to capitalist law. Perhaps in the classic fields of private law—contracts, torts, and property—the metaphor "male" might capture those features of the legal process that feminists and socialists both abhor: the emphasis on individual autonomy, on the exclusivity of rights, on conflict; the division of the world into winners and losers. But in other, more modern branches of our law, the metaphor no longer fits. In many family or administrative law disputes, for instance, capitalist judges no longer operate as

992

principled but heartless arbiters of individual entitlements. They function as managers: address issues in social context rather than in isolation, focus on the future rather than the past, and adjust ongoing relationships to fit people's needs rather than vindicate their rights. All attitudes that one might also call "socialist." But since they are, after all, part of our legal system, it does not make much sense to call them "female," if the feminist analysis of law as patriarchy is to hold up. The gender analogy in these cases no longer advances our understanding.

I find it more helpful to distinguish instead between adversarial and managerial styles of adjudication. Socialist law (and by now much American law) sees the judge as a social-crisis manager rather than as an arbiter of private disputes. The law, in these instances, seeks to solve tasks, rather than to protect individual rights. While rights are best enjoyed alone, tasks are more effectively carried out with the help of others: hence socialist law's emphasis on collectives and the involvement of lay people. Lasting solutions to particular judicial assignments (a divorce, a dismissal case) will often require responses that take social connections into account and that focus on people's needs rather than on their entitlements: hence the cooperative and often nurturing character of socialist adjudication. The analysis explains why East German judges so often sound like social workers rather than jurists....

[I]n any case, the different voice in which East German judges speak is not the voice of women. Rather, it is the voice of subordinates, assistants, administrators. American critics of [Carol] Gilligan have suggested that her analysis does not so much capture the distinctions between women and men as between the dependent and the powerful. Viewed in this fashion, the different-voice analogy applied to East German judges works much better. They speak like people who are not masters of their own decisions, but who carry out tasks set by another, the state.

Despite our law's increasing preoccupation with administrative functions, Western lawyers are still raised in the classic adversarial spirit. It is a fighting spirit, a spirit of self-importance, spelling the "I" with upper case and the "we" with lower case lettering, a spirit always wanting to be right. And our lawyers, accordingly, quite often are people full of themselves. But Peter Stodczyk and his colleagues have been taught to serve a cause supposedly greater than themselves. They considered it their job to follow rules, to keep people housed, employed, and committed to their work, to preserve social peace, and to report to their superiors. They were serving, not self-serving. No wonder that their style is more modest, uncritical, charitable, and cooperative. No wonder also that they are looked down upon by their more self-assertive and quick-witted West German colleagues. But if I had to carry out some unglamorous, burdensome social project, I would love to have Peter Stodczyk on my team.

NOTES AND QUESTIONS

1. Some commentators have criticized Prof. Markovits, on the grounds that she treats too gently what was, indeed, the legal system of a communist

dictatorship, and one which did not hesitate to punish severely those who dared speak out against it—or the *Ausreiser*, those who tried to leave the "socialist paradise."

Markovits does not ignore the political aspects of East German law—she is aware of this harshness; and the way in which party officials violated the rule of law. The courts she described were courts that dealt with ordinary law. "All politically touchy issues investigated by State Security (the *Stasi*) ... were adjudicated by special senates, the infamous IA panels ... which even were physically separated from the rest of the court."

But she is more interested in the ordinary work of the ordinary courts. The essential point she makes is that the type of political structure affects the work of the legal system in many ways that go deeper and further than the differences between capitalist and socialist norms. The whole inner ethos of the law is different. How would you go about trying to prove or disprove this proposition?

2. Prof. Markovits took further advantage of the dismantling of the East German system to study, systematically, how justice operated, through examining court files and records in a town of about 55,000 inhabitants, which she calls "Lüritz" (not its real name). The results of her extensive research have been published in Germany, under the title, *"Gerechtigkeit in Lüritz: Eine ostdeutsche Rechtsgeschichte"* (2006). (She is preparing an English translation). A description of the project, and some of the results can be found in "Justice in Lüritz," 50 *American Journal of Comparative Law* 853 (2002).

Many of the cases she describes in this article seem small-scale, even trivial, and quite personal. And they exemplified a "warmer" way of disputing. She goes on to say: "I have put the word in quotation marks because much of this warmth was make-believe. Are family quarrels 'warmer' than fights between strangers? Because, indeed, much of the civil litigation happening in Lüritz looked like family feuds. In capitalist legal systems, parties to civil suits tend to be socially distant and friends or acquaintances sue each other only if they are sufficiently estranged not to care if the lawsuit ruptures the social bond between them. But in Lüritz, citizens seemed to sue each other not in spite of, but because of their human proximity. In 1982, 43.8% of all civil parties and 61.5% of all parties in lawsuits between individual citizens were either related to each other, had once been married or co-habited, or lived in the same house. People sue in Lüritz because they have to share space or possessions that they would rather use alone. They seem to live too close for comfort."

3. How would you compare the East German legal system, as Markovits describes it, with (a) Weber's notion of substantively irrational justice; and (b) the legal system of a small, close-knit community?

4. Markovits describes the final days of a socialist legal system. What happened afterwards? How easy or difficult is it for a society to make the transition to a free-market system? To what extent had the socialist legal culture become habit for the citizens? To what extent had people become used

to the red tape and corruption of the socialist systems? The Soviet Union lasted more than 70 years. The conversion to capitalism in Russia was sudden, and in many regards painful and frustrating. The subject has been treated in depth by Kathryn Hendley; see, for example, *Trying to Make Law Matter: Labor Law and Legal Reform in Russia* (1996).

(6.4) The Technical Vocabulary of Barotse Jurisprudence

Max Gluckman

61 *American Anthropologist* 743 (1959).

In his great *History of English Law*, Sir William Holdsworth said that primitive law has no technical vocabulary. This is correct if we are thinking of a developed vocabulary to define different kinds of rights and duties arising out of the relations of individuals to property and out of contractual relations between individuals. But we should of course expect this in systems where, as Maine emphasized, there are few contracts and law is dominated by status. But the lack of a technical vocabulary in Holdsworth's sense does not mean that tribal jurisprudence has no technical vocabulary at all: as we should expect in this type of social system, legal terms are elaborated in the definition of status. In addition we find there is a complex vocabulary to name different kinds of property in terms of their significance for relationships of status. I propose to examine here these aspects of Barotse jurisprudence, and to show how the judges operate with virtually a single concept to define relations between persons and things. The Barotse do distinguish sharply between holdings in different kinds of land and holdings in different kinds of chattels, yet they do this with a limited vocabulary to describe proprietorial rights and duties. My main problem is why this situation exists, and how the judges operate in it.

I begin by considering briefly the structure of Barotse land-tenure. The study of tribal land law was for a long time stultified because writers, including some very eminent jurists, wrote in terms of communal land-holding, thus forgetting the basic rule of jurisprudence that persons own not land or things, but rights over property. Therefore, even when we are dealing with situations where groups own joint or coparcenary[2] or other shared rights over land, we have to specify how these rights are distributed between the group as a whole or the various sections or individual members of the group. This is particularly essential when the system which is under study uses only one term to describe the rights of a whole series of individuals and officials in the same piece of land. In Barotse, this term is *mung'a*. I propose to translate it as "owner," though as will become apparent, "ownership (*bung'a*, the abstract form of mung'a) in Barotse law does not confer any absolute title and does not correspond exactly with our everyday conception of ownership....

---

2. "Coparcenary rights are rights in land inherited equally by two or more persons from a common relative (this is also known as 'joint heirship')".

[Another anthropologist who worked in Central Africa argued against translating this concept in English as "owner", and instead used the word "warden" when talking about the leader of a kinship group. But Gluckman notes here that the word "warden" doesn't work well when talking about "ownership" of things. He also points out that the word "owner" has a verbal form ("to own"), which makes it more parallel to the Barotse usage.] "Owner" comes from an Old English form *aegen*, when legal concepts were similar to those of Barotse law, and this lends some traditional sanction to using the word here. I ask that the difficulties of appropriate translation be borne in mind throughout.

Barotse describe their king as *mung'a*, owner, over all Barotseland, and over the people and their cattle. There was a case in which a teacher at a rural school quarreled with a number of immigrants ... and threatened to have them driven out of the land. One of the judges rebuked him: "This affair of driving the people out of the country—soil has no owner! Soil has one owner?—it is the soil of the king" ... [C]orrespondingly, the king has an obligation as owner of the land to give arable and building land to everyone whom he accepts as a subject. This is one of the main duties of the king and his council, and they discharge it faithfully. Nowadays the Barotse council works British civil service hours; and in Northern Rhodesia this means they stop work at 5 P.M. The only time I saw them work after hours was when a suppliant came to ask them for land near the British settlement, so that he could cultivate vegetables for sale to the European residents. Land in this area is of course valuable, and the council could not find land for the suppliant there. The council offered him land in other places, but he refused. The councillors became angry and told him everyone wanted land there and beggars cannot be choosers, but he insisted. They kept discussing the matter til evening, and then adjourned to consult local councillors....

... [T]he king as owner of all land has heavy obligations in addition to rights.... All these rights and powers and privileges of the king are covered by his ownership, his bung'a.

[The king's] ownership also embraces the duty to provide ... land for all subjects, and to allow them access to public fishing-waters, to pasturage, and to wild products. In practice, most residential and arable land, as well as many sites for fishing, are already allocated to villages through their headmen.... The king cannot upset these allocations or take land away from a headman's title without just cause. If he wants land thus allocated, he must beg for it.... The holding of residential and arable land in Barotseland is thus clearly an incident of status: headmen of villages hold from the king rights of administration over land attached to a village, and members of the village hold rights to work and live on land by virtue of their status as villagers, and can transmit these rights to their heirs....

... Thus every parcel of Barotse land is subject to a series of different rights held by a number of different persons in the political and social hierarchy. The products of the land, on the other hand, vest in the individual who cultivates, captures, or collects them, though even these goods are subject to certain claims by superiors and inferiors. . . .

. . . [T]he Barotse describe the king as *mung'a*, owner, as I have translated it for convenience. But they also so describe, as *mung'a*, everyone of the persons—royal or conciliar village head, village headman, villager or villager's dependent—to whom the land has been allocated by a superior. . . . Yet this use of the same term to describe the rights of different persons in the same parcel of land does not lead to any confusion. [I]n a case where the right of a commoner to a piece of land as against the king himself is discussed, the commoner is called mung'a against the king. For example, the king had ordered that a high councilor should take over certain gardens as belonging to his title—i.e., to the king—though the gardens were in cultivation. The cultivators appealed to the court which said that the owners (*beng'i* plural) could not be turned out of their gardens which they had worked for years. . . .

In short, to repeat, the Barotse describe the person who has the strongest claim on a piece of land in a particular case as the *mung'a* of the land as against other particular claimants. Therefore when king or other person is named as *mung'a* of a piece of land, the judges are not asserting that he has any exclusive power over the land, nor are they denying that other persons have enforceable claims on the land. The successful contestant is only *mung'a* in relation to another contestant. In the course of adjudicating the dispute, the judges do not have to enquire into the nature of the rights held by the contestants; their main enquiry is into the status relationship between the litigants, and once they determine this, they know what rights are involved. Hence they are able to work with a single term, mung'a, to cover a series of different rights: the elaboration of their jurisprudence is in the definition of status. For them there is a specific kind of relationship between particular people and a particular type of land, or indeed a particular type of product; and if a dispute arises, determination of the status of the parties immediately clarifies the legal issues.

The legal terminology is secondarily elaborated in the naming of special kinds of gardens or other property. Thus if the king gives a garden to a man, he has no claim on its products. . . . But the king also has special gardens of his own, called *namakau*. . . . [and in similar fashion there are different names for gardens allotted to wives by their husbands, and with this different name come different rights to the crops from the garden]. . . .

I think that we are already in a position to see that Holdsworth was wrong if he meant that primitive legal systems lack any refined and developed vocabulary, even if their terminology for types of rights and duties be relatively simple. It is true, on the Barotse evidence, that there may be only one major term to define relations between persons and property, but there is a complex vocabulary in the Law of Persons. . . . We can add that there is a complex vocabulary to define different kinds of property. . . .

I want to push further the implications of this situation. The essence of the Barotse legal situation is an interest in the Law of Persons, in how people related to one another in terms of status discharge their obligations to each other. People acquire rights in land in virtue of their status as citizens, as villagers, and as kinsfolk. They can only maintain their rights if they discharge their status obligations faithfully; the recalcitrant villager who merits expulsion from the village thereby loses rights in land....

The Barotse council is a court of law, an executive cabinet and legislative assembly, an administrative body, an ecclesiastical chapter, and was formerly a war council.

... [The council is divided into three parts: the most powerful part, composed of commoners, represents the nation; the second part is comprised of those who take care of the royal family, and represent the king; and the third part consists of princes and husbands of princesses, representing the whole royal family. Members of the council have titles that belong to them; but their titles belong as well as to the king and to the "subordinates of the title."] ...

It may seem that I am merely stating at some length that the Barotse say of anyone who is interested in some office or piece of land, that he has a right in it. But what I am trying to emphasize is that the Barotse work with a single concept of ownership of rights as entailing corresponding obligations, because all land and all titles are involved in a complex of social relationships.... [T]he law is interested in property as an incident of social relationship, in addition to the property's material value. To enable social relationships to endure, the law stresses the obligations involved to other persons by holding of property, even beyond its stress on claims to rights over the property. The series of rights of ownership over property constitute an essential part of the status structure of the society; rights in property, and obligations to use property generously, thus define social relationships themselves. Each piece of property, land or title or chattel, may be a link in a complex set of relationships between people who are bound to one another permanently....

In summary, Barotse property law defines not so much the rights of persons over things, as the duties owed between persons in respect of things. Indeed, the critical property rights are demands on other persons in virtue of control over land and chattels—not any set of persons, but persons related in specific ways.... Hence ownership, *bung'a*, is constantly used also in defining social relationships themselves, even where land or things are not immediately involved. This may have given rise to the idea[3] in early writings, and in modern political statements about the position of African women, that persons are chattels in tribal society.

3. Gluckman here describes the kind of ethnocentric misreading of indigenous norms and cultures that comes from an inability to grasp the kind of subtle meanings inherent in language and practices that he here describes. As he attempts to show, the very meaning of "chattel" may not be easily transposed into a particular culture or legal culture. This doesn't mean that there are not forms of gender asymmetry in these societies, as there are in our own. It simply means that we should not assume an easy, transparent translation between Western concepts and those of other societies [ed. note].

In conclusion, therefore, I briefly illustrate this final use of the concept of ownership. Any position in any social relationship may be described as ownership, depending on whose rights to demand the fulfillment of obligations are being emphasized. Dominantly the senior in the relationship is called "owner," for it is usually his rights which are emphasized or called in question. The king, political authorities, senior kinsmen, are all politely addressed as "my owner." The king would never address a subject thus, though in discussion or dispute over constitutional issues the Barotse [say] that the nation is owner of the king, as it is of councillors. But councillors address one another, even juniors, as "my owner," and even a senior councilor may speak thus to a subordinate when he is exhibiting his courtesy. Most strikingly, councillors thus address litigants or accused whom they are reprimanding severely. They do this in order to emphasize that they are discharging an obligation to the wrongdoer by pointing out to him the error of his ways, for they speak not in anger but because the law requires them to do so. . . . Similarly, adults frequently call a child "my owner" as an affectionate endearment, especially if it is fretful or hungry, to emphasize readiness to serve the child. But the adult also uses this address when he is reprimanding the child; thus he states that he reprimands the child as a duty, for he owes it the obligation of bringing it up to be a good citizen. Wives commonly call husbands "my owner"; a husband speaks thus to a wife to mark his respect for her in special circumstances, and above all to placate her if she is angry.

These forms of address stress the constant emphasis of Barotse law on obligation to others which is involved in their concept of ownership. The background to this situation is the complex network of rights and obligations lying between a person and other related social positions, in a society dominated by status. And a court will ascribe ownership to any of these social positions, as against another, depending on who is failing to fill obligations. Thus most commonly a husband is called "owner" of his wife. Where a husband neglected his wife to fornicate with other women, the court called the wife "owner of the husband" and "owner of the marriage," in insisting that the husband must sleep with her a reasonable number of nights. . . . Or the wife may be called "owner of the marriage" if she sues for divorce on grounds of neglect or failure on her husband's part to treat her as a wife, which he commits by entrusting to a kinswoman duties which are his wife's rights, such as receiving visitors. . . .

Similar situations arise in political relationships, but I have not space to set them out. I hope I have demonstrated sufficiently that *bung'a* is ascribed by the Barotse to anyone who has a masterful relationship of responsibility and demands on services over another, in some situation or other. This masterfulness may or may not arise out of property. Barotse jurisprudence sees every situation which arises out of status relationships as containing an essentially similar element, which it calls *bung'a*. They distinguish relatively few forms of *bung'a*, for the rights and duties involved in any particular kind of *bung'a* are defined by the status relationship in dispute, and the main further clarification lies in the multiplying of names for different kinds of property. Suits in court may raise rights, but the courts tend always to lay stress on obligation.

NOTES AND QUESTIONS

1. Consider the contrast that Markovits suggests between East German and U.S. judges. How would Barotse notions of the individual and social responsibility map onto these two positions? Can you find similarities shared by the supposedly more "modern" legal culture in East Germany and the indigenous legal culture described by Gluckman (erroneously described by some scholars as "primitive")?

2. Translation Problems: In this article, Gluckman is focused on describing the way Barotse conceptions of "ownership" differ from those in Anglo–American legal culture. In one sense, he is insisting that we be careful about assuming that a similar concept actually means the same thing in two different societies. But, on the other hand, he is using the same word to describe the concept in both cultures. In this article, Gluckman notes that he does not agree with Paul Bohannon, an anthropologist who argued that "it is, in the long run, the folk classifications that are important to social anthropology, not the 'presence' of torts or contracts which are both folk and analytical concepts in another society." See Paul Bohannon, *Justice and Judgment among the Tiv* (1957). The famous anthropological debate between Bohannon and Gluckman centered on whether it is ever appropriate to use terms derived from one culture (like "torts") to analyze arguably different ideas in other cultures. Gluckman acknowledged that to do this was to sometimes read ideas into other cultures in ways that imposed Western frameworks, but he felt that this was necessary to performing any kind of comparative research. Max Gluckman, *The Judicial Process Among the Barotse of Northern Rhodesia* (1954). What do you think the problems and benefits are of using the same word (e.g., "ownership") to describe quite different legal conceptions in two different societies? Notice that in this article, Gluckman also introduces some of the Barotse's own words (like mung'a) when discussing their system of property. Does that make any difference to his account?

3. Anthropologist Laura Bohannon describes her effort to explain Shakespeare's play Hamlet to her Tiv informants during her fieldwork in West Africa. Laura Bohannon, "Shakespeare in the Bush," in James Spradley and David McCurdy, eds., *Conformity and Conflict: Readings in Cultural Anthropology* (1971). She decided to try to do this to prove her conviction that "human nature is pretty much the same the whole world over" so that "at least the general plot and motivation of the greater tragedies would always be clear" to any audience.

Bohannon, however, ran into difficulties very quickly with her narrative. When she mentioned that Hamlet's mother had remarried her husband's brother (Hamlet's uncle) very quickly after being widowed, the Tiv elder beamed, saying, "He did well ... I told you that if we knew more about Europeans, we would find they really were very like us. In our country also,

... the younger brother marries the elder brother's widow and becomes the father of his children."

Bohannon then attempted to explain that Hamlet was upset by how quickly his mother had remarried, rather than observing the usual two-year mourning period. Again the audience saw things differently, as one women observed that "Two years is too long.... Who will hoe your fields for you while you have no husband?" Bohannon's troubles multiplied as she attempted to explain the appearance of Hamlet's father as a ghost: in the Tiv system of belief, someone who had died could only reappear as an omen (which can't talk) or a zombie (a dead body bewitched to walk around). Her audience was quite shocked to hear that Hamlet wanted to kill his uncle to avenge his father, saying that "For a man to raise his hand against his father's brother and the one who has become his father—that is a terrible thing." By now her listeners had become convinced that Hamlet was behaving quite unreasonably. Of course, if he begins to behave in a crazy way, they conclude it must mean that he has been bewitched. Frustrated, Bohannon offers to stop telling the story. The elder of the group poured her some beer and attempted to soothe her:

> "You tell the story well, and we are listening. But it is clear that the elders of your country have never told you what the story really means. No, don't interrupt! We believe you when you say your marriage customs are different, or your clothes and weapons. But people are the same everywhere; therefore, there are always witches and it is we, the elders, who know how witches work."

By the time Bohannon's story limps to a close, the Tiv men have jumped in to tell the story "correctly," in a form that Shakespeare would probably not have recognized. As she concludes, the elder said encouragingly to her:

> "That was a very good story, ... and you told it with very few mistakes. There was just one more error, at the very end. The poison Hamlet's mother drank was obviously meant for the survivor of the fight, whichever it was.... Sometime ... you must tell us some more stories of your country. We, who are elders, will instruct you in their true meaning, so that when you return to your own land your elders will see that you have not been sitting in the bush, but among those who know things and who have taught you wisdom."

What does this ethnographic account tell us about the relationship between supposedly universal ideas of rights and justice and particular sociocultural settings? What is the relationship here between social structure and legal culture?

4.   Could you call the system described by Gluckman a system of private property owned by individuals? What is the underlying logic of the Barotse system? How does Barotse social organization affect legal claims regarding property? What does Gluckman tell us about the "legal culture" ("legal culture" as defined by Friedman)?

5.   In what situations in modern U.S. law does the status of the parties, or their relationship with each other, determine the rights that can be claimed in court? Think, for example, of family law.

6.   What role does language play in Gluckman's account? Compare his focus on the use of particular words by the Barotse with Markovits' idea of "voice." Does it matter that a single word is used to describe many layers of property relationships among the Barotse? What is the relationship between judges' voices and their legal cultures in Markovits' article? How does each author understand the connection between law, language, and culture?

(6.5) Language, Law, and Social Meanings: Linguistic/Anthropological Contributions to the Study of Law

Elizabeth Mertz

26 *Law & Society Review* 413 (1992).

Ways of Thinking About Language

There have been many different conceptualizations of language in the linguistic and anthropological literature. Some have focused on formal properties of language as an abstract system with its own dynamics. Other approaches have concentrated on language as an instrument effecting social ends. And a number of linguistic anthropologists and sociolinguists have worked to formulate a theory encompassing both formal and functional aspects of language.

. . . For some scholars, attention to language is important because language reflects social contexts. Alternately, language can be viewed as a way of effecting social ends. In either case, language itself is important only because it provides a window on social process; language is understood to be a straightforward expression of its social context. . . .

. . . [F]or example, William Labov found that linguistic variation corresponds with class divisions. In a famous study of New Yorkers' speech, Labov demonstrated that a number of subtle linguistic variations (e.g. pronunciation of the terminal "r" sound in phrases like "fourth floor") mirror divisions in class identity. . . . This [is] a reflectionist view of language as a mirror of social reality. . . .

A similarly straightforward image of the language-society relation is at the heart of an instrumentalist theory of language. According to this theory, people use language transparently to achieve social goals. When we say language is "transparent," we mean that there is no distinctive effect imputed to language; linguistic forms operate as tools through which actors achieve certain social results. Thus, for example, Deborah Tannen views certain linguistic devices [for example, repetition] as "involvement strategies" used to involve and keep the interest of audiences. . . .

1002

Language is certainly used in instrumental fashion to effect social goals, and no integrative theory of language use could neglect consideration of this aspect of language function. However, purposive attempts to use language quite often run up against a resistance or unpredictability that is the result of language's social structuring—that quality of language that results from it being a system that has developed in complex ways over time, a system that is widely shared (in complicated and variable ways) by a community....

If we ask, then, what difference it makes that we pay attention using reflectionist or instrumentalist models, the response is that language is a good diagnostic tool, a good window on social process. But there is an even more compelling answer.... We look to language because the details of how something is said—the shape of a particular verbal exchange or written communication—matters. When attorneys submit briefs and argue to appellate courts, for example, how they write and speak (as well as how they are received) may well to some degree reflect class or gender identities. And attorneys in these settings are almost certainly attempting to use their language in a conscious attempt to effectuate social results. But what happens in the interaction is not always a simple reflection of pre-existing social divisions or a straightforward use of language as a tool. There is a rich and complex dynamic that includes those aspects of language use but also includes the shaping of the interaction by discourse forms (appellate briefs, oral arguments), the complicated speech context of the institutional setting in general (the court), the influence of the particular individuals involved in this instance (the judge, other court personnel, the attorneys, the litigants in this case), the creation of new meanings and relationships and contexts ... and so forth. This is an opportunity to move beyond determinisms that would view legal outcomes as foreordained reflexes of preexisting social structures, while yet not pretending that legal interactions are somehow free of the strong constraints generated by distributions of power and wealth in societies....

Some Past Studies of Language and Law

... I begin with studies focusing on the powerful effects that very slight linguistic differences can have on legal outcomes and then move to studies that have examined more broadly the ways in which legal language can affect relationships and social structures. [Scholars have examined both the "semantics" or content of talk, and the "pragmatics" or contextual structuring of talk—how speech relies on and points to its context of use.]

... [P]sycholinguists have demonstrated that language affects assessments of eyewitness reliability and juries' comprehension of instructions. Certain styles of speech in the courtroom may damage a truthful witness's credibility. In particular, [John] Conley, [William] O'Barr, and [Allan] Lind found that use of a speech style that was characteristic of "powerless" people ... undermined a witness's chance of being believed....

Other work on the language of the law has explored the possibility of still stronger formative effects of legal language on social outcomes and structures.

[. . .] In their study of the language of the lawyer's office, [Austin] Sarat and [William] Felstiner are concerned with how legally circumscribed linguistic interaction frustrates participants' goals. . . . This work employs a careful semantic-level analysis of linguistic interaction to explain the way in which lawyers use language to reinforce their own authority and clients' dependence, remaining deaf to what clients view as the most salient parts of their stories. . . .

[Anthropologists who look at law as a form of dispute resolution have approached the linguistic interactions in legal settings as culturally-laden ways of managing social conflict. For example, different kinds of legal speech—and accompanying legal cultural norms—seem to function differently in egalitarian versus hierarchical societies.]

An appreciation for the formative effect of legal language emerges also from recent work by feminist, critical race theory, and critical legal studies theorists in the legal academy. For example, [Martha] Fineman . . . analyzes legal and political language dealing with poverty and uncovers an ideological vision that attempts to attribute responsibility for poverty to the "pathology" of single motherhood. . . . [Mari] Matsuda describes the power of black women's poetry and of Douglass's and King's re-readings of the Constitution as sources of resistance to social and legal oppression. . . . Each of [these] studies . . . shares a view of language and discourse as formative in some way. In some studies it is the word meaning, the semantics of language, that does the crucial shaping. In others it is both the semantics and the structure of the discourse itself that create strong formative effects.

Conley and O'Barr's Legal Talk, Merry's Social/Legal Discourses

[In this section Mertz compares the findings of two books on U.S. legal language: John Conley and William O'Barr, *Rules versus Relationships: The Ethnography of Legal Discourse* (1990) and Sally Merry, *Getting Justice and Getting Even: Legal Consciousness among Working–Class Americans* (1990).]

Both studies deal with the understandings and discourse of "ordinary people" . . . who are approaching the legal system as non-expert participants. In both cases the basic unit or organizing principle is the pattern emerging from a litigant's encounter with the legal system, rather than a community, case, or legal institution: "My organizing principle is a pattern of court use" (Merry, p. 4); "our unit of analysis is the encounter of the litigant with the legal system" (Conley and O'Barr, p. 29).

However, the two studies employ quite distinct methodologies in attempting to analyze citizens' commonsense understandings of the legal system. Conley and O'Barr look at the language litigants and judges used in small claims courts, focusing on 14 courtrooms in six cities. . . . [Thus] they are able to give us a feeling for broader patterns that emerge in different settings. Merry, on the other hand, examines intensively cases that reached three mediation programs (and sometimes the courts) located in two New England towns—Salem and Cambridge. [Merry observed mediation sessions and court hearings, conducted surveys and ethnographic work in several neighborhoods, performed interviews with court personnel and disputants, and quantitatively analyzed the caseloads of two of the mediation programs.] ... From Merry we get an in-depth vision of the way that legal discourse is grounded in social divisions and needs.... From Conley and O'Barr we get a broader view of the varieties of speech which litigants and judges [use ...]; at the same time, we also see a more detailed linguistic picture of the courtroom exchanges....

A fundamental distinction for Conley and O'Barr is one between "rule-oriented" and "relational" discourses:

> *relational* litigants focus heavily on status and social relationships. They believe that the law is empowered to assign rewards and punishments according to broad notions of social need and entitlement.... By contrast, rule-oriented litigants interpret disputes in terms of rules and principles that apply irrespective of social status. (p. 58)

.... In one landlord-tenant example, Conley and O'Barr contrast the relational account of plaintiffs (who eventually lose) with the more rule-oriented account of the defendant landlords. The plaintiffs rented a "fixer-upper" house from the defendants, thinking that they could repair the home and buy it. They now seek a return of their deposit and $1000 to compensate them for repair work done, claiming that the defendants misrepresented the extent of the work needed on the home. In court the plaintiffs' accounts center on their needs and predicament.... The landlords, by contrast, in an effort to show that the plaintiffs had full knowledge of the condition of the house, focus their account on the crucial legal question of the inspection done before the plaintiffs moved in.

[Conley and O'Barr go on to analyze the language of the judges. Although their study concludes that in general, rule-oriented approaches tend to be more successful in court, they do find that the judges differ in interesting ways—with some judges taking a more relational orientation. Litigants can therefore find that they are in concordant or discordant positions vis-à-vis particular judges. Here is a place where the language and culture of a courtroom can make a difference, even if social divisions such as race and class may frequently determine legal outcomes. Yet in any particular case, it may be that a relationally-oriented judge will listen to disputants' relational accounts with a different ear than would her more rule-oriented colleagues— and this can affect the outcome in the case.]

Sally Merry ... moves yet further in analyzing the role of context.... She concludes that the people who use the lower courts in an attempt to solve "personal problems" are disproportionately from that segment of the working class in New England that lost a secure economic base when major industries (such as textile and leather) closed down. At the time of Merry's study, the area was undergoing economic revitalization.... However, the litigants with whom Merry worked were largely left out of this revitalization.... Thus Merry's informants are neither the poorest and the most recently arrived nor the educated and affluent; they are working-class individuals living in dilapidated and dangerous housing in neighborhoods experiencing the influx of new residents, people surviving without two wage earners in the family and coping with relatively low incomes. They also tend to be people who have lived for one or more generations in the United States (p. 27).

Unlike recent immigrants, these people feel they are entitled to certain rights, including use of the courts for redress of wrongs. . . .

Like many of the plaintiffs in Conley and O'Barr's study, Merry's plaintiffs think in terms of relationships and [general] rights. . . . And the relationships are embedded in wider cultural constructions of self and society, and in social contexts. At every turn, we find connections between the social history with which Merry began and the disputes she analyzes. For example, neighborhood problems center on issues of "shared space" and become more intense where parties cannot avoid one another. . . .

Merry distinguishes the groups of plaintiffs bringing neighborhood and parent/child problems, who tend to be "settled-living" working class people with middle-class aspirations, from those bringing marital and boyfriend/girlfriend problems, who correspond more to the "hard-living" category of poor families who have given up the fight for upward mobility and often suffer the pain of violence, desertion, and substance abuse at close quarters. . . .

Against this backdrop, Merry explicates the way the legal process works for and against these plaintiffs. . . . Merry [describes] three kinds of discourses in the courts and mediation programs she observed: legal, moral, and therapeutic. [She notes that "legal" discourse corresponds with Conley and O'Barr's "rule-oriented" language, while "moral" discourse is similar to their "relational" language—but she also points out that she views these different kinds of language as part of an available repertoire that litigants draw upon differentially, rather than as aspects of the people themselves. So, instead of talking about a rule-oriented litigant, she would prefer to talk about a litigant who draws to a greater extent on "legal" discourse. She does agree, however, that use of "rule-oriented" or "legal" discourse tends to be more successful in court—and that many people leave court feeling unhappy with the treatment they received. On the other hand, she found examples of repeat players who eventually learned to wield "legal discourse" more effectively. In these cases, she argues, we see that learning the language and culture of the court can make a difference.]

NOTES AND QUESTIONS

1. <u>Therapeutic Discourse</u>: In addition to legal and moral discourses, Merry mentions a third kind of language used in the courts and mediation programs she observed—therapeutic discourse, "drawn from the helping professions, one which talks of behavior as environmentally caused rather than based on individual fault." (p. 114) People who engage in offensive

behavior are viewed as having an illness: " 'He is not well. I don't want him to go to jail. I just want him to get help.' The model of illness and disease, which describes difficulties without attaching fault or blame, is the dominant explanation for behavior." In Chapter 3, we encountered a similar shift to therapeutic language in divorce proceedings, as documented in Martha Fineman's research (note 5 following Reading 3.11). How does this kind of language differ from typical legal language? What are the underlying assumptions and goals behind each kind of language? Do you think there could be any difficulties in using therapeutic language for legal goals?

See also Joseph Gusfield's discussion of sick deviants and the appropriate response to them in Reading 4:12 *supra*.

2. <u>Determinism and Creativity in Law</u>: Both O'Barr and Conley's study, and Merry's research focus on the role of language in shaping legal outcomes. As we've seen, some scholars hold very deterministic views of the relationship between law and society, viewing legal outcomes as foreordained reflexes of social or economic structures. Is there a place for a "great woman or man," or for human creativity in these heavily deterministic models? What difference would it make if these more "deterministic" scholars incorporated the model of legal language proposed by O'Barr, Conley, and Merry? How does the "law and language" model presented in the Reading 6.4 compare with Friedman and Ladinsky's view on the issue of determinism in law (that is, on the question of to what degree legal outcomes are predetermined by underlying social developments)?

3. This article stresses the contribution of legal language to the experiences that "ordinary people" have in court. What is the relationship, then, between legal language and legal culture?

4. <u>Jury Research</u>: Research on juries has also highlighted the role of language in legal settings. The Arizona courts recently permitted researchers to study videotapes of actual juror deliberations, in addition to providing videotapes of trials. The Arizona courts permit jurors to submit questions during the trial itself. Shari Diamond, Mary Rose, Beth Murphy, and Sven Smith recently reported initial findings of an ongoing study of these trials and deliberations. Shari Diamond et al., "Juror Questions During Trial: A Window into Juror Thinking," 59 *Vanderbilt Law Review* 1927 (2006). They analyzed 829 questions submitted by jurors during 50 civil jury trials. They summarize their conclusions as follows:

> Our results show that juror questions generally do not add significant time to trials and tend to focus on the primary legal issues in the cases. Jurors not only use questions to clarify the testimony of witnesses and to fill in gaps, but also to assist in evaluating the credibility of witnesses and the plausibility of accounts offered during trial through a process of cross-checking. Talk about answers to juror questions does not dominate deliberations. Rather, the answers to juror questions appear to supplement and deepen juror understanding of the evidence. In particular, the questions jurors submit for experts reveal efforts to grapple with the

content, not merely the trappings, of challenging evidence. Moreover, jurors rarely appear to express an advocacy position through their questions. (p. 1931)

Diamond et al., then, are indicating that the linguistic format used in trials can make a difference in the way the laypeople on the jury process information and come to decisions. (For an argument that the linguistic form of the Anglo–American trial, at its best, advances democratic goals, see Robert Burns, *A Theory of the Trial* (2001).)

This brings us to the question of whether there is a distinctive patterning to legal language, and if so, what the effects of this patterning might be. In the next excerpt, Mertz approaches these questions through the lens provided by an in-depth study of first-year law school teaching. She finds that there is a shared worldview, or "epistemology" that is imparted in all of the classrooms included in the study. (Note that in this article, "epistemology" means the theory of knowledge—of how we know things—that underlies the way lawyers and law professors approach the world around them. This is a form of cultural knowledge, so that we are dealing here with a variety of legal culture.)

(6.6) Teaching Lawyers the Language of Law: Legal and Anthropological Translations

Elizabeth Mertz

34 *John Marshall Law Review* 91 (2000).

I.   Teaching Legal Language: A Persistent Puzzle in Anthropological Perspective

Previous research on law school education has drawn upon a number of different disciplines and approaches. Issues addressed in these studies range from the effects of legal education on students' psychological health, or on their commitment to public interest work, through historical questions about the evolution of legal training in the United States. A number of studies have focused on a distinctive style of pedagogy associated with doctrinal teaching in U.S. law schools. From a number of different vantages, legal scholars and social scientists often remark on a persistent puzzle: the Socratic method and associated approaches to teaching law found in many first-year doctrinal classes do not seem to make sense. These techniques do not appear to convey legal constructs any more effectively than would other methods such as lecturing. Moreover, the Socratic method has been the subject of a great deal of criticism and has been connected to elevated student stress. Additionally, it fails to adequately prepare attorneys for practice. How, then, has doctrinal teaching—particularly doctrinal teaching using a Socratic approach—continued in use for so long?

The study reported in this article examines legal education from a novel standpoint, drawing on the methods and theory of anthropological linguistics.

Anthropological studies of language begin with the premise that it is crucial to actually observe people's use of language in context, rather than to rely on their reports of how they speak. The accuracy of a speaker's perceptions regarding his or her own speech can vary widely, and even when they are correct as to general patterns, such perceptions cannot achieve the level of detail required by anthropological linguists. In order to obtain detailed data on language patterns in first-year classrooms, we taped the entire first semester of Contracts classes in eight different law schools. The schools varied across the prestige hierarchy used to provide school rankings.... Although there were many interesting differences among the classrooms, this research uncovered a shared underlying "message" imparted to law students in all the schools and classrooms examined in the study.

As I will explain, careful examination of this message or worldview helps to explain the puzzle of the "Socratic method" of legal education. The distinctive epistemology that underlies legal language, as it is taught in doctrinal classrooms, fits very well with overall goals and features of the legal system in the United States. Thus, there is a symbolic "fit" that connects teaching method, legal language, the legal system, and that system's underlying worldview. This symbolic connection makes sense of the persistence of certain Socratic aspects of legal teaching, despite ongoing complaints about efficacy, fairness to students of differing backgrounds, and negative impacts on students. The cultural logic entailed by the fundamental worldview taught to law students alters incipient lawyers' orientations concerning human conflict, authority, and morality. A crucial aspect of this changed orientation involves training students to read texts with a new focus, so that they learn to interpret stories of conflict in legal terms. When viewed through this lens, traditional legal pedagogy symbolically mirrors and reinforces an epistemology that is vital to the legal system's legitimacy.

We begin with a brief review of the "puzzle" surrounding the entrenchment of traditional pedagogy in doctrinal classes. I will then summarize the findings of the research, first focusing on features that are found across all of the first-year classrooms in the study. Then I will address the differences among these classrooms in their structures of participation and verbal interaction. Building from these findings, this section will conclude by explaining, in detail, the symbolic fit between pedagogy and legal worldview.

A.   The "Puzzle" of First–Year Doctrinal Teaching

The genealogy of the Socratic method in United States legal education reaches back to the nineteenth century, when Christopher Columbus Langdell brought this distinctive style to the Harvard Law School. Although the intellectual underpinnings of Langdell's approach have long since lost their credibility among legal academics, many aspects of the pedagogy that he developed from those conceptual foundations continued to survive for over a century. Critics of the Socratic method and other traditional methods of teaching law vigorously debate the merits of this tradition. These scholars charge that students either do not absorb moral values or that they absorb largely deleterious values; skeptics have further asserted that this kind of teaching does not even successfully convey legal doctrine, and that students exit law school without adequate preparation for the practice of law. While this last criticism did not end the use of Socratic training, it contributed to a partially successful movement for clinical education in law schools. Some scholars express concern that, historically, as the Socratic method became more popular, legal pedagogy and the legal profession moved further away from a model of lawyers as moral decision-makers. These writers observe that embracing Langdell's scientism entailed an abandonment of moral consider-ations, and a concomitant shift toward an image of law as a field of technical expertise. Moreover, critical legal theorists interpret this emphasis on techni-cal expertise as actually embodying a new morality, one that favors the privileged in society. In addition, multiple studies find that law students tend to lose their desire to pursue altruistic or public interest career goals as they move further into their legal education. Social scientists also criticize the Socratic method from psychological and other perspectives, uncovering its negative effects on self-esteem and interpersonal relationships.

Supporters of the Socratic method, on the other hand, assert that the method mirrors the style of reasoning used by lawyers. Additionally, they argue that it is an efficient system for teaching large classrooms and that it stimulates active student involvement. Supporters also maintain that the Socratic method does not dominate and manipulate any more than do meth-ods used in clinical teaching. Additionally, they maintain that it conveys, at once, the guiding principles and indeterminacy of the law in a way that lectures could not. In this paper, I will demonstrate a different form of congruence between the canonical Socratic method and legal thinking. This is not an argument that the Socratic method has greater efficacy, certainly, given the results of this and other studies, but is rather an argument for a stronger symbolic resonance or "fit."

Social scientists have also studied variations in the teaching methods employed across different law schools as well as differences in the skills imparted by particular methods. Several studies found that differences be-tween law schools correlated with the school's prestige ranking—elite schools being less likely to emphasize rigid rules and more likely to emphasize analytical thinking and theory. [Bryant] Garth, [Joanne] Martin and [Donald] Landon asked urban and rural attorneys to identify the skills taught by law schools that were the most useful in legal practice. Practitioners agreed that legal reasoning is the skill most important to practicing lawyers that law schools address relatively well: "there are some relative successes in teaching the specifically legal skills of legal reasoning, legal research, substantive law, and now also professional responsibility." Similarly, lawyers in a number of studies overwhelmingly agreed that " 'ability to think like a lawyer' was the most important knowledge imparted by law schools." This knowledge would include specific skills such as "fact gathering," the "capacity to marshal facts and order them so that concepts can be applied," and the "ability to understand and interpret opinions, regulations, and statutes." There is still a puzzle as to why the Socratic method of teaching, as opposed to any other approach, should be so important in conveying these skills.

This study analyzes the Socratic method as an oral genre or speech style, using the methods of sociolinguistics and anthropological linguistics. Sociolinguists have developed a considerable literature on the social ramifications of different discourse styles or genres as well as on the role of language in classrooms. In what follows, I will build from this literature and my own initial excavations of law school teaching to provide a detailed analysis of the language of the law school classroom. In addition, I will examine the issue of social inclusion and exclusion, specifically focusing on race, gender, and status.

B.   In the Law School Classroom: Learning a New Language for Telling "Conflict Stories"

As noted earlier, my research on legal education involved taping first semester Contracts classes in eight different law schools. The law schools ranged from those generally recognized as among the elite to those denominated "regional" and "local" by scholars studying legal education. Observers ("in-class coders") in each classroom also tracked the speakers, noting the gender and race of each speaker as well as aspects of the "turn-taking" (for example, did the speaker volunteer or did the professor call on the speaker). The tapes were subsequently transcribed, and transcript coders encoded features of each turn, including length of the turn, who spoke, and whether the turn was part of extended or short dialogue, etc. In addition, both the in-class coders and transcript coders noted qualitative aspects of the interactions.

As a result of access to both qualitative and quantitative findings, this study combines an analysis of the underlying message or worldview imparted to law students with an examination of the patterns of classroom interaction between the professors and students. Despite strong differences in the teaching and participation patterns among the classes, the study finds a similar underlying decontextualized orientation to human conflict, authority, morality, and text across all of the classrooms. We can trace this approach by examining the way in which legal pedagogy deconstructs and analyzes the underlying "conflict stories" (the factual accounts of the underlying conflicts that led to legal intervention) of each case. Although the linguistic structure of Socratic teaching provides a particularly strong mirroring of this orientation, even classrooms that did not employ the Socratic method imparted the same decontextualized orientation to students. Thus, all of these varying

1011

methods of legal instruction manage to impart a shared cultural worldview throughout the notably different classroom environments.

At the core of this legal [world view] is a distinctive orientation toward human social conflict and related notions of authority and morality. Interestingly, achieving this orientation involves the creation of a new relationship with language and text. As law professors teach students to read and discuss legal texts, the students learn to ask new questions and to focus on different aspects of language than they had previously. Indeed, legal education pushes students to direct their attention toward textual and legal authority, casting aside issues of "right" and "wrong," of emotion and empathy—the very feelings most likely to draw the hearts of lay readers as they encounter tales of human conflict. Instead, legal educators rigorously urge law students, as initiates into the legal system, to put aside such considerations—not to stifle them entirely, but push them to the margins of the discourse.

This process of reorientation has parallels in other kinds of initiations. Anthropologists studying initiation rituals describe a process whereby previous orientations and values are broken down, as identity is reformulated. A sociological study of medical school education in the United States suggests that the gross anatomy lab experience during the first year of medical training performs just such a function. As medical students dissect human cadavers in the lab, joking behaviors and other casual approaches to the task violate normal cultural taboos about death and the body. Such detached behavior reorients students so that they can adopt "the clinical attitude." As the days pass, these new markedly different and prosaic approaches to the body being dissected rupture students' earlier more reverential attitudes. This is a crucial part of the students' initiation into their new professional identities.

My study presents data suggesting that first-year law school teaching performs a similar function. However, instead of breaking down attitudes toward the body and death, law professors rupture linguistic norms. Law teaching challenges students' previous attitudes toward speech, reading, and texts—at the same time as it imparts a new approach to conflict, morality, authority, and language. Just as the bodies in the laboratory are the vehicles through which "the clinical attitude" is imparted to medical students, the stories of conflict contained in legal texts and language become vehicles through which the legal "initiates" learn to "think like lawyers." The most canonical form of legal instruction, the "Socratic method," has a linguistic structure that precisely mirrors this reorientation. I would therefore argue that although the Socratic method, as a medium of teaching, may be no more (or even less) effective than others, this approach to legal pedagogy may continue to linger because of a symbolic "fit" between the form and function of language. We begin with an examination of the reorientation toward text, authority, and morality that lies at the heart of first-year legal education.

Then, we consider related concepts of the person, human conflict, and social context that are implicated in this linguistic re-ordering.

1. New Sources of Authority: Reconfiguring the Semantics and Pragmatics of Text

In all the classrooms of this study, law students learn to refocus on new aspects of the legal texts with which they work during their first-year classes. Educational research [in other school settings] demonstrates that during initial educational experiences, teachers encourage the more "able" and elite students, for the most part, to read texts with a focus on content or "semantics." Scholars call this fundamental approach to text "referentialist" ideology, because it privileges referential or semantic content as the "autonomous (fixed, transparent, universally available)" meaning understood as being inherent in the text.

The primary focus in law school pedagogy, by contrast, is on the "pragmatic" or contextual structure of legal texts. More specifically, doctrinal teachers in law school classrooms train their students to notice those aspects of [contextual] structuring that relate most to authority. Instead of putting priority on the content of the factual "conflict stories" told in legal texts, law professors urge their students to analyze how the texts point to (or "index") authority. This focus shifts the students' orientation towards several major sources of authority: (1) the relationship between this text and the language of other texts that provides precedent and authoritative guidance (and correlative issues concerning the authority of the courts, legislatures, or framers who authored those texts); (2) the procedural history of the case, which determines the questions a court can address, the types of standards that are applicable to those questions, and the court's jurisdiction or power to consider the case at all; and (3) the related strategic questions involving framing legal arguments within this authoritative backdrop. When first confronted with stories of conflict between parties, students often begin by concentrating on the drama of the conflict itself. For example, when asked to "start developing for us the arguments for the plaintiff and the defendant," one student begins: "Um, that—the plaintiff was a young, youthful man." This student is starting to "tell the story" of the events in question through the lens of a traditional semantic reading, one focused on character, plot, and content. The professor subsequently admonishes her: "all I'm interested in, Ms. M., is what the arguments are ... all right? I want the arguments, okay?" Throughout the subsequent interchange, the professor repeatedly urges this student to place any "facts" concerning the conflict story of the case within the framework of the relevant precedential legal categories instead of focusing on morality or narrative structure.

This move towards a more "pragmatic" reading of texts requires students to suspend, at least temporarily, their judgments about the emotional or moral character of events. Thus, whether someone was right or wrong, moral or immoral, reprehensible or ethical is not an issue in this pragmatic reading. In another class, a student confronted her professor about whether or not salespeople had to be honest in negotiating with customers. The professor responded by pointing to relevant sections of a key authoritative text for this case:

> Well, if he's made an offer, he's revoked it and unless 2–205 [of the Uniform Commercial Code] is going to be applied and there has to be a signed writing, unless you could argue estoppel, if you're dealing with the code number 1–103, which opens the doors to the common law, you don't have that kind of protection, unless it's a consumer statute, or a federal trade regulation ... regulation, you don't have ... that kind of protection.

When the student responded with an indignant question, "i.e., salespeople can lie?", the professor hastened to disabuse her of any notion that moral indignation or fairness were proper frames for use in deciphering this issue:

> Professor: Huh? Not only. Salespeople can lie; salespeople do lie, constantly.
>
> Student: That's not fair.
>
> Professor: No, no, fairness is not something that I accept as a general proposition, and certainly not in my household.

The clear message here, as it is throughout the classes of this study, is that a legal reading is primarily focused on "what the law says you can or cannot do," rather than on "what's fair." Just as medical training requires a hardening and distancing of students' sensibilities from empathic reactions to death and human bodies, legal training demands a bracketing of emotion and morality in dealing with human conflict and the language of "conflict stories."

Interestingly, if a key aspect of the legal approach to texts is a rupturing of standard semantic readings of "conflict stories," then the Socratic method actually initiates this fracture through its linguistic structure. As I have demonstrated elsewhere, classic Socratic teaching involves a distinctive pattern of interruption and inversion of formal or polite speech norms. In addition, this style uses predominantly negative uptake questions on the part of professors. "Uptake" represents a measure of the degree to which professors incorporate some feature of the student's answer in their subsequent questions. To the extent that professors' questions give little or no recognition to preceding answers, students' responses are, in effect, ignored and have little or no impact on the ongoing conversation.

Typical Socratic questioning frequently involves both a high frequency of interruption and low, or negative, uptake. The primary exceptions ... occur when students answer questions by pointing to procedural history or to precedent. Both represent pragmatic [or contextual] aspects of the hierarchies of textual authority to which students must attend. Thus, instead of explicitly telling students (through the content or semantics of speech) what a new legal reading of text entails, professors use the pragmatic structure of classroom discourse to teach students how to read for a distinctively legal pragmatic structuring of text. For this reason, we can speak of . . . a mirroring connection between the form of speech in the legal classroom and the approach to reading legal text that legal pedagogy seeks to inculcate. The rupturing of normal speech in law school classrooms uses the pragmatic, or contextual, structure of classroom talk to reorient students. This breaks down a more semantic, or content-based, approach to reading stories of human conflict, drawing attention instead to issues of textual form and authority. Professors in Socratic classrooms teach students to focus on the contextual structure of texts using the contextual structure of language in the classroom. This parallel between classroom discourse structure and the legal approach to textual language may help to explain the persistence of Socratic teaching in the face of continuing criticism. Regardless of whether it has any functional advantage in teaching legal reasoning, the Socratic method may simply have a strong symbolic appeal by virtue of pointing to and mirroring the approach to language it promotes.

This issue raises the question of whether there is any possible connection between the orientation to text and authority found in legal education and the [world view] underlying legal thought in the United States. Philosopher Stephen Toumlin uses the term "warrant" to describe the background knowledge that permits us to make assertions. In the legal classroom, professors focus their students' attention on the pragmatic warrants that give legal texts their authority. By redirecting students' attention to hierarchies of authority, professors shift their attention away from the drama of the human conflict and the moral dilemmas inherently involved. As students are socialized to this new reading of legal texts, their increasingly expert gaze moves ever more fluidly through the most wrenching of conflict stories. The "reoriented" students search for those key "facts" and pragmatic cues that allow them to link this story to previous cases and situate it within its current legal context. Indeed, a common approach to law school examinations on the part of professors is to compose their own conflict stories, known as "issue-spotters," through which students must sift in order to select the most legally salient features. Frequently, composing "issue spotters" involves throwing emotionally compelling—but legally irrelevant—cues into the fact pattern. This tests students on their ability to read texts for legal pragmatics rather than for social, emotional, moral, or narrative contexts.

NOTES AND QUESTIONS

1. In her book, *The Language of Law School: Learning to "Think Like a Lawyer"* (2007), Mertz describes in more detail the language used to teach

law students. As noted above, the classic Socratic teaching style involves a pattern in which professors only pick up on students' previous responses ("positive uptake") infrequently. Here is a transcript excerpt in which a law professor fails to pick up on the student's response except when she produces a particular procedural term:

Prof: What errors were alleged in the appeal of *Sullivan v. O'Connor* . . . Ms. *[A]?*

( ) What errors were alleged in the appeal of *Sullivan v. O'Connor?*

Ms. A: Um the defense claimed that um the judge failed in allowing the jury to take into account for damages anything but a claim for out-of-pocket expenses.

Prof: Well that's a rather general statement. How did this get to the appellate court?

Ms. A: Well the um the the patient was a woman who wanted // a //

Prof: // How // did this case get to the appellate court?

Ms. A: The defendant disagreed with the way the damages were awarded in the trial court.

Prof: How did this case get to the appellate court? The Supreme Court once a—I think this is true—they asked some guy who'd never argued a case before the Supreme Court before, they said to him—he was a Southerner—and they said to him ah "Counsel, how did you get here?" [Laughter] * "Well," he said, "I came on the Chesapeake and Ohio River." * (*imitated Southern accent*) [Louder laughter] How did this case get to the supreme judicial court?

Ms. A: It was appealed.

Prof: It was appealed, you say. Did you find that word anywhere except in (the) problem?

[+ positive uptake]

Note that repeating the original question is the purest form of non-uptake: there is no content here to indicate that an intervening response even occurred. Here the professor only incorporates the student's response when she stops trying to "tell the story" in the way a layperson might, and moves to a new focus on the legal framework. This style of teaching in essence pushes students to "learn by doing"—that is, to learn a new approach to reading and talking about stories of conflict by actually using a new form of talking. One important component of that form of talking is an antagonistic or argumentative dialogue, with students required to take and defend points of view (regardless of whether they actually believe in them). Mertz argues that this pushes incipient lawyers to regard language as fundamentally manipulative, and truth as highly contingent. In the process of learning this approach, students close off ways of looking at the world.

However, the new system they are learning does not acknowledge its own limits—its partial character. Instead, the process of "learning to think like a lawyer" teaches students to take almost any social situation imaginable and convert it into a set of legal categories. In first-year law school classrooms, students are generally permitted—even encouraged—to speculate about social context and history without being challenged about the basis for these speculations. Why, for example, would someone want to sell a kidney or other body part? Would the motivations change during wartime? What was the effect of race on a court decision involving an African–American boxer? In law school classes, students and professors draw on anecdote, personal experiences, and imagination to discuss these kinds of questions. At a similar point in a sociology class, students are asked to examine the evidence with care, questioning the methods of studies that might answer such questions. But in law school, this kind of demand for evidence is reserved for assertions about the procedural stance of a case, or the application of a doctrinal category to these particular facts. While legal language gives the appearance of being open to dealing with all kinds of people, ideas, and settings—in fact it is highly limited. The fact that this limitation is essentially rendered invisible during law training means that it may be difficult for lawyers to attain the form of humility that Mertz views as essential to hearing multiple points of view. At the same time, however, it can provide a very powerful tool for translating diverse experiences into a common frame. The key task, then, is for a legal system that operates in this way to balance the benefits of this tool against a self-conscious assessment of its limitations.

2.　To what extent does Mertz' focus on the underlying worldview found in legal language, and in the language of the classroom, represent an aspect of "legal culture" in Friedman's sense? To what extent is it different? According to this account of law and legal training, why should we care about the role of language and culture?

V.　Postlude: A Brief Note About Transnational Law

Each sovereign country has its own legal system; and usually, more than one—either formally or informally. Anthropologists and legal sociologists have talked about "legal pluralism"—they have tried to explode the myth that "the law" in (say) France or Japan consisted entirely of the official formal law emanating from the capital. Anthropologists also have a long tradition of studying the legal systems of small communities and groups. Many of these groups operate within countries that have a formal, official legal system. In many ways, the whole thrust of the sociology of law has been to illustrate that legal systems are complex organisms; that there are many competing norm-systems, within a single polity, and that, as we have noted from time to time, there are many "private" legal systems, alongside the formal, official one.

In our times, there is more and more discussion about what is in some ways the opposite phenomenon: transnational law—law which goes beyond the boundaries of the nation-state, and has a wider scope and reach. There has long been a field called "international law" or the "law of nations." Hugo Grotius, in the 17th century, wrote a book called the *Law of War and Peace;* and this was only the start of a rich literature on the "law of nations." Arguably, however, "international law" or the "law of nations" at that time was not formal law at all; it more closely resembled a collection of informal customs or norms. But these customs could not be enforced, because there was in general no body or institution which could enforce them. It follows that sovereign nations—especially big, powerful ones—could ignore "international law" when it suited their purposes. International law has, of course, a certain moral and rhetorical valence.

But is this really the case in the 21st century? First of all, there are some kinds of transnational law that have more bite and more reality. Countries can enter into treaties with each other; and there are thousands of bilateral and multilateral treaties. Many of these treaties are of enormous importance—consider, for example, NAFTA, the North American Free Trade Agreement, signed by the United States, Mexico, and Canada. These treaties become binding parts of domestic law. There are also organizations, like the World Trade Organization, that are the product of international compacts. Countries are, at least in theory, bound by its decisions, and this organization has mechanisms for hearing complaints and resolving disputes. There is also the United Nations, and its charter; countries which violate the norms that the United Nations stands for can be subjected to sanctions—including, in an extreme case, military power. (On the other hand, as recent events in Iraq demonstrate, it is still the case that powerful sovereign nations can act without much regard for either international law or the United Nations.) There are twenty-seven European countries in the European Union, which has a central bureaucracy in Brussels, a Parliament (of sorts), and a very strong and active court. The European countries have also signed a compact on human rights, which is enforced by another very strong and active court, the European Court of Human Rights. And, as trade and lawyering become more globalized, there is a lot more scope and importance to international arbitration and mediation.

There is an enormous literature on all of this, though most of it is normative and descriptive. Everybody recognizes that globalization is here to stay; and that transnational dealings will only increase in the future. Rigorous, empirical research on the actual behavior of international courts and organizations is only just beginning. See, e.g., John Hagan, *Justice in the Balkans: Prosecuting War Crimes in The Hague Tribunal* (2003); Greg Shaffer, *Defending Interests: Public–Private Partnerships in WTO Litigation* (2003). Transnational law poses many questions of great interest to the social study of law.

For example, on the European Court of Human Rights, there are judges from every European country. Most of these are civil law countries; but

England and Ireland are common law countries. The countries that have signed the treaty on human rights have very different histories and legal traditions—the states include Turkey and Russia, Bulgaria, Malta, Portugal, and Sweden, just to mention some which have very different backgrounds. How, if at all, does background—history and culture—impact the work of the judges who sit on this court?

Moreover, modernization and globalization are powerful processes. We live in a period in which you easily get sushi in Denver, Colorado or Caracas, Venezuela (and it is popular in both cities); and you can find McDonald's in Tokyo as well. American movies are popular in most of the world. So is rock-and-roll. Today you can go on the Internet from Madison, Wisconsin and purchase a recording of the Japanese violinist Midori, playing violin concertos by Bartok with the Berlin Philharmonic, conducted by Zuban Mehta. Museums in New York display African art. The world is, of course, hardly a global village; but if culture and technology converge, at least relatively speaking, does this have an impact on legal systems? Does it have an impact on legal culture?

On all of these global and transnational issues, surely there will be far more interest, and research, in years to come.

*

INDEX

References are to Pages

1021

†